DONALD E. KNUTH *Stanford University*

 ADDISON–WESLEY

THE ART OF
COMPUTER PROGRAMMING

THIRD EDITION

Volume 2 / **Seminumerical Algorithms**

THE ART OF
COMPUTER PROGRAMMING

THIRD EDITION

Boston · Columbus · New York · San Francisco · Amsterdam · Cape Town
Dubai · London · Madrid · Milan · Munich · Paris · Montréal · Toronto · Delhi · Mexico City
São Paulo · Sydney · Hong Kong · Seoul · Singapore · Taipei · Tokyo

TEX is a trademark of the American Mathematical Society

METAFONT is a trademark of Addison–Wesley

The quotation on page 61 is reprinted by permission of Grove Press, Inc.

The author and publisher have taken care in the preparation of this book, but make no expressed or implied warranty of any kind and assume no responsibility for errors or omissions. No liability is assumed for incidental or consequential damages in connection with or arising out of the use of the information or programs contained herein.

For government sales inquiries, please contact governmentsales@pearsoned.com
For questions about sales outside the U.S., please contact intlcs@pearson.com

Visit us on the Web: informit.com/aw

Library of Congress Cataloging-in-Publication Data

```
Knuth, Donald Ervin, 1938-
  The art of computer programming / Donald Ervin Knuth.
  xiv,764 p.   24 cm.
  Includes bibliographical references and index.
  Contents: v. 1. Fundamental algorithms. -- v. 2. Seminumerical
algorithms. -- v. 3. Sorting and searching. -- v. 4a. Combinatorial
algorithms, part 1.
  Contents: v. 2. Seminumerical algorithms. -- 3rd ed.
  ISBN 978-0-201-89683-1 (v. 1, 3rd ed.)
  ISBN 978-0-201-89684-8 (v. 2, 3rd ed.)
  ISBN 978-0-201-89685-5 (v. 3, 2nd ed.)
  ISBN 978-0-201-03804-0 (v. 4a)
  1. Electronic digital computers--Programming.  2. Computer
algorithms.   I. Title.
QA76.6.K64  1997
005.1--DC21                                              97-2147
```

Internet page http://www-cs-faculty.stanford.edu/~knuth/taocp.html contains current information about this book and related books.

Copyright © 1998 by Addison–Wesley

ISBN-13 978-0-201-89684-8
ISBN-10   0-201-89684-2

Forty-eighth printing, December 2023
48 2023

PREFACE

O dear Ophelia!
I am ill at these numbers:
I have not art to reckon my groans.
— HAMLET (Act II, Scene 2, Line 120)

THE ALGORITHMS discussed in this book deal directly with numbers; yet I believe they are properly called *seminumerical*, because they lie on the borderline between numeric and symbolic calculation. Each algorithm not only computes the desired answers to a numerical problem, it also is intended to blend well with the internal operations of a digital computer. In many cases people are not able to appreciate the full beauty of such an algorithm unless they also have some knowledge of a computer's machine language; the efficiency of the corresponding machine program is a vital factor that cannot be divorced from the algorithm itself. The problem is to find the best ways to make computers deal with numbers, and this involves tactical as well as numerical considerations. Therefore the subject matter of this book is unmistakably a part of computer science, as well as of numerical mathematics.

Some people working in "higher levels" of numerical analysis will regard the topics treated here as the domain of system programmers. Other people working in "higher levels" of system programming will regard the topics treated here as the domain of numerical analysts. But I hope that there are a few people left who will want to look carefully at these basic methods. Although the methods reside perhaps on a low level, they underlie all of the more grandiose applications of computers to numerical problems, so it is important to know them well. We are concerned here with the interface between numerical mathematics and computer programming, and it is the mating of both types of skills that makes the subject so interesting.

There is a noticeably higher percentage of mathematical material in this book than in other volumes of this series, because of the nature of the subjects treated. In most cases the necessary mathematical topics are developed here starting almost from scratch (or from results proved in Volume 1), but in several easily recognizable sections a knowledge of calculus has been assumed.

This volume comprises Chapters 3 and 4 of the complete series. Chapter 3 is concerned with "random numbers": It is not only a study of various ways to generate random sequences, it also investigates statistical tests for randomness, as well as the transformation of uniform random numbers into other types of random quantities; the latter subject illustrates how random numbers are used in practice. I have also included a section about the nature of randomness itself. Chapter 4 is my attempt to tell the fascinating story of what people have discovered about the processes of arithmetic, after centuries of progress. It discusses various systems for representing numbers, and how to convert between them; and it treats arithmetic on floating point numbers, high-precision integers, rational fractions, polynomials, and power series, including the questions of factoring and finding greatest common divisors.

Each of Chapters 3 and 4 can be used as the basis of a one-semester college course at the junior to graduate level. Although courses on "Random Numbers" and on "Arithmetic" are not presently a part of many college curricula, I believe the reader will find that the subject matter of these chapters lends itself nicely to a unified treatment of material that has real educational value. My own experience has been that these courses are a good means of introducing elementary probability theory and number theory to college students. Nearly all of the topics usually treated in such introductory courses arise naturally in connection with applications, and the presence of these applications can be an important motivation that helps the student to learn and to appreciate the theory. Furthermore, each chapter gives a few hints of more advanced topics that will whet the appetite of many students for further mathematical study.

For the most part this book is self-contained, except for occasional discussions relating to the MIX computer explained in Volume 1. Appendix B contains a summary of the mathematical notations used, some of which are a little different from those found in traditional mathematics books.

Preface to the Third Edition

When the second edition of this book was completed in 1980, it represented the first major test case for prototype systems of electronic publishing called TEX and METAFONT. I am now pleased to celebrate the full development of those systems by returning to the book that inspired and shaped them. At last I am able to have all volumes of *The Art of Computer Programming* in a consistent format that will make them readily adaptable to future changes in printing and display technology. The new setup has allowed me to make many thousands of improvements that I have been wanting to incorporate for a long time.

In this new edition I have gone over every word of the text, trying to retain the youthful exuberance of my original sentences while perhaps adding some more mature judgment. Dozens of new exercises have been added; dozens of old exercises have been given new and improved answers. Changes appear everywhere, but most significantly in Sections 3.5 (about theoretical guarantees of randomness), 3.6 (about portable random-number generators), 4.5.2 (about the binary gcd algorithm), and 4.7 (about composition and iteration of power series).

The Art of Computer Programming is, however, still a work in progress. Research on seminumerical algorithms continues to grow at a phenomenal rate. Therefore some parts of this book are headed by an "under construction" icon, to apologize for the fact that the material is not up-to-date. My files are bursting with important material that I plan to include in the final, glorious, fourth edition of Volume 2, perhaps 16 years from now; but I must finish Volumes 4 and 5 first, and I do not want to delay their publication any more than absolutely necessary.

I am enormously grateful to the many hundreds of people who have helped me to gather and refine this material during the past 35 years. Most of the hard work of preparing the new edition was accomplished by Silvio Levy, who expertly edited the electronic text, and by Jeffrey Oldham, who converted nearly all of the original illustrations to METAPOST format. I have corrected every error that alert readers detected in the second edition (as well as some mistakes that, alas, nobody else noticed); and I have tried to avoid introducing new errors in the new material. However, I suppose some defects still remain, and I want to fix them as soon as possible. Therefore I will cheerfully award $2.56 to the first finder of each technical, typographical, or historical error. The webpage cited on page iv contains a current listing of all corrections that have been reported to me.

Stanford, California   D. E. K.
July 1997

> When a book has been eight years in the making,
> there are too many colleagues, typists, students,
> teachers, and friends to thank.
> Besides, I have no intention of giving such people
> the usual exoneration from responsibility for errors which remain.
> They should have corrected me!
> And sometimes they are even responsible for ideas
> which may turn out in the long run to be wrong.
> Anyway, to such fellow explorers, my thanks.
>
> — EDWARD F. CAMPBELL, JR. (1975)

> 'Defendit numerus,' [there is safety in numbers]
> is the maxim of the foolish;
> 'Deperdit numerus,' [there is ruin in numbers]
> of the wise.
>
> — C. C. COLTON (1820)

NOTES ON THE EXERCISES

THE EXERCISES in this set of books have been designed for self-study as well as for classroom study. It is difficult, if not impossible, for anyone to learn a subject purely by reading about it, without applying the information to specific problems and thereby being encouraged to think about what has been read. Furthermore, we all learn best the things that we have discovered for ourselves. Therefore the exercises form a major part of this work; a definite attempt has been made to keep them as informative as possible and to select problems that are enjoyable as well as instructive.

In many books, easy exercises are found mixed randomly among extremely difficult ones. A motley mixture is, however, often unfortunate because readers like to know in advance how long a problem ought to take — otherwise they may just skip over all the problems. A classic example of such a situation is the book *Dynamic Programming* by Richard Bellman; this is an important, pioneering work in which a group of problems is collected together at the end of some chapters under the heading "Exercises and Research Problems," with extremely trivial questions appearing in the midst of deep, unsolved problems. It is rumored that someone once asked Dr. Bellman how to tell the exercises apart from the research problems, and he replied, "If you can solve it, it is an exercise; otherwise it's a research problem."

Good arguments can be made for including both research problems and very easy exercises in a book of this kind; therefore, to save the reader from the possible dilemma of determining which are which, *rating numbers* have been provided to indicate the level of difficulty. These numbers have the following general significance:

Rating Interpretation

00 An extremely easy exercise that can be answered immediately if the material of the text has been understood; such an exercise can almost always be worked "in your head."

10 A simple problem that makes you think over the material just read, but is by no means difficult. You should be able to do this in one minute at most; pencil and paper may be useful in obtaining the solution.

20 An average problem that tests basic understanding of the text material, but you may need about fifteen or twenty minutes to answer it completely.

30 A problem of moderate difficulty and/or complexity; this one may involve more than two hours' work to solve satisfactorily, or even more if the TV is on.

40 Quite a difficult or lengthy problem that would be suitable for a term project in classroom situations. A student should be able to solve the problem in a reasonable amount of time, but the solution is not trivial.

50 A research problem that has not yet been solved satisfactorily, as far as the author knew at the time of writing, although many people have tried. If you have found an answer to such a problem, you ought to write it up for publication; furthermore, the author of this book would appreciate hearing about the solution as soon as possible (provided that it is correct).

By interpolation in this "logarithmic" scale, the significance of other rating numbers becomes clear. For example, a rating of *17* would indicate an exercise that is a bit simpler than average. Problems with a rating of *50* that are subsequently solved by some reader may appear with a *40* rating in later editions of the book, and in the errata posted on the Internet (see page iv).

The remainder of the rating number divided by 5 indicates the amount of detailed work required. Thus, an exercise rated *24* may take longer to solve than an exercise that is rated *25*, but the latter will require more creativity. All exercises with ratings of *46* or more are open problems for future research, rated according to the number of different attacks that they've resisted so far.

The author has tried earnestly to assign accurate rating numbers, but it is difficult for the person who makes up a problem to know just how formidable it will be for someone else to find a solution; and everyone has more aptitude for certain types of problems than for others. It is hoped that the rating numbers represent a good guess at the level of difficulty, but they should be taken as general guidelines, not as absolute indicators.

This book has been written for readers with varying degrees of mathematical training and sophistication; as a result, some of the exercises are intended only for the use of more mathematically inclined readers. The rating is preceded by an *M* if the exercise involves mathematical concepts or motivation to a greater extent than necessary for someone who is primarily interested only in programming the algorithms themselves. An exercise is marked with the letters "*HM*" if its solution necessarily involves a knowledge of calculus or other higher mathematics not developed in this book. An "*HM*" designation does *not* necessarily imply difficulty.

Some exercises are preceded by an arrowhead, "▶"; this designates problems that are especially instructive and especially recommended. Of course, no reader/student is expected to work *all* of the exercises, so those that seem to be the most valuable have been singled out. (This distinction is not meant to detract from the other exercises!) Each reader should at least make an attempt to solve all of the problems whose rating is *10* or less; and the arrows may help to indicate which of the problems with a higher rating should be given priority.

Solutions to most of the exercises appear in the answer section. Please use them wisely; do not turn to the answer until you have made a genuine effort to solve the problem by yourself, or unless you absolutely do not have time to work this particular problem. *After* getting your own solution or giving the problem a decent try, you may find the answer instructive and helpful. The solution given will often be quite short, and it will sketch the details under the assumption that you have earnestly tried to solve it by your own means first. Sometimes the solution gives less information than was asked; often it gives more. It is quite possible that you may have a better answer than the one published here, or you may have found an error in the published solution; in such a case, the author will be pleased to know the details. Later printings of this book will give the improved solutions together with the solver's name where appropriate.

When working an exercise you may generally use the answers to previous exercises, unless specifically forbidden from doing so. The rating numbers have been assigned with this in mind; thus it is possible for exercise $n + 1$ to have a lower rating than exercise n, even though it includes the result of exercise n as a special case.

Summary of codes:

▸   Recommended
M   Mathematically oriented
HM   Requiring "higher math"

00   Immediate
10   Simple (one minute)
20   Medium (quarter hour)
30   Moderately hard
40   Term project
50   Research problem

EXERCISES

▸ **1.** [*00*] What does the rating "*M20*" mean?

2. [*10*] Of what value can the exercises in a textbook be to the reader?

3. [*M34*] Leonhard Euler conjectured in 1772 that the equation $w^4 + x^4 + y^4 = z^4$ has no solution in positive integers, but Noam Elkies proved in 1987 that infinitely many solutions exist [see *Math. Comp.* **51** (1988), 825–835]. Find all integer solutions such that $0 \le w \le x \le y < z < 10^6$.

4. [*M50*] Prove that when n is an integer, $n > 4$, the equation $w^n + x^n + y^n = z^n$ has no solution in positive integers w, x, y, z.

> *Exercise is the beste instrument in learnyng.*
> — ROBERT RECORDE, *The Whetstone of Witte* (1557)

CONTENTS

JMK
JSK

CHAPTER THREE

RANDOM NUMBERS

Any one who considers arithmetical
methods of producing random digits
is, of course, in a state of sin.
— JOHN VON NEUMANN (1951)

Lest men suspect your tale untrue,
Keep probability in view.
— JOHN GAY (1727)

There wanted not some beams of light
to guide men in the exercise of their Stocastick faculty.
— JOHN OWEN (1662)

3.1. INTRODUCTION

NUMBERS that are "chosen at random" are useful in many different kinds of applications. For example:

a) *Simulation.* When a computer is being used to simulate natural phenomena, random numbers are required to make things realistic. Simulation covers many fields, from the study of nuclear physics (where particles are subject to random collisions) to operations research (where people come into, say, an airport at random intervals).

b) *Sampling.* It is often impractical to examine all possible cases, but a random sample will provide insight into what constitutes "typical" behavior.

c) *Numerical analysis.* Ingenious techniques for solving complicated numerical problems have been devised using random numbers. Several books have been written on this subject.

d) *Computer programming.* Random values make a good source of data for testing the effectiveness of computer algorithms. More importantly, they are crucial to the operation of *randomized algorithms*, which are often far superior to their deterministic counterparts. This use of random numbers is the primary application of interest to us in this series of books; it accounts for the fact that random numbers are already being considered here in Chapter 3, before most of the other computer algorithms have appeared.

1

e) *Decision making.* There are reports that many executives make their decisions by flipping a coin or by throwing darts, etc. It is also rumored that some college professors prepare their grades on such a basis. Sometimes it is important to make a completely "unbiased" decision. Randomness is also an essential part of optimal strategies in the theory of matrix games.

f) *Cryptography.* A source of unbiased bits is crucial for many types of secure communications, when data needs to be concealed.

g) *Aesthetics.* A little bit of randomness makes computer-generated graphics and music seem more lively. For example, a pattern like

tends to look more appealing than

in certain contexts. [See D. E. Knuth, *Bull. Amer. Math. Soc.* **1** (1979), 369.]

h) *Recreation.* Rolling dice, shuffling decks of cards, spinning roulette wheels, etc., are fascinating pastimes for just about everybody. These traditional uses of random numbers have suggested the name "Monte Carlo method," a general term used to describe any algorithm that employs random numbers.

People who think about this topic almost invariably get into philosophical discussions about what the word "random" means. In a sense, there is no such thing as a random number; for example, is 2 a random number? Rather, we speak of a *sequence of independent random numbers* with a specified *distribution*, and this means loosely that each number was obtained merely by chance, having nothing to do with other numbers of the sequence, and that each number has a specified probability of falling in any given range of values.

A *uniform* distribution on a finite set of numbers is one in which each possible number is equally probable. A distribution is generally understood to be uniform unless some other distribution is specifically mentioned.

Each of the ten digits 0 through 9 will occur about $\frac{1}{10}$ of the time in a (uniform) sequence of random digits. Each pair of two successive digits should occur about $\frac{1}{100}$ of the time, and so on. Yet if we take a truly random sequence of a million digits, it will not always have exactly 100,000 zeros, 100,000 ones, etc. In fact, chances of this are quite slim; a *sequence* of such sequences will have this character on the average.

Any specified sequence of a million digits is as probable as any other. Thus, if we are choosing a million digits at random and if the first 999,999 of them happen to come out to be zero, the chance that the final digit is zero is still exactly $\frac{1}{10}$, in a truly random situation. These statements seem paradoxical to many people, yet no contradiction is really involved.

There are several ways to formulate decent abstract definitions of randomness, and we will return to this interesting subject in Section 3.5; but for the moment, let us content ourselves with an intuitive understanding of the concept.

Many years ago, people who needed random numbers in their scientific work would draw balls out of a "well-stirred urn," or they would roll dice or deal out cards. A table of over 40,000 random digits, "taken at random from census reports," was published in 1927 by L. H. C. Tippett. Since then, a number of devices have been built to generate random numbers mechanically. The first such machine was used in 1939 by M. G. Kendall and B. Babington-Smith to produce a table of 100,000 random digits. The Ferranti Mark I computer, first installed in 1951, had a built-in instruction that put 20 random bits into the accumulator using a resistance noise generator; this feature had been recommended by A. M. Turing. In 1955, the RAND Corporation published a widely used table of a million random digits obtained with the help of another special device. A famous random-number machine called ERNIE has been used for many years to pick the winning numbers in the British Premium Savings Bonds lottery. [F. N. David describes the early history in *Games, Gods, and Gambling* (1962). See also Kendall and Babington-Smith, *J. Royal Stat. Soc.* **A101** (1938), 147–166; **B6** (1939), 51–61; S. H. Lavington's discussion of the Mark I in *CACM* **21** (1978), 4–12; the review of the RAND table in *Math. Comp.* **10** (1956), 39–43; and the discussion of ERNIE by W. E. Thomson, *J. Royal Stat. Soc.* **A122** (1959), 301–333.]

Shortly after computers were introduced, people began to search for efficient ways to obtain random numbers within computer programs. A table could be used, but this method is of limited utility because of the memory space and input time requirement, because the table may be too short, and because it is a bit of a nuisance to prepare and maintain the table. A machine such as ERNIE might be attached to the computer, as in the Ferranti Mark I, but this has proved to be unsatisfactory since it is impossible to reproduce calculations exactly a second time when checking out a program; moreover, such machines have tended to suffer from malfunctions that are extremely difficult to detect. Advances in technology made tables useful again during the 1990s, because a billion well-tested random bytes could easily be made accessible. George Marsaglia helped resuscitate random tables in 1995 by preparing a demonstration disk that contained 650 random megabytes, generated by combining the output of a noise-diode circuit with deterministically scrambled rap music.

The inadequacy of mechanical methods in the early days led to an interest in the production of random numbers using a computer's ordinary arithmetic operations. John von Neumann first suggested this approach in about 1946; his idea was to take the square of the previous random number and to extract the middle digits. For example, if we are generating 10-digit numbers and the previous value was 5772156649, we square it to get

$$33317792380594909201;$$

the next number is therefore 7923805949.

There is a fairly obvious objection to this technique: How can a sequence generated in such a way be random, since each number is completely determined by its predecessor? (See von Neumann's comment at the beginning of this chapter.) The answer is that the sequence *isn't* random, but it *appears* to be. In typical applications the actual relationship between one number and its successor has no physical significance; hence the nonrandom character is not really undesirable. Intuitively, the middle square seems to be a fairly good scrambling of the previous number.

Sequences generated in a deterministic way such as this are often called *pseudorandom* or *quasirandom* sequences in the highbrow technical literature, but in most places of this book we shall simply call them random sequences, with the understanding that they only *appear* to be random. Being "apparently random" is perhaps all that can be said about any random sequence anyway. Random numbers generated deterministically on computers have worked quite well in nearly every application, provided that a suitable method has been carefully selected. Of course, deterministic sequences aren't always the answer; they certainly shouldn't replace ERNIE for the lotteries.

Von Neumann's original "middle-square method" has actually proved to be a comparatively poor source of random numbers. The danger is that the sequence tends to get into a rut, a short cycle of repeating elements. For example, if zero ever appears as a number of the sequence, it will continually perpetuate itself.

Several people experimented with the middle-square method in the early 1950s. Working with numbers that have four digits instead of ten, G. E. Forsythe tried 16 different starting values and found that 12 of them led to sequences ending with the cycle 6100, 2100, 4100, 8100, 6100, ..., while two of them degenerated to zero. More extensive tests were carried out by N. Metropolis, mostly in the binary number system. He showed that when 20-bit numbers are being used, there are 13 different cycles into which the middle-square sequence might degenerate, the longest of which has a period of length 142.

It is fairly easy to restart the middle-square method on a new value when zero has been detected, but long cycles are somewhat harder to avoid. Exercises 6 and 7 discuss some interesting ways to determine the cycles of periodic sequences, using very little memory space.

A theoretical disadvantage of the middle-square method is given in exercises 9 and 10. On the other hand, working with 38-bit numbers, Metropolis obtained a sequence of about 750,000 numbers before degeneracy occurred, and the resulting $750,000 \times 38$ bits satisfactorily passed statistical tests for randomness. [*Symp. on Monte Carlo Methods* (Wiley, 1956), 29–36.] This experience showed that the middle-square method *can* give usable results, but it is rather dangerous to put much faith in it until after elaborate computations have been performed.

Many random number generators in use when this chapter was first written were not very good. People have traditionally tended to avoid learning about such subroutines; old methods that were comparatively unsatisfactory have been passed down blindly from one programmer to another, until the users have no understanding of the original limitations. We shall see in this chapter that the most important facts about random number generators are not difficult to learn, although prudence is necessary to avoid common pitfalls.

It is not easy to invent a foolproof source of random numbers. This fact was convincingly impressed upon the author in 1959, when he attempted to create a fantastically good generator using the following peculiar approach:

Algorithm K (*"Super-random" number generator*). Given a 10-digit decimal number X, this algorithm may be used to change X to the number that should come next in a supposedly random sequence. Although the algorithm might be expected to yield quite a random sequence, reasons given below show that it is not, in fact, very good at all. (The reader need not study this algorithm in great detail except to observe how complicated it is; note, in particular, steps K1 and K2.)

K1. [Choose number of iterations.] Set $Y \leftarrow \lfloor X/10^9 \rfloor$, the most significant digit of X. (We will execute steps K2 through K13 exactly $Y + 1$ times; that is, we will apply randomizing transformations a *random* number of times.)

K2. [Choose random step.] Set $Z \leftarrow \lfloor X/10^8 \rfloor \bmod 10$, the second most significant digit of X. Go to step $K(3 + Z)$. (That is, we now jump to a *random* step in the program.)

K3. [Ensure $\geq 5 \times 10^9$.] If $X < 5000000000$, set $X \leftarrow X + 5000000000$.

K4. [Middle square.] Replace X by $\lfloor X^2/10^5 \rfloor \bmod 10^{10}$, that is, by the middle of the square of X.

K5. [Multiply.] Replace X by $(1001001001\, X) \bmod 10^{10}$.

K6. [Pseudo-complement.] If $X < 100000000$, then set $X \leftarrow X + 9814055677$; otherwise set $X \leftarrow 10^{10} - X$.

K7. [Interchange halves.] Interchange the low-order five digits of X with the high-order five digits; that is, set $X \leftarrow 10^5(X \bmod 10^5) + \lfloor X/10^5 \rfloor$, the middle 10 digits of $(10^{10} + 1)X$.

K8. [Multiply.] Same as step K5.

K9. [Decrease digits.] Decrease each nonzero digit of the decimal representation of X by one.

K10. [99999 modify.] If $X < 10^5$, set $X \leftarrow X^2 + 99999$; otherwise set $X \leftarrow X - 99999$.

K11. [Normalize.] (At this point X cannot be zero.) If $X < 10^9$, set $X \leftarrow 10X$ and repeat this step.

K12. [Modified middle square.] Replace X by $\lfloor X(X - 1)/10^5 \rfloor \bmod 10^{10}$, that is, by the middle 10 digits of $X(X - 1)$.

K13. [Repeat?] If $Y > 0$, decrease Y by 1 and return to step K2. If $Y = 0$, the algorithm terminates with X as the desired "random" value. ∎

(The machine-language program corresponding to this algorithm was intended to be so complicated that a person reading a listing of it without explanatory comments wouldn't know what the program was doing.)

Considering all the contortions of Algorithm K, doesn't it seem plausible that it should produce almost an infinite supply of unbelievably random numbers? No! In fact, when this algorithm was first put onto a computer, it almost immediately converged to the 10-digit value 6065038420, which — by extraordinary

Table 1

A COLOSSAL COINCIDENCE: THE NUMBER 6065038420
IS TRANSFORMED INTO ITSELF BY ALGORITHM K.

Step	X (after)		Step	X (after)	
			K9	1107855700	
K1	6065038420		K10	1107755701	
K3	6065038420		K11	1107755701	
K4	6910360760		K12	1226919902	$Y = 3$
K5	8031120760		K5	0048821902	
K6	1968879240		K6	9862877579	
K7	7924019688		K7	7757998628	
K8	9631707688		K8	2384626628	
K9	8520606577		K9	1273515517	
K10	8520506578		K10	1273415518	
K11	8520506578		K11	1273415518	
K12	0323372207	$Y = 6$	K12	5870802097	$Y = 2$
K6	9676627793		K11	5870802097	
K7	2779396766		K12	3172562687	$Y = 1$
K8	4942162766		K4	1540029446	
K9	3831051655		K5	7015475446	
K10	3830951656		K6	2984524554	
K11	3830951656		K7	2455429845	
K12	1905867781	$Y = 5$	K8	2730274845	
K12	3319967479	$Y = 4$	K9	1620163734	
K6	6680032521		K10	1620063735	
K7	3252166800		K11	1620063735	
K8	2218966800		K12	6065038420	$Y = 0$

coincidence—is transformed into itself by the algorithm (see Table 1). With another starting number, the sequence began to repeat after 7401 values, in a cyclic period of length 3178.

The moral of this story is that *random numbers should not be generated with a method chosen at random.* Some theory should be used.

In the following sections we shall consider random number generators that are superior to the middle-square method and to Algorithm K. The corresponding sequences are guaranteed to have certain desirable random properties, and no degeneracy will occur. We shall explore the reasons for this random-like behavior in some detail, and we shall also consider techniques for manipulating random numbers. For example, one of our investigations will be the shuffling of a simulated deck of cards within a computer program.

Section 3.6 summarizes this chapter and lists several bibliographic sources.

EXERCISES

▶ **1.** [*20*] Suppose that you wish to obtain a decimal digit at random, not using a computer. Which of the following methods would be suitable?

a) Open a telephone directory to a random place by sticking your finger in it some-where, and use the units digit of the first number found on the selected page.

b) Same as (a), but use the units digit of the *page* number.

c) Roll a die that is in the shape of a regular icosahedron, whose twenty faces have been labeled with the digits 0, 0, 1, 1, ..., 9, 9. Use the digit that appears on top, when the die comes to rest. (A felt-covered table with a hard surface is recommended for rolling dice.)

d) Expose a Geiger counter to a source of radioactivity for one minute (shielding yourself) and use the units digit of the resulting count. Assume that the Geiger counter displays the number of counts in decimal notation, and that the count is initially zero.

e) Glance at your wristwatch; and if the position of the second-hand is between $6n$ and $6(n+1)$ seconds, choose the digit n.

f) Ask a friend to think of a random digit, and use that digit.

g) Ask an enemy to think of a random digit, and use that digit.

h) Assume that 10 horses are entered in a race and that you know nothing whatever about their qualifications. Assign to these horses the digits 0 to 9, in arbitrary fashion, and after the race use the winner's digit.

2. [*M22*] In a random sequence of a million decimal digits, what is the probability that there are exactly 100,000 of each possible digit?

3. [*10*] What number follows 1010101010 in the middle-square method?

4. [*20*] (a) Why can't the value of X be zero when step K11 of Algorithm K is performed? What would be wrong with the algorithm if X could be zero? (b) Use Table 1 to deduce what happens when Algorithm K is applied repeatedly with the starting value $X = 3830951656$.

5. [*15*] Explain why, in any case, Algorithm K should not be expected to provide infinitely many random numbers, in the sense that (even if the coincidence given in Table 1 had not occurred) one knows in advance that any sequence generated by Algorithm K will eventually be periodic.

▶ **6.** [*M21*] Suppose that we want to generate a sequence of integers $X_0, X_1, X_2, \ldots$, in the range $0 \le X_n < m$. Let $f(x)$ be any function such that $0 \le x < m$ implies $0 \le f(x) < m$. Consider a sequence formed by the rule $X_{n+1} = f(X_n)$. (Examples are the middle-square method and Algorithm K.)

a) Show that the sequence is ultimately periodic, in the sense that there exist numbers λ and μ for which the values

$$X_0, \ X_1, \ \ldots, \ X_\mu, \ \ldots, \ X_{\mu+\lambda-1}$$

are distinct, but $X_{n+\lambda} = X_n$ when $n \ge \mu$. Find the maximum and minimum possible values of μ and λ.

b) (R. W. Floyd.) Show that there exists an $n > 0$ such that $X_n = X_{2n}$; and the smallest such value of n lies in the range $\mu \le n \le \mu + \lambda$. Furthermore the value of X_n is unique in the sense that if $X_n = X_{2n}$ and $X_r = X_{2r}$, then $X_r = X_n$.

c) Use the idea of part (b) to design an algorithm that calculates μ and λ for any given function f and any given X_0, using only $O(\mu+\lambda)$ steps and only a bounded number of memory locations.

▶ **7.** [*M21*] (R. P. Brent, 1977.) Let $\ell(n)$ be the greatest power of 2 that is less than or equal to n; thus, for example, $\ell(15) = 8$ and $\ell(\ell(n)) = \ell(n)$.

   a) Show that, in terms of the notation in exercise 6, there exists an $n > 0$ such that $X_n = X_{\ell(n)-1}$. Find a formula that expresses the least such n in terms of the periodicity numbers μ and λ.

   b) Apply this result to design an algorithm that can be used in conjunction with any random number generator of the type $X_{n+1} = f(X_n)$, to prevent it from cycling indefinitely. Your algorithm should calculate the period length λ, and it should use only a small amount of memory space — you must not simply store all of the computed sequence values!

8. [*23*] Make a complete examination of the middle-square method in the case of two-digit decimal numbers.

   a) We might start the process out with any of the 100 possible values 00, 01, ..., 99. How many of these values lead ultimately to the repeating cycle 00, 00, ...? [*Example:* Starting with 43, we obtain the sequence 43, 84, 05, 02, 00, 00, 00, ...]

   b) How many possible final cycles are there? How long is the longest cycle?

   c) What starting value or values will give the largest number of distinct elements before the sequence repeats?

9. [*M14*] Prove that the middle-square method using $2n$-digit numbers to the base b has the following disadvantage: If the sequence includes any number whose most significant n digits are zero, the succeeding numbers will get smaller and smaller until zero occurs repeatedly.

10. [*M16*] Under the assumptions of the preceding exercise, what can you say about the sequence of numbers following X if the *least* significant n digits of X are zero? What if the least significant $n + 1$ digits are zero?

▶ **11.** [*M26*] Consider sequences of random number generators having the form described in exercise 6. If we choose $f(x)$ and X_0 at random — in other words, if we assume that each of the m^m possible functions $f(x)$ is equally probable and that each of the m possible values of X_0 is equally probable — what is the probability that the sequence will eventually degenerate into a cycle of length $\lambda = 1$? [*Note:* The assumptions of this problem give a natural way to think of a "random" random number generator of this type. A method such as Algorithm K may be expected to behave somewhat like the generator considered here; the answer to this problem gives a measure of how colossal the coincidence of Table 1 really is.]

▶ **12.** [*M31*] Under the assumptions of the preceding exercise, what is the average length of the final cycle? What is the average length of the sequence before it begins to cycle? (In the notation of exercise 6, we wish to examine the average values of λ and of $\mu + \lambda$.)

13. [*M42*] If $f(x)$ is chosen at random in the sense of exercise 11, what is the average length of the *longest* cycle obtainable by varying the starting value X_0? [*Note:* We have already considered the analogous problem in the case that $f(x)$ is a random permutation; see exercise 1.3.3–23.]

14. [*M38*] If $f(x)$ is chosen at random in the sense of exercise 11, what is the average number of distinct final cycles obtainable by varying the starting value? [See exercise 8(b).]

15. [*M15*] If $f(x)$ is chosen at random in the sense of exercise 11, what is the probability that none of the final cycles has length 1, regardless of the choice of X_0?

16. [*15*] A sequence generated as in exercise 6 must begin to repeat after at most m values have been generated. Suppose we generalize the method so that X_{n+1} depends on X_{n-1} as well as on X_n; formally, let $f(x,y)$ be a function such that $0 \le x, y < m$ implies $0 \le f(x,y) < m$. The sequence is constructed by selecting X_0 and X_1 arbitrarily, and then letting

$$X_{n+1} = f(X_n, X_{n-1}), \qquad \text{for } n > 0.$$

What is the maximum period conceivably attainable in this case?

17. [*10*] Generalize the situation in the previous exercise so that X_{n+1} depends on the preceding k values of the sequence.

18. [*M20*] Invent a method analogous to that of exercise 7 for finding cycles in the general form of random number generator discussed in exercise 17.

19. [*HM47*] Solve the problems of exercises 11 through 15 asymptotically for the more general case that X_{n+1} depends on the preceding k values of the sequence; each of the m^{m^k} functions $f(x_1, \ldots, x_k)$ is to be considered equally probable. [*Note:* The number of functions that yield the *maximum* period is analyzed in exercise 2.3.4.2–23.]

20. [*30*] Find all nonnegative $X < 10^{10}$ that lead ultimately via Algorithm K to the self-reproducing number in Table 1.

21. [*40*] Prove or disprove: The mapping $X \mapsto f(X)$ defined by Algorithm K has exactly five cycles, of lengths 3178, 1606, 1024, 943, and 1.

22. [*21*] (H. Rolletschek.) Would it be a good idea to generate random numbers by using the sequence $f(0), f(1), f(2), \ldots$, where f is a random function, instead of using $x_0, f(x_0), f(f(x_0))$, etc.?

▶ **23.** [*M26*] (D. Foata and A. Fuchs, 1970.) Show that each of the m^m functions $f(x)$ considered in exercise 6 can be represented as a sequence $(x_0, x_1, \ldots, x_{m-1})$ having the following properties:

i) $(x_0, x_1, \ldots, x_{m-1})$ is a permutation of $(f(0), f(1), \ldots, f(m-1))$.

ii) $(f(0), \ldots, f(m-1))$ can be uniquely reconstructed from $(x_0, x_1, \ldots, x_{m-1})$.

iii) The elements that appear in cycles of f are $\{x_0, x_1, \ldots, x_{k-1}\}$, where k is the largest subscript such that these k elements are distinct.

iv) $x_j \notin \{x_0, x_1, \ldots, x_{j-1}\}$ implies $x_{j-1} = f(x_j)$, unless x_j is the smallest element in a cycle of f.

v) $(f(0), f(1), \ldots, f(m-1))$ is a permutation of $(0, 1, \ldots, m-1)$ if and only if $(x_0, x_1, \ldots, x_{m-1})$ represents the *inverse* of that permutation by the "unusual correspondence" of Section 1.3.3.

vi) $x_0 = x_1$ if and only if $(x_1, \ldots, x_{m-1})$ represents an oriented tree by the construction of exercise 2.3.4.4–18, with $f(x)$ the parent of x.

3.2. GENERATING UNIFORM RANDOM NUMBERS

IN THIS SECTION we shall consider methods for generating a sequence of random fractions — random *real numbers* U_n, *uniformly distributed between zero and one*. Since a computer can represent a real number with only finite accuracy, we shall actually be generating integers X_n between zero and some number m; the fraction

$$U_n = X_n/m$$

will then lie between zero and one. Usually m is the word size of the computer, so X_n may be regarded (conservatively) as the integer contents of a computer word with the radix point assumed at the extreme right, and U_n may be regarded (liberally) as the contents of the same word with the radix point assumed at the extreme left.

3.2.1. The Linear Congruential Method

By far the most popular random number generators in use today are special cases of the following scheme, introduced by D. H. Lehmer in 1949. [See *Proc. 2nd Symp. on Large-Scale Digital Calculating Machinery* (Cambridge, Mass.: Harvard University Press, 1951), 141–146.] We choose four magic integers:

$$
\begin{aligned}
&m, &&\text{the modulus;} &&0 < m. \\
&a, &&\text{the multiplier;} &&0 \le a < m. \\
&c, &&\text{the increment;} &&0 \le c < m. \\
&X_0, &&\text{the starting value;} &&0 \le X_0 < m.
\end{aligned}
\tag{1}
$$

The desired sequence of random numbers $\langle X_n \rangle$ is then obtained by setting

$$X_{n+1} = (aX_n + c) \bmod m, \qquad n \ge 0. \tag{2}$$

This is called a *linear congruential sequence*. Taking the remainder mod m is somewhat like determining where a ball will land in a spinning roulette wheel.

For example, the sequence obtained when $m = 10$ and $X_0 = a = c = 7$ is

$$7,\ 6,\ 9,\ 0,\ 7,\ 6,\ 9,\ 0,\ \dots . \tag{3}$$

As this example shows, the sequence is not always "random" for all choices of m, a, c, and X_0; the principles of choosing the magic numbers appropriately will be investigated carefully in later parts of this chapter.

Example (3) illustrates the fact that the congruential sequences always get into a loop: There is ultimately a cycle of numbers that is repeated endlessly. This property is common to all sequences having the general form $X_{n+1} = f(X_n)$, when f transforms a finite set into itself; see exercise 3.1–6. The repeating cycle is called the *period*; sequence (3) has a period of length 4. A useful sequence will of course have a relatively long period.

The special case $c = 0$ deserves explicit mention, since the number generation process is a little faster when $c = 0$ than it is when $c \ne 0$. We shall see later that the restriction $c = 0$ cuts down the length of the period of the sequence, but it is still possible to make the period reasonably long. Lehmer's original generation method had $c = 0$, although he mentioned $c \neq 0$ as a possibility; the fact that $c \neq 0$ can lead to longer periods is due to Thomson [*Comp. J.* **1** (1958), 83, 86] and, independently, to Rotenberg [*JACM* **7** (1960), 75–77]. The terms *multiplicative congruential method* and *mixed congruential method* are used by many authors to denote linear congruential sequences with $c = 0$ and $c \neq 0$, respectively.

The letters m, a, c, and X_0 will be used throughout this chapter in the sense described above. Furthermore, we will find it useful to define

$$b = a - 1,\qquad(4)$$

in order to simplify many of our formulas.

We can immediately reject the case $a = 1$, for this would mean that $X_n = (X_0 + nc) \bmod m$, and the sequence would certainly not behave as a random sequence. The case $a = 0$ is even worse. Hence for practical purposes we may assume that

$$a \geq 2,\qquad b \geq 1.\qquad(5)$$

Now we can prove a generalization of Eq. (2),

$$X_{n+k} = \left(a^k X_n + (a^k - 1)c/b\right) \bmod m,\qquad k \geq 0,\quad n \geq 0,\qquad(6)$$

which expresses the $(n+k)$th term directly in terms of the nth term. (The special case $n = 0$ in this equation is worthy of note.) It follows that the subsequence consisting of every kth term of $\langle X_n \rangle$ is another linear congruential sequence, having the multiplier $a^k \bmod m$ and the increment $\left((a^k - 1)c/b\right) \bmod m$.

An important corollary of (6) is that the general sequence defined by m, a, c, and X_0 can be expressed very simply in terms of the special case where $c = 1$ and $X_0 = 0$. Let

$$Y_0 = 0,\qquad Y_{n+1} = (aY_n + 1) \bmod m.\qquad(7)$$

According to Eq. (6) we will have $Y_k \equiv (a^k - 1)/b$ (modulo m), hence the general sequence defined in (2) satisfies

$$X_n = (AY_n + X_0) \bmod m,\qquad \text{where } A = (X_0 b + c) \bmod m.\qquad(8)$$

EXERCISES

1. [*10*] Example (3) shows a situation in which $X_4 = X_0$, so the sequence begins again from the beginning. Give an example of a linear congruential sequence with $m = 10$ for which X_0 never appears again in the sequence.

▸ **2.** [*M20*] Show that if a and m are relatively prime, the number X_0 will always appear in the period.

3. [*M10*] If a and m are not relatively prime, explain why the sequence will be somewhat handicapped and probably not very random; hence we will generally want the multiplier a to be relatively prime to the modulus m.

4. [*11*] Prove Eq. (6).

5. [*M20*] Equation (6) holds for $k \geq 0$. If possible, give a formula that expresses X_{n+k} in terms of X_n for *negative* values of k.

3.2.1.1. Choice of modulus. Our current goal is to find good values for the parameters that define a linear congruential sequence. Let us first consider the proper choice of the number m. We want m to be rather large, since the period cannot have more than m elements. (Even if we intend to generate only random zeros and ones, we should *not* take $m = 2$, for then the sequence would at best have the form $\ldots, 0, 1, 0, 1, 0, 1, \ldots$! Methods for getting random zeros and ones from linear congruential sequences are discussed in Section 3.4.)

Another factor that influences our choice of m is speed of generation: We want to pick a value so that the computation of $(aX_n + c) \bmod m$ is fast.

Consider MIX as an example. We can compute $y \bmod m$ by putting y in registers A and X and dividing by m; assuming that y and m are positive, we see that $y \bmod m$ will then appear in register X. But division is a comparatively slow operation, and it can be avoided if we take m to be a value that is especially convenient, such as the *word size* of our computer.

Let w be the computer's word size, namely 2^e on an e-bit binary computer or 10^e on an e-digit decimal machine. (In this book we shall often use the letter e to denote an arbitrary integer exponent, instead of the base of natural logarithms, hoping that the context will make our notation unambiguous. Physicists have a similar problem when they use e for the charge on an electron.) The result of an addition operation is usually given modulo w, except on ones'-complement machines; and multiplication mod w is also quite simple, since the desired result is the lower half of the product. Thus, the following program computes the quantity $(aX + c) \bmod w$ efficiently:

```
    LDA   A      rA ← a.
    MUL   X      rAX ← (rA) · X.
    SLAX  5      rA ← rAX mod w.
    ADD   C      rA ← (rA + c) mod w.  ∎
```
(1)

The result appears in register A. The overflow toggle might be on at the conclusion of these instructions; if that is undesirable, the code should be followed by, say, 'JOV *+1' to turn it off.

A clever technique that is less commonly known can be used to perform computations modulo $w + 1$. For reasons to be explained later, we will generally want $c = 0$ when $m = w + 1$, so we merely need to compute $(aX) \bmod (w + 1)$. The following program does this:

```
01  LDAN  X          rA ← −X.
02  MUL   A          rAX ← (rA) · a.
03  STX   TEMP
04  SUB   TEMP       rA ← rA − rX.
05  JANN  *+3        Exit if rA ≥ 0.
06  INCA  2          rA ← rA + 2.
07  ADD   =w − 1=    rA ← rA + w − 1.  ∎
```
(2)

Register A now contains the value $(aX) \bmod (w + 1)$. Of course, this value might lie anywhere between 0 and w, inclusive, so the reader may legitimately wonder how we can represent so many values in the A-register! (The register obviously cannot hold a number larger than $w - 1$.) The answer is that the result equals w if and only if program (2) turns overflow on, assuming that overflow was initially off. We could represent w by 0, since (2) will not normally be used when $X = 0$; but it is most convenient simply to reject the value w if it appears in the congruential sequence modulo $w + 1$. Then we can also avoid overflow, simply by changing lines 05 and 06 of (2) to 'JANN *+4; INCA 2; JAP *-5'.

To prove that code (2) actually does determine $(aX) \bmod (w+1)$, note that in line 04 we are subtracting the lower half of the product from the upper half. No overflow can occur at this step; and if $aX = qw + r$, with $0 \le r < w$, we will have the quantity $r - q$ in register A after line 04. Now

$$aX = q(w + 1) + (r - q),$$

and we have $-w < r - q < w$ since $q < w$; hence $(aX) \bmod (w + 1)$ equals either $r - q$ or $r - q + (w + 1)$, depending on whether $r - q \ge 0$ or $r - q < 0$.

A similar technique can be used to get the product of two numbers modulo $(w - 1)$; see exercise 8.

In later sections we shall require a knowledge of the prime factors of m in order to choose the multiplier a correctly. Table 1 lists the complete factorization of $w \pm 1$ into primes for nearly every known computer word size; the methods of Section 4.5.4 can be used to extend this table if desired.

The reader may well ask why we bother to consider using $m = w \pm 1$, when the choice $m = w$ is so manifestly convenient. The reason is that when $m = w$, the right-hand digits of X_n are much less random than the left-hand digits. If d is a divisor of m, and if

$$Y_n = X_n \bmod d, \tag{3}$$

we can easily show that

$$Y_{n+1} = (aY_n + c) \bmod d. \tag{4}$$

(For $X_{n+1} = aX_n + c - qm$ for some integer q, and taking both sides mod d causes the quantity qm to drop out when d is a factor of m.)

To illustrate the significance of Eq. (4), let us suppose, for example, that we have a binary computer. If $m = w = 2^e$, the low-order four bits of X_n are the numbers $Y_n = X_n \bmod 2^4$. The gist of Eq. (4) is that the low-order four bits of $\langle X_n \rangle$ form a congruential sequence that has a period of length 16 or less. Similarly, the low-order five bits are periodic with a period of at most 32; and the least significant bit of X_n is either constant or strictly alternating.

This situation does not occur when $m = w \pm 1$; in such a case, the low-order bits of X_n will behave just as randomly as the high-order bits do. If, for example, $w = 2^{35}$ and $m = 2^{35} - 1$, the numbers of the sequence will not be very random if we consider only their remainders mod 31, 71, 127, or 122921 (see Table 1); but the low-order bit, which represents the numbers of the sequence taken mod 2, should be satisfactorily random.

Another alternative is to let m be the largest prime number less than w. This prime may be found by using the techniques of Section 4.5.4, and a table of suitably large primes appears in that section.

Table 1

PRIME FACTORIZATIONS OF $w \pm 1$

$2^e - 1$	e	$2^e + 1$
$7 \cdot 31 \cdot 151$	15	$3^2 \cdot 11 \cdot 331$
$3 \cdot 5 \cdot 17 \cdot 257$	16	65537
131071	17	$3 \cdot 43691$
$3^3 \cdot 7 \cdot 19 \cdot 73$	18	$5 \cdot 13 \cdot 37 \cdot 109$
524287	19	$3 \cdot 174763$
$3 \cdot 5^2 \cdot 11 \cdot 31 \cdot 41$	20	$17 \cdot 61681$
$7^2 \cdot 127 \cdot 337$	21	$3^2 \cdot 43 \cdot 5419$
$3 \cdot 23 \cdot 89 \cdot 683$	22	$5 \cdot 397 \cdot 2113$
$47 \cdot 178481$	23	$3 \cdot 2796203$
$3^2 \cdot 5 \cdot 7 \cdot 13 \cdot 17 \cdot 241$	24	$97 \cdot 257 \cdot 673$
$31 \cdot 601 \cdot 1801$	25	$3 \cdot 11 \cdot 251 \cdot 4051$
$3 \cdot 2731 \cdot 8191$	26	$5 \cdot 53 \cdot 157 \cdot 1613$
$7 \cdot 73 \cdot 262657$	27	$3^4 \cdot 19 \cdot 87211$
$3 \cdot 5 \cdot 29 \cdot 43 \cdot 113 \cdot 127$	28	$17 \cdot 15790321$
$233 \cdot 1103 \cdot 2089$	29	$3 \cdot 59 \cdot 3033169$
$3^2 \cdot 7 \cdot 11 \cdot 31 \cdot 151 \cdot 331$	30	$5^2 \cdot 13 \cdot 41 \cdot 61 \cdot 1321$
2147483647	31	$3 \cdot 715827883$
$3 \cdot 5 \cdot 17 \cdot 257 \cdot 65537$	32	$641 \cdot 6700417$
$7 \cdot 23 \cdot 89 \cdot 599479$	33	$3^2 \cdot 67 \cdot 683 \cdot 20857$
$3 \cdot 43691 \cdot 131071$	34	$5 \cdot 137 \cdot 953 \cdot 26317$
$31 \cdot 71 \cdot 127 \cdot 122921$	35	$3 \cdot 11 \cdot 43 \cdot 281 \cdot 86171$
$3^3 \cdot 5 \cdot 7 \cdot 13 \cdot 19 \cdot 37 \cdot 73 \cdot 109$	36	$17 \cdot 241 \cdot 433 \cdot 38737$
$223 \cdot 616318177$	37	$3 \cdot 1777 \cdot 25781083$
$3 \cdot 174763 \cdot 524287$	38	$5 \cdot 229 \cdot 457 \cdot 525313$
$7 \cdot 79 \cdot 8191 \cdot 121369$	39	$3^2 \cdot 2731 \cdot 22366891$
$3 \cdot 5^2 \cdot 11 \cdot 17 \cdot 31 \cdot 41 \cdot 61681$	40	$257 \cdot 4278255361$
$13367 \cdot 164511353$	41	$3 \cdot 83 \cdot 8831418697$
$3^2 \cdot 7^2 \cdot 43 \cdot 127 \cdot 337 \cdot 5419$	42	$5 \cdot 13 \cdot 29 \cdot 113 \cdot 1429 \cdot 14449$
$431 \cdot 9719 \cdot 2099863$	43	$3 \cdot 2932031007403$
$3 \cdot 5 \cdot 23 \cdot 89 \cdot 397 \cdot 683 \cdot 2113$	44	$17 \cdot 353 \cdot 2931542417$
$7 \cdot 31 \cdot 73 \cdot 151 \cdot 631 \cdot 23311$	45	$3^3 \cdot 11 \cdot 19 \cdot 331 \cdot 18837001$
$3 \cdot 47 \cdot 178481 \cdot 2796203$	46	$5 \cdot 277 \cdot 1013 \cdot 1657 \cdot 30269$
$2351 \cdot 4513 \cdot 13264529$	47	$3 \cdot 283 \cdot 165768537521$
$3^2 \cdot 5 \cdot 7 \cdot 13 \cdot 17 \cdot 97 \cdot 241 \cdot 257 \cdot 673$	48	$193 \cdot 65537 \cdot 22253377$
$179951 \cdot 3203431780337$	59	$3 \cdot 2833 \cdot 37171 \cdot 1824726041$
$3^2 \cdot 5^2 \cdot 7 \cdot 11 \cdot 13 \cdot 31 \cdot 41 \cdot 61 \cdot 151 \cdot 331 \cdot 1321$	60	$17 \cdot 241 \cdot 61681 \cdot 4562284561$
$7^2 \cdot 73 \cdot 127 \cdot 337 \cdot 92737 \cdot 649657$	63	$3^3 \cdot 19 \cdot 43 \cdot 5419 \cdot 77158673929$
$3 \cdot 5 \cdot 17 \cdot 257 \cdot 641 \cdot 65537 \cdot 6700417$	64	$274177 \cdot 67280421310721$

$10^e - 1$	e	$10^e + 1$
$3^3 \cdot 7 \cdot 11 \cdot 13 \cdot 37$	6	$101 \cdot 9901$
$3^2 \cdot 239 \cdot 4649$	7	$11 \cdot 909091$
$3^2 \cdot 11 \cdot 73 \cdot 101 \cdot 137$	8	$17 \cdot 5882353$
$3^4 \cdot 37 \cdot 333667$	9	$7 \cdot 11 \cdot 13 \cdot 19 \cdot 52579$
$3^2 \cdot 11 \cdot 41 \cdot 271 \cdot 9091$	10	$101 \cdot 3541 \cdot 27961$
$3^2 \cdot 21649 \cdot 513239$	11	$11^2 \cdot 23 \cdot 4093 \cdot 8779$
$3^3 \cdot 7 \cdot 11 \cdot 13 \cdot 37 \cdot 101 \cdot 9901$	12	$73 \cdot 137 \cdot 99990001$
$3^2 \cdot 11 \cdot 17 \cdot 73 \cdot 101 \cdot 137 \cdot 5882353$	16	$353 \cdot 449 \cdot 641 \cdot 1409 \cdot 69857$

In most applications, the low-order bits are insignificant, and the choice $m = w$ is quite satisfactory — provided that the programmer using the random numbers does so wisely.

Our discussion so far has been based on a "signed magnitude" computer like MIX. Similar ideas apply to machines that use complement notations, although there are some instructive variations. For example, a DECsystem 20 computer has 36 bits with two's complement arithmetic; when it computes the product of two nonnegative integers, the lower half contains the least significant 35 bits with a plus sign. On this machine we should therefore take $w = 2^{35}$, not 2^{36}. The 32-bit two's complement arithmetic on IBM System/370 computers is different: The lower half of a product contains a full 32 bits. Some programmers have felt that this is a disadvantage, since the lower half can be negative when the operands are positive, and it is a nuisance to correct this; but actually it is a distinct *advantage* from the standpoint of random number generation, since we can take $m = 2^{32}$ instead of 2^{31} (see exercise 4).

EXERCISES

1. [*M12*] In exercise 3.2.1–3 we concluded that the best congruential generators will have the multiplier a relatively prime to m. Show that when $m = w$ in this case it is possible to compute $(aX + c) \bmod w$ in just *three* MIX instructions, rather than the four in (1), with the result appearing in register X.

2. [*16*] Write a MIX subroutine having the following characteristics:

       Calling sequence: JMP RANDM

       Entry conditions: Location XRAND contains an integer X.

       Exit conditions: $X \leftarrow \mathrm{rA} \leftarrow (aX + c) \bmod w$, $\mathrm{rX} \leftarrow 0$, overflow off.

(Thus a call on this subroutine will produce the next random number of a linear congruential sequence.)

▸ **3.** [*M25*] Many computers do not provide the ability to divide a two-word number by a one-word number; they provide only operations on single-word numbers, such as $\mathrm{himult}(x, y) = \lfloor xy/w \rfloor$ and $\mathrm{lomult}(x, y) = xy \bmod w$, when x and y are nonnegative integers less than the word size w. Explain how to evaluate $ax \bmod m$ in terms of himult and lomult, assuming that $0 \le a, x < m < w$ and that $m \perp w$. You may use precomputed constants that depend on a, m, and w.

▸ **4.** [*21*] Discuss the calculation of linear congruential sequences with $m = 2^{32}$ on two's-complement machines such as the System/370 series.

5. [*20*] Given that m is less than the word size, and that x and y are nonnegative integers less than m, show that the difference $(x - y) \bmod m$ may be computed in just four MIX instructions, without requiring any division. What is the best code for the sum $(x + y) \bmod m$?

▸ **6.** [*20*] The previous exercise suggests that subtraction mod m is easier to perform than addition mod m. Discuss sequences generated by the rule

$$X_{n+1} = (aX_n - c) \bmod m.$$

Are these sequences essentially different from linear congruential sequences as defined in the text? Are they more suited to efficient computer calculation?

7. [*M24*] What patterns can you spot in Table 1?

▶ **8.** [*20*] Write a MIX program analogous to (2) that computes $(aX) \bmod (w-1)$. The values 0 and $w-1$ are to be treated as equivalent in the input and output of your program.

▶ **9.** [*M25*] Most high-level programming languages do not provide a good way to divide a two-word integer by a one-word integer, nor do they provide the himult operation of exercise 3. The purpose of this exercise is to find a reasonable way to cope with such limitations when we wish to evaluate $ax \bmod m$ for variable x and for constants $0 < a < m$.

   a) Prove that if $q = \lfloor m/a \rfloor$, we have $a(x - (x \bmod q)) = \lfloor x/q \rfloor (m - (m \bmod a))$.
   b) Use the identity of (a) to evaluate $ax \bmod m$ without computing any numbers that exceed m in absolute value, assuming that $a^2 \le m$.

10. [*M26*] The solution to exercise 9(b) sometimes works also when $a^2 > m$. Exactly how many multipliers a are there for which the intermediate results in that method never exceed m, for all x between 0 and m?

11. [*M30*] Continuing exercise 9, show that it is possible to evaluate $ax \bmod m$ using only the following basic operations:

   i) $u \times v$, where $u \ge 0$, $v \ge 0$, and $uv < m$;
   ii) $\lfloor u/v \rfloor$, where $0 < v \le u < m$;
   iii) $(u - v) \bmod m$, where $0 \le u, v < m$.

In fact, it is always possible to do this with at most 12 operations of types (i) and (ii), and with a bounded number of operations of type (iii), not counting the precomputation of constants that depend on a and m. For example, explain how to proceed when a is 62089911 and m is $2^{31} - 1$. (These constants appear in Table 3.3.4–1.)

▶ **12.** [*M28*] Consider computations by pencil and paper or an abacus.
   a) What's a good way to multiply a given 10-digit number by 10, modulo 9999998999?
   b) Same question, but multiply instead by 999999900 (modulo 9999998999).
   c) Explain how to compute the powers $999999900^n \bmod 9999998999$, for $n = 1, 2, 3, \ldots$.
   d) Relate such computations to the decimal expansion of $1/9999998999$.
   e) Show that these ideas make it possible to implement certain kinds of linear congruential generators that have extremely large moduli, using only a few operations per generated number.

13. [*M24*] Repeat the previous exercise, but with modulus 9999999001 and with multipliers 10 and 8999999101.

14. [*M25*] Generalize the ideas of the previous two exercises, obtaining a large family of linear congruential generators with extremely large moduli.

3.2.1.2. Choice of multiplier. In this section we shall consider how to choose the multiplier a so as to produce a *period of maximum length*. A long period is essential for any sequence that is to be used as a source of random numbers; indeed, we would hope that the period contains considerably more numbers than will ever be used in a single application. Therefore we shall concern ourselves in this section with the question of period length. The reader should keep in mind, however, that a long period is only one desirable criterion for the randomness of a linear congruential sequence. For example, when $a = c = 1$, the sequence is simply $X_{n+1} = (X_n + 1) \bmod m$, and this obviously has a period of length m, yet it is anything but random. Other considerations affecting the choice of a multiplier will be given later in this chapter.

Since only m different values are possible, the period surely cannot be longer than m. Can we achieve the maximum length, m? The example above shows that it is always possible, although the choice $a = c = 1$ does not yield a desirable sequence. Let us investigate *all* possible choices of a, c, and X_0 that give a period of length m. It turns out that all such values of the parameters can be characterized very simply; when m is the product of distinct primes, only $a = 1$ will produce the full period, but when m is divisible by a high power of some prime there is considerable latitude in the choice of a. The following theorem makes it easy to tell if the maximum period is achieved.

Theorem A. *The linear congruential sequence defined by m, a, c, and X_0 has period length m if and only if*

i) *c is relatively prime to m;*

ii) *$b = a - 1$ is a multiple of p, for every prime p dividing m;*

iii) *b is a multiple of 4, if m is a multiple of 4.*

Proof. The ideas used in the proof of this theorem go back at least a hundred years. But the first proof of the theorem in this particular form was given by M. Greenberger in the special case $m = 2^e$ [see *JACM* **8** (1961), 163–167], and the sufficiency of conditions (i), (ii), and (iii) in the general case was shown by Hull and Dobell [see *SIAM Review* **4** (1962), 230–254]. To prove the theorem we will first consider some auxiliary number-theoretic results that are of interest in themselves.

Lemma P. *Let p be a prime number, and let e be a positive integer, where $p^e > 2$. If*

$$x \equiv 1 \;(\text{modulo } p^e), \qquad x \not\equiv 1 \;(\text{modulo } p^{e+1}), \tag{1}$$

then

$$x^p \equiv 1 \;(\text{modulo } p^{e+1}), \qquad x^p \not\equiv 1 \;(\text{modulo } p^{e+2}). \tag{2}$$

Proof. We have $x = 1 + qp^e$ for some integer q that is not a multiple of p. By the binomial formula

$$x^p = 1 + \binom{p}{1}qp^e + \cdots + \binom{p}{p-1}q^{p-1}p^{(p-1)e} + q^p p^{pe}$$

$$= 1 + qp^{e+1}\left(1 + \frac{1}{p}\binom{p}{2}qp^e + \frac{1}{p}\binom{p}{3}q^2 p^{2e} + \cdots + \frac{1}{p}\binom{p}{p}q^{p-1}p^{(p-1)e}\right).$$

The quantity in parentheses is an integer, and, in fact, every term inside the parentheses is a multiple of p except the first term. For if $1 < k < p$, the binomial coefficient $\binom{p}{k}$ is divisible by p (see exercise 1.2.6–10); hence

$$\frac{1}{p}\binom{p}{k}q^{k-1}p^{(k-1)e}$$

is divisible by $p^{(k-1)e}$. And the last term is $q^{p-1}p^{(p-1)e-1}$, which is divisible by p since $(p-1)e > 1$ when $p^e > 2$. So $x^p \equiv 1 + qp^{e+1}$ (modulo p^{e+2}), and this completes the proof. (*Note:* A generalization of this result appears in exercise 3.2.2–11(a).) ∎

Lemma Q. *Let the decomposition of m into prime factors be*

$$m = p_1^{e_1} \dots p_t^{e_t}. \tag{3}$$

The length λ of the period of the linear congruential sequence determined by (X_0, a, c, m) is the least common multiple of the lengths λ_j of the periods of the linear congruential sequences $(X_0 \bmod p_j^{e_j}, a \bmod p_j^{e_j}, c \bmod p_j^{e_j}, p_j^{e_j})$, $1 \le j \le t$.

Proof. By induction on t, it suffices to prove that if m_1 and m_2 are relatively prime, the length λ of the period of the linear congruential sequence determined by the parameters $(X_0, a, c, m_1 m_2)$ is the least common multiple of the lengths λ_1 and λ_2 of the periods of the sequences determined by $(X_0 \bmod m_1, a \bmod m_1, c \bmod m_1, m_1)$ and $(X_0 \bmod m_2, a \bmod m_2, c \bmod m_2, m_2)$. We observed in the previous section, Eq. (4), that if the elements of these three sequences are respectively denoted by X_n, Y_n, and Z_n, we will have

$$Y_n = X_n \bmod m_1 \qquad \text{and} \qquad Z_n = X_n \bmod m_2, \qquad \text{for all } n \ge 0.$$

Therefore, by Law D of Section 1.2.4, we find that

$$X_n = X_k \qquad \text{if and only if} \qquad Y_n = Y_k \quad \text{and} \quad Z_n = Z_k. \tag{4}$$

Let λ' be the least common multiple of λ_1 and λ_2; we wish to prove that $\lambda' = \lambda$. Since $X_n = X_{n+\lambda}$ for all suitably large n, we have $Y_n = Y_{n+\lambda}$ (hence λ is a multiple of λ_1) and $Z_n = Z_{n+\lambda}$ (hence λ is a multiple of λ_2), so we must have $\lambda \ge \lambda'$. Furthermore, we know that $Y_n = Y_{n+\lambda'}$ and $Z_n = Z_{n+\lambda'}$ for all suitably large n; therefore, by (4), $X_n = X_{n+\lambda'}$. This proves $\lambda \le \lambda'$. ∎

Now we are ready to prove Theorem A. Lemma Q tells us that it suffices to prove the theorem when m is a power of a prime number, because

$$p_1^{e_1} \dots p_t^{e_t} = \lambda = \mathrm{lcm}(\lambda_1, \dots, \lambda_t) \le \lambda_1 \dots \lambda_t \le p_1^{e_1} \dots p_t^{e_t}$$

will be true if and only if $\lambda_j = p_j^{e_j}$ for $1 \le j \le t$.

Assume therefore that $m = p^e$, where p is prime and e is a positive integer. The theorem is obviously true when $a = 1$, so we may take $a > 1$. The period can be of length m if and only if each possible integer $0 \le x < m$ occurs in the period, since no value occurs in the period more than once. Therefore the period is of length m if and only if the period of the sequence with $X_0 = 0$ is of length m, and we are justified in supposing that $X_0 = 0$. By formula 3.2.1–(6) we have

$$X_n = \left(\frac{a^n - 1}{a - 1} \right) c \bmod m. \tag{5}$$

If c is not relatively prime to m, this value X_n could never be equal to 1, so condition (i) of the theorem is necessary. The period has length m if and only if the smallest positive value of n for which $X_n = X_0 = 0$ is $n = m$. By (5) and condition (i), our theorem now reduces to proving the following fact:

Lemma R. *Assume that $1 < a < p^e$, where p is prime. If λ is the smallest positive integer for which $(a^\lambda - 1)/(a - 1) \equiv 0$ (modulo p^e), then*

$$\lambda = p^e \quad \text{if and only if} \quad \begin{cases} a \equiv 1 \ (\text{modulo } p) & \text{when } p > 2, \\ a \equiv 1 \ (\text{modulo } 4) & \text{when } p = 2. \end{cases}$$

Proof. Assume that $\lambda = p^e$. If $a \not\equiv 1$ (modulo p), then $(a^n - 1)/(a - 1) \equiv 0$ (modulo p^e) if and only if $a^n - 1 \equiv 0$ (modulo p^e). The condition $a^{p^e} - 1 \equiv 0$ (modulo p^e) then implies that $a^{p^e} \equiv 1$ (modulo p); but by Theorem 1.2.4F we have $a^{p^e} \equiv a$ (modulo p), hence $a \not\equiv 1$ (modulo p) leads to a contradiction. And if $p = 2$ and $a \equiv 3$ (modulo 4), we have

$$(a^{2^{e-1}} - 1)/(a - 1) \equiv 0 \ (\text{modulo } 2^e)$$

by exercise 8. These arguments show that it is necessary in general to have $a = 1 + qp^f$, where $p^f > 2$ and q is not a multiple of p, whenever $\lambda = p^e$.

It remains to be shown that this condition is *sufficient* to make $\lambda = p^e$. By repeated application of Lemma P, we find that

$$a^{p^g} \equiv 1 \ (\text{modulo } p^{f+g}), \qquad a^{p^g} \not\equiv 1 \ (\text{modulo } p^{f+g+1}),$$

for all $g \geq 0$, and therefore

$$\begin{aligned} (a^{p^g} - 1)/(a - 1) &\equiv 0 \ (\text{modulo } p^g), \\ (a^{p^g} - 1)/(a - 1) &\not\equiv 0 \ (\text{modulo } p^{g+1}). \end{aligned} \tag{6}$$

In particular, $(a^{p^e} - 1)/(a - 1) \equiv 0$ (modulo p^e). Now the congruential sequence $(0, a, 1, p^e)$ has $X_n = (a^n - 1)/(a - 1) \bmod p^e$; therefore it has a period of length λ, that is, $X_n = 0$ if and only if n is a multiple of λ. Hence p^e is a multiple of λ. This can happen only if $\lambda = p^g$ for some g, and the relations in (6) imply that $\lambda = p^e$, completing the proof. ∎

The proof of Theorem A is now complete. ∎

We will conclude this section by considering the special case of pure multiplicative generators, when $c = 0$. Although the random number generation process is slightly faster in this case, Theorem A shows us that the maximum period length cannot be achieved. In fact, this is quite obvious, since the sequence now satisfies the relation

$$X_{n+1} = aX_n \bmod m, \tag{7}$$

and the value $X_n = 0$ should never appear, lest the sequence degenerate to zero. In general, if d is any divisor of m and if X_n is a multiple of d, all succeeding elements $X_{n+1}, X_{n+2}, \ldots$ of the multiplicative sequence will be multiples of d. So when $c = 0$, we will want X_n to be relatively prime to m for all n, and this limits the length of the period to at most $\varphi(m)$, the number of integers between 0 and m that are relatively prime to m.

It may be possible to achieve an acceptably long period even if we stipulate that $c = 0$. Let us now try to find conditions on the multiplier so that the period is as long as possible in this special case.

According to Lemma Q, the period of the sequence depends entirely on the periods of the sequences when $m = p^e$, so let us consider that situation. We have $X_n = a^n X_0 \bmod p^e$, and it is clear that the period will be of length 1 if a is a multiple of p, so we take a to be relatively prime to p. Then the period is the smallest positive integer λ such that $X_0 = a^\lambda X_0 \bmod p^e$. If the greatest common divisor of X_0 and p^e is p^f, this condition is equivalent to

$$a^\lambda \equiv 1 \pmod{p^{e-f}}. \tag{8}$$

By Euler's theorem (exercise 1.2.4–28), $a^{\varphi(p^{e-f})} \equiv 1 \pmod{p^{e-f}}$; hence λ is a divisor of

$$\varphi(p^{e-f}) = p^{e-f-1}(p-1).$$

When a is relatively prime to m, the smallest positive integer λ for which $a^\lambda \equiv 1 \pmod{m}$ is conventionally called the *order* of a modulo m. Any such value of a that has the *maximum* possible order modulo m is called a *primitive element* modulo m.

Let $\lambda(m)$ denote the order of a primitive element, namely the maximum possible order, modulo m. The remarks above show that $\lambda(p^e)$ is a divisor of $p^{e-1}(p-1)$; with a little care (see exercises 11 through 16 below) we can give the precise value of $\lambda(m)$ in all cases as follows:

$$\lambda(2) = 1, \qquad \lambda(4) = 2, \qquad \lambda(2^e) = 2^{e-2} \quad \text{if} \quad e \geq 3;$$
$$\lambda(p^e) = p^{e-1}(p-1), \qquad \text{if} \quad p > 2; \tag{9}$$
$$\lambda(p_1^{e_1} \ldots p_t^{e_t}) = \text{lcm}\big(\lambda(p_1^{e_1}), \ldots, \lambda(p_t^{e_t})\big).$$

Our remarks may be summarized in the following theorem:

Theorem B. [C. F. Gauss, *Disquisitiones Arithmeticæ* (1801), §90–92.] *The maximum period possible when $c = 0$ is $\lambda(m)$, where $\lambda(m)$ is defined in* (9). *This period is achieved if*

i) X_0 *is relatively prime to* m;

ii) a *is a primitive element modulo* m. ∎

Notice that we can obtain a period of length $m - 1$ if m is prime; this is just one less than the maximum length, so for all practical purposes such a period is as long as we want.

The question now is, how can we find primitive elements modulo m? The exercises at the close of this section tell us that there is a fairly simple answer when m is prime or a power of a prime, namely the results stated in our next theorem.

Theorem C. *Let p be a prime number. The number a is a primitive element modulo p^e if and only if one of the following cases applies:*

i) $p = 2$, $e = 1$, *and a is odd;*

ii) $p = 2$, $e = 2$, and $a \bmod 4 = 3$;

iii) $p = 2$, $e = 3$, and $a \bmod 8 = 3$, 5, or 7;

iv) $p = 2$, $e \geq 4$, and $a \bmod 8 = 3$ or 5;

v) p is odd, $e = 1$, $a \not\equiv 0$ (modulo p), and $a^{(p-1)/q} \not\equiv 1$ (modulo p) for any prime divisor q of $p - 1$;

vi) p is odd, $e > 1$, a satisfies the conditions of (v), and $a^{p-1} \not\equiv 1$ (modulo p^2).

∎

Conditions (v) and (vi) of this theorem are readily tested on a computer for large values of p, by using the efficient methods for evaluating powers discussed in Section 4.6.3, if we know the factors of $p - 1$.

Theorem C applies to powers of primes only. But if we are given values a_j that are primitive modulo $p_j^{e_j}$, it is possible to find a single value a such that $a \equiv a_j$ (modulo $p_j^{e_j}$), for $1 \leq j \leq t$, using the Chinese remainder algorithm discussed in Section 4.3.2; this number a will be a primitive element modulo $p_1^{e_1} \ldots p_t^{e_t}$. Hence there is a reasonably efficient way to construct multipliers satisfying the condition of Theorem B, for any modulus m of moderate size, although the calculations can be somewhat lengthy in the general case.

In the common case $m = 2^e$, with $e \geq 4$, the conditions above simplify to the single requirement that $a \equiv 3$ or 5 (modulo 8). In this case, one-fourth of all possible multipliers will make the period length equal to $m/4$, and $m/4$ is the maximum possible when $c = 0$.

The second most common case is when $m = 10^e$. Using Lemmas P and Q, it is not difficult to obtain necessary and sufficient conditions for the achievement of the maximum period in the case of a decimal computer (see exercise 18):

Theorem D. *If $m = 10^e$, $e \geq 5$, $c = 0$, and X_0 is not a multiple of 2 or 5, the period of the linear congruential sequence is $5 \times 10^{e-2}$ if and only if $a \bmod 200$ equals one of the following 32 values:*

$$3, 11, 13, 19, 21, 27, 29, 37, 53, 59, 61, 67, 69, 77, 83, 91, 109, 117,$$
$$123, 131, 133, 139, 141, 147, 163, 171, 173, 179, 181, 187, 189, 197. \quad ∎ \quad (10)$$

EXERCISES

1. [*10*] What is the length of the period of the linear congruential sequence with $X_0 = 5772156648$, $a = 3141592621$, $c = 2718281829$, and $m = 10000000000$?

2. [*10*] Are the following two conditions sufficient to guarantee the maximum length period, when m is a power of 2? "(i) c is odd; (ii) $a \bmod 4 = 1$."

3. [*13*] Suppose that $m = 10^e$, where $e \geq 2$, and suppose further that c is odd and not a multiple of 5. Show that the linear congruential sequence will have the maximum length period if and only if $a \bmod 20 = 1$.

4. [*M20*] Assume that $m = 2^e$ and $X_0 = 0$. If the numbers a and c satisfy the conditions of Theorem A, what is the value of $X_{2^{e-1}}$?

5. [*14*] Find all multipliers a that satisfy the conditions of Theorem A when $m = 2^{35} + 1$. (The prime factors of m may be found in Table 3.2.1.1–1.)

▶ **6.** [*20*] Find all multipliers a that satisfy the conditions of Theorem A when $m = 10^6 - 1$. (See Table 3.2.1.1–1.)

▶ **7.** [*M23*] The period of a congruential sequence need not start with X_0, but we can always find indices $\mu \geq 0$ and $\lambda > 0$ such that $X_{n+\lambda} = X_n$ whenever $n \geq \mu$, and for which μ and λ are the smallest possible values with this property. (See exercises 3.1–6 and 3.2.1–1.) If μ_j and λ_j are the indices corresponding to the sequences

$$(X_0 \bmod p_j^{e_j},\ a \bmod p_j^{e_j},\ c \bmod p_j^{e_j},\ p_j^{e_j}),$$

and if μ and λ correspond to the composite sequence $(X_0, a, c, p_1^{e_1} \dots p_t^{e_t})$, Lemma Q states that λ is the least common multiple of $\lambda_1, \dots, \lambda_t$. What is the value of μ in terms of the values of $\mu_1, \dots, \mu_t$? What is the maximum possible value of μ obtainable by varying X_0, a, and c, when $m = p_1^{e_1} \dots p_t^{e_t}$ is fixed?

8. [*M20*] Show that if $a \bmod 4 = 3$, we have $(a^{2^{e-1}} - 1)/(a - 1) \equiv 0 \pmod{2^e}$ when $e > 1$. (Use Lemma P.)

▶ **9.** [*M22*] (W. E. Thomson.) When $c = 0$ and $m = 2^e \geq 16$, Theorems B and C say that the period has length 2^{e-2} if and only if the multiplier a satisfies $a \bmod 8 = 3$ or $a \bmod 8 = 5$. Show that every such sequence is essentially a linear congruential sequence with $m = 2^{e-2}$, having *full* period, in the following sense:

a) If $X_{n+1} = (4c + 1)X_n \bmod 2^e$, and $X_n = 4Y_n + 1$, then

$$Y_{n+1} = \big((4c + 1)Y_n + c\big) \bmod 2^{e-2}.$$

b) If $X_{n+1} = (4c - 1)X_n \bmod 2^e$, and $X_n = \big((-1)^n(4Y_n + 1)\big) \bmod 2^e$, then

$$Y_{n+1} = \big((1 - 4c)Y_n - c\big) \bmod 2^{e-2}.$$

[*Note:* In these formulas, c is an odd integer. The literature contains several statements to the effect that sequences with $c = 0$ satisfying Theorem B are somehow more random than sequences satisfying Theorem A, in spite of the fact that the period is only one-fourth as long in the case of Theorem B. This exercise refutes such statements; in essence, we must give up two bits of the word length in order to save the addition of c, when m is a power of 2.]

10. [*M21*] For what values of m is $\lambda(m) = \varphi(m)$?

▶ **11.** [*M28*] Let x be an odd integer greater than 1. (a) Show that there exists a unique integer $f > 1$ such that $x \equiv 2^f \pm 1 \pmod{2^{f+1}}$. (b) Given that $1 < x < 2^e - 1$ and that f is the corresponding integer from part (a), show that the order of x modulo 2^e is 2^{e-f}. (c) In particular, this proves parts (i)–(iv) of Theorem C.

12. [*M26*] Let p be an odd prime. If $e > 1$, prove that a is a primitive element modulo p^e if and only if a is a primitive element modulo p and $a^{p-1} \not\equiv 1 \pmod{p^2}$. (For the purposes of this exercise, assume that $\lambda(p^e) = p^{e-1}(p-1)$. This fact is proved in exercises 14 and 16 below.)

13. [*M22*] Let p be prime. Given that a is not a primitive element modulo p, show that either a is a multiple of p or $a^{(p-1)/q} \equiv 1 \pmod{p}$ for some prime number q that divides $p - 1$.

14. [*M18*] If $e > 1$ and p is an odd prime, and if a is a primitive element modulo p, prove that either a or $a + p$ is a primitive element modulo p^e. [*Hint:* See exercise 12.]

15. [*M29*] (a) Let a_1 and a_2 be relatively prime to m, and let their orders modulo m be λ_1 and λ_2, respectively. If λ is the least common multiple of λ_1 and λ_2, prove that $a_1^{\kappa_1} a_2^{\kappa_2}$ has order λ modulo m, for suitable integers κ_1 and κ_2. [*Hint:* Consider first the case that λ_1 is relatively prime to λ_2.] (b) Let $\lambda(m)$ be the maximum order of any element modulo m. Prove that $\lambda(m)$ is a multiple of the order of each element modulo m; that is, prove that $a^{\lambda(m)} \equiv 1$ (modulo m) whenever a is relatively prime to m. (Do not use Theorem B.)

▶ **16.** [*M24*] (*Existence of primitive roots.*) Let p be a prime number.

a) Consider the polynomial $f(x) = x^n + c_1 x^{n-1} + \cdots + c_n$, where the c's are integers. Given that a is an integer for which $f(a) \equiv 0$ (modulo p), show that there exists a polynomial
$$q(x) = x^{n-1} + q_1 x^{n-2} + \cdots + q_{n-1}$$
with integer coefficients such that $f(x) \equiv (x-a)q(x)$ (modulo p) for all integers x.

b) Let $f(x)$ be a polynomial as in (a). Show that $f(x)$ has at most n distinct "roots" modulo p; that is, there are at most n integers a, with $0 \leq a < p$, such that $f(a) \equiv 0$ (modulo p).

c) Because of exercise 15(b), the polynomial $f(x) = x^{\lambda(p)} - 1$ has $p-1$ distinct roots; hence there is an integer a with order $p - 1$.

17. [*M26*] Not all of the values listed in Theorem D would be found by the text's construction; for example, 11 is not primitive modulo 5^e. How can this be possible, when 11 *is* primitive modulo 10^e, according to Theorem D? Which of the values listed in Theorem D are primitive elements modulo *both* 2^e and 5^e?

18. [*M25*] Prove Theorem D. (See the previous exercise.)

19. [*40*] Make a table of some suitable multipliers, a, for each of the values of m listed in Table 3.2.1.1–1, assuming that $c = 0$.

▶ **20.** [*M24*] (G. Marsaglia.) The purpose of this exercise is to study the period length of an *arbitrary* linear congruential sequence. Let $Y_n = 1 + a + \cdots + a^{n-1}$, so that $X_n = (AY_n + X_0) \bmod m$ for some constant A by Eq. 3.2.1–(8).

a) Prove that the period length of $\langle X_n \rangle$ is the period length of $\langle Y_n \bmod m' \rangle$, where $m' = m/\gcd(A, m)$.

b) Prove that the period length of $\langle Y_n \bmod p^e \rangle$ satisfies the following when p is prime: (i) If $a \bmod p = 0$, it is 1. (ii) If $a \bmod p = 1$, it is p^e, except when $p = 2$ and $e \geq 2$ and $a \bmod 4 = 3$. (iii) If $p = 2$, $e \geq 2$, and $a \bmod 4 = 3$, it is twice the order of a modulo p^e (see exercise 11), unless $a \equiv -1$ (modulo 2^e) when it is 2. (iv) If $a \bmod p > 1$, it is the order of a modulo p^e.

21. [*M25*] In a linear congruential sequence of maximum period, let $X_0 = 0$ and let s be the least positive integer such that $a^s \equiv 1$ (modulo m). Prove that $\gcd(X_s, m) = s$.

▶ **22.** [*M25*] Discuss the problem of finding moduli $m = b^k \pm b^l \pm 1$ so that the subtract-with-borrow and add-with-carry generators of exercise 3.2.1.1–14 will have very long periods.

3.2.1.3. Potency. In the preceding section, we showed that the maximum period can be obtained when $b = a - 1$ is a multiple of each prime dividing m; and b must also be a multiple of 4 if m is a multiple of 4. If z is the radix of the machine being used — so that $z = 2$ for a binary computer, and $z = 10$ for a decimal computer — and if m is the word size z^e, the multiplier

$$a = z^k + 1, \qquad 2 \le k < e \tag{1}$$

satisfies these conditions. Theorem 3.2.1.2A also says that we may take $c = 1$. The recurrence relation now has the form

$$X_{n+1} = \big((z^k + 1)X_n + 1\big) \bmod z^e, \tag{2}$$

and this equation suggests that we can avoid the multiplication; merely shifting and adding will suffice.

For example, suppose we choose $a = B^2 + 1$, where B is the byte size of MIX. The code

$$\text{LDA X;   SLA 2;   ADD X;   INCA 1} \tag{3}$$

can be used in place of the instructions given in Section 3.2.1.1, and the execution time decreases from $16u$ to $7u$.

For this reason, multipliers having form (1) have been widely discussed in the literature, and indeed they have been recommended by many authors. However, the early years of experimentation with this method showed conclusively that *multipliers having the simple form in* (1) *should be avoided.* The generated numbers just aren't random enough.

Later in this chapter we shall be discussing some rather sophisticated theory that accounts for the badness of all the linear congruential random number generators known to be bad. However, some generators $\big($such as (2)$\big)$ are sufficiently awful that a comparatively simple theory can be used to rule them out. This simple theory is related to the concept of "potency," which we shall now discuss.

The *potency* of a linear congruential sequence with maximum period is defined to be the least positive integer s such that

$$b^s \equiv 0 \pmod{m}. \tag{4}$$

(Such an integer s will always exist when the multiplier satisfies the conditions of Theorem 3.2.1.2A, since b is a multiple of every prime dividing m.)

We may analyze the randomness of the sequence by taking $X_0 = 0$, since 0 occurs somewhere in the period. With this assumption, Eq. 3.2.1–(6) reduces to

$$X_n = \big((a^n - 1)c/b\big) \bmod m;$$

and if we expand $a^n - 1 = (b + 1)^n - 1$ by the binomial theorem, we find that

$$X_n = c \left(n + \binom{n}{2} b + \cdots + \binom{n}{s} b^{s-1}\right) \bmod m. \tag{5}$$

All terms in b^s, b^{s+1}, etc., may be ignored, since they are multiples of m.

Equation (5) can be instructive, so we shall consider some special cases. If $a = 1$, the potency is 1; and $X_n \equiv cn \pmod{m}$, as we have already observed, so the sequence is surely not random. If the potency is 2, we have $X_n \equiv cn + cb\binom{n}{2}$, and again the sequence is not very random; indeed,

$$X_{n+1} - X_n \equiv c + cbn$$

in this case, so the differences between consecutively generated numbers change in a simple way from one value of n to the next. The point (X_n, X_{n+1}, X_{n+2}) always lies on one of the four planes

$$x - 2y + z = d + m, \qquad\qquad x - 2y + z = d - m,$$
$$x - 2y + z = d, \qquad\qquad x - 2y + z = d - 2m,$$

in three-dimensional space, where $d = cb \bmod m$.

If the potency is 3, the sequence begins to look somewhat more random, but there is a high degree of dependency between X_n, X_{n+1}, and X_{n+2}; tests show that sequences with potency 3 are still not sufficiently good. Reasonable results have been reported when the potency is 4 or more, but they have been disputed by other people. A potency of at least 5 would seem to be required for sufficiently random values.

Suppose, for example, that $m = 2^{35}$ and $a = 2^k + 1$. Then $b = 2^k$, so we find that the value $b^2 = 2^{2k}$ is a multiple of m when $k \geq 18$: The potency is 2. If $k = 17, 16, \ldots, 12$, the potency is 3, and a potency of 4 is achieved for $k = 11, 10, 9$. The only acceptable multipliers, from the standpoint of potency, therefore have $k \leq 8$. This means $a \leq 257$, and we shall see later that *small* multipliers are also to be avoided. We have now eliminated all multipliers of the form $2^k + 1$ when $m = 2^{35}$.

When m is equal to $w \pm 1$, where w is the word size, m is generally not divisible by high powers of primes, and a high potency is impossible (see exercise 6). So in this case, the maximum-period method should *not* be used; the pure-multiplication method with $c = 0$ should be applied instead.

It must be emphasized that high potency is necessary but not sufficient for randomness; we use the concept of potency only to reject impotent generators, not to accept the potent ones. Linear congruential sequences should pass the "spectral test" discussed in Section 3.3.4 before they are considered to be acceptably random.

EXERCISES

1. [*M10*] Show that, no matter what the byte size B of MIX happens to be, the code (3) yields a random number generator of maximum period.

2. [*10*] What is the potency of the generator represented by the MIX code (3)?

3. [*11*] When $m = 2^{35}$, what is the potency of the linear congruential sequence with $a = 3141592621$? What is the potency if the multiplier is $a = 2^{23} + 2^{13} + 2^2 + 1$?

4. [*15*] Show that if $m = 2^e \geq 8$, maximum potency is achieved when $a \bmod 8 = 5$.

5. [*M20*] Given that $m = p_1^{e_1} \ldots p_t^{e_t}$ and $a = 1 + kp_1^{f_1} \ldots p_t^{f_t}$, where a satisfies the conditions of Theorem 3.2.1.2A and k is relatively prime to m, show that the potency is $\max(\lceil e_1/f_1 \rceil, \ldots, \lceil e_t/f_t \rceil)$.

▶ **6.** [*20*] Which of the values of $m = w \pm 1$ in Table 3.2.1.1–1 can be used in a linear congruential sequence of maximum period whose potency is 4 or more? (Use the result of exercise 5.)

7. [*M20*] When a satisfies the conditions of Theorem 3.2.1.2A, it is relatively prime to m; hence there is a number a' such that $aa' \equiv 1$ (modulo m). Show that a' can be expressed simply in terms of b.

▶ **8.** [*M26*] A random number generator defined by $X_{n+1} = (2^{17} + 3)X_n \bmod 2^{35}$ and $X_0 = 1$ was subjected to the following test: Let $Y_n = \lfloor 20X_n/2^{35} \rfloor$; then Y_n should be a random integer between 0 and 19, and the triples $(Y_{3n}, Y_{3n+1}, Y_{3n+2})$ should take on each of the 8000 possible values from $(0,0,0)$ to $(19,19,19)$ with nearly equal frequency. But with 1,000,000 values of n tested, many triples never occurred, and others occurred much more often than they should have. Can you account for this failure?

3.2.2. Other Methods

Of course, linear congruential sequences are not the only sources of random numbers that have been proposed for computer use. In this section we shall review the most significant alternatives. Some of these methods are quite important, while others are interesting chiefly because they are not as good as a person might expect.

One of the common fallacies encountered in connection with random number generation is the idea that we can take a good generator and modify it a little, in order to get an "even more random" sequence. This is often false. For example, we know that

$$X_{n+1} = (aX_n + c) \bmod m \tag{1}$$

leads to reasonably good random numbers; wouldn't the sequence produced by

$$X_{n+1} = \big((aX_n) \bmod (m+1) + c\big) \bmod m \tag{2}$$

be even *more* random? The answer is, the new sequence is probably a great deal *less* random. For the whole theory breaks down, and in the absence of any theory about the behavior of the sequence (2), we come into the area of generators of the type $X_{n+1} = f(X_n)$ with the function f chosen at random; exercises 3.1–11 through 3.1–15 show that these sequences probably behave much more poorly than the sequences obtained from the more disciplined function (1).

Let us consider another approach, in an attempt to obtain a genuine improvement of sequence (1). The linear congruential method can be generalized to, say, a quadratic congruential method:

$$X_{n+1} = (dX_n^2 + aX_n + c) \bmod m. \tag{3}$$

Exercise 8 generalizes Theorem 3.2.1.2A to obtain necessary and sufficient conditions on a, c, and d such that the sequence defined by (3) has a period of the maximum length m; the restrictions are not much more severe than in the linear method.

An interesting quadratic method has been proposed by R. R. Coveyou when m is a power of two: Let

$$X_0 \bmod 4 = 2, \qquad X_{n+1} = X_n(X_n + 1) \bmod 2^e, \qquad n \geq 0. \tag{4}$$

This sequence can be computed with about the same efficiency as (1), without any worries of overflow. It has an interesting connection with von Neumann's original middle-square method: If we let Y_n be $2^e X_n$, so that Y_n is a double-precision number obtained by placing e zeros to the right of the binary representation of X_n, then Y_{n+1} consists of precisely the middle $2e$ digits of $Y_n^2 + 2^e Y_n$! In other words, Coveyou's method is almost identical to a somewhat degenerate double-precision middle-square method, yet it is guaranteed to have a long period; further evidence of its randomness is proved in Coveyou's paper cited in the answer to exercise 8.

Other generalizations of Eq. (1) also suggest themselves; for example, we might try to extend the period length of the sequence. The period of a linear congruential sequence is fairly long; when m is approximately the word size of the computer, we usually get periods on the order of 10^9 or more, and typical calculations will use only a very small portion of the sequence. On the other hand, when we discuss the idea of "accuracy" in Section 3.3.4 we will see that the period length influences the degree of randomness achievable in a sequence. Therefore it can be desirable to seek a longer period, and several methods are available for this purpose. One technique is to make X_{n+1} depend on both X_n and X_{n-1}, instead of just on X_n; then the period length can be as high as m^2, since the sequence will not begin to repeat until we have $(X_{n+\lambda}, X_{n+\lambda+1}) = (X_n, X_{n+1})$. John Mauchly, in an unpublished paper presented to a statistics conference in 1949, extended the middle square method by using the recurrence $X_n = \text{middle}(X_{n-1} \cdot X_{n-6})$.

The simplest sequence in which X_{n+1} depends on more than one of the preceding values is the Fibonacci sequence,

$$X_{n+1} = (X_n + X_{n-1}) \bmod m. \tag{5}$$

This generator was considered in the early 1950s, and it usually gives a period length greater than m. But tests have shown that the numbers produced by the Fibonacci recurrence are definitely *not* satisfactorily random, and so our main interest in (5) as a source of random numbers is that it makes a nice "bad example." We may also consider generators of the form

$$X_{n+1} = (X_n + X_{n-k}) \bmod m, \tag{6}$$

when k is a comparatively large value. This recurrence was introduced by Green, Smith, and Klem [*JACM* **6** (1959), 527–537], who reported that, when $k \le 15$, the sequence fails to pass the "gap test" described in Section 3.3.2, although when $k = 16$ the test was satisfactory.

A much better type of additive generator was devised in 1958 by G. J. Mitchell and D. P. Moore [unpublished], who suggested the somewhat unusual sequence defined by

$$X_n = (X_{n-24} + X_{n-55}) \bmod m, \qquad n \ge 55, \tag{7}$$

where m is even, and where $X_0, \ldots, X_{54}$ are arbitrary integers not all even. The constants 24 and 55 in this definition were not chosen at random; they are special values that happen to define a sequence whose least significant bits, $\langle X_n \bmod 2 \rangle$, will have a period of length $2^{55} - 1$. Therefore the sequence $\langle X_n \rangle$ must have a period at least this long. Exercise 30 proves that (7) has a period of length exactly $2^{e-1}(2^{55} - 1)$ when $m = 2^e$.

At first glance Eq. (7) may not seem to be extremely well suited to machine implementation, but in fact there is a very efficient way to generate the sequence using a cyclic list:

Algorithm A (*Additive number generator*). Memory cells $Y[1], Y[2], \ldots, Y[55]$ are initially set to the values $X_{54}, X_{53}, \ldots, X_0$, respectively; j is initially equal to 24 and k is 55. Successive performances of this algorithm will produce the numbers $X_{55}, X_{56}, \ldots$ as output.

A1. [Add.] (If we are about to output X_n at this point, $Y[j]$ now equals X_{n-24} and $Y[k]$ equals X_{n-55}.) Set $Y[k] \leftarrow (Y[k] + Y[j]) \bmod 2^e$, and output $Y[k]$.

A2. [Advance.] Decrease j and k by 1. If now $j = 0$, set $j \leftarrow 55$; otherwise if $k = 0$, set $k \leftarrow 55$. (We cannot have both $j = 0$ and $k = 0$.) ∎

This algorithm in MIX is simply the following:

Program A (*Additive number generator*). Assuming that index registers 5 and 6, representing j and k, are not touched by the remainder of the program in which this routine is embedded, the following code performs Algorithm A and leaves the result in register A.

```
LDA   Y,6    A1. Add.
ADD   Y,5    Y_k + Y_j (overflow possible)
STA   Y,6       → Y_k.
DEC5  1      A2. Advance. j ← j - 1.
DEC6  1      k ← k - 1.
J5P   *+2
ENT5  55     If j = 0, set j ← 55.
J6P   *+2
ENT6  55     If k = 0, set k ← 55.   ∎
```

This generator is usually faster than the other methods we have been discussing, since it does not require any multiplication. Besides its speed, it has the longest period we have seen yet, except in exercise 3.2.1.2–22. Furthermore, as Richard Brent has observed, it can be made to work correctly with floating point numbers, avoiding the need to convert between integers and fractions (see exercise 23). Therefore it may well prove to be the very *best* source of random numbers for practical purposes. The main reason why it is difficult to recommend sequences like (7) wholeheartedly is that there is still very little theory to prove that they do or do not have desirable randomness properties; essentially all we know for sure is that the period is very long, and this is not enough. John Reiser [Ph.D. thesis (Stanford University, 1977)] has shown, however, that an additive sequence like (7) will be well distributed in high dimensions, provided that a certain plausible conjecture is true (see exercise 26).

The numbers 24 and 55 in (7) are commonly called *lags*, and the numbers X_n defined by (7) are said to form a *lagged Fibonacci sequence*. Lags like $(24, 55)$ work well because of theoretical results developed in some of the exercises

Table 1

LAGS THAT YIELD LONG PERIODS MOD 2

$(24, 55)$	$(37, 100)$	$(83, 258)$	$(273, 607)$	$(576, 3217)$	$(7083, 19937)$
$(38, 89)$	$(30, 127)$	$(107, 378)$	$(1029, 2281)$	$(4187, 9689)$	$(9739, 23209)$

For extensions of this table, see N. Zierler and J. Brillhart, *Information and Control* **13** (1968), 541–554, **14** (1969), 566–569, **15** (1969), 67–69; Y. Kurita and M. Matsumoto, *Math. Comp.* **56** (1991), 817–821; Heringa, Blöte, and Compagner, *Int. J. Mod. Phys.* **C3** (1992), 561–564.

below. It is of course better to use somewhat larger lags when an application happens to use, say, groups of 55 values at a time; the numbers generated by (7) will never have X_n lying strictly between X_{n-24} and X_{n-55} (see exercise 2). J.-M. Normand, H. J. Herrmann, and M. Hajjar detected slight biases in the numbers generated by (7) when they did extensive high-precision Monte Carlo studies requiring 10^{11} random numbers [*J. Statistical Physics* **52** (1988), 441–446]; but larger values of k decreased the bad effects. Table 1 lists several useful pairs (l, k) for which the sequence $X_n = (X_{n-l} + X_{n-k}) \bmod 2^e$ has period length $2^{e-1}(2^k - 1)$. The case $(l, k) = (30, 127)$ should be large enough for most applications, especially in combination with other randomness-enhancing techniques that we will discuss later.

George Marsaglia [*Comp. Sci. and Statistics: Symposium on the Interface* **16** (1984), 3–10] has suggested replacing (7) by

$$X_n = (X_{n-24} \cdot X_{n-55}) \bmod m, \qquad n \geq 55, \tag{7'}$$

where m is a multiple of 4 and where X_0 through X_{54} are odd, not all congruent to 1 (modulo 4). Then the second-least significant bits have a period of $2^{55} - 1$, while the most significant bits are more thoroughly mixed than before since they depend on all bits of X_{n-24} and X_{n-55} in an essential way. Exercise 31 shows that the period length of sequence (7') is only slightly less than that of (7).

Lagged Fibonacci generators have been used successfully in many situations since 1958, so it came as a shock to discover in the 1990s that they actually fail an extremely simple, non-contrived test for randomness (see exercise 3.3.2–31). A workaround that avoids such problems by discarding appropriate elements of the sequence is described near the end of this section.

Instead of considering purely additive or purely multiplicative sequences, we can construct useful random number generators by taking general linear combinations of $X_{n-1}, \ldots, X_{n-k}$ for small k. In this case the best results occur when the modulus m is a large *prime*; for example, m can be chosen to be the largest prime number that fits in a single computer word (see Table 4.5.4–2). When $m = p$ is prime, the theory of finite fields tells us that it is possible to find multipliers $a_1, \ldots, a_k$ such that the sequence defined by

$$X_n = (a_1 X_{n-1} + \cdots + a_k X_{n-k}) \bmod p \tag{8}$$

has period length $p^k - 1$; here $X_0, \ldots, X_{k-1}$ may be chosen arbitrarily but not all zero. (The special case $k = 1$ corresponds to a multiplicative congruential sequence with prime modulus, with which we are already familiar.) The constants

$a_1, \ldots, a_k$ in (8) have the desired property if and only if the polynomial

$$f(x) = x^k - a_1 x^{k-1} - \cdots - a_k \tag{9}$$

is a "primitive polynomial modulo p," that is, if and only if this polynomial has a root that is a primitive element of the field with p^k elements (see exercise 4.6.2–16).

Of course, the mere fact that suitable constants $a_1, \ldots, a_k$ *exist* giving a period of length $p^k - 1$ is not enough for practical purposes; we must be able to *find* them, and we can't simply try all p^k possibilities, since p is on the order of the computer's word size. Fortunately there are exactly $\varphi(p^k - 1)/k$ suitable choices of $(a_1, \ldots, a_k)$, so there is a fairly good chance of hitting one after making a few random tries. But we also need a way to tell quickly whether or not (9) is a primitive polynomial modulo p; it is certainly unthinkable to generate up to $p^k - 1$ elements of the sequence and wait for a repetition! Methods of testing for primitivity modulo p are discussed by Alanen and Knuth in *Sankhyā* **A26** (1964), 305–328. The following criteria can be used: Let $r = (p^k - 1)/(p - 1)$.

i) $(-1)^{k-1} a_k$ must be a primitive root modulo p. (See Section 3.2.1.2.)

ii) The polynomial x^r must be congruent to $(-1)^{k-1} a_k$, modulo $f(x)$ and p.

iii) The degree of $x^{r/q} \bmod f(x)$, using polynomial arithmetic modulo p, must be positive, for each prime divisor q of r.

Efficient ways to compute the polynomial $x^n \bmod f(x)$, using polynomial arithmetic modulo a given prime p, are discussed in Section 4.6.2.

In order to carry out this test, we need to know the prime factorization of $r = (p^k - 1)/(p - 1)$, and this is the limiting factor in the calculation; r can be factored in a reasonable amount of time when $k = 2, 3$, and perhaps 4, but higher values of k are difficult to handle when p is large. Even $k = 2$ essentially doubles the number of "significant random digits" over what is achievable with $k = 1$, so larger values of k will rarely be necessary.

An adaptation of the spectral test (Section 3.3.4) can be used to rate the sequence of numbers generated by (8); see exercise 3.3.4–24. The considerations of that section show that we should *not* make the obvious choice of $a_1 = +1$ or -1 when a primitive polynomial of that form exists; it is better to pick large, essentially "random" values of $a_1, \ldots, a_k$ that satisfy the conditions, and to verify the choice by applying the spectral test. A significant amount of computation is involved in finding $a_1, \ldots, a_k$, but all known evidence indicates that the result will be a very satisfactory source of random numbers. We essentially achieve the randomness of a linear congruential generator with k-tuple precision, using only single precision operations.

The special case $p = 2$ is of independent interest. Sometimes a random number generator is desired that merely produces a random sequence of *bits* — zeros and ones — instead of fractions between zero and one. There is a simple way to generate a highly random bit sequence on a binary computer, manipulating k-bit words: Start with an arbitrary nonzero binary word X. To get the next random bit of the sequence, do the following operations, shown in MIX's language (see exercise 16):

```
LDA   X     (Assume that overflow is now "off.")
ADD   X     Shift left one bit.
JNOV  *+2   Jump if the high bit was originally zero.          (10)
XOR   A     Otherwise adjust the number with "exclusive or."
STA   X     ▌
```

The fourth instruction here is the "exclusive or" operation found on nearly all binary computers (see exercise 2.5–28 and Section 7.1.3); it changes each bit position of rA in which location A has a "1" bit. The value in location A is the binary constant $(a_1 \ldots a_k)_2$, where $x^k - a_1 x^{k-1} - \cdots - a_k$ is a primitive polynomial modulo 2 as above. After the code (10) has been executed, the next bit of the generated sequence may be taken as the least significant bit of word X. Alternatively, we could consistently use the most significant bit of X, if the most significant bit is more convenient.

```
1011
0101
1010
0111
1110
1111
1101
1001
0001
0010
0100
1000
0011
0110
1100
1011
```

Fig. 1. Successive contents of the computer word X in the binary method, assuming that $k = 4$ and CONTENTS(A) $= (0011)_2$.

For example, consider Fig. 1, which illustrates the sequence generated for $k = 4$ and CONTENTS(A) $= (0011)_2$. This is, of course, an unusually small value for k. The right-hand column shows the sequence of bits of the sequence, namely 1101011110001001..., repeating in a period of length $2^k - 1 = 15$. This sequence is quite random, considering that it was generated with only four bits of memory; to see this, consider the adjacent sets of four bits occurring in the period, namely 1101, 1010, 0101, 1011, 0111, 1111, 1110, 1100, 1000, 0001, 0010, 0100, 1001, 0011, 0110. In general, every possible adjacent set of k bits occurs exactly once in the period, except the set of all zeros, since the period length is $2^k - 1$; thus, adjacent sets of k bits are essentially independent. We shall see in Section 3.5 that this is a very strong criterion for randomness when k is, say, 30 or more. Theoretical results illustrating the randomness of this sequence are given in an article by R. C. Tausworthe, *Math. Comp.* **19** (1965), 201–209.

Primitive polynomials modulo 2 of degree ≤ 168 have been tabulated by W. Stahnke, *Math. Comp.* **27** (1973), 977–980. When $k = 35$, we may take

$$\text{CONTENTS(A)} = (00000000000000000000000000000000101)_2,$$

but the considerations of exercises 18 and 3.3.4–24 imply that it would be better to find "random" constants that define primitive polynomials modulo 2.

Caution: Several people have been trapped into believing that this random bit-generation technique can be used to generate random whole-word fractions $(.X_0X_1 \ldots X_{k-1})_2$, $(.X_kX_{k+1} \ldots X_{2k-1})_2$, $\ldots$; but it is actually a poor source of random fractions, even though the bits are individually quite random. Exercise 18 explains why.

Mitchell and Moore's additive generator (7) is essentially based on the concept of primitive polynomials: The polynomial $x^{55} + x^{24} + 1$ is primitive, and Table 1 is essentially a listing of certain primitive trinomials modulo 2. A generator almost identical to that of Mitchell and Moore was independently discovered in 1971 by T. G. Lewis and W. H. Payne [*JACM* **20** (1973), 456–468], but using "exclusive or" instead of addition; this makes the period length exactly $2^{55} - 1$. Each bit position in the sequence of Lewis and Payne runs through the same periodic sequence, but has its own starting point. Experience has shown that (7) gives better results.

We have now seen that sequences with $0 \le X_n < m$ and period $m^k - 1$ can be constructed without great difficulty, when X_n is a suitable function of $X_{n-1}, \ldots, X_{n-k}$ and when m is prime. The highest conceivable period for *any* sequence defined by a relation of the form

$$X_n = f(X_{n-1}, \ldots, X_{n-k}), \qquad 0 \le X_n < m, \tag{11}$$

is easily seen to be m^k. M. H. Martin [*Bull. Amer. Math. Soc.* **40** (1934), 859–864] was the first person to show that functions achieving this maximum period are possible for all m and k. His method is easy to state (exercise 17) and reasonably efficient to program (exercise 29), but it is unsuitable for random number generation because it changes the value of $X_{n-1} + \cdots + X_{n-k}$ very slowly: All k-tuples occur, but not in a very random order. A better class of functions f that yield the maximum period m^k is considered in exercise 21. The corresponding programs are, in general, not as efficient for random number generation as other methods we have described, but they do give demonstrable randomness when the period as a whole is considered.

Many other schemes have been proposed for random number generation. The most interesting of these alternative methods may well be the *inversive congruential sequences* suggested by Eichenauer and Lehn [*Statistische Hefte* **27** (1986), 315–326]:

$$X_{n+1} = (aX_n^{-1} + c) \bmod p. \tag{12}$$

Here p is prime, X_n ranges over the set $\{0, 1, \ldots, p - 1, \infty\}$, and inverses are defined by $0^{-1} = \infty$, $\infty^{-1} = 0$, otherwise $X^{-1}X \equiv 1$ (modulo p). Since 0 is always followed by ∞ and then by c in this sequence, we could simply define $0^{-1} = 0$ for purposes of implementation; but the theory is cleaner and easier to develop when $0^{-1} = \infty$. Efficient algorithms suitable for hardware implementation are available for computing X^{-1} modulo p; see, for example, exercise 4.5.2–39. Unfortunately, however, this operation is not in the repertoire of most computers. Exercise 35 shows that many choices of a and c yield the maximum period length $p + 1$. Exercise 37 demonstrates the most important property: Inversive congruential sequences are completely free of the lattice structure that is characteristic of linear congruential sequences.

Another important class of techniques deals with the *combination* of random number generators. There will always be people who feel that the linear congruential methods, additive methods, etc., are all too simple to give sufficiently random sequences; and it may never be possible to *prove* that their skepticism is unjustified — indeed, they may be right — so it is pretty useless to argue the point. There are reasonably efficient ways to combine two sequences into a third one that should be haphazard enough to satisfy all but the most hardened skeptic.

Suppose we have two sequences $X_0, X_1, \ldots$ and $Y_0, Y_1, \ldots$ of random numbers between 0 and $m - 1$, preferably generated by two unrelated methods. Then we can, for example, use one random sequence to permute the elements of another, as suggested by M. D. MacLaren and G. Marsaglia [*JACM* **12** (1965), 83–89; see also Marsaglia and Bray, *CACM* **11** (1968), 757–759]:

Algorithm M (*Randomizing by shuffling*). Given methods for generating two sequences $\langle X_n \rangle$ and $\langle Y_n \rangle$, this algorithm will successively output the terms of a "considerably more random" sequence. We use an auxiliary table $V[0]$, $V[1]$, $\ldots$, $V[k-1]$, where k is some number chosen for convenience, usually in the neighborhood of 100. Initially, the V-table is filled with the first k values of the X-sequence.

M1. [Generate X, Y.] Set X and Y equal to the next members of the sequences $\langle X_n \rangle$ and $\langle Y_n \rangle$, respectively.

M2. [Extract j.] Set $j \leftarrow \lfloor kY/m \rfloor$, where m is the modulus used in the sequence $\langle Y_n \rangle$; that is, j is a random value, $0 \le j < k$, determined by Y.

M3. [Exchange.] Output $V[j]$ and then set $V[j] \leftarrow X$. ∎

As an example, assume that Algorithm M is applied to the following two sequences, with $k = 64$:

$$X_0 = 5772156649, \qquad X_{n+1} = (3141592653 X_n + 2718281829) \bmod 2^{35};$$
$$Y_0 = 1781072418, \qquad Y_{n+1} = (2718281829 Y_n + 3141592653) \bmod 2^{35}. \tag{13}$$

On intuitive grounds it appears safe to predict that the sequence obtained by applying Algorithm M to (13) will satisfy virtually *anyone's* requirements for randomness in a computer-generated sequence, because the relationship between nearby terms of the output has been almost entirely obliterated. Furthermore, the time required to generate this sequence is only slightly more than twice as long as it takes to generate the sequence $\langle X_n \rangle$ alone.

Exercise 15 proves that the period length of Algorithm M's output will be the least common multiple of the period lengths of $\langle X_n \rangle$ and $\langle Y_n \rangle$, in most situations of practical interest. In particular, if we reject the value 0 when it occurs in the Y-sequence, so that $\langle Y_n \rangle$ has period length $2^{35} - 1$, the numbers generated by Algorithm M from (13) will have a period of length $2^{70} - 2^{35}$. [See J. Arthur Greenwood, *Computer Science and Statistics: Symposium on the Interface* **9** (1976), 222–227.]

However, there is an even better way to shuffle the elements of a sequence, discovered by Carter Bays and S. D. Durham [*ACM Trans. Math. Software* **2** (1976), 59–64]. Their approach, although it appears to be superficially similar to Algorithm M, can give surprisingly better performance even though it requires only one input sequence $\langle X_n \rangle$ instead of two:

Algorithm B (*Randomizing by shuffling*). Given a method for generating a sequence $\langle X_n \rangle$, this algorithm will successively output the terms of a "considerably more random" sequence, using an auxiliary table $V[0], V[1], \ldots, V[k-1]$ as in Algorithm M. Initially the V-table is filled with the first k values of the X-sequence, and an auxiliary variable Y is set equal to the $(k+1)$st value.

B1. [Extract j.] Set $j \leftarrow \lfloor kY/m \rfloor$, where m is the modulus used in the sequence $\langle X_n \rangle$; that is, j is a random value, $0 \le j < k$, determined by Y.

B2. [Exchange.] Set $Y \leftarrow V[j]$, output Y, and then set $V[j]$ to the next member of the sequence $\langle X_n \rangle$. ∎

The reader is urged to work exercises 3 and 5, in order to get a feeling for the difference between Algorithms M and B.

On MIX we may implement Algorithm B by taking k equal to the byte size, obtaining the following simple generation scheme once the initialization has been done:

LD6	Y(1:1)	$j \leftarrow$ high-order byte of Y.	
LDA	X	$rA \leftarrow X_n$.	
INCA	1	(see exercise 3.2.1.1–1)	
MUL	A	$rX \leftarrow X_{n+1}$.	
STX	X	"$n \leftarrow n+1$."	(14)
LDA	V,6		
STA	Y	$Y \leftarrow V[j]$.	
STX	V,6	$V[j] \leftarrow X_n$. ∎	

The output appears in register A. Notice that Algorithm B requires only four instructions of additional overhead per generated number.

F. Gebhardt [*Math. Comp.* **21** (1967), 708–709] found that satisfactory random sequences were produced by Algorithm M even when it was applied to a sequence as nonrandom as the Fibonacci sequence, with $X_n = F_{2n} \bmod m$ and $Y_n = F_{2n+1} \bmod m$. However, it is also possible for Algorithm M to produce a sequence *less* random than the original sequences, if $\langle X_n \rangle$ and $\langle Y_n \rangle$ are strongly related, as shown in exercise 3. Such problems do not seem to arise with Algorithm B. Since Algorithm B won't make a sequence any less random, and since it enhances the randomness with very little extra cost, it can be recommended for use in combination with any other random number generator.

Shuffling methods have an inherent defect, however: They change only the order of the generated numbers, not the numbers themselves. For most purposes the order is the critical thing, but if a random number generator fails the "birthday spacings" test discussed in Section 3.3.2 or the random walk test of exercise 3.3.2–31 it will not fare much better after it has been shuffled. Shuffling also has the comparative disadvantage that it does not allow us to start at a given place in the period, or to skip quickly from X_n to X_{n+k} for large k.

Many people have therefore suggested combining two sequences $\langle X_n \rangle$ and $\langle Y_n \rangle$ in a much simpler way, which avoids both of the defects of shuffling: We can use a combination like

$$Z_n = (X_n - Y_n) \bmod m \tag{15}$$

when $0 \le X_n < m$ and $0 \le Y_n < m' \le m$. Exercises 13 and 14 discuss the period length of such sequences; exercise 3.3.2–23 shows that (15) tends to enhance the randomness when the seeds X_0 and Y_0 are chosen independently.

An even simpler way to remove the structural biases of arithmetically generated numbers was proposed already in the early days of computing by J. Todd and O. Taussky Todd [*Symp. on Monte Carlo Methods* (Wiley, 1956), 15–28]: We can just throw away some numbers of the sequence. Their suggestion was of little use with linear congruential generators, but it has become quite appropriate nowadays in connection with generators like (7) that have extremely long periods, because we have plenty of numbers to discard.

The simplest way to improve the randomness of (7) is to use only every jth term, for some small j. But a better scheme, which may be even simpler, is to use (7) to produce, say, 500 random numbers in an array and to use only the first 55 of them. After those 55 have been consumed, we generate 500 more in the same way. This idea was proposed by Martin Lüscher [*Computer Physics Communications* **79** (1994), 100–110], motivated by the theory of chaos in dynamical systems: We can regard (7) as a process that maps 55 values $(X_{n-55}, \ldots, X_{n-1})$ into another vector of 55 values $(X_{n+t-55}, \ldots, X_{n+t-1})$. Suppose we generate $t \ge 55$ values and use the first 55 of them. Then if $t = 55$ the new vector of values is rather close to the old; but if $t \approx 500$ there is almost no correlation between old and new (see exercise 33). For the analogous case of add-with-carry or subtract-with-borrow generators (exercise 3.2.1.1–14), the vectors are in fact known to be the radix-b representation of numbers in a linear congruential generator, and the relevant multiplier when we generate t numbers at a time is b^{-t}. Lüscher's theory for this case can therefore be confirmed with the spectral test of Section 3.3.4. A portable random number generator, based on a lagged Fibonacci sequence enhanced with Lüscher's approach, appears in Section 3.6, together with further commentary.

Random number generators typically do only a few multiplications and/or additions to get from one element of the sequence to the next. When such generators are combined as suggested above, common sense tells us that the resulting sequences ought to be indistinguishable from truly random numbers. But intuitive hunches are no substitute for rigorous mathematical proof. If we are willing to do more work — say 1000 or 1000000 times as much — we can obtain sequences for which substantially better theoretical guarantees of randomness are available.

For example, consider the sequence of bits $B_1, B_2, \ldots$ generated by

$$X_{n+1} = X_n^2 \bmod M, \qquad B_n = X_n \bmod 2, \tag{16}$$

[Blum, Blum, and Shub, *SICOMP* **15** (1986), 364–383], or the more elaborate sequence generated by

$$X_{n+1} = X_n^2 \bmod M, \qquad B_n = X_n \cdot Z \bmod 2, \tag{17}$$

where the dot product of r-bit binary numbers $(x_{r-1} \ldots x_0)_2$ and $(z_{r-1} \ldots z_0)_2$ is $x_{r-1}z_{r-1} + \cdots + x_0z_0$; here Z is an r-bit "mask," and r is the number of bits in M. The modulus M should be the product of two large primes of the form $4k + 3$, and the starting value X_0 should be relatively prime to M. Rule (17), suggested by Leonid Levin, is a take-off on von Neumann's original middle-square method; we will call it the *muddle-square method*, because it jumbles the bits of the squares. Rule (16) is, of course, the special case $Z = 1$.

Section 3.5F contains a proof that, when X_0, Z, and M are chosen at random, the sequences generated by (16) and (17) pass all statistical tests for randomness that require no more work than factoring large numbers. In other words, the bits cannot be distinguished from truly random numbers by any computation lasting less than 100 years on today's fastest computers, when M is suitably large, unless it is possible to find the factors of a nontrivial fraction of such numbers much more rapidly than is presently known. Formula (16) is simpler than (17), but the modulus M in (16) has to be somewhat larger than it does in (17) if we want to achieve the same statistical guarantees.

EXERCISES

▶ **1.** [*12*] In practice, we form random numbers using $X_{n+1} = (aX_n+c) \bmod m$, where the X's are *integers*, afterwards treating them as the *fractions* $U_n = X_n/m$. The recurrence relation for U_n is actually

$$U_{n+1} = (aU_n + c/m) \bmod 1.$$

Discuss the generation of random sequences using this relation *directly*, by making use of floating point arithmetic on the computer.

▶ **2.** [*M20*] A good source of random numbers will have $X_{n-1} < X_{n+1} < X_n$ about one-sixth of the time, since each of the six possible relative orders of X_{n-1}, X_n, and X_{n+1} should be equally probable. However, show that the ordering above *never* occurs if the Fibonacci sequence (5) is used.

3. [*23*] (a) What sequence comes from Algorithm M if

$$X_0 = 0, \quad X_{n+1} = (5X_n + 3) \bmod 8, \qquad Y_0 = 0, \quad Y_{n+1} = (5Y_n + 1) \bmod 8,$$

and $k = 4$? (Note that the potency is two, so $\langle X_n \rangle$ and $\langle Y_n \rangle$ aren't extremely random to start with.) (b) What happens if Algorithm B is applied to this same sequence $\langle X_n \rangle$ with $k = 4$?

4. [*00*] Why is the most significant byte used in the first line of program (14), instead of some other byte?

▶ **5.** [*20*] Discuss using $X_n = Y_n$ in Algorithm M, in order to improve the speed of generation. Is the result analogous to Algorithm B?

6. [*10*] In the binary method (10), the text states that the low-order bit of X is random, if the code is performed repeatedly. Why isn't the entire *word* X random?

7. [20] Show that a complete sequence of length 2^e (that is, a sequence in which each of the 2^e possible sets of e adjacent bits occurs just once in the period) may be obtained if program (10) is changed to the following:

```
LDA  X        LDA  A        JNOV *+3        XOR  A
JANZ *+2      ADD  X        JAZ  *+2        STA  X  ▮
```

8. [M39] Prove that the quadratic congruential sequence (3) has period length m if and only if the following conditions are satisfied:

i) c is relatively prime to m;

ii) d and $a - 1$ are both multiples of p, for all odd primes p dividing m;

iii) d is even, and $d \equiv a - 1$ (modulo 4), if m is a multiple of 4;
   $d \equiv a - 1$ (modulo 2), if m is a multiple of 2;

iv) $d \not\equiv 3c$ (modulo 9), if m is a multiple of 9.

[*Hint:* The sequence defined by $X_0 = 0$, $X_{n+1} = dX_n^2 + aX_n + c$ modulo m has a period of length m only if the same sequence modulo any divisor r of m has period length r.]

▶ **9.** [M24] (R. R. Coveyou.) Use the result of exercise 8 to prove that the modified middle-square method (4) has a period of length 2^{e-2}.

10. [M29] Show that if X_0 and X_1 are not both even and if $m = 2^e$, the period of the Fibonacci sequence (5) is $3 \cdot 2^{e-1}$.

11. [M36] The purpose of this exercise is to analyze certain properties of integer sequences satisfying the recurrence relation

$$X_n = a_1 X_{n-1} + \cdots + a_k X_{n-k}, \qquad n \geq k.$$

If we can calculate the period length of this sequence modulo $m = p^e$, when p is prime, the period length with respect to an arbitrary modulus m is the least common multiple of the period lengths for the prime power factors of m.

a) If $f(z)$, $a(z)$, $b(z)$ are polynomials with integer coefficients, let us write $a(z) \equiv b(z)$ (modulo $f(z)$ and m) if $a(z) = b(z) + f(z)u(z) + mv(z)$ for some polynomials $u(z)$ and $v(z)$ with integer coefficients. Prove that the following statement holds when $f(0) = 1$ and $p^e > 2$: If $z^\lambda \equiv 1$ (modulo $f(z)$ and p^e) and $z^\lambda \not\equiv 1$ (modulo $f(z)$ and p^{e+1}), then $z^{p\lambda} \equiv 1$ (modulo $f(z)$ and p^{e+1}) and $z^{p\lambda} \not\equiv 1$ (modulo $f(z)$ and p^{e+2}).

b) Let $f(z) = 1 - a_1 z - \cdots - a_k z^k$, and let

$$G(z) = 1/f(z) = A_0 + A_1 z + A_2 z^2 + \cdots.$$

Let $\lambda(m)$ denote the period length of $\langle A_n \bmod m \rangle$. Prove that $\lambda(m)$ is the smallest positive integer λ such that $z^\lambda \equiv 1$ (modulo $f(z)$ and m).

c) Given that p is prime, $p^e > 2$, and $\lambda(p^e) \neq \lambda(p^{e+1})$, prove that $\lambda(p^{e+r}) = p^r \lambda(p^e)$ for all $r \geq 0$. (Thus, to find the period length of the sequence $\langle A_n \bmod 2^e \rangle$, we can compute $\lambda(4)$, $\lambda(8)$, $\lambda(16)$, ... until we find the smallest $e \geq 3$ such that $\lambda(2^e) \neq \lambda(4)$; then the period length is determined mod 2^e for all e. Exercise 4.6.3–26 explains how to calculate X_n for large n in $O(\log n)$ operations.)

d) Show that any sequence of integers satisfying the recurrence stated at the beginning of this exercise has the generating function $g(z)/f(z)$, for some polynomial $g(z)$ with integer coefficients.

e) Given that the polynomials $f(z)$ and $g(z)$ in part (d) are relatively prime modulo p (see Section 4.6.1), prove that the sequence $\langle X_n \bmod p^e \rangle$ has exactly the same period length as the special sequence $\langle A_n \bmod p^e \rangle$ in (b). (No longer period could be obtained by *any* choice of $X_0, \ldots, X_{k-1}$, since the general sequence is a linear combination of "shifts" of the special sequence.) [*Hint:* By exercise 4.6.2–22 (Hensel's lemma), there exist polynomials such that $a(z)f(z) + b(z)g(z) \equiv 1$ (modulo p^e).]

▶ **12.** [*M28*] Find integers X_0, X_1, a, b, and c such that the sequence

$$X_{n+1} = (aX_n + bX_{n-1} + c) \bmod 2^e, \qquad n \geq 1,$$

has the longest period length of all sequences of this type. [*Hint:* It follows that $X_{n+2} = ((a+1)X_{n+1} + (b-a)X_n - bX_{n-1}) \bmod 2^e$; see exercise 11(c).]

13. [*M20*] Let $\langle X_n \rangle$ and $\langle Y_n \rangle$ be sequences of integers mod m with periods of lengths λ_1 and λ_2, and combine them by letting $Z_n = (X_n + Y_n) \bmod m$. Show that if λ_1 and λ_2 are relatively prime, the sequence $\langle Z_n \rangle$ has a period of length $\lambda_1 \lambda_2$.

14. [*M24*] Let X_n, Y_n, Z_n, λ_1, λ_2 be as in the previous exercise. Suppose that the prime factorization of λ_1 is $2^{e_2} 3^{e_3} 5^{e_5} \ldots$, and similarly suppose that $\lambda_2 = 2^{f_2} 3^{f_3} 5^{f_5} \ldots$. Let $g_p = (\max(e_p, f_p)$ if $e_p \neq f_p$, otherwise 0), and let $\lambda_0 = 2^{g_2} 3^{g_3} 5^{g_5} \ldots$. Show that the period length λ' of the sequence $\langle Z_n \rangle$ is a multiple of λ_0, and it is a divisor of $\lambda = \mathrm{lcm}(\lambda_1, \lambda_2)$. In particular, $\lambda' = \lambda$ if ($e_p \neq f_p$ or $e_p = f_p = 0$) for each prime p.

15. [*M27*] Let the sequence $\langle X_n \rangle$ in Algorithm M have period length λ_1, and assume that all elements of its period are distinct. Let $q_n = \min\{r \mid r > 0$ and $\lfloor kY_{n-r}/m \rfloor = \lfloor kY_n/m \rfloor\}$. Assume that $q_n < \frac{1}{2}\lambda_1$ for all $n \geq n_0$, and that the sequence $\langle q_n \rangle$ has period length λ_2. Let λ be the least common multiple of λ_1 and λ_2. Prove that the output sequence $\langle Z_n \rangle$ produced by Algorithm M has a period of length λ.

▶ **16.** [*M28*] Let CONTENTS(A) in method (10) be $(a_1 a_2 \ldots a_k)_2$ in binary notation. Show that the generated sequence of low-order bits X_0, X_1, ... satisfies the relation

$$X_n = (a_1 X_{n-1} + a_2 X_{n-2} + \cdots + a_k X_{n-k}) \bmod 2.$$

[This may be regarded as another way to define the sequence, although the connection between this relation and the efficient code (10) is not apparent at first glance!]

17. [*M33*] (M. H. Martin, 1934.) Let m and k be positive integers, and let $X_1 = X_2 = \cdots = X_k = 0$. For all $n > 0$, set X_{n+k} equal to the largest nonnegative value $y < m$ such that the k-tuple $(X_{n+1}, \ldots, X_{n+k-1}, y)$ has not already occurred in the sequence; in other words, $(X_{n+1}, \ldots, X_{n+k-1}, y)$ must differ from $(X_{r+1}, \ldots, X_{r+k})$ for $0 \leq r < n$. In this way, each possible k-tuple will occur at most once in the sequence. Eventually the process will terminate, when we reach a value of n such that $(X_{n+1}, \ldots, X_{n+k-1}, y)$ has already occurred in the sequence for all nonnegative $y < m$. For example, if $m = k = 3$ the sequence is 000222122202112102012001110100, and the process terminates at this point. (a) Prove that when the sequence terminates, we have $X_{n+1} = \cdots = X_{n+k-1} = 0$. (b) Prove that *every* k-tuple $(a_1, a_2, \ldots, a_k)$ of elements with $0 \leq a_j < m$ occurs in the sequence; hence the sequence terminates when $n = m^k$. [*Hint:* Prove that the k-tuple $(a_1, \ldots, a_s, 0, \ldots, 0)$ appears, when $a_s \neq 0$, by induction on s.] Note that if we now define $f(X_n, \ldots, X_{n+k-1}) = X_{n+k}$ for $1 \leq n \leq m^k$, setting $X_{m^k+k} = 0$, we obtain a function of maximum possible period.

18. [*M22*] Let $\langle X_n \rangle$ be the sequence of bits generated by method (10), with $k = 35$ and CONTENTS(A) $= (00000000000000000000000000000000101)_2$. Let U_n be the binary fraction $(.X_{nk}X_{nk+1}\ldots X_{nk+k-1})_2$; show that this sequence $\langle U_n \rangle$ fails the serial test on pairs (Section 3.3.2B) when $d = 8$.

19. [*M40*] For each prime p specified by the first two columns of Table 2 in Section 4.5.4, find suitable constants a_1 and a_2 as suggested in the text, such that the period length of (8) is $p^2 - 1$ when $k = 2$. (See Eq. 3.3.4–(39) for an example.)

20. [*M40*] Calculate constants suitable for use as CONTENTS(A) in method (10), having approximately the same number of zeros as ones, for $2 \le k \le 64$.

21. [*M35*] (D. Rees.) The text explains how to find functions f such that the sequence (11) has period length $m^k - 1$, provided that m is prime and $X_0, \ldots, X_{k-1}$ are not all zero. Show that such functions can be modified to obtain sequences of type (11) with period length m^k, for *all* integers m. [*Hints:* Consider the results of exercises 7 and 13, and sequences such as $\langle pX_{2n} + X_{2n+1} \rangle$.]

▶ **22.** [*M24*] The text restricts discussion of the extended linear sequences (8) to the case that m is prime. Prove that reasonably long periods can also be obtained when m is "squarefree," that is, the product of distinct primes. (Examination of Table 3.2.1.1–1 shows that $m = w \pm 1$ often satisfies this hypothesis; many of the results of the text can therefore be carried over to that case, which is somewhat more convenient for calculation.)

▶ **23.** [*20*] Discuss the sequence defined by $X_n = (X_{n-55} - X_{n-24}) \bmod m$ as an alternative to (7).

24. [*M20*] Let $0 < l < k$. Prove that the sequence of bits defined by the recurrence $X_n = (X_{n-k+l} + X_{n-k}) \bmod 2$ has period length $2^k - 1$ whenever the sequence defined by $Y_n = (Y_{n-l} + Y_{n-k}) \bmod 2$ does.

25. [*26*] Discuss the alternative to Program A that changes all 55 entries of the Y table every 55th time a random number is required.

26. [*M48*] (J. F. Reiser.) Let p be prime and let k be a positive integer. Given integers $a_1, \ldots, a_k$ and $x_1, \ldots, x_k$, let λ_α be the period of the sequence $\langle X_n \rangle$ generated by the recurrence

$$X_n = x_n \bmod p^\alpha, \quad 0 \le n < k; \quad X_n = (a_1 X_{n-1} + \cdots + a_k X_{n-k}) \bmod p^\alpha, \quad n \ge k;$$

and let N_α be the number of 0s that occur in the period (the number of indices j such that $\mu_\alpha \le j < \mu_\alpha + \lambda_\alpha$ and $X_j = 0$). Prove or disprove the following conjecture: There exists a constant c (depending possibly on p and k and $a_1, \ldots, a_k$) such that $N_\alpha \le cp^{\alpha(k-2)/(k-1)}$ for all α and all $x_1, \ldots, x_k$.
   [*Notes:* Reiser has proved that if the recurrence has maximum period length mod p (that is, if $\lambda_1 = p^k - 1$), and if the conjecture holds, then the k-dimensional discrepancy of $\langle X_n \rangle$ will be $O(\alpha^k p^{-\alpha/(k-1)})$ as $\alpha \to \infty$; thus an additive generator like (7) would be well distributed in 55 dimensions, when $m = 2^e$ and the entire period is considered. (See Section 3.3.4 for the definition of discrepancy in k dimensions.) The conjecture is a very weak condition, for if $\langle X_n \rangle$ takes on each value about equally often and if $\lambda_\alpha = p^{\alpha-1}(p^k - 1)$, the quantity $N_\alpha \approx (p^k - 1)/p$ does not grow at all as α increases. Reiser has verified the conjecture for $k = 3$. On the other hand he has shown that it is possible to find unusually bad starting values $x_1, \ldots, x_k$ (depending on α) so that $N_{2\alpha} \ge p^\alpha$, provided that $\lambda_\alpha = p^{\alpha-1}(p^k - 1)$ and $k \ge 3$ and α is sufficiently large.]

27. [*M30*] Suppose Algorithm B is being applied to a sequence $\langle X_n \rangle$ whose period length is λ, where $\lambda \gg k$. Show that for fixed k and all sufficiently large λ, the output of the sequence will eventually be periodic with the same period length λ, unless $\langle X_n \rangle$ isn't very random to start with. [*Hint:* Find a pattern of consecutive values of $\lfloor kX_n/m \rfloor$ that causes Algorithm B to "synchronize" its subsequent behavior.]

28. [*40*] (A. G. Waterman.) Experiment with linear congruential sequences with m the square or cube of the computer word size, while a and c are single-precision numbers.

▶ **29.** [*40*] Find a good way to compute the function $f(x_1, \ldots, x_k)$ defined by Martin's sequence in exercise 17, given only the k-tuple $(x_1, \ldots, x_k)$.

30. [*M37*] (R. P. Brent.) Let $f(x) = x^k - a_1 x^{k-1} - \cdots - a_k$ be a primitive polynomial modulo 2, and suppose that $X_0, \ldots, X_{k-1}$ are integers not all even.

a) Prove that the period of the recurrence $X_n = (a_1 X_{n-1} + \cdots + a_k X_{n-k}) \bmod 2^e$ is $2^{e-1}(2^k - 1)$ for all $e \geq 1$ if and only if $f(x)^2 + f(-x)^2 \not\equiv 2f(x^2)$ and $f(x)^2 + f(-x)^2 \not\equiv 2(-1)^k f(-x^2)$ (modulo 8). [*Hint:* We have $x^{2^k} \equiv -x$ (modulo 4 and $f(x)$)) if and only if $f(x)^2 + f(-x)^2 \equiv 2f(x^2)$ (modulo 8).]

b) Prove that this condition always holds when the polynomial $f(x) = x^k \pm x^l \pm 1$ is primitive modulo 2 and $k > 2$.

31. [*M30*] (G. Marsaglia.) What is the period length of the sequence $(7')$ when $m = 2^e \geq 8$? Assume that $X_0, \ldots, X_{54}$ are not all $\equiv \pm 1$ (modulo 8).

32. [*M21*] What recurrences are satisfied by the elements of the subsequences $\langle X_{2n} \rangle$ and $\langle X_{3n} \rangle$, when $X_n = (X_{n-24} + X_{n-55}) \bmod m$?

▶ **33.** [*M23*] (a) Let $g_n(z) = X_{n+30} + X_{n+29}z + \cdots + X_n z^{30} + X_{n+54}z^{31} + \cdots + X_{n+31}z^{54}$, where the X's satisfy the lagged Fibonacci recurrence (7). Find a simple relation between $g_n(z)$ and $g_{n+t}(z)$. (b) Express X_{500} in terms of $X_0, \ldots, X_{54}$.

34. [*M25*] Prove that the inversive congruential sequence (12) has period $p+1$ if and only if the polynomial $f(x) = x^2 - cx - a$ has the following two properties: (i) $x^{p+1} \bmod f(x)$ is a nonzero constant, when computed with polynomial arithmetic modulo p; (ii) $x^{(p+1)/q} \bmod f(x)$ has degree 1 for every prime q that divides $p+1$. [*Hint:* Consider powers of the matrix $\begin{pmatrix} 0 & 1 \\ a & c \end{pmatrix}$.]

35. [*HM35*] How many pairs (a, c) satisfy the conditions of exercise 34?

36. [*M25*] Prove that the inversive congruential sequence $X_{n+1} = (aX_n^{-1} + c) \bmod 2^e$, $X_0 = 1$, $e \geq 3$, has period length 2^{e-1} whenever $a \bmod 4 = 1$ and $c \bmod 4 = 2$.

▶ **37.** [*HM32*] Let p be prime and assume that $X_{n+1} = (aX_n^{-1} + c) \bmod p$ defines an inversive congruential sequence of period $p + 1$. Also let $0 \leq b_1 < \cdots < b_d \leq p$, and consider the set

$$V = \{(X_{n+b_1}, X_{n+b_2}, \ldots, X_{n+b_d}) \mid 0 \leq n \leq p \text{ and } X_{n+b_j} \neq \infty \text{ for } 1 \leq j \leq d\}.$$

This set contains $p + 1 - d$ vectors, any d of which lie in some $(d-1)$-dimensional hyperplane $H = \{(v_1, \ldots, v_d) \mid r_1 v_1 + \cdots + r_d v_d \equiv r_0 \text{ (modulo } p)\}$, where $(r_1, \ldots, r_d) \not\equiv (0, \ldots, 0)$. Prove that no $d + 1$ vectors of V lie in the same hyperplane.

38. [*20*] (H. Nakazawa, 2004.) Show that multiplicative congruential sequences with unbounded moduli can be considered to be "universal" in the following approximate sense: If $\langle x_n \rangle$ is *any* periodic b-ary sequence whatsoever, with $0 \leq x_n < b$ and $x_{n+\lambda} = x_n$ for all $n \geq 0$, let $X = (x_0 x_1 \ldots x_{\lambda-1})_b$. Then the sequence $\langle X_n \rangle$ defined by $X_0 = X/d$, $m = (b^\lambda - 1)/d$, $d = \gcd(X, b^\lambda - 1)$, and $X_{n+1} = bX_n \bmod m$ satisfies $|X_n/m - x_n/b| < 1/b$ for all n.

3.3. STATISTICAL TESTS

OUR MAIN PURPOSE is to obtain sequences that behave as if they are random. So far we have seen how to make the period of a sequence extremely long, indeed long enough that for practical purposes it never will repeat. Period length is an important criterion, but it by no means guarantees that the sequence will be useful in applications. How then are we to decide whether a sequence is sufficiently random?

If we were to give some randomly chosen man a pencil and paper and ask him to write down 100 random decimal digits, chances are very slim that he would produce a satisfactory result. People tend to avoid things that seem nonrandom, such as pairs of equal adjacent digits (although about one out of every 10 digits should equal its predecessor). And if we would show that same man a table of truly random digits, he would quite probably tell us they are not random at all; his eye would spot certain apparent regularities.

According to Dr. I. J. Matrix and Donald C. Rehkopf (as quoted by Martin Gardner in *Scientific American*, January, 1965), "Mathematicians consider the decimal expansion of π a random series, but to a modern numerologist it's rich with remarkable patterns." Dr. Matrix has pointed out, for example, that the first repeated two-digit number in π's expansion is 26, and its second appearance comes in the middle of a curious repetition pattern:

$$3.14159265358979323846264338327950 \tag{1}$$

After listing a dozen or so further properties of these digits, he observed that π, when correctly interpreted, conveys the entire history of the human race!

We all notice patterns in our telephone numbers, license numbers, etc., as aids to memory. The point of these remarks is that we cannot be trusted to judge by ourselves whether a sequence of numbers is random or not. Some unbiased mechanical tests must be applied.

The theory of statistics provides us with some quantitative measures for randomness. There is literally no end to the number of tests that can be conceived; we will discuss the tests that have proved to be most useful, most instructive, and most readily adapted to computer calculation.

If a sequence behaves randomly with respect to tests T_1, T_2, ..., T_n, we cannot be *sure* in general that it will not be a miserable failure when it is subjected to a further test T_{n+1}. Yet each test gives us more and more confidence in the randomness of the sequence. In practice, we apply about half a dozen different kinds of statistical tests to a sequence, and if it passes them satisfactorily we consider it to be random—it is then presumed innocent until proven guilty.

Every sequence that is to be used extensively should be tested carefully, so the following sections explain how to administer the tests in an appropriate way. Two kinds of tests are distinguished: *empirical tests*, for which the computer manipulates groups of numbers of the sequence and evaluates certain statistics; and *theoretical tests*, for which we establish characteristics of the sequence by using number-theoretic methods based on the recurrence rule used to form the sequence.

If the evidence doesn't come out as desired, the reader may wish to try the techniques in *How to Lie With Statistics* by Darrell Huff (Norton, 1954).

3.3.1. General Test Procedures for Studying Random Data

A. "Chi-square" tests. The chi-square test (χ^2 test) is perhaps the best known of all statistical tests, and it is a basic method that is used in connection with many other tests. Before considering the idea in general, let us consider a particular example of the chi-square test as it might be applied to dice throwing. Using two "true" dice (each of which, independently, is assumed to yield the values 1, 2, 3, 4, 5, or 6 with equal probability), the following table gives the probability of obtaining a given total, s, on a single throw:

$$
\begin{array}{cccccccccccc}
\text{value of } s = & 2 & 3 & 4 & 5 & 6 & 7 & 8 & 9 & 10 & 11 & 12 \\
\text{probability, } p_s = & \frac{1}{36} & \frac{1}{18} & \frac{1}{12} & \frac{1}{9} & \frac{5}{36} & \frac{1}{6} & \frac{5}{36} & \frac{1}{9} & \frac{1}{12} & \frac{1}{18} & \frac{1}{36}
\end{array} \tag{1}
$$

For example, a value of 4 can be thrown in three ways: $1 + 3$, $2 + 2$, $3 + 1$; this constitutes $\frac{3}{36} = \frac{1}{12} = p_4$ of the 36 possible outcomes.

If we throw the dice n times, we should obtain the value s approximately np_s times on the average. For example, in 144 throws we should get the value 4 about 12 times. The following table shows what results were *actually* obtained in a particular sequence of 144 throws of the dice:

$$
\begin{array}{crcccccccccc}
\text{value of } s = & 2 & 3 & 4 & 5 & 6 & 7 & 8 & 9 & 10 & 11 & 12 \\
\text{observed number, } Y_s = & 2 & 4 & 10 & 12 & 22 & 29 & 21 & 15 & 14 & 9 & 6 \\
\text{expected number, } np_s = & 4 & 8 & 12 & 16 & 20 & 24 & 20 & 16 & 12 & 8 & 4
\end{array} \tag{2}
$$

Notice that the observed number was different from the expected number in all cases; in fact, random throws of the dice will hardly ever come out with *exactly* the right frequencies. There are 36^{144} possible sequences of 144 throws, all of which are equally likely. One of these sequences consists of all 2s ("snake eyes"), and anyone throwing 144 snake eyes in a row would be convinced that the dice were loaded. Yet the sequence of all 2s is just as probable as any other particular sequence if we specify the outcome of each throw of each die.

In view of this, how can we test whether or not a given pair of dice is loaded? The answer is that we can't make a definite yes-no statement, but we can give a *probabilistic* answer. We can say how probable or improbable certain types of events are.

A fairly natural way to proceed in the example above is to consider the squares of the differences between the observed numbers Y_s and the expected numbers np_s. We can add these together, obtaining

$$
V = (Y_2 - np_2)^2 + (Y_3 - np_3)^2 + \cdots + (Y_{12} - np_{12})^2. \tag{3}
$$

A bad set of dice should result in a relatively high value of V; and for any given value of V we can ask, "What is the probability that V is this high, using true dice?" If this probability is very small, say $\frac{1}{100}$, we would know that only about one time in 100 would true dice give results so far away from the expected numbers, and we would have definite grounds for suspicion. (Remember, however, that even *good* dice would give such a high value of V about one time in a hundred, so a cautious person would repeat the experiment to see if the high value of V is repeated.)

The statistic V in (3) gives equal weight to $(Y_7 - np_7)^2$ and $(Y_2 - np_2)^2$, although $(Y_7 - np_7)^2$ is likely to be a good deal higher than $(Y_2 - np_2)^2$ since 7s occur about six times as often as 2s. It turns out that the "right" statistic, or at least one that has become traditional, will give $(Y_7 - np_7)^2$ only $\frac{1}{6}$ as much weight as $(Y_2 - np_2)^2$, and we should change (3) to the following formula:

$$V = \frac{(Y_2 - np_2)^2}{np_2} + \frac{(Y_3 - np_3)^2}{np_3} + \cdots + \frac{(Y_{12} - np_{12})^2}{np_{12}}. \tag{4}$$

This is called the "chi-square" statistic of the observed quantities $Y_2, \ldots, Y_{12}$ in the dice-throwing experiment. For the data in (2), we find that

$$V = \frac{(2-4)^2}{4} + \frac{(4-8)^2}{8} + \cdots + \frac{(9-8)^2}{8} + \frac{(6-4)^2}{4} = 7\frac{7}{48}. \tag{5}$$

The important question now is, of course, "Does $7\frac{7}{48}$ constitute an improbably high value for V to assume?" Before answering this question, let us consider the general application of the chi-square method.

In general, suppose that every observation can fall into one of k categories. We take n *independent observations*; this means that the outcome of one observation has absolutely no effect on the outcome of any of the others. Let p_s be the probability that each observation falls into category s, and let Y_s be the number of observations that actually *do* fall into category s. We form the statistic

$$V = \sum_{s=1}^{k} \frac{(Y_s - np_s)^2}{np_s}. \tag{6}$$

In our example above, there are eleven possible outcomes of each throw of the dice, so $k = 11$. (Eq. (6) is a slight change of notation from Eq. (4), since we are numbering the possibilities from 1 to k instead of from 2 to 12.)

By expanding $(Y_s - np_s)^2 = Y_s^2 - 2np_sY_s + n^2p_s^2$ in (6), and using the facts that

$$Y_1 + Y_2 + \cdots + Y_k = n,$$
$$p_1 + p_2 + \cdots + p_k = 1, \tag{7}$$

we arrive at the formula

$$V = \frac{1}{n} \sum_{s=1}^{k} \left(\frac{Y_s^2}{p_s} \right) - n, \tag{8}$$

which often makes the computation of V somewhat easier.

Table 1

SELECTED PERCENTAGE POINTS OF THE CHI-SQUARE DISTRIBUTION

	$p = 1\%$	$p = 5\%$	$p = 25\%$	$p = 50\%$	$p = 75\%$	$p = 95\%$	$p = 99\%$
$\nu = 1$	0.00016	0.00393	0.1015	0.4549	1.323	3.841	6.635
$\nu = 2$	0.02010	0.1026	0.5754	1.386	2.773	5.991	9.210
$\nu = 3$	0.1148	0.3518	1.213	2.366	4.108	7.815	11.34
$\nu = 4$	0.2971	0.7107	1.923	3.357	5.385	9.488	13.28
$\nu = 5$	0.5543	1.1455	2.675	4.351	6.626	11.07	15.09
$\nu = 6$	0.8721	1.635	3.455	5.348	7.841	12.59	16.81
$\nu = 7$	1.239	2.167	4.255	6.346	9.037	14.07	18.48
$\nu = 8$	1.646	2.733	5.071	7.344	10.22	15.51	20.09
$\nu = 9$	2.088	3.325	5.899	8.343	11.39	16.92	21.67
$\nu = 10$	2.558	3.940	6.737	9.342	12.55	18.31	23.21
$\nu = 11$	3.053	4.575	7.584	10.34	13.70	19.68	24.72
$\nu = 12$	3.571	5.226	8.438	11.34	14.85	21.03	26.22
$\nu = 15$	5.229	7.261	11.04	14.34	18.25	25.00	30.58
$\nu = 20$	8.260	10.85	15.45	19.34	23.83	31.41	37.57
$\nu = 30$	14.95	18.49	24.48	29.34	34.80	43.77	50.89
$\nu = 50$	29.71	34.76	42.94	49.33	56.33	67.50	76.15
$\nu > 30$	$\nu + \sqrt{2\nu}x_p + \frac{2}{3}x_p^2 - \frac{2}{3} + O\left(1/\sqrt{\nu}\right)$						
$x_p =$	-2.33	-1.64	$-.674$	0.00	0.674	1.64	2.33

(For further values, see *Handbook of Mathematical Functions*, edited by M. Abramowitz and I. A. Stegun (Washington, D.C.: U.S. Government Printing Office, 1964), Table 26.8. See also Eq. (22) and exercise 16.)

Now we turn to the important question, "What constitutes a reasonable value of V?" This is found by referring to a table such as Table 1, which gives values of "the chi-square distribution with ν degrees of freedom" for various values of ν. The line of the table with $\nu = k - 1$ is to be used; *the number of "degrees of freedom" is $k - 1$, one less than the number of categories.* (Intuitively, this means that $Y_1, Y_2, \ldots, Y_k$ are not completely independent, since Eq. (7) shows that Y_k can be computed if $Y_1, \ldots, Y_{k-1}$ are known; hence, $k - 1$ degrees of freedom are present. This argument is not rigorous, but the theory below justifies it.)

If the table entry in row ν under column p is x, it means, "The quantity V in Eq. (8) will be less than or equal to x with approximate probability p, if n is large enough." For example, the 95 percent entry in row 10 is 18.31; we will have $V > 18.31$ only about 5 percent of the time.

Let us assume that our dice-throwing experiment has been simulated on a computer using some sequence of supposedly random numbers, with the following results:

$$\text{value of } s = \quad 2 \quad 3 \quad 4 \quad 5 \quad 6 \quad 7 \quad 8 \quad 9 \quad 10 \quad 11 \quad 12$$
$$\text{Experiment 1,} \quad Y_s = \quad 4 \quad 10 \quad 10 \quad 13 \quad 20 \quad 18 \quad 18 \quad 11 \quad 13 \quad 14 \quad 13 \qquad (9)$$
$$\text{Experiment 2,} \quad Y_s = \quad 3 \quad 7 \quad 11 \quad 15 \quad 19 \quad 24 \quad 21 \quad 17 \quad 13 \quad 9 \quad 5$$

We can compute the chi-square statistic in the first case, getting the value $V_1 = 29\frac{59}{120}$, and in the second case we get $V_2 = 1\frac{17}{120}$. Referring to the table entries for 10 degrees of freedom, we see that V_1 is *much too high*; V will be greater than 23.21 only about one percent of the time! (By using more extensive tables, we find in fact that V will be as high as V_1 only 0.1 percent of the time.) Therefore Experiment 1 represents a significant departure from random behavior.

On the other hand, V_2 is quite low, since the observed values Y_s in Experiment 2 are quite close to the expected values np_s in (2). The chi-square table tells us, in fact, that V_2 is *much too low*: The observed values are so close to the expected values, we cannot consider the result to be random! (Indeed, reference to other tables shows that such a low value of V occurs only 0.03 percent of the time when there are 10 degrees of freedom.) Finally, the value $V = 7\frac{7}{48}$ computed in (5) can also be checked with Table 1. It falls between the entries for 25 percent and 50 percent, so we cannot consider it to be significantly high or significantly low; thus the observations in (2) are satisfactorily random with respect to this test.

It is somewhat remarkable that the same table entries are used no matter what the value of n is, and no matter what the probabilities p_s are. Only the number $\nu = k - 1$ affects the results. In actual fact, however, the table entries are not exactly correct: *The chi-square distribution is an approximation that is valid only for large enough values of n.* How large should n be? A common rule of thumb is to take n large enough so that each of the expected values np_s is five or more; preferably, however, take n much larger than this, to get a more powerful test. In our examples above we took $n = 144$, so np_2 was only 4, violating the stated rule of thumb. This was done only because the author tired of throwing the dice; it makes the entries in Table 1 less accurate for our application. Experiments run on a computer, with $n = 1000$, or 10000, or even 100000, would be much better than this. We could also combine the data for $s = 2$ and $s = 12$; then the test would have only nine degrees of freedom but the chi-square approximation would be more accurate.

We can get an idea of how crude an approximation is involved by considering the case when there are only two categories, having probabilities p_1 and p_2. Suppose $p_1 = \frac{1}{4}$ and $p_2 = \frac{3}{4}$. According to the stated rule of thumb, we should have $n \geq 20$ to have a satisfactory approximation, so let's check that out. When $n = 20$, the possible values of V are $(Y_1 - 5)^2/5 + (5 - Y_1)^2/15 = \frac{4}{15}r^2$ for $-5 \leq r \leq 15$; we wish to know how well the row $\nu = 1$ of Table 1 describes the distribution of V. The chi-square distribution varies continuously, while the actual distribution of V has rather big jumps, so we need some convention for representing the exact distribution. If the distinct possible outcomes of the experiment lead to the values $V_0 \leq V_1 \leq \cdots \leq V_n$ with respective probabilities $\pi_0, \pi_1, \ldots, \pi_n$, suppose that a given percentage p falls in the range $\pi_0 + \cdots + \pi_{j-1} < p < \pi_0 + \cdots + \pi_{j-1} + \pi_j$. We would like to represent p by a "percentage point" x such that V is less than x with probability $\leq p$ and V is greater than x with probability $\leq 1-p$. It is not difficult to see that the only such number is $x = V_j$. In our example for $n = 20$ and $\nu = 1$, it turns out that the percentage points of the exact distribution, corresponding to the approximations in Table 1 for $p = 1\%, 5\%, 25\%, 50\%, 75\%, 95\%,$ and 99%, respectively, are

$$0, \quad 0, \quad .27, \quad .27, \quad 1.07, \quad 4.27, \quad 6.67$$

(to two decimal places). For example, the percentage point for $p = 95\%$ is 4.27, while Table 1 gives the estimate 3.841. The latter value is too low; it tells us (incorrectly) to reject the value $V = \frac{64}{15} \approx 4.27$ at the 95% level, while in fact the probability that $V \geq \frac{64}{15}$ is more than 6.5%. When $n = 21$, the situation changes slightly because the expected values $np_1 = 5.25$ and $np_2 = 15.75$ can never be obtained exactly; the percentage points for $n = 21$ are

$$.02, \quad .02, \quad .14, \quad .40, \quad 1.29, \quad 3.57, \quad 5.73.$$

We would expect Table 1 to be a better approximation when $n = 50$, but the corresponding tableau actually turns out to be further from Table 1 in some respects than it was for $n = 20$:

$$.03, \quad .03, \quad .03, \quad .67, \quad 1.31, \quad 3.23, \quad 6.$$

Here are the values when $n = 300$:

$$0, \quad 0, \quad .07, \quad .44, \quad 1.44, \quad 4, \quad 6.42.$$

Even in this case, when np_s is ≥ 75 in each category, the entries in Table 1 are good to only about one significant digit.

The proper choice of n is somewhat obscure. If the dice are actually biased, the fact will be detected as n gets larger and larger. (See exercise 12.) But large values of n will tend to smooth out *locally* nonrandom behavior, when blocks of numbers with a strong bias are followed by blocks of numbers with the opposite bias. Locally nonrandom behavior is not an issue when actual dice are rolled, since the same dice are used throughout the test, but a sequence of numbers generated by computer might very well display such anomalies. Perhaps a chi-square test should be made for several different values of n. At any rate, n should always be rather large.

We can summarize the chi-square test as follows. A fairly large number, n, of independent observations is made. (It is important to avoid using the chi-square method unless the observations are independent. See, for example, exercise 10, which considers the case when half of the observations depend on the other half.) We count the number of observations falling into each of k categories and compute the quantity V given in Eqs. (6) and (8). Then V is compared with the numbers in Table 1, with $\nu = k - 1$. If V is less than the 1% entry or greater than the 99% entry, we reject the numbers as not sufficiently random. If V lies

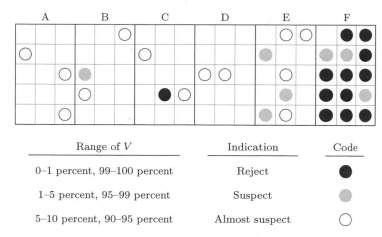

Range of V	Indication	Code
0–1 percent, 99–100 percent	Reject	●
1–5 percent, 95–99 percent	Suspect	◉
5–10 percent, 90–95 percent	Almost suspect	○

Fig. 2. Indications of "significant" deviations in 90 chi-square tests (see also Fig. 5).

between the 1% and 5% entries or between the 95% and 99% entries, the numbers are "suspect"; if (by interpolation in the table) V lies between the 5% and 10% entries, or the 90% and 95% entries, the numbers might be "almost suspect." The chi-square test is often done at least three times on different sets of data, and if at least two of the three results are suspect the numbers are regarded as not sufficiently random.

For example, see Fig. 2, which shows schematically the results of applying five different types of chi-square tests on each of six sequences of random numbers. Each test in this illustration was applied to three different blocks of numbers of the sequence. Generator A is the MacLaren–Marsaglia method (Algorithm 3.2.2M applied to the sequences in 3.2.2–(13)); Generator E is the Fibonacci method, 3.2.2–(5); and the other generators are linear congruential sequences with the following parameters:

Generator B: $X_0 = 0,$ $a = 3141592653,$ $c = 2718281829,$ $m = 2^{35}.$

Generator C: $X_0 = 0,$ $a = 2^7 + 1,$ $c = 1,$ $m = 2^{35}.$

Generator D: $X_0 = 47594118,$ $a = 23,$ $c = 0,$ $m = 10^8 + 1.$

Generator F: $X_0 = 314159265,$ $a = 2^{18} + 1,$ $c = 1,$ $m = 2^{35}.$

From Fig. 2 we conclude that (so far as these tests are concerned) Generators A, B, D are satisfactory, Generator C is on the borderline and should probably be rejected, Generators E and F are definitely unsatisfactory. Generator F has, of course, low potency; Generators C and D have been discussed in the literature, but their multipliers are too small. (Generator D is the original multiplicative generator proposed by Lehmer in 1948; Generator C is the original linear congruential generator with $c \neq 0$ proposed by Rotenberg in 1960.)

Instead of using the "suspect," "almost suspect," etc., criteria for judging the results of chi-square tests, one can employ a less *ad hoc* procedure discussed later in this section.

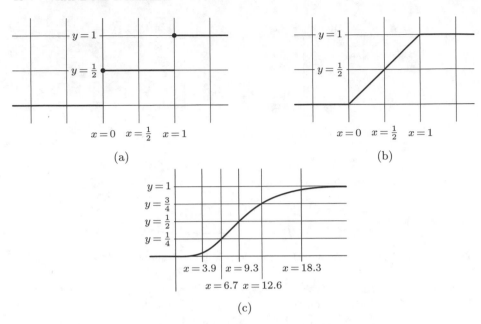

Fig. 3. Examples of distribution functions.

B. The Kolmogorov–Smirnov test. As we have seen, the chi-square test applies to the situation when observations can fall into a finite number of categories. It is not unusual, however, to consider random quantities that range over infinitely many values, such as a random fraction (a random real number between 0 and 1). Even though only finitely many real numbers can be represented in a computer, we want our random values to behave essentially as if all real numbers in $[0 \, . \, . \, 1)$ were equally likely.

A general notation for specifying probability distributions, whether they are finite or infinite, is commonly used in the study of probability and statistics. Suppose we want to specify the distribution of the values of a random quantity, X; we do this in terms of the *distribution function* $F(x)$, where

$$F(x) = \Pr(X \le x) = \text{probability that } (X \le x).$$

Three examples are shown in Fig. 3. First we see the distribution function for a *random bit*, namely for the case when X takes on only the two values 0 and 1, each with probability $\frac{1}{2}$. Part (b) of the figure shows the distribution function for a *uniformly distributed random real number* between zero and one; here the probability that $X \le x$ is simply equal to x when $0 \le x \le 1$. For example, the probability that $X \le \frac{2}{3}$ is, naturally, $\frac{2}{3}$. And part (c) shows the limiting distribution of the value V in the chi-square test (shown here with 10 degrees of freedom); this is a distribution that we have already seen represented in another way in Table 1. Notice that $F(x)$ always increases from 0 to 1 as x increases from $-\infty$ to $+\infty$.

If we make n independent observations of the random quantity X, thereby obtaining the values X_1, X_2, ..., X_n, we can form the *empirical distribution function* $F_n(x)$, where

$$F_n(x) = \frac{\text{number of } X_1, X_2, \ldots, X_n \text{ that are } \leq x}{n}. \qquad (10)$$

Figure 4 illustrates three empirical distribution functions (shown as zigzag lines, although strictly speaking the vertical lines are not part of the graph of $F_n(x)$), superimposed on a graph of the assumed actual distribution function $F(x)$. As n gets large, $F_n(x)$ should be a better and better approximation to $F(x)$.

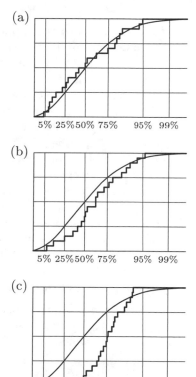

(a)

5% 25% 50% 75%   95% 99%

(b)

5% 25% 50% 75%   95% 99%

(c)

Fig. 4. Examples of empirical distributions. The x value marked "5%" is the percentage point where $F(x) = 0.05$.

5% 25% 50% 75%   95% 99%

The Kolmogorov–Smirnov test (KS test) may be used when $F(x)$ has no jumps. It is based on the *difference between $F(x)$ and $F_n(x)$*. A bad source of random numbers will give empirical distribution functions that do not approximate $F(x)$ sufficiently well. Figure 4(b) shows an example in which the X_i are consistently too high, so the empirical distribution function is too low. Part (c) of the figure shows an even worse example; it is plain that such great deviations between $F_n(x)$ and $F(x)$ are extremely improbable, and the KS test is used to tell us how improbable they are.

To make the KS test, we form the following "supremum" statistics:

$$K_n^+ = \sqrt{n} \sup_{-\infty < x < +\infty} \big(F_n(x) - F(x)\big);$$

$$K_n^- = \sqrt{n} \sup_{-\infty < x < +\infty} \big(F(x) - F_n(x)\big).$$

(11)

Here K_n^+ measures the greatest amount of deviation when F_n is greater than F, and K_n^- measures the maximum deviation when F_n is less than F. The statistics for the examples of Fig. 4 are

	Fig. 4(a)	Fig. 4(b)	Fig. 4(c)	
K_{20}^+	0.492	0.134	0.313	(12)
K_{20}^-	0.536	1.027	2.101	

(*Note:* The factor $\sqrt{n}$ that appears in Eqs. (11) may seem puzzling at first. Exercise 6 shows that, for fixed x, the standard deviation of $F_n(x)$ is proportional to $1/\sqrt{n}$; hence the factor $\sqrt{n}$ magnifies the statistics K_n^+ and K_n^- in such a way that this standard deviation is independent of n.)

As in the chi-square test, we may now look up the values K_n^+, K_n^- in a percentile table to determine if they are significantly high or low. Table 2 may be used for this purpose, both for K_n^+ and K_n^-. For example, the probability is 75 percent that K_{20}^- will be 0.7975 or less. Unlike the chi-square test, the table entries are *not* merely approximations that hold for large values of n; Table 2 gives exact values (except, of course, for roundoff error), and the KS test may be used reliably for any value of n.

As they stand, formulas (11) are not readily adapted to computer calculation, since we are asking for a least upper bound over infinitely many values of x. But from the fact that $F(x)$ is increasing and the fact that $F_n(x)$ increases only in finite steps, we can derive a simple procedure for evaluating the statistics K_n^+ and K_n^-:

Step 1. Obtain independent observations $X_1, X_2, \ldots, X_n$.

Step 2. Rearrange the observations so that they are sorted into ascending order, $X_1 \leq X_2 \leq \cdots \leq X_n$. (Efficient sorting algorithms are the subject of Chapter 5. But it is possible to avoid sorting in this case, as shown in exercise 23.)

Step 3. The desired statistics are now given by the formulas

$$K_n^+ = \sqrt{n} \max_{1 \leq j \leq n} \left(\frac{j}{n} - F(X_j)\right);$$

$$K_n^- = \sqrt{n} \max_{1 \leq j \leq n} \left(F(X_j) - \frac{j-1}{n}\right).$$

(13)

An appropriate choice of the number of observations, n, is slightly easier to make for this test than it is for the χ^2 test, although some of the considerations are similar. If the random variables X_j actually belong to the probability distribution $G(x)$, while they were assumed to belong to the distribution given by $F(x)$, we want n to be comparatively large, in order to reject the hypothesis that $G(x) = F(x)$; for we need n large enough that the empirical distributions

Table 2

SELECTED PERCENTAGE POINTS OF THE DISTRIBUTIONS K_n^+ AND K_n^-

	$p = 1\%$	$p = 5\%$	$p = 25\%$	$p = 50\%$	$p = 75\%$	$p = 95\%$	$p = 99\%$
$n = 1$	0.01000	0.05000	0.2500	0.5000	0.7500	0.9500	0.9900
$n = 2$	0.01400	0.06749	0.2929	0.5176	0.7071	1.0980	1.2728
$n = 3$	0.01699	0.07919	0.3112	0.5147	0.7539	1.1017	1.3589
$n = 4$	0.01943	0.08789	0.3202	0.5110	0.7642	1.1304	1.3777
$n = 5$	0.02152	0.09471	0.3249	0.5245	0.7674	1.1392	1.4024
$n = 6$	0.02336	0.1002	0.3272	0.5319	0.7703	1.1463	1.4144
$n = 7$	0.02501	0.1048	0.3280	0.5364	0.7755	1.1537	1.4246
$n = 8$	0.02650	0.1086	0.3280	0.5392	0.7797	1.1586	1.4327
$n = 9$	0.02786	0.1119	0.3274	0.5411	0.7825	1.1624	1.4388
$n = 10$	0.02912	0.1147	0.3297	0.5426	0.7845	1.1658	1.4440
$n = 11$	0.03028	0.1172	0.3330	0.5439	0.7863	1.1688	1.4484
$n = 12$	0.03137	0.1193	0.3357	0.5453	0.7880	1.1714	1.4521
$n = 15$	0.03424	0.1244	0.3412	0.5500	0.7926	1.1773	1.4606
$n = 20$	0.03807	0.1298	0.3461	0.5547	0.7975	1.1839	1.4698
$n = 30$	0.04354	0.1351	0.3509	0.5605	0.8036	1.1916	1.4801
$n > 30$	$y_p - \frac{1}{6}n^{-1/2} + O(1/n)$, where $y_p^2 = \frac{1}{2}\ln(1/(1-p))$						
$y_p =$	0.07089	0.1601	0.3793	0.5887	0.8326	1.2239	1.5174

(To extend this table, see Eqs. (25) and (26), and the answer to exercise 20.)

$G_n(x)$ and $F_n(x)$ are expected to be observably different. On the other hand, large values of n will tend to average out locally nonrandom behavior, and such undesirable behavior is a significant danger in most computer applications of random numbers; this makes a case for *smaller* values of n. A good compromise would be to take n equal to, say, 1000, and to make a fairly large number of calculations of K_{1000}^+ on different parts of a random sequence, thereby obtaining values

$$K_{1000}^+(1), \qquad K_{1000}^+(2), \qquad \ldots, \qquad K_{1000}^+(r). \tag{14}$$

We can also apply the KS test *again* to *these* results: Let $F(x)$ now be the distribution function for K_{1000}^+, and determine the empirical distribution $F_r(x)$ obtained from the observed values in (14). Fortunately, the function $F(x)$ in this case is very simple; for a large value of n like $n = 1000$, the distribution of K_n^+ is closely approximated by

$$F_\infty(x) = 1 - e^{-2x^2}, \qquad x \geq 0. \tag{15}$$

The same remarks apply to K_n^-, since K_n^+ and K_n^- have the same expected behavior. *This method of using several tests for moderately large n, then combining the observations later in another KS test, will tend to detect both local and global nonrandom behavior.*

For example, the author conducted the following simple experiment while writing this chapter: The "maximum-of-5" test described in the next section was applied to a set of 1000 uniform random numbers, yielding 200 observations X_1, X_2, ..., X_{200} that were supposed to belong to the distribution $F(x) = x^5$ for $0 \leq x \leq 1$. The observations were divided into 20 groups of 10 each, and the statistic K_{10}^+ was computed for each group. The 20 values of K_{10}^+ thus obtained led to the empirical distributions shown in Fig. 4. The smooth curve shown in each of the diagrams in Fig. 4 is the actual distribution the statistic K_{10}^+ should have. Figure 4(a) shows the empirical distribution of K_{10}^+ obtained from the sequence

$$Y_{n+1} = (3141592653Y_n + 2718281829) \bmod 2^{35}, \qquad U_n = Y_n/2^{35},$$

and it is satisfactorily random. Part (b) of the figure came from the Fibonacci method; this sequence has *globally* nonrandom behavior — that is, it can be shown that the observations X_n in the maximum-of-5 test do not have the correct distribution $F(x) = x^5$. Part (c) came from the notorious and impotent linear congruential sequence $Y_{n+1} = \big((2^{18} + 1)Y_n + 1\big) \bmod 2^{35}$, $U_n = Y_n/2^{35}$.

The KS test applied to the data in Fig. 4 gives the results shown in (12). Referring to Table 2 for $n = 20$, we see that the values of K_{20}^+ and K_{20}^- for Fig. 4(b) are almost suspect (they lie at about the 5 percent and 88 percent levels), but they are not quite bad enough to be rejected outright. The value of K_{20}^- for Fig. 4(c) is, of course, completely out of line, so the maximum-of-5 test shows a definite failure of that random number generator.

We would expect the KS test in this experiment to have more difficulty locating global nonrandomness than local nonrandomness, since the basic observations in Fig. 4 were made on samples of only 10 numbers each. If we were to take 20 groups of 1000 numbers each, part (b) would show a much more significant deviation. To illustrate this point, a *single* KS test was applied to all 200 of the observations that led to Fig. 4, and the following results were obtained:

	Fig. 4(a)	Fig. 4(b)	Fig. 4(c)	
K_{200}^+	0.477	1.537	2.819	(16)
K_{200}^-	0.817	0.194	0.058	

The global nonrandomness of the Fibonacci generator has definitely been detected here.

We may summarize the Kolmogorov–Smirnov test as follows. We are given n *independent observations* $X_1, \ldots, X_n$ taken from some distribution specified by a *continuous* function $F(x)$. That is, $F(x)$ must be like the functions shown in Fig. 3(b) and 3(c), having no jumps like those in Fig. 3(a). The procedure explained just before Eqs. (13) is carried out on these observations, and we obtain the statistics K_n^+ and K_n^-. These statistics should be distributed according to Table 2.

Some comparisons between the KS test and the χ^2 test can now be made. In the first place, we should observe that the KS test may be used in conjunction with the χ^2 test, to give a better procedure than the *ad hoc* method we mentioned when summarizing the χ^2 test. (That is, there is a better way to proceed than to make three tests and to consider how many of the results were "suspect.") Suppose we have made, say, 10 independent χ^2 tests on different parts of a random sequence, so that values $V_1, V_2, \ldots, V_{10}$ have been obtained. It is not a good policy simply to count how many of the V's are suspiciously large or small. This procedure will work in extreme cases, and very large or very small values may mean that the sequence has too much local nonrandomness; but a better general method would be to plot the empirical distribution of these 10 values and to compare it to the correct distribution, which may be obtained from Table 1. The empirical distribution gives a clearer picture of the results of the χ^2 tests, and in fact the statistics K_{10}^+ and K_{10}^- could be determined from the empirical χ^2 values as an indication of success or failure. With only 10 values or even as many as 100 this could all be done easily by hand, using graphical methods; with a larger number of V's, a computer subroutine for calculating the chi-square distribution would be necessary. Notice that *all 20 of the observations in Fig. 4(c) fall between the 5 and 95 percent levels*, so we would not have regarded *any* of them as suspicious, individually; yet collectively the empirical distribution shows that these observations are not at all right.

An important difference between the KS test and the chi-square test is that the KS test applies to distributions $F(x)$ having no jumps, while the chi-square test applies to distributions having nothing but jumps (since all observations are divided into k categories). The two tests are thus intended for different sorts of applications. Yet it is possible to apply the χ^2 test even when $F(x)$ is continuous, if we divide the domain of $F(x)$ into k parts and ignore all variations within each part. For example, if we want to test whether or not $U_1, U_2, \ldots, U_n$ can be considered to come from the uniform distribution between zero and one, we want to test if they have the distribution $F(x) = x$ for $0 \le x \le 1$. This is a natural application for the KS test. But we might also divide up the interval from 0 to 1 into $k = 100$ equal parts, count how many U's fall into each part, and apply the chi-square test with 99 degrees of freedom. There are not many theoretical results available at the present time to compare the effectiveness of the KS test versus the chi-square test. The author has found some examples in which the KS test pointed out nonrandomness more clearly than the χ^2 test, and others in which the χ^2 test gave a more significant result. If, for example, the 100 categories mentioned above are numbered 0, 1, $\ldots$, 99, and if the deviations from the expected values are positive in compartments 0 to 49 but negative in compartments 50 to 99, then the empirical distribution function will be much further from $F(x)$ than the χ^2 value would indicate; but if the positive deviations occur in compartments 0, 2, $\ldots$, 98 and the negative ones occur in 1, 3, $\ldots$, 99, the empirical distribution function will tend to hug $F(x)$ much more closely. The

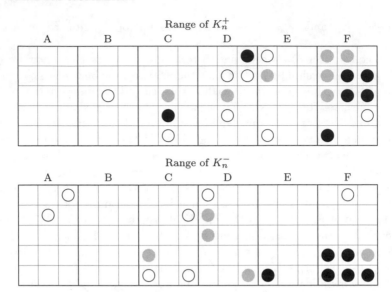

Fig. 5. The KS tests applied to the same data as Fig. 2.

kinds of deviations measured are therefore somewhat different. A χ^2 test was applied to the 200 observations that led to Fig. 4, with $k = 10$, and the respective values of V were 9.4, 17.7, and 39.3; so in this particular case the values were quite comparable to the KS values given in (16). Since the χ^2 test is intrinsically less accurate, and since it requires comparatively large values of n, the KS test has several advantages when a continuous distribution is to be tested.

A further example will also be of interest. The data that led to Fig. 2 were chi-square statistics based on $n = 200$ observations of the maximum-of-t criterion for $1 \leq t \leq 5$, with the range divided into 10 equally probable parts. KS statistics K_{200}^+ and K_{200}^- can be computed from exactly the same sets of 200 observations, and the results can be tabulated in just the same way as we did in Fig. 2 (showing which KS values are beyond the 99-percent level, etc.); the results in this case are shown in Fig. 5. Notice that Generator D (Lehmer's original method) shows up very badly in Fig. 5, while chi-square tests *on the very same data* revealed no difficulty in Fig. 2; contrariwise, Generator E (the Fibonacci method) does not look so bad in Fig. 5. The good generators, A and B, passed all tests satisfactorily. The reasons for the discrepancies between Fig. 2 and Fig. 5 are primarily that (a) the number of observations, 200, is really not large enough for a powerful test, and (b) the "reject," "suspect," "almost suspect" ranking criterion is itself suspect.

(Incidentally, it is not fair to blame Lehmer for using a "bad" random number generator in the 1940s, since his actual use of Generator D was quite valid. The ENIAC computer was a highly parallel machine, programmed by means of a plugboard; Lehmer set it up so that one of its accumulators was repeatedly multiplying its own contents by 23 (modulo $10^8 + 1$), yielding a new value every few milliseconds. Since this multiplier 23 is too small, we know that each value obtained by such a process is too strongly related to the preceding value to be considered sufficiently random; but the durations of time between actual *uses* of the values in the special accumulator by the accompanying program were comparatively long and subject to some fluctuation. So the effective multiplier was 23^k for large, *varying* values of k.)

C. History, bibliography, and theory. The chi-square test was introduced by Karl Pearson in 1900 [*Philosophical Magazine*, Series 5, **50**, 157–175]. Pearson's important paper is regarded as one of the foundations of modern statistics, since before that time people would simply plot experimental results graphically and assert that they were correct. In his paper, Pearson gave several interesting examples of the previous misuse of statistics; and he also proved that certain runs at roulette (which he had experienced during two weeks at Monte Carlo in 1892) were so far from the expected frequencies that odds against the assumption of an honest wheel were some 10^{29} to one! A general discussion of the chi-square test and an extensive bibliography appear in the survey article by William G. Cochran, *Annals Math. Stat.* **23** (1952), 315–345.

Let us now consider a brief derivation of the theory behind the chi-square test. The exact probability that $Y_1 = y_1, \ldots, Y_k = y_k$ is easily seen to be

$$\frac{n!}{y_1! \ldots y_k!} p_1^{y_1} \ldots p_k^{y_k}. \tag{17}$$

If we assume that Y_s has the value y_s with the Poisson probability

$$\frac{e^{-np_s}(np_s)^{y_s}}{y_s!},$$

and that the Y's are independent, then $(Y_1, \ldots, Y_k)$ will equal $(y_1, \ldots, y_k)$ with probability

$$\prod_{s=1}^{k} \frac{e^{-np_s}(np_s)^{y_s}}{y_s!},$$

and $Y_1 + \cdots + Y_k$ will equal n with probability

$$\sum_{\substack{y_1 + \cdots + y_k = n \\ y_1, \ldots, y_k \geq 0}} \prod_{s=1}^{k} \frac{e^{-np_s}(np_s)^{y_s}}{y_s!} = \frac{e^{-n}n^n}{n!}.$$

If we assume that they are independent *except* for the condition $Y_1 + \cdots + Y_k = n$, the probability that $(Y_1, \ldots, Y_k) = (y_1, \ldots, y_k)$ is the quotient

$$\left(\prod_{s=1}^{k} \frac{e^{-np_s}(np_s)^{y_s}}{y_s!} \right) \Big/ \left(\frac{e^{-n}n^n}{n!} \right),$$

which equals (17). *We may therefore regard the Y's as independently Poisson distributed, except for the fact that they have a fixed sum.*

It is convenient to make a change of variables,

$$Z_s = \frac{Y_s - np_s}{\sqrt{np_s}}, \tag{18}$$

so that $V = Z_1^2 + \cdots + Z_k^2$. The condition $Y_1 + \cdots + Y_k = n$ is equivalent to

$$\sqrt{p_1}\, Z_1 + \cdots + \sqrt{p_k}\, Z_k = 0. \tag{19}$$

Let us consider the $(k-1)$-dimensional space S of all vectors $(Z_1, \ldots, Z_k)$ such that (19) holds. For large values of n, each Z_s has *approximately* the normal distribution (see exercise 1.2.10–15; it is at this point in the derivation that the chi-square method becomes only an approximation for large n). Therefore, points in a differential volume $dz_2 \ldots dz_k$ of S occur with probability approximately proportional to $\exp\left(-(z_1^2 + \cdots + z_k^2)/2\right)$, and the probability that $V \le v$ is

$$\frac{\int_{(z_1,\ldots,z_k) \text{ in } S \text{ and } z_1^2 + \cdots + z_k^2 \le v} \exp\left(-(z_1^2 + \cdots + z_k^2)/2\right) dz_2 \ldots dz_k}{\int_{(z_1,\ldots,z_k) \text{ in } S} \exp\left(-(z_1^2 + \cdots + z_k^2)/2\right) dz_2 \ldots dz_k}. \tag{20}$$

Since the hyperplane (19) passes through the origin of k-dimensional space, the numerator in (20) is an integration over a $(k-1)$-dimensional ball centered at the origin. An appropriate transformation to generalized polar coordinates with radius χ and angles $\omega_1, \ldots, \omega_{k-2}$ transforms (20) into

$$\frac{\int_{\chi^2 \le v} e^{-\chi^2/2} \chi^{k-2} f(\omega_1, \ldots, \omega_{k-2})\, d\chi\, d\omega_1 \ldots d\omega_{k-2}}{\int e^{-\chi^2/2} \chi^{k-2} f(\omega_1, \ldots, \omega_{k-2})\, d\chi\, d\omega_1 \ldots d\omega_{k-2}}$$

for some function f (see exercise 15); then integration over the angles $\omega_1, \ldots, \omega_{k-2}$ gives a constant factor that cancels from numerator and denominator. We finally obtain the formula

$$\frac{\int_0^{\sqrt{v}} e^{-\chi^2/2} \chi^{k-2}\, d\chi}{\int_0^{\infty} e^{-\chi^2/2} \chi^{k-2}\, d\chi} \tag{21}$$

for the approximate probability that $V \le v$.

Our derivation of (21) uses the symbol χ to stand for the radial length, just as Pearson did in his original paper; this is how the χ^2 test got its name. Substituting $t = \chi^2/2$, the integrals can be expressed in terms of the incomplete gamma function, which we discussed in Section 1.2.11.3:

$$\lim_{n \to \infty} \Pr(V \le v) = \gamma\left(\frac{k-1}{2}, \frac{v}{2}\right) \Big/ \Gamma\left(\frac{k-1}{2}\right). \tag{22}$$

This is the definition of the chi-square distribution with $k-1$ degrees of freedom.

G. Valiant and P. Valiant recently discovered, to everyone's surprise, that

$$\sum_{s=1}^{k} \frac{(Y_s - np_s)^2 - Y_s}{p_s^{2/3}} \tag{23}$$

is superior to the chi-square statistic (6). [See *SICOMP* **46** (2017), 429–455.]

We now turn to the KS test. In 1933, A. N. Kolmogorov proposed a test based on the statistic

$$K_n = \sqrt{n} \max_{-\infty < x < +\infty} |F_n(x) - F(x)| = \max(K_n^+, K_n^-).$$

N. V. Smirnov discussed several modifications of this test in 1939, including the individual examination of K_n^+ and K_n^- as we have suggested above. There is a large family of similar tests, but the K_n^+ and K_n^- statistics seem to be most convenient for computer application. A comprehensive review of the literature concerning KS tests and their generalizations, including an extensive bibliography, appears in a monograph by J. Durbin, *Regional Conf. Series on Applied Math.* **9** (SIAM, 1973).

To study the distribution of K_n^+ and K_n^-, we begin with the following basic fact: *If X is a random variable with the continuous distribution $F(x)$, then $F(X)$ is a uniformly distributed real number between 0 and 1.* To prove this, we need only verify that if $0 \le y \le 1$ we have $F(X) \le y$ with probability y. Since F is continuous, $F(x_0) = y$ for some x_0; thus the probability that $F(X) \le y$ is the probability that $X \le x_0$. By definition, the latter probability is $F(x_0)$, that is; it is y.

Let $Y_j = nF(X_j)$, for $1 \le j \le n$, where the X's have been sorted as in Step 2 preceding Eq. (13). Then the variables Y_j are essentially the same as independent, uniformly distributed random numbers between 0 and n that have been sorted into nondecreasing order, $Y_1 \le Y_2 \le \cdots \le Y_n$; and the first equation of (13) may be transformed into

$$K_n^+ = \frac{1}{\sqrt{n}} \max(1 - Y_1, 2 - Y_2, \ldots, n - Y_n).$$

If $0 \le t \le n$, the probability that $K_n^+ \le t/\sqrt{n}$ is therefore the probability that $Y_j \ge j - t$ for $1 \le j \le n$. We can express it in terms of n-dimensional integrals,

$$\frac{\int_{\alpha_n}^n dy_n \int_{\alpha_{n-1}}^{y_n} dy_{n-1} \cdots \int_{\alpha_1}^{y_2} dy_1}{\int_0^n dy_n \int_0^{y_n} dy_{n-1} \cdots \int_0^{y_2} dy_1}, \qquad \text{where} \qquad \alpha_j = \max(j - t, 0). \qquad (24)$$

The denominator here is immediately evaluated: It is found to be $n^n/n!$, which makes sense since the hypercube of all vectors $(y_1, y_2, \ldots, y_n)$ with $0 \le y_j < n$ has volume n^n, and it can be divided into $n!$ equal parts corresponding to each possible ordering of the y's. The integral in the numerator is a little more difficult, but it yields to the attack suggested in exercise 17, and we get the general formulas

$$\Pr\left(K_n^+ \le \frac{t}{\sqrt{n}}\right) = \frac{t}{n^n} \sum_{0 \le k \le t} \binom{n}{k} (k - t)^k (t + n - k)^{n-k-1} \qquad (25)$$

$$= 1 - \frac{t}{n^n} \sum_{t < k \le n} \binom{n}{k} (k - t)^k (t + n - k)^{n-k-1}. \qquad (26)$$

The distribution of K_n^- is exactly the same. Equation (26) was first obtained by N. V. Smirnov [*Uspekhi Mat. Nauk* **10** (1944), 179–206]; see also Z. W.

Birnbaum and Fred H. Tingey, *Annals Math. Stat.* **22** (1951), 592–596. Smirnov derived the asymptotic formula

$$\Pr(K_n^+ \leq s) = 1 - e^{-2s^2}\left(1 - \frac{2}{3}s/\sqrt{n} + O(1/n)\right) \tag{27}$$

for all fixed $s \geq 0$; Table 2 shows the resulting approximations for large n.

Abel's binomial theorem, Eq. 1.2.6–(16), proves the equivalence of (25) and (26). We can extend Table 2 using either formula, but there is an interesting tradeoff: Although the sum in (25) has only about $s\sqrt{n}$ terms, when $s = t/\sqrt{n}$ is given, it must be evaluated with multiple-precision arithmetic, because the terms are large and their leading digits cancel out. No such problem arises in (26), since its terms are all positive; but (26) has $n - s\sqrt{n}$ terms.

EXERCISES

1. [*00*] What line of the chi-square table should be used to check whether or not the value $V = 7\frac{7}{48}$ of Eq. (5) is improbably high?

2. [*20*] If two dice are "loaded" so that, on one die, the value 1 will turn up exactly twice as often as any of the other values, and the other die is similarly biased towards 6, compute the probability p_s that a total of exactly s will appear on the two dice, for $2 \leq s \leq 12$.

▶ **3.** [*23*] Some dice that were loaded as described in the previous exercise were rolled 144 times, and the following values were observed:

value of s =	2	3	4	5	6	7	8	9	10	11	12
observed number, Y_s =	2	6	10	16	18	32	20	13	16	9	2

Apply the chi-square test to *these* values, using the probabilities in (1), pretending that the dice are not in fact known to be faulty. Does the chi-square test detect the bad dice? If not, explain why not.

▶ **4.** [*23*] The author actually obtained the data in experiment 1 of (9) by simulating dice in which one was normal, the other was loaded so that it always turned up 1 or 6. (The latter two possibilities were equally probable.) Compute the probabilities that replace (1) in this case, and by using a chi-square test decide if the results of that experiment are consistent with the dice being loaded in this way.

5. [*22*] Let $F(x)$ be the uniform distribution, Fig. 3(b). Find K_{20}^+ and K_{20}^- for the following 20 observations:

0.414, 0.732, 0.236, 0.162, 0.259, 0.442, 0.189, 0.693, 0.098, 0.302,
0.442, 0.434, 0.141, 0.017, 0.318, 0.869, 0.772, 0.678, 0.354, 0.718,

and state whether these observations are significantly different from the expected behavior with respect to either of these two tests.

6. [*M20*] Consider $F_n(x)$, as given in Eq. (10), for fixed x. What is the probability that $F_n(x) = s/n$, given an integer s? What is the mean value of $F_n(x)$? What is the standard deviation?

7. [*M15*] Show that K_n^+ and K_n^- can never be negative. What is the largest possible value K_n^+ can have?

8. [*00*] The text describes an experiment in which 20 values of the statistic K_{10}^+ were obtained in the study of a random sequence. These values were plotted, to obtain

Fig. 4, and a KS statistic was computed from the resulting graph. Why were the table entries for $n = 20$ used to study the resulting statistic, instead of the table entries for $n = 10$?

▶ **9.** [*20*] The experiment described in the text consisted of plotting 20 values of K_{10}^+, computed from the maximum-of-5 test applied to different parts of a random sequence. We could have computed also the corresponding 20 values of K_{10}^-; since K_{10}^- has the same distribution as K_{10}^+, we could lump together the 40 values thus obtained (that is, 20 of the K_{10}^+'s and 20 of the K_{10}^-'s), and a KS test could be applied so that we would get new values K_{40}^+, K_{40}^-. Discuss the merits of this idea.

▶ **10.** [*20*] Suppose a chi-square test is done by making n observations, and the value V is obtained. Now we repeat the test on these same n observations over again (getting, of course, the same results), and we put together the data from both tests, regarding it as a single chi-square test with $2n$ observations. (This procedure violates the text's stipulation that all of the observations must be independent of one another.) How is the second value of V related to the first one?

11. [*10*] Solve exercise 10 substituting the KS test for the chi-square test.

12. [*M28*] Suppose a chi-square test is made on a set of n observations, assuming that p_s is the probability that each observation falls into category s; but suppose that in actual fact the observations have probability $q_s \neq p_s$ of falling into category s. (See exercise 3.) We would, of course, like the chi-square test to detect the fact that the p_s assumption was incorrect. Show that this *will* happen, if n is large enough. Prove also the analogous result for the KS test.

13. [*M24*] Prove that Eqs. (13) are equivalent to Eqs. (11).

▶ **14.** [*HM26*] Let Z_s be given by Eq. (18). Show directly by using Stirling's approximation that the multinomial probability

$$n! p_1^{Y_1} \ldots p_k^{Y_k}/Y_1! \ldots Y_k! = e^{-V/2}/\sqrt{(2n\pi)^{k-1}p_1 \ldots p_k} + O(n^{-k/2}),$$

if $Z_1, Z_2, \ldots, Z_k$ are bounded as $n \to \infty$. (This idea leads to a proof of the chi-square test that is much closer to "first principles," and requires less handwaving, than the derivation in the text.)

15. [*HM24*] Polar coordinates in two dimensions are conventionally defined by the equations $x = r \cos \theta$ and $y = r \sin \theta$. For the purposes of integration, we have $dx \, dy = r \, dr \, d\theta$. More generally, in n-dimensional space we can let

$$x_k = r \sin \theta_1 \ldots \sin \theta_{k-1} \cos \theta_k, \quad 1 \leq k < n, \quad \text{and} \quad x_n = r \sin \theta_1 \ldots \sin \theta_{n-1}.$$

Show that in this case

$$dx_1 \, dx_2 \ldots dx_n = |r^{n-1} \sin^{n-2} \theta_1 \ldots \sin \theta_{n-2} \, dr \, d\theta_1 \ldots d\theta_{n-1}|.$$

▶ **16.** [*HM35*] Generalize Theorem 1.2.11.3A to find the value of

$$\gamma(x + 1, \, x + z\sqrt{2x} + y)/\Gamma(x + 1),$$

for large x and fixed y, z. Disregard terms of the answer that are $O(1/x)$. Use this result to find the approximate solution, t, to the equation

$$\gamma\left(\frac{\nu}{2}, \frac{t}{2}\right) \Big/ \Gamma\left(\frac{\nu}{2}\right) = p,$$

for large ν and fixed p, thereby accounting for the asymptotic formulas indicated in Table 1. [*Hint:* See exercise 1.2.11.3–8.]

17. [*HM26*] Let t be a fixed real number. For $0 \le k \le n$, let

$$P_{nk}(x) = \int_{n-t}^{x} dx_n \int_{n-1-t}^{x_n} dx_{n-1} \cdots \int_{k+1-t}^{x_{k+2}} dx_{k+1} \int_{0}^{x_{k+1}} dx_k \cdots \int_{0}^{x_2} dx_1;$$

by convention, let $P_{00}(x) = 1$. Prove the following relations:

a) $P_{nk}(x) = \int_{n}^{x+t} dx_n \int_{n-1}^{x_n} dx_{n-1} \cdots \int_{k+1}^{x_{k+2}} dx_{k+1} \int_{t}^{x_{k+1}} dx_k \cdots \int_{t}^{x_2} dx_1.$

b) $P_{n0}(x) = (x+t)^n/n! - (x+t)^{n-1}/(n-1)!.$

c) $P_{nk}(x) - P_{n(k-1)}(x) = \dfrac{(k-t)^k}{k!} P_{(n-k)0}(x-k)$, if $1 \le k \le n$.

d) Obtain a general formula for $P_{nk}(x)$, and apply it to the evaluation of Eq. (24).

18. [*M20*] Give a "simple" reason why K_n^- has the same probability distribution as K_n^+.

19. [*HM48*] Develop tests, analogous to the Kolmogorov–Smirnov test, for use with multivariate distributions $F(x_1, \ldots, x_r) = \Pr(X_1 \le x_1, \ldots, X_r \le x_r)$. (Such procedures could be used, for example, in place of the "serial test" in the next section.)

20. [*HM41*] Deduce further terms of the asymptotic behavior of the KS distribution, extending (27).

21. [*M40*] Although the text states that the KS test should be applied only when $F(x)$ is a continuous distribution function, it is, of course, possible to try to compute K_n^+ and K_n^- even when the distribution has jumps. Analyze the probable behavior of K_n^+ and K_n^- for various discontinuous distributions $F(x)$. Compare the effectiveness of the resulting statistical test with the chi-square test on several samples of random numbers.

22. [*HM46*] Investigate the "improved" KS test suggested in the answer to exercise 6.

23. [*M22*] (T. Gonzalez, S. Sahni, and W. R. Franta.) (a) Suppose that the maximum value in formula (13) for the KS statistic K_n^+ occurs at a given index j where $\lfloor nF(X_j) \rfloor = k$. Prove that $F(X_j) = \max_{1 \le i \le n} \{F(X_i) \mid \lfloor nF(X_i) \rfloor = k\}$. (b) Design an algorithm that calculates K_n^+ and K_n^- in $O(n)$ steps (without sorting).

▶ **24.** [*40*] Experiment with various probability distributions (p, q, r) on three categories, where $p + q + r = 1$, by computing the exact distribution of the chi-square statistic V for various n, thereby determining how accurate an approximation the chi-square distribution with two degrees of freedom really is.

25. [*HM26*] Suppose $Y_i = \sum_{j=1}^{n} a_{ij}X_j + \mu_i$ for $1 \le i \le m$, where $X_1, \ldots, X_n$ are independent random variables with mean zero and unit variance, and the matrix $A = (a_{ij})$ has rank n.

a) Express the covariance matrix $C = (c_{ij})$, where $c_{ij} = \mathrm{E}(Y_i - \mu_i)(Y_j - \mu_j)$, in terms of the matrix A.

b) Prove that if $\bar{C} = (\bar{c}_{ij})$ is any matrix such that $C\bar{C}C = C$, the statistic

$$W = \sum_{i=1}^{m} \sum_{j=1}^{m} (Y_i - \mu_i)(Y_j - \mu_j)\bar{c}_{ij}$$

is equal to $X_1^2 + \cdots + X_n^2$. [Consequently, if the X_j have the normal distribution, W has the chi-square distribution with n degrees of freedom.]

The equanimity of your average tosser of coins
depends upon a law ... which ensures that
he will not upset himself by losing too much
nor upset his opponent by winning too often.
— TOM STOPPARD, *Rosencrantz & Guildenstern are Dead* (1966)

3.3.2. Empirical Tests

In this section we shall discuss twelve kinds of specific tests that have traditionally been applied to sequences in order to investigate their randomness. The discussion of each test has two parts: (a) a "plug-in" description of how to perform
the test; and (b) a study of the theoretical basis for the test. (Readers who lack
mathematical training may wish to skip over the theoretical discussions. Conversely, mathematically inclined readers may find the associated theory quite interesting, even if they never intend to test random number generators, since some
instructive combinatorial questions are involved here. Indeed, this section introduces several topics that will be important to us later in quite different contexts.)

Each test is applied to a sequence

$$\langle U_n \rangle = U_0, U_1, U_2, \ldots \tag{1}$$

of real numbers, which purports to be independently and uniformly distributed
between zero and one. Some of the tests are designed primarily for integer-valued
sequences, instead of the real-valued sequence (1). In this case, the auxiliary
sequence

$$\langle Y_n \rangle = Y_0, Y_1, Y_2, \ldots \tag{2}$$

defined by the rule

$$Y_n = \lfloor dU_n \rfloor \tag{3}$$

is used instead. This is a sequence of integers that purports to be independently
and uniformly distributed between 0 and $d - 1$. The number d is chosen for
convenience; for example, we might have $d = 64 = 2^6$ on a binary computer,
so that Y_n represents the six most significant bits of the binary representation
of U_n. The value of d should be large enough so that the test is meaningful, but
not so large that the test becomes impracticably difficult to carry out.

The quantities U_n, Y_n, and d will have the significance stated above throughout this section, although the value of d will probably be different in different
tests.

A. Equidistribution test (Frequency test). The first requirement that
sequence (1) must meet is that its numbers are, in fact, uniformly distributed
between zero and one. There are two ways to make this test: (a) Use the
Kolmogorov–Smirnov test, with $F(x) = x$ for $0 \le x \le 1$. (b) Let d be a
convenient number, such as 100 on a decimal computer, 64 or 128 on a binary
computer, and use the sequence (2) instead of (1). For each integer r, $0 \le r < d$,
count the number of times that $Y_j = r$ for $0 \le j < n$, and then apply the
chi-square test using $k = d$ and probability $p_s = 1/d$ for each category.

The theory behind this test has been covered in Section 3.3.1.

B. Serial test. More generally, we want pairs of successive numbers to be uniformly distributed in an independent manner. The sun comes up just about as often as it goes down, in the long run, but that doesn't make its motion random.

To carry out the serial test, we simply count the number of times that the pair $(Y_{2j}, Y_{2j+1}) = (q, r)$ occurs, for $0 \leq j < n$; these counts are to be made for each pair of integers (q, r) with $0 \leq q, r < d$, and the chi-square test is applied to these $k = d^2$ categories with probability $1/d^2$ in each category. As with the equidistribution test, d may be any convenient number, but it will be somewhat smaller than the values suggested above since a valid chi-square test should have n large compared to k (say $n \geq 5d^2$ at least).

Clearly we can generalize this test to triples, quadruples, etc., instead of pairs (see exercise 2); however, the value of d must then be severely reduced in order to avoid having too many categories. When quadruples and larger numbers of adjacent elements are considered, we therefore make use of less exact tests such as the poker test or the maximum test described below.

Notice that $2n$ numbers of the sequence (2) are used in this test in order to make n observations. It would be a mistake to perform the serial test on the pairs (Y_0, Y_1), (Y_1, Y_2), ..., (Y_{n-1}, Y_n); can the reader see why? We might perform another serial test on the pairs (Y_{2j+1}, Y_{2j+2}), and expect the sequence to pass both tests, remembering that the tests aren't independent of each other. Alternatively, George Marsaglia has proved that, if the pairs (Y_0, Y_1), (Y_1, Y_2), ..., (Y_{n-1}, Y_n) are used, and if we use the usual chi-square method to compute both the statistics V_2 for the serial test and V_1 for the frequency test on $Y_0, \ldots, Y_{n-1}$ with the same value of d, then $V_2 - V_1$ should have the chi-square distribution with $d(d-1)$ degrees of freedom when n is large. (See exercise 24.)

C. Gap test. Another test is used to examine the length of "gaps" between occurrences of U_j in a certain range. If α and β are two real numbers with $0 \leq \alpha < \beta \leq 1$, we want to consider the lengths of consecutive subsequences U_j, U_{j+1}, ..., U_{j+r} in which U_{j+r} lies between α and β but the other U's do not. (This subsequence of $r + 1$ numbers represents a gap of length r.)

Algorithm G (*Data for gap test*). The following algorithm, applied to the sequence (1) for any given values of α and β, counts the number of gaps of lengths 0, 1, ..., $t - 1$ and the number of gaps of length $\geq t$, until n gaps have been tabulated.

G1. [Initialize.] Set $j \leftarrow -1$, $s \leftarrow 0$, and set COUNT$[r] \leftarrow 0$ for $0 \leq r \leq t$.

G2. [Set r zero.] Set $r \leftarrow 0$.

G3. [$\alpha \leq U_j < \beta$?] Increase j by 1. If $U_j \geq \alpha$ and $U_j < \beta$, go to step G5.

G4. [Increase r.] Increase r by one, and return to step G3.

G5. [Record the gap length.] (A gap of length r has now been found.) If $r \geq t$, increase COUNT$[t]$ by one, otherwise increase COUNT$[r]$ by one.

G6. [n gaps found?] Increase s by one. If $s < n$, return to step G2.   ∎

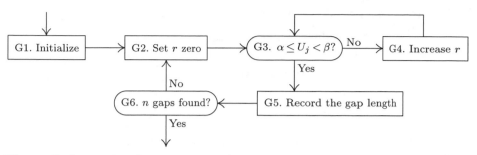

Fig. 6. Gathering data for the gap test. (Algorithms for the "coupon-collector's test" and the "run test" are similar.)

After Algorithm G has been performed, the chi-square test is applied to the $k = t + 1$ values of COUNT[0], COUNT[1], ..., COUNT[t], using the following probabilities:

$$p_r = p(1-p)^r, \quad \text{for } 0 \leq r \leq t-1; \qquad p_t = (1-p)^t. \tag{4}$$

Here $p = \beta - \alpha$ is the probability that $\alpha \leq U_j < \beta$. The values of n and t are to be chosen, as usual, so that each of the values of COUNT[r] is expected to be 5 or more, preferably more.

The gap test is often applied with $\alpha = 0$ or $\beta = 1$ in order to omit one of the comparisons in step G3. The special cases $(\alpha, \beta) = (0, \frac{1}{2})$ or $(\frac{1}{2}, 1)$ give rise to tests that are sometimes called "runs above the mean" and "runs below the mean," respectively.

The probabilities in Eq. (4) are easily deduced, so this derivation is left to the reader. Notice that the gap test as described above observes the lengths of n *gaps*; it does not observe the gap lengths among n *numbers*. If the sequence $\langle U_n \rangle$ is sufficiently nonrandom, Algorithm G might not terminate. Other gap tests that examine a fixed number of U's have also been proposed (see exercise 5).

D. Poker test (Partition test). The "classical" poker test considers n groups of five successive integers, $\{Y_{5j}, Y_{5j+1}, \ldots, Y_{5j+4}\}$ for $0 \leq j < n$, and observes which of the following seven patterns is matched by each (orderless) quintuple:

$$
\begin{aligned}
\text{All different:} &\quad abcde \\
\text{One pair:} &\quad aabcd \\
\text{Two pairs:} &\quad aabbc \\
\text{Three of a kind:} &\quad aaabc \\
\text{Full house:} &\quad aaabb \\
\text{Four of a kind:} &\quad aaaab \\
\text{Five of a kind:} &\quad aaaaa
\end{aligned}
$$

A chi-square test is based on the number of quintuples in each category.

It is reasonable to ask for a somewhat simpler version of this test, to facilitate the programming involved. A good compromise would simply be to count the number of *distinct* values in the set of five. We would then have five categories:

> 5 values = all different;
>
> 4 values = one pair;
>
> 3 values = two pairs, or three of a kind;
>
> 2 values = full house, or four of a kind;
>
> 1 value = five of a kind.

This breakdown is easier to determine systematically, and the test is nearly as good.

In general we can consider n groups of k successive numbers, and we can count the number of k-tuples with r different values. A chi-square test is then made, using the probability

$$
p_r = \frac{d(d-1)\ldots(d-r+1)}{d^k} \left\{ {k \atop r} \right\} \tag{5}
$$

that there are r different. (The Stirling numbers $\left\{ {k \atop r} \right\}$ are defined in Section 1.2.6, and they can readily be computed using the formulas given there.) Since the probability p_r is very small when $r = 1$ or 2, we generally lump a few categories of low probability together before the chi-square test is applied.

To derive the proper formula for p_r, we must count how many of the d^k k-tuples of numbers between 0 and $d-1$ have exactly r different elements, and divide the total by d^k. Since $d(d-1)\ldots(d-r+1)$ is the number of ordered choices of r things from a set of d objects, we need only show that $\left\{ {k \atop r} \right\}$ is the number of ways to partition a set of k elements into exactly r parts. Therefore exercise 1.2.6–64 completes the derivation of Eq. (5).

E. Coupon collector's test. The next test is related to the poker test somewhat as the gap test is related to the frequency test. We use the sequence Y_0, Y_1, ..., and we observe the lengths of segments Y_{j+1}, Y_{j+2}, ..., Y_{j+r} that are required to get a "complete set" of integers from 0 to $d-1$. Algorithm C describes this precisely:

Algorithm C (*Data for coupon collector's test*). Given a sequence of integers Y_0, Y_1, ..., with $0 \le Y_j < d$, this algorithm counts the lengths of n consecutive "coupon collector" segments. At the conclusion of the algorithm, COUNT[r] is the number of segments with length r, for $d \le r < t$, and COUNT[t] is the number of segments with length $\ge t$.

C1. [Initialize.] Set $j \leftarrow -1$, $s \leftarrow 0$, and set COUNT[r] $\leftarrow 0$ for $d \le r \le t$.

C2. [Set q, r zero.] Set $q \leftarrow r \leftarrow 0$, and set OCCURS[$k$] $\leftarrow 0$ for $0 \le k < d$.

C3. [Next observation.] Increase r and j by 1. If OCCURS[Y_j] $\ne 0$, repeat this step.

C4. [Complete set?] Set OCCURS[Y_j] $\leftarrow 1$ and $q \leftarrow q + 1$. (The subsequence observed so far contains q distinct values; if $q = d$, we therefore have a complete set.) If $q < d$, return to step C3.

C5. [Record the length.] If $r \geq t$, increase COUNT[t] by one, otherwise increase COUNT[r] by one.

C6. [n found?] Increase s by one. If $s < n$, return to step C2. ∎

For an example of this algorithm, see exercise 7. We may think of a boy collecting d types of coupons, which are randomly distributed in his breakfast cereal boxes; he must keep eating more cereal until he has one coupon of each type.

A chi-square test is to be applied to COUNT[d], COUNT[d + 1], ..., COUNT[t], with $k = t - d + 1$, after Algorithm C has counted n lengths. The corresponding probabilities are

$$p_r = \frac{d!}{d^r} \left\{ \begin{matrix} r-1 \\ d-1 \end{matrix} \right\}, \qquad d \leq r < t; \qquad p_t = 1 - \frac{d!}{d^{t-1}} \left\{ \begin{matrix} t-1 \\ d \end{matrix} \right\}. \tag{6}$$

To derive these probabilities, we simply note that if q_r denotes the probability that a subsequence of length r is *incomplete*, then

$$q_r = 1 - \frac{d!}{d^r} \left\{ \begin{matrix} r \\ d \end{matrix} \right\}$$

by Eq. (5); for this means we have an r-tuple of elements that do not have all d different values. Then (6) follows from the relations $p_t = q_{t-1}$ and

$$p_r = q_{r-1} - q_r \qquad \text{for } d \leq r < t.$$

For formulas that arise in connection with *generalizations* of the coupon collector's test, see exercises 9 and 10 and also the papers by George Pólya, *Zeitschrift für angewandte Math. und Mech.* **10** (1930), 96–97; Hermann von Schelling, *AMM* **61** (1954), 306–311.

F. Permutation test. Divide the input sequence into n groups of t elements each, that is, $(U_{jt}, U_{jt+1}, \ldots, U_{jt+t-1})$ for $0 \leq j < n$. The elements in each group can have $t!$ possible relative orderings; the number of times each ordering appears is counted, and a chi-square test is applied with $k = t!$ and with probability $1/t!$ for each ordering.

For example, if $t = 3$ we would have six possible categories, according to whether $U_{3j} < U_{3j+1} < U_{3j+2}$ or $U_{3j} < U_{3j+2} < U_{3j+1}$ or $\cdots$ or $U_{3j+2} < U_{3j+1} < U_{3j}$. We assume in this test that equality between U's does not occur; such an assumption is justified, for the probability that two U's are equal is zero.

A convenient way to perform the permutation test on a computer makes use of the following algorithm, which is of interest in itself:

Algorithm P (*Analyze a permutation*). Given a sequence of distinct elements $(U_1, \ldots, U_t)$, we compute an integer $f(U_1, \ldots, U_t)$ such that

$$0 \leq f(U_1, \ldots, U_t) < t!,$$

and $f(U_1, \ldots, U_t) = f(V_1, \ldots, V_t)$ if and only if $(U_1, \ldots, U_t)$ and $(V_1, \ldots, V_t)$ have the same relative ordering.

P1. [Initialize.] Set $r \leftarrow t$, $f \leftarrow 0$. (During this algorithm we will have $0 \leq f < t!/r!$.)

P2. [Find maximum.] Find the maximum of $\{U_1, \ldots, U_r\}$, and suppose that U_s is the maximum. Set $f \leftarrow r \cdot f + s - 1$.

P3. [Exchange.] Exchange $U_r \leftrightarrow U_s$.

P4. [Decrease r.] Decrease r by one. If $r > 1$, return to step P2. ▮

The sequence $(U_1, \ldots, U_t)$ will have been sorted into ascending order when this algorithm stops. To prove that the result f uniquely characterizes the *initial* order of $(U_1, \ldots, U_t)$, we note that Algorithm P can be run backwards:

$$\text{For } r = 2, 3, \ldots, t,$$
$$\text{set } s \leftarrow f \bmod r, \ f \leftarrow \lfloor f/r \rfloor,$$
$$\text{and exchange } U_r \leftrightarrow U_{s+1}.$$

It is easy to see that this will undo the effects of steps P2–P4; hence no two permutations can yield the same value of f, and Algorithm P performs as advertised.

The essential idea that underlies Algorithm P is a mixed-radix representation called the "factorial number system": Every integer in the range $0 \leq f < t!$ can be uniquely written in the form

$$f = \big(\ldots (c_{t-1} \times (t-1) + c_{t-2}) \times (t-2) + \cdots + c_2\big) \times 2 + c_1$$
$$= (t-1)! \, c_{t-1} + (t-2)! \, c_{t-2} + \cdots + 2! \, c_2 + 1! \, c_1 \qquad (7)$$

where the "digits" c_j are integers satisfying

$$0 \leq c_j \leq j, \qquad \text{for } 1 \leq j < t. \qquad (8)$$

In Algorithm P, $c_{r-1} = s - 1$ when step P2 is performed for a given value of r.

G. Run test. A sequence may also be tested for "runs up" and "runs down." This means that we examine the length of *monotone* portions of the original sequence (segments that are increasing or decreasing).

As an example of the precise definition of a run, consider the sequence of ten digits "1298536704". Putting a vertical line at the left and right and between X_j and X_{j+1} whenever $X_j > X_{j+1}$, we obtain

$$|1 \ \ 2 \ \ 9|8|5|3 \ \ 6 \ \ 7|0 \ \ 4|, \qquad (9)$$

which displays the "runs up": There is a run of length 3, followed by two runs of length 1, followed by another run of length 3, followed by a run of length 2. The algorithm of exercise 12 shows how to tabulate the length of "runs up."

Unlike the gap test and the coupon collector's test (which are in many other respects similar to this test), *we should not apply a chi-square test to the run counts*, since adjacent runs are *not* independent. A long run will tend to be followed by a short run, and conversely. This lack of independence is enough to invalidate a straightforward chi-square test. Instead, the following statistic may be computed, when the run lengths have been determined as in exercise 12:

$$V = \frac{1}{n-6} \sum_{1 \le i,j \le 6} (\text{COUNT}[i] - nb_i)(\text{COUNT}[j] - nb_j)a_{ij}, \qquad (10)$$

where n is the length of the sequence, and the matrices of coefficients $A = (a_{ij})_{1 \le i,j \le 6}$ and $B = (b_i)_{1 \le i \le 6}$ are given by

$$A = \begin{pmatrix} 4529.4 & 9044.9 & 13568 & 18091 & 22615 & 27892 \\ 9044.9 & 18097 & 27139 & 36187 & 45234 & 55789 \\ 13568 & 27139 & 40721 & 54281 & 67852 & 83685 \\ 18091 & 36187 & 54281 & 72414 & 90470 & 111580 \\ 22615 & 45234 & 67852 & 90470 & 113262 & 139476 \\ 27892 & 55789 & 83685 & 111580 & 139476 & 172860 \end{pmatrix}, \quad B = \begin{pmatrix} \frac{1}{6} \\ \frac{5}{24} \\ \frac{11}{120} \\ \frac{19}{720} \\ \frac{29}{5040} \\ \frac{1}{840} \end{pmatrix}.$$

$$(11)$$

(The values of a_{ij} shown here are approximate only; exact values can be obtained from formulas derived below.) *The statistic V in* (10) *should have the chi-square distribution with six, not five, degrees of freedom,* when n is large. The value of n should be, say, 4000 or more. The same test can be applied to "runs down."

A vastly simpler and more practical run test appears in exercise 14, so a reader who is interested only in testing random number generators should skip the next few pages and go on to the "maximum-of-t test" after looking at exercise 14. On the other hand it is instructive from a mathematical standpoint to see how a complicated run test with interdependent runs can be treated, so we shall now digress for a moment.

Given any permutation of n elements, let $Z_{pi} = 1$ if position i is the beginning of an ascending run of length p or more, and let $Z_{pi} = 0$ otherwise. For example, consider the permutation (9) with $n = 10$; we have

$$Z_{11} = Z_{21} = Z_{31} = Z_{14} = Z_{15} = Z_{16} = Z_{26} = Z_{36} = Z_{19} = Z_{29} = 1,$$

and all other Z's are zero. With this notation,

$$R'_p = Z_{p1} + Z_{p2} + \cdots + Z_{pn} \qquad (12)$$

is the number of runs of length $\ge p$, and

$$R_p = R'_p - R'_{p+1} \qquad (13)$$

is the number of runs of length p exactly. Our goal is to compute the mean value of R_p, and also the *covariance*

$$\text{covar}(R_p, R_q) = \text{mean}\big((R_p - \text{mean}(R_p))(R_q - \text{mean}(R_q))\big),$$

which measures the interdependence of R_p and R_q. These mean values are to be computed as the average over the set of all $n!$ permutations.

Equations (12) and (13) show that the answers can be expressed in terms of the mean values of Z_{pi} and of $Z_{pi}Z_{qj}$, so as the first step of the derivation we obtain the following results (assuming that $i < j$):

$$\frac{1}{n!} \sum Z_{pi} = \begin{cases} \dfrac{p + \delta_{i1}}{(p+1)!}, & \text{if } i \leq n - p + 1; \\ 0, & \text{otherwise.} \end{cases}$$

$$\frac{1}{n!} \sum Z_{pi}Z_{qj} = \begin{cases} \dfrac{(p + \delta_{i1})q}{(p+1)!\,(q+1)!}, & \text{if } i + p < j \leq n - q + 1; \quad (14) \\ \dfrac{p + \delta_{i1}}{(p+1)!\,q!} - \dfrac{p + q + \delta_{i1}}{(p+q+1)!}, & \text{if } i + p = j \leq n - q + 1; \\ 0, & \text{otherwise.} \end{cases}$$

The $\sum$-signs stand for summation over all possible permutations. To illustrate the calculations involved here, we will work the most difficult case, when $i + p = j \leq n - q + 1$, and when $i > 1$. The quantity $Z_{pi}Z_{qj}$ is either zero or one, so the summation amounts to counting all permutations $U_1 U_2 \ldots U_n$ for which $Z_{pi} = Z_{qj} = 1$, that is, all permutations such that

$$U_{i-1} > U_i < \cdots < U_{i+p-1} > U_{i+p} < \cdots < U_{i+p+q-1}. \quad (15)$$

The number of such permutations may be enumerated as follows: There are $\binom{n}{p+q+1}$ ways to choose the elements for the positions indicated in (15); there are

$$(p+q+1)\binom{p+q}{p} - \binom{p+q+1}{p+1} - \binom{p+q+1}{1} + 1 \quad (16)$$

ways to arrange them in the order (15), as shown in exercise 13; and there are $(n - p - q - 1)!$ ways to arrange the remaining elements. Thus there are $\binom{n}{p+q+1}(n - p - q - 1)!$ times (16) ways in all, and we divide by $n!$ to get the desired formula.

From relations (14) a rather lengthy calculation leads to

$$\text{mean}(R'_p) = (n+1)p/(p+1)! - (p-1)/p!, \qquad 1 \leq p \leq n; \quad (17)$$

$$\begin{aligned} \text{covar}(R'_p, R'_q) &= \text{mean}(R'_p R'_q) - \text{mean}(R'_p)\,\text{mean}(R'_q) \\ &= \sum_{1 \leq i,j \leq n} \frac{1}{n!} \sum Z_{pi}Z_{qj} - \text{mean}(R'_p)\,\text{mean}(R'_q) \\ &= \begin{cases} \text{mean}(R'_t) + f(p,q,n), & \text{if } p + q \leq n, \\ \text{mean}(R'_t) - \text{mean}(R'_p)\,\text{mean}(R'_q), & \text{if } p + q > n, \end{cases} \quad (18) \end{aligned}$$

where $t = \max(p, q)$, $s = p + q$, and

$$f(p,q,n) = (n+1)\left(\frac{s(1 - pq) + pq}{(p+1)!\,(q+1)!} - \frac{2s}{(s+1)!}\right) + 2\left(\frac{s-1}{s!}\right)$$
$$+ \frac{(s^2 - s - 2)pq - s^2 - p^2q^2 + 1}{(p+1)!\,(q+1)!}. \quad (19)$$

This expression for the covariance is unfortunately quite complicated, but it is necessary for a successful run test as described above. From these formulas it is easy to compute

$$\text{mean}(R_p) = \text{mean}(R_p') - \text{mean}(R_{p+1}'),$$

$$\text{covar}(R_p, R_q') = \text{covar}(R_p', R_q') - \text{covar}(R_{p+1}', R_q'), \tag{20}$$

$$\text{covar}(R_p, R_q) = \text{covar}(R_p, R_q') - \text{covar}(R_p, R_{q+1}').$$

In *Annals Math. Stat.* **15** (1944), 163–165, J. Wolfowitz proved that the quantities $R_1, R_2, \ldots, R_{t-1}, R_t'$ become normally distributed as $n \to \infty$, subject to the mean and covariance expressed above; this implies that the following test for runs is valid: Given a sequence of n random numbers, compute the number of runs R_p of length p for $1 \le p < t$, and also the number of runs R_t' of length t or more. Let

$$Q_1 = R_1 - \text{mean}(R_1), \quad \ldots, \quad Q_{t-1} = R_{t-1} - \text{mean}(R_{t-1}),$$
$$Q_t = R_t' - \text{mean}(R_t'). \tag{21}$$

Form the matrix C of the covariances of the R's; for example, $C_{13} = \text{covar}(R_1, R_3)$, while $C_{1t} = \text{covar}(R_1, R_t')$. When $t = 6$, we have

$$C = nC_1 + C_2, \tag{22}$$

where

$$C_1 = \begin{pmatrix}
\frac{23}{180} & \frac{-7}{360} & \frac{-5}{336} & \frac{-433}{60480} & \frac{-13}{5670} & \frac{-121}{181440} \\
\frac{-7}{360} & \frac{2843}{20160} & \frac{-989}{20160} & \frac{-7159}{362880} & \frac{-10019}{1814400} & \frac{-1303}{907200} \\
\frac{-5}{336} & \frac{-989}{20160} & \frac{54563}{907200} & \frac{-21311}{1814400} & \frac{-62369}{19958400} & \frac{-7783}{9979200} \\
\frac{-433}{60480} & \frac{-7159}{362880} & \frac{-21311}{1814400} & \frac{886657}{39916800} & \frac{-257699}{239500800} & \frac{-62611}{239500800} \\
\frac{-13}{5670} & \frac{-10019}{1814400} & \frac{-62369}{19958400} & \frac{-257699}{239500800} & \frac{29874811}{5448643200} & \frac{-1407179}{21794572800} \\
\frac{-121}{181440} & \frac{-1303}{907200} & \frac{-7783}{9979200} & \frac{-62611}{239500800} & \frac{-1407179}{21794572800} & \frac{2134697}{1816214400}
\end{pmatrix},$$

$$C_2 = \begin{pmatrix}
\frac{83}{180} & \frac{-29}{180} & \frac{-11}{210} & \frac{-41}{12096} & \frac{91}{25920} & \frac{41}{18144} \\
\frac{-29}{180} & \frac{-305}{4032} & \frac{319}{20160} & \frac{2557}{72576} & \frac{10177}{604800} & \frac{413}{64800} \\
\frac{-11}{210} & \frac{319}{20160} & \frac{-58747}{907200} & \frac{19703}{604800} & \frac{239471}{19958400} & \frac{39517}{9979200} \\
\frac{-41}{12096} & \frac{2557}{72576} & \frac{19703}{604800} & \frac{-220837}{4435200} & \frac{1196401}{239500800} & \frac{360989}{239500800} \\
\frac{91}{25920} & \frac{10177}{604800} & \frac{239471}{19958400} & \frac{1196401}{239500800} & \frac{-139126639}{7264857600} & \frac{4577641}{10897286400} \\
\frac{41}{18144} & \frac{413}{64800} & \frac{39517}{9979200} & \frac{360989}{239500800} & \frac{4577641}{10897286400} & \frac{-122953057}{21794572800}
\end{pmatrix}$$

if $n \ge 12$. Now form $A = (a_{ij})$, the inverse of the matrix C, and compute $\sum_{i,j=1}^{t} Q_i Q_j a_{ij}$. The result for large n should have approximately the chi-square distribution with t degrees of freedom.

The matrix A given earlier in (11) is the inverse of C_1 to five significant figures. The true inverse, A, is $n^{-1}C_1^{-1} - n^{-2}C_1^{-1}C_2C_1^{-1} + n^{-3}C_1^{-1}C_2C_1^{-1}C_2C_1^{-1} - \cdots$, and it turns out that $C_1^{-1}C_2C_1^{-1}$ is very nearly equal to $-6C_1^{-1}$. Therefore by (10), $V \approx Q^T C_1^{-1} Q/(n-6)$, where $Q = (Q_1 \ldots Q_t)^T$.

H. Maximum-of-t test. For $0 \le j < n$, let $V_j = \max(U_{tj}, U_{tj+1}, \ldots, U_{tj+t-1})$. Now apply the Kolmogorov–Smirnov test to the sequence V_0, V_1, ..., V_{n-1}, with the distribution function $F(x) = x^t$, $0 \le x \le 1$. Alternatively, apply the equidistribution test to the sequence V_0^t, V_1^t, ..., V_{n-1}^t.

To verify this test, we must show that the distribution function for the V_j is $F(x) = x^t$. The probability that $\max(U_1, U_2, \ldots, U_t) \le x$ is the probability that $U_1 \le x$ and $U_2 \le x$ and ... and $U_t \le x$, which is the product of the individual probabilities, namely $xx \ldots x = x^t$.

I. Collision test. Chi-square tests can be made only when a nontrivial number of items are expected in each category. But another kind of test can be used when the number of categories is much larger than the number of observations; this test is related to "hashing," an important method for information retrieval that we shall study in Section 6.4.

Suppose we have m urns and we throw n balls at random into those urns, where m is much greater than n. Most of the balls will land in urns that were previously empty, but if a ball falls into an urn that already contains at least one ball we say that a "collision" has occurred. The collision test counts the number of collisions, and a generator passes this test if it doesn't induce too many or too few collisions.

To fix the ideas, suppose $m = 2^{20}$ and $n = 2^{14}$. Then each urn will receive only one 64th of a ball, on the average. The probability that a given urn will contain exactly k balls is $p_k = \binom{n}{k} m^{-k}(1 - m^{-1})^{n-k}$, so the expected number of collisions per urn is

$$\sum_{k \ge 1}(k-1)p_k = \sum_{k \ge 0} kp_k - \sum_{k \ge 1} p_k = \frac{n}{m} - 1 + p_0.$$

Since $p_0 = (1 - m^{-1})^n = 1 - nm^{-1} + \binom{n}{2}m^{-2} -$ smaller terms, we find that the average total number of collisions taken over all m urns is slightly less than $n^2/(2m) = 128$. (The actual value is ≈ 127.33.)

We can use the collision test to rate a random number generator in a large number of dimensions. For example, when $m = 2^{20}$ and $n = 2^{14}$ we can test the 20-dimensional randomness of a number generator by letting $d = 2$ and forming 20-dimensional vectors $V_j = (Y_{20j}, Y_{20j+1}, \ldots, Y_{20j+19})$ for $0 \le j < n$. We keep a table of $m = 2^{20}$ bits to determine collisions, one bit for each possible value of the vector V_j; on a computer with 32 bits per word, this amounts to 2^{15} words. Initially all 2^{20} bits of this table are cleared to zero; then for each V_j, if the corresponding bit is already 1 we record a collision, otherwise we set the bit to 1. This test can also be used in 10 dimensions with $d = 4$, and so on.

To decide if the test is passed, we can use the following table of percentage points when $m = 2^{20}$ and $n = 2^{14}$:

collisions $\le$	101	108	119	126	134	145	153
with probability	.009	.043	.244	.476	.742	.946	.989

The theory underlying these probabilities is the same we used in the poker test, Eq. (5); the probability that c collisions occur is the probability that $n - c$ urns are occupied, namely

$$\frac{m(m-1)\ldots(m-n+c+1)}{m^n}\left\{\begin{matrix}n\\n-c\end{matrix}\right\}.$$

Although m and n are very large, it is not difficult to compute these probabilities using the following method:

Algorithm S (*Percentage points for collision test*). Given m and n, this algorithm determines the distribution of the number of collisions that occur when n balls are scattered into m urns. An auxiliary array $A[0]$, $A[1]$, ..., $A[n]$ of floating point numbers is used for the computation; actually $A[j]$ will be nonzero only for $j_0 \leq j \leq j_1$, and $j_1 - j_0$ will be at most of order $\log n$, so it would be possible to get by with considerably less storage.

S1. [Initialize.] Set $A[j] \leftarrow 0$ for $0 \leq j \leq n$; then set $A[1] \leftarrow 1$ and $j_0 \leftarrow j_1 \leftarrow 1$. Then do step S2 exactly $n - 1$ times and go on to step S3.

S2. [Update probabilities.] (Performing this step once corresponds to tossing a ball into an urn; $A[j]$ represents the probability that exactly j of the urns are occupied.) Set $j_1 \leftarrow j_1 + 1$. Then for $j \leftarrow j_1, j_1 - 1, \ldots, j_0$ (in this order), set $A[j] \leftarrow (j/m)A[j] + ((1 + 1/m) - (j/m))A[j-1]$. If $A[j]$ has become very small as a result of this calculation, say $A[j] < 10^{-20}$, set $A[j] \leftarrow 0$; and in such a case, decrease j_1 by 1 if $j = j_1$, or increase j_0 by 1 if $j = j_0$.

S3. [Compute the answers.] In this step we make use of an auxiliary table $(T_1, T_2, \ldots, T_{\text{tmax}}) = (.01, .05, .25, .50, .75, .95, .99, 1.00)$ containing the specified percentage points of interest. Set $p \leftarrow 0$, $t \leftarrow 1$, and $j \leftarrow j_0 - 1$. Do the following iteration until $t = \text{tmax}$: Increase j by 1, and set $p \leftarrow p + A[j]$; then if $p > T_t$, output $n - j - 1$ and $1 - p$ (meaning that with probability $1 - p$ there are at most $n - j - 1$ collisions) and repeatedly increase t by 1 until $p \leq T_t$. ∎

J. Birthday spacings test. George Marsaglia introduced a new kind of test in 1984: We throw n balls into m urns, as in the collision test, but now we think of the urns as "days of a year" and the balls as "birthdays." Suppose the birthdays are $(Y_1, \ldots, Y_n)$, where $0 \leq Y_k < m$. Sort them into nondecreasing order $Y_{(1)} \leq \cdots \leq Y_{(n)}$; then define n "spacings" $S_1 = Y_{(2)} - Y_{(1)}, \ldots, S_{n-1} = Y_{(n)} - Y_{(n-1)}$, $S_n = Y_{(1)} + m - Y_{(n)}$; finally sort the spacings into order, $S_{(1)} \leq \cdots \leq S_{(n)}$. Let R be the number of equal spacings, namely the number of indices j such that $1 < j \leq n$ and $S_{(j)} = S_{(j-1)}$. When $m = 2^{25}$ and $n = 512$, we should have

$R =$	0	1	2	3 or more
with probability	.368801577	.369035243	.183471182	.078691997

(The average number of equal spacings for this choice of m and n should be approximately 1.) Repeat the test 1000 times, say, and do a chi-square test with 3 degrees of freedom to compare the empirical R's with the correct distribution; this will tell whether or not the generator produces reasonably random birthday spacings. Exercises 28–30 develop the theory behind this test and formulas for other values of m and n.

Such a test of birthday spacings is important primarily because of the remarkable fact that lagged Fibonacci generators consistently *fail* it, although they pass the other traditional tests quite nicely. [Dramatic examples of such failures were reported by Marsaglia, Zaman, and Tsang in *Stat. and Prob. Letters* **9** (1990), 35–39.] Consider, for example, the sequence

$$X_n = (X_{n-24} + X_{n-55}) \bmod m$$

of Eq. 3.2.2–(7). The numbers of this sequence satisfy

$$X_n + X_{n-86} \equiv X_{n-24} + X_{n-31} \quad (\text{modulo } m)$$

because both sides are congruent to $X_{n-24} + X_{n-55} + X_{n-86}$. Therefore two pairs of differences are equal:

$$X_n - X_{n-24} \equiv X_{n-31} - X_{n-86},$$

and

$$X_n - X_{n-31} \equiv X_{n-24} - X_{n-86}.$$

Whenever X_n is reasonably close to X_{n-24} or X_{n-31} (as it should be in a truly random sequence), the difference has a good chance of showing up in two of the spacings. So we get significantly more cases of equality — typically $R \approx 2$ on the average, not 1. But if we discount from R any equal spacings that arise from the stated congruence, the resulting statistic R' usually does pass the birthday test. (One way to avoid failure is to discard certain elements of the sequence, using for example only X_0, X_2, X_4, ... as random numbers; then we never get all four elements of the set $\{X_n, X_{n-24}, X_{n-31}, X_{n-86}\}$, and the birthday spacings are no problem. An even better way to avoid the problem is to discard consecutive batches of numbers, as suggested by Lüscher; see Section 3.2.2.) Similar remarks apply to the subtract-with-borrow and add-with-carry generators of exercise 3.2.1.1–14.

K. Serial correlation test. We may also compute the following statistic:

$$C = \frac{n(U_0 U_1 + U_1 U_2 + \cdots + U_{n-2} U_{n-1} + U_{n-1} U_0) - (U_0 + U_1 + \cdots + U_{n-1})^2}{n(U_0^2 + U_1^2 + \cdots + U_{n-1}^2) - (U_0 + U_1 + \cdots + U_{n-1})^2}. \quad (23)$$

This is the "serial correlation coefficient," a measure of the extent to which U_{j+1} depends on U_j.

Correlation coefficients appear frequently in statistical work. If we have n quantities U_0, U_1, ..., U_{n-1} and n others V_0, V_1, ..., V_{n-1}, the correlation coefficient between them is defined to be

$$C = \frac{n \sum (U_j V_j) - \left(\sum U_j\right)\left(\sum V_j\right)}{\sqrt{\left(n \sum U_j^2 - \left(\sum U_j\right)^2\right)\left(n \sum V_j^2 - \left(\sum V_j\right)^2\right)}}. \quad (24)$$

All summations in this formula are to be taken over the range $0 \le j < n$; Eq. (23) is the special case $V_j = U_{(j+1) \bmod n}$. The denominator of (24) is zero when $U_0 = U_1 = \cdots = U_{n-1}$ or $V_0 = V_1 = \cdots = V_{n-1}$; we exclude that case from discussion.

A correlation coefficient always lies between -1 and $+1$. When it is zero or very small, it indicates that the quantities U_j and V_j are (relatively speaking) independent of each other, whereas a value of ± 1 indicates total linear dependence. In fact, $V_j = \alpha \pm \beta U_j$ for all j in the latter case, for some constants α and β. (See exercise 17.)

Therefore it is desirable to have C in Eq. (23) close to zero. In actual fact, since $U_0 U_1$ is not completely independent of $U_1 U_2$, the serial correlation coefficient is not expected to be *exactly* zero. (See exercise 18.) A "good" value of C will be between $\mu_n - 2\sigma_n$ and $\mu_n + 2\sigma_n$, where

$$\mu_n = \frac{-1}{n-1}, \qquad \sigma_n^2 = \frac{n^2}{(n-1)^2(n-2)}, \qquad n > 2. \tag{25}$$

We expect C to be between these limits about 95 percent of the time.

The formula for σ_n^2 in (25) is an upper bound, valid for serial correlations between independent random variables from an arbitrary distribution. When the U's are uniformly distributed, the true variance is obtained by subtracting $\frac{24}{5} n^{-2} + O(n^{-7/3} \log n)$. (See exercise 20.)

Instead of simply computing the correlation coefficient between the observations $(U_0, U_1, \ldots, U_{n-1})$ and their immediate successors $(U_1, \ldots, U_{n-1}, U_0)$, we can also compute it between $(U_0, U_1, \ldots, U_{n-1})$ and any cyclically shifted sequence $(U_q, \ldots, U_{n-1}, U_0, \ldots, U_{q-1})$; the cyclic correlations should be small for $0 < q < n$. A straightforward computation of Eq. (24) for all q would require about n^2 multiplications, but it is actually possible to compute all the correlations in only $O(n \log n)$ steps by using "fast Fourier transforms." (See Section 4.6.4; see also L. P. Schmid, *CACM* **8** (1965), 115.)

L. Tests on subsequences. External programs often call for random numbers in batches. For example, if a program works with three random variables X, Y, and Z, it may consistently invoke the generation of three random numbers at a time. In such applications it is important that the subsequences consisting of every *third* term of the original sequence be random. If the program requires q numbers at a time, the sequences

$$U_0, U_q, U_{2q}, \ldots; \quad U_1, U_{q+1}, U_{2q+1}, \ldots; \quad \ldots; \quad U_{q-1}, U_{2q-1}, U_{3q-1}, \ldots$$

can each be put through the tests described above for the original sequence U_0, U_1, U_2, $\ldots$.

Experience with linear congruential sequences has shown that these derived sequences rarely if ever behave less randomly than the original sequence, unless q has a large factor in common with the period length. On a binary computer with m equal to the word size, for example, a test of the subsequences for $q = 8$ will tend to give the poorest randomness for all $q < 16$; and on a decimal computer, $q = 10$ yields the subsequences most likely to be unsatisfactory. (This can be explained somewhat on the grounds of potency, since such values of q will tend to lower the potency. Exercise 3.2.1.2–20 provides a more detailed explanation.)

M. Historical remarks and further discussion. Statistical tests arose naturally in the course of scientists' efforts to "prove" or "disprove" hypotheses about various observed data. The best-known early papers dealing with the testing of artificially generated numbers for randomness are two articles by M. G. Kendall and B. Babington-Smith in the *Journal of the Royal Statistical Society* **101** (1938), 147–166, and in the supplement to that journal, **6** (1939), 51–61. Those papers were concerned with the testing of random digits between 0 and 9, rather than random real numbers; for this purpose, the authors discussed the frequency test, serial test, gap test, and poker test, although they misapplied the serial test. Kendall and Babington-Smith also used a variant of the coupon collector's test; the method described in this section was introduced by R. E. Greenwood in *Math. Comp.* **9** (1955), 1–5.

The run test has a rather interesting history. Originally, tests were made on runs up and down at once: A run up would be followed by a run down, then another run up, and so on. Note that the run test and the permutation test do not depend on the uniform distribution of the U's, but only on the fact that $U_i = U_j$ occurs with probability zero when $i \neq j$; therefore these tests can be applied to many types of random sequences. The run test in primitive form was originated by J. Bienaymé [*Comptes Rendus Acad. Sci.* **81** (Paris, 1875), 417–423]. Some sixty years later, W. O. Kermack and A. G. McKendrick published two extensive papers on the subject [*Proc. Royal Society Edinburgh* **57** (1937), 228–240, 332–376]; as an example they stated that Edinburgh rainfall between the years 1785 and 1930 was "entirely random in character" with respect to the run test (although they examined only the mean and standard deviation of the run lengths). Several other people began using the test, but it was not until 1944 that the use of the chi-square method in connection with this test was shown to be incorrect. A paper by H. Levene and J. Wolfowitz in *Annals Math. Stat.* **15** (1944), 58–69, introduced the correct run test (for runs up and down, alternately) and discussed the fallacies in earlier misuses of that test. Separate tests for runs up and runs down, as proposed in the text above, are more suited to computer application, so we have not given the more complex formulas for the alternate-up-and-down case. See the survey paper by D. E. Barton and C. L. Mallows, *Annals Math. Stat.* **36** (1965), 236–260.

Of all the tests we have discussed, the frequency test and the serial correlation test seem to be the weakest, in the sense that nearly all random number generators pass them. Theoretical grounds for the weakness of these tests are discussed briefly in Section 3.5 (see exercise 3.5–26). The run test, on the other hand, is rather strong: The results of exercises 3.3.3–23 and 24 suggest that linear congruential generators tend to have runs somewhat longer than normal if the multiplier is not large enough, so the run test of exercise 14 is definitely to be recommended.

The collision test is also highly recommended, since it has been specially designed to detect the deficiencies of many poor generators that have unfortunately become widespread. Based on ideas of H. Delgas Christiansen [Inst. Math. Stat. and Oper. Res., Tech. Univ. Denmark (October 1975), unpublished], this test was the first to be developed after the advent of computers; it is specifically intended for computer use, and unsuitable for hand calculation.

The reader probably wonders, *"Why are there so many tests?"* It has been said that more computer time is spent testing random numbers than using them in applications! This is untrue, although it is possible to go overboard in testing.

The need for making several tests has been amply documented. People have found, for example, that some numbers generated by a variant of the middle-square method have passed the frequency test, gap test, and poker test, yet flunked the serial test. Linear congruential sequences with small multipliers have been known to pass many tests, yet fail on the run test because there are too few runs of length one. The maximum-of-t test has also been used to ferret out some bad generators that otherwise seemed to perform respectably. A subtract-with-borrow generator fails the gap test when the maximum gap length exceeds the largest lag; see Vattulainen, Kankaala, Saarinen, and Ala-Nissila, *Computer Physics Communications* **86** (1995), 209–226, where a variety of other tests are also reported. Lagged Fibonacci generators, which are theoretically guaranteed to have equally distributed least-significant bits, still fail some simple variants of the 1-bit equidistribution test (see exercises 31 and 35, also 3.6–14).

Perhaps the main reason for doing extensive testing on random number generators is that people misusing Mr. X's random number generator will hardly ever admit that their programs are at fault: They will blame the generator, until Mr. X can *prove* to them that his numbers are sufficiently random. On the other hand, if the source of random numbers is only for Mr. X's personal use, he might decide not to bother to test them, since the techniques recommended in this chapter have a high probability of being satisfactory.

As computers become faster, more random numbers are consumed than ever before, and random number generators that once were satisfactory are no longer good enough for sophisticated applications in physics, combinatorics, stochastic geometry, etc. George Marsaglia has therefore introduced a number of *stringent tests*, which go well beyond classical methods like the gap and poker tests, in order to meet the new challenges. For example, he found that the sequence $X_{n+1} = (62605X_n + 113218009) \bmod 2^{29}$ had a noticeable bias in the following experiment: Generate 2^{21} random numbers X_n and extract their 10 leading bits $Y_n = \lfloor X_n/2^{19} \rfloor$. Count how many of the 2^{20} possible pairs (y, y') of 10-bit numbers do *not* occur among (Y_1, Y_2), (Y_2, Y_3), ..., $(Y_{2^{21}-1}, Y_{2^{21}})$. There ought to be about 141909.33 missing pairs, with standard deviation ≈ 290.46 (see exercise 34). But six consecutive trials, starting with $X_1 = 1234567$, produced counts that were all between 1.5 and 3.5 standard deviations too low. The distribution was a bit too "flat" to be random — probably because 2^{21} numbers is a significant fraction, $1/256$, of the entire period. A similar generator with multiplier 69069 and modulus 2^{30} proved to be better. Marsaglia and Zaman call this procedure a "monkey test," because it counts the number of two-character combinations that a monkey will miss after typing randomly on a keyboard with 1024 keys; see *Computers and Math.* **26**, 9 (November 1993), 1–10, for the analysis of several monkey tests.

EXERCISES

1. [*10*] Why should the serial test described in part B be applied to (Y_0, Y_1), (Y_2, Y_3), ..., (Y_{2n-2}, Y_{2n-1}) instead of to (Y_0, Y_1), (Y_1, Y_2), ..., (Y_{n-1}, Y_n)?

2. [*10*] State an appropriate way to generalize the serial test to triples, quadruples, etc., instead of pairs.

▶ **3.** [*M20*] How many U's need to be examined in the gap test (Algorithm G) before n gaps have been found, on the average, assuming that the sequence is random? What is the standard deviation of this quantity?

4. [*M12*] Prove that the probabilities in (4) are correct for the gap test.

5. [*M23*] The "classical" gap test used by Kendall and Babington-Smith considers the numbers U_0, U_1, ..., U_{N-1} to be a cyclic sequence with U_{N+j} identified with U_j. Here N is a fixed number of U's that are to be subjected to the test. If n of the numbers U_0, ..., U_{N-1} fall into the range $\alpha \le U_j < \beta$, there are n gaps in the cyclic sequence. Let Z_r be the number of gaps of length r, for $0 \le r < t$, and let Z_t be the number of gaps of length $\ge t$; show that the quantity $V = \sum_{0 \le r \le t}(Z_r - np_r)^2/np_r$ should have the chi-square distribution with t degrees of freedom, in the limit as N goes to infinity, where p_r is given in Eq. (4).

6. [*40*] (H. Geiringer.) A frequency count of the first 2000 decimal digits in the representation of $e = 2.71828\ldots$ gave a χ^2 value of 1.06, indicating that the actual frequencies of the digits 0, 1, ..., 9 are much too close to their expected values to be considered randomly distributed. (In fact, $\chi^2 \ge 1.15$ with probability 99.9 percent.) The same test applied to the first 10,000 digits of e gives the reasonable value $\chi^2 = 8.61$; but the fact that the first 2000 digits are so evenly distributed is still surprising. Does the same phenomenon occur in the representation of e to other bases? [See *AMM* **72** (1965), 483–500.]

7. [*08*] Apply the coupon collector's test procedure (Algorithm C), with $d = 3$ and $n = 7$, to the sequence 1101221022120202001212201010201121. What lengths do the seven subsequences have?

▶ **8.** [*M22*] How many U's need to be examined in the coupon collector's test, on the average, before n complete sets have been found by Algorithm C, assuming that the sequence is random? What is the standard deviation? [*Hint:* See Eq. 1.2.9–(28).]

9. [*M21*] Generalize the coupon collector's test so that the search stops as soon as w distinct values have been found, where w is a fixed positive integer less than or equal to d. What probabilities should be used in place of (6)?

10. [*M23*] Solve exercise 8 for the more general coupon collector's test described in exercise 9.

11. [*00*] The "runs up" in a particular permutation are displayed in (9); what are the "runs down" in that permutation?

12. [*20*] Let U_0, U_1, ..., U_{n-1} be n distinct numbers. Write an algorithm that determines the lengths of all ascending runs in the sequence. When your algorithm terminates, `COUNT[r]` should be the number of runs of length r, for $1 \le r \le 5$, and `COUNT[6]` should be the number of runs of length 6 or more.

13. [*M23*] Show that (16) is the number of permutations of $p+q+1$ distinct elements having the pattern (15).

▶ **14.** [*M15*] If we "throw away" the element that immediately follows a run, so that when X_j is greater than X_{j+1} we start the next run with X_{j+2}, the run lengths are independent, and a simple chi-square test may be used (instead of the horribly complicated method derived in the text). What are the appropriate run-length probabilities for this simple run test?

15. [*M10*] In the maximum-of-t test, why are V_0^t, V_1^t, ..., V_{n-1}^t supposed to be uniformly distributed between zero and one?

▶ **16.** [*15*] Mr. J. H. Quick (a student) wanted to perform the maximum-of-t test for several different values of t.

  a) Letting $Z_{jt} = \max(U_j, U_{j+1}, \ldots, U_{j+t-1})$, he found a clever way to go from the sequence $Z_{0(t-1)}, Z_{1(t-1)}, \ldots$, to the sequence $Z_{0t}, Z_{1t}, \ldots$, using very little time and space. What was his bright idea?

  b) He decided to modify the maximum-of-t method so that the jth observation would be $\max(U_j, \ldots, U_{j+t-1})$; in other words, he took $V_j = Z_{jt}$ instead of $V_j = Z_{(tj)t}$ as the text says. He reasoned that *all* of the Z's should have the same distribution, so the test is even stronger if each Z_{jt}, $0 \le j < n$, is used instead of just every tth one. But when he tried a chi-square equidistribution test on the values of V_j^t, he got extremely high values of the statistic V, which got even higher as t increased. Why did this happen?

17. [*M25*] Given any numbers $U_0, \ldots, U_{n-1}, V_0, \ldots, V_{n-1}$, let their mean values be

$$\bar{u} = \frac{1}{n} \sum_{0 \le k < n} U_k, \qquad \bar{v} = \frac{1}{n} \sum_{0 \le k < n} V_k.$$

  a) Let $U_k' = U_k - \bar{u}$, $V_k' = V_k - \bar{v}$. Show that the correlation coefficient C given in Eq. (24) is equal to

$$\sum_{0 \le k < n} U_k' V_k' \Big/ \sqrt{\sum_{0 \le k < n} U_k'^2} \sqrt{\sum_{0 \le k < n} V_k'^2}.$$

  b) Let $C = N/D$, where N and D denote the numerator and denominator of the expression in part (a). Show that $N^2 \le D^2$, hence $-1 \le C \le 1$; and obtain a formula for the difference $D^2 - N^2$. [*Hint:* See exercise 1.2.3–30.]

  c) If $C = \pm 1$, show that $\alpha U_k + \beta V_k = \tau$, $0 \le k < n$, for some constants α, β, and τ, not all zero.

18. [*M20*] (a) Show that if $n = 2$, the serial correlation coefficient (23) is always equal to -1 (unless the denominator is zero). (b) Similarly, show that when $n = 3$, the serial correlation coefficient always equals $-\frac{1}{2}$. (c) Show that the denominator in (23) is zero if and only if $U_0 = U_1 = \cdots = U_{n-1}$.

19. [*M30*] (J. P. Butler.) Let U_0, ..., U_{n-1} be independent random variables having the same distribution. Prove that the expected value of the serial correlation coefficient (23), averaged over all cases with nonzero denominator, is $-1/(n-1)$.

20. [*HM41*] Continuing the previous exercise, prove that the variance of (23) is equal to $n^2/(n-1)^2(n-2) - n^3 \, \mathrm{E}((U_0-U_1)^4/D^2)/2(n-2)$, where D is the denominator of (23) and E denotes the expected value over all cases with $D \ne 0$. What is the asymptotic value of $\mathrm{E}((U_0 - U_1)^4/D^2)$ when each U_j is uniformly distributed?

21. [*19*] What value of f is computed by Algorithm P if it is presented with the permutation $(1, 2, 9, 8, 5, 3, 6, 7, 0, 4)$?

22. [*18*] For what permutation of $\{0, 1, 2, 3, 4, 5, 6, 7, 8, 9\}$ will Algorithm P produce the value $f = 1024$?

23. [*M22*] Let $\langle Y_n \rangle$ and $\langle Y_n' \rangle$ be integer sequences having period lengths λ and λ', respectively, with $0 \leq Y_n, Y_n' < d$; also let $Z_n = (Y_n + Y_{n+r}') \bmod d$, where r is chosen at random between 0 and $\lambda' - 1$. Show that $\langle Z_n \rangle$ passes the t-dimensional serial test at least as well as $\langle Y_n \rangle$ does, in the following sense: Let $P(x_1, \ldots, x_t)$ and $Q(x_1, \ldots, x_t)$ be the probabilities that the t-tuple $(x_1, \ldots, x_t)$ occurs in $\langle Y_n \rangle$ and $\langle Z_n \rangle$:

$$P(x_1, \ldots, x_t) = \frac{1}{\lambda} \sum_{n=0}^{\lambda-1} [(Y_n, \ldots, Y_{n+t-1}) = (x_1, \ldots, x_t)];$$

$$Q(x_1, \ldots, x_t) = \frac{1}{\lambda\lambda'} \sum_{n=0}^{\lambda-1} \sum_{r=0}^{\lambda'-1} [(Z_n, \ldots, Z_{n+t-1}) = (x_1, \ldots, x_t)].$$

Then $\displaystyle\sum_{(x_1,\ldots,x_t)} (Q(x_1, \ldots, x_t) - d^{-t})^2 \leq \sum_{(x_1,\ldots,x_t)} (P(x_1, \ldots, x_t) - d^{-t})^2.$

24. [*HM37*] (G. Marsaglia.) Show that the serial test on n overlapping t-tuples $(Y_1, Y_2, \ldots, Y_t)$, $(Y_2, Y_3, \ldots, Y_{t+1})$, $\ldots$, $(Y_n, Y_1, \ldots, Y_{t-1})$ can be carried out as follows: For each string $\alpha = a_1 \ldots a_m$ with $0 \leq a_i < d$, let $N(\alpha)$ be the number of times α occurs as a substring of $Y_1 Y_2 \ldots Y_n Y_1 \ldots Y_{m-1}$, and let $P(\alpha) = P(a_1) \ldots P(a_m)$ be the probability that α occurs at any given position; individual digits may occur with differing probabilities $P(0), P(1), \ldots, P(d-1)$. Compute the statistic

$$V = \frac{1}{n} \sum_{|\alpha|=t} \frac{N(\alpha)^2}{P(\alpha)} - \frac{1}{n} \sum_{|\alpha|=t-1} \frac{N(\alpha)^2}{P(\alpha)}.$$

Then V should have the chi-square distribution with $d^t - d^{t-1}$ degrees of freedom when n is large. [*Hint:* Use exercise 3.3.1–25.]

25. [*M46*] Why is $C_1^{-1} C_2 C_1^{-1} \approx -6 C_1^{-1}$, when C_1 and C_2 are the matrices defined after (22)?

26. [*HM30*] Let $U_1, U_2, \ldots, U_n$ be independent uniform deviates in $[0 \mathinner{.\,.} 1)$, and let $U_{(1)} \leq U_{(2)} \leq \cdots \leq U_{(n)}$ be their values after sorting; also define the spacings $S_1 = U_{(2)} - U_{(1)}, \ldots, S_{n-1} = U_{(n)} - U_{(n-1)}, S_n = U_{(1)} + 1 - U_{(n)}$ and sorted spacings $S_{(1)} \leq \cdots \leq S_{(n)}$ as in the birthday spacings test. It is convenient in the following calculations to use the notation x_+^n as an abbreviation for the expression $x^n[x \geq 0]$.

a) Given any real numbers $s_1, s_2, \ldots, s_n$, prove that the simultaneous inequalities $S_1 \geq s_1, S_2 \geq s_2, \ldots, S_n \geq s_n$ occur with probability $(1 - s_1 - s_2 - \cdots - s_n)_+^{n-1}$.

b) Consequently the smallest spacing $S_{(1)}$ is $\leq s$ with probability $1 - (1 - ns)_+^{n-1}$.

c) What are the distribution functions $F_k(s) = \Pr(S_{(k)} \leq s)$, for $1 \leq k \leq n$?

d) Calculate the mean and variance of each $S_{(k)}$.

▶ **27.** [*HM26*] (*Iterated spacings.*) In the notation of the previous exercise, show that the numbers $S_1' = nS_{(1)}$, $S_2' = (n-1)(S_{(2)} - S_{(1)})$, $\ldots$, $S_n' = 1(S_{(n)} - S_{(n-1)})$ have the same joint probability distribution as the original spacings $S_1, \ldots, S_n$ of n uniform deviates. Therefore we can sort them into order, $S_{(1)}' \leq \cdots \leq S_{(n)}'$, and repeat this transformation to get yet another set of random spacings $S_1'', \ldots, S_n''$, etc. Each successive set of spacings $S_1^{(k)}, \ldots, S_n^{(k)}$ can be subjected to the Kolmogorov–Smirnov test, using

$$K_{n-1}^+ = \sqrt{n-1} \max_{1 \le j < n} \left(\frac{j}{n-1} - S_1^{(k)} - \cdots - S_j^{(k)} \right),$$

$$K_{n-1}^- = \sqrt{n-1} \max_{1 \le j < n} \left(S_1^{(k)} + \cdots + S_j^{(k)} - \frac{j-1}{n-1} \right).$$

Examine the transformation from $(S_1, \ldots, S_n)$ to $(S_1', \ldots, S_n')$ in detail in the cases $n = 2$ and $n = 3$; explain why continued repetition of this process will break down eventually when it is applied to computer-generated numbers with finite precision. (One way to compare random number generators is to see how long they can continue to survive such a torture test.)

28. [*M26*] Let $b_{nrs}(m)$ be the number of n-tuples $(y_1, \ldots, y_n)$ with $0 \le y_j < m$ that have exactly r equal spacings and s zero spacings. Thus, the probability that $R = r$ in the birthday spacings test is $\sum_{s=0}^{r+1} b_{nrs}(m)/m^n$. Also let $p_n(m)$ be the number of partitions of m into at most n parts (exercise 5.1.1–15). (a) Express $b_{n00}(m)$ in terms of partitions. [*Hint:* Consider cases with small m and n.] (b) Show that there is a simple relation between $b_{nrs}(m)$ and $b_{(n-s)(r+1-s)0}(m)$ when $s > 0$. (c) Deduce an explicit formula for the probability that no spacings are equal.

29. [*M35*] Continuing exercise 28, find simple expressions for the generating functions $b_{nr}(z) = \sum_{m \ge 0} b_{nr0}(m) z^m/m$, when $r = 0$, 1, and 2.

30. [*HM41*] Continuing the previous exercises, prove that if $m = n^3/\alpha$ we have

$$p_n(m) = \frac{m^{n-1} e^{\alpha/4}}{n! \, (n-1)!} \left(1 - \frac{13\alpha^2}{288n} + \frac{169\alpha^4 + 2016\alpha^3 - 1728\alpha^2 - 41472\alpha}{165888n^2} + O(n^{-3}) \right)$$

for fixed α as $n \to \infty$. Find a similar formula for $q_n(m)$, the number of partitions of m into n *distinct* positive parts. Deduce the asymptotic probabilities that the birthday spacings test finds R equal to 0, 1, and 2, to within $O(1/n)$.

▶ **31.** [*M21*] The recurrence $Y_n = (Y_{n-24} + Y_{n-55}) \bmod 2$, which describes the least significant bits of the lagged Fibonacci generator 3.2.2–(7) as well as the second-least significant bits of 3.2.2–(7'), is known to have period length $2^{55} - 1$; hence every possible nonzero pattern of bits $(Y_n, Y_{n+1}, \ldots, Y_{n+54})$ occurs equally often. Nevertheless, prove that if we generate 79 consecutive random bits $Y_n, \ldots, Y_{n+78}$ starting at a random point in the period, the probability is more than 51% that there are more 1s than 0s. If we use such bits to define a "random walk" that moves to the right when the bit is 1 and to the left when the bit is 0, we'll finish to the right of our starting point significantly more than half of the time. [*Hint:* Find the generating function $\sum_{k=0}^{79} \Pr(Y_n + \cdots + Y_{n+78} = k) z^k$.]

32. [*M20*] True or false: If X and Y are independent, identically distributed random variables with mean 0, and if they are more likely to be positive than negative, then $X + Y$ is more likely to be positive than negative.

33. [*HM32*] Find the asymptotic value of the probability that $k + l$ consecutive bits generated by the recurrence $Y_n = (Y_{n-l} + Y_{n-k}) \bmod 2$ have more 1s than 0s, when $k > 2l$ and the period length of this recurrence is $2^k - 1$, assuming that k is large.

34. [*HM29*] Explain how to estimate the mean and variance of the number of two-letter combinations that do not occur consecutively in a random string of length n on an m-letter alphabet. Assume that m is large and $n \approx 2m^2$.

▶ **35.** [*HM32*] (J. H. Lindholm, 1968.) Suppose we generate random bits $\langle Y_n \rangle$ using the recurrence

$$Y_n = (a_1 Y_{n-1} + a_2 Y_{n-2} + \cdots + a_k Y_{n-k}) \bmod 2,$$

for some choice of $a_1, \ldots, a_k$ such that the period length is $2^k - 1$; start with $Y_0 = 1$ and $Y_1 = \cdots = Y_{k-1} = 0$. Let $Z_n = (-1)^{Y_n+1} = 2Y_n - 1$ be a random sign, and consider the statistic $S_m = Z_n + Z_{n+1} + \cdots + Z_{n+m-1}$, where n is a random point in the period.

a) Prove that $\mathrm{E}\,S_m = m/N$, where $N = 2^k - 1$.

b) What is $\mathrm{E}\,S_m^2$? Assume that $m \le N$. *Hint:* See exercise 3.2.2–16.

c) What would $\mathrm{E}\,S_m$ and $\mathrm{E}\,S_m^2$ be if the Z's were truly random?

d) Assuming that $m \le N$, prove that $\mathrm{E}\,S_m^3 = m^3/N - 6B(N+1)/N$, where

$$B = \sum_{0 < i < j < m} \left[(Y_{i+1}Y_{i+2}\ldots Y_{i+k-1})_2 = (Y_{j+1}Y_{j+2}\ldots Y_{j+k-1})_2 \right] (m - j).$$

e) Evaluate B in the special case considered in exercise 31: $m = 79$ and $Y_n = (Y_{n-24} + Y_{n-55}) \bmod 2$.

*3.3.3. Theoretical Tests

Although it is always possible to test a random number generator using the methods in the previous section, it is far better to have *a priori* tests: theoretical results that tell us in advance how well those tests will come out. Such theoretical results give us much more understanding about the generation methods than empirical, trial-and-error results do. In this section we shall study the linear congruential sequences in more detail; if we know what the results of certain tests will be before we actually generate the numbers, we have a better chance of choosing a, m, and c properly.

The development of this kind of theory is quite difficult, although some progress has been made. The results obtained so far are generally for *statistical tests made over the entire period.* Not all statistical tests make sense when they are applied over a full period — for example, the equidistribution test will give results that are too perfect — but the serial test, gap test, permutation test, maximum test, etc., can be fruitfully analyzed in this way. Such studies will detect *global* nonrandomness of a sequence, that is, improper behavior in very large samples.

The theory we shall discuss is quite illuminating, but it does not eliminate the need for testing local nonrandomness by the methods of Section 3.3.2. Indeed, the task of proving anything useful about short subsequences appears to be very hard. Only a few theoretical results are known about the behavior of linear congruential sequences over less than a full period; they will be discussed at the end of Section 3.3.4. (See also exercise 18.)

Let us begin with a proof of a simple *a priori* law, for the least complicated case of the permutation test. The gist of our first theorem is that we have $X_{n+1} < X_n$ about half the time, provided that the sequence has high potency.

Theorem P. *Let a, c, and m generate a linear congruential sequence with maximum period; let $b = a - 1$ and let d be the greatest common divisor of m and b. The probability that $X_{n+1} < X_n$ is equal to $\frac{1}{2} + r$, where*

$$r = \left(2(c \bmod d) - d \right)/2m; \tag{1}$$

hence $|r| < d/2m$.

Proof. The proof of this theorem involves some techniques that are of interest in themselves. First we define

$$s(x) = (ax + c) \bmod m. \tag{2}$$

Thus, $X_{n+1} = s(X_n)$, and the theorem reduces to counting the number of integers x such that $0 \le x < m$ and $s(x) < x$, since every such integer occurs somewhere in the period. We want to show that this number is

$$\tfrac{1}{2}\big(m + 2(c \bmod d) - d\big). \tag{3}$$

The function $\lceil (x - s(x))/m \rceil$ is equal to 1 when $x > s(x)$, and it is 0 otherwise; hence the count we wish to obtain can be written simply as

$$\sum_{0 \le x < m} \left\lceil \frac{x - s(x)}{m} \right\rceil = \sum_{0 \le x < m} \left\lceil \frac{x}{m} - \left(\frac{ax + c}{m} - \left\lfloor \frac{ax + c}{m} \right\rfloor \right) \right\rceil$$

$$= \sum_{0 \le x < m} \left(\left\lfloor \frac{ax + c}{m} \right\rfloor - \left\lfloor \frac{bx + c}{m} \right\rfloor \right). \tag{4}$$

(Recall that $\lceil -y \rceil = -\lfloor y \rfloor$ and $b = a - 1$.) Such sums can be evaluated by the method of exercise 1.2.4–37, where we have proved that

$$\sum_{0 \le j < k} \left\lfloor \frac{hj + c}{k} \right\rfloor = \frac{(h-1)(k-1)}{2} + \frac{g-1}{2} + g\lfloor c/g \rfloor, \qquad g = \gcd(h, k), \tag{5}$$

whenever h and k are integers and $k > 0$. Since a is relatively prime to m, this formula yields

$$\sum_{0 \le x < m} \left\lfloor \frac{ax + c}{m} \right\rfloor = \frac{(a-1)(m-1)}{2} + c,$$

$$\sum_{0 \le x < m} \left\lfloor \frac{bx + c}{m} \right\rfloor = \frac{(b-1)(m-1)}{2} + \frac{d-1}{2} + c - (c \bmod d),$$

and (3) follows immediately. ∎

The proof of Theorem P indicates that *a priori* tests can indeed be carried out, provided that we are able to deal satisfactorily with sums involving the $\lfloor \ \rfloor$ and $\lceil \ \rceil$ functions. In many cases the most powerful technique for dealing with floor and ceiling functions is to replace them by two somewhat more symmetrical operations:

$$\delta(x) = \lfloor x \rfloor + 1 - \lceil x \rceil = [x \text{ is an integer}]; \tag{6}$$

$$((x)) = x - \lfloor x \rfloor - \tfrac{1}{2} + \tfrac{1}{2}\delta(x) = x - \lceil x \rceil + \tfrac{1}{2} - \tfrac{1}{2}\delta(x) = x - \tfrac{1}{2}\big(\lfloor x \rfloor + \lceil x \rceil\big). \tag{7}$$

The latter function is a "sawtooth" function familiar in the study of Fourier series; its graph is shown in Fig. 7. The reason for choosing to work with $((x))$ rather than $\lfloor x \rfloor$ or $\lceil x \rceil$ is that $((x))$ possesses several very useful properties:

$$((-x)) = -((x)); \tag{8}$$

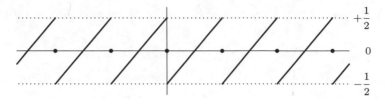

Fig. 7. The sawtooth function $((x))$.

$$((x+n)) = ((x)), \quad \text{integer } n; \tag{9}$$

$$((nx)) = ((x)) + \left(\left(x + \frac{1}{n}\right)\right) + \cdots + \left(\left(x + \frac{n-1}{n}\right)\right), \quad \text{integer } n \geq 1. \tag{10}$$

(See exercises 1.2.4–38 and 1.2.4–39(a,b,g).)

In order to get some practice working with these functions, let us prove Theorem P again, this time without relying on exercise 1.2.4–37. With the help of Eqs. (7), (8), (9), we can show that

$$\left\lceil \frac{x - s(x)}{m} \right\rceil = \frac{x - s(x)}{m} - \left(\left(\frac{x - s(x)}{m}\right)\right) + \frac{1}{2} - \frac{1}{2}\delta\left(\frac{x - s(x)}{m}\right)$$

$$= \frac{x - s(x)}{m} - \left(\left(\frac{x - (ax + c)}{m}\right)\right) + \frac{1}{2}$$

$$= \frac{x - s(x)}{m} + \left(\left(\frac{bx + c}{m}\right)\right) + \frac{1}{2} \tag{11}$$

since $\big(x - s(x)\big)/m$ is never an integer. Now

$$\sum_{0 \leq x < m} \frac{x - s(x)}{m} = 0$$

since both x and $s(x)$ take on each value of $\{0, 1, \ldots, m-1\}$ exactly once; hence (11) yields

$$\sum_{0 \leq x < m} \left\lceil \frac{x - s(x)}{m} \right\rceil = \sum_{0 \leq x < m} \left(\left(\frac{bx + c}{m}\right)\right) + \frac{m}{2}. \tag{12}$$

Let $b = b_0 d$, $m = m_0 d$, where b_0 and m_0 are relatively prime. We know that $(b_0 x) \bmod m_0$ takes on the values $\{0, 1, \ldots, m_0 - 1\}$ in some order as x varies from 0 to $m_0 - 1$. By (9) and (10) and the fact that

$$\left(\left(\frac{b(x + m_0) + c}{m}\right)\right) = \left(\left(\frac{bx + c}{m}\right)\right)$$

we have

$$\sum_{0 \leq x < m} \left(\left(\frac{bx + c}{m}\right)\right) = d \sum_{0 \leq x < m_0} \left(\left(\frac{bx + c}{m}\right)\right)$$

$$= d \sum_{0 \le x < m_0} \left(\left(\frac{c}{m} + \frac{b_0 x}{m_0} \right) \right) = d \left(\left(\frac{c}{d} \right) \right). \tag{13}$$

Theorem P follows immediately from (12) and (13).

One consequence of Theorem P is that practically *any* choice of a and c will give a reasonable probability that $X_{n+1} < X_n$, at least over the entire period, except those that have large d. A large value of d corresponds to low potency, and we already know that generators of low potency are undesirable.

The next theorem gives us a more stringent condition for the choice of the parameters a and c; we will consider the *serial correlation test* applied over the entire period. The quantity C defined in Section 3.3.2, Eq. (23), is

$$C = \left(m \sum_{0 \le x < m} x \, s(x) - \left(\sum_{0 \le x < m} x \right)^2 \right) \Big/ \left(m \sum_{0 \le x < m} x^2 - \left(\sum_{0 \le x < m} x \right)^2 \right). \tag{14}$$

Let x' be the element such that $s(x') = 0$. We have

$$s(x) = m \left(\left(\frac{ax + c}{m} \right) \right) + \frac{m}{2} [x \ne x']. \tag{15}$$

The formulas we are about to derive can be expressed most easily in terms of the sum

$$\sigma(h, k, c) = 12 \sum_{0 \le j < k} \left(\left(\frac{j}{k} \right) \right) \left(\left(\frac{hj + c}{k} \right) \right), \tag{16}$$

an important function that arises in several mathematical problems. It is called a *generalized Dedekind sum*, since Richard Dedekind introduced the function $\sigma(h, k, 0)$ in 1876 when commenting on one of Riemann's incomplete manuscripts. [See B. Riemann's *Gesammelte math. Werke*, 2nd ed. (1892), 466–478.]

Using the well-known formulas

$$\sum_{0 \le x < m} x = \frac{m(m-1)}{2} \qquad \text{and} \qquad \sum_{0 \le x < m} x^2 = \frac{m(m-\frac{1}{2})(m-1)}{3},$$

it is a straightforward matter to transform Eq. (14) into

$$C = \frac{m\sigma(a, m, c) - 3 + 6(m - x' - c)}{m^2 - 1}. \tag{17}$$

(See exercise 5.) Since m is usually very large, we may discard terms of order $1/m$, and we have the approximation

$$C \approx \sigma(a, m, c) / m, \tag{18}$$

with an error of less than $6/m$ in absolute value.

The serial correlation test now reduces to determining the value of the Dedekind sum $\sigma(a, m, c)$. Evaluating $\sigma(a, m, c)$ directly from its definition (16) is hardly any easier than evaluating the correlation coefficient itself directly, but fortunately there are simple methods available for computing Dedekind sums quite rapidly.

Lemma B ("Reciprocity law" for Dedekind sums). *Let h, k, c be integers. If $0 \leq c < k$, $0 < h \leq k$, and if h is relatively prime to k, then*

$$\sigma(h, k, c) + \sigma(k, h, c) = \frac{h}{k} + \frac{k}{h} + \frac{1}{hk} + \frac{6c^2}{hk} - 6\left\lfloor \frac{c}{h} \right\rfloor - 3e(h, c), \quad (19)$$

where

$$e(h, c) = [c = 0] + [c \bmod h \neq 0]. \quad (20)$$

Proof. We leave it to the reader to prove that, under these hypotheses,

$$\sigma(h, k, c) + \sigma(k, h, c) = \sigma(h, k, 0) + \sigma(k, h, 0) + \frac{6c^2}{hk} - 6\left\lfloor \frac{c}{h} \right\rfloor - 3e(h, c) + 3. \quad (21)$$

(See exercise 6.) The lemma now must be proved only in the case $c = 0$.

The proof we will give, based on complex roots of unity, is essentially due to L. Carlitz. There is actually a simpler proof that uses only elementary manipulations of sums (see exercise 7) — but the following method reveals more of the mathematical tools that are available for problems of this kind and it is therefore much more instructive.

Let $f(x)$ and $g(x)$ be polynomials defined as follows:

$$
\begin{aligned}
f(x) &= 1 + x + \cdots + x^{k-1} = (x^k - 1)/(x - 1) \\
g(x) &= x + 2x^2 + \cdots + (k-1)x^{k-1} \\
&= xf'(x) = kx^k/(x-1) - x(x^k - 1)/(x-1)^2.
\end{aligned}
\quad (22)
$$

If ω is the complex kth root of unity $e^{2\pi i/k}$, we have by Eq. 1.2.9–(13)

$$\frac{1}{k} \sum_{0 \leq j < k} \omega^{-jr} g(\omega^j x) = rx^r, \quad \text{if } 0 \leq r < k. \quad (23)$$

Set $x = 1$; then $g(\omega^j x) = k/(\omega^j - 1)$ if $j \neq 0$, otherwise it equals $k(k-1)/2$. Therefore

$$r \bmod k = \sum_{0 < j < k} \frac{\omega^{-jr}}{\omega^j - 1} + \tfrac{1}{2}(k - 1), \quad \text{if } r \text{ is an integer.}$$

(Eq. (23) shows that the right-hand side equals r when $0 \leq r < k$, and it is unchanged when multiples of k are added to r.) Hence

$$\left(\!\left(\frac{r}{k}\right)\!\right) = \frac{1}{k} \sum_{0 < j < k} \frac{\omega^{-jr}}{\omega^j - 1} - \frac{1}{2k} + \frac{1}{2}\delta\!\left(\frac{r}{k}\right). \quad (24)$$

This important formula, which holds whenever r is an integer, allows us to reduce many calculations involving $((r/k))$ to sums involving kth roots of unity, and it brings a whole new range of techniques into the picture. In particular, we get the following formula when $h \perp k$:

$$\sigma(h, k, 0) + \frac{3(k-1)}{k^2} = \frac{12}{k^2} \sum_{0 < r < k} \sum_{0 < i < k} \sum_{0 < j < k} \frac{\omega^{-ir}}{\omega^i - 1} \frac{\omega^{-jhr}}{\omega^j - 1}. \quad (25)$$

The right-hand side of this formula may be simplified by carrying out the sum on r; we have $\sum_{0 \le r < k} \omega^{rs} = f(\omega^s) = 0$ if $s \bmod k \ne 0$. Equation (25) now reduces to

$$\sigma(h, k, 0) + \frac{3(k-1)}{k} = \frac{12}{k} \sum_{0 < j < k} \frac{1}{(\omega^{-jh} - 1)(\omega^j - 1)}. \qquad (26)$$

A similar formula is obtained for $\sigma(k, h, 0)$, with $\zeta = e^{2\pi i/h}$ replacing ω.

It is not obvious what we can do with the sum in (26), but there is an elegant way to proceed, based on the fact that each term of the sum is a function of ω^j, where $0 < j < k$; hence the sum is essentially taken over the kth roots of unity other than 1. Whenever $x_1, x_2, \ldots, x_n$ are distinct complex numbers, we have the identity

$$\sum_{j=1}^{n} \frac{1}{(x_j - x_1) \ldots (x_j - x_{j-1})(x - x_j)(x_j - x_{j+1}) \ldots (x_j - x_n)}$$

$$= \frac{1}{(x - x_1) \ldots (x - x_n)}, \qquad (27)$$

which follows from the usual method of expanding the right-hand side into partial fractions. Moreover, if $q(x) = (x - y_1)(x - y_2) \ldots (x - y_m)$, we have

$$q'(y_j) = (y_j - y_1) \ldots (y_j - y_{j-1})(y_j - y_{j+1}) \ldots (y_j - y_m); \qquad (28)$$

this identity may often be used to simplify expressions like those in the left-hand side of (27). When h and k are relatively prime, the numbers $\omega, \omega^2, \ldots, \omega^{k-1}, \zeta, \zeta^2, \ldots, \zeta^{h-1}$ are all distinct; we can therefore consider formula (27) in the special case of the polynomial $(x - \omega) \ldots (x - \omega^{k-1})(x - \zeta) \ldots (x - \zeta^{h-1}) = (x^k - 1)(x^h - 1)/(x - 1)^2$, obtaining the following identity in x:

$$\frac{1}{h} \sum_{0 < j < h} \frac{\zeta^j (\zeta^j - 1)^2}{(\zeta^{jk} - 1)(x - \zeta^j)} + \frac{1}{k} \sum_{0 < j < k} \frac{\omega^j (\omega^j - 1)^2}{(\omega^{jh} - 1)(x - \omega^j)} = \frac{(x - 1)^2}{(x^h - 1)(x^k - 1)}. \qquad (29)$$

This identity has many interesting consequences, and it leads to numerous reciprocity formulas for sums of the type given in Eq. (26). For example, if we differentiate (29) twice with respect to x and let $x \to 1$, we find that

$$\frac{2}{h} \sum_{0 < j < h} \frac{\zeta^j (\zeta^j - 1)^2}{(\zeta^{jk} - 1)(1 - \zeta^j)^3} + \frac{2}{k} \sum_{0 < j < k} \frac{\omega^j (\omega^j - 1)^2}{(\omega^{jh} - 1)(1 - \omega^j)^3}$$

$$= \frac{1}{6} \left(\frac{h}{k} + \frac{k}{h} + \frac{1}{hk} \right) + \frac{1}{2} - \frac{1}{2h} - \frac{1}{2k}.$$

Replace j by $h - j$ and by $k - j$ in these sums and use (26) to get

$$\frac{1}{6} \left(\sigma(k, h, 0) + \frac{3(h-1)}{h} \right) + \frac{1}{6} \left(\sigma(h, k, 0) + \frac{3(k-1)}{k} \right)$$

$$= \frac{1}{6} \left(\frac{h}{k} + \frac{k}{h} + \frac{1}{hk} \right) + \frac{1}{2} - \frac{1}{2h} - \frac{1}{2k},$$

which is equivalent to the desired result. ∎

Lemma B gives us an explicit function $f(h, k, c)$ such that

$$\sigma(h, k, c) = f(h, k, c) - \sigma(k, h, c) \tag{30}$$

whenever $0 < h \leq k$, $0 \leq c < k$, and h is relatively prime to k. From the definition (16) it is clear that

$$\sigma(k, h, c) = \sigma(k \bmod h, h, c \bmod h). \tag{31}$$

Therefore we can use (30) iteratively to evaluate $\sigma(h, k, c)$, using a process that reduces the parameters as in Euclid's algorithm.

Further simplifications occur when we examine this iterative procedure more closely. Let us set $m_1 = k$, $m_2 = h$, $c_1 = c$, and form the following tableau:

$$\begin{aligned}
m_1 &= a_1 m_2 + m_3 & c_1 &= b_1 m_2 + c_2 \\
m_2 &= a_2 m_3 + m_4 & c_2 &= b_2 m_3 + c_3 \\
m_3 &= a_3 m_4 + m_5 & c_3 &= b_3 m_4 + c_4 \\
m_4 &= a_4 m_5 & c_4 &= b_4 m_5 + c_5
\end{aligned} \tag{32}$$

Here

$$\begin{aligned}
a_j &= \lfloor m_j / m_{j+1} \rfloor, & b_j &= \lfloor c_j / m_{j+1} \rfloor, \\
m_{j+2} &= m_j \bmod m_{j+1}, & c_{j+1} &= c_j \bmod m_{j+1},
\end{aligned} \tag{33}$$

and it follows that

$$0 \leq m_{j+1} < m_j, \qquad 0 \leq c_j < m_j. \tag{34}$$

We have assumed for convenience that Euclid's algorithm terminates in (32) after four iterations; this assumption will reveal the pattern that holds in the general case. Since h and k were relatively prime to start with, we must have $m_5 = 1$ and $c_5 = 0$ in (32).

Let us assume also that $c_3 \neq 0$ but $c_4 = 0$, in order to get a feeling for the effect this has on the recurrence. Equations (30) and (31) yield

$$\begin{aligned}
\sigma(h, k, c) &= \sigma(m_2, m_1, c_1) \\
&= f(m_2, m_1, c_1) - \sigma(m_3, m_2, c_2) \\
&= \cdots \\
&= f(m_2, m_1, c_1) - f(m_3, m_2, c_2) + f(m_4, m_3, c_3) - f(m_5, m_4, c_4).
\end{aligned}$$

The first part, $h/k + k/h$, of the formula for $f(h, k, c)$ in (19) contributes

$$\frac{m_2}{m_1} + \frac{m_1}{m_2} - \frac{m_3}{m_2} - \frac{m_2}{m_3} + \frac{m_4}{m_3} + \frac{m_3}{m_4} - \frac{m_5}{m_4} - \frac{m_4}{m_5}$$

to the total, and this simplifies to

$$\frac{h}{k} + \frac{m_1 - m_3}{m_2} - \frac{m_2 - m_4}{m_3} + \frac{m_3 - m_5}{m_4} - \frac{m_4}{m_5} = \frac{h}{k} + a_1 - a_2 + a_3 - a_4.$$

The next part of (19), $1/hk$, also leads to a simple contribution; according to Eq. 4.5.3–(9) and other formulas in Section 4.5.3, we have

$$\frac{1}{m_1 m_2} - \frac{1}{m_2 m_3} + \frac{1}{m_3 m_4} - \frac{1}{m_4 m_5} = \frac{h'}{k} - 1, \tag{35}$$

where h' is the unique integer satisfying

$$h'h \equiv 1 \pmod{k}, \quad 0 < h' \le k. \tag{36}$$

Adding up all the contributions, and remembering our assumption that $c_4 = 0$ $\big($so that $e(m_4, c_3) = 0$, see $(20)\big)$, we find that

$$\sigma(h, k, c) = \frac{h + h'}{k} + (a_1 - a_2 + a_3 - a_4) - 6(b_1 - b_2 + b_3 - b_4)$$
$$+ 6\left(\frac{c_1^2}{m_1 m_2} - \frac{c_2^2}{m_2 m_3} + \frac{c_3^2}{m_3 m_4} - \frac{c_4^2}{m_4 m_5}\right) + 2,$$

in terms of the assumed tableau (32). Similar results hold in general:

Theorem D. *Let h, k, c be integers with $0 < h \le k$, $0 \le c < k$, and h relatively prime to k. Form the "Euclidean tableau" as defined in (33) above, and assume that the process stops after t steps with $m_{t+1} = 1$. Let s be the smallest subscript such that $c_s = 0$, and let h' be defined by (36). Then*

$$\sigma(h, k, c) = \frac{h + h'}{k} + \sum_{1 \le j \le t} (-1)^{j+1}\left(a_j - 6b_j + 6\frac{c_j^2}{m_j m_{j+1}}\right)$$
$$+ 3\big((-1)^s + \delta_{s1}\big) - 2 + (-1)^t. \quad \blacksquare$$

Euclid's algorithm is analyzed carefully in Section 4.5.3; the quantities a_1, a_2, $\ldots$, a_t are called the *partial quotients* of h/k. Theorem 4.5.3F tells us that the number of iterations, t, will never exceed $\log_\phi k$; hence Dedekind sums can be evaluated rapidly. The terms $c_j^2/m_j m_{j+1}$ can be simplified further, and an efficient algorithm for evaluating $\sigma(h, k, c)$ appears in exercise 17.

Now that we have analyzed generalized Dedekind sums, let us apply our knowledge to the determination of serial correlation coefficients.

Example 1. *Find the serial correlation when $m = 2^{35}$, $a = 2^{34} + 1$, $c = 1$.*

Solution. We have

$$C = \big(2^{35}\sigma(2^{34} + 1, 2^{35}, 1) - 3 + 6(2^{35} - (2^{34} - 1) - 1)\big)/(2^{70} - 1),$$

by Eq. (17). To evaluate $\sigma(2^{34} + 1, 2^{35}, 1)$, we can form the tableau

$m_1 = 2^{35}$		$c_1 = 1$	
$m_2 = 2^{34} + 1$	$a_1 = 1$	$c_2 = 1$	$b_1 = 0$
$m_3 = 2^{34} - 1$	$a_2 = 1$	$c_3 = 1$	$b_2 = 0$
$m_4 = 2$	$a_3 = 2^{33} - 1$	$c_4 = 1$	$b_3 = 0$
$m_5 = 1$	$a_4 = 2$	$c_5 = 0$	$b_4 = 1$

Since $h' = 2^{34} + 1$, the value according to Theorem D comes to $2^{33} - 3 + 2^{-32}$. Thus

$$C = (2^{68} + 5)/(2^{70} - 1) = \tfrac{1}{4} + \epsilon, \qquad |\epsilon| < 2^{-67}. \tag{37}$$

Such a correlation is much, much too high for randomness. Of course, this generator has very low potency, and we have already rejected it as nonrandom.

Example 2. *Find the approximate serial correlation when* $m = 10^{10}$, $a = 10001$, $c = 2113248653$.

Solution. We have $C \approx \sigma(a, m, c)/m$, and the computation proceeds as follows:

$m_1 = 10000000000$			$c_1 = 2113248653$		
$m_2 = 10001$	$a_1 = 999900$		$c_2 = 7350$	$b_1 = 211303$	
$m_3 = 100$	$a_2 = 100$		$c_3 = 50$	$b_2 = 73$	
$m_4 = 1$	$a_3 = 100$		$c_4 = 0$	$b_3 = 50$	

$$\sigma(m_2, m_1, c_1) = -31.6926653544; \qquad C \approx -3 \cdot 10^{-9}. \tag{38}$$

This is a very respectable value of C indeed. But the generator has a potency of only 3, *so it is not really a very good source of random numbers in spite of the fact that it has low serial correlation.* It is necessary to have a low serial correlation, but not sufficient.

Example 3. *Estimate the serial correlation for general* a, m, *and* c.

Solution. If we consider just one application of (30), we have

$$\sigma(a, m, c) \approx \frac{m}{a} + 6\frac{c^2}{am} - 6\frac{c}{a} - \sigma(m, a, c).$$

Now $|\sigma(m, a, c)| < a$ by exercise 12, and therefore

$$C \approx \frac{\sigma(a, m, c)}{m} \approx \frac{1}{a}\left(1 - 6\frac{c}{m} + 6\left(\frac{c}{m}\right)^2\right). \tag{39}$$

The error in this approximation is less than $(a + 6)/m$ in absolute value.

The estimate in (39) was the first theoretical result known about the randomness of congruential generators. R. R. Coveyou [*JACM* **7** (1960), 72–74] obtained it by averaging over all *real* numbers x between 0 and m instead of considering only the integer values (see exercise 21); then Martin Greenberger [*Math. Comp.* **15** (1961), 383–389] gave a rigorous derivation including an estimate of the error term.

So began one of the saddest chapters in the history of computer science! Although the approximation above is quite correct, it has been grievously misapplied in practice; people abandoned the perfectly good generators they had been using and replaced them by terrible generators that looked good from the standpoint of (39). For more than a decade, the most common random number generators in daily use were seriously deficient, solely because of a theoretical advance.

> A little Learning *is a dang'rous Thing.*
> — ALEXANDER POPE, *An Essay on Criticism*, 215 (1711)

If we are to learn by past mistakes, we had better look carefully at how (39) has been misused. In the first place people assumed uncritically that a small serial correlation over the whole period would be a pretty good guarantee of randomness; but in fact it doesn't even ensure a small serial correlation for 1000 consecutive elements of the sequence (see exercise 14).

Secondly, (39) and its error term will ensure a relatively small value of C only when $a \approx \sqrt{m}$; therefore people suggested choosing multipliers near $\sqrt{m}$. In fact, we shall see that nearly all multipliers give a value of C that is substantially less than $1/\sqrt{m}$, hence (39) is not a very good approximation to the true behavior. Minimizing a crude upper bound for C does not minimize C.

In the third place, people observed that (39) yields its best estimate when

$$c/m \approx \tfrac{1}{2} \pm \tfrac{1}{6}\sqrt{3}, \tag{40}$$

since these values are the roots of $1 - 6x + 6x^2 = 0$. "In the absence of any other criterion for choosing c, we might as well use this one." The latter statement is not incorrect, but it is misleading at best, since experience has shown that the value of c has hardly any influence on the true value of the serial correlation when a is a good multiplier; the choice (40) reduces C substantially only in cases like Example 2 above. And we are fooling ourselves in such cases, since the bad multiplier will reveal its deficiencies in other ways.

Clearly we need a better estimate than (39); and such an estimate is now available thanks to Theorem D, which stems principally from the work of Ulrich Dieter [*Math. Comp.* **25** (1971), 855–883]. Theorem D implies that $\sigma(a, m, c)$ *will be small if the partial quotients of a/m are small.* Indeed, by analyzing generalized Dedekind sums still more closely, it is possible to obtain quite a sharp estimate:

Theorem K. *Under the assumptions of Theorem D, we always have*

$$-\frac{1}{2} \sum_{\substack{1 \le j \le t \\ j \text{ odd}}} a_j - \sum_{\substack{1 \le j \le t \\ j \text{ even}}} a_j \le \sigma(h, k, c) \le \sum_{\substack{1 \le j \le t \\ j \text{ odd}}} a_j + \frac{1}{2} \sum_{\substack{1 \le j \le t \\ j \text{ even}}} a_j - \frac{1}{2}. \tag{41}$$

Proof. See D. E. Knuth, *Acta Arithmetica* **33** (1977), 297–325, where it is shown further that these bounds are essentially the best possible when large partial quotients are present. ∎

Example 4. *Estimate the serial correlation for* $a = 3141592621$, $m = 2^{35}$, c *odd.*

Solution. The partial quotients of a/m are 10, 1, 14, 1, 7, 1, 1, 1, 3, 3, 3, 5, 2, 1, 8, 7, 1, 4, 1, 2, 4, 2; hence by Theorem K

$$-55 \le \sigma(a, m, c) \le 67.5,$$

and the serial correlation is guaranteed to be extremely low for all c.

Note that this bound is considerably better than we could obtain from (39), since the error in (39) is of order a/m; our "random" multiplier has turned out to be much better than one specifically chosen to look good on the basis of (39). In fact, it is possible to show that the *average* value of $\sum_{j=1}^{t} a_j$, taken over all multipliers a relatively prime to m, is

$$\frac{6}{\pi^2}(\ln m)^2 + O\big((\log m)(\log\log m)^4\big)$$

(see exercise 4.5.3–35). Therefore the probability that a random multiplier has large $\sum_{j=1}^{t} a_j$, say larger than $(\log m)^{2+\epsilon}$ for some fixed $\epsilon > 0$, approaches zero as $m \to \infty$. This substantiates the empirical evidence that almost all linear congruential sequences have extremely low serial correlation over the entire period.

The exercises below show that other *a priori* tests, such as the serial test over the entire period, can also be expressed in terms of a few generalized Dedekind sums. It follows from Theorem K that linear congruential sequences will pass those tests provided that certain specified fractions (depending on a and m but not on c) have small partial quotients. In particular, the result of exercise 19 implies that *the serial test on pairs will be passed satisfactorily if and only if a/m has no large partial quotients.*

The book *Dedekind Sums* by Hans Rademacher and Emil Grosswald (Math. Assoc. of America, Carus Monograph No. 16, 1972) discusses the history and properties of Dedekind sums and their generalizations. Further theoretical tests, including the serial test in higher dimensions, are discussed in Section 3.3.4.

EXERCISES — First Set

1. [*M10*] Express $x \bmod y$ in terms of the sawtooth and δ functions.

2. [*HM22*] What is the Fourier series expansion (in terms of sines and cosines) of the function $((x))$?

3. [*M23*] (N. J. Fine.) Prove that $|\sum_{k=0}^{n-1}((2^k x + \frac{1}{2}))| < 1$ for all real numbers x.

▶ **4.** [*M19*] If $m = 10^{10}$, what is the highest possible value of d (in the notation of Theorem P), given that the potency of the generator is 10?

5. [*M21*] Carry out the derivation of Eq. (17).

6. [*M27*] Assume that $hh' + kk' = 1$.
a) Show, without using Lemma B, that

$$\sigma(h,k,c) = \sigma(h,k,0) + 12 \sum_{0<j<c} \left(\!\left(\frac{h'j}{k}\right)\!\right) + 6\left(\!\left(\frac{h'c}{k}\right)\!\right)$$

for all integers $c \geq 0$.

b) Show that $\left(\!\left(\dfrac{h'j}{k}\right)\!\right) + \left(\!\left(\dfrac{k'j}{h}\right)\!\right) = \dfrac{j}{hk} - \dfrac{1}{2}\delta\left(\dfrac{j}{h}\right)$ if $0 < j < k$.

c) Under the assumptions of Lemma B, prove Eq. (21).

▶ **7.** [*M24*] Give a proof of the reciprocity law (19), when $c = 0$, by using the general reciprocity law of exercise 1.2.4–45.

▶ **8.** [*M34*] (L. Carlitz.) Let

$$\rho(p,q,r) = 12 \sum_{0 \leq j < r} \left(\!\left(\frac{jp}{r}\right)\!\right)\left(\!\left(\frac{jq}{r}\right)\!\right).$$

By generalizing the method of proof used in Lemma B, prove the following beautiful identity due to H. Rademacher: If each of p, q, r is relatively prime to the other two,

$$\rho(p, q, r) + \rho(q, r, p) + \rho(r, p, q) = \frac{p}{qr} + \frac{q}{rp} + \frac{r}{pq} - 3.$$

(The reciprocity law for Dedekind sums, with $c = 0$, is the special case $r = 1$.)

9. [*M40*] Is there a simple proof of Rademacher's identity (exercise 8) along the lines of the proof in exercise 7 of a special case?

10. [*M20*] Show that when $0 < h < k$ it is possible to express $\sigma(k - h, k, c)$ and $\sigma(h, k, -c)$ easily in terms of $\sigma(h, k, c)$.

11. [*M30*] The formulas given in the text show us how to evaluate $\sigma(h, k, c)$ when h and k are relatively prime and c is an integer. For the general case, prove that

a) $\sigma(dh, dk, dc) = \sigma(h, k, c)$, for integer $d > 0$;

b) $\sigma(h, k, c + \theta) = \sigma(h, k, c) + 6((h'c/k))$, for integer c, real $0 < \theta < 1$, $h \perp k$, and $hh' \equiv 1$ (modulo k).

12. [*M24*] Show that if h is relatively prime to k and c is an integer, $|\sigma(h, k, c)| \leq (k - 1)(k - 2)/k$.

13. [*M24*] Generalize Eq. (26) so that it gives an expression for $\sigma(h, k, c)$.

▶ **14.** [*M20*] The linear congruential generator that has $m = 2^{35}$, $a = 2^{18} + 1$, $c = 1$, was given the serial correlation test on three batches of 1000 consecutive numbers, and the result was a very high correlation, between 0.2 and 0.3, in each case. What is the serial correlation of this generator, taken over all 2^{35} numbers of the period?

15. [*M21*] Generalize Lemma B so that it applies to all *real* values of c, $0 \leq c < k$.

16. [*M24*] Given the Euclidean tableau defined in (33), let $p_0 = 1$, $p_1 = a_1$, and $p_j = a_j p_{j-1} + p_{j-2}$ for $1 < j \leq t$. Show that the complicated portion of the sum in Theorem D can be rewritten as follows, making it possible to avoid noninteger computations:

$$\sum_{1 \leq j \leq t} (-1)^{j+1} \frac{c_j^2}{m_j m_{j+1}} = \frac{1}{m_1} \sum_{1 \leq j \leq t} (-1)^{j+1} b_j (c_j + c_{j+1}) p_{j-1}.$$

[*Hint:* Prove that $\sum_{1 \leq j \leq r} (-1)^{j+1}/m_j m_{j+1} = (-1)^{r+1} p_{r-1}/m_1 m_{r+1}$ for $1 \leq r \leq t$.]

17. [*M22*] Design an algorithm that evaluates $\sigma(h, k, c)$ for integers h, k, c satisfying the hypotheses of Theorem D. Your algorithm should use only integer arithmetic (of unlimited precision), and it should produce the answer in the form $A + B/k$ where A and B are integers. (See exercise 16.) If possible, use only a finite number of variables for temporary storage, instead of maintaining arrays such as $a_1, a_2, \ldots, a_t$.

▶ **18.** [*M23*] (U. Dieter.) Given positive integers h, k, z, let

$$S(h, k, c, z) = \sum_{0 \leq j < z} \left(\left(\frac{hj + c}{k}\right)\right).$$

Show that this sum can be evaluated in closed form, in terms of generalized Dedekind sums and the sawtooth function. [*Hint:* When $z \leq k$, the quantity $\lfloor j/k \rfloor - \lfloor (j - z)/k \rfloor$ equals 1 for $0 \leq j < z$, and it equals 0 for $z \leq j < k$, so we can introduce this factor and sum over $0 \leq j < k$.]

▶ **19.** [*M23*] Show that the *serial test* can be analyzed over the full period, in terms of generalized Dedekind sums, by finding a formula for the probability that $\alpha \le X_n < \beta$ and $\alpha' \le X_{n+1} < \beta'$ when $\alpha, \beta, \alpha', \beta'$ are given integers with $0 \le \alpha < \beta \le m$ and $0 \le \alpha' < \beta' \le m$. [*Hint:* Consider the quantity $\lfloor (x-\alpha)/m \rfloor - \lfloor (x-\beta)/m \rfloor$.]

20. [*M29*] (U. Dieter.) Extend Theorem P by obtaining a formula for the probability that $X_n > X_{n+1} > X_{n+2}$, in terms of generalized Dedekind sums.

EXERCISES — Second Set

In many cases, exact computations with integers are quite difficult to carry out, but we can attempt to study the probabilities that arise when we take the average over all real values of x instead of restricting the calculation to integer values. Although these results are only approximate, they shed some light on the subject.

It is convenient to deal with numbers U_n between zero and one; for linear congruential sequences, $U_n = X_n/m$, and we have $U_{n+1} = \{aU_n + \theta\}$, where $\theta = c/m$ and $\{x\}$ denotes $x \bmod 1$. For example, the formula for serial correlation now becomes

$$C = \left(\int_0^1 x\{ax+\theta\}\,dx - \left(\int_0^1 x\,dx \right)^2 \right) \bigg/ \left(\int_0^1 x^2\,dx - \left(\int_0^1 x\,dx \right)^2 \right).$$

▶ **21.** [*HM23*] (R. R. Coveyou.) What is the value of C in the formula just given?

▶ **22.** [*M22*] Let a be an integer, and let $0 \le \theta < 1$. If x is a random real number, uniformly distributed between 0 and 1, and if $s(x) = \{ax+\theta\}$, what is the probability that $s(x) < x$? (This is the "real number" analog of Theorem P.)

23. [*M28*] The previous exercise gives the probability that $U_{n+1} < U_n$. What is the probability that $U_{n+2} < U_{n+1} < U_n$, assuming that U_n is a random real number between zero and one?

24. [*M29*] Under the assumptions of the preceding problem, except with $\theta = 0$, show that $U_n > U_{n+1} > \cdots > U_{n+t-1}$ occurs with probability

$$\frac{1}{t!}\left(1+\frac{1}{a}\right)\cdots\left(1+\frac{t-2}{a}\right).$$

What is the average length of a descending run starting at U_n, assuming that U_n is selected at random between zero and one?

▶ **25.** [*M25*] Let $\alpha, \beta, \alpha', \beta'$ be real numbers with $0 \le \alpha < \beta \le 1$, $0 \le \alpha' < \beta' \le 1$. Under the assumptions of exercise 22, what is the probability that $\alpha \le x < \beta$ and $\alpha' \le s(x) < \beta'$? (This is the "real number" analog of exercise 19.)

26. [*M21*] Consider a "Fibonacci" generator, where $U_{n+1} = \{U_n + U_{n-1}\}$. Assuming that U_1 and U_2 are independently chosen at random between 0 and 1, find the probability that $U_1 < U_2 < U_3$, $U_1 < U_3 < U_2$, $U_2 < U_1 < U_3$, etc. [*Hint:* Divide the unit square $\{(x,y) \mid 0 \le x, y < 1\}$ into six parts, depending on the relative order of x, y, and $\{x+y\}$, and determine the area of each part.]

27. [*M32*] In the Fibonacci generator of the preceding exercise, let U_0 and U_1 be chosen independently in the unit square except that $U_0 > U_1$. Determine the probability that U_1 is the beginning of an upward run of length k, so that $U_0 > U_1 < \cdots < U_k > U_{k+1}$. Compare this with the corresponding probabilities for a random sequence.

28. [*M35*] According to Eq. 3.2.1.3–(5), a linear congruential generator with potency 2 satisfies the condition $X_{n-1} - 2X_n + X_{n+1} \equiv (a-1)c$ (modulo m). Consider a generator that abstracts this situation: Let $U_{n+1} = \{\alpha + 2U_n - U_{n-1}\}$. As in exercise 26, divide the unit square into parts that show the relative order of U_1, U_2, and U_3 for each pair (U_1, U_2). Are there any values of α for which all six possible orders are achieved with probability $\frac{1}{6}$, assuming that U_1 and U_2 are chosen at random in the unit square?

3.3.4. The Spectral Test

In this section we shall study an especially important way to check the quality of linear congruential random number generators. Not only do all good generators pass this test, all generators now known to be bad actually *fail* it. Thus it is by far the most powerful test known, and it deserves particular attention. Our discussion will also bring out some fundamental limitations on the degree of randomness that we can expect from linear congruential sequences and their generalizations.

The spectral test embodies aspects of both the empirical and theoretical tests studied in previous sections: It is like the theoretical tests because it deals with properties of the full period of the sequence, and it is like the empirical tests because it requires a computer program to determine the results.

A. Ideas underlying the test. The most important randomness criteria seem to rely on properties of the joint distribution of t consecutive elements of the sequence, and the spectral test deals directly with this distribution. If we have a sequence $\langle U_n \rangle$ of period m, the basic idea is to analyze the set of all m points

$$\{ (U_n, U_{n+1}, \ldots, U_{n+t-1}) \mid 0 \le n < m \} \tag{1}$$

in t-dimensional space.

For simplicity we shall assume that we have a linear congruential sequence (X_0, a, c, m) of maximum period length m (so that $c \ne 0$), or that m is prime and $c = 0$ and the period length is $m - 1$. In the latter case we shall add the point $(0, 0, \ldots, 0)$ to the set (1), so that there are always m points in all; this extra point has a negligible effect when m is large, and it makes the theory much simpler. Under these assumptions, (1) can be rewritten as

$$\left\{ \frac{1}{m} \left(x, s(x), s(s(x)), \ldots, s^{[t-1]}(x) \right) \;\middle|\; 0 \le x < m \right\}, \tag{2}$$

where

$$s(x) = (ax + c) \bmod m \tag{3}$$

is the successor of x. We are considering only the set of all such points in t dimensions, not the order in which those points are actually generated. But the order of generation is reflected in the dependence between components of the vectors; and the spectral test studies such dependence for various dimensions t by dealing with the totality of all points (2).

For example, Fig. 8 shows a typical small case in 2 and 3 dimensions, for the generator with

$$s(x) = (137x + 187) \bmod 256. \tag{4}$$

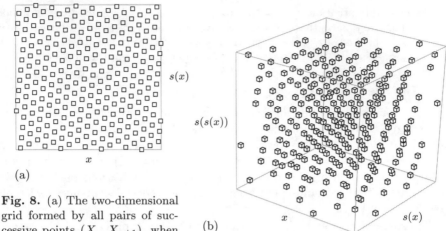

Fig. 8. (a) The two-dimensional grid formed by all pairs of successive points (X_n, X_{n+1}), when $X_{n+1} = (137X_n + 187) \bmod 256$. (b) The three-dimensional grid of triplets (X_n, X_{n+1}, X_{n+2}).

Of course a generator with period length 256 will hardly be random, but 256 is small enough that we can draw the diagram and gain some understanding before we turn to the larger m's that are of practical interest.

Perhaps the most striking thing about the pattern of boxes in Fig. 8(a) is that we can cover them all by a fairly small number of parallel lines; indeed, there are many different families of parallel lines that will hit all the points. For example, a set of 20 nearly vertical lines will do the job, as will a set of 21 lines that tilt upward at roughly a 30° angle. We commonly observe similar patterns when driving past farmlands that have been planted in a systematic manner.

If the same generator is considered in three dimensions, we obtain 256 points in a cube, obtained by appending a "height" component $s(s(x))$ to each of the 256 points $\bigl(x, s(x)\bigr)$ in the plane of Fig. 8(a), as shown in Fig. 8(b). Let's imagine that this 3-D crystal structure has been made into a physical model, a cube that we can turn in our hands; as we rotate it, we will notice various families of parallel planes that encompass all of the points. In the words of Wallace Givens, the random numbers stay "mainly in the planes."

At first glance we might think that such systematic behavior is so nonrandom as to make congruential generators quite worthless; but more careful reflection, remembering that m is quite large in practice, provides a better insight. The regular structure in Fig. 8 is essentially the "grain" we see when examining our random numbers under a high-power microscope. If we take truly random numbers between 0 and 1, and round or truncate them to finite accuracy so that each is an integer multiple of $1/\nu$ for some given number ν, then the t-dimensional points (1) we obtain will have an extremely regular character when viewed through a microscope.

Let $1/\nu_2$ be the maximum distance between lines, taken over all families of parallel straight lines that cover the points $\bigl\{\bigl(x/m, s(x)/m\bigr)\bigr\}$ in two dimensions. We shall call ν_2 the two-dimensional *accuracy* of the random number generator, since the pairs of successive numbers have a fine structure that is essentially good to one part in ν_2. Similarly, let $1/\nu_3$ be the maximum distance between planes, taken over all families of parallel planes that cover all points $\{(x/m, s(x)/m, s(s(x))/m)\}$; we shall call ν_3 the accuracy in three dimensions. The t-dimensional accuracy ν_t is the reciprocal of the maximum distance between hyperplanes, taken over all families of parallel $(t - 1)$-dimensional hyperplanes that cover all points $\{(x/m, s(x)/m, \ldots, s^{[t-1]}(x)/m)\}$.

The essential difference between periodic sequences and truly random sequences that have been truncated to multiples of $1/\nu$ is that the accuracy of truly random sequences is the same in all dimensions, while that of periodic sequences decreases as t increases. Indeed, since there are only m points in the t-dimensional cube when m is the period length, we can't achieve a t-dimensional accuracy of more than about $m^{1/t}$.

When the independence of t consecutive values is considered, computer-generated random numbers will behave essentially as if we took truly random numbers and truncated them to $\lg \nu_t$ bits, where ν_t decreases with increasing t. In practice, such varying accuracy is usually all we need. We don't insist that the 10-dimensional accuracy be 2^{32}, in the sense that all $(2^{32})^{10}$ possible 10-tuples $(U_n, U_{n+1}, \ldots, U_{n+9})$ should be equally likely on a 32-bit machine; for such large values of t we want only a few of the leading bits of $(U_n, U_{n+1}, \ldots, U_{n+t-1})$ to behave as if they were independently random.

On the other hand when an application demands high resolution of the random number sequence, simple linear congruential sequences will necessarily be inadequate. A generator with longer period should be used instead, even though only a small fraction of the period will actually be generated. Squaring the period length will essentially square the accuracy in higher dimensions; that is, it will double the effective number of bits of precision.

The spectral test is based on the values of ν_t for small t, say $2 \leq t \leq 6$. Dimensions 2, 3, and 4 seem to be adequate to detect important deficiencies in a sequence, but since we are considering the entire period it is wise to be somewhat cautious and go up into another dimension or two; on the other hand the values of ν_t for $t \geq 10$ seem to be of no practical significance whatever. (This is fortunate, because it appears to be rather difficult to calculate the accuracy ν_t precisely when $t \geq 10$.)

There is a vague relation between the spectral test and the serial test; for example, a special case of the serial test, taken over the entire period as in exercise 3.3.3–19, counts the number of boxes in each of 64 subsquares of Fig. 8(a). The main difference is that the spectral test rotates the dots so as to discover the least favorable orientation. We shall return to the serial test later in this section.

It may appear at first that we should apply the spectral test only for one suitably high value of t; if a generator passes the test in three dimensions, it seems plausible that it should also pass the 2-D test, hence we might as well omit the latter. The fallacy in this reasoning occurs because we apply more stringent conditions in lower dimensions. A similar situation occurs with the serial test:

Consider a generator that (quite properly) has almost the same number of points in each subcube of the unit cube, when the unit cube has been divided into 64 subcubes of size $\frac{1}{4} \times \frac{1}{4} \times \frac{1}{4}$; this same generator might yield completely *empty* subsquares of the unit square, when the unit square has been divided into 64 subsquares of size $\frac{1}{8} \times \frac{1}{8}$. Since we increase our expectations in lower dimensions, a separate test for each dimension is required.

It is not always true that $\nu_t \leq m^{1/t}$, although this upper bound is valid when the points form a rectangular grid. For example, it turns out that $\nu_2 = \sqrt{274} > \sqrt{256}$ in Fig. 8, because a nearly hexagonal structure brings the m points closer together than would be possible in a strictly rectangular arrangement.

In order to develop an algorithm that computes ν_t efficiently, we must look more deeply at the associated mathematical theory. Therefore a reader who is not mathematically inclined is advised to skip to part D of this section, where the spectral test is presented as a "plug-in" method accompanied by several examples. But the mathematics behind the spectral test requires only some elementary manipulations of vectors.

Some authors have suggested using the minimum number N_t of parallel covering lines or hyperplanes as the criterion, instead of the maximum distance $1/\nu_t$ between them. However, this number N_t does not appear to be as important as the concept of accuracy defined above, because it is biased by how nearly the slope of the lines or hyperplanes matches the coordinate axes of the cube. For example, the 20 nearly vertical lines that cover all the points of Fig. 8(a) are actually $1/\sqrt{328}$ units apart, according to Eq. (14) below with $(u_1, u_2) = (18, -2)$; this might falsely imply an accuracy of one part in $\sqrt{328}$, or perhaps even an accuracy of one part in 20. The true accuracy of only one part in $\sqrt{274}$ is realized only for the larger family of 21 lines with a slope of $7/15$; another family of 24 lines, with a slope of $-11/13$, also has a greater inter-line distance than the 20-line family, since $1/\sqrt{290} > 1/\sqrt{328}$. The precise way in which families of lines act at the boundaries of the unit hypercube does not seem to be an especially "clean" or significant criterion. However, for those people who prefer to count hyperplanes, it is possible to compute N_t using a method quite similar to the way in which we shall calculate ν_t (see exercise 16).

*B. Theory behind the test. In order to analyze the basic set (2), we start with the observation that

$$\frac{1}{m} s^{[j]}(x) = \left(\frac{a^j x + (1 + a + \cdots + a^{j-1})c}{m} \right) \bmod 1. \tag{5}$$

We can get rid of the "mod 1" operation by extending the set periodically, making infinitely many copies of the original t-dimensional hypercube, proceeding in all directions. This gives us the set

$$\begin{aligned} L &= \left\{ \left(\frac{x}{m} + k_1, \frac{s(x)}{m} + k_2, \ldots, \frac{s^{[t-1]}(x)}{m} + k_t \right) \;\middle|\; \text{integer } x, k_1, k_2, \ldots, k_t \right\} \\ &= \left\{ V_0 + \left(\frac{x}{m} + k_1, \frac{ax}{m} + k_2, \ldots, \frac{a^{t-1}x}{m} + k_t \right) \;\middle|\; \text{integer } x, k_1, k_2, \ldots, k_t \right\}, \end{aligned}$$

where

$$V_0 = \frac{1}{m} \left(0, c, (1+a)c, \ldots, (1+a+\cdots+a^{t-2})c\right) \qquad (6)$$

is a constant vector. The variable k_1 is redundant in this representation of L, because we can change $(x, k_1, k_2, \ldots, k_t)$ to $(x+k_1 m, 0, k_2-ak_1, \ldots, k_t-a^{t-1}k_1)$, reducing k_1 to zero without loss of generality. Therefore we obtain the comparatively simple formula

$$L = \{V_0 + y_1 V_1 + y_2 V_2 + \cdots + y_t V_t \mid \text{integer } y_1, y_2, \ldots, y_t\}, \qquad (7)$$

where

$$V_1 = \frac{1}{m}(1, a, a^2, \ldots, a^{t-1}); \qquad (8)$$

$$V_2 = (0, 1, 0, \ldots, 0), \quad V_3 = (0, 0, 1, \ldots, 0), \quad \ldots, \quad V_t = (0, 0, 0, \ldots, 1). \qquad (9)$$

The points $(x_1, x_2, \ldots, x_t)$ of L that satisfy $0 \le x_j < 1$ for all j are precisely the m points of our original set (2).

Notice that the increment c appears only in V_0, and the effect of V_0 is merely to shift all elements of L without changing their relative distances; hence c does not affect the spectral test in any way, and we might as well assume that $V_0 = (0, 0, \ldots, 0)$ when we are calculating ν_t. When V_0 is the zero vector we have a *lattice* of points

$$L_0 = \{y_1 V_1 + y_2 V_2 + \cdots + y_t V_t \mid \text{integer } y_1, y_2, \ldots, y_t\}, \qquad (10)$$

and our goal is to study the distances between adjacent $(t-1)$-dimensional hyperplanes, in families of parallel hyperplanes that cover all the points of L_0.

A family of parallel $(t-1)$-dimensional hyperplanes can be defined by a nonzero vector $U = (u_1, \ldots, u_t)$ that is perpendicular to all of them; and the set of points on a particular hyperplane is then

$$\{(x_1, \ldots, x_t) \mid x_1 u_1 + \cdots + x_t u_t = q\}, \qquad (11)$$

where q is a different constant for each hyperplane in the family. In other words, each hyperplane is the set of all vectors X for which the *dot product* $X \cdot U$ has a given value q. In our case the hyperplanes are all separated by a fixed distance, and one of them contains $(0, 0, \ldots, 0)$; hence we can adjust the magnitude of U so that the set of all *integer* values q gives all the hyperplanes in the family. Then the distance between neighboring hyperplanes is the minimum distance from $(0, 0, \ldots, 0)$ to the hyperplane for $q = 1$, namely

$$\min_{\text{real } x_1, \ldots, x_t} \left\{ \sqrt{x_1^2 + \cdots + x_t^2} \mid x_1 u_1 + \cdots + x_t u_t = 1 \right\}. \qquad (12)$$

Cauchy's inequality (see exercise 1.2.3–30) tells us that

$$(x_1 u_1 + \cdots + x_t u_t)^2 \le (x_1^2 + \cdots + x_t^2)(u_1^2 + \cdots + u_t^2), \qquad (13)$$

hence the minimum in (12) occurs when each $x_j = u_j/(u_1^2 + \cdots + u_t^2)$; the distance between neighboring hyperplanes is

$$1/\sqrt{u_1^2 + \cdots + u_t^2} = 1/\text{length}(U). \tag{14}$$

In other words, the quantity ν_t that we seek is precisely the length of the shortest vector U that defines a family of hyperplanes $\{X \cdot U = q \mid \text{integer } q\}$ containing all the elements of L_0.

Such a vector $U = (u_1, \ldots, u_t)$ must be nonzero, and it must satisfy $V \cdot U = $ integer for all V in L_0. In particular, since the points $(1, 0, \ldots, 0)$, $(0, 1, \ldots, 0)$, $\ldots$, $(0, 0, \ldots, 1)$ are all in L_0, all of the u_j must be integers. Furthermore since V_1 is in L_0, we must have $\frac{1}{m}(u_1 + au_2 + \cdots + a^{t-1}u_t) = $ integer, i.e.,

$$u_1 + au_2 + \cdots + a^{t-1}u_t \equiv 0 \pmod{m}. \tag{15}$$

Conversely, any nonzero integer vector $U = (u_1, \ldots, u_t)$ satisfying (15) defines a family of hyperplanes with the required properties, since all of L_0 will be covered: The dot product $(y_1 V_1 + \cdots + y_t V_t) \cdot U$ will be an integer for all integers $y_1, \ldots, y_t$. We have proved that

$$\begin{aligned}
\nu_t^2 &= \min_{(u_1, \ldots, u_t) \neq (0, \ldots, 0)} \{u_1^2 + \cdots + u_t^2 \mid u_1 + au_2 + \cdots + a^{t-1}u_t \equiv 0 \pmod{m}\} \\
&= \min_{(x_1, \ldots, x_t) \neq (0, \ldots, 0)} \left((mx_1 - ax_2 - a^2 x_3 - \cdots - a^{t-1}x_t)^2 + x_2^2 + x_3^2 + \cdots + x_t^2\right).
\end{aligned} \tag{16}$$

C. Deriving a computational method. We have now reduced the spectral test to the problem of finding the minimum value (16); but how on earth can we determine that minimum value in a reasonable amount of time? A brute-force search is out of the question, since m is very large in cases of practical interest.

It will be interesting and probably more useful if we develop a computational method for solving an even more general problem: *Find the minimum value of the quantity*

$$f(x_1, \ldots, x_t) = (u_{11}x_1 + \cdots + u_{t1}x_t)^2 + \cdots + (u_{1t}x_1 + \cdots + u_{tt}x_t)^2 \tag{17}$$

over all nonzero integer vectors $(x_1, \ldots, x_t)$, given any nonsingular matrix of coefficients $U = (u_{ij})$. The expression (17) is called a "positive definite quadratic form" in t variables. Since U is nonsingular, (17) cannot be zero unless the x_j are all zero.

Let us write $U_1, \ldots, U_t$ for the rows of U. Then (17) may be written

$$f(x_1, \ldots, x_t) = (x_1 U_1 + \cdots + x_t U_t) \cdot (x_1 U_1 + \cdots + x_t U_t), \tag{18}$$

the square of the length of the vector $x_1 U_1 + \cdots + x_t U_t$. The nonsingular matrix U has an inverse, which means that we can find uniquely determined vectors $V_1, \ldots, V_t$ such that

$$U_i \cdot V_j = \delta_{ij}, \qquad 1 \leq i, j \leq t. \tag{19}$$

For example, in the special form (16) that arises in the spectral test, we have

$$U_1 = (\quad m, 0, 0, \dots, 0), \qquad\qquad V_1 = \tfrac{1}{m}(1, a, a^2, \dots, a^{t-1}),$$
$$U_2 = (\quad -a, 1, 0, \dots, 0), \qquad\qquad V_2 = \quad(0, 1, \ 0, \dots, \quad 0),$$
$$U_3 = (\ -a^2, 0, 1, \dots, 0), \qquad\qquad V_3 = \quad(0, 0, \ 1, \dots, \quad 0), \qquad (20)$$

$$\cdot \quad \cdot \quad \cdot \quad \cdot \quad \cdot \quad \cdot \quad \cdot \quad \cdot \quad \cdot \quad \cdot$$

$$U_t = (-a^{t-1}, 0, 0, \dots, 1), \qquad\qquad V_t = \quad(0, 0, \ 0, \dots, \quad 1).$$

These V_j are precisely the vectors (8), (9) that we used to define our original lattice L_0. As the reader may well suspect, this is not a coincidence — indeed, if we had begun with an arbitrary lattice L_0, defined by any set of linearly independent vectors $V_1, \dots, V_t$, the argument we have used above can be generalized to show that the maximum separation between hyperplanes in a covering family is equivalent to minimizing (17), where the coefficients u_{ij} are defined by (19). (See exercise 2.)

Our first step in minimizing (18) is to reduce it to a finite problem, namely to show that we won't need to test infinitely many vectors $(x_1, \dots, x_t)$ when finding the minimum. This is where the vectors $V_1, \dots, V_t$ come in handy; we have

$$x_k = (x_1 U_1 + \dots + x_t U_t) \cdot V_k,$$

and Cauchy's inequality tells us that

$$\big((x_1 U_1 + \dots + x_t U_t) \cdot V_k\big)^2 \le f(x_1, \dots, x_t)(V_k \cdot V_k).$$

Hence we have derived a useful upper bound on each coordinate x_k:

Lemma A. *Let* $(x_1, \dots, x_t)$ *be a nonzero vector that minimizes* (18) *and let* $(y_1, \dots, y_t)$ *be any nonzero integer vector. Then*

$$x_k^2 \le f(y_1, \dots, y_t)(V_k \cdot V_k), \qquad \text{for } 1 \le k \le t. \qquad (21)$$

In particular, letting $y_i = \delta_{ij}$ *for all* i,

$$x_k^2 \le (U_j \cdot U_j)(V_k \cdot V_k), \qquad \text{for } 1 \le j, k \le t. \quad \blacksquare \qquad (22)$$

Lemma A reduces the problem to a finite search, but the right-hand side of (21) is usually much too large to make an exhaustive search feasible; we need at least one more idea. On such occasions, an old maxim provides sound advice: "If you can't solve a problem as it is stated, change it into a simpler problem that has the same answer." For example, Euclid's algorithm has this form; if we don't know the gcd of the input numbers, we change them into smaller numbers having the same gcd. (In fact, a slightly more general approach probably underlies the discovery of nearly all algorithms: "If you can't solve a problem directly, change it into one or more simpler problems, from whose solution you can solve the original one.")

In our case, a simpler problem is one that requires less searching because the right-hand side of (22) is smaller. The key idea we shall use is that it is possible to change one quadratic form into another one that is equivalent for all practical purposes. Let j be any fixed subscript, $1 \le j \le t$; let $(q_1, \ldots, q_{j-1}, q_{j+1}, \ldots, q_t)$ be any sequence of $t - 1$ integers; and consider the following transformation of the vectors:

$$V_i' = V_i - q_i V_j, \qquad x_i' = x_i - q_i x_j, \qquad U_i' = U_i, \qquad \text{for } i \ne j;$$
$$V_j' = V_j, \qquad\qquad x_j' = x_j, \qquad\qquad U_j' = U_j + \sum_{i \ne j} q_i U_i. \qquad (23)$$

It is easy to see that the new vectors $U_1', \ldots, U_t'$ define a quadratic form f' for which $f'(x_1', \ldots, x_t') = f(x_1, \ldots, x_t)$; furthermore the basic orthogonality condition (19) remains valid, because it is easy to check that $U_i' \cdot V_j' = \delta_{ij}$. As $(x_1, \ldots, x_t)$ runs through all nonzero integer vectors, so does $(x_1', \ldots, x_t')$; hence the new form f' has the same minimum as f.

Our goal is to use transformation (23), replacing U_i by U_i' and V_i by V_i' for all i, in order to make the right-hand side of (22) small; and the right-hand side of (22) will be small when both $U_j \cdot U_j$ and $V_k \cdot V_k$ are small. Therefore it is natural to ask the following two questions about the transformation (23):

a) *What choice of q_i makes $V_i' \cdot V_i'$ as small as possible?*

b) *What choice of $q_1, \ldots, q_{j-1}, q_{j+1}, \ldots, q_t$ makes $U_j' \cdot U_j'$ as small as possible?*

It is easiest to solve these questions first for *real* values of the q_i. Question (a) is quite simple, since

$$(V_i - q_i V_j) \cdot (V_i - q_i V_j) = V_i \cdot V_i - 2q_i\, V_i \cdot V_j + q_i^2\, V_j \cdot V_j$$
$$= (V_j \cdot V_j)\left(q_i - (V_i \cdot V_j / V_j \cdot V_j)\right)^2 + V_i \cdot V_i - (V_i \cdot V_j)^2 / V_j \cdot V_j,$$

and the minimum occurs when

$$q_i = V_i \cdot V_j \,/\, V_j \cdot V_j. \qquad (24)$$

Geometrically, we are asking what multiple of V_j should be subtracted from V_i so that the resulting vector V_i' has minimum length, and the answer is to choose q_i so that V_i' is perpendicular to V_j (that is, to make $V_i' \cdot V_j = 0$); the following diagram makes this plain.

$$(25)$$

Turning to question (b), we want to choose the q_i so that $U_j + \sum_{i \ne j} q_i U_i$ has minimum length; geometrically, we want to start with U_j and add some vector in the $(t - 1)$-dimensional hyperplane whose points are the sums of multiples of $\{U_i \mid i \ne j\}$. Again the best solution is to choose things so that U_j' is perpendicular to the hyperplane, making $U_j' \cdot U_k = 0$ for all $k \ne j$:

$$U_j \cdot U_k + \sum_{i \ne j} q_i (U_i \cdot U_k) = 0, \qquad 1 \le k \le t, \qquad k \ne j. \qquad (26)$$

(See exercise 12 for a rigorous proof that a solution to question (b) must satisfy these $t - 1$ equations.)

Now that we have answered questions (a) and (b), we are in a bit of a quandary; should we choose the q_i according to (24), so that the $V_i' \cdot V_i'$ are minimized, or according to (26), so that $U_j' \cdot U_j'$ is minimized? Either of these alternatives makes an improvement in the right-hand side of (22), so it is not immediately clear which choice should get priority. Fortunately, there is a very simple answer to this dilemma: Conditions (24) and (26) are exactly the same! (See exercise 7.) Therefore questions (a) and (b) have the same answer; we have a happy state of affairs in which we can reduce the length of both the U's and the V's simultaneously. Indeed, we have just rediscovered the *Gram–Schmidt orthogonalization process* [see *Crelle* **94** (1883), 41–73].

Our joy must be tempered with the realization that we have dealt with questions (a) and (b) only for *real* values of the q_i. Our application restricts us to integer values, so we cannot make V_i' exactly perpendicular to V_j. The best we can do for question (a) is to let q_i be the *nearest integer* to $V_i \cdot V_j \, / \, V_j \cdot V_j$ $\bigl($see (25)$\bigr)$. It turns out that this is *not* always the best solution to question (b); in fact U_j' may at times be longer than U_j. However, the bound (21) is never increased, since we can remember the smallest value of $f(y_1, \ldots, y_t)$ found so far. Thus a choice of q_i based solely on question (a) is quite satisfactory.

If we apply transformation (23) repeatedly in such a way that none of the vectors V_i gets longer and at least one gets shorter, we can never get into a loop; that is, we will never be considering the same quadratic form again after a sequence of nontrivial transformations of this kind. But eventually we will get stuck, in the sense that none of the transformations (23) for $1 \le j \le t$ will be able to shorten any of the vectors $V_1, \ldots, V_t$. At that point we can revert to an exhaustive search, using the bounds of Lemma A, which will now be quite small in most cases. Occasionally these bounds (21) will be poor, and another type of transformation will usually get the algorithm unstuck again and reduce the bounds (see exercise 18). However, transformation (23) by itself has proved to be quite adequate for the spectral test; in fact, it has proved to be amazingly powerful when the computations are arranged as in the algorithm discussed below.

*D. How to perform the spectral test. Here now is an efficient computational procedure that follows from our considerations. R. W. Gosper and U. Dieter have observed that it is possible to use the results of lower dimensions to make the spectral test significantly faster in higher dimensions. This refinement has been incorporated into the following algorithm, together with Gauss's significant simplification of the two-dimensional case (exercise 5).

Algorithm S (*The spectral test*). This algorithm determines the value of

$$\nu_t = \min\left\{ \sqrt{x_1^2 + \cdots + x_t^2} \;\middle|\; x_1 + ax_2 + \cdots + a^{t-1}x_t \equiv 0 \pmod{m} \right\} \quad (27)$$

for $2 \le t \le T$, given a, m, and T, where $0 < a < m$ and a is relatively prime to m. (The minimum is taken over all nonzero integer vectors $(x_1, \ldots, x_t)$, and the number ν_t measures the t-dimensional accuracy of random number generators, as discussed in the text above.) All arithmetic within this algorithm is done on integers whose magnitudes rarely if ever exceed m^2, except in step S7; in fact, nearly all of the integer variables will be less than m in absolute value during the computation.

When ν_t is being calculated for $t \geq 3$, the algorithm works with two $t \times t$ matrices U and V, whose row vectors are denoted by $U_i = (u_{i1}, \ldots, u_{it})$ and $V_i = (v_{i1}, \ldots, v_{it})$ for $1 \leq i \leq t$. These vectors satisfy the conditions

$$u_{i1} + au_{i2} + \cdots + a^{t-1}u_{it} \equiv 0 \pmod{m}, \qquad 1 \leq i \leq t; \qquad (28)$$

$$U_i \cdot V_j = m\delta_{ij}, \qquad 1 \leq i, j \leq t. \qquad (29)$$

(Thus the V_j of our previous discussion have been multiplied by m, to ensure that their components are integers.) There are three other auxiliary vectors, $X = (x_1, \ldots, x_t)$, $Y = (y_1, \ldots, y_t)$, and $Z = (z_1, \ldots, z_t)$. During the entire algorithm, r will denote $a^{t-1} \bmod m$ and s will denote the smallest upper bound for ν_t^2 that has been discovered so far.

S1. [Initialize.] Set $t \leftarrow 2$, $h \leftarrow a$, $h' \leftarrow m$, $p \leftarrow 1$, $p' \leftarrow 0$, $r \leftarrow a$, $s \leftarrow 1 + a^2$. (The first steps of this algorithm handle the case $t = 2$ by a special method, very much like Euclid's algorithm; we will have

$$h - ap \equiv h' - ap' \equiv 0 \pmod{m} \qquad \text{and} \qquad hp' - h'p = \pm m \qquad (30)$$

during this phase of the calculation.)

S2. [Euclidean step.] Set $q \leftarrow \lfloor h'/h \rfloor$, $u \leftarrow h' - qh$, $v \leftarrow p' - qp$. If $u^2 + v^2 < s$, set $s \leftarrow u^2 + v^2$, $h' \leftarrow h$, $h \leftarrow u$, $p' \leftarrow p$, $p \leftarrow v$, and repeat step S2.

S3. [Compute ν_2.] Set $u \leftarrow u - h$, $v \leftarrow v - p$; and if $u^2 + v^2 < s$, set $s \leftarrow u^2 + v^2$, $h' \leftarrow u$, $p' \leftarrow v$. Then output $\sqrt{s} = \nu_2$. (The validity of this calculation for the two-dimensional case is proved in exercise 5. Now we will set up the U and V matrices satisfying (28) and (29), in preparation for calculations in higher dimensions.) Set

$$U \leftarrow \begin{pmatrix} -h & p \\ -h' & p' \end{pmatrix}, \qquad V \leftarrow \pm \begin{pmatrix} p' & h' \\ -p & -h \end{pmatrix},$$

where the $-$ sign is chosen for V if and only if $p' > 0$.

S4. [Advance t.] If $t = T$, the algorithm terminates. (Otherwise we want to increase t by 1. At this point U and V are $t \times t$ matrices satisfying (28) and (29), and we must enlarge them by adding an appropriate new row and column.) Set $t \leftarrow t + 1$ and $r \leftarrow (ar) \bmod m$. Set U_t to the new row $(-r, 0, 0, \ldots, 0, 1)$ of t elements, and set $u_{it} \leftarrow 0$ for $1 \leq i < t$. Set V_t to the new row $(0, 0, 0, \ldots, 0, m)$. Finally, for $1 \leq i < t$, set $q \leftarrow \text{round}(v_{i1}r/m)$, $v_{it} \leftarrow v_{i1}r - qm$, and $U_t \leftarrow U_t + qU_i$. (Here "round$(x)$" denotes the nearest integer to x, e.g., $\lfloor x + 1/2 \rfloor$. We are essentially setting $v_{it} \leftarrow v_{i1}r$ and immediately applying transformation (23) with $j = t$, since the numbers $|v_{i1}r|$ are so large they ought to be reduced at once.) Finally set $s \leftarrow \min(s, U_t \cdot U_t)$, $k \leftarrow t$, and $j \leftarrow 1$. (In the following steps, j denotes the current row index for transformation (23), and k denotes the last such index where the transformation shortened at least one of the V_i.)

S5. [Transform.] For $1 \le i \le t$, do the following operations: If $i \ne j$ and $2|V_i \cdot V_j| > V_j \cdot V_j$, set $q \leftarrow \mathrm{round}(V_i \cdot V_j \,/\, V_j \cdot V_j)$, $V_i \leftarrow V_i - qV_j$, $U_j \leftarrow U_j + qU_i$, $s \leftarrow \min(s, U_j \cdot U_j)$, and $k \leftarrow j$. (We omit the transformation when $2|V_i \cdot V_j|$ exactly equals $V_j \cdot V_j$; exercise 19 shows that this precaution keeps the algorithm from looping endlessly.)

S6. [Advance j.] If $j = t$, set $j \leftarrow 1$; otherwise set $j \leftarrow j + 1$. Now if $j \ne k$, return to step S5. (If $j = k$, we have gone through $t - 1$ consecutive cycles of no transformation, so the transformation process is stuck.)

S7. [Prepare for search.] (Now the absolute minimum will be determined, using an exhaustive search over all $(x_1, \ldots, x_t)$ satisfying condition (21) of Lemma A.) Set $X \leftarrow Y \leftarrow (0, \ldots, 0)$, set $k \leftarrow t$, and set

$$ z_j \leftarrow \left\lfloor \sqrt{\lfloor (V_j \cdot V_j) s / m^2 \rfloor} \right\rfloor, \qquad \text{for } 1 \le j \le t. \tag{31} $$

(We will examine all $X = (x_1, \ldots, x_t)$ with $|x_j| \le z_j$ for $1 \le j \le t$. Usually $|z_j| \le 1$, but L. C. Killingbeck noticed in 1999 that larger values occur for about 0.00001 of all multipliers when $m = 2^{64}$. During the exhaustive search, the vector Y will always be equal to $x_1 U_1 + \cdots + x_t U_t$, so that $f(x_1, \ldots, x_t) = Y \cdot Y$. Since $f(-x_1, \ldots, -x_t) = f(x_1, \ldots, x_t)$, we shall examine only vectors whose first nonzero component is positive. The method is essentially that of counting in steps of one, regarding $(x_1, \ldots, x_t)$ as the digits in a balanced number system with mixed radices $(2z_1+1, \ldots, 2z_t+1)$; see Section 4.1.)

S8. [Advance x_k.] If $x_k = z_k$, go to S10. Otherwise increase x_k by 1 and set $Y \leftarrow Y + U_k$.

S9. [Advance k.] Set $k \leftarrow k+1$. Then if $k \le t$, set $x_k \leftarrow -z_k$, $Y \leftarrow Y - 2z_k U_k$, and repeat step S9. But if $k > t$, set $s \leftarrow \min(s, Y \cdot Y)$.

S10. [Decrease k.] Set $k \leftarrow k - 1$. If $k \ge 1$, return to S8. Otherwise output $\nu_t = \sqrt{s}$ (the exhaustive search is completed) and return to S4. ∎

In practice Algorithm S is applied for $T = 5$ or 6, say; it usually works reasonably well when $T = 7$ or 8, but it can be terribly slow when $T \ge 9$ since the exhaustive search tends to make the running time grow as 3^T. (If the minimum value ν_t occurs at many different points, the exhaustive search will hit them all; hence we typically find that all $z_k = 1$ for large t. As remarked above, the values of ν_t are generally irrelevant for practical purposes when t is large.)

An example will help to make Algorithm S clear. Consider the linear congruential sequence defined by

$$ m = 10^{10}, \qquad a = 3141592621, \qquad c = 1, \qquad X_0 = 0. \tag{32} $$

Six cycles of the Euclidean algorithm in steps S2 and S3 suffice to prove that the minimum nonzero value of $x_1^2 + x_2^2$ with

$$ x_1 + 3141592621 x_2 \equiv 0 \pmod{10^{10}} $$

occurs for $x_1 = 67654$, $x_2 = 226$; hence the two-dimensional accuracy of this generator is

$$\nu_2 = \sqrt{67654^2 + 226^2} \approx 67654.37748.$$

Passing to three dimensions, we seek the minimum nonzero value of $x_1^2 + x_2^2 + x_3^2$ such that

$$x_1 + 3141592621 x_2 + 3141592621^2 x_3 \equiv 0 \pmod{10^{10}}. \tag{33}$$

Step S4 sets up the matrices

$$U = \begin{pmatrix} -67654 & -226 & 0 \\ -44190611 & 191 & 0 \\ 5793866 & 33 & 1 \end{pmatrix}, \quad V = \begin{pmatrix} -191 & -44190611 & 2564918569 \\ -226 & 67654 & 1307181134 \\ 0 & 0 & 10000000000 \end{pmatrix}.$$

The first iteration of step S5, with $q = 1$ for $i = 2$ and $q = 4$ for $i = 3$, changes them to

$$U = \begin{pmatrix} -21082801 & 97 & 4 \\ -44190611 & 191 & 0 \\ 5793866 & 33 & 1 \end{pmatrix}, \quad V = \begin{pmatrix} -191 & -44190611 & 2564918569 \\ -35 & 44258265 & -1257737435 \\ 764 & 176762444 & -259674276 \end{pmatrix}.$$

(The first row U_1 has actually gotten longer in this transformation, although eventually the rows of U should get shorter.)

The next fourteen iterations of step S5 have $(j, q_1, q_2, q_3) = (2, -2, *, 0)$, $(3, 0, 3, *)$, $(1, *, -10, -1)$, $(2, -1, *, -6)$, $(3, -1, 0, *)$, $(1, *, 0, 2)$, $(2, 0, *, -1)$, $(3, 3, 4, *)$, $(1, *, 0, 0)$, $(2, -5, *, 0)$, $(3, 1, 0, *)$, $(1, *, -3, -1)$, $(2, 0, *, 0)$, $(3, 0, 0, *)$. Now the transformation process is stuck, but the rows of the matrices have become significantly shorter:

$$U = \begin{pmatrix} -1479 & 616 & -2777 \\ -3022 & 104 & 918 \\ -227 & -983 & -130 \end{pmatrix}, \quad V = \begin{pmatrix} -888874 & 601246 & -2994234 \\ -2809871 & 438109 & 1593689 \\ -854296 & -9749816 & -1707736 \end{pmatrix}. \tag{34}$$

The search limits (z_1, z_2, z_3) in step S7 turn out to be $(0, 0, 1)$, so U_3 is the shortest solution to (33); we have

$$\nu_3 = \sqrt{227^2 + 983^2 + 130^2} \approx 1017.21089.$$

Only a few iterations were needed to find this value, although condition (33) looks quite formidable at first glance. Our computation has proved that all points (U_n, U_{n+1}, U_{n+2}) produced by the random number generator (32) lie on a family of parallel planes about 0.001 units apart, but not on any family of planes that differ by more than 0.001 units.

The exhaustive search in steps S8–S10 reduces the value of s only rarely. One such case, found in 1982 by R. Carling and K. Levine, occurs when $a = 464680339$, $m = 2^{29}$, and $t = 5$; another case arose when the author calculated ν_6^2 for line 21 of Table 1, later in this section.

E. Ratings for various generators. So far we haven't really given a criterion that tells us whether or not a particular random number generator passes or flunks the spectral test. In fact, spectral success depends on the application, since some applications demand higher resolution than others. It appears that

$\nu_t \geq 2^{30/t}$ for $2 \leq t \leq 6$ will be quite adequate for most purposes (although the author must admit choosing this criterion partly because 30 is conveniently divisible by 2, 3, 5, and 6).

For some purposes we would like a criterion that is relatively independent of m, so we can say that a particular multiplier is good or bad with respect to the set of all other multipliers for the given m, without examining any others. A reasonable figure of merit for rating the goodness of a particular multiplier seems to be the volume of the ellipsoid in t-space defined by the relation

$$(x_1 m - x_2 a - \cdots - x_t a^{t-1})^2 + x_2^2 + \cdots + x_t^2 \leq \nu_t^2,$$

since this volume tends to indicate how likely it is that nonzero *integer* points $(x_1, \ldots, x_t)$ — corresponding to solutions of (15) — are in the ellipsoid. We therefore propose to calculate this volume, namely

$$\mu_t = \frac{\pi^{t/2} \nu_t^t}{(t/2)! \, m}, \tag{35}$$

as an indication of the effectiveness of the multiplier a for the given m. In this formula,

$$\left(\frac{t}{2}\right)! = \left(\frac{t}{2}\right)\left(\frac{t}{2} - 1\right) \cdots \left(\frac{1}{2}\right) \sqrt{\pi}, \qquad \text{for } t \text{ odd.} \tag{36}$$

Thus, in six or fewer dimensions the merit is computed as follows:

$$\mu_2 = \pi \nu_2^2/m, \qquad \mu_3 = \tfrac{4}{3}\pi \nu_3^3/m, \qquad \mu_4 = \tfrac{1}{2}\pi^2 \nu_4^4/m,$$
$$\mu_5 = \tfrac{8}{15}\pi^2 \nu_5^5/m, \qquad \mu_6 = \tfrac{1}{6}\pi^3 \nu_6^6/m.$$

We might say that the multiplier a passes the spectral test if μ_t is 0.1 or more for $2 \leq t \leq 6$, and it "passes with flying colors" if $\mu_t \geq 1$ for all these t. A low value of μ_t means that we have probably picked a very unfortunate multiplier, since very few lattices will have integer points so close to the origin. Conversely, a high value of μ_t means that we have found an unusually good multiplier for the given m; but it does not mean that the random numbers are necessarily very good, since m might be too small. Only the values ν_t truly indicate the degree of randomness.

Table 1 shows what sorts of values occur in typical sequences. Each line of the table considers a particular generator, and lists ν_t^2, μ_t, and the "number of bits of accuracy" $\lg \nu_t$. Lines 1 through 4 show the generators that were the subject of Figs. 2 and 5 in Section 3.3.1. The generators in lines 1 and 2 suffer from too small a multiplier; a diagram like Fig. 8 will have a nearly vertical "stripes" when a is small. The terrible generator in line 3 has a good μ_2 but very poor μ_3 and μ_4; like nearly all generators of potency 2, it has $\nu_3 = \sqrt{6}$ and $\nu_4 = 2$ (see exercise 3). Line 4 shows a "random" multiplier; this generator has satisfactorily passed numerous empirical tests for randomness, but it does not have especially high values of $\mu_2, \ldots, \mu_6$. In fact, the value of μ_5 flunks our criterion.

Line 5 shows the generator of Fig. 8. It passes the spectral test with very high-flying colors, when μ_2 through μ_6 are considered, but of course m is so small that the numbers can hardly be called random; the ν_t values are terribly low.

Table 1

SAMPLE RESULTS OF THE SPECTRAL TEST

Line	a	m	ν_2^2	ν_3^2	ν_4^2	ν_5^2	ν_6^2
1	23	10^8+1	530	530	530	530	447
2	2^7+1	2^{35}	16642	16642	16642	15602	252
3	$2^{18}+1$	2^{35}	34359738368	6	4	4	4
4	3141592653	2^{35}	2997222016	1026050	27822	1118	1118
5	137	256	274	30	14	6	4
6	3141592621	10^{10}	4577114792	1034718	62454	1776	542
7	3141592221	10^{10}	4293881050	276266	97450	3366	2382
8	4219755981	10^{10}	10721093248	2595578	49362	5868	820
9	4160984121	10^{10}	9183801602	4615650	16686	6840	1344
10	$2^{24}+2^{13}+5$	2^{35}	8364058	8364058	21476	16712	1496
11	5^{13}	2^{35}	33161885770	2925242	113374	13070	2256
12	$2^{16}+3$	2^{29}	536936458	118	116	116	116
13	1812433253	2^{32}	4326934538	1462856	15082	4866	906
14	1566083941	2^{32}	4659748970	2079590	44902	4652	662
15	69069	2^{32}	4243209856	2072544	52804	6990	242
16	2650845021	2^{32}	4938969760	2646962	68342	8778	1506
17	314159269	$2^{31}-1$	1432232969	899290	36985	3427	1144
18	62089911	$2^{31}-1$	1977289717	1662317	48191	6101	1462
19	16807	$2^{31}-1$	282475250	408197	21682	4439	895
20	48271	$2^{31}-1$	1990735345	1433881	47418	4404	1402
21	40692	$2^{31}-249$	1655838865	1403422	42475	6507	1438
22	44485709377909	2^{46}	5.6×10^{13}	1180915002	1882426	279928	26230
23	31167285	2^{48}	3.2×10^{14}	4111841446	17341510	306326	59278
24	see (38)		2.4×10^{18}	4.7×10^{11}	1.9×10^9	3194548	1611610
25	see (39)		$(2^{31}-1)^2$	1.4×10^{12}	643578623	12930027	837632
26	see the text	2^{64}	8.8×10^{18}	6.4×10^{12}	4.1×10^9	45662836	1846368
27	see the text	$\approx 2^{78}$	$2^{62}+1$	4281084902	2.2×10^9	1.8×10^9	1862407
28	$2^{-24\cdot389}$	$\approx 2^{576}$	1.8×10^{173}	3.5×10^{115}	4.4×10^{86}	2×10^{69}	5×10^{57}
29	$(2^{32}-5)^{-400}$	$\approx 2^{1376}$	1.6×10^{414}	8.6×10^{275}	1×10^{207}	2×10^{165}	8×10^{137}

Line 6 is the generator discussed in (32) above. Line 7 is a similar example, having an abnormally low value of μ_3. Line 8 shows a nonrandom multiplier for the same modulus m; all of its partial quotients are 1, 2, or 3. Such multipliers have been suggested by I. Borosh and H. Niederreiter because the Dedekind sums are likely to be especially small and because they produce best results in the two-dimensional serial test (see Section 3.3.3 and exercise 30). The particular example in line 8 has only one '3' as a partial quotient; there is no multiplier congruent to 1 modulo 20 whose partial quotients with respect to 10^{10} are only 1s and 2s. The generator in line 9 shows another multiplier chosen with malice aforethought, following a suggestion by A. G. Waterman that guarantees a reasonably high value of μ_2 (see exercise 11). Line 10 is interesting because it has high μ_3 in spite of very low μ_2 (see exercise 8).

Line 11 of Table 1 is a reminder of the good old days—it once was used extensively, following a suggestion of O. Taussky in the early 1950s. But computers for which 2^{35} was an appropriate modulus began to fade in importance during the late 60s, and they disappeared almost completely in the 80s, as machines

$$(\epsilon = \tfrac{1}{10})$$

$\lg \nu_2$	$\lg \nu_3$	$\lg \nu_4$	$\lg \nu_5$	$\lg \nu_6$	μ_2	μ_3	μ_4	μ_5	μ_6	Line
4.5	4.5	4.5	4.5	4.4	$2\epsilon^5$	$5\epsilon^4$	0.01	0.34	4.62	1
7.0	7.0	7.0	7.0	4.0	$2\epsilon^6$	$3\epsilon^4$	0.04	4.66	$2\epsilon^3$	2
17.5	1.3	1.0	1.0	1.0	3.14	$2\epsilon^9$	$2\epsilon^9$	$5\epsilon^9$	ϵ^8	3
15.7	10.0	7.4	5.1	5.1	0.27	0.13	0.11	0.01	0.21	4
4.0	2.5	1.9	1.3	1.0	3.36	2.69	3.78	1.81	1.29	5
16.0	10.0	8.0	5.4	4.5	1.44	0.44	1.92	0.07	0.08	6
16.0	9.0	8.3	5.9	5.6	1.35	0.06	4.69	0.35	6.98	7
16.7	10.7	7.8	6.3	4.8	3.37	1.75	1.20	1.39	0.28	8
16.5	11.1	7.0	6.4	5.2	2.89	4.15	0.14	2.04	1.25	9
11.5	11.5	7.2	7.0	5.3	$8\epsilon^4$	2.95	0.07	5.53	0.50	10
17.5	10.7	8.4	6.8	5.6	3.03	0.61	1.85	2.99	1.73	11
14.5	3.4	3.4	3.4	3.4	3.14	ϵ^5	ϵ^4	ϵ^3	0.02	12
16.0	10.2	6.9	6.1	4.9	3.16	1.73	0.26	2.02	0.89	13
16.1	10.5	7.7	6.1	4.7	3.41	2.92	2.32	1.81	0.35	14
16.0	10.5	7.8	6.4	4.0	3.10	2.91	3.20	5.01	0.02	15
16.1	10.7	8.0	6.6	5.3	3.61	4.20	5.37	8.85	4.11	16
15.2	9.9	7.6	5.9	5.1	2.10	1.66	3.14	1.69	3.60	17
15.4	10.3	7.8	6.3	5.3	2.89	4.18	5.34	7.13	7.52	18
14.0	9.3	7.2	6.1	4.9	0.41	0.51	1.08	3.22	1.73	19
15.4	10.2	7.8	6.1	5.2	2.91	3.35	5.17	3.15	6.63	20
15.3	10.2	7.7	6.3	5.2	2.42	3.24	4.15	8.37	7.16	21
22.8	15.1	10.4	9.0	7.3	2.48	2.42	0.25	3.10	1.33	22
24.1	16.0	12.0	9.1	7.9	3.60	3.92	5.27	0.97	3.82	23
30.5	19.4	15.4	10.8	10.3	1.65	0.29	3.88	0.02	4.69	24
31.0	20.2	14.6	11.8	9.8	3.14	1.49	0.44	0.69	0.66	25
31.5	21.3	16.0	12.7	10.4	1.50	3.68	4.52	4.02	1.76	26
31.0	16.0	15.5	15.4	10.4	$5\epsilon^5$	$4\epsilon^9$	$8\epsilon^5$	2.56	ϵ^4	27
288.	192.	144.	115.	95.9	2.27	3.46	3.92	2.49	2.98	28
688.	458.	344.	275.	229.	3.10	2.04	2.85	1.15	1.33	29

upper bounds from (40): 3.63   5.92   9.87   14.89   23.87

with 32-bit arithmetic began to proliferate. This switch to a comparatively small word size called for comparatively greater care. Line 12 was, alas, the generator actually used on such machines in most of the world's scientific computing centers for more than a decade; its very name RANDU is enough to bring dismay into the eyes and stomachs of many computer scientists! The actual generator is defined by

$$X_0 \text{ odd}, \qquad X_{n+1} = (65539 X_n) \bmod 2^{31}, \qquad (37)$$

and exercise 20 indicates that 2^{29} is the appropriate modulus for the spectral test. Since $9X_n - 6X_{n+1} + X_{n+2} \equiv 0 \pmod{2^{31}}$, the generator fails most three-dimensional criteria for randomness, and it should never have been used. Almost any multiplier $\equiv 5 \pmod 8$ would be better. (A curious fact about RANDU, noticed by R. W. Gosper, is that $\nu_4 = \nu_5 = \nu_6 = \nu_7 = \nu_8 = \nu_9 = \sqrt{116}$, hence μ_9 is a spectacular 11.98.) Lines 13 and 14 are the Borosh–Niederreiter and Waterman multipliers for modulus 2^{32}. Line 16 was found by L. C. Killingbeck, who carried out an exhaustive search of all multipliers $a \equiv 1 \bmod 4$ when $m = 2^{32}$. Line 23, similarly, was found by M. Lavaux and F. Janssens in a (nonexhaustive) computer search for spectrally good multipliers having a very high μ_2. Line 22 is for the multiplier used with $c = 0$ and $m = 2^{48}$ in the Cray X-MP library; line 26 (whose excellent multiplier 6364136223846793005 is too big to fit in the column) is due to C. E. Haynes. Line 15 was nominated by George Marsaglia as "a candidate for the best of all multipliers," after a computer search for nearly cubical lattices in dimensions 2 through 5, partly because it is easy to remember [*Applications of Number Theory to Numerical Analysis*, edited by S. K. Zaremba (New York: Academic Press, 1972), 275].

Line 17 uses a random primitive root, modulo the prime $2^{31}-1$, as multiplier. Line 18 shows the spectrally best primitive root for $2^{31}-1$, found in an exhaustive search by G. S. Fishman and L. R. Moore III [*SIAM J. Sci. Stat. Comput.* **7** (1986), 24–45]. The adequate but less outstanding multiplier $16807 = 7^5$ in line 19 is actually used most often for that modulus, after being proposed by Lewis, Goodman, and Miller in *IBM Systems J.* **8** (1969), 136–146; it has been one of the main generators in the popular IMSL subroutine library since 1971. The main reason for continued use of $a = 16807$ is that a^2 is less than the modulus m, hence $ax \bmod m$ can be implemented with reasonable efficiency in high-level languages using the technique of exercise 3.2.1.1–9. However, such small multipliers have known defects. S. K. Park and K. W. Miller noticed that the same implementation technique applies also to certain multipliers greater than $\sqrt{m}$, so they asked G. S. Fishman to find the best "efficiently portable" multiplier in this wider class; the result appears in line 20 [*CACM* **31** (1988), 1192–1201]. Line 21 shows another good multiplier, due to P. L'Ecuyer [*CACM* **31** (1988), 742–749, 774]; this one uses a slightly smaller prime modulus.

When the generators of lines 20 and 21 are combined by subtraction as suggested in Eq. 3.2.2–(15), so that the generated numbers $\langle Z_n \rangle$ satisfy

$$X_{n+1} = 48271 X_n \bmod (2^{31} - 1), \qquad Y_{n+1} = 40692 Y_n \bmod (2^{31} - 249),$$
$$Z_n = (X_n - Y_n) \bmod (2^{31} - 1), \tag{38}$$

exercise 32 shows that it is reasonable to rate $\langle Z_n \rangle$ with the spectral test for $m = (2^{31}-1)(2^{31}-249)$ and $a = 1431853894371298687$. (This value of a satisfies $a \bmod (2^{31} - 1) = 48271$ and $a \bmod (2^{31} - 249) = 40692$.) The results appear on line 24. We needn't worry too much about the low value of μ_5, since $\nu_5 > 1000$. Generator (38) has a period of length $(2^{31} - 2)(2^{31} - 250)/62 \approx 7 \times 10^{16}$.

Line 25 of the table represents the sequence

$$X_n = (271828183 X_{n-1} - 314159269 X_{n-2}) \bmod (2^{31} - 1), \tag{39}$$

which can be shown to have period length $(2^{31} - 1)^2 - 1$; it has been analyzed with the generalized spectral test of exercise 24.

The last three lines of Table 1 are based on add-with-carry and subtract-with-borrow methods, which simulate linear congruential sequences that have extremely large moduli (see exercise 3.2.1.1–14). Line 27 is for the generator

$$X_n = (X_{n-1} + 65430 X_{n-2} + C_n) \bmod 2^{31},$$
$$C_{n+1} = \lfloor (X_{n-1} + 65430 X_{n-2} + C_n)/2^{31} \rfloor,$$

which corresponds to $\mathcal{X}_{n+1} = (65430 \cdot 2^{31} + 1)\mathcal{X}_n \bmod (65430 \cdot 2^{62} + 2^{31} - 1)$; the numbers in the table refer to the "super-values"

$$\mathcal{X}_n = (65430 \cdot 2^{31} + 1)X_{n-1} + 65430X_{n-2} + C_n$$

rather than to the values X_n actually computed and used as random numbers. Line 28 represents a more typical subtract-with-borrow generator

$$X_n = (X_{n-10} - X_{n-24} - C_n) \bmod 2^{24}, \quad C_{n+1} = [X_{n-10} < X_{n-24} + C_n],$$

but modified by generating 389 elements of the sequence and then using only the first (or last) 24. This generator, called RANLUX, was recommended by Martin Lüscher after it passed many stringent tests that previous generators failed [*Computer Physics Communications* **79** (1994), 100–110]. A similar sequence,

$$X_n = (X_{n-22} - X_{n-43} - C_n) \bmod (2^{32} - 5), \quad C_{n+1} = [X_{n-22} < X_{n-43} + C_n],$$

with 43 elements used after 400 are generated, appears in line 29; this sequence is discussed in the answer to exercise 3.2.1.2–22. In both cases the table entries refer to the spectral test on multiprecision numbers $\mathcal{X}_n$ instead of to the individual "digits" X_n, but the high μ values indicate that the process of generating 389 or 400 numbers before selecting 24 or 43 is an excellent way to remove biases due to the extreme simplicity of the generation scheme.

Theoretical upper bounds on μ_t, which can never be transcended for any m, are shown just below Table 1; it is known that every lattice with m points per unit volume has

$$\nu_t \leq \gamma_t^{1/2} m^{1/t}, \tag{40}$$

where γ_t takes the respective values

$$(4/3)^{1/2}, \quad 2^{1/3}, \quad 2^{1/2}, \quad 2^{3/5}, \quad (64/3)^{1/6}, \quad 4^{3/7}, \quad 2 \tag{41}$$

for $t = 2, \ldots, 8$. [See exercise 9 and J. W. S. Cassels, *Introduction to the Geometry of Numbers* (Berlin: Springer, 1959), 332; J. H. Conway and N. J. A. Sloane, *Sphere Packings, Lattices and Groups* (New York: Springer, 1988), 20.] These bounds hold for lattices generated by vectors with arbitrary real coordinates. For example, the optimum lattice for $t = 2$ is hexagonal, and it is generated by vectors of length $2/\sqrt{3m}$ that form two sides of an equilateral triangle. In three dimensions the optimum lattice is generated by vectors V_1, V_2, V_3 that can be rotated into the form $(v, v, -v)$, $(v, -v, v)$, $(-v, v, v)$, where $v = 1/\sqrt[3]{4m}$.

*F. Relation to the serial test. In a series of important papers published during the 1970s, Harald Niederreiter showed how to analyze the distribution of the t-dimensional vectors (1) by means of exponential sums. One of the main consequences of his theory is that the serial test in several dimensions will be passed by any generator that passes the spectral test, even when we consider only a sufficiently large part of the period instead of the whole period. We shall now turn briefly to a study of his interesting methods, in the case of linear congruential sequences (X_0, a, c, m) of period length m.

The first idea we need is the notion of *discrepancy* in t dimensions, a quantity that we shall define as the difference between the expected number and the actual number of t-dimensional vectors $(x_n, x_{n+1}, \ldots, x_{n+t-1})$ falling into a hyper-rectangular region, maximized over all such regions. To be precise, let $\langle x_n \rangle$ be a sequence of integers in the range $0 \le x_n < m$. We define

$$D_N^{(t)} = \max_R \left| \frac{\text{number of } (x_n, \ldots, x_{n+t-1}) \text{ in } R \text{ for } 0 \le n < N}{N} - \frac{\text{volume of } R}{m^t} \right| \tag{42}$$

where R ranges over all sets of points of the form

$$R = \{(y_1, \ldots, y_t) \mid \alpha_1 \le y_1 < \beta_1, \ldots, \alpha_t \le y_t < \beta_t\}; \tag{43}$$

here α_j and β_j are integers in the range $0 \le \alpha_j < \beta_j \le m$, for $1 \le j \le t$. The volume of R is clearly $(\beta_1 - \alpha_1) \ldots (\beta_t - \alpha_t)$. To get the discrepancy $D_N^{(t)}$, we imagine looking at all these sets R and finding the one with the greatest excess or deficiency of points $(x_n, \ldots, x_{n+t-1})$.

An upper bound for the discrepancy can be found by using exponential sums. Let $\omega = e^{2\pi i/m}$ be a primitive mth root of unity. If $(x_1, \ldots, x_t)$ and $(y_1, \ldots, y_t)$ are two vectors with all components in the range $0 \le x_j, y_j < m$, we have

$$\sum_{0 \le u_1, \ldots, u_t < m} \omega^{(x_1 - y_1)u_1 + \cdots + (x_t - y_t)u_t} = \begin{cases} m^t & \text{if } (x_1, \ldots, x_t) = (y_1, \ldots, y_t), \\ 0 & \text{if } (x_1, \ldots, x_t) \ne (y_1, \ldots, y_t). \end{cases}$$

Therefore the number of vectors $(x_n, \ldots, x_{n+t-1})$ in R for $0 \le n < N$, when R is defined by (43), can be expressed as

$$\frac{1}{m^t} \sum_{0 \le n < N} \sum_{0 \le u_1, \ldots, u_t < m} \omega^{x_n u_1 + \cdots + x_{n+t-1} u_t} \sum_{\alpha_1 \le y_1 < \beta_1} \cdots \sum_{\alpha_t \le y_t < \beta_t} \omega^{-(y_1 u_1 + \cdots + y_t u_t)}.$$

When $u_1 = \cdots = u_t = 0$ in this sum, we get N/m^t times the volume of R; hence we can express $D_N^{(t)}$ as the maximum over R of

$$\left| \frac{1}{N m^t} \sum_{0 \le n < N} \sum_{\substack{0 \le u_1, \ldots, u_t < m \\ (u_1, \ldots, u_t) \ne (0, \ldots, 0)}} \omega^{x_n u_1 + \cdots + x_{n+t-1} u_t} \sum_{\alpha_1 \le y_1 < \beta_1} \cdots \sum_{\alpha_t \le y_t < \beta_t} \omega^{-(y_1 u_1 + \cdots + y_t u_t)} \right|.$$

Since complex numbers satisfy $|w + z| \le |w| + |z|$ and $|wz| = |w||z|$, it follows that

$$D_N^{(t)} \le \max_R \frac{1}{m^t} \sum_{\substack{0 \le u_1, \ldots, u_t < m \\ (u_1, \ldots, u_t) \ne (0, \ldots, 0)}} \left| \sum_{\alpha_1 \le y_1 < \beta_1} \cdots \sum_{\alpha_t \le y_t < \beta_t} \omega^{-(y_1 u_1 + \cdots + y_t u_t)} \right| g(u_1, \ldots, u_t)$$

$$\le \frac{1}{m^t} \sum_{\substack{0 \le u_1, \ldots, u_t < m \\ (u_1, \ldots, u_t) \ne (0, \ldots, 0)}} \max_R \left| \sum_{\alpha_1 \le y_1 < \beta_1} \cdots \sum_{\alpha_t \le y_t < \beta_t} \omega^{-(y_1 u_1 + \cdots + y_t u_t)} \right| g(u_1, \ldots, u_t)$$

$$= \sum_{\substack{0 \le u_1,\ldots,u_t < m \\ (u_1,\ldots,u_t) \ne (0,\ldots,0)}} f(u_1,\ldots,u_t)\, g(u_1,\ldots,u_t), \tag{44}$$

where

$$g(u_1,\ldots,u_t) = \left| \frac{1}{N} \sum_{0 \le n < N} \omega^{x_n u_1 + \cdots + x_{n+t-1} u_t} \right|;$$

$$f(u_1,\ldots,u_t) = \max_R \frac{1}{m^t} \left| \sum_{\alpha_1 \le y_1 < \beta_1} \cdots \sum_{\alpha_t \le y_t < \beta_t} \omega^{-(y_1 u_1 + \cdots + y_t u_t)} \right|$$

$$= \max_R \left| \frac{1}{m} \sum_{\alpha_1 \le y_1 < \beta_1} \omega^{-u_1 y_1} \right| \cdots \left| \frac{1}{m} \sum_{\alpha_t \le y_t < \beta_t} \omega^{-u_t y_t} \right|.$$

Both f and g can be simplified further in order to get a good upper bound on $D_N^{(t)}$. We have

$$\left| \frac{1}{m} \sum_{\alpha \le y < \beta} \omega^{-uy} \right| = \frac{1}{m} \left| \frac{\omega^{-\beta u} - \omega^{-\alpha u}}{\omega^{-u} - 1} \right| \le \frac{2}{m\,|\omega^u - 1|} = \frac{1}{m \sin(\pi u/m)}$$

when $u \ne 0$, and the sum is ≤ 1 when $u = 0$; hence

$$f(u_1,\ldots,u_t) \le r(u_1,\ldots,u_t), \tag{45}$$

where

$$r(u_1,\ldots,u_t) = \prod_{\substack{1 \le k \le t \\ u_k \ne 0}} \frac{1}{m \sin(\pi u_k/m)}. \tag{46}$$

Furthermore, when $\langle x_n \rangle$ is generated modulo m by a linear congruential sequence, we have

$$x_n u_1 + \cdots + x_{n+t-1} u_t = x_n u_1 + (ax_n + c)u_2 + \cdots + \left(a^{t-1} x_n + c(a^{t-2} + \cdots + 1)\right) u_t$$

$$= (u_1 + au_2 + \cdots + a^{t-1} u_t) x_n + h(u_1,\ldots,u_t)$$

where $h(u_1,\ldots,u_t)$ is independent of n; hence

$$g(u_1,\ldots,u_t) = \left| \frac{1}{N} \sum_{0 \le n < N} \omega^{q(u_1,\ldots,u_t)x_n} \right|, \tag{47}$$

where

$$q(u_1,\ldots,u_t) = u_1 + au_2 + \cdots + a^{t-1} u_t. \tag{48}$$

Now here is where the connection to the spectral test comes in: We will show that the sum $g(u_1,\ldots,u_t)$ is rather small unless $q(u_1,\ldots,u_t) \equiv 0$ (modulo m); in other words, the contributions to (44) arise mainly from the solutions to (15). Furthermore exercise 27 shows that $r(u_1,\ldots,u_t)$ is rather small when $(u_1,\ldots,u_t)$ is a "large" solution to (15). Hence the discrepancy $D_N^{(t)}$ will be rather small when (15) has only "large" solutions, namely when the spectral test is passed. Our remaining task is to quantify these qualitative statements by making careful calculations.

In the first place, let's consider the size of $g(u_1, \ldots, u_t)$. When $N = m$, so that the sum (47) is over an entire period, we have $g(u_1, \ldots, u_t) = 0$ except when $(u_1, \ldots, u_t)$ satisfies (15), so the discrepancy is bounded above in this case by the sum of $r(u_1, \ldots, u_t)$ taken over all the nonzero solutions of (15). But let's consider also what happens in a sum like (47) when N is less than m and $q(u_1, \ldots, u_t)$ is not a multiple of m. We have

$$\sum_{0 \le n < N} \omega^{x_n} = \sum_{0 \le n < N} \frac{1}{m} \sum_{0 \le k < m} \omega^{-nk} \sum_{0 \le j < m} \omega^{x_j + jk}$$

$$= \sum_{0 \le k < m} \left(\frac{1}{m} \sum_{0 \le n < N} \omega^{-nk} \right) S_{k0}, \qquad (49)$$

where

$$S_{kl} = \sum_{0 \le j < m} \omega^{x_{j+l} + jk}. \qquad (50)$$

Now $S_{kl} = \omega^{-lk} S_{k0}$, so $|S_{kl}| = |S_{k0}|$ for all l, and we can calculate this common value by further exponential-summery:

$$|S_{k0}|^2 = \frac{1}{m} \sum_{0 \le l < m} |S_{kl}|^2$$

$$= \frac{1}{m} \sum_{0 \le l < m} \sum_{0 \le j < m} \omega^{x_{j+l} + jk} \sum_{0 \le i < m} \omega^{-x_{i+l} - ik}$$

$$= \frac{1}{m} \sum_{0 \le i,j < m} \omega^{(j-i)k} \sum_{0 \le l < m} \omega^{x_{j+l} - x_{i+l}}$$

$$= \frac{1}{m} \sum_{0 \le i < m, \; i \le j < m+i} \omega^{(j-i)k} \sum_{0 \le l < m} \omega^{(a^{j-i} - 1)x_{i+l} + (a^{j-i} - 1)c/(a-1)}.$$

Let s be minimum such that $a^s \equiv 1$ (modulo m), and let

$$s' = (a^s - 1)c/(a - 1) \bmod m.$$

Then s is a divisor of m (see Lemma 3.2.1.2P), and $x_{n+js} \equiv x_n + js'$ (modulo m). The sum on l vanishes unless $j - i$ is a multiple of s, so we find that

$$|S_{k0}|^2 = m \sum_{0 \le j < m/s} \omega^{jsk + js'}.$$

We have $s' = q's$ where q' is relatively prime to m (see exercise 3.2.1.2–21), so it turns out that

$$|S_{k0}| = \begin{cases} 0 & \text{if } k + q' \not\equiv 0 \pmod{m/s}, \\ m/\sqrt{s} & \text{if } k + q' \equiv 0 \pmod{m/s}. \end{cases} \qquad (51)$$

Putting this information back into (49), and recalling the derivation of (45), shows that

$$\left| \sum_{0 \le n < N} w^{x_n} \right| \le \frac{m}{\sqrt{s}} \sum_{k} r(k), \tag{52}$$

where the sum is over $0 \le k < m$ such that $k + q' \equiv 0 \pmod{m/s}$. Exercise 25 can now be used to estimate the remaining sum, and we find that

$$\left| \sum_{0 \le n < N} w^{x_n} \right| \le \frac{2}{\pi} \sqrt{s} \ln s + O\left(\frac{m}{\sqrt{s}} \right). \tag{53}$$

The same upper bound applies also to $|\sum_{0 \le n < N} w^{q x_n}|$ for any $q \not\equiv 0 \pmod{m}$, since the effect is to replace m in this derivation by a divisor of m. In fact, the upper bound gets even smaller when q has a factor in common with m, since s and $m/\sqrt{s}$ generally become smaller. (See exercise 26.)

We have now proved that the $g(u_1, \dots, u_t)$ part of our upper bound (44) on the discrepancy is small, if N is large enough and if $(u_1, \dots, u_t)$ does not satisfy the spectral test congruence (15). Exercise 27 proves that the $f(u_1, \dots, u_t)$ part of our upper bound is small, when summed over all the nonzero vectors $(u_1, \dots, u_t)$ satisfying (15), provided that all such vectors are far away from $(0, \dots, 0)$. Putting these results together leads to the following theorem of Niederreiter:

Theorem N. *Let $\langle X_n \rangle$ be a linear congruential sequence (X_0, a, c, m) of period length $m > 1$, and let s be the least positive integer such that $a^s \equiv 1 \pmod{m}$. Then the t-dimensional discrepancy $D_N^{(t)}$ corresponding to the first N values of $\langle X_n \rangle$, as defined in (42), satisfies*

$$D_N^{(t)} = O\left(\frac{\sqrt{s} \log s \, (\log m)^t}{N} \right) + O\left(\frac{m (\log m)^t}{N \sqrt{s}} \right) + O((\log m)^t \, r_{\max}); \tag{54}$$

$$D_m^{(t)} = O((\log m)^t \, r_{\max}). \tag{55}$$

Here $r_{\max}$ is the maximum value of the quantity $r(u_1, \dots, u_t)$ defined in (46), taken over all nonzero integer vectors $(u_1, \dots, u_t)$ satisfying (15).

Proof. The first two O-terms in (54) come from vectors $(u_1, \dots, u_t)$ in (44) that do not satisfy (15), since exercise 25 proves that $f(u_1, \dots, u_t)$ summed over all $(u_1, \dots, u_t)$ is $O(((2/\pi) \ln m)^t)$ and exercise 26 bounds each $g(u_1, \dots, u_t)$. (These terms are missing from (55) since $g(u_1, \dots, u_t) = 0$ in that case.) The remaining O-term in (54) and (55) comes from nonzero vectors $(u_1, \dots, u_t)$ that do satisfy (15), using the bound derived in exercise 27. (By examining this proof carefully, we could replace each O in these formulas by an explicit function of t.) ∎

Eq. (55) relates to the serial test in t dimensions over the entire period, while Eq. (54) gives us useful information about the distribution of the first N generated values when N is less than m, provided that N is not too small.

Notice that (54) will guarantee low discrepancy only when s is sufficiently large, otherwise the $m/\sqrt{s}$ term will dominate. If $m = p_1^{e_1} \dots p_r^{e_r}$ and $\gcd(a-1, m) = p_1^{f_1} \dots p_r^{f_r}$, then s equals $p_1^{e_1-f_1} \dots p_r^{e_r-f_r}$ by Lemma 3.2.1.2P; thus, the largest values of s correspond to high potency. In the common case $m = 2^e$ and $a \equiv 5$ (modulo 8), we have $s = \frac{1}{4}m$, so $D_N^{(t)}$ is $O\big(\sqrt{m}\,(\log m)^{t+1}/N\big) + O\big((\log m)^t r_{\max}\big)$. It is not difficult to prove that

$$r_{\max} \leq \frac{1}{\sqrt{8}\,\nu_t} \tag{56}$$

(see exercise 29). Therefore Eq. (54) says in particular that the discrepancy will be low in t dimensions if the spectral test is passed and if N is somewhat larger than $\sqrt{m}\,(\log m)^{t+1}$.

In a sense Theorem N is almost too strong, for the result in exercise 30 shows that linear congruential sequences like those in lines 8 and 13 of Table 1 have a discrepancy of order $(\log m)^2/m$ in two dimensions. The discrepancy in this case is extremely small in spite of the fact that there are parallelogram-shaped regions of area $\approx 1/\sqrt{m}$ containing no points (U_n, U_{n+1}). The fact that discrepancy can change so drastically when the points are rotated warns us that the serial test may not be as meaningful a measure of randomness as the rotation-invariant spectral test.

G. Historical remarks. In 1959, while deriving upper bounds for the error in the evaluation of t-dimensional integrals by the Monte Carlo method, N. M. Korobov devised a way to rate the multiplier of a linear congruential sequence. His rather complicated formula is related to the spectral test, since it is strongly influenced by "small" solutions to (15); but it is not quite the same. Korobov's test has been the subject of an extensive literature, surveyed by Kuipers and Niederreiter in *Uniform Distribution of Sequences* (New York: Wiley, 1974), §2.5.

The spectral test was originally formulated by R. R. Coveyou and R. D. MacPherson [*JACM* **14** (1967), 100–119], who introduced it in an interesting indirect way. Instead of working with the grid structure of successive points, they considered random number generators as sources of t-dimensional "waves." The numbers $\sqrt{x_1^2 + \dots + x_t^2}$ such that $x_1 + \dots + a^{t-1}x_t \equiv 0$ (modulo m) in their original treatment were the wave "frequencies," or points in the "spectrum" defined by the random number generator, with low-frequency waves being the most damaging to randomness; hence the name *spectral test*. Coveyou and MacPherson introduced a procedure analogous to Algorithm S for performing their test, based on the principle of Lemma A. However, their original procedure (which used matrices UU^T and VV^T instead of U and V) dealt with extremely large numbers; the idea of working directly with U and V was independently suggested by F. Janssens and by U. Dieter. [See *Math. Comp.* **29** (1975), 827–833.]

Several other authors pointed out that the spectral test could be understood in far more concrete terms; by introducing the study of the grid and lattice structures corresponding to linear congruential sequences, the fundamental limitations on randomness became graphically clear. See G. Marsaglia, *Proc. Nat. Acad. Sci.*

61 (1968), 25–28; W. W. Wood, *J. Chem. Phys.* **48** (1968), 427; R. R. Coveyou, *Studies in Applied Math.* **3** (Philadelphia: SIAM, 1969), 70–111; W. A. Beyer, R. B. Roof, and D. Williamson, *Math. Comp.* **25** (1971), 345–360; G. Marsaglia and W. A. Beyer, *Applications of Number Theory to Numerical Analysis*, edited by S. K. Zaremba (New York: Academic Press, 1972), 249–285, 361–370.

R. G. Stoneham showed, by using estimates of exponential sums, that $p^{1/2+\epsilon}$ or more elements of the sequence $a^k X_0 \bmod p$ have asymptotically small discrepancy, when a is a primitive root modulo the prime p [*Acta Arithmetica* **22** (1973), 371–389]. This work was extended as explained above in a number of papers by Harald Niederreiter [*Math. Comp.* **28** (1974), 1117–1132; **30** (1976), 571–597; *Advances in Math.* **26** (1977), 99–181; *Bull. Amer. Math. Soc.* **84** (1978), 957–1041]. See also Niederreiter's book *Random Number Generation and Quasi-Monte Carlo Methods* (Philadelphia: SIAM, 1992).

EXERCISES

1. [*M10*] To what does the spectral test reduce in *one* dimension? (In other words, what happens when $t = 1$?)

2. [*HM20*] Let $V_1, \ldots, V_t$ be linearly independent vectors in t-space, let L_0 be the lattice of points defined by (10), and let $U_1, \ldots, U_t$ be defined by (19). Prove that the maximum distance between $(t-1)$-dimensional hyperplanes, over all families of parallel hyperplanes that cover L_0, is $1/\min\{f(x_1, \ldots, x_t)^{1/2} \mid (x_1, \ldots, x_t) \neq (0, \ldots, 0)\}$, where f is defined in (17).

3. [*M24*] Determine ν_3 and ν_4 for all linear congruential generators of potency 2 and period length m.

▸ **4.** [*M23*] Let $u_{11}, u_{12}, u_{21}, u_{22}$ be elements of a 2×2 integer matrix such that $u_{11} + au_{12} \equiv u_{21} + au_{22} \equiv 0$ (modulo m) and $u_{11}u_{22} - u_{21}u_{12} = m$.

   a) Prove that all integer solutions (y_1, y_2) to the congruence $y_1 + ay_2 \equiv 0$ (modulo m) have the form $(y_1, y_2) = (x_1 u_{11} + x_2 u_{21}, x_1 u_{12} + x_2 u_{22})$ for integer x_1, x_2.

   b) If, in addition, $2|u_{11}u_{21} + u_{12}u_{22}| \leq u_{11}^2 + u_{12}^2 \leq u_{21}^2 + u_{22}^2$, prove that $(y_1, y_2) = (u_{11}, u_{12})$ minimizes $y_1^2 + y_2^2$ over all nonzero solutions to the congruence.

5. [*M30*] Prove that steps S1 through S3 of Algorithm S correctly perform the spectral test in two dimensions. [*Hint:* See exercise 4, and prove that $(h' + h)^2 + (p' + p)^2 \geq h^2 + p^2$ at the beginning of step S2.]

6. [*M30*] Let $a_0, a_1, \ldots, a_{t-1}$ be the partial quotients of a/m as defined in Section 3.3.3, and let $A = \max_{0 \leq j < t} a_j$. Prove that $\mu_2 > 2\pi/(A + 1 + 1/A)$.

7. [*HM22*] Prove that questions (a) and (b) following Eq. (23) have the same solution for real values of $q_1, \ldots, q_{j-1}, q_{j+1}, \ldots, q_t$ (see (24) and (26)).

8. [*M18*] Line 10 of Table 1 has a very low value of μ_2, yet μ_3 is quite satisfactory. What is the highest possible value of μ_3 when $\mu_2 = 10^{-6}$ and $m = 10^{10}$?

9. [*HM32*] (C. Hermite, 1846.) Let $f(x_1, \ldots, x_t)$ be a positive definite quadratic form, defined by the matrix U as in (17), and let θ be the minimum value of f at nonzero integer points. Prove that $\theta \leq (\frac{4}{3})^{(t-1)/2} |\det U|^{2/t}$. [*Hints:* If W is any integer matrix of determinant 1, the matrix WU defines a form equivalent to f; and if S is any orthogonal matrix (that is, if $S^{-1} = S^T$), the matrix US defines a form identically equal to f. Show that there is an equivalent form g whose minimum θ occurs at

$(1, 0, \ldots, 0)$. Then prove the general result by induction on t, writing $g(x_1, \ldots, x_t) = \theta(x_1 + \beta_2 x_2 + \cdots + \beta_t x_t)^2 + h(x_2, \ldots, x_t)$ where h is a positive definite quadratic form in $t - 1$ variables.]

10. [*M28*] Let y_1 and y_2 be relatively prime integers such that $y_1 + a y_2 \equiv 0$ (modulo m) and $y_1^2 + y_2^2 < \sqrt{4/3}\, m$. Show that there exist integers u_1 and u_2 such that $u_1 + a u_2 \equiv 0$ (modulo m), $u_1 y_2 - u_2 y_1 = m$, $2|u_1 y_1 + u_2 y_2| \le \min(u_1^2 + u_2^2, y_1^2 + y_2^2)$, and $(u_1^2 + u_2^2) \times (y_1^2 + y_2^2) \ge m^2$. (Hence $\nu_2^2 = \min(u_1^2 + u_2^2, y_1^2 + y_2^2)$ by exercise 4.)

▶ **11.** [*HM30*] (Alan G. Waterman, 1974.) Invent a reasonably efficient procedure that computes multipliers $a \equiv 1$ (modulo 4) for which there exists a relatively prime solution to the congruence $y_1 + a y_2 \equiv 0$ (modulo m) with $y_1^2 + y_2^2 = \sqrt{4/3}\, m - \epsilon$, where $\epsilon > 0$ is as small as possible, given $m = 2^e$. (By exercise 10, this choice of a will guarantee that $\nu_2^2 \ge m^2/(y_1^2 + y_2^2) > \sqrt{3/4}\, m$, and there is a chance that ν_2^2 will be near its optimum value $\sqrt{4/3}\, m$. In practice we will compute several such multipliers having small ϵ, choosing the one with best spectral values ν_2, ν_3, $\ldots$.)

12. [*HM23*] Prove, without geometrical handwaving, that any solution to question (b) following Eq. (23) must also satisfy the set of equations (26).

13. [*HM22*] Lemma A uses the fact that U is nonsingular to prove that a positive definite quadratic form attains a definite, nonzero minimum value at nonzero integer points. Show that this hypothesis is necessary, by exhibiting a quadratic form (19) whose matrix of coefficients is singular, and for which the values of $f(x_1, \ldots, x_t)$ get arbitrarily near zero (but never reach it) at nonzero integer points $(x_1, \ldots, x_t)$.

14. [*24*] Perform Algorithm S by hand, for $m = 100$, $a = 41$, $T = 3$.

▶ **15.** [*M20*] Let U be an integer vector satisfying (15). How many of the $(t - 1)$-dimensional hyperplanes defined by U intersect the unit hypercube $\{(x_1, \ldots, x_t) \mid 0 \le x_j < 1$ for $1 \le j \le t\}$? (This is approximately the number of hyperplanes in the family that will suffice to cover L_0.)

16. [*M30*] (U. Dieter.) Show how to modify Algorithm S in order to calculate the minimum number N_t of parallel hyperplanes intersecting the unit hypercube as in exercise 15, over all U satisfying (15). [*Hint:* What are appropriate analogs to positive definite quadratic forms and to Lemma A?]

17. [*20*] Modify Algorithm S so that, in addition to computing the quantities ν_t, it outputs all integer vectors $(u_1, \ldots, u_t)$ satisfying (15) such that $u_1^2 + \cdots + u_t^2 = \nu_t^2$, for $2 \le t \le T$.

18. [*M30*] This exercise is about the worst case of Algorithm S.

   a) By considering "combinatorial matrices," whose elements have the form $y + x\delta_{ij}$ (see exercise 1.2.3–39), find 3×3 matrices of integers U and V satisfying (29) such that the transformation of step S5 does nothing for any j, but the corresponding values of z_k in (31) are so huge that exhaustive search is out of the question. (The matrix U need not satisfy (28); we are interested here in *arbitrary* positive definite quadratic forms of determinant m.)

   b) Although transformation (23) is of no use for the matrices constructed in (a), find another transformation that does produce a substantial reduction.

▶ **19.** [*HM25*] Suppose step S5 were changed slightly, so that a transformation with $q = 1$ would be performed when $2 V_i \cdot V_j = V_j \cdot V_j$. (Thus, $q = \lfloor (V_i \cdot V_j / V_j \cdot V_j) + \frac{1}{2} \rfloor$ whenever $i \ne j$.) Would it be possible for Algorithm S to get into an infinite loop?

20. [*M23*] Discuss how to carry out an appropriate spectral test for linear congruential sequences having $c = 0$, X_0 odd, $m = 2^e$, $a \bmod 8 = 3$ or 5. (See exercise 3.2.1.2–9.)

21. [*M20*] (R. W. Gosper.) A certain application uses random numbers in batches of four, but "throws away" the second of each set. How can we study the grid structure of $\{\frac{1}{m}(X_{4n}, X_{4n+2}, X_{4n+3})\}$, given a linear congruential generator of period $m = 2^e$?

22. [*M46*] What is the best upper bound on μ_3, given that μ_2 is very near its maximum value $\sqrt{4/3}\,\pi$? What is the best upper bound on μ_2, given that μ_3 is very near its maximum value $\frac{4}{3}\pi\sqrt{2}$?

23. [*M46*] Let U_i, V_j be vectors of real numbers with $U_i \cdot V_j = \delta_{ij}$ for $1 \le i, j \le t$, and such that $U_i \cdot U_i = 1$, $2|U_i \cdot U_j| \le 1$, $2|V_i \cdot V_j| \le V_j \cdot V_j$ for $i \ne j$. How large can $V_1 \cdot V_1$ be? (This question relates to the bounds in step S7, if both (23) and the transformation of exercise 18(b) fail to make any reductions. The maximum value known to be achievable is $(t+2)/3$, which occurs when $U_1 = I_1$, $U_j = \frac{1}{2}I_1 + \frac{1}{2}\sqrt{3}\,I_j$, $V_1 = I_1 - (I_2 + \cdots + I_t)/\sqrt{3}$, $V_j = 2I_j/\sqrt{3}$, for $2 \le j \le t$, where $(I_1, \ldots, I_t)$ is the identity matrix; this construction is due to B. V. Alexeev.)

▶ **24.** [*M28*] Generalize the spectral test to second-order sequences of the form $X_n = (aX_{n-1} + bX_{n-2}) \bmod p$, having period length $p^2 - 1$. (See Eq. 3.2.2–(8).) How should Algorithm S be modified?

25. [*HM24*] Let d be a divisor of m and let $0 \le q < d$. Prove that $\sum r(k)$, summed over all $0 \le k < m$ such that $k \bmod d = q$, is at most $(2/d\pi)\ln(m/d) + O(1)$. (Here $r(k)$ is defined in Eq. (46) when $t = 1$.)

26. [*M22*] Explain why the derivation of (53) leads to a similar bound on

$$\left| \sum_{0 \le n < N} \omega^{qx_n} \right|$$

for $0 < q < m$.

27. [*HM39*] (E. Hlawka, H. Niederreiter.) Let $r(u_1, \ldots, u_t)$ be the function defined in (46). Prove that $\sum r(u_1, \ldots, u_t)$, summed over all $0 \le u_1, \ldots, u_t < m$ such that $(u_1, \ldots, u_t) \ne (0, \ldots, 0)$ and (15) holds, is at most $2((\pi + 2\pi \lg m)^t\, r_{\max})$, where $r_{\max}$ is the maximum term $r(u_1, \ldots, u_t)$ in the sum.

▶ **28.** [*M28*] (H. Niederreiter.) Find an analog of Theorem N for the case $m = $ prime, $c = 0$, $a = $ primitive root modulo m, $X_0 \ne 0$ (modulo m). [*Hint:* Your exponential sums should involve $\zeta = e^{2\pi i/(m-1)}$ as well as ω.] Prove that in this case the "average" primitive root has discrepancy $D_{m-1}^{(t)} = O\left(t(\log m)^t/\varphi(m-1)\right)$, hence good primitive roots exist for all m.

29. [*HM22*] Prove that the quantity $r_{\max}$ of exercise 27 is never larger than $1/(\sqrt{8}\,\nu_t)$.

30. [*M33*] (S. K. Zaremba.) Prove that $r_{\max} = O(\max(a_1, \ldots, a_s)/m)$ in two dimensions, where $a_1, \ldots, a_s$ are the partial quotients obtained when Euclid's algorithm is applied to m and a. [*Hint:* We have $a/m = /\!/a_1, \ldots, a_s/\!/$, in the notation of Section 4.5.3; apply exercise 4.5.3–42.]

31. [*HM48*] (I. Borosh and H. Niederreiter.) Prove that for all sufficiently large m there exists a number a relatively prime to m such that all partial quotients of a/m are ≤ 3. Furthermore the set of all m satisfying this condition but with all partial quotients ≤ 2 has positive density.

▸ **32.** [*M21*] Let $m_1 = 2^{31} - 1$ and $m_2 = 2^{31} - 249$ be the moduli of generator (38).
  a) Show that if $U_n = (X_n/m_1 - Y_n/m_2) \bmod 1$, we have $U_n \approx Z_n/m_1$.
  b) Let $W_0 = (X_0 m_2 - Y_0 m_1) \bmod m$ and $W_{n+1} = a W_n \bmod m$, where a and m have
     the values stated in the text following (38). Prove that there is a simple relation
     between W_n and U_n.

⬦ *In the next edition of this book, I plan to introduce a new Section 3.3.5,
  entitled "The L^3 Algorithm." It will be a digression from the general topic of
  Random Numbers, but it will continue the discussion of lattice basis reduction in
  Section 3.3.4. Its main topic will be the now-classic algorithm of A. K. Lenstra,
  H. W. Lenstra, Jr., and L. Lovász [Math. Annalen **261** (1982), 515–534] for
  finding a near-optimum set of basis vectors, and improvements to that algorithm
  made subsequently by other researchers. Examples of the latter can be found
  in the following papers and their bibliographies: M. Seysen, Combinatorica **13**
  (1993), 363–375; C. P. Schnorr and H. H. Hörner, Lecture Notes in Comp. Sci.
  921 (1995), 1–12.*

3.4. OTHER TYPES OF RANDOM QUANTITIES

WE HAVE NOW SEEN how to make a computer generate a sequence of numbers U_0, U_1, U_2, ... that behaves as if each number were independently selected at random between zero and one with the uniform distribution. Applications of random numbers often call for other kinds of distributions, however; for example, if we want to make a random choice from among k alternatives, we want a random *integer* between 1 and k. If some simulation process calls for a random waiting time between occurrences of independent events, a random number with the *exponential distribution* is desired. Sometimes we don't even want random *numbers* — we want a random *permutation* (a random arrangement of n objects) or a random *combination* (a random choice of k objects from a collection of n).

In principle, any of these other random quantities can be obtained from the uniform deviates U_0, U_1, U_2, ...; people have devised a number of important "random tricks" for the efficient transformation of uniform deviates. A study of these techniques also gives us insight into the proper use of random numbers in any Monte Carlo application.

It is conceivable that someday somebody will invent a random number generator that produces one of these other random quantities *directly*, instead of getting it indirectly via the uniform distribution. But no direct methods have as yet proved to be practical, except for the "random bit" generator described in Section 3.2.2. (See also exercise 3.4.1–31, where the uniform distribution is used primarily for initialization, after which the method is almost entirely direct.)

The discussion in the following section assumes the existence of a random sequence of uniformly distributed real numbers between zero and one. A new uniform deviate U is generated whenever we need it. These numbers are usually represented in a computer word with the radix point assumed at the left.

3.4.1. Numerical Distributions

This section summarizes the best techniques known for producing numbers from various important distributions. Many of the methods were originally suggested by John von Neumann in the early 1950s, and they have gradually been improved upon by other people, notably George Marsaglia, J. H. Ahrens, and U. Dieter.

A. Random choices from a finite set. The simplest and most common type of distribution required in practice is a random *integer*. An integer between 0 and 7 can be extracted from three bits of U on a binary computer; in such a case, these bits should be extracted from the *most significant* (left-hand) part of the computer word, since the least significant bits by many random number generators are not sufficiently random. (See the discussion in Section 3.2.1.1.)

In general, to get a random integer X between 0 and $k - 1$, we can *multiply* by k, and let $X = \lfloor kU \rfloor$. On MIX, we would write

$$
\begin{array}{ll}
\text{LDA} & \text{U} \\
\text{MUL} & \text{K}
\end{array}
\qquad (1)
$$

and after these two instructions have been executed the desired integer will appear in register A. If a random integer between 1 and k is desired, we add one to this result. (The instruction 'INCA 1' would follow (1).)

This method gives each integer with nearly equal probability. There is a slight error because the computer word size is finite (see exercise 2); but the error is quite negligible if k is small, for example if $k/m < 1/10000$.

In a more general situation we might want to give different weights to different integers. Suppose that the value $X = x_1$ is to be obtained with probability p_1, and $X = x_2$ with probability p_2, ..., $X = x_k$ with probability p_k. We can generate a uniform number U and let

$$
X = \begin{cases}
x_1, & \text{if } 0 \le U < p_1; \\
x_2, & \text{if } p_1 \le U < p_1 + p_2; \\
\ \vdots \\
x_k, & \text{if } p_1 + p_2 + \cdots + p_{k-1} \le U < 1.
\end{cases}
\tag{2}
$$

(Note that $p_1 + p_2 + \cdots + p_k = 1$.)

There is a "best possible" way to do the comparisons of U against various values of $p_1 + p_2 + \cdots + p_s$, as implied in (2); this situation is discussed in Section 2.3.4.5. Special cases can be handled by more efficient methods; for example, to obtain one of the eleven values 2, 3, ..., 12 with the respective "dice" probabilities $\frac{1}{36}$, $\frac{2}{36}$, ..., $\frac{6}{36}$, ..., $\frac{2}{36}$, $\frac{1}{36}$, we could compute two independent random integers between 1 and 6 and add them together.

However, there is actually a faster way to select x_1, ..., x_k with arbitrarily given probabilities, based on an ingenious approach introduced by A. J. Walker [*Electronics Letters* **10**, 8 (1974), 127–128; *ACM Trans. Math. Software* **3** (1977), 253–256]. Suppose we form kU and consider the integer part $K = \lfloor kU \rfloor$ and fraction part $V = (kU) \bmod 1$ separately; for example, after the code (1) we will have K in register A and V in register X. Then we can always obtain the desired distribution by doing the operations

$$ \text{if} \quad V < P_K \quad \text{then} \quad X \leftarrow x_{K+1} \quad \text{otherwise} \quad X \leftarrow Y_K, \tag{3} $$

for some appropriate tables $(P_0, \ldots, P_{k-1})$ and $(Y_0, \ldots, Y_{k-1})$. Exercise 7 shows how such tables can be computed in general. Walker's method is sometimes called the method of "aliases."

On a binary computer it is usually helpful to assume that k is a power of 2, so that multiplication can be replaced by shifting; this can be done without loss of generality by introducing additional x's that occur with probability zero. For example, let's consider dice again; suppose we want $X = j$ to occur with the following 16 probabilities:

$j =$	0	1	2	3	4	5	6	7	8	9	10	11	12	13	14	15
$p_j =$	0	0	$\frac{1}{36}$	$\frac{2}{36}$	$\frac{3}{36}$	$\frac{4}{36}$	$\frac{5}{36}$	$\frac{6}{36}$	$\frac{5}{36}$	$\frac{4}{36}$	$\frac{3}{36}$	$\frac{2}{36}$	$\frac{1}{36}$	0	0	0

We can do this using (3), if $k = 16$ and $x_{j+1} = j$ for $0 \le j < 16$, and if the P and Y tables are set up as follows:

$j =$	0	1	2	3	4	5	6	7	8	9	10	11	12	13	14	15
$P_j =$	0	0	$\frac{4}{9}$	$\frac{8}{9}$	1	$\frac{7}{9}$	1	1	1	$\frac{7}{9}$	$\frac{7}{9}$	$\frac{8}{9}$	$\frac{4}{9}$	0	0	0
$Y_j =$	5	9	7	4	*	6	*	*	*	8	4	7	10	6	7	8

(When $P_j = 1$, Y_j is not used.) For example, the value 7 occurs with probability $\frac{1}{16} \cdot \big((1 - P_2) + P_7 + (1 - P_{11}) + (1 - P_{14})\big) = \frac{6}{36}$ as required. It is a peculiar way to throw dice, but the results are indistinguishable from the real thing.

The probabilities p_j can be represented implicitly by nonnegative weights $w_1, w_2, \ldots, w_k$; if we denote the sum of the weights by W, then $p_j = w_j/W$. In many applications the individual weights vary dynamically. Matias, Vitter, and Ni [*SODA* **4** (1993), 361–370] have shown how to update a weight and generate X in constant expected time.

B. General methods for continuous distributions. The most general real-valued distribution can be expressed in terms of its "distribution function" $F(x)$, which specifies the probability that a random quantity X will not exceed x:

$$F(x) = \Pr(X \le x). \tag{4}$$

This function always increases monotonically from zero to one; that is,

$$F(x_1) \le F(x_2), \quad \text{if } x_1 \le x_2; \qquad F(-\infty) = 0, \qquad F(+\infty) = 1. \tag{5}$$

Examples of distribution functions are given in Section 3.3.1, Fig. 3. If $F(x)$ is continuous and strictly increasing (so that $F(x_1) < F(x_2)$ when $x_1 < x_2$), it takes on all values between zero and one, and there is an *inverse function* $F^{[-1]}(y)$ such that, for $0 < y < 1$,

$$y = F(x) \qquad \text{if and only if} \qquad x = F^{[-1]}(y). \tag{6}$$

In general, when $F(x)$ is continuous and strictly increasing, we can compute a random quantity X with distribution $F(x)$ by setting

$$X = F^{[-1]}(U), \tag{7}$$

where U is uniform. This works because the probability that $X \le x$ is the probability that $F^{[-1]}(U) \le x$, namely the probability that $U \le F(x)$, namely $F(x)$.

The problem now reduces to one of numerical analysis, namely to find good methods for evaluating $F^{[-1]}(U)$ to the desired accuracy. Numerical analysis lies outside the scope of this seminumerical book; yet a number of important shortcuts are available to speed up the general approach of (7), and we will consider them here.

In the first place, if X_1 is a random variable having the distribution $F_1(x)$ and if X_2 is an independent random variable with the distribution $F_2(x)$, then

$$
\begin{aligned}
\max(X_1, X_2) \quad &\text{has the distribution} \quad F_1(x)F_2(x), \\
\min(X_1, X_2) \quad &\text{has the distribution} \quad F_1(x) + F_2(x) - F_1(x)F_2(x).
\end{aligned}
\tag{8}
$$

(See exercise 4.) For example, a uniform deviate U has the distribution $F(x) = x$, for $0 \leq x \leq 1$; if $U_1, U_2, \ldots, U_t$ are independent uniform deviates, then $\max(U_1, U_2, \ldots, U_t)$ has the distribution function $F(x) = x^t$, for $0 \leq x \leq 1$. This formula is the basis of the "maximum-of-t test" given in Section 3.3.2; the inverse function is $F^{[-1]}(y) = \sqrt[t]{y}$. In the special case $t = 2$, we see therefore that the two formulas

$$X = \sqrt{U} \qquad \text{and} \qquad X = \max(U_1, U_2) \tag{9}$$

will give equivalent distributions to the random variable X, although this is not obvious at first glance. We need not take the square root of a uniform deviate.

The number of tricks like this is endless: *Any* algorithm that employs random numbers as input will give a random quantity with *some* distribution as output. The problem is to find general methods for constructing the algorithm, given the distribution function of the output. Instead of discussing such methods in purely abstract terms, we shall study how they can be applied in important cases.

C. The normal distribution. Perhaps the most important nonuniform, continuous distribution is the *normal distribution with mean zero and standard deviation one*:

$$F(x) = \frac{1}{\sqrt{2\pi}} \int_{-\infty}^{x} e^{-t^2/2}\, dt. \tag{10}$$

The significance of this distribution was indicated in Section 1.2.10. In this case the inverse function $F^{[-1]}$ is not especially easy to compute; but we shall see that several other techniques are available.

1) *The polar method*, due to G. E. P. Box, M. E. Muller, and G. Marsaglia. (See *Annals Math. Stat.* **29** (1958), 610–611; and Boeing Scientific Res. Lab. report D1-82-0203 (1962).)

Algorithm P (*Polar method for normal deviates*). This algorithm calculates two independent normally distributed variables, X_1 and X_2.

P1. [Get uniform variables.] Generate two independent random variables, U_1 and U_2, uniformly distributed between zero and one. Set $V_1 \leftarrow 2U_1 - 1$, $V_2 \leftarrow 2U_2 - 1$. (Now V_1 and V_2 are uniformly distributed between -1 and $+1$. On most computers it will be preferable to have V_1 and V_2 represented in floating point form.)

P2. [Compute S.] Set $S \leftarrow V_1^2 + V_2^2$.

P3. [Is $S \geq 1$?] If $S \geq 1$, return to step P1. (Steps P1 through P3 are executed 1.27 times on the average, with a standard deviation of 0.59; see exercise 6.)

P4. [Compute X_1, X_2.] If $S = 0$, set $X_1 \leftarrow X_2 \leftarrow 0$; otherwise set

$$X_1 \leftarrow V_1 \sqrt{\frac{-2 \ln S}{S}}, \qquad X_2 \leftarrow V_2 \sqrt{\frac{-2 \ln S}{S}}. \tag{11}$$

These are the normally distributed variables desired. ∎

To prove the validity of this method, we use elementary analytic geometry and calculus: If $S < 1$ in step P3, the point in the plane with Cartesian coordinates (V_1, V_2) *is a random point uniformly distributed inside the unit circle*. Transforming to polar coordinates $V_1 = R \cos \Theta$, $V_2 = R \sin \Theta$, we find

$$S = R^2, \quad X_1 = \sqrt{-2 \ln S} \cos \Theta, \quad X_2 = \sqrt{-2 \ln S} \sin \Theta.$$

Using also the polar coordinates $X_1 = R' \cos \Theta'$, $X_2 = R' \sin \Theta'$, we find that $\Theta' = \Theta$ and $R' = \sqrt{-2 \ln S}$. It is clear that R' and Θ' are independent, since R and Θ are independent inside the unit circle. Also, Θ' is uniformly distributed between 0 and 2π; and the probability that $R' \leq r$ is the probability that $-2 \ln S \leq r^2$, namely the probability that $S \geq e^{-r^2/2}$. This equals $1 - e^{-r^2/2}$, since $S = R^2$ is uniformly distributed between zero and one. The probability that R' lies between r and $r + dr$ is therefore the differential of $1 - e^{-r^2/2}$, namely $re^{-r^2/2} dr$. Similarly, the probability that Θ' lies between θ and $\theta + d\theta$ is $(1/2\pi) d\theta$. The joint probability that $X_1 \leq x_1$ and that $X_2 \leq x_2$ now can be computed; it is

$$\int_{\{(r,\theta) \mid r \cos \theta \leq x_1, \, r \sin \theta \leq x_2\}} \frac{1}{2\pi} e^{-r^2/2} r \, dr \, d\theta$$

$$= \frac{1}{2\pi} \int_{\{(x,y) \mid x \leq x_1, \, y \leq x_2\}} e^{-(x^2+y^2)/2} \, dx \, dy$$

$$= \left(\sqrt{\frac{1}{2\pi}} \int_{-\infty}^{x_1} e^{-x^2/2} \, dx \right) \left(\sqrt{\frac{1}{2\pi}} \int_{-\infty}^{x_2} e^{-y^2/2} \, dy \right).$$

This calculation proves that X_1 and X_2 are independent and normally distributed, as desired.

2) *The rectangle-wedge-tail method*, introduced by G. Marsaglia. Here we use the function

$$F(x) = \operatorname{erf}(x/\sqrt{2}) = \sqrt{\frac{2}{\pi}} \int_0^x e^{-t^2/2} \, dt, \qquad x \geq 0, \tag{12}$$

which gives the distribution of the *absolute value* of a normal deviate. After X has been computed according to distribution (12), we will attach a random sign to its value, and this will make it a true normal deviate.

The rectangle-wedge-tail approach is based on several important general techniques that we shall explore as we develop the algorithm. The first key idea is to regard $F(x)$ as a *mixture* of several other functions, namely to write

$$F(x) = p_1 F_1(x) + p_2 F_2(x) + \cdots + p_n F_n(x), \tag{13}$$

where F_1, F_2, ..., F_n are appropriate distributions and p_1, p_2, ..., p_n are nonnegative probabilities that sum to 1. If we generate a random variable X by choosing distribution F_j with probability p_j, it is easy to see that X will have distribution F overall. Some of the distributions $F_j(x)$ may be rather difficult to handle, even harder than F itself, but we can usually arrange things so that the

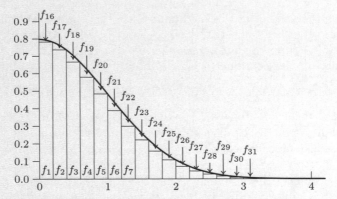

Fig. 9. The density function divided into 31 parts. The area of each part represents the average number of times a random number with that density is to be computed.

probability p_j is very small in that case. Most of the distributions $F_j(x)$ will be quite easy to accommodate, since they will be trivial modifications of the uniform distribution. The resulting method yields an extremely efficient program, since its *average* running time is very small.

It is easier to understand the method if we work with the *derivatives* of the distributions instead of the distributions themselves. Let

$$f(x) = F'(x), \qquad f_j(x) = F_j'(x)$$

be the *density functions* of the probability distributions. Equation (13) becomes

$$f(x) = p_1 f_1(x) + p_2 f_2(x) + \cdots + p_n f_n(x). \tag{14}$$

Each $f_j(x)$ is ≥ 0, and the total area under the graph of $f_j(x)$ is 1; so there is a convenient graphical way to display the relation (14): The area under $f(x)$ is divided into n parts, with the part corresponding to $f_j(x)$ having area p_j. See Fig. 9, which illustrates the situation in the case of interest to us here, with $f(x) = F'(x) = \sqrt{2/\pi}\, e^{-x^2/2}$; the area under this curve has been divided into $n = 31$ parts. There are 15 rectangles, which represent $p_1 f_1(x), \ldots, p_{15} f_{15}(x)$; there are 15 wedge-shaped pieces, which represent $p_{16} f_{16}(x), \ldots, p_{30} f_{30}(x)$; and the remaining part $p_{31} f_{31}(x)$ is the "tail," namely the entire graph of $f(x)$ for $x \geq 3$.

The rectangular parts $f_1(x), \ldots, f_{15}(x)$ represent *uniform distributions*. For example, $f_3(x)$ represents a random variable uniformly distributed between $\frac{2}{5}$ and $\frac{3}{5}$. The altitude of $p_j f_j(x)$ is $f(j/5)$, hence the area of the jth rectangle is

$$p_j = \frac{1}{5} f(j/5) = \sqrt{\frac{2}{25\pi}}\, e^{-j^2/50}, \qquad \text{for } 1 \leq j \leq 15. \tag{15}$$

In order to generate such rectangular portions of the distribution, we simply compute

$$X = \tfrac{1}{5}U + S, \tag{16}$$

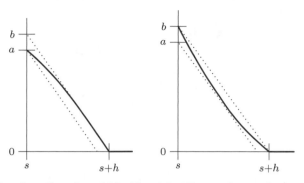

Fig. 10. Density functions for which Algorithm L may be used to generate random numbers.

where U is uniform and S takes the value $(j - 1)/5$ with probability p_j. Since $p_1 + \cdots + p_{15} = .9183$, we can use simple uniform deviates like this about 92 percent of the time.

In the remaining 8 percent, we will usually have to generate one of the wedge-shaped distributions $F_{16}, \ldots, F_{30}$. Typical examples of what we need to do are shown in Fig. 10. When $x < 1$, the curved part is concave, and when $x > 1$ it is convex, but in each case the curved part is reasonably close to a straight line, and it can be enclosed in two parallel lines as shown.

To handle these wedge-shaped distributions, we will rely on yet another general technique, von Neumann's *rejection method* for obtaining a complicated density from another one that "encloses" it. The polar method described above is a simple example of such an approach: Steps P1–P3 obtain a random point inside the unit circle by first generating a random point in a larger square, rejecting it and starting over again if the point was outside the circle.

The general rejection method is even more powerful than this. To generate a random variable X with density f, let g be another probability density function such that

$$f(t) \leq cg(t) \tag{17}$$

for all t, where c is a constant. Now generate X according to density g, and also generate an independent uniform deviate U. If $U \geq f(X)/cg(X)$, reject X and start again with another X and U. When the condition $U < f(X)/cg(X)$ finally occurs, the resulting X will have density f as desired. [*Proof:* $X \leq x$ will occur with probability $p(x) = \int_{-\infty}^{x} \left(g(t)\, dt \cdot f(t)/cg(t) \right) + qp(x)$, where the quantity $q = \int_{-\infty}^{\infty} \left(g(t)\, dt \cdot (1 - f(t)/cg(t)) \right) = 1 - 1/c$ is the probability of rejection; hence $p(x) = \int_{-\infty}^{x} f(t)\, dt.$]

The rejection technique is most efficient when c is small, since there will be c iterations on the average before a value is accepted. (See exercise 6.) In some cases $f(x)/cg(x)$ is always 0 or 1; then U need not be generated. In other cases if $f(x)/cg(x)$ is hard to compute, we may be able to "squeeze" it between two bounding functions

$$r(x) \leq f(x)/cg(x) \leq s(x) \tag{18}$$

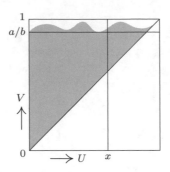

Fig. 11. Region of "acceptance" in Algorithm L.

that are much simpler, and the exact value of $f(x)/cg(x)$ need not be calculated unless $r(x) \le U < s(x)$. The following algorithm solves the wedge problem by developing the rejection method still further.

Algorithm L (*Nearly linear densities*). This algorithm may be used to generate a random variable X for any distribution whose density $f(x)$ satisfies the following conditions (see Fig. 10):

$$f(x) = 0, \qquad \text{for } x < s \text{ and for } x > s + h;$$
$$a - b(x - s)/h \le f(x) \le b - b(x - s)/h, \qquad \text{for } s \le x \le s + h. \tag{19}$$

L1. [Get $U \le V$.] Generate two independent random variables U and V, uniformly distributed between zero and one. If $U > V$, exchange $U \leftrightarrow V$.

L2. [Easy case?] If $V \le a/b$, go to L4.

L3. [Try again?] If $V > U + (1/b)f(s + hU)$, go back to step L1. (If a/b is close to 1, this step of the algorithm will not be necessary very often.)

L4. [Compute X.] Set $X \leftarrow s + hU$. ∎

When step L4 is reached, the point (U, V) is a random point in the area shaded in Fig. 11, namely, $0 \le U \le V \le U + (1/b)f(s + hU)$. Conditions (19) ensure that

$$\frac{a}{b} \le U + \frac{1}{b}f(s + hU) \le 1.$$

Now the probability that $X \le s + hx$, for $0 \le x \le 1$, is the area that lies to the left of the vertical line $U = x$ in Fig. 11, divided by the total area, namely

$$\int_0^x \frac{1}{b}f(s + hu)\, du \bigg/ \int_0^1 \frac{1}{b}f(s + hu)\, du = \int_s^{s+hx} f(v)\, dv;$$

therefore X has the correct distribution.

With appropriate constants a_j, b_j, s_j, Algorithm L will take care of the wedge-shaped densities f_{j+15} of Fig. 9, for $1 \le j \le 15$. The final distribution, F_{31}, needs to be treated only about one time in 370; it is used whenever a result $X \ge 3$ is to be computed. Exercise 11 shows that a standard rejection scheme can be used for this "tail." We are ready to consider the procedure in its entirety:

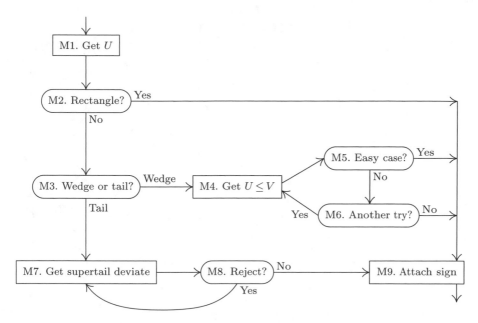

Fig. 12. The "rectangle-wedge-tail" algorithm for generating normal deviates.

Algorithm M (*Rectangle-wedge-tail method for normal deviates*). For this algorithm we use auxiliary tables $(P_0, \ldots, P_{31})$, $(Q_1, \ldots, Q_{15})$, $(Y_0, \ldots, Y_{31})$, $(Z_0, \ldots, Z_{31})$, $(S_1, \ldots, S_{16})$, $(D_{16}, \ldots, D_{30})$, $(E_{16}, \ldots, E_{30})$, constructed as explained in exercise 10; examples appear in Table 1. We assume that a binary computer is being used; a similar procedure could be worked out for decimal machines.

M1. [Get U.] Generate a uniform random number $U = (.b_0 b_1 b_2 \ldots b_t)_2$. (Here the b's are the bits in the binary representation of U. For reasonable accuracy, t should be at least 24.) Set $\psi \leftarrow b_0$. (Later, ψ will be used to determine the sign of the result.)

M2. [Rectangle?] Set $j \leftarrow (b_1 b_2 b_3 b_4 b_5)_2$, a binary number determined by the leading bits of U, and set $f \leftarrow (.b_6 b_7 \ldots b_t)_2$, the fraction determined by the remaining bits. If $f \geq P_j$, set $X \leftarrow Y_j + f Z_j$ and go to M9. Otherwise if $j \leq 15$ (that is, $b_1 = 0$), set $X \leftarrow S_j + f Q_j$ and go to M9. (This is an adaptation of Walker's alias method (3).)

M3. [Wedge or tail?] (Now $16 \leq j \leq 31$, and each particular value j occurs with probability p_j.) If $j = 31$, go to M7.

M4. [Get $U \leq V$.] Generate two new uniform deviates, U and V; if $U > V$, exchange $U \leftrightarrow V$. (We are now performing a special case of Algorithm L.) Set $X \leftarrow S_{j-15} + \frac{1}{5} U$.

M5. [Easy case?] If $V \leq D_j$, go to M9.

Table 1

EXAMPLE OF TABLES USED WITH ALGORITHM M*

j	P_j	P_{j+16}	Q_j	Y_j	Y_{j+16}	Z_j	Z_{j+16}	S_{j+1}	D_{j+15}	E_{j+15}
0	.000	.067		0.00	0.59	0.20	0.21	0.0		
1	.849	.161	.236	− 0.92	0.96	1.32	0.24	0.2	.505	25.00
2	.970	.236	.206	− 5.86	−0.06	6.66	0.26	0.4	.773	12.50
3	.855	.285	.234	− 0.58	0.12	1.38	0.28	0.6	.876	8.33
4	.994	.308	.201	−33.16	1.31	34.96	0.29	0.8	.939	6.25
5	.995	.304	.201	−39.51	0.31	41.31	0.29	1.0	.986	5.00
6	.933	.280	.214	− 2.57	1.12	2.97	0.28	1.2	.995	4.06
7	.923	.241	.217	− 1.61	0.54	2.61	0.26	1.4	.987	3.37
8	.727	.197	.275	0.67	0.75	0.73	0.25	1.6	.979	2.86
9	1.000	.152	.200		0.56		0.24	1.8	.972	2.47
10	.691	.112	.289	0.35	0.17	0.65	0.23	2.0	.966	2.16
11	.454	.079	.440	− 0.17	0.38	0.37	0.22	2.2	.960	1.92
12	.287	.052	.698	0.92	−0.01	0.28	0.21	2.4	.954	1.71
13	.174	.033	1.150	0.36	0.39	0.24	0.21	2.6	.948	1.54
14	.101	.020	1.974	− 0.02	0.20	0.22	0.20	2.8	.942	1.40
15	.057	.086	3.526	0.19	0.78	0.21	0.22	3.0	.936	1.27

*In practice, this data would be given with much greater precision; the table shows only enough figures so that interested readers will be able to test their own algorithms for computing the values more accurately. The values of Q_0, Y_9, Z_9, D_{15}, and E_{15} are not used.

M6. [Another try?] If $V > U + E_j(e^{(S_{j-14}^2 - X^2)/2} - 1)$, go back to step M4; otherwise go to M9. (This step is executed with low probability.)

M7. [Get supertail deviate.] Generate two new independent uniform deviates, U and V, and set $X \leftarrow \sqrt{9 - 2\ln V}$.

M8. [Reject?] If $UX \geq 3$, go back to step M7. (This will occur only about one-twelfth as often as we reach step M8.)

M9. [Attach sign.] If $\psi = 1$, set $X \leftarrow -X$. ∎

This algorithm is a very pretty example of mathematical theory intimately interwoven with programming ingenuity — a fine illustration of the art of computer programming! Only steps M1, M2, and M9 need to be performed most of the time, and the other steps aren't terribly slow either. The first publications of the rectangle-wedge-tail method were by G. Marsaglia, *Annals Math. Stat.* **32** (1961), 894–899; G. Marsaglia, M. D. MacLaren, and T. A. Bray, *CACM* **7** (1964), 4–10. Further refinements of Algorithm M have been developed by G. Marsaglia, K. Ananthanarayanan, and N. J. Paul, *Inf. Proc. Letters* **5** (1976), 27–30.

3) *The odd-even method*, due to G. E. Forsythe. An amazingly simple technique for generating random deviates with a density of the general exponential form

$$f(x) = Ce^{-h(x)} \; [a \leq x < b], \qquad (20)$$

when

$$0 \leq h(x) \leq 1 \qquad \text{for } a \leq x < b, \qquad (21)$$

was discovered by John von Neumann and G. E. Forsythe about 1950. The idea is based on the rejection method described earlier, letting $g(x)$ be the uniform distribution on $[a \mathinner{.\,.} b)$: We set $X \leftarrow a + (b - a)U$, where U is a uniform deviate, and then we want to accept X with probability $e^{-h(X)}$. The latter operation could be done by comparing $e^{-h(X)}$ to V, or $h(X)$ to $-\ln V$, when V is another uniform deviate, but the job can be done without applying any transcendental functions in the following interesting way. Set $V_0 \leftarrow h(X)$, then generate uniform deviates $V_1, V_2, \ldots$ until finding some $K \geq 1$ with $V_{K-1} < V_K$. For fixed X and k, the probability that $h(X) \geq V_1 \geq \cdots \geq V_k$ is $1/k!$ times the probability that $\max(V_1, \ldots, V_k) \leq h(X)$, namely $h(X)^k/k!$; hence the probability that $K = k$ is $h(X)^{k-1}/(k-1)! - h(X)^k/k!$, and the probability that K is odd is

$$\sum_{k \text{ odd}, k \geq 1} \left(\frac{h(X)^{k-1}}{(k-1)!} - \frac{h(X)^k}{k!} \right) = e^{-h(X)}. \qquad (22)$$

Therefore we reject X and try again if K is even; we accept X as a random variable with density (20) if K is odd. We usually won't have to generate many V's in order to determine K, since the average value of K (given X) is $\sum_{k \geq 0} \Pr(K > k) = \sum_{k \geq 0} h(X)^k/k! = c^{h(X)} \leq e$.

Forsythe realized some years later that this approach leads to an efficient method for calculating normal deviates, without the need for any auxiliary routines to calculate square roots or logarithms as in Algorithms P and M. His procedure, with an improved choice of intervals $[a \mathinner{.\,.} b)$ due to J. H. Ahrens and U. Dieter, can be summarized as follows.

Algorithm F (*Odd-even method for normal deviates*). This algorithm generates normal deviates on a binary computer, assuming approximately $t + 1$ bits of accuracy. It requires a table of values $d_j = a_j - a_{j-1}$, for $1 \leq j \leq t+1$, where a_j is defined by the relation

$$\sqrt{\frac{2}{\pi}} \int_{a_j}^{\infty} e^{-x^2/2} \, dx = \frac{1}{2^j}. \qquad (23)$$

F1. [Get U.] Generate a uniform random number $U = (.b_0 b_1 \ldots b_t)_2$, where b_0, $b_1, \ldots, b_t$ denote the bits in binary notation. Set $\psi \leftarrow b_0$, $j \leftarrow 1$, and $a \leftarrow 0$.

F2. [Find first zero b_j.] If $b_j = 1$, set $a \leftarrow a + d_j$, $j \leftarrow j + 1$, and repeat this step. (If $j = t + 1$, treat b_j as zero.)

F3. [Generate candidate.] (Now $a = a_{j-1}$, and the current value of j occurs with probability $\approx 2^{-j}$. We will generate X in the range $[a_{j-1} \mathinner{.\,.} a_j)$, using the rejection method above, with $h(x) = x^2/2 - a^2/2 = y^2/2 + ay$ where $y = x - a$. Exercise 12 proves that $h(x) \leq 1$ as required in (21).) Set $Y \leftarrow d_j$ times $(.b_{j+1} \ldots b_t)_2$ and $V \leftarrow (\frac{1}{2}Y + a)Y$. (Since the average value of j is 2, there will usually be enough significant bits in $(.b_{j+1} \ldots b_t)_2$ to provide decent accuracy. The calculations are readily done in fixed point arithmetic.)

F4. [Reject?] Generate a uniform deviate U. If $V < U$, go on to step F5. Otherwise set V to a new uniform deviate; and repeat step F4 if the new V is $\leq U$. Otherwise (that is, if K is even, in the discussion above), replace U by a new uniform deviate $(.b_0 b_1 \ldots b_t)_2$ and go back to F3.

F5. [Return X.] Set $X \leftarrow a + Y$. If $\psi = 1$, set $X \leftarrow -X$. ∎

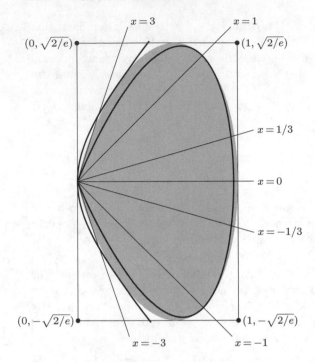

Fig. 13. Region of "acceptance" in the ratio-of-uniforms method for normal deviates. Lengths of lines with coordinate ratio x have the normal distribution.

Values of d_j for $1 \leq j \leq 47$ appear in a paper by Ahrens and Dieter, *Math. Comp.* **27** (1973), 927–937; their paper discusses refinements of the algorithm that improve its speed at the expense of more tables. Algorithm F is attractive since it is almost as fast as Algorithm M and it is easier to implement. The average number of uniform deviates per normal deviate is 2.53947; R. P. Brent [*CACM* **17** (1974), 704–705] has shown how to reduce this number to 1.37446 at the expense of two subtractions and one division per uniform deviate saved.

4) *Ratios of uniform deviates.* There is yet another good way to generate normal deviates, discovered by A. J. Kinderman and J. F. Monahan in 1976. Their idea is to generate a random point (U, V) in the region defined by

$$0 < u \leq 1, \qquad -2u\sqrt{\ln(1/u)} \leq v \leq 2u\sqrt{\ln(1/u)}, \qquad (24)$$

and then to output the ratio $X \leftarrow V/U$. The shaded area of Fig. 13 is the magic region (24) that makes this all work. Before we study the associated theory, let us first state the algorithm so that its efficiency and simplicity are manifest:

Algorithm R (*Ratio method for normal deviates*). This algorithm generates normal deviates X.

R1. [Get U, V.] Generate two independent uniform deviates U and V, where U is nonzero, and set $X \leftarrow \sqrt{8/e}\,(V - \frac{1}{2})/U$. (Now X is the ratio of the coordinates $(U, \sqrt{8/e}\,(V - \frac{1}{2}))$ of a random point in the rectangle that encloses the shaded region in Fig. 13. We will accept X if the corresponding point actually lies "in the shade," otherwise we will try again.)

R2. [Optional upper bound test.] If $X^2 \leq 5 - 4e^{1/4}U$, output X and terminate the algorithm. (This step can be omitted if desired; it tests whether or not the selected point is in the interior region of Fig. 13, making it unnecessary to calculate a logarithm.)

R3. [Optional lower bound test.] If $X^2 \geq 4e^{-1.35}/U + 1.4$, go back to R1. (This step could also be omitted; it tests whether or not the selected point is outside the exterior region of Fig. 13, making it unnecessary to calculate a logarithm.)

R4. [Final test.] If $X^2 \leq -4\ln U$, output X and terminate the algorithm. Otherwise go back to R1. ∎

Exercises 20 and 21 work out the timing analysis; four different algorithms are analyzed, since steps R2 and R3 can be included or omitted depending on one's preference. The following table shows how many times each step will be performed, on the average, depending on which of the optional tests is applied:

Step	Neither	R2 only	R3 only	Both
R1	1.369	1.369	1.369	1.369
R2	0	1.369	0	1.369
R3	0	0	1.369	0.467
R4	1.369	0.467	1.134	0.232

$$(25)$$

Thus it pays to omit the optional tests if there is a very fast logarithm operation, but if the log routine is rather slow it pays to include them.

But why does it work? One reason is that we can calculate the probability that $X \leq x$, and it turns out to be the correct value (10). But such a calculation isn't very easy unless one happens to hit on the right trick, and anyway it is better to understand how the algorithm might have been discovered in the first place. Kinderman and Monahan derived it by working out the following theory that can be used with any well-behaved density function $f(x)$ [see *ACM Trans. Math. Software* **3** (1977), 257–260].

In general, suppose that a point (U, V) has been generated uniformly over the region of the (u, v)-plane defined by

$$u > 0, \qquad u^2 \leq g(v/u) \qquad (26)$$

for some nonnegative integrable function g. If we set $X \leftarrow V/U$, the probability that $X \leq x$ can be calculated by integrating $du\,dv$ over the region defined by the two relations in (26) plus the auxiliary condition $v/u \leq x$, then dividing by the same integral without this extra condition. Letting $v = tu$, so that $dv = u\,dt$, the integral becomes

$$\int_{-\infty}^{x} dt \int_{0}^{\sqrt{g(t)}} u\,du = \frac{1}{2} \int_{-\infty}^{x} g(t)\,dt.$$

Hence the probability that $X \leq x$ is

$$\int_{-\infty}^{x} g(t)\,dt \bigg/ \int_{-\infty}^{+\infty} g(t)\,dt. \qquad (27)$$

The normal distribution comes out when $g(t) = e^{-t^2/2}$; and the condition $u^2 \leq g(v/u)$ simplifies in this case to $(v/u)^2 \leq -4 \ln u$. It is easy to see that the set of all such pairs (u, v) is entirely contained in the rectangle of Fig. 13.

The bounds in steps R2 and R3 define interior and exterior regions with simpler boundary equations. The well-known inequality

$$e^x \geq 1 + x,$$

which holds for all real numbers x, can be used to show that

$$1 + \ln c - cu \; \leq \; -\ln u \; \leq \; 1/(cu) - 1 + \ln c \tag{28}$$

for any constant $c > 0$. Exercise 21 proves that $c = e^{1/4}$ is the best possible constant to use in step R2. The situation is more complicated in step R3, and there doesn't seem to be a simple expression for the optimum c in that case, but computational experiments show that the best value for R3 is $\approx e^{1.35}$. The approximating curves (28) are tangent to the true boundary when $u = 1/c$.

With an improved approximation to the acceptance region [see J. L. Leva, *ACM Trans. Math. Software* **18** (1992), 449–455] we can, in fact, reduce the expected number of logarithm computations to only 0.012.

It is possible to obtain a faster method by partitioning the region into subregions, most of which can be handled more quickly. Of course, this means that auxiliary tables will be needed, as in Algorithms M and F. An interesting alternative that requires fewer auxiliary table entries has been suggested by Ahrens and Dieter in *CACM* **31** (1988), 1330–1337.

5) *Normal deviates from normal deviates.* Exercise 31 discusses an interesting approach that saves time by working directly with normal deviates instead of basing everything on uniform deviates. This method, introduced by C. S. Wallace in 1996, has comparatively little theoretical support at the present time, but it has successfully passed a number of empirical tests.

6) *Variations of the normal distribution.* So far we have considered the normal distribution with mean zero and standard deviation one. If X has this distribution, then

$$Y = \mu + \sigma X \tag{29}$$

has the normal distribution with mean μ and standard deviation σ. Furthermore, if X_1 and X_2 are independent normal deviates with mean zero and standard deviation one, and if

$$Y_1 = \mu_1 + \sigma_1 X_1, \qquad Y_2 = \mu_2 + \sigma_2 \left(\rho X_1 + \sqrt{1 - \rho^2}\, X_2\right), \tag{30}$$

then Y_1 and Y_2 are *dependent* random variables, normally distributed with means μ_1, μ_2 and standard deviations σ_1, σ_2, and with correlation coefficient ρ. (For a generalization to n variables, see exercise 13.)

D. The exponential distribution. After uniform deviates and normal deviates, the next most important random quantity is an *exponential deviate.* Such numbers occur in "arrival time" situations; for example, if a radioactive substance emits alpha particles at a rate such that one particle is emitted every μ seconds on the average, then the time between two successive emissions has the exponential distribution with mean μ. This distribution is defined by the formula

$$F(x) = 1 - e^{-x/\mu}, \qquad x \geq 0. \tag{31}$$

1) *Logarithm method.* Clearly, if $y = F(x) = 1 - e^{-x/\mu}$, then $x = F^{[-1]}(y) = -\mu \ln(1-y)$. Therefore $-\mu \ln(1-U)$ has the exponential distribution by Eq. (7). Since $1 - U$ is uniformly distributed when U is, we conclude that

$$X = -\mu \ln U \tag{32}$$

is exponentially distributed with mean μ. (The case $U = 0$ must be treated specially; we can substitute any convenient value ϵ for 0, since the probability of this case is extremely small.)

2) *Random minimization method.* We saw in Algorithm F that there are simple and fast alternatives to calculating the logarithm of a uniform deviate. The following especially efficient approach has been developed by G. Marsaglia, M. Sibuya, and J. H. Ahrens [see *CACM* **15** (1972), 876–877]:

Algorithm S (*Exponential distribution with mean μ*). This algorithm produces exponential deviates on a binary computer, using uniform deviates with $(t+1)$-bit accuracy. The constants

$$Q[k] = \frac{\ln 2}{1!} + \frac{(\ln 2)^2}{2!} + \cdots + \frac{(\ln 2)^k}{k!}, \qquad k \geq 1, \tag{33}$$

should be precomputed, extending until $Q[k] > 1 - 2^{-t}$.

S1. [Get U and shift.] Generate a $(t+1)$-bit uniform random binary fraction $U = (.b_0 b_1 b_2 \ldots b_t)_2$; locate the first zero bit b_j, and shift off the leading $j+1$ bits, setting $U \leftarrow (.b_{j+1} \ldots b_t)_2$. (As in Algorithm F, the average number of discarded bits is 2.)

S2. [Immediate acceptance?] If $U < \ln 2$, set $X \leftarrow \mu(j \ln 2 + U)$ and terminate the algorithm. (Note that $Q[1] = \ln 2$.)

S3. [Minimize.] Find the least $k \geq 2$ such that $U < Q[k]$. Generate k new uniform deviates $U_1, \ldots, U_k$ and set $V \leftarrow \min(U_1, \ldots, U_k)$.

S4. [Deliver the answer.] Set $X \leftarrow \mu(j + V) \ln 2$.   ∎

Alternative ways to generate exponential deviates (for example, a ratio of uniforms as in Algorithm R) might also be used.

E. Other continuous distributions. Let us now consider briefly how to handle some other distributions that arise reasonably often in practice.

1) *The gamma distribution* of order $a > 0$ is defined by

$$F(x) = \frac{1}{\Gamma(a)} \int_0^x t^{a-1} e^{-t} \, dt, \qquad x \geq 0. \tag{34}$$

When $a = 1$, this is the exponential distribution with mean 1; when $a = \frac{1}{2}$, it is the distribution of $\frac{1}{2}Z^2$, where Z has the normal distribution (mean 0, variance 1). If X and Y are independent gamma-distributed random variables, of order a and b, respectively, then $X + Y$ has the gamma distribution of order $a + b$. Thus, for example, the sum of k independent exponential deviates with mean 1 has the gamma distribution of order k. If the logarithm method (32) is being used to generate these exponential deviates, we need compute only one logarithm: $X \leftarrow -\ln(U_1 \ldots U_k)$, where $U_1, \ldots, U_k$ are nonzero uniform deviates. This technique handles all integer orders a; to complete the picture, a suitable method for $0 < a < 1$ appears in exercise 16.

The simple logarithm method is much too slow when a is large, since it requires $\lfloor a \rfloor$ uniform deviates. Moreover, there is a substantial risk that the product $U_1 \ldots U_{\lfloor a \rfloor}$ will cause floating point underflow. For large a, the following algorithm due to J. H. Ahrens is reasonably efficient, and it is easy to write in terms of standard subroutines. [See *Ann. Inst. Stat. Math.* **13** (1962), 231–237.]

Algorithm A (*Gamma distribution of order $a > 1$*).

A1. [Generate candidate.] Set $Y \leftarrow \tan(\pi U)$, where U is a uniform deviate, and set $X \leftarrow \sqrt{2a-1}\, Y + a - 1$. (In place of $\tan(\pi U)$ we could use a polar method, calculating a ratio V_2/V_1 as in step P4 of Algorithm P.)

A2. [Accept?] If $X \leq 0$, return to A1. Otherwise generate a uniform deviate V, and return to A1 if $V > (1 + Y^2)\exp\big((a-1)\ln(X/(a-1)) - \sqrt{2a-1}\,Y\big)$. Otherwise accept X. ∎

The average number of times step A1 is performed is < 1.902 when $a \geq 3$.

There is also an attractive approach for large a based on the remarkable fact that gamma deviates are approximately equal to aX^3, where X is normally distributed with mean $1 - 1/(9a)$ and standard deviation $1/\sqrt{9a}$; see E. B. Wilson and M. M. Hilferty, *Proc. Nat. Acad. Sci.* **17** (1931), 684–688; G. Marsaglia, *Computers and Math.* **3** (1977), 321–325.*

For a somewhat complicated but significantly faster algorithm, which generates a gamma deviate in about twice the time to generate a normal deviate, see J. H. Ahrens and U. Dieter, *CACM* **25** (1982), 47–54. This article contains an instructive discussion of the design principles used to construct the algorithm.

2) *The beta distribution* with positive parameters a and b is defined by

$$F(x) = \frac{\Gamma(a+b)}{\Gamma(a)\,\Gamma(b)} \int_0^x t^{a-1}(1-t)^{b-1}\, dt, \qquad 0 \leq x \leq 1. \qquad (35)$$

Let X_1 and X_2 be independent gamma deviates of order a and b, respectively, and set $X \leftarrow X_1/(X_1 + X_2)$. Another method, useful for small a and b, is to set

$$Y_1 \leftarrow U_1^{1/a} \qquad \text{and} \qquad Y_2 \leftarrow U_2^{1/b}$$

repeatedly until $Y_1 + Y_2 \leq 1$; then $X \leftarrow Y_1/(Y_1 + Y_2)$. [See M. D. Jöhnk, *Metrika* **8** (1964), 5–15.] Still another approach, if a and b are integers and not

---

* Change "$+(3a-1)$" to "$-(3a-1)$" in Step 3 of the algorithm on page 323.

too large, is to set X to the bth largest of $a + b - 1$ independent uniform deviates (see exercise 9 at the beginning of Chapter 5). See also the more direct method described by R. C. H. Cheng, *CACM* **21** (1978), 317–322.

3) *The chi-square distribution* with ν degrees of freedom (Eq. 3.3.1–(22)) is obtained by setting $X \leftarrow 2Y$, where Y is a random variable having the gamma distribution of order $\nu/2$.

4) *The F-distribution* (variance-ratio distribution) with ν_1 and ν_2 degrees of freedom is defined by

$$F(x) = \frac{\nu_1^{\nu_1/2} \, \nu_2^{\nu_2/2} \, \Gamma\big((\nu_1 + \nu_2)/2\big)}{\Gamma(\nu_1/2) \, \Gamma(\nu_2/2)} \int_0^x t^{\nu_1/2 - 1} (\nu_2 + \nu_1 t)^{-\nu_1/2 - \nu_2/2} \, dt, \quad (36)$$

where $x \geq 0$. Let Y_1 and Y_2 be independent, having the chi-square distribution with ν_1 and ν_2 degrees of freedom, respectively; set $X \leftarrow Y_1 \nu_2 / Y_2 \nu_1$. Or set $X \leftarrow \nu_2 Y / \nu_1 (1 - Y)$, where Y is a beta deviate with parameters $\nu_1/2$ and $\nu_2/2$.

5) *Student's t-distribution* with ν degrees of freedom is defined by

$$F(x) = \frac{\Gamma\big((\nu + 1)/2\big)}{\sqrt{\pi \nu} \, \Gamma(\nu/2)} \int_{-\infty}^x (1 + t^2/\nu)^{-(\nu+1)/2} \, dt. \quad (37)$$

Let Y_1 be a normal deviate (mean 0, variance 1) and let Y_2 be independent of Y_1, having the chi-square distribution with ν degrees of freedom; set $X \leftarrow Y_1/\sqrt{Y_2/\nu}$. Alternatively, when $\nu > 2$, let Y_1 be a normal deviate and let Y_2 independently have the exponential distribution with mean $2/(\nu - 2)$; set $Z \leftarrow Y_1^2/(\nu - 2)$ and reject (Y_1, Y_2) if $e^{-Y_2 - Z} \geq 1 - Z$, otherwise set

$$X \leftarrow Y_1/\sqrt{(1 - 2/\nu)(1 - Z)}.$$

The latter method is due to George Marsaglia, *Math. Comp.* **34** (1980), 235–236. [See also A. J. Kinderman, J. F. Monahan, and J. G. Ramage, *Math. Comp.* **31** (1977), 1009–1018.]

6) *Random point on the surface of an n-dimensional ball with radius one.* Let $X_1, X_2, \ldots, X_n$ be independent normal deviates (mean 0, variance 1); the desired point on the unit sphere is

$$(X_1/r, X_2/r, \ldots, X_n/r), \qquad \text{where } r = \sqrt{X_1^2 + X_2^2 + \cdots + X_n^2}. \quad (38)$$

If the X's are calculated using the polar method, Algorithm P, we compute two independent X's each time, and we have $X_1^2 + X_2^2 = -2 \ln S$ in the notation of that algorithm; this saves a little of the time needed to evaluate r. The validity of (38) comes from the fact that the distribution function for the point $(X_1, \ldots, X_n)$ has a density that depends only on its distance from the origin, so when it is projected onto the unit sphere it has the uniform distribution. This method was first suggested by G. W. Brown, in *Modern Mathematics for the Engineer*, First series, edited by E. F. Beckenbach (New York: McGraw–Hill,

1956), 302. To get a random point *inside* the n-ball, R. P. Brent suggests taking a point on the surface and multiplying it by $U^{1/n}$.

In three dimensions a significantly simpler method can be used, since each individual coordinate is uniformly distributed between -1 and 1: Find V_1, V_2, and S by steps P1–P3 of Algorithm P; then the desired random point on the surface of a globe is $(\alpha V_1, \alpha V_2, 2S - 1)$, where $\alpha = 2\sqrt{1 - S}$. [Robert E. Knop, *CACM* **13** (1970), 326.]

F. Important integer-valued distributions. A probability distribution that is nonzero only at integer values can essentially be handled by the techniques described at the beginning of this section; but some of these distributions are so important in practice, they deserve special mention here.

1) *The geometric distribution.* If some event occurs with probability p, the number N of independent trials needed between occurrences of the event (or until the event occurs for the first time) has the geometric distribution. We have $N = 1$ with probability p, $N = 2$ with probability $(1 - p)p$, $\ldots$, $N = n$ with probability $(1 - p)^{n-1}p$. This is essentially the situation we have already considered in the gap test of Section 3.3.2; it is also directly related to the number of times certain loops in the algorithms of this section are executed, like steps P1–P3 of the polar method.

A convenient way to generate a variable with this distribution is to set

$$N \leftarrow \lceil \ln U / \ln(1 - p) \rceil. \tag{39}$$

To check this formula, we observe that $\lceil \ln U / \ln(1 - p) \rceil = n$ if and only if $n - 1 < \ln U / \ln(1 - p) \le n$, that is, $(1 - p)^{n-1} > U \ge (1 - p)^n$, and this happens with probability $(1 - p)^{n-1}p$ as required. The quantity $\ln U$ can optionally be replaced by $-Y$, where Y has the exponential distribution with mean 1.

The special case $p = \frac{1}{2}$ is quite simple on a binary computer, since formula (39) reduces to setting $N \leftarrow \lceil -\lg U \rceil$; that is, N is one more than the number of leading zero bits in the binary representation of U.

2) *The binomial distribution* (t, p). If some event occurs with probability p, and if we carry out t independent trials, the total number N of occurrences equals n with probability $\binom{t}{n} p^n (1 - p)^{t-n}$. (See Section 1.2.10.) In other words if we generate $U_1, \ldots, U_t$, we want to count how many of these are $< p$. For small t we can obtain N in exactly this way.

For large t, we can generate a beta deviate X with integer parameters a and b where $a + b - 1 = t$; this effectively gives us the bth largest of t elements, without bothering to generate the other elements. Now if $X \ge p$, we set $N \leftarrow N_1$ where N_1 has the binomial distribution $(a-1, p/X)$, since this tells us how many of $a - 1$ random numbers in the range $[0 .. X]$ are $< p$; and if $X < p$, we set $N \leftarrow a + N_1$ where N_1 has the binomial distribution $\big(b - 1, (p - X)/(1 - X)\big)$, since N_1 tells us how many of $b-1$ random numbers in the range $[X .. 1)$ are $< p$. By choosing $a = 1 + \lfloor t/2 \rfloor$, the parameter t will be reduced to a reasonable size after about $\lg t$ reductions of this kind. (This approach is due to J. H. Ahrens, who has also suggested an alternative for medium-sized t; see exercise 27.)

3) *The Poisson distribution* with mean μ. The Poisson distribution is related to the exponential distribution as the binomial distribution is related to the geometric: It represents the number of occurrences, per unit time, of an event that can occur at any instant of time. For example, the number of alpha particles emitted by a radioactive substance in a single second has a Poisson distribution.

According to this principle, we can produce a Poisson deviate N by generating independent exponential deviates X_1, X_2, ... with mean $1/\mu$, stopping as soon as $X_1 + \cdots + X_m \geq 1$; then $N \leftarrow m - 1$. The probability that $X_1 + \cdots + X_m \geq 1$ is the probability that a gamma deviate of order m is $\geq \mu$, and this comes to $\int_\mu^\infty t^{m-1}e^{-t} \, dt/(m-1)!$; hence the probability that $N = n$ is

$$\frac{1}{n!} \int_\mu^\infty t^n e^{-t} \, dt - \frac{1}{(n-1)!} \int_\mu^\infty t^{n-1}e^{-t} \, dt = e^{-\mu}\frac{\mu^n}{n!}, \qquad n \geq 0. \qquad (40)$$

If we generate exponential deviates by the logarithm method, the recipe above tells us to stop when $-(\ln U_1 + \cdots + \ln U_m)/\mu \geq 1$. Simplifying this expression, we see that the desired Poisson deviate can be obtained by calculating $e^{-\mu}$, converting it to a fixed point representation, then generating one or more uniform deviates U_1, U_2, ... until the product satisfies $U_1 \ldots U_m \leq e^{-\mu}$, finally setting $N \leftarrow m-1$. On the average this requires the generation of $\mu+1$ uniform deviates, so it is a very useful approach when μ is not too large.

When μ is large, we can obtain a method of order $\log \mu$ by using the fact that we know how to handle the gamma and binomial distributions for large orders: First generate X with the gamma distribution of order $m = \lfloor \alpha\mu \rfloor$, where α is a suitable constant. (Since X is equivalent to $-\ln(U_1 \ldots U_m)$, we are essentially bypassing m steps of the previous method.) If $X < \mu$, set $N \leftarrow m + N_1$, where N_1 is a Poisson deviate with mean $\mu - X$; and if $X \geq \mu$, set $N \leftarrow N_1$, where N_1 has the binomial distribution $(m - 1, \mu/X)$. This method is due to J. H. Ahrens and U. Dieter, whose experiments suggest that $\frac{7}{8}$ is a good choice for α.

The validity of the stated reduction when $X \geq \mu$ is a consequence of the following important principle: "Let X_1, ..., X_m be independent exponential deviates with the same mean; let $S_j = X_1 + \cdots + X_j$ and let $V_j = S_j/S_m$ for $1 \leq j \leq m$. Then the distribution of V_1, V_2, ..., V_{m-1} is the same as the distribution of $m - 1$ independent uniform deviates sorted into increasing order." To establish this principle formally, we compute the probability that $V_1 \leq v_1$, ..., $V_{m-1} \leq v_{m-1}$, given the value of $S_m = s$, for arbitrary values $0 \leq v_1 \leq \cdots \leq v_{m-1} \leq 1$: Let $f(v_1, v_2, \ldots, v_{m-1})$ be the $(m-1)$-fold integral

$$\int_0^{v_1 s} \mu e^{-t_1/\mu} \, dt_1 \int_0^{v_2 s - t_1} \mu e^{-t_2/\mu} \, dt_2 \cdots$$
$$\times \int_0^{v_{m-1}s - t_1 - \cdots - t_{m-2}} \mu e^{-t_{m-1}/\mu} \, dt_{m-1} \cdot \mu e^{-(s-t_1-\cdots-t_{m-1})/\mu};$$

then

$$\frac{f(v_1, v_2, \ldots, v_{m-1})}{f(1, 1, \ldots, 1)} = \frac{\int_0^{v_1} du_1 \int_{u_1}^{v_2} du_2 \cdots \int_{u_{m-2}}^{v_{m-1}} du_{m-1}}{\int_0^1 du_1 \int_{u_1}^1 du_2 \cdots \int_{u_{m-2}}^1 du_{m-1}},$$

by making the substitution $t_1 = su_1$, $t_1 + t_2 = su_2$, ..., $t_1 + \cdots + t_{m-1} = su_{m-1}$. The latter ratio is the corresponding probability that uniform deviates $U_1, \ldots, U_{m-1}$ satisfy $U_1 \leq v_1, \ldots, U_{m-1} \leq v_{m-1}$, given that they also satisfy $U_1 \leq \cdots \leq U_{m-1}$.

A more efficient but somewhat more complicated technique for binomial and Poisson deviates is sketched in exercise 22.

G. For further reading. A facsimile of a letter from von Neumann dated May 21, 1947, in which the rejection method first saw the light of day, appears in *Stanislaw Ulam 1909–1984*, a special issue of *Los Alamos Science* (Los Alamos National Lab., 1987), 135–136. The book *Non-Uniform Random Variate Generation* by L. Devroye (Springer, 1986) discusses many more algorithms for the generation of random variables with nonuniform distributions, together with a careful consideration of the efficiency of each technique on typical computers.

W. Hörmann and G. Derflinger [*ACM Trans. Math. Software* **19** (1993), 489–495] have pointed out that it can be dangerous to use the rejection method in connection with linear congruential generators that have small multipliers $a \approx \sqrt{m}$.

From a theoretical point of view it is interesting to consider *optimal* ways to generate random variables with a given distribution, in the sense that the method produces the desired result from the minimum possible number of random bits. For the beginnings of a theory dealing with such questions, see D. E. Knuth and A. C. Yao, *Algorithms and Complexity*, edited by J. F. Traub (New York: Academic Press, 1976), 357–428.

Exercise 16 is recommended as a review of many of the techniques in this section.

EXERCISES

1. [*10*] If α and β are real numbers with $\alpha < \beta$, how would you generate a random real number uniformly distributed between α and β?

2. [*M16*] Assuming that mU is a random integer between 0 and $m - 1$, what is the *exact* probability that $\lfloor kU \rfloor = r$, if $0 \leq r < k$? Compare this with the desired probability $1/k$.

▶ **3.** [*14*] Discuss treating U as an integer and computing its *remainder* mod k to get a random integer between 0 and $k - 1$, instead of multiplying as suggested in the text. Thus (1) would be changed to

```
ENTA 0;   LDX U;   DIV K,
```

with the result appearing in register X. Is this a good method?

4. [*M20*] Prove the two relations in (8).

▶ **5.** [*21*] Suggest an efficient way to compute a random variable with the distribution $F(x) = px + qx^2 + rx^3$, where $p \geq 0$, $q \geq 0$, $r \geq 0$, and $p + q + r = 1$.

6. [*HM21*] A quantity X is computed by the following method:

> **Step 1.** Generate two independent uniform deviates U and V.
>
> **Step 2.** If $U^2 + V^2 \geq 1$, return to step 1; otherwise set $X \leftarrow U$.

What is the distribution function of X? How many times will step 1 be performed?
(Give the mean and standard deviation.)

▶ **7.** [*20*] (A. J. Walker.) Suppose we have a bunch of cubes of k different colors, say
n_j cubes of color C_j for $1 \le j \le k$, and we also have k boxes $\{B_1, \dots, B_k\}$ each of
which can hold exactly n cubes. Furthermore $n_1 + \dots + n_k = kn$, so the cubes will
just fit in the boxes. Prove (constructively) that there is always a way to put the cubes
into the boxes so that each box contains at most two different colors of cubes; in fact,
there is a way to do it so that, whenever box B_j contains two colors, one of those colors
is C_j. Show how to use this principle to compute the P and Y tables required in (3),
given a probability distribution $(p_1, \dots, p_k)$.

8. [*M15*] Show that operation (3) could be changed to

$$\text{if} \quad U < P_K \quad \text{then} \quad X \leftarrow x_{K+1} \quad \text{otherwise} \quad X \leftarrow Y_K$$

(thus using the original value of U instead of V) if this were more convenient, by
suitably modifying $P_0, P_1, \dots, P_{k-1}$.

9. [*HM10*] Why is the curve $f(x)$ of Fig. 9 concave for $x < 1$, convex for $x > 1$?

▶ **10.** [*HM24*] Explain how to calculate auxiliary constants $P_j, Q_j, Y_j, Z_j, S_j, D_j, E_j$
so that Algorithm M delivers answers with the correct distribution.

▶ **11.** [*HM27*] Prove that steps M7–M8 of Algorithm M generate a random variable
with the appropriate tail of the normal distribution; in other words, the probability
that $X \le x$ should be exactly

$$\int_3^x e^{-t^2/2}\, dt \bigg/ \int_3^\infty e^{-t^2/2}\, dt, \qquad x \ge 3.$$

[*Hint:* Show that it is a special case of the rejection method, with $g(t) = Cte^{-t^2/2}$ for
some C.]

12. [*HM23*] (R. P. Brent.) Prove that the numbers a_j defined in (23) satisfy the
relation

$$a_j^2 - a_{j-1}^2 < 2\ln 2 \qquad \text{for all } j \ge 1.$$

[*Hint:* If $f(x) = e^{x^2/2} \int_x^\infty e^{-t^2/2}\, dt$, show that $f(x) > f(y)$ for $0 \le x < y$.]

13. [*HM25*] Given a set of n independent normal deviates, $X_1, X_2, \dots, X_n$, with
mean 0 and variance 1, show how to find constants b_j and a_{ij}, $1 \le j \le i \le n$, so that if

$$Y_1 = b_1 + a_{11}X_1, \quad Y_2 = b_2 + a_{21}X_1 + a_{22}X_2, \quad \dots, \quad Y_n = b_n + a_{n1}X_1 + \dots + a_{nn}X_n,$$

then $Y_1, Y_2, \dots, Y_n$ are dependent normally distributed variables, Y_j has mean μ_j,
and the Y's have a given covariance matrix (c_{ij}). (The covariance, c_{ij}, of Y_i and Y_j is
defined to be the average value of $(Y_i - \mu_i)(Y_j - \mu_j)$. In particular, c_{jj} is the variance
of Y_j, the square of its standard deviation. Not all matrices (c_{ij}) can be covariance
matrices, and your construction is, of course, only supposed to work whenever a solution
to the given conditions is possible.)

14. [*M21*] If X is a random variable with the continuous distribution $F(x)$, and if c
is a (possibly negative) constant, what is the distribution of cX?

15. [*HM21*] If X_1 and X_2 are independent random variables with the respective
distributions $F_1(x)$ and $F_2(x)$, and with densities $f_1(x) = F_1'(x)$, $f_2(x) = F_2'(x)$, what
are the distribution and density functions of the quantity $X_1 + X_2$?

▶ **16.** [*HM22*] (J. H. Ahrens.) Develop an algorithm for gamma deviates of order a when $0 < a \leq 1$, using the rejection method with $cg(t) = t^{a-1}/\Gamma(a)$ for $0 < t < 1$, and with $cg(t) = e^{-t}/\Gamma(a)$ for $t \geq 1$.

▶ **17.** [*M24*] What is the *distribution function* $F(x)$ for the geometric distribution with probability p? What is the *generating function* $G(z)$? What are the mean and standard deviation of this distribution?

18. [*M24*] Suggest a method to compute a random integer N for which N takes the value n with probability $np^2(1-p)^{n-1}$, $n \geq 0$. (The case of particular interest is when p is rather small.)

19. [*22*] The *negative binomial distribution* (t, p) has integer values $N = n$ with probability $\binom{t-1+n}{n} p^t (1-p)^n$. (Unlike the ordinary binomial distribution, t need not be an integer, since this quantity is nonnegative for all n whenever $t > 0$.) Generalizing exercise 18, explain how to generate integers N with this distribution when t is a small positive integer. What method would you suggest if $t = p = \frac{1}{2}$?

20. [*M20*] Let A be the area of the shaded region in Fig. 13, and let R be the area of the enclosing rectangle. Let I be the area of the interior region recognized by step R2, and let E be the area between the exterior region rejected in step R3 and the outer rectangle. Determine the number of times each step of Algorithm R is performed, for each of its four variants as in (25), in terms of A, R, I, and E.

21. [*HM29*] Derive formulas for the quantities A, R, I, and E defined in exercise 20. (For I and especially E you may wish to use an interactive computer algebra system.) Show that $c = e^{1/4}$ is the best possible constant in step R2 for tests of the form "$X^2 \leq 4(1 + \ln c) - 4cU$."

22. [*HM40*] Can the exact Poisson distribution for large μ be obtained by generating an appropriate normal deviate, converting it to an integer in some convenient way, and applying a (possibly complicated) correction a small percent of the time?

23. [*HM23*] (J. von Neumann.) Are the following two ways to generate a random quantity X equivalent (that is, does the quantity X have the same distribution)?

> **Method 1:** Set $X \leftarrow \sin((\pi/2)U)$, where U is uniform.
>
> **Method 2:** Generate two uniform deviates, U and V; if $U^2 + V^2 \geq 1$, repeat until $U^2 + V^2 < 1$. Then set $X \leftarrow |U^2 - V^2|/(U^2 + V^2)$.

24. [*HM40*] (S. Ulam, J. von Neumann.) Let V_0 be a randomly selected real number between 0 and 1, and define the sequence $\langle V_n \rangle$ by the rule $V_{n+1} = 4V_n(1 - V_n)$. If this computation is done with perfect accuracy, the result should be a sequence with the distribution $\sin^2 \pi U$, where U is uniform, that is, with distribution function $F(x) = \int_0^x dx/\sqrt{2\pi x(1-x)}$. For if we write $V_n = \sin^2 \pi U_n$, we find that $U_{n+1} = (2U_n) \bmod 1$; and by the fact that almost all real numbers have a random binary expansion (see Section 3.5), this sequence U_n is equidistributed. But if the computation of V_n is done with only finite accuracy, the argument breaks down because we soon are dealing with noise from the roundoff error. [See von Neumann's *Collected Works* **5**, 768–770.]

Analyze the sequence $\langle V_n \rangle$ defined in the preceding paragraph, when only finite accuracy is present, both empirically (for various different choices of V_0) and theoretically. Does the sequence have a distribution resembling the expected distribution?

25. [*M25*] Let X_1, X_2, ..., X_5 be binary words each of whose bits is independently 0 or 1 with probability $\frac{1}{2}$. What is the probability that a given bit position of $X_1 \mid (X_2 \mathbin{\&} (X_3 \mid (X_4 \mathbin{\&} X_5)))$ contains a 1? Generalize.

26. [*M18*] Let N_1 and N_2 be independent Poisson deviates with means μ_1 and μ_2, where $\mu_1 > \mu_2 \geq 0$. Prove or disprove: (a) $N_1 + N_2$ has the Poisson distribution with mean $\mu_1 + \mu_2$. (b) $N_1 - N_2$ has the Poisson distribution with mean $\mu_1 - \mu_2$.

27. [*22*] (J. H. Ahrens.) On most binary computers there is an efficient way to count the number of 1s in a binary word (see Section 7.1.3). Hence there is a nice way to obtain the binomial distribution (t, p) when $p = \frac{1}{2}$, simply by generating t random bits and counting the number of 1s.

Design an algorithm that produces the binomial distribution (t, p) for *arbitrary* p, using only a subroutine for the special case $p = \frac{1}{2}$ as a source of random data. [*Hint:* Simulate a process that first looks at the most significant bits of t uniform deviates, then at the second bit of those deviates whose leading bit is not sufficient to determine whether or not their value is $< p$, etc.]

28. [*HM35*] (R. P. Brent.) Develop a method to generate a random point on the surface of the ellipsoid defined by $\sum a_k x_k^2 = 1$, where $a_1 \geq \cdots \geq a_n > 0$.

29. [*M20*] (J. L. Bentley and J. B. Saxe.) Find a simple way to generate n numbers $X_1, \ldots, X_n$ that are uniform between 0 and 1 except for the fact that they are sorted: $X_1 \leq \cdots \leq X_n$. Your algorithm should take only $O(n)$ steps.

30. [*M30*] Explain how to generate a set of random points (X_j, Y_j) such that, if R is any rectangle of area α contained in the unit square, the number of (X_j, Y_j) lying in R has the Poisson distribution with mean $\alpha\mu$.

31. [*HM39*] (*Direct generation of normal deviates.*)
  a) Prove that if $a_1^2 + \cdots + a_k^2 = 1$ and if $X_1, \ldots, X_k$ are independent normal deviates with mean 0 and variance 1, then $a_1 X_1 + \cdots + a_k X_k$ is a normal deviate with mean 0 and variance 1.
  b) The result of (a) suggests that we can generate new normal deviates from old ones, just as we obtain new uniform deviates from old ones. For example, we might use the idea of 3.2.2–(7), but with a recurrence like

$$X_n = (X_{n-24} + X_{n-55})/\sqrt{2} \quad \text{or} \quad X_n = \tfrac{3}{5} X_{n-24} + \tfrac{4}{5} X_{n-55},$$

  after a set of normal deviates $X_0, \ldots, X_{54}$ has been computed initially. Explain why this is *not* a good idea.
  c) Show, however, that there *is* a suitable way to generate normal deviates quickly from other normal deviates, by using a refinement of the idea in (a) and (b). [*Hint:* If X and Y are independent normal deviates, so are $X' = X \cos \theta + Y \sin \theta$ and $Y' = -X \sin \theta + Y \cos \theta$, for any angle θ.]

32. [*HM30*] (C. S. Wallace.) Let X and Y be independent exponential deviates with mean 1. Show that X' and Y' are, likewise, independent exponential deviates with mean 1, if we obtain them from X and Y in any of the following ways:
  a) Given $0 < \lambda < 1$,

$$X' = (1 - \lambda)X - \lambda Y + (X + Y)[(1 - \lambda)X < \lambda Y], \qquad Y' = X + Y - X'.$$

  b) $(X', Y') = \begin{cases} (2X, Y - X), & \text{if } X \leq Y; \\ (2Y, X - Y), & \text{if } X > Y. \end{cases}$

  c) If $X = (\ldots x_2 x_1 x_0 . x_{-1} x_{-2} x_{-3} \ldots)_2$ and $Y = (\ldots y_2 y_1 y_0 . y_{-1} y_{-2} y_{-3} \ldots)_2$ in binary notation, then X' and Y' have the "shuffled" values

$$X' = (\ldots x_2 y_1 x_0 . y_{-1} x_{-2} y_{-3} \ldots)_2, \qquad Y' = (\ldots y_2 x_1 y_0 . x_{-1} y_{-2} x_{-3} \ldots)_2.$$

33. [*20*] Algorithms P, M, F, and R generate normal deviates by consuming an un-known number of uniform random variables $U_1, U_2, \ldots$. How can they be modified so that the output is a function of just one U?

3.4.2. Random Sampling and Shuffling

Many data processing applications call for an unbiased choice of n records at random from a file containing N records. This problem arises, for example, in quality control or other statistical calculations where sampling is needed. Usually N is very large, so that it is impossible to contain all the data in memory at once; and the individual records themselves are often very large, so that we can't even hold n records in memory. Therefore we seek an efficient procedure for selecting n records by deciding either to accept or to reject each record as it comes along, writing the accepted records onto an output file.

Several methods have been devised for this problem. The most obvious approach is to select each record with probability n/N; this may sometimes be appropriate, but it gives only an *average* of n records in the sample. The standard deviation is $\sqrt{n(1 - n/N)}$, and the sample might turn out to be either too large for the desired application or too small to give the necessary results.

Fortunately, a simple modification of the "obvious" procedure gives us what we want: The $(t+1)$st record should be selected with probability $(n-m)/(N-t)$, if m items have already been selected. This is the appropriate probability, since of all the possible ways to choose n things from N such that m values occur in the first t, exactly

$$\binom{N-t-1}{n-m-1} \Big/ \binom{N-t}{n-m} = \frac{n-m}{N-t} \tag{1}$$

of them select the $(t + 1)$st element.

The idea developed in the preceding paragraph leads immediately to the following algorithm:

Algorithm S (*Selection sampling technique*). To select n records at random from a set of N, where $0 < n \le N$.

S1. [Initialize.] Set $t \leftarrow 0$, $m \leftarrow 0$. (During this algorithm, m represents the number of records selected so far, and t is the total number of input records that we have dealt with.)

S2. [Generate U.] Generate a random number U, uniformly distributed between zero and one.

S3. [Test.] If $(N - t)U \ge n - m$, go to step S5.

S4. [Select.] Select the next record for the sample, and increase m and t by 1. If $m < n$, go to step S2; otherwise the sample is complete and the algorithm terminates.

S5. [Skip.] Skip the next record (do not include it in the sample), increase t by 1, and go back to step S2. ∎

This algorithm may appear to be unreliable at first glance and, in fact, to be incorrect; but a careful analysis (see the exercises below) shows that it is completely trustworthy. It is not difficult to verify that

a) At most N records are input (we never run off the end of the file before choosing n items).

b) The sample is completely unbiased. In particular, the probability that any given element is selected, such as the last element of the file, is n/N.

Statement (b) is true in spite of the fact that we are *not* selecting the $(t+1)$st item with probability n/N, but rather with the probability in Eq. (1)! This has caused some confusion in the published literature. Can the reader explain this seeming contradiction?

(*Note:* When using Algorithm S, one should be careful to use a different source of random numbers U each time the program is run, to avoid connections between the samples obtained on different days. This can be done, for example, by choosing a different value of X_0 for the linear congruential method each time. The seed value X_0 could be set to the current date, or to the last random number X that was generated on the previous run of the program.)

We will usually not have to pass over all N records. In fact, since (b) above says that the last record is selected with probability n/N, we will terminate the algorithm *before* considering the last record exactly $(1 - n/N)$ of the time. The average number of records considered when $n = 2$ is about $\frac{2}{3}N$, and the general formulas are given in exercises 5 and 6.

Algorithm S and a number of other sampling techniques are discussed in a paper by C. T. Fan, Mervin E. Muller, and Ivan Rezucha, *J. Amer. Stat. Assoc.* **57** (1962), 387–402. The method was independently discovered by T. G. Jones, *CACM* **5** (1962), 343.

A problem arises if we don't know the value of N in advance, since the precise value of N is crucial in Algorithm S. Suppose we want to select n items at random from a file, without knowing exactly how many are present in that file. We could first go through and count the records, then take a second pass to select them; but it is generally better to sample $m \geq n$ of the original items on the first pass, where m is much less than N, so that only m items must be considered on the second pass. The trick, of course, is to do this in such a way that the final result is a truly random sample of the original file.

Since we don't know when the input is going to end, we must keep track of a random sample of the input records seen so far, thus always being prepared for the end. As we read the input we will construct a "reservoir" that contains only the records that have appeared among the previous samples. The first n records always go into the reservoir. When the $(t+1)$st record is being input, for $t \geq n$, we will have in memory a table of n indices pointing to the records that we have chosen from among the first t. The problem is to maintain this situation with t increased by one, namely to find a new random sample from among the $t + 1$ records now known to be present. It is not hard to see that we should include the new record in the new sample with probability $n/(t+1)$, and in such a case it should replace a random element of the previous sample.

Thus, the following procedure does the job:

Algorithm R (*Reservoir sampling*). To select n records at random from a file of unknown size $\geq n$, given $n > 0$. An auxiliary file called the "reservoir" contains all records that are candidates for the final sample. The algorithm uses a table of distinct indices $I[j]$ for $1 \leq j \leq n$, each of which points to one of the records in the reservoir.

R1. [Initialize.] Input the first n records and copy them to the reservoir. Set $I[j] \leftarrow j$ for $1 \leq j \leq n$, and set $t \leftarrow m \leftarrow n$. (If the file being sampled has fewer than n records, it will of course be necessary to abort the algorithm and report failure. During this algorithm, indices $I[1], \ldots, I[n]$ point to the records in the current sample; m is the size of the reservoir; and t is the number of input records dealt with so far.)

R2. [End of file?] If there are no more records to be input, go to step R6.

R3. [Generate and test.] Increase t by 1, then generate a random integer M between 1 and t (inclusive). If $M > n$, go to R5.

R4. [Add to reservoir.] Copy the next record of the input file to the reservoir, increase m by 1, and set $I[M] \leftarrow m$. (The record previously pointed to by $I[M]$ is being replaced in the sample by the new record.) Go back to R2.

R5. [Skip.] Skip over the next record of the input file (do not include it in the reservoir), and return to step R2.

R6. [Second pass.] Sort the I table entries so that $I[1] < \cdots < I[n]$; then go through the reservoir, copying the records with these indices into the output file that is to hold the final sample. ∎

Algorithm R is due to Alan G. Waterman. The reader may wish to work out the example of its operation that appears in exercise 9.

If the records are sufficiently short, it is of course unnecessary to have a reservoir at all; we can keep the n records of the current sample in memory at all times, and the algorithm becomes much simpler (see exercise 10).

The natural question to ask about Algorithm R is, "What is the expected size of the reservoir?" Exercise 11 shows that the average value of m is exactly $n(1 + H_N - H_n)$; this is approximately $n(1 + \ln(N/n))$. So if $N/n = 1000$, the reservoir will contain only about $1/125$ as many items as the original file.

Notice that Algorithms S and R can be used to obtain samples for several independent categories simultaneously. For example, if we have a large file of names and addresses of U.S. residents, we could pick random samples of exactly 10 people from each of the 50 states without making 50 passes through the file, and without first sorting the file by state.

Significant improvements to both Algorithms S and R are possible, when n/N is small, if we generate a single random variable to tell us how many records should be skipped instead of deciding whether or not to skip each record. (See exercise 8.)

The sampling problem can be regarded as the computation of a random *combination*, according to the conventional definition of combinations of N things taken n at a time (see Section 1.2.6). Now let us consider the problem of computing a random *permutation* of t objects; we will call this the *shuffling* problem, since shuffling a deck of cards is nothing more than subjecting the deck to a random permutation.

A moment's reflection is enough to convince any card player that traditional shuffling procedures are miserably inadequate. There is no hope of obtaining each of the $t!$ permutations with anywhere near equal probability by such methods. Expert bridge players reportedly make use of this fact when deciding whether or not to finesse. At least seven "riffle shuffles" of a 52-card deck are needed to reach a distribution within 10% of uniform, and 14 random riffles are guaranteed to do so [see Aldous and Diaconis, *AMM* **93** (1986), 333–348].

If t is small, we can obtain a random permutation very quickly by generating a random integer between 1 and $t!$. For example, when $t = 4$, a random number between 1 and 24 suffices to select a random permutation from a table of all possibilities. But for large t, it is necessary to be more careful if we want to claim that each permutation is equally likely, since $t!$ is much larger than the accuracy of individual random numbers.

A suitable shuffling procedure can be obtained by recalling Algorithm 3.3.2P, which gives a simple correspondence between each of the $t!$ possible permutations and a sequence of numbers $(c_1, c_2, \ldots, c_{t-1})$, with $0 \le c_j \le j$. It is easy to compute such a set of numbers at random, and we can use the correspondence to produce a random permutation.

Algorithm P (*Shuffling*). Let $(X_1, X_2, \ldots, X_t)$ be a sequence of t numbers to be shuffled.

P1. [Initialize.] Set $j \leftarrow t$.

P2. [Generate U.] Generate a random number U, uniformly distributed between zero and one.

P3. [Exchange.] Set $k \leftarrow \lfloor jU \rfloor + 1$. (Now k is a random integer, between 1 and j. Exercise 3.4.1–3 explains that k should *not* be computed by taking a remainder modulo j.) Exchange $X_k \leftrightarrow X_j$.

P4. [Decrease j.] Decrease j by 1. If $j > 1$, return to step P2. ▮

This algorithm was first published by R. A. Fisher and F. Yates [*Statistical Tables* (London, 1938), Example 12], in ordinary language, and by R. Durstenfeld [*CACM* **7** (1964), 420] in computer language. If we merely wish to generate a random permutation of $\{1, \ldots, t\}$ instead of shuffling a given sequence $(X_1, \ldots, X_t)$, we can avoid the exchange operation $X_k \leftrightarrow X_j$ by letting j increase from 1 to t and setting $X_j \leftarrow X_k$, $X_k \leftarrow j$; see D. E. Knuth, *The Stanford GraphBase* (New York: ACM Press, 1994), 104.

R. Salfi [*COMPSTAT 1974* (Vienna: 1974), 28–35] has pointed out that Algorithm P cannot possibly generate more than m distinct permutations when we obtain the uniform U's with a linear congruential sequence of modulus m, or indeed whenever we use a recurrence $U_{n+1} = f(U_n)$ for which U_n can take only m different values, because the final permutation in such cases is entirely determined by the value of the first U that is generated. Thus, for example, if $m = 2^{32}$, certain permutations of 13 elements will never occur, since $13! \approx 1.45 \times 2^{32}$. In most applications we don't really *want* to see all $13!$ permutations; yet it is disconcerting to know that the excluded ones are determined by a fairly simple mathematical rule such as a lattice structure (see Section 3.3.4).

This problem does not arise when we use a lagged Fibonacci generator like 3.2.2–(7) with a sufficiently long period. But even with such methods we cannot get all permutations uniformly unless we are able to specify at least $t!$ different seed values to initialize the generator. In other words, we can't get $\lg t!$ truly random bits out unless we put $\lg t!$ truly random bits in. Section 3.5 shows that we need not despair about this.

Algorithm P can easily be modified to yield a random permutation of a random combination (see exercise 15). For a discussion of random combinatorial objects of other kinds (e.g., partitions), see Section 7.2 and/or the book *Combinatorial Algorithms* by Nijenhuis and Wilf (New York: Academic Press, 1975).

EXERCISES

1. [*M12*] Explain Eq. (1).

2. [*20*] Prove that Algorithm S never tries to read more than N records of its input file.

▶ **3.** [*22*] The $(t+1)$st item in Algorithm S is selected with probability $(n-m)/(N-t)$, not n/N, yet the text claims that the sample is unbiased; thus each item should be selected with the *same* probability. How can both of these statements be true?

4. [*M23*] Let $p(m, t)$ be the probability that exactly m items are selected from among the first t in the selection sampling technique. Show directly from Algorithm S that

$$ p(m, t) = \binom{t}{m}\binom{N-t}{n-m} \bigg/ \binom{N}{n}, \qquad \text{for } 0 \le t \le N. $$

5. [*M24*] What is the average value of t when Algorithm S terminates? (In other words, how many of the N records have been passed, on the average, before the sample is complete?)

6. [*M24*] What is the standard deviation of the value computed in exercise 5?

7. [*M25*] Prove that any *given* choice of n records from the set of N is obtained by Algorithm S with probability $1/\binom{N}{n}$. Therefore the sample is completely unbiased.

▶ **8.** [*M39*] (J. S. Vitter.) Algorithm S computes one uniform deviate for each input record it handles. The purpose of this exercise is to consider a more efficient approach in which we calculate more quickly the proper number X of input records to skip before the first selection is made.

a) What is the probability that $X \ge k$, given k?
b) Show that the result of (a) allows us to calculate X by generating only one uniform U and then doing $O(X)$ other calculations.
c) Show that we may also set $X \leftarrow \min(Y_N, Y_{N-1}, \ldots, Y_{N-n+1})$, where the Y's are independent and each Y_t is a random integer in the range $0 \le Y_t < t$.

d) For maximum speed, show that X can also be calculated in $O(1)$ steps, on the average, using a "squeeze method" like Eq. 3.4.1–(18).

9. [*12*] Let $n = 3$. If Algorithm R is applied to a file containing 20 records numbered 1 thru 20, and if the random numbers generated in step R3 are respectively

$$4, 1, 6, 7, 5, 3, 5, 11, 11, 3, 7, 9, 3, 11, 4, 5, 4,$$

which records go into the reservoir? Which are in the final sample?

10. [*15*] Modify Algorithm R so that the reservoir is eliminated, assuming that the n records of the current sample can be held in memory.

▶ **11.** [*M25*] Let p_m be the probability that exactly m elements are put into the reservoir during the first pass of Algorithm R. Determine the generating function $G(z) = \sum_m p_m z^m$, and find the mean and standard deviation. (Use the ideas of Section 1.2.10.)

12. [*M26*] The gist of Algorithm P is that any permutation π can be uniquely written as a product of transpositions in the form $\pi = (a_t t) \ldots (a_3 3)(a_2 2)$, where $1 \le a_j \le j$ for $t \ge j > 1$. Prove that there is also a unique representation of the form $\pi = (b_2 2)(b_3 3) \ldots (b_t t)$, where $1 \le b_j \le j$ for $1 < j \le t$, and design an algorithm that computes the b's from the a's in $O(t)$ steps.

13. [*M23*] (S. W. Golomb.) One of the most common ways to shuffle cards is to divide the deck into two parts as equal as possible, and to "riffle" them together. (According to the discussion of card-playing etiquette in Hoyle's rules of card games, "A shuffle of this sort should be made about three times to mix the cards thoroughly.") Consider a deck of $2n - 1$ cards $X_1, X_2, \ldots, X_{2n-1}$; a "perfect shuffle" s divides this deck into $X_1, X_2, \ldots, X_n$ and $X_{n+1}, \ldots, X_{2n-1}$, then perfectly interleaves them to obtain X_1, $X_{n+1}, X_2, X_{n+2}, \ldots, X_{2n-1}, X_n$. The "cut" operation c^j changes $X_1, X_2, \ldots, X_{2n-1}$ into $X_{j+1}, \ldots, X_{2n-1}, X_1, \ldots, X_j$. Show that by combining perfect shuffles and cuts, at most $(2n - 1)(2n - 2)$ different arrangements of the deck are possible, if $n > 1$.

14. [*22*] A cut-and-riffle permutation of $a_0 a_1 \ldots a_{n-1}$ changes it to a sequence that contains the subsequences

$$a_x\, a_{(x+1) \bmod n} \cdots a_{(y-1) \bmod n} \quad \text{and} \quad a_y\, a_{(y+1) \bmod n} \cdots a_{(x-1) \bmod n}$$

intermixed in some way, for some x and y. Thus, 3890145267 is a cut-and-riffle of 0123456789, with $x = 3$ and $y = 8$.

a) Beginning with 52 playing cards arranged in the standard order

2 3 4 5 6 7 8 9 10 J Q K A ♣ 2 3 4 5 6 7 8 9 10 J Q K A ♦ 2 3 4 5 6 7 8 9 10 J Q K A ♥ 2 3 4 5 6 7 8 9 10 J Q K A ♠,

Mr. J. H. Quick (a student) did a random cut-and-riffle; then he removed the leftmost card and inserted it in a random place, obtaining the sequence

9 10 K J Q A K A 2 Q 3 2 3 4 5 6 7 4 8 9 5 10 6 J 7 Q 8 K 9 10 J Q A K 2 3 A 4 2 3 4 5 6 5 6 7 8 7 9 10 J 8.

Which card did he move from the leftmost position?

b) Starting again with the deck in its original order, Quick now did *three* cut-and-riffles before moving the leftmost card to a new place:

10 J Q 3 4 5 6 J J Q 4 6 K A 2 3 K 4 7 5 6 Q A 7 5 A 8 7 6 K K 9 A 7 8 9 10 8 10 8 2 5 J 2 3 Q 4 9 3 2 9 10.

Which card did he move this time?

▶ **15.** [*30*] (Ole-Johan Dahl.) If $X_k = k$ for $1 \le k \le t$ at the start of Algorithm P, and if we terminate the algorithm when j reaches the value $t - n$, the sequence X_{t-n+1}, ..., X_t is a random permutation of a random combination of n elements. Show how to simulate the effect of this procedure using only $O(n)$ cells of memory.

▶ **16.** [*M25*] Devise a way to compute a random sample of n records from N, given N and n, based on the idea of hashing (Section 6.4). Your method should use $O(n)$ storage locations and an average of $O(n)$ units of time, and it should present the sample as a sorted set of integers $1 \le X_1 < X_2 < \cdots < X_n \le N$.

17. [*M22*] (R. W. Floyd.) Prove that the following algorithm generates a random sample S of n integers from $\{1, \ldots, N\}$: Set $S \leftarrow \emptyset$; then for $j \leftarrow N - n + 1, N - n + 2$, ..., N (in this order), set $k \leftarrow \lfloor jU \rfloor + 1$ and

$$S \leftarrow \begin{cases} S \cup \{k\}, & \text{if } k \notin S; \\ S \cup \{j\}, & \text{if } k \in S. \end{cases}$$

▶ **18.** [*M32*] People sometimes try to shuffle n items $(X_1, X_2, \ldots, X_n)$ by successively interchanging

$$X_1 \leftrightarrow X_{k_1}, \quad X_2 \leftrightarrow X_{k_2}, \quad \ldots, \quad X_n \leftrightarrow X_{k_n},$$

where the indices k_j are independent and uniformly random between 1 and n.

Consider the directed graph with vertices $\{1, 2, \ldots, n\}$ and with arcs from j to k_j for $1 \le j \le n$. Describe the digraphs of this type for which, if we start with the elements $(X_1, X_2, \ldots, X_n) = (1, 2, \ldots, n)$, the stated interchanges produce the respective permutations (a) $(n, 1, 2, \ldots)$; (b) $(1, 2, \ldots, n)$; (c) $(2, \ldots, n, 1)$. Conclude that these three permutations are obtained with wildly different probabilities.

▶ **19.** [*M28*] (*Priority sampling.*) Consider a file of N items in which the kth item has a positive weight w_k. Let $q_k = U_k/w_k$ for $1 \le k \le N$, where $\{U_1, \ldots, U_N\}$ are independent uniform deviates in $[0 \mathbin{..} 1)$. If r is any real number, define

$$\widehat{w}_k^{(r)} = \begin{cases} \max(w_k, 1/r), & \text{if } q_k < r; \\ 0, & \text{if } q_k \ge r. \end{cases} \qquad \widehat{w}_k^{(r+)} = \begin{cases} \max(w_k, 1/r), & \text{if } q_k \le r; \\ 0, & \text{if } q_k > r. \end{cases}$$

   a) If r is the nth smallest element of $\{q_1, \ldots, q_N\}$, prove that the expected value $\mathrm{E}\, \widehat{w}_1^{(r)} \widehat{w}_2^{(r)} \ldots w_k^{(r)}$ is $w_1 w_2 \ldots w_k$, for $1 \le k < n \le N$. *Hint:* Show that, if s is the $(n-k)$th smallest element of $\{q_{k+1}, \ldots, q_N\}$, we have $\widehat{w}_1^{(r)} \ldots \widehat{w}_k^{(r)} = \widehat{w}_1^{(s+)} \ldots \widehat{w}_k^{(s+)}$. (Notice that the quantity s is independent of $\{U_1, \ldots, U_k\}$.)

   b) Consequently $\mathrm{E}\, \widehat{w}_{j_1}^{(r)} \ldots \widehat{w}_{j_k}^{(r)} = w_{j_1} \ldots w_{j_k}$ when $j_1 < \cdots < j_k$.

   c) Show that, if $n > 2$, the variance $\mathrm{Var}(\widehat{w}_{j_1}^{(r)} + \cdots + \widehat{w}_{j_k}^{(r)})$ is $\mathrm{Var}(\widehat{w}_{j_1}^{(r)}) + \cdots + \mathrm{Var}(\widehat{w}_{j_k}^{(r)})$.

   d) Given n, explain how to modify the reservoir sampling method so that the value of r and the $n - 1$ items with subscripts $\{j \mid q_j < r\}$ can be obtained with one pass through a file of unknown size N. *Hint:* Use a priority queue of size n.

*3.5. WHAT IS A RANDOM SEQUENCE?

A. Introductory remarks. We have seen in this chapter how to generate sequences

$$\langle U_n \rangle = U_0, \; U_1, \; U_2, \; \ldots \tag{1}$$

of real numbers in the range $0 \leq U_n < 1$, and we have called them "random" sequences even though they are completely deterministic in character. To justify this terminology, we claimed that the numbers "behave as if they are truly random." Such a statement may be satisfactory for practical purposes (at the present time), but it sidesteps a very important philosophical and theoretical question: Precisely what do we mean by "random behavior"? A quantitative definition is needed. It is undesirable to talk about concepts that we do not really understand, especially since many apparently paradoxical statements can be made about random numbers.

The mathematical theory of probability and statistics scrupulously avoids the issue. It refrains from making absolute statements, and instead expresses everything in terms of how much *probability* is to be attached to statements involving random sequences of events. The axioms of probability theory are set up so that abstract probabilities can be computed readily, but nothing is said about what probability really signifies, or how this concept can be applied meaningfully to the actual world. In the book *Probability, Statistics, and Truth* (New York: Macmillan, 1957), R. von Mises discusses this situation in detail, and presents the view that a proper definition of probability depends on obtaining a proper definition of a random sequence.

Let us paraphrase here some statements made by two of the many authors who have commented on the subject.

> *D. H. Lehmer* (1951): "A random sequence is a vague notion embodying the idea of a sequence in which each term is unpredictable to the uninitiated and whose digits pass a certain number of tests, traditional with statisticians and depending somewhat on the uses to which the sequence is to be put."

> *J. N. Franklin* (1962): "The sequence (1) is random if it has every property that is shared by all infinite sequences of independent samples of random variables from the uniform distribution."

Franklin's statement essentially generalizes Lehmer's to say that the sequence must satisfy *all* statistical tests. His definition is not completely precise, and we will see later that a reasonable interpretation of his statement leads us to conclude that there is no such thing as a random sequence! So let us begin with Lehmer's less restrictive statement and attempt to make *it* precise. What we really want is a relatively short list of mathematical properties, each of which is satisfied by our intuitive notion of a random sequence; furthermore, the list is to be complete enough so that we are willing to agree that *any* sequence satisfying these properties is "random." In this section, we will develop what seems to be an adequate definition of randomness according to these criteria, although many interesting questions remain to be answered.

Let u and v be real numbers, $0 \leq u < v \leq 1$. If U is a random variable that is uniformly distributed between 0 and 1, the probability that $u \leq U < v$ is equal to $v - u$. For example, the probability that $\frac{1}{5} \leq U < \frac{3}{5}$ is $\frac{2}{5}$. How can we translate this property of the single number U into a property of the infinite sequence $U_0, U_1, U_2, \ldots$? The obvious answer is to count how many times U_n lies between u and v, and the average number of times should equal $v - u$. Our intuitive idea of probability is based in this way on the frequency of occurrence.

More precisely, let $\nu(n)$ be the number of values of j, $0 \leq j < n$, such that $u \leq U_j < v$; we want the ratio $\nu(n)/n$ to approach the value $v - u$ as n approaches infinity:

$$\lim_{n \to \infty} \frac{\nu(n)}{n} = v - u. \tag{2}$$

If this condition holds for all choices of u and v, the sequence is said to be *equidistributed*.

Let $S(n)$ be a statement about the integer n and the sequence $U_0, U_1, \ldots$; for example, $S(n)$ might be the statement considered above, "$u \leq U_n < v$." We can generalize the idea used in the preceding paragraph to define the probability that $S(n)$ is true with respect to a particular infinite sequence.

Definition A. *Let $\nu(n)$ be the number of values of j, $0 \leq j < n$, such that $S(j)$ is true. We say that $S(n)$ is true with probability λ if the limit as n tends to infinity of $\nu(n)/n$ equals λ. Symbolically:* $\Pr\bigl(S(n)\bigr) = \lambda$ *if* $\lim_{n \to \infty} \nu(n)/n = \lambda$. ∎

In terms of this notation, the sequence $U_0, U_1, \ldots$ is equidistributed if and only if $\Pr(u \leq U_n < v) = v - u$, for all real numbers u, v with $0 \leq u < v \leq 1$.

A sequence might be equidistributed without being random. For example, if $U_0, U_1, \ldots$ and $V_0, V_1, \ldots$ are equidistributed sequences, it is not hard to show that the sequence

$$W_0, W_1, W_2, W_3, \ldots = \tfrac{1}{2}U_0, \ \tfrac{1}{2} + \tfrac{1}{2}V_0, \ \tfrac{1}{2}U_1, \ \tfrac{1}{2} + \tfrac{1}{2}V_1, \ \ldots \tag{3}$$

is also equidistributed, since the subsequence $\tfrac{1}{2}U_0, \tfrac{1}{2}U_1, \ldots$ is equidistributed between 0 and $\frac{1}{2}$, while the alternate terms $\frac{1}{2} + \frac{1}{2}V_0, \frac{1}{2} + \frac{1}{2}V_1, \ldots$, are equidistributed between $\frac{1}{2}$ and 1. But in the sequence of W's, a value less than $\frac{1}{2}$ is always followed by a value greater than or equal to $\frac{1}{2}$, and conversely; hence the sequence is not random by any reasonable definition. A stronger property than equidistribution is needed.

A natural generalization of the equidistribution property, which removes the objection stated in the preceding paragraph, is to consider adjacent pairs of numbers of our sequence. We can require the sequence to satisfy the condition

$$\Pr(u_1 \leq U_n < v_1 \ \text{and} \ u_2 \leq U_{n+1} < v_2) = (v_1 - u_1)(v_2 - u_2) \tag{4}$$

for any four numbers u_1, v_1, u_2, v_2 with $0 \leq u_1 < v_1 \leq 1$, $0 \leq u_2 < v_2 \leq 1$. And in general, for any positive integer k we can require our sequence to be *k-distributed* in the following sense:

Definition B. *The sequence* (1) *is said to be k-distributed if*

$$\Pr(u_1 \leq U_n < v_1, \ \ldots, \ u_k \leq U_{n+k-1} < v_k) = (v_1 - u_1)\ldots(v_k - u_k) \quad (5)$$

for all choices of real numbers u_j, v_j, with $0 \leq u_j < v_j \leq 1$ for $1 \leq j \leq k$. ∎

An equidistributed sequence is a 1-distributed sequence. Notice that if $k > 1$, a k-distributed sequence is always $(k - 1)$-distributed, since we may set $u_k = 0$ and $v_k = 1$ in Eq. (5). Thus, in particular, any sequence that is known to be 4-distributed must also be 3-distributed, 2-distributed, and equidistributed. We can investigate the largest k for which a given sequence is k-distributed; and this leads us to formulate a stronger property:

Definition C. *A sequence is said to be ∞-distributed if it is k-distributed for all positive integers k.* ∎

So far we have considered "$[0..1)$ sequences," that is, sequences of real numbers lying between zero and one. The same ideas apply to integer-valued sequences; let us say that the sequence $\langle X_n \rangle = X_0, X_1, X_2, \ldots$ is a *b-ary sequence* if each X_n is one of the integers $0, 1, \ldots, b-1$. Thus, a 2-ary (binary) sequence is a sequence of zeros and ones.

We also define a k-digit *b-ary number* as a string of k integers $x_1 x_2 \ldots x_k$, where $0 \leq x_j < b$ for $1 \leq j \leq k$.

Definition D. *A b-ary sequence is said to be k-distributed if*

$$\Pr(X_n X_{n+1} \ldots X_{n+k-1} = x_1 x_2 \ldots x_k) = 1/b^k \quad (6)$$

for all b-ary numbers $x_1 x_2 \ldots x_k$. ∎

It is clear from this definition that if $U_0, U_1, \ldots$ is a k-distributed $[0..1)$ sequence, then the sequence $\lfloor bU_0 \rfloor, \lfloor bU_1 \rfloor, \ldots$ is a k-distributed b-ary sequence. (If we set $u_j = x_j/b$, $v_j = (x_j + 1)/b$, $X_n = \lfloor bU_n \rfloor$, Eq. (5) becomes Eq. (6).) Furthermore, every k-distributed b-ary sequence is also $(k - 1)$-distributed, if $k > 1$: We add together the probabilities for the b-ary numbers $x_1 \ldots x_{k-1} 0$, $x_1 \ldots x_{k-1} 1, \ldots, x_1 \ldots x_{k-1}(b - 1)$ to obtain

$$\Pr(X_n \ldots X_{n+k-2} = x_1 \ldots x_{k-1}) = 1/b^{k-1}.$$

(Probabilities for disjoint events are additive; see exercise 4.) It therefore is natural to speak of an ∞-distributed b-ary sequence, as in Definition C above.

The representation of a positive real number in the radix-b number system may be regarded as a b-ary sequence; for example, π corresponds to the 10-ary sequence 3, 1, 4, 1, 5, 9, 2, 6, 5, 3, 5, 8, 9, ... People have conjectured that this sequence is ∞-distributed, but nobody has yet been able to prove that it is even 1-distributed.

Let us analyze these concepts a little more closely in the case when k equals a million. A binary sequence that is 1000000-distributed is going to have runs of a million zeros in a row! Similarly, a $[0..1)$ sequence that is 1000000-distributed is going to have runs of a million consecutive values each of which is less than $\frac{1}{2}$.

It is true that this will happen only $(\frac{1}{2})^{1000000}$ of the time, on the average, but the fact is that it *does* happen. Indeed, this phenomenon will occur in any truly random sequence, using our intuitive notion of "truly random." One can easily imagine that such a situation will have a drastic effect if this set of a million "truly random" numbers is being used in a computer-simulation experiment; there would be good reason to complain about the random number generator. However, if we have a sequence of numbers that never has runs of a million consecutive U's less than $\frac{1}{2}$, the sequence is not random, and it will not be a suitable source of numbers for other conceivable applications that use extremely long blocks of U's as input. In summary, *a truly random sequence will exhibit local nonrandomness.* Local nonrandomness is necessary in some applications, but it is disastrous in others. We are forced to conclude that no sequence of "random" numbers can be adequate for every application.

In a similar vein, one may argue that it is impossible to judge whether a *finite* sequence is random or not; any particular sequence is just as likely as any other one. These facts are definitely stumbling blocks if we are ever to have a useful definition of randomness, but they are not really cause for alarm. It is still possible to give a definition for the randomness of infinite sequences of real numbers in such a way that the corresponding theory (viewed properly) will give us a great deal of insight concerning the ordinary finite sequences of rational numbers that are actually generated on a computer. Furthermore, we shall see later in this section that there are several plausible definitions of randomness for finite sequences.

B. ∞-distributed sequences. Let us now make a brief study of the theory of sequences that are ∞-distributed. To describe the theory adequately, we will need to use a bit of higher mathematics, so we assume in the remainder of this subsection that the reader knows the material ordinarily taught in an "advanced calculus" course.

First it is convenient to generalize Definition A, since the limit appearing there does not exist for all sequences. We define

$$\overline{\Pr}\big(S(n)\big) = \limsup_{n\to\infty} \frac{\nu(n)}{n}, \qquad \underline{\Pr}\big(S(n)\big) = \liminf_{n\to\infty} \frac{\nu(n)}{n}. \tag{7}$$

Then $\Pr\big(S(n)\big)$, if it exists, is the common value of $\underline{\Pr}\big(S(n)\big)$ and $\overline{\Pr}\big(S(n)\big)$.

We have seen that a k-distributed $[0 \mathinner{.\,.} 1)$ sequence leads to a k-distributed b-ary sequence, if U is replaced by $\lfloor bU \rfloor$. Our first theorem shows that a converse result is also true.

Theorem A. *Let $\langle U_n \rangle = U_0, U_1, U_2, \ldots$ be a $[0 \mathinner{.\,.} 1)$ sequence. If the sequence*

$$\langle \lfloor b_j U_n \rfloor \rangle = \lfloor b_j U_0 \rfloor, \lfloor b_j U_1 \rfloor, \lfloor b_j U_2 \rfloor, \ldots$$

is a k-distributed b_j-ary sequence for all b_j in an infinite sequence of integers $1 < b_1 < b_2 < b_3 < \cdots$, then the original sequence $\langle U_n \rangle$ is k-distributed.

As an example of this theorem, suppose that $b_j = 2^j$. The sequence $\lfloor 2^j U_0 \rfloor, \lfloor 2^j U_1 \rfloor, \ldots$ is essentially the sequence of the first j bits of the binary representations of U_0, U_1, ... If all these 2^j-ary sequences are k-distributed, in the sense of Definition D, then the real-valued sequence U_0, U_1, ... must also be k-distributed in the sense of Definition B.

Proof of Theorem A. If the sequence $\lfloor bU_0 \rfloor$, $\lfloor bU_1 \rfloor$, ... is k-distributed, it follows by the addition of probabilities that Eq. (5) holds whenever each u_j and v_j is a rational number with denominator b. Now let u_j, v_j be any real numbers, and let u'_j, v'_j be rational numbers with denominator b such that

$$u'_j \le u_j < u'_j + 1/b, \qquad v'_j \le v_j < v'_j + 1/b.$$

Let $S(n)$ be the statement that $u_1 \le U_n < v_1, \ldots, u_k \le U_{n+k-1} < v_k$. We have

$$\overline{\Pr}\bigl(S(n)\bigr) \le \Pr\left(u'_1 \le U_n < v'_1 + \frac{1}{b}, \ \ldots, \ u'_k \le U_{n+k-1} < v'_k + \frac{1}{b}\right)$$
$$= \left(v'_1 - u'_1 + \frac{1}{b}\right) \ldots \left(v'_k - u'_k + \frac{1}{b}\right);$$

$$\underline{\Pr}\bigl(S(n)\bigr) \ge \Pr\left(u'_1 + \frac{1}{b} \le U_n < v'_1, \ \ldots, \ u'_k + \frac{1}{b} \le U_{n+k-1} < v'_k\right)$$
$$= \left(v'_1 - u'_1 - \frac{1}{b}\right) \ldots \left(v'_k - u'_k - \frac{1}{b}\right).$$

Now $\bigl|(v'_j - u'_j \pm 1/b) - (v_j - u_j)\bigr| \le 2/b$. Since our inequalities hold for all $b = b_j$, and since $b_j \to \infty$ as $j \to \infty$, we have

$$(v_1 - u_1) \ldots (v_k - u_k) \le \underline{\Pr}\bigl(S(n)\bigr) \le \overline{\Pr}\bigl(S(n)\bigr) \le (v_1 - u_1) \ldots (v_k - u_k). \quad \blacksquare$$

The next theorem is our main tool for proving things about k-distributed sequences.

Theorem B. *Suppose that $\langle U_n \rangle$ is a k-distributed $[0 \mathinner{.\,.} 1)$ sequence, and let $f(x_1, x_2, \ldots, x_k)$ be a Riemann-integrable function of k variables; then*

$$\lim_{n \to \infty} \frac{1}{n} \sum_{0 \le j < n} f(U_j, U_{j+1}, \ldots, U_{j+k-1}) = \int_0^1 \cdots \int_0^1 f(x_1, x_2, \ldots, x_k)\, dx_1 \ldots dx_k. \tag{8}$$

Proof. The definition of a k-distributed sequence states that this result is true in the special case that

$$f(x_1, \ldots, x_k) = [u_1 \le x_1 < v_1, \ \ldots, \ u_k \le x_k < v_k] \tag{9}$$

for some constants u_1, v_1, $\ldots$, u_k, v_k. Therefore Eq. (8) is true whenever $f = a_1 f_1 + a_2 f_2 + \cdots + a_m f_m$ and when each f_j is a function of type (9); in other words, Eq. (8) holds whenever f is a "step-function" obtained by partitioning the unit k-dimensional cube into subcells whose faces are parallel to the coordinate axes, and assigning a constant value to f on each subcell.

Now let f be any Riemann-integrable function. If ϵ is any positive number, we know (by the definition of Riemann-integrability) that there exist step functions $\underline{f}$ and $\overline{f}$ such that $\underline{f}(x_1, \ldots, x_k) \le f(x_1, \ldots, x_k) \le \overline{f}(x_1, \ldots, x_k)$, and such that the difference of the integrals of $\underline{f}$ and $\overline{f}$ is less than ϵ. Since Eq. (8) holds for $\underline{f}$ and $\overline{f}$, and since

$$\frac{1}{n} \sum_{0 \le j < n} \underline{f}(U_j, \ldots, U_{j+k-1}) \le \frac{1}{n} \sum_{0 \le j < n} f(U_j, \ldots, U_{j+k-1})$$

$$\le \frac{1}{n} \sum_{0 \le j < n} \overline{f}(U_j, \ldots, U_{j+k-1}),$$

we conclude that Eq. (8) is true also for f. ∎

Theorem B can be applied, for example, to the *permutation test* of Section 3.3.2. Let $(p_1, p_2, \ldots, p_k)$ be any permutation of the numbers $\{1, 2, \ldots, k\}$; we want to show that

$$\Pr(U_{n+p_1-1} < U_{n+p_2-1} < \cdots < U_{n+p_k-1}) = 1/k!. \tag{10}$$

To prove this, assume that the sequence $\langle U_n \rangle$ is k-distributed, and let

$$f(x_1, \ldots, x_k) = [x_{p_1} < x_{p_2} < \cdots < x_{p_k}].$$

We have

$$\Pr(U_{n+p_1-1} < U_{n+p_2-1} < \cdots < U_{n+p_k-1})$$

$$= \int_0^1 \cdots \int_0^1 f(x_1, \ldots, x_k) \, dx_1 \ldots dx_k$$

$$= \int_0^1 dx_{p_k} \int_0^{x_{p_k}} \cdots \int_0^{x_{p_3}} dx_{p_2} \int_0^{x_{p_2}} dx_{p_1} = \frac{1}{k!}.$$

Corollary P. *If a* $[0\,..\,1)$ *sequence is k-distributed, it satisfies the permutation test of order k, in the sense of Eq. (10).* ∎

We can also show that the *serial correlation test* is satisfied:

Corollary S. *If a* $[0\,..\,1)$ *sequence is $(k+1)$-distributed, the serial correlation coefficient between U_n and U_{n+k} tends to zero:*

$$\lim_{n \to \infty} \frac{\frac{1}{n} \sum U_j U_{j+k} - \left(\frac{1}{n} \sum U_j\right)\left(\frac{1}{n} \sum U_{j+k}\right)}{\sqrt{\left(\frac{1}{n} \sum U_j^2 - \left(\frac{1}{n} \sum U_j\right)^2\right)\left(\frac{1}{n} \sum U_{j+k}^2 - \left(\frac{1}{n} \sum U_{j+k}\right)^2\right)}} = 0.$$

(All summations here are for $0 \le j < n$.)

Proof. By Theorem B, the quantities

$$\frac{1}{n} \sum U_j U_{j+k}, \qquad \frac{1}{n} \sum U_j^2, \qquad \frac{1}{n} \sum U_{j+k}^2, \qquad \frac{1}{n} \sum U_j, \qquad \frac{1}{n} \sum U_{j+k}$$

tend to the respective limits $\frac{1}{4}, \frac{1}{3}, \frac{1}{3}, \frac{1}{2}, \frac{1}{2}$ as $n \to \infty$. ∎

Let us now consider some slightly more general distribution properties of sequences. We have defined the notion of k-distribution by considering all of the adjacent k-tuples; for example, a sequence is 2-distributed if and only if the points

$$(U_0, U_1), \ (U_1, U_2), \ (U_2, U_3), \ (U_3, U_4), \ (U_4, U_5), \ \ldots$$

are equidistributed in the unit square. It is quite possible, however, that this can happen while alternate pairs of points (U_1, U_2), (U_3, U_4), (U_5, U_6), $\ldots$ are *not* equidistributed; if the density of points (U_{2n-1}, U_{2n}) is deficient in some area, the other points (U_{2n}, U_{2n+1}) might compensate. For example, the periodic binary sequence

$$\langle X_n \rangle = 0,0,0,1, \ \ 0,0,0,1, \ \ 1,1,0,1, \ \ 1,1,0,1, \ \ 0,0,0,1, \ \ \ldots, \qquad (11)$$

with a period of length 16, is seen to be 3-distributed; yet the sequence of even-numbered elements $\langle X_{2n} \rangle = 0, 0, 0, 0, 1, 0, 1, 0, \ldots$ has three times as many zeros as ones, while the subsequence of odd-numbered elements $\langle X_{2n+1} \rangle = 0, 1,$ 0, 1, 1, 1, 1, 1, $\ldots$ has three times as many ones as zeros.

Suppose the sequence $\langle U_n \rangle$ is ∞-distributed. Example (11) shows that the subsequence of alternate terms $\langle U_{2n} \rangle = U_0, U_2, U_4, U_6, \ldots$ is not obviously guaranteed to be ∞-distributed or even 1-distributed. But we shall see that $\langle U_{2n} \rangle$ is, in fact, ∞-distributed, and much more is true.

Definition E. *A $[0..1)$ sequence $\langle U_n \rangle$ is said to be (m, k)-distributed if*

$$\Pr(u_1 \leq U_{mn+j} < v_1, \ u_2 \leq U_{mn+j+1} < v_2, \ \ldots, \ u_k \leq U_{mn+j+k-1} < v_k)$$
$$= (v_1 - u_1) \ldots (v_k - u_k)$$

for all choices of real numbers u_r, v_r with $0 \leq u_r < v_r \leq 1$ for $1 \leq r \leq k$, and for all integers j with $0 \leq j < m$. ∎

Thus a k-distributed sequence is the special case $m = 1$ in Definition E; the case $m = 2$ means that the k-tuples starting in even positions must have the same density as the k-tuples starting in odd positions, etc.

The following properties of Definition E are obvious:

An (m, k)-distributed sequence is (m, κ)-distributed for $1 \leq \kappa \leq k$. $\qquad (12)$

An (m, k)-distributed sequence is (d, k)-distributed for all divisors d of m. $\quad (13)$

(See exercise 8.) We can also define the concept of an (m, k)-distributed b-ary sequence, as in Definition D; and the proof of Theorem A remains valid for (m, k)-distributed sequences.

The next theorem, which is in many ways rather surprising, shows that the property of being ∞-distributed is very strong indeed, much stronger than we imagined it to be when we first considered the definition of the concept.

Theorem C (Ivan Niven and H. S. Zuckerman). *An ∞-distributed sequence is (m, k)-distributed for all positive integers m and k.*

Proof. It suffices to prove the theorem for b-ary sequences, by using the generalization of Theorem A just mentioned. Furthermore, we may assume that $m = k$, because (12) and (13) tell us that the sequence will be (m, k)-distributed if it is (mk, mk)-distributed.

So we will prove that *any ∞-distributed b-ary sequence $X_0, X_1, \ldots$ is (m, m)-distributed for all positive integers m.* Our proof is a simplified version of the original one given by Niven and Zuckerman in *Pacific J. Math.* **1** (1951), 103–109.

The key idea we shall use is an important technique that applies to many situations in mathematics: "If the sum of m quantities and the sum of their squares are both consistent with the hypothesis that the m quantities are equal, then that hypothesis is true." In a strong form, this principle may be stated as follows:

Lemma E. *Given m sequences of numbers $\langle y_{jn} \rangle = y_{j0}, y_{j1}, \ldots$ for $1 \leq j \leq m$, suppose that*

$$\lim_{n \to \infty} (y_{1n} + y_{2n} + \cdots + y_{mn}) = m\alpha,$$

$$\limsup_{n \to \infty} (y_{1n}^2 + y_{2n}^2 + \cdots + y_{mn}^2) \leq m\alpha^2. \qquad (14)$$

Then for each j, $\lim_{n \to \infty} y_{jn}$ exists and equals α.

An incredibly simple proof of this lemma is given in exercise 9.   ∎

Resuming our proof of Theorem C, let $x = x_1 x_2 \ldots x_m$ be a b-ary number, and say that x *occurs at position* p if $X_{p-m+1} X_{p-m+2} \ldots X_p = x$. Let $\nu_j(n)$ be the number of occurrences of x at position p when $p < n$ and $p \bmod m = j$. Let $y_{jn} = \nu_j(n)/n$; we wish to prove that

$$\lim_{n \to \infty} y_{jn} = \frac{1}{m b^m}. \qquad (15)$$

First we know that

$$\lim_{n \to \infty} (y_{0n} + y_{1n} + \cdots + y_{(m-1)n}) = \frac{1}{b^m}, \qquad (16)$$

since the sequence is m-distributed. By Lemma E and Eq. (16), the theorem will be proved if we can show that

$$\limsup_{n \to \infty} (y_{0n}^2 + y_{1n}^2 + \cdots + y_{(m-1)n}^2) \leq \frac{1}{m b^{2m}}. \qquad (17)$$

This inequality is not obvious yet; some rather delicate maneuvering is necessary before we can prove it. Let q be a multiple of m, and consider

$$C(n) = \sum_{0 \leq j < m} \binom{\nu_j(n) - \nu_j(n - q)}{2}. \qquad (18)$$

This is the number of pairs of occurrences of x in positions p_1 and p_2 for which $n - q \leq p_1 < p_2 < n$ and $p_2 - p_1$ is a multiple of m. Consider now the sum

$$S_N = \sum_{n=1}^{N+q} C(n). \qquad (19)$$

Each pair of occurrences of x in positions p_1 and p_2 with $p_1 < p_2 < p_1 + q$, where $p_2 - p_1$ is a multiple of m and $p_1 \le N$, is counted exactly $p_1 + q - p_2$ times in the total S_N (namely, when $p_2 < n \le p_1 + q$); and the pairs of such occurrences with $N < p_1 < p_2 < N + q$ are counted exactly $N + q - p_2$ times.

Let $d_t(n)$ be the number of pairs of occurrences of x in positions p_1 and p_2 with $p_1 + t = p_2 < n$. The analysis above shows that

$$\sum_{0 < t < q/m} (q - mt) d_{mt}(N + q) \ge S_N \ge \sum_{0 < t < q/m} (q - mt) d_{mt}(N). \qquad (20)$$

Since the original sequence is q-distributed,

$$\lim_{N \to \infty} \frac{1}{N} d_{mt}(N) = \frac{1}{b^{2m}} \qquad (21)$$

for all t, $0 < t < q/m$, and therefore by (20) we have

$$\lim_{N \to \infty} \frac{S_N}{N} = \sum_{0 < t < q/m} \frac{q - mt}{b^{2m}} = \frac{q(q - m)}{2mb^{2m}}. \qquad (22)$$

This fact will prove the theorem, after some manipulation.

By definition,

$$2S_N = \sum_{n=1}^{N+q} \sum_{0 \le j < m} \left((\nu_j(n) - \nu_j(n - q))^2 - (\nu_j(n) - \nu_j(n - q)) \right),$$

and we can remove the unsquared terms by applying (16) to get

$$\lim_{N \to \infty} \frac{T_N}{N} = \frac{q(q - m)}{mb^{2m}} + \frac{q}{b^m}, \qquad (23)$$

where

$$T_N = \sum_{n=1}^{N+q} \sum_{0 \le j < m} \left(\nu_j(n) - \nu_j(n - q) \right)^2.$$

Using the inequality

$$\frac{1}{r} \left(\sum_{j=1}^{r} a_j \right)^2 \le \sum_{j=1}^{r} a_j^2$$

(see exercise 1.2.3–30), we find that

$$\limsup_{N \to \infty} \sum_{0 \le j < m} \frac{1}{N(N + q)} \left(\sum_{n=1}^{N+q} (\nu_j(n) - \nu_j(n - q)) \right)^2 \le \frac{q(q - m)}{mb^{2m}} + \frac{q}{b^m}. \qquad (24)$$

We also have

$$q \nu_j(N) \le \sum_{N < n \le N+q} \nu_j(n) = \sum_{n=1}^{N+q} (\nu_j(n) - \nu_j(n - q)) \le q \nu_j(N + q),$$

and putting this into (24) gives

$$\limsup_{N \to \infty} \sum_{0 \le j < m} \left(\frac{\nu_j(N)}{N} \right)^2 \le \frac{q - m}{q m b^{2m}} + \frac{1}{q b^m}. \tag{25}$$

This formula has been established whenever q is a multiple of m; and if we let $q \to \infty$ we obtain (17), completing the proof.

For a possibly simpler proof, see J. W. S. Cassels, *Pacific J. Math.* **2** (1952), 555–557. ∎

Exercises 29 and 30 illustrate the nontriviality of this theorem, and they also demonstrate the fact that a q-distributed sequence will have probabilities deviating from the true (m, m)-distribution probabilities by essentially $1/\sqrt{q}$ at most. (See (25).) The full hypothesis of ∞-distribution is necessary for the proof of the theorem.

As a result of Theorem C, we can prove that an ∞-distributed sequence passes the serial test, the maximum-of-t test, the collision test, the birthday spacings test, and the tests on subsequences mentioned in Section 3.3.2. It is not hard to show that the gap test, the poker test, and the run test are also satisfied (see exercises 12 through 14). The coupon collector's test is considerably more difficult to deal with, but it too is passed (see exercises 15 and 16).

The existence of ∞-distributed sequences of a rather simple type is guaranteed by the next theorem.

Theorem F (J. N. Franklin). *The* $[0 \mathinner{.\,.} 1)$ *sequence* $U_0, U_1, U_2, \dots$ *with*

$$U_n = \theta^n \bmod 1 \tag{26}$$

is ∞-distributed for almost all real numbers $\theta > 1$. That is, the set

$$\{\theta \mid \theta > 1 \text{ and } (26) \text{ is not } \infty\text{-distributed}\}$$

is of measure zero.

The proofs of this theorem and some generalizations are given in *Math. Comp.* **17** (1963), 28–59. ∎

Franklin has shown that θ must be a transcendental number for (26) to be ∞-distributed. Early in the 1960s, the powers $\langle \pi^n \bmod 1 \rangle$ were laboriously computed for $n \le 10000$ using multiple-precision arithmetic; and the most significant 35 bits of each of these numbers, stored on a disk file, were used successfully as a source of uniform deviates. According to Theorem F, the probability that the powers $\langle \pi^n \bmod 1 \rangle$ are ∞-distributed is equal to 1; yet there are uncountably many real numbers, so the theorem gives us no information about whether the sequence for π is really ∞-distributed or not. It is a fairly safe bet that nobody in our lifetimes will ever *prove* that this particular sequence is *not* ∞-distributed; but it might not be. Because of these considerations, one may legitimately wonder if there is any *explicit* sequence that is ∞-distributed: *Is there an algorithm to compute real numbers U_n for all $n \ge 0$, such that* *the sequence* $\langle U_n \rangle$ *is* ∞-*distributed?* The answer is yes, as shown for example by D. E. Knuth in *BIT* **5** (1965), 246–250. The sequence constructed there consists entirely of rational numbers; in fact, each number U_n has a terminating representation in the binary number system. Another construction of an explicit ∞-distributed sequence, somewhat more complicated than the sequence just cited, follows from Theorem W below. See also N. M. Korobov, *Izv. Akad. Nauk SSSR* **20** (1956), 649–660.

C. Does ∞-distributed = random? In view of all the theoretical results about ∞-distributed sequences, we can be sure of one thing: The concept of an ∞-distributed sequence is an important one in mathematics. There is also a good deal of evidence that the following statement might be a valid formulation of the intuitive idea of randomness:

Definition R1. *A* $[0..1)$ *sequence is defined to be "random" if it is an* ∞-*distributed sequence.* ∎

We have seen that sequences meeting this definition will satisfy all the statistical tests of Section 3.3.2 and many more.

Let us attempt to criticize this definition objectively. First of all, is every "truly random" sequence ∞-distributed? There are uncountably many sequences $U_0, U_1, \ldots$ of real numbers between zero and one. If a truly random number generator is sampled to give values $U_0, U_1, \ldots$, any of the possible sequences may be considered equally likely, and some of the sequences (indeed, uncountably many of them) are not even equidistributed. On the other hand, using any reasonable definition of probability on this space of all possible sequences leads us to conclude that a random sequence is ∞-distributed *with probability one*. We are therefore led to formalize Franklin's definition of randomness (as given at the beginning of this section) in the following way:

Definition R2. *A* $[0..1)$ *sequence* $\langle U_n \rangle$ *is defined to be "random" if, whenever P is a property such that* $P(\langle V_n \rangle)$ *holds with probability one for a sequence* $\langle V_n \rangle$ *of independent samples of random variables from the uniform distribution, then* $P(\langle U_n \rangle)$ *is true.* ∎

Is it perhaps possible that Definition R1 is equivalent to Definition R2? Let us try out some possible objections to Definition R1, and see whether these criticisms are valid.

In the first place, Definition R1 deals only with limiting properties of the sequence as $n \to \infty$. There are ∞-distributed sequences in which the first million elements are all zero; should such a sequence be considered random?

This objection is not very substantial. If ϵ is any positive number, there is no reason why the first million elements of a sequence should not all be less than ϵ. With probability one, a truly random sequence contains infinitely many runs of a million consecutive elements less than ϵ, so why can't this happen at the beginning of the sequence?

On the other hand, consider Definition R2 and let P be the property that all elements of the sequence are distinct; P is true with probability one, so any sequence with a million zeros is not random by *this* criterion.

Now let P be the property that *no* element of the sequence is equal to zero; again, P is true with probability one, so by Definition R2 any sequence with a zero element is nonrandom. More generally, however, let x_0 be any fixed number between zero and one, and let P be the property that no element of the sequence is equal to x_0; Definition R2 now says that no random sequence may contain the element x_0! We can now prove that *no sequence satisfies the condition of Definition R2.* (For if $U_0, U_1, \ldots$ is such a sequence, take $x_0 = U_0$.)

Therefore if R1 is too weak a definition, R2 is certainly too strong. The "right" definition must be less strict than R2. We have not really shown that R1 is too weak, however, so let us continue to attack it some more. As mentioned above, an ∞-distributed sequence of *rational* numbers has been constructed. (Indeed, this is not so surprising; see exercise 18.) Almost all real numbers are irrational; perhaps we should insist that

$$\Pr(U_n \text{ is rational}) = 0$$

for a random sequence.

The definition of equidistribution, Eq. (2), says that $\Pr(u \le U_n < v) = v - u$. There is an obvious way to generalize this definition, using measure theory: "If $S \subseteq [0\,..\,1)$ is a set of measure μ, then

$$\Pr(U_n \in S) = \mu, \tag{27}$$

for all random sequences $\langle U_n \rangle$." In particular, if S is the set of rationals, it has measure zero, so no sequence of rational numbers is equidistributed in this generalized sense. It is reasonable to expect that Theorem B could be extended to Lebesgue integration instead of Riemann integration, if property (27) is stipulated. However, once again we find that definition (27) is too strict, for *no* sequence satisfies that property. If $U_0, U_1, \ldots$ is any sequence, the set $S = \{U_0, U_1, \ldots\}$ is of measure zero, yet $\Pr(U_n \in S) = 1$. Thus, by the force of the same argument we used to exclude rationals from random sequences, we can exclude all random sequences.

So far Definition R1 has proved to be defensible. There are, however, some quite valid objections to it. For example, if we have a random sequence in the intuitive sense, the infinite subsequence

$$U_0, \ U_1, \ U_4, \ U_9, \ \ldots, \ U_{n^2}, \ \ldots \tag{28}$$

should also be a random sequence. This is not always true for an ∞-distributed sequence. In fact, if we take any ∞-distributed sequence and set $U_{n^2} \leftarrow 0$ for all n, the counts $\nu_k(n)$ that appear in the test of k-distributivity are changed by at most $\sqrt{n}$, so the limits of the ratios $\nu_k(n)/n$ remain unchanged. Definition R1 unfortunately fails to satisfy this randomness criterion.

Perhaps we should strengthen R1 as follows:

Definition R3. *A* $[0..1)$ *sequence is said to be "random" if each of its infinite subsequences is ∞-distributed.* ∎

Once again, however, the definition turns out to be too strict; any equidistributed sequence $\langle U_n \rangle$ has a monotonic subsequence with $U_{s_0} < U_{s_1} < U_{s_2} < \cdots$.

The secret is to restrict the subsequences so that they could be defined by a person who does not look at U_n before deciding whether or not it is to be in the subsequence. The following definition now suggests itself:

Definition R4. *A* $[0..1)$ *sequence $\langle U_n \rangle$ is said to be "random" if, for every effective algorithm that specifies an infinite sequence of distinct nonnegative integers s_n for $n \geq 0$, the subsequence $U_{s_0}, U_{s_1}, U_{s_2}, \ldots$ corresponding to this algorithm is ∞-distributed.* ∎

The algorithms referred to in Definition R4 are effective procedures that compute s_n, given n. (See the discussion in Section 1.1.) Thus, for example, the sequence $\langle \pi^n \bmod 1 \rangle$ will *not* satisfy R4, since it is either not equidistributed or there is an effective algorithm that determines an infinite subsequence s_n with $(\pi^{s_0} \bmod 1) < (\pi^{s_1} \bmod 1) < (\pi^{s_2} \bmod 1) < \cdots$. Similarly, *no explicitly defined sequence can satisfy Definition R4*; this is appropriate, if we agree that no explicitly defined sequence can really be random. The explicit-looking sequence $\langle \theta^n \bmod 1 \rangle$ actually does, however, satisfy Definition R4, for almost all real numbers $\theta > 1$; this is no contradiction, since almost all θ are uncomputable by algorithms. J. F. Koksma proved that $\langle \theta^{s_n} \bmod 1 \rangle$ is 1-distributed for almost all $\theta > 1$, if $\langle s_n \rangle$ is any sequence of distinct positive integers [*Compositio Math.* **2** (1935), 250–258]; H. Niederreiter and R. F. Tichy strengthened Koksma's theorem, replacing "1-distributed" by "∞-distributed" [*Mathematika* **32** (1985), 26–32]. Only countably many sequences $\langle s_n \rangle$ are effectively definable, so $\langle \theta^n \bmod 1 \rangle$ almost always satisfies R4.

Definition R4 is much stronger than Definition R1; but it is still reasonable to claim that Definition R4 is too weak. For example, let $\langle U_n \rangle$ be a truly random sequence, and define the subsequence $\langle U_{s_n} \rangle$ by the following rules: $s_0 = 0$; and if $n > 0$, s_n is the smallest integer $\geq n$ for which $U_{s_n-1}, U_{s_n-2}, \ldots, U_{s_n-n}$ are all less than $\frac{1}{2}$. Thus we are considering the subsequence of values following the first consecutive run of n values less than $\frac{1}{2}$. Suppose that "$U_n < \frac{1}{2}$" corresponds to the value "heads" in the flipping of a coin. Gamblers tend to feel that a long run of "heads" makes the opposite condition, "tails," more probable, assuming that a true coin is being used; and the subsequence $\langle U_{s_n} \rangle$ just defined corresponds to a gambling system for a man who places his nth bet on the coin toss following the first run of n consecutive "heads." The gambler may think that $\Pr(U_{s_n} \geq \frac{1}{2})$ is more than $\frac{1}{2}$, but of course in a truly random sequence $\langle U_{s_n} \rangle$ will be completely random. No gambling system will ever be able to beat the odds! Definition R4 says nothing about subsequences formed according to such a gambling system, so apparently we need something more.

Let us define a "subsequence rule" $\mathcal{R}$ as an infinite sequence of functions $\langle f_n(x_1, \ldots, x_n) \rangle$ where, for $n \geq 0$, f_n is a function of n variables, and the value of $f_n(x_1, \ldots, x_n)$ is either 0 or 1. Here $x_1, \ldots, x_n$ are elements of some set S. (Thus, in particular, f_0 is a constant function, either 0 or 1.) A subsequence rule $\mathcal{R}$ defines a subsequence of any infinite sequence $\langle X_n \rangle$ of elements of S as follows: *The nth term X_n is in the subsequence $\langle X_n \rangle \mathcal{R}$ if and only if $f_n(X_0, X_1, \ldots, X_{n-1}) = 1$.* Note that the subsequence $\langle X_n \rangle \mathcal{R}$ thus defined is not necessarily infinite, and it may in fact contain no elements at all.

For example, the gambler's subsequence just described corresponds to the following subsequence rule: "$f_0 = 1$; and for $n > 0$, $f_n(x_1, \ldots, x_n) = 1$ if and only if there is some k in the range $0 < k \leq n$ such that the k consecutive parameters $x_m, x_{m-1}, \ldots, x_{m-k+1}$ are all $< \frac{1}{2}$ when $m = n$ but not when $k \leq m < n$."

A subsequence rule $\mathcal{R}$ is said to be *computable* if there is an effective algorithm that determines the value of $f_n(x_1, \ldots, x_n)$, when n and $x_1, \ldots, x_n$ are given as input. We had better restrict ourselves to computable subsequence rules when trying to define randomness, lest we obtain an overly restrictive definition like R3 above. But effective algorithms cannot deal nicely with arbitrary real numbers as inputs; for example, if a real number x is specified by an infinite radix-10 expansion, there is no algorithm to determine if x is $< \frac{1}{3}$ or not, since all digits of the number $0.333\ldots$ have to be examined. Therefore computable subsequence rules do not apply to all $[0 \,..\, 1)$ sequences, and it is convenient to base our next definition on b-ary sequences.

Definition R5. *A b-ary sequence is said to be "random" if every infinite subsequence defined by a computable subsequence rule is 1-distributed.* ∎

A $[0 \,..\, 1)$ sequence $\langle U_n \rangle$ is said to be "random" if the b-ary sequence $\langle \lfloor bU_n \rfloor \rangle$ is "random" for all integers $b \geq 2$.

Note that Definition R5 says only "1-distributed," not "∞-distributed." It is interesting to verify that this may be done without loss of generality. For we may define an obviously computable subsequence rule $\mathcal{R}(a_1 \ldots a_k)$ as follows, given any b-ary number $a_1 \ldots a_k$: Let $f_n(x_1, \ldots, x_n) = 1$ if and only if $n \geq k - 1$ and $x_{n-k+1} = a_1, \ldots, x_{n-1} = a_{k-1}, x_n = a_k$. Now if $\langle X_n \rangle$ is a k-distributed b-ary sequence, this rule $\mathcal{R}(a_1 \ldots a_k)$ — which selects the subsequence consisting of those terms just following an occurrence of $a_1 \ldots a_k$ — defines an infinite subsequence; and if this subsequence is 1-distributed, each of the $(k+1)$-tuples $a_1 \ldots a_k a_{k+1}$ for $0 \leq a_{k+1} < b$ occurs with probability $1/b^{k+1}$ in $\langle X_n \rangle$. Thus we can prove that a sequence satisfying Definition R5 is k-distributed for all k, by induction on k. Similarly, by considering the "composition" of subsequence rules — if $\mathcal{R}_1$ defines an infinite subsequence $\langle X_n \rangle \mathcal{R}_1$, then we can define $\mathcal{R}_1 \mathcal{R}_2$ to be the subsequence rule for which $\langle X_n \rangle \mathcal{R}_1 \mathcal{R}_2 = (\langle X_n \rangle \mathcal{R}_1) \mathcal{R}_2$ — we find that all subsequences considered in Definition R5 are ∞-distributed. (See exercise 32.)

The fact that ∞-distribution comes out of Definition R5 as a very special case is encouraging, and it is a good indication that we may at last have found the definition of randomness we have been seeking. But alas, there still is a problem. It is not clear that sequences satisfying Definition R5 must satisfy Definition R4. The "computable subsequence rules" we have just specified always enumerate subsequences $\langle X_{s_n} \rangle$ for which $s_0 < s_1 < \cdots$, but $\langle s_n \rangle$ does not have to be monotone in R4; it must only satisfy the condition $s_n \neq s_m$ for $n \neq m$.

To meet this objection, we may combine Definitions R4 and R5 as follows:

Definition R6. *A b-ary sequence $\langle X_n \rangle$ is said to be "random" if, for every effective algorithm that specifies an infinite sequence of distinct nonnegative integers $\langle s_n \rangle$ as a function of n and the values of $X_{s_0}, \ldots, X_{s_{n-1}}$, the subsequence $\langle X_{s_n} \rangle$ corresponding to this algorithm is "random" in the sense of Definition R5.*

A $[0 .. 1)$ sequence $\langle U_n \rangle$ is said to be "random" if the b-ary sequence $\langle \lfloor b U_n \rfloor \rangle$ is "random" for all integers $b \geq 2$. ∎

The author contends[*] that this definition surely meets all reasonable philosophical requirements for randomness, so it provides an answer to the principal question posed in this section.

D. Existence of random sequences. We have seen that Definition R3 is too strong, in the sense that no sequence can satisfy that definition; and the formulation of Definitions R4, R5, and R6 above was carried out in an attempt to recapture the essential characteristics of Definition R3. In order to show that Definition R6 is not overly restrictive, it is still necessary for us to prove that sequences satisfying all these conditions exist. Intuitively, we feel quite sure that there is no problem, because we believe that a truly random sequence exists and satisfies R6; but a proof is really necessary to show that the definition is consistent.

An interesting method for constructing sequences satisfying Definition R5 has been found by A. Wald, starting with a very simple 1-distributed sequence.

Lemma T. *Let the sequence of real numbers $\langle V_n \rangle$ be defined in terms of the binary system as follows:*

$$V_0 = 0, \quad V_1 = .1, \quad V_2 = .01, \quad V_3 = .11, \quad V_4 = .001, \quad \cdots$$
$$V_n = .c_r \ldots c_1 1 \quad \text{if } n = 2^r + c_1 2^{r-1} + \cdots + c_r. \tag{29}$$

Let $I_{b_1 \ldots b_r}$ denote the set of all real numbers in $[0 .. 1)$ whose binary representation begins with $0.b_1 \ldots b_r$; thus

$$I_{b_1 \ldots b_r} = \left[(0.b_1 \ldots b_r)_2 \,..\, (0.b_1 \ldots b_r)_2 + 2^{-r} \right). \tag{30}$$

Then if $\nu(n)$ denotes the number of V_k in $I_{b_1 \ldots b_r}$ for $0 \leq k < n$, we have

$$\left| \nu(n)/n - 2^{-r} \right| \leq 1/n. \tag{31}$$

Proof. Since $\nu(n)$ is the number of k for which $k \bmod 2^r = (b_r \ldots b_1)_2$, we have $\nu(n) = t$ or $t + 1$ when $\lfloor n/2^r \rfloor = t$. Hence $\left| \nu(n) - n/2^r \right| \leq 1$. ∎

It follows from (31) that the sequence $\langle \lfloor 2^r V_n \rfloor \rangle$ is an equidistributed 2^r-ary sequence; hence by Theorem A, $\langle V_n \rangle$ is an equidistributed $[0 .. 1)$ sequence. Indeed, it is pretty clear that $\langle V_n \rangle$ is about as equidistributed as a $[0 .. 1)$ sequence can be. (For further discussion of this and related sequences, see J. G. van der

---

[*] At least, he made such a contention when originally preparing this material in 1966.

Corput, *Proc. Koninklijke Nederl. Akad. Wetenschappen* **38** (1935), 813–821, 1058–1066; J. H. Halton, *Numerische Math.* **2** (1960), 84–90, 196; S. Haber, *J. Research National Bur. Standards* **B70** (1966), 127–136; R. Béjian and H. Faure, *Comptes Rendus Acad. Sci.* **A285** (Paris, 1977), 313–316; H. Faure, *J. Number Theory* **22** (1986), 4–20; S. Tezuka, *ACM Trans. Modeling and Comp. Simul.* **3** (1993), 99–107. L. H. Ramshaw has shown that the sequence $\langle \phi n \bmod 1 \rangle$ is slightly more equally distributed than $\langle V_n \rangle$; see *J. Number Theory* **13** (1981), 138–175.)

Now let $\mathcal{R}_1, \mathcal{R}_2, \ldots$ be infinitely many subsequence rules; we seek a sequence $\langle U_n \rangle$ for which all the infinite subsequences $\langle U_n \rangle \mathcal{R}_j$ are equidistributed.

Algorithm W (*Wald sequence*). Given an infinite sequence of subsequence rules $\mathcal{R}_1, \mathcal{R}_2, \ldots$ that define subsequences of $[0 \mathinner{.\,.} 1)$ sequences of rational numbers, this procedure defines a $[0 \mathinner{.\,.} 1)$ sequence $\langle U_n \rangle$. The computation involves infinitely many auxiliary variables $C[a_1, \ldots, a_r]$, where $r \geq 1$ and where $a_j = 0$ or 1 for $1 \leq j \leq r$. These variables are initially all zero.

W1. [Initialize n.] Set $n \leftarrow 0$.

W2. [Initialize r.] Set $r \leftarrow 1$.

W3. [Test $\mathcal{R}_r$.] If the element U_n is to be in the subsequence defined by $\mathcal{R}_r$, based on the values of U_k for $0 \leq k < n$, set $a_r \leftarrow 1$; otherwise set $a_r \leftarrow 0$.

W4. [Is case $[a_1, \ldots, a_r]$ unfinished?] If $C[a_1, \ldots, a_r] < 3 \cdot 4^{r-1}$, go to W6.

W5. [Increase r.] Set $r \leftarrow r + 1$ and return to W3.

W6. [Set U_n.] Increase the value of $C[a_1, \ldots, a_r]$ by 1 and let k be its new value. Set $U_n \leftarrow V_k$, where V_k is defined in Lemma T above.

W7. [Advance n.] Increase n by 1 and return to W2. ∎

Strictly speaking, this is not an algorithm, since it doesn't terminate; but we could of course easily modify the procedure to make it stop when n reaches a given value. In order to grasp the idea of the construction, the reader is advised to try it out manually, replacing the number $3 \cdot 4^{r-1}$ of step W4 by 2^r during this exercise.

Algorithm W is not meant to be a practical source of random numbers. It is intended to serve only a theoretical purpose:

Theorem W. *Let $\langle U_n \rangle$ be the sequence of rational numbers defined by Algorithm W, and let k be a positive integer. If the subsequence $\langle U_n \rangle \mathcal{R}_k$ is infinite, it is 1-distributed.*

Proof. Let $A[a_1, \ldots, a_r]$ denote the (possibly empty) subsequence of $\langle U_n \rangle$ containing precisely those elements U_n that, for all $j \leq r$, belong to subsequence $\langle U_n \rangle \mathcal{R}_j$ if $a_j = 1$ and do not belong to subsequence $\langle U_n \rangle \mathcal{R}_j$ if $a_j = 0$.

It suffices to prove, for all $r \geq 1$ and all pairs of binary numbers $a_1 \ldots a_r$ and $b_1 \ldots b_r$, that $\Pr(U_n \in I_{b_1 \ldots b_r}) = 2^{-r}$ with respect to the subsequence $A[a_1, \ldots, a_r]$, whenever the latter is infinite. (See Eq. (30).) For if $r \geq k$, the infinite sequence $\langle U_n \rangle \mathcal{R}_k$ is the finite union of the disjoint subsequences

$A[a_1, \ldots, a_r]$ for $a_k = 1$ and $a_j = 0$ or 1 for $1 \leq j \leq r$, $j \neq k$; and it follows that $\Pr(U_n \in I_{b_1 \ldots b_r}) = 2^{-r}$ with respect to $\langle U_n \rangle \mathcal{R}_k$. (See exercise 33.) This is enough to show that the sequence is 1-distributed, by Theorem A.

Let $B[a_1, \ldots, a_r]$ denote the subsequence of $\langle U_n \rangle$ that consists of the values for those n in which $C[a_1, \ldots, a_r]$ is increased by one in step W6 of the algorithm. By the algorithm, $B[a_1, \ldots, a_r]$ is a finite sequence with at most $3 \cdot 4^{r-1}$ elements. All but a finite number of the members of $A[a_1, \ldots, a_r]$ come from the subsequences $B[a_1, \ldots, a_r, \ldots, a_t]$, where $a_j = 0$ or 1 for $r < j \leq t$.

Now assume that $A[a_1, \ldots, a_r]$ is infinite, and let $A[a_1, \ldots, a_r] = \langle U_{s_n} \rangle$, where $s_0 < s_1 < s_2 < \cdots$. If N is a large integer, with $4^r \leq 4^q < N \leq 4^{q+1}$, it follows that the number of values of $k < N$ for which U_{s_k} is in $I_{b_1 \ldots b_r}$ is (except for finitely many elements at the beginning of the subsequence)

$$\nu(N) = \nu(N_1) + \cdots + \nu(N_m).$$

Here m is the number of subsequences $B[a_1, \ldots, a_t]$ listed above in which U_{s_k} appears for some $k < N$; N_j is the number of values of k with U_{s_k} in the corresponding subsequence; and $\nu(N_j)$ is the number of such values that are also in $I_{b_1 \ldots b_r}$. Therefore by Lemma T,

$$\left| \nu(N) - 2^{-r} N \right| = \left| \nu(N_1) - 2^{-r} N_1 + \cdots + \nu(N_m) - 2^{-r} N_m \right|$$
$$\leq \left| \nu(N_1) - 2^{-r} N_1 \right| + \cdots + \left| \nu(N_m) - 2^{-r} N_m \right|$$
$$\leq m \leq 1 + 2 + 4 + \cdots + 2^{q-r+1} < 2^{q+1}.$$

The inequality on m follows here from the fact that, by our choice of N, the element U_{s_N} is in $B[a_1, \ldots, a_t]$ for some $t \leq q+1$.

We have proved that $|\nu(N)/N - 2^{-r}| \leq 2^{q+1}/N < 2/\sqrt{N}$.   ∎

To show finally that sequences satisfying Definition R5 exist, we note first that if $\langle U_n \rangle$ is a $[0 \mathinner{.\,.} 1)$ sequence of rational numbers and if $\mathcal{R}$ is a computable subsequence rule for a b-ary sequence, we can make $\mathcal{R}$ into a computable subsequence rule $\mathcal{R}'$ for $\langle U_n \rangle$ by letting $f_n'(x_1, \ldots, x_n)$ in $\mathcal{R}'$ equal $f_n(\lfloor bx_1 \rfloor, \ldots, \lfloor bx_n \rfloor)$ in $\mathcal{R}$. If the $[0 \mathinner{.\,.} 1)$ sequence $\langle U_n \rangle \mathcal{R}'$ is equidistributed, so is the b-ary sequence $\langle \lfloor bU_n \rfloor \rangle \mathcal{R}$. Now the set of all computable subsequence rules for b-ary sequences, for all values of b, is countable (since only countably many effective algorithms are possible), so they may be listed in some sequence $\mathcal{R}_1, \mathcal{R}_2, \ldots$; therefore Algorithm W defines a $[0 \mathinner{.\,.} 1)$ sequence that is random in the sense of Definition R5.

This brings us to a somewhat paradoxical situation. As we mentioned earlier, no effective algorithm can define a sequence that satisfies Definition R4, and for the same reason there is no effective algorithm that defines a sequence satisfying Definition R5. A proof of the existence of such random sequences is necessarily nonconstructive; how then can Algorithm W construct such a sequence?

There is no contradiction here; we have merely stumbled on the fact that the set of all effective algorithms cannot be enumerated by an effective algorithm. In other words, there is no effective algorithm to select the jth computable subsequence rule $\mathcal{R}_j$; this happens because there is no effective algorithm to determine if a computational method ever terminates. But important large classes of algorithms *can* be systematically enumerated; thus, for example, Algorithm W shows that it is possible to construct, with an effective algorithm, a sequence that satisfies Definition R5 if we restrict consideration to subsequence rules that are "primitive recursive."

By modifying step W6 of Algorithm W, so that it sets $U_n \leftarrow V_{k+t}$ instead of V_k, where t is any nonnegative integer depending on $a_1, \ldots, a_r$, we can show that there are *uncountably* many $[0 \,..\, 1)$ sequences satisfying Definition R5.

The following theorem shows still another way to prove the existence of uncountably many random sequences, using a less direct argument based on measure theory, even if the strong definition R6 is used:

Theorem M. *Let the real number x, $0 \leq x < 1$, correspond to the binary sequence $\langle X_n \rangle$ if the binary representation of x is $(0.X_0 X_1 \ldots)_2$. Under this correspondence, almost all x correspond to binary sequences that are random in the sense of Definition R6.* (In other words, the set of all real x that correspond to a binary sequence that is nonrandom by Definition R6 has measure zero.)

Proof. Let $\mathcal{S}$ be an effective algorithm that determines an infinite sequence of distinct nonnegative integers $\langle s_n \rangle$, where the choice of s_n depends only on n and X_{s_k} for $0 \leq k < n$; and let $\mathcal{R}$ be a computable subsequence rule. Then any binary sequence $\langle X_n \rangle$ leads to a subsequence $\langle X_{s_n} \rangle \mathcal{R}$, and Definition R6 says this subsequence must either be finite or 1-distributed. It suffices to prove that for fixed $\mathcal{R}$ and $\mathcal{S}$ the set $N(\mathcal{R}, \mathcal{S})$ of all real x corresponding to $\langle X_n \rangle$, such that $\langle X_{s_n} \rangle \mathcal{R}$ is infinite and not 1-distributed, has measure zero. For x has a nonrandom binary representation if and only if x is in $\bigcup N(\mathcal{R}, \mathcal{S})$, taken over the countably many choices of $\mathcal{R}$ and $\mathcal{S}$.

Therefore let $\mathcal{R}$ and $\mathcal{S}$ be fixed. Consider the set $T(a_1 a_2 \ldots a_r)$ defined for all binary numbers $a_1 a_2 \ldots a_r$ as the set of all x corresponding to $\langle X_n \rangle$, such that $\langle X_{s_n} \rangle \mathcal{R}$ has $\geq r$ elements whose first r elements are respectively equal to $a_1, a_2, \ldots, a_r$. Our first result is that

$$T(a_1 a_2 \ldots a_r) \text{ has measure} \leq 2^{-r}. \tag{32}$$

To prove this, we start by observing that $T(a_1 a_2 \ldots a_r)$ is a measurable set: Each element of $T(a_1 a_2 \ldots a_r)$ is a real number $x = (0.X_0 X_1 \ldots)_2$ for which there exists an integer m such that algorithm $\mathcal{S}$ determines distinct values $s_0, s_1, \ldots, s_m$, and rule $\mathcal{R}$ determines a subsequence of $X_{s_0}, X_{s_1}, \ldots, X_{s_m}$ such that X_{s_m} is the rth element of this subsequence. The set of all real $y = (0.Y_0 Y_1 \ldots)_2$ such that $Y_{s_k} = X_{s_k}$ for $0 \leq k \leq m$ also belongs to $T(a_1 a_2 \ldots a_r)$, and this is a measurable set consisting of the finite union of dyadic subintervals $I_{b_1 \ldots b_t}$. Since there are only countably many such dyadic intervals, we see that $T(a_1 a_2 \ldots a_r)$ is a countable union of dyadic intervals, and it is therefore measurable. Furthermore, this argument can be extended to show that the measure of $T(a_1 \ldots a_{r-1} 0)$ equals the measure of $T(a_1 \ldots a_{r-1} 1)$, since the latter is a union of dyadic intervals obtained from the former by requiring that $Y_{s_k} = X_{s_k}$ for $0 \le k < m$ and $Y_{s_m} \ne X_{s_m}$. Now since

$$T(a_1 \ldots a_{r-1} 0) \cup T(a_1 \ldots a_{r-1} 1) \subseteq T(a_1 \ldots a_{r-1}),$$

the measure of $T(a_1 a_2 \ldots a_r)$ is at most one-half the measure of $T(a_1 \ldots a_{r-1})$. The inequality (32) follows by induction on r.

Now that (32) has been established, the remainder of the proof is essentially to show that the binary representations of almost all real numbers are equidistributed. For $0 < \epsilon < 1$, let $B(r, \epsilon)$ be $\bigcup T(a_1 \ldots a_r)$, where the union is taken over all binary strings $a_1 \ldots a_r$ for which the number $\nu(r)$ of ones among $a_1 \ldots a_r$ satisfies

$$\left| \nu(r) - \tfrac{1}{2}r \right| \ge \epsilon r.$$

The number of such binary strings is $C(r, \epsilon) = \sum \binom{r}{k}$ summed over all values of k with $|k - \tfrac{1}{2}r| \ge \epsilon r$. Exercise 1.2.10–21 proves that $C(r, \epsilon) \le 2^{r+1} e^{-\epsilon^2 r}$; hence by (32),

$$B(r, \epsilon) \text{ has measure} \le 2^{-r} C(r, \epsilon) \le 2e^{-\epsilon^2 r}. \tag{33}$$

The next step is to define

$$B^*(r, \epsilon) = B(r, \epsilon) \cup B(r+1, \epsilon) \cup B(r+2, \epsilon) \cup \cdots.$$

The measure of $B^*(r, \epsilon)$ is at most $\sum_{k \ge r} 2e^{-\epsilon^2 k}$, and this is the remainder of a convergent series, so

$$\lim_{r \to \infty} \left(\text{measure of } B^*(r, \epsilon) \right) = 0. \tag{34}$$

Now if x is a real number whose binary expansion $(0.X_0 X_1 \ldots)_2$ leads to an infinite sequence $\langle X_{s_n} \rangle \mathcal{R}$ that is not 1-distributed, and if $\nu(r)$ denotes the number of ones in the first r elements of the latter sequence, then

$$\left| \nu(r)/r - \tfrac{1}{2} \right| \ge \epsilon,$$

for some $\epsilon > 0$ and infinitely many r. This means x is in $B^*(r, \epsilon)$ for all r. So finally we find that

$$N(\mathcal{R}, \mathcal{S}) = \bigcup_{t \ge 2} \bigcap_{r \ge 1} B^*(r, 1/t);$$

and, by (34), $\bigcap_{r \ge 1} B^*(r, 1/t)$ has measure zero for all t. Hence $N(\mathcal{R}, \mathcal{S})$ has measure zero. ∎

From the existence of *binary* sequences satisfying Definition R6, we can show the existence of $[0 \mathinner{.\,.} 1)$ sequences that are random in this sense. For details, see exercise 36. The consistency of Definition R6 is thereby established.

E. Random finite sequences. An argument was given above to indicate that it is impossible to define the concept of randomness for finite sequences: Any given finite sequence is as likely as any other. Still, nearly everyone would agree that the sequence 011101001 is "more random" than 101010101, and even the latter sequence is "more random" than 000000000. Although it is true that truly random sequences will exhibit locally nonrandom behavior, we would expect such behavior only in a long finite sequence, not in a short one.

Several ways to define the randomness of a finite sequence have been proposed, and only a few of the ideas will be sketched here. For simplicity, we shall restrict our consideration to the case of b-ary sequences.

Given a b-ary sequence X_0, X_1, ..., X_{N-1}, we can say that

$$\Pr\big(S(n)\big) \approx p, \qquad \text{if } |\nu(N)/N - p| \leq 1/\sqrt{N}, \tag{35}$$

where $\nu(n)$ is the quantity appearing in Definition A at the beginning of this section. The sequence above can be called "k-distributed" if

$$\Pr(X_n X_{n+1} \ldots X_{n+k-1} = x_1 x_2 \ldots x_k) \approx 1/b^k \tag{36}$$

for all b-ary numbers $x_1 x_2 \ldots x_k$. (Compare with Definition D. Unfortunately a sequence might turn out to be k-distributed by this new definition when it is not $(k-1)$-distributed.)

A definition of randomness may now be given analogous to Definition R1, as follows:

Definition Q1. *A b-ary sequence of length N is "random" if it is k-distributed (in the sense above) for all positive integers $k \leq \log_b N$.* ∎

According to this definition, for example, there are 178 nonrandom binary sequences of length 11:

00000001111	10000000111	11000000011	11100000001	11110000000
00000001110	10000000110	11000000010	11100000000	11010000000
00000001101	10000000101	11000000001	10100000001	10110000000
00000001011	10000000011	01000000011	01100000001	01110000000
00000000111				

plus 01010101010 and all sequences with nine or more zeros, plus all sequences obtained from the preceding sequences by interchanging ones and zeros.

Similarly, we can formulate a definition for finite sequences analogous to Definition R6. Let $\mathbf{A}$ be a set of algorithms, each of which is a selection-and-choice procedure that gives a subsequence $\langle X_{s_n} \rangle \mathcal{R}$ as in the proof of Theorem M.

Definition Q2. *The b-ary sequence X_0, X_1, ..., X_{N-1} is (n, ϵ)-random with respect to a set of algorithms $\mathbf{A}$, if for every subsequence X_{t_1}, X_{t_2}, ..., X_{t_m} determined by an algorithm of $\mathbf{A}$ we have either $m < n$ or*

$$\left| \frac{1}{m} \nu_a(X_{t_1}, \ldots, X_{t_m}) - \frac{1}{b} \right| \leq \epsilon \qquad \text{for } 0 \leq a < b.$$

Here $\nu_a(x_1, \ldots, x_m)$ is the number of a's in the sequence $x_1, \ldots, x_m$. ∎

(In other words, every sufficiently long subsequence determined by an algorithm of $\mathbf{A}$ must be approximately equidistributed.) The basic idea in this case is to let $\mathbf{A}$ be a set of "simple" algorithms; the number (and the complexity) of the algorithms in $\mathbf{A}$ can grow as N grows.

As an example of Definition Q2, let us consider binary sequences, and let **A** be just the following four algorithms:

a) Take the whole sequence.
b) Take alternate terms of the sequence, starting with the first.
c) Take the terms of the sequence following a zero.
d) Take the terms of the sequence following a one.

Now a sequence $X_0, X_1, \ldots, X_7$ is $(4, \frac{1}{8})$-random with respect to **A** if:

by (a), $\left|\frac{1}{8}(X_0 + X_1 + \cdots + X_7) - \frac{1}{2}\right| \leq \frac{1}{8}$, that is, if there are 3, 4, or 5 ones;

by (b), $\left|\frac{1}{4}(X_0 + X_2 + X_4 + X_6) - \frac{1}{2}\right| \leq \frac{1}{8}$, that is, if there are exactly 2 ones in even-numbered positions;

by (c), there are three possibilities depending on how many zeros occupy positions $X_0, \ldots, X_6$: If there are 2 or 3 zeros here, there is no condition to test (since $n = 4$); if there are 4 zeros, they must respectively be followed by two zeros and two ones; and if there are 5 zeros, they must respectively be followed by two or three zeros;

by (d), we get conditions similar to those implied by (c).

It turns out that only the following binary sequences of length 8 are $(4, \frac{1}{8})$-random with respect to these rules:

00001011	00101001	01001110	01101000
00011010	00101100	01011011	01101100
00011011	00110010	01011110	01101101
00100011	00110011	01100010	01110010
00100110	00110110	01100011	01110110
00100111	00111001	01100110	

plus those obtained by interchanging 0 and 1 consistently.

It is clear that we could make the set of algorithms so large that no sequences satisfy the definition, when n and ϵ are reasonably small. A. N. Kolmogorov has proved that an (n, ϵ)-random binary sequence *will* always exist, for any given N, if the number of algorithms in **A** does not exceed

$$\frac{1}{2}e^{2n\epsilon^2(1-\epsilon)}. \tag{37}$$

This result is not nearly strong enough to show that sequences satisfying Definition Q1 will exist, but the latter can be constructed efficiently using the procedure of Rees in exercise 3.2.2–21. A generalized spectral test, based on discrete Fourier transforms, can be used to test how well a sequence measures up to Definition Q1 [see A. Compagner, *Physical Rev.* **E52** (1995), 5634–5645].

Still another interesting approach to a definition of randomness has been taken by Per Martin-Löf [*Information and Control* **9** (1966), 602–619]. Given a finite b-ary sequence $X_1, \ldots, X_N$, let $l(X_1, \ldots, X_N)$ be the length of the shortest Turing machine program that generates this sequence. (Alternatively, we could use other classes of effective algorithms, such as those discussed in Section 1.1.) Then $l(X_1, \ldots, X_N)$ is a measure of the "patternlessness" of the sequence, and we may equate this idea with randomness. The sequences of length N that maximize $l(X_1, \ldots, X_N)$ may be called random. (From the standpoint of practical random number generation by computer, this is, of course, the worst definition of "randomness" that can be imagined!)

Essentially the same definition of randomness was given independently by G. Chaitin at about the same time; see *JACM* **16** (1969), 145–159. It is interesting to note that even though this definition makes no reference to equidistribution properties as our other definitions have, Martin-Löf and Chaitin have proved that random sequences of this type also have the expected equidistribution properties. In fact, Martin-Löf has demonstrated that such sequences satisfy *all* computable statistical tests for randomness, in an appropriate sense.

For further developments in the definition of random finite sequences, see A. K. Zvonkin and L. A. Levin, *Uspekhi Mat. Nauk* **25**, 6 (November 1970), 85–127 [English translation in *Russian Math. Surveys* **25**, 6 (November 1970), 83–124]; L. A. Levin, *Doklady Akad. Nauk SSSR* **212** (1973), 548–550; L. A. Levin, *Information and Control* **61** (1984), 15–37.

F. Pseudorandom numbers. It is comforting from a theoretical standpoint to know that random finite sequences of various flavors exist, but such theorems don't answer the questions faced by real-world programmers. More recent developments have led to a more relevant theory, based on the study of *sets* of finite sequences. More precisely, we consider *multisets* in which sequences may appear more than once.

Let S be a multiset containing bit strings (binary sequences) of length N; we call S an *N-source*. Let $\$_N$ denote the special N-source that contains all 2^N possible N-bit strings. Each element of S represents a sequence that we might use as a source of pseudorandom bits; choosing different "seed" values leads to different elements of S. For example, S might be

$$\{B_1 B_2 \ldots B_N \mid B_j \text{ is the most significant bit of } X_j\} \qquad (38)$$

in the linear congruential sequence defined by $X_{j+1} = (aX_j + c) \bmod 2^e$, where there is one string $B_1 B_2 \ldots B_N$ for each of the 2^e starting values X_0.

The basic idea of pseudorandom sequences, as we have seen throughout this chapter, is to get N bits that appear to be random, although we rely only on a few "truly random" bits when we choose the seed value. In the example just considered, we need e truly random bits to select X_0; in general, selecting a member of S amounts to using $\lg |S|$ truly random bits, after which we proceed deterministically. If $N = 10^6$ and $|S| = 2^{32}$, we are getting more than 30,000 "apparently random" bits for each truly random bit expended. With $\$_N$ instead of S, we get no such amplification, because $\lg |\$_N| = N$.

What does it mean to be "apparently random"? A. C. Yao proposed a good definition in 1982: Consider any algorithm A that looks at a bit string $B = B_1 \ldots B_N$ and outputs the value $A(B) = 0$ or 1. We may think of A as a test for randomness; for example, A might compute the distribution of runs of consecutive 0s and 1s, outputting 1 if the run lengths differ significantly from the expected distribution. Whatever A does, we can consider the probability $P(A, S)$ that $A(B) = 1$ when B is a randomly chosen element of S, and we can compare it to the probability $P(A, \$_N)$ that $A(B) = 1$ when B is a truly random bit string of length N. If $P(A, S)$ is extremely close to $P(A, \$_N)$ for all statistical tests A, we cannot tell the difference between the sequences of S and truly random binary sequences.

Definition P. *We say that an N-source S passes statistical test A with tolerance ϵ if $\bigl|P(A, S) - P(A, \$_N)\bigr| < \epsilon$. It fails the test if $\bigl|P(A, S) - P(A, \$_N)\bigr| \geq \epsilon$.* ∎

The algorithm A need not be designed by statisticians. *Any* algorithm can be considered a statistical test for randomness, according to Definition P. We allow A to flip coins (that is, to use truly random bits) as it performs its calculations. The only requirement is that A must output 0 or 1.

Well, actually there is another requirement: We insist that A must deliver its output in a reasonable time, at least on the average. We're not interested in algorithms that will take many years to run, because we will never notice any disparities between S and $\$_N$ if our computers cannot detect them during our lifetime. The sequences of S contain only $\lg |S|$ bits of information, so there surely are algorithms that will eventually detect the redundancy; but we don't care, as long as S is able to pass all the tests that really matter.

These qualitative ideas can be quantified, as we will now see. The theory is rather subtle, but it is sufficiently beautiful and important that readers who take the time to study the details carefully will be amply rewarded.

In the following discussion, the *running time* $T(A)$ of an algorithm A on N-bit strings is defined to be the maximum of the expected number of steps needed to output $A(B)$, maximized over all $B \in \$_N$; the expected number is averaged over all coin flips made by the algorithm.

The first step in our quantitative analysis is to show that we may restrict the tests to be of a very special kind. Let A_k be an algorithm that depends only on the first k bits of the input string $B = B_1 \ldots B_N$, where $0 \leq k < N$, and let $A_k^P(B) = \bigl(A_k(B) + B_{k+1} + 1\bigr) \bmod 2$. Thus A_k^P outputs 1 if and only if A_k has successfully predicted B_{k+1}; we call A_k^P a *prediction* test.

Lemma P1. *Let S be an N-source. If S fails test A with tolerance ϵ, there is an integer $k \in \{0, 1, \ldots, N-1\}$ and a prediction test A_k^P with $T(A_k^P) \leq T(A) + O(N)$ such that S fails A_k^P with tolerance ϵ/N.*

Proof. By complementing the output of A, if necessary, we may assume that $P(A, S) - P(A, \$_N) \geq \epsilon$. Consider the algorithms F_k that begin by flipping $N - k$ coins and replacing $B_{k+1} \ldots B_N$ by random bits $B'_{k+1} \ldots B'_N$ before executing A. Algorithm F_N is the same as A, while F_0 acts on S as if A were acting on $\$_N$. Let $p_k = P(F_k, S)$. Since $\sum_{k=0}^{N-1} (p_{k+1} - p_k) = p_N - p_0 = P(A, S) - P(A, \$_N) \geq \epsilon$, there is some k such that $p_{k+1} - p_k \geq \epsilon/N$.

Let A_k^P be the algorithm that performs the computations of F_k and predicts the value $\bigl(F_k(B) + B'_{k+1} + 1\bigr) \bmod 2$; in other words, it outputs

$$A_k^P(B) = \bigl(F_k(B) + B_{k+1} + B'_{k+1}\bigr) \bmod 2. \tag{39}$$

A careful analysis of probabilities shows that $P(A_k^P, S) - P(A_k^P, \$_N) = p_{k+1} - p_k$. (See exercise 40.)   ∎

Most N-sources S of practical interest are *shift-symmetric* in the sense that every substring $B_1 \ldots B_k$, $B_2 \ldots B_{k+1}$, $\ldots$, $B_{N-k+1} \ldots B_N$ of length k has the same probability distribution. This holds, for example, when S corresponds to a linear congruential sequence as in (38). In such cases we can improve on Lemma P1 by taking $k = N - 1$:

Lemma P2. *If S is a shift-symmetric N-source that fails test A with tolerance ϵ, there is an algorithm A' with $T(A') \leq T(A) + O(N)$ that predicts B_N from $B_1 \ldots B_{N-1}$ with probability at least $\frac{1}{2} + \epsilon/N$.*

Proof. If $P(A, S) > P(A, \$_N)$, let A' be the A_k^P in the proof of Lemma P1, but applied to $B_{N-k} \ldots B_{N-1}0 \ldots 0$ instead of $B_1 \ldots B_N$. Then A' has the same average behavior, because of shift-symmetry. If $P(A, S) < P(A, \$_N)$, let A' be $1 - A_k^P$ in the same fashion. Clearly $P(A', \$_N) = \frac{1}{2}$.   ∎

Now let's specialize S even more, by supposing that each of the sequences $B_1 B_2 \ldots B_N$ has the form $f\big(g(X_0)\big) f\big(g(g(X_0))\big) \ldots f\big(g^{[N]}(X_0)\big)$ as X_0 ranges over some set X, where g is a permutation of X and $f(x)$ is 0 or 1 for all $x \in X$. Our linear congruential example satisfies this restriction, with $X = \{0, 1, \ldots, 2^e - 1\}$, $g(x) = (ax + c) \bmod 2^e$, and $f(x) =$ most significant bit of x. Such N-sources will be called *iterative*.

Lemma P3. *If S is an iterative N-source that fails test A with tolerance ϵ, there is an algorithm A' with $T(A') \leq T(A) + O(N)$ that predicts B_1 from $B_2 \ldots B_N$ with probability at least $\frac{1}{2} + \epsilon/N$.*

Proof. An iterative N-source is shift-symmetric, and so is its reflection $S^R = \{B_N \ldots B_1 \mid B_1 \ldots B_N \in S\}$. Therefore Lemma P2 applies to S^R.   ∎

The permutation $g(x) = (ax + c) \bmod 2^e$ is easy to invert, in the sense that we can determine x from $g(x)$ whenever a is odd. But many easily computed permutation functions are "one-way" — hard to invert — and we will see that this makes them provably good sources of pseudorandom numbers.

Lemma P4. *Let S be an iterative N-source corresponding to f, g, and X. If S fails test A with tolerance ϵ, there is an algorithm G that correctly guesses $f(x)$, given $g(x)$, with probability $\geq \frac{1}{2} + \epsilon/N$, when x is a random element of X. The running time $T(G)$ is at most $T(A) + O(N)\big(T(f) + T(g)\big)$.*

Proof. Given the value of $g(x)$, the desired algorithm G successively computes $B_2 = f\big(g(x)\big)$, $B_3 = f\big(g(g(x))\big)$, $\ldots$, $B_N = f\big(g^{[N-1]}(x)\big)$ and applies the algorithm A' of Lemma P3. It guesses $f(x) = B_1$ with probability $\geq \frac{1}{2} + \epsilon/N$, because g is a permutation of X, and $B_1 \ldots B_N$ is the element of S corresponding to the seed value X_0 for which we have $g(X_0) = x$.   ∎

In order to use Lemma P4, we need to amplify the ability to guess a single bit $f(x)$ to an ability to guess x itself, given only the value of $g(x)$. There is a nice general way to do this, using the properties of Boolean functions, if we extend S so that many different functions $f(x)$ need to be guessed. (However, the method is somewhat technical, so the first-time reader may want to skip down to Theorem G before looking closely at the details that follow.)

Suppose $G(z_1 \ldots z_R)$ is a binary-valued function on R-bit strings that is good at guessing a function of the form $f(z_1 \ldots z_R) = (x_1 z_1 + \cdots + x_R z_R) \bmod 2$ for some fixed $x = x_1 \ldots x_R$. It is convenient to measure the success of G by computing the expected value

$$s = \mathrm{E}\big((-1)^{G(z_1 \ldots z_R) + x_1 z_1 + \cdots + x_R z_R}\big), \qquad (40)$$

averaged over all possibilities for $z_1 \ldots z_R$. This is the sum of correct guesses minus incorrect guesses, divided by 2^R; so if p is the probability that G is correct, we have $s = p - (1 - p)$, or $p = \frac{1}{2} + \frac{1}{2} s$.

For example, suppose $R = 4$ and $G(z_1 z_2 z_3 z_4) = [z_1 \neq z_2][z_3 + z_4 < 2]$. This function has success rate $s = \frac{3}{4}$ (and $p = \frac{7}{8}$) if $x = 1100$, because it equals $x \cdot z \bmod 2 = (z_1 + z_2) \bmod 2$ for all 4-bit strings z except 0111 or 1011. It also has success rate $\frac{1}{4}$ when $x = 0000, 0011, 1101$, or 1110; so there are five plausible possibilities for x. The other eleven x's make $s \leq 0$.

The following algorithm magically discovers x in most cases when G is a successful guesser in the sense just described. More precisely, the algorithm constructs a short list that has a good chance of containing x.

Algorithm L (*Amplification of linear guesses*). Given a binary-valued function $G(z_1 \ldots z_R)$ and a positive integer k, this algorithm outputs a list of 2^k binary sequences $x = x_1 \ldots x_R$ with the property that x is likely to be output when $G(z_1 \ldots z_R)$ is a good approximation to the function $(x_1 z_1 + \cdots + x_R z_R) \bmod 2$.

L1. [Construct a random matrix.] Generate random bits B_{ij} for $1 \leq i \leq k$ and $1 \leq j \leq R$.

L2. [Compute signs.] For $1 \leq i \leq R$, and for all bit strings $b = b_1 \ldots b_k$, compute

$$h_i(b) = \sum_{c \neq 0} (-1)^{b \cdot c + G(cB + e_i)} \qquad (41)$$

where e_i is the R-bit string $0 \ldots 010 \ldots 0$ having 1 in position i, and where cB is the string $d_1 \ldots d_R$ with $d_j = (B_{1j} c_1 + \cdots + B_{kj} c_k) \bmod 2$. (In other words the binary vector $c_1 \ldots c_k$ is multiplied by the $k \times R$ binary matrix B.) The sum is taken over all $2^k - 1$ bit strings $c_1 \ldots c_k \neq 0 \ldots 0$. It can be evaluated for each i with $k \cdot 2^k$ additions and subtractions, using Yates's method for the Hadamard transform; see the remarks following Eq. 4.6.4–(38).

L3. [Output the guesses.] For all 2^k choices of $b = b_1 \ldots b_k$, output the string $x(b) = [h_1(b) < 0] \ldots [h_R(b) < 0]$. ∎

To prove that Algorithm L works properly, we must show that a given string x will probably be output whenever it deserves to be. Notice first that if we change G to G', where $G'(z) = (G(z) + z_j) \bmod 2$, the original $G(z)$ is a good approximation to $x \cdot z \bmod 2$ if and only if the new $G'(z)$ is a good approximation to $(x + e_j) \cdot z \bmod 2$, where e_j is the unit-vector string defined in step L2. Moreover, if we apply the algorithm to G' instead of G, we get

$$h_i'(b) = \sum_{c \neq 0} (-1)^{b \cdot c + G(cB + e_i) + (cB + e_i) \cdot e_j} = (-1)^{\delta_{ij}} h_i\big((b + B_j) \bmod 2\big),$$

where B_j is column j of B. Therefore step L3 outputs the vectors $x'(b) = x\big((b + B_j) \bmod 2\big) + e_j$, modulo 2. As b runs through all k-bit strings, so does $(b + B_j) \bmod 2$, and the effect is to complement bit j of every x in the output.

We need therefore prove only that the vector $x = 0 \ldots 0$ is likely to be output whenever $G(z)$ is a good approximation to the constant function 0. We will show, in fact, that $x(0 \ldots 0)$ equals $0 \ldots 0$ in step L3 with high probability, whenever $G(z)$ is a lot more likely to be 0 than 1 and k is sufficiently large. More precisely, the condition

$$\sum_{c \neq 0} (-1)^{G(cB + e_i)} > 0$$

holds for $1 \leq i \leq R$ with probability $> \frac{1}{2}$, if $s = \mathrm{E}\big((-1)^{G(z)}\big)$ is positive when averaged over all 2^R possibilities for z and if k is large enough.

The key observation is that, for each fixed $c = c_1 \ldots c_k \neq 0 \ldots 0$, the string $d = cB$ is uniformly distributed: Every value of d occurs with probability $1/2^R$, because the bits of B are random. Furthermore, when $c \neq c' = c_1' \ldots c_k'$, the strings $d = cB$ and $d' = c'B$ are *independent*: Every value of the pair (d, d') occurs with probability $1/2^{2R}$. Therefore we can argue as in the proof of Chebyshev's inequality that, for any fixed i, the sum $\sum_{c \neq 0} (-1)^{G(cB + e_i)}$ is negative with probability at most $1/((2^k - 1)s^2)$. (Exercise 42 contains the details.) It follows that $R/((2^k - 1)s^2)$ is an upper bound on the probability that $x(0)$ is nonzero in step L3.

Theorem G. *If $s = \mathrm{E}\big((-1)^{G(z) + x \cdot z}\big) > 0$ and $2^k > \lceil 2R/s^2 \rceil$, Algorithm L outputs x with probability $\geq \frac{1}{2}$. The running time is $O(k 2^k R)$ plus the time to make $2^k R$ evaluations of G.* ▮

Now we are ready to prove that the muddle-square sequence of Eq. 3.2.2–(17) is a good source of (pseudo)random numbers. Suppose $2^{R-1} < M = PQ < 2^R$, where P and Q are prime numbers of the form $4k + 3$ in the respective ranges $2^{(R-2)/2} < P < 2^{(R-1)/2}$, $2^{R/2} < Q < 2^{(R+1)/2}$. We will call M an R-bit *Blum integer*, because the importance of such numbers for cryptography was first pointed out by Manuel Blum [*COMPCON* **24** (Spring 1982), 133–137]. Blum originally suggested that P and Q both have $R/2$ bits, but Algorithm 4.5.4D shows that it is better to choose P and Q as stated here so that $Q - P > .29 \times 2^{R/2}$.

Choose X_0 at random in the range $0 < X_0 < M$, with $X_0 \perp M$; also let Z be a random R-bit mask. We can construct an iterative N-source S by letting X be the set of all (x, z, m) that are possibilities for (X_0, Z, M), with the further restriction that $x \equiv a^2$ (modulo m) for some a. The function $g(x, z, m) = (x^2 \bmod m, z, m)$ is easily shown to be a permutation of X (see, for example, exercise 4.5.4–35). The function $f(x, z, m)$ that extracts bits in this iterative source is $x \cdot z \bmod 2$. Our starting value (X_0, Z, M) isn't necessarily in X, but $g(X_0, Z, M)$ is uniformly distributed in X, because exactly four values of X_0 have a given square $X_0^2 \bmod M$.

Theorem P. *Let S be the N-source defined by the muddle-square method on R-bit moduli, and suppose S fails some statistical test A with tolerance $\epsilon \geq 1/2^N$. Then we can construct an algorithm F that finds factors of random R-bit Blum integers $M = PQ$ having the form described above, with success probability at least $\epsilon/(4N)$ and with running time $T(F) = O(N^2 R^2 \epsilon^{-2} T(A) + N^3 R^4 \epsilon^{-2})$.*

Proof. Multiplication mod M can be done in $O(R^2)$ steps; hence $T(f) + T(g) = O(R^2)$. Lemma P4 therefore asserts the existence of a guessing algorithm G with success rate ϵ/N and $T(G) \leq T(A) + O(NR^2)$. We can construct G from A using the method of exercise 41. This algorithm G has the property that $s = \mathrm{E}\big((-1)^{G(y,z,m)+z\cdot x}\big) \geq (\frac{1}{2} + \epsilon/N) - (\frac{1}{2} - \epsilon/N) = 2\epsilon/N$, where the expected value is taken over all $(x, z, m) \in X$, and where $(y, z, m) = g(x, z, m)$.

The desired algorithm F proceeds as follows. Given a random $M = PQ$ with unknown P and Q, it computes a random X_0 between 0 and M, and stops immediately with a known factorization if $\gcd(X_0, M) \neq 1$. Otherwise it applies Algorithm L with $G(z) = G(X_0^2 \bmod M, z, M)$ and $k = \lceil \lg(1 + 2N^2 R/\epsilon^2) \rceil$. If one of the 2^k values x output by that algorithm satisfies $x^2 \equiv X_0^2$ (modulo M), there is a 50:50 chance that $x \not\equiv \pm X_0$; then $\gcd(X_0 - x, M)$ and $\gcd(X_0 + x, M)$ are the prime factors of M. (See Rabin's "SQRT box" in Section 4.5.4.)

The running time of this algorithm is clearly $O(N^2 R^2 \epsilon^{-2} T(A) + N^3 R^4 \epsilon^{-2})$, since $\epsilon \geq 2^{-N}$. The probability that it succeeds in factoring M can be estimated as follows. Let $n = |X|/2^R$ be the number of choices of (x, m), and let $s_{xm} = 2^{-R} \sum (-1)^{G(y,z,m)+z\cdot x}$ summed over all R-bit numbers z; thus $s = \sum_{x,m} s_{xm}/n \geq 2\epsilon/N$. Let t be the number of (x, m) such that $s_{xm} \geq \epsilon/N$. The probability that our algorithm deals with such a pair (x, m) is

$$\frac{t}{n} \geq \sum_{x,m}[s_{xm} \geq \epsilon/N]\frac{s_{xm}}{n} = \sum_{x,m}(1 - [s_{xm} < \epsilon/N])\frac{s_{xm}}{n}$$

$$\geq \frac{2\epsilon}{N} - \sum_{x,m}[s_{xm} < \epsilon/N]\frac{s_{xm}}{n} \geq \frac{\epsilon}{N}.$$

And in such a case it finds x with probability $\geq \frac{1}{2}$, by Theorem G, since we have $2^k > \lceil 2R/s_{xm}^2 \rceil$; so it finds a factor with probability $\geq \frac{1}{4}$. ∎

What does Theorem P imply, from a practical standpoint? Our proof shows that the constant implied by the O is small; let us assume that the running time for factoring is at most $10(N^2 R^2 \epsilon^{-2} T(A) + N^3 R^4 \epsilon^{-2})$. Many of the world's greatest mathematicians have worked on the problem of factoring large numbers, especially after factoring was shown to be highly relevant to cryptography in the late 1970s. Since they haven't found a good solution, we have excellent reason to believe that factoring is hard; hence Theorem P will show that $T(A)$ must be large on all algorithms that detect nonrandomness of muddle-square bits.

Long computations are conveniently measured in MIP-years, the number of instructions executed per Gregorian year by a machine that performs a million instructions per Gregorian second — namely $31{,}556{,}952{,}000{,}000 \approx 3.16 \times 10^{13}$. In 1995, the time to factor a number of 120 decimal digits (400 bits), using the most highly tuned algorithms, was more than 250 MIP-years. The most optimistic researchers who have worked on factorization would be astonished if an algorithm were discovered that requires only $\exp\bigl(R^{1/4}(\ln R)^{3/4}\bigr)$ instructions as $R \to \infty$. But let us assume that such a breakthrough has been achieved, for at least a not-too-small fraction of the R-bit Blum integers M. Then we could factor many numbers of about 50000 bits (15000 digits) in 2×10^{25} MIP-years. If we generate $N = 1000$ random bits by muddle-square with $R = 50000$, and if we assume that all algorithms that are good enough to factor at least $\frac{1}{400000}$ of the 50000-bit Blum integers must run at least 2×10^{25} MIP-years, Theorem P tells us that every such set of 1000 bits will pass all statistical tests for randomness whose running time $T(A)$ is less than 70000 MIP-years: No such algorithm A will be able to distinguish such bits from a truly random sequence with probability $\geq \epsilon = \frac{1}{100}$.

Impressive? No. Such a result is hardly surprising, since we need to specify about 150000 truly random bits just to start up the muddle-square method with X_0, Z, and M when $R = 50000$. Of *course* we should be able to get 1000 random bits back from such an investment!

But in general, the formula becomes

$$T(A) \geq \frac{1}{100000} N^{-2} R^{-2} \exp\bigl(R^{1/4}(\ln R)^{3/4}\bigr) - NR^2,$$

under our conservative assumptions, when $\epsilon = \frac{1}{100}$; the NR^2 term is negligible when R is large. So let's set $R = 200000$ and $N = 10^{10}$. Then we get ten billion pseudorandom muddle-bits from $\approx 3R = 600000$ truly random bits, passing all statistical tests that require fewer than 7.486×10^{10} MIP-years $= 74.86$ gigaMIP-years. With $R = 333333$ and $N = 10^{13}$ the computation time needed to detect any statistical bias increases to 535 teraMIP-years.

The simple pseudorandom generator 3.2.2–(16), which avoids the random mask Z, can also be shown to pass all polynomial-time tests for randomness if factoring is intractable. (See exercise 4.5.4–43.) But the known performance guarantees for the simpler method are somewhat weaker than for muddle-square; currently they are $O\bigl(N^4 R\epsilon^{-4} \log(NR\epsilon^{-1})\bigr)$ versus the $O(N^2 R^2 \epsilon^{-2})$ of Theorem P.

Everyone believes that there is no usable factoring algorithm for R-bit numbers whose running time is polynomial in R. If that conjecture is true in a stronger form, so that we cannot even factor $1/R^k$ of the R-bit Blum integers in polynomial time for any fixed k, Theorem P proves that the muddle-square method generates pseudorandom numbers that pass all usable polynomial-time statistical tests for randomness.

Stating this another way: If you generate random bits with the muddle-square method for suitably chosen N and R, you either get numbers that pass all reasonable statistical tests, or you get fame and fortune for discovering a new factorization algorithm.

G. Summary, history, and bibliography. We have defined several degrees of randomness that a sequence might possess.

An infinite sequence that is ∞-distributed satisfies a great many useful properties that are expected of random sequences, and there is a rich theory concerning ∞-distributed sequences. (The exercises below develop several important properties of such sequences that have not been mentioned in the text.) Definition R1 is therefore an appropriate basis for theoretical studies of randomness.

The concept of an ∞-distributed b-ary sequence was introduced in 1909 by Emile Borel. He essentially defined the concept of an (m, k)-distributed sequence, and showed that the b-ary representations of almost all real numbers are (m, k)-distributed for all m and k. He called such numbers *entirely normal* to base b, and he stated Theorem C informally without apparently realizing that it required proof [*Rendiconti Circ. Mat. Palermo* **27** (1909), 247–271, §12.]

The notion of an ∞-distributed sequence of *real* numbers, also called a *completely equidistributed sequence*, first appeared in a note by N. M. Korobov in *Doklady Akad. Nauk SSSR* **62** (1948), 21–22. Korobov and several of his colleagues developed the theory of such sequences quite extensively in a series of papers during the 1950s. Completely equidistributed sequences were independently studied by Joel N. Franklin, *Math. Comp.* **17** (1963), 28–59, in a paper that is particularly noteworthy because it was inspired by the problem of random number generation. The book *Uniform Distribution of Sequences* by L. Kuipers and H. Niederreiter (New York: Wiley, 1974) is an extraordinarily complete source of information about the rich mathematical literature concerning k-distributed sequences of all kinds.

We have seen, however, that ∞-distributed sequences need not be sufficiently haphazard to qualify completely as "random." Three definitions, R4, R5, and R6, were formulated above to provide the additional conditions; and Definition R6, in particular, seems to be an appropriate way to define the concept of an infinite random sequence. It is a precise, quantitative statement that may well coincide with the intuitive idea of true randomness.

Historically, the development of these definitions was primarily influenced by the quest of R. von Mises for a good definition of "probability." In *Math. Zeitschrift* **5** (1919), 52–99, von Mises proposed a definition similar in spirit to Definition R5, although stated too strongly (like our Definition R3) so that no sequences satisfying the conditions could possibly exist. Many people noticed this discrepancy, and A. H. Copeland [*Amer. J. Math.* **50** (1928), 535–552] suggested weakening von Mises's definition by substituting what he called "admissible numbers" (or Bernoulli sequences). These are equivalent to ∞-distributed $[0 . . 1)$ sequences in which all entries U_n have been replaced by 1 if $U_n < p$ or by 0 if $U_n \geq p$, for a given probability p. Thus Copeland was essentially suggesting a return to Definition R1. Then Abraham Wald showed that it is not necessary to weaken von Mises's definition so drastically, and he proposed substituting a countable set of subsequence rules. In an important paper [*Ergebnisse eines math. Kolloquiums* **8** (Vienna: 1937), 38–72], Wald essentially proved Theorem W, although he made the erroneous assertion that the sequence constructed by Algorithm W also satisfies the stronger condition that $\Pr(U_n \in A)$ = measure of A, for all Lebesgue measurable $A \subseteq [0 \mathrel{..} 1)$. We have observed that no sequence can satisfy this property.

The concept of "computability" was still very much in its infancy when Wald wrote his paper, and A. Church [*Bull. Amer. Math. Soc.* **46** (1940), 130–135] showed how the precise notion of "effective algorithm" could be added to Wald's theory to make his definitions completely rigorous. The extension to Definition R6 was due essentially to A. N. Kolmogorov [*Sankhyā* **A25** (1963), 369–376], who proposed Definition Q2 for finite sequences at the same time. Another definition of randomness for finite sequences, somewhere "between" Definitions Q1 and Q2, had been formulated many years earlier by A. S. Besicovitch [*Math. Zeitschrift* **39** (1934), 146–156].

The publications of Church and Kolmogorov considered only binary sequences for which $\Pr(X_n = 1) = p$ for a given probability p. Our discussion in this section has been slightly more general, since a $[0 \mathrel{..} 1)$ sequence essentially represents all p at once. The von Mises–Wald–Church definition has been refined in yet another interesting way by J. V. Howard, *Zeitschr. für math. Logik und Grundlagen der Math.* **21** (1975), 215–224.

Another important contribution was made by Donald W. Loveland [*Zeitschr. für math. Logik und Grundlagen der Math.* **12** (1966), 279–294], who discussed Definitions R4, R5, R6, and several intermediate concepts. Loveland proved that there are R5-random sequences that do not satisfy R4, thereby establishing the need for a stronger definition such as R6. In fact, he defined a rather simple permutation $\langle f(n) \rangle$ of the nonnegative integers, and an Algorithm W' analogous to Algorithm W, such that

$$\overline{\Pr}(U_{f(n)} \geq \tfrac{1}{2}) - \underline{\Pr}(U_{f(n)} \geq \tfrac{1}{2}) \geq \tfrac{1}{2}$$

for every R5-random sequence $\langle U_n \rangle$ produced by Algorithm W' when it is given an infinite set of subsequence rules $\mathcal{R}_k$.

Although Definition R6 is intuitively much stronger than R4, it is apparently not a simple matter to prove this rigorously, and for several years it was an open question whether or not R4 implies R6. Finally Thomas Herzog and James C. Owings, Jr., discovered how to construct a large family of sequences that satisfy R4 but not R6. [See *Zeitschr. für math. Logik und Grundlagen der Math.* **22** (1976), 385–389.]

Kolmogorov wrote another significant paper [*Problemy Peredači Informatsii* **1** (1965), 3–11] in which he considered the problem of defining the "information content" of a sequence, and this work led to Chaitin and Martin-Löf's interesting definition of finite random sequences via "patternlessness." [See *IEEE Trans.* **IT-14** (1968), 662–664.] The ideas can also be traced to R. J. Solomonoff, *Information and Control* **7** (1964), 1–22, 224–254; *IEEE Trans.* **IT-24** (1978), 422–432; *J. Computer and System Sciences* **55** (1997), 73–88.

For a philosophical discussion of random sequences, see K. R. Popper, *The Logic of Scientific Discovery* (London, 1959), especially the interesting construction on pages 162–163, which he first published in 1934.

Further connections between random sequences and recursive function theory have been explored by D. W. Loveland, *Trans. Amer. Math. Soc.* **125** (1966), 497–510. See also C.-P. Schnorr [*Zeitschr. Wahr. verw. Geb.* **14** (1969), 27–35], who found strong relations between random sequences and the "species of measure zero" defined by L. E. J. Brouwer in 1919. Schnorr's subsequent book *Zufälligkeit und Wahrscheinlichkeit* [*Lecture Notes in Math.* **218** (Berlin: Springer, 1971)] gives a detailed treatment of the entire subject of randomness and makes an excellent introduction to the ever-growing advanced literature on the topic. Important developments during the next two decades are surveyed in *An Introduction to Kolmogorov Complexity and Its Applications* (Springer, 1993), by Ming Li and Paul M. B. Vitányi.

The foundations of the theory of pseudorandom sequences and effective information were laid by Manuel Blum, Silvio Micali, and Andrew Yao [*FOCS* **23** (1982), 80–91, 112–117; *SICOMP* **13** (1984), 850–864], who constructed the first explicit sequences that pass all feasible statistical tests. Blum and Micali introduced the notion of a "hard-core bit," a Boolean function f such that $f(x)$ and $g(x)$ are easily computed although $f\big(g^{[-1]}(x)\big)$ is not; their paper was the origin of Lemma P4. Leonid Levin developed the theory further [*Combinatorica* **7** (1987), 357–363], then he and Oded Goldreich [*STOC* **21** (1989), 25–32] analyzed algorithms such as the muddle-square method and showed that similar use of a mask yields hard-core bits in many further cases. Finally Charles Rackoff refined the methods of that paper by introducing and analyzing Algorithm L [see L. Levin, *J. Symbolic Logic* **58** (1993), 1102–1103].

Many other authors have contributed to the theory—notably Impagliazzo, Levin, Luby, and Håstad, who showed [*SICOMP* **28** (1999), 1364–1396] that pseudorandom sequences can be constructed from any one-way function—but such results are beyond the scope of this book. The practical implications of theoretical work on pseudorandomness were first investigated empirically by P. L'Ecuyer and R. Proulx, *Proc. Winter Simulation Conf.* **22** (1989), 467–476.

> *If the numbers are not random,*
> *they are at least higgledy-piggledy.*
> — GEORGE MARSAGLIA (1984)

EXERCISES

1. [*10*] Can a periodic sequence be equidistributed?

2. [*10*] Consider the periodic binary sequence 0, 0, 1, 1, 0, 0, 1, 1, …. Is it 1-distributed? Is it 2-distributed? Is it 3-distributed?

3. [*M22*] Construct a periodic ternary sequence that is 3-distributed.

4. [*HM14*] Prove that $\Pr\big(S(n) \text{ and } T(n)\big) + \Pr\big(S(n) \text{ or } T(n)\big) = \Pr(S(n)) + \Pr(T(n))$, for any two statements $S(n)$ and $T(n)$, provided that at least three of the limits exist. For example, if a sequence is 2-distributed, we would find that

$$\Pr(u_1 \le U_n < v_1 \text{ or } u_2 \le U_{n+1} < v_2) = v_1 - u_1 + v_2 - u_2 - (v_1 - u_1)(v_2 - u_2).$$

▶ **5.** [*HM22*] Let $U_n = (2^{\lfloor \lg(n+1) \rfloor}/3) \bmod 1$. What is $\Pr(U_n < \frac{1}{2})$?

6. [*HM23*] Let $S_1(n), S_2(n), \ldots$ be an infinite sequence of statements about mutually disjoint events; that is, $S_i(n)$ and $S_j(n)$ cannot simultaneously be true if $i \neq j$. Assume that $\Pr(S_j(n))$ exists for each $j \geq 1$. Show that $\underline{\Pr}(S_j(n)$ is true for some $j \geq 1) \geq \sum_{j \geq 1} \Pr(S_j(n))$, and give an example to show that equality need not hold.

7. [*HM27*] Let $\{S_{ij}(n)\}$ be a family of statements such that $\Pr(S_{ij}(n))$ exists for all $i, j \geq 1$. Assume that for all $n > 0$, $S_{ij}(n)$ is true for exactly one pair of integers i, j. If $\sum_{i,j \geq 1} \Pr(S_{ij}(n)) = 1$, does it follow that "$\Pr(S_{ij}(n)$ is true for some $j \geq 1)$" exists for all $i \geq 1$, and that it equals $\sum_{j \geq 1} \Pr(S_{ij}(n))$?

8. [*M15*] Prove (13).

9. [*HM20*] Prove Lemma E. [*Hint:* Consider $\sum_{j=1}^{m}(y_{jn} - \alpha)^2$.]

▶ **10.** [*HM22*] Where was the fact that m divides q used in the proof of Theorem C?

11. [*M10*] Use Theorem C to prove that if a sequence $\langle U_n \rangle$ is ∞-distributed, so is the subsequence $\langle U_{2n} \rangle$.

12. [*HM20*] Show that a k-distributed sequence passes the "maximum-of-k test," in the following sense: $\Pr\big(u \leq \max(U_n, U_{n+1}, \ldots, U_{n+k-1}) < v\big) = v^k - u^k$.

▶ **13.** [*HM27*] Show that an ∞-distributed $[0 \ldots 1)$ sequence passes the "gap test" in the following sense: If $0 \leq \alpha < \beta \leq 1$ and $p = \beta - \alpha$, let $f(0) = 0$, and for $n \geq 1$ let $f(n)$ be the smallest integer $m > f(n-1)$ such that $\alpha \leq U_m < \beta$; then

$$\Pr\big(f(n) - f(n-1) = k\big) = p(1-p)^{k-1}.$$

14. [*HM25*] Show that an ∞-distributed sequence passes the "run test" in the following sense: If $f(0) = 0$ and if, for $n \geq 1$, $f(n)$ is the smallest integer $m > f(n-1)$ such that $U_{m-1} > U_m$, then

$$\Pr\big(f(n) - f(n-1) = k\big) = 2k/(k+1)! - 2(k+1)/(k+2)!.$$

▶ **15.** [*HM30*] Show that an ∞-distributed sequence passes the "coupon-collector's test" when there are only two kinds of coupons, in the following sense: Let $X_1, X_2, \ldots$ be an ∞-distributed binary sequence. Let $f(0) = 0$, and for $n \geq 1$ let $f(n)$ be the smallest integer $m > f(n-1)$ such that $\{X_{f(n-1)+1}, \ldots, X_m\}$ is the set $\{0, 1\}$. Prove that $\Pr\big(f(n) - f(n-1) = k\big) = 2^{1-k}$, for $k \geq 2$. (See exercise 7.)

16. [*HM38*] Does the coupon-collector's test hold for ∞-distributed sequences when there are more than two kinds of coupons? (See the previous exercise.)

17. [*HM50*] If r is any given rational number, Franklin has proved that the sequence $\langle r^n \bmod 1 \rangle$ is not 2-distributed. But is there any rational number r for which this sequence is equidistributed? In particular, is the sequence equidistributed when $r = \frac{3}{2}$? [See K. Mahler, *Mathematika* **4** (1957), 122–124.]

▶ **18.** [*HM22*] Prove that if $U_0, U_1, \ldots$ is k-distributed, so is the sequence $V_0, V_1, \ldots$, where $V_n = \lfloor nU_n \rfloor /n$.

19. [*HM35*] Consider a modification of Definition R4 that requires the subsequences to be only 1-distributed instead of ∞-distributed. Is there a sequence that satisfies this weaker definition, but that is not ∞-distributed? (Is the weaker definition really weaker?)

▶ **20.** [*HM36*] (N. G. de Bruijn and P. Erdős.) The first n points of any $[0 . . 1)$ sequence $\langle U_n \rangle$ with $U_0 = 0$ divide the interval $[0 . . 1)$ into n subintervals; let those subintervals have lengths $l_n^{(1)} \geq l_n^{(2)} \geq \cdots \geq l_n^{(n)}$. Clearly $l_n^{(1)} \geq \frac{1}{n} \geq l_n^{(n)}$, because $l_n^{(1)} + \cdots + l_n^{(n)} = 1$. One way to measure the equitability of the distribution of $\langle U_n \rangle$ is to consider

$$\bar{L} = \limsup_{n \to \infty} n l_n^{(1)} \quad \text{and} \quad \underline{L} = \liminf_{n \to \infty} n l_n^{(n)}.$$

a) What are $\bar{L}$ and $\underline{L}$ for van der Corput's sequence (29)?

b) Show that $l_{n+k-1}^{(1)} \geq l_n^{(k)}$ for $1 \leq k \leq n$. Use this result to prove that $\bar{L} \geq 1/\ln 2$.

c) Prove that $\underline{L} \leq 1/\ln 4$. [*Hint:* For each n there are numbers $a_1, \ldots, a_{2n}$ such that $l_{2n}^{(k)} \geq l_{n+a_k}^{(n+a_k)}$ for $1 \leq k \leq 2n$. Moreover, each integer $2, \ldots, n$ occurs at most twice in $\{a_1, \ldots, a_{2n}\}$.]

d) Show that the sequence $\langle W_n \rangle$ defined by $W_n = \lg(2n+1) \bmod 1$ satisfies $1/\ln 2 > n l_n^{(1)} \geq n l_n^{(n)} > 1/\ln 4$ for all n; hence it achieves the optimum $\bar{L}$ and $\underline{L}$.

21. [*HM40*] (L. H. Ramshaw.)

a) Continuing the previous exercise, is the sequence $\langle W_n \rangle$ equidistributed?

b) Show that $\langle W_n \rangle$ is the only $[0 . . 1)$ sequence for which we have $\sum_{j=1}^k l_n^{(j)} \leq \lg(1 + k/n)$ whenever $1 \leq k \leq n$.

c) Let $\langle f_n(l_1, \ldots, l_n) \rangle$ be any sequence of continuous functions on the sets of n-tuples $\{(l_1, \ldots, l_n) \mid l_1 \geq \cdots \geq l_n \text{ and } l_1 + \cdots + l_n = 1\}$, satisfying the following two properties:

$$f_{mn}(\tfrac{1}{m} l_1, \ldots, \tfrac{1}{m} l_1, \tfrac{1}{m} l_2, \ldots, \tfrac{1}{m} l_2, \ldots, \tfrac{1}{m} l_n, \ldots, \tfrac{1}{m} l_n) = f_n(l_1, \ldots, l_n);$$

$$\text{if} \quad \sum_{j=1}^k l_j \geq \sum_{j=1}^k l'_j \text{ for } 1 \leq k \leq n \quad \text{then} \quad f_n(l_1, \ldots, l_n) \geq f_n(l'_1, \ldots, l'_n).$$

[Examples are: $n l_n^{(1)}$; $-n l_n^{(n)}$; $l_n^{(1)}/l_n^{(n)}$; $n(l_n^{(1)2} + \cdots + l_n^{(n)2})$.] Let

$$\bar{F} = \limsup_{n \to \infty} f_n(l_n^{(1)}, \ldots, l_n^{(n)})$$

for the sequence $\langle W_n \rangle$. Show that $f_n(l_n^{(1)}, \ldots, l_n^{(n)}) \leq \bar{F}$ for all n, with respect to $\langle W_n \rangle$; also $\limsup_{n \to \infty} f_n(l_n^{(1)}, \ldots, l_n^{(n)}) \geq \bar{F}$ with respect to every other $[0 . . 1)$ sequence.

▶ **22.** [*HM30*] (Hermann Weyl.) Show that the $[0 . . 1)$ sequence $\langle U_n \rangle$ is k-distributed if and only if

$$\lim_{N \to \infty} \frac{1}{N} \sum_{0 \leq n < N} \exp(2\pi i(c_1 U_n + \cdots + c_k U_{n+k-1})) = 0$$

for every set of integers $c_1, c_2, \ldots, c_k$ not all zero.

23. [*M32*] (a) Show that a $[0 . . 1)$ sequence $\langle U_n \rangle$ is k-distributed if and only if all of the sequences $\langle (c_1 U_n + c_2 U_{n+1} + \cdots + c_k U_{n+k-1}) \bmod 1 \rangle$ are 1-distributed, whenever $c_1, c_2, \ldots, c_k$ are integers not all zero. (b) Show that a b-ary sequence $\langle X_n \rangle$ is k-distributed if and only if all of the sequences $\langle (c_1 X_n + c_2 X_{n+1} + \cdots + c_k X_{n+k-1}) \bmod b \rangle$ are 1-distributed, whenever $c_1, c_2, \ldots, c_k$ are integers with $\gcd(c_1, \ldots, c_k) = 1$.

▶ **24.** [*M35*] (J. G. van der Corput.) (a) Prove that the $[0 . . 1)$ sequence $\langle U_n \rangle$ is equidistributed whenever the sequences $\langle (U_{n+k} - U_n) \bmod 1 \rangle$ are equidistributed for all $k > 0$. (b) Consequently $\langle (\alpha_d n^d + \cdots + \alpha_1 n + \alpha_0) \bmod 1 \rangle$ is equidistributed, when $d > 0$ and α_d is irrational.

25. [*HM20*] A sequence is called a "white sequence" if all serial correlations are zero; that is, if the equation in Corollary S is true for *all* $k \geq 1$. (By Corollary S, an ∞-distributed sequence is white.) Show that if a $[0 \mathinner{\ldotp\ldotp} 1)$ sequence is equidistributed, it is white if and only if

$$\lim_{n \to \infty} \frac{1}{n} \sum_{0 \leq j < n} (U_j - \tfrac{1}{2})(U_{j+k} - \tfrac{1}{2}) = 0, \qquad \text{for all } k \geq 1.$$

26. [*HM34*] (J. Franklin.) A white sequence, as defined in the previous exercise, can definitely fail to be random. Let $U_0, U_1, \ldots$ be an ∞-distributed sequence, and define the sequence $V_0, V_1, \ldots$ as follows:

$$\begin{aligned}(V_{2n-1}, V_{2n}) &= (U_{2n-1}, U_{2n}) && \text{if } (U_{2n-1}, U_{2n}) \in G,\\(V_{2n-1}, V_{2n}) &= (U_{2n}, U_{2n-1}) && \text{if } (U_{2n-1}, U_{2n}) \notin G,\end{aligned}$$

where G is the set

$$\{(x, y) \mid x - \tfrac{1}{2} \leq y \leq x \text{ or } x + \tfrac{1}{2} \leq y\}.$$

Show that (a) $V_0, V_1, \ldots$ is equidistributed and white; (b) $\Pr(V_n > V_{n+1}) = \tfrac{5}{8}$. (This points out the weakness of the serial correlation test.)

27. [*HM48*] What is the highest possible value for $\Pr(V_n > V_{n+1})$ in an equidistributed, white sequence? (D. Coppersmith has constructed such a sequence achieving the value $\tfrac{7}{8}$.)

▶ **28.** [*HM21*] Use the sequence (11) to construct a $[0 \mathinner{\ldotp\ldotp} 1)$ sequence that is 3-distributed, for which $\Pr(U_{2n} \geq \tfrac{1}{2}) = \tfrac{3}{4}$.

29. [*HM34*] Let $X_0, X_1, \ldots$ be a $(2k)$-distributed binary sequence. Show that

$$\overline{\Pr}(X_{2n} = 0) \leq \frac{1}{2} + \binom{2k-1}{k} \Big/ 2^{2k}.$$

▶ **30.** [*M39*] Construct a binary sequence that is $(2k)$-distributed, and for which

$$\Pr(X_{2n} = 0) = \frac{1}{2} + \binom{2k-1}{k} \Big/ 2^{2k}.$$

(Therefore the inequality in the previous exercise is the best possible.)

31. [*M30*] Show that $[0 \mathinner{\ldotp\ldotp} 1)$ sequences exist that satisfy Definition R5, yet $\nu_n/n \geq \tfrac{1}{2}$ for all $n > 0$, where ν_n is the number of $j < n$ for which $U_j < \tfrac{1}{2}$. (This might be considered a nonrandom property of the sequence.)

32. [*M24*] Given that $\langle X_n \rangle$ is a "random" b-ary sequence according to Definition R5, and that $\mathcal{R}$ is a computable subsequence rule that specifies an infinite subsequence $\langle X_n \rangle \mathcal{R}$, show that the latter subsequence is not only 1-distributed, it is "random" by Definition R5.

33. [*HM22*] Let $\langle U_{r_n} \rangle$ and $\langle U_{s_n} \rangle$ be infinite disjoint subsequences of a sequence $\langle U_n \rangle$. (Thus, $r_0 < r_1 < r_2 < \cdots$ and $s_0 < s_1 < s_2 < \cdots$ are increasing sequences of integers and $r_m \neq s_n$ for any m, n.) Let $\langle U_{t_n} \rangle$ be the combined subsequence, so that $t_0 < t_1 < t_2 < \cdots$ and the set $\{t_n\} = \{r_n\} \cup \{s_n\}$. Show that if $\Pr(U_{r_n} \in A) = \Pr(U_{s_n} \in A) = p$, then $\Pr(U_{t_n} \in A) = p$.

▶ **34.** [*M25*] Define subsequence rules $\mathcal{R}_1, \mathcal{R}_2, \mathcal{R}_3, \ldots$ such that Algorithm W can be used with these rules to give an effective algorithm to construct a $[0 \mathinner{\ldotp\ldotp} 1)$ sequence satisfying Definition R1.

▶ **35.** [*HM35*] (D. W. Loveland.) Show that if a binary sequence $\langle X_n \rangle$ is R5-random, and if $\langle s_n \rangle$ is any computable sequence as in Definition R4, then $\overline{\Pr}(X_{s_n} = 1) \geq \frac{1}{2}$ and $\underline{\Pr}(X_{s_n} = 1) \leq \frac{1}{2}$.

36. [*HM30*] Let $\langle X_n \rangle$ be a binary sequence that is "random" according to Definition R6. Show that the $[0 \, . \, . \, 1)$ sequence $\langle U_n \rangle$ defined in binary notation by the scheme

$$U_0 = (0.X_0)_2, \quad U_1 = (0.X_1 X_2)_2, \quad U_2 = (0.X_3 X_4 X_5)_2, \quad U_3 = (0.X_6 X_7 X_8 X_9)_2, \quad \dots$$

is random in the sense of Definition R6.

37. [*M37*] (D. Coppersmith.) Define a sequence that satisfies Definition R4 but not Definition R5. [*Hint:* Consider changing U_0, U_1, U_4, U_9, $\dots$ in a truly random sequence.]

38. [*M49*] (A. N. Kolmogorov.) Given N, n, and ϵ, what is the smallest number of algorithms in a set $\mathbf{A}$ such that no (n, ϵ)-random binary sequences of length N exist with respect to $\mathbf{A}$? (If exact formulas cannot be given, can asymptotic formulas be found? The point of this problem is to discover how close the bound (37) comes to being "best possible.")

39. [*HM42*] (W. M. Schmidt.) Let U_n be a $[0 \, . \, . \, 1)$ sequence, and let $\nu_n(u)$ be the number of nonnegative integers $j \leq n$ such that $0 \leq U_j < u$. Prove that there is a positive constant c such that, for any N and for any $[0 \, . \, . \, 1)$ sequence $\langle U_n \rangle$, we have

$$|\nu_n(u) - un| > c \ln N$$

for some n and u with $0 \leq n < N$, $0 \leq u < 1$. (In other words, no $[0 \, . \, . \, 1)$ sequence can be *too* equidistributed.)

40. [*M28*] Complete the proof of Lemma P1.

41. [*M21*] Lemma P2 shows the existence of a prediction test, but its proof relies on the existence of a suitable k without explaining how we could find k constructively from A. Show that any algorithm A can be converted into an algorithm A' with $T(A') \leq T(A) + O(N)$ that predicts B_N from $B_1 \dots B_{N-1}$ with probability at least $\frac{1}{2} + \big(P(A, S) - P(A, \$_N)\big)/N$ on any shift-symmetric N-source S.

▶ **42.** [*M28*] (*Pairwise independence.*)

a) Let X_1, $\dots$, X_n be random variables having mean value $\mu = \mathrm{E}\, X_j$ and variance $\sigma^2 = \mathrm{E}\, X_j^2 - (\mathrm{E}\, X_j)^2$ for $1 \leq j \leq n$. Prove Chebyshev's inequality

$$\Pr\big((X_1 + \dots + X_n - n\mu)^2 \geq tn\sigma^2\big) \leq 1/t,$$

under the additional assumption that $\mathrm{E}(X_i X_j) = (\mathrm{E}\, X_i)(\mathrm{E}\, X_j)$ whenever $i \neq j$.

b) Let B be a random $k \times R$ binary matrix. Prove that if c and c' are fixed nonzero k-bit vectors, with $c \neq c'$, the vectors cB and $c'B$ are independent random R-bit vectors (modulo 2).

c) Apply (a) and (b) to the analysis of Algorithm L.

43. [*20*] It seems just as difficult to find the factors of any *fixed* R-bit Blum integer M as to find the factors of a *random* R-bit integer. Why then is Theorem P stated for random M instead of fixed M?

▶ **44.** [*16*] (I. J. Good.) Can a valid table of random digits contain just one misprint?

3.6. SUMMARY

WE HAVE COVERED a fairly large number of topics in this chapter: How to generate random numbers, how to test them, how to modify them in applications, and how to derive theoretical facts about them. Perhaps the main question in many readers' minds will be, "What is the result of all this theory? What is a simple, virtuous generator that I can use in my programs in order to have a reliable source of random numbers?"

The detailed investigations in this chapter suggest that the following procedure gives the simplest random number generator for the machine language of most computers: At the beginning of the program, set an integer variable X to some value X_0. This variable X is to be used only for the purpose of random number generation. Whenever a new random number is required by the program, set

$$X \leftarrow (aX + c) \bmod m \tag{1}$$

and use the new value of X as the random value. It is necessary to choose X_0, a, c, and m properly, and to use the random numbers wisely, according to the following principles:

i) The "seed" number X_0 may be chosen arbitrarily. If the program is run several times and a different source of random numbers is desired each time, set X_0 to the last value attained by X on the preceding run; or (if more convenient) set X_0 to the current date and time. If the program may need to be rerun later with the *same* random numbers (for example, when debugging), be sure to print out X_0 if it isn't otherwise known.

ii) The number m should be large, say at least 2^{30}. It may conveniently be taken as the computer's word size, since this makes the computation of $(aX + c) \bmod m$ quite efficient. Section 3.2.1.1 discusses the choice of m in more detail. The computation of $(aX + c) \bmod m$ must be done *exactly*, with no roundoff error.

iii) If m is a power of 2 (that is, if a binary computer is being used), pick a so that $a \bmod 8 = 5$. If m is a power of 10 (that is, if a decimal computer is being used), choose a so that $a \bmod 200 = 21$. This choice of a together with the choice of c given below ensures that the random number generator will produce all m different possible values of X before it starts to repeat (see Section 3.2.1.2) and ensures high "potency" (see Section 3.2.1.3).

iv) The multiplier a should preferably be chosen between $.01m$ and $.99m$, and its binary or decimal digits should *not* have a simple, regular pattern. By choosing some haphazard constant like $a = 3141592621$ (which satisfies both of the conditions in (iii)), one almost always obtains a reasonably good multiplier. Further testing should of course be done if the random number generator is to be used extensively; for example, there should be no large quotients when Euclid's algorithm is used to find the gcd of a and m (see Section 3.3.3). The multiplier should pass the spectral test (Section 3.3.4) and several tests of Section 3.3.2, before it is considered to have a truly clean bill of health.

v) The value of c is immaterial when a is a good multiplier, except that c must have no factor in common with m when m is the computer's word size. Thus we may choose $c = 1$ or $c = a$. (People who use $c = 0$ together with $m = 2^e$ are sacrificing two bits of accuracy and half of the seed values just to save a few nanoseconds of running time; see exercise 3.2.1.2–9.)

vi) The least significant (right-hand) digits of X are not very random, so decisions based on the number X should always be influenced primarily by the most significant digits. It is generally best to think of X as a random fraction X/m between 0 and 1, that is, to visualize X with a radix point at its left, rather than to regard X as a random integer between 0 and $m - 1$. To compute a random integer between 0 and $k - 1$, one should multiply by k and truncate the result. (Don't divide by k; see exercise 3.4.1–3.)

vii) An important limitation on the randomness of sequence (1) is discussed in Section 3.3.4, where it is shown that the "accuracy" in t dimensions will be only about one part in $\sqrt[t]{m}$. Monte Carlo applications requiring higher resolution can improve the randomness by employing techniques discussed in Section 3.2.2.

viii) At most about $m/1000$ numbers should be generated; otherwise the future will behave more and more like the past. If $m = 2^{32}$, this means that a new scheme (for example, a new multiplier a) should be adopted after every few million random numbers are consumed.

The comments above apply primarily to machine-language coding. Some of the ideas work fine also in higher-level languages for programming; for example, (1) becomes just 'X=a*X+c' in the C language, if X is of type **unsigned long** and if m is the modulus of **unsigned long** arithmetic (usually 2^{32} or 2^{64}). But C gives us no good way to regard X as a fraction, as required in (vi) above, unless we convert to double-precision floating point numbers.

Another variant of (1) is therefore often used in languages like C: We choose m to be a prime number near the largest easily computed integer, and we let a be a primitive root of m; the appropriate increment c for this case is zero. Then (1) can be implemented entirely with simple arithmetic on numbers that remain between $-m$ and $+m$, using the technique of exercise 3.2.1.1–9. For example, when $a = 48271$ and $m = 2^{31} - 1$ (see line 20 of Table 3.3.4–1), we can compute $X \leftarrow aX \bmod m$ with the following C code:

```
#define MM 2147483647          /* a Mersenne prime */
#define AA 48271    /* this does well in the spectral test */
#define QQ 44488    /* MM / AA */
#define RR 3399     /* MM % AA; it is important that RR<QQ */
X=AA*(X%QQ)-RR*(X/QQ);
if (X<0) X+=MM;
```

Here X is type **long**, and X should be initialized to a nonzero seed value less than MM. Since MM is prime, the least-significant bits of X are just as random as the most-significant bits, so the precautions of (vi) no longer need to be taken.

If you need millions and millions of random numbers, you can combine that routine with another, as in Eq. 3.3.4–(38), by writing some additional code:

```
#define MMM 2147483399              /* a non-Mersenne prime */
#define AAA 40692        /* another spectral success story */
#define QQQ 52774        /* MMM / AAA */
#define RRR 3791         /* MMM % AAA; again less than QQQ */
Y=AAA*(Y%QQQ)-RRR*(Y/QQQ);
if (Y<0) Y+=MMM;
Z=X-Y; if (Z<=0) Z+=MM-1;
```

Like X, the variable Y needs to be initially nonzero. This code deviates slightly from 3.3.4–(38) so that the output, Z, always lies strictly between 0 and $2^{31} - 1$, as recommended by Liviu Lalescu. The period length of the Z sequence is about 74 quadrillion, and its numbers now have about twice as many bits of accuracy as the X numbers do.

This method is portable and fairly simple, but not very fast. An alternative scheme based on lagged Fibonacci sequences with subtraction (exercise 3.2.2–23) is even more attractive, because it not only allows easy portability between computers, it is considerably faster, and it delivers random numbers of better quality because the t-dimensional accuracy is probably good for $t \leq 100$. Here is a C subroutine $ran\_array(\textbf{long}\ aa[],\ \textbf{int}\ n)$ that generates n new random numbers and places them into a given array aa, using the recurrence

$$X_j = (X_{j-100} - X_{j-37}) \bmod 2^{30}. \tag{2}$$

This recurrence is particularly well suited to modern computers. The value of n must be at least 100; larger values like 1000 are recommended.

```
#define KK 100                             /* the long lag */
#define LL  37                             /* the short lag */
#define MM (1L<<30)                         /* the modulus */
#define mod_diff(x,y) (((x)-(y))&(MM-1))   /* (x-y) mod MM */
long ran_x[KK];                       /* the generator state */
void ran_array(long aa[],int n) { /* put n new values in aa */
  register int i,j;
  for (j=0;j<KK;j++) aa[j]=ran_x[j];
  for (;j<n;j++) aa[j]=mod_diff(aa[j-KK],aa[j-LL]);
  for (i=0;i<LL;i++,j++) ran_x[i]=mod_diff(aa[j-KK],aa[j-LL]);
  for (;i<KK;i++,j++) ran_x[i]=mod_diff(aa[j-KK],ran_x[i-LL]);
}
```

All information about numbers that will be generated by future calls to ran_array appears in ran_x, so you can make a copy of that array in the midst of a computation if you want to restart at the same point later without going all the way back to the beginning of the sequence. The tricky thing about using a recurrence like (2) is, of course, to get everything started properly in the first place, by setting up suitable values of X_0, ..., X_{99}. The following subroutine *ran_start*(**long** *seed*) initializes the generator nicely when given any seed number between 0 and $2^{30} - 3 = 1,073,741,821$ inclusive:

```
#define TT  70        /* guaranteed separation between streams */
#define is_odd(x)  ((x)&1)                /* the units bit of x */
void ran_start(long seed) { /* use this to set up ran_array */
  register int t,j;
  long x[KK+KK-1];                        /* the preparation buffer */
  register long ss=(seed+2)&(MM-2);
  for (j=0;j<KK;j++) {
    x[j]=ss;                              /* bootstrap the buffer */
    ss<<=1; if (ss>=MM) ss-=MM-2;  /* cyclic shift 29 bits */
  }
  x[1]++;                      /* make x[1] (and only x[1]) odd */
  for (ss=seed&(MM-1),t=TT-1; t; ) {
    for (j=KK-1;j>0;j--)
      x[j+j]=x[j], x[j+j-1]=0;                  /* "square" */
    for (j=KK+KK-2;j>=KK;j--)
      x[j-(KK-LL)]=mod_diff(x[j-(KK-LL)],x[j]),
      x[j-KK]=mod_diff(x[j-KK],x[j]);
    if (is_odd(ss)) {                      /* "multiply by z" */
      for (j=KK;j>0;j--)  x[j]=x[j-1];
      x[0]=x[KK];             /* shift the buffer cyclically */
      x[LL]=mod_diff(x[LL],x[KK]);
    }
    if (ss) ss>>=1; else t--;
  }
  for (j=0;j<LL;j++) ran_x[j+KK-LL]=x[j];
  for (;j<KK;j++) ran_x[j-LL]=x[j];
  for (j=0;j<10;j++) ran_array(x,KK+KK-1);    /* warm it up */
}
```

(This program incorporates improvements to the author's original *ran_start* routine, recommended by Richard Brent and Pedro Gimeno in November 2001.)

The somewhat curious maneuverings of *ran_start* are explained in exercise 9, which proves that the sequences of numbers generated from different starting seeds are independent of each other: *Every block of 100 consecutive values X_n, X_{n+1}, ..., X_{n+99} in the subsequent output of ran_array will be distinct from the blocks that occur with another seed.* (Strictly speaking, this is known to be true only when $n < 2^{70}$; but there are fewer than 2^{55} nanoseconds in a year.) Several processes can therefore start in parallel with different seeds and be sure that they are doing independent calculations; different groups of scientists working on a problem in different computer centers can be sure that they are not duplicating the work of others if they restrict themselves to disjoint sets of seeds. Thus, more than one billion essentially disjoint batches of random numbers are provided by the single routines *ran_array* and *ran_start*. And if that is not enough, you can replace the program parameters 100 and 37 by other values from Table 3.2.2–1.

These C routines use the bitwise-and operation '&' for efficiency, so they are not strictly portable unless the computer uses two's complement representation for integers. Almost all modern computers are based on two's complement arithmetic, but '&' is not really necessary for this algorithm. Exercise 10 shows how to get exactly the same sequences of numbers in FORTRAN, using no such tricks. Although the programs illustrated here are designed to generate 30-bit integers, they are easily modified to generate random 52-bit fractions between 0 and 1, on computers that have reliable floating point arithmetic; see exercise 11.

You may wish to include *ran_array* in a library of subroutines, or you may find that somebody else has already done so. One way to check whether an implementation of *ran_array* and *ran_start* conforms with the code above is to run the following rudimentary test program:

```
int main() { register int m; long a[2009];
   ran_start(310952L);
   for (m=0;m<2009;m++) ran_array(a,1009);
   printf("%ld\n", ran_x[0]);
   ran_start(310952L);
   for (m=0;m<1009;m++) ran_array(a,2009);
   printf("%ld\n", ran_x[0]); return 0;
}
```

The printed output should be 995235265 (twice).

Caution: The numbers generated by *ran_array* fail the birthday spacings test of Section 3.3.2J, and they have other deficiencies that sometimes show up in high-resolution simulations (see exercises 3.3.2–31 and 3.3.2–35). One way to avoid the birthday spacings problem is simply to use only half of the numbers (skipping the odd-numbered elements); but that doesn't cure the other problems. An even better procedure is to follow Martin Lüscher's suggestion, discussed in Section 3.2.2: Use *ran_array* to generate, say, 1009 numbers, but use only the first 100 of these. (See exercise 15.) *This method has modest theoretical support and no known defects.* Most users will not need such a precaution, but it is definitely less risky, and it allows a convenient tradeoff between randomness and speed.

A great deal is known about linear congruential sequences like (1), but comparatively little has yet been proved about the randomness properties of lagged Fibonacci sequences like (2). Both approaches seem to be reliable in practice, if they are used with the caveats already stated.

When this chapter was first written in the late 1960s, a truly horrible random number generator called RANDU was commonly used on most of the world's computers (see Section 3.3.4). The authors of many contributions to the science of random number generation have often been unaware that particular methods they were advocating would prove to be inadequate. A particularly noteworthy example was the experience of Alan M. Ferrenberg and his colleagues, reported in *Physical Review Letters* **69** (1992), 3382–3384: They tested their algorithms for a three-dimensional problem by considering first a related two-dimensional problem with a known answer, and discovered that supposedly super-quality modern random number generators gave wrong results in the fifth decimal place. By contrast, an old-fashioned run-of-the-mill linear congruential generator, $X \leftarrow 16807X \bmod (2^{31} - 1)$, worked fine. Perhaps further research will show that even the random number generators recommended here are unsatisfactory; we hope this is not the case, but the history of the subject warns us to be cautious. The most prudent policy for a person to follow is to run each Monte Carlo program at least twice using quite different sources of random numbers, before taking the answers of the program seriously; this will not only give an indication of the stability of the results, it also will guard against the danger of trusting in a generator with hidden deficiencies. (Every random number generator will fail in at least one application.)

Excellent bibliographies of the pre-1972 literature on random number generation have been compiled by Richard E. Nance and Claude Overstreet, Jr., *Computing Reviews* **13** (1972), 495–508, and by E. R. Sowey, *International Stat. Review* **40** (1972), 355–371. The period 1972–1984 is covered by Sowey in *International Stat. Review* **46** (1978), 89–102; *J. Royal Stat. Soc.* **A149** (1986), 83–107. Subsequent developments are discussed by Shu Tezuka, *Uniform Random Numbers* (Boston: Kluwer, 1995).

For a detailed study of the use of random numbers in numerical analysis, see J. M. Hammersley and D. C. Handscomb, *Monte Carlo Methods* (London: Methuen, 1964). This book shows that some numerical methods are enhanced by using numbers that are "quasirandom," designed specifically for a certain purpose (not necessarily satisfying the statistical tests we have discussed). The origins of Monte Carlo methods for computers are discussed by N. Metropolis and R. Eckhardt in *Stanislaw Ulam 1909–1984*, a special issue of *Los Alamos Science* **15** (1987), 125–137.

Every reader is urged to work exercise 6 in the following set of problems.

> *Almost all good computer programs*
> *contain at least one random-number generator.*
> — DONALD E. KNUTH, *Seminumerical Algorithms* (1969)

EXERCISES

1. [*21*] Write a `MIX` subroutine with the following characteristics, using method (1):

Calling sequence: `JMP RANDI`

Entry conditions: rA = k, a positive integer < 5000.

Exit conditions: rA ← a random integer Y, $1 \leq Y \leq k$, with each integer about equally probable; rX =?; overflow off.

▶ **2.** [*15*] Some people have been afraid that computers will someday take over the world; but they are reassured by the statement that a machine cannot do anything really new, since it is only obeying the commands of its master, the programmer. Lady Lovelace wrote in 1844, "The Analytical Engine has no pretensions to *originate* anything. It can do *whatever we know how to order it* to perform." Her statement has been elaborated further by many philosophers. Discuss this topic, with random number generators in mind.

3. [*32*] (*A dice game.*) Write a program that simulates a roll of two dice, each of which takes on the values 1, 2, ..., 6 with equal probability. If the total is 7 or 11 on the first roll, the game is won; a total of 2, 3, or 12 loses; and on any other total, call that total the "point" and continue rolling dice until either a 7 occurs (a loss) or the point occurs again (a win).

Play ten games. The result of each roll of the dice should be printed in the form *m n*, where *m* and *n* are the contents of the two dice, followed by some appropriate comment (like "snake eyes" or "little Joe" or "the hard way", etc.).

4. [*40*] (*Solitaire or patience.*) Some people spend a lot of valuable time playing card games of solitaire, and perhaps automation will make an important inroad in this area. Write a program that (i) shuffles a simulated deck of cards; (ii) plays some common game of solitaire based on the order of the cards in the deck; and (iii) displays the result of the game, showing how close the program came to winning. Cumulative statistics should be kept. The program might be set up to "cheat" upon request.

5. [*46*] (*Creative writing by computer.*) A television program entitled "The Thinking Machine," broadcast by the CBS television network on October 26, 1960, featured (among other things) two Western-style playlets that were written by a computer program. Here are the two scripts as they were printed out by the computer:

Saga #1. (The gun is in the right hand; the money is in the left hand; the glass is on the table; the bottle is on the table; the holster is on the robber; the sheriff's gun is in the sheriff's right hand; the sheriff's holster is on the sheriff.)

ROBBER: (The robber is at the window.) Go to door; open door; go thru door; close door; go to corner; put money down at corner; go to table; put gun on table; sit and fidget; sit at table; pick up glass with right hand (empty); put glass on table; pick up bottle with right hand; pour; put bottle on table; pick up glass with right hand; take a drink from glass; put glass on table; pick up bottle with right hand; sit at table; sit at table; go to corner; go to window; go to table; put bottle on table; sit and fidget; sit at table; sit and fidget; go to window; go to table; pick up glass with right hand.

SHERIFF: (The sheriff is at the window.) See robber; (robber sees sheriff); go to door.

ROBBER: Put glass on table; pick up gun with right hand; check gun.

SHERIFF: Wait; open door; see robber; (robber sees sheriff); go thru door.

ROBBER: Go to window; aim; fire; SHERIFF NICKED.

SHERIFF: Go to window; aim; fire; MISSED; go to door; go to window.

ROBBER: Go to door; aim; aim.

SHERIFF: Aim; fire; MISSED.

ROBBER: Fire; SHERIFF NICKED.

SHERIFF: Go to door; aim; fire; MISSED; go thru door; aim.

ROBBER: Aim; fire; MISSED; aim; fire; MISSED.

SHERIFF: Fire; MISSED; go to window; aim; fire; MISSED.

ROBBER: Aim; fire; MISSED; aim; fire; MISSED; aim; fire; SHERIFF NICKED.

SHERIFF: Aim; fire; ROBBER HIT.

ROBBER: Drop gun; robber dies.

SHERIFF: Put gun in holster; go to table; pick up glass with right hand (empty); take glass from right hand with left hand; pick up bottle with right hand; pour; put bottle on table; take glass from left hand with right hand; take a drink from glass; take glass from right hand with left hand; pick up bottle with right hand; pour; put bottle on table; take glass from left hand with right hand; take a drink from glass; put glass on table; go to corner; pick up money with right hand; go to door; go thru door; close door. CURTAIN.

Saga #2. (The gun is in the right hand; the money is in the left hand; the glass is on the table; the bottle is on the table; the holster is on the robber; the sheriff's gun is in the sheriff's right hand; the sheriff's holster is on the sheriff.)

ROBBER: (The robber is at the window.) Go to door; open door; go thru door; close door; go to corner; put money down at corner; go to window; put gun down at window; lean on window and look; lean on window and look; go to corner; count money; go to table; pick up glass with right hand (empty); take glass from right hand with left hand; pick up bottle with right hand; pour; put bottle on table; take glass from left hand with right hand; take a drink from glass; put glass on table; pick up bottle with right hand; pour; go to corner; put bottle down at corner; go to window; pick up gun with right hand; check gun; put gun in holster; go to table; pick up glass with right hand; take a drink from glass; go to window; put glass down at window.

SHERIFF: (The sheriff is at the window.) See robber; (robber sees sheriff); go to door.

ROBBER: Take gun from holster with right hand; check gun; go to door; check gun; put gun down at door.

SHERIFF: Open door; see robber; (robber sees sheriff); go thru door; go to window.

ROBBER: Pick up gun with right hand.

SHERIFF: Go to table.

ROBBER: Aim; fire; MISSED; aim; fire; SHERIFF HIT; blow out barrel; put gun in holster.

SHERIFF: Drop gun; sheriff dies.

ROBBER: Go to corner; pick up money with right hand; go to door; go thru door; close door. CURTAIN.

A careful reading of these scripts reveals the highly intense drama present here. The computer program was careful to keep track of the locations of each player, the contents of his hands, etc. Actions taken by the players were random, governed by certain probabilities; the probability of a foolish action was increased depending on how much that player had had to drink and on how often he had been nicked by a shot. The reader will be able to deduce further properties of the program by studying the sample scripts.

Of course, even the best scripts are rewritten before they are produced, and this is especially true when an inexperienced writer has prepared the original draft. Here are the scripts just as they were actually used in the show:

Saga #1.   Music up.
MS Robber peering thru window of shack.
CU Robber's face.
MS Robber entering shack.
CU Robber sees whiskey bottle on table.
CU Sheriff outside shack.
MS Robber sees sheriff.
LS Sheriff in doorway over shoulder of robber, both draw.
MS Sheriff drawing gun.
LS Shooting it out. Robber gets shot.
MS Sheriff picking up money bags.
MS Robber staggering.
MS Robber dying. Falls across table, after trying to take last shot at sheriff.
MS Sheriff walking thru doorway with money.
MS of robber's body, now still, lying across table top. Camera dollies back. (Laughter)

Saga #2.   Music up.
CU of window. Robber appears.
MS Robber entering shack with two sacks of money.
MS Robber puts money bags on barrel.
CU Robber — sees whiskey on table.
MS Robber pouring himself a drink at table. Goes to count money. Laughs.
MS Sheriff outside shack.
MS thru window.
MS Robber sees sheriff thru window.
LS Sheriff entering shack. Draw. Shoot it out.
CU Sheriff. Writhing from shot.
M/2 shot Sheriff staggering to table for a drink . . . falls dead.
MS Robber leaves shack with money bags.*

[*Note:* CU = "close up", MS = "medium shot", etc. The details above were kindly furnished to the author by Thomas H. Wolf, producer of the television show, who suggested the idea of a computer-written playlet in the first place, and also by Douglas T. Ross and Harrison R. Morse who produced the computer program.]

In the summer of 1952, Christopher Strachey had used the hardware random number generator of the Ferranti Mark I to compose the following letter:

Honey Dear
   My sympathetic affection beautifully attracts your affectionate enthusiasm. You are my loving adoration: my breathless adoration. My fellow feeling breathlessly hopes for your dear eagerness. My lovesick adoration cherishes your avid ardour.
                                                             Yours wistfully,
                                                             M. U. C.

[*Encounter* **3** (1954), 4, 25–31; another example appears in the article on Electronic Computers in the 64th edition of *Pears Cyclopedia* (London, 1955), 190–191.]

---

   * © 1962 by Columbia Broadcasting System, Inc. All Rights Reserved. Used by permission. For further information, see J. E. Pfeiffer, *The Thinking Machine* (New York: J. B. Lippincott, 1962).

The reader will undoubtedly have many ideas about how to teach a computer to do creative writing; and that is the point of this exercise.

▶ **6.** [*40*] Look at the subroutine library of each computer installation in your organization, and replace the random number generators by good ones. Try to avoid being too shocked at what you find.

▶ **7.** [*M40*] A programmer decided to encipher his files by using a linear congruential sequence $\langle X_n \rangle$ of period 2^{32} generated by (1) with $m = 2^{32}$. He took the most significant bits $\lfloor X_n/2^{16} \rfloor$ and exclusive-or'ed them onto his data, but kept the parameters a, c, and X_0 secret.

Show that this isn't a very secure scheme, by devising a method that deduces the multiplier a and the first difference $X_1 - X_0$ in a reasonable amount of time, given only the values of $\lfloor X_n/2^{16} \rfloor$ for $0 \le n < 150$.

8. [*M15*] Suggest a good way to test whether an implementation of linear congruential generators is working properly.

9. [*HM32*] Let X_0, X_1, ... be the numbers produced by *ran_array* after *ran_start* has initialized the generation process with seed s, and consider the polynomials

$$P_n(z) = X_{n+62}z^{99} + X_{n+61}z^{98} + \cdots + X_n z^{37} + X_{n+99}z^{36} + \cdots + X_{n+64}z + X_{n+63}.$$

a) Prove that $P_n(z) \equiv z^{h(s)-n}$ (modulo 2 and $z^{100} + z^{37} + 1$), for some exponent $h(s)$.
b) Express $h(s)$ in terms of the binary representation of s.
c) Prove that if X_0', X_1', ... is the sequence of numbers produced by the same routines from the seed $s' \ne s$, we have $X_{n+k} \equiv X_{n'+k}'$ (modulo 2) for $0 \le k < 100$ only if $|n - n'| \ge 2^{70} - 1$.

10. [*22*] Convert the C code for *ran_array* and *ran_start* to FORTRAN 77 subroutines that generate exactly the same sequences of numbers.

▶ **11.** [*M25*] Assuming that floating point arithmetic on numbers of type **double** is properly rounded in the sense of Section 4.2.2 (hence exact when the values are suitably restricted), convert the C routines *ran_array* and *ran_start* to similar programs that deliver double-precision random fractions in the range $[0 . . 1)$, instead of 30-bit integers.

▶ **12.** [*M21*] What random number generator would be suitable for a minicomputer that does arithmetic only on integers in the range $[-32768 . . 32767]$?

13. [*M25*] Compare the subtract-with-borrow generators of exercise 3.2.1.1–12 to the lagged Fibonacci generators implemented in the programs of this section.

▶ **14.** [*M35*] (*The future versus the past.*) Let $X_n = (X_{n-37} + X_{n-100}) \bmod 2$ and consider the sequence

$$\langle Y_0, Y_1, \ldots \rangle = \langle X_0, X_1, \ldots, X_{99}, X_{200}, X_{201}, \ldots, X_{299}, X_{400}, X_{401}, \ldots, X_{499}, X_{600}, \ldots \rangle.$$

(This sequence corresponds to calling *ran_array*$(a, 200)$ repeatedly and looking only at the least significant bits, after discarding half of the elements.) The following experiment was repeated one million times using the sequence $\langle Y_n \rangle$: "Generate 100 random bits; then if 60 or more of them were 0, generate one more bit and print it." The result was to print 14527 0s and 13955 1s; but the probability that 28482 random bits contain at most 13955 1s is only about .000358.

Give a mathematical explanation why so many 0s were output.

▶ **15.** [*25*] Write C code that makes it convenient to generate the random integers obtained from *ran_array* by discarding all but the first 100 of every 1009 elements, as recommended in the text.

CHAPTER FOUR

ARITHMETIC

*Seeing there is nothing (right well beloued Students in the Mathematickes)
that is so troublesome to Mathematicall practise, nor that doth more molest
and hinder Calculators, then the Multiplications, Diuisions, square and
cubical Extractions of great numbers, which besides the tedious
expence of time, are for the most part subiect to many slippery errors.
I began therefore to consider in my minde, by what certaine and
ready Art I might remoue those hindrances.*

— JOHN NEPAIR [NAPIER] (1616)

I do hate sums. There is no greater mistake than to call arithmetic an exact
*science. There are . . . hidden laws of Number which it requires a mind
like mine to perceive. For instance, if you add a sum from the bottom up,
and then again from the top down, the result is always different.*

— M. P. LA TOUCHE (1878)

*I cannot conceive that anybody will require multiplications at the rate
of 40,000, or even 4,000 per hour; such a revolutionary change as the
octonary scale should not be imposed upon mankind in general
for the sake of a few individuals.*

— F. H. WALES (1936)

Most numerical analysts have no interest in arithmetic.

— B. PARLETT (1979)

THE CHIEF PURPOSE of this chapter is to make a careful study of the four
basic processes of arithmetic: addition, subtraction, multiplication, and division. Many people regard arithmetic as a trivial thing that children learn and
computers do, but we will see that arithmetic is a fascinating topic with many
interesting facets. It is important to make a thorough study of efficient methods for calculating with numbers, since arithmetic underlies so many computer
applications.

Arithmetic is, in fact, a lively subject that has played an important part in
the history of the world, and it still is undergoing rapid development. In this
chapter, we shall analyze algorithms for doing arithmetic operations on many
types of quantities, such as "floating point" numbers, extremely large numbers,
fractions (rational numbers), polynomials, and power series; and we will also
discuss related topics such as radix conversion, factoring of numbers, and the
evaluation of polynomials.

4.1. POSITIONAL NUMBER SYSTEMS

THE WAY WE DO ARITHMETIC is intimately related to the way we represent the numbers we deal with, so it is appropriate to begin our study of the subject with a discussion of the principal means for representing numbers.

Positional notation using base b (or *radix b*) is defined by the rule

$$(\ldots a_3a_2a_1a_0.a_{-1}a_{-2}\ldots)_b$$
$$= \cdots + a_3b^3 + a_2b^2 + a_1b^1 + a_0 + a_{-1}b^{-1} + a_{-2}b^{-2} + \cdots; \qquad (1)$$

for example, $(520.3)_6 = 5 \cdot 6^2 + 2 \cdot 6^1 + 0 + 3 \cdot 6^{-1} = 192\frac{1}{2}$. Our conventional decimal number system is, of course, the special case when b is ten, and when the a's are chosen from the "decimal digits" 0, 1, 2, 3, 4, 5, 6, 7, 8, 9; in this case the subscript b in (1) may be omitted.

The simplest generalizations of the decimal number system are obtained when we take b to be an integer greater than 1 and when we require the a's to be integers in the range $0 \leq a_k < b$. This gives us the standard binary $(b = 2)$, ternary $(b = 3)$, quaternary $(b = 4)$, quinary $(b = 5)$, ... number systems. In general, we could take b to be any nonzero number, and we could choose the a's from any specified set of numbers; this leads to some interesting situations, as we shall see.

The dot that appears between a_0 and a_{-1} in (1) is called the *radix point*. (When $b = 10$, it is also called the decimal point, and when $b = 2$, it is sometimes called the binary point, etc.) Continental Europeans often use a comma instead of a dot to denote the radix point; the English formerly used a raised dot.

The a's in (1) are called the *digits* of the representation. A digit a_k for large k is often said to be "more significant" than the digits a_k for small k; accordingly, the leftmost or "leading" digit is referred to as the *most significant digit* and the rightmost or "trailing" digit is referred to as the *least significant digit*. In the standard binary system the binary digits are often called *bits*; in the standard hexadecimal system (radix sixteen) the hexadecimal digits zero through fifteen are usually denoted by

$$\text{either} \quad 0, 1, 2, 3, 4, 5, 6, 7, 8, 9, a, b, c, d, e, f$$
$$\text{or} \quad 0, 1, 2, 3, 4, 5, 6, 7, 8, 9, A, B, C, D, E, F.$$

The historical development of number representations is a fascinating story, since it parallels the development of civilization itself. We would be going far afield if we were to examine this history in minute detail, but it will be instructive to look at its main features here.

The earliest forms of number representations, still found in primitive cultures, are generally based on groups of fingers, piles of stones, etc., usually with special conventions about replacing a larger pile or group of, say, five or ten objects by one object of a special kind or in a special place. Such systems lead naturally to the earliest ways of representing numbers in written form, as in the systems of Babylonian, Egyptian, Greek, Chinese, and Roman numerals; but such notations are comparatively inconvenient for performing arithmetic operations except in the simplest cases.

During the twentieth century, historians of mathematics have made extensive studies of early cuneiform tablets found by archæologists in the Middle East. These studies show that the Babylonian people actually had two distinct systems of number representation: The numbers used in everyday business transactions were written in a notation based on grouping by tens, hundreds, etc.; this notation was inherited from earlier Mesopotamian civilizations, and large numbers were seldom required. When more difficult mathematical problems were considered, however, Babylonian mathematicians made extensive use of a sexagesimal (radix sixty) positional notation that was highly developed at least as early as 1750 B.C. This notation was unique in that it was actually a *floating point* form of representation with exponents omitted; the proper scale factor or power of sixty was to be supplied by the context, so that, for example, the numbers 2, 120, 7200, and $\frac{1}{30}$ were all written in an identical manner. The notation was especially convenient for multiplication and division, using auxiliary tables, since radix-point alignment had no effect on the answer. As examples of this Babylonian notation, consider the following excerpts from early tables: The square of 30 is 15 (which may also be read, "The square of $\frac{1}{2}$ is $\frac{1}{4}$"); the reciprocal of $81 = (1\ 21)_{60}$ is $(44\ 26\ 40)_{60}$; and the square of the latter is $(32\ 55\ 18\ 31\ 6\ 40)_{60}$. The Babylonians had a symbol for zero, but because of their "floating point" philosophy, it was used only within numbers, not at the right end to denote a scale factor. For the interesting story of early Babylonian mathematics, see O. Neugebauer, *The Exact Sciences in Antiquity* (Princeton, N. J.: Princeton University Press, 1952), and B. L. van der Waerden, *Science Awakening*, translated by A. Dresden (Groningen: P. Noordhoff, 1954); see also D. E. Knuth, *CACM* **15** (1972), 671–677; **19** (1976), 108.

Fixed point positional notation was apparently first conceived by the Maya Indians in central America some 2000 years ago; their radix-20 system was highly developed, especially in connection with astronomical records and calendar dates. They began to use a written sign for zero about A.D. 200. But the Spanish conquerors destroyed nearly all of the Maya books on history and science, so we have comparatively little knowledge about the degree of sophistication that native Americans had reached in arithmetic. Special-purpose multiplication tables have been found, but no examples of division are known. [See J. Eric S. Thompson, *Contrib. to Amer. Anthropology and History* **7** (Carnegie Inst. of Washington, 1941), 37–67; J. Justeson, "Pratiche di calcolo nell'antica mesoamerica," *Storia della Scienza* **2** (Rome: Istituto della Enciclopedia Italiana, 2001), 976–990.]

Several centuries before Christ, the Greek people employed an early form of the abacus to do their arithmetical calculations, using sand or pebbles on a board that had rows or columns corresponding in a natural way to our decimal system. It is perhaps surprising to us that the same positional notation was never adapted to written forms of numbers, since we are so accustomed to decimal reckoning with pencil and paper; but the greater ease of calculating by abacus (since handwriting was not a common skill, and since abacus users need not memorize addition and multiplication tables) probably made the Greeks feel it would be silly even to suggest that computing could be done better on "scratch paper." At the same time Greek astronomers did make use of a sexagesimal positional notation for fractions, which they had learned from the Babylonians.

Our decimal notation, which differs from the more ancient forms primarily because of its fixed radix point, together with its symbol for zero to mark an empty position, was developed first in India within the Hindu culture. The exact date when this notation first appeared is quite uncertain; about A.D. 600 seems to be a good guess. Hindu science was highly developed at that time, particularly in astronomy. The earliest known Hindu manuscripts that show decimal notation have numbers written backwards (with the most significant digit at the right), but soon it became standard to put the most significant digit at the left.

The Hindu principles of decimal arithmetic were brought to Persia about A.D. 750, as several important works were translated into Arabic; a picturesque account of this development is given in a Hebrew document by Abraham Ibn Ezra, which has been translated into English in *AMM* **25** (1918), 99–108. Not long after this, al-Khwārizmī wrote his Arabic textbook on the subject. (As noted in Chapter 1, our word "algorithm" comes from al-Khwārizmī's name.) His work was translated into Latin and was a strong influence on Leonardo Pisano (Fibonacci), whose book on arithmetic (A.D. 1202) played a major role in the spreading of Hindu-Arabic numerals into Europe. It is interesting to note that the left-to-right order of writing numbers was unchanged during these two transitions, although Arabic is written from right to left while Hindu and Latin scholars generally wrote from left to right. A detailed account of the subsequent propagation of decimal numeration and arithmetic into all parts of Europe during the period 1200–1600 has been given by David Eugene Smith in his *History of Mathematics* **1** (Boston: Ginn and Co., 1923), Chapters 6 and 8.

Decimal notation was applied at first only to integer numbers, not to fractions. Arabic astronomers, who required fractions in their star charts and other tables, continued to use the notation of Ptolemy (the famous Greek astronomer), a notation based on sexagesimal fractions. This system still survives today in our trigonometric units of degrees, minutes, and seconds, and also in our units of time, as a remnant of the original Babylonian sexagesimal notation. Early European mathematicians also used sexagesimal fractions when dealing with noninteger numbers; for example, Fibonacci gave the value

$$1° \ 22' \ 7'' \ 42''' \ 33^{IV} \ 4^{V} \ 40^{VI}$$

as an approximation to the root of the equation $x^3 + 2x^2 + 10x = 20$. (The correct answer is $1° \ 22' \ 7'' \ 42''' \ 33^{IV} \ 4^{V} \ 38^{VI} \ 30^{VII} \ 50^{VIII} \ 15^{IX} \ 43^{X} \ \dots$.)

The use of decimal notation also for tenths, hundredths, etc., in a similar way seems to be a comparatively minor change; but, of course, it is hard to break with tradition, and sexagesimal fractions have an advantage over decimal fractions because numbers such as $\frac{1}{3}$ can be expressed exactly, in a simple way.

Chinese mathematicians — who used sexagesimals only rarely — were apparently the first people to work with the equivalent of decimal fractions, although their numeral system (lacking zero) was not originally a positional number system in the strict sense. Chinese units of weights and measures were decimal, so that Tsu Ch'ung-Chih (who died in A.D. 500 or 501) was able to express an approximation to π in the following form:

3 chang, 1 ch'in, 4 ts'un, 1 fen, 5 li, 9 hao, 2 miao, 7 hu.

Here chang, ..., hu are units of length; 1 hu (the diameter of a silk thread) equals 1/10 miao, etc. The use of such decimal-like fractions was fairly widespread in China after about 1250.

An embryonic form of truly positional decimal fractions appeared in a 10th-century arithmetic text, written in Damascus by an obscure mathematician named al-Uqlīdisī ("the Euclidean"). He occasionally marked the place of a decimal point, for example in connection with a problem about compound interest, the computation of 135 times $(1.1)^n$ for $1 \leq n \leq 5$. [See A. S. Saidan, *The Arithmetic of al-Uqlīdisī* (Dordrecht: D. Reidel, 1975), 110, 114, 343, 355, 481–485.] But he did not develop the idea very fully, and his trick was soon forgotten. Al-Samaw'al of Baghdad and Baku, writing in 1172, understood that $\sqrt{10} = 3.162277\ldots$, but he had no convenient way to write such approximations down. Several centuries passed before decimal fractions were reinvented by a Persian mathematician, al-Kāshī, who died in 1429. Al-Kāshī was a highly skillful calculator, who gave the value of 2π as follows, correct to 16 decimal places:

integer		fractions															
0	6	2	8	3	1	8	5	3	0	7	1	7	9	5	8	6	5

This was by far the best approximation to π known until Ludolph van Ceulen laboriously calculated 35 decimal places during the period 1586–1610. (In India, al-Kāshī's contemporary Mādhava had computed $9 \cdot 10^{11}\pi \approx 2827433388233$, according to Nīlakantha's commentary on Gaṇita §10 of the *Āryabhaṭīya*.)

Decimal fractions began to appear sporadically in Europe; for example, a so-called "Turkish method" was used to compute $153.5 \times 16.25 = 2494.375$. Giovanni Bianchini developed them further, with applications to surveying, prior to 1450; but like al-Uqlīdisī, his work seems to have had little influence. Christof Rudolff and François Viète suggested the idea again in 1525 and 1579. Finally, an arithmetic text by Simon Stevin, who independently hit on the idea of decimal fractions in 1585, became popular. Stevin's work, and the discovery of logarithms soon afterwards, made decimal fractions commonplace in Europe during the 17th century. [For further remarks and references, see D. E. Smith, *History of Mathematics* **2** (1925), 228–247; V. J. Katz, *A History of Mathematics* (1993), 225–228, 345–348; and G. Rosińska, *Quart. J. Hist. Sci. Tech.* **40** (1995), 17–32.]

The binary system of notation has its own interesting history. Many primitive tribes in existence today are known to use a binary or "pair" system of counting (making groups of two instead of five or ten), but they do not count in a true radix-2 system, since they do not treat powers of 2 in a special manner. See *The Diffusion of Counting Practices* by Abraham Seidenberg, *Univ. of Calif. Publ. in Math.* **3** (1960), 215–300, for interesting details about primitive number systems. Another "primitive" example of an essentially binary system is the conventional musical notation for expressing rhythms and durations of time.

Nondecimal number systems were discussed in Europe during the seventeenth century. For many years astronomers had occasionally used sexagesimal arithmetic both for the integer and the fractional parts of numbers, primarily when performing multiplication [see John Wallis, *Treatise of Algebra* (Oxford: 1685), 18–22, 30]. The fact that *any* integer greater than 1 could serve as radix was apparently first stated in print by Blaise Pascal in *De Numeris Multiplicibus*, which was written about 1658 [see Pascal's *Œuvres Complètes* (Paris: 1963), 84–89]. Pascal wrote [in Latin], "The decimal system has been established, somewhat foolishly to be sure, according to human custom, not from a natural necessity as most people think." He stated that the duodecimal (radix twelve) system would be a welcome change, and he gave a rule for testing a duodecimal number for divisibility by nine. Erhard Weigel tried to drum up enthusiasm for the quaternary (radix four) system in a series of publications beginning in 1673. A detailed discussion of radix-twelve arithmetic was given by Joshua Jordaine, *Duodecimal Arithmetick* (London: 1687).

Although decimal notation was almost exclusively used for arithmetic during that era, other systems of weights and measures were rarely if ever based on multiples of 10, and business transactions required a good deal of skill in adding quantities such as pounds, shillings, and pence. For centuries merchants had therefore learned to compute sums and differences of quantities expressed in peculiar units of currency, weights, and measures; thus they were doing arithmetic in nondecimal number systems. The common units of liquid measure in England, dating from the 13th century or earlier, are particularly noteworthy:

<table>
<tr><td>2 gills = 1 chopin</td><td>2 demibushels = 1 bushel or firkin</td></tr>
<tr><td>2 chopins = 1 pint</td><td>2 firkins = 1 kilderkin</td></tr>
<tr><td>2 pints = 1 quart</td><td>2 kilderkins = 1 barrel</td></tr>
<tr><td>2 quarts = 1 pottle</td><td>2 barrels = 1 hogshead</td></tr>
<tr><td>2 pottles = 1 gallon</td><td>2 hogsheads = 1 pipe</td></tr>
<tr><td>2 gallons = 1 peck</td><td>2 pipes = 1 tun</td></tr>
<tr><td>2 pecks = 1 demibushel</td><td></td></tr>
</table>

Quantities of liquid expressed in gallons, pottles, quarts, pints, etc. were essentially written in binary notation. Perhaps the true inventors of binary arithmetic were British wine merchants!

The first known appearance of pure binary notation was about 1605 in some unpublished manuscripts of Thomas Harriot (1560–1621). Harriot was a creative man who first became famous by coming to America as a representative of Sir Walter Raleigh. He invented (among other things) a notation like that now used for "less than" and "greater than" relations; but for some reason he chose not to publish many of his discoveries. Excerpts from his notes on binary arithmetic have been reproduced by John W. Shirley, *Amer. J. Physics* **19** (1951), 452–454; Harriot's discovery of binary notation was first cited by Frank Morley in *The Scientific Monthly* **14** (1922), 60–66.

The first published treatment of the binary system appeared in the work of a prominent Cistercian bishop, Juan Caramuel de Lobkowitz, *Mathesis Biceps* **1** (Campaniæ: 1670), 45–48. Caramuel discussed the representation of numbers in radices 2, 3, 4, 5, 6, 7, 8, 9, 10, 12, and 60 at some length, but gave no examples of arithmetic operations in nondecimal systems except in the sexagesimal case.

Ultimately, an article by G. W. Leibniz [*Mémoires de l'Académie Royale des Sciences* (Paris: 1703), 110–116], which illustrated binary addition, subtraction, multiplication, and division, really brought binary notation into the limelight, and his article is usually referred to as the birth of radix-2 arithmetic. Leibniz referred to the binary system quite frequently in letters to friends. He didn't recommend it for practical calculations; but he stressed its importance in number-theoretical investigations, since patterns in number sequences are often easier to see in binary notation than they are in decimal. He also saw a mystical significance in the fact that everything is expressible in terms of zero and one. Leibniz's unpublished manuscripts show that he had been interested in binary notation already in 1679 or earlier, and that he often experimented with radix-16 numbers.

A careful study of Leibniz's early work with binary numbers has been made by Hans J. Zacher, *Die Hauptschriften zur Dyadik von G. W. Leibniz* (Frankfurt am Main: 1973), and extended by L. Strickland and H. Lewis (Cambridge, Mass.: MIT Press, 2022), who have provided English translations. Zacher pointed out that Leibniz was familiar with John Napier's so-called "local arithmetic," a way for calculating with stones that amounts to using a radix-2 abacus. [Napier had published the idea of local arithmetic as part three of his little book *Rabdologiæ* in 1617; it may be called the world's first "binary computer," and it is surely the world's cheapest, although Napier felt that it was more amusing than practical. See Martin Gardner's discussion in *Knotted Doughnuts and Other Mathematical Entertainments* (New York: Freeman, 1986), Chapter 8.]

It is interesting to note that the important concept of negative powers to the right of the radix point was not yet well understood at that time. Leibniz asked James Bernoulli to calculate π in the binary system, and Bernoulli "solved" the problem by taking a 35-place approximation to π, multiplying it by 10^{35}, and then expressing this integer in the binary system as his answer. On a smaller scale this would be like saying that $\pi \approx 3.14$, and $(314)_{10} = (100111010)_2$; hence π in binary is 100111010! [See Leibniz, *Math. Schriften*, edited by C. I. Gerhardt, **3** (Halle: 1855), 97; two of the 118 bits in the answer are incorrect, due to computational errors.] Bernoulli and Leibniz were hoping to discover a simple pattern in this representation of π.

Charles XII of Sweden, whose talent for mathematics perhaps exceeded that of all other kings in the history of the world, hit on the idea of radix-8 arithmetic about 1717. This was probably his own invention, although he had met Leibniz briefly in 1707. Charles felt that radix 8 or 64 would be more convenient for calculation than the decimal system, and he considered introducing octal arithmetic into Sweden; but he died in battle before decreeing such a change. [See *The Works of Voltaire* **21** (Paris: E. R. DuMont, 1901), 49; E. Swedenborg, *Gentleman's Magazine* **24** (1754), 423–424.]

Octal notation was proposed also in colonial America before 1750, by the Rev. Hugh Jones, professor at the College of William and Mary [see *Gentleman's Magazine* **15** (1745), 377–379; H. R. Phalen, *AMM* **56** (1949), 461–465].

The eccentric British schoolmaster T. W. Hill spent more than 50 years of his life experimenting with radix 16. His public lecture in 1845, published posthumously, described ingenious ways to say and to write hexadecimal numbers and fractions [*Selections from the Papers of the Late Thomas Wright Hill, Esq. F.R.A.S.* (London: 1860), 63–85]. But he gave no examples of arithmetic.

Independently, a prominent Swedish-American civil engineer named John W. Nystrom decided to carry Charles XII's plans a step further, by devising a complete system of numeration, weights, and measures based on radix 16. He wrote, "I am not afraid, or do not hesitate, to advocate a binary system of arithmetic and metrology. I know I have nature on my side; if I do not succeed to impress upon you its utility and great importance to mankind, it will reflect that much less credit upon our generation, upon our scientific men and philosophers." Nystrom devised his own way to pronounce hexadecimal numbers; for example, $(C0160)_{16}$ was to be read "vybong, bysanton." His entire system was called the Tonal System, and it is described in *J. Franklin Inst.* **46** (1863), 263–275, 337–348, 402–407. A similar system, but using radix 8, was worked out by Alfred B. Taylor [*Proc. Amer. Pharmaceutical Assoc.* **8** (1859), 115–216; *Proc. Amer. Philosophical Soc.* **24** (1887), 296–366]. Increased use of the French (metric) system of weights and measures prompted extensive debate about the merits of decimal arithmetic during that era; indeed, octal arithmetic was even being proposed in France [J. D. Collenne, *Le Système Octaval* (Paris: 1845); Aimé Mariage, *Numération par Huit* (Paris: Le Nonnant, 1857)].

The binary system was well known as a curiosity ever since Leibniz's time, and about 20 early references to it have been compiled by R. C. Archibald [*AMM* **25** (1918), 139–142]. It was applied chiefly to the calculation of powers, as explained in Section 4.6.3, and to the analysis of certain games and puzzles. Giuseppe Peano [*Atti della R. Accademia delle Scienze di Torino* **34** (1898), 47–55] used binary notation as the basis of a "logical" character set of 256 symbols. Joseph Bowden [*Special Topics in Theoretical Arithmetic* (Garden City: 1936), 49] gave his own system of nomenclature for hexadecimal numbers.

Much of the recent history of number systems is connected with the development of calculating machines. Charles Babbage's notebooks for 1838 show that he considered using nondecimal numbers in his Analytical Engine [see M. V. Wilkes, *Historia Math.* **4** (1977), 421]. Increased interest in mechanical devices for arithmetic, especially for multiplication, led several people in the 1930s to consider the binary system for this purpose. A particularly delightful account of such activity appears in the article "Binary Calculation" by E. William Phillips [*J. Institute of Actuaries* **67** (1936), 187–221] together with a record of the discussion that followed a lecture he gave on the subject. Phillips began by saying, "The ultimate aim [of this paper] is to persuade the whole civilized world to abandon decimal numeration and to use octonal [that is, radix 8] numeration in its place."

Modern readers of Phillips's article will perhaps be surprised to discover that a radix-8 number system was properly referred to as "octonary" or "octonal," according to all dictionaries of the English language at that time, just as the radix-10 number system is properly called either "denary" or "decimal"; the word "octal" did not appear in English language dictionaries until 1961, and it apparently originated as a term for the base of a certain class of vacuum tubes. The word "hexadecimal," which has crept into our language even more recently, is a mixture of Greek and Latin stems; more proper terms would be "senidenary" or "sedecimal" or even "sexdecimal," but the latter is perhaps too risqué for computer programmers.

The comment by Mr. Wales that is quoted at the beginning of this chapter has been taken from the discussion printed with Phillips's paper. Another man who attended the same lecture objected to the octal system for business purposes: "5% becomes $3.\dot{1}46\dot{3}$ per 64, which sounds rather horrible."

Phillips got the inspiration for his proposals from an electronic circuit that was capable of counting in binary [C. E. Wynn-Williams, *Proc. Roy. Soc. London* **A136** (1932), 312–324]. Electromechanical and electronic circuitry for general arithmetic operations was developed during the late 1930s, notably by John V. Atanasoff and George R. Stibitz in the U.S.A., L. Couffignal and R. Valtat in France, Helmut Schreyer and Konrad Zuse in Germany. All of these inventors used the binary system, although Stibitz later developed excess-3 binary-coded-decimal notation. A fascinating account of these early developments, including reprints and translations of important contemporary documents, appears in Brian Randell's book *The Origins of Digital Computers* (Berlin: Springer, 1973).

The first American high-speed computers, built in the early 1940s, used decimal arithmetic. But in 1946, an important memorandum by A. W. Burks, H. H. Goldstine, and J. von Neumann, in connection with the design of the first stored-program computers, gave detailed reasons for making a radical departure from tradition and using base-two notation [see John von Neumann, *Collected Works* **5**, 41–65]. Since then binary computers have multiplied. After a dozen years of experience with binary machines, a discussion of the relative advantages and disadvantages of radix-2 notation was given by W. Buchholz in his paper "Fingers or Fists?" [*CACM* **2**, 12 (December 1959), 3–11].

The MIX computer used in this book has been defined so that it can be either binary or decimal. It is interesting to note that nearly all MIX programs can be expressed without knowing whether binary or decimal notation is being used — even when we are doing calculations involving multiple-precision arithmetic. Thus we find that the choice of radix does not significantly influence computer programming. (Noteworthy exceptions to this statement, however, are the "Boolean" algorithms discussed in Section 7.1; see also Algorithm 4.5.2B.)

There are several different ways to represent *negative* numbers in a computer, and this sometimes influences the way arithmetic is done. In order to understand these notations, let us first consider MIX as if it were a decimal computer; then each word contains 10 digits and a sign, for example

$$-12345\ 67890. \tag{2}$$

This is called the *signed magnitude* representation. Such a representation agrees with common notational conventions, so it is preferred by many programmers. A potential disadvantage is that minus zero and plus zero can both be represented, while they usually should mean the same number; this possibility requires some care in practice, although it turns out to be useful at times.

Most mechanical calculators that do decimal arithmetic use another system called *ten's complement* notation. If we subtract 1 from 00000 00000, we get 99999 99999 in this notation; in other words, no explicit sign is attached to the number, and calculation is done modulo 10^{10}. The number $-12345\ 67890$ would appear as

$$87654\ 32110 \qquad (3)$$

in ten's complement notation. It is conventional to regard any number whose leading digit is 5, 6, 7, 8, or 9 as a negative value in this notation, although with respect to addition and subtraction there is no harm in regarding (3) as the number $+87654\ 32110$ if it is convenient to do so. Notice that there is no problem of minus zero in such a system.

The major difference between signed magnitude and ten's complement notations in practice is that shifting right, in the latter, does not always divide the magnitude by ten. For example, the number $-11 = \ldots 99989$, shifted right one, gives $\ldots 99998 = -2$ (assuming that a shift to the right inserts "9" as the leading digit when the number shifted is negative). In general, x shifted right one digit in ten's complement notation will give $\lfloor x/10 \rfloor$, whether x is positive or negative.

A possible disadvantage of the ten's complement system is the fact that it is not symmetric about zero; the p-digit negative number $500\ldots 0$ is not the negative of any p-digit positive number. Thus it is possible that changing x to $-x$ will cause overflow. (See exercises 7 and 31 for a discussion of radix-complement notation with *infinite* precision.)

Another notation that has been used since the earliest days of high-speed computers is called *nines' complement* representation. In this case the number $-12345\ 67890$ would appear as

$$87654\ 32109. \qquad (4)$$

Each digit of a negative number $(-x)$ is equal to 9 minus the corresponding digit of x. It is not difficult to see that the nines' complement notation for a negative number is always one less than the corresponding ten's complement notation. Addition and subtraction are done modulo $10^{10} - 1$, which means that a carry off the left end is to be added at the right end. (See the discussion of arithmetic modulo $w - 1$ in Section 3.2.1.1.) Again there is a potential problem with minus zero, since 99999 99999 and 00000 00000 denote the same value.

The ideas just explained for radix-10 arithmetic apply in a similar way to radix-2 arithmetic, where we have *signed magnitude, two's complement*, and *ones' complement* notations. Two's complement arithmetic on n-bit numbers is arithmetic modulo 2^n; ones' complement arithmetic is modulo $2^n - 1$. The MIX computer, as used in the examples of this chapter, deals only with signed magnitude arithmetic; however, alternative procedures for complement notations are discussed in the accompanying text when it is important to do so.

Detail-oriented readers and copy editors should notice the position of the apostrophe in terms like "two's complement" and "ones' complement": A two's complement number is complemented with respect to a single power of 2, while a ones' complement number is complemented with respect to a long sequence of 1s. Indeed, there is also a "twos' complement notation," which has radix 3 and complementation with respect to $(2 \ldots 22)_3$.

Descriptions of machine language often tell us that a computer's circuitry is set up with the radix point at a particular place within each numeric word. Such statements should usually be disregarded. It is better to learn the rules concerning where the radix point will appear in the result of an instruction if we assume that it lies in a certain place beforehand. For example, in the case of MIX we could regard our operands either as integers with the radix point at the extreme right, or as fractions with the radix point at the extreme left, or as some mixture of these two extremes; the rules for the appearance of the radix point after addition, subtraction, multiplication, or division are straightforward.

It is easy to see that there is a simple relation between radix b and radix b^k:

$$(\ldots a_3 a_2 a_1 a_0 . a_{-1} a_{-2} \ldots)_b = (\ldots A_3 A_2 A_1 A_0 . A_{-1} A_{-2} \ldots)_{b^k}, \qquad (5)$$

where

$$A_j = (a_{kj+k-1} \ldots a_{kj+1} a_{kj})_b;$$

see exercise 8. Thus we have simple techniques for converting at sight between, say, binary and hexadecimal notation.

Many interesting variations on positional number systems are possible in addition to the standard b-ary systems discussed so far. For example, we might have numbers in base (-10), so that

$$(\ldots a_3 a_2 a_1 a_0 . a_{-1} a_{-2} \ldots)_{-10}$$
$$= \cdots + a_3 (-10)^3 + a_2 (-10)^2 + a_1 (-10)^1 + a_0 + \cdots$$
$$= \cdots - 1000 a_3 + 100 a_2 - 10 a_1 + a_0 - \tfrac{1}{10} a_{-1} + \tfrac{1}{100} a_{-2} - \cdots.$$

Here the individual digits satisfy $0 \le a_k \le 9$ just as in the decimal system. The number 12345 67890 appears in the "negadecimal" system as

$$(1\ 93755\ 73910)_{-10}, \qquad (6)$$

since the latter represents $10305070900 - 9070503010$. It is interesting to note that the negative of this number, $-12345\ 67890$, would be written

$$(28466\ 48290)_{-10}, \qquad (7)$$

and, in fact, *every real number whether positive or negative can be represented without a sign* in the -10 system.

Negative-base systems were first considered by Vittorio Grünwald [*Giornale di Matematiche di Battaglini* **23** (1885), 203–221, 367], who explained how to perform the four arithmetic operations in such systems; Grünwald also discussed root extraction, divisibility tests, and radix conversion. However, his work seems to have had no effect on other research, since it was published in a rather obscure journal, and it was soon forgotten. The next publication about negative-base systems was apparently by A. J. Kempner [*AMM* **43** (1936), 610–617], who discussed the properties of noninteger radices and remarked in a footnote that negative radices would be feasible too. After twenty more years the idea was rediscovered again, this time by Z. Pawlak and A. Wakulicz [*Bulletin de l'Académie Polonaise des Sciences*, Classe III, **5** (1957), 233–236; Série des sciences techniques **7** (1959), 713–721], and also by L. Wadel [*IRE Transactions* **EC-6** (1957), 123]. Experimental computers called SKRZAT 1 and BINEG, which used −2 as the radix of arithmetic, were built in Poland in the late 1950s; see N. M. Blachman, *CACM* **4** (1961), 257; R. W. Marczyński, *Ann. Hist. Computing* **2** (1980), 37–48. For further references see *IEEE Transactions* **EC-12** (1963), 274–277; *Computer Design* **6** (May 1967), 52–63. There is evidence that the idea of negative bases occurred independently to quite a few people. For example, D. E. Knuth had discussed negative-radix systems in 1955, together with a further generalization to complex-valued bases, in a short paper submitted to a "science talent search" contest for high-school seniors.

The base $2i$ gives rise to a system called the "quater-imaginary" number system (by analogy with "quaternary"), which has the unusual feature that *every complex number can be represented with the digits* 0, 1, 2, *and* 3 *without a sign.* [See D. E. Knuth, *CACM* **3** (1960), 245–247; **4** (1961), 355.] For example,

$$(11210.31)_{2i} = 1 \cdot 16 + 1 \cdot (-8i) + 2 \cdot (-4) + 1 \cdot (2i) + 3 \cdot (-\tfrac{1}{2}i) + 1(-\tfrac{1}{4}) = 7\tfrac{3}{4} - 7\tfrac{1}{2}i.$$

Here the number $(a_{2n} \ldots a_1 a_0 . a_{-1} \ldots a_{-2k})_{2i}$ is equal to

$$(a_{2n} \ldots a_2 a_0 . a_{-2} \ldots a_{-2k})_{-4} + 2i(a_{2n-1} \ldots a_3 a_1 . a_{-1} \ldots a_{-2k+1})_{-4},$$

so conversion to and from quater-imaginary notation reduces to conversion to and from negative quaternary representation of the real and imaginary parts. The interesting property of this system is that it allows multiplication and division of complex numbers to be done in a fairly unified manner without treating real and imaginary parts separately. For example, we can multiply two numbers in this system much as we do with any base, merely using a different carry rule: Whenever a digit exceeds 3 we subtract 4 and carry −1 two columns to the left; when a digit is negative, we add 4 to it and carry +1 two columns to the left. The following example shows this peculiar carry rule at work:

```
              1 2 2 3 1      [9 − 10i]
          ×   1 2 2 3 1      [9 − 10i]
          ─────────────
              1 2 2 3 1
      1 0 3 2 0 2 1 3
          1 3 0 2 2
        1 3 0 2 2
      1 2 2 3 1
      ─────────────────────
      0 2 1 3 3 3 1 2 1      [−19 − 180i]
```

A similar system that uses just the digits 0 and 1 may be based on $\sqrt{2}\,i$, but this requires an infinite nonrepeating expansion for the simple number "i" itself. Vittorio Grünwald proposed using the digits 0 and $1/\sqrt{2}$ in odd-numbered positions, to avoid such a problem; but that actually spoils the whole system [see *Commentari dell'Ateneo di Brescia* (1886), 43–54].

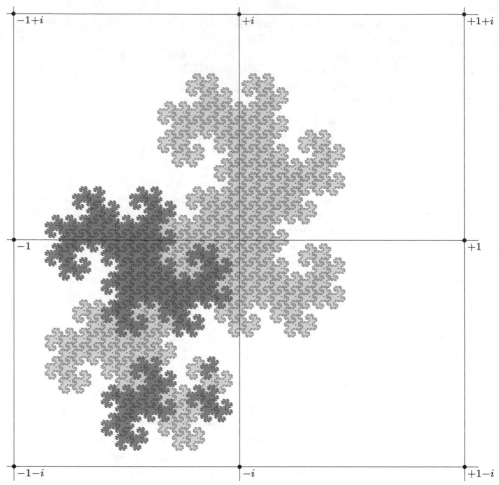

Fig. 1. The fractal set S called the "twindragon."

Another "binary" complex number system may be obtained by using the base $i - 1$, as suggested by W. Penney [*JACM* **12** (1965), 247–248]:

$$(\ldots a_4 a_3 a_2 a_1 a_0 . a_{-1} \ldots)_{i-1}$$
$$= \cdots - 4a_4 + (2i+2)a_3 - 2ia_2 + (i-1)a_1 + a_0 - \tfrac{1}{2}(i+1)a_{-1} + \cdots.$$

In this system, only the digits 0 and 1 are needed. One way to demonstrate that every complex number has such a representation is to consider the interesting set S shown in Fig. 1; this set is, by definition, all points that can be written as $\sum_{k \geq 1} a_k (i - 1)^{-k}$, for an infinite sequence a_1, a_2, a_3, ... of zeros and ones. It is also known as the "twindragon fractal" [see M. F. Barnsley, *Fractals Everywhere*, second edition (Academic Press, 1993), 306, 310]. Figure 1 shows that S can be decomposed into 256 pieces congruent to $\frac{1}{16}S$. Notice that if the diagram of S is rotated counterclockwise by 135°, we obtain two adjacent sets congruent to

$(1/\sqrt{2})\,S$, because $(i-1)S = S \cup (S+1)$. For details of a proof that S contains all complex numbers that are of sufficiently small magnitude, see exercise 18.

Perhaps the prettiest number system of all is the *balanced ternary* notation, which consists of radix-3 representation using -1, 0, and $+1$ as "trits" (ternary digits) instead of 0, 1, and 2. If we let the symbol $\bar{1}$ stand for -1, we have the following examples of balanced ternary numbers:

Balanced ternary	Decimal
$10\bar{1}$	8
$1\bar{1}0.\bar{1}\bar{1}$	$32\frac{5}{9}$
$\bar{1}\bar{1}0.11$	$-32\frac{5}{9}$
$\bar{1}\bar{1}10$	-33
$0.11111\ldots$	$\frac{1}{2}$

One way to find the representation of a number in the balanced ternary system is to start by representing it in ordinary ternary notation; for example,

$$208.3 = (21201.022002200220\ldots)_3.$$

(A very simple pencil-and-paper method for converting to ternary notation is given in exercise 4.4–12.) Now add the infinite number $\ldots 11111.11111\ldots$ in ternary notation; we obtain, in the example above, the infinite number

$$(\ldots 11111210012.210121012101\ldots)_3.$$

Finally, subtract $\ldots 11111.11111\ldots$ by decrementing each digit; we get

$$208.3 = (10\bar{1}\bar{1}01.10\bar{1}010\bar{1}010\bar{1}0\ldots)_3. \tag{8}$$

This process may clearly be made rigorous if we replace the artificial infinite number $\ldots 11111.11111\ldots$ by a number with suitably many ones.

The balanced ternary number system has many pleasant properties:

a) The negative of a number is obtained by interchanging 1 and $\bar{1}$.

b) The sign of a number is given by its most significant nonzero trit, and in general we can compare any two numbers by reading them from left to right and using lexicographic order, as in the decimal system.

c) The operation of rounding to the nearest integer is identical to truncation; in other words, we simply delete everything to the right of the radix point.

Addition in the balanced ternary system is quite simple, using the table

$\bar{1}$	$\bar{1}$	$\bar{1}$	$\bar{1}$	$\bar{1}$	$\bar{1}$	$\bar{1}$	$\bar{1}$	$\bar{1}$	0	0	0	0	0	0	0	0	0	1	1	1	1	1	1	1	1	1
$\bar{1}$	$\bar{1}$	$\bar{1}$	0	0	0	1	1	1	$\bar{1}$	$\bar{1}$	$\bar{1}$	0	0	0	1	1	1	$\bar{1}$	$\bar{1}$	$\bar{1}$	0	0	0	1	1	1
$\bar{1}$	0	1	$\bar{1}$	0	1	$\bar{1}$	0	1	$\bar{1}$	0	1	$\bar{1}$	0	1	$\bar{1}$	0	1	$\bar{1}$	0	1	$\bar{1}$	0	1	$\bar{1}$	0	1
$\bar{1}0$	$\bar{1}\bar{1}$	$\bar{1}$	$\bar{1}\bar{1}$	$\bar{1}$	0	$\bar{1}$	0	1	$\bar{1}\bar{1}$	$\bar{1}$	0	$\bar{1}$	0	1	0	1	1$\bar{1}$	$\bar{1}$	0	1	0	1	1$\bar{1}$	1	1$\bar{1}$	10

(The three inputs to the addition are the digits of the numbers to be added and the carry digit.) Subtraction is negation followed by addition. Multiplication also reduces to negation and addition, as in the following example:

$$
\begin{array}{r}
1\ \bar 1\ 0\ \bar 1 \quad [17] \\
\times\ 1\ \bar 1\ 0\ \bar 1 \quad [17] \\
\hline
\bar 1\ 1\ 0\ 1 \\
\bar 1\ 1\ 0\ 1 \\
1\ \bar 1\ 0\ \bar 1 \\
\hline
0\ 1\ 1\ \bar 1\ \bar 1\ 0\ 1 \quad [289]
\end{array}
$$

Representation of numbers in the balanced ternary system is implicitly present in a famous mathematical puzzle, commonly called "Bachet's problem of weights" — although it was already stated by Fibonacci four centuries before Bachet wrote his book, and by Ṭabarī in Persia more than 100 years before Fibonacci. [See W. Ahrens, *Mathematische Unterhaltungen und Spiele* **1** (Leipzig: Teubner, 1910), Section 3.4; H. Hermelink, *Janus* **65** (1978), 105–117.] Positional number systems with negative digits were invented by J. Colson [*Philos. Trans.* **34** (1726), 161–173], then forgotten and rediscovered about 100 years later by Sir John Leslie [*The Philosophy of Arithmetic* (Edinburgh: 1817); see pages 33–34, 54, 64–65, 117, 150], and by A. Cauchy [*Comptes Rendus Acad. Sci.* **11** (Paris, 1840), 789–798]. Cauchy pointed out that negative digits make it unnecessary for a person to memorize the multiplication table past 5×5. A claim that such number systems were known in India long ago [J. Bharati, *Vedic Mathematics* (Delhi: Motilal Banarsidass, 1965)] has been refuted by K. S. Shukla [*Mathematical Education* **5**, 3 (1989), 129–133]. The first true appearance of "pure" balanced ternary notation was in an article by Léon Lalanne [*Comptes Rendus Acad. Sci.* **11** (Paris, 1840), 903–905], who was a designer of mechanical devices for arithmetic. Thomas Fowler independently invented and constructed a balanced ternary calculator at about the same time [see *Report British Assoc. Adv. Sci.* **10** (1840), 55; **11** (1841), 39–40]. The balanced ternary number system was mentioned only rarely for the next 100 years, until the development of the first electronic computers at the Moore School of Electrical Engineering in 1945–1946; at that time it was given serious consideration as a possible replacement for the decimal system. The complexity of arithmetic circuitry for balanced ternary arithmetic is not much greater than it is for the binary system, and a given number requires only $\ln 2 / \ln 3 \approx 63\%$ as many digit positions for its representation. Discussions of the balanced ternary system appear in *AMM* **57** (1950), 90–93, and in *High-speed Computing Devices*, Engineering Research Associates (McGraw–Hill, 1950), 287–289. The experimental Russian computer SETUN was based on balanced ternary notation [see *CACM* **3** (1960), 149–150], and perhaps the symmetric properties and simple arithmetic of this number system will prove to be quite important someday — when the "flip-flop" is replaced by a "flip-flap-flop."

Positional notation generalizes in another important way to a *mixed-radix* system. Given a sequence of numbers $\langle b_n \rangle$ (where n may be negative), we define

$$
\begin{bmatrix}
\ldots, a_3, a_2, a_1, a_0; \ a_{-1},\ a_{-2}, \ldots \\
\ldots, b_3, b_2, b_1, b_0; \ b_{-1},\ b_{-2}, \ldots
\end{bmatrix}
$$
$$
= \cdots + a_3 b_2 b_1 b_0 + a_2 b_1 b_0 + a_1 b_0 + a_0 + a_{-1}/b_{-1} + a_{-2}/b_{-1} b_{-2} + \cdots . \tag{9}
$$

In the simplest mixed-radix systems, we work only with integers; we let b_0, b_1, b_2, ... be integers greater than one, and deal only with numbers that have no radix point, where a_n is required to lie in the range $0 \le a_n < b_n$.

One of the most important mixed-radix systems is the *factorial number system*, where $b_n = n + 2$. Using this system [C.-A. Laisant, *Bull. Soc. Math. France* **16** (1888), 176–183], we can represent every positive integer uniquely in the form

$$c_n \, n! + c_{n-1} \, (n-1)! + \cdots + c_2 \, 2! + c_1, \tag{10}$$

where $0 \le c_k \le k$ for $1 \le k \le n$, and $c_n \ne 0$. (See Algorithms 3.3.2P and 3.4.2P. Section 7.2.1.7 traces the origin of this system to 13th-century India.)

Mixed-radix systems are familiar in everyday life, when we deal with units of measure. For example, the quantity "3 weeks, 2 days, 9 hours, 22 minutes, 57 seconds, and 492 milliseconds" is equal to

$$\begin{bmatrix} 3, & 2, & 9, & 22, & 57; & 492 \\ & 7, & 24, & 60, & 60; & 1000 \end{bmatrix} \text{ seconds.}$$

The quantity "10 pounds, 6 shillings, and thruppence ha'penny" was once equal to $\begin{bmatrix} 10, & 6, & 3; & 1 \\ & 20, & 12; & 2 \end{bmatrix}$ pence in British currency, before Great Britain changed to a purely decimal monetary system.

It is possible to add and subtract mixed-radix numbers by using a straightforward generalization of the usual addition and subtraction algorithms, provided of course that the same mixed-radix system is being used for both operands (see exercise 4.3.1–9). Similarly, we can easily multiply or divide a mixed-radix number by small integer constants, using simple extensions of the familiar pencil-and-paper methods.

Mixed-radix systems were first discussed in full generality by Georg Cantor [*Zeitschrift für Math. und Physik* **14** (1869), 121–128]. Exercises 26 and 29 give further information about them.

Intriguing questions concerning *irrational* radices have been investigated by A. Rényi, *Acta Math. Acad. Sci. Hung.* **8** (1957), 477–493; W. Parry, *Acta Math. Acad. Sci. Hung.* **11** (1960), 401–416.

Besides the systems described in this section, several other important ways to represent numbers are mentioned elsewhere in this series of books: the combinatorial number system (exercise 1.2.6–56); the Fibonacci number system (exercises 1.2.8–34, 5.4.2–10); the phi number system (exercise 1.2.8–35); modular representations (Section 4.3.2); regular continued fractions (Section 4.5.3); Gray codes (Section 7.2.1.1); and Roman numerals (Section 9.1).

EXERCISES

1. [*15*] Express -10, -9, ..., 9, 10 in the number system whose radix is -2.

▶ **2.** [*24*] Consider the following four number systems: (a) binary (signed magnitude), (b) negabinary (radix -2); (c) balanced ternary; and (d) radix $b = \frac{1}{10}$. Use each of these four number systems to express each of the following three numbers: (i) -49; (ii) $-3\frac{1}{7}$ (show the repeating cycle); (iii) π (to a few significant figures).

3. [*20*] Express $-49 + i$ in the quater-imaginary system.

4. [*15*] Assume that we have a `MIX` program in which location `A` contains a number for which the radix point lies between bytes 3 and 4, while location `B` contains a number whose radix point lies between bytes 2 and 3. (The leftmost byte is number 1.) Where will the radix point be, in registers A and X, after the following instructions?

(a) `LDA A;   MUL B`   (b) `LDA A;   SRAX 5;   DIV B`

5. [*00*] Explain why a negative integer in nines' complement notation has a representation in ten's complement notation that is always one greater, if the representations are regarded as positive.

6. [*16*] What are the largest and smallest p-bit integers that can be represented in (a) signed magnitude binary notation (including one bit for the sign), (b) two's complement notation, (c) ones' complement notation?

7. [*M20*] The text defines ten's complement notation only for integers represented in a single computer word. Is there a way to define a ten's complement notation *for all real numbers*, having "infinite precision," analogous to the text's definition? Is there a similar way to define a nines' complement notation for all real numbers?

8. [*M10*] Prove Eq. (5).

▸ **9.** [*15*] Change the following *octal* numbers to *hexadecimal* notation, using the hexadecimal digits 0, 1, ..., 9, A, B, C, D, E, F: *12*; *5655*; *2550276*; *76545336*; *3726755*.

10. [*M22*] Generalize Eq. (5) to mixed-radix notation as in (9).

11. [*22*] Design an algorithm that uses the -2 number system to compute the sum of $(a_n \ldots a_1 a_0)_{-2}$ and $(b_n \ldots b_1 b_0)_{-2}$, obtaining the answer $(c_{n+2} \ldots c_1 c_0)_{-2}$.

12. [*23*] Specify algorithms that convert (a) the binary signed magnitude number $\pm(a_n \ldots a_0)_2$ to its negabinary form $(b_{n+2} \ldots b_0)_{-2}$; and (b) the negabinary number $(b_{n+1} \ldots b_0)_{-2}$ to its signed magnitude form $\pm(a_{n+1} \ldots a_0)_2$.

▸ **13.** [*M21*] In the decimal system there are some numbers with two infinite decimal expansions; for example, $2.3599999\ldots = 2.3600000\ldots$. Does the *negadecimal* (base -10) system have unique expansions, or are there real numbers with two different infinite expansions in this base also?

14. [*14*] Multiply $(11321)_{2i}$ by itself in the quater-imaginary system using the method illustrated in the text.

15. [*M24*] What are the sets $S = \{\sum_{k \geq 1} a_k b^{-k} \mid a_k \text{ an allowable digit}\}$, analogous to Fig. 1, for the negative decimal and for the quater-imaginary number systems?

16. [*M24*] Design an algorithm to add 1 to $(a_n \ldots a_1 a_0)_{i-1}$ in the $i-1$ number system.

17. [*M30*] It may seem peculiar that $i - 1$ has been suggested as a number-system base, instead of the similar but intuitively simpler number $i + 1$. Can every complex number $a + bi$, where a and b are integers, be represented in a positional number system to base $i + 1$, using only the digits 0 and 1?

18. [*HM32*] Show that the twindragon of Fig. 1 is a closed set that contains a neighborhood of the origin. (Consequently, every complex number has a binary representation with radix $i - 1$.)

▸ **19.** [*23*] (David W. Matula.) Let D be a set of b integers, containing exactly one solution to the congruence $x \equiv j$ (modulo b) for $0 \leq j < b$. Prove that all integers m (positive, negative, or zero) can be represented in the form $m = (a_n \ldots a_0)_b$, where all the a_j are in D, if and only if all integers in the range $l \leq m \leq u$ can be so represented, where $l = -\max\{a \mid a \in D\}/(b - 1)$ and $u = -\min\{a \mid a \in D\}/(b - 1)$. For example,

$D = \{-1, 0, \ldots, b-2\}$ satisfies the conditions for all $b \geq 3$. [*Hint:* Design an algorithm that constructs a suitable representation.]

20. [*HM28*] (David W. Matula.) Consider a decimal number system that uses the digits $D = \{-1, 0, 8, 17, 26, 35, 44, 53, 62, 71\}$ instead of $\{0, 1, \ldots, 9\}$. The result of exercise 19 implies (as in exercise 18) that all real numbers have an infinite decimal expansion using digits from D.

In the usual decimal system, exercise 13 points out that some numbers have two representations. (a) Find a real number that has *more* than two D-decimal representations. (b) Show that no real number has infinitely many D-decimal representations. (c) Show that uncountably many numbers have two or more D-decimal representations.

▶ **21.** [*M22*] (C. E. Shannon.) Can every real number (positive, negative, or zero) be expressed in a "balanced decimal" system, that is, in the form $\sum_{k \leq n} a_k 10^k$, for some integer n and some sequence $a_n, a_{n-1}, a_{n-2}, \ldots$, where each a_k is one of the ten numbers $\{-4\frac{1}{2}, -3\frac{1}{2}, -2\frac{1}{2}, -1\frac{1}{2}, -\frac{1}{2}, \frac{1}{2}, 1\frac{1}{2}, 2\frac{1}{2}, 3\frac{1}{2}, 4\frac{1}{2}\}$? (Although zero is not one of the allowed digits, we implicitly assume that $a_{n+1}, a_{n+2}, \ldots$ are zero.) Find all representations of zero in this number system, and find all representations of unity.

22. [*HM25*] Let $\alpha = -\sum_{m \geq 1} 10^{-m^2}$. Given $\epsilon > 0$ and any real number x, prove that there is a "decimal" representation such that $0 < |x - \sum_{k=0}^{n} a_k 10^k| < \epsilon$, where each a_k is allowed to be only one of the three values 0, 1, or α. (No negative powers of 10 are used in this representation!)

23. [*HM30*] Let D be a set of b real numbers such that every positive real number has a representation $\sum_{k \leq n} a_k b^k$ with all $a_k \in D$. Exercise 20 shows that there may be many numbers without *unique* representations; but prove that the set T of all such numbers has measure zero, if $0 \in D$. Show that this conclusion need not be true if $0 \notin D$.

24. [*M35*] Find infinitely many different sets D of ten nonnegative integers satisfying the following three conditions: (i) $\gcd(D) = 1$; (ii) $0 \in D$; (iii) every positive real number can be represented in the form $\sum_{k \leq n} a_k 10^k$ with all $a_k \in D$.

25. [*M25*] (S. A. Cook.) Let b, u, and v be positive integers, where $b \geq 2$ and $0 < v < b^m$. Show that the radix-b representation of u/v does not contain a run of m consecutive digits equal to $b - 1$, anywhere to the right of the radix point. (By convention, no runs of infinitely many $(b - 1)$'s are permitted in the standard radix-b representation.)

▶ **26.** [*HM30*] (N. S. Mendelsohn.) Let $\langle \beta_n \rangle$ be a sequence of real numbers defined for all integers n, $-\infty < n < \infty$, such that

$$\beta_n < \beta_{n+1}; \qquad \lim_{n \to \infty} \beta_n = \infty; \qquad \lim_{n \to -\infty} \beta_n = 0.$$

Let $\langle c_n \rangle$ be an arbitrary sequence of positive integers that is defined for all integers n, $-\infty < n < \infty$. Let us say that a number x has a "generalized representation" if there is an integer n and an infinite sequence of integers $a_n, a_{n-1}, a_{n-2}, \ldots$ such that $x = \sum_{k \leq n} a_k \beta_k$, where $a_n \neq 0$, $0 \leq a_k \leq c_k$, and $a_k < c_k$ for infinitely many k.

Show that every positive real number x has exactly one generalized representation if and only if

$$\beta_{n+1} = \sum_{k \leq n} c_k \beta_k \qquad \text{for all } n.$$

(Consequently, the mixed-radix systems with integer bases all have this property; and mixed-radix systems with $\beta_1 = (c_0 + 1)\beta_0$, $\beta_2 = (c_1 + 1)(c_0 + 1)\beta_0$, $\ldots$, $\beta_{-1} = \beta_0/(c_{-1} + 1)$, $\ldots$ are the most general number systems of this type.)

27. [*M21*] Show that every nonzero integer has a unique "reversing binary representation"

$$2^{e_0} - 2^{e_1} + \cdots + (-1)^t 2^{e_t},$$

where $e_0 < e_1 < \cdots < e_t$.

▶ **28.** [*M24*] Show that every nonzero complex number of the form $a + bi$ where a and b are integers has a unique "revolving binary representation"

$$(1+i)^{e_0} + i(1+i)^{e_1} - (1+i)^{e_2} - i(1+i)^{e_3} + \cdots + i^t(1+i)^{e_t},$$

where $e_0 < e_1 < \cdots < e_t$. (Compare with exercise 27.)

29. [*M35*] (N. G. de Bruijn.) Let S_0, S_1, S_2, ... be sets of nonnegative integers; we will say that the collection $\{S_0, S_1, S_2, \ldots\}$ has Property B if every nonnegative integer n can be written in the form

$$n = s_0 + s_1 + s_2 + \cdots, \qquad s_j \in S_j,$$

in exactly one way. (Property B implies that $0 \in S_j$ for all j, since $n = 0$ can only be represented as $0 + 0 + 0 + \cdots$.) Any mixed-radix number system with radices b_0, b_1, b_2, ... provides an example of a collection of sets satisfying Property B, if we let $S_j = \{0, B_j, \ldots, (b_j - 1)B_j\}$, where $B_j = b_0 b_1 \ldots b_{j-1}$; here the representation of $n = s_0 + s_1 + s_2 + \cdots$ corresponds in an obvious manner to its mixed-radix representation (9). Furthermore, if the collection $\{S_0, S_1, S_2, \ldots\}$ has Property B, and if A_0, A_1, A_2, ... is any partition of the nonnegative integers (so that we have $A_0 \cup A_1 \cup A_2 \cup \cdots = \{0, 1, 2, \ldots\}$ and $A_i \cap A_j = \emptyset$ for $i \neq j$; some A_j's may be empty), then the "collapsed" collection $\{T_0, T_1, T_2, \ldots\}$ also has Property B, where T_j is the set of all sums $\sum_{i \in A_j} s_i$ taken over all possible choices of $s_i \in S_i$.

Prove that *any* collection $\{T_0, T_1, T_2, \ldots\}$ that satisfies Property B may be obtained by collapsing some collection $\{S_0, S_1, S_2, \ldots\}$ that corresponds to a mixed-radix number system.

30. [*M39*] (N. G. de Bruijn.) The negabinary number system shows us that every integer (positive, negative, or zero) has a unique representation of the form

$$(-2)^{e_1} + (-2)^{e_2} + \cdots + (-2)^{e_t}, \qquad e_1 > e_2 > \cdots > e_t \geq 0, \qquad t \geq 0.$$

The purpose of this exercise is to explore generalizations of this phenomenon.

a) Let b_0, b_1, b_2, ... be a sequence of integers such that every integer n has a unique representation of the form

$$n = b_{e_1} + b_{e_2} + \cdots + b_{e_t}, \qquad e_1 > e_2 > \cdots > e_t \geq 0, \qquad t \geq 0.$$

(Such a sequence $\langle b_n \rangle$ is called a "binary basis.") Show that there is an index j such that b_j is odd, but b_k is even for all $k \neq j$.

b) Prove that a binary basis $\langle b_n \rangle$ can always be rearranged into the form d_0, $2d_1$, $4d_2$, $\ldots = \langle 2^n d_n \rangle$, where each d_k is odd.

c) If each of d_0, d_1, d_2, ... in (b) is ± 1, prove that $\langle b_n \rangle$ is a binary basis if and only if there are infinitely many $+1$'s and infinitely many -1's.

d) Prove that 7, $-13 \cdot 2$, $7 \cdot 2^2$, $-13 \cdot 2^3$, $\ldots$, $7 \cdot 2^{2k}$, $-13 \cdot 2^{2k+1}$, $\ldots$ is a binary basis, and find the representation of $n = 1$.

▶ **31.** [*M35*] A generalization of two's complement arithmetic, called "2-adic numbers," was introduced by K. Hensel in *Jahresbreicht der Deutschen Mathematiker-Vereinigung* **6** (1897), 83–88. (In fact he treated *p-adic numbers*, for any prime p.) A 2-adic number may be regarded as a binary number

$$u = (\dots u_3 u_2 u_1 u_0 . u_{-1} \dots u_{-n})_2,$$

whose representation extends infinitely far to the left of the binary point, but only finitely many places to the right. Addition, subtraction, and multiplication of 2-adic numbers are done according to the ordinary procedures of arithmetic, which can in principle be extended indefinitely to the left. For example,

$$7 = (\dots 000000000000111)_2 \qquad \tfrac{1}{7} = (\dots 110110110110111)_2$$
$$-7 = (\dots 111111111111001)_2 \qquad -\tfrac{1}{7} = (\dots 001001001001001)_2$$
$$\tfrac{7}{4} = (\dots 000000000000001.11)_2 \qquad \tfrac{1}{10} = (\dots 110011001100110.1)_2$$
$$\sqrt{-7} = (\dots 100000010110101)_2 \quad \text{or} \quad (\dots 011111101001011)_2.$$

Here 7 appears as the ordinary binary integer seven, while -7 is its two's complement (extending infinitely to the left); it is easy to verify that the ordinary procedure for addition of binary numbers will give $-7 + 7 = (\dots 00000)_2 = 0$, when the procedure is continued indefinitely. The values of $\tfrac{1}{7}$ and $-\tfrac{1}{7}$ are the unique 2-adic numbers that, when formally multiplied by 7, give 1 and -1, respectively. The values of $\tfrac{7}{4}$ and $\tfrac{1}{10}$ are examples of 2-adic numbers that are not 2-adic "integers," since they have nonzero bits to the right of the binary point. The two values of $\sqrt{-7}$, which are negatives of each other, are the only 2-adic numbers that, when formally squared, yield the value $(\dots 111111111111001)_2$.

a) Prove that any 2-adic number u can be divided by any nonzero 2-adic number v to obtain a unique 2-adic number w satisfying $u = vw$. (Hence the set of 2-adic numbers forms a "field"; see Section 4.6.1.)

b) Prove that the 2-adic representation of the rational number $-1/(2n+1)$ may be obtained as follows, when n is a positive integer: First find the ordinary binary expansion of $+1/(2n+1)$, which has the periodic form $(0.\alpha\alpha\alpha\dots)_2$ for some string α of 0s and 1s. Then $-1/(2n+1)$ is the 2-adic number $(\dots\alpha\alpha\alpha)_2$.

c) Prove that the representation of a 2-adic number u is ultimately periodic (that is, $u_{N+\lambda} = u_N$ for all large N, for some $\lambda \geq 1$) if and only if u is rational (that is, $u = m/n$, for some integers m and n).

d) Prove that, when n is an integer, $\sqrt{n}$ is a 2-adic number if and only if it satisfies $n \bmod 2^{2k+3} = 2^{2k}$ for some nonnegative integer k. (Thus, the possibilities are either $n \bmod 8 = 1$, or $n \bmod 32 = 4$, etc.)

32. [*M40*] (I. Z. Ruzsa.) Construct infinitely many integers whose ternary representation uses only 0s and 1s and whose quinary representation uses only 0s, 1s, and 2s.

33. [*M40*] (D. A. Klarner.) Let D be any set of integers, let b be any positive integer, and let k_n be the number of distinct integers that can be written as n-digit numbers $(a_{n-1}\dots a_1 a_0)_b$ to base b with digits a_i in D. Prove that the sequence $\langle k_n \rangle$ satisfies a linear recurrence relation, and explain how to compute the generating function $\sum_n k_n z^n$. Illustrate your algorithm by showing that k_n is a Fibonacci number in the case $b = 3$ and $D = \{-1, 0, 3\}$.

▶ **34.** [*22*] (G. W. Reitwiesner, 1960.) Explain how to represent a given integer n in the form $(\dots a_2 a_1 a_0)_2$, where each a_j is -1, 0, or 1, using the fewest nonzero digits.

4.2. FLOATING POINT ARITHMETIC

IN THIS SECTION we shall study the basic principles of arithmetic operations on "floating point" numbers, by analyzing the internal mechanisms underlying such calculations. Perhaps many readers will have little interest in this subject, since their computers either have built-in floating point instructions or their operating systems include suitable subroutines. But, in fact, the material of this section should not merely be the concern of computer-design engineers or of a small clique of people who write library subroutines for new machines; *every* well-rounded programmer ought to have a knowledge of what goes on during the elementary steps of floating point arithmetic. This subject is not at all as trivial as most people think, and it involves a surprising amount of interesting information.

4.2.1. Single-Precision Calculations

A. Floating point notation. We have discussed "fixed point" notation for numbers in Section 4.1; in such a case the programmer knows where the radix point is assumed to lie in the numbers being manipulated. For many purposes, however, it is considerably more convenient to let the position of the radix point be dynamically variable or "floating" as a program is running, and to carry with each number an indication of its current radix point position. This idea has been used for many years in scientific calculations, especially for expressing very large numbers like Avogadro's number $N = 6.02214076 \times 10^{23}$ mol^{-1}, or very small numbers like Planck's constant $h = 6.62607015 \times 10^{-34}$ J s.

In this section we shall work with *base b, excess q, floating point numbers with p digits*: Such numbers will be represented by pairs of values (e, f), denoting

$$(e, f) = f \times b^{e-q}. \tag{1}$$

Here e is an integer having a specified range, and f is a signed fraction. We will adopt the convention that

$$|f| < 1;$$

in other words, the radix point appears at the left of the positional representation of f. More precisely, the stipulation that we have p-digit numbers means that $b^p f$ is an integer, and that

$$-b^p < b^p f < b^p. \tag{2}$$

The term "floating binary" implies that $b = 2$, "floating decimal" implies $b = 10$, etc. Using excess-50 floating decimal numbers with 8 digits, we can write, for example,

$$\begin{aligned}
\text{Avogadro's number} \quad & N = (74, +.60221408); \\
\text{Planck's constant} \quad & h = (17, +.66260702).
\end{aligned} \tag{3}$$

The two components e and f of a floating point number are called the *exponent* and the *fraction* parts, respectively. (Other names are occasionally used for this purpose, notably "characteristic" and "mantissa"; but it is an abuse of terminology to call the fraction part a mantissa, since that term has quite a different meaning in connection with logarithms. Furthermore the English word mantissa means "a worthless addition.")

The MIX computer assumes that its floating point numbers have the form

$$\boxed{\pm \,|\, e \,|\, f \,|\, f \,|\, f \,|\, f} \,. \tag{4}$$

Here we have base b, excess q, floating point notation with four bytes of precision, where b is the byte size (e.g., $b = 64$ or $b = 100$), and q is equal to $\lfloor \frac{1}{2} b \rfloor$. The fraction part is $\pm f f f f$, and e is the exponent, which lies in the range $0 \le e < b$. This internal representation is typical of the conventions in most existing computers, although b is a much larger base than usual.

B. Normalized calculations. A floating point number (e, f) is *normalized* if the most significant digit of the representation of f is nonzero, so that

$$1/b \le |f| < 1; \tag{5}$$

or if $f = 0$ and e has its smallest possible value. It is possible to tell which of two normalized floating point numbers has a greater magnitude by comparing the exponent parts first, and then testing the fraction parts only if the exponents are equal.

Most floating point routines now in use deal almost entirely with normalized numbers: Inputs to the routines are assumed to be normalized, and the outputs are always normalized. Under these conventions we lose the ability to represent a few numbers of very small magnitude — for example, the value $(0, .00000001)$ can't be normalized without producing a negative exponent — but we gain in speed, uniformity, and the ability to give relatively simple bounds on the relative error in our computations. (Unnormalized floating point arithmetic is discussed in Section 4.2.2.)

Let us now study the normalized floating point operations in detail. At the same time we can consider the construction of subroutines for these operations, assuming that we have a computer without built-in floating point hardware.

Machine-language subroutines for floating point arithmetic are usually written in a very machine-dependent manner, using many of the wildest idiosyncrasies of the computer at hand. Therefore floating point addition subroutines for two different machines usually bear little superficial resemblance to each other. Yet a careful study of numerous subroutines for both binary and decimal computers reveals that these programs actually have quite a lot in common, and it is possible to discuss the topics in a machine-independent way.

The first (and by far the most difficult!) algorithm we shall discuss in this section is a procedure for floating point addition,

$$(e_u, f_u) \oplus (e_v, f_v) = (e_w, f_w). \tag{6}$$

Since floating point arithmetic is inherently approximate, not exact, we will use "round" symbols

$$\oplus, \quad \ominus, \quad \otimes, \quad \oslash$$

to stand for floating point addition, subtraction, multiplication, and division, respectively, in order to distinguish approximate operations from the true ones.

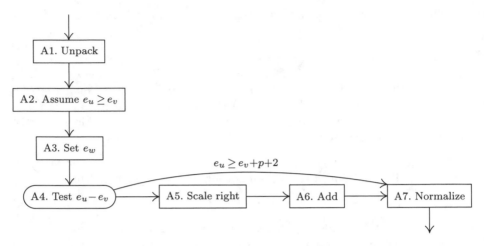

Fig. 2. Floating point addition.

The basic idea involved in floating point addition is fairly simple: Assuming that $e_u \geq e_v$, we take $e_w = e_u$, $f_w = f_u + f_v/b^{e_u-e_v}$ (thereby aligning the radix points for a meaningful addition), and normalize the result. But several situations can arise that make this process nontrivial, and the following algorithm explains the method more precisely.

Algorithm A (*Floating point addition*). Given base b, excess q, p-digit, normalized floating point numbers $u = (e_u, f_u)$ and $v = (e_v, f_v)$, this algorithm forms the sum $w = u \oplus v$. The same procedure may be used for floating point subtraction, if $-v$ is substituted for v.

A1. [Unpack.] Separate the exponent and fraction parts of the representations of u and v.

A2. [Assume $e_u \geq e_v$.] If $e_u < e_v$, interchange u and v. (In many cases, it is best to combine step A2 with step A1 or with some of the later steps.)

A3. [Set e_w.] Set $e_w \leftarrow e_u$.

A4. [Test $e_u - e_v$.] If $e_u - e_v \geq p+2$ (large difference in exponents), set $f_w \leftarrow f_u$ and go to step A7. (Actually, since we are assuming that u is normalized, we could terminate the algorithm; but it is occasionally useful to be able to normalize a possibly unnormalized number by adding zero to it.)

A5. [Scale right.] Shift f_v to the right $e_u - e_v$ places; that is, divide it by $b^{e_u-e_v}$. [*Note:* This will be a shift of up to $p + 1$ places, and the next step (which adds f_u to f_v) thereby requires an accumulator capable of holding $2p + 1$ base-b digits to the right of the radix point. If such a large accumulator is not available, it is possible to shorten the requirement to $p + 2$ or $p + 3$ places if proper precautions are taken; the details are given in exercise 5.]

A6. [Add.] Set $f_w \leftarrow f_u + f_v$.

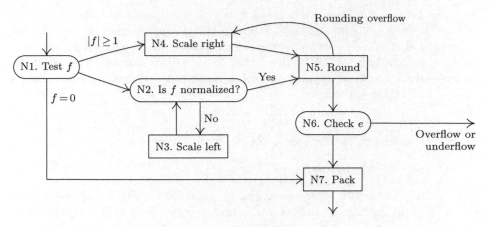

Fig. 3. Normalization of (e, f).

A7. [Normalize.] (At this point (e_w, f_w) represents the sum of u and v, but $|f_w|$ may have more than p digits, and it may be greater than unity or less than $1/b$.) Perform Algorithm N below, to normalize and round (e_w, f_w) into the final answer. ▌

Algorithm N (*Normalization*). A "raw exponent" e and a "raw fraction" f are converted to normalized form, rounding if necessary to p digits. This algorithm assumes that $|f| < b$.

N1. [Test f.] If $|f| \geq 1$ ("fraction overflow"), go to step N4. If $f = 0$, set e to its lowest possible value and go to step N7.

N2. [Is f normalized?] If $|f| \geq 1/b$, go to step N5.

N3. [Scale left.] Shift f to the left by one digit position (that is, multiply it by b), and decrease e by 1. Return to step N2.

N4. [Scale right.] Shift f to the right by one digit position (that is, divide it by b), and increase e by 1.

N5. [Round.] Round f to p places. (We take this to mean that f is changed to the nearest multiple of b^{-p}. It is possible that $(b^p f) \bmod 1 = \frac{1}{2}$ so that there are *two* nearest multiples; if b is even, we change f to the nearest multiple f' of b^{-p} such that $b^p f' + \frac{1}{2}b$ is odd. Further discussion of rounding appears in Section 4.2.2.) It is important to note that this rounding operation can make $|f| = 1$ ("rounding overflow"); in such a case, return to step N4.

N6. [Check e.] If e is too large, that is, greater than its allowed range, an *exponent overflow* condition is sensed. If e is too small, an *exponent underflow* condition is sensed. (See the discussion below; since the result cannot be expressed as a normalized floating point number in the required range, special action is necessary.)

N7. [Pack.] Put e and f together into the desired output representation. ▌

Some simple examples of floating point addition are given in exercise 4.

The following MIX subroutines, for addition and subtraction of numbers having the form (4), show how Algorithms A and N can be expressed as computer programs. The subroutines below are designed to take one input u from symbolic location ACC, and the other input v comes from register A upon entrance to the subroutine. The output w appears both in register A and location ACC. Thus, a fixed point coding sequence

$$\text{LDA A; ADD B; SUB C; STA D} \tag{7}$$

would correspond to the floating point coding sequence

$$\text{LDA A, STA ACC; LDA B, JMP FADD; LDA C, JMP FSUB; STA D.} \tag{8}$$

Program A (*Addition, subtraction, and normalization*). The following program is a subroutine for Algorithm A, and it is also designed so that the normalization portion can be used by other subroutines that appear later in this section. In this program and in many others throughout this chapter, OFLO stands for a subroutine that prints out a message to the effect that MIX's overflow toggle was unexpectedly found to be on. The byte size b is assumed to be a multiple of 4. The normalization routine NORM assumes that $rI2 = e$ and $rAX = f$, where $rA = 0$ implies $rX = 0$ and $rI2 < b$.

00	BYTE	EQU	1(4:4)	Byte size b
01	EXP	EQU	1:1	Definition of exponent field
02	FSUB	STA	TEMP	Floating point subtraction subroutine:
03		LDAN	TEMP	Change sign of operand.
04	FADD	STJ	EXITF	Floating point addition subroutine:
05		JOV	OFLO	Ensure that overflow is off.
06		STA	TEMP	TEMP $\leftarrow v$.
07		LDX	ACC	$rX \leftarrow u$.
08		CMPA	ACC(EXP)	<u>Steps A1, A2, A3 are combined here:</u>
09		JGE	1F	Jump if $e_v \geq e_u$.
10		STX	FU(0:4)	FU $\leftarrow \pm f f f f 0$.
11		LD2	ACC(EXP)	$rI2 \leftarrow e_w$.
12		STA	FV(0:4)	
13		LD1N	TEMP(EXP)	$rI1 \leftarrow -e_v$.
14		JMP	4F	
15	1H	STA	FU(0:4)	FU $\leftarrow \pm f f f f 0$ $(u, v$ interchanged).
16		LD2	TEMP(EXP)	$rI2 \leftarrow e_w$.
17		STX	FV(0:4)	
18		LD1N	ACC(EXP)	$rI1 \leftarrow -e_v$.
19	4H	INC1	0,2	$rI1 \leftarrow e_u - e_v$. (Step A4 unnecessary.)
20	5H	LDA	FV	<u>A5. Scale right.</u>
21		ENTX	0	Clear rX.
22		SRAX	0,1	Shift right $e_u - e_v$ places.
23	6H	ADD	FU	<u>A6. Add.</u>
24		JOV	N4	<u>A7. Normalize.</u> Jump if fraction overflow.
25		JXZ	NORM	Easy case?
26		LD1	FV(0:1)	Check for opposite signs.
27		JAP	1F	

28		J1N	N2	If not, normalize.
29		JMP	2F	
30	1H	J1P	N2	
31	2H	SRC	5	$\lvert rX\rvert \leftrightarrow \lvert rA\rvert$.
32		DECX	1	(rX is positive.)
33		STA	TEMP	(The operands had opposite signs;
34		STA	HALF(0:0)	we must adjust the registers
35		LDAN	TEMP	before rounding and normalization.)
36		ADD	HALF	
37		ADD	HALF	Complement the least significant portion.
38		SRC	5	Jump into normalization routine.
39		JMP	N2	
40	HALF	CON	1//2	Half of the word size (Sign varies)
41	FU	CON	0	Fraction part f_u
42	FV	CON	0	Fraction part f_v
43	NORM	JAZ	ZRO	*N1. Test f.*
44	N2	CMPA	=0=(1:1)	*N2. Is f normalized?*
45		JNE	N5	To N5 if leading byte nonzero.
46	N3	SLAX	1	*N3. Scale left.*
47		DEC2	1	Decrease e by 1.
48		JMP	N2	Return to N2.
49	N4	ENTX	1	*N4. Scale right.*
50		SRC	1	Shift right, insert "1" with proper sign.
51		INC2	1	Increase e by 1.
52	N5	CMPA	=BYTE/2=(5:5)	*N5. Round.*
53		JL	N6	Is $\lvert\text{tail}\rvert < \frac{1}{2}b$?
54		JG	5F	
55		JXNZ	5F	Is $\lvert\text{tail}\rvert > \frac{1}{2}b$?
56		STA	TEMP	$\lvert\text{tail}\rvert = \frac{1}{2}b$; round to odd.
57		LDX	TEMP(4:4)	
58		JXO	N6	To N6 if rX is odd.
59	5H	STA	*+1(0:0)	Store sign of rA.
60		INCA	BYTE	Add b^{-4} to $\lvert f\rvert$. (Sign varies)
61		JOV	N4	Check for rounding overflow.
62	N6	J2N	EXPUN	*N6. Check e.* Underflow if $e < 0$.
63	N7	ENTX	0,2	*N7. Pack.* rX $\leftarrow e$.
64		SRC	1	
65	ZRO	DEC2	BYTE	rI2 $\leftarrow e - b$.
66	8H	STA	ACC	
67	EXITF	J2N	*	Exit, unless $e \geq b$.
68	EXPOV	HLT	2	Exponent overflow detected
69	EXPUN	HLT	1	Exponent underflow detected
70	ACC	CON	0	Floating point accumulator ∎

The rather long section of code from lines 26 to 40 is needed because MIX has only a 5-byte accumulator for adding signed numbers while in general $2p + 1 = 9$ places of accuracy are required by Algorithm A. The program could be shortened to about half its present length if we were willing to sacrifice a little bit of its accuracy, but we shall see in the next section that full accuracy is important. Line 58 uses a nonstandard MIX instruction defined in Section 4.5.2. The running time for floating point addition and subtraction depends on several factors that are analyzed in Section 4.2.4.

Now let us consider multiplication and division, which are simpler than addition, and somewhat similar to each other.

Algorithm M (*Floating point multiplication or division*). Given base b, excess q, p-digit, normalized floating point numbers $u = (e_u, f_u)$ and $v = (e_v, f_v)$, this algorithm forms the product $w = u \otimes v$ or the quotient $w = u \oslash v$.

M1. [Unpack.] Separate the exponent and fraction parts of the representations of u and v. (Sometimes it is convenient, but not necessary, to test the operands for zero during this step.)

M2. [Operate.] Set

$$e_w \leftarrow e_u + e_v - q, \qquad f_w \leftarrow f_u f_v \qquad \text{for multiplication;}$$
$$e_w \leftarrow e_u - e_v + q + 1, \quad f_w \leftarrow (b^{-1} f_u)/f_v \quad \text{for division.}$$

(9)

(Since the input numbers are assumed to be normalized, it follows that either $f_w = 0$, or $1/b^2 \le |f_w| < 1$, or a division-by-zero error has occurred.) If necessary, the representation of f_w may be reduced to $p+2$ or $p+3$ digits at this point, as in exercise 5.

M3. [Normalize.] Perform Algorithm N on (e_w, f_w) to normalize, round, and pack the result. (*Note:* Normalization is simpler in this case, since scaling left occurs at most once, and since rounding overflow cannot occur after division.) ∎

The following MIX subroutines, intended to be used in connection with Program A, illustrate the machine considerations that arise in Algorithm M.

Program M (*Floating point multiplication and division*).

```
01 Q      EQU  BYTE/2      q is half the byte size
02 FMUL   STJ  EXITF       Floating point multiplication subroutine:
03        JOV  OFLO        Ensure that overflow is off.
04        STA  TEMP        TEMP ← v.
05        LDX  ACC         rX ← u.
06        STX  FU(0:4)     FU ← ±f f f f 0.
07        LD1  TEMP(EXP)
08        LD2  ACC(EXP)
09        INC2 -Q,1        rI2 ← eu + ev − q.
10        SLA  1
11        MUL  FU          Multiply fu times fv.
12        JMP  NORM        Normalize, round, and exit.
13 FDIV   STJ  EXITF       Floating point division subroutine:
14        JOV  OFLO        Ensure that overflow is off.
15        STA  TEMP        TEMP ← v.
16        STA  FV(0:4)     FV ← ±f f f f 0.
17        LD1  TEMP(EXP)
18        LD2  ACC(EXP)
19        DEC2 -Q,1        rI2 ← eu − ev + q.
```

```
20          ENTX  0
21          LDA   ACC
22          SLA   1              rA ← fᵤ.
23          CMPA  FV(1:5)
24          JL    *+3            Jump if |fᵤ| < |fᵥ|.
25          SRA   1              Otherwise, scale fᵤ right
26          INC2  1                  and increase rI2 by 1.
27          DIV   FV             Divide.
28          JNOV  NORM           Normalize, round, and exit.
29  DVZRO   HLT   3              Unnormalized or zero divisor  ▮
```

The most noteworthy feature of this program is the provision for division in lines 23–26, which is made in order to ensure enough accuracy to round the answer. If $|f_u| < |f_v|$, straightforward application of Algorithm M would leave a result of the form "$\pm 0\,f\,f\,f\,f$" in register A, and this would not allow a proper rounding without a careful analysis of the remainder (which appears in register X). So the program computes $f_w \leftarrow f_u/f_v$ in this case, ensuring that f_w is either zero or normalized in all cases; rounding can proceed with five significant bytes, possibly testing whether the remainder is zero.

We occasionally need to convert values between fixed and floating point representations. A "fix-to-float" routine is easily obtained with the help of the normalization algorithm above; for example, in MIX, the following subroutine converts an integer to floating point form:

```
01  FLOT STJ   EXITF    Assume that rA = u, an integer.
02       JOV   OFLO     Ensure that overflow is off.
03       ENT2  Q+5      Set raw exponent.                      (10)
04       ENTX  0
05       JMP   NORM     Normalize, round, and exit.  ▮
```

A "float-to-fix" subroutine is the subject of exercise 14.

The debugging of floating point subroutines is usually a difficult job, since there are so many cases to consider. Here is a list of common pitfalls that often trap a programmer or machine designer who is preparing floating point routines:

1) *Losing the sign.* On many machines (not MIX), shift instructions between registers will affect the sign, and the shifting operations used in normalizing and scaling numbers must be carefully analyzed. The sign is also lost frequently when minus zero is present. (For example, Program A is careful to retain the sign of register A in lines 33–37. See also exercise 6.)

2) *Failure to treat exponent underflow or overflow properly.* The size of e_w should not be checked until *after* the rounding and normalization, because preliminary tests may give an erroneous indication. Exponent underflow and overflow can occur on floating point addition and subtraction, not only during multiplication and division; and even though this is a rather rare occurrence, it must be tested each time. Enough information should be retained so that meaningful corrective actions are possible after overflow or underflow has occurred.

It has unfortunately become customary in many instances to ignore exponent underflow and simply to set underflowed results to zero with no indication of error. This causes a serious loss of accuracy in most cases (indeed, it is the loss of *all* the significant digits), and the assumptions underlying floating point arithmetic have broken down; so the programmer really must be told when underflow has occurred. Setting the result to zero is appropriate only in certain cases when the result is later to be added to a significantly larger quantity. When exponent underflow is not detected, we find mysterious situations in which $(u \otimes v) \otimes w$ is zero, but $u \otimes (v \otimes w)$ is not, since $u \otimes v$ results in exponent underflow but $u \otimes (v \otimes w)$ can be calculated without any exponents falling out of range. Similarly, we can find positive numbers a, b, c, d, and y such that

$$(a \otimes y \oplus b) \oslash (c \otimes y \oplus d) \approx \tfrac{2}{3},$$

$$(a \oplus b \oslash y) \oslash (c \oplus d \oslash y) = 1$$

(11)

if exponent underflow is not detected. (See exercise 9.) Even though floating point routines are not precisely accurate, such a disparity as (11) is certainly unexpected when a, b, c, d, and y are all *positive*! Exponent underflow is usually not anticipated by a programmer, so it needs to be reported.*

3) *Inserted garbage.* When scaling to the left it is important to keep from introducing anything but zeros at the right. For example, note the 'ENTX 0' instruction in line 21 of Program A, and the all-too-easily-forgotten 'ENTX 0' instruction in line 04 of the FLOT subroutine (10). (But it would be a mistake to clear register X after line 27 in the division subroutine.)

4) *Unforeseen rounding overflow.* When a number like .999999997 is rounded to 8 digits, a carry will occur to the left of the decimal point, and the result must be scaled to the right. Many people have mistakenly concluded that rounding overflow is impossible during multiplication, since they look at the maximum value of $|f_u f_v|$, which is $1 - 2b^{-p} + b^{-2p}$; and this cannot round up to 1. The fallacy in this reasoning is exhibited in exercise 11. Curiously, it turns out that the phenomenon of rounding overflow *is* impossible during floating point division (see exercise 12).

---

* On the other hand, we must admit that today's high-level programming languages give the programmer little or no satisfactory way to make use of the information that a floating point routine wants to provide; and the MIX programs in this section, which simply halt when errors are detected, are even worse. There are numerous important applications in which exponent underflow is relatively harmless, and it is desirable to find a way for programmers to cope with such situations easily and safely. The practice of silently replacing underflows by zero has been thoroughly discredited, but there is another alternative that has recently been gaining much favor, namely to modify the definition that we have given for floating point numbers, allowing an unnormalized fraction part when the exponent has its smallest possible value. This idea of "gradual underflow," which was first embodied in the hardware of the Electrologica X8 computer, adds only a small amount of complexity to the algorithms, and it makes exponent underflow impossible during addition or subtraction. The simple formulas for relative error in Section 4.2.2 no longer hold in the presence of gradual underflow, so the topic is beyond the scope of this book. However, by using formulas like round$(x) = x(1-\delta)+\epsilon$, where $|\delta| < b^{1-p}/2$ and $|\epsilon| < b^{-p-q}/2$, one can show that gradual underflow succeeds in many important cases. See W. M. Kahan and J. Palmer, *ACM SIGNUM Newsletter* (October 1979), 13–21.

There is a school of thought that says it is harmless to "round" a value like
.999999997 to .99999999 instead of to 1.0000000, since this does not increase
the worst-case bounds on relative error. The floating decimal number 1.0000000
may be said to represent all real values in the interval

$$[1.0000000 - 5 \times 10^{-8} .. 1.0000000 + 5 \times 10^{-8}],$$

while .99999999 represents all values in the much smaller interval

$$(.99999999 - 5 \times 10^{-9} ... .99999999 + 5 \times 10^{-9}).$$

Even though the latter interval does not contain the original value .999999997,
each number of the second interval is contained in the first, so subsequent
calculations with the second interval are no less accurate than with the first. This
ingenious argument is, however, incompatible with the mathematical philosophy
of floating point arithmetic expressed in Section 4.2.2.

5) *Rounding before normalizing.* Inaccuracies are caused by premature rounding in the wrong digit position. This error is obvious when rounding is being done
to the left of the appropriate position; but it is also dangerous in the less obvious
cases where rounding is first done too far to the right, followed by rounding in the
true position. For this reason it is a mistake to round during the "scaling-right"
operation in step A5, except as prescribed in exercise 5. (The special case of
rounding in step N5, then rounding again after rounding overflow has occurred,
is harmless, however, because rounding overflow always yields ± 1.0000000 and
such values are unaffected by the subsequent rounding process.)

6) *Failure to retain enough precision in intermediate calculations.* Detailed
analyses of the accuracy of floating point arithmetic, made in the next section,
suggest strongly that normalizing floating point routines should always deliver
a properly rounded result to the maximum possible accuracy. There should
be no exceptions to this dictum, even in cases that occur with extremely low
probability; the appropriate number of significant digits should be retained
throughout the computations, as stated in Algorithms A and M.

C. Floating point hardware. Nearly every large computer intended for
scientific calculations includes floating point arithmetic as part of its repertoire of
built-in operations. Unfortunately, the design of such hardware usually includes
some anomalies that result in dismally poor behavior in certain circumstances,
and we hope that future computer designers will pay more attention to providing
the proper behavior than they have in the past. It costs only a little more
to build the machine right, and considerations in the following section show
that substantial benefits will be gained. Yesterday's compromises are no longer
appropriate for modern machines, based on what we know now.

The MIX computer, which is being used as an example of a "typical" machine
in this series of books, has an optional "floating point attachment" (available at
extra cost) that includes the following seven operations:

• FADD, FSUB, FMUL, FDIV, FLOT, FCMP ($C = 1, 2, 3, 4, 5, 56$, respectively; $F = 6$).
The contents of rA after the operation 'FADD V' are precisely the same as the

contents of rA after the operations

$$\texttt{STA ACC; \quad LDA V; \quad JMP FADD}$$

where `FADD` is the subroutine that appears earlier in this section, except that both operands are automatically normalized before entry to the subroutine if they were not already in normalized form. (If exponent underflow occurs during this pre-normalization, but not during the normalization of the answer, no underflow is signalled.) Similar remarks apply to `FSUB`, `FMUL`, and `FDIV`. The contents of rA after the operation 'FLOT' are the contents after 'JMP FLOT' in the subroutine (10) above.

The contents of rA are unchanged by the operation 'FCMP V'. This instruction sets the comparison indicator to LESS, EQUAL, or GREATER, depending on whether the contents of rA are "definitely less than," "approximately equal to," or "definitely greater than" V, as discussed in the next section. The precise action is defined by the subroutine `FCMP` of exercise 4.2.2–17 with `EPSILON` in location 0.

No register other than rA is affected by any of the floating point operations. If exponent overflow or underflow occurs, the overflow toggle is turned on and the exponent of the answer is given modulo the byte size. Division by zero leaves undefined garbage in rA. Execution times: $4u, 4u, 9u, 11u, 3u, 4u$, respectively.

• FIX ($C = 5$; $F = 7$). The contents of rA are replaced by the integer "round(rA)", rounding to the nearest integer as in step N5 of Algorithm N. However, if this answer is too large to fit in the register, the overflow toggle is set on and the result is undefined. Execution time: $3u$.

Sometimes it is helpful to use floating point operators in a nonstandard way. For example, if the operation `FLOT` had not been included as part of MIX's floating point attachment, we could easily achieve its effect on 4-byte numbers by writing

```
FLOT STJ   9F
     SLA   1
     ENTX  Q+4
     SRC   1
     FADD  =0=
9H   JMP   *
```
$$(12)$$

This routine is not strictly equivalent to the `FLOT` operator, since it assumes that the 1:1 byte of rA is zero, and it destroys rX. The handling of more general situations is a little tricky, because rounding overflow can occur even during a `FLOT` operation.

Similarly, suppose MIX had a `FADD` operation but not `FIX`. If we wanted to round a number u from floating point form to the nearest fixed point integer, and if we knew that the number was nonnegative and would fit in at most three bytes, we could write

$$\texttt{FADD \quad FUDGE}$$

where location FUDGE contains the constant

+	Q+4	1	0	0	0

;

the result in rA would be

+	Q+4	1	round(u)

. $\qquad$ (13)

D. History and bibliography. The origins of floating point notation can be traced back to Babylonian mathematicians (1800 B.C. or earlier), who made extensive use of radix-60 floating point arithmetic but did not have a notation for the exponents. The appropriate exponent was always somehow "understood" by whoever was doing the calculations. At least one case has been found in which the wrong answer was given because addition was performed with improper alignment of the operands, but such examples are very rare; see O. Neugebauer, *The Exact Sciences in Antiquity* (Princeton, N. J.: Princeton University Press, 1952), 26–27. Another early contribution to floating point notation is due to the Greek mathematician Apollonius (3rd century B.C.), who apparently was the first to explain how to simplify multiplication by collecting powers of 10 separately from their coefficients, at least in simple cases. [For a discussion of Apollonius's method, see Pappus, *Mathematical Collections* (4th century A.D.).] After the Babylonian civilization died out, the first significant uses of floating point notation for products and quotients did not emerge until much later, about the time logarithms were invented (1600) and shortly afterwards when Oughtred invented the slide rule (1630). The modern notation " x^n " for exponents was being introduced at about the same time; separate symbols for x squared, x cubed, etc., had been in use before this.

Floating point arithmetic was incorporated into the design of some of the earliest computers. It was independently proposed by Leonardo Torres y Quevedo in Madrid, 1914; by Konrad Zuse in Berlin, 1936; and by George Stibitz in New Jersey, 1939. Zuse's machines used a floating binary representation that he called "semi-logarithmic notation"; he also incorporated conventions for dealing with special quantities like "∞" and "undefined." The first American computers to operate with floating point arithmetic hardware were the Bell Laboratories' Model V and the Harvard Mark II, both of which were relay calculators designed in 1944. [See B. Randell, *The Origins of Digital Computers* (Berlin: Springer, 1973), 100, 155, 163–164, 259–260; *Proc. Symp. Large-Scale Digital Calculating Machinery* (Harvard, 1947), 41–68, 69–79; *Datamation* **13** (April 1967), 35–44 (May 1967), 45–49; *Zeit. für angew. Math. und Physik* **1** (1950), 345–346.]

The use of floating binary arithmetic was seriously considered in 1944–1946 by researchers at the Moore School in their plans for the first *electronic* digital computers, but they found that floating point circuitry was much harder to implement with tubes than with relays. The group realized that scaling was a problem in programming; but they knew that it was only a very small part of a total programming job in those days. Indeed, explicit fixed-point scaling seemed to be well worth the time and trouble it took, since it tended to keep programmers aware of the numerical accuracy they were getting. Furthermore, the machine designers argued that floating point representation would consume valuable memory space, since the exponents must be stored; and they noted that floating point hardware was not readily adapted to multiple-precision calculations. [See von Neumann's *Collected Works* **5** (New York: Macmillan, 1963), 43, 73–74.] At that time, of course, they were designing the first stored-program computer and the second electronic computer, and their choice had to be *either* fixed point *or* floating point arithmetic, not both. They anticipated the coding of floating binary subroutines, and in fact "shift left" and "shift right" instructions were put into their design primarily to make such routines more efficient. The first machine to have both kinds of arithmetic in its hardware was apparently a computer developed at General Electric Company [see *Proc. 2nd Symp. Large-Scale Digital Calculating Machinery* (Cambridge, Mass.: Harvard University Press, 1951), 65–69].

Floating point subroutines and interpretive systems for early machines were coded by D. J. Wheeler and others, and the first publication of such routines was in *The Preparation of Programs for an Electronic Digital Computer* by Wilkes, Wheeler, and Gill (Reading, Mass.: Addison–Wesley, 1951), subroutines A1–A11, pages 35–37 and 105–117. It is interesting to note that floating *decimal* subroutines are described here, although a binary computer was being used; in other words, the numbers were represented as $10^e f$, not $2^e f$, and therefore the scaling operations required multiplication or division by 10. On this particular machine such decimal scaling was almost as easy as shifting, and the decimal approach greatly simplified input/output conversions.

Most published references to the details of floating point arithmetic routines are scattered in technical memorandums distributed by various computer manufacturers, but there have been occasional appearances of these routines in the open literature. Besides the reference above, the following are of historical interest: R. H. Stark and D. B. MacMillan, *Math. Comp.* **5** (1951), 86–92, where a plugboard-wired program is described; D. McCracken, *Digital Computer Programming* (New York: Wiley, 1957), 121–131; J. W. Carr III, *CACM* **2**, 5 (May 1959), 10–15; W. G. Wadey, *JACM* **7** (1960), 129–139; D. E. Knuth, *JACM* **8** (1961), 119–128; O. Kesner, *CACM* **5** (1962), 269–271; F. P. Brooks and K. E. Iverson, *Automatic Data Processing* (New York: Wiley, 1963), 184–199. For a discussion of floating point arithmetic from a computer designer's standpoint, see "Floating point operation" by S. G. Campbell, in *Planning a Computer System*, edited by W. Buchholz (New York: McGraw–Hill, 1962), 92–121; A. Padegs, *IBM Systems J.* **7** (1968), 22–29. Additional references, which deal primarily with the accuracy of floating point methods, are given in Section 4.2.2.

A revolutionary change in floating point hardware took place when most manufacturers began to adopt ANSI/IEEE Standard 754 during the late 1980s. Relevant references are: *IEEE Micro* **4** (1984), 86–100; W. J. Cody, *Comp. Sci. and Statistics: Symp. on the Interface* **15** (1983), 133–139; W. M. Kahan, *Mini/Micro West-83 Conf. Record* (1983), Paper 16/1; D. Goldberg, *Computing Surveys* **23** (1991), 5–48, 413; W. J. Cody and J. T. Coonen, *ACM Trans. Math. Software* **19** (1993), 443–451.

The MMIX *computer, which will replace* MIX *in the next edition of this book, will naturally conform to the new standard.*

EXERCISES

1. [*10*] How would Avogadro's number and Planck's constant (3) be represented in base 100, excess 50, four-digit floating point notation? (This would be the representation used by MIX, as in (4), when the byte size is 100.)

2. [*12*] Assume that the exponent e is constrained to lie in the range $0 \le e \le E$; what are the largest and smallest positive values that can be written as base b, excess q, p-digit floating point numbers? What are the largest and smallest positive values that can be written as *normalized* floating point numbers with these specifications?

3. [*11*] (K. Zuse, 1936.) Show that if we are using normalized floating binary arithmetic, there is a way to increase the precision slightly without loss of memory space: A p-bit fraction part can be represented using only $p - 1$ bit positions of a computer word, if the range of exponent values is decreased very slightly.

▶ **4.** [*16*] Assume that $b = 10$, $p = 8$. What result does Algorithm A give for $(50, +.98765432) \oplus (49, +.33333333)$? For $(53, -.99987654) \oplus (54, +.10000000)$? For $(45, -.50000001) \oplus (54, +.10000000)$?

▶ **5.** [*24*] Let us say that $x \sim y$ (with respect to a given radix b) if x and y are real numbers satisfying the following conditions:

$$\lfloor x/b \rfloor = \lfloor y/b \rfloor;$$
$$x \bmod b = 0 \iff y \bmod b = 0;$$
$$0 < x \bmod b < \tfrac{1}{2}b \iff 0 < y \bmod b < \tfrac{1}{2}b;$$
$$x \bmod b = \tfrac{1}{2}b \iff y \bmod b = \tfrac{1}{2}b;$$
$$\tfrac{1}{2}b < x \bmod b < b \iff \tfrac{1}{2}b < y \bmod b < b.$$

Prove that if f_v is replaced by $b^{-p-2}F_v$ between steps A5 and A6 of Algorithm A, where $F_v \sim b^{p+2}f_v$, the result of that algorithm will be unchanged. (If F_v is an integer and b is even, this operation essentially truncates f_v to $p+2$ places while remembering whether any nonzero digits have been dropped, thereby minimizing the length of register that is needed for the addition in step A6.)

6. [*20*] If the result of a FADD instruction is zero, what will be the sign of rA, according to the definitions of MIX's floating point attachment given in this section?

7. [*27*] Discuss floating point arithmetic using balanced ternary notation.

8. [*20*] Give examples of normalized eight-digit floating decimal numbers u and v for which addition yields (a) exponent underflow, (b) exponent overflow, assuming that exponents must satisfy $0 \le e < 100$.

9. [*M24*] (W. M. Kahan.) Assume that the occurrence of exponent underflow causes the result to be replaced by zero, with no error indication given. Using excess zero, eight-digit floating decimal numbers with e in the range $-50 \le e < 50$, find positive values of a, b, c, d, and y such that (11) holds.

10. [*12*] Give an example of normalized eight-digit floating decimal numbers u and v for which rounding overflow occurs in addition.

▶ **11.** [*M20*] Give an example of normalized, excess 50, eight-digit floating decimal numbers u and v for which rounding overflow occurs in multiplication.

12. [*M25*] Prove that rounding overflow cannot occur during the normalization phase of floating point division.

13. [*30*] When doing "interval arithmetic" we don't want to round the results of a floating point computation; we want rather to implement operations such as $\bigtriangledown$ and $\bigtriangleup$, which give the tightest possible representable bounds on the true sum:

$$u \bigtriangledown v \le u + v \le u \bigtriangleup v.$$

How should the algorithms of this section be modified for such a purpose?

14. [*25*] Write a `MIX` subroutine that begins with an arbitrary floating point number in register A, not necessarily normalized, and converts it to the nearest fixed point integer (or determines that the number is too large in absolute value to make such a conversion possible).

▶ **15.** [*28*] Write a `MIX` subroutine, to be used in connection with the other subroutines of this section, that calculates u (mod) 1, namely $u - \lfloor u \rfloor$ rounded to the nearest floating point number, given a floating point number u. Notice that when u is a very small negative number, u (mod) 1 should be rounded so that the result is unity (even though u mod 1 has been defined to be always *less* than unity, as a real number).

16. [*HM21*] (Robert L. Smith.) Design an algorithm to compute the real and imaginary parts of the complex number $(a + bi)/(c + di)$, given real floating point values a, b, c, and d with $c + di \ne 0$. Avoid the computation of $c^2 + d^2$, since it would cause floating point overflow even when $|c|$ or $|d|$ is approximately the square root of the maximum allowable floating point value.

17. [*40*] (John Cocke.) Explore the idea of extending the range of floating point numbers by defining a single-word representation in which the precision of the fraction decreases as the magnitude of the exponent increases.

18. [*25*] Consider a binary computer with 36-bit words, on which positive floating binary numbers are represented as $(0\,e_1 e_2 \ldots e_8 f_1 f_2 \ldots f_{27})_2$; here $(e_1 e_2 \ldots e_8)_2$ is an excess $(10000000)_2$ exponent and $(f_1 f_2 \ldots f_{27})_2$ is a 27-bit fraction. Negative floating point numbers are represented by the *two's complement* of the corresponding positive representation (see Section 4.1). Thus, 1.5 is $201|600000000$ in octal notation, while -1.5 is $576|200000000$; the octal representations of 1.0 and -1.0 are $201|400000000$ and $576|400000000$, respectively. (A vertical line is used here to show the boundary between exponent and fraction.) Note that bit f_1 of a normalized positive number is always 1, while it is almost always zero for negative numbers; the exceptional cases are representations of -2^k.

Suppose that the exact result of a floating point operation has the octal code $572|740000000|01$; this (negative) 33-bit fraction must be normalized and rounded to 27 bits. If we shift left until the leading fraction bit is zero, we get $576|000000000|20$, but this rounds to the illegal value $576|000000000$; we have over-normalized, since the correct answer is $575|400000000$. On the other hand if we start (in some other problem) with the value $572|740000000|05$ and stop before over-normalizing it, we get $575|400000000|50$, which rounds to the unnormalized number $575|400000001$; subsequent normalization yields $576|000000002$ while the correct answer is $576|000000001$.

Give a simple, correct rounding rule that resolves this dilemma on such a machine (without abandoning two's complement notation).

19. [*24*] What is the running time for the `FADD` subroutine in Program A, in terms of relevant characteristics of the data? What is the maximum running time, over all inputs that do not cause exponent overflow or underflow?

Round numbers are always false.
— SAMUEL JOHNSON (1750)

I shall speak in round numbers, not absolutely accurate,
yet not so wide from truth as to vary the result materially.
— THOMAS JEFFERSON (1824)

4.2.2. Accuracy of Floating Point Arithmetic

Floating point computation is by nature inexact, and programmers can easily misuse it so that the computed answers consist almost entirely of "noise." One of the principal problems of numerical analysis is to determine how accurate the results of certain numerical methods will be. There's a credibility gap: We don't know how much of the computer's answers to believe. Novice computer users solve this problem by implicitly trusting in the computer as an infallible authority; they tend to believe that all digits of a printed answer are significant. Disillusioned computer users have just the opposite approach; they are constantly afraid that their answers are almost meaningless. Many serious mathematicians have attempted to analyze a sequence of floating point operations rigorously, but have found the task so formidable that they have tried to be content with plausibility arguments instead.

A thorough examination of error analysis techniques is beyond the scope of this book, but in the present section we shall study some of the low-level characteristics of floating point arithmetic errors. Our goal is to discover how to perform floating point arithmetic in such a way that reasonable analyses of error propagation are facilitated as much as possible.

A rough (but reasonably useful) way to express the behavior of floating point arithmetic can be based on the concept of "significant figures" or *relative error*. If we are representing an exact real number x inside a computer by using the approximation $\hat{x} = x(1 + \epsilon)$, the quantity $\epsilon = (\hat{x} - x)/x$ is called the relative error of approximation. Roughly speaking, the operations of floating point multiplication and division do not magnify the relative error by very much; but floating point subtraction of nearly equal quantities (and floating point addition, $u \oplus v$, where u is nearly equal to $-v$) can very greatly increase the relative error. So we have a general rule of thumb, that a substantial loss of accuracy is expected from such additions and subtractions, but not from multiplications and divisions. On the other hand, the situation is somewhat paradoxical and needs to be understood properly, since the "bad" additions and subtractions are always performed with perfect accuracy! (See exercise 25.)

One of the consequences of the possible unreliability of floating point addition is that the associative law breaks down:

$$(u \oplus v) \oplus w \neq u \oplus (v \oplus w), \qquad \text{for many } u, v, w. \tag{1}$$

For example,

$(11111113. \oplus -11111111.) \oplus 7.5111111 = 2.0000000 \oplus 7.5111111 = 9.5111111;$
$11111113. \oplus (-11111111. \oplus 7.5111111) = 11111113. \oplus -11111103. = 10.000000.$

(All examples in this section are given in eight-digit floating decimal arithmetic, with exponents indicated by an explicit decimal point. Recall that, as in Section 4.2.1, the symbols $\oplus$, $\ominus$, $\otimes$, $\oslash$ are used to stand for floating point operations that correspond to the exact operations $+$, $-$, $\times$, $/$.)

In view of the failure of the associative law, the comment of Mrs. La Touche that appears at the beginning of this chapter makes a good deal of sense with respect to floating point arithmetic. Mathematical notations like "$a_1 + a_2 + a_3$" or "$\sum_{k=1}^{n} a_k$" are inherently based upon the assumption of associativity, so a programmer must be especially careful not to assume implicitly that the associative law is valid.

A. An axiomatic approach. Although the associative law is not valid, the commutative law

$$u \oplus v = v \oplus u \tag{2}$$

does hold, and this law can be a valuable conceptual asset in programming and in the analysis of programs. Equation (2) suggests that we should look for additional examples of important laws that *are* satisfied by $\oplus$, $\ominus$, $\otimes$, and $\oslash$; it is not unreasonable to say that *floating point routines should be designed to preserve as many of the ordinary mathematical laws as possible.* If more axioms are valid, it becomes easier to write good programs, and programs also become more portable from machine to machine.

Let us therefore consider some of the other basic laws that are valid for normalized floating point operations as described in the previous section. First we have

$$u \ominus v = u \oplus -v; \tag{3}$$
$$-(u \oplus v) = -u \oplus -v; \tag{4}$$
$$u \oplus v = 0 \qquad \text{if and only if} \qquad v = -u; \tag{5}$$
$$u \oplus 0 = u. \tag{6}$$

From these laws we can derive further identities; for example (exercise 1),

$$u \ominus v = -(v \ominus u). \tag{7}$$

Identities (2) to (6) are easily deduced from the algorithms in Section 4.2.1. The following rule is slightly less obvious:

$$\text{if} \qquad u \leq v \qquad \text{then} \qquad u \oplus w \leq v \oplus w. \tag{8}$$

Instead of attempting to prove this rule by analyzing Algorithm 4.2.1A, let us go back to the basic principle by which that algorithm was designed. (Algorithmic proofs aren't always easier than mathematical ones.) Our idea was that the floating point operations should satisfy

$$\begin{aligned}
u \oplus v = \text{round}(u + v), \qquad u \ominus v = \text{round}(u - v), \\
u \otimes v = \text{round}(u \times v), \qquad u \oslash v = \text{round}(u \ / \ v),
\end{aligned} \tag{9}$$

where round(x) denotes the best floating point approximation to x as defined in Algorithm 4.2.1N. We have

$$\text{round}(-x) = -\text{round}(x), \qquad (10)$$

$$x \leq y \quad \text{implies} \quad \text{round}(x) \leq \text{round}(y), \qquad (11)$$

and these fundamental relations yield properties (2) through (8) immediately. We can also write down several more identities:

$$u \otimes v = v \otimes u, \qquad (-u) \otimes v = -(u \otimes v), \qquad 1 \otimes v = v;$$

$$u \otimes v = 0 \qquad \text{if and only if} \qquad u = 0 \text{ or } v = 0;$$

$$(-u) \oslash v = u \oslash (-v) = -(u \oslash v);$$

$$0 \oslash v = 0, \qquad u \oslash 1 = u, \qquad u \oslash u = 1.$$

If $u \leq v$ and $w > 0$, then $u \otimes w \leq v \otimes w$ and $u \oslash w \leq v \oslash w$; also $w \oslash u \geq w \oslash v$ when $v \geq u > 0$. If $u \oplus v = u + v$, then $(u \oplus v) \ominus v = u$; and if $u \otimes v = u \times v \neq 0$, then $(u \otimes v) \oslash v = u$. We see that a good deal of regularity is present in spite of the inexactness of the floating point operations, when things have been defined properly. (These laws assume, of course, that there's no overflow or underflow.)

Several familiar rules of algebra are still conspicuously absent from the collection of identities above. For instance, the associative law for floating point multiplication is not strictly true, as shown in exercise 3; and the distributive law between $\otimes$ and $\oplus$ can fail rather badly: Let $u = 20000.000$, $v = -6.0000000$, and $w = 6.0000003$; then

$$(u \otimes v) \oplus (u \otimes w) = -120000.00 \oplus 120000.01 = .010000000$$

$$u \otimes (v \oplus w) = 20000.000 \otimes .00000030000000 = .0060000000$$

so

$$u \otimes (v \oplus w) \neq (u \otimes v) \oplus (u \otimes w). \qquad (12)$$

On the other hand we do have $b \otimes (v \oplus w) = (b \otimes v) \oplus (b \otimes w)$, when b is the floating point radix, since

$$\text{round}(bx) = b \, \text{round}(x). \qquad (13)$$

(Strictly speaking, the identities and inequalities we are considering in this section implicitly assume that exponent underflow and overflow do not occur. The function round(x) is undefined when $|x|$ is too small or too large, and equations such as (13) hold only when both sides are defined.)

The failure of Cauchy's fundamental inequality

$$(x_1^2 + \cdots + x_n^2)(y_1^2 + \cdots + y_n^2) \geq (x_1 y_1 + \cdots + x_n y_n)^2$$

is another important example of the breakdown of traditional algebra in the presence of floating point arithmetic. Exercise 7 shows that Cauchy's inequality can fail even in the simple case $n = 2$, $x_1 = x_2 = 1$. Novice programmers who calculate the standard deviation of some observations by using the textbook formula

$$\sigma = \sqrt{\left(n \sum_{1 \le k \le n} x_k^2 - \left(\sum_{1 \le k \le n} x_k \right)^2 \right) \Big/ n(n-1)} \qquad (14)$$

often find themselves taking the square root of a negative number! A much better way to calculate means and standard deviations with floating point arithmetic is to use the recurrence formulas

$$M_1 = x_1, \qquad M_k = M_{k-1} \oplus (x_k \ominus M_{k-1}) \oslash k, \qquad (15)$$

$$S_1 = 0, \qquad S_k = S_{k-1} \oplus (x_k \ominus M_{k-1}) \otimes (x_k \ominus M_k), \qquad (16)$$

for $2 \le k \le n$, where $\sigma = \sqrt{S_n/(n-1)}$. [See B. P. Welford, *Technometrics* **4** (1962), 419–420.] With this method S_n can never be negative, and we avoid other serious problems encountered by the naïve method of accumulating sums, as shown in exercise 16. (See exercise 19 for a summation technique that provides an even better guarantee on the accuracy.)

Although algebraic laws do not always hold exactly, we can often show that they aren't too far off base. When $b^{e-1} \le |x| < b^e$ we have round$(x) = x + \rho(x)$, where $|\rho(x)| \le \frac{1}{2} b^{e-p}$; hence

$$\text{round}(x) = x\bigl(1 + \delta(x)\bigr), \qquad (17)$$

where the relative error is bounded independently of x:

$$|\delta(x)| = \frac{|\rho(x)|}{|x|} \le \frac{|\rho(x)|}{b^{e-1} + |\rho(x)|} \le \frac{\frac{1}{2} b^{e-p}}{b^{e-1} + \frac{1}{2} b^{e-p}} < \frac{1}{2} b^{1-p}. \qquad (18)$$

We can use this inequality to estimate the relative error of normalized floating point calculations in a simple way, since $u \oplus v = (u+v)\bigl(1 + \delta(u+v)\bigr)$, etc.

As an example of typical error-estimation procedures, let us consider the associative law for multiplication. Exercise 3 shows that $(u \otimes v) \otimes w$ is not in general equal to $u \otimes (v \otimes w)$; but the situation in this case is much better than it was with respect to the associative law of addition (1) and the distributive law (12). In fact, we have

$$(u \otimes v) \otimes w = \bigl((uv)(1 + \delta_1)\bigr) \otimes w = uvw(1 + \delta_1)(1 + \delta_2),$$

$$u \otimes (v \otimes w) = u \otimes \bigl((vw)(1 + \delta_3)\bigr) = uvw(1 + \delta_3)(1 + \delta_4),$$

for some $\delta_1, \delta_2, \delta_3, \delta_4$, provided that no exponent underflow or overflow occurs, where $|\delta_j| < \frac{1}{2} b^{1-p}$ for each j. Hence

$$\frac{(u \otimes v) \otimes w}{u \otimes (v \otimes w)} = \frac{(1 + \delta_1)(1 + \delta_2)}{(1 + \delta_3)(1 + \delta_4)} = 1 + \delta,$$

where

$$|\delta| < 2b^{1-p} \Big/ \bigl(1 - \tfrac{1}{2} b^{1-p}\bigr)^2. \qquad (19)$$

The number b^{1-p} occurs so often in such analyses, it has been given a special name, one *ulp*, meaning one unit in the last place of the fraction part. Floating point operations are correct to within half an ulp, and the calculation of uvw by two floating point multiplications will be correct within about one ulp (ignoring second-order terms). Hence the associative law for multiplication holds to within about two ulps of relative error.

We have shown that $(u \otimes v) \otimes w$ is approximately equal to $u \otimes (v \otimes w)$, except when exponent overflow or underflow is a problem. It is worthwhile to study this intuitive idea of approximate equality in more detail; can we make such a statement more precise in a reasonable way?

Programmers who use floating point arithmetic almost never want to test if two computed values are exactly equal to each other (or at least they hardly ever should try to do so), because this is an extremely improbable occurrence. For example, if a recurrence relation

$$x_{n+1} = f(x_n)$$

is being used, where the theory in some textbook says that x_n approaches a limit as $n \to \infty$, it is usually a mistake to wait until $x_{n+1} = x_n$ for some n, since the sequence x_n might be periodic with a longer period due to the rounding of intermediate results. The proper procedure is to wait until $|x_{n+1} - x_n| < \delta$, for some suitably chosen number δ; but since we don't necessarily know the order of magnitude of x_n in advance, it is even better to wait until

$$|x_{n+1} - x_n| \le \epsilon|x_n|; \tag{20}$$

now ϵ is a number that is much easier to select. Relation (20) is another way of saying that x_{n+1} and x_n are approximately equal; and our discussion indicates that a relation of "approximately equal" would be more useful than the traditional relation of equality, when floating point computations are involved, if we could only define a suitable approximation relation.

In other words, the fact that strict equality of floating point values is of little importance implies that we ought to have a new operation, *floating point comparison*, which is intended to help assess the relative values of two floating point quantities. The following definitions seem to be appropriate for base b, excess q, floating point numbers $u = (e_u, f_u)$ and $v = (e_v, f_v)$:

$$u \prec v \quad (\epsilon) \qquad \text{if and only if} \qquad v - u > \epsilon \max(b^{e_u - q}, b^{e_v - q}); \tag{21}$$

$$u \sim v \quad (\epsilon) \qquad \text{if and only if} \qquad |v - u| \le \epsilon \max(b^{e_u - q}, b^{e_v - q}); \tag{22}$$

$$u \succ v \quad (\epsilon) \qquad \text{if and only if} \qquad u - v > \epsilon \max(b^{e_u - q}, b^{e_v - q}); \tag{23}$$

$$u \approx v \quad (\epsilon) \qquad \text{if and only if} \qquad |v - u| \le \epsilon \min(b^{e_u - q}, b^{e_v - q}). \tag{24}$$

These definitions apply to unnormalized values as well as to normalized ones. Notice that exactly one of the conditions $u \prec v$ (definitely less than), $u \sim v$ (approximately equal to), or $u \succ v$ (definitely greater than) must always hold for any given pair of values u and v. The relation $u \approx v$ is somewhat stronger than $u \sim v$, and it might be read "u is essentially equal to v." All of the relations are specified in terms of a positive real number ϵ that measures the degree of approximation being considered.

One way to view the definitions above is to associate a "neighborhood" set $N(u) = \{x \mid |x - u| \le \epsilon b^{e_u - q}\}$ with each floating point number u; thus, $N(u)$ represents a set of values near u based on the exponent of u's floating point representation. In these terms, we have $u \prec v$ if and only if $N(u) < v$ and $u < N(v)$; $u \sim v$ if and only if $u \in N(v)$ or $v \in N(u)$; $u \succ v$ if and only if $u > N(v)$ and $N(u) > v$; $u \approx v$ if and only if $u \in N(v)$ and $v \in N(u)$. (Here we are assuming that the parameter ϵ, which measures the degree of approximation, is a constant; a more complete notation would indicate the dependence of $N(u)$ upon ϵ.)

Here are some simple consequences of definitions (21)–(24):

$$\text{if} \quad u \prec v \quad (\epsilon) \qquad \text{then} \qquad v \succ u \quad (\epsilon); \tag{25}$$

$$\text{if} \quad u \approx v \quad (\epsilon) \qquad \text{then} \qquad u \sim v \quad (\epsilon); \tag{26}$$

$$u \approx u \quad (\epsilon); \tag{27}$$

$$\text{if} \quad u \prec v \quad (\epsilon) \qquad \text{then} \qquad u < v; \tag{28}$$

$$\text{if} \quad u \prec v \quad (\epsilon_1) \quad \text{and} \quad \epsilon_1 \ge \epsilon_2 \qquad \text{then} \qquad u \prec v \quad (\epsilon_2); \tag{29}$$

$$\text{if} \quad u \sim v \quad (\epsilon_1) \quad \text{and} \quad \epsilon_1 \le \epsilon_2 \qquad \text{then} \qquad u \sim v \quad (\epsilon_2); \tag{30}$$

$$\text{if} \quad u \approx v \quad (\epsilon_1) \quad \text{and} \quad \epsilon_1 \le \epsilon_2 \qquad \text{then} \qquad u \approx v \quad (\epsilon_2); \tag{31}$$

$$\text{if} \quad u \prec v \quad (\epsilon_1) \quad \text{and} \quad v \prec w \quad (\epsilon_2) \qquad \text{then} \qquad u \prec w \quad (\min(\epsilon_1, \epsilon_2)); \tag{32}$$

$$\text{if} \quad u \approx v \quad (\epsilon_1) \quad \text{and} \quad v \approx w \quad (\epsilon_2) \qquad \text{then} \qquad u \sim w \quad (\epsilon_1 + \epsilon_2). \tag{33}$$

Moreover, we can prove without difficulty that

$$|u - v| \le \epsilon|u| \quad \text{and} \quad |u - v| \le \epsilon|v| \qquad \text{implies} \qquad u \approx v \quad (\epsilon); \tag{34}$$

$$|u - v| \le \epsilon|u| \quad \text{or} \quad |u - v| \le \epsilon|v| \qquad \text{implies} \qquad u \sim v \quad (\epsilon); \tag{35}$$

and conversely, for *normalized* floating point numbers u and v, when $\epsilon < 1$,

$$u \approx v \quad (\epsilon) \qquad \text{implies} \qquad |u - v| \le b\epsilon|u| \quad \text{and} \quad |u - v| \le b\epsilon|v|; \tag{36}$$

$$u \sim v \quad (\epsilon) \qquad \text{implies} \qquad |u - v| \le b\epsilon|u| \quad \text{or} \quad |u - v| \le b\epsilon|v|. \tag{37}$$

Let $\epsilon_0 = b^{1-p}$ be one ulp. The derivation of (17) establishes the inequality $|x - \text{round}(x)| = |\rho(x)| < \frac{1}{2}\epsilon_0 \min(|x|, |\text{round}(x)|)$, hence

$$x \approx \text{round}(x) \quad (\tfrac{1}{2}\epsilon_0); \tag{38}$$

it follows that $u \oplus v \approx u + v$ $(\frac{1}{2}\epsilon_0)$, etc. The approximate associative law for multiplication derived above can be recast as follows: We have

$$\left| (u \otimes v) \otimes w - u \otimes (v \otimes w) \right| < \frac{2\epsilon_0}{(1 - \frac{1}{2}\epsilon_0)^2} \left| u \otimes (v \otimes w) \right|$$

by (19), and the same inequality is valid with $(u \otimes v) \otimes w$ and $u \otimes (v \otimes w)$ interchanged. Hence by (34),

$$(u \otimes v) \otimes w \approx u \otimes (v \otimes w) \quad (\epsilon) \tag{39}$$

whenever $\epsilon \ge 2\epsilon_0/(1 - \frac{1}{2}\epsilon_0)^2$. For example, if $b = 10$ and $p = 8$ we may take $\epsilon = 0.00000021$.

The relations $\prec$, $\sim$, $\succ$, and $\approx$ are useful within numerical algorithms, and it is therefore a good idea to provide routines for comparing floating point numbers as well as for doing arithmetic on them.

Let us now shift our attention back to the question of finding *exact* relations that are satisfied by the floating point operations. It is interesting to note that floating point addition and subtraction are not completely intractable from an axiomatic standpoint, since they do satisfy the nontrivial identities stated in the following theorems.

Theorem A. *Let u and v be normalized floating point numbers. Then*

$$((u \oplus v) \ominus u) + ((u \oplus v) \ominus ((u \oplus v) \ominus u)) = u \oplus v, \tag{40}$$

provided that no exponent overflow or underflow occurs.

This rather cumbersome-looking identity can be rewritten in a simpler manner: Let

$$u' = (u \oplus v) \ominus v, \qquad v' = (u \oplus v) \ominus u;$$
$$u'' = (u \oplus v) \ominus v', \qquad v'' = (u \oplus v) \ominus u'. \tag{41}$$

Intuitively, u' and u'' should be approximations to u, and v' and v'' should be approximations to v. Theorem A tells us that

$$u \oplus v = u' + v'' = u'' + v'. \tag{42}$$

This is a stronger statement than the identity

$$u \oplus v = u' \oplus v'' = u'' \oplus v', \tag{43}$$

which follows by rounding (42).

Proof. Let us say that t is a *tail* of x modulo b^e if

$$t \equiv x \pmod{b^e}, \qquad |t| \le \tfrac{1}{2} b^e; \tag{44}$$

thus, $x - \text{round}(x)$ is always a tail of x. The proof of Theorem A rests largely on the following simple fact proved in exercise 11:

Lemma T. *If t is a tail of the floating point number x, then $x \ominus t = x - t$.* ∎

Let $w = u \oplus v$. Theorem A holds trivially when $w = 0$. By multiplying all variables by a suitable power of b, we may assume without loss of generality that $e_w = p$. Then $u + v = w + r$, where r is a tail of $u + v$ modulo 1. Furthermore $u' = \text{round}(w - v) = \text{round}(u - r) = u - r - t$, where t is a tail of $u - r$ modulo b^e and $e = e_{u'} - p$.

If $e \le 0$, then $t \equiv u - r \equiv -v \pmod{b^e}$, hence t is a tail of $-v$ and $v'' = \text{round}(w - u') = \text{round}(v + t) = v + t$; this proves (40). If $e > 0$, then $|u - r| \ge b^p - \tfrac{1}{2}$; and since $|r| \le \tfrac{1}{2}$, we have $|u| \ge b^p - 1$. It follows that u is an integer, so r is a tail of v modulo 1. If $u' = u$, then $t = -r$ is a tail of $-v$. Otherwise the relation $\text{round}(u - r) \ne u$ implies that $|u| = b^p - 1$, $|r| = \tfrac{1}{2}$, $|u'| = b^p$, $t = r$; again t is a tail of $-v$. ∎

Theorem A exhibits a regularity property of floating point addition, but it doesn't seem to be an especially useful result. The following identity is more significant:

Theorem B. *Under the hypotheses of Theorem A and* (41),

$$u + v = (u \oplus v) + \big((u \ominus u') \oplus (v \ominus v'')\big). \tag{45}$$

Proof. In fact, we can show that $u \ominus u' = u - u'$, $v \ominus v'' = v - v''$, and $(u - u') \oplus (v - v'') = (u - u') + (v - v'')$, hence (45) will follow from Theorem A. Using the notation of the preceding proof, these relations are respectively equivalent to

$$\text{round}(t + r) = t + r, \qquad \text{round}(t) = t, \qquad \text{round}(r) = r. \tag{46}$$

Exercise 12 establishes the theorem in the special case $|e_u - e_v| \geq p$. Otherwise $u + v$ has at most $2p$ significant digits and it is easy to see that $\text{round}(r) = r$. If now $e > 0$, the proof of Theorem A shows that $t = -r$ or $t = r = \pm\frac{1}{2}$. If $e \leq 0$ we have $t + r \equiv u$ and $t \equiv -v$ (modulo b^e); this is enough to prove that $t + r$ and t round to themselves, provided that $e_u \geq e$ and $e_v \geq e$. But either $e_u < 0$ or $e_v < 0$ would contradict our hypothesis that $|e_u - e_v| < p$, since $e_w = p$. ∎

Theorem B gives *an explicit formula for the difference* between $u + v$ and $u \oplus v$, in terms of quantities that can be calculated directly using five operations of floating point arithmetic. If the radix b is 2 or 3, we can improve on this result, obtaining the exact value of the correction term with only two floating point operations and one (fixed point) comparison of absolute values:

Theorem C. *If $b \leq 3$ and $|u| \geq |v|$, then*

$$u + v = (u \oplus v) + \big(u \ominus (u \oplus v)\big) \oplus v. \tag{47}$$

Proof. Following the conventions of preceding proofs again, we wish to show that $v \ominus v' = r$. It suffices to show that $v' = w - u$, because (46) will then yield $v \ominus v' = \text{round}(v - v') = \text{round}(u + v - w) = \text{round}(r) = r$.

We shall in fact prove (47) whenever $b \leq 3$ and $e_u \geq e_v$. If $e_u \geq p$, then r is a tail of v modulo 1, hence $v' = w \ominus u = v \ominus r = v - r = w - u$ as desired. If $e_u < p$, then we must have $e_u = p - 1$, and $w - u$ is a multiple of b^{-1}; it will therefore round to itself if its magnitude is less than $b^{p-1} + b^{-1}$. Since $b \leq 3$, we have indeed $|w - u| \leq |w - u - v| + |v| \leq \frac{1}{2} + (b^{p-1} - b^{-1}) < b^{p-1} + b^{-1}$. This completes the proof. ∎

The proofs of Theorems A, B, and C do not rely on the precise definitions of $\text{round}(x)$ in the ambiguous cases when x is exactly midway between consecutive floating point numbers; any way of resolving the ambiguity will suffice for the validity of everything we have proved so far.

No rounding rule can be best for every application. For example, we generally want a special rule when computing our income tax. But for most numerical calculations the best policy appears to be the rounding scheme specified in Algorithm 4.2.1N, which insists that the least significant digit should always be made even (or always odd) when an ambiguous value is rounded. This is not a trivial technicality, of interest only to nit-pickers; it is an important practical consideration, since the ambiguous case arises surprisingly often and a biased rounding rule produces significantly poor results. For example, consider decimal arithmetic and assume that remainders of 5 are always rounded upwards. Then if $u = 1.0000000$ and $v = 0.55555555$ we have $u \oplus v = 1.5555556$; and if we floating-subtract v from this result we get $u' = 1.0000001$. Adding and subtracting v from u' gives 1.0000002, and the next time we get 1.0000003, etc.; the result keeps growing although we are adding and subtracting the same value.

This phenomenon, called *drift,* will not occur when we use a stable rounding rule based on the parity of the least significant digit. More precisely:

Theorem D. $\big(((u \oplus v) \ominus v) \oplus v\big) \ominus v = (u \oplus v) \ominus v.$

For example, if $u = 1.2345679$ and $v = -0.23456785$, we find

$$u \oplus v = 1.0000000, \qquad\qquad (u \oplus v) \ominus v = 1.2345678,$$
$$((u \oplus v) \ominus v) \oplus v = 0.99999995, \qquad (((u \oplus v) \ominus v) \oplus v) \ominus v = 1.2345678.$$

The proof for general u and v seems to require a case analysis even more detailed than that in the theorems above; see the references below.   ∎

Theorem D is valid both for "round to even" and "round to odd"; how should we choose between these possibilities? When the radix b is odd, ambiguous cases never arise except during floating point division, and the rounding in such cases is comparatively unimportant. For *even* radices, there is reason to prefer the following rule: "Round to even when $b/2$ is odd, round to odd when $b/2$ is even." The least significant digit of a floating point fraction occurs frequently as a remainder to be rounded off in subsequent calculations, and this rule avoids generating the digit $b/2$ in the least significant position whenever possible; its effect is to provide some memory of an ambiguous rounding so that subsequent rounding will tend to be unambiguous. For example, if we were to round to odd in the decimal system, repeated rounding of the number 2.44445 to one less place each time leads to the sequence 2.4445, 2.445, 2.45, 2.5, 3; if we round to even, such situations do not occur, although repeated rounding of a number like 2.5454 will lead to almost as much error. [See Roy A. Keir, *Inf. Proc. Letters* **3** (1975), 188–189.] Some people prefer rounding to even in all cases, so that the least significant digit will tend to be 0 more often. Exercise 23 demonstrates this advantage of round-to-even. Neither alternative conclusively dominates the other; fortunately the base is usually $b = 2$ or $b = 10$, when everyone agrees that round-to-even is best.

A reader who has checked some of the details of the proofs above will realize the immense simplification that has been afforded by the simple rule $u \oplus v = \text{round}(u + v)$. If our floating point addition routine would fail to give this result even in a few rare cases, the proofs would become enormously more complicated and perhaps they would even break down completely.

Theorem B fails if truncation arithmetic is used in place of rounding, that is, if we let $u \oplus v = \text{trunc}(u + v)$ and $u \ominus v = \text{trunc}(u - v)$, where $\text{trunc}(x)$ for a positive real x is the largest floating point number $\leq x$. An exception to Theorem B would then occur for cases such as $(20, +.10000001) \oplus (10, -.10000001) = (20, +.10000000)$, when the difference between $u+v$ and $u \oplus v$ cannot be expressed exactly as a floating point number; and also for cases such as $12345678 \oplus .012345678$, when it can be.

Many people feel that, since floating point arithmetic is inexact by nature, there is no harm in making it just a little bit less exact in certain rather rare cases, if it is convenient to do so. This policy saves a few cents in the design of computer hardware, or a small percentage of the average running time of a subroutine. But our discussion shows that such a policy is mistaken. We could save about five percent of the running time of the FADD subroutine, Program 4.2.1A, and about 25 percent of its space, if we took the liberty of rounding incorrectly in a few cases, but we are much better off leaving it as it is. The reason is not to glorify "bit chasing"; a more fundamental issue is at stake here: *Numerical subroutines should deliver results that satisfy simple, useful mathematical laws whenever possible.* The crucial formula $u \oplus v = \text{round}(u + v)$ is a regularity property that makes a great deal of difference between whether mathematical analysis of computational algorithms is worth doing or worth avoiding. Without any underlying symmetry properties, the job of proving interesting results becomes extremely unpleasant. *The enjoyment of one's tools is an essential ingredient of successful work.*

B. Unnormalized floating point arithmetic. The policy of normalizing all floating point numbers may be construed in two ways: We may look on it favorably by saying that it is an attempt to get the maximum possible accuracy obtainable with a given degree of precision, or we may consider it to be potentially dangerous since it tends to imply that the results are more accurate than they really are. When we normalize the result of $(1, +.31428571) \ominus (1, +.31415927)$ to $(-2, +.12644000)$, we are suppressing information about the possibly greater inaccuracy of the latter quantity. Such information would be retained if the answer were left as $(1, +.00012644)$.

The input data to a problem is frequently not known as precisely as the floating point representation allows. Before 2019, for example, the values of Avogadro's number and Planck's constant were not known to eight significant digits, and it would have been more appropriate to denote them, respectively, by

$$(26, +.00602214) \qquad \text{and} \qquad (-30, +.00066261)$$

instead of by $(24, +.60221408)$ and $(-33, +.66260702)$. It would be nice if we could give our input data for each problem in an unnormalized form that expresses how much precision is assumed, and if the output would indicate just how much precision is known in the answer. Unfortunately, this is a terribly difficult problem, although the use of unnormalized arithmetic can help to give some indication. For example, we can say with a fair degree of certainty that the product of Avogadro's number by Planck's constant is $(-6, +.00039903)$, and that their sum is $(26, +.00602214)$. (The purpose of this example is not to suggest that any important physical significance should be attached to the sum and product of these fundamental constants; the point is that it is possible to preserve a little of the information about precision in the result of calculations with imprecise quantities, when the original operands are independent of each other.)

The rules for unnormalized arithmetic are simply this: Let l_u be the number of leading zeros in the fraction part of $u = (e_u, f_u)$, so that l_u is the largest integer $\leq p$ with $|f_u| < b^{-l_u}$. Then addition and subtraction are performed just as in Algorithm 4.2.1A, except that all scaling to the left is suppressed. Multiplication and division are performed as in Algorithm 4.2.1M, except that the answer is scaled right or left so that precisely $\max(l_u, l_v)$ leading zeros appear. Essentially the same rules have been used in manual calculation for many years.

It follows that, for unnormalized computations,

$$e_{u \oplus v}, \ e_{u \ominus v} = \max(e_u, e_v) + (0 \text{ or } 1) \tag{48}$$

$$e_{u \otimes v} = e_u + e_v - q - \min(l_u, l_v) - (0 \text{ or } 1) \tag{49}$$

$$e_{u \oslash v} = e_u - e_v + q - l_u + l_v + \max(l_u, l_v) + (0 \text{ or } 1). \tag{50}$$

When the result of a calculation is zero, an unnormalized zero (often called an "order of magnitude zero") is given as the answer; this indicates that the answer may not truly be zero, we just don't know any of its significant digits.

Error analysis takes a somewhat different form with unnormalized floating point arithmetic. Let us define

$$\delta_u = \tfrac{1}{2} b^{e_u - q - p} \qquad \text{if } u = (e_u, f_u). \tag{51}$$

This quantity depends on the representation of u, not just on the value $b^{e_u - q} f_u$. Our rounding rule tells us that

$$\left| u \oplus v - (u + v) \right| \leq \delta_{u \oplus v}, \qquad \left| u \ominus v - (u - v) \right| \leq \delta_{u \ominus v},$$

$$\left| u \otimes v - (u \times v) \right| \leq \delta_{u \otimes v}, \qquad \left| u \oslash v - (u \ / \ v) \right| \leq \delta_{u \oslash v}.$$

These inequalities apply to normalized as well as unnormalized arithmetic; the main difference between the two types of error analysis is the definition of the exponent of the result of each operation $\bigl($Eqs. (48) to (50)$\bigr)$.

We have remarked that the relations $\prec$, $\sim$, $\succ$, and $\approx$ defined earlier in this section are valid and meaningful for unnormalized numbers as well as for normalized numbers. As an example of the use of these relations, let us prove an approximate associative law for unnormalized addition, analogous to (39):

$$(u \oplus v) \oplus w \approx u \oplus (v \oplus w) \quad (\epsilon), \tag{52}$$

for suitable ϵ. We have

$$|(u \oplus v) \oplus w - (u + v + w)| \leq \left| (u \oplus v) \oplus w - \bigl((u \oplus v) + w \bigr) \right| + |u \oplus v - (u + v)|$$

$$\leq \delta_{(u \oplus v) \oplus w} + \delta_{u \oplus v}$$

$$\leq 2\delta_{(u \oplus v) \oplus w}.$$

A similar formula holds for $|u \oplus (v \oplus w) - (u + v + w)|$. Now since $e_{(u \oplus v) \oplus w} = \max(e_u, e_v, e_w) + (0, 1, \text{ or } 2)$, we have $\delta_{(u \oplus v) \oplus w} \leq b^2 \delta_{u \oplus (v \oplus w)}$. Therefore we find that (52) is valid when $\epsilon \geq b^{2-p} + b^{-p}$; unnormalized addition is not as erratic as normalized addition with respect to the associative law.

It should be emphasized that unnormalized arithmetic is by no means a panacea. There are examples where it indicates greater accuracy than is present (for example, addition of a great many small quantities of about the same magnitude, or evaluation of x^n for large n); and there are many more examples when it indicates poor accuracy while normalized arithmetic actually does produce good results. There is an important reason why no straightforward one-operation-at-a-time method of error analysis can be completely satisfactory, namely the fact that operands are usually not independent of each other. This means that errors tend to cancel or reinforce each other in strange ways. For example, suppose that x is approximately $1/2$, and suppose that we have an approximation $y = x + \delta$ with absolute error δ. If we now wish to compute $x(1 - x)$, we can form $y(1 - y)$; if $x = \frac{1}{2} + \epsilon$ we find $y(1 - y) = x(1 - x) - 2\epsilon\delta - \delta^2$, so the absolute error has decreased substantially: It has been multiplied by a factor of $2\epsilon + \delta$. This is just one case where multiplication of imprecise quantities can lead to a quite accurate result when the operands are not independent of each other. A more obvious example is the computation of $x \ominus x$, which can be obtained with perfect accuracy regardless of how bad an approximation to x we begin with.

The extra information that unnormalized arithmetic gives us can often be more important than the information it destroys during an extended calculation, but (as usual) we must use it with care. Examples of the proper use of unnormalized arithmetic are discussed by R. L. Ashenhurst and N. Metropolis in *Computers and Computing, AMM* **72**, 2, part 2, Slaught Memorial Papers No. 10 (February 1965), 47–59; by N. Metropolis in *Numer. Math.* **7** (1965), 104–112; and by R. L. Ashenhurst in *Error in Digital Computation* **2**, edited by L. B. Rall (New York: Wiley, 1965), 3–37. Appropriate methods for computing standard mathematical functions with both input and output in unnormalized form are given by R. L. Ashenhurst in *JACM* **11** (1964), 168–187. An extension of unnormalized arithmetic, which remembers that certain values are known to be *exact*, has been discussed by N. Metropolis in *IEEE Trans.* **C-22** (1973), 573–576.

C. Interval arithmetic. Another approach to the problem of error determination is the so-called interval or range arithmetic, in which rigorous upper and lower bounds on each number are maintained during the calculations. Thus, for example, if we know that $u_0 \leq u \leq u_1$ and $v_0 \leq v \leq v_1$, we represent this by the interval notation $u = [u_0 .. u_1]$, $v = [v_0 .. v_1]$. The sum $u \oplus v$ is $[u_0 \triangledown v_0 .. u_1 \triangle v_1]$, where $\triangledown$ denotes "lower floating point addition," the greatest representable number less than or equal to the true sum, and $\triangle$ is defined similarly (see exercise 4.2.1–13). Furthermore $u \ominus v = [u_0 \triangledown v_1 .. u_1 \triangle v_0]$; and if u_0 and v_0 are positive, we have $u \otimes v = [u_0 \triangledown v_0 .. u_1 \triangle v_1]$, $u \oslash v = [u_0 \triangledown v_1 .. u_1 \triangle v_0]$. For example, we might represent Avogadro's number and Planck's constant as

$$N = \big[(24, +.60221407) .. (24, +.60221408)\big],$$
$$h = \big[(-33, +.66260701) .. (-33, +.66260702)\big];$$

their sum and product would then turn out to be

$$N \oplus h = \left[(24, +.60221407) .. (24, +.60221408)\right],$$
$$N \otimes h = \left[(-9, +.39903126) .. (-9, +.39903128)\right].$$

If we try to divide by $[v_0 .. v_1]$ when $v_0 < 0 < v_1$, there is a possibility of division by zero. Since the philosophy underlying interval arithmetic is to provide rigorous error estimates, a divide-by-zero error should be signalled in this case. However, overflow and underflow need not be treated as fatal errors in interval arithmetic, if special conventions are introduced as discussed in exercise 24.

Interval arithmetic takes only about twice as long as ordinary arithmetic, and it provides truly reliable error estimates. Considering the difficulty of mathematical error analyses, this is indeed a small price to pay. Since the intermediate values in a calculation often depend on each other, as explained above, the final estimates obtained with interval arithmetic will tend to be pessimistic; and iterative numerical methods often have to be redesigned if we want to deal with intervals. However, the prospects for effective use of interval arithmetic look very good, so efforts should be made to increase its availability and to make it as user-friendly as possible.

D. History and bibliography. Jules Tannery's classic treatise on decimal calculations, *Leçons d'Arithmétique* (Paris: Colin, 1894), stated that positive numbers should be rounded upwards if the first discarded digit is 5 or more; since exactly half of the decimal digits are 5 or more, he felt that this rule would round upwards exactly half of the time, on the average, so it would produce compensating errors. The idea of "round to even" in the ambiguous cases seems to have been mentioned first by James B. Scarborough in the first edition of his pioneering book *Numerical Mathematical Analysis* (Baltimore: Johns Hopkins Press, 1930), 2; in the second (1950) edition he amplified his earlier remarks, stating that "It should be obvious to any thinking person that when a 5 is cut off, the preceding digit should be increased by 1 in only *half* the cases," and he recommended round-to-even in order to achieve this.

The first analysis of floating point arithmetic was given by F. L. Bauer and K. Samelson, *Zeitschrift für angewandte Math. und Physik* **4** (1953), 312–316. The next publication was not until over five years later: J. W. Carr III, *CACM* **2**, 5 (May 1959), 10–15. See also P. C. Fischer, *Proc. ACM Nat. Meeting* **13** (1958), Paper 39. The book *Rounding Errors in Algebraic Processes* (Englewood Cliffs: Prentice–Hall, 1963), by J. H. Wilkinson, shows how to apply error analysis of the individual arithmetic operations to the error analysis of large-scale problems; see also his treatise on *The Algebraic Eigenvalue Problem* (Oxford: Clarendon Press, 1965).

Additional early work on floating point accuracy is summarized in two important papers that can be especially recommended for further study: W. M. Kahan, *Proc. IFIP Congress* (1971), **2**, 1214–1239; R. P. Brent, *IEEE Trans.* **C-22** (1973), 601–607. Both papers include useful theory and demonstrate that it pays off in practice.

The relations $\prec$, $\sim$, $\succ$, $\approx$ introduced in this section are similar to ideas published by A. van Wijngaarden in *BIT* **6** (1966), 66–81. Theorems A and B above were inspired by some related work of Ole Møller, *BIT* **5** (1965), 37–50, 251–255; Theorem C is due to T. J. Dekker, *Numer. Math.* **18** (1971), 224–242. Extensions and refinements of all three theorems have been published by S. Linnainmaa, *BIT* **14** (1974), 167–202. W. M. Kahan introduced Theorem D in some unpublished notes; for a complete proof and further commentary, see J. F. Reiser and D. E. Knuth, *Inf. Proc. Letters* **3** (1975), 84–87, 164.

Unnormalized floating point arithmetic was recommended by F. L. Bauer and K. Samelson in the article cited above, and it was independently used by J. W. Carr III at the University of Michigan in 1953. Several years later, the MANIAC III computer was designed to include both kinds of arithmetic in its hardware; see R. L. Ashenhurst and N. Metropolis, *JACM* **6** (1959), 415–428, *IEEE Trans.* **EC-12** (1963), 896–901; R. L. Ashenhurst, *Proc. Spring Joint Computer Conf.* **21** (1962), 195–202. See also H. L. Gray and C. Harrison, Jr., *Proc. Eastern Joint Computer Conf.* **16** (1959), 244–248, and W. G. Wadey, *JACM* **7** (1960), 129–139, for further early discussions of unnormalized arithmetic.

For early developments in interval arithmetic, and some modifications, see A. Gibb, *CACM* **4** (1961), 319–320; B. A. Chartres, *JACM* **13** (1966), 386–403; and the book *Interval Analysis* by Ramon E. Moore (Prentice–Hall, 1966). The subsequent flourishing of this subject is described in Moore's later book, *Methods and Applications of Interval Analysis* (Philadelphia: SIAM, 1979).

An extension of the Pascal language that allows variables to be of type "interval" was developed at the University of Karlsruhe in the early 1980s. For a description of this language, which also includes numerous other features for scientific computing, see *Pascal-SC* by Bohlender, Ullrich, Wolff von Gudenberg, and Rall (New York: Academic Press, 1987).

The book *Grundlagen des numerischen Rechnens: Mathematische Begründung der Rechnerarithmetik* by Ulrich Kulisch (Mannheim: Bibl. Inst., 1976) is entirely devoted to the study of floating point arithmetic systems. See also Kulisch's article in *IEEE Trans.* **C-26** (1977), 610–621, and his more recent book written jointly with W. L. Miranker, entitled *Computer Arithmetic in Theory and Practice* (New York: Academic Press, 1981).

An excellent summary of more recent work on floating point error analysis appears in the book *Accuracy and Stability of Numerical Algorithms* by N. J. Higham (Philadelphia: SIAM, 1996).

EXERCISES

Note: Normalized floating point arithmetic is assumed unless the contrary is specified.

1. [*M18*] Prove that identity (7) is a consequence of (2) through (6).

2. [*M20*] Use identities (2) through (8) to prove that $(u \oplus x) \oplus (v \oplus y) \geq u \oplus v$ whenever $x \geq 0$ and $y \geq 0$.

3. [*M20*] Find eight-digit floating decimal numbers u, v, and w such that

$$u \otimes (v \otimes w) \neq (u \otimes v) \otimes w,$$

and such that no exponent overflow or underflow occurs during the computations.

4. [*10*] Is it possible to have floating point numbers u, v, and w for which exponent overflow occurs during the calculation of $u \otimes (v \otimes w)$ but not during the calculation of $(u \otimes v) \otimes w$?

5. [*M20*] Is $u \oslash v = u \otimes (1 \oslash v)$ an identity, for all floating point numbers u and $v \neq 0$ such that no exponent overflow or underflow occurs?

6. [*M22*] Are either of the following two identities valid for all floating point numbers u? (a) $0 \ominus (0 \ominus u) = u$; (b) $1 \oslash (1 \oslash u) = u$.

7. [*M21*] Let $u^{\circled{2}}$ stand for $u \otimes u$. If possible, find floating binary numbers u and v such that $(u \oplus v)^{\circled{2}} > 2(u^{\circled{2}} \oplus v^{\circled{2}})$.

▶ **8.** [*20*] Let $\epsilon = 0.0001$; which of the relations

$$ u \prec v \quad (\epsilon), \qquad u \sim v \quad (\epsilon), \qquad u \succ v \quad (\epsilon), \qquad u \approx v \quad (\epsilon) $$

hold for the following pairs of base 10, excess 0, eight-digit floating point numbers?

a) $u = (1, +.31415927)$, $v = (1, +.31416000)$;
b) $u = (0, +.99997000)$, $v = (1, +.10000039)$;
c) $u = (24, +.60221400)$, $v = (27, +.00060221)$;
d) $u = (24, +.60221400)$, $v = (31, +.00000006)$;
e) $u = (24, +.60221400)$, $v = (28, +.00000000)$.

9. [*M22*] Prove (33), and explain why the conclusion cannot be strengthened to the relation $u \approx w$ $(\epsilon_1 + \epsilon_2)$.

▶ **10.** [*M25*] (W. M. Kahan.) A certain computer performs floating point arithmetic without proper rounding, and, in fact, its floating point multiplication routine ignores all but the first p most significant digits of the $2p$-digit product $f_u f_v$. (Thus when $f_u f_v < 1/b$, the least-significant digit of $u \otimes v$ always comes out to be zero, due to subsequent normalization.) Show that this causes the monotonicity of multiplication to fail; in other words, exhibit positive normalized floating point numbers u, v, and w such that $u < v$ but $u \otimes w > v \otimes w$ on this machine.

11. [*M20*] Prove Lemma T.

12. [*M24*] Carry out the proof of Theorem B and (46) when $|e_u - e_v| \geq p$.

▶ **13.** [*M25*] Some programming languages (and even some computers) make use of floating point arithmetic only, with no provision for exact calculations with integers. If operations on integers are desired, we can, of course, represent an integer as a floating point number; and when the floating point operations satisfy the basic definitions in (9), we know that all floating point operations will be exact, provided that the operands and the answer can each be represented exactly with p significant digits. Therefore — so long as we know that the numbers aren't too large — we can add, subtract, or multiply integers with no inaccuracy due to rounding errors.

But suppose that a programmer wants to determine if m is an exact multiple of n, when m and $n \neq 0$ are integers. Suppose further that a subroutine is available to calculate the quantity $\text{round}(u \bmod 1) = u \circled{mod} 1$ for any given floating point number u, as in exercise 4.2.1–15. One good way to determine whether or not m is a multiple of n might be to test whether or not $(m \oslash n) \circled{mod} 1 = 0$, using the assumed subroutine; but perhaps rounding errors in the floating point calculations will invalidate this test in certain cases.

Find suitable conditions on the range of integer values $n \neq 0$ and m, such that m is a multiple of n if and only if $(m \oslash n) \circled{mod} 1 = 0$. In other words, show that if m and n are not too large, this test is valid.

14. [*M27*] Find a suitable ϵ such that $(u \otimes v) \otimes w \approx u \otimes (v \otimes w)$ (ϵ), when *unnormalized* multiplication is being used. (This generalizes (39), since unnormalized multiplication is exactly the same as normalized multiplication when the input operands u, v, and w are normalized.)

▶ **15.** [*M24*] (H. Björk.) Does the computed midpoint of an interval always lie between the endpoints? (In other words, does $u \le v$ imply that $u \le (u \oplus v) \oslash 2 \le v$?)

16. [*M28*] (a) What is $\left(\cdots ((x_1 \oplus x_2) \oplus x_3) \oplus \cdots \oplus x_n \right)$ when $n = 10^6$ and $x_k = 1.1111111$ for all k, using eight-digit floating decimal arithmetic? (b) What happens when Eq. (14) is used to calculate the standard deviation of these particular values x_k? What happens when Eqs. (15) and (16) are used instead? (c) Prove that $S_k \ge 0$ in (16), for all choices of $x_1, \ldots, x_k$.

17. [*28*] Write a MIX subroutine, FCMP, that compares the floating point number u in location ACC with the floating point number v in register A, setting the comparison indicator to LESS, EQUAL, or GREATER according as $u \prec v$, $u \sim v$, or $u \succ v$ (ϵ); here ϵ is stored in location EPSILON as a nonnegative fixed point quantity with the radix point assumed at the left of the word. Assume normalized inputs.

18. [*M40*] In unnormalized arithmetic is there a suitable number ϵ such that

$$u \otimes (v \oplus w) \approx (u \otimes v) \oplus (u \otimes w) \quad (\epsilon)\,?$$

▶ **19.** [*M30*] (W. M. Kahan.) Consider the following procedure for floating point summation of $x_1, x_2, \ldots, x_n$:

$$s_0 = c_0 = 0;$$
$$y_k = x_k \ominus c_{k-1}, \quad s_k = s_{k-1} \oplus y_k, \quad c_k = (s_k \ominus s_{k-1}) \ominus y_k, \qquad \text{for } 1 \le k \le n.$$

Let the relative errors in these operations be defined by the equations

$$y_k = (x_k - c_{k-1})(1 + \eta_k), \qquad s_k = (s_{k-1} + y_k)(1 + \sigma_k),$$
$$c_k = ((s_k - s_{k-1})(1 + \gamma_k) - y_k)(1 + \delta_k),$$

where $|\eta_k|, |\sigma_k|, |\gamma_k|, |\delta_k| \le \epsilon$. Prove that $s_n - c_n = \sum_{k=1}^{n} (1 + \theta_k) x_k$, where $|\theta_k| \le 2\epsilon + O(n\epsilon^2)$. [Theorem C says that if $b = 2$ and $|s_{k-1}| \ge |y_k|$ we have $s_{k-1} + y_k = s_k - c_k$ exactly. But in this exercise we want to obtain an estimate that is valid *even when floating point operations are not carefully rounded*, assuming only that each operation has bounded relative error.]

20. [*25*] (S. Linnainmaa.) Find all u and v for which $|u| \ge |v|$ and (47) fails.

21. [*M35*] (T. J. Dekker.) Theorem C shows how to do exact addition of floating binary numbers. Explain how to do *exact multiplication*: Express the product uv in the form $w + w'$, where w and w' are computed from two given floating binary numbers u and v, using only the operations $\oplus$, $\ominus$, and $\otimes$.

22. [*M30*] Can drift occur in floating point multiplication/division? Consider the sequence $x_0 = u$, $x_{2n+1} = x_{2n} \otimes v$, $x_{2n+2} = x_{2n+1} \oslash v$, given u and $v \ne 0$; what is the largest subscript k such that $x_k \ne x_{k+2}$ is possible?

▶ **23.** [*M26*] Prove or disprove: $u \ominus (u \bmod 1) = \lfloor u \rfloor$, for all floating point u.

24. [*M27*] Consider the set of all intervals $[u_l \mathinner{.\,.} u_r]$, where u_l and u_r are either nonzero floating point numbers or the special symbols $+0$, -0, $+\infty$, $-\infty$; each interval must have $u_l \leq u_r$, and $u_l = u_r$ is allowed only when u_l is finite and nonzero. The interval $[u_l \mathinner{\ldotp\ldotp} u_r]$ stands for all floating point x such that $u_l \leq x \leq u_r$, where we agree that

$$-\infty < -x < -0 < 0 < +0 < +x < +\infty$$

for all positive x. (Thus, $[1 \mathinner{\ldotp\ldotp} 2]$ means $1 \leq x \leq 2$; $[+0 \mathinner{\ldotp\ldotp} 1]$ means $0 < x \leq 1$; $[-0 \mathinner{\ldotp\ldotp} 1]$ means $0 \leq x \leq 1$; $[-0 \mathinner{\ldotp\ldotp} +0]$ denotes the single value 0; and $[-\infty \mathinner{\ldotp\ldotp} +\infty]$ stands for everything.) Show how to define appropriate arithmetic operations on all such intervals, without resorting to overflow or underflow or other anomalous indications except when dividing by an interval that includes zero.

▶ **25.** [*15*] When people speak about inaccuracy in floating point arithmetic they often ascribe errors to "cancellation" that occurs during the subtraction of nearly equal quantities. But when u and v are approximately equal, the difference $u \ominus v$ is obtained exactly, with no error. What do these people really mean?

26. [*M21*] Given that u, u', v, and v' are positive floating point numbers with $u \sim u'$ (ϵ) and $v \sim v'$ (ϵ), prove that there's a small ϵ' such that $u \oplus v \sim u' \oplus v'$ (ϵ'), assuming normalized arithmetic.

27. [*M27*] (W. M. Kahan.) Prove that $1 \oslash (1 \oslash (1 \oslash u)) = 1 \oslash u$ for all $u \neq 0$.

28. [*HM30*] (H. G. Diamond.) Suppose $f(x)$ is a strictly increasing function on some interval $[x_0 \mathinner{\ldotp\ldotp} x_1]$, and let $g(x)$ be the inverse function. (For example, f and g might be "exp" and "ln", or "tan" and "arctan".) If x is a floating point number such that $x_0 \leq x \leq x_1$, let $\hat{f}(x) = \mathrm{round}(f(x))$, and if y is another such that $f(x_0) \leq y \leq f(x_1)$, let $\hat{g}(y) = \mathrm{round}(g(y))$; furthermore, let $h(x) = \hat{g}(\hat{f}(x))$, whenever this is defined. Although $h(x)$ won't always be equal to x, due to rounding, we expect $h(x)$ to be fairly near x.

Prove that if the precision b^p is at least 3, and if f is strictly concave or strictly convex (that is, $f''(x)$ has the same sign for all x in $[x_0 \mathinner{\ldotp\ldotp} x_1]$), then repeated application of h will be *stable* in the sense that

$$h(h(h(x))) = h(h(x)),$$

for all x such that both sides of this equation are defined. In other words, there will be no "drift" if the subroutines are properly implemented.

▶ **29.** [*M25*] Give an example to show that the condition $b^p \geq 3$ is necessary in the previous exercise.

▶ **30.** [*M30*] (W. M. Kahan.) Let $f(x) = 1 + x + \cdots + x^{106} = (1 - x^{107})/(1 - x)$ for $x < 1$, and let $g(y) = f((\frac{1}{3} - y^2)(3 + 3.45y^2))$ for $0 < y < 1$. Evaluate $g(y)$ on one or more pocket calculators, for $y = 10^{-3}$, 10^{-4}, 10^{-5}, 10^{-6}, and explain all inaccuracies in the results you obtain. (Since most present-day calculators do not round correctly, the results are often surprising. Note that $g(\epsilon) = 107 - 10491.35\epsilon^2 + 659749.9625\epsilon^4 - 30141386.26625\epsilon^6 + O(\epsilon^8)$.)

31. [*M25*] (U. Kulisch.) When the polynomial $2y^2 + 9x^4 - y^4$ is evaluated for $x = 408855776$ and $y = 708158977$ using standard 53-bit double-precision floating point arithmetic, the result is $\approx -3.7 \times 10^{19}$. Evaluating it in the alternative form $2y^2 + (3x^2 - y^2)(3x^2 + y^2)$ gives $\approx +1.0 \times 10^{18}$. The true answer, however, is 1.0 (exactly). Explain how to construct similar examples of numerical instability.

32. [*M21*] For what pairs (a, b) is round_to_even$(x) = \lfloor ax + b \rfloor + \lceil ax - b \rceil$ for all x?

*4.2.3. Double-Precision Calculations

Up to now we have considered "single-precision" floating point arithmetic, which essentially means that the floating point values we have dealt with can be stored in a single machine word. When single-precision floating point arithmetic does not yield sufficient accuracy for a given application, the precision can be increased by suitable programming techniques that use two or more words of memory to represent each number.

Although we shall discuss the general question of high-precision calculations in Section 4.3, it is appropriate to give a separate discussion of double-precision here. Special techniques apply to double precision that are comparatively inappropriate for higher precisions; and double precision is a reasonably important topic in its own right, since it is the first step beyond single precision and it is applicable to many problems that do not require extremely high precision.

> *Well, that paragraph was true when the author wrote the first edition of this book in the 1960s. But computers have evolved in such a way that the old motivations for double-precision floating point have mostly disappeared; the present section is therefore primarily of historical interest. In the planned fourth edition of this book, Section 4.2.1 will be renamed "Normalized Calculations," and the present Section 4.2.3 will be replaced by a discussion of "Exceptional Numbers." The new material will focus on special aspects of ANSI/IEEE Standard 754: subnormal numbers, infinities, and the so-called NaNs that represent undefined or otherwise unusual quantities. (See the references at the end of Section 4.2.1.) Meanwhile, let us take one last look at the older ideas, in order to see what lessons they can still teach us.*

Double-precision calculations are almost always required for floating point rather than fixed point arithmetic, except perhaps in statistical work where fixed point double-precision is commonly used to calculate sums of squares and cross products; since fixed point versions of double-precision arithmetic are simpler than floating point versions, we shall confine our discussion here to the latter.

Double precision is quite frequently desired not only to extend the precision of the fraction parts of floating point numbers, but also to increase the range of the exponent part. Thus we shall deal in this section with the following two-word format for double-precision floating point numbers in the MIX computer:

$$\boxed{\pm \mid e \mid e \mid f \mid f \mid f} \qquad \boxed{ \mid f \mid f \mid f \mid f \mid f}. \qquad (1)$$

Here two bytes are used for the exponent and eight bytes are used for the fraction. The exponent is "excess $b^2/2$," where b is the byte size. The sign will appear in the most significant word; it is convenient to ignore the sign of the other word completely.

Our discussion of double-precision arithmetic will be quite machine-oriented, because it is only by studying the problems involved in coding these routines that a person can properly appreciate the subject. A careful study of the MIX programs below is therefore essential to the understanding of the material.

In this section we shall depart from the idealistic goals of accuracy stated in the previous two sections; our double-precision routines will *not* round their results, and a little bit of error will sometimes be allowed to creep in. Users dare not trust these routines too much. There was ample reason to squeeze out every possible drop of accuracy in the single-precision case, but now we face a different situation: (a) The extra programming required to ensure true double-precision rounding in all cases is considerable; fully accurate routines would take, say, twice as much space and half again as much time. It was comparatively easy to make our single-precision routines perfect, but double precision brings us face to face with our machine's limitations. A similar situation occurs with respect to other floating point subroutines; we can't expect the cosine routine to compute round($\cos x$) exactly for all x, since that turns out to be virtually impossible. Instead, the cosine routine should provide the best relative error it can achieve with reasonable speed, for all reasonable values of x. Of course, the designer of the routine should try to make the computed function satisfy simple mathematical laws whenever possible — for example,

$$\cos(-x) = \cos x; \quad |\cos x| \le 1; \quad \cos x \ge \cos y \text{ for } 0 \le x \le y < \pi.$$

(b) Single-precision arithmetic is a "staple food" that everybody who wants to employ floating point arithmetic must use, but double precision is usually for situations where such clean results aren't as important. The difference between seven- and eight-place accuracy can be noticeable, but we rarely care about the difference between 15- and 16-place accuracy. Double precision is most often used for intermediate steps during the calculation of single-precision results; its full potential isn't needed. (c) It will be instructive for us to analyze these procedures in order to see how inaccurate they can be, since they typify the types of short cuts generally taken in bad single-precision routines (see exercises 7 and 8).

Let us now consider addition and subtraction operations from this standpoint. Subtraction is, of course, converted to addition by changing the sign of the second operand. Addition is performed by separately adding together the least-significant halves and the most-significant halves, propagating "carries" appropriately.

A difficulty arises, however, since we are doing signed magnitude arithmetic: it is possible to add the least-significant halves and to get the wrong sign (namely, when the signs of the operands are opposite and the least-significant half of the smaller operand is bigger than the least-significant half of the larger operand). The simplest solution is to anticipate the correct sign; so in step A2 of Algorithm 4.2.1A we will now assume not only that $e_u \ge e_v$ but also that $|u| \ge |v|$. Then we can be sure that the final sign will be the sign of u. In other respects, double-precision addition is very much like its single-precision counterpart, except that everything needs to be done twice.

Program A (*Double-precision addition*). The subroutine DFADD adds a double-precision floating point number v, having the form (1), to a double-precision floating point number u, assuming that v is initially in rAX (registers A and X), and that u is initially stored in locations ACC and ACCX. The answer appears both in rAX and in (ACC, ACCX). The subroutine DFSUB subtracts v from u under the same conventions.

Both input operands are assumed to be normalized, and the answer is normalized. The last portion of this program is a double-precision normalization procedure that is used by other subroutines of this section. Exercise 5 shows how to improve the program significantly.

01	ABS	EQU	1:5	Field definition for absolute value
02	SIGN	EQU	0:0	Field definition for sign
03	EXPD	EQU	1:2	Double-precision exponent field
04	DFSUB	STA	TEMP	Double-precision subtraction:
05		LDAN	TEMP	Change sign of v.
06	DFADD	STJ	EXITDF	Double-precision addition:
07		CMPA	ACC(ABS)	Compare $|v|$ with $|u|$.
08		JG	1F	
09		JL	2F	
10		CMPX	ACCX(ABS)	
11		JLE	2F	
12	1H	STA	ARG	If $|v| > |u|$, interchange $u \leftrightarrow v$.
13		STX	ARGX	
14		LDA	ACC	
15		LDX	ACCX	
16		ENT1	ACC	(ACC and ACCX are in consecutive
17		MOVE	ARG(2)	locations.)
18	2H	STA	TEMP	
19		LD1N	TEMP(EXPD)	$rI1 \leftarrow -e_v$.
20		LD2	ACC(EXPD)	$rI2 \leftarrow e_u$.
21		INC1	0,2	$rI1 \leftarrow e_u - e_v$.
22		SLAX	2	Remove exponent.
23		SRAX	1,1	Scale right.
24		STA	ARG	$0\ v_1\ v_2\ v_3\ v_4$
25		STX	ARGX	$v_5\ v_6\ v_7\ v_8\ v_9$
26		STA	ARGX(SIGN)	Store true sign of v in both halves.
27		LDA	ACC	(We know that u has the sign of the answer.)
28		LDX	ACCX	$rAX \leftarrow u$.
29		SLAX	2	Remove exponent.
30		STA	ACC	$u_1\ u_2\ u_3\ u_4\ u_5$
31		SLAX	4	
32		ENTX	1	
33		STX	EXPO	EXPO $\leftarrow 1$ (see below).
34		SRC	1	$1\ u_5\ u_6\ u_7\ u_8$
35		STA	1F(SIGN)	A trick, see comments in text.
36		ADD	ARGX(0:4)	Add $0\ v_5\ v_6\ v_7\ v_8$.
37		SRAX	4	
38	1H	DECA	1	Recover from inserted 1. (Sign varies)
39		ADD	ACC(0:4)	Add most significant halves.
40		ADD	ARG	(Overflow cannot occur)

```
41  DNORM   JANZ  1F              Normalization routine:
42          JXNZ  1F              f_w in rAX, e_w = EXPO + rI2.
43  DZERO   STA   ACC             If f_w = 0, set e_w ← 0.
44          JMP   9F
45  2H      SLAX  1               Normalize to the left.
46          DEC2  1
47  1H      CMPA  =0=(1:1)        Is the leading byte zero?
48          JE    2B
49          SRAX  2               (Rounding omitted)
50          STA   ACC
51          LDA   EXPO            Compute final exponent.
52          INCA  0,2
53          JAN   EXPUND          Is it negative?
54          STA   ACC(EXPD)
55          CMPA  =1(3:3)=        Is it more than two bytes?
56          JL    8F
57  EXPOVD  HLT   20
58  EXPUND  HLT   10
59  8H      LDA   ACC             Bring answer into rA.
60  9H      STX   ACCX
61  EXITDF  JMP   *               Exit from subroutine.
62  ARG     CON   0
63  ARGX    CON   0
64  ACC     CON   0               Floating point accumulator
65  ACCX    CON   0
66  EXPO    CON   0               Part of "raw exponent"  ∎
```

When the least-significant halves are added together in this program, an extra digit "1" is inserted at the left of the word that is known to have the correct sign. After the addition, this byte can be 0, 1, or 2, depending on the circumstances, and all three cases are handled simultaneously in this way. (Compare this with the rather cumbersome method of complementation that is used in Program 4.2.1A.)

It is worth noting that register A can be zero after the instruction on line 40 has been performed; and, because of the way MIX defines the sign of a zero result, the accumulator contains the correct sign that is to be attached to the result if register X is nonzero. If lines 39 and 40 were interchanged, the program would be incorrect, even though both instructions are 'ADD'!

Now let us consider double-precision multiplication. The product has four components, shown schematically in Fig. 4. Since we need only the leftmost eight bytes, it is convenient to ignore the digits to the right of the vertical line in the diagram; in particular, we need not even compute the product of the two least-significant halves.

Program M (*Double-precision multiplication*). The input and output conventions for this subroutine are the same as for Program A.

```
01  BYTE  EQU  1(4:4)        Byte size
02  QQ    EQU  BYTE*BYTE/2   Excess of double-precision exponent
```

$$
\begin{array}{ccccccccccc}
u & u & u & u & u & & u & u & u & 0 & 0 & = u_m + \epsilon u_l \\
v & v & v & v & v & & v & v & v & 0 & 0 & = v_m + \epsilon v_l \\
\hline
& & & & & & x & x & x & x & x & x & 0 & 0 & 0 & 0 & = \epsilon^2 u_l \times v_l
\end{array}
$$

$$
\begin{array}{lll}
u\;u\;u\;u\;u \qquad u\;u\;u\;0\;0 & = u_m + \epsilon u_l \\
v\;v\;v\;v\;v \qquad v\;v\;v\;0\;0 & = v_m + \epsilon v_l \\
\hline
\qquad\qquad\quad x\;x\;x\;x\;x\;0\;0\;0\;0 & = \epsilon^2 u_l \times v_l \\
x\;x\;x\;x\,|\,x \qquad x\;x\;x\;0\;0 & = \epsilon\,u_m \times v_l \\
x\;x\;x\;x\,|\,x \qquad x\;x\;x\;0\;0 & = \epsilon\,u_l \times v_m \\
x\;x\;x\;x\;x \quad x\;x\;x\;x\,|\,x & = u_m \times v_m \\
\hline
w\;w\;w\;w\;w \quad w\;w\;w\;w\,|\,w \qquad w\;w\;w\;w \quad w\;0\;0\;0\;0
\end{array}
$$

Fig. 4. Double-precision multiplication of eight-byte fraction parts.

```
03  DFMUL  STJ   EXITDF              Double-precision multiplication:
04         STA   TEMP
05         SLAX  2                   Remove exponent.
06         STA   ARG                 v_m
07         STX   ARGX                v_l
08         LDA   TEMP(EXPD)
09         ADD   ACC(EXPD)
10         STA   EXPO                EXPO ← e_u + e_v.
11         ENT2  -QQ                 rI2 ← −QQ.
12         LDA   ACC
13         LDX   ACCX
14         SLAX  2                   Remove exponent.
15         STA   ACC                 u_m
16         STX   ACCX                u_l
17         MUL   ARGX                u_m × v_l
18         STA   TEMP
19         LDA   ARG(ABS)
20         MUL   ACCX(ABS)           |v_m × u_l|
21         SRA   1                   0 x x x x
22         ADD   TEMP(1:4)           (Overflow cannot occur)
23         STA   TEMP
24         LDA   ARG
25         MUL   ACC                 v_m × u_m
26         STA   TEMP(SIGN)          Store true sign of result.
27         STA   ACC                 Now prepare to add all the
28         STX   ACCX                    partial products together.
29         LDA   ACCX(0:4)           0 x x x x
30         ADD   TEMP                (Overflow cannot occur)
31         SRAX  4
32         ADD   ACC                 (Overflow cannot occur)
33         JMP   DNORM               Normalize and exit.  █
```

Notice the careful treatment of signs in this program, and note also the fact that the range of exponents makes it impossible to compute the final exponent using an index register. Program M is perhaps too slipshod in accuracy, since it uses only the information to the left of the vertical line in Fig. 4; this can make the least significant byte as much as 2 in error. A little more accuracy can be achieved as discussed in exercise 4.

Double-precision floating division is the most difficult routine, or at least the most frightening prospect we have encountered so far in this chapter. Actually, it is not terribly complicated, once we see how to do it; let us write the numbers to be divided in the form $(u_m + \epsilon u_l)/(v_m + \epsilon v_l)$, where ϵ is the reciprocal of the word size of the computer, and where v_m is assumed to be normalized. The fraction can now be expanded as follows:

$$
\frac{u_m + \epsilon u_l}{v_m + \epsilon v_l} = \frac{u_m + \epsilon u_l}{v_m} \left(\frac{1}{1 + \epsilon(v_l/v_m)} \right)
$$
$$
= \frac{u_m + \epsilon u_l}{v_m} \left(1 - \epsilon \left(\frac{v_l}{v_m} \right) + \epsilon^2 \left(\frac{v_l}{v_m} \right)^2 - \cdots \right). \tag{2}
$$

Since $0 \le |v_l| < 1$ and $1/b \le |v_m| < 1$, we have $|v_l/v_m| < b$, and the error from dropping terms involving ϵ^2 can be disregarded. Our method therefore is to compute $w_m + \epsilon w_l = (u_m + \epsilon u_l)/v_m$, and then to subtract ϵ times $w_m v_l/v_m$ from the result.

In the following program, lines 27–32 do the lower half of a double-precision addition, using another method for forcing the appropriate sign as an alternative to the trick of Program A.

Program D (*Double-precision division*). This program adheres to the same conventions as Programs A and M.

```
01  DFDIV  STJ   EXITDF          Double-precision division:
02         JOV   OFLO            Ensure that overflow is off.
03         STA   TEMP
04         SLAX  2               Remove exponent.
05         STA   ARG             vm
06         STX   ARGX            vl
07         LDA   ACC(EXPD)
08         SUB   TEMP(EXPD)
09         STA   EXPO            EXPO ← eu − ev.
10         ENT2  QQ+1            rI2 ← QQ + 1.
11         LDA   ACC
12         LDX   ACCX
13         SLAX  2               Remove exponent.
14         SRAX  1               (See Algorithm 4.2.1M)
15         DIV   ARG             If overflow, it is detected below.
16         STA   ACC             wm
17         SLAX  5               Use remainder in further division.
18         DIV   ARG
19         STA   ACCX            ±wl
20         LDA   ARGX(1:4)
21         ENTX  0
22         DIV   ARG(ABS)        rA ← ⌊|b⁴vl/vm|⌋/b⁵.
23         JOV   DVZROD          Did division cause overflow?
24         MUL   ACC(ABS)        rAX ← |wm vl/bvm|, approximately.
25         SRAX  4               Multiply by b, and save
26         SLC   5                   the leading byte in rX.
```

27		SUB	ACCX(ABS)	Subtract $|w_l|$.
28		DECA	1	Force minus sign.
29		SUB	WM1	
30		JOV	*+2	If no overflow, carry one more
31		INCX	1	to upper half.
32		SLC	5	(Now rA $\leq$ 0)
33		ADD	ACC(ABS)	rA $\leftarrow$ $|w_m|$ $-$ $|$rA$|$.
34		STA	ACC(ABS)	(Now rA $\geq$ 0)
35		LDA	ACC	rA $\leftarrow$ w_m with correct sign.
36		JMP	DNORM	Normalize and exit.
37	DVZROD	HLT	30	Unnormalized or zero divisor
38	1H	EQU	1(1:1)	
39	WM1	CON	1B-1,BYTE-1(1:1)	Word size minus one █

Here is a table of the approximate average computation times for these double-precision subroutines, compared to the single-precision subroutines that appear in Section 4.2.1:

	Single precision	Double precision
Addition	$45.5u$	$84u$
Subtraction	$49.5u$	$88u$
Multiplication	$48u$	$109u$
Division	$52u$	$126.5u$

For extension of the methods of this section to triple-precision floating point fraction parts, see Y. Ikebe, *CACM* **8** (1965), 175–177.

EXERCISES

1. [*16*] Try the double-precision division technique by hand, with $\epsilon = \frac{1}{1000}$, when dividing 180000 by 314159. (Thus, let $(u_m, u_l) = (.180, .000)$ and $(v_m, v_l) = (.314, .159)$, and find the quotient using the method suggested in the text following (2).)

2. [*20*] Would it be a good idea to insert the instruction 'ENTX 0' between lines 30 and 31 of Program M, in order to keep unwanted information left over in register X from interfering with the accuracy of the results?

3. [*M20*] Explain why overflow cannot occur during Program M.

4. [*22*] How should Program M be changed so that extra accuracy is achieved, essentially by moving the vertical line in Fig. 4 over to the right one position? Specify all changes that are required, and determine the difference in execution time caused by these changes.

▶ **5.** [*24*] How should Program A be changed so that extra accuracy is achieved, essentially by working with a nine-byte accumulator instead of an eight-byte accumulator to the right of the radix point? Specify all changes that are required, and determine the difference in execution time caused by these changes.

6. [*23*] Assume that the double-precision subroutines of this section and the single-precision subroutines of Section 4.2.1 are being used in the same main program. Write a subroutine that converts a single-precision floating point number into double-precision form (1), and write another subroutine that converts a double-precision floating point number into single-precision form (reporting exponent overflow or underflow if the conversion is impossible).

▶ **7.** [*M30*] Estimate the accuracy of the double-precision subroutines in this section, by finding bounds δ_1, δ_2, and δ_3 on the relative errors

$$\left|((u \oplus v) - (u + v))/(u + v)\right|, \qquad \left|((u \otimes v) - (u \times v))/(u \times v)\right|,$$
$$\left|((u \oslash v) - (u/v))/(u/v)\right|.$$

8. [*M28*] Estimate the accuracy of the "improved" double-precision subroutines of exercises 4 and 5, in the sense of exercise 7.

9. [*M42*] T. J. Dekker [*Numer. Math.* **18** (1971), 224–242] has suggested an alternative approach to double precision, based entirely on single-precision floating binary calculations. For example, Theorem 4.2.2C states that $u + v = w + r$, where $w = u \oplus v$ and $r = (u \ominus w) \oplus v$, if $|u| \geq |v|$ and the radix is 2; here $|r| \leq |w|/2^p$, so the pair (w, r) may be considered a double-precision version of $u + v$. To add two such pairs $(u, u') \oplus (v, v')$, where $|u'| \leq |u|/2^p$ and $|v'| \leq |v|/2^p$ and $|u| \geq |v|$, Dekker suggests computing $u + v = w + r$ (exactly), then $s = (r \oplus v') \oplus u'$ (an approximate remainder), and finally returning the value $(w \oplus s, (w \ominus (w \oplus s)) \oplus s)$.

Study the accuracy and efficiency of this approach when it is used recursively to produce quadruple-precision calculations.

4.2.4. Distribution of Floating Point Numbers

In order to analyze the average behavior of floating point arithmetic algorithms (and in particular to determine their average running time), we need some statistical information that allows us to determine how often various cases arise. The purpose of this section is to discuss the empirical and theoretical properties of the distribution of floating point numbers.

A. Addition and subtraction routines. The execution time for a floating point addition or subtraction depends largely on the initial difference of exponents, and also on the number of normalization steps required (to the left or to the right). No way is known to give a good theoretical model that tells what characteristics to expect, but extensive empirical investigations have been made by D. W. Sweeney [*IBM Systems J.* **4** (1965), 31–42].

By means of a special tracing routine, Sweeney ran six "typical" large-scale numerical programs, selected from several different computing laboratories, and examined each floating addition or subtraction operation very carefully. Over 250,000 floating point addition-subtractions were involved in gathering this data. About one out of every ten instructions executed by the tested programs was either FADD or FSUB.

Subtraction is the same as addition preceded by negating the second operand, so we can give all the statistics as if we were merely doing addition. Sweeney's results can be summarized as follows:

One of the two operands to be added was found to be equal to zero about 9 percent of the time, and this was usually the accumulator (ACC). The other 91 percent of the cases split about equally between operands of the same or of

Table 1

EMPIRICAL DATA FOR OPERAND ALIGNMENTS BEFORE ADDITION

$|e_u - e_v|$	$b = 2$	$b = 10$	$b = 16$	$b = 64$
0	0.33	0.47	0.47	0.56
1	0.12	0.23	0.26	0.27
2	0.09	0.11	0.10	0.04
3	0.07	0.03	0.02	0.02
4	0.07	0.01	0.01	0.02
5	0.04	0.01	0.02	0.00
over 5	0.28	0.13	0.11	0.09
average	3.1	0.9	0.8	0.5

Table 2

EMPIRICAL DATA FOR NORMALIZATION AFTER ADDITION

	$b = 2$	$b = 10$	$b = 16$	$b = 64$
Shift right 1	0.20	0.07	0.06	0.03
No shift	0.59	0.80	0.82	0.87
Shift left 1	0.07	0.08	0.07	0.06
Shift left 2	0.03	0.02	0.01	0.01
Shift left 3	0.02	0.00	0.01	0.00
Shift left 4	0.02	0.01	0.00	0.01
Shift left > 4	0.06	0.02	0.02	0.02

opposite signs, and about equally between cases where $|u| \leq |v|$ or $|v| \leq |u|$. The computed answer was zero about 1.4 percent of the time.

The difference between exponents had a behavior approximately given by the probabilities shown in Table 1, for various radices b. (The "over 5" line of that table includes essentially all of the cases when one operand was zero, but the "average" line does not include these cases.)

When u and v have the same sign and are normalized, then $u + v$ either requires one shift to the *right* (for fraction overflow), or no normalization shifts whatever. When u and v have opposite signs, we have zero or more *left* shifts during the normalization. Table 2 gives the observed number of shifts required; the last line of that table includes all cases where the result was zero. The average number of left shifts per normalization was about 0.9 when $b = 2$; about 0.2 when $b = 10$ or 16; and about 0.1 when $b = 64$.

B. The fraction parts. Further analysis of floating point routines can be based on the *statistical distribution of the fraction parts* of randomly chosen normalized floating point numbers. The facts are quite surprising, and there is an interesting theory that accounts for the unusual phenomena that are observed.

For convenience let us assume temporarily that we are dealing with floating *decimal* arithmetic (radix 10); modifications of the following discussion to any other positive integer base b will be very straightforward. Suppose we are given a "random" positive normalized number $(e, f) = 10^e \cdot f$. Since f is normalized, we know that its leading digit is 1, 2, 3, 4, 5, 6, 7, 8, or 9, and we might naturally expect each of these nine possible leading digits to occur about one-ninth of the time. But, in fact, the behavior in practice is quite different. For example, the leading digit tends to be equal to 1 more than 30 percent of the time!

One way to test the assertion just made is to take a table of physical constants (like the speed of light or the acceleration of gravity) from some standard reference. If we look at the *Handbook of Mathematical Functions* (U.S. Dept. of Commerce, 1964), for example, we find that 8 of the 28 different physical constants given in Table 2.3, roughly 29 percent, have leading digit equal to 1. The decimal values of $n!$ for $1 \leq n \leq 100$ include exactly 30 entries beginning with 1; so do the decimal values of 2^n and of F_n, for $1 \leq n \leq 100$. We might also try looking at census reports, or a Farmer's Almanack (but not a telephone directory).

In the days before pocket calculators, the pages in well-used tables of logarithms tended to get quite dirty in the front, while the last pages stayed relatively clean and neat. This phenomenon was apparently first mentioned in print by the astronomer Simon Newcomb [*Amer. J. Math.* **4** (1881), 39–40], who gave good grounds for believing that the leading digit d occurs with probability $\log_{10}(1 + 1/d)$. The same distribution was discovered empirically, many years later, by Frank Benford, who reported the results of 20,229 observations taken from many different sources [*Proc. Amer. Philosophical Soc.* **78** (1938), 551–572].

In order to account for this leading-digit law, let's take a closer look at the way we write numbers in floating point notation. If we take any positive number u, its fraction part is determined by the formula $10f_u = 10^{(\log_{10} u) \bmod 1}$; hence its leading digit is less than d if and only if

$$(\log_{10} u) \bmod 1 < \log_{10} d. \qquad (1)$$

Now if we have a "random" positive number U, chosen from some reasonable distribution that might occur in nature, we might expect that $(\log_{10} U) \bmod 1$ would be uniformly distributed between zero and one, at least to a very good approximation. (Similarly, we expect $U \bmod 1$, $U^2 \bmod 1$, $\sqrt{U + \pi} \bmod 1$, etc., to be uniformly distributed. We expect a roulette wheel to be unbiased, for essentially the same reason.) Therefore by (1) the leading digit will be 1 with probability $\log_{10} 2 \approx 30.103$ percent; it will be 2 with probability $\log_{10} 3 - \log_{10} 2 \approx 17.609$ percent; and, in general, if r is any real value between 1 and 10, we ought to have $10f_U \leq r$ approximately $\log_{10} r$ of the time.

The fact that leading digits tend to be small makes the most obvious techniques of "average error" estimation for floating point calculations invalid. The relative error due to rounding is usually a little more than expected.

Of course, it may justly be said that the heuristic argument above does not prove the stated law. It merely shows us a plausible reason why the leading digits behave the way they do. An interesting approach to the analysis of leading digits has been suggested by R. Hamming: Let $p(r)$ be the probability that $10f_U \leq r$, where $1 \leq r \leq 10$ and f_U is the normalized fraction part of a random normalized floating point number U. If we think of random quantities in the real world, we observe that they are measured in terms of arbitrary units; and if we were to change the definition of a meter or a gram, many of the fundamental physical constants would have different values. Suppose then that all of the numbers in the universe are suddenly multiplied by a constant factor c; our universe of random floating point quantities should be essentially unchanged by this transformation, so $p(r)$ should not be affected.

Multiplying everything by c has the effect of transforming $(\log_{10} U) \bmod 1$ into $(\log_{10} U + \log_{10} c) \bmod 1$. It is now time to set up formulas that describe the desired behavior; we may assume that $1 \le c \le 10$. By definition,

$$p(r) = \Pr\big((\log_{10} U) \bmod 1 \le \log_{10} r\big).$$

By our assumption, we should also have

$$p(r) = \Pr\big((\log_{10} U + \log_{10} c) \bmod 1 \le \log_{10} r\big)$$

$$= \begin{cases} \Pr\big((\log_{10} U \bmod 1) \le \log_{10} r - \log_{10} c \\ \qquad \text{or } (\log_{10} U \bmod 1) \ge 1 - \log_{10} c\big), & \text{if } c \le r; \\ \Pr\big((\log_{10} U \bmod 1) \le \log_{10} r + 1 - \log_{10} c \\ \qquad \text{and } (\log_{10} U \bmod 1) \ge 1 - \log_{10} c\big), & \text{if } c \ge r; \end{cases}$$

$$= \begin{cases} p(r/c) + 1 - p(10/c), & \text{if } c \le r; \\ p(10r/c) - p(10/c), & \text{if } c \ge r. \end{cases} \tag{2}$$

Let us now extend the function $p(r)$ to values outside the range $1 \le r \le 10$, by defining $p(10^n r) = p(r) + n$; then if we replace $10/c$ by d, the last equation of (2) may be written

$$p(rd) = p(r) + p(d). \tag{3}$$

If our assumption about invariance of the distribution under multiplication by a constant factor is valid, then Eq. (3) must hold for all $r > 0$ and $1 \le d \le 10$. The facts that $p(1) = 0$ and $p(10) = 1$ now imply that

$$1 = p(10) = p\big((\sqrt[n]{10})^n\big) = p(\sqrt[n]{10}) + p\big((\sqrt[n]{10})^{n-1}\big) = \cdots = np(\sqrt[n]{10});$$

hence we deduce that $p(10^{m/n}) = m/n$ for all positive integers m and n. If we now decide to require that p is continuous, we are forced to conclude that $p(r) = \log_{10} r$, and this is the desired law.

Although this argument may be more convincing than the first one, it doesn't really hold up under scrutiny if we stick to conventional notions of probability. The traditional way to make the argument above rigorous is to assume that there is some underlying distribution of numbers $F(u)$ such that a given positive number U is $\le u$ with probability $F(u)$; then the probability of concern to us is

$$p(r) = \sum_m \big(F(10^m r) - F(10^m)\big), \tag{4}$$

summed over all values $-\infty < m < \infty$. Our assumptions about scale invariance and continuity have led us to conclude that

$$p(r) = \log_{10} r.$$

Using the same argument, we could "prove" that

$$\sum_{m} \left(F(b^m r) - F(b^m) \right) = \log_b r, \tag{5}$$

for each integer $b \geq 2$, when $1 \leq r \leq b$. But there *is* no distribution function F that satisfies this equation for all such b and r! (See exercise 7.)

One way out of the difficulty is to regard the logarithm law $p(r) = \log_{10} r$ as only a very close *approximation* to the true distribution. The true distribution itself may perhaps be changing as the universe expands, becoming a better and better approximation as time goes on; and if we replace 10 by an arbitrary base b, the approximation might be less accurate (at any given time) as b gets larger. Another rather appealing way to resolve the dilemma, by abandoning the traditional idea of a distribution function, has been suggested by R. A. Raimi, *AMM* **76** (1969), 342–348.

The hedging in the last paragraph is probably a very unsatisfactory explanation, and so the following further calculation (which sticks to rigorous mathematics and avoids any intuitive, yet paradoxical, notions of probability) should be welcome. Let us consider the distribution of the leading digits of the *positive integers*, instead of the distribution for some imagined set of real numbers. The investigation of this topic is quite interesting, not only because it sheds some light on the probability distributions of floating point data, but also because it makes a particularly instructive example of how to combine the methods of discrete mathematics with the methods of infinitesimal calculus.

In the following discussion, let r be a fixed real number, $1 \leq r \leq 10$; we will attempt to make a reasonable definition of $p(r)$, the "probability" that the representation $10^{e_N} \cdot f_N$ of a "random" positive integer N has $10 f_N < r$, assuming infinite precision.

To start, let us try to find the probability using a limiting method like the definition of "Pr" in Section 3.5. One nice way to rephrase that definition is to define

$$P_0(n) = [n = 10^e \cdot f \text{ where } 10f < r] = \left[(\log_{10} n) \bmod 1 < \log_{10} r \right]. \tag{6}$$

Now $P_0(1)$, $P_0(2)$, ... is an infinite sequence of zeros and ones, with ones to represent the cases that contribute to the probability we are seeking. We can try to "average out" this sequence, by defining

$$P_1(n) = \frac{1}{n} \sum_{k=1}^{n} P_0(k). \tag{7}$$

Thus if we generate a random integer between 1 and n using the techniques of Chapter 3, and convert it to floating decimal form (e, f), the probability that $10f < r$ is exactly $P_1(n)$. It is natural to let $\lim_{n \to \infty} P_1(n)$ be the "probability" $p(r)$ we are after, and that is just what we did in Definition 3.5A.

But in this case the limit does not exist. For example, let us consider the subsequence

$$P_1(s), P_1(10s), P_1(100s), \ldots, P_1(10^n s), \ldots,$$

where s is a real number, $1 \le s \le 10$. If $s \le r$, we find that

$$P_1(10^n s) = \frac{1}{10^n s}\big(\lceil r \rceil - 1 + \lceil 10r \rceil - 10 + \cdots + \lceil 10^{n-1}r \rceil - 10^{n-1} + \lfloor 10^n s \rfloor + 1 - 10^n \big)$$

$$= \frac{1}{10^n s}\big(r(1 + 10 + \cdots + 10^{n-1}) + O(n) + \lfloor 10^n s \rfloor - 1 - 10 - \cdots - 10^n\big)$$

$$= \frac{1}{10^n s}\big(\tfrac{1}{9}(10^n r - 10^{n+1}) + \lfloor 10^n s \rfloor + O(n)\big). \tag{8}$$

As $n \to \infty$, $P_1(10^n s)$ therefore approaches the limiting value $1 + (r - 10)/9s$. The same calculation is valid for the case $s > r$ if we replace $\lfloor 10^n s \rfloor + 1$ by $\lceil 10^n r \rceil$; thus we obtain the limiting value $10(r - 1)/9s$ when $s \ge r$. [See J. Franel, *Naturforschende Gesellschaft, Vierteljahrsschrift* **62** (Zürich: 1917), 286–295.]

In other words, the sequence $\langle P_1(n) \rangle$ has subsequences $\langle P_1(10^n s) \rangle$ whose limit goes from $(r - 1)/9$ up to $10(r - 1)/9r$ and down again to $(r - 1)/9$, as s goes from 1 to r to 10. We see that $P_1(n)$ has no limit as $n \to \infty$; and the values of $P_1(n)$ for large n are not particularly good approximations to our conjectured limit $\log_{10} r$ either!

Since $P_1(n)$ doesn't approach a limit, we can try to use the same idea as (7) once again, to "average out" the anomalous behavior. In general, let

$$P_{m+1}(n) = \frac{1}{n} \sum_{k=1}^{n} P_m(k). \tag{9}$$

Then $P_{m+1}(n)$ will tend to be a more well-behaved sequence than $P_m(n)$. Let us try to confirm this with quantitative calculations; our experience with the special case $m = 0$ indicates that it might be worthwhile to consider the subsequence $P_{m+1}(10^n s)$. The following results can, in fact, be derived:

Lemma Q. *For any integer $m \ge 1$ and any real number $\epsilon > 0$, there are functions $Q_m(s)$, $R_m(s)$ and an integer $N_m(\epsilon)$, such that whenever $n > N_m(\epsilon)$ and $1 \le s \le 10$, we have*

$$|P_m(10^n s) - Q_m(s) - R_m(s)[s > r]| < \epsilon. \tag{10}$$

Furthermore the functions $Q_m(s)$ and $R_m(s)$ satisfy the relations

$$Q_m(s) = \frac{1}{s}\Big(\frac{1}{9}\int_1^{10} Q_{m-1}(t)\, dt + \int_1^s Q_{m-1}(t)\, dt + \frac{1}{9}\int_r^{10} R_{m-1}(t)\, dt\Big);$$

$$R_m(s) = \frac{1}{s}\int_r^s R_{m-1}(t)\, dt; \tag{11}$$

$$Q_0(s) = 1, \qquad R_0(s) = -1.$$

Proof. Consider the functions $Q_m(s)$ and $R_m(s)$ defined by (11), and let

$$S_m(t) = Q_m(t) + R_m(t)[t > r]. \tag{12}$$

We will prove the lemma by induction on m.

First note that $Q_1(s) = \big(1 + (s-1) - (10-r)/9\big)/s = 1 + (r-10)/9s$, and $R_1(s) = (r-s)/s$. From (8) we find that $|P_1(10^n s) - S_1(s)| = O(n)/10^n$; this establishes the lemma when $m = 1$.

Now for $m > 1$, we have

$$P_m(10^n s) = \frac{1}{s}\left(\sum_{0 \le j < n} \frac{1}{10^{n-j}} \sum_{10^j \le k < 10^{j+1}} \frac{1}{10^j} P_{m-1}(k) + \sum_{10^n \le k \le 10^n s} \frac{1}{10^n} P_{m-1}(k) \right),$$

and we want to approximate this quantity. By induction, the difference

$$\left| \sum_{10^j \le k \le 10^j q} \frac{1}{10^j} P_{m-1}(k) - \sum_{10^j \le k \le 10^j q} \frac{1}{10^j} S_{m-1}\left(\frac{k}{10^j}\right) \right| \tag{13}$$

is less than $q\epsilon$ when $1 \le q \le 10$ and $j > N_{m-1}(\epsilon)$. Since $S_{m-1}(t)$ is continuous, it is a Riemann-integrable function; and the difference

$$\left| \sum_{10^j \le k \le 10^j q} \frac{1}{10^j} S_{m-1}\left(\frac{k}{10^j}\right) - \int_1^q S_{m-1}(t)\, dt \right| \tag{14}$$

is less than ϵ for all j greater than some number N, independent of q, by the definition of integration. We may choose N to be $> N_{m-1}(\epsilon)$. Therefore for $n > N$, the difference

$$\left| P_m(10^n s) - \frac{1}{s}\left(\sum_{0 \le j < n} \frac{1}{10^{n-j}} \int_1^{10} S_{m-1}(t)\, dt + \int_1^s S_{m-1}(t)\, dt \right) \right| \tag{15}$$

is bounded by $\sum_{j=0}^{N}(M/10^{n-j}) + \sum_{N<j<n}(11\epsilon/10^{n-j}) + 11\epsilon$, if M is an upper bound for $(13) + (14)$ that is valid for all positive integers j. Finally, the sum $\sum_{0 \le j < n}(1/10^{n-j})$, which appears in (15), is equal to $(1 - 1/10^n)/9$; so

$$\left| P_m(10^n s) - \frac{1}{s}\left(\frac{1}{9} \int_1^{10} S_{m-1}(t)\, dt + \int_1^s S_{m-1}(t)\, dt \right) \right|$$

can be made smaller than, say, 20ϵ, if n is taken large enough. Comparing this with (10) and (11) completes the proof. ∎

The gist of Lemma Q is that we have the limiting relationship

$$\lim_{n \to \infty} P_m(10^n s) = S_m(s). \tag{16}$$

Also, since $S_m(s)$ is not constant as s varies, the limit

$$\lim_{n \to \infty} P_m(n)$$

(which would be our desired "probability") does not exist for any m. The situation is shown in Fig. 5, which shows the values of $S_m(s)$ when m is small and $r = 2$.

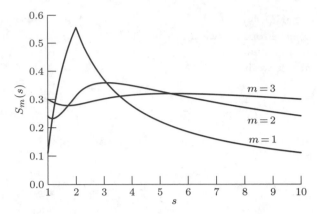

Fig. 5. The probability that the leading digit is 1.

Even though $S_m(s)$ is not a constant, so that we do not have a definite limit for $P_m(n)$, notice that already for $m = 3$ in Fig. 5 the value of $S_m(s)$ stays very close to $\log_{10} 2 \approx 0.30103$. Therefore we have good reason to suspect that $S_m(s)$ is very close to $\log_{10} r$ for all large m, and, in fact, that the sequence of functions $\langle S_m(s) \rangle$ converges uniformly to the constant function $\log_{10} r$.

It is interesting to prove this conjecture by explicitly calculating $Q_m(s)$ and $R_m(s)$ for all m, as in the proof of the following theorem:

Theorem F. *Let $S_m(s)$ be the limit defined in* (16). *For all $\epsilon > 0$, there exists a number $N(\epsilon)$ such that*

$$|S_m(s) - \log_{10} r| < \epsilon, \qquad \text{for } 1 \le s \le 10, \tag{17}$$

whenever $m > N(\epsilon)$.

Proof. In view of Lemma Q, we can prove this result if we can show that there is a number M depending on ϵ such that, for $1 \le s \le 10$ and for all $m > M$, we have

$$|Q_m(s) - \log_{10} r| < \epsilon \qquad \text{and} \qquad |R_m(s)| < \epsilon. \tag{18}$$

It is not difficult to solve the recurrence formula (11) for R_m: We have $R_0(s) = -1$, $R_1(s) = -1 + r/s$, $R_2(s) = -1 + (r/s)(1 + \ln(s/r))$, and in general

$$R_m(s) = -1 + \frac{r}{s}\left(1 + \frac{1}{1!}\ln\frac{s}{r} + \cdots + \frac{1}{(m-1)!}\left(\ln\frac{s}{r}\right)^{m-1}\right). \tag{19}$$

For the stated range of s, this converges uniformly to $-1 + (r/s)\exp\left(\ln(s/r)\right) = 0$.

The recurrence (11) for Q_m takes the form

$$Q_m(s) = \frac{1}{s}\left(c_m + 1 + \int_1^s Q_{m-1}(t)\, dt\right), \tag{20}$$

where

$$c_m = \frac{1}{9}\left(\int_1^{10} Q_{m-1}(t)\, dt + \int_r^{10} R_{m-1}(t)\, dt\right) - 1. \tag{21}$$

And the solution to recurrence (20) is easily found by trying out the first few cases and guessing at a formula that can be proved by induction; we find that

$$Q_m(s) = 1 + \frac{1}{s}\left(c_m + \frac{1}{1!}c_{m-1}\ln s + \cdots + \frac{1}{(m-1)!}c_1(\ln s)^{m-1}\right). \qquad (22)$$

It remains for us to calculate the coefficients c_m, which by (19), (21), and (22) satisfy the relations

$$c_1 = (r-10)/9;$$

$$\begin{aligned}
c_{m+1} = \frac{1}{9}&\left(c_m \ln 10 + \frac{1}{2!}c_{m-1}(\ln 10)^2 + \cdots + \frac{1}{m!}c_1(\ln 10)^m\right. \\
&\left.+ r\left(1 + \frac{1}{1!}\ln\frac{10}{r} + \cdots + \frac{1}{m!}\left(\ln\frac{10}{r}\right)^m\right) - 10\right).
\end{aligned} \qquad (23)$$

This sequence appears at first to be very complicated, but actually we can analyze it without difficulty with the help of generating functions. Let

$$C(z) = c_1 z + c_2 z^2 + c_3 z^3 + \cdots;$$

then since $10^z = 1 + z\ln 10 + (1/2!)(z\ln 10)^2 + \cdots$, we deduce that

$$\begin{aligned}
c_{m+1} &= \frac{1}{10}c_{m+1} + \frac{9}{10}c_{m+1} \\
&= \frac{1}{10}\left(c_{m+1} + c_m\ln 10 + \cdots + \frac{1}{m!}c_1(\ln 10)^m\right) + \frac{r}{10}\left(1 + \cdots + \frac{1}{m!}\left(\ln\frac{10}{r}\right)^m\right) - 1
\end{aligned}$$

is the coefficient of z^{m+1} in the function

$$\frac{1}{10}C(z)10^z + \frac{r}{10}\left(\frac{10}{r}\right)^z\left(\frac{z}{1-z}\right) - \frac{z}{1-z}. \qquad (24)$$

This condition holds for all values of m, so (24) must equal $C(z)$, and we obtain the explicit formula

$$C(z) = \frac{-z}{1-z}\left(\frac{(10/r)^{z-1}-1}{10^{z-1}-1}\right). \qquad (25)$$

We want to study asymptotic properties of the coefficients of $C(z)$, to complete our analysis. The large parenthesized factor in (25) approaches $\ln(10/r)/\ln 10 = 1 - \log_{10} r$ as $z \to 1$, so we see that

$$C(z) + \frac{1 - \log_{10} r}{1 - z} = R(z) \qquad (26)$$

is an analytic function of the complex variable z in the circle

$$|z| < \left|1 + \frac{2\pi i}{\ln 10}\right|.$$

In particular, $R(z)$ converges for $z = 1$, so its coefficients approach zero. This proves that the coefficients of $C(z)$ behave like those of $(\log_{10} r - 1)/(1 - z)$, that is,

$$\lim_{m \to \infty} c_m = \log_{10} r - 1.$$

Finally, we may combine this with (22), to show that $Q_m(s)$ approaches

$$1 + \frac{\log_{10} r - 1}{s}\left(1 + \ln s + \frac{1}{2!}(\ln s)^2 + \cdots\right) = \log_{10} r$$

uniformly for $1 \le s \le 10$.   ∎

Therefore we have established the logarithmic law for integers by direct calculation, at the same time seeing that it is an extremely good approximation to the average behavior although it is never precisely achieved.

The proofs of Lemma Q and Theorem F given above are slight simplifications and amplifications of methods due to B. J. Flehinger, *AMM* **73** (1966), 1056–1061. Many authors have written about the distribution of initial digits, showing that the logarithmic law is a good approximation for many underlying distributions; see the surveys by Ralph A. Raimi, *AMM* **83** (1976), 521–538, and Peter Schatte, *J. Information Processing and Cybernetics* **24** (1988), 443–455, for a comprehensive review of the literature.

Exercise 17 discusses an approach to the definition of probability under which the logarithmic law holds exactly, over the integers. Furthermore, exercise 18 demonstrates that *any* reasonable definition of probability over the integers must lead to the logarithmic law, if it assigns a value to the probability of leading digits.

Floating point computations operate primarily on noninteger numbers, of course; we have studied integers because of their familiarity and their simplicity. When arbitrary real numbers are considered, theoretical results are more difficult to obtain, but evidence is accumulating that the same statistics apply, in the sense that repeated calculations with real numbers will nearly always tend to yield better and better approximations to a logarithmic distribution of fraction parts. For example, Peter Schatte [*Zeitschrift für angewandte Math. und Mechanik* **53** (1973), 553–565] showed that, under mild restrictions, the products of independent, identically distributed random real variables approach the logarithmic distribution. The sums of such variables do too, but only in the sense of repeated averaging. Similar results have been obtained by J. L. Barlow and E. H. Bareiss, *Computing* **34** (1985), 325–347. See also A. Berger, L. A. Bunimovich, and T. P. Hill, *Trans. Amer. Math. Soc.* **357** (2004), 197–219.

EXERCISES

1. [*13*] Given that u and v are nonzero floating decimal numbers *with the same sign*, what is the approximate probability that fraction overflow occurs during the calculation of $u \oplus v$, according to Tables 1 and 2?

2. [*42*] Make further tests of floating point addition and subtraction, to confirm or improve on the accuracy of Tables 1 and 2.

3. [*15*] What is the probability that the two leading digits of a floating decimal number are "23", according to the logarithmic law?

4. [*M18*] The text points out that the front pages of a well-used table of logarithms get dirtier than the back pages do. What if we had an *antilogarithm* table instead, namely a table that tells us the value of x when $\log_{10} x$ is given; which pages of such a table would be the dirtiest?

▶ **5.** [*M20*] Let U be a random real number that is uniformly distributed in the interval $0 < U < 1$. What is the distribution of the leading digits of U?

6. [*23*] If we have binary computer words containing $n + 1$ bits, we might use p bits for the fraction part of floating binary numbers, one bit for the sign, and $n - p$ bits for the exponent. This means that the range of values representable, namely the ratio of the largest positive normalized value to the smallest, is essentially $2^{2^{n-p}}$. The same computer word could be used to represent floating *hexadecimal* numbers, that is, floating point numbers with radix 16, with $p + 2$ bits for the fraction part $((p+2)/4$ hexadecimal digits) and $n - p - 2$ bits for the exponent; then the range of values would be $16^{2^{n-p-2}} = 2^{2^{n-p}}$, the same as before, and with more bits in the fraction part. This may sound as if we are getting something for nothing, but the normalization condition for base 16 is weaker in that there may be up to three leading zero bits in the fraction part; thus not all of the $p + 2$ bits are "significant."

On the basis of the logarithmic law, what are the probabilities that the fraction part of a positive normalized radix 16 floating point number has exactly 0, 1, 2, and 3 leading zero bits? Discuss the desirability of hexadecimal versus binary.

7. [*HM28*] Prove that there is no distribution function $F(u)$ that satisfies (5) for each integer $b \geq 2$, and for all real values r in the range $1 \leq r \leq b$.

8. [*HM23*] Does (10) hold when $m = 0$ for suitable $N_0(\epsilon)$?

9. [*HM25*] (P. Diaconis.) Let $P_1(n)$, $P_2(n)$, ... be any sequence of functions defined by repeatedly averaging a given function $P_0(n)$ according to Eq. (9). Prove that $\lim_{m \to \infty} P_m(n) = P_0(1)$ for all fixed n.

▶ **10.** [*HM28*] The text shows that $c_m = \log_{10} r - 1 + \epsilon_m$, where ϵ_m approaches zero as $m \to \infty$. Obtain the next term in the asymptotic expansion of c_m.

11. [*M15*] Given that U is a random variable distributed according to the logarithmic law, prove that $1/U$ is also.

12. [*HM25*] (R. W. Hamming.) The purpose of this exercise is to show that the result of floating point multiplication tends to obey the logarithmic law more perfectly than the operands do. Let U and V be random, normalized, positive floating point numbers, whose fraction parts are independently distributed with the respective density functions $f(x)$ and $g(x)$. Thus, $f_u \leq r$ and $f_v \leq s$ with probability $\int_{1/b}^{r} \int_{1/b}^{s} f(x)g(y)\, dy\, dx$, for $1/b \leq r, s \leq 1$. Let $h(x)$ be the density function of the fraction part of $U \times V$ (unrounded). Define the *abnormality* $A(f)$ of a density function f to be the maximum relative error,

$$A(f) = \max_{1/b \leq x \leq 1} \left| \frac{f(x) - l(x)}{l(x)} \right|,$$

where $l(x) = 1/(x \ln b)$ is the density of the logarithmic distribution.

Prove that $A(h) \leq \min(A(f), A(g))$. (In particular, if either factor has logarithmic distribution the product does also.)

▶ **13.** [*M20*] The floating point multiplication routine, Algorithm 4.2.1M, requires zero or one left shifts during normalization, depending on whether $f_u f_v \geq 1/b$ or not. Assuming that the input operands are independently distributed according to the logarithmic law, what is the probability that no left shift is needed for normalization of the result?

▶ **14.** [*HM30*] Let U and V be random, normalized, positive floating point numbers whose fraction parts are independently distributed according to the logarithmic law, and let p_k be the probability that the difference in their exponents is k. Assuming that the distribution of the exponents is independent of the fraction parts, give an equation for the probability that "fraction overflow" occurs during the floating point addition of $U \oplus V$, in terms of the base b and the quantities p_0, p_1, p_2, ... Compare this result with exercise 1. (Ignore rounding.)

15. [*HM28*] Let U, V, p_0, p_1, ... be as in exercise 14, and assume that radix 10 arithmetic is being used. Show that regardless of the values of p_0, p_1, p_2, ..., the sum $U \oplus V$ will *not* obey the logarithmic law exactly, and in fact the probability that $U \oplus V$ has leading digit 1 is always strictly *less* than $\log_{10} 2$.

16. [*HM28*] (P. Diaconis.) Let $P_0(n)$ be 0 or 1 for each n, and define "probabilities" $P_{m+1}(n)$ by repeated averaging, as in (9). Show that if $\lim_{n\to\infty} P_1(n)$ does not exist, neither does $\lim_{n\to\infty} P_m(n)$ for any m. [*Hint:* Prove that $a_n \to 0$ whenever we have $(a_1 + \cdots + a_n)/n \to 0$ and $a_{n+1} \leq a_n + M/n$, for some fixed constant $M > 0$.]

▶ **17.** [*HM25*] (M. Tsuji.) Another way to define the value of $\Pr(S(n))$ is to evaluate the quantity $\lim_{n\to\infty}(H_n^{-1}\sum_{k=1}^{n}[S(k)]/k)$; it can be shown that this *harmonic probability* exists and is equal to $\Pr(S(n))$, whenever the latter exists according to Definition 3.5A. Prove that the harmonic probability of the statement "$(\log_{10} n) \bmod 1 < r$" exists and equals r. (Thus, initial digits of integers satisfy the logarithmic law *exactly* in this sense.)

▶ **18.** [*HM30*] Let $P(S)$ be any real-valued function defined on sets S of positive integers, but not necessarily on all such sets, satisfying the following rather weak axioms:

   i) If $P(S)$ and $P(T)$ are defined and $S \cap T = \emptyset$, then $P(S \cup T) = P(S) + P(T)$.
  ii) If $P(S)$ is defined, then $P(S + 1) = P(S)$, where $S + 1 = \{n + 1 \mid n \in S\}$.
 iii) If $P(S)$ is defined, then $P(2S) = \frac{1}{2}P(S)$, where $2S = \{2n \mid n \in S\}$.
 iv) If S is the set of *all* positive integers, then $P(S) = 1$.
  v) If $P(S)$ is defined, then $P(S) \geq 0$.

Assume furthermore that $P(L_a)$ is defined for all positive integers a, where L_a is the set of all integers whose decimal representation begins with a:

$$L_a = \{n \mid 10^m a \leq n < 10^m(a + 1) \text{ for some integer } m\} .$$

(In this definition, m may be negative; for example, 1 is an element of L_{10}, but not of L_{11}.) Prove that $P(L_a) = \log_{10}(1 + 1/a)$ for all integers $a \geq 1$.

19. [*HM25*] (R. L. Duncan.) Prove that the leading digits of Fibonacci numbers obey the logarithmic law of fraction parts: $\Pr(10 f_{F_n} < r) = \log_{10} r$.

20. [*HM40*] Sharpen (16) by finding the asymptotic behavior of $P_m(10^n s) - S_m(s)$ as $n \to \infty$.

4.3. MULTIPLE-PRECISION ARITHMETIC

LET US NOW consider operations on numbers that have arbitrarily high precision. For simplicity in exposition, we shall assume that we are working with integers, instead of with numbers that have an embedded radix point.

4.3.1. The Classical Algorithms

In this section we shall discuss algorithms for

a) addition or subtraction of n-place integers, giving an n-place answer and a carry;

b) multiplication of an m-place integer by an n-place integer, giving an $(m+n)$-place answer;

c) division of an $(m+n)$-place integer by an n-place integer, giving an $(m+1)$-place quotient and an n-place remainder.

These may be called *the classical algorithms*, since the word "algorithm" was used only in connection with these processes for several centuries. The term "n-place integer" means any nonnegative integer less than b^n, where b is the radix of ordinary positional notation in which the numbers are expressed; such numbers can be written using at most n "places" in this notation.

It is a straightforward matter to apply the classical algorithms for integers to numbers with embedded radix points or to extended-precision floating point numbers, in the same way that arithmetic operations defined for integers in MIX are applied to these more general problems.

In this section we shall study algorithms that do operations (a), (b), and (c) above for integers expressed in radix b notation, where b is any given integer that is 2 or more. Thus the algorithms are quite general definitions of arithmetic processes, and as such they are unrelated to any particular computer. But the discussion in this section will also be somewhat machine-oriented, since we are chiefly concerned with efficient methods for doing high-precision calculations by computer. Although our examples are based on the mythical MIX, essentially the same considerations apply to nearly every other machine.

The most important fact to understand about extended-precision numbers is that they may be regarded as numbers written in radix w notation, where w is the computer's word size. For example, an integer that fills 10 words on a computer whose word size is $w = 10^{10}$ has 100 decimal digits; but we will consider it to be a 10-place number to the base 10^{10}. This viewpoint is justified for the same reason that we may convert, say, from binary to hexadecimal notation, simply by grouping the bits together. (See Eq. 4.1–(5).)

In these terms, we are given the following primitive operations to work with:

a_0) addition or subtraction of one-place integers, giving a one-place answer and a carry;

b_0) multiplication of a one-place integer by another one-place integer, giving a two-place answer;

c_0) division of a two-place integer by a one-place integer, provided that the quotient is a one-place integer, and yielding also a one-place remainder.

By adjusting the word size, if necessary, nearly all computers will have these three operations available; so we will construct algorithms (a), (b), and (c) mentioned above in terms of the primitive operations (a_0), (b_0), and (c_0).

Since we are visualizing extended-precision integers as base b numbers, it is sometimes helpful to think of the situation when $b = 10$, and to imagine that we are doing the arithmetic by hand. Then operation (a_0) is analogous to memorizing the addition table; (b_0) is analogous to memorizing the multiplication table; and (c_0) is essentially memorizing the multiplication table in reverse. The more complicated operations (a), (b), (c) on high-precision numbers can now be done using the simple addition, subtraction, multiplication, and long-division procedures that children are taught in elementary school. In fact, most of the algorithms we shall discuss in this section are essentially nothing more than mechanizations of familiar pencil-and-paper operations. Of course, we must state the algorithms much more precisely than they have ever been stated in the fifth grade, and we should also attempt to minimize computer memory and running time requirements.

To avoid a tedious discussion and cumbersome notations, we shall assume first that all the numbers we deal with are *nonnegative*. The additional work of computing the signs, etc., is quite straightforward, although some care is necessary when dealing with complemented numbers on computers that do not use a signed magnitude representation. Such issues are discussed near the end of this section.

First comes addition, which of course is very simple, but it is worth careful study since the same ideas occur also in the other algorithms.

Algorithm A (*Addition of nonnegative integers*). Given nonnegative n-place integers $(u_{n-1} \dots u_1 u_0)_b$ and $(v_{n-1} \dots v_1 v_0)_b$, this algorithm forms their radix-b sum, $(w_n w_{n-1} \dots w_1 w_0)_b$. Here w_n is the carry, and it will always be equal to 0 or 1.

A1. [Initialize.] Set $j \leftarrow 0$, $k \leftarrow 0$. (The variable j will run through the various digit positions, and the variable k will keep track of carries at each step.)

A2. [Add digits.] Set $w_j \leftarrow (u_j + v_j + k) \bmod b$, and $k \leftarrow \lfloor (u_j + v_j + k)/b \rfloor$. (By induction on the computation, we will always have

$$u_j + v_j + k \le (b-1) + (b-1) + 1 < 2b.$$

Thus k is being set to 1 or 0, depending on whether a carry occurs or not; equivalently, $k \leftarrow [u_j + v_j + k \ge b]$.)

A3. [Loop on j.] Increase j by one. Now if $j < n$, go back to step A2; otherwise set $w_n \leftarrow k$ and terminate the algorithm. ∎

For a formal proof that Algorithm A is valid, see exercise 4.

A MIX program for this addition process might take the following form:

Program A (*Addition of nonnegative integers*). Let $\text{LOC}(u_j) \equiv \text{U} + j$, $\text{LOC}(v_j) \equiv \text{V} + j$, $\text{LOC}(w_j) \equiv \text{W} + j$, $\text{rI1} \equiv j - n$, $\text{rA} \equiv k$, word size $\equiv b$, $\text{N} \equiv n$.

01		ENN1	N	1	*A1. Initialize.* $j \leftarrow 0$.
02		JOV	OFLO	1	Ensure that overflow is off.
03	1H	ENTA	0	$N+1-K$	$k \leftarrow 0$.
04		J1Z	3F	$N+1-K$	Exit the loop if $j = n$.
05	2H	ADD	U+N,1	N	*A2. Add digits.*
06		ADD	V+N,1	N	
07		STA	W+N,1	N	
08		INC1	1	N	*A3. Loop on j.* $j \leftarrow j+1$.
09		JNOV	1B	N	If no overflow, set $k \leftarrow 0$.
10		ENTA	1	K	Otherwise, set $k \leftarrow 1$.
11		J1N	2B	K	To A2 if $j < n$.
12	3H	STA	W+N	1	Store final carry in w_n. ∎

The running time for this program is $10N + 6$ cycles, independent of the number of carries, K. The quantity K is analyzed in detail at the close of this section.

Many modifications of Algorithm A are possible, and only a few of these are mentioned in the exercises below. A chapter on generalizations of this algorithm might be entitled "How to design addition circuits for a digital computer."

The problem of subtraction is similar to addition, but the differences are worth noting:

Algorithm S (*Subtraction of nonnegative integers*). Given nonnegative n-place integers $(u_{n-1} \ldots u_1 u_0)_b \geq (v_{n-1} \ldots v_1 v_0)_b$, this algorithm forms their nonnegative radix-b difference, $(w_{n-1} \ldots w_1 w_0)_b$.

S1. [Initialize.] Set $j \leftarrow 0$, $k \leftarrow 0$.

S2. [Subtract digits.] Set $w_j \leftarrow (u_j - v_j + k) \bmod b$, and $k \leftarrow \lfloor (u_j - v_j + k)/b \rfloor$. (In other words, k is set to -1 or 0, depending on whether a borrow occurs or not, namely whether $u_j - v_j + k < 0$ or not. In the calculation of w_j, we must have $-b = 0 - (b-1) + (-1) \leq u_j - v_j + k \leq (b-1) - 0 + 0 < b$; hence $0 \leq u_j - v_j + k + b < 2b$, and this suggests the method of computer implementation explained below.)

S3. [Loop on j.] Increase j by one. Now if $j < n$, go back to step S2; otherwise terminate the algorithm. (When the algorithm terminates, we should have $k = 0$; the condition $k = -1$ will occur if and only if $(v_{n-1} \ldots v_1 v_0)_b > (u_{n-1} \ldots u_1 u_0)_b$, contrary to the given assumptions. See exercise 12.) ∎

In a MIX program to implement subtraction, it is most convenient to retain the value $1 + k$ instead of k throughout the algorithm, so that we can calculate $u_j - v_j + (1 + k) + (b - 1)$ in step S2. (Recall that b is the word size.) This is illustrated in the following code.

Program S (*Subtraction of nonnegative integers*). This program is analogous to the code in Program A, but with rA $\equiv 1 + k$. Here, as in other programs of this section, location WM1 contains the constant $b - 1$, the largest possible value that can be stored in a MIX word; see Program 4.2.3D, lines 38–39.

01		ENN1	N	1	*S1. Initialize.* $j \leftarrow 0$.
02		JOV	OFLO	1	Ensure that overflow is off.

03	1H	J1Z	DONE	$K+1$	Terminate if $j = n$.
04		ENTA	1	K	Set $k \leftarrow 0$.
05	2H	ADD	U+N,1	N	*S2. Subtract digits.*
06		SUB	V+N,1	N	Compute $u_j - v_j + k + b$.
07		ADD	WM1	N	
08		STA	W+N,1	N	(May be minus zero)
09		INC1	1	N	*S3. Loop on j.* $j \leftarrow j + 1$.
10		JOV	1B	N	If overflow, set $k \leftarrow 0$.
11		ENTA	0	$N - K$	Otherwise set $k \leftarrow -1$.
12		J1N	2B	$N - K$	Back to S2 if $j < n$.
13		HLT	5		(Error, $v > u$) ▮

The running time for this program is $12N + 3$ cycles, slightly longer than the corresponding amount for Program A.

The reader may wonder if it would not be worthwhile to have a combined addition-subtraction routine in place of the two algorithms A and S. But an examination of the code shows that it is generally better to use two different routines, so that the inner loops of the computations can be performed as rapidly as possible, since the programs are so short.

Our next problem is multiplication, and here we carry the ideas used in Algorithm A a little further:

Algorithm M (*Multiplication of nonnegative integers*).   Given nonnegative integers $(u_{m-1} \ldots u_1 u_0)_b$ and $(v_{n-1} \ldots v_1 v_0)_b$, this algorithm forms their radix-b product $(w_{m+n-1} \ldots w_1 w_0)_b$.   (The conventional pencil-and-paper method is based on forming the partial products $(u_{m-1} \ldots u_1 u_0)_b \times v_j$ first, for $0 \leq j < n$, and then adding these products together with appropriate scale factors; but in a computer it is simpler to do the addition concurrently with the multiplication, as described in this algorithm.)

M1. [Initialize.] Set $w_{m-1}, w_{m-2}, \ldots, w_0$ all to zero. Set $j \leftarrow 0$. (If those positions were not cleared to zero in this step, one can show that the steps below would set

$$(w_{m+n-1} \ldots w_0)_b \leftarrow (u_{m-1} \ldots u_0)_b \times (v_{n-1} \ldots v_0)_b + (w_{m-1} \ldots w_0)_b.$$

This more general multiply-and-add operation is often useful.)

M2. [Zero multiplier?] If $v_j = 0$, set $w_{j+m} \leftarrow 0$ and go to step M6. (This test might save time if there is a reasonable chance that v_j is zero, but it may be omitted without affecting the validity of the algorithm.)

M3. [Initialize i.] Set $i \leftarrow 0$, $k \leftarrow 0$.

M4. [Multiply and add.] Set $t \leftarrow u_i \times v_j + w_{i+j} + k$; then set $w_{i+j} \leftarrow t \bmod b$ and $k \leftarrow \lfloor t/b \rfloor$. (Here the carry k will always be in the range $0 \leq k < b$; see below.)

M5. [Loop on i.] Increase i by one. Now if $i < m$, go back to step M4; otherwise set $w_{j+m} \leftarrow k$.

M6. [Loop on j.] Increase j by one. Now if $j < n$, go back to step M2; otherwise the algorithm terminates. ▮

Table 1

MULTIPLICATION OF 914 BY 84

Step	i	j	u_i	v_j	t	w_4	w_3	w_2	w_1	w_0
M5	0	0	4	4	16	.	.	0	0	6
M5	1	0	1	4	05	.	.	0	5	6
M5	2	0	9	4	36	.	.	6	5	6
M6	3	0	.	4	36	.	3	6	5	6
M5	0	1	4	8	37	.	3	6	7	6
M5	1	1	1	8	17	.	3	7	7	6
M5	2	1	9	8	76	.	6	7	7	6
M6	3	1	.	8	76	7	6	7	7	6

Algorithm M is illustrated in Table 1, assuming that $b = 10$, by showing the states of the computation at the beginning of steps M5 and M6. A proof of Algorithm M appears in the answer to exercise 14.

The two inequalities

$$0 \le t < b^2, \qquad 0 \le k < b \qquad (1)$$

are crucial for an efficient implementation of this algorithm, since they point out how large a register is needed for the computations. These inequalities may be proved by induction as the algorithm proceeds, for if we have $k < b$ at the start of step M4, we have

$$u_i \times v_j + w_{i+j} + k \le (b-1) \times (b-1) + (b-1) + (b-1) = b^2 - 1 < b^2.$$

The following MIX program shows the considerations that are necessary when Algorithm M is implemented on a computer. The coding for step M4 would be a little simpler if our computer had a "multiply-and-add" instruction, or if it had a double-length accumulator for addition.

Program M (*Multiplication of nonnegative integers*). This program is analogous to Program A. $\text{rI1} \equiv i - m$, $\text{rI2} \equiv j - n$, $\text{rI3} \equiv i + j$, CONTENTS(CARRY) $\equiv k$.

01		ENT1	M-1	1	M1. Initialize.
02		JOV	OFLO	1	Ensure that overflow is off.
03		STZ	W,1	M	$w_{\text{rI1}} \leftarrow 0$.
04		DEC1	1	M	
05		J1NN	*-2	M	Repeat for $m > \text{rI1} \ge 0$.
06		ENN2	N	1	$j \leftarrow 0$.
07	1H	LDX	V+N,2	N	M2. Zero multiplier?
08		JXZ	8F	N	If $v_j = 0$, set $w_{j+m} \leftarrow 0$ and go to M6.
09		ENN1	M	$N - Z$	M3. Initialize i. $i \leftarrow 0$.
10		ENT3	N,2	$N - Z$	$(i + j) \leftarrow j$.
11		ENTX	0	$N - Z$	$k \leftarrow 0$.
12	2H	STX	CARRY	$(N - Z)M$	M4. Multiply and add.
13		LDA	U+M,1	$(N - Z)M$	
14		MUL	V+N,2	$(N - Z)M$	$\text{rAX} \leftarrow u_i \times v_j$.
15		SLC	5	$(N - Z)M$	Interchange $\text{rA} \leftrightarrow \text{rX}$.
16		ADD	W,3	$(N - Z)M$	Add w_{i+j} to lower half.

17		JNOV	*+2	$(N-Z)M$	Did overflow occur?
18		INCX	1	K	If so, carry 1 into upper half.
19		ADD	CARRY	$(N-Z)M$	Add k to lower half.
20		JNOV	*+2	$(N-Z)M$	Did overflow occur?
21		INCX	1	K'	If so, carry 1 into upper half.
22		STA	W,3	$(N-Z)M$	$w_{i+j} \leftarrow t \bmod b$.
23		INC1	1	$(N-Z)M$	M5. Loop on i. $i \leftarrow i+1$.
24		INC3	1	$(N-Z)M$	$(i+j) \leftarrow (i+j)+1$.
25		J1N	2B	$(N-Z)M$	Back to M4 with rX $= \lfloor t/b \rfloor$ if $i < m$.
26	8H	STX	W+M+N,2	N	Set $w_{j+m} \leftarrow k$.
27		INC2	1	N	M6. Loop on j. $j \leftarrow j+1$.
28		J2N	1B	N	Repeat until $j = n$. ▮

The execution time of Program M depends on the number of places, M, in the multiplicand u; the number of places, N, in the multiplier v; the number of zeros, Z, in the multiplier; and the number of carries, K and K', that occur during the addition to the lower half of the product in the computation of t. If we approximate both K and K' by the reasonable (although somewhat pessimistic) values $\frac{1}{2}(N-Z)M$, we find that the total running time comes to $28MN + 4M + 10N + 3 - Z(28M + 3)$ cycles. If step M2 were deleted, the running time would be $28MN + 4M + 7N + 3$ cycles, so that step is advantageous only if the density of zero positions within the multiplier is $Z/N > 3/(28M + 3)$. If the multiplier is chosen completely at random, the ratio Z/N is expected to be only about $1/b$, which is extremely small. We conclude that step M2 is usually *not* worthwhile, unless b is small.

Algorithm M is not the fastest way to multiply when m and n are large, although it has the advantage of simplicity. Speedier but more complicated methods are discussed in Section 4.3.3; it is possible to multiply numbers faster than Algorithm M even when $m = n = 4$.

The final algorithm of concern to us in this section is long division, in which we want to divide $(m + n)$-place integers by n-place integers. Here the ordinary pencil-and-paper method involves a certain amount of guesswork and ingenuity on the part of the person doing the division; we must either eliminate this guesswork from the algorithm or develop some theory to explain it more carefully.

A moment's reflection about the ordinary process of long division shows that the general problem breaks down into simpler steps, each of which is the division of an $(n + 1)$-place dividend u by the n-place divisor v, where $0 \le u/v < b$; the remainder r after each step is less than v, so we may use the quantity $rb + $ (next place of dividend) as the new u in the succeeding step. For example, if we are asked to divide 3142 by 53, we first divide 314 by 53, getting 5 and a remainder of 49; then we divide 492 by 53, getting 9 and a remainder of 15; thus we have a quotient of 59 and a remainder of 15. It is clear that this same idea works in general, and so our search for an appropriate division algorithm reduces to the following problem (Fig. 6):

Let $u = (u_n u_{n-1} \ldots u_1 u_0)_b$ and $v = (v_{n-1} \ldots v_1 v_0)_b$ be nonnegative integers in radix-b notation, where $u/v < b$. Find an algorithm to determine $q = \lfloor u/v \rfloor$.

$$q$$
$$v_{n-1} \ldots v_1 v_0 \overline{)\, u_n u_{n-1} \ldots u_1 u_0}$$

$$\xleftarrow{\hspace{1.2cm}} qv \xrightarrow{\hspace{1.2cm}}$$

$$\xleftarrow{\hspace{1.5cm}} r \xrightarrow{\hspace{1.5cm}}$$

Fig. 6. Wanted: a way to determine q rapidly.

We may observe that the condition $u/v < b$ is equivalent to the condition that $u/b < v$, which is the same as $\lfloor u/b \rfloor < v$. This is simply the condition that $(u_n u_{n-1} \ldots u_1)_b < (v_{n-1} v_{n-2} \ldots v_0)_b$. Furthermore, if we write $r = u - qv$, then q is the unique integer such that $0 \le r < v$.

The most obvious approach to this problem is to make a guess about q, based on the most significant digits of u and v. It isn't obvious that such a method will be reliable enough, but it is worth investigating; let us therefore set

$$\hat{q} = \min \left(\left\lfloor \frac{u_n b + u_{n-1}}{v_{n-1}} \right\rfloor, \, b - 1 \right). \tag{2}$$

This formula says that $\hat{q}$ is obtained by dividing the two leading digits of u by the leading digit of v; and if the result is b or more we can replace it by $(b-1)$.

It is a remarkable fact, which we will now investigate, that this value $\hat{q}$ is always a very good approximation to the desired answer q, so long as v_{n-1} is reasonably large. In order to analyze how close $\hat{q}$ comes to q, we will first prove that $\hat{q}$ is never too small.

Theorem A. *In the notation above, $\hat{q} \ge q$.*

Proof. Since $q \le b - 1$, the theorem is certainly true if $\hat{q} = b - 1$. Otherwise we have $\hat{q} = \lfloor (u_n b + u_{n-1})/v_{n-1} \rfloor$, hence $\hat{q} v_{n-1} \ge u_n b + u_{n-1} - v_{n-1} + 1$. It follows that

$$u - \hat{q} v \le u - \hat{q} v_{n-1} b^{n-1}$$
$$\le u_n b^n + \cdots + u_0 - (u_n b^n + u_{n-1} b^{n-1} - v_{n-1} b^{n-1} + b^{n-1})$$
$$= u_{n-2} b^{n-2} + \cdots + u_0 - b^{n-1} + v_{n-1} b^{n-1} < v_{n-1} b^{n-1} \le v.$$

Since $u - \hat{q} v < v$, we must have $\hat{q} \ge q$. ∎

We will now prove that $\hat{q}$ cannot be much larger than q in practical situations. Assume that $\hat{q} \ge q + 3$. We have

$$\hat{q} \le \frac{u_n b + u_{n-1}}{v_{n-1}} = \frac{u_n b^n + u_{n-1} b^{n-1}}{v_{n-1} b^{n-1}} \le \frac{u}{v_{n-1} b^{n-1}} < \frac{u}{v - b^{n-1}}.$$

(The case $v = b^{n-1}$ is impossible, for if $v = (100 \ldots 0)_b$ then $q = \hat{q}$.) Furthermore, the relation $q > (u/v) - 1$ implies that

$$3 \le \hat{q} - q < \frac{u}{v - b^{n-1}} - \frac{u}{v} + 1 = \frac{u}{v} \left(\frac{b^{n-1}}{v - b^{n-1}} \right) + 1.$$

Therefore

$$\frac{u}{v} > 2 \left(\frac{v - b^{n-1}}{b^{n-1}} \right) \ge 2(v_{n-1} - 1).$$

Finally, since $b - 4 \geq \hat{q} - 3 \geq q = \lfloor u/v \rfloor \geq 2(v_{n-1} - 1)$, we have $v_{n-1} < \lfloor b/2 \rfloor$. This proves the result we seek:

Theorem B. *If* $v_{n-1} \geq \lfloor b/2 \rfloor$, *then* $\hat{q} - 2 \leq q \leq \hat{q}$. ∎

The most important part of this theorem is that *the conclusion is independent of* b; no matter how large the radix is, the trial quotient $\hat{q}$ will never be more than 2 in error.

The condition that $v_{n-1} \geq \lfloor b/2 \rfloor$ is very much like a normalization requirement; in fact, it is exactly the condition of floating-binary normalization in a binary computer. One simple way to ensure that v_{n-1} is sufficiently large is to multiply both u and v by $\lfloor b/(v_{n-1} + 1) \rfloor$; this does not change the value of u/v, nor does it increase the number of places in v, and exercise 23 proves that it will always make the new value of v_{n-1} large enough. (Another way to normalize the divisor is discussed in exercise 28.)

Now that we have armed ourselves with all of these facts, we are in a position to write the desired long-division algorithm. This algorithm uses a slightly improved choice of $\hat{q}$ in step D3, which guarantees that $q = \hat{q}$ or $\hat{q} - 1$; in fact, the improved choice of $\hat{q}$ made here is almost always accurate.

Algorithm D (*Division of nonnegative integers*). Given nonnegative integers $u = (u_{m+n-1} \ldots u_1 u_0)_b$ and $v = (v_{n-1} \ldots v_1 v_0)_b$, where $v_{n-1} \neq 0$ and $n > 1$, we form the radix-b quotient $\lfloor u/v \rfloor = (q_m q_{m-1} \ldots q_0)_b$ and the remainder $u \bmod v = (r_{n-1} \ldots r_1 r_0)_b$. (When $n = 1$, the simpler algorithm of exercise 16 should be used.)

D1. [Normalize.] Set $d \leftarrow \lfloor b/(v_{n-1} + 1) \rfloor$. Then set $(u_{m+n} u_{m+n-1} \ldots u_1 u_0)_b$ equal to $(u_{m+n-1} \ldots u_1 u_0)_b$ times d; similarly, set $(v_{n-1} \ldots v_1 v_0)_b$ equal to $(v_{n-1} \ldots v_1 v_0)_b$ times d. (Notice the introduction of a new digit position u_{m+n} at the left of u_{m+n-1}; if $d = 1$, all we need to do in this step is to set $u_{m+n} \leftarrow 0$. On a binary computer it may be preferable to choose d to be a power of 2 instead of using the value suggested here; any value of d that results in $v_{n-1} \geq \lfloor b/2 \rfloor$ will suffice. See also exercise 37.)

D2. [Initialize j.] Set $j \leftarrow m$. (The loop on j, steps D2 through D7, will be essentially a division of $(u_{j+n} \ldots u_{j+1} u_j)_b$ by $(v_{n-1} \ldots v_1 v_0)_b$ to get a single quotient digit q_j; see Fig. 6.)

D3. [Calculate $\hat{q}$.] Set $\hat{q} \leftarrow \lfloor (u_{j+n}b + u_{j+n-1})/v_{n-1} \rfloor$ and let $\hat{r}$ be the remainder, $(u_{j+n}b + u_{j+n-1}) \bmod v_{n-1}$. Now test if $\hat{q} \geq b$ or $\hat{q}v_{n-2} > b\hat{r} + u_{j+n-2}$; if so, decrease $\hat{q}$ by 1, increase $\hat{r}$ by v_{n-1}, and repeat this test if $\hat{r} < b$. (The test on v_{n-2} determines at high speed most of the cases in which the trial value $\hat{q}$ is one too large, and it eliminates *all* cases where $\hat{q}$ is two too large; see exercises 19, 20, 21.)

D4. [Multiply and subtract.] Replace $(u_{j+n} u_{j+n-1} \ldots u_j)_b$ by

$$(u_{j+n} u_{j+n-1} \ldots u_j)_b - \hat{q}(0 v_{n-1} \ldots v_1 v_0)_b.$$

This computation (analogous to steps M3, M4, and M5 of Algorithm M) consists of a simple multiplication by a one-place number, combined with

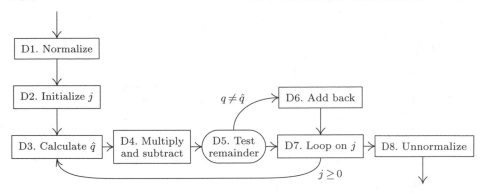

Fig. 7. Long division.

a subtraction. The digits $(u_{j+n}, u_{j+n-1}, \ldots, u_j)$ should be kept positive; if the result of this step is actually negative, $(u_{j+n}u_{j+n-1}\ldots u_j)_b$ should be left as the true value plus b^{n+1}, namely as the b's complement of the true value, and a "borrow" to the left should be remembered.

D5. [Test remainder.] Set $q_j \leftarrow \hat{q}$. If the result of step D4 was negative, go to step D6; otherwise go on to step D7.

D6. [Add back.] (The probability that this step is necessary is very small, on the order of only $2/b$, as shown in exercise 21; test data to activate this step should therefore be specifically contrived when debugging. See exercise 22.) Decrease q_j by 1, and add $(0 v_{n-1} \ldots v_1 v_0)_b$ to $(u_{j+n}u_{j+n-1}\ldots u_{j+1}u_j)_b$. (A carry will occur to the left of u_{j+n}, and it should be ignored since it cancels with the borrow that occurred in D4.)

D7. [Loop on j.] Decrease j by one. Now if $j \geq 0$, go back to D3.

D8. [Unnormalize.] Now $(q_m \ldots q_1 q_0)_b$ is the desired quotient, and the desired remainder may be obtained by dividing $(u_{n-1} \ldots u_1 u_0)_b$ by d. ∎

The representation of Algorithm D as a MIX program has several points of interest:

Program D (*Division of nonnegative integers*). The conventions of this program are analogous to Program A; $\text{rI1} \equiv i - n$, $\text{rI2} \equiv j$, $\text{rI3} \equiv i + j$.

001	D1	JOV	OFLO	1	*D1. Normalize.*
	...				(See exercise 25)
039	D2	ENT2	M	1	*D2. Initialize j. $j \leftarrow m$.*
040		STZ	V+N	1	Set $v_n \leftarrow 0$, for convenience in D4.
041	D3	LDA	U+N,2(1:5)	$M+1$	*D3. Calculate $\hat{q}$.*
042		LDX	U+N-1,2	$M+1$	$\text{rAX} \leftarrow u_{j+n}b + u_{j+n-1}$.
043		DIV	V+N-1	$M+1$	$\text{rA} \leftarrow \lfloor \text{rAX}/v_{n-1} \rfloor$.
044		JOV	1F	$M+1$	Jump if quotient $\geq b$.
045		STA	QHAT	$M+1$	$\hat{q} \leftarrow \text{rA}$.
046		STX	RHAT	$M+1$	$\hat{r} \leftarrow u_{j+n}b + u_{j+n-1} - \hat{q}v_{n-1}$
047		JMP	2F	$M+1$	$= (u_{j+n}b + u_{j+n-1}) \bmod v_{n-1}$.

048	1H LDX	WM1		rX ← $b - 1$.
049	LDA	U+N-1,2		rA ← u_{j+n-1}. (Here $u_{j+n} = v_{n-1}$.)
050	JMP	4F		
051	3H LDX	QHAT	E	
052	DECX	1	E	Decrease $\hat{q}$ by one.
053	LDA	RHAT	E	Adjust $\hat{r}$ accordingly:
054	4H STX	QHAT	E	$\hat{q}$ ← rX.
055	ADD	V+N-1	E	rA ← $\hat{r} + v_{n-1}$.
056	JOV	D4	E	(If $\hat{r}$ will be $\geq b$, $\hat{q}v_{n-2}$ will be $< \hat{r}b$.)
057	STA	RHAT	E	$\hat{r}$ ← rA.
058	LDA	QHAT	E	
059	2H MUL	V+N-2	$M + E + 1$	
060	CMPA	RHAT	$M + E + 1$	Test if $\hat{q}v_{n-2} \leq \hat{r}b + u_{j+n-2}$.
061	JL	D4	$M + E + 1$	
062	JG	3B	E	
063	CMPX	U+N-2,2		
064	JG	3B		If not, $\hat{q}$ is too large.
065	D4 ENTX	1	$M + 1$	*D4. Multiply and subtract.*
066	ENN1	N	$M + 1$	i ← 0.
067	ENT3	0,2	$M + 1$	$(i + j)$ ← j.
068	2H STX	CARRY	$(M + 1)(N + 1)$	(Here $1 - b < $ rX $\leq +1$.)
069	LDAN	V+N,1	$(M + 1)(N + 1)$	
070	MUL	QHAT	$(M + 1)(N + 1)$	rAX ← $-\hat{q}v_i$.
071	SLC	5	$(M + 1)(N + 1)$	Interchange rA ↔ rX.
072	ADD	CARRY	$(M + 1)(N + 1)$	Add the contribution from the
073	JNOV	*+2	$(M + 1)(N + 1)$	digit to the right, plus 1.
074	DECX	1	K	If sum is $\leq -b$, carry -1.
075	ADD	U,3	$(M + 1)(N + 1)$	Add u_{i+j}.
076	ADD	WM1	$(M + 1)(N + 1)$	Add $b - 1$ to force $+$ sign.
077	JNOV	*+2	$(M + 1)(N + 1)$	If no overflow, carry -1.
078	INCX	1	K'	rX $\equiv$ carry $+ 1$.
079	STA	U,3	$(M + 1)(N + 1)$	u_{i+j} ← rA (may be minus zero).
080	INC1	1	$(M + 1)(N + 1)$	
081	INC3	1	$(M + 1)(N + 1)$	
082	J1NP	2B	$(M + 1)(N + 1)$	Repeat for $0 \leq i \leq n$.
083	D5 LDA	QHAT	$M + 1$	*D5. Test remainder.*
084	STA	Q,2	$M + 1$	Set q_j ← $\hat{q}$.
085	JXP	D7	$M + 1$	(Here rX = 0 or 1, since $v_n = 0$.)
086	D6 DECA	1		*D6. Add back.*
087	STA	Q,2		Set q_j ← $\hat{q} - 1$.
088	ENN1	N		i ← 0.
089	ENT3	0,2		$(i + j)$ ← j.
090	1H ENTA	0		(This is essentially Program A.)
091	2H ADD	U,3		
092	ADD	V+N,1		
093	STA	U,3		
094	INC1	1		
095	INC3	1		
096	JNOV	1B		

```
097        ENTA  1
098        J1NP  2B
099   D7   DEC2  1              M + 1          D7. Loop on j.
100        J2NN  D3             M + 1          Repeat for m ≥ j ≥ 0.
101   D8  ···                                  (See exercise 26)   ▌
```

Note how easily the rather complex-appearing calculations and decisions of step D3 can be handled inside the machine. Notice also that the program for step D4 is analogous to Program M, except that the ideas of Program S have also been incorporated.

The running time for Program D can be estimated by considering the quantities M, N, E, K, and K' shown in the program. (These quantities ignore several situations that occur only with very low probability; for example, we may assume that lines 048–050, 063–064, and step D6 are never executed.) Here $M + 1$ is the number of words in the quotient; N is the number of words in the divisor; E is the number of times $\hat{q}$ is adjusted downwards in step D3; K and K' are the number of times certain carry adjustments are made during the multiply-subtract loop. If we assume that $K + K'$ is approximately $(N + 1)(M + 1)$, and that E is approximately $\frac{1}{2}M$, we get a total running time of approximately $30MN + 30N + 89M + 111$ cycles, plus $67N + 23.5M + 4$ more if $d > 1$. (The program segments of exercises 25 and 26 are included in these totals.) When M and N are large, this is only about seven percent longer than the time needed by Program M to multiply the quotient by the divisor.

When the radix b is comparatively small, so that b^2 is less than the computer's word size, multiprecision division can be speeded up by not reducing individual digits of intermediate results to the range $[0..b)$; see D. M. Smith, *Math. Comp.* **65** (1996), 157–163. Further commentary on Algorithm D appears in the exercises at the close of this section.

It is possible to debug programs for multiple-precision arithmetic by using the multiplication and addition routines to check the result of the division routine, etc. The following type of test data is occasionally useful:

$$(t^m - 1)(t^n - 1) = t^{m+n} - t^n - t^m + 1.$$

If $m < n$, this number has the radix-t expansion

$$\underbrace{(t-1) \quad \cdots \quad (t-1)}_{m-1 \text{ places}} \; (t-2) \; \underbrace{(t-1) \quad \cdots \quad (t-1)}_{n-m \text{ places}} \; \underbrace{0 \quad \cdots \quad 0}_{m-1 \text{ places}} \; 1;$$

for example, $(10^3 - 1)(10^8 - 1) = 99899999001$. In the case of Program D, it is also necessary to find some test cases that cause the rarely executed parts of the program to be exercised; some portions of that program would probably never get tested even if a million random test cases were tried. (See exercise 22.)

Now that we have seen how to operate with signed magnitude numbers, let us consider what approach should be taken to the same problems when a computer with complement notation is being used. For two's complement and ones' complement notations, it is usually best to let the radix b be just *half* of the word size; thus for a 32-bit computer word we would use $b = 2^{31}$ in the algorithms above. The sign bit of all but the most significant word of a multiple-precision number will be zero, so that no anomalous sign correction takes place during the computer's multiplication and division operations. In fact, the basic meaning of complement notation requires that we consider all but the most significant word to be nonnegative. For example, assuming an 8-bit word, the two's complement number

$$11011111 \quad 1111110 \quad 1101011$$

(where the sign bit is shown only in the most significant word) is properly thought of as

$$-2^{21} + (1011111)_2 \cdot 2^{14} + (1111110)_2 \cdot 2^7 + (1101011)_2.$$

On the other hand, some binary computers that work with two's complement notation also provide true unsigned arithmetic as well. For example, let x and y be 32-bit operands. A computer might regard them as two's complement numbers in the range $-2^{31} \leq x, y < 2^{31}$, or as unsigned numbers in the range $0 \leq x, y < 2^{32}$. If we ignore overflow, the 32-bit sum $(x + y) \bmod 2^{32}$ is the same under either interpretation; but overflow occurs in different circumstances when we change the assumed range. If the computer allows easy computation of the carry bit $\lfloor (x + y)/2^{32} \rfloor$ in the unsigned interpretation, and if it provides a full 64-bit product of unsigned 32-bit integers, we can use $b = 2^{32}$ instead of $b = 2^{31}$ in our high-precision algorithms.

Addition of signed numbers is slightly easier when complement notations are being used, since the routine for adding n-place nonnegative integers can be used for arbitrary n-place integers; the sign appears only in the first word, so the less significant words may be added together irrespective of the actual sign. (Special attention must be given to the leftmost carry when ones' complement notation is being used, however; it must be added into the least significant word, and possibly propagated further to the left.) Similarly, we find that subtraction of signed numbers is slightly simpler with complement notation. On the other hand, multiplication and division seem to be done most easily by working with nonnegative quantities and doing suitable complementation operations beforehand to make sure that both operands are nonnegative. It may be possible to avoid this complementation by devising some tricks for working directly with negative numbers in a complement notation, and it is not hard to see how this could be done in double-precision multiplication; but care should be taken not to slow down the inner loops of the subroutines when high precision is required.

Let us now turn to an analysis of the quantity K that arises in Program A, namely the number of carries that occur when two n-place numbers are being added together. Although K has no effect on the total running time of Program A, it does affect the running time of the Program A's counterparts that deal with complement notations, and its analysis is interesting in itself as a significant application of generating functions.

Suppose that u and v are independent random n-place integers, uniformly distributed in the range $0 \leq u, v < b^n$. Let p_{nk} be the probability that exactly k carries occur in the addition of u to v, *and* that one of these carries occurs in the most significant position (so that $u + v \geq b^n$). Similarly, let q_{nk} be the probability that exactly k carries occur, but that there is no carry in the most significant position. Then it is not hard to see that, for all k and n,

$$p_{0k} = 0, \qquad p_{(n+1)(k+1)} = \frac{b+1}{2b} p_{nk} + \frac{b-1}{2b} q_{nk},$$

$$q_{0k} = \delta_{0k}, \qquad q_{(n+1)k} = \frac{b-1}{2b} p_{nk} + \frac{b+1}{2b} q_{nk}; \tag{3}$$

this happens because $(b-1)/2b$ is the probability that $u_{n-1} + v_{n-1} \geq b$ and $(b+1)/2b$ is the probability that $u_{n-1} + v_{n-1} + 1 \geq b$, when u_{n-1} and v_{n-1} are independently and uniformly distributed integers in the range $0 \leq u_{n-1}, v_{n-1} < b$.

To obtain further information about these quantities p_{nk} and q_{nk}, we set up the generating functions

$$P(z,t) = \sum_{k,n} p_{nk} z^k t^n, \qquad Q(z,t) = \sum_{k,n} q_{nk} z^k t^n. \tag{4}$$

From (3) we have the basic relations

$$P(z,t) = zt \left(\frac{b+1}{2b} P(z,t) + \frac{b-1}{2b} Q(z,t) \right),$$

$$Q(z,t) = 1 + t \left(\frac{b-1}{2b} P(z,t) + \frac{b+1}{2b} Q(z,t) \right).$$

These two equations are readily solved for $P(z,t)$ and $Q(z,t)$; and if we let

$$G(z,t) = P(z,t) + Q(z,t) = \sum_n G_n(z) t^n,$$

where $G_n(z)$ is the generating function for the total number of carries when n-place numbers are added, we find that

$$G(z,t) = (b - zt)/p(z,t), \quad \text{where } p(z,t) = b - \tfrac{1}{2}(1+b)(1+z)t + zt^2. \tag{5}$$

Note that $G(1,t) = 1/(1-t)$, and this checks with the fact that $G_n(1)$ must equal 1 (it is the sum of all the possible probabilities). Taking partial derivatives of (5) with respect to z, we find that

$$\frac{\partial G}{\partial z} = \sum_n G'_n(z) t^n = \frac{-t}{p(z,t)} + \frac{t(b-zt)(b+1-2t)}{2p(z,t)^2};$$

$$\frac{\partial^2 G}{\partial z^2} = \sum_n G''_n(z) t^n = \frac{-t^2(b+1-2t)}{p(z,t)^2} + \frac{t^2(b-zt)(b+1-2t)^2}{2p(z,t)^3}.$$

Now let us put $z = 1$ and expand in partial fractions:

$$\sum_n G'_n(1) t^n = \frac{t}{2} \left(\frac{1}{(1-t)^2} - \frac{1}{(b-1)(1-t)} + \frac{1}{(b-1)(b-t)} \right),$$

$$\sum_n G''_n(1) t^n = \frac{t^2}{2} \left(\frac{1}{(1-t)^3} - \frac{1}{(b-1)^2(1-t)} + \frac{1}{(b-1)^2(b-t)} + \frac{1}{(b-1)(b-t)^2} \right).$$

It follows that the average number of carries, the mean value of K, is

$$G'_n(1) = \frac{1}{2}\left(n - \frac{1}{b-1}\left(1 - \left(\frac{1}{b}\right)^n\right)\right); \tag{6}$$

the variance, $G''_n(1) + G'_n(1) - G'_n(1)^2$, is

$$\frac{1}{4}\left(n + \frac{2n}{b-1} - \frac{2b+1}{(b-1)^2} + \frac{2b+2}{(b-1)^2}\left(\frac{1}{b}\right)^n - \frac{1}{(b-1)^2}\left(\frac{1}{b}\right)^{2n}\right). \tag{7}$$

So the number of carries is just slightly less than $\frac{1}{2}n$ under these assumptions.

History and bibliography.   The early history of the classical algorithms described in this section is left as an interesting project for the reader, and only the history of their implementation on computers will be traced here.

D. N. Lehmer and J. P. Ballantine, *AMM* **30** (1923), 67–69, discussed the use of 10^n as an assumed radix when multiplying large numbers mechanically.

Double-precision arithmetic on digital computers was first treated by J. von Neumann and H. H. Goldstine in their introductory notes on programming, originally published in 1947 [J. von Neumann, *Collected Works* **5**, 142–151]. Theorems A and B above are due to D. A. Pope and M. L. Stein [*CACM* **3** (1960), 652–654], whose paper also contains a bibliography of earlier work on double-precision routines. Other ways of choosing the trial quotient $\hat{q}$ have been discussed by A. G. Cox and H. A. Luther, *CACM* **4** (1961), 353 [divide by $v_{n-1}+1$ instead of v_{n-1}], and by M. L. Stein, *CACM* **7** (1964), 472–474 [divide by v_{n-1} or $v_{n-1}+1$ according to the magnitude of v_{n-2}]; E. V. Krishnamurthy [*CACM* **8** (1965), 179–181] showed that examination of the single-precision remainder in the latter method leads to an improvement over Theorem B. Krishnamurthy and Nandi [*CACM* **10** (1967), 809–813] suggested a way to replace the normalization and unnormalization operations of Algorithm D by a calculation of $\hat{q}$ based on several leading digits of the operands. G. E. Collins and D. R. Musser have carried out an interesting analysis of the original Pope and Stein algorithm [*Information Processing Letters* **6** (1977), 151–155].

Several alternative approaches to division have also been suggested:

1) "Fourier division" [J. Fourier, *Analyse des Équations Déterminées* (Paris: 1831), §2.21]. This method, which was often used on desk calculators, essentially obtains each new quotient digit by increasing the precision of the divisor and the dividend at each step. Some rather extensive tests by the author have indicated that such a method is inferior to the divide-and-correct technique above, but there may be some applications in which Fourier division is practical. See D. H. Lehmer, *AMM* **33** (1926), 198–206; J. V. Uspensky, *Theory of Equations* (New York: McGraw–Hill, 1948), 159–164.

2) "Newton's method" for evaluating the reciprocal of a number was extensively used in early computers when there was no single-precision division instruction. The idea is to find some initial approximation x_0 to the number $1/v$, then to let $x_{n+1} = 2x_n - vx_n^2$. This method converges rapidly to $1/v$, since $x_n = (1 - \epsilon)/v$ implies that $x_{n+1} = (1 - \epsilon^2)/v$. Convergence to third order, with ϵ replaced by

$O(\epsilon^3)$ at each step, can be obtained using the formula

$$x_{n+1} = x_n \left(1 + (1 - vx_n)(1 + (1 - vx_n))\right),$$

and similar formulas hold for fourth-order convergence, etc.; see P. Rabinowitz, *CACM* **4** (1961), 98. For calculations on extremely large numbers, Newton's second-order method and subsequent multiplication by u can actually be considerably faster than Algorithm D, if we increase the precision of x_n at each step and if we also use the fast multiplication routines of Section 4.3.3. (See Algorithm 4.3.3R for details.) Some related iterative schemes have been discussed by E. V. Krishnamurthy, *IEEE Trans.* **C-19** (1970), 227–231.

N. Möller and T. Granlund, *IEEE Trans.* **C-60** (2011), 165–175, have developed highly tuned methods that work well on modern machines.

3) Division methods have also been based on the evaluation of

$$\frac{u}{v + \epsilon} = \frac{u}{v}\left(1 - \left(\frac{\epsilon}{v}\right) + \left(\frac{\epsilon}{v}\right)^2 - \left(\frac{\epsilon}{v}\right)^3 + \cdots\right).$$

See H. H. Laughlin, *AMM* **37** (1930), 287–293. We have used this idea in the double-precision case $\left(\text{Eq. 4.2.3–(2)}\right)$.

Besides the references just cited, the following early articles concerning multiple-precision arithmetic are also of interest: High-precision routines for floating point calculations using ones' complement arithmetic were described by A. H. Stroud and D. Secrest, *Comp. J.* **6** (1963), 62–66. Extended-precision subroutines for use in FORTRAN programs were described by B. I. Blum, *CACM* **8** (1965), 318–320, and for use in ALGOL by M. Tienari and V. Suokonautio, *BIT* **6** (1966), 332–338. Arithmetic on integers with *unlimited* precision, making use of linked memory allocation techniques, was elegantly introduced by G. E. Collins, *CACM* **9** (1966), 578–589. For a much larger repertoire of multiple-precision operations, including logarithms and trigonometric functions, see R. P. Brent, *ACM Trans. Math. Software* **4** (1978), 57–81; D. M. Smith, *ACM Trans. Math. Software* **17** (1991), 273–283, **24** (1998), 359–367.

Human progress in calculation has traditionally been measured by the number of decimal digits of π that were known at a given point in history. Section 4.1 mentions some of the early developments; by 1719, Thomas Fantet de Lagny had computed π to 127 decimal places [*Mémoires Acad. Sci.* (Paris, 1719), 135–145; a typographical error affected the 113th digit]. After better formulas were discovered, a famous mental calculator from Hamburg named Zacharias Dase needed less than two months to calculate 200 decimal digits correctly in 1844 [*Crelle* **27** (1844), 198]. Then William Shanks published 607 decimals of π in 1853, and continued to extend his calculations until he had obtained 707 digits in 1873. [See W. Shanks, *Contributions to Mathematics* (London: 1853); *Proc. Royal Soc. London* **21** (1873), 318–319; **22** (1873), 45–46; J. C. V. Hoffmann, *Zeit. für math. und naturwiss. Unterricht* **26** (1895), 261–264.] Shanks's 707-place value was widely quoted in mathematical reference books for many years, but D. F. Ferguson noticed in 1945 that it contained several mistakes beginning at the 528th decimal place [*Math. Gazette* **30** (1946), 89–90]. G. Reitwiesner and his colleagues used 70 hours of computing time on ENIAC during Labor Day weekend in 1949 to obtain 2037 correct decimals [*Math. Tables and Other Aids to Comp.* **4** (1950), 11–15]. F. Genuys reached 10,000 digits in 1958, after 100 minutes on an IBM 704 [*Chiffres* **1** (1958), 17–22]; shortly afterwards, the first 100,000 digits were published by D. Shanks [no relation to William] and J. W. Wrench, Jr. [*Math. Comp.* **16** (1962), 76–99], after about 8 hours on an IBM 7090 and another 4.5 hours for checking. Their check actually revealed a transient hardware error, which went away when the computation was repeated. One million digits of π were computed by Jean Guilloud and Martine Bouyer of the French Atomic Energy Commission in 1973, after nearly 24 hours of computer time on a CDC 7600 [see A. Shibata, *Surikagaku* **20** (1982), 65–73]. Amazingly, Dr. I. J. Matrix had correctly predicted seven years earlier that the millionth digit would turn out to be "5" [Martin Gardner, *New Mathematical Diversions* (Simon and Schuster, 1966), addendum to Chapter 8]. The billion-digit barrier was passed in 1989 by Gregory V. Chudnovsky and David V. Chudnovsky, and independently by Yasumasa Kanada and Yoshiaki Tamura; the Chudnovskys extended their calculation to two billion digits in 1991, after 250 hours of computation on a home-built parallel machine. [See Richard Preston, *The New Yorker* **68**, 2 (2 March 1992), 36–67. The novel formula used by the Chudnovskys is described in *Proc. Nat. Acad. Sci.* **86** (1989), 8178–8182.] Yasumasa Kanada and Daisuke Takahashi obtained more than 51.5 billion digits in July, 1997, using two independent methods that required respectively 29.0 and 37.1 hours on a HITACHI SR2201 computer with 1024 processing elements. By 14 March 2019 the world record had risen to 31,415,926,535,897 digits(!), obtained by A. J. Yee and E. H. Iwao using the Chudnovsky formula together with exercise 39. That computation, which involved 170 terabytes of data, took 121 days on 25 cloud-based virtual machines.

We have restricted our discussion in this section to arithmetic techniques for use in computer programming. Many algorithms for *hardware* implementation of arithmetic operations are also quite interesting, but they appear to be inapplicable to high-precision software routines; see, for example, G. W. Reitwiesner, "Binary Arithmetic," *Advances in Computers* **1** (New York: Academic Press, 1960), 231–308; O. L. MacSorley, *Proc. IRE* **49** (1961), 67–91; G. Metze, *IRE Trans.* **EC-11** (1962), 761–764; H. L. Garner, "Number Systems and Arithmetic," *Advances in Computers* **6** (New York: Academic Press, 1965), 131–194. An infamous but very instructive bug in the division routine of the 1994 Pentium chip is discussed by A. Edelman in *SIAM Review* **39** (1997), 54–67. The minimum achievable execution time for hardware addition and multiplication operations has been investigated by S. Winograd, *JACM* **12** (1965), 277–285, **14** (1967), 793–802; by R. P. Brent, *IEEE Trans.* **C-19** (1970), 758–759; and by R. W. Floyd, *FOCS* **16** (1975), 3–5. See also Section 4.3.3E.

EXERCISES

1. [*42*] Study the early history of the classical algorithms for arithmetic by looking up the writings of, say, Sun Tsǔ, al-Khwārizmī, al-Uqlīdisī, Fibonacci, and Robert

Recorde, and by translating their methods as faithfully as possible into precise algorithmic notation.

2. [*15*] Generalize Algorithm A so that it does "column addition," obtaining the sum of m nonnegative n-place integers. (Assume that $m \le b$.)

3. [*21*] Write a MIX program for the algorithm of exercise 2, and estimate its running time as a function of m and n.

4. [*M21*] Give a formal proof of the validity of Algorithm A, using the method of inductive assertions explained in Section 1.2.1.

5. [*21*] Algorithm A adds the two inputs by going from right to left, but sometimes the data is more readily accessible from left to right. Design an algorithm that produces the same answer as Algorithm A, but that generates the digits of the answer from left to right, going back to change previous values if a carry occurs to make a previous value incorrect. [*Note:* Early Hindu and Arabic manuscripts dealt with addition from left to right in this way, probably because it was customary to work from left to right on an abacus; the right-to-left addition algorithm was a refinement due to al-Uqlīdisī, perhaps because Arabic is written from right to left.]

▶ **6.** [*22*] Design an algorithm that adds from left to right (as in exercise 5), but never stores a digit of the answer until this digit cannot possibly be affected by future carries; there is to be no changing of any answer digit once it has been stored. [*Hint:* Keep track of the number of consecutive $(b-1)$'s that have not yet been stored in the answer.] This sort of algorithm would be appropriate, for example, in a situation where the input and output numbers are to be read and written from left to right on magnetic tapes, or if they appear in straight linear lists.

7. [*M26*] Determine the average number of times the algorithm of exercise 5 will find that a carry makes it necessary to go back and change k digits of the partial answer, for $k = 1, 2, \ldots, n$. (Assume that both inputs are independently and uniformly distributed between 0 and $b^n - 1$.)

8. [*M26*] Write a MIX program for the algorithm of exercise 5, and determine its average running time based on the expected number of carries as computed in the text.

▶ **9.** [*21*] Generalize Algorithm A to obtain an algorithm that adds two n-place numbers in a *mixed-radix* number system, with bases b_0, b_1, ... (from right to left). Thus the least significant digits lie between 0 and $b_0 - 1$, the next digits lie between 0 and $b_1 - 1$, etc.; see Eq. 4.1–(9).

10. [*18*] Would Program S work properly if the instructions on lines 06 and 07 were interchanged? If the instructions on lines 05 and 06 were interchanged?

11. [*10*] Design an algorithm that compares two nonnegative n-place integers $u = (u_{n-1} \ldots u_1 u_0)_b$ and $v = (v_{n-1} \ldots v_1 v_0)_b$, to determine whether $u < v$, $u = v$, or $u > v$.

12. [*16*] Algorithm S assumes that we know which of the two input operands is the larger; if this information is not known, we could go ahead and perform the subtraction anyway, and we would find that an extra borrow is still present at the end of the algorithm. Design another algorithm that could be used (if there is a borrow present at the end of Algorithm S) to complement $(w_{n-1} \ldots w_1 w_0)_b$ and therefore to obtain the absolute value of the difference of u and v.

13. [*21*] Write a MIX program that multiplies $(u_{n-1} \ldots u_1 u_0)_b$ by v, where v is a single-precision number (that is, $0 \le v < b$), producing the answer $(w_n \ldots w_1 w_0)_b$. How much running time is required?

▶ **14.** [*M22*] Give a formal proof of the validity of Algorithm M, using the method of inductive assertions explained in Section 1.2.1. (See exercise 4.)

15. [*M20*] If we wish to form the product of two n-place fractions, $(.u_1u_2 \ldots u_n)_b \times (.v_1v_2 \ldots v_n)_b$, and to obtain only an n-place approximation $(.w_1w_2 \ldots w_n)_b$ to the result, Algorithm M could be used to obtain a $2n$-place answer that is subsequently rounded to the desired approximation. But this involves about twice as much work as is necessary for reasonable accuracy, since the products u_iv_j for $i+j > n+2$ contribute very little to the answer.

Give an estimate of the maximum error that can occur, if these products u_iv_j for $i+j > n+2$ are not computed during the multiplication, but are assumed to be zero.

▶ **16.** [*20*] (*Short division.*) Design an algorithm that divides a nonnegative n-place integer $(u_{n-1} \ldots u_1u_0)_b$ by v, where v is a single-precision number (that is, $0 < v < b$), producing the quotient $(w_{n-1} \ldots w_1w_0)_b$ and remainder r.

17. [*M20*] In the notation of Fig. 6, assume that $v_{n-1} \geq \lfloor b/2 \rfloor$; show that if $u_n = v_{n-1}$, we must have $q = b - 1$ or $b - 2$.

18. [*M20*] In the notation of Fig. 6, show that if $q' = \lfloor (u_nb+u_{n-1})/(v_{n-1}+1) \rfloor$, then $q' \leq q$.

▶ **19.** [*M21*] In the notation of Fig. 6, let $\hat{q}$ be an approximation to q, and let $\hat{r} = u_nb + u_{n-1} - \hat{q}v_{n-1}$. Assume that $v_{n-1} > 0$. Show that if $\hat{q}v_{n-2} > b\hat{r} + u_{n-2}$, then $q < \hat{q}$. [*Hint:* Strengthen the proof of Theorem A by examining the influence of v_{n-2}.]

20. [*M22*] Using the notation and assumptions of exercise 19, show that if $\hat{q}v_{n-2} \leq b\hat{r} + u_{n-2}$ and $\hat{q} < b$, then $\hat{q} = q$ or $q = \hat{q} - 1$.

▶ **21.** [*M23*] Show that if $v_{n-1} \geq \lfloor b/2 \rfloor$, and if $\hat{q}v_{n-2} \leq b\hat{r} + u_{n-2}$ but $\hat{q} \neq q$ in the notation of exercises 19 and 20, then $u \bmod v \geq (1 - 2/b)v$. (The latter event occurs with approximate probability $2/b$, so that when b is the word size of a computer we must have $q_j = \hat{q}$ in Algorithm D except in very rare circumstances.)

▶ **22.** [*24*] Find an example of a four-digit number divided by a three-digit number for which step D6 is necessary in Algorithm D, when the radix b is 10.

23. [*M23*] Given that v and b are integers, and that $1 \leq v < b$, prove that we always have $\lfloor b/2 \rfloor \leq v \lfloor b/(v+1) \rfloor < (v+1) \lfloor b/(v+1) \rfloor \leq b$.

24. [*M20*] Using the law of the distribution of leading digits explained in Section 4.2.4, give an approximate formula for the probability that $d = 1$ in Algorithm D. (When $d = 1$, we can omit most of the calculation in steps D1 and D8.)

25. [*26*] Write a MIX routine for step D1, which is needed to complete Program D.

26. [*21*] Write a MIX routine for step D8, which is needed to complete Program D.

27. [*M20*] Prove that at the beginning of step D8 in Algorithm D, the unnormalized remainder $(u_{n-1} \ldots u_1u_0)_b$ is always an exact multiple of d.

28. [*M30*] (A. Svoboda, *Stroje na Zpracování Informací* **9** (1963), 25–32.) Let $v = (v_{n-1} \ldots v_1v_0)_b$ be any radix b integer, where $v_{n-1} \neq 0$. Perform the following operations:

N1. If $v_{n-1} < b/2$, multiply v by $\lfloor (b+1)/(v_{n-1}+1) \rfloor$. Let the result of this step be $(v_nv_{n-1} \ldots v_1v_0)_b$.

N2. If $v_n = 0$, set $v \leftarrow v + (1/b)\lfloor b(b - v_{n-1})/(v_{n-1}+1) \rfloor v$; let the result of this step be $(v_nv_{n-1} \ldots v_0.v_{-1} \ldots)_b$. Repeat step N2 until $v_n \neq 0$. ∎

Prove that step N2 will be performed at most three times, and that we must always have $v_n = 1$, $v_{n-1} = 0$ at the end of the calculations.

[*Note:* If u and v are both multiplied by the constants above, we do not change the value of the quotient u/v, and the divisor has been converted into the form $(10v_{n-2} \ldots v_0.v_{-1}v_{-2}v_{-3})_b$. This form of the divisor is very convenient because, in the notation of Algorithm D, we may simply take $\hat{q} = u_{j+n}$ as a trial divisor at the beginning of step D3, or $\hat{q} = b - 1$ when $(u_{j+n+1}, u_{j+n}) = (1, 0)$.]

29. [*15*] Prove or disprove: At the beginning of step D7 of Algorithm D, we always have $u_{j+n} = 0$.

▶ **30.** [*22*] If memory space is limited, it may be desirable to use the same storage locations for both input and output during the performance of some of the algorithms in this section. Is it possible to have $w_0, w_1, \ldots, w_{n-1}$ stored in the same respective locations as $u_0, \ldots, u_{n-1}$ or $v_0, \ldots, v_{n-1}$ during Algorithm A or S? Is it possible to have the quotient $q_0, \ldots, q_m$ occupy the same locations as $u_n, \ldots, u_{m+n}$ in Algorithm D? Is there any permissible overlap of memory locations between input and output in Algorithm M?

31. [*28*] Assume that $b = 3$ and that $u = (u_{m+n-1} \ldots u_1 u_0)_3$, $v = (v_{n-1} \ldots v_1 v_0)_3$ are integers in *balanced ternary* notation (see Section 4.1), $v_{n-1} \neq 0$. Design a long-division algorithm that divides u by v, obtaining a remainder whose absolute value does not exceed $\frac{1}{2}|v|$. Try to find an algorithm that would be efficient if incorporated into the arithmetic circuitry of a balanced ternary computer.

32. [*M40*] Assume that $b = 2i$ and that u and v are complex numbers expressed in the quater-imaginary number system. Design algorithms that divide u by v, perhaps obtaining a suitable remainder of some sort, and compare their efficiency.

33. [*M40*] Design an algorithm for taking square roots, analogous to Algorithm D and to the traditional pencil-and-paper method for extracting square roots.

34. [*40*] Develop a set of computer subroutines for doing the four arithmetic operations on arbitrary integers, putting no constraint on the size of the integers except for the implicit assumption that the total memory capacity of the computer should not be exceeded. (Use linked memory allocation, so that no time is wasted in finding room to put the results.)

35. [*40*] Develop a set of computer subroutines for "decuple-precision floating point" arithmetic, using excess 0, base b, nine-place floating point number representation, where b is the computer word size, and allowing a full word for the exponent. (Thus each floating point number is represented in 10 words of memory, and all scaling is done by moving full words instead of by shifting within the words.)

36. [*M25*] Explain how to compute $\ln \phi$ to high precision, given a suitably precise approximation to ϕ, using only multiprecision addition, subtraction, and division by small numbers.

▶ **37.** [*20*] (E. Salamin.) Explain how to avoid the normalization and unnormalization steps of Algorithm D, when d is a power of 2 on a binary computer, without changing the sequence of trial quotient digits computed by that algorithm. (How can $\hat{q}$ be computed in step D3 if the normalization of step D1 hasn't been done?)

38. [*M35*] Suppose u and v are integers in the range $0 \leq u, v < 2^n$. Devise a way to compute the geometric mean $\lfloor \sqrt{uv} + \frac{1}{2} \rfloor$ by doing $O(n)$ operations of addition, subtraction, and comparison of $(n+2)$-bit numbers. [*Hint:* Use a "pipeline" to combine the classical methods of multiplication and square rooting.]

39. [*25*] (D. Bailey, P. Borwein, and S. Plouffe, 1996.) Explain how to compute the nth bit of the binary representation of π without knowing the previous $n - 1$ bits, by using the identity

$$\pi = \sum_{k \geq 0} \frac{1}{16^k} \left(\frac{4}{8k+1} - \frac{2}{8k+4} - \frac{1}{8k+5} - \frac{1}{8k+6} \right)$$

and doing $O(n \log n)$ arithmetic operations on $O(\log n)$-bit integers. (Assume that the binary digits of π do not have surprisingly long stretches of consecutive 0s or 1s.)

40. [*M24*] Sometimes we want to divide u by v when we know that the remainder will be zero. Show that if u is a $2n$-place number and v is an n-place number with $u \bmod v = 0$, we can save about 75% of the work of Algorithm D if we compute half of the quotient from left to right and the other half from right to left.

▶ **41.** [*M26*] Many applications of high-precision arithmetic require repeated calculations modulo a fixed n-place number w, where w is relatively prime to the base b. We can speed up such calculations by using a trick due to Peter L. Montgomery [*Math. Comp.* **44** (1985), 519–521], which streamlines the remaindering process by essentially working from right to left instead of left to right.

   a) Given $u = \pm(u_{m+n-1} \ldots u_1 u_0)_b$, $w = (w_{n-1} \ldots w_1 w_0)_b$, and a number w' such that $w_0 w' \bmod b = 1$, show how to compute $v = \pm(v_{n-1} \ldots v_1 v_0)_b$ such that $b^m v \bmod w = u \bmod w$.

   b) Given n-place signed integers u, v, w with $|u|, |v| < w$, and given w' as in (a), show how to calculate an n-place integer t such that $|t| < w$ and $b^n t \equiv uv$ (modulo w).

   c) How do the algorithms of (a) and (b) facilitate arithmetic mod w?

42. [*HM35*] Given m and b, let P_{nk} be the probability that $\lfloor (u_1 + \cdots + u_m)/b^n \rfloor = k$, when $u_1, \ldots, u_m$ are random n-place integers in radix b. (This is the distribution of w_n in the column addition algorithm of exercise 2.) Show that $P_{nk} = \frac{1}{m!} \left\langle {m \atop k} \right\rangle + O(b^{-n})$, where $\left\langle {m \atop k} \right\rangle$ is an Eulerian number (see Section 5.1.3).

▶ **43.** [*22*] Shades of gray or components of color values in digitized images are usually represented as 8-bit numbers u in the range $[0 .. 255]$, denoting the fraction $u/255$. Given two such fractions $u/255$ and $v/255$, graphical algorithms often need to compute their approximate product $w/255$, where w is the nearest integer to $uv/255$. Prove that w can be obtained from the efficient formula

$$t = uv + 128, \qquad w = \lfloor (\lfloor t/256 \rfloor + t)/256 \rfloor.$$

*4.3.2. Modular Arithmetic

Another interesting alternative is available for doing arithmetic on large integer numbers, based on some simple principles of number theory. The idea is to have several *moduli* $m_1, m_2, \ldots, m_r$ that contain no common factors, and to work indirectly with *residues* $u \bmod m_1$, $u \bmod m_2$, $\ldots$, $u \bmod m_r$ instead of directly with the number u.

For convenience in notation throughout this section, let

$$u_1 = u \bmod m_1, \qquad u_2 = u \bmod m_2, \qquad \ldots, \qquad u_r = u \bmod m_r. \qquad (1)$$

It is easy to compute $(u_1, u_2, \ldots, u_r)$ from an integer number u by means of division; and it is important to note that no information is lost in this process (if

u isn't too large), since we can recompute u from $(u_1, u_2, \ldots, u_r)$. For example, if $0 \le u < v \le 1000$, it is impossible to have $(u \bmod 7,\ u \bmod 11,\ u \bmod 13)$ equal to $(v \bmod 7,\ v \bmod 11,\ v \bmod 13)$. This is a consequence of the "Chinese remainder theorem" stated below.

We may therefore regard $(u_1, u_2, \ldots, u_r)$ as a new type of internal computer representation, a "modular representation," of the integer u.

The advantages of a modular representation are that addition, subtraction, and multiplication are very simple:

$$(u_1, \ldots, u_r) + (v_1, \ldots, v_r) = \big((u_1 + v_1) \bmod m_1,\ \ldots,\ (u_r + v_r) \bmod m_r\big), \quad (2)$$

$$(u_1, \ldots, u_r) - (v_1, \ldots, v_r) = \big((u_1 - v_1) \bmod m_1,\ \ldots,\ (u_r - v_r) \bmod m_r\big), \quad (3)$$

$$(u_1, \ldots, u_r) \times (v_1, \ldots, v_r) = \big((u_1 \times v_1) \bmod m_1,\ \ldots,\ (u_r \times v_r) \bmod m_r\big). \quad (4)$$

To derive (4), for example, we need to show that

$$uv \bmod m_j = (u \bmod m_j)(v \bmod m_j) \bmod m_j$$

for each modulus m_j. But this is a basic fact of elementary number theory: $x \bmod m_j = y \bmod m_j$ if and only if $x \equiv y$ (modulo m_j); furthermore if $x \equiv x'$ and $y \equiv y'$, then $xy \equiv x'y'$ (modulo m_j); hence $(u \bmod m_j)(v \bmod m_j) \equiv uv$ (modulo m_j).

The main disadvantage of a modular representation is that we cannot easily test whether $(u_1, \ldots, u_r)$ is greater than $(v_1, \ldots, v_r)$. It is also difficult to test whether or not overflow has occurred as the result of an addition, subtraction, or multiplication, and it is even more difficult to perform division. When such operations are required frequently in conjunction with addition, subtraction, and multiplication, the use of modular arithmetic can be justified only if fast means of conversion to and from the modular representation are available. Therefore conversion between modular and positional notation is one of the principal topics of interest to us in this section.

The processes of addition, subtraction, and multiplication using (2), (3), and (4) are called residue arithmetic or *modular arithmetic*. The range of numbers that can be handled by modular arithmetic is equal to $m = m_1 m_2 \ldots m_r$, the product of the moduli; and if each m_j is near our computer's word size we can deal with n-place numbers when $r \approx n$. Therefore we see that the amount of time required to add, subtract, or multiply n-place numbers using modular arithmetic is essentially proportional to n (not counting the time to convert in and out of modular representation). This is no advantage at all when addition and subtraction are considered, but it can be a considerable advantage with respect to multiplication since the conventional method of Section 4.3.1 requires an execution time proportional to n^2.

Moreover, on a computer that allows many operations to take place simultaneously, modular arithmetic can be a significant advantage even for addition and subtraction; the operations with respect to different moduli can all be done at the same time, so we obtain a substantial increase in speed. The same kind of decrease in execution time could not be achieved by the conventional techniques discussed in the previous section, since carry propagation must be considered. Perhaps highly parallel computers will someday make simultaneous operations commonplace, so that modular arithmetic will be of significant importance in "real-time" calculations when a quick answer to a single problem requiring high precision is needed. (With highly parallel computers, it is often preferable to run k *separate* programs simultaneously, instead of running a *single* program k times as fast, since the latter alternative is more complicated but does not utilize the machine any more efficiently. "Real-time" calculations are exceptions that make the inherent parallelism of modular arithmetic more significant.)

Now let us examine the basic fact that underlies the modular representation of numbers:

Theorem C (Chinese Remainder Theorem). *Let m_1, m_2, ..., m_r be positive integers that are relatively prime in pairs; that is,*

$$m_j \perp m_k \qquad \text{when } j \neq k. \tag{5}$$

Let $m = m_1 m_2 \ldots m_r$, and let a, u_1, u_2, ..., u_r be integers. Then there is exactly one integer u that satisfies the conditions

$$a \leq u < a + m, \qquad \text{and} \qquad u \equiv u_j \ (\text{modulo } m_j) \quad \text{for } 1 \leq j \leq r. \tag{6}$$

Proof. If $u \equiv v$ (modulo m_j) for $1 \leq j \leq r$, then $u - v$ is a multiple of m_j for all j, so (5) implies that $u - v$ is a multiple of $m = m_1 m_2 \ldots m_r$. This argument shows that there is *at most* one solution of (6). To complete the proof we must now show the existence of *at least* one solution, and this can be done in two simple ways:

Method 1 ("Nonconstructive" proof). As u runs through the m distinct values $a \leq u < a + m$, the r-tuples $(u \bmod m_1, \ldots, u \bmod m_r)$ must also run through m distinct values, since (6) has at most one solution. But there are exactly $m_1 m_2 \ldots m_r$ possible r-tuples $(v_1, \ldots, v_r)$ such that $0 \leq v_j < m_j$. Therefore each r-tuple must occur exactly once, and there must be some value of u for which $(u \bmod m_1, \ldots, u \bmod m_r) = (u_1, \ldots, u_r)$.

Method 2 ("Constructive" proof). We can find numbers M_j for $1 \leq j \leq r$ such that

$$M_j \equiv 1 \ (\text{modulo } m_j) \qquad \text{and} \qquad M_j \equiv 0 \ (\text{modulo } m_k) \quad \text{for } k \neq j. \tag{7}$$

This follows because (5) implies that m_j and m/m_j are relatively prime, so we may take

$$M_j = (m/m_j)^{\varphi(m_j)} \tag{8}$$

by Euler's theorem (exercise 1.2.4–28). Now the number

$$u = a + \big((u_1 M_1 + u_2 M_2 + \cdots + u_r M_r - a) \bmod m \big) \tag{9}$$

satisfies all the conditions of (6). ∎

A very special case of this theorem was stated by the Chinese mathematician Sun Tsŭ, probably some time after A.D. 280 and some time before A.D. 473. Mathematicians in mediæval India developed the techniques further, with their methods of *kuṭṭaka* (see Section 4.5.2); but Theorem C was first stated and proved in its proper generality by Ch'in Chiu-Shao in his *Shu Shu Chiu Chang* (1247). Ch'in called it ta-yen-shu (the "great generalization procedure"), and considered also the case where the moduli might have common factors, as in exercise 3. [See J. Needham, *Science and Civilisation in China* **3** (Cambridge University Press, 1959), 33–34, 119–120; Y. Li and S. Du, *Chinese Mathematics* (Oxford: Clarendon, 1987), 92–94, 105, 161–166; K. Shen, *Archive for History of Exact Sciences* **38** (1988), 285–305.] Numerous early contributions to this theory have been summarized by L. E. Dickson in his *History of the Theory of Numbers* **2** (Carnegie Inst. of Washington, 1920), 57–64.

As a consequence of Theorem C, we may use modular representation for numbers in any consecutive interval of $m = m_1 m_2 \ldots m_r$ integers. For example, we could take $a = 0$ in (6), and work only with nonnegative integers u less than m. On the other hand, when addition and subtraction are being done, as well as multiplication, it is usually most convenient to assume that all of the moduli $m_1, m_2, \ldots, m_r$ are odd numbers, so that $m = m_1 m_2 \ldots m_r$ is odd, and to work with integers in the range

$$-\frac{m}{2} < u < \frac{m}{2}, \tag{10}$$

which is completely symmetrical about zero.

In order to perform the basic operations listed in (2), (3), and (4), we need to compute $(u_j + v_j) \bmod m_j$, $(u_j - v_j) \bmod m_j$, and $u_j v_j \bmod m_j$, when $0 \le u_j, v_j < m_j$. If m_j is a single-precision number, it is most convenient to form $u_j v_j \bmod m_j$ by doing a multiplication and then a division operation. For addition and subtraction, the situation is a little simpler, since no division is necessary; the following formulas may conveniently be used:

$$(u_j + v_j) \bmod m_j = u_j + v_j - m_j[u_j + v_j \ge m_j]. \tag{11}$$

$$(u_j - v_j) \bmod m_j = u_j - v_j + m_j[u_j < v_j]. \tag{12}$$

(See Section 3.2.1.1.) Since we want m to be as large as possible, it is easiest to let m_1 be the largest odd number that fits in a computer word, to let m_2 be the largest odd number $< m_1$ that is relatively prime to m_1, to let m_3 be the largest odd number $< m_2$ that is relatively prime to both m_1 and m_2, and so on until enough m_j's have been found to give the desired range m. Efficient ways to determine whether or not two integers are relatively prime are discussed in Section 4.5.2.

As a simple example, suppose that we have a decimal computer whose words hold only two digits, so that the word size is 100. Then the procedure described in the previous paragraph would give

$$m_1 = 99, \quad m_2 = 97, \quad m_3 = 95, \quad m_4 = 91, \quad m_5 = 89, \quad m_6 = 83, \tag{13}$$

and so on.

On binary computers it is sometimes desirable to choose the m_j in a different way, by selecting

$$m_j = 2^{e_j} - 1. \tag{14}$$

In other words, each modulus is one less than a power of 2. Such a choice of m_j often makes the basic arithmetic operations simpler, because it is relatively easy to work modulo $2^{e_j} - 1$, as in ones' complement arithmetic. When the moduli are chosen according to this strategy, it is helpful to relax the condition $0 \le u_j < m_j$ slightly, so that we require only

$$0 \le u_j < 2^{e_j}, \qquad u_j \equiv u \ (\text{modulo } 2^{e_j} - 1). \tag{15}$$

Thus, the value $u_j = m_j = 2^{e_j} - 1$ is allowed as an optional alternative to $u_j = 0$; this does not affect the validity of Theorem C, and it means we are allowing u_j to be any e_j-bit binary number. Under this assumption, the operations of addition and multiplication modulo m_j become the following:

$$u_j \oplus v_j = \big((u_j + v_j) \bmod 2^{e_j}\big) + [u_j + v_j \ge 2^{e_j}]. \tag{16}$$

$$u_j \otimes v_j = (u_j v_j \bmod 2^{e_j}) \ \oplus \ \lfloor u_j v_j / 2^{e_j} \rfloor. \tag{17}$$

(Here $\oplus$ and $\otimes$ refer to the operations done on the individual components of $(u_1, \dots, u_r)$ and $(v_1, \dots, v_r)$ when adding or multiplying, respectively, using the convention (15).) Equation (12) is still good for subtraction, or we can use

$$u_j \ominus v_j = \big((u_j - v_j) \bmod 2^{e_j}\big) - [u_j < v_j]. \tag{18}$$

These operations can be performed efficiently even when 2^{e_j} is larger than the computer's word size, since it is a simple matter to compute the remainder of a positive number modulo a power of 2, or to divide a number by a power of 2. In (17) we have the sum of the "upper half" and the "lower half" of the product, as discussed in exercise 3.2.1.1–8.

If moduli of the form $2^{e_j} - 1$ are to be used, we must know under what conditions the number $2^e - 1$ is relatively prime to the number $2^f - 1$. Fortunately, there is a very simple rule:

$$\gcd(2^e - 1, \ 2^f - 1) = 2^{\gcd(e,f)} - 1. \tag{19}$$

This formula states in particular that *$2^e - 1$ and $2^f - 1$ are relatively prime if and only if e and f are relatively prime.* Equation (19) follows from Euclid's algorithm and the identity

$$(2^e - 1) \bmod (2^f - 1) = 2^{e \bmod f} - 1. \tag{20}$$

(See exercise 6.) On a computer with word size 2^{32}, we could therefore choose $m_1 = 2^{32} - 1$, $m_2 = 2^{31} - 1$, $m_3 = 2^{29} - 1$, $m_4 = 2^{27} - 1$, $m_5 = 2^{25} - 1$; this would permit efficient addition, subtraction, and multiplication of integers in a range of size $m_1 m_2 m_3 m_4 m_5 > 2^{143}$.

As we have already observed, the operations of conversion to and from modular representation are very important. If we are given a number u, its modular representation $(u_1, \dots, u_r)$ may be obtained by simply dividing u by

$m_1, \ldots, m_r$ and saving the remainders. A possibly more attractive procedure, if $u = (v_m v_{m-1} \ldots v_0)_b$, is to evaluate the polynomial

$$\left(\ldots (v_m b + v_{m-1}) b + \cdots \right) b + v_0$$

using modular arithmetic. When $b = 2$ and when the modulus m_j has the special form $2^{e_j} - 1$, both of these methods reduce to quite a simple procedure: Consider the binary representation of u with blocks of e_j bits grouped together,

$$u = a_t A^t + a_{t-1} A^{t-1} + \cdots + a_1 A + a_0, \tag{21}$$

where $A = 2^{e_j}$ and $0 \le a_k < 2^{e_j}$ for $0 \le k \le t$. Then

$$u \equiv a_t + a_{t-1} + \cdots + a_1 + a_0 \pmod{2^{e_j} - 1}, \tag{22}$$

since $A \equiv 1$, so we obtain u_j by adding the e_j-bit numbers $a_t \oplus \cdots \oplus a_1 \oplus a_0$, using (16). This process is similar to the familiar device of "casting out nines" that determines $u \bmod 9$ when u is expressed in the decimal system.

Conversion back from modular form to positional notation is somewhat more difficult. It is interesting in this regard to notice how the study of computation changes our viewpoint towards mathematical proofs: Theorem C tells us that the conversion from $(u_1, \ldots, u_r)$ to u is possible, and two proofs are given. The first proof we considered is a classical one that relies only on very simple concepts, namely the facts that

i) any number that is a multiple of m_1, of m_2, $\ldots$, and of m_r, must be a multiple of $m_1 m_2 \ldots m_r$ when the m_j's are pairwise relatively prime; and

ii) if m pigeons are put into m pigeonholes with no two pigeons in the same hole, then there must be one in each hole.

By traditional notions of mathematical aesthetics, this is no doubt the nicest proof of Theorem C; but from a computational standpoint it is completely worthless. It amounts to saying, "Try $u = a, a+1, \ldots$ until you find a value for which $u \equiv u_1 \pmod{m_1}$, $\ldots$, $u \equiv u_r \pmod{m_r}$."

The second proof of Theorem C is more explicit; it shows how to compute r new constants $M_1, \ldots, M_r$, and to get the solution in terms of these constants by formula (9). This proof uses more complicated concepts (for example, Euler's theorem), but it is much more satisfactory from a computational standpoint, since the constants $M_1, \ldots, M_r$ need to be determined only once. On the other hand, the determination of M_j by Eq. (8) is certainly not trivial, since the evaluation of Euler's φ-function requires, in general, the factorization of m_j into prime powers. There are much better ways to compute M_j than to use (8); in this respect we can see again the distinction between mathematical elegance and computational efficiency. But even if we find M_j by the best possible method, we're stuck with the fact that M_j is a multiple of the huge number m/m_j. Thus, (9) forces us to do a lot of high-precision calculation, and such calculation is just what we wished to avoid by modular arithmetic in the first place.

So we need an even *better* proof of Theorem C if we are going to have a really usable method of conversion from $(u_1, \ldots, u_r)$ to u. Such a method was suggested by H. L. Garner in 1958; it can be carried out using $\binom{r}{2}$ constants c_{ij} for $1 \leq i < j \leq r$, where

$$c_{ij} m_i \equiv 1 \pmod{m_j}. \tag{23}$$

These constants c_{ij} are readily computed using Euclid's algorithm, since for any given i and j Algorithm 4.5.2X will determine a and b such that $am_i + bm_j = \gcd(m_i, m_j) = 1$, and we may take $c_{ij} = a$. When the moduli have the special form $2^{e_j} - 1$, a simple method of determining c_{ij} is given in exercise 6.

Once the c_{ij} have been determined satisfying (23), we can set

$$
\begin{aligned}
v_1 &\leftarrow u_1 \bmod m_1, \\
v_2 &\leftarrow (u_2 - v_1)\, c_{12} \bmod m_2, \\
v_3 &\leftarrow \big((u_3 - v_1)\, c_{13} - v_2\big)\, c_{23} \bmod m_3, \\
&\ \ \vdots \\
v_r &\leftarrow \big(\ldots((u_r - v_1)\, c_{1r} - v_2)\, c_{2r} - \cdots - v_{r-1}\big)\, c_{(r-1)r} \bmod m_r.
\end{aligned}
\tag{24}
$$

Then

$$u = v_r m_{r-1} \ldots m_2 m_1 + \cdots + v_3 m_2 m_1 + v_2 m_1 + v_1 \tag{25}$$

is a number satisfying the conditions

$$0 \leq u < m, \qquad u \equiv u_j \pmod{m_j} \quad \text{for } 1 \leq j \leq r. \tag{26}$$

(See exercise 8; another way of rewriting (24) that does not involve as many auxiliary constants is given in exercise 7.) Equation (25) is a *mixed-radix representation* of u, which can be converted to binary or decimal notation using the methods of Section 4.4. If $0 \leq u < m$ is not the desired range, an appropriate multiple of m can be added or subtracted after the conversion process.

The advantage of the computation shown in (24) is that the calculation of v_j can be done using only arithmetic mod m_j, which is already built into the modular arithmetic algorithms. Furthermore, (24) allows parallel computation: We can start with $(v_1, \ldots, v_r) \leftarrow (u_1 \bmod m_1, \ldots, u_r \bmod m_r)$, then at time j for $1 \leq j < r$ we simultaneously set $v_k \leftarrow (v_k - v_j) c_{jk} \bmod m_k$ for $j < k \leq r$. An alternative way to compute the mixed-radix representation, allowing similar possibilities for parallelism, has been discussed by A. S. Fraenkel, *Proc. ACM Nat. Conf.* **19** (Philadelphia: 1964), E1.4.

It is important to observe that the mixed-radix representation (25) is sufficient to compare the magnitudes of two modular numbers. For if we know that $0 \leq u < m$ and $0 \leq u' < m$, then we can tell if $u < u'$ by first doing the conversion to $(v_1, \ldots, v_r)$ and $(v'_1, \ldots, v'_r)$, then testing if $v_r < v'_r$, or if $v_r = v'_r$ and $v_{r-1} < v'_{r-1}$, etc., according to lexicographic order. It is not necessary to convert all the way to binary or decimal notation if we only want to know whether $(v_1, \ldots, v_r)$ is less than $(v'_1, \ldots, v'_r)$.

The operation of comparing two numbers, or of deciding if a modular number is negative, is intuitively very simple, so we would expect to have a much easier way to make this test than the conversion to mixed-radix form. But the following theorem shows that there is little hope of finding a substantially better method, since the range of a modular number depends essentially on all bits of all the residues $(u_1, \ldots, u_r)$:

Theorem S (Nicholas Szabó, 1961). *In terms of the notation above, assume that $m_1 < \sqrt{m}$, and let L be any value in the range*

$$m_1 \leq L \leq m - m_1. \tag{27}$$

Let g be any function such that the set $\{g(0), g(1), \ldots, g(m_1 - 1)\}$ contains fewer than m_1 values. Then there are numbers u and v such that

$$g(u \bmod m_1) = g(v \bmod m_1), \quad u \bmod m_j = v \bmod m_j \text{ for } 2 \leq j \leq r; \tag{28}$$

$$0 \leq u < L \leq v < m. \tag{29}$$

Proof. By hypothesis, there must exist numbers $u \neq v$ satisfying (28), since g must take on the same value for two different residues. Let (u, v) be a pair of values with $0 \leq u < v < m$ satisfying (28), for which u is a minimum. Since $u' = u - m_1$ and $v' = v - m_1$ also satisfy (28), we must have $u' < 0$ by the minimality of u. Hence $u < m_1 \leq L$; and if (29) does not hold, we must have $v < L$. But $v > u$, and $v - u$ is a multiple of $m_2 \ldots m_r = m/m_1$, so $v \geq v - u \geq m/m_1 > m_1$. Therefore, if (29) does not hold for (u, v), it will be satisfied for the pair $(u'', v'') = (v - m_1, u + m - m_1)$. ∎

Of course, a similar result can be proved for any m_j in place of m_1; and we could also replace (29) by the condition "$a \leq u < a + L \leq v < a + m$" with only minor changes in the proof. Therefore Theorem S shows that many simple functions cannot be used to determine the range of a modular number.

Let us now reiterate the main points of the discussion in this section: Modular arithmetic can be a significant advantage for applications in which the predominant calculations involve exact multiplication (or raising to a power) of large integers, combined with addition and subtraction, but where there is very little need to divide or compare numbers, *or to test whether intermediate results "overflow" out of range.* (It is important not to forget the latter restriction; methods are available to test for overflow, as in exercise 12, but they are so complicated that they nullify the advantages of modular arithmetic.) Several applications of modular computations have been discussed by H. Takahasi and Y. Ishibashi, *Information Proc. in Japan* **1** (1961), 28–42.

An example of such an application is the exact solution of linear equations with rational coefficients. For various reasons it is desirable in this case to assume that the moduli $m_1, m_2, \ldots, m_r$ are all prime numbers; the linear equations can be solved independently modulo each m_j. A detailed discussion of this procedure has been given by I. Borosh and A. S. Fraenkel [*Math. Comp.* **20** (1966), 107–112], with further improvements by A. S. Fraenkel and D. Loewenthal [*J. Res. National Bureau of Standards* **75B** (1971), 67–75]. By means of their method, the nine independent solutions of a system of 111 linear equations in 120 unknowns were obtained exactly in less than 20 minutes on a CDC 1604 computer. The same procedure is worthwhile also for solving simultaneous linear equations with floating point coefficients, when the matrix of coefficients is ill-conditioned. The modular technique (treating the given floating point coefficients as exact rational numbers) gives a method for obtaining the *true* answers in less time than conventional methods can produce reliable *approximate* answers! [See M. T. McClellan, *JACM* **20** (1973), 563–588, for further developments of this approach; and see also E. H. Bareiss, *J. Inst. Math. and Appl.* **10** (1972), 68–104, for a discussion of its limitations.]

The published literature concerning modular arithmetic is mostly oriented towards hardware design, since the carry-free properties of modular arithmetic make it attractive from the standpoint of high-speed operation. The idea was first published by A. Svoboda and M. Valach in the Czechoslovakian journal *Stroje na Zpracování Informací* (*Information Processing Machines*) **3** (1955), 247–295; then independently by H. L. Garner [*IRE Trans.* **EC-8** (1959), 140–147]. The use of moduli of the form $2^{e_j} - 1$ was suggested by A. S. Fraenkel [*JACM* **8** (1961), 87–96], and several advantages of such moduli were demonstrated by A. Schönhage [*Computing* **1** (1966), 182–196]. See the book *Residue Arithmetic and Its Applications to Computer Technology* by N. S. Szabó and R. I. Tanaka (New York: McGraw–Hill, 1967), for additional information and a comprehensive bibliography of the subject. A Russian book published in 1968 by I. Y. Akushsky and D. I. Yuditsky includes a chapter about complex moduli [see *Rev. Roumaine de Math. Pures et Appl.* **15** (1970), 159–160].

Further discussion of modular arithmetic can be found in Section 4.3.3B.

> *The notice-board had said he was in Room 423,*
> *but the numbering system, nominally consecutive,*
> *seemed to have been applied on a plan that could only*
> *have been the work of a lunatic or a mathematician.*
> — ROBERT BARNARD, *The Case of the Missing Brontë* (1983)

EXERCISES

1. [*20*] Find all integers u that satisfy all of the following conditions: $u \bmod 7 = 1$, $u \bmod 11 = 6$, $u \bmod 13 = 5$, $0 \le u < 1000$.

2. [*M20*] Would Theorem C still be true if we allowed $a, u_1, u_2, \ldots, u_r$ and u to be arbitrary real numbers (not just integers)?

▶ **3.** [*M26*] (*Generalized Chinese Remainder Theorem.*) Let $m_1, m_2, \ldots, m_r$ be positive integers. Let m be the least common multiple of $m_1, m_2, \ldots, m_r$, and let $a, u_1, u_2, \ldots, u_r$ be any integers. Prove that there is exactly one integer u that satisfies the conditions

$$a \le u < a + m, \qquad u \equiv u_j \pmod{m_j}, \qquad 1 \le j \le r,$$

provided that

$$u_i \equiv u_j \pmod{\gcd(m_i, m_j)}, \qquad 1 \le i < j \le r;$$

and there is no such integer u when the latter condition fails to hold.

4. [*20*] Continue the process shown in (13); what would $m_7, m_8, m_9, \ldots$ be?

▶ **5.** [*M23*] (a) Suppose that the method of (13) is continued until no more m_j can be chosen. Does this "greedy" method give the largest attainable value $m_1 m_2 \ldots m_r$ such

that the m_j are odd positive integers less than 100 that are relatively prime in pairs?
(b) What is the largest possible $m_1 m_2 \ldots m_r$ when each residue u_j must fit in eight
bits of memory?

6. [*M22*] Let e, f, and g be nonnegative integers.
a) Show that $2^e \equiv 2^f$ (modulo $2^g - 1$) if and only if $e \equiv f$ (modulo g).
b) Given that $e \bmod f = d$ and $ce \bmod f = 1$, prove the identity

$$\left((1 + 2^d + \cdots + 2^{(c-1)d}) \cdot (2^e - 1)\right) \bmod (2^f - 1) = 1.$$

(Thus, we have a comparatively simple formula for the inverse of $2^e - 1$, modulo
$2^f - 1$, as required in (23).)

▶ **7.** [*M21*] Show that (24) can be rewritten as follows:

$$v_1 \leftarrow u_1 \bmod m_1,$$
$$v_2 \leftarrow (u_2 - v_1)\, c_{12} \bmod m_2,$$
$$v_3 \leftarrow (u_3 - (v_1 + m_1 v_2))\, c_{13} c_{23} \bmod m_3,$$

$$\vdots$$

$$v_r \leftarrow (u_r - (v_1 + m_1(v_2 + m_2(v_3 + \cdots + m_{r-2} v_{r-1}) \ldots)))\, c_{1r} \ldots c_{(r-1)r} \bmod m_r.$$

If the formulas are rewritten in this way, we see that only $r - 1$ constants $C_j = c_{1j} \ldots c_{(j-1)j} \bmod m_j$ are needed instead of $r(r-1)/2$ constants c_{ij} as in (24). Discuss
the relative merits of this version of the formula as compared to (24), from the stand-
point of computer calculation.

8. [*M21*] Prove that the number u defined by (24) and (25) satisfies (26).

9. [*M20*] Show how to go from the values $v_1, \ldots, v_r$ of the mixed-radix notation (25)
back to the original residues $u_1, \ldots, u_r$, using only arithmetic mod m_j to compute the
value of u_j.

10. [*M25*] An integer u that lies in the symmetrical range (10) might be represented
by finding the numbers $u_1, \ldots, u_r$ such that $u \equiv u_j$ (modulo m_j) and $-m_j/2 < u_j < m_j/2$, instead of insisting that $0 \le u_j < m_j$ as in the text. Discuss the modular
arithmetic procedures that would be appropriate in connection with such a symmetrical
representation (including the conversion process, (24)).

11. [*M23*] Assume that all the m_j are odd, and that $u = (u_1, \ldots, u_r)$ is known to be
even, where $0 \le u < m$. Find a reasonably fast method to compute $u/2$ using modular
arithmetic.

12. [*M10*] Prove that, if $0 \le u, v < m$, the modular addition of u and v causes overflow
(lies outside the range allowed by the modular representation) if and only if the sum
is less than u. (Thus the overflow detection problem is equivalent to the comparison
problem.)

▶ **13.** [*M25*] (*Automorphic numbers.*) An n-digit decimal number $x > 1$ is called an
"automorph" by recreational mathematicians if the last n digits of x^2 are equal to x.
For example, 9376 is a 4-digit automorph, since $9376^2 = 87909376$. [See *Scientific
American* **218**, 1 (January 1968), 125.]

    a) Prove that an n-digit number $x > 1$ is an automorph if and only if $x \bmod 5^n = 0$ or 1 and $x \bmod 2^n = 1$ or 0, respectively. (Thus, if $m_1 = 2^n$ and $m_2 = 5^n$, the
only two n-digit automorphs are the numbers M_1 and M_2 in (7).)

b) Prove that if x is an n-digit automorph, then $(3x^2 - 2x^3) \bmod 10^{2n}$ is a $2n$-digit automorph.

c) Given that $cx \equiv 1 \pmod{y}$, find a simple formula for a number c' depending on c and x but not on y, such that $c'x^2 \equiv 1 \pmod{y^2}$.

▶ **14.** [*M30*] (*Mersenne multiplication.*) The cyclic convolution of $(x_0, x_1, \ldots, x_{n-1})$ and $(y_0, y_1, \ldots, y_{n-1})$ is defined to be $(z_0, z_1, \ldots, z_{n-1})$, where

$$z_k = \sum_{i+j \equiv k \,(\text{modulo } n)} x_i y_j, \qquad \text{for } 0 \le k < n.$$

We will study efficient algorithms for cyclic convolution in Sections 4.3.3 and 4.6.4.

Consider q-bit integers u and v that are represented in the form

$$u = \sum_{k=0}^{n-1} u_k 2^{\lfloor kq/n \rfloor}, \qquad v = \sum_{k=0}^{n-1} v_k 2^{\lfloor kq/n \rfloor},$$

where $0 \le u_k, v_k < 2^{\lfloor (k+1)q/n \rfloor - \lfloor kq/n \rfloor}$. (This representation is a mixture of radices $2^{\lfloor q/n \rfloor}$ and $2^{\lceil q/n \rceil}$.) Suggest a good way to find the representation of

$$w = (uv) \bmod (2^q - 1),$$

using an appropriate cyclic convolution. [*Hint:* Do not be afraid of floating point arithmetic.]

*4.3.3. How Fast Can We Multiply?

The conventional procedure for multiplication in positional number systems, Algorithm 4.3.1M, requires approximately cmn operations to multiply an m-place number by an n-place number, where c is a constant. In this section, let us assume for convenience that $m = n$, and let us consider the following question: *Does every general computer algorithm for multiplying two n-place numbers require an execution time proportional to n^2, as n increases?*

(In this question, a "general" algorithm means one that accepts, as input, the number n and two arbitrary n-place numbers in positional notation; the algorithm is supposed to output their product in positional form. Certainly if we were allowed to choose a different algorithm for each value of n, the question would be of no interest, since multiplication could be done for any specific value of n by a "table-lookup" operation in some huge table. The term "computer algorithm" is meant to imply an algorithm that is suitable for implementation on a digital computer like MIX, and the execution time is to be the time it takes to perform the algorithm on such a computer.)

A. Digital methods. The answer to the question above is, rather surprisingly, "No," and, in fact, it is not very difficult to see why. For convenience, let us assume throughout this section that we are working with integers expressed in binary notation. If we have two $2n$-bit numbers $u = (u_{2n-1} \ldots u_1 u_0)_2$ and $v = (v_{2n-1} \ldots v_1 v_0)_2$, we can write

$$u = 2^n U_1 + U_0, \qquad v = 2^n V_1 + V_0, \tag{1}$$

where $U_1 = (u_{2n-1} \ldots u_n)_2$ is the "most significant half" of the number u and $U_0 = (u_{n-1} \ldots u_0)_2$ is the "least significant half"; similarly $V_1 = (v_{2n-1} \ldots v_n)_2$ and $V_0 = (v_{n-1} \ldots v_0)_2$. Now we have

$$uv = (2^{2n} + 2^n)U_1V_1 + 2^n(U_1 - U_0)(V_0 - V_1) + (2^n + 1)U_0V_0. \qquad (2)$$

This formula reduces the problem of multiplying $2n$-bit numbers to three multiplications of n-bit numbers, namely U_1V_1, $(U_1 - U_0)(V_0 - V_1)$, and U_0V_0, plus some simple shifting and adding operations.

Formula (2) can be used to multiply double-precision inputs when we want a quadruple-precision result, and it will be just a little faster than the traditional method on many machines. But the main advantage of (2) is that we can use it to define a recursive process for multiplication that is significantly faster than the familiar order-n^2 method when n is large: If $T(n)$ is the time required to perform multiplication of n-bit numbers, we have

$$T(2n) \le 3T(n) + cn \qquad (3)$$

for some constant c, since the right-hand side of (2) uses just three multiplications plus some additions and shifts. Relation (3) implies by induction that

$$T(2^k) \le c(3^k - 2^k), \qquad k \ge 1, \qquad (4)$$

if we choose c to be large enough so that this inequality is valid when $k = 1$; therefore we have

$$T(n) \le T\left(2^{\lceil \lg n \rceil}\right) \le c\left(3^{\lceil \lg n \rceil} - 2^{\lceil \lg n \rceil}\right) < 3c \cdot 3^{\lg n} = 3cn^{\lg 3}. \qquad (5)$$

Relation (5) shows that the running time for multiplication can be reduced from order n^2 to order $n^{\lg 3} \approx n^{1.585}$, so the recursive method is much faster than the traditional method when n is large. Exercise 18 discusses an implementation of this approach.

(A similar but slightly more complicated method for doing multiplication with running time of order $n^{\lg 3}$ was apparently first suggested by A. Karatsuba [see *Doklady Akad. Nauk SSSR* **145** (1962), 293–294; English translation in *Soviet Physics–Doklady* **7** (1963), 595–596]. Curiously, this idea does not seem to have been discovered before 1960: None of the "calculating prodigies" who have become famous for their ability to multiply large numbers mentally have been reported to use any such method, although formula (2) adapted to decimal notation would seem to lead to a reasonably easy way to multiply eight-digit numbers in one's head.)

The running time can be reduced still further, in the limit as n approaches infinity, if we observe that the method just used is essentially the special case $r = 1$ of a more general method that yields

$$T\left((r + 1)n\right) \le (2r + 1)T(n) + cn \qquad (6)$$

for any fixed r. This more general method can be obtained as follows: Let

$$u = (u_{(r+1)n-1} \ldots u_1 u_0)_2 \qquad \text{and} \qquad v = (v_{(r+1)n-1} \ldots v_1 v_0)_2$$

be broken into $r + 1$ pieces,

$$u = U_r 2^{rn} + \cdots + U_1 2^n + U_0, \qquad v = V_r 2^{rn} + \cdots + V_1 2^n + V_0, \qquad (7)$$

where each U_j and each V_j is an n-bit number. Consider the polynomials

$$U(x) = U_r x^r + \cdots + U_1 x + U_0, \qquad V(x) = V_r x^r + \cdots + V_1 x + V_0, \qquad (8)$$

and let

$$W(x) = U(x)V(x) = W_{2r} x^{2r} + \cdots + W_1 x + W_0. \qquad (9)$$

Since $u = U(2^n)$ and $v = V(2^n)$, we have $uv = W(2^n)$, so we can easily compute uv if we know the coefficients of $W(x)$. The problem is to find a good way to compute the coefficients of $W(x)$ by using only $2r + 1$ multiplications of n-bit numbers plus some further operations that involve only an execution time proportional to n. This can be done by computing

$$U(0)V(0) = W(0), \quad U(1)V(1) = W(1), \quad \ldots, \quad U(2r)V(2r) = W(2r). \qquad (10)$$

The coefficients of a polynomial of degree $2r$ can be written as a linear combination of the values of that polynomial at $2r + 1$ distinct points; computing such a linear combination requires an execution time at most proportional to n. (Actually, the products $U(j)V(j)$ are not strictly products of n-bit numbers, but they are products of at most $(n + t)$-bit numbers, where t is a fixed value depending on r. It is easy to design a multiplication routine for $(n + t)$-bit numbers that requires only $T(n) + c_1 n$ operations, where $T(n)$ is the number of operations needed for n-bit multiplications, since two products of t-bit by n-bit numbers can be done in $c_2 n$ operations when t is fixed.) Therefore we obtain a method of multiplication satisfying (6).

Relation (6) implies that $T(n) \le c_3 n^{\log_{r+1}(2r+1)} < c_3 n^{1+\log_{r+1} 2}$, if we argue as in the derivation of (5), so we have now proved the following result:

Theorem A. *Given $\epsilon > 0$, there exists a multiplication algorithm such that the number of elementary operations $T(n)$ needed to multiply two n-bit numbers satisfies*

$$T(n) < c(\epsilon) n^{1+\epsilon}, \qquad (11)$$

for some constant $c(\epsilon)$ independent of n. ∎

This theorem is still not the result we are after. It is unsatisfactory for practical purposes because the method becomes quite complicated as $\epsilon \to 0$ (and therefore as $r \to \infty$), causing $c(\epsilon)$ to grow so rapidly that extremely huge values of n are needed before we have any significant improvement over (5). And it is unsatisfactory for theoretical purposes because it does not make use of the full power of the polynomial method on which it is based. We can obtain a better result if we let r *vary* with n, choosing larger and larger values of r as n increases. This idea is due to A. L. Toom [*Doklady Akad. Nauk SSSR* **150** (1963), 496–498, English translation in *Soviet Mathematics* **4** (1963), 714–716], who used it to show that computer circuitry for the multiplication of n-bit numbers can be constructed with a fairly small number of components as n grows. S. A. Cook [*On the Minimum Computation Time of Functions* (Thesis, Harvard University, 1966), 51–77] showed later that Toom's method can be adapted to fast computer programs.

Before we discuss the Toom–Cook algorithm any further, let us study a small example of the transition from $U(x)$ and $V(x)$ to the coefficients of $W(x)$. This example will not demonstrate the efficiency of the method, since the numbers are too small, but it reveals some useful simplifications that we can make in the general case. Suppose that we want to multiply $u = 1234$ times $v = 2341$; in binary notation this is

$$u = (0100\ 1101\ 0010)_2 \text{ times } v = (1001\ 0010\ 0101)_2. \tag{12}$$

Let $r = 2$; the polynomials $U(x)$ and $V(x)$ in (8) are

$$U(x) = 4x^2 + 13x + 2, \qquad V(x) = 9x^2 + 2x + 5.$$

Hence we find, for $W(x) = U(x)V(x)$,

$$
\begin{array}{llllll}
U(0) = & 2, & U(1) = & 19, & U(2) = & 44, & U(3) = & 77, & U(4) = & 118; \\
V(0) = & 5, & V(1) = & 16, & V(2) = & 45, & V(3) = & 92, & V(4) = & 157; \\
W(0) = & 10, & W(1) = 304, & W(2) = 1980, & W(3) = 7084, & W(4) = 18526. & (13)
\end{array}
$$

Our job is to compute the five coefficients of $W(x)$ from the latter five values.

An attractive little algorithm can be used to compute the coefficients of a polynomial $W(x) = W_{m-1}x^{m-1} + \cdots + W_1 x + W_0$ when the values $W(0)$, $W(1)$, ..., $W(m-1)$ are given. Let us first write

$$W(x) = a_{m-1}x^{\underline{m-1}} + a_{m-2}x^{\underline{m-2}} + \cdots + a_1 x^{\underline{1}} + a_0, \tag{14}$$

where $x^{\underline{k}} = x(x-1)\ldots(x-k+1)$, and where the coefficients a_j are unknown. The falling factorial powers have the important property that

$$W(x+1) - W(x) = (m-1)a_{m-1}x^{\underline{m-2}} + (m-2)a_{m-2}x^{\underline{m-3}} + \cdots + a_1;$$

hence by induction we find that, for all $k \geq 0$,

$$\frac{1}{k!}\left(W(x+k) - \binom{k}{1}W(x+k-1) + \binom{k}{2}W(x+k-2) - \cdots + (-1)^k W(x)\right)$$

$$= \binom{m-1}{k}a_{m-1}x^{\underline{m-1-k}} + \binom{m-2}{k}a_{m-2}x^{\underline{m-2-k}} + \cdots + \binom{k}{k}a_k. \tag{15}$$

Denoting the left-hand side of (15) by $(1/k!)\,\Delta^k W(x)$, we see that

$$\frac{1}{k!}\Delta^k W(x) = \frac{1}{k}\left(\frac{1}{(k-1)!}\Delta^{k-1}W(x+1) - \frac{1}{(k-1)!}\Delta^{k-1}W(x)\right)$$

and $(1/k!)\,\Delta^k W(0) = a_k$. So the coefficients a_j can be evaluated using a very simple method, illustrated here for the polynomial $W(x)$ in (13):

$$
\begin{array}{cccccc}
10 & & & & & \\
 & 294 & & & & \\
304 & & 1382/2 = \ 691 & & & \\
 & 1676 & & 1023/3 = 341 & & \\
1980 & & 3428/2 = 1714 & & 144/4 = 36 & \quad(16) \\
 & 5104 & & 1455/3 = 485 & & \\
7084 & & 6338/2 = 3169 & & & \\
 & 11442 & & & & \\
18526 & & & & &
\end{array}
$$

The leftmost column of this tableau is a listing of the given values of $W(0)$, $W(1)$, $\ldots$, $W(4)$; the kth succeeding column is obtained by computing the difference between successive values of the preceding column and dividing by k. The coefficients a_j appear at the top of the columns, so that $a_0 = 10$, $a_1 = 294$, $\ldots$, $a_4 = 36$, and we have

$$W(x) = 36x^4 + 341x^3 + 691x^2 + 294x^1 + 10$$
$$= \big(\big((36(x-3) + 341)(x-2) + 691\big)(x-1) + 294\big)x + 10. \qquad(17)$$

In general, we can write

$$W(x) = \big(\ldots\big((a_{m-1}(x-m+2) + a_{m-2})(x-m+3) + a_{m-3}\big)(x-m+4) + \cdots + a_1\big)x + a_0,$$

and this formula shows how the coefficients $W_{m-1}, \ldots, W_1, W_0$ can be obtained from the a's:

$$
\begin{array}{ccccc}
36 & 341 & & & \\
 & -3 \cdot 36 & & & \\
36 & 233 & 691 & & \\
 & -2 \cdot 36 & -2 \cdot 233 & & \quad(18)\\
36 & 161 & 225 & 294 & \\
 & -1 \cdot 36 & -1 \cdot 161 & -1 \cdot 225 & \\
36 & 125 & 64 & 69 & 10
\end{array}
$$

Here the numbers below the horizontal lines successively show the coefficients of the polynomials

$$a_{m-1},$$
$$a_{m-1}(x - m + 2) + a_{m-2},$$
$$\big(a_{m-1}(x - m + 2) + a_{m-2}\big)(x - m + 3) + a_{m-3}, \qquad \text{etc.}$$

From this tableau we have

$$W(x) = 36x^4 + 125x^3 + 64x^2 + 69x + 10, \qquad(19)$$

so the answer to our original problem is $1234 \cdot 2341 = W(16) = 2888794$, where $W(16)$ is obtained by adding and shifting. A generalization of this method for obtaining coefficients is discussed in Section 4.6.4.

The basic Stirling number identity of Eq. 1.2.6–(45),

$$x^n = \left\{ {n \atop n} \right\} x^{\underline{n}} + \cdots + \left\{ {n \atop 1} \right\} x^{\underline{1}} + \left\{ {n \atop 0} \right\},$$

shows that if the coefficients of $W(x)$ are nonnegative, so are the numbers a_j, and in such a case *all of the intermediate results in the computation above are nonnegative.* This further simplifies the Toom–Cook multiplication algorithm, which we will now consider in detail. (Impatient readers should, however, skip to subsection C below.)

Algorithm T (*High-precision multiplication of binary numbers*). Given a positive integer n and two nonnegative n-bit integers u and v, this algorithm forms their $2n$-bit product, w. Four auxiliary stacks are used to hold the long numbers that are manipulated during the procedure:

> Stacks U, V: Temporary storage of $U(j)$ and $V(j)$ in step T4.
> Stack C: Numbers to be multiplied, and control codes.
> Stack W: Storage of $W(j)$.

These stacks may contain either binary numbers or special control symbols called code-1, code-2, and code-3. The algorithm also constructs an auxiliary table of numbers q_k, r_k; this table is maintained in such a manner that it may be stored as a linear list, where a single pointer that traverses the list (moving back and forth) can be used to access the current table entry of interest.

(Stacks C and W are used to control the recursive mechanism of this multiplication algorithm in a reasonably straightforward manner that is a special case of general procedures discussed in Chapter 8.)

T1. [Compute q, r tables.] Set stacks U, V, C, and W empty. Set

$$k \leftarrow 1, \qquad q_0 \leftarrow q_1 \leftarrow 16, \qquad r_0 \leftarrow r_1 \leftarrow 4, \qquad Q \leftarrow 4, \qquad R \leftarrow 2.$$

Now if $q_{k-1} + q_k < n$, set

$$k \leftarrow k+1, \qquad Q \leftarrow Q+R, \qquad R \leftarrow \lfloor \sqrt{Q} \rfloor, \qquad q_k \leftarrow 2^Q, \qquad r_k \leftarrow 2^R,$$

and repeat this operation until $q_{k-1} + q_k \geq n$. $\bigl($*Note:* The calculation of $R \leftarrow \lfloor \sqrt{Q} \rfloor$ does not require a square root to be taken, since we may simply set $R \leftarrow R + 1$ if $(R+1)^2 \leq Q$ and leave R unchanged if $(R+1)^2 > Q$; see exercise 2. In this step we build the sequences

$k =$	0	1	2	3	4	5	6	$\cdots$
$q_k =$	2^4	2^4	2^6	2^8	2^{10}	2^{13}	2^{16}	$\cdots$
$r_k =$	2^2	2^2	2^2	2^2	2^3	2^3	2^4	$\cdots$

The multiplication of 70000-bit numbers would cause this step to terminate with $k = 6$, since $70000 < 2^{13} + 2^{16}$.$\bigr)$

T2. [Put u, v on stack.] Put code-1 on stack C, then place u and v onto stack C as numbers of exactly $q_{k-1} + q_k$ bits each.

T3. [Check recursion level.] Decrease k by 1. If $k = 0$, the top of stack C now contains two 32-bit numbers, u and v; remove them, set $w \leftarrow uv$ using a built-in routine for multiplying 32-bit numbers, and go to step T10. If $k > 0$, set $r \leftarrow r_k$, $q \leftarrow q_k$, $p \leftarrow q_{k-1} + q_k$, and go on to step T4.

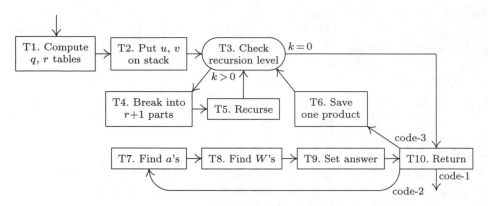

Fig. 8. The Toom–Cook algorithm for high-precision multiplication.

T4. [Break into $r+1$ parts.] Let the number at the top of stack C be regarded as a list of $r+1$ numbers with q bits each, $(U_r \ldots U_1 U_0)_{2^q}$. (The top of stack C now contains an $(r+1)q = (q_k + q_{k+1})$-bit number.) For $j = 0, 1, \ldots, 2r$, compute the p-bit numbers

$$\big(\ldots (U_r j + U_{r-1})j + \cdots + U_1\big)j + U_0 = U(j)$$

and successively put these values onto stack U. (The bottom of stack U now contains $U(0)$, then comes $U(1)$, etc., with $U(2r)$ on top. We have

$$U(j) \le U(2r) < 2^q\big((2r)^r + (2r)^{r-1} + \cdots + 1\big) < 2^{q+1}(2r)^r \le 2^p,$$

by exercise 3.) Then remove $U_r \ldots U_1 U_0$ from stack C.

Now the top of stack C contains another list of $r+1$ q-bit numbers, $V_r \ldots V_1 V_0$, and the p-bit numbers

$$\big(\ldots (V_r j + V_{r-1})j + \cdots + V_1\big)j + V_0 = V(j)$$

should be put onto stack V in the same way. After this has been done, remove $V_r \ldots V_1 V_0$ from stack C.

T5. [Recurse.] Successively put the following items onto stack C, at the same time emptying stacks U and V:

$$\text{code-2, } V(2r), U(2r), \text{ code-3, } V(2r-1), U(2r-1), \ldots,$$
$$\text{code-3, } V(1), U(1), \text{ code-3, } V(0), U(0).$$

Go back to step T3.

T6. [Save one product.] (At this point the multiplication algorithm has set w to one of the products $W(j) = U(j)V(j)$.) Put w onto stack W. (This number w contains $2(q_k + q_{k-1})$ bits.) Go back to step T3.

T7. [Find a's.] Set $r \leftarrow r_k$, $q \leftarrow q_k$, $p \leftarrow q_{k-1} + q_k$. (At this point stack W contains a sequence of numbers ending with $W(0), W(1), \ldots, W(2r)$ from bottom to top, where each $W(j)$ is a $2p$-bit number.)

Now for $j = 1, 2, 3, \ldots, 2r$, perform the following loop: For $t = 2r$, $2r - 1$, $2r - 2$, $\ldots$, j, set $W(t) \leftarrow (W(t) - W(t-1))/j$. (Here j must increase and t must decrease. The quantity $(W(t) - W(t-1))/j$ will always be a nonnegative integer that fits in $2p$ bits; see (16).)

T8. [Find W's.] For $j = 2r - 1, 2r - 2, \ldots, 1$, perform the following loop: For $t = j, j+1, \ldots, 2r - 1$, set $W(t) \leftarrow W(t) - jW(t+1)$. (Here j must decrease and t must increase. The result of this operation will again be a nonnegative $2p$-bit integer; see (18).)

T9. [Set answer.] Set w to the $2(q_k + q_{k+1})$-bit integer

$$(\ldots (W(2r)2^q + W(2r - 1))2^q + \cdots + W(1))2^q + W(0).$$

Remove $W(2r), \ldots, W(0)$ from stack W.

T10. [Return.] Set $k \leftarrow k + 1$. Remove the top of stack C. If it is code-3, go to step T6. If it is code-2, put w onto stack W and go to step T7. And if it is code-1, terminate the algorithm (w is the answer). ∎

Let us now estimate the running time, $T(n)$, for Algorithm T, in terms of some things we shall call "cycles," that is, elementary machine operations. Step T1 takes $O(q_k)$ cycles, even if we represent the number q_k internally as a long string of q_k bits followed by some delimiter, since $q_k + q_{k-1} + \cdots + q_0$ will be $O(q_k)$. Step T2 obviously takes $O(q_k)$ cycles.

Now let t_k denote the amount of computation required to get from step T3 to step T10 for a particular value of k (after k has been decreased at the beginning of step T3). Step T3 requires $O(q)$ cycles at most. Step T4 involves r multiplications of q-bit numbers by $(\lg 2r)$-bit numbers, and r additions of p-bit numbers, all repeated $4r + 2$ times. Thus we need a total of $O(r^2 q \log r)$ cycles. Step T5 requires moving $4r+2$ p-bit numbers, so it involves $O(rq)$ cycles. Step T6 requires $O(q)$ cycles, and it is done $2r + 1$ times per iteration. The recursion involved when the algorithm essentially invokes itself (by returning to step T3) requires t_{k-1} cycles, $2r + 1$ times. Step T7 requires $O(r^2)$ subtractions of p-bit numbers and divisions of $2p$-bit by $(\lg 2r)$-bit numbers, so it requires $O(r^2 q \log r)$ cycles. Similarly, step T8 requires $O(r^2 q \log r)$ cycles. Step T9 involves $O(rq)$ cycles, and T10 takes hardly any time at all.

Summing up, we have $T(n) = O(q_k) + O(q_k) + t_{k-1}$, where (if $q = q_k$ and $r = r_k$) the main contribution to the running time satisfies

$$t_k = O(q) + O(r^2 q \log r) + O(rq) + (2r + 1)O(q) + O(r^2 q \log r)$$
$$+ O(r^2 q \log r) + O(rq) + O(q) + (2r + 1)t_{k-1}$$

$$= O(r^2 q \log r) + (2r + 1)t_{k-1}.$$

Thus there is a constant c such that

$$t_k \leq c r_k^2 q_k \lg r_k + (2r_k + 1)t_{k-1}.$$

To complete the estimation of t_k we can prove by brute force that

$$t_k \leq C q_{k+1} 2^{2.5\sqrt{\lg q_{k+1}}} \tag{20}$$

for some constant C. Let us choose $C > 20c$, and let us also take C large enough so that (20) is valid for $k \le k_0$, where k_0 will be specified below. Then when $k > k_0$, let $Q_k = \lg q_k$, $R_k = \lg r_k$; we have by induction

$$t_k \le c q_k r_k^2 \lg r_k + (2r_k + 1)C q_k 2^{2.5\sqrt{Q_k}} = C q_{k+1} 2^{2.5\sqrt{\lg q_{k+1}}}(\eta_1 + \eta_2),$$

where

$$\eta_1 = \frac{c}{C} R_k 2^{R_k - 2.5\sqrt{Q_{k+1}}} < \frac{1}{20} R_k 2^{-R_k} < 0.05,$$

$$\eta_2 = \left(2 + \frac{1}{r_k}\right) 2^{2.5(\sqrt{Q_k} - \sqrt{Q_{k+1}})} \to 2^{-1/4} < 0.85,$$

since

$$\sqrt{Q_{k+1}} - \sqrt{Q_k} = \sqrt{Q_k + \lfloor\sqrt{Q_k}\rfloor} - \sqrt{Q_k} \to \tfrac{1}{2}$$

as $k \to \infty$. It follows that we can find k_0 such that $\eta_2 < 0.95$ for all $k > k_0$, and this completes the proof of (20) by induction.

Finally, therefore, we are ready to estimate $T(n)$. Since $n > q_{k-1} + q_{k-2}$, we have $q_{k-1} < n$; hence

$$r_{k-1} = 2^{\lfloor\sqrt{\lg q_{k-1}}\rfloor} < 2^{\sqrt{\lg n}}, \qquad \text{and} \qquad q_k = r_{k-1} q_{k-1} < n 2^{\sqrt{\lg n}}.$$

Thus

$$t_{k-1} \le C q_k 2^{2.5\sqrt{\lg q_k}} < C n 2^{\sqrt{\lg n} + 2.5(\sqrt{\lg n} + 1)},$$

and, since $T(n) = O(q_k) + t_{k-1}$, we have derived the following theorem:

Theorem B. *There is a constant c_0 such that the execution time of Algorithm T is less than $c_0 n 2^{3.5\sqrt{\lg n}}$ cycles.* ∎

Since $n 2^{3.5\sqrt{\lg n}} = n^{1+3.5/\sqrt{\lg n}}$, this result is noticeably stronger than Theorem A. By adding a few complications to the algorithm, pushing the ideas to their apparent limits (see exercise 5), we can improve the estimated execution time to

$$T(n) = O(n 2^{\sqrt{2\lg n}} \log n). \tag{21}$$

*B. A modular method. There is another way to multiply large numbers very rapidly, based on the ideas of modular arithmetic as presented in Section 4.3.2. It is very hard to believe at first that this method can be of advantage, since a multiplication algorithm based on modular arithmetic must include the choice of moduli and the conversion of numbers into and out of modular representation, besides the actual multiplication operation itself. In spite of these formidable difficulties, A. Schönhage discovered that all of these operations can be carried out quite rapidly.

In order to understand the essential mechanism of Schönhage's method, we shall look at a special case. Consider the sequence defined by the rules

$$q_0 = 1, \qquad q_{k+1} = 3q_k - 1, \tag{22}$$

so that $q_k = 3^k - 3^{k-1} - \cdots - 1 = \tfrac{1}{2}(3^k + 1)$. We will study a procedure that multiplies p_k-bit numbers, where $p_k = (18q_k + 8)$, in terms of a method for multiplying p_{k-1}-bit numbers. Thus, if we know how to multiply numbers having $p_0 = 26$ bits, the procedure to be described will show us how to multiply numbers of $p_1 = 44$ bits, then 98 bits, then 260 bits, etc., eventually increasing the number of bits by almost a factor of 3 at each step.

When multiplying p_k-bit numbers, the idea is to use the six moduli

$$m_1 = 2^{6q_k-1} - 1, \qquad m_2 = 2^{6q_k+1} - 1, \qquad m_3 = 2^{6q_k+2} - 1,$$
$$m_4 = 2^{6q_k+3} - 1, \qquad m_5 = 2^{6q_k+5} - 1, \qquad m_6 = 2^{6q_k+7} - 1. \tag{23}$$

These moduli are relatively prime, by Eq. 4.3.2–(19), since the exponents

$$6q_k - 1, \quad 6q_k + 1, \quad 6q_k + 2, \quad 6q_k + 3, \quad 6q_k + 5, \quad 6q_k + 7 \tag{24}$$

are always relatively prime (see exercise 6). The six moduli in (23) are capable of representing numbers up to $m = m_1 m_2 m_3 m_4 m_5 m_6 > 2^{36q_k+16} = 2^{2p_k}$, so there is no chance of overflow in the multiplication of p_k-bit numbers u and v. Thus we can use the following method, when $k > 0$:

a) Compute $u_1 = u \bmod m_1$, ..., $u_6 = u \bmod m_6$; and $v_1 = v \bmod m_1$, ..., $v_6 = v \bmod m_6$.

b) Multiply u_1 by v_1, u_2 by v_2, ..., u_6 by v_6. These are numbers of at most $6q_k + 7 = 18q_{k-1} + 1 < p_{k-1}$ bits, so the multiplications can be performed by using the assumed p_{k-1}-bit multiplication procedure.

c) Compute $w_1 = u_1 v_1 \bmod m_1$, $w_2 = u_2 v_2 \bmod m_2$, ..., $w_6 = u_6 v_6 \bmod m_6$.

d) Compute w such that $0 \le w < m$, $w \bmod m_1 = w_1$, ..., $w \bmod m_6 = w_6$.

Let t_k be the amount of time needed for this process. It is not hard to see that operation (a) takes $O(p_k)$ cycles, since the determination of $u \bmod (2^e - 1)$ is quite simple (like "casting out nines"), as shown in Section 4.3.2. Similarly, operation (c) takes $O(p_k)$ cycles. Operation (b) requires essentially $6t_{k-1}$ cycles. This leaves us with operation (d), which seems to be quite a difficult computation; but Schönhage has found an ingenious way to perform step (d) in $O(p_k \log p_k)$ cycles, and this is the crux of the method. As a consequence, we have

$$t_k = 6t_{k-1} + O(p_k \log p_k).$$

Since $p_k = 3^{k+2} + 17$, we can show that the time for n-bit multiplication is

$$T(n) = O(n^{\log_3 6}) = O(n^{1.631}). \tag{25}$$

(See exercise 7.)

Although the modular method is more complicated than the $O(n^{\lg 3})$ procedure discussed at the beginning of this section, Eq. (25) shows that it does, in fact, lead to an execution time substantially better than $O(n^2)$ for the multiplication of n-bit numbers. Thus we have seen how to improve on the classical method by using either of two completely different approaches.

Let us now analyze operation (d) above. Assume that we are given a set of positive integers $e_1 < e_2 < \cdots < e_r$, relatively prime in pairs; let

$$m_1 = 2^{e_1} - 1, \qquad m_2 = 2^{e_2} - 1, \qquad \ldots, \qquad m_r = 2^{e_r} - 1. \tag{26}$$

We are also given numbers $w_1, \ldots, w_r$ such that $0 \leq w_j \leq m_j$. Our job is to determine the binary representation of the number w that satisfies the conditions

$$0 \leq w < m_1 m_2 \ldots m_r,$$

$$w \equiv w_1 \pmod{m_1}, \qquad \ldots, \qquad w \equiv w_r \pmod{m_r}. \tag{27}$$

The method is based on (24) and (25) of Section 4.3.2. First we compute

$$w'_j = \big(\ldots ((w_j - w'_1) c_{1j} - w'_2) c_{2j} - \cdots - w'_{j-1}\big) c_{(j-1)j} \bmod m_j, \tag{28}$$

for $j = 2, \ldots, r$, where $w'_1 = w_1 \bmod m_1$; then we compute

$$w = \big(\ldots (w'_r m_{r-1} + w'_{r-1}) m_{r-2} + \cdots + w'_2\big) m_1 + w'_1. \tag{29}$$

Here c_{ij} is a number such that $c_{ij} m_i \equiv 1 \pmod{m_j}$; these numbers c_{ij} are not given, they must be determined from the e_j's.

The calculation of (28) for all j involves $\binom{r}{2}$ additions modulo m_j, each of which takes $O(e_r)$ cycles, plus $\binom{r}{2}$ multiplications by c_{ij}, modulo m_j. The calculation of w by formula (29) involves r additions and r multiplications by m_j; it is easy to multiply by m_j, since this is just adding, shifting, and subtracting, so it is clear that the evaluation of Eq. (29) takes $O(r^2 e_r)$ cycles. We will soon see that each of the multiplications by c_{ij}, modulo m_j, requires only $O(e_r \log e_r)$ cycles, and therefore *it is possible to complete the entire job of conversion in $O(r^2 e_r \log e_r)$ cycles.*

These observations leave us with the following problem to solve: Given relatively prime positive integers e and f with $e < f$, and a nonnegative integer $u < 2^f$, compute the value of $(cu) \bmod (2^f - 1)$, where c is the number such that $(2^e - 1)c \equiv 1 \pmod{2^f - 1}$; this entire computation must be done in $O(f \log f)$ cycles. The result of exercise 4.3.2–6 gives a formula for c that suggests a suitable procedure. First we find the least positive integer b such that

$$be \equiv 1 \pmod{f}. \tag{30}$$

Euclid's algorithm will discover b in $O((\log f)^3)$ cycles, since it requires $O(\log f)$ iterations when applied to e and f, and each iteration requires $O((\log f)^2)$ cycles. Alternatively, we could be very sloppy here without violating the total time constraint, by simply trying $b = 1, 2$, etc., until (30) is satisfied; such a process would take $O(f \log f)$ cycles in all. Once b has been found, exercise 4.3.2–6 tells us that

$$c = c[b] = \left(\sum_{0 \leq j < b} 2^{je} \right) \bmod (2^f - 1). \tag{31}$$

A brute-force multiplication of $(cu) \bmod (2^f - 1)$ would not be good enough to solve the problem, since we do not know how to multiply general f-bit numbers in $O(f \log f)$ cycles. But the special form of c provides a clue: The binary representation of c is composed of bits in a regular pattern, and Eq. (31) shows that the number $c[2b]$ can be obtained in a simple way from $c[b]$. This suggests that we can rapidly multiply a number u by $c[b]$ if we build $c[b]u$ up in $\lg b$ steps in a suitably clever manner, such as the following: Suppose b is

$$b = (b_s \ldots b_2 b_1 b_0)_2$$

in binary notation; we can calculate four sequences a_k, d_k, u_k, v_k defined by

$$
\begin{aligned}
a_0 &= e, & a_k &= 2a_{k-1} \bmod f; \\
d_0 &= b_0 e, & d_k &= (d_{k-1} + b_k a_k) \bmod f; \\
u_0 &= u, & u_k &= (u_{k-1} + 2^{a_{k-1}} u_{k-1}) \bmod (2^f - 1); \\
v_0 &= b_0 u, & v_k &= (v_{k-1} + b_k 2^{d_{k-1}} u_k) \bmod (2^f - 1).
\end{aligned}
\tag{32}
$$

It is easy to prove by induction on k that

$$
\begin{aligned}
a_k &= (2^k e) \bmod f; & u_k &= (c[2^k] u) \bmod (2^f - 1); \\
d_k &= ((b_k \ldots b_1 b_0)_2\, e) \bmod f; & v_k &= (c[(b_k \ldots b_1 b_0)_2] u) \bmod (2^f - 1).
\end{aligned}
\tag{33}
$$

Hence the desired result, $(c[b]u) \bmod (2^f - 1)$, is v_s. The calculation of a_k, d_k, u_k, and v_k from a_{k-1}, d_{k-1}, u_{k-1}, v_{k-1} takes $O(\log f) + O(\log f) + O(f) + O(f) = O(f)$ cycles; consequently the entire calculation can be done in $s\,O(f) = O(f \log f)$ cycles as desired.

The reader will find it instructive to study the ingenious method represented by (32) and (33) very carefully. Similar techniques are discussed in Section 4.6.3.

Schönhage's paper [*Computing* **1** (1966), 182–196] shows that these ideas can be extended to the multiplication of n-bit numbers using $r \approx 2^{\sqrt{2\lg n}}$ moduli, obtaining a method analogous to Algorithm T. We shall not dwell on the details here, since Algorithm T is always superior; in fact, an even better method is next on our agenda.

C. Discrete Fourier transforms. The critical problem in high-precision multiplication is the determination of "convolution products" such as

$$u_r v_0 + u_{r-1} v_1 + \cdots + u_0 v_r, \tag{34}$$

and there is an intimate relation between convolutions and an important mathematical concept called "Fourier transformation." If $\omega = \exp(2\pi i / K)$ is a Kth root of unity, the one-dimensional Fourier transform of the sequence of complex numbers $(u_0, u_1, \ldots, u_{K-1})$ is defined to be the sequence $(\hat{u}_0, \hat{u}_1, \ldots, \hat{u}_{K-1})$, where

$$\hat{u}_s = \sum_{0 \le t < K} \omega^{st} u_t, \qquad 0 \le s < K. \tag{35}$$

Letting $(\hat{v}_0, \hat{v}_1, \ldots, \hat{v}_{K-1})$ be defined in the same way, as the Fourier transform of $(v_0, v_1, \ldots, v_{K-1})$, it is not difficult to see that $(\hat{u}_0 \hat{v}_0, \hat{u}_1 \hat{v}_1, \ldots, \hat{u}_{K-1} \hat{v}_{K-1})$ is the transform of $(w_0, w_1, \ldots, w_{K-1})$, where

$$
\begin{aligned}
w_r &= u_r v_0 + u_{r-1} v_1 + \cdots + u_0 v_r + u_{K-1} v_{r+1} + \cdots + u_{r+1} v_{K-1} \\
&= \sum_{i+j \equiv r \pmod{K}} u_i v_j.
\end{aligned}
\tag{36}
$$

When $K \geq 2n - 1$ and $u_n = u_{n+1} = \cdots = u_{K-1} = v_n = v_{n+1} = \cdots = v_{K-1} = 0$, the w's are just what we need for multiplication, since the terms $u_{K-1}v_{r+1} + \cdots + u_{r+1}v_{K-1}$ vanish when $0 \leq r \leq 2n - 2$. In other words, *the transform of a convolution product is the ordinary product of the transforms.* This idea is actually a special case of Toom's use of polynomials (see (10)), with x replaced by roots of unity.

If K is a power of 2, the discrete Fourier transform (35) can be obtained quite rapidly when the computations are arranged in a certain way, and so can the inverse transform (determining the w's from the $\hat{w}$'s). This property of Fourier transforms was exploited by V. Strassen in 1968, who discovered how to multiply large numbers faster than was possible under all previously known schemes. He and A. Schönhage later refined the method and published improved procedures in *Computing* **7** (1971), 281–292. Similar ideas, but with all-integer methods, had been worked out independently by J. M. Pollard [*Math. Comp.* **25** (1971), 365–374]. In order to understand their approach to the problem, let us first take a look at the mechanism of fast Fourier transforms.

Given a sequence of $K = 2^k$ complex numbers $(u_0, \ldots, u_{K-1})$, and given the complex number

$$\omega = \exp(2\pi i / K), \tag{37}$$

the sequence $(\hat{u}_0, \ldots, \hat{u}_{K-1})$ defined in (35) can be calculated rapidly by carrying out the following scheme. (In these formulas the parameters s_j and t_j are either 0 or 1, so that each "pass" represents 2^k elementary computations.)

Pass 0. Let $A^{[0]}(t_{k-1}, \ldots, t_0) = u_t$, where $t = (t_{k-1} \ldots t_0)_2$.

Pass 1. Set $A^{[1]}(s_{k-1}, t_{k-2}, \ldots, t_0) \leftarrow$
$$A^{[0]}(0, t_{k-2}, \ldots, t_0) + \omega^{2^{k-1}s_{k-1}} A^{[0]}(1, t_{k-2}, \ldots, t_0).$$

Pass 2. Set $A^{[2]}(s_{k-1}, s_{k-2}, t_{k-3}, \ldots, t_0) \leftarrow$
$$A^{[1]}(s_{k-1}, 0, t_{k-3}, \ldots, t_0) + \omega^{2^{k-2}(s_{k-2}s_{k-1})_2} A^{[1]}(s_{k-1}, 1, t_{k-3}, \ldots, t_0).$$

$\cdots$

Pass k. Set $A^{[k]}(s_{k-1}, \ldots, s_1, s_0) \leftarrow$
$$A^{[k-1]}(s_{k-1}, \ldots, s_1, 0) + \omega^{(s_0 s_1 \ldots s_{k-1})_2} A^{[k-1]}(s_{k-1}, \ldots, s_1, 1).$$

It is fairly easy to prove by induction that we have

$$A^{[j]}(s_{k-1}, \ldots, s_{k-j}, t_{k-j-1}, \ldots, t_0) = \sum_{0 \leq t_{k-1}, \ldots, t_{k-j} \leq 1} \omega^{2^{k-j}(s_{k-j} \ldots s_{k-1})_2 (t_{k-1} \ldots t_{k-j})_2} u_t, \tag{38}$$

where $t = (t_{k-1} \ldots t_1 t_0)_2$, so that

$$A^{[k]}(s_{k-1}, \ldots, s_1, s_0) = \hat{u}_s, \qquad \text{where } s = (s_0 s_1 \ldots s_{k-1})_2. \tag{39}$$

(It is important to notice that the binary digits of s are reversed in the final result (39). Section 4.6.4 contains further discussion of transforms such as this.)

To get the inverse Fourier transform $(u_0, \ldots, u_{K-1})$ from the values of $(\hat{u}_0, \ldots, \hat{u}_{K-1})$, notice that the "double transform" is

$$\hat{\hat{u}}_r = \sum_{0 \le s < K} w^{rs} \hat{u}_s = \sum_{0 \le s,t < K} w^{rs} w^{st} u_t$$

$$= \sum_{0 \le t < K} u_t \left(\sum_{0 \le s < K} w^{s(t+r)} \right) = K u_{(-r) \bmod K}, \qquad (40)$$

since the geometric series $\sum_{0 \le s < K} w^{sj}$ sums to zero unless j is a multiple of K. Therefore the inverse transform can be computed in the same way as the transform itself, except that the final results must be divided by K and shuffled slightly.

Returning to the problem of integer multiplication, suppose we wish to compute the product of two n-bit integers u and v. As in Algorithm T we shall work with groups of bits; let

$$2n \le 2^k l < 4n, \qquad K = 2^k, \qquad L = 2^l, \qquad (41)$$

and write

$$u = (U_{K-1} \ldots U_1 U_0)_L, \qquad v = (V_{K-1} \ldots V_1 V_0)_L, \qquad (42)$$

regarding u and v as K-place numbers in radix L so that each digit U_j or V_j is an l-bit integer. Actually the leading digits U_j and V_j are zero for all $j \ge K/2$, because $2^{k-1} l \ge n$. We will select appropriate values for k and l later; at the moment our goal is to see what happens in general, so that we can choose k and l intelligently when all the facts are before us.

The next step of the multiplication procedure is to compute the Fourier transforms $(\hat{u}_0, \ldots, \hat{u}_{K-1})$ and $(\hat{v}_0, \ldots, \hat{v}_{K-1})$ of the sequences $(u_0, \ldots, u_{K-1})$ and $(v_0, \ldots, v_{K-1})$, where we define

$$u_t = U_t / 2^{k+l}, \qquad v_t = V_t / 2^{k+l}. \qquad (43)$$

This scaling is done for convenience so that each u_t and v_t is less than 2^{-k}, ensuring that the absolute values $|\hat{u}_s|$ and $|\hat{v}_s|$ will be less than 1 for all s.

An obvious problem arises here, since the complex number w can't be represented exactly in binary notation. How are we going to compute a reliable Fourier transform? By a stroke of good luck, it turns out that everything will work properly if we do the calculations with only a modest amount of precision. For the moment let us bypass this question and assume that infinite-precision calculations are being performed; we shall analyze later how much accuracy is actually needed.

Once the $\hat{u}_s$ and $\hat{v}_s$ have been found, we let $\hat{w}_s = \hat{u}_s \hat{v}_s$ for $0 \le s < K$ and determine the inverse Fourier transform $(w_0, \ldots, w_{K-1})$. As explained above, we now have

$$w_r = \sum_{i+j=r} u_i v_j = \sum_{i+j=r} U_i V_j / 2^{2k+2l},$$

Table 1
MULTIPLICATION VIA DISCRETE FOURIER TRANSFORMATION

s	$2^7\hat{u}_s$	$2^7\hat{v}_s$	$2^{14}\hat{w}_s$	$2^{14}\hat{\hat{w}}_s$	$2^{14}w_s = W_s$
0	19	16	304	80	10
1	$2 + 4i + 13\omega$	$5 + 9i + 2\omega$	$-26 + 64i + 69\omega - 125\bar{\omega}$	0	69
2	$-2 + 13i$	$-4 + 2i$	$-18 - 56i$	0	64
3	$2 - 4i - 13\bar{\omega}$	$5 - 9i - 2\bar{\omega}$	$-26 - 64i + 125\omega - 69\bar{\omega}$	0	125
4	-7	12	-84	288	36
5	$2 + 4i - 13\omega$	$5 + 9i - 2\omega$	$-26 + 64i - 69\omega + 125\bar{\omega}$	1000	0
6	$-2 - 13i$	$-4 - 2i$	$-18 + 56i$	512	0
7	$2 - 4i + 13\bar{\omega}$	$5 - 9i + 2\bar{\omega}$	$-26 - 64i - 125\omega + 69\bar{\omega}$	552	0

so the integers $W_r = 2^{2k+2l}w_r$ are the coefficients in the desired product

$$u \cdot v = W_{K-2}L^{K-2} + \cdots + W_1L + W_0. \tag{44}$$

Since $0 \le W_r < (r+1)L^2 < KL^2$, each W_r has at most $k + 2l$ bits, so it will not be difficult to compute the binary representation when the W's are known unless k is large compared to l.

For example, suppose we want to multiply $u = 1234$ times $v = 2341$ when the parameters are $k = 3$ and $l = 4$. The computation of $(\hat{u}_0, \ldots, \hat{u}_7)$ from u proceeds as follows (see (12)):

$(r,s,t) =$	$(0,0,0)$	$(0,0,1)$	$(0,1,0)$	$(0,1,1)$	$(1,0,0)$	$(1,0,1)$	$(1,1,0)$	$(1,1,1)$
$2^7A^{[0]}(r,s,t) =$	2	13	4	0	0	0	0	0
$2^7A^{[1]}(r,s,t) =$	2	13	4	0	2	13	4	0
$2^7A^{[2]}(r,s,t) =$	6	13	-2	13	$2 + 4i$	13	$2 - 4i$	13
$2^7A^{[3]}(r,s,t) =$	19	-7	$-2 + 13i$	$-2 - 13i$	$\alpha + \beta$	$\alpha - \beta$	$\bar{\alpha} - \bar{\beta}$	$\bar{\alpha} + \bar{\beta}$

Here $\alpha = 2 + 4i$, $\beta = 13\omega$, and $\omega = (1 + i)/\sqrt{2}$; this gives us the column headed $2^7\hat{u}_s$ in Table 1. The column for $2^7\hat{v}_s$ is obtained from v in the same way; then we multiply $\hat{u}_s$ by $\hat{v}_s$ to get $\hat{w}_s$. Transforming again gives us w_s and W_s, using relation (40). Once again we obtain the convolution products in (19), this time using complex numbers instead of sticking to an all-integer method.

Let us try to estimate how much time this method takes on large numbers, if m-bit fixed point arithmetic is used in calculating the Fourier transforms. Exercise 10 shows that all of the quantities $A^{[j]}$ during all the passes of the transform calculations will be less than 1 in magnitude because of the scaling (43), hence it suffices to deal with m-bit fractions $(.a_{-1} \ldots a_{-m})_2$ for the real and imaginary parts of all the intermediate quantities. Simplifications are possible because the inputs u_t and v_t are real-valued; only K real values instead of $2K$ need to be carried in each step (see exercise 4.6.4–14). We will ignore such refinements in order to keep complications to a minimum.

The first job is to compute ω and its powers. For simplicity we shall make a table of the values $\omega^0, \ldots, \omega^{K-1}$. Let

$$\omega_r = \exp(2\pi i/2^r), \tag{45}$$

so that $\omega_1 = -1$, $\omega_2 = i$, $\omega_3 = (1+i)/\sqrt{2}$, ..., $\omega_k = \omega$. If $\omega_r = x_r + iy_r$ and $r \geq 2$, we have $\omega_{r+1} = x_{r+1} + iy_{r+1}$ where

$$x_{r+1} = \sqrt{\frac{1+x_r}{2}}, \qquad y_{r+1} = \frac{y_r}{2x_{r+1}}. \tag{46}$$

[See S. R. Tate, *IEEE Transactions* **SP-43** (1995), 1709–1711.] The calculation of ω_1, ω_2, ..., ω_k takes negligible time compared with the other computations we need, so we can use any straightforward algorithm for square roots. Once the ω_r have been calculated we can compute all of the powers ω^j by noting that

$$\omega^j = \omega_1^{j_{k-1}} \ldots \omega_{k-1}^{j_1} \omega_k^{j_0} \qquad \text{if } j = (j_{k-1} \ldots j_1 j_0)_2. \tag{47}$$

This method of calculation keeps errors from propagating, since each ω^j is a product of at most k of the ω_r's. The total time to calculate all the ω^j is $O(KM)$, where M is the time to do an m-bit complex multiplication, because only one multiplication is needed to obtain each ω^j from a previously computed value. The subsequent steps will require more than $O(KM)$ cycles, so the powers of ω have been computed at negligible cost.

Each of the three Fourier transformations comprises k passes, each of which involves K operations of the form $a \leftarrow b + \omega^j c$, so the total time to calculate the Fourier transforms is

$$O(kKM) = O(Mnk/l).$$

Finally, the work involved in computing the binary digits of $u \cdot v$ using (44) is $O\big(K(k+l)\big) = O(n + nk/l)$. Summing over all operations, we find that the total time to multiply n-bit numbers u and v will be $O(n) + O(Mnk/l)$.

Now let's see how large the intermediate precision m needs to be, so that we know how large M needs to be. For simplicity we shall be content with safe estimates of the accuracy, instead of finding the best possible bounds. It will be convenient to compute all the ω^j in such a way that our approximations $(\omega^j)'$ will satisfy $|(\omega^j)'| \leq 1$; this condition is easy to guarantee if we truncate towards zero instead of rounding, because $x_{r+1}^2 + y_{r+1}^2 = (1 + x_r^2 + y_r^2 + 2x_r)/(2 + 2x_r)$ in (46). The operations we need to perform with m-bit fixed point complex arithmetic are all obtained by replacing an exact computation of the form $a \leftarrow b + \omega^j c$ by the approximate computation

$$a' \leftarrow \text{truncate}\big(b' + (\omega^j)'c'\big), \tag{48}$$

where b', $(\omega^j)'$, and c' are previously computed approximations; all of these complex numbers and their approximations are bounded by 1 in absolute value. If $|b' - b| \leq \delta_1$, $|(\omega^j)' - \omega^j| \leq \delta_2$, and $|c' - c| \leq \delta_3$, it is not difficult to see that we will have $|a' - a| < \delta + \delta_1 + \delta_2 + \delta_3$, where

$$\delta = |2^{-m} + 2^{-m}i| = 2^{1/2-m}, \tag{49}$$

because we have $\big|(\omega^j)'c' - \omega^j c\big| = \big|((\omega^j)' - \omega^j)c' + \omega^j(c' - c)\big| \leq \delta_2 + \delta_3$, and δ exceeds the maximum truncation error. The approximations $(\omega^j)'$ are obtained by starting with approximations ω_r' to the numbers defined in (46), and we may assume that (46) is performed with sufficient precision to make $|\omega_r' - \omega_r| < \delta$. Then (47) implies that $|(\omega^j)' - \omega^j| < (2k-1)\delta$ for all j, because the error is due to at most k approximations and $k-1$ truncations.

If we have errors of at most ϵ before any pass of the fast Fourier transform, the operations of that pass therefore have the form (48) where $\delta_1 = \delta_3 = \epsilon$ and $\delta_2 = (2k-1)\delta$; the errors after the pass will then be at most $2\epsilon + 2k\delta$. There is no error in Pass 0, so we find by induction on j that the maximum error after Pass j is bounded by $(2^j - 1) \cdot 2k\delta$, and the computed values of $\hat{u}_s$ will satisfy $|(\hat{u}_s)' - \hat{u}_s| < (2^k - 1) \cdot 2k\delta$. A similar formula will hold for $(\hat{v}_s)'$; and we will have

$$|(\hat{w}_s)' - \hat{w}_s| < 2(2^k - 1) \cdot 2k\delta + \delta < (4k2^k - 2k)\delta.$$

During the inverse transformation there is an additional accumulation of errors, but the division by $K = 2^k$ ameliorates most of this; by the same argument we find that the computed values w_r' will satisfy

$$|(\hat{w}_r)' - \hat{w}_r| < 2^k(4k2^k - 2k)\delta + (2^k - 1)2k\delta; \quad |w_r' - w_r| < 4k2^k\delta. \tag{50}$$

We need enough precision to make $2^{2k+2l}w_r'$ round to the correct integer W_r, hence we need

$$2^{2k+2l+2+\lg k+k+1/2-m} \le \tfrac{1}{2}; \tag{51}$$

that is, $m \ge 3k + 2l + \lg k + 7/2$. This will hold if we simply require that

$$k \ge 7 \qquad \text{and} \qquad m \ge 4k + 2l. \tag{52}$$

Relations (41) and (52) can be used to determine parameters k, l, m so that multiplication takes $O(n) + O(Mnk/l)$ units of time, where M is the time to multiply m-bit fractions.

If we are using MIX, for example, suppose we want to multiply binary numbers having $n = 2^{13} = 8192$ bits each. We can choose $k = 11$, $l = 8$, $m = 60$, so that the necessary m-bit operations are nothing more than double-precision arithmetic. The running time M needed to do fixed point m-bit complex multiplication will therefore be comparatively small. With triple-precision operations we can go up for example to $k = l = 15$, $n \le 15 \cdot 2^{14}$, which takes us way beyond MIX's memory capacity. On a larger machine we could multiply a pair of gigabit numbers if we took $k = l = 27$ and $m = 144$.

Further study of the choice of k, l, and m leads in fact to a rather surprising conclusion: *For all practical purposes we can assume that M is constant, and the Schönhage–Strassen multiplication technique will have a running time linearly proportional to n.* The reason is that we can choose $k = l$ and $m = 6k$; this choice of k is always less than $\lg n$, so we will never need to use more than sextuple precision unless n is larger than the word size of our computer. (In particular, n would have to be larger than the capacity of an index register, so we probably couldn't fit the numbers u and v in main memory.)

The practical problem of fast multiplication is therefore solved, except for improvements in the constant factor. In fact, the all-integer convolution algorithm of exercise 4.6.4–59 is probably a better choice for practical high-precision multiplication. Our interest in multiplying large numbers is partly theoretical, however, because it is interesting to explore the ultimate limits of computational complexity. So let's forget practical considerations momentarily and suppose that n is extremely huge, perhaps much larger than the number of atoms in the universe. We can let m be approximately $6 \lg n$, and use the same algorithm recursively to do the m-bit multiplications. The running time will satisfy $T(n) = O(nT(\log n))$; hence

$$T(n) \leq C\, n (C \lg n)(C \lg \lg n)(C \lg \lg \lg n) \ldots , \tag{53}$$

where the product continues until reaching a factor with $\lg \ldots \lg n \leq 2$.

Schönhage and Strassen showed how to improve this theoretical upper bound to $O(n \log n \log \log n)$ in their paper, by using *integer* numbers ω to carry out fast Fourier transforms on integers, modulo numbers of the form $2^e + 1$. This upper bound applies to Turing machines, namely to computers with bounded memory and a finite number of arbitrarily long tapes.

If we allow ourselves a more powerful computer, with random access to any number of words of bounded size, Schönhage has pointed out that the upper bound drops to $O(n \log n)$. For we can choose $k = l$ and $m = 6k$, and we have time to build a complete multiplication table of all possible products xy for $0 \leq x, y < 2^{\lceil m/12 \rceil}$. (The number of such products is 2^k or 2^{k+1}, and we can compute each table entry by addition from one of its predecessors in $O(k)$ steps, hence $O(k2^k) = O(n)$ steps will suffice for the calculation.) In this case M is the time needed to do 12-place arithmetic in radix $2^{\lceil m/12 \rceil}$, and it follows that $M = O(k) = O(\log n)$ because 1-place multiplication can be done by table lookup. (The time to access a word of memory is assumed to be proportional to the number of bits in the address of that word.)

In fact, $O(n \log n)$ bit operations suffice also in the ordinary Turing machine model, as shown by D. Harvey and J. van der Hoeven [*Ann. Math.* (2) **193** (2021), 563–617], using asymptotically fast transforms on multivariate polynomials.

Moreover, Schönhage discovered in 1979 that a *pointer machine* can carry out n-bit multiplication in $O(n)$ steps; see exercise 12. Such devices (which are also called "storage modification machines" and "linking automata") seem to provide the best models of computation when $n \to \infty$, as discussed at the end of Section 2.6. In this sense we can conclude that multiplication in $O(n)$ steps is possible for theoretical purposes as well as in practice.

An unusual general-purpose computer called Little Fermat, with a special ability to multiply large integers rapidly, was designed in 1986 by D. V. Chudnovsky, G. V. Chudnovsky, M. M. Denneau, and S. G. Younis. Its hardware featured fast arithmetic modulo $2^{256} + 1$ on 257-bit words; a convolution of 256-word arrays could then be done using 256 single-word multiplications, together with three discrete transforms that required only addition, subtraction, and shifting. This made it possible to multiply two 10^6-bit integers in less than 0.1 second, based on a pipelined cycle time of approximately 60 nanoseconds [*Proc. Third International Conf. on Supercomputing* **2** (International Supercomputing Institute, 1988), 498–499; *Contemporary Math.* **143** (1993), 136].

D. Division.   Now that we have efficient routines for multiplication, let's consider the inverse problem. It turns out that division can be performed just as fast as multiplication, except for a constant factor.

To divide an n-bit number u by an n-bit number v, we can first find an n-bit approximation to $1/v$, then multiply by u to get an approximation $\hat{q}$ to u/v; finally, we can make the slight correction necessary to $\hat{q}$ to ensure that $0 \le u - qv < v$ by using another multiplication. From this reasoning, we see that it suffices to have an efficient way to approximate the reciprocal of an n-bit number. The following algorithm does this, using "Newton's method" as explained at the end of Section 4.3.1.

Algorithm R (*High-precision reciprocal*).   Let v have the binary representation $v = (0.v_1v_2v_3 \ldots)_2$, where $v_1 = 1$. This algorithm computes an approximation z to $1/v$, such that

$$|z - 1/v| \le 2^{-n}. \tag{54}$$

R1. [Initial approximation.] Set $z \leftarrow \frac{1}{4}\lfloor 32/(4v_1 + 2v_2 + v_3)\rfloor$ and $k \leftarrow 0$.

R2. [Newtonian iteration.]   (At this point we have a number z of the binary form $(xx.xx \ldots x)_2$ with $2^k + 1$ places after the radix point, and $z \le 2$.) Calculate $z^2 = (xxx.xx \ldots x)_2$ exactly, using a high-speed multiplication routine. Then calculate $V_k z^2$ exactly, where $V_k = (0.v_1v_2 \ldots v_{2^{k+1}+3})_2$. Then set $z \leftarrow 2z - V_k z^2 + r$, where $0 \le r < 2^{-2^{k+1}-1}$ is added if necessary to round z up so that it is a multiple of $2^{-2^{k+1}-1}$. Finally, set $k \leftarrow k + 1$.

R3. [Done?] If $2^k < n$, go back to step R2; otherwise z is the answer.   ∎

This algorithm is based on a suggestion by S. A. Cook. A similar technique has been used in computer hardware [see Anderson, Earle, Goldschmidt, and Powers, *IBM J. Res. Dev.* **11** (1967), 48–52]. Of course, it is necessary to check the accuracy of Algorithm R quite carefully, because it comes very close to being inaccurate. We will prove by induction that

$$z \le 2 \quad \text{and} \quad |z - 1/v| \le 2^{-2^k} \tag{55}$$

at the beginning and end of step R2.

For this purpose, let $\delta_k = 1/v - z_k$, where z_k is the value of z after k iterations of step R2. To start the induction on k, we have

$$\delta_0 = 1/v - 8/v' + (32/v' - \lfloor 32/v'\rfloor)/4 = \eta_1 + \eta_2,$$

where $v' = (v_1v_2v_3)_2$ and $\eta_1 = (v' - 8v)/vv'$, so that we have $-\frac{1}{2} < \eta_1 \le 0$ and $0 \le \eta_2 < \frac{1}{4}$. Hence $|\delta_0| < \frac{1}{2}$. Now suppose that (55) has been verified for k; then

$$\delta_{k+1} = 1/v - z_{k+1} = 1/v - z_k - z_k(1 - z_kV_k) - r$$
$$= \delta_k - z_k(1 - z_kv) - z_k^2(v - V_k) - r$$
$$= v\delta_k^2 - z_k^2(v - V_k) - r.$$

Now $0 \le v\delta_k^2 < \delta_k^2 \le (2^{-2^k})^2 = 2^{-2^{k+1}}$, and

$$0 \le z^2(v - V_k) + r < 4(2^{-2^{k+1}-3}) + 2^{-2^{k+1}-1} = 2^{-2^{k+1}},$$

so $|\delta_{k+1}| \leq 2^{-2^{k+1}}$. We must still verify the first inequality of (55); to show that $z_{k+1} \leq 2$, there are three cases:

a) $V_k = \frac{1}{2}$; then $z_{k+1} = 2$.

b) $V_k \neq \frac{1}{2} = V_{k-1}$; then $z_k = 2$, so $2z_k - z_k^2 V_k \leq 2 - 2^{-2^{k+1}-1}$.

c) $V_{k-1} \neq \frac{1}{2}$; then $z_{k+1} = 1/v - \delta_{k+1} < 2 - 2^{-2^{k+1}} \leq 2$, since $k > 0$.

The running time of Algorithm R is bounded by

$$2T(4n) + 2T(2n) + 2T(n) + 2T(\tfrac{1}{2}n) + \cdots + O(n)$$

steps, where $T(n)$ is an upper bound on the time needed to do a multiplication of n-bit numbers. If $T(n)$ has the form $nf(n)$ for some monotonically nondecreasing function $f(n)$, we have

$$T(4n) + T(2n) + T(n) + \cdots < T(8n), \tag{56}$$

so division can be done with a speed comparable to that of multiplication except for a constant factor.

R. P. Brent has shown that functions such as $\log x$, $\exp x$, and $\arctan x$ can be evaluated to n significant bits in $O\big(M(n)\log n\big)$ steps, if it takes $M(n)$ units of time to multiply n-bit numbers [*JACM* **23** (1976), 242–251].

E. Multiplication in real time. It is natural to wonder if multiplication of n-bit numbers can be accomplished in just n steps. We have come from order n^2 down to order n, so perhaps we can squeeze the time down to the absolute minimum. In fact, it is actually possible to output the answer as fast as we input the digits, if we leave the domain of conventional computer programming and allow ourselves to build a computer that has an unlimited number of components all acting at once.

A *linear iterative array* of automata is a set of devices M_1, M_2, M_3, ... that can each be in a finite set of "states" at each step of a computation. The machines M_2, M_3, ... all have *identical* circuitry, and their state at time $t + 1$ is a function of their own state at time t as well as the states of their left and right neighbors at time t. The first machine M_1 is slightly different: Its state at time $t + 1$ is a function of its own state and that of M_2, at time t, and also of the *input* at time t. The *output* of a linear iterative array is a function defined on the states of M_1.

Let $u = (u_{n-1} \ldots u_1 u_0)_2$, $v = (v_{n-1} \ldots v_1 v_0)_2$, and $q = (q_{n-1} \ldots q_1 q_0)_2$ be binary numbers, and let $uv + q = w = (w_{2n-1} \ldots w_1 w_0)_2$. It is a remarkable fact that a linear iterative array can be constructed, independent of n, that will output w_0, w_1, w_2, ... at times 1, 2, 3, ..., if it is given the inputs (u_0, v_0, q_0), (u_1, v_1, q_1), (u_2, v_2, q_2), ... at times 0, 1, 2, ...

We can state this phenomenon in the language of computer hardware by saying that it is possible to design a single integrated circuit module with the following property: If we wire together sufficiently many of these chips in a straight line, with each module communicating only with its left and right neighbors, the resulting circuitry will produce the $2n$-bit product of n-bit numbers in exactly $2n$ clock pulses.

Table 2
MULTIPLICATION IN A LINEAR ITERATIVE ARRAY

In each module, the x_0/y_0, x_1/y_1, and x/y columns show x-value over y-value (written here as x/y); the z column shows z_2,z_1,z_0 from top to bottom (written here as $z_2\,z_1\,z_0$).

Time	u_j v_j	q_j	M_1 c	M_1 x_0/y_0	M_1 x_1/y_1	M_1 x/y	M_1 $z_2z_1z_0$	M_2 c	M_2 x_0/y_0	M_2 x_1/y_1	M_2 x/y	M_2 $z_2z_1z_0$	M_3 c	M_3 x_0/y_0	M_3 x_1/y_1	M_3 x/y	M_3 $z_2z_1z_0$
0	1 1	1	0	0/0	0/0	0/0	0 0 0	0	0/0	0/0	0/0	0 0 0	0	0/0	0/0	0/0	0 0 0
1	1 1	1	1	1/1	0/0	0/0	0 1 0	0	0/0	0/0	0/0	0 0 0	0	0/0	0/0	0/0	0 0 0
2	1 1	0	2	1/1	1/1	0/0	1 0 0	0	0/0	0/0	0/0	0 0 0	0	0/0	0/0	0/0	0 0 0
3	0 0	1	3	1/1	1/1	1/1	0 1 1	0	0/0	0/0	0/0	0 0 1	0	0/0	0/0	0/0	0 0 0
4	1 1	0	3	1/1	1/1	0/0	1 0 1	1	1/1	0/0	0/0	0 0 1	0	0/0	0/0	0/0	0 0 0
5	0 0	0	3	1/1	1/1	1/1	0 1 1	2	1/1	0/0	0/0	0 0 1	0	0/0	0/0	0/0	0 0 0
6	0 0	0	3	1/1	1/1	0/0	1 0 0	3	1/1	0/0	1/1	0 1 0	0	0/0	0/0	0/0	0 0 0
7	0 0	0	3	1/1	1/1	0/0	0 0 0	3	1/1	0/0	0/0	0 1 0	1	1/1	0/0	0/0	0 0 1
8	0 0	0	3	1/1	1/1	0/0	0 0 0	3	1/1	0/0	0/0	0 1 0	2	1/1	0/0	0/0	0 0 0
9	0 0	0	3	1/1	1/1	0/0	0 0 0	3	1/1	0/0	0/0	0 0 1	3	1/1	0/0	0/0	0 0 0
10	0 0	0	3	1/1	1/1	0/0	0 0 1	3	1/1	0/0	0/0	0 0 0	3	1/1	0/0	0/0	0 0 0
11	0 0	0	3	1/1	1/1	0/0	0 0 0	3	1/1	0/0	0/0	0 0 0	3	1/1	0/0	0/0	0 0 0

The basic idea can be understood as follows. At time 0, machine M_1 senses (u_0, v_0, q_0) and it therefore is able to output $(u_0v_0 + q_0) \bmod 2$ at time 1. Then it sees (u_1, v_1, q_1) and it can output $(u_0v_1 + u_1v_0 + q_1 + k_1) \bmod 2$, where k_1 is the "carry" left over from the previous step, at time 2. Next it sees (u_2, v_2, q_2) and outputs $(u_0v_2 + u_1v_1 + u_2v_0 + q_2 + k_2) \bmod 2$; furthermore, its state holds the values of u_2 and v_2 so that machine M_2 will be able to sense these values at time 3, and M_2 will be able to compute u_2v_2 for the benefit of M_1 at time 4. Machine M_1 essentially arranges to start M_2 multiplying the sequence $(u_2, v_2), (u_3, v_3)$, ..., and M_2 will ultimately give M_3 the job of multiplying $(u_4, v_4), (u_5, v_5)$, etc. Fortunately, things just work out so that no time is lost. The reader will find it interesting to deduce further details from the formal description that follows.

Each automaton has 2^{11} states $(c, x_0, y_0, x_1, y_1, x, y, z_2, z_1, z_0)$, where $0 \le c < 4$ and each of the x's, y's, and z's is either 0 or 1. Initially, all the devices are in state $(0,0,0,0,0,0,0,0,0,0)$. Suppose that a machine M_j, for $j > 1$, is in state $(c, x_0, y_0, x_1, y_1, x, y, z_2, z_1, z_0)$ at time t, and its left neighbor M_{j-1} is in state $(c^l, x_0^l, y_0^l, x_1^l, y_1^l, x^l, y^l, z_2^l, z_1^l, z_0^l)$ while its right neighbor M_{j+1} is in state $(c^r, x_0^r, y_0^r, x_1^r, y_1^r, x^r, y^r, z_2^r, z_1^r, z_0^r)$ at that time. Then machine M_j will go into state $(c', x_0', y_0', x_1', y_1', x', y', z_2', z_1', z_0')$ at time $t+1$, where

$$\begin{aligned}
c' &= \min(c+1, 3) &&\text{if } c^l = 3, &&0 &&\text{otherwise;} \\
(x_0', y_0') &= (x^l, y^l) &&\text{if } c = 0, &&(x_0, y_0) &&\text{otherwise;} \\
(x_1', y_1') &= (x^l, y^l) &&\text{if } c = 1, &&(x_1, y_1) &&\text{otherwise;} \\
(x', y') &= (x^l, y^l) &&\text{if } c \ge 2, &&(x, y) &&\text{otherwise;}
\end{aligned} \tag{57}$$

and $(z_2' z_1' z_0')_2$ is the binary notation for

$$z_0^r + z_1 + z_2^l + \begin{cases}
x^l y^l & \text{if } c = 0; \\
x_0 y^l + x^l y_0 & \text{if } c = 1; \\
x_0 y^l + x_1 y_1 + x^l y_0 & \text{if } c = 2; \\
x_0 y^l + x_1 y + x y_1 + x^l y_0 & \text{if } c = 3.
\end{cases} \tag{58}$$

The leftmost machine M_1 behaves in almost the same way as the others; it acts exactly as if there were a machine to its left in state $(3, 0, 0, 0, 0, u, v, q, 0, 0)$ when it is receiving the inputs (u, v, q). The output of the array is the z_0 component of M_1.

Table 2 shows an example of this array acting on the inputs

$$u = v = (\dots 00010111)_2, \qquad q = (\dots 00001011)_2.$$

The output sequence appears in the lower right portion of the states of M_1:

$$0, \ 0, \ 1, \ 1, \ 1, \ 0, \ 0, \ 0, \ 0, \ 1, \ 0, \ \dots,$$

representing the number $(\dots 01000011100)_2$ from right to left.

This construction is based on a similar one first published by A. J. Atrubin, *IEEE Trans.* **EC-14** (1965), 394–399.

Fast as it is, the iterative array is optimum only when the input bits arrive one at a time. If the input bits are all present simultaneously, we prefer parallel circuitry that will obtain the product of two n-bit numbers after $O(\log n)$ levels of delay. Efficient circuits of that kind have been described, for example, by C. S. Wallace, *IEEE Trans.* **EC-13** (1964), 14–17; D. E. Knuth, *The Stanford GraphBase* (New York: ACM Press, 1994), 270–279.

S. Winograd [*JACM* **14** (1967), 793–802] has investigated the minimum multiplication time achievable in a logical circuit when n is given and when the inputs are available all at once in arbitrarily coded form. For similar questions when multiplication and addition must both be supported simultaneously, see A. C. Yao, *STOC* **13** (1981), 308–311; Mansour, Nisan, and Tiwari, *STOC* **22** (1990), 235–243.

> *Multiplication is mie vexation,*
> *And Division is quite as bad:*
> *The Golden Rule is mie stumbling stule,*
> *And Practice drives me mad.*
>
> — Manuscript collected by J. O. HALLIWELL (c. 1570)

EXERCISES

1. [*22*] The idea expressed in (2) can be generalized to the decimal system, if the radix 2 is replaced by 10. Using this generalization, calculate 1234 times 2341 (reducing this product of four-digit numbers to three products of two-digit numbers, and reducing each of the latter to products of one-digit numbers).

2. [*M22*] Prove that, in step T1 of Algorithm T, the value of R either stays the same or increases by one when we set $R \leftarrow \lfloor \sqrt{Q} \rfloor$. (Therefore, as observed in that step, we need not calculate a square root.)

3. [*M22*] Prove that the sequences q_k and r_k defined in Algorithm T satisfy the inequality $2^{q_k+1}(2r_k)^{r_k} \leq 2^{q_{k-1}+q_k}$, when $k > 0$.

▸ **4.** [*28*] (K. Baker.) Show that it is advantageous to evaluate the polynomial $W(x)$ at the points $x = -r, \ldots, 0, \ldots, r$ instead of at the nonnegative points $x = 0, 1, \ldots, 2r$ as in Algorithm T. The polynomial $U(x)$ can be written

$$U(x) = U_e(x^2) + xU_o(x^2),$$

and similarly $V(x)$ and $W(x)$ can be expanded in this way; show how to exploit this idea, obtaining faster calculations in steps T7 and T8.

▸ **5.** [*35*] Show that if in step T1 of Algorithm T we set $R \leftarrow \lceil \sqrt{2Q} \rceil + 1$ instead of setting $R \leftarrow \lfloor \sqrt{Q} \rfloor$, with suitable initial values of q_0, q_1, r_0, and r_1, then (20) can be improved to $t_k \leq q_{k+1} 2^{\sqrt{2 \lg q_{k+1}}} (\lg q_{k+1})$.

6. [*M23*] Prove that the six numbers in (24) are relatively prime in pairs.

7. [*M23*] Prove (25).

8. [*M20*] True or false: We can ignore the bit reversal $(s_{k-1}, \ldots, s_0) \to (s_0, \ldots, s_{k-1})$ in (39), because the inverse Fourier transform will reverse the bits again anyway.

9. [*M15*] Suppose the Fourier transformation method of the text is applied with all occurrences of ω replaced by ω^q, where q is some fixed integer. Find a simple relation between the numbers $(\tilde{u}_0, \tilde{u}_1, \ldots, \tilde{u}_{K-1})$ obtained by this general procedure and the numbers $(\hat{u}_0, \hat{u}_1, \ldots, \hat{u}_{K-1})$ obtained when $q = 1$.

10. [*M26*] The scaling in (43) makes it clear that all the complex numbers $A^{[j]}$ computed by pass j of the transformation subroutine will be less than 2^{j-k} in absolute value, during the calculations of $\hat{u}_s$ and $\hat{v}_s$ in the Schönhage–Strassen multiplication algorithm. Show that all of the $A^{[j]}$ will be less than 1 in absolute value during the *third* Fourier transformation (the calculation of $\hat{w}_r$).

▶ **11.** [*M26*] If n is fixed, how many of the automata in the linear iterative array defined by (57) and (58) are needed to compute the product of n-bit numbers? (Notice that the automaton M_j is influenced only by the component z_0^r of the machine on its right, so we may remove all automata whose z_0 component is always zero whenever the inputs are n-bit numbers.)

▶ **12.** [*M41*] (A. Schönhage.) The purpose of this exercise is to prove that a simple form of pointer machine can multiply n-bit numbers in $O(n)$ steps. The machine has no built-in facilities for arithmetic; all it does is work with nodes and pointers. Each node has the same finite number of link fields, and there are finitely many link registers. The only operations this machine can do are:

i) read one bit of input and jump if that bit is 0;
ii) output 0 or 1;
iii) load a register with the contents of another register or with the contents of a link field in a node pointed to by a register;
iv) store the contents of a register into a link field in a node pointed to by a register;
v) jump if two registers are equal;
vi) create a new node and make a register point to it;
vii) halt.

Implement the Fourier-transform multiplication method efficiently on such a machine. [*Hints:* First show that if N is any positive integer, it is possible to create N nodes representing the integers $\{0, 1, \ldots, N-1\}$, where the node representing p has pointers to the nodes representing $p+1$, $\lfloor p/2 \rfloor$, and $2p$. These nodes can be created in $O(N)$ steps. Show that arithmetic with radix N can now be simulated without difficulty: For example, it takes $O(\log N)$ steps to find the node for $(p+q) \bmod N$ and to determine if $p+q \geq N$, given pointers to p and q; and multiplication can be simulated in $O(\log N)^2$ steps. Now consider the algorithm in the text, with $k = l$ and $m = 6k$ and $N = 2^{\lceil m/13 \rceil}$, so that all quantities in the fixed point arithmetic calculations are 13-place integers with radix N. Finally, show that each pass of the fast Fourier transformations can be done in $O(K + (N \log N)^2) = O(K)$ steps, using the following idea: Each of the K necessary assignments can be "compiled" into a bounded list of instructions for a simulated MIX-like computer whose word size is N, and instructions for K such machines acting in parallel can be simulated in $O(K + (N \log N)^2)$ steps if they are first sorted so that all identical instructions are performed together. (Two instructions are identical if they have the same operation code, the same register contents, and the same memory operand contents.) Note that $N^2 = O(n^{12/13})$, so $(N \log N)^2 = O(K)$.]

13. [*M25*] (A. Schönhage.) What is a good upper bound on the time needed to multiply an m-bit number by an n-bit number, when both m and n are very large but n is much larger than m, based on the results discussed in this section for the case $m = n$?

14. [*M42*] Write a program for Algorithm T, incorporating the improvements of exercise 4. Compare it with a program for Algorithm 4.3.1M and with a program based on (2), to see how large n must be before Algorithm T is an improvement.

15. [*M49*] (S. A. Cook.) A multiplication algorithm is said to be *online* if the $(k+1)$st input bits of the operands, from right to left, are not read until the kth output bit has been produced. What are the fastest possible online multiplication algorithms achievable on various species of automata?

▶ **16.** [*25*] Prove that it takes only $O(K \log K)$ arithmetic operations to evaluate the discrete Fourier transform (35), even when K is not a power of 2. [*Hint:* Rewrite (35) in the form

$$\hat{u}_s = \omega^{-s^2/2} \sum_{0 \le t < K} \omega^{(s+t)^2/2} \omega^{-t^2/2} u_t$$

and express this sum as a convolution product.]

17. [*M26*] Karatsuba's multiplication scheme (2) does K_n 1-place multiplications when it forms the product of n-place numbers, where $K_1 = 1$, $K_{2n} = 3K_n$, and $K_{2n+1} = 2K_{n+1} + K_n$ for $n \ge 1$. "Solve" this recurrence by finding an explicit formula for K_n when $n = 2^{e_1} + 2^{e_2} + \cdots + 2^{e_t}$, $e_1 > e_2 > \cdots > e_t \ge 0$.

▶ **18.** [*M30*] Devise a scheme to allocate memory for the intermediate results when multiplication is performed by a recursive algorithm based on (2): Given two N-place integers u and v, each in N consecutive places of memory, show how to arrange the computation so that the product uv appears in the least significant $2N$ places of a $(3N + O(\log N))$-place area of working storage.

▶ **19.** [*M23*] Show how to compute $uv \bmod m$ with a bounded number of operations that meet the ground rules of exercise 3.2.1.1–11, if you are also allowed to test whether one operand is less than another. Both u and v are variable, but m is constant. *Hint:* Consider the decomposition in (2).

4.4. RADIX CONVERSION

IF OUR ANCESTORS had invented arithmetic by counting with their two fists or their eight fingers, instead of their ten "digits," we would never have to worry about writing binary-decimal conversion routines. (And we would perhaps never have learned as much about number systems.) In this section, we shall discuss the conversion of numbers from positional notation with one radix into positional notation with another radix; this process is, of course, most important on binary computers when converting decimal input data into binary form, and converting binary answers into decimal form.

A. The four basic methods. Binary-decimal conversion is one of the most machine-dependent operations of all, since computer designers keep inventing different ways to provide for it in the hardware. Therefore we shall discuss only the general principles involved, from which programmers can select the procedures that are best suited to their machines.

We shall assume that only nonnegative numbers enter into the conversion, since the manipulation of signs is easily accounted for.

Let us assume that we are converting from radix b to radix B. (Mixed-radix generalizations are considered in exercises 1 and 2.) Most radix-conversion routines are based on multiplication and division, using one of the four methods below. The first two methods apply to integers (radix point at the right), and the others to fractions (radix point at the left). It is often impossible to express a terminating radix-b fraction $(0.u_{-1}u_{-2}\ldots u_{-m})_b$ *exactly* as a terminating radix-B fraction $(0.U_{-1}U_{-2}\ldots U_{-M})_B$. For example, the fraction $\frac{1}{10}$ has the infinite binary representation $(0.0001100110011\ldots)_2$. Therefore methods of rounding the result to M places are sometimes necessary.

Method 1a (Division by B using radix-b arithmetic). Given an integer u, we can obtain its radix-B representation $(\ldots U_2U_1U_0)_B$ as follows:

$$U_0 = u \bmod B, \qquad U_1 = \lfloor u/B \rfloor \bmod B, \qquad U_2 = \lfloor \lfloor u/B \rfloor /B \rfloor \bmod B, \qquad \ldots,$$

stopping when $\lfloor \ldots \lfloor \lfloor u/B \rfloor /B \rfloor \ldots /B \rfloor = 0$.

Method 1b (Multiplication by b using radix-B arithmetic). If u has the radix-b representation $(u_m \ldots u_1 u_0)_b$, we can use radix-B arithmetic to evaluate the polynomial $u_m b^m + \cdots + u_1 b + u_0 = u$ in the form

$$((\ldots (u_m b + u_{m-1}) b + \cdots) b + u_1) b + u_0.$$

Method 2a (Multiplication by B using radix-b arithmetic). Given a fractional number u, we can obtain the digits of its radix-B representation $(.U_{-1}U_{-2}\ldots)_B$ as follows:

$$U_{-1} = \lfloor uB \rfloor, \qquad U_{-2} = \lfloor \{uB\}B \rfloor, \qquad U_{-3} = \lfloor \{\{uB\}B\}B \rfloor, \qquad \ldots,$$

where $\{x\}$ denotes $x \bmod 1 = x - \lfloor x \rfloor$. If it is desired to round the result to M places, the computation can be stopped after U_{-M} has been calculated, and U_{-M} should be increased by unity if $\{\ldots\{\{uB\}B\}\ldots B\}$ is greater than $\frac{1}{2}$. (Note, however, that this may cause carries to propagate, and these carries must be incorporated into the answer using radix-B arithmetic. It would be simpler to add the constant $\frac{1}{2}B^{-M}$ to the original number u before the calculation begins, but this may lead to an incorrect answer when $\frac{1}{2}B^{-M}$ cannot be represented exactly as a radix-b number inside the computer. Note further that it is possible for the answer to round up to $(1.00\ldots0)_B$, if $b^m \geq 2B^M$.)

Exercise 3 shows how to extend this method so that M is *variable*, just large enough to represent the original number to a specified accuracy. In this case the problem of carries does not occur.

Method 2b (Division by b using radix-B arithmetic). If u has the radix-b representation $(0.u_{-1}u_{-2}\ldots u_{-m})_b$, we can use radix-$B$ arithmetic to evaluate $u_{-1}b^{-1} + u_{-2}b^{-2} + \cdots + u_{-m}b^{-m}$ in the form

$$\bigl((\ldots(u_{-m}/b + u_{1-m})/b + \cdots + u_{-2})/b + u_{-1}\bigr)/b.$$

Care should be taken to control errors that might occur due to truncation or rounding in the division by b; these are often negligible, but not always.

To summarize, Methods 1a, 1b, 2a, and 2b give us two ways to convert integers and two ways to convert fractions; and it is certainly possible to convert between integers and fractions by multiplying or dividing by an appropriate power of b or B. Therefore there are at least four methods to choose from when trying to do radix conversion.

B. Single-precision conversion.   To illustrate these four methods, let us assume that MIX is a binary computer, and suppose that we want to convert a nonnegative binary integer u to a decimal integer. Thus $b = 2$ and $B = 10$. Method 1a could be programmed as follows:

```
      ENT1 0        Set j ← 0.
      LDX  U
      ENTA 0        Set rAX ← u.
1H    DIV  =10=     (rA,rX) ← (⌊rAX/10⌋,rAX mod 10).
      STX  ANSWER,1 Uj ← rX.
      INC1 1        j ← j + 1.
      SRAX 5        rAX ← rA.
      JXP  1B       Repeat until result is zero.  ∎
```
                                                                                  (1)

This requires $18M + 4$ cycles to obtain M digits.

Method 1a uses division by 10; Method 2a uses *multiplication* by 10, so it might be a little faster. But in order to use Method 2a, we must deal with fractions, and this leads to an interesting situation. Let w be the word size of the computer, and assume that $u < 10^n < w$. With a single division we can find q and r, where

$$wu = 10^n q + r, \qquad 0 \leq r < 10^n. \tag{2}$$

Now if we apply Method 2a to the fraction $(q+1)/w$, we will obtain the digits of u from left to right, in n steps, since

$$\left\lfloor 10^n \frac{q+1}{w} \right\rfloor = \left\lfloor u + \frac{10^n - r}{w} \right\rfloor = u. \tag{3}$$

(This idea is due to P. A. Samet, *Software Practice & Experience* **1** (1971), 93–96.)

Here is the corresponding MIX program:

```
        JOV   OFLO        Ensure that overflow is off.
        LDA   U
        LDX   =10ⁿ=       rAX ← wu + 10ⁿ.
        DIV   =10ⁿ=       rA ← q + 1, rX ← r.
        JOV   ERROR       Jump if u ≥ 10ⁿ.
        ENT1  n-1         Set j ← n − 1.                        (4)
2H      MUL   =10=        Now imagine the radix point at the left, rA = x.
        STA   ANSWER,1    Set Uⱼ ← ⌊10x⌋.
        SLAX  5           x ← {10x}.
        DEC1  1           j ← j − 1.
        J1NN  2B          Repeat for n > j ≥ 0.   ▌
```

This slightly longer routine requires $16n + 19$ cycles, so it is a little faster than program (1) if $n = M \geq 8$; when leading zeros are present, (1) will be faster.

Program (4) as it stands cannot be used to convert integers $u \geq 10^m$ when $10^m < w < 10^{m+1}$, since we would need to take $n = m + 1$. In this case we can obtain the leading digit of u by computing $\lfloor u/10^m \rfloor$; then $u \bmod 10^m$ can be converted as above with $n = m$.

The fact that the answer digits are obtained from left to right may be an advantage in some applications (for example, when typing out an answer one digit at a time). Thus we see that a fractional method can be used for conversion of integers, although the use of inexact division makes a little bit of numerical analysis necessary.

We can avoid the division by 10 in Method 1a if we do two multiplications instead. This alternative can be important, because radix conversion is often done by "satellite" computers that have no built-in division capability. If we let x be an approximation to $\frac{1}{10}$, so that

$$\frac{1}{10} < x < \frac{1}{10} + \frac{1}{w},$$

it is easy to prove (see exercise 7) that $\lfloor ux \rfloor = \lfloor u/10 \rfloor$ or $\lfloor u/10 \rfloor + 1$, so long as $0 \leq u < w$. Therefore, if we compute $u - 10\lfloor ux \rfloor$, we will be able to determine the value of $\lfloor u/10 \rfloor$:

$$\lfloor u/10 \rfloor = \lfloor ux \rfloor - [u < 10\lfloor ux \rfloor]. \tag{5}$$

At the same time we will have determined $u \bmod 10$. A MIX program for conversion using (5) appears in exercise 8; it requires about 33 cycles per digit.

If the computer has neither division nor multiplication in its repertoire of built-in instructions, we can still use Method 1a for conversion by judiciously shifting and adding, as explained in exercise 9.

Another way to convert from binary to decimal is to use Method 1b, but to do this we need to simulate doubling in a *decimal* number system. This approach is generally most suitable for incorporation into computer hardware; however, it is possible to program the doubling process for decimal numbers, using binary addition, binary shifting, and binary extraction or masking (bitwise AND) as shown in Table 1, which was suggested by Peter L. Montgomery.

Table 1

DOUBLING A BINARY-CODED DECIMAL NUMBER

Operation	*General form*	*Example*
1. Given number	$u_{11}\, u_{10}\, u_9\, u_8\ \ u_7\, u_6\, u_5\, u_4\ \ u_3\, u_2\, u_1\, u_0$	$0011\,0110\,1001 = 369$
2. Add 3 to each digit	$v_{11}\, v_{10}\, v_9\, v_8\ \ v_7\, v_6\, v_5\, v_4\ \ v_3\, v_2\, v_1\, v_0$	$0110\,1001\,1100$
3. Extract each high bit	$v_{11}\ 0\ \ 0\ \ 0\ \ v_7\ 0\ \ 0\ \ 0\ \ v_3\ 0\ \ 0\ \ 0$	$0000\,1000\,1000$
4. Shift right 2 and subtract	$0\ \ v_{11}\, v_{11}0\ \ 0\ \ v_7\, v_7\ 0\ \ 0\ \ v_3\, v_3\ 0$	$0000\,0110\,0110$
5. Add original number	$w_{11} w_{10} w_9 w_8\ \ w_7 w_6 w_5 w_4\ \ w_3 w_2 w_1 w_0$	$0011\,1100\,1111$
6. Add original number	$x_{12}\, x_{11}\, x_{10}\, x_9\, x_8\ \ x_7\, x_6\, x_5\, x_4\ \ x_3\, x_2\, x_1\, x_0$	$0\,0111\,0011\,1000 = 738$

This method changes each individual digit d into $2d$ when $0 \le d \le 4$, and into $6 + 2d = (2d - 10) + 2^4$ when $5 \le d \le 9$; and that is just what is needed to double decimal numbers encoded with 4 bits per digit.

Another related idea is to keep a table of the powers of two in decimal form, and to add the appropriate powers together by simulating decimal addition. A survey of bit-manipulation techniques appears in Section 7.1.3.

Finally, even Method 2b can be used for the conversion of binary integers to decimal integers. We can find q as in (2), and then we can simulate the decimal division of $q + 1$ by w, using a "halving" process (exercise 10) that is similar to the doubling process just described, retaining only the first n digits to the right of the radix point in the answer. In this situation, Method 2b does not seem to offer advantages over the other three methods already discussed, but we have confirmed the remark made earlier that at least four distinct methods are available for converting integers from one radix to another.

Now let us consider decimal-to-binary conversion (so that $b = 10$, $B = 2$). Method 1a simulates a decimal division by 2; this is feasible (see exercise 10), but it is primarily suitable for incorporation in hardware instead of programs.

Method 1b is the most practical method for decimal-to-binary conversion in the great majority of cases. The following MIX code assumes that there are at least two digits in the number $(u_m \ldots u_1 u_0)_{10}$ being converted, and that $10^{m+1} < w$ so that overflow is not an issue:

```
    ENT1 M-1      Set j ← m − 1.
    LDA  INPUT+M  Set U ← u_m.
1H  MUL  =10=
    SLAX 5                                        (6)
    ADD  INPUT,1  U ← 10U + u_j.
    DEC1 1
    J1NN 1B       Repeat for m > j ≥ 0.  ∎
```

The multiplication by 10 could be replaced by shifting and adding.

A trickier but perhaps faster method, which uses about $\lg m$ multiplications, extractions, and additions instead of $m - 1$ multiplications and additions, is described in exercise 19.

For the conversion of decimal fractions $(0.u_{-1}u_{-2} \ldots u_{-m})_{10}$ to binary form, we can use Method 2b; or, more commonly, we can first convert the integer $(u_{-1}u_{-2} \ldots u_{-m})_{10}$ by Method 1b and then divide by 10^m.

C. Hand calculation. It is occasionally necessary for computer programmers to convert numbers by hand, and since this is a subject not yet taught in elementary schools, it may be worthwhile to examine it briefly here. There are simple pencil-and-paper methods for converting between decimal and octal notations, and these methods are easily learned, so they should be more widely known.

Converting octal integers to decimal. The simplest conversion is from octal to decimal; this technique was apparently first published by Walter Soden, *Math. Comp.* **7** (1953), 273–274. To do the conversion, write down the given octal number, inserting a radix point after the leading digit. Then at the kth step, double the leading digits left of the point, using decimal arithmetic; and subtract this from the leading digits after shifting the point right, again using decimal arithmetic. The process terminates in m steps if the given number has $m + 1$ digits. The radix point clarifies which digits are to be doubled.

Example 1. Convert $(1234567)_8$ to decimal.

$$
\begin{array}{r}
1.2\ 3\ 4\ 5\ 6\ 7 \\
-\quad 2 \\
\hline
1\ 0.3\ 4\ 5\ 6\ 7 \\
-\quad 2\ 0 \\
\hline
8\ 3.4\ 5\ 6\ 7 \\
-\quad 1\ 6\ 6 \\
\hline
6\ 6\ 8.5\ 6\ 7 \\
-\quad 1\ 3\ 3\ 6 \\
\hline
5\ 3\ 4\ 9.6\ 7 \\
-\quad 1\ 0\ 6\ 9\ 8 \\
\hline
4\ 2\ 7\ 9\ 8.7 \\
-\quad 8\ 5\ 5\ 9\ 6 \\
\hline
3\ 4\ 2\ 3\ 9\ 1
\end{array}
$$

Answer: $(342391)_{10}$.

A reasonably good check on the computations may be had by "casting out nines": The sum of the digits of the decimal number must be congruent modulo 9 to the alternating sum and difference of the digits of the octal number, with the rightmost digit of the latter given a plus sign. In the example above, we have $3 + 4 + 2 + 3 + 9 + 1 = 22$, and $7 - 6 + 5 - 4 + 3 - 2 + 1 = 4$; the difference is 18 (a multiple of 9). If this test fails, it can be applied to the digits left of the point after each step, and the error can be located using a "binary search" procedure; in other words, we can locate the error by first checking the middle result, then using the same procedure on the first or second half of the calculation, depending on whether the middle result is incorrect or correct.

The "casting-out-nines" process is only about 89 percent reliable, because there is one chance in nine that two *random* integers will differ by a multiple of nine. An even better check is to convert the answer back to octal by using an inverse method, which we shall now consider.

Converting decimal integers to octal. A similar procedure can be used for the opposite conversion: Write down the given decimal number, inserting a radix point after the leading digit. Then at the kth step, double the leading digits left of the point, using *octal* arithmetic; and *add* these to the leading digits after shifting the point right, again using *octal* arithmetic. The process terminates in m steps if the given number has $m + 1$ digits.

Example 2. Convert $(342391)_{10}$ to octal.

$$
\begin{array}{r}
3.4\ 2\ 3\ 9\ 1 \\
+\quad 6 \\
\hline
4\ 2.2\ 3\ 9\ 1 \\
+\quad 1\ 0\ 4 \\
\hline
5\ 2\ 6.3\ 9\ 1 \\
+\quad 1\ 2\ 5\ 4 \\
\hline
6\ 5\ 3\ 7.9\ 1 \\
+\quad 1\ 5\ 2\ 7\ 6 \\
\hline
1\ 0\ 2\ 6\ 7\ 7.1 \\
+\quad 2\ 0\ 5\ 5\ 7\ 6 \\
\hline
1\ 2\ 3\ 4\ 5\ 6\ 7
\end{array}
$$

Answer: $(1234567)_8$.

(Notice that the nonoctal digits 8 and 9 might enter into this octal computation.) The answer can be checked as discussed above. This method was published by Charles P. Rozier, *IEEE Trans.* **EC-11** (1962), 708–709.

The two procedures just given are essentially Method 1b of the general radix-conversion procedures. Doubling and subtracting in decimal notation is like multiplying by $10 - 2 = 8$; doubling and adding in octal notation is like multiplying by $8 + 2 = 10$. There is a similar method for hexadecimal/decimal conversions, but it is a little more difficult since it involves multiplication by 6 instead of by 2.

To keep these two methods straight in our minds, it is not hard to remember that we must subtract to go from octal to decimal, since the decimal representation of a number is smaller; similarly we must add to go from decimal to octal. The computations are performed using the radix of the *answer*, not the radix of the given number, otherwise we couldn't get the desired answer.

Converting fractions. No equally fast method of converting fractions manually is known. The best way seems to be Method 2a, with doubling and adding or subtracting to simplify the multiplications by 10 or by 8. In this case, we reverse the addition-subtraction criterion, adding when we convert to decimal and subtracting when we convert to octal; we also use the radix of the given input number, *not* the radix of the answer, in this computation (see Examples 3 and 4). The process is about twice as hard as the method that we used for integers.

Example 3. Convert $(.14159)_{10}$ to octal.

$$
\begin{array}{r}
.1\ 4\ 1\ 5\ 9 \\
2\ 8\ 3\ 1\ 8- \\
\hline
1.1\ 3\ 2\ 7\ 2 \\
2\ 6\ 5\ 4\ 4- \\
\hline
1.0\ 6\ 1\ 7\ 6 \\
1\ 2\ 3\ 5\ 2- \\
\hline
0.4\ 9\ 4\ 0\ 8 \\
9\ 8\ 8\ 1\ 6- \\
\hline
3.9\ 5\ 2\ 6\ 4 \\
1\ 9\ 0\ 5\ 2\ 8- \\
\hline
7.6\ 2\ 1\ 1\ 2 \\
1\ 2\ 4\ 2\ 2\ 4- \\
\hline
4.9\ 6\ 8\ 9\ 6
\end{array}
$$

Answer: $(.110374\ldots)_8$.

Example 4. Convert $(.110374)_8$ to decimal.

$$
\begin{array}{r}
.1\ 1\ 0\ 3\ 7\ 4 \\
2\ 2\ 0\ 7\ 7\ 0+ \\
\hline
1.3\ 2\ 4\ 7\ 3\ 0 \\
6\ 5\ 1\ 6\ 6\ 0+ \\
\hline
4.1\ 2\ 1\ 1\ 6\ 0 \\
2\ 4\ 2\ 3\ 4\ 0+ \\
\hline
1.4\ 5\ 4\ 1\ 4\ 0 \\
1\ 1\ 3\ 0\ 3\ 0\ 0+ \\
\hline
5.6\ 7\ 1\ 7\ 0\ 0 \\
1\ 5\ 6\ 3\ 6\ 0\ 0+ \\
\hline
8.5\ 0\ 2\ 6\ 0\ 0 \\
1\ 2\ 0\ 5\ 4\ 0\ 0+ \\
\hline
6.2\ 3\ 3\ 4\ 0\ 0
\end{array}
$$

Answer: $(.141586\ldots)_{10}$.

D. Floating point conversion. When floating point values are to be converted, it is necessary to deal with both the exponent and the fraction parts simultaneously, since conversion of the exponent will affect the fraction part. Given the number $f \cdot 2^e$ to be converted to decimal, we may express 2^e in the form $F \cdot 10^E$ (usually by means of auxiliary tables), and then convert Ff to decimal. Alternatively, we can multiply e by $\log_{10} 2$ and round this to the nearest integer E; then divide $f \cdot 2^e$ by 10^E and convert the result. Conversely, given the number $F \cdot 10^E$ to be converted to binary, we may convert F and then multiply it by the floating point number 10^E (again by using auxiliary tables). Obvious techniques can be used to reduce the maximum size of the auxiliary tables by using several multiplications and/or divisions, although this can cause rounding errors to propagate. Exercise 17 considers the minimization of error.

E. Multiple-precision conversion. When converting extremely long numbers, it is most convenient to start by converting blocks of digits, which can be handled by single-precision techniques, and then to combine these blocks by using simple multiple-precision techniques. For example, suppose that 10^n is the highest power of 10 less than the computer word size. Then:

a) To convert a multiple-precision *integer* from binary to decimal, divide it repeatedly by 10^n (thus converting from binary to radix 10^n by Method 1a). Single-precision operations will give the n decimal digits for each place of the radix-10^n representation.

b) To convert a multiple-precision *fraction* from binary to decimal, proceed similarly, multiplying by 10^n (that is, using Method 2a with $B = 10^n$).

c) To convert a multiple-precision integer from decimal to binary, convert blocks of n digits first; then use Method 1b to convert from radix 10^n to binary.

d) To convert a multiple-precision fraction from decimal to binary, convert first to radix 10^n as in (c), then use Method 2b.

F. History and Bibliography. Radix-conversion techniques implicitly originated in ancient problems dealing with weights, measures, and currencies, where mixed-radix systems were generally involved. Auxiliary tables were usually prepared to help people make the conversions. During the seventeenth century, when sexagesimal fractions were being supplanted by decimal fractions, it was necessary to convert between the two systems in order to use existing books of astronomical tables; a systematic method to transform fractions from radix 60 to radix 10 and vice versa was given in the 1667 edition of William Oughtred's *Clavis Mathematicæ*, Chapter 6, Section 18. (This material was not present in the original 1631 edition of Oughtred's book.) Conversion rules had already been given by al-Kāshī of Samarkand in his *Key to Arithmetic* (1427), where Methods 1a, 1b, and 2a are clearly explained [*Istoriko-Mat. Issled.* **7** (1954), 126–135], but his work was unknown in Europe. The 18th century American mathematician Hugh Jones used the words "octavation" and "decimation" to describe octal/decimal conversions, but his methods were not as clever as his terminology. A. M. Legendre [*Théorie des Nombres* (Paris: 1798), 229] noted that positive integers may be conveniently converted to binary form if they are repeatedly divided by 64.

In 1946, H. H. Goldstine and J. von Neumann gave prominent consideration to radix conversion in their classic memoir, *Planning and Coding Problems for an Electronic Computing Instrument*, because it was necessary to justify the use of binary arithmetic; see John von Neumann, *Collected Works* **5** (New York: Macmillan, 1963), 127–142. Another early discussion of radix conversion on binary computers was published by F. Koons and S. Lubkin, *Math. Comp.* **3** (1949), 427–431, who suggested a rather unusual method. The first discussion of floating point conversion was given somewhat later by F. L. Bauer and K. Samelson [*Zeit. für angewandte Math. und Physik* **4** (1953), 312–316].

The following articles are, similarly, of historic interest: A note by G. T. Lake [*CACM* **5** (1962), 468–469] mentioned some hardware techniques for conversion and gave clear examples. A. H. Stroud and D. Secrest [*Comp. J.* **6** (1963), 62–66] discussed conversion of multiple-precision floating point numbers. The conversion of *unnormalized* floating point numbers, preserving the amount of "significance" implied by the representation, was discussed by H. Kanner [*JACM* **12** (1965), 242–246] and by N. Metropolis and R. L. Ashenhurst [*Math. Comp.* **19** (1965), 435–441]. See also K. Sikdar, *Sankhyā* **B30** (1968), 315–334, and the references cited in his paper.

Detailed subroutines for formatted input and output of integers and floating point numbers in the C programming language have been given by P. J. Plauger in *The Standard C Library* (Prentice–Hall, 1992), 301–331.

See T. Granlund and P. L. Montgomery, *SIGPLAN Notices* **29**, 6 (June 1994), 61–72, for state-of-the-art techniques that convert binary integers to decimal strings without division.

EXERCISES

▶ **1.** [*25*] Generalize Method 1b so that it works with arbitrary mixed-radix notations, converting

$$a_m b_{m-1} \ldots b_1 b_0 + \cdots + a_1 b_0 + a_0 \quad \text{into} \quad A_M B_{M-1} \ldots B_1 B_0 + \cdots + A_1 B_0 + A_0,$$

where $0 \le a_j < b_j$ and $0 \le A_J < B_J$ for $0 \le j < m$ and $0 \le J < M$.

Give an example of your generalization by manually converting "3 days, 9 hours, 12 minutes, and 37 seconds" into long tons, hundredweights, stones, pounds, and ounces. (Let one second equal one ounce. The British system of weights has 1 stone = 14 pounds, 1 hundredweight = 8 stone, 1 long ton = 20 hundredweight.) In other words, let $b_0 = 60$, $b_1 = 60$, $b_2 = 24$, $m = 3$, $B_0 = 16$, $B_1 = 14$, $B_2 = 8$, $B_3 = 20$, $M = 4$; the problem is to find A_4, $\ldots$, A_0 in the proper ranges such that $3b_2 b_1 b_0 + 9b_1 b_0 + 12b_0 + 37 = A_4 B_3 B_2 B_1 B_0 + A_3 B_2 B_1 B_0 + A_2 B_1 B_0 + A_1 B_0 + A_0$, using a systematic method that generalizes Method 1b. (All arithmetic is to be done in a mixed-radix system.)

2. [*25*] Generalize Method 1a so that it works with mixed-radix notations, as in exercise 1, and give an example of your generalization by manually solving the same conversion problem stated in exercise 1.

▶ **3.** [*25*] (D. Taranto.) When fractions are being converted, there is no obvious way to decide how many digits to give in the answer. Design a simple generalization of Method 2a that, given two positive radix-b fractions u and ϵ between 0 and 1, converts u to a rounded radix-B equivalent U that has just enough places M to the right of the radix point to ensure that $|U - u| < \epsilon$. (In particular if u is a multiple of b^{-m} and $\epsilon = b^{-m}/2$, the value of U will have just enough digits so that u can be recomputed exactly, given U and m. Note that M might be zero; for example, if $\epsilon \leq \frac{1}{2}$ and $u > 1 - \epsilon$, the proper answer is $U = 1$.)

4. [*M21*] (a) Prove that every real number with a terminating *binary* representation also has a terminating *decimal* representation. (b) Find a simple condition on the positive integers b and B that is satisfied if and only if every real number that has a terminating radix-b representation also has a terminating radix-B representation.

5. [*M20*] Show that program (4) would still work if the instruction 'LDX =10^n=' were replaced by 'LDX =c=' for certain other constants c.

6. [*30*] Discuss using Methods 1a, 1b, 2a, and 2b when b or B is -2.

7. [*M18*] Given that $0 < \alpha \leq x \leq \alpha + 1/w$ and $0 \leq u \leq w$, where u is an integer, prove that $\lfloor ux \rfloor$ is equal to either $\lfloor \alpha u \rfloor$ or $\lfloor \alpha u \rfloor + 1$. Furthermore $\lfloor ux \rfloor = \lfloor \alpha u \rfloor$ exactly, if $u < \alpha w$ and α^{-1} is an integer.

8. [*24*] Write a MIX program analogous to (1) that uses (5) and includes no division instructions.

▶ **9.** [*M29*] The purpose of this exercise is to compute $\lfloor u/10 \rfloor$ with binary shifting and addition operations only, when u is a nonnegative integer. Let $v_0(u) = 3\lfloor u/2 \rfloor + 3$ and

$$v_{k+1}(u) = v_k(u) + \lfloor v_k(u)/2^{2^{k+2}} \rfloor \qquad \text{for } k \geq 0.$$

Given k, what is the smallest nonnegative integer u such that $\lfloor v_k[u]/16 \rfloor \neq \lfloor u/10 \rfloor$?

10. [*22*] Table 1 shows how a binary-coded decimal number can be doubled by using various shifting, extracting, and addition operations on a binary computer. Give an analogous method that computes *half* of a binary-coded decimal number (throwing away the remainder if the number is odd).

11. [*18*] Convert $(21446)_8$ to decimal, and back again to octal.

▶ **12.** [*22*] Invent a rapid pencil-and-paper method for converting integers from ternary notation to decimal, and illustrate your method by converting $(1212011210210)_3$ into decimal. How would you go from decimal to ternary?

▶ **13.** [*25*] Assume that locations $U + 1$, $U + 2$, $\ldots$, $U + m$ contain a multiple-precision fraction $(.u_{-1}u_{-2} \ldots u_{-m})_b$, where b is the word size of MIX. Write a MIX routine that converts this fraction to decimal notation, truncating it to 180 decimal digits. The answer should be printed on two lines, with the digits grouped into 20 blocks of nine each separated by blanks. (Use the CHAR instruction.)

▶ **14.** [*M27*] (A. Schönhage.) The text's method of converting multiple-precision integers requires an execution time of order n^2 to convert an n-place integer, when n is large. Show that it is possible to convert n-digit decimal integers into binary notation in $O(M(n) \log n)$ steps, where $M(n)$ is an upper bound on the number of steps needed to multiply n-bit binary numbers that satisfies the "smoothness condition" $M(2n) \geq 2M(n)$.

15. [*M47*] Can the upper bound on the time to convert large integers given in the preceding exercise be substantially lowered? (See exercise 4.3.3–12.)

16. [*41*] Construct a fast linear iterative array for radix conversion from decimal to binary (see Section 4.3.3E).

17. [*M40*] Design "ideal" floating point conversion subroutines, taking p-digit decimal numbers into P-digit binary numbers and vice versa, in both cases producing a true rounded result in the sense of Section 4.2.2.

18. [*HM34*] (David W. Matula.) Let $\text{round}_b(u, p)$ be the function of b, u, and p that represents the best p-digit base b floating point approximation to u, in the sense of Section 4.2.2. Under the assumption that $\log_B b$ is irrational and that the range of exponents is unlimited, prove that

$$u = \text{round}_b(\text{round}_B(u, P), p)$$

holds for all p-digit base b floating point numbers u if and only if $B^{P-1} \geq b^p$. (In other words, an "ideal" input conversion of u into an independent base B, followed by an "ideal" output conversion of this result, will always yield u again if and only if the intermediate precision P is suitably large, as specified by the formula above.)

▶ **19.** [*M23*] Let the decimal number $u = (u_7 \ldots u_1 u_0)_{10}$ be represented as the binary-coded decimal number $U = (u_7 \ldots u_1 u_0)_{16}$. Find appropriate constants c_i and masks m_i so that the operation $U \leftarrow U - c_i(U \mathbin{\&} m_i)$, repeated for $i = 1, 2, 3$, will convert U to the binary representation of u, where "$\&$" denotes extraction (bitwise AND).

4.5. RATIONAL ARITHMETIC

IT IS OFTEN IMPORTANT to know that the answer to some numerical problem is exactly $1/3$, not a floating point number that gets printed as "0.333333574". If arithmetic is done on fractions instead of on approximations to fractions, many computations can be done entirely *without any accumulated rounding errors*. This results in a comfortable feeling of security that is often lacking when floating point calculations have been made, and it means that the accuracy of the calculation cannot be improved upon.

Irrationality is the square root of all evil.
— DOUGLAS HOFSTADTER, *Metamagical Themas* (1983)

4.5.1. Fractions

When fractional arithmetic is desired, the numbers can be represented as pairs of integers, (u/u'), where u and u' are relatively prime to each other and $u' > 0$. The number zero is represented as $(0/1)$. In this form, $(u/u') = (v/v')$ if and only if $u = v$ and $u' = v'$.

Multiplication of fractions is, of course, easy; to form $(u/u') \times (v/v') = (w/w')$, we can simply compute uv and $u'v'$. The two products uv and $u'v'$ might not be relatively prime, but if $d = \gcd(uv, u'v')$, the desired answer is $w = uv/d$, $w' = u'v'/d$. (See exercise 2.) Efficient algorithms to compute the greatest common divisor are discussed in Section 4.5.2.

Another way to perform the multiplication is to find $d_1 = \gcd(u, v')$ and $d_2 = \gcd(u', v)$; then the answer is $w = (u/d_1)(v/d_2)$, $w' = (u'/d_2)(v'/d_1)$. (See exercise 3.) This method requires two gcd calculations, but it is not really slower than the former method; the gcd process involves a number of iterations that is essentially proportional to the logarithm of its inputs, so the total number of iterations needed to evaluate both d_1 and d_2 is essentially the same as the number of iterations during the single calculation of d. Furthermore, each iteration in the evaluation of d_1 and d_2 is potentially faster, because comparatively small numbers are being examined. If u, u', v, and v' are single-precision quantities, this method has the advantage that no double-precision numbers appear in the calculation unless it is impossible to represent both of the answers w and w' in single-precision form.

Division may be done in a similar manner; see exercise 4.

Addition and subtraction are slightly more complicated. The obvious procedure is to set $(u/u') \pm (v/v') = \big((uv' \pm u'v)/u'v'\big)$ and then to reduce this fraction to lowest terms by calculating $d = \gcd(uv' \pm u'v, u'v')$, as in the first multiplication method. But again it is possible to avoid working with such large numbers, if we start by calculating $d_1 = \gcd(u', v')$. If $d_1 = 1$, then the desired numerator and denominator are $w = uv' \pm u'v$ and $w' = u'v'$. (According to Theorem 4.5.2D, d_1 will be 1 about 61 percent of the time, if the denominators u' and v' are randomly distributed, so it is wise to single out this case.) If $d_1 > 1$, then let $t = u(v'/d_1) \pm v(u'/d_1)$ and calculate $d_2 = \gcd(t, d_1)$; finally the answer is $w = t/d_2$, $w' = (u'/d_1)(v'/d_2)$. (Exercise 6 proves that these values of w and w' are relatively prime to each other.) If single-precision numbers are being used, this method requires only single-precision operations, except that t may be a double-precision number or slightly larger (see exercise 7); since $\gcd(t, d_1) = \gcd(t \bmod d_1, d_1)$, the calculation of d_2 does not require double precision.

For example, to compute $(7/66) + (17/12)$, we form $d_1 = \gcd(66, 12) = 6$; then $t = 7 \cdot 2 + 17 \cdot 11 = 201$, and $d_2 = \gcd(201, 6) = 3$, so the answer is

$$\frac{201}{3} \bigg/ \left(\frac{66}{6} \cdot \frac{12}{3}\right) = 67/44.$$

To help check out subroutines for rational arithmetic, inversion of matrices with known inverses (like Cauchy matrices, exercise 1.2.3–41) is suggested.

Experience with fractional calculations shows that in many cases the numbers grow to be quite large. So if u and u' are intended to be single-precision numbers for each fraction (u/u'), it is important to include tests for overflow in each of the addition, subtraction, multiplication, and division subroutines. For numerical problems in which perfect accuracy is important, a set of subroutines for fractional arithmetic with *arbitrary* precision allowed in numerator and denominator is very useful.

The methods of this section extend also to other number fields besides the rational numbers; for example, we could do arithmetic on quantities of the form $(u + u'\sqrt{5})/u''$, where u, u', u'' are integers, $\gcd(u, u', u'') = 1$, and $u'' > 0$; or on quantities of the form $(u + u'\sqrt[3]{2} + u''\sqrt[3]{4})/u'''$, etc.

Instead of insisting on exact calculations with fractions, it is interesting to consider also "fixed slash" and "floating slash" numbers, which are analogous to floating point numbers but based on rational fractions instead of radix-oriented fractions. In a binary fixed-slash scheme, the numerator and denominator of a representable fraction each consist of at most p bits, for some given p. In a floating-slash scheme, the *sum* of numerator bits plus denominator bits must be a total of at most q, for some given q, and another field of the representation is used to indicate how many of these q bits belong to the numerator. Infinity can be represented as $(1/0)$. To do arithmetic on such numbers, we define $x \oplus y = \text{round}(x+y)$, $x \ominus y = \text{round}(x-y)$, etc., where $\text{round}(x) = x$ if x is representable, otherwise it is one of the two representable numbers that surround x.

It may seem at first that the best definition of $\text{round}(x)$ would be to choose the representable number that is closest to x, by analogy with the way we round in floating point arithmetic. But experience has shown that it is best to bias our rounding towards "simple" numbers, since numbers with small numerator and denominator occur much more often than complicated fractions do. We want more numbers to round to $\frac{1}{2}$ than to $\frac{127}{255}$. The rounding rule that turns out to be most successful in practice is called "mediant rounding": If (u/u') and (v/v') are adjacent representable numbers, so that whenever $u/u' \leq x \leq v/v'$ we must have $\text{round}(x)$ equal to (u/u') or (v/v'), the mediant rounding rule says that

$$\text{round}(x) = \frac{u}{u'} \text{ for } x < \frac{u+v}{u'+v'}, \quad \text{round}(x) = \frac{v}{v'} \text{ for } x > \frac{u+v}{u'+v'}. \tag{1}$$

If $x = (u+v)/(u'+v')$ exactly, we let $\mathrm{round}(x)$ be the neighboring fraction with the smallest denominator (or, if $u' = v'$, with the smallest numerator). Exercise 4.5.3–43 shows that it is not difficult to implement mediant rounding efficiently.

For example, suppose we are doing fixed slash arithmetic with $p = 8$, so that the representable numbers (u/u') have $-128 < u < 128$ and $0 \leq u' < 256$ and $u \perp u'$. This isn't much precision, but it is enough to give us a feel for slash arithmetic. The numbers adjacent to $0 = (0/1)$ are $(-1/255)$ and $(1/255)$; according to the mediant rounding rule, we will therefore have $\mathrm{round}(x) = 0$ if and only if $|x| \leq 1/256$. Suppose we have a calculation that would take the overall form $\frac{22}{7} = \frac{314}{159} + \frac{1300}{1113}$ if we were working in exact rational arithmetic, but the intermediate quantities have had to be rounded to representable numbers. In this case $\frac{314}{159}$ would round to $(79/40)$ and $\frac{1300}{1113}$ would round to $(7/6)$. The rounded terms sum to $\frac{79}{40} + \frac{7}{6} = \frac{377}{120}$, which rounds to $(22/7)$; so we have obtained the correct answer even though three roundings were required. This example was not specially contrived. When the answer to a problem is a simple fraction, slash arithmetic tends to make the intermediate rounding errors cancel out.

Exact representation of fractions within a computer was first discussed in the literature by P. Henrici, *JACM* **3** (1956), 6–9. Fixed and floating slash arithmetic were proposed by David W. Matula, in *Applications of Number Theory to Numerical Analysis*, edited by S. K. Zaremba (New York: Academic Press, 1972), 486–489. Further developments of the idea are discussed by Matula and Kornerup in *Proc. IEEE Symp. Computer Arith.* **4** (1978), 29–38, 39–47; *Lecture Notes in Comp. Sci.* **72** (1979), 383–397; *Computing*, Suppl. **2** (1980), 85–111; *IEEE Trans.* **C-32** (1983), 378–388; *IEEE Trans.* **C-34** (1985), 3–18; *IEEE Trans.* **C-39** (1990), 1106–1115.

EXERCISES

1. [*15*] Suggest a reasonable computational method for comparing two fractions, to test whether or not $(u/u') < (v/v')$.

2. [*M15*] Prove that if $d = \gcd(u, v)$ then u/d and v/d are relatively prime.

3. [*M20*] Prove that $u \perp u'$ and $v \perp v'$ implies $\gcd(uv, u'v') = \gcd(u, v') \gcd(u', v)$.

4. [*11*] Design a division algorithm for fractions, analogous to the second multiplication method of the text. (Note that the sign of v must be considered.)

5. [*10*] Compute $(17/120) + (-27/70)$ by the method recommended in the text.

▶ **6.** [*M23*] Show that $u \perp u'$ and $v \perp v'$ implies $\gcd(uv' + vu', u'v') = d_1 d_2$, where $d_1 = \gcd(u', v)$ and $d_2 = \gcd(d_1, u(v'/d_1) + v(u'/d_1))$. (Hence if $d_1 = 1$ we have $(uv' + vu') \perp u'v'$.)

7. [*M22*] How large can the absolute value of the quantity t become, in the addition-subtraction method recommended in the text, if the numerators and denominators of the inputs are less than N in absolute value?

▶ **8.** [*22*] Discuss using $(1/0)$ and $(-1/0)$ as representations for ∞ and $-\infty$, and/or as representations of overflow.

9. [*M23*] If $1 \leq u', v' < 2^n$, show that $\lfloor 2^{2n} u/u' \rfloor = \lfloor 2^{2n} v/v' \rfloor$ implies $u/u' = v/v'$.

10. [*41*] Extend the subroutines suggested in exercise 4.3.1–34 so that they deal with "arbitrary" rational numbers.

11. [*M23*] Consider fractions of the form $(u + u'\sqrt{5})/u''$, where u, u', u'' are integers, $\gcd(u, u', u'') = 1$, and $u'' > 0$. Explain how to divide two such fractions and to obtain a quotient having the same form.

12. [*M16*] What is the largest finite floating slash number, given a bound q on the numerator length plus the denominator length? Which numbers round to $(0/1)$?

13. [*20*] (Matula and Kornerup.) Discuss the representation of floating slash numbers in a 32-bit word.

14. [*M23*] Explain how to compute the exact number of pairs of integers (u, u') such that $M_1 < u \le M_2$ and $N_1 < u' \le N_2$ and $u \perp u'$. (This can be used to determine how many numbers are representable in slash arithmetic. According to Theorem 4.5.2D, the number will be approximately $(6/\pi^2)(M_2 - M_1)(N_2 - N_1)$.)

15. [*42*] Modify one of the compilers at your installation so that it will replace all floating point calculations by floating slash calculations. Experiment with the use of slash arithmetic by running existing programs that were written by programmers who actually had floating point arithmetic in mind. (When special subroutines like square root or logarithm are called, your system should automatically convert slash numbers to floating point form before the subroutine is invoked, then back to slash form again afterwards. There should be a new option to print slash numbers in a fractional format; however, you should also print slash numbers in decimal notation as usual, if no changes are made to a user's source program.) Are the results better or worse, when floating slash numbers are substituted?

16. [*40*] Experiment with interval arithmetic on slash numbers.

4.5.2. The Greatest Common Divisor

If u and v are integers, not both zero, we say that their *greatest common divisor*, $\gcd(u, v)$, is the largest integer that evenly divides both u and v. This definition makes sense, because if $u \ne 0$ then no integer greater than $|u|$ can evenly divide u, but the integer 1 does divide both u and v; hence there must be a largest integer that divides them both. When u and v are both zero, every integer evenly divides zero, so the definition above does not apply; it is convenient to set

$$\gcd(0, 0) = 0. \tag{1}$$

The definitions just given obviously imply that

$$\gcd(u, v) = \gcd(v, u), \tag{2}$$

$$\gcd(u, v) = \gcd(-u, v), \tag{3}$$

$$\gcd(u, 0) = |u|. \tag{4}$$

In the previous section, we reduced the problem of expressing a rational number in lowest terms to the problem of finding the greatest common divisor of its numerator and denominator. Other applications of the greatest common divisor have been mentioned for example in Sections 3.2.1.2, 3.3.3, 4.3.2, 4.3.3. So the concept of $\gcd(u, v)$ is important and worthy of serious study.

The *least common multiple* of two integers u and v, written $\text{lcm}(u, v)$, is a related idea that is also important. It is defined to be the smallest positive integer that is an integer multiple of both u and v; and $\text{lcm}(u, 0) = \text{lcm}(0, v) = 0$. The classical method for teaching children how to add fractions $u/u' + v/v'$ is to train them to find the "least common denominator," which is $\text{lcm}(u', v')$.

According to the "fundamental theorem of arithmetic" (proved in exercise 1.2.4–21), each positive integer u can be expressed in the form

$$u = 2^{u_2} 3^{u_3} 5^{u_5} 7^{u_7} 11^{u_{11}} \ldots = \prod_{p \text{ prime}} p^{u_p}, \tag{5}$$

where the exponents u_2, u_3, ... are uniquely determined nonnegative integers, and where all but a finite number of the exponents are zero. From this canonical factorization of a positive integer, we immediately obtain one way to compute the greatest common divisor of u and v: By (2), (3), and (4), we may assume that u and v are positive integers, and if both of them have been canonically factored into primes we have

$$\gcd(u, v) = \prod_{p \text{ prime}} p^{\min(u_p, v_p)}, \tag{6}$$

$$\text{lcm}(u, v) = \prod_{p \text{ prime}} p^{\max(u_p, v_p)}. \tag{7}$$

Thus, for example, the greatest common divisor of $u = 7000 = 2^3 \cdot 5^3 \cdot 7$ and $v = 4400 = 2^4 \cdot 5^2 \cdot 11$ is $2^{\min(3,4)} 5^{\min(3,2)} 7^{\min(1,0)} 11^{\min(0,1)} = 2^3 \cdot 5^2 = 200$. The least common multiple of the same two numbers is $2^4 \cdot 5^3 \cdot 7 \cdot 11 = 154000$.

From formulas (6) and (7) we can easily prove a number of basic identities concerning the gcd and the lcm:

$$\gcd(u, v)w = \gcd(uw, vw), \qquad \text{if } w \geq 0; \tag{8}$$

$$\text{lcm}(u, v)w = \text{lcm}(uw, vw), \qquad \text{if } w \geq 0; \tag{9}$$

$$u \cdot v = \gcd(u, v) \cdot \text{lcm}(u, v), \qquad \text{if } u, v \geq 0; \tag{10}$$

$$\gcd\big(\text{lcm}(u, v), \text{lcm}(u, w)\big) = \text{lcm}\big(u, \gcd(v, w)\big); \tag{11}$$

$$\text{lcm}\big(\gcd(u, v), \gcd(u, w)\big) = \gcd\big(u, \text{lcm}(v, w)\big). \tag{12}$$

The latter two formulas are "distributive laws" analogous to the familiar identity $uv + uw = u(v + w)$. Equation (10) reduces the calculation of $\gcd(u, v)$ to the calculation of $\text{lcm}(u, v)$, and conversely.

Euclid's algorithm. Although Eq. (6) is useful for theoretical purposes, it is generally no help for calculating a greatest common divisor in practice, because it requires that we first determine the canonical factorization of u and v. There is no known way to find the prime factors of an integer very rapidly (see Section 4.5.4). But fortunately the greatest common divisor of two integers can be found efficiently without factoring, and in fact such a method was discovered more than 2300 years ago; it is *Euclid's algorithm*, which we have already examined in Sections 1.1 and 1.2.1.

Euclid's algorithm is found in Book 7, Propositions 1 and 2 of his *Elements* (c. 300 B.C.), but it probably wasn't his own invention. Some scholars believe that the method was known up to 200 years earlier, at least in its subtractive form, and it was almost certainly known to Eudoxus (c. 375 B.C.); see K. von Fritz, *Ann. Math.* (2) **46** (1945), 242–264. Aristotle (c. 330 B.C.) hinted at it in his *Topics*, 158b, 29–35. However, very little hard evidence about such early history has survived [see W. R. Knorr, *The Evolution of the Euclidean Elements* (Dordrecht: 1975)].

We might call Euclid's method the granddaddy of all algorithms, because it is the oldest nontrivial algorithm that has survived to the present day. (The chief rival for this honor is perhaps the ancient Egyptian method for multiplication, which was based on doubling and adding, and which forms the basis for efficient calculation of nth powers as explained in Section 4.6.3. But the Egyptian manuscripts merely give examples that are not completely systematic, and the examples were certainly not stated systematically; the Egyptian method is therefore not quite deserving of the name "algorithm." Several ancient Babylonian methods, for doing such things as solving special sets of quadratic equations in two variables, are also known. Genuine algorithms are involved in this case, not just special solutions to the equations for certain input parameters; even though the Babylonians invariably presented each method in conjunction with an example worked with particular input data, they regularly explained the general procedure in the accompanying text. [See D. E. Knuth, *CACM* **15** (1972), 671–677; **19** (1976), 108.] Many of these Babylonian algorithms predate Euclid by 1500 years, and they are the earliest known instances of written procedures for mathematics. But they do not have the stature of Euclid's algorithm, since they do not involve iteration and since they have been superseded by modern algebraic methods.)

In view of the importance of Euclid's algorithm, for historical as well as practical reasons, let us now consider how Euclid himself treated it. Paraphrased into modern terminology, this is essentially what he wrote:

Proposition. *Given two positive integers, find their greatest common divisor.*

Let A and C be the two given positive integers; it is required to find their greatest common divisor. If C divides A, then C is a common divisor of C and A, since it also divides itself. And it clearly is in fact the greatest, since no greater number than C will divide C.

But if C does not divide A, then continually subtract the lesser of the numbers A, C from the greater, until some number is left that divides the previous one. This will eventually happen, for if unity is left, it will divide the previous number.

Now let E be the positive remainder of A divided by C; let F be the positive remainder of C divided by E; and suppose that F is a divisor of E. Since F divides E and E divides $C - F$, F also divides $C - F$; but it also divides itself, so it divides C. And C divides $A - E$; therefore F also divides $A - E$. But it also divides E; therefore it divides A. Hence it is a common divisor of A and C.

I now claim that it is also the greatest. For if F is not the greatest common divisor of A and C, some larger number will divide them both. Let such a number be G.

Now since G divides C while C divides $A - E$, G divides $A - E$. G also divides the whole of A, so it divides the remainder E. But E divides $C - F$; therefore G also divides $C - F$. And G also divides the whole of C, so it divides the remainder F; that is, a greater number divides a smaller one. This is impossible.

Therefore no number greater than F will divide A and C, so F is their greatest common divisor.

Corollary. This argument makes it evident that any number dividing two numbers divides their greatest common divisor. *Q.E.D.*

Euclid's statements have been simplified here in one nontrivial respect: Greek mathematicians did not regard unity as a "divisor" of another positive integer. Two positive integers were either both equal to unity, or they were relatively prime, or they had a greatest common divisor. In fact, unity was not even considered to be a "number," and zero was of course nonexistent. These rather awkward conventions made it necessary for Euclid to duplicate much of his discussion, and he gave two separate propositions that are each essentially like the one appearing here.

In his discussion, Euclid first suggests subtracting the smaller of the two current numbers from the larger, repeatedly, until we get two numbers where one is a multiple of the other. But in the proof he really relies on taking the remainder of one number divided by another; and since he has no simple concept of zero, he cannot speak of the remainder when one number divides the other. It is reasonable to say that he imagines each *division* (not the individual subtractions) as a single step of the algorithm, and hence an "authentic" rendition of his algorithm can be phrased as follows:

Algorithm E (*Original Euclidean algorithm*). Given two integers A and C greater than unity, this algorithm finds their greatest common divisor.

E1. [Is A divisible by C?] If C divides A, the algorithm terminates with C as the answer.

E2. [Replace A by remainder.] If $A \bmod C$ is equal to unity, the given numbers were relatively prime, so the algorithm terminates. Otherwise replace the pair of values (A, C) by $(C, A \bmod C)$ and return to step E1. ▌

Euclid's "proof" quoted above is especially interesting because it is not really a proof at all! He verifies the result of the algorithm only if step E1 is performed once or thrice. Surely he must have realized that step E1 could take place more than three times, although he made no mention of such a possibility. Not having the notion of a proof by mathematical induction, he could only give a proof for a finite number of cases. (In fact, he often proved only the case $n = 3$ of a theorem that he wanted to establish for general n.) Although Euclid is justly famous for the great advances he made in the art of logical deduction, techniques for giving valid proofs by induction were not discovered until many centuries later, and the crucial ideas for proving the validity of *algorithms* are only now becoming really clear. (See Section 1.2.1 for a complete proof of Euclid's algorithm, together with a short discussion of general proof procedures for algorithms.)

It is worth noting that this algorithm for finding the greatest common divisor was chosen by Euclid to be the very first step in his development of the theory of numbers. The same order of presentation is still in use today in modern textbooks. Euclid also gave a method (Proposition 34) to find the least common multiple of two integers u and v, namely to divide u by $\gcd(u, v)$ and to multiply the result by v; this is equivalent to Eq. (10).

If we avoid Euclid's bias against the numbers 0 and 1, we can reformulate Algorithm E in the following way.

Algorithm A (*Modern Euclidean algorithm*). Given nonnegative integers u and v, this algorithm finds their greatest common divisor. (*Note:* The greatest common divisor of *arbitrary* integers u and v may be obtained by applying this algorithm to $|u|$ and $|v|$, because of Eqs. (2) and (3).)

A1. [$v = 0$?] If $v = 0$, the algorithm terminates with u as the answer.

A2. [Take $u \bmod v$.] Set $r \leftarrow u \bmod v$, $u \leftarrow v$, $v \leftarrow r$, and return to A1. (The operations of this step decrease the value of v, but they leave $\gcd(u, v)$ unchanged.) ∎

For example, we may calculate $\gcd(40902, 24140)$ as follows:

$$\gcd(40902, 24140) = \gcd(24140, 16762) = \gcd(16762, 7378)$$
$$= \gcd(7378, 2006) = \gcd(2006, 1360) = \gcd(1360, 646)$$
$$= \gcd(646, 68) = \gcd(68, 34) = \gcd(34, 0) = 34.$$

The validity of Algorithm A follows readily from Eq. (4) and the fact that

$$\gcd(u, v) = \gcd(v, u - qv), \qquad (13)$$

if q is any integer. Equation (13) holds because any common divisor of u and v is a divisor of both v and $u - qv$, and, conversely, any common divisor of v and $u - qv$ must divide both u and v.

The following MIX program illustrates the fact that Algorithm A can easily be implemented on a computer:

Program A (*Euclid's algorithm*). Assume that u and v are single-precision, nonnegative integers, stored respectively in locations U and V; this program puts $\gcd(u, v)$ into rA.

```
         LDX  U      1      rX ← u.
         JMP  2F     1
   1H    STX  V      T      v ← rX.
         SRAX 5      T      rAX ← rA.
         DIV  V      T      rX ← rAX mod v.
   2H    LDA  V     1+T     rA ← v.
         JXNZ 1B    1+T     Done if rX = 0.  ∎
```

The running time for this program is $19T + 6$ cycles, where T is the number of divisions performed. The discussion in Section 4.5.3 shows that we may take $T = 0.842766 \ln N + 0.06$ as an approximate average value, when u and v are independently and uniformly distributed in the range $1 \le u, v \le N$.

A binary method. Since Euclid's patriarchal algorithm has been used for so many centuries, it is rather surprising that it might not be the best way to find the greatest common divisor after all. A quite different gcd algorithm, primarily suited to binary arithmetic, was devised by Josef Stein in 1961 [see *J. Comp. Phys.* **1** (1967), 397–405]. This new algorithm requires no division instruction; it relies solely on the operations of subtraction, parity testing, and halving of even numbers (which corresponds to a right shift in binary notation).

The binary gcd algorithm is based on four simple facts about positive integers u and v:

a) If u and v are both even, then $\gcd(u, v) = 2\gcd(u/2, v/2)$. [See Eq. (8).]
b) If u is even and v is odd, then $\gcd(u, v) = \gcd(u/2, v)$. [See Eq. (6).]
c) As in Euclid's algorithm, $\gcd(u, v) = \gcd(u - v, v)$. [See Eqs. (13), (2).]
d) If u and v are both odd, then $u - v$ is even, and $|u - v| < \max(u, v)$.

Algorithm B (*Binary gcd algorithm*). Given positive integers u and v, this algorithm finds their greatest common divisor.

B1. [Find power of 2.] Set $k \leftarrow 0$, and then repeatedly set $k \leftarrow k + 1$, $u \leftarrow u/2$, $v \leftarrow v/2$, zero or more times until u and v are not both even.

B2. [Initialize.] (Now the original values of u and v have been divided by 2^k, and at least one of their present values is odd.) If u is odd, set $t \leftarrow -v$ and go to B4. Otherwise set $t \leftarrow u$.

B3. [Halve t.] (At this point, t is even, and nonzero.) Set $t \leftarrow t/2$.

B4. [Is t even?] If t is even, go back to B3.

B5. [Reset $\max(u, v)$.] If $t > 0$, set $u \leftarrow t$; otherwise set $v \leftarrow -t$. (The larger of u and v has been replaced by $|t|$, except perhaps during the first time this step is performed.)

B6. [Subtract.] Set $t \leftarrow u - v$. If $t \neq 0$, go back to B3. Otherwise the algorithm terminates with $u \cdot 2^k$ as the output. ∎

As an example of Algorithm B, let us consider $u = 40902$, $v = 24140$, the same numbers we used when trying out Euclid's algorithm. Step B1 sets $k \leftarrow 1$, $u \leftarrow 20451$, $v \leftarrow 12070$. Then t is set to -12070, and replaced by -6035; then v is replaced by 6035, and the computation proceeds as follows:

u	v	t
20451	6035	$+14416, +7208, +3604, +1802, +901;$
901	6035	$-5134, -2567;$
901	2567	$-1666, -833;$
901	833	$+68, +34, +17;$
17	833	$-816, -408, -204, -102, -51;$
17	51	$-34, -17;$
17	17	$0.$

The answer is $17 \cdot 2^1 = 34$. A few more iterations were necessary here than we needed with Algorithm A, but each iteration was somewhat simpler since no division steps were used.

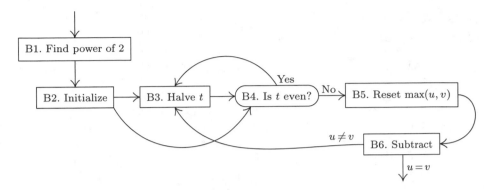

Fig. 9. Binary algorithm for the greatest common divisor.

A MIX program for Algorithm B requires a bit more code than for Algorithm A, but the steps are elementary. In order to make such a program fairly typical of a binary computer's representation of Algorithm B, let us assume that MIX is extended to include the following operators:

• SLB (shift left AX binary). C = 6; F = 6.
The contents of registers A and X are "shifted left" M binary places; that is, $|rAX| \leftarrow |2^M rAX| \bmod B^{10}$, where B is the byte size. (As with all MIX shift commands, the signs of rA and rX are not affected.)

• SRB (shift right AX binary). C = 6; F = 7.
The contents of registers A and X are "shifted right" M binary places; that is, $|rAX| \leftarrow \lfloor |rAX|/2^M \rfloor$.

• JAE, JAO (jump A even, jump A odd). C = 40; F = 6, 7, respectively.
A JMP occurs if rA is even or odd, respectively.

• JXE, JXO (jump X even, jump X odd). C = 47; F = 6, 7, respectively.
Analogous to JAE, JAO.

Program B (*Binary gcd algorithm*). Assume that u and v are single-precision positive integers, stored respectively in locations U and V; this program uses Algorithm B to put $\gcd(u, v)$ into rA. Register assignments: rA ≡ t, rI1 ≡ k.

01	ABS	EQU	1:5		
02	B1	ENT1 0	1	*B1. Find power of 2.*
03		LDX U	1	rX ← u.
04		LDAN V	1	rA ← −v.
05		JMP 1F	1	
06	2H	SRB 1	A	Halve rA, rX.
07		INC1 1	A	k ← k + 1.
08		STX U	A	u ← u/2.
09		STA V(ABS)	A	v ← v/2.
10	1H	JXO B4	1 + A	To B4 with t ← −v if u is odd.
11	B2	JAE 2B	B + A	*B2. Initialize.*

12		LDA	U	B	$t \leftarrow u.$
13	B3	SRB	1	D	B3. Halve t.
14	B4	JAE	B3	$1 - B + D$	B4. Is t even?
15	B5	JAN	1F	C	B5. Reset $\max(u,v)$.
16		STA	U	E	If $t > 0$, set $u \leftarrow t.$
17		SUB	V	E	$t \leftarrow u - v.$
18		JMP	2F	E	
19	1H	STA	V(ABS)	$C - E$	If $t < 0$, set $v \leftarrow -t.$
20	B6	ADD	U	$C - E$	B6. Subtract.
21	2H	JANZ	B3	C	To B3 if $t \neq 0.$
22		LDA	U	1	$rA \leftarrow u.$
23		ENTX	0	1	$rX \leftarrow 0.$
24		SLB	0,1	1	$rA \leftarrow 2^k \cdot rA.$ ∎

The running time of this program is

$$9A + 2B + 6C + 3D + E + 13$$

units, where $A = k$, $B = 1$ if $t \leftarrow u$ in step B2 (otherwise $B = 0$), C is the number of subtraction steps, D is the number of halvings in step B3, and E is the number of times $t > 0$ in step B5. Calculations discussed later in this section imply that we may take $A = \frac{1}{3}$, $B = \frac{1}{3}$, $C = 0.71N - 0.5$, $D = 1.41N - 2.7$, and $E = 0.35N - 0.4$ as average values for these quantities, assuming random inputs u and v in the range $1 \leq u, v < 2^N$. The total running time is therefore about $8.8N + 5.2$ cycles, compared to about $11.1N + 7.1$ for Program A under the same assumptions. The worst possible running time for u and v in this range occurs when $A = 0$, $B = 1$, $C = N$, $D = 2N - 2$, $E = N - 1$; this amounts to $13N + 8$ cycles. (The corresponding value for Program A is $26.8N + 19$.)

Thus the greater speed of the iterations in Program B, due to the simplicity of the operations, compensates for the greater number of iterations required. We have found that the binary algorithm is about 20 percent faster than Euclid's algorithm on the MIX computer. Of course, the situation may be different on other computers, and in any event both programs are quite efficient; but it appears that not even a procedure as venerable as Euclid's algorithm can withstand progress.

The binary gcd algorithm itself might have a distinguished pedigree, since it may well have been known in ancient China. Chapter 1, Section 6 of a classic text called *Chiu Chang Suan Shu*, the "Nine Chapters on Arithmetic" (c. 1st century A.D.), gives the following method for reducing a fraction to lowest terms:

> If halving is possible, take half.
>
> Otherwise write down the denominator and the numerator, and subtract the smaller from the greater.
>
> Repeat until both numbers are equal.
>
> Simplify with this common value.

If the repeat instruction means to go back to the halving step instead of to repeat the subtraction step—this point isn't clear—the method is essentially Algorithm B. [See Y. Mikami, *The Development of Mathematics in China and Japan* (Leipzig: 1913), 11; K. Vogel, *Neun Bücher arithmetischer Technik* (Braunschweig: Vieweg, 1968), 8.]

V. C. Harris [*Fibonacci Quarterly* **8** (1970), 102–103; see also V. A. Lebesgue, *J. Math. Pures Appl.* **12** (1847), 497–520] has suggested an interesting cross between Euclid's algorithm and the binary algorithm. If u and v are odd, with $u \geq v > 0$, we can always write

$$u = qv \pm r$$

where $0 \leq r < v$ and r is even; if $r \neq 0$ we set $r \leftarrow r/2$ until r is odd, then set $u \leftarrow v$, $v \leftarrow r$ and repeat the process. In subsequent iterations, $q \geq 3$.

Extensions. We can extend the methods used to calculate $\gcd(u, v)$ in order to solve some slightly more difficult problems. For example, assume that we want to compute the greatest common divisor of n integers $u_1, u_2, \ldots, u_n$.

One way to calculate $\gcd(u_1, u_2, \ldots, u_n)$, assuming that the u's are all nonnegative, is to extend Euclid's algorithm in the following way: If all u_j are zero, the greatest common divisor is taken to be zero; otherwise if only one u_j is nonzero, it is the greatest common divisor; otherwise replace u_k by $u_k \bmod u_j$ for all $k \neq j$, where u_j is the minimum of the nonzero u's, and repeat the process.

The algorithm sketched in the preceding paragraph is a natural generalization of Euclid's method, and it can be justified in a similar manner. But there is a simpler method available, based on the easily verified identity

$$\gcd(u_1, u_2, \ldots, u_n) = \gcd\big(u_1, \gcd(u_2, \ldots, u_n)\big). \tag{14}$$

To calculate $\gcd(u_1, u_2, \ldots, u_n)$, we may therefore proceed as follows:

Algorithm C (*Greatest common divisor of n integers*). Given integers $u_1, u_2, \ldots, u_n$, where $n \geq 1$, this algorithm computes their greatest common divisor, using an algorithm for the case $n = 2$ as a subroutine.

C1. Set $d \leftarrow u_n$, $k \leftarrow n - 1$.

C2. If $d \neq 1$ and $k > 0$, set $d \leftarrow \gcd(u_k, d)$ and $k \leftarrow k - 1$ and repeat this step. Otherwise $d = \gcd(u_1, \ldots, u_n)$. ∎

This method reduces the calculation of $\gcd(u_1, \ldots, u_n)$ to repeated calculations of the greatest common divisor of two numbers at a time. It makes use of the fact that $\gcd(u_1, \ldots, u_k, 1) = 1$; and this will be helpful, since we will already have $\gcd(u_{n-1}, u_n) = 1$ more than 60 percent of the time, if u_{n-1} and u_n are chosen at random. In most cases the value of d will decrease rapidly during the first few stages of the calculation, and this will make the remainder of the computation quite fast. Here Euclid's algorithm has an advantage over Algorithm B, because its running time is primarily governed by the value of $\min(u, v)$, while the running time for Algorithm B is primarily governed by $\max(u, v)$; it would be reasonable to perform one iteration of Euclid's algorithm, replacing u by $u \bmod v$ if u is much larger than v, and then to continue with Algorithm B.

The assertion that $\gcd(u_{n-1}, u_n)$ will be equal to unity more than 60 percent of the time for random inputs is a consequence of the following well-known result of number theory:

Theorem D. [G. Lejeune Dirichlet, *Abhandlungen Königlich Preuß. Akad. Wiss.* (1849), 69–83.] *If u and v are integers chosen at random, the probability that $\gcd(u, v) = 1$ is $6/\pi^2 \approx .60793$.*

A precise formulation of this theorem, which defines carefully what is meant by being "chosen at random," appears in exercise 10 with a rigorous proof. Let us content ourselves here with a heuristic argument that shows why the theorem is plausible.

If we assume, without proof, the existence of a well-defined probability p that $u \perp v$, then we can determine the probability that $\gcd(u, v) = d$ for any positive integer d, because $\gcd(u, v) = d$ if and only if u is a multiple of d and v is a multiple of d and $u/d \perp v/d$. Thus the probability that $\gcd(u, v) = d$ is equal to $1/d$ times $1/d$ times p, namely p/d^2. Now let us sum these probabilities over all possible values of d; we should get

$$1 = \sum_{d \geq 1} p/d^2 = p\left(1 + \tfrac{1}{4} + \tfrac{1}{9} + \tfrac{1}{16} + \cdots\right).$$

Since the sum $1 + \tfrac{1}{4} + \tfrac{1}{9} + \cdots = H_\infty^{(2)}$ is equal to $\pi^2/6$ by Eq. 1.2.7–(7), we need $p = 6/\pi^2$ in order to make this equation come out right. ∎

Euclid's algorithm can be extended in another important way: We can calculate integers u' and v' such that

$$uu' + vv' = \gcd(u, v) \tag{15}$$

at the same time $\gcd(u, v)$ is being calculated. This extension of Euclid's algorithm can be described conveniently in vector notation:

Algorithm X (*Extended Euclid's algorithm*). Given nonnegative integers u and v, this algorithm determines a vector (u_1, u_2, u_3) such that $uu_1 + vu_2 = u_3 = \gcd(u, v)$. The computation makes use of auxiliary vectors (v_1, v_2, v_3), (t_1, t_2, t_3); all vectors are manipulated in such a way that the relations

$$ut_1 + vt_2 = t_3, \qquad uu_1 + vu_2 = u_3, \qquad uv_1 + vv_2 = v_3 \tag{16}$$

hold throughout the calculation.

X1. [Initialize.] Set $(u_1, u_2, u_3) \leftarrow (1, 0, u)$, $(v_1, v_2, v_3) \leftarrow (0, 1, v)$.

X2. [Is $v_3 = 0$?] If $v_3 = 0$, the algorithm terminates.

X3. [Divide, subtract.] Set $q \leftarrow \lfloor u_3/v_3 \rfloor$, and then set

$$(t_1, t_2, t_3) \leftarrow (u_1, u_2, u_3) - (v_1, v_2, v_3)q,$$
$$(u_1, u_2, u_3) \leftarrow (v_1, v_2, v_3), \qquad (v_1, v_2, v_3) \leftarrow (t_1, t_2, t_3).$$

Return to step X2. ∎

For example, let $u = 40902$, $v = 24140$. At step X2 we have

q	u_1	u_2	u_3	v_1	v_2	v_3
—	1	0	40902	0	1	24140
1	0	1	24140	1	−1	16762
1	1	−1	16762	−1	2	7378
2	−1	2	7378	3	−5	2006
3	3	−5	2006	−10	17	1360
1	−10	17	1360	13	−22	646
2	13	−22	646	−36	61	68
9	−36	61	68	337	−571	34
2	337	−571	34	−710	1203	0

The solution is therefore $337 \cdot 40902 - 571 \cdot 24140 = 34 = \gcd(40902, 24140)$.

Algorithm X can be traced to the *Āryabhatīya* (c. 500) by Āryabhaṭa of northern India. His description was rather cryptic, but later commentators such as Bhāskara I in the seventh century clarified the rule, which was called *kuṭṭaka* ("the pulverizer"). [See B. Datta and A. N. Singh, *History of Hindu Mathematics* **2** (Lahore: Motilal Banarsi Das, 1938), 89–116.] Its validity follows from (16) and the fact that the algorithm is identical to Algorithm A with respect to its manipulation of u_3 and v_3; a detailed proof of Algorithm X is discussed in Section 1.2.1. Gordon H. Bradley has observed that we can avoid a good deal of the calculation in Algorithm X by suppressing u_2, v_2, and t_2; then u_2 can be determined afterwards using the relation $uu_1 + vu_2 = u_3$.

Exercise 15 shows that the values of $|u_1|$, $|u_2|$, $|v_1|$, and $|v_2|$ remain bounded by the size of the inputs u and v. Algorithm B, which computes the greatest common divisor using properties of binary notation, can be extended in a similar way; see exercise 39. For some instructive extensions to Algorithm X, see exercises 18 and 19 in Section 4.6.1.

The ideas underlying Euclid's algorithm can also be applied to find a *general solution in integers* of any set of linear equations with integer coefficients. For example, suppose that we want to find all integers w, x, y, z that satisfy the two equations

$$10w + 3x + 3y + 8z = 1, \tag{17}$$
$$6w - 7x \qquad - 5z = 2. \tag{18}$$

We can introduce a new variable

$$\lfloor 10/3 \rfloor w + \lfloor 3/3 \rfloor x + \lfloor 3/3 \rfloor y + \lfloor 8/3 \rfloor z = 3w + x + y + 2z = t_1,$$

and use it to eliminate y; Eq. (17) becomes

$$(10 \bmod 3)w + (3 \bmod 3)x + 3t_1 + (8 \bmod 3)z = w + 3t_1 + 2z = 1, \tag{19}$$

and Eq. (18) remains unchanged. The new equation (19) may be used to eliminate w, and (18) becomes

$$6(1 - 3t_1 - 2z) - 7x - 5z = 2;$$

that is,

$$7x + 18t_1 + 17z = 4. \tag{20}$$

Now as before we introduce a new variable

$$x + 2t_1 + 2z = t_2$$

and eliminate x from (20):

$$7t_2 + 4t_1 + 3z = 4. \tag{21}$$

Another new variable can be introduced in the same fashion, in order to eliminate the variable z, which has the smallest coefficient:

$$2t_2 + t_1 + z = t_3.$$

Eliminating z from (21) yields

$$t_2 + t_1 + 3t_3 = 4, \tag{22}$$

and this equation, finally, can be used to eliminate t_2. We are left with two independent variables, t_1 and t_3; substituting back for the original variables, we obtain the general solution

$$\begin{aligned}
w &= 17 - 5t_1 - 14t_3, \\
x &= 20 - 5t_1 - 17t_3, \\
y &= -55 + 19t_1 + 45t_3, \\
z &= -8 + t_1 + 7t_3.
\end{aligned} \tag{23}$$

In other words, all integer solutions (w, x, y, z) to the original equations (17) and (18) are obtained from (23) by letting t_1 and t_3 independently run through all integers.

The general method that has just been illustrated is based on the following procedure: Find a nonzero coefficient c of smallest absolute value in the system of equations. Suppose that this coefficient appears in an equation having the form

$$cx_0 + c_1x_1 + \cdots + c_kx_k = d; \tag{24}$$

and assume for simplicity that $c > 0$. If $c = 1$, use this equation to eliminate the variable x_0 from the other equations remaining in the system; then repeat the procedure on the remaining equations. (If no more equations remain, the computation stops, and a general solution in terms of the variables not yet eliminated has essentially been obtained.) If $c > 1$, then if $c_1 \bmod c = \cdots = c_k \bmod c = 0$ check that $d \bmod c = 0$, otherwise there is no integer solution; then divide both sides of (24) by c and eliminate x_0 as in the case $c = 1$. Finally, if $c > 1$ and not all of $c_1 \bmod c, \ldots, c_k \bmod c$ are zero, then introduce a new variable

$$\lfloor c/c \rfloor x_0 + \lfloor c_1/c \rfloor x_1 + \cdots + \lfloor c_k/c \rfloor x_k = t; \tag{25}$$

eliminate the variable x_0 from the other equations, in favor of t, and replace the original equation (24) by

$$ct + (c_1 \bmod c)x_1 + \cdots + (c_k \bmod c)x_k = d. \qquad (26)$$

(See (19) and (21) in the example above.)

This process must terminate, since each step reduces either the number of equations or the size of the smallest nonzero coefficient in the system. When this procedure is applied to the equation $ux + vy = 1$, for specific integers u and v, it runs through essentially the steps of Algorithm X.

The transformation-of-variables procedure just explained is a simple and straightforward way to solve linear equations when the variables are allowed to take on integer values only, but it isn't the best method available for this problem. Substantial refinements are possible, but beyond the scope of this book. [See Henri Cohen, *A Course in Computational Algebraic Number Theory* (New York: Springer, 1993), Chapter 2.]

Variants of Euclid's algorithm can be used also with Gaussian integers $u+iu'$ and in certain other quadratic number fields. See, for example, A. Hurwitz, *Acta Math.* **11** (1887), 187–200; E. Kaltofen and H. Rolletschek, *Math. Comp.* **53** (1989), 697–720; A. Knopfmacher and J. Knopfmacher, *BIT* **31** (1991), 286–292.

High-precision calculation. If u and v are very large integers, requiring a multiple-precision representation, the binary method (Algorithm B) is a simple and fairly efficient means of calculating their greatest common divisor, since it involves only subtractions and shifting.

By contrast, Euclid's algorithm seems much less attractive, since step A2 requires a multiple-precision division of u by v. But this difficulty is not really as bad as it seems, since we will prove in Section 4.5.3 that the quotient $\lfloor u/v \rfloor$ is almost always very small. For example, assuming random inputs, the quotient $\lfloor u/v \rfloor$ will be less than 1000 approximately 99.856 percent of the time. Therefore it is almost always possible to find $\lfloor u/v \rfloor$ and $(u \bmod v)$ using single-precision calculations, together with the comparatively simple operation of calculating $u - qv$ where q is a single-precision number. Furthermore, if it does turn out that u is much larger than v (for instance, the initial input data might have this form), we don't really mind having a large quotient q, since Euclid's algorithm makes a great deal of progress when it replaces u by $u \bmod v$ in such a case.

A significant improvement in the speed of Euclid's algorithm when high-precision numbers are involved can be achieved by using a method due to D. H. Lehmer [*AMM* **45** (1938), 227–233]. Working only with the leading digits of large numbers, it is possible to do most of the calculations with single-precision arithmetic, and to make a substantial reduction in the number of multiple-precision operations involved. The idea is to save time by doing a "virtual" calculation instead of the actual one.

For example, let us consider the pair of eight-digit numbers $u = 27182818$, $v = 10000000$, assuming that we are using a machine with only four-digit words.

Let $u' = 2718$, $v' = 1001$, $u'' = 2719$, $v'' = 1000$; then u'/v' and u''/v'' are approximations to u/v, with

$$u'/v' < u/v < u''/v''. \tag{27}$$

The ratio u/v determines the sequence of quotients obtained in Euclid's algorithm. If we perform Euclid's algorithm simultaneously on the single-precision values (u', v') and (u'', v'') until we get a different quotient, it is not difficult to see that the same sequence of quotients would have appeared to this point if we had worked with the multiple-precision numbers (u, v). Thus, consider what happens when Euclid's algorithm is applied to (u', v') and to (u'', v''):

u'	v'	q'		u''	v''	q''
2718	1001	2		2719	1000	2
1001	716	1		1000	719	1
716	285	2		719	281	2
285	146	1		281	157	1
146	139	1		157	124	1
139	7	19		124	33	3

The first five quotients are the same in both cases, so they must be the true ones. But on the sixth step we find that $q' \neq q''$, so the single-precision calculations are suspended. We have gained the knowledge that the calculation would have proceeded as follows if we had been working with the original multiple-precision numbers:

u	v	q	
u_0	v_0	2	
v_0	$u_0 - 2v_0$	1	
$u_0 - 2v_0$	$-u_0 + 3v_0$	2	(28)
$-u_0 + 3v_0$	$3u_0 - 8v_0$	1	
$3u_0 - 8v_0$	$-4u_0 + 11v_0$	1	
$-4u_0 + 11v_0$	$7u_0 - 19v_0$	?	

(The next quotient lies somewhere between 3 and 19.) No matter how many digits are in u and v, the first five steps of Euclid's algorithm would be the same as (28), so long as (27) holds. We can therefore avoid the multiple-precision operations of the first five steps, and replace them all by a multiple-precision calculation of $-4u_0 + 11v_0$ and $7u_0 - 19v_0$. In this case we obtain $u = 1268728$, $v = 279726$; the calculation can now continue in a similar manner with $u' = 1268$, $v' = 280$, $u'' = 1269$, $v'' = 279$, etc. If we had a larger accumulator, more steps could be done by single-precision calculations. Our example showed that only five cycles of Euclid's algorithm were combined into one multiple step, but with (say) a word size of 10 digits we could do about twelve cycles at a time. Results proved in Section 4.5.3 imply that the number of multiple-precision cycles that can be replaced at each iteration is essentially proportional to the number of digits used in the single-precision calculations.

Lehmer's method can be formulated as follows:

Algorithm L (*Euclid's algorithm for large numbers*). Let u and v be nonnegative integers, with $u \geq v$, represented in multiple precision. This algorithm computes the greatest common divisor of u and v, making use of auxiliary single-precision p-digit variables $\hat{u}$, $\hat{v}$, A, B, C, D, T, q, and auxiliary multiple-precision variables t and w.

L1. [Initialize.] If v is small enough to be represented as a single-precision value, calculate $\gcd(u, v)$ by Algorithm A and terminate the computation. Otherwise, let $\hat{u}$ be the p leading digits of u, and let $\hat{v}$ be the corresponding digits of v; in other words, if radix-b notation is being used, $\hat{u} \leftarrow \lfloor u/b^k \rfloor$ and $\hat{v} \leftarrow \lfloor v/b^k \rfloor$, where k is as small as possible consistent with the condition $\hat{u} < b^p$.

Set $A \leftarrow 1$, $B \leftarrow 0$, $C \leftarrow 0$, $D \leftarrow 1$. (These variables represent the coefficients in (28), where

$$u = Au_0 + Bv_0, \quad \text{and} \quad v = Cu_0 + Dv_0, \tag{29}$$

in the equivalent actions of Algorithm A on multiple-precision numbers. We also have

$$u' = \hat{u} + B, \qquad v' = \hat{v} + D, \qquad u'' = \hat{u} + A, \qquad v'' = \hat{v} + C \tag{30}$$

in terms of the notation in the example worked above.)

L2. [Test quotient.] Set $q \leftarrow \lfloor (\hat{u} + A)/(\hat{v} + C) \rfloor$. If $q \neq \lfloor (\hat{u} + B)/(\hat{v} + D) \rfloor$, go to step L4. (This step tests if $q' \neq q''$, in the notation of the example above. Single-precision overflow can occur in special circumstances during the computation in this step, but only when $\hat{u} = b^p - 1$ and $A = 1$ or when $\hat{v} = b^p - 1$ and $D = 1$; the conditions

$$0 \leq \hat{u} + A \leq b^p, \qquad 0 \leq \hat{v} + C < b^p,$$
$$0 \leq \hat{u} + B < b^p, \qquad 0 \leq \hat{v} + D \leq b^p \tag{31}$$

will always hold, because of (30). It is possible to have $\hat{v} + C = 0$ or $\hat{v} + D = 0$, but not both simultaneously; therefore division by zero in this step is taken to mean "Go directly to L4.")

L3. [Emulate Euclid.] Set $T \leftarrow A - qC$, $A \leftarrow C$, $C \leftarrow T$, $T \leftarrow B - qD$, $B \leftarrow D$, $D \leftarrow T$, $T \leftarrow \hat{u} - q\hat{v}$, $\hat{u} \leftarrow \hat{v}$, $\hat{v} \leftarrow T$, and go back to step L2. (These single-precision calculations are the equivalent of multiple-precision operations, as in (28), under the conventions of (29).)

L4. [Multiprecision step.] If $B = 0$, set $t \leftarrow u \bmod v$, $u \leftarrow v$, $v \leftarrow t$, using multiple-precision division. (This happens only if the single-precision operations cannot simulate any of the multiple-precision ones. It implies that Euclid's algorithm requires a very large quotient, and this is an extremely rare occurrence.) Otherwise, set $t \leftarrow Au$, $t \leftarrow t + Bv$, $w \leftarrow Cu$, $w \leftarrow w + Dv$, $u \leftarrow t$, $v \leftarrow w$ (using straightforward multiple-precision operations). Go back to step L1. ∎

The values of A, B, C, D remain as single-precision numbers throughout this calculation, because of (31).

Algorithm L requires a somewhat more complicated program than Algorithm B, but with large numbers it will be faster on many computers. The binary technique of Algorithm B can, however, be speeded up in a similar way (see exercise 38), to the point where it continues to win. Algorithm L has the advantage that it determines the sequence of quotients obtained in Euclid's algorithm, and this sequence has numerous applications (see, for example, exercises 43, 47, 49, and 51 in Section 4.5.3). See also exercise 4.5.3–46.

*Analysis of the binary algorithm. Let us conclude this section by studying the running time of Algorithm B, in order to justify the formulas stated earlier.

An exact determination of Algorithm B's behavior appears to be exceedingly difficult to derive, but we can begin to study it by means of an approximate model. Suppose that u and v are odd numbers, with $u > v$ and

$$\lfloor \lg u \rfloor = m, \qquad \lfloor \lg v \rfloor = n. \tag{32}$$

(Thus, u is an $(m + 1)$-bit number, and v is an $(n + 1)$-bit number.) Consider a subtract-and-shift cycle of Algorithm B, namely an operation that starts at step B6 and then stops after step B5 is finished. Every subtract-and-shift cycle with $u > v$ forms $u - v$ and shifts this quantity right until obtaining an odd number u' that replaces u. Under random conditions, we would expect to have $u' = (u - v)/2$ about one-half of the time, $u' = (u - v)/4$ about one-fourth of the time, $u' = (u - v)/8$ about one-eighth of the time, and so on. We have

$$\lfloor \lg u' \rfloor = m - k - r, \tag{33}$$

where k is the number of places that $u - v$ is shifted right, and where r is $\lfloor \lg u \rfloor - \lfloor \lg(u - v) \rfloor$, the number of bits lost at the left during the subtraction of v from u. Notice that $r \leq 1$ when $m \geq n + 2$, and $r \geq 1$ when $m = n$.

The interaction between k and r is quite messy (see exercise 20). But Richard Brent discovered a nice way to analyze the approximate behavior by assuming that u and v are large enough that a continuous distribution describes the ratio v/u, while k varies discretely. [See *Algorithms and Complexity*, edited by J. F. Traub (New York: Academic Press, 1976), 321–355.] Let us assume that u and v are large integers that are essentially random, except that they are odd and their ratio has a certain probability distribution. Then the least significant bits of the quantity $t = u - v$ in step B6 will be essentially random, except that t will be even. Hence t will be an odd multiple of 2^k with probability 2^{-k}; this is the approximate probability that k right shifts will be needed in the subtract-and-shift cycle. In other words, we obtain a reasonable approximation to the behavior of Algorithm B if we assume that step B4 always branches to B3 with probability $1/2$.

Let $G_n(x)$ be the probability that $\min(u,v)/\max(u,v)$ is $\geq x$ after n subtract-and-shift cycles have been performed under this assumption. If $u \geq v$ and if exactly k right shifts are performed, the ratio $X = v/u$ is changed to $X' =$

$\min(2^k v/(u-v), (u-v)/2^k v) = \min(2^k X/(1-X), (1-X)/2^k X)$. Thus we will have $X' \geq x$ if and only if $2^k X/(1-X) \geq x$ and $(1-X)/2^k X \geq x$; and this is the same as

$$\frac{1}{1+2^k/x} \leq X \leq \frac{1}{1+2^k x}. \tag{34}$$

Therefore $G_n(x)$ satisfies the interesting recurrence

$$G_{n+1}(x) = \sum_{k \geq 1} 2^{-k} \left(G_n\left(\frac{1}{1+2^k/x}\right) - G_n\left(\frac{1}{1+2^k x}\right) \right), \tag{35}$$

where $G_0(x) = 1 - x$ for $0 \leq x \leq 1$. Computational experiments indicate that $G_n(x)$ converges rapidly to a limiting distribution $G_\infty(x) = G(x)$, although a formal proof of convergence seems to be difficult. We shall assume that $G(x)$ exists; hence it satisfies

$$G(x) = \sum_{k \geq 1} 2^{-k} \left(G\left(\frac{1}{1+2^k/x}\right) - G\left(\frac{1}{1+2^k x}\right) \right), \quad \text{for } 0 < x \leq 1; \tag{36}$$

$$G(0) = 1; \qquad\qquad G(1) = 0. \tag{37}$$

Let

$$S(x) = \frac{1}{2}G\left(\frac{1}{1+2x}\right) + \frac{1}{4}G\left(\frac{1}{1+4x}\right) + \frac{1}{8}G\left(\frac{1}{1+8x}\right) + \cdots$$

$$= \sum_{k \geq 1} 2^{-k} G\left(\frac{1}{1+2^k x}\right); \tag{38}$$

then we have

$$G(x) = S(1/x) - S(x). \tag{39}$$

It is convenient to define

$$G(1/x) = -G(x), \tag{40}$$

so that (39) holds for all $x > 0$. As x runs from 0 to ∞, $S(x)$ increases from 0 to 1, hence $G(x)$ decreases from $+1$ to -1. Of course $G(x)$ is no longer a probability when $x > 1$; but it is meaningful nevertheless (see exercise 23). We will assume that there are power series $\alpha(x)$, $\beta(x)$, $\gamma_m(x)$, $\delta_m(x)$, $\lambda(x)$, $\mu(x)$, $\sigma_m(x)$, $\tau_m(x)$, and $\rho(x)$ such that

$$G(x) = \alpha(x)\lg x + \beta(x) + \sum_{m=1}^{\infty} (\gamma_m(x)\cos 2\pi m\lg x + \delta_m(x)\sin 2\pi m\lg x), \tag{41}$$

$$S(x) = \lambda(x)\lg x + \mu(x) + \sum_{m=1}^{\infty} (\sigma_m(x)\cos 2\pi m\lg x + \tau_m(x)\sin 2\pi m\lg x), \tag{42}$$

$$\rho(x) = G(1+x) = \rho_1 x + \rho_2 x^2 + \rho_3 x^3 + \rho_4 x^4 + \rho_5 x^5 + \rho_6 x^6 + \cdots, \tag{43}$$

because it can be shown that the solutions $G_n(x)$ to (35) have this property for $n \geq 1$. (See, for example, exercise 30.) The power series converge for $|x| < 1$.

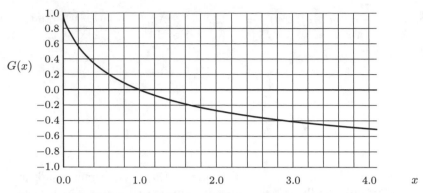

Fig. 10. The limiting distribution of ratios in the binary gcd algorithm.

What can we deduce about $\alpha(x), \ldots, \rho(x)$ from equations (36)–(43)? In the first place we have

$$2S(x) = G\big(1/(1+2x)\big) + S(2x) = S(2x) - \rho(2x) \qquad (44)$$

from (38), (40), and (43). Consequently Eq. (42) holds if and only if

$$2\lambda(x) = \lambda(2x); \qquad (45)$$
$$2\mu(x) = \mu(2x) + \lambda(2x) - \rho(2x); \qquad (46)$$
$$2\sigma_m(x) = \sigma_m(2x), \qquad 2\tau_m(x) = \tau_m(2x), \qquad \text{for } m \geq 1. \qquad (47)$$

Relation (45) tells us that $\lambda(x)$ is simply a constant multiple of x; we will write

$$\lambda(x) = -\lambda x \qquad (48)$$

because the constant is negative. (The relevant coefficient turns out to be

$$\lambda = 0.39792\,26811\,88316\,64407\,67071\,61142\,65498\,23098+, \qquad (49)$$

but no easy way to compute it is known.) Relation (46) tells us that $\rho_1 = -\lambda$, and that $2\mu_k = 2^k\mu_k - 2^k\rho_k$ when $k > 1$; in other words,

$$\mu_k = \rho_k/(1 - 2^{1-k}), \qquad \text{for } k \geq 2. \qquad (50)$$

We also know from (47) that the two families of power series

$$\sigma_m(x) = \sigma_m x, \qquad \tau_m(x) = \tau_m x \qquad (51)$$

are simply linear functions. (This is not true for $\gamma_m(x)$ and $\delta_m(x)$.)

Replacing x by $1/2x$ in (44) yields

$$2S(1/2x) = S(1/x) + G(x/(1+x)), \qquad (52)$$

and (39) converts this equation to a relation between G and S when x is near 0:

$$2G(2x) + 2S(2x) = G(x) + S(x) + G(x/(1+x)). \qquad (53)$$

The coefficients of $\lg x$ must agree when both sides of this equation are expanded in power series, hence

$$2\alpha(2x) - 4\lambda x = \alpha(x) - \lambda x + \alpha(x/(1+x)). \qquad (54)$$

Equation (54) is a recurrence that defines $\alpha(x)$. In fact, let us consider the function $\psi(z)$ that satisfies

$$\psi(z) = \frac{1}{2}\left(z + \psi\left(\frac{z}{2}\right) + \psi\left(\frac{z}{2+z}\right)\right), \qquad \psi(0) = 0, \quad \psi'(0) = 1. \qquad (55)$$

Then (54) says that

$$\alpha(x) = \frac{3}{2}\lambda\psi(x). \qquad (56)$$

Moreover, iteration of (55) yields

$$\psi(z) = \frac{z}{2}\left(\frac{1}{1} + \frac{1}{2}\left(\frac{1}{2} + \frac{1}{2+z}\right) + \frac{1}{4}\left(\frac{1}{4} + \frac{1}{4+z} + \frac{1}{4+2z} + \frac{1}{4+3z}\right) + \cdots\right)$$

$$= \frac{z}{2}\sum_{k\geq 0}\frac{1}{2^k}\sum_{0\leq j<2^k}\frac{1}{2^k + jz}. \qquad (57)$$

It follows that the power series expansion of $\psi(z)$ is

$$\psi(z) = \sum_{n\geq 1}(-1)^{n-1}\psi_n z^n, \qquad \psi_n = \frac{1}{2n}\sum_{k=0}^{n-1}\frac{(-1)^k B_k}{2^{k+1}-1}\binom{n}{k} + \frac{\delta_{n1}}{2}; \qquad (58)$$

see exercise 27. This formula for ψ_n is surprisingly similar to an expression that arises in connection with digital search tree algorithms, Eq. 6.3–(18). Exercise 28 proves that $\psi_n = \Theta(n^{-2})$.

We now know $\alpha(x)$, except for the constant $\lambda = -\rho_1$, and (50) relates $\mu(x)$ to $\rho(x)$ except for the coefficient μ_1. The answer to exercise 25 shows that the coefficients of $\rho(x)$ can all be expressed in terms of $\rho_1, \rho_3, \rho_5, \ldots$; moreover, the constants σ_m and τ_m can be computed by the method used to solve exercise 29, and complicated relations also hold between the coefficients of the functions $\gamma_m(x)$ and $\delta_m(x)$. However, there seems to be no way to compute all the coefficients of the various functions that enter into $G(x)$ except to iterate the recurrence (36) by elaborate numerical methods.

Once we have computed a good approximation to $G(x)$, we can estimate the asymptotic average running time of Algorithm B as follows: If $u \geq v$ and if k right shifts are performed, the quantity $Y = uv$ is changed to $Y' = (u - v)v/2^k$; hence the ratio Y/Y' is $2^k/(1-X)$, where $X = v/u$ is $\geq x$ with probability $G(x)$. Therefore the number of bits in uv decreases on the average by the constant

$$b = \mathrm{E}\lg(Y/Y') = \sum_{k\geq 1}2^{-k}\left(f_k(0) + \int_0^1 G(x)f_k'(x)\,dx\right),$$

where $f_k(x) = \lg(2^k/(1-x))$; we have

$$b = \sum_{k\geq 1}2^{-k}\left(k + \int_0^1\frac{G(x)\,dx}{(1-x)\ln 2}\right) = 2 + \int_0^1\frac{G(x)\,dx}{(1-x)\ln 2}. \qquad (59)$$

When eventually $u = v$, the expected value of $\lg uv$ will be approximately 0.9779 (see exercise 14); therefore the total number of subtract-and-shift cycles of Algorithm B will be approximately $1/b$ times the initial value of $\lg uv$. By symmetry, this is about $2/b$ times the initial value of $\lg u$. Numerical computations carried out by Richard Brent in 1997 give the value

$$2/b = 0.70597\,12461\,01916\,39152\,93141\,35852\,88176\,66677+ \qquad (60)$$

for this fundamental constant.

All of these calculations are highly plausible, but they rely on unproved assumptions. By introducing a slightly different model, and applying deep methods from the theory of dynamical systems, Brigitte Vallée was finally able to complete the first rigorous analysis of Algorithm B [see *Algorithmica* **22** (1998), 660–685]. Her results led her to suspect that the constants λ and b might be related by the remarkable formula

$$\frac{\lambda}{b} = \frac{2\ln 2}{\pi^2}; \qquad (61)$$

and indeed, she was right! More than a decade later, Ian D. Morris found a proof of (61), as a byproduct of an analytic *tour de force* with which he successfully demonstrated the complete validity of Brent's model [see exercise 34].

Let us return to our assumption in (32) that u and v are odd and in the ranges $2^m \le u < 2^{m+1}$ and $2^n \le v < 2^{n+1}$. Empirical tests of Algorithm B with several million random inputs and with various values of m and n in the range $29 \le m, n \le 37$ indicate that the actual average behavior of the algorithm is given by

$$\begin{aligned} C &\approx \tfrac{1}{2}m + 0.203n + 1.9 - 0.4(0.6)^{m-n}, \\ D &\approx \quad m + 0.41n\; - 0.5 - 0.7(0.6)^{m-n}, \end{aligned} \qquad m \ge n, \qquad (62)$$

with a rather small standard deviation from these observed average values. The coefficients $\frac{1}{2}$ and 1 of m in (62) can be verified rigorously (see exercise 21).

If we assume instead that u and v are to be *any* integers, independently and uniformly distributed over the ranges

$$1 \le u < 2^N, \qquad 1 \le v < 2^N, \qquad (63)$$

then we can calculate the average values of C and D from the data already given:

$$C \approx 0.70N + O(1), \qquad D \approx 1.41N + O(1). \qquad (64)$$

(See exercise 22.) This agrees perfectly with the results of further empirical tests, made on several million random inputs for $N \le 30$; the latter tests show that we may take

$$C = 0.70N - 0.5, \qquad D = 1.41N - 2.7 \qquad (65)$$

as decent estimates of the values, given this distribution of the inputs u and v.

The theoretical analysis in Brent's continuous model of Algorithm B predicts that C and D will be asymptotically equal to $2N/b$ and $4N/b$ under assumption (63), where $2/b \approx 0.70597$ is the constant in (60). The agreement with experiment is so good that Brent's constant $2/b$ must be the true value of the number "0.70" in (65), and we should replace 0.203 by 0.206 in (62).

This completes our study of the average values of C and D. The other three quantities that appear in the running time of Algorithm B are quite easy to analyze; see exercises 6, 7, and 8.

Now that we know approximately how Algorithm B behaves on the average, let's consider a "worst case" scenario: What values of u and v are in some sense the hardest to handle? If we assume as before that

$$\lfloor \lg u \rfloor = m \quad \text{and} \quad \lfloor \lg v \rfloor = n,$$

we want to find u and v that make the algorithm run most slowly. The subtractions take somewhat longer than the shifts, when the auxiliary bookkeeping is considered, so this question may be rephrased by asking for the inputs u and v that require the most subtractions. The answer is somewhat surprising; the maximum value of C is exactly

$$\max(m, n) + 1, \tag{66}$$

although a naïve analysis would predict that substantially higher values of C are possible (see exercise 35). The derivation of the worst case (66) is quite interesting, so it has been left as an amusing problem for readers to work out for themselves (see exercises 36 and 37).

EXERCISES

1. [*M21*] How can (8), (9), (10), (11), and (12) be derived easily from (6) and (7)?

2. [*M22*] Given that u divides $v_1 v_2 \ldots v_n$, prove that u divides

$$\gcd(u, v_1) \gcd(u, v_2) \ldots \gcd(u, v_n).$$

3. [*M23*] Show that the number of ordered pairs of positive integers (u, v) such that $\text{lcm}(u, v) = n$ is the number of divisors of n^2.

4. [*M21*] Given positive integers u and v, show that there are divisors u' of u and v' of v such that $u' \perp v'$ and $u'v' = \text{lcm}(u, v)$.

▶ **5.** [*M26*] Invent an algorithm (analogous to Algorithm B) for calculating the greatest common divisor of two integers based on their *balanced ternary* representation. Demonstrate your algorithm by applying it to the calculation of $\gcd(40902, 24140)$.

6. [*M22*] Given that u and v are random positive integers, find the mean and the standard deviation of the quantity A that enters into the timing of Program B. (This is the number of right shifts applied to both u and v during the preparatory phase.)

7. [*M20*] Analyze the quantity B that enters into the timing of Program B.

▶ **8.** [*M25*] Show that in Program B, the average value of E is approximately equal to $\frac{1}{2} C_{\text{ave}}$, where C_{ave} is the average value of C.

9. [*18*] Using Algorithm B and hand calculation, find $\gcd(31408, 2718)$. Also find integers m and n such that $31408m + 2718n = \gcd(31408, 2718)$, using Algorithm X.

▶ **10.** [*HM24*] Let q_n be the number of ordered pairs of integers (u, v) lying in the range $1 \le u, v \le n$ such that $u \perp v$. The object of this exercise is to prove that we have $\lim_{n \to \infty} q_n/n^2 = 6/\pi^2$, thereby establishing Theorem D.

a) Use the principle of inclusion and exclusion (Section 1.3.3) to show that

$$q_n = n^2 - \sum_{p_1} \lfloor n/p_1 \rfloor^2 + \sum_{p_1 < p_2} \lfloor n/p_1 p_2 \rfloor^2 - \cdots,$$

where the sums are taken over all *prime* numbers p_i.

b) The *Möbius function* $\mu(n)$ is defined by the rules $\mu(1) = 1$, $\mu(p_1 p_2 \ldots p_r) = (-1)^r$ if $p_1, p_2, \ldots, p_r$ are distinct primes, and $\mu(n) = 0$ if n is divisible by the square of a prime. Show that $q_n = \sum_{k \ge 1} \mu(k) \lfloor n/k \rfloor^2$.

c) As a consequence of (b), prove that $\lim_{n \to \infty} q_n/n^2 = \sum_{k \ge 1} \mu(k)/k^2$.

d) Prove that $(\sum_{k \ge 1} \mu(k)/k^2)(\sum_{m \ge 1} 1/m^2) = 1$. *Hint:* When the series are absolutely convergent we have

$$\left(\sum_{k \ge 1} a_k/k^z \right) \left(\sum_{m \ge 1} b_m/m^z \right) = \sum_{n \ge 1} \left(\sum_{d \backslash n} a_d b_{n/d} \right) \bigg/ n^z.$$

11. [*M22*] What is the probability that $\gcd(u, v) \le 3$? (See Theorem D.) What is the *average* value of $\gcd(u, v)$?

12. [*M24*] (E. Cesàro.) If u and v are random positive integers, what is the average number of (positive) divisors they have in common? [*Hint:* See the identity in exercise 10(d), with $a_k = b_m = 1$.]

13. [*HM23*] Given that u and v are random *odd* positive integers, show that they are relatively prime with probability $8/\pi^2$.

▶ **14.** [*HM25*] What is the expected value of $\ln \gcd(u, v)$ when u and v are (a) random positive integers? (b) random positive odd integers?

15. [*M21*] What are the values of v_1 and v_2 when Algorithm X terminates?

▶ **16.** [*M22*] Design an algorithm to *divide u by v modulo m*, given positive integers u, v, and m, with v relatively prime to m. In other words, your algorithm should find w, in the range $0 \le w < m$, such that $u \equiv vw$ (modulo m).

▶ **17.** [*M20*] Given two integers u and v such that $uv \equiv 1$ (modulo 2^e), explain how to compute an integer u' such that $u'v \equiv 1$ (modulo 2^{2e}). [This leads to a fast algorithm for computing the reciprocal of an odd number modulo a power of 2, since we can start with a table of all such reciprocals for $e = 8$ or $e = 16$.]

▶ **18.** [*M24*] Show how Algorithm L can be extended (as Algorithm A was extended to Algorithm X) to obtain solutions of (15) when u and v are large.

19. [*21*] Use the text's method to find a general solution in integers to the following sets of equations:

a) $3x + 7y + 11z = 1$
    $5x + 7y - 5z = 3$

b) $3x + 7y + 11z = 1$
    $5x + 7y - 5z = -3$

20. [*M37*] Let u and v be odd integers, independently and uniformly distributed in the ranges $2^m \le u < 2^{m+1}$, $2^n \le v < 2^{n+1}$. What is the *exact* probability that a single subtract-and-shift cycle in Algorithm B reduces u and v to the ranges $2^{m'} \le u < 2^{m'+1}$, $2^{n'} \le v < 2^{n'+1}$, as a function of m, n, m', and n'?

21. [*HM26*] Let C_{mn} and D_{mn} be the average number of subtraction steps and shift steps, respectively, in Algorithm B, when u and v are odd, $\lfloor \lg u \rfloor = m$, $\lfloor \lg v \rfloor = n$. Show that for fixed n, $C_{mn} = \frac{1}{2}m + O(1)$ and $D_{mn} = m + O(1)$ as $m \to \infty$.

22. [*M28*] Continuing the previous exercise, show that if $C_{mn} = \alpha m + \beta n + \gamma$ for some constants α, β, and γ, then

$$\sum_{1 \le n < m \le N} (N - m)(N - n)2^{m+n-2}C_{mn} = 2^{2N}\left(\tfrac{11}{27}(\alpha + \beta)N + O(1)\right),$$

$$\sum_{1 \le n \le N} (N - n)^2 2^{2n-2}C_{nn} = 2^{2N}\left(\tfrac{5}{27}(\alpha + \beta)N + O(1)\right).$$

▶ **23.** [*M20*] What is the probability that $v/u \le x$ after n subtract-and-shift cycles of Algorithm B, when the algorithm begins with large random integers? (Here x is any real number ≥ 0; we do not assume that $u \ge v$.)

24. [*M20*] Suppose $u > v$ in step B6, and assume that the ratio v/u has Brent's limiting distribution G. What is the probability that $u < v$ the next time step B6 is encountered?

25. [*M21*] Equation (46) implies that $\rho_1 = -\lambda$; prove that $\rho_2 = \lambda/2$.

26. [*M22*] Prove that when $G(x)$ satisfies (36)–(40) we have

$$2G(x) - 5G(2x) + 2G(4x) = G(1 + 2x) - 2G(1 + 4x) + 2G(1 + 1/x) - G(1 + 1/2x).$$

27. [*M22*] Prove (58), which expresses ψ_n in terms of Bernoulli numbers.

28. [*HM36*] Study the asymptotic behavior of ψ_n. *Hint:* See exercise 6.3–34.

▶ **29.** [*HM26*] (R. P. Brent.) Find $G_1(x)$, the distribution of $\min(u, v)/\max(u, v)$ after the first subtract-and-shift cycle of Algorithm B as defined in (35). *Hint:* Let $S_{n+1}(x) = \sum_{k=1}^{\infty} 2^{-k}G_n(1/(1+2^kx))$, and use the method of Mellin transforms for harmonic sums [see P. Flajolet, X. Gourdon, and P. Dumas, *Theor. Comp. Sci.* **144** (1995), 3–58].

30. [*HM39*] Continuing the previous exercise, determine $G_2(x)$.

31. [*HM46*] Prove or disprove the "wild conjecture" in the answer to exercise 25.

32. [*HM42*] Is there a unique continuous function $G(x)$ that satisfies (36) and (37)?

33. [*M46*] Analyze Harris's "binary Euclidean algorithm," stated after Program B.

34. [*HM44*] Find a rigorous proof that Brent's model describes the asymptotic behavior of Algorithm B, and indeed that $G(z)$ is an analytic function when $\Re z > 0$.

35. [*M23*] Consider a directed graph with vertices (m, n) for all nonnegative integers $m, n \ge 0$, having arcs from (m, n) to (m', n') whenever it is possible for a subtract-and-shift cycle of Algorithm B to transform integers u and v with $\lfloor \lg u \rfloor = m$ and $\lfloor \lg v \rfloor = n$ into integers u' and v' with $\lfloor \lg u' \rfloor = m'$ and $\lfloor \lg v' \rfloor = n'$; there also is a special "Stop" vertex, with arcs from (n, n) to Stop for all $n \ge 0$. What is the length of the longest path from (m, n) to Stop? (This gives an upper bound on the maximum running time of Algorithm B.)

▶ **36.** [*M28*] Given $m \ge n \ge 1$, find values of u and v with $\lfloor \lg u \rfloor = m$ and $\lfloor \lg v \rfloor = n$ such that Algorithm B requires $m + 1$ subtraction steps.

37. [*M32*] Prove that the subtraction step B6 of Algorithm B is never executed more than $1 + \lfloor \lg \max(u, v) \rfloor$ times.

▶ **38.** [*M32*] (R. W. Gosper.) Demonstrate how to modify Algorithm B for large numbers, using ideas analogous to those in Algorithm L.

▸ **39.** [*M28*] (V. R. Pratt.) Extend Algorithm B to an Algorithm Y that is analogous to Algorithm X.

▸ **40.** [*M25*] (R. P. Brent and H. T. Kung.) The following variant of the binary gcd algorithm is better than Algorithm B from the standpoint of hardware implementation, because it does not require testing the sign of $u - v$. Assume that u is odd; u and v can be either positive or negative.

> **K1.** [Initialize.] Set $c \leftarrow 0$. (This counter estimates the difference between $\lg |u|$ and $\lg |v|$.)
>
> **K2.** [Done?] If $v = 0$, terminate with $|u|$ as the answer.
>
> **K3.** [Make v odd.] Set $v \leftarrow v/2$ and $c \leftarrow c + 1$ zero or more times, until v is odd.
>
> **K4.** [Make $c \leq 0$.] If $c > 0$, interchange $u \leftrightarrow v$ and set $c \leftarrow -c$.
>
> **K5.** [Reduce.] Set $w \leftarrow (u+v)/2$. If w is even, set $v \leftarrow w$; otherwise set $v \leftarrow w - v$. Return to step K2. ∎

Prove that step K2 is performed at most $2 + 2\lg\max(|u|, |v|)$ times.

41. [*M22*] Use Euclid's algorithm to find a simple formula for $\gcd(10^m - 1, 10^n - 1)$ when m and n are nonnegative integers.

42. [*M30*] Evaluate the determinant

$$\begin{vmatrix} \gcd(1,1) & \gcd(1,2) & \cdots & \gcd(1,n) \\ \gcd(2,1) & \gcd(2,2) & \cdots & \gcd(2,n) \\ \vdots & \vdots & & \vdots \\ \gcd(n,1) & \gcd(n,2) & \cdots & \gcd(n,n) \end{vmatrix}.$$

*4.5.3. Analysis of Euclid's Algorithm

The execution time of Euclid's algorithm depends on T, the number of times the division step A2 is performed. (See Algorithm 4.5.2A and Program 4.5.2A.) The quantity T is also an important factor in the running time of other algorithms, such as the evaluation of functions satisfying a reciprocity formula (see Section 3.3.3). We shall see in this section that the mathematical analysis of this quantity T is interesting and instructive.

Relation to continued fractions. Euclid's algorithm is intimately connected with *continued fractions*, which are expressions of the form

$$\cfrac{b_1}{a_1 + \cfrac{b_2}{a_2 + \cfrac{b_3}{\cdots \cfrac{}{a_{n-1} + \cfrac{b_n}{a_n}}}}} = b_1 / \big(a_1 + b_2/(a_2 + b_3/(\cdots/(a_{n-1} + b_n/a_n)\ldots))\big). \tag{1}$$

Continued fractions have a beautiful theory that is the subject of several classic books, such as O. Perron, *Die Lehre von den Kettenbrüchen*, 3rd edition (Stuttgart: Teubner, 1954), 2 volumes; A. Khinchin, *Continued Fractions*, translated by Peter Wynn (Groningen: P. Noordhoff, 1963); and H. S. Wall, *Analytic Theory* of *Continued Fractions* (New York: Van Nostrand, 1948). See also Claude Brezinski, *History of Continued Fractions and Padé Approximants* (Springer, 1991), for the early history of the subject. It is necessary to limit ourselves to a comparatively brief treatment of the theory here, studying only those aspects that give us more insight into the behavior of Euclid's algorithm.

The continued fractions of primary interest to us are those in which all of the b's in (1) are equal to unity. For convenience in notation, let us define

$$//x_1, x_2, \ldots, x_n// = 1/\big(x_1 + 1/(x_2 + 1/(\cdots/(x_{n-1} + 1/x_n)\ldots))\big). \qquad (2)$$

Thus, for example,

$$//x_1// = \frac{1}{x_1}, \qquad //x_1, x_2// = \frac{1}{x_1 + 1/x_2} = \frac{x_2}{x_1 x_2 + 1}. \qquad (3)$$

If $n = 0$, the symbol $//x_1, \ldots, x_n//$ is taken to mean 0. Let us also define the so-called *continuant polynomials* $K_n(x_1, x_2, \ldots, x_n)$ of n variables, for $n \geq 0$, by the rule

$$K_n(x_1, x_2, \ldots, x_n) = \begin{cases} 1, & \text{if } n = 0; \\ x_1, & \text{if } n = 1; \\ x_1 K_{n-1}(x_2, \ldots, x_n) + K_{n-2}(x_3, \ldots, x_n), & \text{if } n > 1. \end{cases} \qquad (4)$$

Thus $K_2(x_1, x_2) = x_1 x_2 + 1$, $K_3(x_1, x_2, x_3) = x_1 x_2 x_3 + x_1 + x_3$, etc. In general, as noted by L. Euler in the eighteenth century, $K_n(x_1, x_2, \ldots, x_n)$ is the sum of all terms obtainable by starting with $x_1 x_2 \ldots x_n$ and deleting zero or more nonoverlapping pairs of consecutive variables $x_j x_{j+1}$; there are F_{n+1} such terms.

The basic property of continuants is the explicit formula

$$//x_1, x_2, \ldots, x_n// = K_{n-1}(x_2, \ldots, x_n)/K_n(x_1, x_2, \ldots, x_n), \qquad n \geq 1. \qquad (5)$$

This can be proved by induction, since it implies that

$$x_0 + //x_1, \ldots, x_n// = K_{n+1}(x_0, x_1, \ldots, x_n)/K_n(x_1, \ldots, x_n);$$

hence $//x_0, x_1, \ldots, x_n//$ is the reciprocal of the latter quantity.

The K-polynomials are symmetrical in the sense that

$$K_n(x_1, x_2, \ldots, x_n) = K_n(x_n, \ldots, x_2, x_1). \qquad (6)$$

This follows from Euler's observation above, and as a consequence we have

$$K_n(x_1, \ldots, x_n) = x_n K_{n-1}(x_1, \ldots, x_{n-1}) + K_{n-2}(x_1, \ldots, x_{n-2}) \qquad (7)$$

for $n > 1$. The K-polynomials also satisfy the important identity

$$K_n(x_1, \ldots, x_n) K_n(x_2, \ldots, x_{n+1}) - K_{n+1}(x_1, \ldots, x_{n+1}) K_{n-1}(x_2, \ldots, x_n)$$
$$= (-1)^n, \qquad n \geq 1. \qquad (8)$$

(See exercise 4.) The latter equation in connection with (5) implies that

$$//x_1, \ldots, x_n// = \frac{1}{q_0 q_1} - \frac{1}{q_1 q_2} + \frac{1}{q_2 q_3} - \cdots + \frac{(-1)^{n-1}}{q_{n-1} q_n},$$
$$\text{where } q_k = K_k(x_1, \ldots, x_k). \qquad (9)$$

Thus the K-polynomials are intimately related to continued fractions.

Every real number X in the range $0 \le X < 1$ has a *regular continued fraction* defined as follows: Let $X_0 = X$, and for all $n \ge 0$ such that $X_n \ne 0$ let

$$A_{n+1} = \lfloor 1/X_n \rfloor, \qquad X_{n+1} = 1/X_n - A_{n+1}. \tag{10}$$

If $X_n = 0$, the quantities A_{n+1} and X_{n+1} are not defined, and the regular continued fraction for X is $/\!/A_1, \ldots, A_n/\!/$. If $X_n \ne 0$, this definition guarantees that $0 \le X_{n+1} < 1$, so each of the A's is a positive integer. Definition (10) also implies that

$$X = X_0 = \cfrac{1}{A_1 + X_1} = \cfrac{1}{A_1 + 1/(A_2 + X_2)} = \cdots ;$$

hence

$$X = /\!/A_1, \ldots, A_{n-1}, A_n + X_n/\!/ \tag{11}$$

for all $n \ge 1$, whenever X_n is defined. In particular, we have $X = /\!/A_1, \ldots, A_n/\!/$ when $X_n = 0$. If $X_n \ne 0$, the number X always lies *between* $/\!/A_1, \ldots, A_n/\!/$ and $/\!/A_1, \ldots, A_n + 1/\!/$, since by (7) the quantity $q_n = K_n(A_1, \ldots, A_n + X_n)$ increases monotonically from $K_n(A_1, \ldots, A_n)$ up to $K_n(A_1, \ldots, A_n + 1)$ as X_n increases from 0 to 1, and by (9) the continued fraction increases or decreases when q_n increases, according as n is even or odd. In fact,

$$
\begin{aligned}
|X - /\!/A_1, \ldots, A_n/\!/| &= |/\!/A_1, \ldots, A_n + X_n/\!/ - /\!/A_1, \ldots, A_n/\!/| \\
&= |/\!/A_1, \ldots, A_n, 1/X_n/\!/ - /\!/A_1, \ldots, A_n/\!/| \\
&= \left| \frac{K_n(A_2, \ldots, A_n, 1/X_n)}{K_{n+1}(A_1, \ldots, A_n, 1/X_n)} - \frac{K_{n-1}(A_2, \ldots, A_n)}{K_n(A_1, \ldots, A_n)} \right| \\
&= 1/\big(K_n(A_1, \ldots, A_n) K_{n+1}(A_1, \ldots, A_n, 1/X_n)\big) \\
&\le 1/\big(K_n(A_1, \ldots, A_n) K_{n+1}(A_1, \ldots, A_n, A_{n+1})\big) \tag{12}
\end{aligned}
$$

by (5), (7), (8), and (10). Therefore $/\!/A_1, \ldots, A_n/\!/$ is an extremely close approximation to X, unless n is small. If X_n is nonzero for all n, we obtain an *infinite continued fraction* $/\!/A_1, A_2, A_3, \ldots /\!/$, whose value is defined to be

$$\lim_{n \to \infty} /\!/A_1, A_2, \ldots, A_n/\!/;$$

from inequality (12) it is clear that this limit equals X.

The regular continued fraction expansion of real numbers has several properties analogous to the representation of numbers in the decimal system. If we use the formulas above to compute the regular continued fraction expansions of some familiar real numbers, we find, for example, that

$$\tfrac{8}{29} = /\!/3, 1, 1, 1, 2/\!/;$$
$$\sqrt{\tfrac{8}{29}} = /\!/1, 1, 9, 2, 2, 3, 2, 2, 9, 1, 2, 1, 9, 2, 2, 3, 2, 2, 9, 1, 2, 1, 9, 2, 2, 3, 2, 2, 9, 1, \ldots /\!/;$$
$$\sqrt[3]{2} = 1 + /\!/3, 1, 5, 1, 1, 4, 1, 1, 8, 1, 14, 1, 10, 2, 1, 4, 12, 2, 3, 2, 1, 3, 4, 1, 1, 2, 14, 3, \ldots /\!/;$$
$$\pi = 3 + /\!/7, 15, 1, 292, 1, 1, 1, 2, 1, 3, 1, 14, 2, 1, 1, 2, 2, 2, 2, 1, 84, 2, 1, 1, 15, 3, 13, \ldots /\!/;$$

$$e = 2 + //1, 2, 1, 1, 4, 1, 1, 6, 1, 1, 8, 1, 1, 10, 1, 1, 12, 1, 1, 14, 1, 1, 16, 1, 1, 18, 1, \ldots //;$$

$$\gamma = //1, 1, 2, 1, 2, 1, 4, 3, 13, 5, 1, 1, 8, 1, 2, 4, 1, 1, 40, 1, 11, 3, 7, 1, 7, 1, 1, 5, 1, 49, \ldots //;$$

$$\phi = 1 + //1, 1, 1, 1, 1, 1, 1, 1, 1, 1, 1, 1, 1, 1, 1, 1, 1, 1, 1, 1, 1, 1, 1, 1, 1, 1, 1, 1, \ldots //. \quad (13)$$

The numbers A_1, A_2, ... are called the *partial quotients* of X. Notice the regular pattern that appears in the partial quotients for $\sqrt{8/29}$, ϕ, and e; the reasons for this behavior are discussed in exercises 12 and 16. There is no apparent pattern in the partial quotients for $\sqrt[3]{2}$, π, or γ.

It is interesting to note that the ancient Greeks' first definition of real numbers, once they had discovered the existence of irrationals, was essentially stated in terms of infinite continued fractions. (Later they adopted the suggestion of Eudoxus that $x = y$ should be defined instead as "$x < r$ if and only if $y < r$, for all rational r.") See O. Becker, *Quellen und Studien zur Geschichte der Mathematik, Astronomie und Physik* **B2** (1933), 311–333.

When X is a rational number, the regular continued fraction corresponds in a natural way to Euclid's algorithm. Let us assume that $X = v/u$, where $u > v \geq 0$. The regular continued fraction process starts with $X_0 = X$; let us define $U_0 = u$, $V_0 = v$. Assuming that $X_n = V_n/U_n \neq 0$, (10) becomes

$$A_{n+1} = \lfloor U_n/V_n \rfloor, \qquad X_{n+1} = U_n/V_n - A_{n+1} = (U_n \bmod V_n)/V_n. \quad (14)$$

Therefore, if we define

$$U_{n+1} = V_n, \qquad V_{n+1} = U_n \bmod V_n, \quad (15)$$

the condition $X_n = V_n/U_n$ holds throughout the process. Furthermore, (15) is precisely the transformation made on the variables u and v in Euclid's algorithm (see Algorithm 4.5.2A, step A2). For example, since $\frac{8}{29} = //3, 1, 1, 1, 2//$, we know that Euclid's algorithm applied to $u = 29$ and $v = 8$ will require exactly five division steps, and the quotients $\lfloor u/v \rfloor$ in step A2 will be successively 3, 1, 1, 1, and 2. The last partial quotient A_n must always be 2 or more when $X_n = 0$ and $n \geq 1$, since X_{n-1} is less than unity.

From this correspondence with Euclid's algorithm we can see that the regular continued fraction for X terminates at some step with $X_n = 0$ if and only if X is rational; for it is obvious that X_n cannot be zero if X is irrational, and, conversely, we know that Euclid's algorithm always terminates. If the partial quotients obtained during Euclid's algorithm are A_1, A_2, ..., A_n, then we have, by (5),

$$\frac{v}{u} = \frac{K_{n-1}(A_2, \ldots, A_n)}{K_n(A_1, A_2, \ldots, A_n)}. \quad (16)$$

This formula holds also if Euclid's algorithm is applied for $u < v$, when $A_1 = 0$. Furthermore, because of relation (8), the continuants $K_{n-1}(A_2, \ldots, A_n)$ and $K_n(A_1, A_2, \ldots, A_n)$ are relatively prime, and the fraction on the right-hand side of (16) is in lowest terms; therefore

$$u = K_n(A_1, A_2, \ldots, A_n)d, \qquad v = K_{n-1}(A_2, \ldots, A_n)d, \quad (17)$$

where $d = \gcd(u, v)$.

The worst case. We can now apply these observations to determine the behavior of Euclid's algorithm in the worst case, or in other words to give an upper bound on the number of division steps. The worst case occurs when the inputs are consecutive Fibonacci numbers:

Theorem F. *For $n \geq 1$, let u and v be integers with $u > v > 0$ such that Euclid's algorithm applied to u and v requires exactly n division steps, and such that u is as small as possible satisfying these conditions. Then $u = F_{n+2}$ and $v = F_{n+1}$.*

Proof. By (17), we must have $u = K_n(A_1, A_2, \ldots, A_n)d$, where A_1, A_2, $\ldots$, A_n, and d are positive integers and $A_n \geq 2$. Since K_n is a polynomial with nonnegative coefficients, involving all of the variables, the minimum value is achieved only when $A_1 = 1$, $\ldots$, $A_{n-1} = 1$, $A_n = 2$, $d = 1$. Putting these values in (17) yields the desired result. ▌

This theorem has the historical claim of being the first practical application of the Fibonacci sequence; since then many other applications of Fibonacci numbers to algorithms and to the study of algorithms have been discovered. The result is essentially due to T. F. de Lagny [*Mém. Acad. Sci.* **11** (Paris, 1733), 363–364], who tabulated the first several continuants and observed that Fibonacci numbers give the smallest numerator and denominator for continued fractions of a given length. He did not explicitly mention gcd calculation, however; the connection between Fibonacci numbers and Euclid's algorithm was first pointed out by É. Léger [*Correspondance Math. et Physique* **9** (1837), 483–485.]

Shortly afterwards, P. J. É. Finck [*Traité Élémentaire d'Arithmétique* (Strasbourg: 1841), 44] proved by another method that $\gcd(u, v)$ takes at most $2 \lg v + 1$ steps, when $u > v > 0$; and G. Lamé [*Comptes Rendus Acad. Sci.* **19** (Paris, 1844), 867–870] improved this to $5\lceil \log_{10}(v + 1) \rceil$. Full details about these pioneering studies in the analysis of algorithms appear in an interesting review by J. O. Shallit, *Historia Mathematica* **21** (1994), 401–419. A more precise estimate of the worst case is, however, a direct consequence of Theorem F:

Corollary L. *If $0 \leq v < N$, the number of division steps required when Algorithm 4.5.2A is applied to u and v is at most $\lfloor \log_\phi (3 - \phi)N \rfloor$.*

Proof. After step A1 we have $v > u \bmod v$. Therefore by Theorem F, the maximum number of steps, n, occurs when $v = F_{n+1}$ and $u \bmod v = F_n$. Since $F_{n+1} < N$, we have $\phi^{n+1}/\sqrt{5} < N$ (see Eq. 1.2.8–(15)); thus $\phi^n < (\sqrt{5}/\phi)N = (3 - \phi)N$. ▌

The quantity $\log_\phi (3 - \phi)N$ is approximately equal to $2.078 \ln N + .6723 \approx 4.785 \log_{10} N + .6723$. See exercises 31, 36, and 38 for extensions of Theorem F.

An approximate model. Now that we know the maximum number of division steps that can occur, let us attempt to find the *average* number. Let $T(m, n)$ be the number of division steps that occur when $u = m$ and $v = n$ are input to Euclid's algorithm. Thus

$$T(m, 0) = 0; \qquad T(m, n) = 1 + T(n, m \bmod n) \qquad \text{if } n \geq 1. \qquad (18)$$

Let T_n be the average number of division steps when $v = n$ and when u is chosen at random; since only the value of $u \bmod v$ affects the algorithm after the first division step, we have

$$T_n = \frac{1}{n} \sum_{0 \leq k < n} T(k, n). \qquad (19)$$

For example, $T(0, 5) = 1$, $T(1, 5) = 2$, $T(2, 5) = 3$, $T(3, 5) = 4$, $T(4, 5) = 3$, so

$$T_5 = \tfrac{1}{5}(1 + 2 + 3 + 4 + 3) = 2\tfrac{3}{5}.$$

Our goal is to estimate T_n for large n. One idea is to try an approximation suggested by R. W. Floyd: We might assume that, for $0 \leq k < n$, the value of n is essentially "random" modulo k, so that we can set

$$T_n \approx 1 + \frac{1}{n}(T_0 + T_1 + \cdots + T_{n-1}).$$

Then $T_n \approx S_n$, where the sequence $\langle S_n \rangle$ is the solution to the recurrence relation

$$S_0 = 0, \qquad S_n = 1 + \frac{1}{n}(S_0 + S_1 + \cdots + S_{n-1}), \qquad n \geq 1. \qquad (20)$$

This recurrence is easy to solve by noting that

$$S_{n+1} = 1 + \frac{1}{n+1}(S_0 + S_1 + \cdots + S_{n-1} + S_n)$$

$$= 1 + \frac{1}{n+1}\left(n(S_n - 1) + S_n\right) = S_n + \frac{1}{n+1};$$

hence S_n is $1 + \frac{1}{2} + \cdots + \frac{1}{n} = H_n$, a harmonic number. The approximation $T_n \approx S_n$ now suggests that we might have $T_n \approx \ln n + O(1)$.

Comparison of this approximation with tables of the true value of T_n show, however, that $\ln n$ is too large; T_n does not grow this fast. Our tentative assumption that n is random modulo k must therefore be too pessimistic. And indeed, a closer look shows that the average value of $n \bmod k$ is less than the average value of $\frac{1}{2}k$, in the range $1 \leq k \leq n$:

$$\frac{1}{n} \sum_{1 \leq k \leq n} (n \bmod k) = \frac{1}{n} \sum_{1 \leq k, q \leq n} (n - qk) \left[\lfloor n/(q+1) \rfloor < k \leq \lfloor n/q \rfloor\right]$$

$$= n - \frac{1}{n} \sum_{1 \leq q \leq n} q \left(\binom{\lfloor n/q \rfloor + 1}{2} - \binom{\lfloor n/(q+1) \rfloor + 1}{2}\right)$$

$$= n - \frac{1}{n} \sum_{1 \leq q \leq n} \binom{\lfloor n/q \rfloor + 1}{2}$$

$$= \left(1 - \frac{\pi^2}{12}\right)n + O(\log n) \qquad (21)$$

$\bigl($see exercise 4.5.2–10(c)$\bigr)$. This is only about $.1775n$, not $.25n$; so the value of $n \bmod k$ tends to be smaller than Floyd's model predicts, and Euclid's algorithm works faster than we might expect.

A continuous model. The behavior of Euclid's algorithm with $v = N$ is essentially determined by the behavior of the regular continued fraction process when $X = 0/N, 1/N, \ldots, (N-1)/N$. When N is very large, we therefore want to study the behavior of regular continued fractions when X is essentially a random real number, uniformly distributed in $[0 \mathinner{.\,.} 1)$. Consider the distribution function

$$F_n(x) = \Pr(X_n \le x), \qquad \text{for } 0 \le x \le 1, \tag{22}$$

given a uniform distribution of $X = X_0$. By the definition of regular continued fractions, we have $F_0(x) = x$, and

$$F_{n+1}(x) = \sum_{k \ge 1} \Pr(k \le 1/X_n \le k + x)$$

$$= \sum_{k \ge 1} \Pr\bigl(1/(k + x) \le X_n \le 1/k\bigr)$$

$$= \sum_{k \ge 1} \bigl(F_n(1/k) - F_n\bigl(1/(k + x)\bigr)\bigr). \tag{23}$$

If the distributions $F_0(x)$, $F_1(x)$, ... defined by these formulas approach a limiting distribution $F_\infty(x) = F(x)$, we will have

$$F(x) = \sum_{k \ge 1} \bigl(F(1/k) - F\bigl(1/(k + x)\bigr)\bigr). \tag{24}$$

(An analogous relation, 4.5.2–(36), arose in our study of the binary gcd algorithm.) One function that satisfies (24) is $F(x) = \log_b(1+x)$, for any base $b > 1$; see exercise 19. The further condition $F(1) = 1$ implies that we should take $b = 2$. Thus it is reasonable to make a guess that $F(x) = \lg(1 + x)$, and that $F_n(x)$ approaches this behavior.

We might conjecture, for example, that $F(\frac{1}{2}) = \lg(\frac{3}{2}) \approx 0.58496$; let us see how close $F_n(\frac{1}{2})$ comes to this value for small n. We have $F_0(\frac{1}{2}) = 0.50000$, and

$$F_1(x) = \sum_{k \ge 1} \left(\frac{1}{k} - \frac{1}{k + x}\right) = H_x;$$

$$F_1(\tfrac{1}{2}) = H_{1/2} = 2 - 2\ln 2 \approx 0.61371;$$

$$F_2(\tfrac{1}{2}) = H_{2/2} - H_{2/3} + H_{2/4} - H_{2/5} + H_{2/6} - H_{2/7} + \cdots.$$

(See Table 3 of Appendix A.) The power series expansion

$$H_x = \zeta(2)x - \zeta(3)x^2 + \zeta(4)x^3 - \zeta(5)x^4 + \cdots \tag{25}$$

makes it feasible to compute the numerical value

$$F_2(\tfrac{1}{2}) = 0.57655\,93276\,99914\,08418\,82618\,72122\,27055\,92452 - . \tag{26}$$

We're getting closer to 0.58496; but it is not immediately clear how to get a good estimate of $F_n(\frac{1}{2})$ for $n = 3$, much less for really large values of n.

The distributions $F_n(x)$ were first studied by C. F. Gauss, who first thought of the problem on the 5th day of February in 1799. His notebook for 1800 lists various recurrence relations and gives a brief table of values, including the (inaccurate) approximation $F_2(\frac{1}{2}) \approx 0.5748$. After performing these calculations, Gauss wrote, "Tam complicatæ evadunt, ut nulla spes superesse videatur"; i.e., "They come out so complicated that no hope appears to be left." Twelve years later, he wrote a letter to Laplace in which he posed the problem as one he could not resolve to his satisfaction. He said, "I found by very simple reasoning that, for n infinite, $F_n(x) = \log(1+x)/\log 2$. But the efforts that I made since then in my inquiries to assign $F_n(x) - \log(1+x)/\log 2$ for very large but not infinite values of n were fruitless." He never published his "very simple reasoning," and it is not completely clear that he had found a rigorous proof. [See Gauss's *Werke*, vol. 10^1, 552–556.] More than 100 years went by before a proof was finally published, by R. O. Kuz'min [*Atti del Congresso Internazionale dei Matematici* **6** (Bologna, 1928), 83–89], who showed that

$$F_n(x) = \lg(1+x) + O(e^{-A\sqrt{n}})$$

for some positive constant A. The error term was improved to $O(e^{-An})$ by Paul Lévy shortly afterwards [*Bull. Soc. Math. de France* **57** (1929), 178–194]*; but Gauss's problem, namely to find the asymptotic behavior of $F_n(x) - \lg(1+x)$, was not really resolved until 1974, when Eduard Wirsing published a beautiful analysis of the situation [*Acta Arithmetica* **24** (1974), 507–528]. We shall study the simplest aspects of Wirsing's approach here, since his method is an instructive use of linear operators.

If G is any function of x defined for $0 \le x \le 1$, let SG be the function defined by

$$SG(x) = \sum_{k\ge 1}\left(G\left(\frac{1}{k}\right) - G\left(\frac{1}{k+x}\right)\right). \tag{27}$$

Thus, S is an operator that changes one function into another. In particular, by (23) we have $F_{n+1}(x) = SF_n(x)$, hence

$$F_n = S^n F_0. \tag{28}$$

(In this discussion F_n stands for a distribution function, *not* for a Fibonacci number.) Notice that S is a "linear operator"; that is, $S(cG) = c(SG)$ for all constants c, and $S(G_1 + G_2) = SG_1 + SG_2$.

Now if G has a bounded first derivative, we can differentiate (27) term by term to show that

$$(SG)'(x) = \sum_{k\ge 1}\frac{1}{(k+x)^2}G'\left(\frac{1}{k+x}\right); \tag{29}$$

hence SG also has a bounded first derivative. (Term-by-term differentiation of a convergent series is justified when the series of derivatives is uniformly

---

* An exposition of Lévy's interesting proof appeared in the first edition of this book.

convergent; see, for example, K. Knopp, *Theory and Application of Infinite Series* (Glasgow: Blackie, 1951), §47.)

Let $H = SG$, and let $g(x) = (1 + x)G'(x)$, $h(x) = (1 + x)H'(x)$. It follows that

$$h(x) = \sum_{k \geq 1} \frac{1 + x}{(k + x)^2} \left(1 + \frac{1}{k + x}\right)^{-1} g\left(\frac{1}{k + x}\right)$$

$$= \sum_{k \geq 1} \left(\frac{k}{k + 1 + x} - \frac{k - 1}{k + x}\right) g\left(\frac{1}{k + x}\right).$$

In other words, $h = Tg$, where T is the linear operator defined by

$$Tg(x) = \sum_{k \geq 1} \left(\frac{k}{k + 1 + x} - \frac{k - 1}{k + x}\right) g\left(\frac{1}{k + x}\right). \tag{30}$$

Continuing, we see that if g has a bounded first derivative, we can differentiate term by term to show that Tg does also:

$$(Tg)'(x) = -\sum_{k \geq 1} \left(\left(\frac{k}{(k + 1 + x)^2} - \frac{k - 1}{(k + x)^2}\right) g\left(\frac{1}{k + x}\right)\right.$$

$$\left. + \left(\frac{k}{k + 1 + x} - \frac{k - 1}{k + x}\right) \frac{1}{(k + x)^2} g'\left(\frac{1}{k + x}\right)\right)$$

$$= -\sum_{k \geq 1} \left(\frac{k}{(k + 1 + x)^2} \left(g\left(\frac{1}{k + x}\right) - g\left(\frac{1}{k + 1 + x}\right)\right)\right.$$

$$\left. + \frac{1 + x}{(k + x)^3(k + 1 + x)} g'\left(\frac{1}{k + x}\right)\right).$$

There is consequently a third linear operator, U, such that $(Tg)' = -U(g')$, namely

$$U\varphi(x) = \sum_{k \geq 1} \left(\frac{k}{(k + 1 + x)^2} \int_{1/(k+1+x)}^{1/(k+x)} \varphi(t)\,dt + \frac{1 + x}{(k + x)^3(k + 1 + x)} \varphi\left(\frac{1}{k + x}\right)\right). \tag{31}$$

What is the relevance of all this to our problem? Well, if we set

$$F_n(x) = \lg(1 + x) + R_n\big(\lg(1 + x)\big), \tag{32}$$

$$f_n(x) = (1 + x) F_n'(x) = \frac{1}{\ln 2}\big(1 + R_n'\big(\lg(1 + x)\big)\big), \tag{33}$$

we have

$$f_n'(x) = R_n''\big(\lg(1 + x)\big)/\big((\ln 2)^2(1 + x)\big); \tag{34}$$

the effect of the $\lg(1 + x)$ term disappears, after these transformations. Furthermore, since $F_n = S^n F_0$, we have $f_n = T^n f_0$ and $f_n' = (-1)^n U^n f_0'$. Both F_n and f_n have bounded derivatives, by induction on n. Thus (34) becomes

$$(-1)^n R_n''\big(\lg(1 + x)\big) = (1 + x)(\ln 2)^2 U^n f_0'(x). \tag{35}$$

Now $F_0(x) = x$, $f_0(x) = 1 + x$, and $f_0'(x)$ is the constant function 1. We are going to show that the operator U^n takes the constant function into a function with very small values, hence $|R_n''(x)|$ must be very small for $0 \leq x \leq 1$. Finally we can clinch the argument by showing that $R_n(x)$ itself is small: Since we have $R_n(0) = R_n(1) = 0$, it follows from a well-known interpolation formula (see exercise 4.6.4–15 with $x_0 = 0$, $x_1 = x$, $x_2 = 1$) that

$$R_n(x) = -\frac{x(1-x)}{2} R_n''(\xi_n(x)) \tag{36}$$

for some function $\xi_n(x)$, where $0 \leq \xi_n(x) \leq 1$ when $0 \leq x \leq 1$.

Thus everything hinges on our being able to prove that U^n produces small function values, where U is the linear operator defined in (31). Notice that U is a *positive* operator, in the sense that $U\varphi(x) \geq 0$ for all x if $\varphi(x) \geq 0$ for all x. It follows that U is order-preserving: If $\varphi_1(x) \leq \varphi_2(x)$ for all x then we have $U\varphi_1(x) \leq U\varphi_2(x)$ for all x.

One way to exploit this property is to find a function φ for which we can calculate $U\varphi$ exactly, and to use constant multiples of this function to bound the ones that we are really interested in. First let us look for a function g such that Tg is easy to compute. If we consider functions defined for all $x \geq 0$, instead of only on $[0..1]$, it is easy to remove the summation from (27) by observing that

$$SG(x+1) - SG(x) = G\left(\frac{1}{1+x}\right) - \lim_{k \to \infty} G\left(\frac{1}{k+x}\right) = G\left(\frac{1}{1+x}\right) - G(0) \tag{37}$$

when G is continuous. Since $T((1+x)G') = (1+x)(SG)'$, it follows (see exercise 20) that

$$\frac{Tg(x)}{1+x} - \frac{Tg(1+x)}{2+x} = \left(\frac{1}{1+x} - \frac{1}{2+x}\right) g\left(\frac{1}{1+x}\right). \tag{38}$$

If we set $Tg(x) = 1/(1+x)$, we find that the corresponding value of $g(x)$ is $1 + x - 1/(1+x)$. Let $\varphi(x) = g'(x) = 1 + 1/(1+x)^2$, so that $U\varphi(x) = -(Tg)'(x) = 1/(1+x)^2$; this is the function φ we have been looking for.

For this choice of φ we have $2 \leq \varphi(x)/U\varphi(x) = (1+x)^2 + 1 \leq 5$ for $0 \leq x \leq 1$, hence

$$\tfrac{1}{5}\varphi \leq U\varphi \leq \tfrac{1}{2}\varphi.$$

By the positivity of U and φ we can apply U to this inequality again, obtaining $\tfrac{1}{25}\varphi \leq \tfrac{1}{5}U\varphi \leq U^2\varphi \leq \tfrac{1}{2}U\varphi \leq \tfrac{1}{4}\varphi$; and after $n - 1$ applications we have

$$5^{-n}\varphi \leq U^n\varphi \leq 2^{-n}\varphi \tag{39}$$

for this particular φ. Let $\chi(x) = f_0'(x) = 1$ be the constant function; then for $0 \leq x \leq 1$ we have $\tfrac{5}{4}\chi \leq \varphi \leq 2\chi$, hence

$$\tfrac{5}{8}5^{-n}\chi \leq \tfrac{1}{2}5^{-n}\varphi \leq \tfrac{1}{2}U^n\varphi \leq U^n\chi \leq \tfrac{4}{5}U^n\varphi \leq \tfrac{4}{5}2^{-n}\varphi \leq \tfrac{8}{5}2^{-n}\chi.$$

It follows by (35) that

$$\tfrac{5}{8}(\ln 2)^2 5^{-n} \leq (-1)^n R_n''(x) \leq \tfrac{16}{5}(\ln 2)^2 2^{-n}, \qquad \text{for } 0 \leq x \leq 1;$$

hence by (32) and (36) we have proved the following result:

Theorem W. *The distribution $F_n(x)$ equals $\lg(1+x) + O(2^{-n})$ as $n \to \infty$. In fact, $F_n(x) - \lg(1+x)$ lies between $\frac{5}{16}(-1)^{n+1}5^{-n}\big(\ln(1+x)\big)\big(\ln 2/(1+x)\big)$ and $\frac{8}{5}(-1)^{n+1}2^{-n}\big(\ln(1+x)\big)\big(\ln 2/(1+x)\big)$, for $0 \le x \le 1$.* ∎

With a slightly different choice of φ, we can obtain tighter bounds (see exercise 21). In fact, Wirsing went much further in his paper, proving that

$$F_n(x) = \lg(1+x) + (-\lambda)^n \Psi(x) + O\big(x(1-x)(\lambda - 0.031)^n\big), \tag{40}$$

where

$$\begin{aligned}
\lambda &= 0.30366\,30028\,98732\,65859\,74481\,21901\,55623\,31109- \\
&= /\!/3,3,2,2,3,13,1,174,1,1,1,2,2,2,1,1,1,2,2,1,\ldots/\!/
\end{aligned} \tag{41}$$

is a fundamental constant (apparently unrelated to more familiar constants), and where Ψ is an interesting function that is analytic in the entire complex plane except for the negative real axis from -1 to $-\infty$. Wirsing's function satisfies $\Psi(0) = \Psi(1) = 0$, $\Psi'(0) < 0$, and $S\Psi = -\lambda\Psi$; thus by (37) it satisfies the identity

$$\Psi(z) - \Psi(z+1) = \frac{1}{\lambda}\Psi\left(\frac{1}{1+z}\right). \tag{42}$$

Furthermore, Wirsing demonstrated that

$$\Psi\left(-\frac{u}{v} + \frac{i}{N}\right) = c\lambda^{-n}\log N + O(1) \qquad \text{as } N \to \infty, \tag{43}$$

where c is a constant and $n = T(u,v)$ is the number of iterations when Euclid's algorithm is applied to the integers $u > v > 0$.

A complete solution to Gauss's problem was found a few years later by K. I. Babenko [*Doklady Akad. Nauk SSSR* **238** (1978), 1021–1024], who used powerful techniques of functional analysis to prove that

$$F_n(x) = \lg(1+x) + \sum_{j \ge 2} \lambda_j^n \Psi_j(x) \tag{44}$$

for all $0 \le x \le 1$, $n \ge 1$. Here $|\lambda_2| > |\lambda_3| \ge |\lambda_4| \ge \cdots$, and each $\Psi_j(z)$ is an analytic function in the complex plane except for a cut at $[-\infty \ldots -1]$. The function Ψ_2 is Wirsing's Ψ, and $\lambda_2 = -\lambda$, while $\lambda_3 \approx 0.10088$, $\lambda_4 \approx -0.03550$, $\lambda_5 \approx 0.01284$, $\lambda_6 \approx -0.00472$, $\lambda_7 \approx 0.00175$. Babenko also established further properties of the eigenvalues λ_j, proving in particular that they are exponentially small as $j \to \infty$, and that the sum for $j \ge k$ in (44) is bounded by $(\pi^2/6)|\lambda_k|^{n-1}\min(x, 1-x)$. [Further information appears in papers by Babenko and Yuriev, *Doklady Akad. Nauk SSSR* **240** (1978), 1273–1276; Mayer and Roepstorff, *J. Statistical Physics* **47** (1987), 149–171; **50** (1988), 331–344; D. Hensley, *J. Number Theory* **49** (1994), 142–182; Daudé, Flajolet, and Vallée, *Combinatorics, Probability and Computing* **6** (1997), 397–433; Flajolet and Vallée, *Theoretical Comp. Sci.* **194** (1998), 1–34.] The 40-place value of λ in (41) was computed by John Hershberger.

From continuous to discrete. We have now derived results about the probability distributions for continued fractions when X is a real number uniformly distributed in the interval $[0 .. 1)$. But a real number is rational with probability zero — almost all numbers are irrational — so these results do not apply directly to Euclid's algorithm. Before we can apply Theorem W to our problem, some technicalities must be overcome. Consider the following observation based on elementary measure theory:

Lemma M. *Let* $I_1, I_2, \ldots, J_1, J_2, \ldots$ *be pairwise disjoint intervals contained in the interval* $[0 .. 1)$, *and let*

$$\mathcal{I} = \bigcup_{k \geq 1} I_k, \qquad \mathcal{J} = \bigcup_{k \geq 1} J_k, \qquad \mathcal{K} = [0 .. 1] \setminus (\mathcal{I} \cup \mathcal{J}).$$

Assume that $\mathcal{K}$ *has measure zero. Let* P_n *be the set* $\{0/n, 1/n, \ldots, (n-1)/n\}$. *Then*

$$\lim_{n \to \infty} \frac{|\mathcal{I} \cap P_n|}{n} = \mu(\mathcal{I}). \tag{45}$$

Here $\mu(\mathcal{I})$ *is the Lebesgue measure of* $\mathcal{I}$, *namely,* $\sum_{k \geq 1} \text{length}(I_k)$; *and* $|\mathcal{I} \cap P_n|$ *denotes the number of elements in the set* $\mathcal{I} \cap P_n$.

Proof. Let $\mathcal{I}_N = \bigcup_{1 \leq k \leq N} I_k$ and $\mathcal{J}_N = \bigcup_{1 \leq k \leq N} J_k$. Given $\epsilon > 0$, find N large enough so that $\mu(\mathcal{I}_N) + \mu(\mathcal{J}_N) \geq 1 - \epsilon$, and let

$$\mathcal{K}_N = \mathcal{K} \cup \bigcup_{k > N} I_k \cup \bigcup_{k > N} J_k.$$

If I is an interval, having any of the forms $(a .. b)$ or $[a .. b)$ or $(a .. b]$ or $[a .. b]$, it is clear that $\mu(I) = b - a$ and

$$n\mu(I) - 1 \leq |I \cap P_n| \leq n\mu(I) + 1.$$

Now let $r_n = |\mathcal{I}_N \cap P_n|$, $s_n = |\mathcal{J}_N \cap P_n|$, $t_n = |\mathcal{K}_N \cap P_n|$; we have

$$r_n + s_n + t_n = n;$$
$$n\mu(\mathcal{I}_N) - N \leq r_n \leq n\mu(\mathcal{I}_N) + N;$$
$$n\mu(\mathcal{J}_N) - N \leq s_n \leq n\mu(\mathcal{J}_N) + N.$$

Furthermore $r_n \leq |\mathcal{I} \cap P_n| \leq r_n + t_n$, because $\mathcal{I}_N \subseteq \mathcal{I} \subseteq \mathcal{I}_N \cup \mathcal{K}$. Consequently

$$\mu(\mathcal{I}) - \frac{N}{n} - \epsilon \leq \mu(\mathcal{I}_N) - \frac{N}{n} \leq \frac{r_n}{n} \leq \frac{r_n + t_n}{n}$$

$$= 1 - \frac{s_n}{n} \leq 1 - \mu(\mathcal{J}_N) + \frac{N}{n} \leq \mu(\mathcal{I}) + \frac{N}{n} + \epsilon.$$

Given ϵ, this holds for all n; so $\lim_{n \to \infty} r_n/n = \lim_{n \to \infty} (r_n + t_n)/n = \mu(\mathcal{I})$. ∎

Exercise 25 shows that Lemma M is not trivial, in the sense that some rather restrictive hypotheses are needed to prove (45).

Distribution of partial quotients. Now we put Theorem W and Lemma M together to derive some solid facts about Euclid's algorithm.

Theorem E. *Let $p_k(a, n)$ be the probability that the $(k+1)$st quotient A_{k+1} in Euclid's algorithm is equal to a, when $u = n$ and when v is equally likely to be any of the numbers $\{0, 1, \ldots, n-1\}$. Then*

$$\lim_{n \to \infty} p_k(a, n) = F_k\left(\frac{1}{a}\right) - F_k\left(\frac{1}{a+1}\right),$$

where $F_k(x)$ is the distribution function (22).

Proof. The set $\mathcal{I}$ of all X in $[0 \mathinner{\ldotp\ldotp} 1)$ for which $A_{k+1} = a$ is a union of disjoint intervals, and so is the set $\mathcal{J}$ of all X for which $A_{k+1} \neq a$. Lemma M therefore applies, with $\mathcal{K}$ the set of all X for which A_{k+1} is undefined. Furthermore, $F_k(1/a) - F_k(1/(a+1))$ is the probability that $1/(a+1) < X_k \leq 1/a$, which is $\mu(\mathcal{I})$, the probability that $A_{k+1} = a$. ∎

As a consequence of Theorems E and W, we can say that a quotient equal to a occurs with the approximate probability

$$\lg(1 + 1/a) - \lg(1 + 1/(a+1)) = \lg\big((a+1)^2/((a+1)^2 - 1)\big).$$

Thus

a quotient of 1 occurs about $\lg(\frac{4}{3}) \approx 41.504$ percent of the time;

a quotient of 2 occurs about $\lg(\frac{9}{8}) \approx 16.993$ percent of the time;

a quotient of 3 occurs about $\lg(\frac{16}{15}) \approx 9.311$ percent of the time;

a quotient of 4 occurs about $\lg(\frac{25}{24}) \approx 5.889$ percent of the time.

Actually, if Euclid's algorithm produces the quotients A_1, A_2, $\ldots$, A_t, the nature of the proofs above will guarantee this behavior only for A_k when k is comparatively small with respect to t; the values A_{t-1}, A_{t-2}, $\ldots$ are not covered by this proof. But we can in fact show that the distribution of the last quotients A_{t-1}, A_{t-2}, $\ldots$ is essentially the same as the first.

For example, consider the regular continued fraction expansions for the set of all proper fractions whose denominator is 29:

$$\frac{1}{29} = /\!/\,29\,/\!/ \qquad \frac{8}{29} = /\!/\,3,1,1,1,2\,/\!/ \qquad \frac{15}{29} = /\!/\,1,1,14\,/\!/ \qquad \frac{22}{29} = /\!/\,1,3,7\,/\!/$$
$$\frac{2}{29} = /\!/\,14,2\,/\!/ \qquad \frac{9}{29} = /\!/\,3,4,2\,/\!/ \qquad \frac{16}{29} = /\!/\,1,1,4,3\,/\!/ \qquad \frac{23}{29} = /\!/\,1,3,1,5\,/\!/$$
$$\frac{3}{29} = /\!/\,9,1,2\,/\!/ \qquad \frac{10}{29} = /\!/\,2,1,9\,/\!/ \qquad \frac{17}{29} = /\!/\,1,1,2,2,2\,/\!/ \qquad \frac{24}{29} = /\!/\,1,4,1,4\,/\!/$$
$$\frac{4}{29} = /\!/\,7,4\,/\!/ \qquad \frac{11}{29} = /\!/\,2,1,1,1,3\,/\!/ \qquad \frac{18}{29} = /\!/\,1,1,1,1,1,3\,/\!/ \qquad \frac{25}{29} = /\!/\,1,6,4\,/\!/$$
$$\frac{5}{29} = /\!/\,5,1,4\,/\!/ \qquad \frac{12}{29} = /\!/\,2,2,2,2\,/\!/ \qquad \frac{19}{29} = /\!/\,1,1,1,9\,/\!/ \qquad \frac{26}{29} = /\!/\,1,8,1,2\,/\!/$$
$$\frac{6}{29} = /\!/\,4,1,5\,/\!/ \qquad \frac{13}{29} = /\!/\,2,4,3\,/\!/ \qquad \frac{20}{29} = /\!/\,1,2,4,2\,/\!/ \qquad \frac{27}{29} = /\!/\,1,13,2\,/\!/$$
$$\frac{7}{29} = /\!/\,4,7\,/\!/ \qquad \frac{14}{29} = /\!/\,2,14\,/\!/ \qquad \frac{21}{29} = /\!/\,1,2,1,1,1,2\,/\!/ \qquad \frac{28}{29} = /\!/\,1,28\,/\!/$$

Several things can be observed in this table.

a) As mentioned earlier, the last quotient is always 2 or more. Furthermore, we have the obvious identity

$$/\!/\,x_1, \ldots, x_{n-1}, x_n + 1\,/\!/ = /\!/\,x_1, \ldots, x_{n-1}, x_n, 1\,/\!/, \qquad (46)$$

which shows how continued fractions whose last quotient is unity are related to regular continued fractions.

b) The values in the right-hand columns have a simple relationship to the values in the left-hand columns; can the reader see the correspondence before reading any further? The relevant identity is

$$1 - //x_1, x_2, \ldots, x_n// = //1, x_1 - 1, x_2, \ldots, x_n//; \tag{47}$$

see exercise 9.

c) There is symmetry between left and right in the first two columns: If $//A_1, A_2, \ldots, A_t//$ occurs, so does $//A_t, \ldots, A_2, A_1//$. This will always be the case (see exercise 26).

d) If we examine all of the quotients in the table, we find that there are 96 in all, of which $\frac{39}{96} \approx 40.6$ percent are equal to 1, $\frac{21}{96} \approx 21.9$ percent are equal to 2, $\frac{8}{96} \approx 8.3$ percent are equal to 3; this agrees reasonably well with the probabilities listed above.

The number of division steps. Let us now return to our original problem and investigate T_n, the average number of division steps when $v = n$. (See Eq. (19).) Here are some sample values of T_n:

$n =$	95	96	97	98	99	100	101	102	103	104	105
$T_n =$	5.0	4.4	5.3	4.8	4.7	4.6	5.3	4.6	5.3	4.7	4.6

$n =$	996	997	998	999	1000	1001	$\cdots$	9999	10000	10001
$T_n =$	6.5	7.3	7.0	6.8	6.4	6.7	$\cdots$	8.6	8.3	9.1

$n =$	49998	49999	50000	50001	$\cdots$	99999	100000	100001
$T_n =$	9.8	10.6	9.7	10.0	$\cdots$	10.7	10.3	11.0

Notice the somewhat erratic behavior; T_n tends to be larger than its neighbors when n is prime, and it is correspondingly lower when n has many divisors. (In this list, 97, 101, 103, 997, and 49999 are primes; $10001 = 73 \cdot 137$; $49998 = 2 \cdot 3 \cdot 13 \cdot 641$; $50001 = 3 \cdot 7 \cdot 2381$; $99999 = 3 \cdot 3 \cdot 41 \cdot 271$; and $100001 = 11 \cdot 9091$.) It is not difficult to understand why this happens: If $\gcd(u, v) = d$, Euclid's algorithm applied to u and v behaves essentially the same as if it were applied to u/d and v/d. Therefore, when $v = n$ has several divisors, there are many choices of u for which n behaves as if it were smaller.

Accordingly let us consider *another* quantity, τ_n, which is the average number of division steps when $v = n$ and when u is *relatively prime* to n. Thus

$$\tau_n = \frac{1}{\varphi(n)} \sum_{\substack{0 \le m < n \\ m \perp n}} T(m, n). \tag{48}$$

It follows that

$$T_n = \frac{1}{n} \sum_{d \backslash n} \varphi(d)\tau_d. \tag{49}$$

Here is a table of τ_n for the same values of n considered above:

$n =$	95	96	97	98	99	100	101	102	103	104	105
$\tau_n =$	5.4	5.3	5.3	5.6	5.2	5.2	5.4	5.3	5.4	5.3	5.6

$n =$	996	997	998	999	1000	1001	$\cdots$	9999	10000	10001
$\tau_n =$	7.2	7.3	7.3	7.3	7.3	7.4	$\cdots$	9.21	9.21	9.22

$n =$	49998	49999	50000	50001	$\cdots$	99999	100000	100001
$\tau_n =$	10.59	10.58	10.57	10.59	$\cdots$	11.170	11.172	11.172

Clearly τ_n is much more well-behaved than T_n, and it should be more susceptible to analysis. Inspection of a table of τ_n for small n reveals some curious anomalies; for example, $\tau_{50} = \tau_{100}$ and $\tau_{60} = \tau_{120}$. But as n grows, the values of τ_n behave quite regularly indeed, as the table indicates, and they show no significant relation to the factorization properties of n. If these values τ_n are plotted as functions of $\ln n$ on graph paper, for the values of τ_n given above, they lie very nearly on the straight line

$$\tau_n \approx 0.843 \ln n + 1.47. \tag{50}$$

We can account for this behavior if we study the regular continued fraction process a little further. In Euclid's algorithm as expressed in (15) we have

$$\frac{V_0}{U_0} \frac{V_1}{U_1} \cdots \frac{V_{t-1}}{U_{t-1}} = \frac{V_{t-1}}{U_0},$$

since $U_{k+1} = V_k$; therefore if $U = U_0$ and $V = V_0$ are relatively prime, and if there are t division steps, we have

$$X_0 X_1 \ldots X_{t-1} = 1/U.$$

Setting $U = N$ and $V = m < N$, we find that

$$\ln X_0 + \ln X_1 + \cdots + \ln X_{t-1} = -\ln N. \tag{51}$$

We know the approximate distribution of X_0, X_1, X_2, $\ldots$, so we can use this equation to estimate

$$t = T(N, m) = T(m, N) - 1.$$

Returning to the formulas preceding Theorem W, we find that the average value of $\ln X_n$, when X_0 is a real number uniformly distributed in $[0 \ldots 1)$, is

$$\int_0^1 \ln x \, F_n'(x) \, dx = \int_0^1 \ln x \, f_n(x) \, dx / (1 + x), \tag{52}$$

where $f_n(x)$ is defined in (33). Now

$$f_n(x) = \frac{1}{\ln 2} + O(2^{-n}), \tag{53}$$

using the facts we have derived earlier (see exercise 23); hence the average value of $\ln X_n$ is very well approximated by

$$\frac{1}{\ln 2}\int_0^1 \frac{\ln x}{1+x}\,dx = -\frac{1}{\ln 2}\int_0^\infty \frac{ue^{-u}}{1+e^{-u}}\,du$$

$$= -\frac{1}{\ln 2}\sum_{k\geq 1}(-1)^{k+1}\int_0^\infty ue^{-ku}\,du$$

$$= -\frac{1}{\ln 2}\left(1 - \frac{1}{4} + \frac{1}{9} - \frac{1}{16} + \frac{1}{25} - \cdots\right)$$

$$= -\frac{1}{\ln 2}\left(1 + \frac{1}{4} + \frac{1}{9} + \cdots - 2\left(\frac{1}{4} + \frac{1}{16} + \frac{1}{36} + \cdots\right)\right)$$

$$= -\frac{1}{2\ln 2}\left(1 + \frac{1}{4} + \frac{1}{9} + \cdots\right)$$

$$= -\pi^2/(12\ln 2).$$

By (51) we therefore expect to have the approximate formula

$$-t\pi^2/(12\ln 2) \approx -\ln N;$$

that is, t should be approximately equal to $\big((12\ln 2)/\pi^2\big)\ln N$. This constant $(12\ln 2)/\pi^2 = 0.842765913\ldots$ agrees perfectly with the empirical formula (50) obtained earlier, so we have good reason to believe that the formula

$$\tau_n \approx \frac{12\ln 2}{\pi^2}\ln n + 1.47 \tag{54}$$

indicates the true asymptotic behavior of τ_n as $n \to \infty$.

If we assume that (54) is valid, we obtain the formula

$$T_n \approx \frac{12\ln 2}{\pi^2}\left(\ln n - \sum_{d\backslash n}\frac{\Lambda(d)}{d}\right) + 1.47, \tag{55}$$

where $\Lambda(d)$ is *von Mangoldt's function* defined by the rules

$$\Lambda(n) = \begin{cases} \ln p, & \text{if } n = p^r \text{ for } p \text{ prime and } r \geq 1; \\ 0, & \text{otherwise.} \end{cases} \tag{56}$$

(See exercise 27.) For example,

$$T_{100} \approx \frac{12\ln 2}{\pi^2}\left(\ln 100 - \frac{\ln 2}{2} - \frac{\ln 2}{4} - \frac{\ln 5}{5} - \frac{\ln 5}{25}\right) + 1.47$$

$$\approx (0.843)(4.605 - 0.347 - 0.173 - 0.322 - 0.064) + 1.47$$

$$\approx 4.59;$$

the exact value of T_{100} is 4.56.

We can also estimate the average number of division steps when u and v are both uniformly distributed between 1 and N, by calculating

$$\frac{1}{N^2} \sum_{m=1}^{N} \sum_{n=1}^{N} T(m,n) = \frac{2}{N^2} \sum_{n=1}^{N} nT_n - \frac{1}{2} - \frac{1}{2N}. \tag{57}$$

Assuming formula (55), exercise 29 shows that this sum has the form

$$\frac{12 \ln 2}{\pi^2} \ln N + O(1), \tag{58}$$

and empirical calculations with the same numbers used to derive Eq. 4.5.2–(65) show good agreement with the formula

$$\frac{12 \ln 2}{\pi^2} \ln N + 0.06. \tag{59}$$

Of course we have not yet *proved* anything about T_n and τ_n in general; so far we have only been considering plausible reasons why certain formulas ought to hold. Fortunately it is now possible to supply rigorous proofs, based on a careful analysis by several mathematicians.

The leading coefficient $12\pi^{-2} \ln 2$ in the formulas above was established first, in independent studies by Gustav Lochs, John D. Dixon, and Hans A. Heilbronn. Lochs [*Monatshefte für Math.* **65** (1961), 27–52] derived a formula equivalent to the fact that (57) equals $(12\pi^{-2} \ln 2) \ln N + a + O(N^{-1/2})$, where $a \approx 0.065$. Unfortunately his paper remained essentially unknown for many years, perhaps because it computed only an average value from which we cannot derive definite information about T_n for any particular n. Dixon [*J. Number Theory* **2** (1970), 414–422] developed the theory of the $F_n(x)$ distributions to show that individual partial quotients are essentially independent of each other in an appropriate sense, and proved that for all positive ϵ we have $|T(m,n) - (12\pi^{-2} \ln 2) \ln n| < (\ln n)^{(1/2)+\epsilon}$ except for $\exp(-c(\epsilon)(\log N)^{\epsilon/2}) N^2$ values of m and n in the range $1 \le m < n \le N$, where $c(\epsilon) > 0$. Heilbronn's approach was completely different, working entirely with integers instead of continuous variables. His idea, which is presented in slightly modified form in exercises 33 and 34, is based on the fact that τ_n can be related to the number of ways to represent n in a certain manner. Furthermore, his paper [*Number Theory and Analysis*, edited by Paul Turán (New York: Plenum, 1969), 87–96] shows that the distribution of individual partial quotients 1, 2, ... that we have discussed above actually applies to the entire collection of partial quotients belonging to the fractions having a given denominator; this is a sharper form of Theorem E. A still sharper result was obtained several years later by J. W. Porter [*Mathematika* **22** (1975), 20–28], who established that

$$\tau_n = \frac{12 \ln 2}{\pi^2} \ln n + C + O(n^{-1/6+\epsilon}), \tag{60}$$

where $C \approx 1.46707\,80794$ is the constant

$$\frac{6 \ln 2}{\pi^2} \left(3 \ln 2 + 4\gamma - \frac{24}{\pi^2} \zeta'(2) - 2 \right) - \frac{1}{2}; \tag{61}$$

see D. E. Knuth, *Computers and Math. with Applic.* **2** (1976), 137–139. Thus the conjecture (50) is fully proved. Using (60), Graham H. Norton [*J. Symbolic Computation* **10** (1990), 53–58] extended the calculations of exercise 29 to confirm Lochs's work, proving that the empirical constant 0.06 in (59) is actually

$$\frac{6\ln 2}{\pi^2}\left(3\ln 2 + 4\gamma - \frac{12}{\pi^2}\zeta'(2) - 3\right) - 1 = 0.06535\,14259\ldots. \tag{62}$$

D. Hensley proved in *J. Number Theory* **49** (1994), 142–182, that the variance of τ_n is proportional to $\log n$.

The average running time for Euclid's algorithm on multiple-precision integers, using classical algorithms for arithmetic, was shown to be of order

$$\left(1 + \log\left(\max(u,v)/\gcd(u,v)\right)\right)\log\min(u,v) \tag{63}$$

by G. E. Collins, in *SICOMP* **3** (1974), 1–10.

Summary. We have found that the worst case of Euclid's algorithm occurs when its inputs u and v are consecutive Fibonacci numbers (Theorem F); the number of division steps when $0 \le v < N$ will never exceed $\lceil 4.8\log_{10} N - 0.32\rceil$. We have determined the frequency of the values of various partial quotients, showing, for example, that the division step finds $\lfloor u/v\rfloor = 1$ about 41 percent of the time (Theorem E). And, finally, the theorems of Heilbronn and Porter prove that the average number T_n of division steps when $v = n$ is approximately

$$\left((12\ln 2)/\pi^2\right)\ln n \approx 1.9405\log_{10} n,$$

minus a correction term based on the divisors of n as shown in Eq. (55).

EXERCISES

▶ **1.** [*20*] Since the quotient $\lfloor u/v\rfloor$ is equal to unity more than 40 percent of the time in Algorithm 4.5.2A, it may be advantageous on some computers to make a test for this case and to avoid the division when the quotient is unity. Is the following MIX program for Euclid's algorithm more efficient than Program 4.5.2A?

```
      LDX   U    rX ← u.              SRAX 5    rAX ← rA.
      JMP   2F                        JL    2F  Is u − v < v?
1H    STX   V    v ← rX.              DIV  V    rX ← rAX mod v.
      SUB   V    rA ← u − v.       2H LDA  V    rA ← v.
      CMPA  V                         JXNZ 1B   Done if rX = 0.  ∎
```

2. [*M21*] Evaluate the matrix product $\begin{pmatrix} x_1 & 1 \\ 1 & 0 \end{pmatrix}\begin{pmatrix} x_2 & 1 \\ 1 & 0 \end{pmatrix}\cdots\begin{pmatrix} x_n & 1 \\ 1 & 0 \end{pmatrix}$.

3. [*M21*] What is the value of $\det\begin{pmatrix} x_1 & 1 & 0 & \cdots & 0 \\ -1 & x_2 & 1 & & 0 \\ 0 & -1 & x_3 & 1 & \vdots \\ \vdots & & -1 & \ddots & 1 \\ 0 & 0 & \cdots & -1 & x_n \end{pmatrix}$?

4. [*M20*] Prove Eq. (8).

5. [*HM25*] Let x_1, x_2, ... be a sequence of real numbers that are each greater than some positive real number ϵ. Prove that the infinite continued fraction $/\!\!/x_1, x_2, \ldots/\!\!/ = \lim_{n \to \infty} /\!\!/x_1, \ldots, x_n/\!\!/$ exists. Show also that $/\!\!/x_1, x_2, \ldots/\!\!/$ need not exist if we assume only that $x_j > 0$ for all j.

6. [*M23*] Prove that the regular continued fraction expansion of a number is *unique* in the following sense: If B_1, B_2, ... are positive integers, then the infinite continued fraction $/\!\!/B_1, B_2, \ldots/\!\!/$ is an irrational number X between 0 and 1 whose regular continued fraction has $A_n = B_n$ for all $n \geq 1$; and if B_1, ..., B_m are positive integers with $B_m > 1$, then the regular continued fraction for $X = /\!\!/B_1, \ldots, B_m/\!\!/$ has $A_n = B_n$ for $1 \leq n \leq m$.

7. [*M26*] Find all permutations $p(1)p(2) \ldots p(n)$ of the integers $\{1, 2, \ldots, n\}$ such that $K_n(x_1, x_2, \ldots, x_n) = K_n(x_{p(1)}, x_{p(2)}, \ldots, x_{p(n)})$ is an identity for all $x_1, x_2, \ldots, x_n$.

8. [*M20*] Show that $-1/X_n = /\!\!/A_n, \ldots, A_1, -X/\!\!/$, whenever X_n is defined, in the regular continued fraction process.

9. [*M21*] Show that continued fractions satisfy the following identities:

a) $/\!\!/x_1, \ldots, x_n/\!\!/ = /\!\!/x_1, \ldots, x_k + /\!\!/x_{k+1}, \ldots, x_n/\!\!/ /\!\!/$, $1 \leq k \leq n$;

b) $/\!\!/0, x_1, x_2, \ldots, x_n/\!\!/ = x_1 + /\!\!/x_2, \ldots, x_n/\!\!/$, $n \geq 1$;

c) $/\!\!/x_1, \ldots, x_{k-1}, x_k, 0, x_{k+1}, x_{k+2}, \ldots, x_n/\!\!/ = /\!\!/x_1, \ldots, x_{k-1}, x_k + x_{k+1}, x_{k+2}, \ldots, x_n/\!\!/$,
   $1 \leq k < n$;

d) $1 - /\!\!/x_1, x_2, \ldots, x_n/\!\!/ = /\!\!/1, x_1 - 1, x_2, \ldots, x_n/\!\!/$, $n \geq 1$.

10. [*M28*] By the result of exercise 6, every irrational real number X has a unique regular continued fraction representation of the form

$$X = A_0 + /\!\!/A_1, A_2, A_3, A_4, \ldots/\!\!/,$$

where A_0 is an integer and A_1, A_2, A_3, A_4, ... are positive integers. Show that if X has this representation then the regular continued fraction for $1/X$ is

$$1/X = B_0 + /\!\!/B_1, \ldots, B_m, A_5, A_6, \ldots/\!\!/$$

for suitable integers B_0, B_1, ..., B_m. (The case $A_0 < 0$ is, of course, the most interesting.) Explain how to determine the B's in terms of A_0, A_1, A_2, A_3, and A_4.

11. [*M30*] (J.-A. Serret, 1850.) Let $X = A_0 + /\!\!/A_1, A_2, A_3, A_4, \ldots/\!\!/$ and $Y = B_0 + /\!\!/B_1, B_2, B_3, B_4, \ldots/\!\!/$ be the regular continued fraction representations of two real numbers X and Y, in the sense of exercise 10. Show that these representations "eventually agree," in the sense that $A_{m+k} = B_{n+k}$ for some m and n and for all $k \geq 0$, if and only if we have $X = (qY + r)/(sY + t)$ for some integers q, r, s, t with $|qt - rs| = 1$. (This theorem is the analog, for continued fraction representations, of the simple result that the representations of X and Y in the decimal system eventually agree if and only if $X = (10^q Y + r)/10^s$ for some integers q, r, and s.)

▶ **12.** [*M30*] A *quadratic irrationality* is a number of the form $(\sqrt{D} - U)/V$, where D, U, and V are integers, $D > 0$, $V \neq 0$, and D is not a perfect square. We may assume without loss of generality that V is a divisor of $D - U^2$, for otherwise the number may be rewritten as $(\sqrt{DV^2} - U|V|)/(V|V|)$.

a) Prove that the regular continued fraction expansion (in the sense of exercise 10) of a quadratic irrationality $X = (\sqrt{D} - U)/V$ is obtained by the following formulas:

$$V_0 = V, \qquad\qquad A_0 = \lfloor X \rfloor, \qquad\qquad U_0 = U + A_0 V;$$

$$V_{n+1} = (D - U_n^2)/V_n, \quad A_{n+1} = \lfloor (\sqrt{D} + U_n)/V_{n+1} \rfloor, \quad U_{n+1} = A_{n+1} V_{n+1} - U_n.$$

b) Prove that $0 < U_n < \sqrt{D}$, $0 < V_n < 2\sqrt{D}$, for all $n > N$, where N is some integer depending on X; hence the regular continued fraction representation of every quadratic irrationality is eventually periodic. [*Hint:* Show that

$$(-\sqrt{D} - U)/V = A_0 + /\!/A_1, \ldots, A_n, -V_n/(\sqrt{D} + U_n)/\!/,$$

and use Eq. (5) to prove that $(\sqrt{D} + U_n)/V_n$ is positive when n is large.]

c) Letting $p_n = K_{n+1}(A_0, A_1, \ldots, A_n)$ and $q_n = K_n(A_1, \ldots, A_n)$, prove the identity $Vp_n^2 + 2Up_nq_n + ((U^2 - D)/V)q_n^2 = (-1)^{n+1}V_{n+1}$.

d) Prove that the regular continued fraction representation of an irrational number X is eventually periodic if and only if X is a quadratic irrationality. (This is the continued fraction analog of the fact that the decimal expansion of a real number X is eventually periodic if and only if X is rational.)

13. [*M40*] (J. Lagrange, 1767.) Let $f(x) = a_nx^n + \cdots + a_0$, $a_n > 0$, be a polynomial having exactly one real root $\xi > 1$, where ξ is irrational and $f'(\xi) \neq 0$. Experiment with a computer program to find the first thousand or so partial quotients of ξ, using the following algorithm (which essentially involves only addition):

L1. Set $A \leftarrow 1$.

L2. For $k = 0, 1, \ldots, n-1$ (in this order) and for $j = n-1, \ldots, k$ (in this order), set $a_j \leftarrow a_{j+1} + a_j$. (This step replaces $f(x)$ by $g(x) = f(x+1)$, a polynomial whose roots are one less than those of f.)

L3. If $a_n + a_{n-1} + \cdots + a_0 < 0$, set $A \leftarrow A + 1$ and return to L2.

L4. Output A (which is the value of the next partial quotient). Replace the coefficients $(a_n, a_{n-1}, \ldots, a_0)$ by $(-a_0, -a_1, \ldots, -a_n)$ and return to L1. (This step replaces $f(x)$ by a polynomial whose roots are reciprocals of those of f.) ∎

For example, starting with $f(x) = x^3 - 2$, the algorithm will output "1" (changing $f(x)$ to $x^3 - 3x^2 - 3x - 1$); then "3" (changing $f(x)$ to $10x^3 - 6x^2 - 6x - 1$); etc.

14. [*M22*] (A. Hurwitz, 1891.) Show that the following rules make it possible to find the regular continued fraction expansion of $2X$, given the partial quotients of X:

$$2/\!/\, 2a, b, c, \ldots /\!/ = /\!/\, a, 2b + 2/\!/c, \ldots /\!/\, /\!/;$$
$$2/\!/\, 2a + 1, b, c, \ldots /\!/ = /\!/\, a, 1, 1 + 2/\!/b - 1, c, \ldots /\!/\, /\!/.$$

Use this idea to find the regular continued fraction expansion of $\frac{1}{2}e$, given the expansion of e in (13).

▶ **15.** [*M31*] (R. W. Gosper.) Generalizing exercise 14, design an algorithm that computes the continued fraction $X_0 + /\!/X_1, X_2, \ldots /\!/$ for $(ax + b)/(cx + d)$, given the continued fraction $x_0 + /\!/x_1, x_2, \ldots /\!/$ for x, and given integers a, b, c, d with $ad \neq bc$. Make your algorithm an "online coroutine" that outputs as many X_k as possible before inputting each x_j. Demonstrate how your algorithm computes $(97x + 39)/(-62x - 25)$ when $x = -1 + /\!/5, 1, 1, 1, 2, 1, 2/\!/$.

16. [*HM30*] (L. Euler, 1731.) Let $f_0(z) = (e^z - e^{-z})/(e^z + e^{-z}) = \tanh z$, and let $f_{n+1}(z) = 1/f_n(z) - (2n + 1)/z$. Prove that, for all n, $f_n(z)$ is an analytic function of the complex variable z in a neighborhood of the origin, and it satisfies the differential equation $f_n'(z) = 1 - f_n(z)^2 - 2nf_n(z)/z$. Use this fact to prove that

$$\tanh z = /\!/z^{-1}, 3z^{-1}, 5z^{-1}, 7z^{-1}, \ldots /\!/;$$

then apply Hurwitz's rule (exercise 14) to prove that

$$e^{-1/n} = /\!\!/ \, \overline{1, (2m+1)n - 1, 1} /\!\!/, \qquad m \geq 0.$$

(This notation denotes the infinite continued fraction $/\!\!/ \, 1, \, n - 1, \, 1, \, 1, \, 3n - 1, \, 1, \, 1,$ $5n - 1, \, 1, \, \ldots /\!\!/$.) Also find the regular continued fraction expansion of $e^{-2/n}$ when $n > 0$ is odd.

▶ **17.** [*M23*] (a) Prove that $/\!\!/ x_1, -x_2 /\!\!/ = /\!\!/ x_1 - 1, 1, x_2 - 1 /\!\!/$. (b) Generalize this identity, obtaining a formula for $/\!\!/ x_1, -x_2, x_3, -x_4, x_5, -x_6, \ldots, x_{2n-1}, -x_{2n} /\!\!/$ in which all partial quotients are positive integers when the x's are large positive integers. (c) The result of exercise 16 implies that $\tan 1 = /\!\!/ 1, -3, 5, -7, \ldots /\!\!/$. Find the regular continued fraction expansion of $\tan 1$.

18. [*M25*] Show that $/\!\!/ a_1, a_2, \ldots, a_m, x_1, a_1, a_2, \ldots, a_m, x_2, a_1, a_2, \ldots, a_m, x_3, \ldots /\!\!/ -$ $/\!\!/ a_m, \ldots, a_2, a_1, x_1, a_m, \ldots, a_2, a_1, x_2, a_m, \ldots, a_2, a_1, x_3, \ldots /\!\!/$ does not depend on x_1, x_2, x_3, ... *Hint:* Multiply both continued fractions by $K_m(a_1, a_2, \ldots, a_m)$.

19. [*M20*] Prove that $F(x) = \log_b(1 + x)$ satisfies Eq. (24).

20. [*HM20*] Derive (38) from (37).

21. [*HM29*] (E. Wirsing.) The bounds (39) were obtained for a function φ corresponding to g with $Tg(x) = 1/(x + 1)$. Show that the function corresponding to $Tg(x) = 1/(x + c)$ yields better bounds, when $c > 0$ is an appropriate constant.

22. [*HM46*] (K. I. Babenko.) Develop efficient means to calculate accurate approximations to the quantities λ_j and $\Psi_j(x)$ in (44), for small $j \geq 3$ and for $0 \leq x \leq 1$.

23. [*HM23*] Prove (53), using results from the proof of Theorem W.

24. [*M22*] What is the average value of a partial quotient A_n in the regular continued fraction expansion of a random real number?

25. [*HM25*] Find an example of a set $\mathcal{I} = I_1 \cup I_2 \cup I_3 \cup \cdots \subseteq [0 \, . \, . \, 1]$, where the I's are disjoint intervals, for which (45) does not hold.

26. [*M23*] Show that if the numbers $\{1/n, 2/n, \ldots, \lfloor n/2 \rfloor / n\}$ are expressed as regular continued fractions, the result is symmetric between left and right, in the sense that $/\!\!/ A_t, \ldots, A_2, A_1 /\!\!/$ appears whenever $/\!\!/ A_1, A_2, \ldots, A_t /\!\!/$ does.

27. [*M21*] Derive (55) from (49) and (54).

28. [*M23*] Prove the following identities involving the three number-theoretic functions $\varphi(n)$, $\mu(n)$, $\Lambda(n)$:

a) $\displaystyle\sum_{d \backslash n} \mu(d) = \delta_{n1}.$ b) $\displaystyle\ln n = \sum_{d \backslash n} \Lambda(d), \qquad n = \sum_{d \backslash n} \varphi(d).$

c) $\displaystyle\Lambda(n) = \sum_{d \backslash n} \mu\left(\frac{n}{d}\right) \ln d, \qquad \varphi(n) = \sum_{d \backslash n} \mu\left(\frac{n}{d}\right) d.$

29. [*M23*] Assuming that T_n is given by (55), show that (57) equals (58).

▶ **30.** [*HM32*] The following "greedy" variant of Euclid's algorithm is often suggested: Instead of replacing v by $u \bmod v$ during the division step, replace it by $|(u \bmod v) - v|$ if $u \bmod v > \frac{1}{2}v$. Thus, for example, if $u = 26$ and $v = 7$, we have $\gcd(26, 7) = \gcd(-2, 7) = \gcd(7, 2)$; -2 is the *remainder of smallest magnitude* when multiples of 7 are subtracted from 26. Compare this procedure with Euclid's algorithm; estimate the number of division steps this method saves, on the average.

▶ **31.** [*M35*] Find the worst case of the modification of Euclid's algorithm suggested in exercise 30: What are the smallest inputs $u > v > 0$ that require n division steps?

32. [*20*] (a) A Morse code sequence of length n is a string of r dots and s dashes, where $r + 2s = n$. For example, the Morse code sequences of length 4 are

$$\bullet\bullet\bullet\bullet, \quad \bullet\bullet-, \quad \bullet-\bullet, \quad -\bullet\bullet, \quad --.$$

Noting that the continuant $K_4(x_1, x_2, x_3, x_4)$ is $x_1 x_2 x_3 x_4 + x_1 x_2 + x_1 x_4 + x_3 x_4 + 1$, find and prove a simple relation between $K_n(x_1, \ldots, x_n)$ and Morse code sequences of length n. (b) (L. Euler, *Novi Comm. Acad. Sci. Pet.* **9** (1762), 53–69.) Prove that

$$K_{m+n}(x_1, \ldots, x_{m+n}) = K_m(x_1, \ldots, x_m) K_n(x_{m+1}, \ldots, x_{m+n})$$
$$+ K_{m-1}(x_1, \ldots, x_{m-1}) K_{n-1}(x_{m+2}, \ldots, x_{m+n}).$$

33. [*M32*] Let $h(n)$ be the number of representations of n in the form

$$n = xx' + yy', \qquad x > y > 0, \qquad x' > y' > 0, \qquad x \perp y, \qquad \text{integer } x, x', y, y'.$$

a) Show that if the conditions are relaxed to allow $x' = y'$, the number of representations is $h(n) + \lfloor (n-1)/2 \rfloor$.

b) Show that for fixed $y > 0$ and $0 < t \le y$, where $t \perp y$, and for each fixed x' in the range $0 < x' < n/(y+t)$ such that $x't \equiv n$ (modulo y), there is exactly one representation of n satisfying the restrictions of (a) and the condition $x \equiv t$ (modulo y).

c) Consequently, $h(n) = \sum \lceil (n/(y+t) - t')/y \rceil - \lfloor (n-1)/2 \rfloor$, where the sum is over all positive integers y, t, t' such that $t \perp y$, $t \le y$, $t' \le y$, $tt' \equiv n$ (modulo y).

d) Show that each of the $h(n)$ representations can be expressed uniquely in the form

$$x = K_m(x_1, \ldots, x_m), \qquad y = K_{m-1}(x_1, \ldots, x_{m-1}),$$
$$x' = K_k(x_{m+1}, \ldots, x_{m+k}) d, \qquad y' = K_{k-1}(x_{m+2}, \ldots, x_{m+k}) d,$$

where m, k, d, and the x_j are positive integers with $x_1 \ge 2$, $x_{m+k} \ge 2$, and d is a divisor of n. The identity of exercise 32 now implies that $n/d = K_{m+k}(x_1, \ldots, x_{m+k})$. Conversely, any given sequence of positive integers $x_1, \ldots, x_{m+k}$ such that $x_1 \ge 2$, $x_{m+k} \ge 2$, and $K_{m+k}(x_1, \ldots, x_{m+k})$ divides n, corresponds in this way to $m+k-1$ representations of n.

e) Therefore $nT_n = \lfloor (5n-3)/2 \rfloor + 2h(n)$.

34. [*HM40*] (H. Heilbronn.) Let $h_d(n)$ be the number of representations of n as in exercise 33 such that $xd < x'$, plus half the number of representations with $xd = x'$.

a) Let $g(n)$ be the number of representations without the requirement that $x \perp y$. Prove that

$$h(n) = \sum_{d \backslash n} \mu(d) g\left(\frac{n}{d}\right), \qquad g(n) = 2 \sum_{d \backslash n} h_d\left(\frac{n}{d}\right).$$

b) Generalizing exercise 33(b), show that for $d \ge 1$, $h_d(n) = \sum (n/(y(y+t))) + O(n)$, where the sum is over all integers y and t such that $t \perp y$ and $0 < t \le y < \sqrt{n/d}$.

c) Show that $\sum (y/(y+t)) = \varphi(y) \ln 2 + O(\sigma_{-1}(y))$, where the sum is over the range $0 < t \le y$, $t \perp y$, and where $\sigma_{-1}(y) = \sum_{d \backslash y} (1/d)$.

d) Show that $\sum_{y=1}^n \varphi(y)/y^2 = \sum_{d=1}^n \mu(d) H_{\lfloor n/d \rfloor}/d^2$.

e) Hence we have the asymptotic formula

$$T_n = ((12 \ln 2)/\pi^2)(\ln n - \sum_{d \backslash n} \Lambda(d)/d) + O(\sigma_{-1}(n)^2).$$

35. [*HM41*] (A. C. Yao and D. E. Knuth.) Prove that the sum of all partial quotients for the fractions m/n, for $1 \le m < n$, is equal to $2(\sum \lfloor x/y \rfloor + \lfloor n/2 \rfloor)$, where the sum is over all representations $n = xx' + yy'$ satisfying the conditions of exercise 33(a). Show that $\sum \lfloor x/y \rfloor = 3\pi^{-2} n (\ln n)^2 + O(n \log n \, (\log \log n)^2)$, and apply this to the "ancient" form of Euclid's algorithm that uses only subtraction instead of division.

36. [*M25*] (G. H. Bradley.) What is the smallest value of u_n such that the calculation of $\gcd(u_1, \ldots, u_n)$ by Algorithm 4.5.2C requires N divisions, if Euclid's algorithm is used throughout? Assume that $N \ge n \ge 3$.

37. [*M38*] (T. S. Motzkin and E. G. Straus.) Let $a_1, \ldots, a_n$ be positive integers. Show that $\max K_n(a_{p(1)}, \ldots, a_{p(n)})$, over all permutations $p(1) \ldots p(n)$ of $\{1, 2, \ldots, n\}$, occurs when $a_{p(1)} \ge a_{p(n)} \ge a_{p(2)} \ge a_{p(n-1)} \ge \cdots$; and the minimum occurs when $a_{p(1)} \le a_{p(n)} \le a_{p(3)} \le a_{p(n-2)} \le a_{p(5)} \le \cdots \le a_{p(6)} \le a_{p(n-3)} \le a_{p(4)} \le a_{p(n-1)} \le a_{p(2)}$.

38. [*M25*] (J. Mikusiński.) Let $L(n) = \max_{m \ge 0} T(m, n)$. Theorem F shows that $L(n) \le \log_\phi(\sqrt{5}\, n + 1) - 2$; prove that $2L(n) \ge \log_\phi(\sqrt{5}\, n + 1) - 2$.

▸ **39.** [*M25*] (R. W. Gosper.) If a baseball player's batting average is .334, what is the smallest possible number of times he has been at bat? [Note for non-baseball-fans: Batting average = (number of hits)/(times at bat), rounded to three decimal places.]

▸ **40.** [*M28*] (*The Stern–Brocot tree.*) Consider an infinite binary tree in which each node is labeled with the fraction $(p_l + p_r)/(q_l + q_r)$, where p_l/q_l is the label of the node's nearest left ancestor and p_r/q_r is the label of the node's nearest right ancestor. (A left ancestor is one that precedes a node in symmetric order, while a right ancestor follows the node. See Section 2.3.1 for the definition of symmetric order.) If the node has no left ancestors, $p_l/q_l = 0/1$; if it has no right ancestors, $p_r/q_r = 1/0$. Thus the label of the root is $1/1$; the labels of its two children are $1/2$ and $2/1$; the labels of the four nodes on level 2 are $1/3$, $2/3$, $3/2$, and $3/1$, from left to right; the labels of the eight nodes on level 3 are $1/4$, $2/5$, $3/5$, $3/4$, $4/3$, $5/3$, $5/2$, $4/1$; and so on.

Prove that p is relatively prime to q in each label p/q; furthermore, the node labeled p/q precedes the node labeled p'/q' in symmetric order if and only if the labels satisfy $p/q < p'/q'$. Find a connection between the continued fraction for the label of a node and the path to that node, thereby showing that each positive rational number appears as the label of exactly one node in the tree.

41. [*M40*] (J. Shallit, 1979.) Show that the regular continued fraction expansion of

$$\frac{1}{2^1} + \frac{1}{2^3} + \frac{1}{2^7} + \cdots = \sum_{n \ge 1} \frac{1}{2^{2^n - 1}}$$

contains only 1s and 2s and has a fairly simple pattern. Prove that the partial quotients of Liouville's numbers $\sum_{n \ge 1} l^{-n!}$ also have a regular pattern, when l is any integer ≥ 2. [The latter numbers, introduced by J. Liouville in *J. de Math. Pures et Appl.* **16** (1851), 133–142, were the first explicitly defined numbers to be proved *transcendental*. The former number and similar constants were first proved transcendental by A. J. Kempner, *Trans. Amer. Math. Soc.* **17** (1916), 476–482.]

42. [*M30*] (J. Lagrange, 1798.) Let X have the regular continued fraction expansion $/\!/A_1, A_2, \ldots /\!/$, and let $q_n = K_n(A_1, \ldots, A_n)$. Let $\|x\|$ denote the distance from x to the nearest integer, namely $\min_p |x - p|$. Show that $\|qX\| \ge \|q_{n-1}X\|$ for $1 \le q < q_n$. (Thus the denominators q_n of the so-called convergents $p_n/q_n = /\!/A_1, \ldots, A_n /\!/$ are the "record-breaking" integers that make $\|qX\|$ achieve new lows.)

43. [*M30*] (D. W. Matula.) Show that the "mediant rounding" rule for fixed slash or floating slash numbers, Eq. 4.5.1–(1), can be implemented simply as follows, when the number $x > 0$ is not representable: Let the regular continued fraction expansion of x be $a_0 + /\!/a_1, a_2, \ldots /\!/$, and let $p_n = K_{n+1}(a_0, \ldots, a_n)$, $q_n = K_n(a_1, \ldots, a_n)$ be its convergents. Then $\text{round}(x) = (p_i/q_i)$, where (p_i/q_i) is representable but (p_{i+1}/q_{i+1}) is not. [*Hint:* See exercise 40.]

44. [*M25*] Suppose we are doing fixed slash arithmetic with mediant rounding, where the fraction (u/u') is representable if and only if $|u| < M$ and $0 \le u' < N$ and $u \perp u'$. Prove or disprove the identity $((u/u') \oplus (v/v')) \ominus (v/v') = (u/u')$ for all representable (u/u') and (v/v'), provided that $u' < \sqrt{N}$ and no overflow occurs.

45. [*M25*] Show that Euclid's algorithm (Algorithm 4.5.2A) applied to two n-bit binary numbers requires $O(n^2)$ units of time, as $n \to \infty$. (The same upper bound obviously holds for Algorithm 4.5.2B.)

46. [*M43*] Can the upper bound $O(n^2)$ in exercise 45 be decreased, if another algorithm for calculating the greatest common divisor is used?

47. [*M40*] Develop a computer program to find as many partial quotients of x as possible, when x is a real number given with high precision. Use your program to calculate the first several thousand partial quotients of Euler's constant γ, which can be calculated as explained by D. W. Sweeney in *Math. Comp.* **17** (1963), 170–178. (If γ is a rational number, you might discover its numerator and denominator, thereby resolving a famous problem in mathematics. According to the theory in the text, we expect to get about 0.97 partial quotients per decimal digit, when the given number is random. Multiprecision division is not necessary; see Algorithm 4.5.2L and the article by J. W. Wrench, Jr. and D. Shanks, *Math. Comp.* **20** (1966), 444–447.)

48. [*M21*] Let $T_0 = (1, 0, u)$, $T_1 = (0, 1, v)$, $\ldots$, $T_{n+1} = ((-1)^{n+1}v/d, (-1)^n u/d, 0)$ be the sequence of vectors computed by Algorithm 4.5.2X (the extended Euclidean algorithm), and let $/\!/a_1, \ldots, a_n/\!/$ be the regular continued fraction for v/u. Express T_j in terms of continuants involving $a_1, \ldots, a_n$, for $1 < j \le n$.

49. [*M33*] By adjusting the final iteration of Algorithm 4.5.2X so that a_n is optionally replaced by two partial quotients $(a_n - 1, 1)$, we can assume that the number of iterations, n, has a given parity. Continuing the previous exercise, let λ and μ be arbitrary positive real numbers and let $\theta = \sqrt{\lambda\mu v/d}$, where $d = \gcd(u, v)$. Prove that if n is even, and if $T_j = (x_j, y_j, z_j)$, we have $\min_{j=1}^{n+1} |\lambda x_j + \mu z_j - [j \text{ even}]\theta| \le \theta$.

▶ **50.** [*M25*] Given an irrational number $\alpha \in (0 \mathinner{.\,.} 1)$ and real numbers β and γ with $0 \le \beta < \gamma < 1$, let $f(\alpha, \beta, \gamma)$ be the smallest nonnegative integer n such that $\beta \le \alpha n \bmod 1 < \gamma$. (Such an integer exists because of Weyl's theorem, exercise 3.5–22.) Design an algorithm to compute $f(\alpha, \beta, \gamma)$.

▶ **51.** [*M30*] (*Rational reconstruction.*) The number 28481 turns out to be equal to 41/316 (modulo 199999), in the sense that $316 \cdot 28481 \equiv 41$. How could a person discover this? Given integers a and m with $m > a > 1$, explain how to find integers x and y such that $ax \equiv y$ (modulo m), $x \perp y$, $0 < x \le \sqrt{m/2}$, and $|y| \le \sqrt{m/2}$, or to determine that no such x and y exist. Can there be more than one solution?

▶ **52.** [*M21*] (A. Ostrowski, 1922.) Let $a_1, a_2, \ldots$ be a sequence of positive integers, and let $q_n = K_n(a_1, \ldots, a_n)$ as in exercise 42 and other exercises. Prove that every nonnegative integer n has a unique representation of the form

$$n = c_0 q_0 + c_1 q_1 + c_2 q_2 + \cdots, \qquad 0 \le c_k \le a_{k+1},$$

where $c_k = a_{k+1}$ implies that $k > 0$ and $c_{k-1} = 0$. (When $a_k = 1$ for all k, this is the Fibonacci number system of exercise 1.2.8–34.)

4.5.4. Factoring into Primes

Several of the computational methods we have encountered in this book rest on the fact that every positive integer n can be expressed in a unique way in the form

$$n = p_1 p_2 \ldots p_t, \qquad p_1 \leq p_2 \leq \cdots \leq p_t, \qquad (1)$$

where each p_k is prime. (When $n = 1$, this equation holds for $t = 0$.) It is unfortunately not a simple matter to find this prime factorization of n, or to determine whether or not n is prime. So far as anyone knows, it is a great deal harder to factor a large number n than to compute the greatest common divisor of two large numbers m and n; therefore we should avoid factoring large numbers whenever possible. But several ingenious ways to speed up the factoring process have been discovered, and we will now investigate some of them. [A comprehensive history of factoring before 1950 has been compiled by H. C. Williams and J. O. Shallit, *Proc. Symp. Applied Math.* **48** (1993), 481–531.]

Divide and factor. First let us consider the most obvious algorithm for factorization: If $n > 1$, we can divide n by successive primes $p = 2, 3, 5, \ldots$ until discovering the smallest p for which $n \bmod p = 0$. Then p is the smallest prime factor of n, and the same process may be applied to $n \leftarrow n/p$ in an attempt to divide this new value of n by p and by higher primes. If at any stage we find that $n \bmod p \neq 0$ but $\lfloor n/p \rfloor \leq p$, we can conclude that n is prime; for if n is not prime, then by (1) we must have $n \geq p_1^2$, but $p_1 > p$ implies that $p_1^2 \geq (p+1)^2 > p(p+1) > p^2 + (n \bmod p) \geq \lfloor n/p \rfloor p + (n \bmod p) = n$. This leads us to the following procedure:

Algorithm A (*Factoring by division*). Given a positive integer N, this algorithm finds the prime factors $p_1 \leq p_2 \leq \cdots \leq p_t$ of N as in Eq. (1). The method makes use of an auxiliary sequence of trial divisors

$$2 = d_0 < d_1 < d_2 < d_3 < \cdots, \qquad (2)$$

which includes all prime numbers $\leq \sqrt{N}$ (and possibly values that are *not* prime, if convenient). The sequence of d's must also include at least one value such that $d_k \geq \sqrt{N}$.

A1. [Initialize.] Set $t \leftarrow 0$, $k \leftarrow 0$, $n \leftarrow N$. (During this algorithm the variables t, k, n are related by the following condition: "$n = N/p_1 \ldots p_t$, and n has no prime factors less than d_k.")

A2. [$n = 1$?] If $n = 1$, the algorithm terminates.

A3. [Divide.] Set $q \leftarrow \lfloor n/d_k \rfloor$, $r \leftarrow n \bmod d_k$. (Here q and r are the quotient and remainder obtained when n is divided by d_k.)

A4. [Zero remainder?] If $r \neq 0$, go to step A6.

A5. [Factor found.] Increase t by 1, and set $p_t \leftarrow d_k$, $n \leftarrow q$. Return to step A2.

A6. [Low quotient?] If $q > d_k$, increase k by 1 and return to step A3.

A7. [n is prime.] Increase t by 1, set $p_t \leftarrow n$, and terminate the algorithm. ∎

As an example of Algorithm A, consider the factorization of the number $N = 25852$. We find immediately that $N = 2 \cdot 12926$; hence $p_1 = 2$. Furthermore,

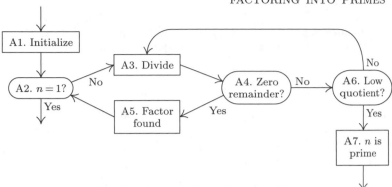

Fig. 11. A simple factoring algorithm.

$12926 = 2 \cdot 6463$, so $p_2 = 2$. But now $n = 6463$ is not divisible by 2, 3, 5, $\ldots$, 19; we find that $n = 23 \cdot 281$, hence $p_3 = 23$. Finally $281 = 12 \cdot 23 + 5$ and $12 \le 23$; hence $p_4 = 281$. The determination of 25852's factors has therefore involved a total of 12 division operations; on the other hand, if we had tried to factor the slightly smaller number 25849 (which is prime), at least 38 division operations would have been performed. This illustrates the fact that Algorithm A requires a running time roughly proportional to $\max(p_{t-1}, \sqrt{p_t})$. (If $t = 1$, this formula is valid if we adopt the convention $p_0 = 1$.)

The sequence d_0, d_1, d_2, $\ldots$ of trial divisors used in Algorithm A can be taken to be simply 2, 3, 5, 7, 11, 13, 17, 19, 23, 25, 29, 31, 35, $\ldots$, where we alternately add 2 and 4 after the first three terms. This sequence contains all numbers that are not multiples of 2 or 3; it also includes numbers such as 25, 35, 49, etc., which are not prime, but the algorithm will still give the correct answer. A further savings of 20 percent in computation time can be made by removing the numbers $30m \pm 5$ from the list for $m \ge 1$, thereby eliminating all of the spurious multiples of 5. The exclusion of multiples of 7 shortens the list by 14 percent more, etc. A compact bit table can be used to govern the choice of trial divisors.

If N is known to be small, it is reasonable to have a table of all the necessary primes as part of the program. For example, if N is less than a million, we need only include the 168 primes less than a thousand (followed by the value $d_{168} = 1000$, to terminate the list in case N is a prime larger than 997^2). Such a table can be set up by means of a short auxiliary program; see, for example, Algorithm 1.3.2P or exercise 8.

How many trial divisions are necessary in Algorithm A? Let $\pi(x)$ be the number of primes $\le x$, so that $\pi(2) = 1$, $\pi(10) = 4$; the asymptotic behavior of this function has been studied extensively by many of the world's greatest mathematicians, beginning with Legendre in 1798. Numerous advances made during the nineteenth century culminated in 1899, when Charles de La Vallée Poussin proved that, for some $A > 0$,

$$\pi(x) = \int_2^x \frac{dt}{\ln t} + O\!\left(x e^{-A\sqrt{\log x}}\right). \tag{3}$$

[*Mém. Couronnés Acad. Roy. Belgique* **59** (1899), 1–74; see also J. Hadamard, *Bull. Soc. Math. de France* **24** (1896), 199–220.] Integrating by parts yields

$$\pi(x) = \frac{x}{\ln x} + \frac{x}{(\ln x)^2} + \frac{2!\,x}{(\ln x)^3} + \cdots + \frac{r!\,x}{(\ln x)^{r+1}} + O\left(\frac{x}{(\log x)^{r+2}}\right) \quad (4)$$

for all fixed $r \geq 0$. The error term in (3) has subsequently been improved; for example, it can be replaced by $O\big(x \exp(-A(\log x)^{3/5}/(\log\log x)^{1/5})\big)$. [See A. Walfisz, *Weyl'sche Exponentialsummen in der neueren Zahlentheorie* (Berlin: 1963), Chapter 5.] Bernhard Riemann conjectured in 1859 that

$$\pi(x) \approx \sum_{k=1}^{\lg x} \frac{\mu(k)}{k} L\big(\sqrt[k]{x}\big) = L(x) - \frac{1}{2}L\big(\sqrt{x}\big) - \frac{1}{3}L\big(\sqrt[3]{x}\big) + \cdots \quad (5)$$

where $L(x) = \int_2^x dt/\ln t$, and his formula agrees well with actual counts when x is of reasonable size:

x	$\pi(x)$	$L(x)$	Riemann's formula
10^3	168	176.6	168.3
10^6	78498	78626.5	78527.4
10^9	50847534	50849233.9	50847455.4
10^{12}	37607912018	37607950279.8	37607910542.2
10^{15}	29844570422669	29844571475286.5	29844570495886.9
10^{18}	24739954287740860	24739954309690414.0	24739954284239494.4

(See exercise 41.) However, the distribution of large primes is not that simple, and Riemann's conjecture (5) was disproved by J. E. Littlewood in 1914; see Hardy and Littlewood, *Acta Math.* **41** (1918), 119–196, where it is shown that there is a positive constant C such that

$$\pi(x) > L(x) + C\sqrt{x}\,\log\log\log x/\log x$$

for infinitely many x. Littlewood's result shows that prime numbers are inherently somewhat mysterious, and it will be necessary to develop deep properties of mathematics before their distribution is really understood. Riemann made another much more plausible conjecture, the famous "Riemann hypothesis," which states that the complex function $\zeta(z)$ is zero only when the real part of z is equal to $1/2$, except in the trivial cases where z is a negative even integer. This hypothesis, if true, would imply that $\pi(x) = L(x) + O\big(\sqrt{x}\log x\big)$; see exercise 25. Richard Brent has used a method of D. H. Lehmer to verify Riemann's hypothesis computationally for all "small" values of z, by showing that $\zeta(z)$ has exactly 75,000,000 zeros whose imaginary part is in the range $0 < \Im z < 32585736.4$; all of these zeros have $\Re z = \frac{1}{2}$ and $\zeta'(z) \neq 0$. [*Math. Comp.* **33** (1979), 1361–1372.]

In order to analyze the average behavior of Algorithm A, we would like to know how large the largest prime factor p_t will tend to be. This question was first investigated by Karl Dickman [*Arkiv för Mat., Astron. och Fys.* **22A**, 10 (1930), 1–14], who studied the probability that a random integer between 1 and x will have its largest prime factor $\leq x^\alpha$. Dickman gave a heuristic argument to show that this probability approaches the limiting value $F(\alpha)$ as $x \to \infty$, where F can be calculated from the functional equation

$$F(\alpha) = \int_0^\alpha F\left(\frac{t}{1-t}\right) \frac{dt}{t}, \quad \text{for } 0 \le \alpha \le 1; \qquad F(\alpha) = 1, \quad \text{for } \alpha \ge 1. \qquad (6)$$

His argument was essentially this: Given $0 < t < 1$, the number of integers less than x whose largest prime factor is between x^t and x^{t+dt} is $xF'(t)\,dt$. The number of primes p in that range is $\pi(x^{t+dt}) - \pi(x^t) = \pi(x^t + (\ln x)x^t\, dt) - \pi(x^t) = x^t\, dt/t$. For every such p, the number of integers n such that "$np \le x$ and the largest prime factor of n is $\le p$" is the number of $n \le x^{1-t}$ whose largest prime factor is $\le (x^{1-t})^{t/(1-t)}$, namely $x^{1-t} F\big(t/(1-t)\big)$. Hence $xF'(t)\,dt = (x^t\, dt/t)\big(x^{1-t}F\big(t/(1-t)\big)\big)$, and (6) follows by integration. This heuristic argument can be made rigorous; V. Ramaswami [*Bull. Amer. Math. Soc.* **55** (1949), 1122–1127] showed that the probability in question for fixed α is asymptotically $F(\alpha) + O(1/\log x)$, as $x \to \infty$, and many other authors have extended the analysis [see the survey by Karl K. Norton, *Memoirs Amer. Math. Soc.* **106** (1971), 9–27].

If $\frac{1}{2} \le \alpha \le 1$, formula (6) simplifies to

$$F(\alpha) = 1 - \int_\alpha^1 F\left(\frac{t}{1-t}\right) \frac{dt}{t} = 1 - \int_\alpha^1 \frac{dt}{t} = 1 + \ln \alpha.$$

Thus, for example, the probability that a random positive integer $\le x$ has a prime factor $> \sqrt{x}$ is $1 - F(\frac{1}{2}) = \ln 2$, about 69 percent. In all such cases, Algorithm A must work hard.

The net result of this discussion is that Algorithm A will give the answer rather quickly if we want to factor a six-digit number; but for large N the amount of computer time for factorization by trial division will rapidly exceed practical limits, unless we are unusually lucky.

Later in this section we will see that there are fairly good ways to determine whether or not a reasonably large number n is prime, without trying all divisors up to $\sqrt{n}$. Therefore Algorithm A would often run faster if we inserted a primality test between steps A2 and A3; the running time for this improved algorithm would then be roughly proportional to p_{t-1}, the *second-largest* prime factor of N, instead of to $\max(p_{t-1}, \sqrt{p_t})$. By an argument analogous to Dickman's (see exercise 18), we can show that the second-largest prime factor of a random integer $\le x$ will be $\le x^\beta$ with approximate probability $G(\beta)$, where

$$G(\beta) = \int_0^\beta \left(G\left(\frac{t}{1-t}\right) - F\left(\frac{t}{1-t}\right)\right) \frac{dt}{t}, \quad \text{for } 0 \le \beta \le \tfrac{1}{2}. \qquad (7)$$

Clearly $G(\beta) = 1$ for $\beta \ge \frac{1}{2}$. (See Fig. 12.) Numerical evaluation of (6) and (7) yields the following "percentage points":

$F(\alpha), G(\beta) =$	.01	.05	.10	.20	.35	.50	.65	.80	.90	.95	.99
$\alpha \approx$	.2697	.3348	.3785	.4430	.5220	.6065	.7047	.8187	.9048	.9512	.9900
$\beta \approx$	.0056	.0273	.0531	.1003	.1611	.2117	.2582	.3104	.3590	.3967	.4517

Thus, the second-largest prime factor will be $\le x^{.2117}$ about half the time, etc.

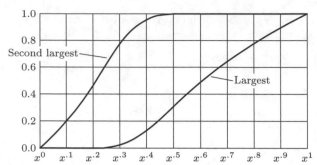

Fig. 12. Probability distribution functions for the
two largest prime factors of a random integer $\leq x$.

The *total number of prime factors*, t, has also been intensively analyzed.
Obviously $1 \leq t \leq \lg N$, but these lower and upper bounds are seldom achieved.
It is possible to prove that if N is chosen at random between 1 and x, the
probability that $t \leq \ln \ln x + c \sqrt{\ln \ln x}$ approaches

$$\frac{1}{\sqrt{2\pi}} \int_{-\infty}^{c} e^{-u^2/2} \, du \tag{8}$$

as $x \to \infty$, for any fixed c. In other words, the distribution of t is essentially
normal, with mean and variance $\ln \ln x$; about 99.73 percent of all the large
integers $\leq x$ have $|t - \ln \ln x| \leq 3\sqrt{\ln \ln x}$. Furthermore the average value of
$t - \ln \ln x$ for $1 \leq N \leq x$ is known to approach

$$\gamma + \sum_{p \text{ prime}} \left(\ln(1 - 1/p) + 1/(p-1) \right) = \gamma + \sum_{n \geq 2} \frac{\varphi(n) \ln \zeta(n)}{n}$$

$$= 1.03465\,38818\,97437\,91161\,97942\,98464\,63825\,46703+ . \tag{9}$$

[See G. H. Hardy and E. M. Wright, *An Introduction to the Theory of Numbers*,
5th edition (Oxford, 1979), §22.11; see also P. Erdös and M. Kac, *Amer. J. Math.*
62 (1940), 738–742.]

The size of prime factors has a remarkable connection with permutations:
The average number of bits in the kth largest prime factor of a random n-bit
integer is asymptotically the same as the average length of the kth largest cycle
of a random n-element permutation, as $n \to \infty$. [See D. E. Knuth, *Selected
Papers on Analysis of Algorithms* (2000), 329–330, 336–337, for references to
the relevant literature.] It follows that Algorithm A usually finds a few small
factors and then begins a long-drawn-out search for the big ones that are left.

An excellent exposition of the probability distribution of the prime factors
of a random integer has been given by Patrick Billingsley, *AMM* **80** (1973),
1099–1115; see also his paper in *Annals of Probability* **2** (1974), 749–791.

Factoring by pseudorandom cycles. Near the beginning of Chapter 3, we
observed that "a random number generator chosen at random isn't very random."
This principle, which worked against us in that chapter, has the redeeming virtue

that it leads to a surprisingly efficient method of factorization, discovered by
J. M. Pollard [*BIT* **15** (1975), 331–334]. The number of computational steps
in Pollard's method is on the order of $\sqrt{p_{t-1}}$, so it is significantly faster than
Algorithm A when N is large. According to (7) and Fig. 12, the running time
will usually be well under $N^{1/4}$.

Let $f(x)$ be any polynomial with integer coefficients, and consider the two
sequences defined by

$$x_0 = y_0 = A; \qquad x_{m+1} = f(x_m) \bmod N, \qquad y_{m+1} = f(y_m) \bmod p, \qquad (10)$$

where p is any prime factor of N. It follows that

$$y_m = x_m \bmod p, \qquad \text{for } m \geq 1. \qquad (11)$$

Now exercise 3.1–7 shows that we will have $y_m = y_{\ell(m)-1}$ for some $m \geq 1$,
where $\ell(m)$ is the greatest power of 2 that is $\leq m$. Thus $x_m - x_{\ell(m)-1}$ will
be a multiple of p. Furthermore if $f(y) \bmod p$ behaves as a random mapping
from the set $\{0, 1, \ldots, p-1\}$ into itself, exercise 3.1–12 shows that the average
value of the least such m will be of order $\sqrt{p}$. In fact, exercise 4 below shows
that this average value for random mappings is less than $1.625\,Q(p)$, where the
function $Q(p) \approx \sqrt{\pi p/2}$ was defined in Section 1.2.11.3. If the different prime
divisors of N correspond to different values of m (as they almost surely will, when
N is large), we will be able to find them by calculating $\gcd(x_m - x_{\ell(m)-1}, N)$
for $m = 1, 2, 3, \ldots$, until the unfactored residue is prime. Pollard called his
technique the "rho method," because an eventually periodic sequence such as
$y_0, y_1, \ldots$ is reminiscent of the Greek letter ρ.

From the theory in Chapter 3, we know that a linear polynomial $f(x) =
ax + c$ will not be sufficiently random for our purposes. The next-simplest
case is quadratic, say $f(x) = x^2 + 1$. We don't *know* that this function is
sufficiently random, but our lack of knowledge tends to support the hypothesis
of randomness, and empirical tests show that this f does work essentially as
predicted. In fact, f is probably slightly *better* than random, since $x^2 + 1$ takes
on only $\frac{1}{2}(p+1)$ distinct values mod p; see Arney and Bender, *Pacific J. Math.*
103 (1982), 269–294. Therefore the following procedure is reasonable:

Algorithm B (*Factoring by the rho method*). This algorithm outputs the prime
factors of a given integer $N \geq 2$, with high probability, although there is a chance
that it will fail.

B1. [Initialize.] Set $x \leftarrow 5$, $x' \leftarrow 2$, $k \leftarrow 1$, $l \leftarrow 1$, $n \leftarrow N$. (During this
algorithm, n is the unfactored part of N, and the variables x and x' represent
the quantities $x_m \bmod n$ and $x_{\ell(m)-1} \bmod n$ in (10), where $f(x) = x^2 + 1$,
$A = 2$, $l = \ell(m)$, and $k = 2l - m$.)

B2. [Test primality.] If n is prime (see the discussion below), output n; the
algorithm terminates.

B3. [Factor found?] Set $g \leftarrow \gcd(x' - x, n)$. If $g = 1$, go on to step B4; otherwise
output g. Now if $g = n$, the algorithm terminates (and it has failed, because

we know that n isn't prime). Otherwise set $n \leftarrow n/g$, $x \leftarrow x \bmod n$, $x' \leftarrow x' \bmod n$, and return to step B2. (Note that g may not be prime; this should be tested. In the rare event that g isn't prime, its prime factors won't be determinable with this algorithm.)

B4. [Advance.] Set $k \leftarrow k - 1$. If $k = 0$, set $x' \leftarrow x$, $l \leftarrow 2l$, $k \leftarrow l$. Set $x \leftarrow (x^2 + 1) \bmod n$ and return to B3. ∎

As an example of Algorithm B, let's try to factor $N = 25852$ again. The third execution of step B3 will output $g = 4$ (which isn't prime). After six more iterations the algorithm finds the factor $g = 23$. Algorithm B has not distinguished itself in this example, but of course it was designed to factor *big* numbers. Algorithm A takes much longer to find large prime factors, but it can't be beat when it comes to removing the small ones. In practice, we should run Algorithm A awhile before switching over to Algorithm B.

We can get a better idea of Algorithm B's prowess by considering the ten largest six-digit primes. The number of iterations, $m(p)$, that Algorithm B needs to find the factor p is given in the following table:

$p =$	999863	999883	999907	999917	999931	999953	999959	999961	999979	999983
$m(p) =$	276	409	2106	1561	1593	1091	474	1819	395	814

Experiments by Tomás Oliveira e Silva indicate that $m(p)$ has an average value of about $2\sqrt{p}$, and it never exceeds $16\sqrt{p}$ when $p < 1000000000$. The maximum $m(p)$ for $p < 10^9$ is $m(850112303) = 416784$; and the maximum of $m(p)/\sqrt{p}$ occurs when $p = 695361131$, $m(p) = 406244$. According to these experimental results, almost all 18-digit numbers can be factored in fewer than 64,000 iterations of Algorithm B (compared to roughly 50,000,000 divisions in Algorithm A).

The time-consuming operations in each iteration of Algorithm B are the multiple-precision multiplication and division in step B4, and the gcd in step B3. The technique of "Montgomery multiplication" (exercise 4.3.1–41) will speed this up. Moreover, if the gcd operation is slow, Pollard suggests gaining speed by accumulating the product mod n of, say, ten consecutive $(x' - x)$ values before taking each gcd; this replaces 90 percent of the gcd operations by a single multiplication mod N while only slightly increasing the chance of failure. He also suggests starting with $m = q$ instead of $m = 1$ in step B1, where q is, say, one tenth of the number of iterations you are planning to use.

In those rare cases where failure occurs for large N, we could try using $f(x) = x^2 + c$ for some $c \neq 0$ or 1. The value $c = -2$ should also be avoided, since the recurrence $x_{m+1} = x_m^2 - 2$ has solutions of the form $x_m = r^{2^m} + r^{-2^m}$. Other values of c do not seem to lead to simple relationships mod p, and they should all be satisfactory when used with suitable starting values.

Richard Brent used a modification of Algorithm B to discover the prime factor 1238926361552897 of $2^{256} + 1$. [See *Math. Comp.* **36** (1981), 627–630; **38** (1982), 253–255.]

Fermat's method. Another approach to the factoring problem, which was used by Pierre de Fermat in 1643, is more suited to finding large factors than small ones. [Fermat's original description of his method, translated into English, can be found in L. E. Dickson's monumental *History of the Theory of Numbers* **1** (Carnegie Inst. of Washington, 1919), 357. An equivalent idea had in fact been used already by Nārāyaṇa Paṇḍita in his remarkable book *Gaṇita Kaumudī* (1356); see Parmanand Singh, *Gaṇita Bhāratī* **22** (2000), 72–74.]

Assume that $N = uv$, where $u \leq v$. For practical purposes we may assume that N is odd; this means that u and v are odd, and we can let

$$x = (u+v)/2, \qquad y = (v-u)/2, \tag{12}$$
$$N = x^2 - y^2, \qquad 0 \leq y < x \leq N. \tag{13}$$

Fermat's method searches systematically for integers x and y that satisfy Equation (13). The following algorithm shows how factoring can therefore be done *without using any multiplication or division:*

Algorithm C (*Factoring by addition and subtraction*). Given an odd number N, this algorithm determines the largest factor of N less than or equal to $\sqrt{N}$.

C1. [Initialize.] Set $a \leftarrow 2\lfloor \sqrt{N} \rfloor + 1$, $b \leftarrow 1$, $r \leftarrow \lfloor \sqrt{N} \rfloor^2 - N$. (During this algorithm a, b, and r correspond respectively to $2x+1$, $2y+1$, and $x^2 - y^2 - N$ as we search for a solution to (13); we will have $|r| < a$ and $b < a$.)

C2. [Done?] If $r = 0$, the algorithm terminates; we have

$$N = \big((a-b)/2\big)\big((a+b-2)/2\big),$$

and $(a-b)/2$ is the largest factor of N less than or equal to $\sqrt{N}$.

C3. [Increase a.] Set $r \leftarrow r + a$ and $a \leftarrow a + 2$.

C4. [Increase b.] Set $r \leftarrow r - b$ and $b \leftarrow b + 2$.

C5. [Test r.] Return to step C4 if $r > 0$, otherwise go back to C2. ∎

The reader may find it amusing to find the factors of 377 by hand, using this algorithm. The number of steps needed to find the factors u and v of $N = uv$ is essentially proportional to $(a+b-2)/2 - \lfloor \sqrt{N} \rfloor = v - \lfloor \sqrt{N} \rfloor$; this can, of course, be a very large number, although each step can be done very rapidly on most computers. An improvement that requires only $O(N^{1/3})$ operations in the worst case has been developed by R. S. Lehman [*Math. Comp.* **28** (1974), 637–646].

It is not quite correct to call Algorithm C "Fermat's method," since Fermat used a somewhat more streamlined approach. Algorithm C's main loop is quite fast on computers, but it is not very suitable for hand calculation. Fermat didn't actually maintain the running value of y; he would look at $x^2 - N$ and guess whether or not this quantity was a perfect square by looking at its least significant digits. (The last two digits of a perfect square must be 00, $e1$, $e4$, 25, $o6$, or $e9$, where e is an even digit and o is an odd digit.) Therefore he avoided the operations of steps C4 and C5, replacing them by an occasional determination that a certain number is not a perfect square.

Fermat's method of looking at the rightmost digits can, of course, be generalized by using other moduli. Suppose for clarity that $N = 8616460799$, a number whose historic significance is explained below, and consider the following table:

m	if $x \bmod m$ is	then $x^2 \bmod m$ is	and $(x^2 - N) \bmod m$ is
3	$0, 1, 2$	$0, 1, 1$	$1, 2, 2$
5	$0, 1, 2, 3, 4$	$0, 1, 4, 4, 1$	$1, 2, 0, 0, 2$
7	$0, 1, 2, 3, 4, 5, 6$	$0, 1, 4, 2, 2, 4, 1$	$5, 6, 2, 0, 0, 2, 6$
8	$0, 1, 2, 3, 4, 5, 6, 7$	$0, 1, 4, 1, 0, 1, 4, 1$	$1, 2, 5, 2, 1, 2, 5, 2$
11	$0, 1, 2, 3, 4, 5, 6, 7, 8, 9, 10$	$0, 1, 4, 9, 5, 3, 3, 5, 9, 4, 1$	$10, 0, 3, 8, 4, 2, 2, 4, 8, 3, 0$

If $x^2 - N$ is to be a perfect square y^2, it must have a residue mod m consistent with this fact, for all m. For example, if $N = 8616460799$ and $x \bmod 3 \neq 0$, then $(x^2 - N) \bmod 3 = 2$, so $x^2 - N$ cannot be a perfect square; therefore x must be a multiple of 3 whenever $N = x^2 - y^2$. The table tells us, in fact, that

$$\begin{aligned}
x \bmod 3 &= 0; \\
x \bmod 5 &= 0, 2, \text{ or } 3; \\
x \bmod 7 &= 2, 3, 4, \text{ or } 5; \\
x \bmod 8 &= 0 \text{ or } 4 \text{ (hence } x \bmod 4 = 0); \\
x \bmod 11 &= 1, 2, 4, 7, 9, \text{ or } 10.
\end{aligned} \qquad (14)$$

This narrows down the search for x considerably. For example, x must be a multiple of 12. We must have $x \geq \lceil \sqrt{N} \rceil = 92825$, and the least such multiple of 12 is 92832. This value has residues $(2, 5, 3)$ modulo $(5, 7, 11)$ respectively, so it fails (14) with respect to modulus 11. Increasing x by 12 changes the residue mod 5 by 2, mod 7 by 5, and mod 11 by 1; so it is easy to see that the first value of $x \geq 92825$ that satisfies all of the conditions in (14) is $x = 92880$. Now $92880^2 - N = 10233601$, and the pencil-and-paper method for square root tells us that $10233601 = 3199^2$ is indeed a perfect square. Therefore we have found the desired solution $x = 92880$, $y = 3199$, and the factorization is

$$8616460799 = (x - y)(x + y) = 89681 \cdot 96079.$$

This value of N is interesting because the English economist and logician W. S. Jevons introduced it as follows in a well-known book: "Given any two numbers, we may by a simple and infallible process obtain their product, but it is quite another matter when a large number is given to determine its factors. Can the reader say what two numbers multiplied together will produce the number 8,616,460,799? I think it unlikely that anyone but myself will ever know." [*The Principles of Science* (1874), Chapter 7.] We have just seen, however, that Fermat could have factored N in less than 10 minutes, on the back of an envelope! Jevons's point about the difficulty of factoring versus multiplying is well taken, but only if we form the product of numbers that aren't so close to each other.

In place of the moduli considered in (14), we can use any powers of distinct primes. For example, if we had used 25 in place of 5, we would find that the only permissible values of $x \bmod 25$ are 0, 5, 7, 10, 15, 18, and 20. This gives more information than (14). In general, we will get more information modulo p^2 than we do modulo p, for odd primes p, whenever $x^2 - N \equiv 0$ (modulo p) has a solution x. Individual primes p and q are, however, preferable to moduli like p^2 unless p is quite small, because we tend to get even more information mod pq.

The modular method just used is called a *sieve procedure*, since we can imagine passing all integers through a "sieve" for which only those values with $x \bmod 3 = 0$ come out, then sifting these numbers through another sieve that allows only numbers with $x \bmod 5 = 0$, 2, or 3 to pass, etc. Each sieve by itself will remove about half of the remaining values (see exercise 6); and when we sieve with respect to moduli that are relatively prime in pairs, each sieve is independent of the others because of the Chinese remainder theorem (Theorem 4.3.2C). So if we sieve with respect to, say, 30 different primes, only about one value in every 2^{30} will need to be examined to see if $x^2 - N$ is a perfect square y^2.

Algorithm D (*Factoring with sieves*). Given an odd number N, this algorithm determines the largest factor of N less than or equal to $\sqrt{N}$. The procedure uses moduli $m_1, m_2, \ldots, m_r$ that are relatively prime to each other in pairs and relatively prime to N. We assume that we have access to r *sieve tables* $S[i, j]$ for $0 \le j < m_i$, $1 \le i \le r$, where

$$S[i, j] = \big[j^2 - N \equiv y^2 \text{ (modulo } m_i) \text{ has a solution } y \big].$$

D1. [Initialize.] Set $x \leftarrow \lceil \sqrt{N} \rceil$, and set $k_i \leftarrow (-x) \bmod m_i$ for $1 \le i \le r$. (Throughout this algorithm the index variables $k_1, k_2, \ldots, k_r$ will be set so that $k_i = (-x) \bmod m_i$.)

D2. [Sieve.] If $S[i, k_i] = 1$ for $1 \le i \le r$, go to step D4.

D3. [Step x.] Set $x \leftarrow x + 1$, and set $k_i \leftarrow (k_i - 1) \bmod m_i$ for $1 \le i \le r$. Return to step D2.

D4. [Test $x^2 - N$.] Set $y \leftarrow \lfloor \sqrt{x^2 - N} \rfloor$ or to $\lceil \sqrt{x^2 - N} \rceil$. If $y^2 = x^2 - N$, then $(x - y)$ is the desired factor, and the algorithm terminates. Otherwise return to step D3. ∎

There are several ways to make this procedure run fast. For example, we have seen that if $N \bmod 3 = 2$, then x must be a multiple of 3; we can set $x = 3x'$, and use a different sieve corresponding to x', increasing the speed threefold. If $N \bmod 9 = 1$, 4, or 7, then x must be congruent respectively to ± 1, ± 2, or ± 4 (modulo 9); so we run two sieves (one for x' and one for x'', where $x = 9x' + a$ and $x = 9x'' - a$) to increase the speed by a factor of $4\frac{1}{2}$. If $N \bmod 4 = 3$, then $x \bmod 4$ is known and the speed is increased by an additional factor of 4; in the other case, when $N \bmod 4 = 1$, x must be odd so the speed may be doubled. Another way to double the speed of the algorithm (at the expense of storage space) is to combine pairs of moduli, using $m_{r-k} m_k$ in place of m_k for $1 \le k < \frac{1}{2}r$.

An even more important method of speeding up Algorithm D is to use the Boolean operations found on most binary computers. Let us assume, for example, that MIX is a binary computer with 30 bits per word. The tables $S[i, k_i]$ can be kept in memory with one bit per entry; thus 30 values can be stored in a single word. The operation AND, which replaces the kth bit of the accumulator by zero if the kth bit of a specified word in memory is zero, for $1 \le k \le 30$, can be used to process 30 values of x at once! For convenience, we can make several copies of the tables $S[i, j]$ so that the table entries for m_i involve $\text{lcm}(m_i, 30)$ bits; then the sieve tables for each modulus fill an integral number of words. Under these assumptions, 30 executions of the main loop in Algorithm D are equivalent to code of the following form:

```
D2 LD1   K1     rI1 ← k'₁.
   LDA   S1,1   rA ← S'[1, rI1].
   DEC1  1      rI1 ← rI1 − 1.
   J1NN  *+2
   INC1  M1     If rI1 < 0, set rI1 ← rI1 + lcm(m₁, 30).
   ST1   K1     k'₁ ← rI1.
   LD1   K2     rI1 ← k'₂.
   AND   S2,1   rA ← rA & S'[2, rI1].
   DEC1  1      rI1 ← rI1 − 1.
   J1NN  *+2
   INC1  M2     If rI1 < 0, set rI1 ← rI1 + lcm(m₂, 30).
   ST1   K2     k'₂ ← rI1.
   LD1   K3     rI1 ← k'₃.
   ...          (m₃ through mᵣ are like m₂)
   ST1   Kr     k'ᵣ ← rI1.
   INCX  30     x ← x + 30.
   JAZ   D2     Repeat if all sieved out.   ∎
```

The number of cycles for 30 iterations is essentially $2 + 8r$; if $r = 11$, this means three cycles are being used on each iteration, just as in Algorithm C, and Algorithm C involves $y = \frac{1}{2}(v - u)$ more iterations.

If the table entries for m_i do not come out to be an integral number of words, further shifting of the table entries would be necessary on each iteration in order to align the bits properly. This would add quite a lot of coding to the main loop and it would probably make the program too slow to compete with Algorithm C unless $v/u \leq 100$ (see exercise 7).

Sieve procedures can be applied to a variety of other problems, not necessarily having much to do with arithmetic. A survey of these techniques has been prepared by Marvin C. Wunderlich, *JACM* **14** (1967), 10–19.

F. W. Lawrence proposed the construction of special sieve machines for factorization in the 19th century [*Quart. J. of Pure and Applied Math.* **28** (1896), 285–311], and E. O. Carissan completed such a device with 14 moduli in 1919. [See Shallit, Williams, and Morain, *Math. Intelligencer* **17**, 3 (1995), 41–47, for the interesting story of how Carissan's long-lost sieve was rediscovered and preserved for posterity.] D. H. Lehmer and his associates constructed and used many different sieve devices during the period 1926–1989, beginning with bicycle chains and later using photoelectric cells and other kinds of technology; see, for example, *AMM* **40** (1933), 401–406. Lehmer's electronic delay-line sieve, which began operating in 1965, processed one million numbers per second. By 1995 it was possible to construct a machine that sieved 6144 million numbers per second, performing 256 iterations of steps D2 and D3 in about 5.2 nanoseconds [see Lukes, Patterson, and Williams, *Nieuw Archief voor Wiskunde* (4) **13** (1995),

113–139]. Another way to factor with sieves was described by D. H. and Emma Lehmer in *Math. Comp.* **28** (1974), 625–635.

Primality testing. None of the algorithms we have discussed so far is an efficient way to determine that a large number n is prime. Fortunately, there are other methods available for settling this question; efficient techniques have been devised by É. Lucas and others, notably D. H. Lehmer [see *Bull. Amer. Math. Soc.* **33** (1927), 327–340].

According to Fermat's theorem (Theorem 1.2.4F), we have

$$x^{p-1} \bmod p = 1$$

whenever p is prime and x is not a multiple of p. Furthermore, there are efficient ways to calculate $x^{n-1} \bmod n$, requiring only $O(\log n)$ operations of multiplication mod n. (We shall study them in Section 4.6.3 below.) Therefore we can often determine that n is *not* prime when this relationship fails.

For example, Fermat once verified that the numbers $2^1 + 1$, $2^2 + 1$, $2^4 + 1$, $2^8 + 1$, and $2^{16} + 1$ are prime. In a letter to Mersenne written in 1640, Fermat conjectured that $2^{2^n} + 1$ is always prime, but said he was unable to determine definitely whether the number $4294967297 = 2^{32} + 1$ is prime or not. Neither Fermat nor Mersenne ever resolved this problem, although they could have done it as follows: The number $3^{2^{32}} \bmod (2^{32} + 1)$ can be computed by doing 32 operations of squaring modulo $2^{32} + 1$, and the answer is 3029026160; therefore (by Fermat's own theorem, which he discovered in the same year 1640!) the number $2^{32} + 1$ is *not* prime. This argument gives us absolutely no idea what the factors are, but it answers Fermat's question.

Fermat's theorem is a powerful test for showing nonprimality of a given number. When n is not prime, it is always possible to find a value of $x < n$ such that $x^{n-1} \bmod n \neq 1$; experience shows that, in fact, such a value can almost always be found very quickly. There are some rare values of n for which $x^{n-1} \bmod n$ is frequently equal to unity, but then n has a factor less than $\sqrt[3]{n}$; see exercise 9.

The same method can be extended to prove that a large prime number n really *is* prime, by using the following idea: *If there is a number x for which the order of x modulo n is equal to $n - 1$, then n is prime.* (The order of x modulo n is the smallest positive integer k such that $x^k \bmod n = 1$; see Section 3.2.1.2.) For this condition implies that the numbers $x^1 \bmod n$, ..., $x^{n-1} \bmod n$ are distinct and relatively prime to n, so they must be the numbers 1, 2, ..., $n-1$ in some order; thus n has no proper divisors. If n is prime, such a number x (called a *primitive root* of n) will always exist; see exercise 3.2.1.2–16. In fact, primitive roots are rather numerous. There are $\varphi(n-1)$ of them, and this is quite a substantial number, since $n/\varphi(n-1) = O(\log \log n)$.

It is unnecessary to calculate $x^k \bmod n$ for all $k \leq n-1$ to determine if the order of x is $n-1$ or not. The order of x will be $n-1$ if and only if

i) $x^{n-1} \bmod n = 1$;

ii) $x^{(n-1)/p} \bmod n \neq 1$ for all primes p that divide $n - 1$.

For $x^s \bmod n = 1$ if and only if s is a multiple of the order of x modulo n. If the two conditions hold, and if k is the order of x modulo n, we therefore know that k is a divisor of $n - 1$, but not a divisor of $(n - 1)/p$ for any prime factor p of $n - 1$; the only remaining possibility is $k = n - 1$. This completes the proof that conditions (i) and (ii) suffice to establish the primality of n.

Exercise 10 shows that we can in fact use different values of x for each of the primes p, and n will still be prime. We may restrict consideration to prime values of x, since the order of uv modulo n divides the least common multiple of the orders of u and v by exercise 3.2.1.2–15. Conditions (i) and (ii) can be tested efficiently by using the rapid methods for evaluating powers of numbers discussed in Section 4.6.3. But it is necessary to know the prime factors of $n-1$, so we have an interesting situation in which the factorization of n depends on that of $n - 1$.

An example. The study of a reasonably typical large factorization will help to fix the ideas we have discussed so far. Let us try to find the prime factors of $2^{214} + 1$, a 65-digit number. The factorization can be initiated with a bit of clairvoyance if we notice that

$$2^{214} + 1 = (2^{107} - 2^{54} + 1)(2^{107} + 2^{54} + 1); \qquad (15)$$

this is a special case of the factorization $4x^4 + 1 = (2x^2 + 2x + 1)(2x^2 - 2x + 1)$, which Euler communicated to Goldbach in 1742 [P. H. Fuss, *Correspondance Math. et Physique* **1** (1843), 145]. The problem now boils down to examining each of the 33-digit factors in (15).

A computer program readily discovers that $2^{107} - 2^{54} + 1 = 5 \cdot 857 \cdot n_0$, where

$$n_0 = 37866809061660057264219253397 \qquad (16)$$

is a 29-digit number having no prime factors less than 1000. A multiple-precision calculation using Algorithm 4.6.3A shows that

$$3^{n_0 - 1} \bmod n_0 = 1,$$

so we suspect that n_0 is prime. It is certainly out of the question to prove that n_0 is prime by trying the 10 million million or so potential divisors, but the method discussed above gives a feasible test for primality: Our next goal is to factor $n_0 - 1$. With little difficulty, our computer will tell us that

$$n_0 - 1 = 2 \cdot 2 \cdot 19 \cdot 107 \cdot 353 \cdot n_1, \qquad n_1 = 13191270754108226049301.$$

Here $3^{n_1 - 1} \bmod n_1 \neq 1$, so n_1 is not prime; by continuing Algorithm A or Algorithm B we obtain another factor,

$$n_1 = 91813 \cdot n_2, \qquad n_2 = 143675413657196977.$$

This time $3^{n_2 - 1} \bmod n_2 = 1$, so we will try to prove that n_2 is prime. Casting out factors < 1000 yields $n_2 - 1 = 2 \cdot 2 \cdot 2 \cdot 2 \cdot 3 \cdot 3 \cdot 547 \cdot n_3$, where $n_3 = 1824032775457$. Since $3^{n_3 - 1} \bmod n_3 \neq 1$, we know that n_3 cannot be prime, and Algorithm A finds that $n_3 = 1103 \cdot n_4$, where $n_4 = 1653701519$. The number n_4 behaves like a prime (that is, $3^{n_4 - 1} \bmod n_4 = 1$), so we calculate

$$n_4 - 1 = 2 \cdot 7 \cdot 19 \cdot 23 \cdot 137 \cdot 1973.$$

Good; this is our first complete factorization. We are now ready to backtrack to the previous subproblem, proving that n_4 is prime. Using the procedure suggested by exercise 10, we compute the following values:

x	p	$x^{(n_4-1)/p} \bmod n_4$	$x^{n_4-1} \bmod n_4$	
2	2	1	(1)	
2	7	766408626	(1)	
2	19	332952683	(1)	
2	23	1154237810	(1)	(17)
2	137	373782186	(1)	
2	1973	490790919	(1)	
3	2	1	(1)	
5	2	1	(1)	
7	2	1653701518	1	

(Here "(1)" means a result of 1 that needn't be computed since it can be deduced from previous calculations.) Thus n_4 is prime, and $n_2 - 1$ has been completely factored. A similar calculation shows that n_2 is prime, and this complete factorization of $n_0 - 1$ finally shows, after still another calculation like (17), that n_0 is prime.

The last three lines of (17) represent a search for an integer x that satisfies $x^{(n_4-1)/2} \not\equiv x^{n_4-1} \equiv 1$ (modulo n_4). If n_4 is prime, we have only a 50-50 chance of success, so the case $p = 2$ is typically the hardest one to verify. We could streamline this part of the calculation by using the law of quadratic reciprocity (see exercise 23), which tells us for example that $5^{(q-1)/2} \equiv 1$ (modulo q) whenever q is a prime congruent to ± 1 (modulo 5). Merely calculating $n_4 \bmod 5$ would have told us right away that $x = 5$ could not possibly help in showing that n_4 is prime. In fact, however, the result of exercise 26 implies that the case $p = 2$ doesn't really need to be considered at all when testing n for primality, unless $n - 1$ is divisible by a high power of 2, so we could have dispensed with the last three lines of (17) entirely.

The next quantity to be factored is the other half of (15), namely

$$n_5 = 2^{107} + 2^{54} + 1.$$

Since $3^{n_5-1} \bmod n_5 \neq 1$, we know that n_5 is not prime, and Algorithm B shows that $n_5 = 843589 \cdot n_6$, where $n_6 = 19234399314027729309649191917$. Unfortunately, $3^{n_6-1} \bmod n_6 \neq 1$, so we are left with a 27-digit nonprime. Continuing Algorithm B might well exhaust our patience (not our budget — we're using idle time on a weekend rather than "prime time"). But the sieve method of Algorithm D will be able to crack n_6 into its two factors,

$$n_6 = 8174912477117 \cdot 23528569104401.$$

(It turns out that Algorithm B would also have succeeded, after 6,432,966 iterations.) The factors of n_6 could *not* have been discovered by Algorithm A in a reasonable length of time.

Now the computation is complete: $2^{214} + 1$ has the prime factorization

$$5 \cdot 857 \cdot 843589 \cdot 8174912477117 \cdot 23528569104401 \cdot n_0,$$

where n_0 is the 29-digit prime in (16). A certain amount of good fortune entered into these calculations, for if we had not started with the known factorization (15) it is quite probable that we would first have cast out the small factors, reducing n to $n_6 n_0$. This 55-digit number would have been much more difficult to factor — Algorithm D would be useless and Algorithm B would have to work overtime because of the high precision necessary.

Dozens of further numerical examples can be found in an article by John Brillhart and J. L. Selfridge, *Math. Comp.* **21** (1967), 87–96.

Improved primality tests. The procedure just illustrated requires the complete factorization of $n-1$ before we can prove that n is prime, so it will bog down for large n. Another technique, which uses the factorization of $n + 1$ instead, is described in exercise 15; if $n - 1$ turns out to be too hard, $n + 1$ might be easier.

Significant improvements are available for dealing with large n. For example, it is not difficult to prove a stronger converse of Fermat's theorem that requires only a partial factorization of $n - 1$. Exercise 26 shows that we could have avoided most of the calculations in (17); the three conditions $2^{n_4 - 1} \bmod n_4 =$ $\gcd(2^{(n_4-1)/23} - 1, n_4) = \gcd(2^{(n_4-1)/1973} - 1, n_4) = 1$ are sufficient by themselves to prove that n_4 is prime. Brillhart, Lehmer, and Selfridge have in fact developed a method that works when the numbers $n - 1$ and $n + 1$ have been only partially factored [*Math. Comp.* **29** (1975), 620–647, Corollary 11]: Suppose $n - 1 = f^- r^-$ and $n + 1 = f^+ r^+$, where we know the complete factorizations of f^- and f^+, and we also know that all factors of r^- and r^+ are $\geq b$. If the product $\left(b^3 f^- f^+ \max(f^-, f^+)\right)$ is greater than $2n$, a small amount of additional computation, described in their paper, will determine whether or not n is prime. Therefore numbers of up to 35 digits can usually be tested for primality in a fraction of a second, simply by casting out all prime factors < 30030 from $n \pm 1$ [see J. L. Selfridge and M. C. Wunderlich, *Congressus Numerantium* **12** (1974), 109–120]. The partial factorization of other quantities like $n^2 \pm n + 1$ and $n^2 + 1$ can be used to improve this method still further [see H. C. Williams and J. S. Judd, *Math. Comp.* **30** (1976), 157–172, 867–886].

In practice, when n has no small prime factors and $3^{n-1} \bmod n = 1$, further calculations almost always show that n is prime. (One of the rare exceptions in the author's experience is $n = \frac{1}{7}(2^{28} - 9) = 2341 \cdot 16381$.) On the other hand, some nonprime values of n are definitely bad news for the primality test we have discussed, because it might happen that $x^{n-1} \bmod n = 1$ for all x relatively prime to n (see exercise 9). The smallest such number is $n = 3 \cdot 11 \cdot 17 = 561$; here $\lambda(n) = \mathrm{lcm}(2, 10, 16) = 80$ in the notation of Eq. 3.2.1.2–(9), so $x^{80} \bmod 561 = 1 = x^{560} \bmod 561$ whenever x is relatively prime to 561. Our procedure would repeatedly fail to show that such an n is nonprime, until we had stumbled across one of its divisors. To improve the method, we need a quick way to determine the nonprimality of nonprime n, even in such pathological cases.

The following surprisingly simple procedure is guaranteed to do the job with high probability:

Algorithm P (*Probabilistic primality test*). Given an odd integer n, this algorithm attempts to decide whether or not n is prime. By repeating the algorithm several times, as explained in the remarks below, it is possible to be extremely confident about the primality of n, in a precise sense, yet the primality will not be rigorously proved. Let $n = 1 + 2^k q$, where q is odd.

P1. [Generate x.] Let x be a random integer in the range $1 < x < n$.

P2. [Exponentiate.] Set $j \leftarrow 0$ and $y \leftarrow x^q \bmod n$. (As in our previous primality test, $x^q \bmod n$ should be calculated in $O(\log q)$ steps; see Section 4.6.3.)

P3. [Done?] (Now $y = x^{2^j q} \bmod n$.) If $y = n-1$, or if $y = 1$ and $j = 0$, terminate the algorithm and say "n is probably prime." If $y = 1$ and $j > 0$, go to P5.

P4. [Increase j.] Increase j by 1. If $j < k$, set $y \leftarrow y^2 \bmod n$ and return to P3.

P5. [Not prime.] Terminate and say "n is definitely not prime." ∎

The idea underlying Algorithm P is that if $x^q \bmod n \neq 1$ and $n = 1 + 2^k q$ is prime, the sequence of values

$$x^q \bmod n, \quad x^{2q} \bmod n, \quad x^{4q} \bmod n, \quad \ldots, \quad x^{2^k q} \bmod n$$

will end with 1, and the value just preceding the first appearance of 1 will be $n - 1$. (The only solutions to $y^2 \equiv 1$ (modulo p) are $y \equiv \pm 1$, when p is prime, since $(y - 1)(y + 1)$ must be a multiple of p.)

Exercise 22 proves the basic fact that Algorithm P will be wrong at most $1/4$ of the time, for all n. Actually it will rarely fail at all, for most n; but the crucial point is that the probability of failure is bounded *regardless* of the value of n.

Suppose we invoke Algorithm P repeatedly, choosing x independently and at random whenever we get to step P1. If the algorithm ever reports that n is nonprime, we can be sure this is so. But if the algorithm reports 25 times in a row that n is "probably prime," we can say that n is "almost surely prime." For the probability is less than $(1/4)^{25}$ that such a 25-times-in-a-row procedure gives the wrong information about its input. This is less than one chance in a quadrillion; even if we tested a billion different numbers with such a procedure, the expected number of mistakes would be less than $\frac{1}{1000000}$. It's much more likely that our computer has dropped a bit in its calculations, due to hardware malfunctions or cosmic radiations, than that Algorithm P has repeatedly guessed wrong!

Probabilistic algorithms like this lead us to question our traditional standards of reliability. Do we really *need* to have a rigorous proof of primality? For people unwilling to abandon traditional notions of proof, Gary L. Miller has demonstrated (in slightly weaker form) that if a certain well-known conjecture in number theory called the Extended Riemann Hypothesis can be proved, then either n is prime or there is an $x < 2(\ln n)^2$ such that Algorithm P will discover the nonprimality of n. [See *J. Comp. System Sci.* **13** (1976), 300–317. The constant 2 in this upper bound is due to Eric Bach, *Math. Comp.* **55** (1990), 355–380. See Chapter 8 of *Algorithmic Number Theory 1* by E. Bach and J. O.

Shallit (MIT Press, 1996), for an exposition of various generalizations of the Riemann hypothesis.] Thus, we would have a rigorous way to test primality in $O(\log n)^5$ elementary operations, as opposed to a probabilistic method whose running time is $O(\log n)^3$, if the Extended Riemann Hypothesis were proved. But one might well ask whether any purported proof of that hypothesis will ever be as reliable as repeated application of Algorithm P on random x's.

A probabilistic test for primality was proposed in 1974 by R. Solovay and V. Strassen, who devised the interesting but more complicated test described in exercise 23(b). [See *SICOMP* **6** (1977), 84–85; **7** (1978), 118.] Algorithm P is a simplified version of a procedure due to M. O. Rabin, based in part on ideas of Gary L. Miller [see *Algorithms and Complexity* (1976), 35–36], and independently discovered by J. L. Selfridge. B. Arazi [*Comp. J.* **37** (1994), 219–222] has observed that Algorithm P can be speeded up significantly for large n by using Montgomery's fast method for remainders (exercise 4.3.1–41).

A completely rigorous and deterministic way to test for primality in polynomial time was finally discovered in 2002 by Manindra Agrawal, Neeraj Kayal, and Nitin Saxena, who proved the following result:

Theorem A. *Let r be an integer such that $n \perp r$ and the order of n modulo r exceeds $(\lg n)^2$. Then n is prime if and only if the polynomial congruence*

$$(z + a)^n \equiv z^n + a \qquad (\text{modulo } z^r - 1 \text{ and } n)$$

holds for $0 \le z \le \sqrt{r}\,\lg n$. (See exercise 3.2.2–11(a).) ∎

An excellent exposition of this theorem has been prepared by Andrew Granville [*Bull. Amer. Math. Soc.* **42** (2005), 3–38], who presents an elementary proof that it yields a primality test with running time $\Omega(\log n)^6$ and $O(\log n)^{11}$. He also explains a subsequent improvement due to H. Lenstra and C. Pomerance, who showed that the running time can be reduced to $O(\log n)^{6+\epsilon}$ if the polynomial $z^r - 1$ is replaced by a more general family of polynomials. And he discusses refinements by P. Berrizbeitia, Q. Cheng, P. Mihăilescu, R. Avanzi, and D. Bernstein, leading to a probabilistic algorithm by which a proof of primality can almost surely be found in $O(\log n)^{4+\epsilon}$ steps whenever n is prime.

Factoring via continued fractions. The factorization procedures we have discussed so far will often balk at numbers of 30 digits or more, and another idea is needed if we are to go much further. Fortunately there is such an idea; in fact, there were two ideas, due respectively to A. M. Legendre and M. Kraïtchik, which led D. H. Lehmer and R. E. Powers to devise a new technique many years ago [*Bull. Amer. Math. Soc.* **37** (1931), 770–776]. However, the method was not used at the time because it was comparatively unsuitable for desk calculators. This negative judgment prevailed until the late 1960s, when John Brillhart found that the Lehmer–Powers approach deserved to be resurrected, since it was quite well suited to computer programming. In fact, he and Michael A. Morrison later developed it into the champion of all multiprecision factorization methods that were known in the 1970s. Their program would handle typical 25-digit numbers in about 30 seconds, and 40-digit numbers in about 50 minutes, on an IBM

360/91 computer [see *Math. Comp.* **29** (1975), 183–205]. The method had its first triumphant success in 1970, discovering that $2^{128} + 1 = 59649589127497217 \cdot 5704689200685129054721$.

The basic idea is to search for numbers x and y such that

$$x^2 \equiv y^2 \ (\text{modulo } N), \qquad 0 < x, y < N, \qquad x \neq y, \qquad x + y \neq N. \tag{18}$$

Fermat's method imposes the stronger requirement $x^2 - y^2 = N$, but actually the congruence (18) is enough to split N into factors: It implies that N is a divisor of $x^2 - y^2 = (x - y)(x + y)$, yet N divides neither $x - y$ nor $x + y$; hence $\gcd(N, x - y)$ and $\gcd(N, x + y)$ are proper factors of N that can be found by the efficient methods of Section 4.5.2.

One way to discover solutions of (18) is to look for values of x such that $x^2 \equiv a \ (\text{modulo } N)$, for small values of $|a|$. As we will see, it is often a simple matter to piece together solutions of this congruence to obtain solutions of (18). Now if $x^2 = a + kNd^2$ for some k and d, with small $|a|$, the fraction x/d is a good approximation to $\sqrt{kN}$; conversely, if x/d is an especially good approximation to $\sqrt{kN}$, the difference $|x^2 - kNd^2|$ will be small. This observation suggests looking at the continued fraction expansion of $\sqrt{kN}$, since we have seen in Eq. 4.5.3–(12) and exercise 4.5.3–42 that continued fractions yield good rational approximations.

Continued fractions for quadratic irrationalities have many pleasant properties, which are proved in exercise 4.5.3–12. The algorithm below makes use of these properties to derive solutions to the congruence

$$x^2 \equiv (-1)^{e_0} p_1^{e_1} p_2^{e_2} \dots p_m^{e_m} \ (\text{modulo } N). \tag{19}$$

Here we use a fixed set of small primes $p_1 = 2$, $p_2 = 3$, ..., up to p_m; only primes p such that either $p = 2$ or $(kN)^{(p-1)/2} \bmod p \leq 1$ should appear in this list, since other primes will never be factors of the numbers generated by the algorithm (see exercise 14). If $(x_1, e_{01}, e_{11}, \dots, e_{m1})$, ..., $(x_r, e_{0r}, e_{1r}, \dots, e_{mr})$ are solutions of (19) such that the vector sum

$$(e_{01}, e_{11}, \dots, e_{m1}) + \dots + (e_{0r}, e_{1r}, \dots, e_{mr}) = (2e_0', 2e_1', \dots, 2e_m') \tag{20}$$

is *even* in each component, then

$$x = (x_1 \dots x_r) \bmod N, \qquad y = \left((-1)^{e_0'} p_1^{e_1'} \dots p_m^{e_m'}\right) \bmod N \tag{21}$$

yields a solution to (18), except for the possibility that $x \equiv \pm y$. Condition (20) essentially says that the vectors are linearly dependent modulo 2, so we must have a solution to (20) if we have found at least $m + 2$ solutions to (19).

Algorithm E (*Factoring via continued fractions*). Given a positive integer N and a positive integer k such that kN is not a perfect square, this algorithm attempts to discover solutions to the congruence (19) for a given sequence of primes p_1, ..., p_m, by analyzing the convergents of the continued fraction for $\sqrt{kN}$. (Another algorithm, which uses the outputs to discover factors of N, is the subject of exercise 12.)

Table 1

AN ILLUSTRATION OF ALGORITHM E

$N = 197209$, $k = 1$, $m = 3$, $p_1 = 2$, $p_2 = 3$, $p_3 = 5$

	U	V	A	P	S	T	Output
After E1:	876	73	12	5329	1	—	
After E4:	882	145	6	5329	0	29	
After E4:	857	37	23	32418	1	37	
After E4:	751	720	1	159316	0	1	$159316^2 \equiv +2^4 \cdot 3^2 \cdot 5^1$
After E4:	852	143	5	191734	1	143	
After E4:	681	215	3	131941	0	43	
After E4:	863	656	1	193139	1	41	
After E4:	883	33	26	127871	0	11	
After E4:	821	136	6	165232	1	17	
After E4:	877	405	2	133218	0	1	$133218^2 \equiv +2^0 \cdot 3^4 \cdot 5^1$
After E4:	875	24	36	37250	1	1	$37250^2 \equiv -2^3 \cdot 3^1 \cdot 5^0$
After E4:	490	477	1	93755	0	53	

E1. [Initialize.] Set $D \leftarrow kN$, $R \leftarrow \lfloor\sqrt{D}\rfloor$, $R' \leftarrow 2R$, $U' \leftarrow R'$, $V \leftarrow D - R^2$, $V' \leftarrow 1$, $A \leftarrow \lfloor R'/V \rfloor$, $U \leftarrow R' - (R' \bmod V)$, $P' \leftarrow R$, $P \leftarrow (AR+1) \bmod N$, $S \leftarrow 1$. (This algorithm follows the general procedure of exercise 4.5.3–12, finding the continued fraction expansion of $\sqrt{kN}$. The variables U, U', V, V', P, P', A, and S represent, respectively, what that exercise calls $\lfloor\sqrt{D}\rfloor + U_n$, $\lfloor\sqrt{D}\rfloor + U_{n-1}$, V_n, V_{n-1}, $p_n \bmod N$, $p_{n-1} \bmod N$, A_n, and $n \bmod 2$, where n is initially 1. We will always have $0 < V \le U \le R'$, so the highest precision is needed only for P and P'.)

E2. [Advance U, V, S.] Set $T \leftarrow V$, $V \leftarrow A(U' - U) + V'$, $V' \leftarrow T$, $A \leftarrow \lfloor U/V \rfloor$, $U' \leftarrow U$, $U \leftarrow R' - (U \bmod V)$, $S \leftarrow 1 - S$.

E3. [Factor V.] (Now we have $P^2 - kNQ^2 = (-1)^S V$, for some Q relatively prime to P, by exercise 4.5.3–12(c).) Set $(e_0, e_1, \ldots, e_m) \leftarrow (S, 0, \ldots, 0)$, $T \leftarrow V$. Now do the following, for $1 \le j \le m$: If $T \bmod p_j = 0$, set $T \leftarrow T/p_j$ and $e_j \leftarrow e_j + 1$, and repeat this process until $T \bmod p_j \ne 0$.

E4. [Solution?] If $T = 1$, output the values $(P, e_0, e_1, \ldots, e_m)$, which comprise a solution to (19). (If enough solutions have been generated, we may terminate the algorithm now.)

E5. [Advance P, P'.] If $V \ne 1$, set $T \leftarrow P$, $P \leftarrow (AP + P') \bmod N$, $P' \leftarrow T$, and return to step E2. Otherwise the continued fraction process has started to repeat its cycle, except perhaps for S, so the algorithm terminates. (The cycle will usually be so long that this doesn't happen.) ∎

We can illustrate the application of Algorithm E to relatively small numbers by considering the case $N = 197209$, $k = 1$, $m = 3$, $p_1 = 2$, $p_2 = 3$, $p_3 = 5$. The computation begins as shown in Table 1.

Continuing the computation gives 25 outputs in the first 100 iterations; in other words, the algorithm is finding solutions quite rapidly. But some of the solutions are trivial. For example, if the computation above were continued 14 more times, we would obtain the output $197197^2 \equiv 2^4 \cdot 3^2 \cdot 5^0$, which is of no interest since $197197 \equiv -12$. The first two solutions above are already enough to complete the factorization: We have found that

$$(159316 \cdot 133218)^2 \equiv (2^2 \cdot 3^3 \cdot 5^1)^2 \text{ (modulo } 197209);$$

thus (18) holds with $x = (159316 \cdot 133218) \bmod 197209 = 126308$, $y = 540$. By Euclid's algorithm, $\gcd(126308 - 540, 197209) = 199$; hence we obtain the pretty factorization

$$197209 = 199 \cdot 991.$$

We can get some understanding of why Algorithm E factors large numbers so successfully by considering a heuristic analysis of its running time, following unpublished ideas that R. Schroeppel communicated to the author in 1975. Let us assume for convenience that $k = 1$. The number of outputs needed to produce a factorization of N will be roughly proportional to the number m of small primes being cast out. Each execution of step E3 takes about order $m \log N$ units of time, so the total running time will be roughly proportional to $m^2 \log N/P$, where P is the probability of a successful output per iteration. If we make the conservative assumption that V is randomly distributed between 0 and $2\sqrt{N}$, the probability P is $(2\sqrt{N})^{-1}$ times the number of integers $< 2\sqrt{N}$ whose prime factors are all in the set $\{p_1, \ldots, p_m\}$. Exercise 29 gives a lower bound for P, from which we conclude that the running time is at most of order

$$\frac{2\sqrt{N}\, m^2 \log N}{m^r/r!}, \qquad \text{where } r = \left\lfloor \frac{\log 2\sqrt{N}}{\log p_m} \right\rfloor. \tag{22}$$

If we let $\ln m$ be approximately $\frac{1}{2}\sqrt{\ln N \ln \ln N}$, we have $r \approx \sqrt{\ln N/\ln \ln N} - 1$, assuming that $p_m = O(m \log m)$, so formula (22) reduces to

$$\exp\left(2\sqrt{(\ln N)(\ln \ln N)} + O\left((\log N)^{1/2}(\log \log N)^{-1/2}(\log \log \log N)\right)\right).$$

Stating this another way, the running time of Algorithm E is expected to be at most $N^{\epsilon(N)}$ under reasonably plausible assumptions, where the exponent $\epsilon(N) \approx 2\sqrt{\ln \ln N/\ln N}$ goes to 0 as $N \to \infty$.

When N is in a practical range, we should of course be careful not to take such asymptotic estimates too seriously. For example, if $N = 10^{50}$ we have $N^{1/\alpha} = (\lg N)^\alpha$ when $\alpha \approx 4.75$, and the same relation holds for $\alpha \approx 8.42$ when $N = 10^{200}$. The function $N^{\epsilon(N)}$ has an order of growth that is sort of a cross between $N^{1/\alpha}$ and $(\lg N)^\alpha$; but all three of these forms are about the same, unless N is intolerably large. Extensive computational experiments by M. C. Wunderlich have shown that a well-tuned version of Algorithm E performs much better than our estimate would indicate [see *Lecture Notes in Math.* **751** (1979), 328–342]; although $2\sqrt{\ln \ln N/\ln N} \approx .41$ when $N = 10^{50}$, he obtained running times of about $N^{0.15}$ while factoring thousands of numbers in the range $10^{13} \le N \le 10^{42}$.

Algorithm E begins its attempt to factorize N by essentially replacing N by kN, and this is a rather curious way to proceed (if not downright stupid).

"Excuse me, do you mind if I multiply your number by 3 before I try to factor it?" Nevertheless, it turns out to be a good idea, since certain values of k will make the V numbers potentially divisible by more small primes, hence they will be more likely to factor completely in step E3. On the other hand, a large value of k will make the V numbers larger, hence they will be less likely to factor completely; we want to balance these tendencies by choosing k wisely. Consider, for example, the divisibility of V by powers of 5. We have $P^2 - kNQ^2 = (-1)^S V$ in step E3, so if 5 divides V we have $P^2 \equiv kNQ^2$ (modulo 5). In this congruence Q cannot be a multiple of 5, since it is relatively prime to P, so we may write $(P/Q)^2 \equiv kN$ (modulo 5). If we assume that P and Q are random relatively prime integers, so that the 24 possible pairs $(P \bmod 5, Q \bmod 5) \neq (0, 0)$ are equally likely, the probability that 5 divides V is therefore $\frac{4}{24}$, $\frac{8}{24}$, 0, 0, or $\frac{8}{24}$ according as $kN \bmod 5$ is 0, 1, 2, 3, or 4. Similarly the probability that 25 divides V is 0, $\frac{40}{600}$, 0, 0, $\frac{40}{600}$ respectively, unless kN is a multiple of 25. In general, given an odd prime p with $(kN)^{(p-1)/2} \bmod p = 1$, we find that V is a multiple of p^e with probability $2/\big(p^{e-1}(p+1)\big)$; and the average number of times p divides V comes to $2p/(p^2-1)$. This analysis, suggested by R. Schroeppel, suggests that the best choice of k is the value that maximizes

$$\sum_{j=1}^{m} f(p_j, kN) \log p_j - \frac{1}{2} \log k, \tag{23}$$

where f is the function defined in exercise 28, since this is essentially the expected value of $\ln(\sqrt{N}/T)$ when we reach step E4.

Best results will be obtained with Algorithm E when both k and m are well chosen. The proper choice of m can only be made by experimental testing, since the asymptotic analysis we have made is too crude to give sufficiently precise information, and since a variety of refinements to the algorithm tend to have unpredictable effects. For example, we can make an important improvement by comparing step E3 with Algorithm A: The factoring of V can stop whenever we find $T \bmod p_j \neq 0$ and $\lfloor T/p_j \rfloor \leq p_j$, since T will then be either 1 or prime. If T is a prime greater than p_m (it will be at most $p_m^2 + p_m - 1$ in such a case), we can still output $(P, e_0, \ldots, e_m, T)$, since a complete factorization has been obtained. The second phase of the algorithm will use only those outputs whose prime T's have occurred at least twice. This modification gives the effect of a much longer list of primes, without increasing the factorization time. Wunderlich's experiments indicate that $m \approx 150$ works well in the presence of this refinement, when N is in the neighborhood of 10^{40}.

Since step E3 is by far the most time-consuming part of the algorithm, Morrison, Brillhart, and Schroeppel have suggested several ways to abort this step when success becomes improbable: (a) Whenever T changes to a single-precision value, continue only if $\lfloor T/p_j \rfloor > p_j$ and $3^{T-1} \bmod T \neq 1$. (b) Give up if T is still $> p_m^2$ after casting out factors $< \frac{1}{10}p_m$. (c) Cast out factors only up to p_5, say, for batches of 100 or so consecutive V's; continue the factorization later, but only on the V from each batch that has produced the smallest residual T. (Before casting out the factors up to p_5, it is wise to calculate $V \bmod p_1^{f_1} p_2^{f_2} p_3^{f_3} p_4^{f_4} p_5^{f_5}$, where the f's are small enough to make $p_1^{f_1} p_2^{f_2} p_3^{f_3} p_4^{f_4} p_5^{f_5}$ fit in single precision, but large enough to make $V \bmod p_i^{f_i+1} = 0$ unlikely. One single-precision remainder will therefore characterize the value of V modulo five small primes.)

For estimates of the cycle length in the output of Algorithm E, see H. C. Williams, *Math. Comp.* **36** (1981), 593–601.

*A theoretical upper bound. From the standpoint of computational complexity, we would like to know if there is any method of factorization whose expected running time can be proved to be $O(N^{\epsilon(N)})$, where $\epsilon(N) \to 0$ as $N \to \infty$. We have seen that Algorithm E probably has such behavior, but it seems hopeless to find a rigorous proof, because continued fractions are not sufficiently well disciplined. The first proof that a good factorization algorithm exists in this sense was discovered by John Dixon in 1978; Dixon showed, in fact, that it suffices to consider a simplified version of Algorithm E, in which the continued fraction apparatus is removed but the basic idea of (18) remains.

Dixon's method [*Math. Comp.* **36** (1981), 255–260] is simply this, assuming that N is known to have at least two distinct prime factors, and that N is not divisible by the first m primes $p_1, p_2, \ldots, p_m$: Choose a random integer X in the range $0 < X < N$, and let $V = X^2 \bmod N$. If $V = 0$, the number $\gcd(X, N)$ is a proper factor of N. Otherwise cast out all of the small prime factors of V as in step E3; in other words, express V in the form

$$V = p_1^{e_1} \ldots p_m^{e_m} T, \tag{24}$$

where T is not divisible by any of the first m primes. If $T = 1$, the algorithm proceeds as in step E4 to output $(X, e_1, \ldots, e_m)$, which represents a solution to (19) with $e_0 = 0$. This process continues with new random values of X until there are sufficiently many outputs to discover a factor of N by the method of exercise 12.

In order to analyze this algorithm, we want to find bounds on (a) the probability that a random X will yield an output, and (b) the probability that a large number of outputs will be required before a factor is found. Let $P(m, N)$ be the probability (a), namely the probability that $T = 1$ when X is chosen at random. After M values of X have been tried, we will obtain $MP(m, N)$ outputs, on the average; and the number of outputs has a binomial distribution, so the standard deviation is less than the square root of the mean. The probability (b) is fairly easy to deal with, since exercise 13 proves that the algorithm needs more than $m + k$ outputs with probability $\leq 2^{-k}$.

Exercise 30 proves that $P(m, N) \geq m^r/(r!\,N)$ when $r = 2\lfloor \log N/(2 \log p_m) \rfloor$, so we can estimate the running time almost as we did in (22) but with the quantity $2\sqrt{N}$ replaced by N. This time we choose

$$r = \sqrt{2 \ln N / \ln \ln N} + \theta,$$

where $|\theta| \leq 1$ and r is even, and we choose m so that

$$r = \ln N / \ln p_m + O(1/\log \log N);$$

this means

$$\ln p_m = \sqrt{\frac{\ln N \ln \ln N}{2}} - \frac{\theta}{2} \ln \ln N + O(1),$$

$$\ln m = \ln \pi(p_m) = \ln p_m - \ln \ln p_m + O(1/\log p_m)$$

$$= \sqrt{\frac{\ln N \ln \ln N}{2}} - \frac{\theta + 1}{2} \ln \ln N + O(\log \log \log N),$$

$$\frac{m^r}{r! N} = \exp\left(-\sqrt{2 \ln N \ln \ln N} + O(r \log \log \log N)\right).$$

We will choose M so that $Mm^r/(r!N) \geq 4m$; thus the expected number of outputs $MP(m, N)$ will be at least $4m$. The running time of the algorithm is of order $Mm \log N$, plus $O(m^3)$ steps for exercise 12; it turns out that $O(m^3)$ is less than $Mm \log N$, which is

$$\exp\left(\sqrt{8(\ln N)(\ln \ln N)} + O\left((\log N)^{1/2}(\log \log N)^{-1/2}(\log \log \log N)\right)\right).$$

The probability that this method fails to find a factor is negligibly small, since the probability is at most $e^{-m/2}$ that fewer than $2m$ outputs are obtained (see exercise 31), while the probability is at most 2^{-m} that no factors are found from the first $2m$ outputs, and $m \gg \ln N$. We have proved the following slight strengthening of Dixon's original theorem:

Theorem D. *There is an algorithm whose running time is $O(N^{\epsilon(N)})$, where $\epsilon(N) = c\sqrt{\ln \ln N / \ln N}$ and c is any constant greater than $\sqrt{8}$, that finds a nontrivial factor of N with probability $1 - O(1/N)$, whenever N has at least two distinct prime divisors.* ∎

Other approaches. Another factorization technique was suggested by John M. Pollard [*Proc. Cambridge Phil. Soc.* **76** (1974), 521–528], who gave a practical way to discover prime factors p of N when $p - 1$ has no large prime factors. The latter algorithm (see exercise 19) is probably the first thing to try after Algorithms A and B have run too long on a large N.

A survey paper by R. K. Guy, written in collaboration with J. H. Conway, *Congressus Numerantium* **16** (1976), 49–89, gave a unique perspective on the developments up till that time. Guy stated, "I shall be surprised if anyone regularly factors numbers of size 10^{80} without special form during the present century"; and he was indeed destined to be surprised many times during the next 20 years.

Tremendous advances in factorization techniques for large numbers were made during the 1980s, beginning with Carl Pomerance's *quadratic sieve method* of 1981 [see *Lecture Notes in Comp. Sci.* **209** (1985), 169–182]. Then Hendrik Lenstra devised the *elliptic curve method* [*Annals of Math.* (2) **126** (1987), 649–673], which heuristically is expected to take about $\exp\left(\sqrt{(2 + \epsilon)(\ln p)(\ln \ln p)}\right)$ multiplications to find a prime factor p. This is asymptotically the square root of the running time in our estimate for Algorithm E when $p \approx \sqrt{N}$, and it becomes even better when N has relatively small prime factors. An excellent exposition of this method has been given by Joseph H. Silverman and John Tate in *Rational Points on Elliptic Curves* (New York: Springer, 1992), Chapter 4.

John Pollard came back in 1988 with another new technique, which has become known as the *number field sieve*; see *Lecture Notes in Math.* **1554** (1993) for a series of papers about this method, which is the current champion for factoring extremely large integers. Its running time is predicted to be of order

$$\exp\left((64/9 + \epsilon)^{1/3}(\ln N)^{1/3}(\ln \ln N)^{2/3}\right) \tag{25}$$

as $N \to \infty$. The crossover point at which a well-tuned version of the number field sieve begins to beat a well-tuned version of the quadratic sieve appears to be at $N \approx 10^{112}$, according to A. K. Lenstra.

Details of the new methods are beyond the scope of this book, but we can get an idea of their effectiveness by noting some of the early success stories in which unfactored Fermat numbers of the form $2^{2^k} + 1$ were cracked. For example, the factorization

$$2^{512} + 1 = 2424833 \cdot$$

$$7455602825647884208337395736200454918783366342657 \cdot p_{99}$$

was found by the number field sieve, after four months of computation that occupied otherwise idle time on about 700 workstations [Lenstra, Lenstra, Manasse, and Pollard, *Math. Comp.* **61** (1993), 319–349; **64** (1995), 1357]; here p_{99} denotes a 99-digit prime number. The next Fermat number has twice as many digits, but it yielded to the elliptic curve method on October 20, 1995:

$$2^{1024} + 1 = 45592577 \cdot 6487031809 \cdot$$

$$4659775785220018543264560743076778192897 \cdot p_{252}.$$

[Richard Brent, *Math. Comp.* **68** (1999), 429–451.] In fact, Brent had already used the elliptic curve method to resolve the next case as early as 1988:

$$2^{2048} + 1 = 319489 \cdot 974849 \cdot$$

$$167988556341760475137 \cdot 3560841906445833920513 \cdot p_{564};$$

by a stroke of good luck, all but one of the prime factors was $< 10^{22}$, so the elliptic curve method was a winner.

What about $2^{4096} + 1$? At present, that number seems completely out of reach. It has five factors $< 10^{16}$, but the unfactored residual has 1187 decimal digits. The next case, $2^{8192} + 1$, has four known factors $< 10^{27}$ [Crandall and Fagin, *Math. Comp.* **62** (1994), 321; Brent, Crandall, Dilcher, and van Halewyn, *Math. Comp.* **69** (2000), 1297–1304] and a huge unfactored residual.

Secret factors. Worldwide interest in the problem of factorization increased dramatically in 1977, when R. L. Rivest, A. Shamir, and L. Adleman discovered a way to encode messages that can apparently be decoded only by knowing the factors of a large number N, even though the method of encoding is known to everyone. Since a significant number of the world's greatest mathematicians have been unable to find efficient methods of factoring, this scheme [*CACM* **21** (1978), 120–126] almost certainly provides a secure way to protect confidential data and communications in computer networks.

Let us imagine a small electronic device called an *RSA box* that has two large prime numbers p and q stored in its memory. We will assume that $p-1$ and $q-1$ are not divisible by 3. The RSA box is connected somehow to a computer, and it has told the computer the product $N = pq$; however, no human being will be able to discover the values of p and q except by factoring N, since the RSA box is cleverly designed to self-destruct if anybody tries to tamper with it. In other words, it will erase its memory if it is jostled or if it is subjected to any radiation that could change or read out the data stored inside. Furthermore, the RSA box is sufficiently reliable that it never needs to be maintained; we simply would discard it and buy another, if an emergency arose or if it wore out. The prime factors p and q were generated by the RSA box itself, using some scheme based on truly random phenomena in nature like cosmic rays. The important point is that *nobody* knows p or q, not even a person or organization that owns or has access to this RSA box; there is no point in bribing or blackmailing anyone or holding anybody hostage in order to discover N's factors.

To send a secret message to the owner of an RSA box whose product number is N, you break the message up into a sequence of numbers $(x_1, \ldots, x_k)$, where each x_i lies in the range $0 \le x_i < N$; then you transmit the numbers

$$(x_1^3 \bmod N, \ \ldots, \ x_k^3 \bmod N).$$

The RSA box, knowing p and q, can decode the message, because it has pre-computed a number $d < N$ such that $3d \equiv 1 \ \big(\text{modulo } (p-1)(q-1)\big)$; it can now compute each secret component $(x_i^3 \bmod N)^d \bmod N = x_i$ in a reasonable amount of time, using the method of Section 4.6.3. Naturally the RSA box keeps this magic number d to itself; in fact, the RSA box might choose to remember only d instead of p and q, because its only duties after having computed N are to protect its secrets and to take cube roots mod N.

Such an encoding scheme is ineffective if $x < \sqrt[3]{N}$, since $x^3 \bmod N = x^3$ and the cube root will easily be found. The logarithmic law of leading digits in Section 4.2.4 implies that the leading place x_1 of a k-place message $(x_1, \ldots, x_k)$ will be less than $\sqrt[3]{N}$ about $\frac{1}{3}$ of the time, so this is a problem that needs to be resolved. Exercise 32 presents one way to avoid the difficulty.

The security of the RSA encoding scheme relies on the fact that nobody has been able to discover how to take cube roots quickly mod N without knowing N's factors. It seems likely that no such method will be found, but we cannot be absolutely sure. So far all that can be said for certain is that all of the ordinary ways to discover cube roots will fail. For example, there is essentially no point in trying to compute the number d as a function of N; the reason is that if d is known, or in fact if any number m of reasonable size is known such that $x^m \bmod N = 1$ holds for a significant number of x's, then we can find the factors of N in a few more steps (see exercise 34). Thus, any method of attack based explicitly or implicitly on finding such an m can be no better than factoring.

Some precautions are necessary, however. If the same message is sent to three different people on a computer network, a person who knows x^3 modulo N_1, N_2, and N_3 could reconstruct $x^3 \bmod N_1 N_2 N_3 = x^3$ by the Chinese remainder theorem, so x would no longer be a secret. In fact, even if a "time-stamped" message $(2^{\lceil \lg t_i \rceil} x + t_i)^3 \bmod N_i$ is sent to seven different people, with known or guessable t_i, the value of x can be deduced (see exercise 44). Therefore some cryptographers have recommended encoding with the exponent $2^{16} + 1 = 65537$ instead of 3; this exponent is prime, and the computation of $x^{65537} \bmod N$ takes only about 8.5 times as long as the computation of $x^3 \bmod N$. [*CCITT Recommendations Blue Book* (Geneva: International Telecommunication Union, 1989), Fascicle VIII.8, Recommendation X.509, Annex C, pages 74–76.] The original proposal of Rivest, Shamir, and Adleman was to encode x by $x^a \bmod N$ where a is any exponent prime to $\varphi(N)$, not just $a = 3$; in practice, however, we prefer an exponent for which encoding is faster than decoding.

The numbers p and q shouldn't merely be "random" primes in order to make the RSA scheme effective. We have mentioned that $p - 1$ and $q - 1$ should not be divisible by 3, since we want to ensure that unique cube roots exist modulo N. Another condition is that $p - 1$ should have at least one very large prime factor, and so should $q - 1$; otherwise N can be factored using the algorithm of exercise 19. In fact, that algorithm essentially relies on finding a fairly small number m with the property that $x^m \bmod N$ is frequently equal to 1, and we have just seen that such an m is dangerous. When $p - 1$ and $q - 1$ have large prime factors p_1 and q_1, the theory in exercise 34 implies that m is either a multiple of $p_1 q_1$ (hence m will be hard to discover) or the probability that $x^m \equiv 1$ will be less than $1/p_1 q_1$ (hence $x^m \bmod N$ will almost never be 1). Besides this condition, we don't want p and q to be close to each other, lest Algorithm D succeed in discovering them; in fact, we don't want the ratio p/q to be near a simple fraction, otherwise Lehman's generalization of Algorithm C could find them.

The following procedure for generating p and q is almost surely unbreakable: Start with a truly random number p_0 between, say, 10^{80} and 10^{81}. Search for the first prime number p_1 greater than p_0; this will require testing about $\frac{1}{2} \ln p_0 \approx 90$ odd numbers, and it will be sufficient to have p_1 a "probable prime" with probability $> 1 - 2^{-100}$ after 50 trials of Algorithm P. Then choose another truly random number p_2 between, say, 10^{39} and 10^{40}. Search for the first prime number p of the form $kp_1 + 1$ where $k \geq p_2$, k is even, and $k \equiv p_1$ (modulo 3). This will require testing about $\frac{1}{3} \ln p_1 p_2 \approx 90$ numbers before a prime p is found. The prime p will be about 120 digits long; a similar construction can be used to find a prime q about 130 digits long. For extra security, it is probably advisable to check that neither $p + 1$ nor $q + 1$ consists entirely of rather small prime factors (see exercise 20). The product $N = pq$, whose order of magnitude will be about 10^{250}, now meets all of our requirements, and it is inconceivable at this time that such an N could be factored.

For example, suppose we knew a method that could factor a 250-digit number N in $N^{0.1}$ microseconds. This amounts to 10^{25} microseconds, and there are only 31,556,952,000,000 μs per year, so we would need more than 3×10^{11} years of CPU time to complete the factorization. Even if a government agency purchased 10 billion computers and set them all to working on this problem, it would take more than 31 years before one of them would crack N into factors;

meanwhile the fact that the government had purchased so many specialized machines would leak out, and people would start using 300-digit N's.

Since the encoding method $x \mapsto x^3 \bmod N$ is known to everyone, there are additional advantages besides the fact that the code can be cracked only by the RSA box. Such "public key" systems were first published by W. Diffie and M. E. Hellman in *IEEE Trans.* **IT-22** (1976), 644–654. As an example of what can be done when the encoding method is public knowledge, suppose Alice wants to communicate with Bob securely via electronic mail, *signing* her letter so that Bob can be sure nobody else has forged it. Let $E_A(M)$ be the encoding function for messages M sent to Alice, let $D_A(M)$ be the decoding done by Alice's RSA box, and let $E_B(M)$, $D_B(M)$ be the corresponding encoding and decoding functions for Bob's RSA box. Then Alice can send a signed message by affixing her name and the date to some confidential message, then transmitting $E_B(D_A(M))$ to Bob, using her machine to compute $D_A(M)$. When Bob gets this message, his RSA box converts it to $D_A(M)$, and he knows E_A so he can compute $M = E_A(D_A(M))$. This should convince him that the message did indeed come from Alice; nobody else could have sent the message $D_A(M)$. (Well, Bob himself now knows $D_A(M)$, so he could impersonate Alice by passing $E_X(D_A(M))$ to Xavier. To defeat any such attempted forgery, the content of M should clearly indicate that it is for Bob's eyes only.)

We might ask, how do Alice and Bob know each other's encoding functions E_A and E_B? It wouldn't do simply to have them stored in a public file, since some Charlie could tamper with that file, substituting an N that he has computed by himself; Charlie could then surreptitiously intercept and decode a private message before Alice or Bob would discover that something is amiss. The solution is to keep the product numbers N_A and N_B in a special public directory that has its own RSA box and its own widely publicized product number N_D. When Alice wants to know how to communicate with Bob, she asks the directory for Bob's product number; the directory computer sends her a *signed* message giving the value of N_B. Nobody can forge such a message, so it must be legitimate.

An interesting alternative to the RSA scheme has been proposed by Michael Rabin [M.I.T. Lab. for Comp. Sci., report TR-212 (1979)], who suggests encoding by the function $x^2 \bmod N$ instead of $x^3 \bmod N$. In this case the decoding mechanism, which we can call a SQRT box, returns four different messages; the reason is that four different numbers have the same square modulo N, namely x, $-x$, $fx \bmod N$, and $(-fx) \bmod N$, where

$$f = (p^{q-1} - q^{p-1}) \bmod N.$$

If we agree in advance that x is even, or that $x < \frac{1}{2}N$, then the ambiguity drops to two messages, presumably only one of which makes any sense. The ambiguity can in fact be eliminated entirely, as shown in exercise 35. Rabin's scheme has the important property that it is provably as difficult to find square roots mod N as to find the factorization $N = pq$; for by taking the square root of $x^2 \bmod N$ when x is chosen at random, we have a 50-50 chance of finding a value y such that $x^2 \equiv y^2$ and $x \not\equiv \pm y$, after which $\gcd(x - y, N) = p$ or q. However, the system has a fatal flaw that does not seem to be present in the RSA scheme (see exercise 33): Anyone with access to a SQRT box can easily determine the factors of its N. This not only permits cheating by dishonest employees, or threats of extortion, it also allows people to reveal their p and q, after which they might claim that their "signature" on some transmitted document was a forgery. Thus it is clear that the goal of secure communication leads to subtle problems quite different from those we usually face in the design and analysis of algorithms.

Historical note: It was revealed in 1997 that Clifford Cocks had considered the encoding of messages by the transformation $x^{pq} \bmod pq$ already in 1973, but his work was kept secret.

The largest known primes. We have discussed several computational methods elsewhere in this book that require the use of large prime numbers, and the techniques just described can be used to discover primes of up to, say, 25 digits or fewer, with relative ease. Table 2 shows the ten largest primes that are less than the word size of typical computers. (Some other useful primes appear in the answers to exercises 3.2.1.2–22 and 4.6.4–57.)

Actually much larger primes of special forms are known, and it is occasionally important to find primes that are as large as possible. Let us therefore conclude this section by investigating the interesting manner in which the largest explicitly known primes have been discovered. Such primes are of the form $2^n - 1$, for various special values of n, and so they are especially suited to certain applications of binary computers.

A number of the form $2^n - 1$ cannot be prime unless n is prime, since $2^{uv} - 1$ is divisible by $2^u - 1$. In 1644, Marin Mersenne astonished his contemporaries by stating, in essence, that the numbers $2^p - 1$ are prime for $p = 2, 3, 5, 7, 13, 17,$ 19, 31, 67, 127, 257, and for no other p less than 257. (This statement appeared in connection with a discussion of perfect numbers in the preface to his *Cogitata Physico-Mathematica*. Curiously, he also made the following remark: "To tell if a given number of 15 or 20 digits is prime or not, all time would not suffice for the test, whatever use is made of what is already known.") Mersenne, who had corresponded frequently with Fermat, Descartes, and others about similar topics in previous years, gave no proof of his assertions, and for over 200 years nobody knew whether he was correct. Euler showed that $2^{31} - 1$ is prime in 1772, after having tried unsuccessfully to prove this in previous years. About 100 years later, É. Lucas discovered that $2^{127} - 1$ is prime, but $2^{67} - 1$ was questionable; therefore Mersenne might not be completely accurate. Then I. M. Pervushin proved in 1883 that $2^{61} - 1$ is prime [see *Istoriko-Mat. Issledovaniĭa* **6** (1953), 559], and this touched off speculation that Mersenne had only made a copying error, writing 67 for 61. Eventually other errors in Mersenne's statement were discovered; R. E. Powers [*AMM* **18** (1911), 195] showed that $2^{89} - 1$ is prime, as had been conjectured by some earlier writers, and three years later he proved that $2^{107} - 1$ also is prime. M. Kraïtchik found in 1922 that $2^{257} - 1$ is *not* prime [see his *Recherches sur la Théorie des Nombres* (Paris: 1924), 21]; computational errors may have crept in to his calculations, but his conclusion has turned out to be correct.

Table 2

USEFUL PRIME NUMBERS

N	a_1	a_2	a_3	a_4	a_5	a_6	a_7	a_8	a_9	a_{10}
2^{15}	19	49	51	55	61	75	81	115	121	135
2^{16}	15	17	39	57	87	89	99	113	117	123
2^{17}	1	9	13	31	49	61	63	85	91	99
2^{18}	5	11	17	23	33	35	41	65	75	93
2^{19}	1	19	27	31	45	57	67	69	85	87
2^{20}	3	5	17	27	59	69	129	143	153	185
2^{21}	9	19	21	55	61	69	105	111	121	129
2^{22}	3	17	27	33	57	87	105	113	117	123
2^{23}	15	21	27	37	61	69	135	147	157	159
2^{24}	3	17	33	63	75	77	89	95	117	167
2^{25}	39	49	61	85	91	115	141	159	165	183
2^{26}	5	27	45	87	101	107	111	117	125	135
2^{27}	39	79	111	115	135	187	199	219	231	235
2^{28}	57	89	95	119	125	143	165	183	213	273
2^{29}	3	33	43	63	73	75	93	99	121	133
2^{30}	35	41	83	101	105	107	135	153	161	173
2^{31}	1	19	61	69	85	99	105	151	159	171
2^{32}	5	17	65	99	107	135	153	185	209	267
2^{33}	9	25	49	79	105	285	301	303	321	355
2^{34}	41	77	113	131	143	165	185	207	227	281
2^{35}	31	49	61	69	79	121	141	247	309	325
2^{36}	5	17	23	65	117	137	159	173	189	233
2^{37}	25	31	45	69	123	141	199	201	351	375
2^{38}	45	87	107	131	153	185	191	227	231	257
2^{39}	7	19	67	91	135	165	219	231	241	301
2^{40}	87	167	195	203	213	285	293	299	389	437
2^{41}	21	31	55	63	73	75	91	111	133	139
2^{42}	11	17	33	53	65	143	161	165	215	227
2^{43}	57	67	117	175	255	267	291	309	319	369
2^{44}	17	117	119	129	143	149	287	327	359	377
2^{45}	55	69	81	93	121	133	139	159	193	229
2^{46}	21	57	63	77	167	197	237	287	305	311
2^{47}	115	127	147	279	297	339	435	541	619	649
2^{48}	59	65	89	93	147	165	189	233	243	257
2^{59}	55	99	225	427	517	607	649	687	861	871
2^{60}	93	107	173	179	257	279	369	395	399	453
2^{63}	25	165	259	301	375	387	391	409	457	471
2^{64}	59	83	95	179	189	257	279	323	353	363
10^{6}	17	21	39	41	47	69	83	93	117	137
10^{7}	9	27	29	57	63	69	71	93	99	111
10^{8}	11	29	41	59	69	153	161	173	179	213
10^{9}	63	71	107	117	203	239	243	249	261	267
10^{10}	33	57	71	119	149	167	183	213	219	231
10^{11}	23	53	57	93	129	149	167	171	179	231
10^{12}	11	39	41	63	101	123	137	143	153	233
10^{16}	63	83	113	149	183	191	329	357	359	369

The ten largest primes less than N are $N - a_1, \ldots, N - a_{10}$.

Numbers of the form $2^p - 1$ are now called *Mersenne numbers*, and it is known that Mersenne primes are obtained for p equal to

$$2, 3, 5, 7, 13, 17, 19, 31, 61, 89, 107, 127, 521, 607, 1279, 2203, 2281, 3217,$$
$$4253, 4423, 9689, 9941, 11213, 19937, 21701, 23209, 44497, 86243, 110503,$$
$$132049, 216091, 756839, 859433, 1257787, 1398269, 2976221, 3021377, 6972593,$$
$$13466917, 20996011, 24036583, 25964951, 30402457, 32582657, 37156667,$$
$$42643801, 43112609, 57885161, 74207281, 77232917, 82589933, \dots . \quad (26)$$

The first entries above 100000 were found by David Slowinski and associates while testing new supercomputers [see *J. Recreational Math.* **11** (1979), 258–261]; he found 756839, 859433, and 1257787 in collaboration with Paul Gage during the 1990s. But the remaining exponents, beginning with 1398269, were found respectively by Joël Armengaud, Gordon Spence, Roland Clarkson, Nayan Hajratwala, Michael Cameron, Michael Shafer, Josh Findley, Martin Nowak, Curtis Cooper/Steven Boone, Hans-Michael Elvenich, Odd Magnar Strindmo, Edson Smith, Jonathan Pace, and Patrick Laroche, using off-the-shelf personal computers, most recently in 2018. They used a program by George Woltman, who launched the Great Internet Mersenne Prime Search project (GIMPS) in 1996, with Internet software contributed subsequently by Scott Kurowski.

Notice that the prime $8191 = 2^{13} - 1$ does not occur in (26); Mersenne had stated that $2^{8191} - 1$ is prime, and others had conjectured that any Mersenne prime could perhaps be used in the exponent.

The search for large primes has not been systematic, because people have generally tried to set a hard-to-beat world record instead of spending time with smaller exponents. For example, $2^{132049} - 1$ was proved prime in 1983, and $2^{216091} - 1$ in 1984, but the case $2^{110503} - 1$ was not discovered until 1988. Therefore one or more unknown Mersenne primes less than $2^{82589933} - 1$ might still exist. According to Woltman, all exponents $< 65,610,011$ were checked as of November 8, 2023; his volunteers are systematically filling the remaining gaps.

Since $2^{82589933} - 1$ has more than 24 million decimal digits, it is clear that some special techniques have been used to prove that such numbers are prime. An efficient way to test the primality of a given Mersenne number $2^p - 1$ was first devised by É. Lucas [*Amer. J. Math.* **1** (1878), 184–239, 289–321, especially page 316] and improved by D. H. Lehmer [*Annals of Math.* (2) **31** (1930), 419–448, especially page 443]. The Lucas–Lehmer test, which is a special case of the method now used for testing the primality of n when the factors of $n + 1$ are known, is the following:

Theorem L. *Let q be an odd prime, and define the sequence $\langle L_n \rangle$ by the rule*

$$L_0 = 4, \qquad L_{n+1} = (L_n^2 - 2) \bmod (2^q - 1). \quad (27)$$

Then $2^q - 1$ is prime if and only if $L_{q-2} = 0$.

For example, $2^3 - 1$ is prime since $L_1 = (4^2 - 2) \bmod 7 = 0$. This test is particularly well suited to binary computers, since calculation mod $(2^q - 1)$ is so convenient; see Section 4.3.2. Exercise 4.3.2–14 explains how to save time when q is extremely large.

Proof. We will prove Theorem L using only very simple principles of number theory, by investigating several features of recurring sequences that are of independent interest. Consider the sequences $\langle U_n \rangle$ and $\langle V_n \rangle$ defined by

$$U_0 = 0, \qquad U_1 = 1, \qquad U_{n+1} = 4U_n - U_{n-1};$$
$$V_0 = 2, \qquad V_1 = 4, \qquad V_{n+1} = 4V_n - V_{n-1}. \tag{28}$$

The following equations are readily proved by induction:

$$V_n = U_{n+1} - U_{n-1}; \tag{29}$$
$$U_n = \big((2 + \sqrt{3}\,)^n - (2 - \sqrt{3}\,)^n\big)/\sqrt{12}; \tag{30}$$
$$V_n = (2 + \sqrt{3}\,)^n + (2 - \sqrt{3}\,)^n; \tag{31}$$
$$U_{m+n} = U_m U_{n+1} - U_{m-1} U_n. \tag{32}$$

Let us now prove an auxiliary result, when p is prime and $e \geq 1$:

$$\text{if} \qquad U_n \equiv 0 \ (\text{modulo } p^e) \qquad \text{then} \qquad U_{np} \equiv 0 \ (\text{modulo } p^{e+1}). \tag{33}$$

This follows from the more general considerations of exercise 3.2.2–11, but a direct proof can be given for sequence (28). Assume that $U_n = bp^e$, $U_{n+1} = a$. By (32) and (28), $U_{2n} = bp^e(2a - 4bp^e) \equiv 2aU_n$ (modulo p^{e+1}), while we have $U_{2n+1} = U_{n+1}^2 - U_n^2 \equiv a^2$. Similarly, $U_{3n} = U_{2n+1}U_n - U_{2n}U_{n-1} \equiv 3a^2 U_n$ and $U_{3n+1} = U_{2n+1}U_{n+1} - U_{2n}U_n \equiv a^3$. In general,

$$U_{kn} \equiv ka^{k-1}U_n \qquad \text{and} \qquad U_{kn+1} \equiv a^k \ (\text{modulo } p^{e+1}),$$

so (33) follows if we take $k = p$.

From formulas (30) and (31) we can obtain other expressions for U_n and V_n, expanding $(2 \pm \sqrt{3}\,)^n$ by the binomial theorem:

$$U_n = \sum_k \binom{n}{2k+1} 2^{n-2k-1} 3^k, \qquad V_n = \sum_k \binom{n}{2k} 2^{n-2k+1} 3^k. \tag{34}$$

Now if we set $n = p$, where p is an odd prime, and if we use the fact that $\binom{p}{k}$ is a multiple of p except when $k = 0$ or $k = p$, we find that

$$U_p \equiv 3^{(p-1)/2}, \qquad V_p \equiv 4 \qquad (\text{modulo } p). \tag{35}$$

If $p \neq 3$, Fermat's theorem tells us that $3^{p-1} \equiv 1$; hence $(3^{(p-1)/2} - 1) \times (3^{(p-1)/2} + 1) \equiv 0$, and $3^{(p-1)/2} \equiv \pm 1$. When $U_p \equiv -1$, we have $U_{p+1} = 4U_p - U_{p-1} = 4U_p + V_p - U_{p+1} \equiv -U_{p+1}$; hence $U_{p+1} \bmod p = 0$. When $U_p \equiv +1$, we have $U_{p-1} = 4U_p - U_{p+1} = 4U_p - V_p - U_{p-1} \equiv -U_{p-1}$; hence $U_{p-1} \bmod p = 0$. We have proved that, for all primes p, there is an integer $\epsilon(p)$ such that

$$U_{p+\epsilon(p)} \bmod p = 0, \qquad |\epsilon(p)| \leq 1. \tag{36}$$

Now if N is any positive integer, and if $m = m(N)$ is the smallest positive integer such that $U_{m(N)} \bmod N = 0$, we have

$$U_n \bmod N = 0 \qquad \text{if and only if} \qquad n \text{ is a multiple of } m(N). \tag{37}$$

(This number $m(N)$ is called the *rank of apparition* of N in the sequence.) To prove (37), observe that the sequence $U_m, U_{m+1}, U_{m+2}, \ldots$ is congruent (modulo N) to aU_0, aU_1, aU_2, ..., where $a = U_{m+1} \bmod N$ is relatively prime to N because $\gcd(U_n, U_{n+1}) = 1$.

With these preliminaries out of the way, we are ready to prove Theorem L. By (27) and induction,

$$L_n = V_{2^n} \bmod (2^q - 1). \tag{38}$$

Furthermore, the identity $2U_{n+1} = 4U_n + V_n$ implies that $\gcd(U_n, V_n) \le 2$, since any common factor of U_n and V_n must divide U_n and $2U_{n+1}$, while $U_n \perp U_{n+1}$. So U_n and V_n have no odd factor in common, and if $L_{q-2} = 0$ we must have

$$U_{2^{q-1}} = U_{2^{q-2}} V_{2^{q-2}} \equiv 0 \ (\text{modulo } 2^q - 1),$$
$$U_{2^{q-2}} \not\equiv 0 \ (\text{modulo } 2^q - 1).$$

Now if $m = m(2^q - 1)$ is the rank of apparition of $2^q - 1$, it must be a divisor of 2^{q-1} but not of 2^{q-2}; thus $m = 2^{q-1}$. We will prove that $n = 2^q - 1$ must therefore be prime: Let the factorization of n be $p_1^{e_1} \ldots p_r^{e_r}$. All primes p_j are greater than 3, since n is odd and congruent to $(-1)^q - 1 = -2 \ (\text{modulo } 3)$. From (33), (36), and (37) we know that $U_t \equiv 0 \ (\text{modulo } 2^q - 1)$, where

$$t = \mathrm{lcm}\big(p_1^{e_1-1}(p_1 + \epsilon_1), \ldots, p_r^{e_r-1}(p_r + \epsilon_r)\big),$$

and each ϵ_j is ± 1. It follows that t is a multiple of $m = 2^{q-1}$. Let $n_0 = \prod_{j=1}^r p_j^{e_j-1}(p_j + \epsilon_j)$; we have $n_0 \le \prod_{j=1}^r p_j^{e_j-1}(p_j + \tfrac{1}{5}p_j) = (\tfrac{6}{5})^r n$. Also, because $p_j + \epsilon_j$ is even, $t \le n_0/2^{r-1}$, since a factor of two is lost each time the least common multiple of two even numbers is taken. Combining these results, we have $m \le t \le 2(\tfrac{3}{5})^r n < 4(\tfrac{3}{5})^r m < 3m$; hence $r \le 2$ and $t = m$ or $t = 2m$, a power of 2. Therefore $e_1 = 1$, $e_r = 1$, and if n is not prime we must have $n = 2^q - 1 = (2^k + 1)(2^l - 1)$ where $2^k + 1$ and $2^l - 1$ are prime. The latter factorization is obviously impossible when q is odd, so n is prime.

Conversely, suppose that $n = 2^q - 1$ is prime; we must show that $V_{2^{q-2}} \equiv 0 \ (\text{modulo } n)$. For this purpose it suffices to prove that $V_{2^{q-1}} \equiv -2 \ (\text{modulo } n)$, since $V_{2^{q-1}} = (V_{2^{q-2}})^2 - 2$. Now

$$V_{2^{q-1}} = \big((\sqrt{2} + \sqrt{6})/2\big)^{n+1} + \big((\sqrt{2} - \sqrt{6})/2\big)^{n+1}$$

$$= 2^{-n} \sum_k \binom{n+1}{2k} \sqrt{2}^{\,n+1-2k} \sqrt{6}^{\,2k} = 2^{(1-n)/2} \sum_k \binom{n+1}{2k} 3^k.$$

Since n is an odd prime, the binomial coefficient

$$\binom{n+1}{2k} = \binom{n}{2k} + \binom{n}{2k-1}$$

is divisible by n except when $2k = 0$ and $2k = n + 1$; hence

$$2^{(n-1)/2} V_{2^{q-1}} \equiv 1 + 3^{(n+1)/2} \ (\text{modulo } n).$$

Here $2 \equiv (2^{(q+1)/2})^2$, so $2^{(n-1)/2} \equiv (2^{(q+1)/2})^{(n-1)} \equiv 1$ by Fermat's theorem. Finally, by a simple case of the law of quadratic reciprocity (see exercise 23), $3^{(n-1)/2} \equiv -1$, since $n \bmod 3 = 1$ and $n \bmod 4 = 3$. This means $V_{2^{q-1}} \equiv -2$, so we must have $V_{2^{q-2}} \equiv 0$ as desired. ∎

An anonymous author whose works are now preserved in Italian libraries had discovered by 1460 that $2^{17} - 1$ and $2^{19} - 1$ are prime. Ever since then, the world's largest explicitly known prime numbers have almost always been Mersenne primes. But the situation might change, since Mersenne primes are getting harder to find, and since exercise 27 presents an efficient test for primes of other forms. [See E. Picutti, *Historia Math.* **16** (1989), 123–136; Hugh C. Williams, *Édouard Lucas and Primality Testing* (1998), Chapter 2.]

EXERCISES

1. [*10*] If the sequence d_0, d_1, d_2, ... of trial divisors in Algorithm A contains a number that is not prime, why will it never appear in the output?

2. [*15*] If it is known that the input N to Algorithm A is equal to 3 or more, could step A2 be eliminated?

3. [*M20*] Show that there is a number P with the following property: If $1000 \le n \le 1000000$, then n is prime if and only if $\gcd(n, P) = 1$.

4. [*M29*] In the notation of exercise 3.1–7 and Section 1.2.11.3, prove that the average value of the least n such that $X_n = X_{\ell(n)-1}$ lies between $1.5Q(m) - 0.5$ and $1.625Q(m) - 0.5$.

5. [*21*] Use Fermat's method (Algorithm D) to find the factors of 11111 by hand, when the moduli are 3, 5, 7, 8, and 11.

6. [*M24*] If p is an odd prime and if N is not a multiple of p, prove that the number of integers x such that $0 \le x < p$ and $x^2 - N \equiv y^2$ (modulo p) has a solution y is equal to $(p \pm 1)/2$.

7. [*25*] Discuss the problems of programming the sieve of Algorithm D on a binary computer when the table entries for modulus m_i do not exactly fill an integral number of memory words.

▶ **8.** [*23*] (*The sieve of Eratosthenes*, 3rd century B.C.) The following procedure evidently discovers all odd prime numbers less than a given integer N, since it removes all the nonprime numbers: Start with all the odd numbers between 1 and N; then successively strike out the multiples p_k^2, $p_k(p_k + 2)$, $p_k(p_k + 4)$, ..., of the kth prime p_k, for $k = 2, 3, 4, \ldots$, until reaching a prime p_k with $p_k^2 > N$.

Show how to adapt the procedure just described into an algorithm that is directly suited to efficient computer calculation, using no multiplication.

9. [*M25*] Let n be an odd number, $n \ge 3$. Show that if the number $\lambda(n)$ of Theorem 3.2.1.2B is a divisor of $n-1$ but not equal to $n-1$, then n must have the form $p_1 p_2 \ldots p_t$ where the p's are distinct primes and $t \ge 3$.

▶ **10.** [*M26*] (John Selfridge.) Prove that if, for each prime divisor p of $n - 1$, there is a number x_p such that $x_p^{(n-1)/p} \bmod n \ne 1$ but $x_p^{n-1} \bmod n = 1$, then n is prime.

11. [*M20*] What outputs does Algorithm E give when $N = 197209$, $k = 5$, $m = 1$? [*Hint:* $\sqrt{5 \cdot 197209} = 992 + //\overline{1, 495, 2, 495, 1, 1984}//.$]

▶ **12.** [*M28*] Design an algorithm that uses the outputs of Algorithm E to find a proper factor of N, if Algorithm E has produced enough outputs to deduce a solution of (18).

13. [*HM25*] (J. D. Dixon.) Prove that whenever the algorithm of exercise 12 is presented with a solution $(x, e_0, \ldots, e_m)$ whose exponents are linearly dependent modulo 2 on the exponents of previous solutions, the probability is 2^{1-d} that a factorization will not be found, when N has d distinct prime factors and x is chosen at random.

14. [*M20*] Prove that the number T in step E3 of Algorithm E will never be a multiple of an odd prime p for which $(kN)^{(p-1)/2} \bmod p > 1$.

▶ **15.** [*M34*] (Lucas and Lehmer.) Let P and Q be relatively prime integers, and let $U_0 = 0$, $U_1 = 1$, $U_{n+1} = PU_n - QU_{n-1}$ for $n \geq 1$. Prove that if N is a positive integer relatively prime to $2P^2 - 8Q$, and if $U_{N+1} \bmod N = 0$, while $U_{(N+1)/p} \bmod N \neq 0$ for each prime p dividing $N + 1$, then N is prime. (This gives a test for primality when the factors of $N + 1$ are known instead of the factors of $N - 1$. We can evaluate U_m in $O(\log m)$ steps as in exercise 4.6.3–26.) [*Hint:* See the proof of Theorem L.]

16. [*M50*] Are there infinitely many Mersenne primes?

17. [*M25*] (V. R. Pratt.) A complete proof of primality by the converse of Fermat's theorem takes the form of a tree whose nodes have the form (q, x), where q and x are positive integers satisfying the following arithmetic conditions: (i) If $(q_1, x_1), \ldots,$ (q_t, x_t) are the children of (q, x) then $q = q_1 \ldots q_t + 1$. [In particular, if (q, x) is childless, then $q = 2$.] (ii) If (r, y) is a child of (q, x), then $x^{(q-1)/r} \bmod q \neq 1$. (iii) For each node (q, x), we have $x^{q-1} \bmod q = 1$. From these conditions it follows that q is prime and x is a primitive root modulo q, for all nodes (q, x). [For example, the tree

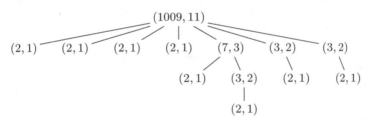

demonstrates that 1009 is prime.] Prove that such a tree with root (q, x) has at most $f(q)$ nodes, where f is a rather slowly growing function.

▶ **18.** [*HM23*] Give a heuristic proof of (7), analogous to the text's derivation of (6). What is the approximate probability that $p_{t-1} \leq \sqrt{p_t}$?

▶ **19.** [*M25*] (J. M. Pollard.) Show how to compute a number M that is divisible by all odd primes p such that $p - 1$ is a divisor of some given number D. [*Hint:* Consider numbers of the form $a^n - 1$.] Such an M is useful in factorization, for by computing $\gcd(M, N)$ we may discover a factor of N. Extend this idea to an efficient method that has high probability of discovering prime factors p of a given large number N, when all prime power factors of $p - 1$ are less than 10^3 except for at most one prime factor less than 10^5. [For example, the second-largest prime dividing (15) would be detected by this method, since it is $1 + 2^4 \cdot 5^2 \cdot 67 \cdot 107 \cdot 199 \cdot 41231$.]

20. [*M40*] Consider exercise 19 with $p + 1$ replacing $p - 1$.

21. [*M49*] (R. K. Guy.) Let $m(p)$ be the number of iterations required by Algorithm B to cast out the prime factor p. Is $m(p) = O(\sqrt{p} \log p)$ as $p \to \infty$?

▶ **22.** [*M30*] (M. O. Rabin.) Let p_n be the probability that Algorithm P guesses wrong, when n is an odd integer ≥ 3. Show that $p_n < \frac{1}{4}$ for all n.

23. [*M35*] The *Jacobi symbol* $\left(\frac{p}{q}\right)$ is defined to be -1, 0, or $+1$ for all integers $p \geq 0$ and all odd integers $q > 1$ by the rules $\left(\frac{p}{q}\right) \equiv p^{(q-1)/2}$ (modulo q) when q is prime;

$\left(\frac{p}{q}\right) = \left(\frac{p}{q_1}\right) \ldots \left(\frac{p}{q_t}\right)$ when q is the product $q_1 \ldots q_t$ of t primes (not necessarily distinct). Thus it generalizes the Legendre symbol of exercise 1.2.4–47.

a) Prove that $\left(\frac{p}{q}\right)$ satisfies the following relationships, hence it can be computed efficiently: $\left(\frac{0}{q}\right) = 0$; $\left(\frac{1}{q}\right) = 1$; $\left(\frac{p}{q}\right) = \left(\frac{p \bmod q}{q}\right)$; $\left(\frac{2}{q}\right) = (-1)^{(q^2-1)/8}$; $\left(\frac{pp'}{q}\right) = \left(\frac{p}{q}\right)\left(\frac{p'}{q}\right)$; $\left(\frac{p}{q}\right) = (-1)^{(p-1)(q-1)/4}\left(\frac{q}{p}\right)$ if both p and q are odd. [The latter law, which is a reciprocity relation reducing the evaluation of $\left(\frac{p}{q}\right)$ to the evaluation of $\left(\frac{q}{p}\right)$, has been proved in exercise 1.2.4–47(d) when both p and q are prime, so you may assume its validity in that special case.]

b) (Solovay and Strassen.) Prove that if n is odd but not prime, the number of integers x such that $1 \leq x < n$ and $0 \neq \left(\frac{x}{n}\right) \equiv x^{(n-1)/2}$ (modulo n) is at most $\frac{1}{2}\varphi(n)$. (Thus, the following testing procedure correctly determines whether or not a given n is prime, with probability at least $1/2$ for all fixed n: "Generate x at random with $1 \leq x < n$. If $0 \neq \left(\frac{x}{n}\right) \equiv x^{(n-1)/2}$ (modulo n), say that n is probably prime, otherwise say that n is definitely not prime.")

c) (L. Monier.) Prove that if n and x are numbers for which Algorithm P concludes that "n is probably prime," then $0 \neq \left(\frac{x}{n}\right) \equiv x^{(n-1)/2}$ (modulo n). [Hence Algorithm P is always superior to the test in (b).]

▶ **24.** [*M25*] (L. Adleman.) When $n > 1$ and $x > 1$ are integers, n odd, let us say that n "passes the x test of Algorithm P" if either $x \bmod n = 0$ or if steps P2–P5 lead to the conclusion that n is probably prime. Prove that, for any N, there exists a set of positive integers $x_1, \ldots, x_m \leq N$ with $m \leq \lfloor \lg N \rfloor$ such that a positive odd integer in the range $1 < n \leq N$ is prime if and only if it passes the x test of Algorithm P for $x = x_1 \bmod n, \ldots, x = x_m \bmod n$. Thus, the probabilistic test for primality can in principle be converted into an efficient test that leaves nothing to chance. (You need not show how to compute the x_j efficiently; just prove that they exist.)

25. [*HM41*] (B. Riemann.) Prove that

$$\pi(x) + \frac{\pi(x^{1/2})}{2} + \frac{\pi(x^{1/3})}{3} + \cdots = \int_2^x \frac{dt}{\ln t} - 2\sum \int_{-\infty}^\sigma \frac{e^{(t+i\tau)\ln x}\,dt}{t+i\tau} + O(1),$$

where the sum is over all complex $\sigma + i\tau$ such that $\tau > 0$ and $\zeta(\sigma + i\tau) = 0$.

▶ **26.** [*M25*] (H. C. Pocklington, 1914.) Let $N = fr + 1$, where $0 < r \leq f + 1$. Prove that N is prime if, for every prime divisor p of f, there is an integer x_p such that $x_p^{N-1} \bmod N = \gcd\left(x_p^{(N-1)/p} - 1, N\right) = 1$.

▶ **27.** [*M30*] Show that there is a way to test numbers of the form $N = 5\cdot 2^n + 1$ for primality, using approximately the same number of squarings mod N as the Lucas–Lehmer test for Mersenne primes in Theorem L. [*Hint:* See the previous exercise.]

28. [*M27*] Given a prime p and a positive integer d, what is the value of $f(p,d)$, the average number of times that p divides $A^2 - dB^2$ (counting multiplicity), when A and B are random integers that are independent except for the condition $A \perp B$?

29. [*M25*] Prove that the number of positive integers $\leq n$ whose prime factors are all contained in a given set of primes $\{p_1, \ldots, p_m\}$ is at least $m^r/r!$, when $r = \lfloor \log n / \log p_m \rfloor$ and $p_1 < \cdots < p_m$.

30. [*HM35*] (J. D. Dixon and Claus-Peter Schnorr.) Let $p_1 < \cdots < p_m$ be primes that do not divide the odd number N, and let r be an even integer $\leq \log N / \log p_m$. Prove that the number of integers X in the range $0 \leq X < N$ such that $X^2 \bmod N =$

$p_1^{e_1} \ldots p_m^{e_m}$ is at least $m^r/r!$. *Hint:* Let the prime factorization of N be $q_1^{f_1} \ldots q_d^{f_d}$. Show that a sequence of exponents $(e_1, \ldots, e_m)$ leads to 2^d solutions X whenever we have $e_1 + \cdots + e_m \le r$ and $p_1^{e_1} \ldots p_m^{e_m}$ is a quadratic residue modulo q_i for $1 \le i \le d$. Such exponent sequences can be obtained as ordered pairs $(e_1', \ldots, e_m'; e_1'', \ldots, e_m'')$ where $e_1' + \cdots + e_m' \le \frac{1}{2}r$ and $e_1'' + \cdots + e_m'' \le \frac{1}{2}r$ and

$$(p_1^{e_1'} \ldots p_m^{e_m'})^{(q_i-1)/2} \equiv (p_1^{e_1''} \ldots p_m^{e_m''})^{(q_i-1)/2} \pmod{q_i} \qquad \text{for } 1 \le i \le d.$$

31. [*M20*] Use exercise 1.2.10–21 to estimate the probability that Dixon's factorization algorithm (as described preceding Theorem D) obtains fewer than $2m$ outputs.

▸ **32.** [*M21*] Show how to modify the RSA encoding scheme so that there is no problem with messages $< \sqrt[3]{N}$, in such a way that the length of messages is not substantially increased.

33. [*M50*] Prove or disprove: If a reasonably efficient algorithm exists that has a nonnegligible probability of being able to find $x \bmod N$, given a number $N = pq$ whose prime factors satisfy $p \equiv q \equiv 2 \pmod 3$ and given the value of $x^3 \bmod N$, then there is a reasonably efficient algorithm that has a nonnegligible probability of being able to find the factors of N. [If this could be proved, it would not only show that the cube root problem is as difficult as factoring, it would also show that the RSA scheme has the same fatal flaw as the SQRT scheme.]

34. [*M30*] (Peter Weinberger.) Suppose $N = pq$ in the RSA scheme, and suppose you know a number m such that $x^m \bmod N = 1$ for at least 10^{-12} of all positive integers x. Explain how you could go about factoring N without great difficulty, if m is not too large (say $m < N^{10}$).

▸ **35.** [*M25*] (H. C. Williams, 1979.) Let N be the product of two primes p and q, where $p \bmod 8 = 3$ and $q \bmod 8 = 7$. Prove that the Jacobi symbol satisfies $\left(\frac{-x}{N}\right) = \left(\frac{x}{N}\right) = -\left(\frac{2x}{N}\right)$, and use this property to design an encoding/decoding scheme analogous to Rabin's SQRT box but with no ambiguity of messages.

36. [*HM24*] The asymptotic analysis following (22) is too coarse to give meaningful values unless N is extremely large, since $\ln \ln N$ is always rather small when N is in a practical range. Carry out a more precise analysis that gives insight into the behavior of (22) for reasonable values of N; also explain how to choose a value of $\ln m$ that minimizes (22) except for a factor of size at most $\exp(O(\log \log N))$.

37. [*M27*] Prove that the square root of every positive integer D has a periodic continued fraction of the form

$$\sqrt{D} = R + /\!\!/ a_1, \ldots, a_n, 2R, a_1, \ldots, a_n, 2R, a_1, \ldots, a_n, 2R, \ldots /\!\!/,$$

unless D is a perfect square, where $R = \lfloor \sqrt{D} \rfloor$ and $(a_1, \ldots, a_n)$ is a *palindrome* (that is, $a_i = a_{n+1-i}$ for $1 \le i \le n$).

38. [*25*] (*Useless primes.*) For $0 \le d \le 9$, find P_d, the largest 50-digit prime number that has the maximum possible number of decimal digits equal to d. (First maximize the number of d's, then find the largest such prime.)

39. [*40*] Many primes p have the property that $2p + 1$ is also prime; for example, $5 \to 11 \to 23 \to 47$. More generally, say that q is a *successor* of p if p and q are both prime and $q = 2^k p + 1$ for some $k \ge 0$. For example, $2 \to 3 \to 7 \to 29 \to 59 \to 1889 \to 3779 \to 7559 \to 4058207223809 \to 32465657790473 \to 44620460305026929 71872257 \to 95\langle 30 \text{ omitted digits}\rangle 37 \to \cdots$; the smallest successor of $95 \ldots 37$ has 103 digits.

   Find the longest chain of successive primes that you can.

▶ **40.** [*M36*] (A. Shamir.) Consider an abstract computer that can perform the operations $x + y$, $x - y$, $x \cdot y$, and $\lfloor x/y \rfloor$ on integers x and y of arbitrary length, in just one unit of time, no matter how large those integers are. The machine stores integers in a random-access memory and it can select different program steps depending on whether or not $x = y$, given x and y. The purpose of this exercise is to demonstrate that there is an amazingly fast way to factorize numbers on such a computer. (Therefore it will probably be quite difficult to show that factorization is inherently complicated on *real* machines, although we suspect that it is.)

    a) Find a way to compute $n!$ in $O(\log n)$ steps on such a computer, given an integer value $n \geq 2$. [*Hint:* If A is a sufficiently large integer, the binomial coefficients $\binom{m}{k} = m!/(m-k)!\,k!$ can be computed readily from the value of $(A+1)^m$.]

    b) Show how to compute a number $f(n)$ in $O(\log n)$ steps on such a computer, given an integer value $n \geq 2$, having the following properties: $f(n) = n$ if n is prime, otherwise $f(n)$ is a proper (but not necessarily prime) divisor of n. [*Hint:* If $n \neq 4$, one such function $f(n)$ is $\gcd(m(n), n)$, where $m(n) = \min\{m \mid m! \bmod n = 0\}$.]

(As a consequence of (b), we can completely factor a given number n by doing only $O(\log n)^2$ arithmetic operations on arbitrarily large integers: Given a partial factorization $n = n_1 \ldots n_r$, each nonprime n_i can be replaced by $f(n_i) \cdot (n_i/f(n_i))$ in $\sum O(\log n_i) = O(\log n)$ steps, and this refinement can be repeated until all n_i are prime.)

▶ **41.** [*M28*] (Lagarias, Miller, and Odlyzko.) The purpose of this exercise is to show that the number of primes less than N^3 can be calculated by looking only at the primes less than N^2, and thus to evaluate $\pi(N^3)$ in $O(N^{2+\epsilon})$ steps.

Say that an "m-survivor" is a positive integer whose prime factors all exceed m; thus, an m-survivor remains in the sieve of Eratosthenes (exercise 8) after all multiples of primes $\leq m$ have been sieved out. Let $f(x, m)$ be the number of m-survivors that are $\leq x$, and let $f_k(x, m)$ be the number of such survivors that have exactly k prime factors (counting multiplicity).

    a) Prove that $\pi(N^3) = \pi(N) + f(N^3, N) - 1 - f_2(N^3, N)$.

    b) Explain how to compute $f_2(N^3, N)$ from the values of $\pi(x)$ for $x \leq N^2$. Use your method to evaluate $f_2(1000, 10)$ by hand.

    c) Same question as (b), but evaluate $f(N^3, N)$ instead of $f_2(N^3, N)$. [*Hint:* Use the identity $f(x, p_j) = f(x, p_{j-1}) - f(x/p_j, p_{j-1})$, where p_j is the jth prime and $p_0 = 1$.]

    d) Discuss data structures for the efficient evaluation of the quantities in (b) and (c).

42. [*M35*] (H. W. Lenstra, Jr.) Given $0 < r < s < N$ with $r \perp s$ and $N \perp s$, show that it is possible to find all divisors of N that are $\equiv r$ (modulo s) by performing $O(\lceil N/s^3 \rceil^{1/2} \log s)$ well-chosen arithmetic operations on $(\lg N)$-bit numbers. [*Hint:* Apply exercise 4.5.3–49.]

▶ **43.** [*M43*] Let $m = pq$ be an r-bit Blum integer as in Theorem 3.5P, and let $Q_m = \{y \mid y = x^2 \bmod m$ for some $x\}$. Then Q_m has $(p+1)(q+1)/4$ elements, and every element $y \in Q_m$ has a unique square root $x = \sqrt{y}$ such that $x \in Q_m$. Suppose $G(y)$ is an algorithm that correctly guesses $\sqrt{y} \bmod 2$ with probability $\geq \frac{1}{2} + \epsilon$, when y is a random element of Q_m. The goal of this exercise is to prove that the problem solved by G is almost as hard as the problem of factoring m.

    a) Construct an algorithm $A(G, m, \epsilon, y, \delta)$ that uses random numbers and algorithm G to guess whether a given integer y is in Q_m, without necessarily computing $\sqrt{y}$. Your algorithm should guess correctly with probability $\geq 1 - \delta$, and its running time $T(A)$ should be at most $O(\epsilon^{-2}(\log \delta^{-1})T(G))$, assuming that $T(G) \geq r^2$. (If $T(G) < r^2$, replace $T(G)$ by $(T(G) + r^2)$ in this formula.)

b) Construct an algorithm $F(G, m, \epsilon)$ that finds the factors of m with expected running time $T(F) = O(r^2(\epsilon^{-6} + \epsilon^{-4}(\log \epsilon^{-1})T(G)))$.

Hints: For fixed $y \in Q_m$, and for $0 \leq v < m$, let $\tau v = v\sqrt{y} \bmod m$ and $\lambda v = \tau v \bmod 2$. Notice that $\lambda(-v) + \lambda v = 1$ and $\lambda(v_1 + \cdots + v_n) = (\lambda v_1 + \cdots + \lambda v_n + \lfloor(\tau v_1 + \cdots + \tau v_m)/m\rfloor) \bmod 2$. Furthermore we have $\tau(\frac{1}{2}v) = \frac{1}{2}(\tau v + m\lambda v)$; here $\frac{1}{2}v$ stands for $(\frac{m+1}{2}v) \bmod m$. If $\pm v \in Q_m$ we have $\tau(\pm v) = \sqrt{v^2 y}$; therefore algorithm G gives us a way to guess λv for about half of all v.

44. [*M35*] (J. Håstad.) Show that it is not difficult to find x when $a_{i0} + a_{i1}x + a_{i2}x^2 + a_{i3}x^3 \equiv 0$ (modulo m_i), $0 < x < m_i$, $\gcd(a_{i0}, a_{i1}, a_{i2}, a_{i3}, m_i) = 1$, and $m_i > 10^{27}$ for $1 \leq i \leq 7$, if $m_i \perp m_j$ for $1 \leq i < j \leq 7$. (All variables are integers; all but x are known.) *Hint:* When L is any nonsingular matrix of real numbers, the algorithm of Lenstra, Lenstra, and Lovász [*Mathematische Annalen* **261** (1982), 515–534] efficiently finds a nonzero integer vector $v = (v_1, \ldots, v_n)$ such that $\text{length}(vL) \leq \sqrt{n2^n} |\det L|^{1/n}$.

▶ **45.** [*M41*] (J. M. Pollard and Claus-Peter Schnorr.) Find an efficient way to solve the congruence
$$x^2 - ay^2 \equiv b \pmod{n}$$
for integers x and y, given integers a, b, and n with $ab \perp n$ and n odd, even if the factorization of n is unknown. [*Hint:* Use the identity $(x_1^2 - ay_1^2)(x_2^2 - ay_2^2) = x^2 - ay^2$, where $x = x_1 x_2 - ay_1 y_2$ and $y = x_1 y_2 + x_2 y_1$.]

46. [*HM30*] (L. Adleman.) Let p be a rather large prime number and let a be a primitive root modulo p; thus, all integers b in the range $1 \leq b < p$ can be written $b = a^n \bmod p$, for some unique n with $1 \leq n < p$.

Design an algorithm that almost always finds n, given b, in $O(p^\epsilon)$ steps for all $\epsilon > 0$, using ideas similar to those of Dixon's factoring algorithm. [*Hint:* Start by building a repertoire of numbers n_i such that $a^{n_i} \bmod p$ has only small prime factors.]

47. [*M50*] A certain literary quotation $x = x_1 x_2$, represented in ASCII code, has the enciphered value $(x_1^3 \bmod N, x_2^3 \bmod N) =$

(8372e6cadf564a9ee347092daefc242058b8044228597e5f2326bbbff1583ea4200d895d9564d39229c79af8
72a72e38bb92852a22679080e269c30690fab0ec19f78e9ef8bae74b600f4ebef42a1dd5a6d806dc70b96de2
bf4a6c7d2ebb51bfd156dd8ac3cb0ae1c1c38d76a3427bcc3f12af7d4d04314c0d8377a0c79db1b1f0cd1702,
2aabcd0f9f1f9fb382313246de168bae6a28d177963a8ebe6023f1c5bd8632caee9604f63c6a6e33ceb1e1bd
4732a2973f5021e96e05e0da932b5b1d2bc618351ca584bb6e49255ba22dca55ebd6b93a9c94d8749bb53be2
90650878b17f4fe30bbb08453929a94a2efe3367e2cd92ea31a5e0d9f466870b162272e9e164e8c3238da519)

in hexadecimal notation, where N is

c97d1cbcc3b67d1ba197100df7dbd2d2864c4fef4a78e62ddd1423d972bc7a420f66046386462d260d68a8b2
3fbf12354705d874f79c22698f750c1b4435bc99174e58180bd18560a5c69c4eafb573446f79f588f624ec18
4c3e7098e65ac7b88f89e1fadcdc3558c878dde6bc7c32be57c5e7e8d95d697ad3c6c343485132dcbb74f411.

What is x?

> *The problem of distinguishing prime numbers from composites,*
> *and of resolving composite numbers into their prime factors,*
> *is one of the most important and useful in all of arithmetic.*
> *... The dignity of science seems to demand that every aid to the solution*
> *of such an elegant and celebrated problem be zealously cultivated.*
> — C. F. GAUSS, *Disquisitiones Arithmeticæ*, Article 329 (1801)

4.6. POLYNOMIAL ARITHMETIC

THE TECHNIQUES we have been studying apply in a natural way to many types of mathematical quantities, not simply to numbers. In this section we shall deal with polynomials, which are the next step up from numbers. Formally speaking, a *polynomial over* S is an expression of the form

$$u(x) = u_n x^n + \cdots + u_1 x + u_0, \tag{1}$$

where the *coefficients* u_n, $\ldots$, u_1, u_0 are elements of some algebraic system S, and the *variable* x may be regarded as a formal symbol with an indeterminate meaning. We will assume that the algebraic system S is a *commutative ring with identity*; this means that S admits the operations of addition, subtraction, and multiplication, satisfying the customary properties: Addition and multiplication are binary operations defined on S; they are associative and commutative, and multiplication distributes over addition. There is an additive identity element 0 and a multiplicative identity element 1, such that $a + 0 = a$ and $a \cdot 1 = a$ for all a in S. Subtraction is the inverse of addition, but we assume nothing about the possibility of division as an inverse to multiplication. The polynomial $0x^{n+m} + \cdots + 0x^{n+1} + u_n x^n + \cdots + u_1 x + u_0$ is regarded as the same polynomial as (1), although its expression is formally different.

We say that (1) is a polynomial of *degree n* and *leading coefficient* u_n if $u_n \neq 0$; and in this case we write

$$\deg(u) = n, \qquad \ell(u) = u_n. \tag{2}$$

By convention, we also set

$$\deg(0) = -\infty, \qquad \ell(0) = 0, \tag{3}$$

where "0" denotes the zero polynomial whose coefficients are all zero. We say that $u(x)$ is a *monic polynomial* if its leading coefficient $\ell(u)$ is 1.

Arithmetic on polynomials consists primarily of addition, subtraction, and multiplication; in some cases, further operations such as division, exponentiation, factoring, and taking the greatest common divisor are important. Addition, subtraction, and multiplication are defined in a natural way, as though the variable x were an element of S: We add or subtract polynomials by adding or subtracting the coefficients of like powers of x. Multiplication is done by the rule

$$(u_r x^r + \cdots + u_0)(v_s x^s + \cdots + v_0) = w_{r+s} x^{r+s} + \cdots + w_0,$$

where

$$w_k = u_0 v_k + u_1 v_{k-1} + \cdots + u_{k-1} v_1 + u_k v_0. \tag{4}$$

In the latter formula u_i or v_j are treated as zero if $i > r$ or $j > s$.

The algebraic system S is usually the set of integers, or the rational numbers; or it may itself be a set of polynomials (in variables other than x), in which case (1) is a *multivariate* polynomial, a polynomial in several variables. Another important case occurs when the algebraic system S consists of the integers 0, 1, $\ldots$, $m - 1$, with addition, subtraction, and multiplication performed mod m

(see Eq. 4.3.2–(11)); this is called *polynomial arithmetic modulo m.* Polynomial arithmetic modulo 2, when each of the coefficients is 0 or 1, is especially important.

The reader should note the similarity between polynomial arithmetic and multiple-precision arithmetic (Section 4.3.1), where the radix b is substituted for x. The chief difference is that the coefficient u_k of x^k in polynomial arithmetic bears no essential relation to its neighboring coefficients $u_{k\pm1}$, so the idea of "carrying" from one place to the next is absent. In fact, polynomial arithmetic modulo b is essentially identical to multiple-precision arithmetic with radix b, except that all carries are suppressed. For example, compare the multiplication of $(1101)_2$ by $(1011)_2$ in the binary number system with the analogous multiplication of $x^3 + x^2 + 1$ by $x^3 + x + 1$ modulo 2:

Binary system	Polynomials modulo 2
1101	1101
× 1011	× 1011
1101	1101
1101	1101
1101	1101
10001111	1111111

The product of these polynomials modulo 2 is obtained by suppressing all carries, and it is $x^6 + x^5 + x^4 + x^3 + x^2 + x + 1$. If we had multiplied the same polynomials over the integers, without taking residues modulo 2, the result would have been $x^6 + x^5 + x^4 + 3x^3 + x^2 + x + 1$; again carries are suppressed, but in this case the coefficients can get arbitrarily large.

In view of this strong analogy with multiple-precision arithmetic, it is unnecessary to discuss polynomial addition, subtraction, and multiplication much further in this section. However, we should point out some aspects that often make polynomial arithmetic somewhat different from multiple-precision arithmetic in practice: There is often a tendency to have a large number of zero coefficients, and polynomials of huge degrees, so special forms of representation are desirable; see Section 2.2.4. Furthermore, arithmetic on polynomials in several variables leads to routines that are best understood in a recursive framework; this situation is discussed in Chapter 8.

Although the techniques of polynomial addition, subtraction, and multiplication are comparatively straightforward, several other important aspects of polynomial arithmetic deserve special examination. The following subsections therefore discuss *division* of polynomials, with associated techniques such as finding greatest common divisors and factoring. We shall also discuss the problem of efficient *evaluation* of polynomials, namely the task of finding the value of $u(x)$ when x is a given element of S, using as few operations as possible. The special case of evaluating x^n rapidly when n is large is quite important by itself, so it is discussed in detail in Section 4.6.3.

The first major set of computer subroutines for doing polynomial arithmetic was the ALPAK system [W. S. Brown, J. P. Hyde, and B. A. Tague, *Bell System*

Tech. J. **42** (1963), 2081–2119; **43** (1964), 785–804, 1547–1562]. Another early landmark in this field was the PM system of George Collins [*CACM* **9** (1966), 578–589]; see also C. L. Hamblin, *Comp. J.* **10** (1967), 168–171.

EXERCISES

1. [*10*] If we are doing polynomial arithmetic modulo 10, what is $7x+2$ minus x^2+5? What is $6x^2 + x + 3$ times $5x^2 + 2$?

2. [*17*] True or false: (a) The product of monic polynomials is monic. (b) The product of polynomials of degrees m and n has degree $m+n$. (c) The sum of polynomials of degrees m and n has degree $\max(m, n)$.

3. [*M20*] If each of the coefficients $u_r, \ldots, u_0, v_s, \ldots, v_0$ in (4) is an integer satisfying the conditions $|u_i| \le m_1, |v_j| \le m_2$, what is the maximum absolute value of the product coefficients w_k?

▸ **4.** [*21*] Can the multiplication of polynomials modulo 2 be facilitated by using the ordinary arithmetic operations on a binary computer, if coefficients are packed into computer words?

▸ **5.** [*M21*] Show how to multiply two polynomials of degree $\le n$, modulo 2, with an execution time proportional to $O(n^{\lg 3})$ when n is large, by adapting Karatsuba's method (see Section 4.3.3).

4.6.1. Division of Polynomials

It is possible to divide one polynomial by another in essentially the same way that we divide one multiple-precision integer by another, when arithmetic is being done on polynomials over a *field*. A field S is a commutative ring with identity, in which exact division is possible as well as the operations of addition, subtraction, and multiplication; this means as usual that whenever u and v are elements of S, and $v \ne 0$, there is an element w in S such that $u = vw$. The most important fields of coefficients that arise in applications are

a) the rational numbers (represented as fractions, see Section 4.5.1);
b) the real or complex numbers (represented within a computer by means of floating point approximations; see Section 4.2);
c) the integers modulo p where p is prime (where division can be implemented as suggested in exercise 4.5.2–16);
d) *rational functions* over a field, that is, quotients of two polynomials whose coefficients are in that field, the denominator being monic.

Of special importance is the field of integers modulo 2, whose only elements are 0 and 1. Polynomials over this field (namely polynomials modulo 2) have many analogies to integers expressed in binary notation; and rational functions over this field have striking analogies to rational numbers whose numerator and denominator are represented in binary notation.

Given two polynomials $u(x)$ and $v(x)$ over a field, with $v(x) \ne 0$, we can divide $u(x)$ by $v(x)$ to obtain a quotient polynomial $q(x)$ and a remainder polynomial $r(x)$ satisfying the conditions

$$u(x) = q(x) \cdot v(x) + r(x), \qquad \deg(r) < \deg(v). \tag{1}$$

It is easy to see that there is at most one pair of polynomials $(q(x), r(x))$ satisfying these relations; for if $(q_1(x), r_1(x))$ and $(q_2(x), r_2(x))$ both satisfy (1) with respect to the same polynomials $u(x)$ and $v(x)$, then $q_1(x)v(x) + r_1(x) = q_2(x)v(x) + r_2(x)$, so $(q_1(x) - q_2(x))v(x) = r_2(x) - r_1(x)$. Now if $q_1(x) - q_2(x)$ is nonzero, we have $\deg((q_1 - q_2) \cdot v) = \deg(q_1 - q_2) + \deg(v) \geq \deg(v) > \deg(r_2 - r_1)$, a contradiction. Hence $q_1(x) - q_2(x) = 0$ and $r_1(x) = r_2(x)$.

The following algorithm, which is essentially the same as Algorithm 4.3.1D for multiple-precision division but without any concerns of carries, may be used to determine $q(x)$ and $r(x)$:

Algorithm D (*Division of polynomials over a field*). Given polynomials

$$u(x) = u_m x^m + \cdots + u_1 x + u_0, \qquad v(x) = v_n x^n + \cdots + v_1 x + v_0$$

over a field S, where $v_n \neq 0$ and $m \geq n \geq 0$, this algorithm finds the polynomials

$$q(x) = q_{m-n} x^{m-n} + \cdots + q_0, \qquad r(x) = r_{n-1} x^{n-1} + \cdots + r_0$$

over S that satisfy (1).

D1. [Iterate on k.] Do step D2 for $k = m - n$, $m - n - 1$, ..., 0; then terminate the algorithm with $(r_{n-1}, \ldots, r_0) = (u_{n-1}, \ldots, u_0)$.

D2. [Division loop.] Set $q_k \leftarrow u_{n+k}/v_n$, and then set $u_j \leftarrow u_j - q_k v_{j-k}$ for $j = n + k - 1$, $n + k - 2$, ..., k. (The latter operation amounts to replacing $u(x)$ by $u(x) - q_k x^k v(x)$, a polynomial of degree $< n + k$.) ∎

An example of Algorithm D appears below in (5). The number of arithmetic operations is essentially proportional to $n(m - n + 1)$. Note that explicit division of coefficients is done only at the beginning of step D2, and the divisor is always v_n; thus if $v(x)$ is a monic polynomial (with $v_n = 1$), there is no actual division at all. If multiplication is easier to perform than division it will be preferable to compute $1/v_n$ at the beginning of the algorithm and to multiply by this quantity in step D2.

We shall often write $u(x) \bmod v(x)$ for the remainder $r(x)$ in (1).

Unique factorization domains. If we restrict consideration to polynomials over a field, we are not coming to grips with many important cases, such as polynomials over the integers or polynomials in several variables. Let us therefore now consider the more general situation that the algebraic system S of coefficients is a *unique factorization domain*, not necessarily a field. This means that S is a commutative ring with identity, and that

i) $uv \neq 0$, whenever u and v are nonzero elements of S;
ii) every nonzero element u of S is either a *unit* or has a "unique" representation as a product of *primes* p_1, ..., p_t:

$$u = p_1 \ldots p_t, \qquad t \geq 1. \tag{2}$$

A *unit* is an element that has a reciprocal, namely an element u such that $uv = 1$ for some v in S; and a *prime* is a nonunit element p such that the equation $p = qr$

can be true only if either q or r is a unit. The representation (2) is to be unique in the sense that if $p_1 \ldots p_t = q_1 \ldots q_s$, where all the p's and q's are primes, then $s = t$ and there is a permutation $\pi_1 \ldots \pi_t$ of $\{1, \ldots, t\}$ such that $p_1 = a_1 q_{\pi_1}, \ldots,$ $p_t = a_t q_{\pi_t}$ for some units $a_1, \ldots, a_t$. In other words, factorization into primes is unique, except for unit multiples and except for the order of the factors.

Any field is a unique factorization domain, in which each nonzero element is a unit and there are no primes. The integers form a unique factorization domain in which the units are $+1$ and -1, and the primes are $\pm 2, \pm 3, \pm 5, \pm 7, \pm 11$, etc. The case that S is the set of all integers is of principal importance, because it is often preferable to work with integer coefficients instead of arbitrary rational coefficients.

One of the key facts about polynomials (see exercise 10) is that *the polynomials over a unique factorization domain form a unique factorization domain.* A polynomial that is prime in this domain is usually called an *irreducible polynomial.* By using the unique factorization theorem repeatedly, we can prove that multivariate polynomials over the integers, or over any field, in any number of variables, can be uniquely factored into irreducible polynomials. For example, the multivariate polynomial $90x^3 - 120x^2y + 18x^2yz - 24xy^2z$ over the integers is the product of five irreducible polynomials $2 \cdot 3 \cdot x \cdot (3x - 4y) \cdot (5x + yz)$. The same polynomial, as a polynomial over the rationals, is the product of three irreducible polynomials $(6x) \cdot (3x - 4y) \cdot (5x + yz)$; this factorization can also be written $x \cdot (90x - 120y) \cdot (x + \frac{1}{5}yz)$ and in infinitely many other ways, although the factorization is essentially unique.

As usual, we say that $u(x)$ is a *multiple* of $v(x)$, and that $v(x)$ is a *divisor* of $u(x)$, if $u(x) = v(x)q(x)$ for some polynomial $q(x)$. If we have an algorithm to tell whether or not u is a multiple of v for arbitrary nonzero elements u and v of a unique factorization domain S, and to determine w if $u = v \cdot w$, then Algorithm D gives us a method to tell whether or not $u(x)$ is a multiple of $v(x)$ for arbitrary nonzero polynomials $u(x)$ and $v(x)$ over S. For if $u(x)$ is a multiple of $v(x)$, it is easy to see that u_{n+k} must be a multiple of v_n each time we get to step D2, hence the quotient $u(x)/v(x)$ will be found. Applying this observation recursively, we obtain an algorithm that decides if a given polynomial over S, in any number of variables, is a multiple of another given polynomial over S, and the algorithm will find the quotient when it exists.

A set of elements of a unique factorization domain is said to be *relatively prime* if no prime of that unique factorization domain divides all of them. A polynomial over a unique factorization domain is called *primitive* if its coefficients are relatively prime. (This concept should not be confused with the quite different idea of "primitive polynomials modulo p" discussed in Section 3.2.2.) The following fact, introduced for the case of polynomials over the integers by C. F. Gauss in article 42 of his celebrated book *Disquisitiones Arithmeticæ* (Leipzig: 1801), is of prime importance:

Lemma G (Gauss's Lemma). *The product of primitive polynomials over a unique factorization domain is primitive.*

Proof. Let $u(x) = u_m x^m + \cdots + u_0$ and $v(x) = v_n x^n + \cdots + v_0$ be primitive polynomials. If p is any prime of the domain, we must show that p does not divide all the coefficients of $u(x)v(x)$. By assumption, there is an index j such that u_j is not divisible by p, and an index k such that v_k is not divisible by p. Let j and k be as small as possible; then the coefficient of x^{j+k} in $u(x)v(x)$ is

$$u_j v_k + u_{j+1} v_{k-1} + \cdots + u_{j+k} v_0 + u_{j-1} v_{k+1} + \cdots + u_0 v_{k+j},$$

and it is easy to see that this is not a multiple of p (since its first term isn't, but all of its other terms are). ∎

If a nonzero polynomial $u(x)$ over a unique factorization domain S is not primitive, we can write $u(x) = p_1 \cdot u_1(x)$, where p_1 is a prime of S dividing all the coefficients of $u(x)$, and where $u_1(x)$ is another nonzero polynomial over S. All of the coefficients of $u_1(x)$ have one less prime factor than the corresponding coefficients of $u(x)$. Now if $u_1(x)$ is not primitive, we can write $u_1(x) = p_2 \cdot u_2(x)$, etc.; this process must ultimately terminate in a representation $u(x) = c \cdot u_k(x)$, where c is an element of S and $u_k(x)$ is primitive. In fact, we have the following companion to Lemma G:

Lemma H. *Any nonzero polynomial $u(x)$ over a unique factorization domain S can be factored in the form $u(x) = c \cdot v(x)$, where c is in S and $v(x)$ is primitive. Furthermore, this representation is unique, in the sense that if $u = c_1 \cdot v_1(x) = c_2 \cdot v_2(x)$, then $c_1 = a c_2$ and $v_2(x) = a v_1(x)$ where a is a unit of S.*

Proof. We have shown that such a representation exists, so only the uniqueness needs to be proved. Assume that $c_1 \cdot v_1(x) = c_2 \cdot v_2(x)$, where $v_1(x)$ and $v_2(x)$ are primitive. Let p be any prime of S. If p^k divides c_1, then p^k also divides c_2; otherwise p^k would divide all the coefficients of $c_2 \cdot v_2(x)$, so p would divide all the coefficients of $v_2(x)$, a contradiction. Similarly, p^k divides c_2 only if p^k divides c_1. Hence, by unique factorization, $c_1 = a c_2$ where a is a unit; and $0 = a c_2 \cdot v_1(x) - c_2 \cdot v_2(x) = c_2 \cdot \big(a v_1(x) - v_2(x)\big)$, so $a v_1(x) - v_2(x) = 0$. ∎

Therefore we may write any nonzero polynomial $u(x)$ as

$$u(x) = \text{cont}(u) \cdot \text{pp}\big(u(x)\big), \tag{3}$$

where $\text{cont}(u)$, the *content* of u, is an element of S, and $\text{pp}\big(u(x)\big)$, the *primitive part* of $u(x)$, is a primitive polynomial over S. When $u(x) = 0$, it is convenient to define $\text{cont}(u) = \text{pp}\big(u(x)\big) = 0$. Combining Lemmas G and H gives us the relations

$$\text{cont}(u \cdot v) = a \, \text{cont}(u) \, \text{cont}(v),$$
$$\text{pp}\big(u(x) \cdot v(x)\big) = b \, \text{pp}\big(u(x)\big) \, \text{pp}\big(v(x)\big), \tag{4}$$

where a and b are units, depending on the way contents are calculated, with $ab = 1$. When we are working with polynomials over the integers, the only units are $+1$ and -1, and it is conventional to define $\text{pp}\big(u(x)\big)$ so that its leading coefficient is positive; then (4) is true with $a = b = 1$. When working with polynomials over a field we may take $\text{cont}(u) = \ell(u)$, so that $\text{pp}\big(u(x)\big)$ is monic; in this case again (4) holds with $a = b = 1$, for all $u(x)$ and $v(x)$.

For example, if we are dealing with polynomials over the integers, let $u(x) = -26x^2 + 39$ and $v(x) = 21x + 14$. Then

$$\text{cont}(u) = -13, \qquad \text{pp}\big(u(x)\big) = 2x^2 - 3,$$
$$\text{cont}(v) = +7, \qquad \text{pp}\big(v(x)\big) = 3x + 2,$$
$$\text{cont}(u \cdot v) = -91, \qquad \text{pp}\big(u(x) \cdot v(x)\big) = 6x^3 + 4x^2 - 9x - 6.$$

Greatest common divisors. When there is unique factorization, it makes sense to speak of a *greatest common divisor* of two elements; this is a common divisor that is divisible by as many primes as possible. (See Eq. 4.5.2–(6).) Since a unique factorization domain may have many units, however, there is ambiguity in this definition of greatest common divisor; if w is a greatest common divisor of u and v, so is $a \cdot w$, when a is any unit. Conversely, the assumption of unique factorization implies that if w_1 and w_2 are both greatest common divisors of u and v, then $w_1 = a \cdot w_2$ for some unit a. In other words it does not make sense, in general, to speak of "the" greatest common divisor of u and v; there is a set of greatest common divisors, each one being a unit multiple of the others.

Let us now consider the problem of finding a greatest common divisor of two given polynomials over an algebraic system S, a question originally raised by the Portuguese mathematician Pedro Nuñez in his *Libro de Algebra* (Antwerp: 1567). If S is a field, the problem is relatively simple; our division algorithm, Algorithm D, can be extended to an algorithm that computes greatest common divisors, just as Euclid's algorithm (Algorithm 4.5.2A) yields the greatest common divisor of two given integers based on a division algorithm for integers:

If $v(x) = 0$, then $\gcd\big(u(x), v(x)\big) = u(x)$;
otherwise $\gcd\big(u(x), v(x)\big) = \gcd\big(v(x), r(x)\big)$,

where $r(x)$ is given by (1). This procedure is called Euclid's algorithm for polynomials over a field. It was first used by the Flemish mathematician Simon Stevin in *L'Arithmetique* (Leiden: 1585); see A. Girard, *Les Œuvres Mathématiques de Simon Stevin* **1** (Leiden: 1634), 56.

For example, let us determine the gcd of $x^8 + x^6 + 10x^4 + 10x^3 + 8x^2 + 2x + 8$ and $3x^6 + 5x^4 + 9x^2 + 4x + 8$, mod 13, by using Euclid's algorithm for polynomials over the integers modulo 13. First, writing only the coefficients to show the steps of Algorithm D, we have

$$
\begin{array}{r}
9\ \ 0\ \ 7 \\
3\ 0\ 5\ 0\ 9\ 4\ 8\ \overline{\big)\ 1\ 0\ 1\ 0\ 10\ 10\ \ 8\ 2\ 8} \\
\underline{1\ 0\ 6\ 0\ \ 3\ 10\ \ 7} \\
0\ 8\ 0\ \ 7\ \ 0\ \ 1\ 2\ 8 \\
\underline{8\ 0\ \ 9\ \ 0\ 11\ 2\ 4} \\
0\ 11\ \ 0\ \ 3\ 0\ 4
\end{array}
\qquad (5)
$$

so that $x^8 + x^6 + 10x^4 + 10x^3 + 8x^2 + 2x + 8$ equals

$$(9x^2 + 7)(3x^6 + 5x^4 + 9x^2 + 4x + 8) + (11x^4 + 3x^2 + 4).$$

Similarly,

$$3x^6 + 5x^4 + 9x^2 + 4x + 8 = (5x^2 + 5)(11x^4 + 3x^2 + 4) + (4x + 1);$$
$$11x^4 + 3x^2 + 4 = (6x^3 + 5x^2 + 6x + 5)(4x + 1) + 12;$$
$$4x + 1 = (9x + 12) \cdot 12 + 0. \tag{6}$$

(The equality sign here means congruence modulo 13, since all arithmetic on the coefficients has been done mod 13.) This computation shows that 12 is a greatest common divisor of the two original polynomials. Now any nonzero element of a field is a unit of the domain of polynomials over that field, so it is conventional in the case of fields to divide the result of the algorithm by its leading coefficient, producing a *monic* polynomial that is called *the* greatest common divisor of the two given polynomials. The gcd computed in (6) is accordingly taken to be 1, not 12. The last step in (6) could have been omitted, for if $\deg(v) = 0$, then $\gcd(u(x), v(x)) = 1$, no matter what polynomial is chosen for $u(x)$. Exercise 4 determines the average running time for Euclid's algorithm on random polynomials modulo p.

Let us now turn to the more general situation in which our polynomials are given over a unique factorization domain that is not a field. From Eqs. (4) we can deduce the important relations

$$\operatorname{cont}(\gcd(u, v)) = a \cdot \gcd(\operatorname{cont}(u), \operatorname{cont}(v)),$$
$$\operatorname{pp}(\gcd(u(x), v(x))) = b \cdot \gcd(\operatorname{pp}(u(x)), \operatorname{pp}(v(x))), \tag{7}$$

where a and b are units. Here $\gcd(u(x), v(x))$ denotes any particular polynomial in x that is a greatest common divisor of $u(x)$ and $v(x)$. Equations (7) reduce the problem of finding greatest common divisors of arbitrary polynomials to the problem of finding greatest common divisors of *primitive* polynomials.

Algorithm D for division of polynomials over a field can be generalized to a *pseudo-division* of polynomials over any algebraic system that is a commutative ring with identity. We can observe that Algorithm D requires explicit division only by $\ell(v)$, the leading coefficient of $v(x)$, and that step D2 is carried out exactly $m - n + 1$ times; thus if $u(x)$ and $v(x)$ start with integer coefficients, and if we are working over the rational numbers, then the only denominators that appear in the coefficients of $q(x)$ and $r(x)$ are divisors of $\ell(v)^{m-n+1}$. This suggests that we can always find polynomials $q(x)$ and $r(x)$ such that

$$\ell(v)^{m-n+1} u(x) = q(x)v(x) + r(x), \qquad \deg(r) < n, \tag{8}$$

where $m = \deg(u)$ and $n = \deg(v)$, for any polynomials $u(x)$ and $v(x) \neq 0$, provided that $m \geq n$.

Algorithm R (*Pseudo-division of polynomials*). Given polynomials

$$u(x) = u_m x^m + \cdots + u_1 x + u_0, \qquad v(x) = v_n x^n + \cdots + v_1 x + v_0,$$

where $v_n \neq 0$ and $m \geq n \geq 0$, this algorithm finds polynomials $q(x) = q_{m-n}x^{m-n} + \cdots + q_0$ and $r(x) = r_{n-1}x^{n-1} + \cdots + r_0$ satisfying (8).

R1. [Iterate on k.] Do step R2 for $k = m - n,\ m - n - 1,\ \ldots,\ 0$; then terminate the algorithm with $(r_{n-1}, \ldots, r_0) = (u_{n-1}, \ldots, u_0)$.

R2. [Multiplication loop.] Set $q_k \leftarrow u_{n+k}v_n^k$, and set $u_j \leftarrow v_n u_j - u_{n+k}v_{j-k}$ for $j = n + k - 1,\ n + k - 2,\ \ldots,\ 0$. (When $j < k$ this means that $u_j \leftarrow v_n u_j$, since we treat $v_{-1}, v_{-2}, \ldots$ as zero. These multiplications could have been avoided if we had started the algorithm by replacing u_t by $v_n^{m-n-t}u_t$, for $0 \le t < m - n$.) ▌

An example calculation appears below in (10). It is easy to prove the validity of Algorithm R by induction on $m - n$, since each execution of step R2 essentially replaces $u(x)$ by $\ell(v)u(x) - \ell(u)x^k v(x)$, where $k = \deg(u) - \deg(v)$. Notice that no division whatever is used in this algorithm; the coefficients of $q(x)$ and $r(x)$ are themselves certain polynomial functions of the coefficients of $u(x)$ and $v(x)$. If $v_n = 1$, the algorithm is identical to Algorithm D. If $u(x)$ and $v(x)$ are polynomials over a unique factorization domain, we can prove as before that the polynomials $q(x)$ and $r(x)$ are unique; therefore another way to do the pseudo-division over a unique factorization domain is to multiply $u(x)$ by v_n^{m-n+1} and apply Algorithm D, knowing that all the quotients in step D2 will exist.

Algorithm R can be extended to a "generalized Euclidean algorithm" for primitive polynomials over a unique factorization domain, in the following way: Let $u(x)$ and $v(x)$ be primitive polynomials with $\deg(u) \ge \deg(v)$, and determine the polynomial $r(x)$ satisfying (8) by means of Algorithm R. Now we can prove that $\gcd\big(u(x), v(x)\big) = \gcd\big(v(x), r(x)\big)$: Any common divisor of $u(x)$ and $v(x)$ divides $v(x)$ and $r(x)$; conversely, any common divisor of $v(x)$ and $r(x)$ divides $\ell(v)^{m-n+1}u(x)$, and it must be primitive $\big($since $v(x)$ is primitive$\big)$ so it divides $u(x)$. If $r(x) = 0$, we therefore have $\gcd\big(u(x), v(x)\big) = v(x)$; on the other hand if $r(x) \ne 0$, we have $\gcd\big(v(x), r(x)\big) = \gcd\big(v(x), \mathrm{pp}\big(r(x)\big)\big)$ since $v(x)$ is primitive, so the process can be iterated.

Algorithm E (*Generalized Euclidean algorithm*). Given nonzero polynomials $u(x)$ and $v(x)$ over a unique factorization domain S, this algorithm calculates a greatest common divisor of $u(x)$ and $v(x)$. We assume that auxiliary algorithms exist to calculate greatest common divisors of elements of S, and to divide a by b in S when $b \ne 0$ and a is a multiple of b.

E1. [Reduce to primitive.] Set $d \leftarrow \gcd\big(\mathrm{cont}(u), \mathrm{cont}(v)\big)$, using the assumed algorithm for calculating greatest common divisors in S. $\big($By definition, $\mathrm{cont}(u)$ is a greatest common divisor of the coefficients of $u(x)$.$\big)$ Replace $u(x)$ by the polynomial $u(x)/\mathrm{cont}(u) = \mathrm{pp}\big(u(x)\big)$; similarly, replace $v(x)$ by $\mathrm{pp}\big(v(x)\big)$.

E2. [Pseudo-division.] Calculate $r(x)$ using Algorithm R. $\big($It is unnecessary to calculate the quotient polynomial $q(x)$.$\big)$ If $r(x) = 0$, go to E4. If $\deg(r) = 0$, replace $v(x)$ by the constant polynomial "1" and go to E4.

E3. [Make remainder primitive.] Replace $u(x)$ by $v(x)$ and replace $v(x)$ by $\mathrm{pp}\big(r(x)\big)$. Go back to step E2. (This is the "Euclidean step," analogous to the other instances of Euclid's algorithm that we have seen.)

E4. [Attach the content.] The algorithm terminates, with $d \cdot v(x)$ as the desired answer. ∎

As an example of Algorithm E, let us calculate the gcd of the polynomials

$$u(x) = x^8 + x^6 - 3x^4 - 3x^3 + 8x^2 + 2x - 5,$$
$$v(x) = 3x^6 + 5x^4 - 4x^2 - 9x + 21, \tag{9}$$

over the integers. These polynomials are primitive, so step E1 sets $d \leftarrow 1$. In step E2 we have the pseudo-division

```
                                          1    0    −6
3 0 5 0 −4 −9 21  )  1 0    1 0  −3 −3   8   2    −5
                     3 0    3 0  −9 −9  24   6   −15
                     3 0    5 0  −4 −9  21

                      0  −2 0   −5    0   3   6   −15
                      0  −6 0  −15    0   9  18   −45       (10)
                      0    0 0    0    0   0   0     0

                          −6 0  −15    0   9  18   −45
                         −18 0  −45    0  27  54  −135
                         −18 0  −30    0  24  54  −126

                          −15    0   3   0    −9
```

Here the quotient $q(x)$ is $1 \cdot 3^2 x^2 + 0 \cdot 3^1 x + -6 \cdot 3^0$; we have

$$27u(x) = v(x)(9x^2 - 6) + (-15x^4 + 3x^2 - 9). \tag{11}$$

Now step E3 replaces $u(x)$ by $v(x)$ and $v(x)$ by $\mathrm{pp}\big(r(x)\big) = 5x^4 - x^2 + 3$. The subsequent calculation is summarized in the following table, where only the coefficients are shown:

$u(x)$	$v(x)$	$r(x)$
$1, 0, 1, 0, -3, -3, 8, 2, -5$	$3, 0, 5, 0, -4, -9, 21$	$-15, 0, 3, 0, -9$
$3, 0, 5, 0, -4, -9, 21$	$5, 0, -1, 0, 3$	$-585, -1125, 2205$
$5, 0, -1, 0, 3$	$13, 25, -49$	$-233150, 307500$
$13, 25, -49$	$4663, -6150$	143193869 (12)

It is instructive to compare this calculation with the computation of the same greatest common divisor over the *rational* numbers, instead of over the integers, by using Euclid's algorithm for polynomials over a field as described earlier in this section. The following surprisingly complicated sequence appears:

$u(x)$	$v(x)$
$1, 0, 1, 0, -3, -3, 8, 2, -5$	$3, 0, 5, 0, -4, -9, 21$
$3, 0, 5, 0, -4, -9, 21$	$-\frac{5}{9}, 0, \frac{1}{9}, 0, -\frac{1}{3}$
$-\frac{5}{9}, 0, \frac{1}{9}, 0, -\frac{1}{3}$	$-\frac{117}{25}, -9, \frac{441}{25}$
$-\frac{117}{25}, -9, \frac{441}{25}$	$\frac{233150}{19773}, -\frac{102500}{6591}$
$\frac{233150}{19773}, -\frac{102500}{6591}$	$-\frac{1288744821}{543589225}$ (13)

To improve that algorithm, we can reduce $u(x)$ and $v(x)$ to monic polynomials at each step, since this removes unit factors that make the coefficients more complicated than necessary; this is actually Algorithm E over the rationals:

$$
\begin{array}{cc}
u(x) & v(x) \\
1, 0, 1, 0, -3, -3, 8, 2, -5 & 1, 0, \frac{5}{3}, 0, -\frac{4}{3}, -3, 7 \\
1, 0, \frac{5}{3}, 0, -\frac{4}{3}, -3, 7 & 1, 0, -\frac{1}{5}, 0, \frac{3}{5} \\
1, 0, -\frac{1}{5}, 0, \frac{3}{5} & 1, \frac{25}{13}, -\frac{49}{13} \\
1, \frac{25}{13}, -\frac{49}{13} & 1, -\frac{6150}{4663} \\
1, -\frac{6150}{4663} & 1
\end{array}
\qquad (14)
$$

In both (13) and (14) the sequence of polynomials is essentially the same as (12), which was obtained by Algorithm E over the integers; the only difference is that the polynomials have been multiplied by certain rational numbers. Whether we have $5x^4 - x^2 + 3$ or $-\frac{5}{9}x^4 + \frac{1}{9}x^2 - \frac{1}{3}$ or $x^4 - \frac{1}{5}x^2 + \frac{3}{5}$, the computations are essentially the same. But either algorithm using rational arithmetic tends to run slower than the all-integer Algorithm E, since rational arithmetic usually requires more evaluations of integer gcds within each step when the polynomials have large degree.

It is instructive to compare (12), (13), and (14) with (6) above, where we determined the gcd of the same polynomials $u(x)$ and $v(x)$ modulo 13 with considerably less labor. Since $\ell(u)$ and $\ell(v)$ are not multiples of 13, the fact that $\gcd\bigl(u(x), v(x)\bigr) = 1$ modulo 13 is sufficient to prove that $u(x)$ and $v(x)$ are relatively prime over the integers (and therefore over the rational numbers). We will return to this time-saving observation at the close of Section 4.6.2.

The subresultant algorithm. An ingenious algorithm that is generally superior to Algorithm E, and that gives us further information about Algorithm E's behavior, was discovered by George E. Collins [*JACM* **14** (1967), 128–142] and subsequently improved by W. S. Brown and J. F. Traub [*JACM* **18** (1971), 505–514; see also W. S. Brown, *ACM Trans. Math. Software* **4** (1978), 237–249]. This algorithm avoids the calculation of primitive parts in step E3, dividing instead by an element of S that is known to be a factor of $r(x)$:

Algorithm C (*Greatest common divisor over a unique factorization domain*). This algorithm has the same input and output assumptions as Algorithm E, and has the advantage that fewer calculations of greatest common divisors of coefficients are needed.

C1. [Reduce to primitive.] As in step E1 of Algorithm E, set $d \leftarrow \gcd\bigl(\mathrm{cont}(u), \mathrm{cont}(v)\bigr)$, and replace $\bigl(u(x), v(x)\bigr)$ by $\bigl(\mathrm{pp}(u(x)), \mathrm{pp}(v(x))\bigr)$. Set $g \leftarrow h \leftarrow 1$.

C2. [Pseudo-division.] Set $\delta \leftarrow \deg(u) - \deg(v)$. Calculate $r(x)$ using Algorithm R. If $r(x) = 0$, go to C4. If $\deg(r) = 0$, replace $v(x)$ by the constant polynomial "1" and go to C4.

C3. [Adjust remainder.] Replace the polynomial $u(x)$ by $v(x)$, and replace $v(x)$ by $r(x)/gh^\delta$. (At this point all coefficients of $r(x)$ are multiples of gh^δ.)

Then set $g \leftarrow \ell(u)$, $h \leftarrow h^{1-\delta}g^\delta$ and return to C2. (The new value of h will be in the domain S, even if $\delta > 1$.)

C4. [Attach the content.] Return $d \cdot \mathrm{pp}(v(x))$ as the answer. ▮

If we apply this algorithm to the polynomials (9) considered earlier, the following sequence of results is obtained at the beginning of step C2:

$u(x)$	$v(x)$	g	h	
$1, 0, 1, 0, -3, -3, 8, 2, -5$	$3, 0, 5, 0, -4, -9, 21$	1	1	
$3, 0, 5, 0, -4, -9, 21$	$-15, 0, 3, 0, -9$	3	9	
$-15, 0, 3, 0, -9$	$65, 125, -245$	-15	25	
$65, 125, -245$	$-9326, 12300$	65	169	(15)

At the conclusion of the algorithm, $r(x)/gh^\delta = 260708$.

The sequence of polynomials consists of integral multiples of the polynomials in the sequence produced by Algorithm E. In spite of the fact that the polynomials are not reduced to primitive form, the coefficients are kept to a reasonable size because of the reduction factor in step C3.

In order to analyze Algorithm C and to prove that it is valid, let us call the sequence of polynomials it produces $u_1(x)$, $u_2(x)$, $u_3(x)$, $\ldots$, where $u_1(x) = u(x)$ and $u_2(x) = v(x)$. Let $\delta_j = n_j - n_{j+1}$ for $j \geq 1$, where $n_j = \deg(u_j)$; and let $g_1 = h_1 = 1$, $g_j = \ell(u_j)$, $h_j = h_{j-1}^{1-\delta_{j-1}}g_j^{\delta_{j-1}}$ for $j \geq 2$. Then we have

$$g_2^{\delta_1+1}u_1(x) = u_2(x)q_1(x) + g_1h_1^{\delta_1}u_3(x), \qquad n_3 < n_2;$$
$$g_3^{\delta_2+1}u_2(x) = u_3(x)q_2(x) + g_2h_2^{\delta_2}u_4(x), \qquad n_4 < n_3; \qquad (16)$$
$$g_4^{\delta_3+1}u_3(x) = u_4(x)q_3(x) + g_3h_3^{\delta_3}u_5(x), \qquad n_5 < n_4;$$

and so on. The process terminates when $n_{k+1} = \deg(u_{k+1}) \leq 0$. We must show that $u_3(x)$, $u_4(x)$, $\ldots$, have coefficients in S, namely that the factors $g_j h_j^{\delta_j}$ exactly divide all coefficients of the remainders, and we must also show that the h_j values all belong to S. The proof is rather involved, and it can be most easily understood by considering an example.

Suppose, as in (15), that $n_1 = 8$, $n_2 = 6$, $n_3 = 4$, $n_4 = 2$, $n_5 = 1$, $n_6 = 0$, so that $\delta_1 = \delta_2 = \delta_3 = 2$, $\delta_4 = \delta_5 = 1$. Let us write $u_1(x) = a_8x^8 + a_7x^7 + \cdots + a_0$, $u_2(x) = b_6x^6 + b_5x^5 + \cdots + b_0$, $\ldots$, $u_5(x) = e_1x + e_0$, $u_6(x) = f_0$, so that $h_1 = 1$, $h_2 = b_6^2$, $h_3 = c_4^2/b_6^2$, $h_4 = d_2^2b_6^2/c_4^2$. In these terms it is helpful to consider the array shown in Table 1. For concreteness, let us assume that the coefficients of the polynomials are integers. We have $b_6^3u_1(x) = u_2(x)q_1(x) + u_3(x)$; so if we multiply row A_5 by b_6^3 and subtract appropriate multiples of rows B_7, B_6, and B_5 (corresponding to the coefficients of $q_1(x)$) we will get row C_5. If we also multiply row A_4 by b_6^3 and subtract multiples of rows B_6, B_5, and B_4, we get row C_4. In a similar way, we have $c_4^3u_2(x) = u_3(x)q_2(x) + b_6^5u_4(x)$; so we can multiply row B_3 by c_4^3, subtract integer multiples of rows C_5, C_4, and C_3, then divide by b_6^5 to obtain row D_3.

In order to prove that $u_4(x)$ has integer coefficients, let us consider the matrix

$$
\begin{matrix}
A_2 \\
A_1 \\
A_0 \\
B_4 \\
B_3 \\
B_2 \\
B_1 \\
B_0
\end{matrix}
\begin{pmatrix}
a_8 & a_7 & a_6 & a_5 & a_4 & a_3 & a_2 & a_1 & a_0 & 0 & 0 \\
0 & a_8 & a_7 & a_6 & a_5 & a_4 & a_3 & a_2 & a_1 & a_0 & 0 \\
0 & 0 & a_8 & a_7 & a_6 & a_5 & a_4 & a_3 & a_2 & a_1 & a_0 \\
b_6 & b_5 & b_4 & b_3 & b_2 & b_1 & b_0 & 0 & 0 & 0 & 0 \\
0 & b_6 & b_5 & b_4 & b_3 & b_2 & b_1 & b_0 & 0 & 0 & 0 \\
0 & 0 & b_6 & b_5 & b_4 & b_3 & b_2 & b_1 & b_0 & 0 & 0 \\
0 & 0 & 0 & b_6 & b_5 & b_4 & b_3 & b_2 & b_1 & b_0 & 0 \\
0 & 0 & 0 & 0 & b_6 & b_5 & b_4 & b_3 & b_2 & b_1 & b_0
\end{pmatrix} = M. \qquad (17)
$$

The indicated row operations and a permutation of rows will transform M into

$$
\begin{matrix}
B_4 \\
B_3 \\
B_2 \\
B_1 \\
C_2 \\
C_1 \\
C_0 \\
D_0
\end{matrix}
\begin{pmatrix}
b_6 & b_5 & b_4 & b_3 & b_2 & b_1 & b_0 & 0 & 0 & 0 & 0 \\
0 & b_6 & b_5 & b_4 & b_3 & b_2 & b_1 & b_0 & 0 & 0 & 0 \\
0 & 0 & b_6 & b_5 & b_4 & b_3 & b_2 & b_1 & b_0 & 0 & 0 \\
0 & 0 & 0 & b_6 & b_5 & b_4 & b_3 & b_2 & b_1 & b_0 & 0 \\
0 & 0 & 0 & 0 & c_4 & c_3 & c_2 & c_1 & c_0 & 0 & 0 \\
0 & 0 & 0 & 0 & 0 & c_4 & c_3 & c_2 & c_1 & c_0 & 0 \\
0 & 0 & 0 & 0 & 0 & 0 & c_4 & c_3 & c_2 & c_1 & c_0 \\
0 & 0 & 0 & 0 & 0 & 0 & 0 & 0 & d_2 & d_1 & d_0
\end{pmatrix} = M'. \qquad (18)
$$

Because of the way M' has been derived from M, we must have

$$
b_6^3 \cdot b_6^3 \cdot b_6^3 \cdot (c_4^3/b_6^5) \cdot \det M_0 = \pm \det M_0',
$$

if M_0 and M_0' represent any square matrices obtained by selecting eight corresponding columns from M and M'. For example, let us select the first seven columns and the column containing d_1; then

$$
b_6^3 \cdot b_6^3 \cdot b_6^3 \cdot (c_4^3/b_6^5) \cdot \det
\begin{pmatrix}
a_8 & a_7 & a_6 & a_5 & a_4 & a_3 & a_2 & 0 \\
0 & a_8 & a_7 & a_6 & a_5 & a_4 & a_3 & a_0 \\
0 & 0 & a_8 & a_7 & a_6 & a_5 & a_4 & a_1 \\
b_6 & b_5 & b_4 & b_3 & b_2 & b_1 & b_0 & 0 \\
0 & b_6 & b_5 & b_4 & b_3 & b_2 & b_1 & 0 \\
0 & 0 & b_6 & b_5 & b_4 & b_3 & b_2 & 0 \\
0 & 0 & 0 & b_6 & b_5 & b_4 & b_3 & b_0 \\
0 & 0 & 0 & 0 & b_6 & b_5 & b_4 & b_1
\end{pmatrix} = \pm b_6^4 \cdot c_4^3 \cdot d_1.
$$

Since $b_6 c_4 \neq 0$, this proves that d_1 is an integer. Similarly, d_2 and d_0 are integers.

In general, we can show that $u_{j+1}(x)$ has integer coefficients in a similar manner. If we start with the matrix M consisting of rows $A_{n_2-n_j}$ through A_0 and $B_{n_1-n_j}$ through B_0, and if we perform the row operations indicated in Table 1, we will obtain a matrix M' consisting in some order of rows $B_{n_1-n_j}$ through $B_{n_3-n_j+1}$, then $C_{n_2-n_j}$ through $C_{n_4-n_j+1}$, $\ldots$, $P_{n_{j-2}-n_j}$ through P_1, then $Q_{n_{j-1}-n_j}$ through Q_0, and finally R_0 $\big($a row containing the coefficients of $u_{j+1}(x)\big)$. Extracting appropriate columns shows that

$$
(g_2^{\delta_1+1}/g_1 h_1^{\delta_1})^{n_2-n_j+1} (g_3^{\delta_2+1}/g_2 h_2^{\delta_2})^{n_3-n_j+1} \cdots (g_j^{\delta_{j-1}+1}/g_{j-1} h_{j-1}^{\delta_{j-1}})^{n_j-n_j+1}
$$

$$
\times \det M_0 = \pm g_2^{n_1-n_3} g_3^{n_2-n_4} \cdots g_{j-1}^{n_{j-2}-n_j} g_j^{n_{j-1}-n_j+1} r_t, \qquad (19)
$$

Table 1

COEFFICIENTS THAT ARISE IN ALGORITHM C

Row name	Row														Multiply by	Replace by row
A_5	a_8	a_7	a_6	a_5	a_4	a_3	a_2	a_1	a_0	0	0	0	0	0	b_6^3	C_5
A_4	0	a_8	a_7	a_6	a_5	a_4	a_3	a_2	a_1	a_0	0	0	0	0	b_6^3	C_4
A_3	0	0	a_8	a_7	a_6	a_5	a_4	a_3	a_2	a_1	a_0	0	0	0	b_6^3	C_3
A_2	0	0	0	a_8	a_7	a_6	a_5	a_4	a_3	a_2	a_1	a_0	0	0	b_6^3	C_2
A_1	0	0	0	0	a_8	a_7	a_6	a_5	a_4	a_3	a_2	a_1	a_0	0	b_6^3	C_1
A_0	0	0	0	0	0	a_8	a_7	a_6	a_5	a_4	a_3	a_2	a_1	a_0	b_6^3	C_0
B_7	b_6	b_5	b_4	b_3	b_2	b_1	b_0	0	0	0	0	0	0	0		
B_6	0	b_6	b_5	b_4	b_3	b_2	b_1	b_0	0	0	0	0	0	0		
B_5	0	0	b_6	b_5	b_4	b_3	b_2	b_1	b_0	0	0	0	0	0		
B_4	0	0	0	b_6	b_5	b_4	b_3	b_2	b_1	b_0	0	0	0	0		
B_3	0	0	0	0	b_6	b_5	b_4	b_3	b_2	b_1	b_0	0	0	0	c_4^3/b_6^5	D_3
B_2	0	0	0	0	0	b_6	b_5	b_4	b_3	b_2	b_1	b_0	0	0	c_4^3/b_6^5	D_2
B_1	0	0	0	0	0	0	b_6	b_5	b_4	b_3	b_2	b_1	b_0	0	c_4^3/b_6^5	D_1
B_0	0	0	0	0	0	0	0	b_6	b_5	b_4	b_3	b_2	b_1	b_0	c_4^3/b_6^5	D_0
C_5	0	0	0	0	c_4	c_3	c_2	c_1	c_0	0	0	0	0	0		
C_4	0	0	0	0	0	c_4	c_3	c_2	c_1	c_0	0	0	0	0		
C_3	0	0	0	0	0	0	c_4	c_3	c_2	c_1	c_0	0	0	0		
C_2	0	0	0	0	0	0	0	c_4	c_3	c_2	c_1	c_0	0	0		
C_1	0	0	0	0	0	0	0	0	c_4	c_3	c_2	c_1	c_0	0	$d_2^3 b_6^4/c_4^5$	E_1
C_0	0	0	0	0	0	0	0	0	0	c_4	c_3	c_2	c_1	c_0	$d_2^3 b_6^4/c_4^5$	E_0
D_3	0	0	0	0	0	0	0	0	d_2	d_1	d_0	0	0	0		
D_2	0	0	0	0	0	0	0	0	0	d_2	d_1	d_0	0	0		
D_1	0	0	0	0	0	0	0	0	0	0	d_2	d_1	d_0	0		
D_0	0	0	0	0	0	0	0	0	0	0	0	d_2	d_1	d_0	$e_1^2 c_4^2/d_2^3 b_6^2$	F_0
E_1	0	0	0	0	0	0	0	0	0	0	0	e_1	e_0	0		
E_0	0	0	0	0	0	0	0	0	0	0	0	0	e_1	e_0		
F_0	0	0	0	0	0	0	0	0	0	0	0	0	0	f_0		

where r_t is a given coefficient of $u_{j+1}(x)$ and M_0 is a submatrix of M. The h's have been chosen very cleverly so that this equation simplifies to

$$\det M_0 = \pm r_t \qquad (20)$$

(see exercise 24). Therefore *every coefficient of $u_{j+1}(x)$ can be expressed as the determinant of an $(n_1+n_2-2n_j+2) \times (n_1+n_2-2n_j+2)$ matrix whose elements are coefficients of $u(x)$ and $v(x)$.*

It remains to be shown that the cleverly chosen h's also are integers. A similar technique applies: Let's look, for example, at the matrix

$$
\begin{array}{c}
A_1 \\
A_0 \\
B_3 \\
B_2 \\
B_1 \\
B_0
\end{array}
\begin{pmatrix}
a_8 & a_7 & a_6 & a_5 & a_4 & a_3 & a_2 & a_1 & a_0 & 0 \\
0 & a_8 & a_7 & a_6 & a_5 & a_4 & a_3 & a_2 & a_1 & a_0 \\
b_6 & b_5 & b_4 & b_3 & b_2 & b_1 & b_0 & 0 & 0 & 0 \\
0 & b_6 & b_5 & b_4 & b_3 & b_2 & b_1 & b_0 & 0 & 0 \\
0 & 0 & b_6 & b_5 & b_4 & b_3 & b_2 & b_1 & b_0 & 0 \\
0 & 0 & 0 & b_6 & b_5 & b_4 & b_3 & b_2 & b_1 & b_0
\end{pmatrix} = M. \qquad (21)
$$

Row operations as specified in Table 1, and permutation of rows, leads to

$$
\begin{array}{c}
B_3 \\
B_2 \\
B_1 \\
B_0 \\
C_1 \\
C_0
\end{array}
\begin{pmatrix}
b_6 & b_5 & b_4 & b_3 & b_2 & b_1 & b_0 & 0 & 0 & 0 \\
0 & b_6 & b_5 & b_4 & b_3 & b_2 & b_1 & b_0 & 0 & 0 \\
0 & 0 & b_6 & b_5 & b_4 & b_3 & b_2 & b_1 & b_0 & 0 \\
0 & 0 & 0 & b_6 & b_5 & b_4 & b_3 & b_2 & b_1 & b_0 \\
0 & 0 & 0 & 0 & c_4 & c_3 & c_2 & c_1 & c_0 & 0 \\
0 & 0 & 0 & 0 & 0 & c_4 & c_3 & c_2 & c_1 & c_0
\end{pmatrix}
= M'; \tag{22}
$$

hence if we consider any submatrices M_0 and M_0' obtained by selecting six corresponding columns of M and M' we have $b_6^3 \cdot b_6^3 \cdot \det M_0 = \pm \det M_0'$. When M_0 is chosen to be the first six columns of M, we find that $\det M_0 = \pm c_4^2 / b_6^2 = \pm h_3$, so h_3 is an integer.

In general, to show that h_j is an integer for $j \geq 3$, we start with the matrix M consisting of rows $A_{n_2 - n_j - 1}$ through A_0 and $B_{n_1 - n_j - 1}$ through B_0; then we perform appropriate row operations until obtaining a matrix M' consisting of rows $B_{n_1 - n_j - 1}$ through $B_{n_3 - n_j}$, then $C_{n_2 - n_j - 1}$ through $C_{n_4 - n_j}, \ldots, P_{n_{j-2} - n_j - 1}$ through P_0, then $Q_{n_{j-1} - n_j - 1}$ through Q_0. Letting M_0 be the first $n_1 + n_2 - 2n_j$ columns of M, we obtain

$$
(g_2^{\delta_1 + 1} / g_1 h_1^{\delta_1})^{n_2 - n_j} (g_3^{\delta_2 + 1} / g_2 h_2^{\delta_2})^{n_3 - n_j} \cdots (g_j^{\delta_{j-1} + 1} / g_{j-1} h_{j-1}^{\delta_{j-1}})^{n_j - n_j} \det M_0
$$
$$
= \pm g_2^{n_1 - n_3} g_3^{n_2 - n_4} \cdots g_{j-1}^{n_{j-2} - n_j} g_j^{n_{j-1} - n_j}, \tag{23}
$$

an equation that neatly simplifies to

$$
\det M_0 = \pm h_j. \tag{24}
$$

(This proof, although stated for the domain of integers, obviously applies to any unique factorization domain.)

In the process of verifying Algorithm C, we have also learned that every element of S dealt with by the algorithm can be expressed as a determinant whose entries are the coefficients of the primitive parts of the original polynomials. A well-known theorem of Hadamard (see exercise 15) states that

$$
|\det(a_{ij})| \leq \prod_{1 \leq i \leq n} \left(\sum_{1 \leq j \leq n} a_{ij}^2 \right)^{1/2}; \tag{25}
$$

therefore every coefficient appearing in the polynomials computed by Algorithm C is at most

$$
N^{m+n} (m+1)^{n/2} (n+1)^{m/2}, \tag{26}
$$

if all coefficients of the given polynomials $u(x)$ and $v(x)$ are bounded by N in absolute value. This same upper bound applies to the coefficients of all polynomials $u(x)$ and $v(x)$ computed during the execution of Algorithm E, since the polynomials obtained in Algorithm E are always divisors of the polynomials obtained in Algorithm C.

This upper bound on the coefficients is extremely gratifying, because it is much better than we would ordinarily have a right to expect. For example, consider what happens if we avoid the corrections in steps E3 and C3, merely replacing $v(x)$ by $r(x)$. This is the simplest gcd algorithm, and it is the one that traditionally appears in textbooks on algebra (for theoretical purposes, not intended for practical calculations). If we suppose that $\delta_1 = \delta_2 = \cdots = 1$, we find that the coefficients of $u_3(x)$ are bounded by N^3, the coefficients of $u_4(x)$ are bounded by N^7, those of $u_5(x)$ by N^{17}, $\ldots$; the coefficients of $u_k(x)$ are bounded by N^{a_k}, where $a_k = 2a_{k-1} + a_{k-2}$. Thus the upper bound, in place of (26) for $m = n + 1$, would be approximately

$$N^{0.5(2.414)^n}, \tag{27}$$

and experiments show that the simple algorithm does in fact have this behavior; the number of digits in the coefficients grows exponentially at each step! In Algorithm E, by contrast, the growth in the number of digits is only slightly more than linear at most.

Another byproduct of our proof of Algorithm C is the fact that the degrees of the polynomials will almost always decrease by 1 at each step, so that the number of iterations of step C2 (or E2) will usually be $\deg(v)$ if the given polynomials are "random." In order to see why this happens, notice for example that we could have chosen the first eight columns of M and M' in (17) and (18); then we would have found that $u_4(x)$ has degree less than 3 if and only if $d_3 = 0$, that is, if and only if

$$\det \begin{pmatrix} a_8 & a_7 & a_6 & a_5 & a_4 & a_3 & a_2 & a_1 \\ 0 & a_8 & a_7 & a_6 & a_5 & a_4 & a_3 & a_2 \\ 0 & 0 & a_8 & a_7 & a_6 & a_5 & a_4 & a_3 \\ b_6 & b_5 & b_4 & b_3 & b_2 & b_1 & b_0 & 0 \\ 0 & b_6 & b_5 & b_4 & b_3 & b_2 & b_1 & b_0 \\ 0 & 0 & b_6 & b_5 & b_4 & b_3 & b_2 & b_1 \\ 0 & 0 & 0 & b_6 & b_5 & b_4 & b_3 & b_2 \\ 0 & 0 & 0 & 0 & b_6 & b_5 & b_4 & b_3 \end{pmatrix} = 0.$$

In general, δ_j will be greater than 1 for $j > 1$ if and only if a similar determinant in the coefficients of $u(x)$ and $v(x)$ is zero. Since such a determinant is a nonzero multivariate polynomial in the coefficients, it will be nonzero "almost always," or "with probability 1." (See exercise 16 for a more precise formulation of this statement, and see exercise 4 for a related proof.) The example polynomials in (15) have both δ_2 and δ_3 equal to 2, so they are exceptional indeed.

The considerations above can be used to derive the well-known fact that two polynomials are relatively prime if and only if their *resultant* is nonzero; the resultant is a determinant having the form of rows A_5 through A_0 and B_7 through B_0 in Table 1. (This is "Sylvester's determinant"; see exercise 12. Further properties of resultants are discussed in B. L. van der Waerden, *Modern Algebra*, translated by Fred Blum (New York: Ungar, 1949), Sections 27–28.) From the standpoint discussed above, we could say that the gcd is "almost always" of degree zero, since Sylvester's determinant is almost never zero. But many calculations of practical interest would never be undertaken if there weren't some reasonable chance that the gcd would be a polynomial of positive degree.

We can see exactly what happens during Algorithms E and C when the gcd is not 1 by considering $u(x) = w(x)u_1(x)$ and $v(x) = w(x)u_2(x)$, where $u_1(x)$ and $u_2(x)$ are relatively prime and $w(x)$ is primitive. Then if the polynomials $u_1(x)$, $u_2(x)$, $u_3(x)$, ... are obtained when Algorithm E works on $u(x) = u_1(x)$ and $v(x) = u_2(x)$, it is easy to see that the sequence obtained for $u(x) = w(x)u_1(x)$ and $v(x) = w(x)u_2(x)$ is simply $w(x)u_1(x)$, $w(x)u_2(x)$, $w(x)u_3(x)$, $w(x)u_4(x)$, etc. With Algorithm C the behavior is different: If the polynomials $u_1(x)$, $u_2(x)$, $u_3(x)$, ... are obtained when Algorithm C is applied to $u(x) = u_1(x)$ and $v(x) = u_2(x)$, and if we assume that $\deg(u_{j+1}) = \deg(u_j) - 1$ (which is almost always true when $j > 1$), then the sequence

$$w(x)u_1(x),\ w(x)u_2(x),\ \ell^2 w(x)u_3(x),\ \ell^4 w(x)u_4(x),\ \ell^6 w(x)u_5(x),\ \ldots \quad (28)$$

is obtained when Algorithm C is applied to $u(x) = w(x)u_1(x)$ and $v(x) = w(x)u_2(x)$, where $\ell = \ell(w)$. (See exercise 13.) Even though these additional ℓ-factors are present, Algorithm C will be superior to Algorithm E, because it is easier to deal with slightly larger polynomials than to calculate primitive parts repeatedly.

Polynomial remainder sequences such as those in Algorithms C and E are not useful merely for finding greatest common divisors and resultants. Another important application is to the enumeration of real roots, for a given polynomial in a given interval, according to the famous theorem of J. Sturm [*Mém. Présentés par Divers Savants* **6** (Paris, 1835), 271–318]. Let $u(x)$ be a polynomial over the real numbers, having distinct complex roots. We shall see in the next section that the roots are distinct if and only if $\gcd(u(x), u'(x)) = 1$, where $u'(x)$ is the derivative of $u(x)$; accordingly, there is a polynomial remainder sequence proving that $u(x)$ is relatively prime to $u'(x)$. We set $u_0(x) = u(x)$, $u_1(x) = u'(x)$, and (following Sturm) we negate the sign of all remainders, obtaining

$$c_1 u_0(x) = u_1(x)q_1(x) - d_1 u_2(x),$$
$$c_2 u_1(x) = u_2(x)q_2(x) - d_2 u_3(x),$$
$$\vdots \qquad\qquad\qquad\qquad\qquad (29)$$
$$c_k u_{k-1}(x) = u_k(x)q_k(x) - d_k u_{k+1}(x),$$

for some positive constants c_j and d_j, where $\deg(u_{k+1}) = 0$. We say that the *variation* $V(u, a)$ of $u(x)$ at a is the number of changes of sign in the sequence $u_0(a)$, $u_1(a)$, ..., $u_{k+1}(a)$, not counting zeros. For example, if the sequence of signs is $0, +, -, -, 0, +, +, -$, we have $V(u, a) = 3$. Sturm's theorem asserts that *the number of roots of $u(x)$ in the interval $a < x \le b$ is $V(u, a) - V(u, b)$*; and the proof is surprisingly short (see exercise 22).

Although Algorithms C and E are interesting, they aren't the whole story. Important alternative ways to calculate polynomial gcds over the integers are discussed at the end of Section 4.6.2. There is also a general determinant-evaluation algorithm that may be said to include Algorithm C as a special case; see E. H. Bareiss, *Math. Comp.* **22** (1968), 565–578.

⚑ In the fourth edition of this book I plan to redo the exposition of the present section, taking into proper account the 19th-century research on determinants, as well as the work of W. Habicht, *Comm. Math. Helvetici* **21** (1948), 99–116. An excellent discussion of the latter has been given by R. Loos in *Computing, Supplement 4* (1982), 115–137. An interesting method for evaluating determinants, published in 1853 by Felice Chiò and rediscovered by C. L. Dodgson (aka Lewis Carroll), is also highly relevant. See D. E. Knuth, *Electronic J. Combinatorics* **3**, 2 (1996), #R5, 1–13, §3, for a summary of the early history of identities between determinants of submatrices.

EXERCISES

1. [*10*] Compute the pseudo-quotient $q(x)$ and pseudo-remainder $r(x)$, namely the polynomials satisfying (8), when $u(x) = x^6 + x^5 - x^4 + 2x^3 + 3x^2 - x + 2$ and $v(x) = 2x^3 + 2x^2 - x + 3$, over the integers.

2. [*15*] What is the greatest common divisor of $3x^6 + x^5 + 4x^4 + 4x^3 + 3x^2 + 4x + 2$ and its "reverse" $2x^6 + 4x^5 + 3x^4 + 4x^3 + 4x^2 + x + 3$, modulo 7?

▶ **3.** [*M25*] Show that Euclid's algorithm for polynomials over a field S can be extended to find polynomials $U(x)$ and $V(x)$ over S such that

$$u(x)V(x) + U(x)v(x) = \gcd(u(x), v(x)).$$

(See Algorithm 4.5.2X.) What are the degrees of the polynomials $U(x)$ and $V(x)$ that are computed by this extended algorithm? Prove that if S is the field of rational numbers, and if $u(x) = x^m - 1$ and $v(x) = x^n - 1$, then the extended algorithm yields polynomials $U(x)$ and $V(x)$ having *integer* coefficients. Find $U(x)$ and $V(x)$ when $u(x) = x^{21} - 1$ and $v(x) = x^{13} - 1$.

▶ **4.** [*M30*] Let p be prime, and suppose that Euclid's algorithm applied to the polynomials $u(x)$ and $v(x)$ modulo p yields a sequence of polynomials having respective degrees $m, n, n_1, \ldots, n_t, -\infty$, where $m = \deg(u)$, $n = \deg(v)$, and $n_t \geq 0$. Assume that $m \geq n$. If $u(x)$ and $v(x)$ are monic polynomials, independently and uniformly distributed over all the p^{m+n} pairs of monic polynomials having respective degrees m and n, what are the average values of the three quantities t, $n_1 + \cdots + n_t$, and $(n - n_1)n_1 + \cdots + (n_{t-1} - n_t)n_t$, as functions of m, n, and p? (These three quantities are the fundamental factors in the running time of Euclid's algorithm applied to polynomials modulo p, assuming that division is done by Algorithm D.) [*Hint:* Show that $u(x) \bmod v(x)$ is uniformly distributed and independent of $v(x)$.]

5. [*M22*] What is the probability that $u(x)$ and $v(x)$ are relatively prime modulo p, if $u(x)$ and $v(x)$ are independently and uniformly distributed monic polynomials of degree n?

6. [*M23*] We have seen that Euclid's Algorithm 4.5.2A for integers can be directly adapted to an algorithm for the greatest common divisor of polynomials. Can the binary gcd algorithm, Algorithm 4.5.2B, be adapted in an analogous way to an algorithm that applies to polynomials?

7. [*M10*] What are the units in the domain of all polynomials over a unique factorization domain S?

▶ **8.** [*M22*] Show that if a polynomial with integer coefficients is irreducible over the domain of integers, it is irreducible when considered as a polynomial over the field of rational numbers.

9. [*M25*] Let $u(x)$ and $v(x)$ be primitive polynomials over a unique factorization domain S. Prove that $u(x)$ and $v(x)$ are relatively prime if and only if there are polynomials $U(x)$ and $V(x)$ over S such that $u(x)V(x) + U(x)v(x)$ is a polynomial of degree zero. [*Hint:* Extend Algorithm E, as Algorithm 4.5.2A is extended in exercise 3.]

10. [*M28*] Prove that the polynomials over a unique factorization domain form a unique factorization domain. [*Hint:* Use the result of exercise 9 to help show that there is at most one kind of factorization possible.]

11. [*M22*] What row names would have appeared in Table 1 if the sequence of degrees had been 9, 6, 5, 2, $-\infty$ instead of 8, 6, 4, 2, 1, 0?

▶ **12.** [*M24*] Let $u_1(x)$, $u_2(x)$, $u_3(x)$, ... be a sequence of polynomials obtained during a run of Algorithm C. "Sylvester's matrix" is the square matrix formed from rows A_{n_2-1} through A_0 and B_{n_1-1} through B_0 (in a notation analogous to that of Table 1). Show that if $u_1(x)$ and $u_2(x)$ have a common factor of positive degree, then the determinant of Sylvester's matrix is zero. Conversely, given that $\deg(u_k) = 0$ for some k, show that the determinant of Sylvester's matrix is nonzero by deriving a formula for its absolute value in terms of $\ell(u_j)$ and $\deg(u_j)$, $1 \leq j \leq k$.

13. [*M22*] Show that the leading coefficient ℓ of the primitive part of $\gcd(u(x), v(x))$ enters into Algorithm C's polynomial sequence as shown in (28), when $\delta_1 = \delta_2 = \cdots = \delta_{k-1} = 1$. What is the behavior for general δ_j?

14. [*M29*] Let $r(x)$ be the pseudo-remainder when $u(x)$ is pseudo-divided by $v(x)$. If $\deg(u) \geq \deg(v) + 2$ and $\deg(v) \geq \deg(r) + 2$, show that $r(x)$ is a multiple of $\ell(v)$.

15. [*M26*] Prove Hadamard's inequality (25). [*Hint:* Consider the matrix AA^T.]

▶ **16.** [*M22*] Let $f(x_1, \ldots, x_n)$ be a multivariate polynomial that is not identically zero, and let $r(S_1, \ldots, S_n)$ be the set of roots $(x_1, \ldots, x_n)$ of $f(x_1, \ldots, x_n) = 0$ such that $x_1 \in S_1$, ..., $x_n \in S_n$. If the degree of f is at most $d_j \leq |S_j|$ in the variable x_j, prove that
$$|r(S_1, \ldots, S_n)| \leq |S_1| \ldots |S_n| - (|S_1| - d_1) \ldots (|S_n| - d_n).$$
Therefore the probability of finding a root at random, $|r(S_1, \ldots, S_n)|/|S_1| \ldots |S_n|$, approaches zero as the sets S_j get bigger. [This inequality has many applications in the design of randomized algorithms, because it provides a good way to test whether a complicated sum of products of sums is identically zero without expanding out all the terms.]

17. [*M32*] (*P. M. Cohn's algorithm for division of string polynomials.*) Let A be an *alphabet*, that is, a set of symbols. A *string* α on A is a sequence of $n \geq 0$ symbols, $\alpha = a_1 \ldots a_n$, where each a_j is in A. The *length* of α, denoted by $|\alpha|$, is the number n of symbols. A *string polynomial* on A is a finite sum $U = \sum_k r_k \alpha_k$, where each r_k is a nonzero rational number and each α_k is a string on A; we assume that $\alpha_j \neq \alpha_k$ when $j \neq k$. The *degree* of U, $\deg(U)$, is defined to be $-\infty$ if $U = 0$ (that is, if the sum is empty), otherwise $\deg(U) = \max |\alpha_k|$. The sum and product of string polynomials are defined in an obvious manner; thus, $(\sum_j r_j \alpha_j)(\sum_k s_k \beta_k) = \sum_{j,k} r_j s_k \alpha_j \beta_k$, where the product of two strings is obtained by simply juxtaposing them, after which we collect like terms. For example, if $A = \{a, b\}$, $U = ab + ba - 2a - 2b$, and $V = a + b - 1$, then $\deg(U) = 2$, $\deg(V) = 1$, $V^2 = aa + ab + ba + bb - 2a - 2b + 1$, and $V^2 - U = aa + bb + 1$. Clearly $\deg(UV) = \deg(U) + \deg(V)$, and $\deg(U + V) \leq \max(\deg(U), \deg(V))$, with equality in the latter formula if $\deg(U) \neq \deg(V)$. (String polynomials may be regarded as ordinary multivariate polynomials over the field of rational numbers, except that the variables are *not commutative* under multiplication. In the conventional language of pure mathematics, the set of string polynomials with the operations defined here is the "free associative algebra" generated by A over the rationals.)

a) Let Q_1, Q_2, U, and V be string polynomials with $\deg(U) \geq \deg(V)$ and such that $\deg(Q_1 U - Q_2 V) < \deg(Q_1 U)$. Give an algorithm to find a string polynomial Q such that $\deg(U - QV) < \deg(U)$. (Thus if we are given U and V such that $Q_1 U = Q_2 V + R$ and $\deg(R) < \deg(Q_1 U)$, for some Q_1 and Q_2, then there is a solution to these conditions with $Q_1 = 1$.)

b) Given that U and V are string polynomials with $\deg(V) > \deg(Q_1 U - Q_2 V)$ for some Q_1 and Q_2, show that the result of (a) can be improved to find a quotient Q such that $U = QV + R$, $\deg(R) < \deg(V)$. (This is the analog of (1) for string polynomials; part (a) showed that we can make $\deg(R) < \deg(U)$, under weaker hypotheses.)

c) A *homogeneous polynomial* is one whose terms all have the same degree (length). If U_1, U_2, V_1, V_2 are homogeneous string polynomials with $U_1 V_1 = U_2 V_2$ and $\deg(V_1) \geq \deg(V_2)$, show that there is a homogeneous string polynomial U such that $U_2 = U_1 U$ and $V_1 = U V_2$.

d) Given that U and V are homogeneous string polynomials with $UV = VU$, prove that there is a homogeneous string polynomial W such that $U = rW^m$, $V = sW^n$ for some integers m, n and rational numbers r, s. Give an algorithm to compute such a W having the largest possible degree. (This algorithm is of interest, for example, when $U = \alpha$ and $V = \beta$ are strings satisfying $\alpha\beta = \beta\alpha$; then W is simply a string γ. When $U = x^m$ and $V = x^n$, the solution of largest degree is the string $W = x^{\gcd(m,n)}$, so this algorithm includes a gcd algorithm for integers as a special case.)

▶ **18.** [*M24*] (*Euclidean algorithm for string polynomials.*) Let V_1 and V_2 be string polynomials, not both zero, having a *common left multiple*. (This means that there exist string polynomials U_1 and U_2, not both zero, such that $U_1 V_1 = U_2 V_2$.) The purpose of this exercise is to find an algorithm to compute their *greatest common right divisor* $\gcd(V_1, V_2)$ and their *least common left multiple* $\operatorname{lclm}(V_1, V_2)$. The latter quantities are defined as follows: $\gcd(V_1, V_2)$ is a common right divisor of V_1 and V_2 (that is, $V_1 = W_1 \gcd(V_1, V_2)$ and $V_2 = W_2 \gcd(V_1, V_2)$ for some W_1 and W_2), and any common right divisor of V_1 and V_2 is a right divisor of $\gcd(V_1, V_2)$; $\operatorname{lclm}(V_1, V_2) = Z_1 V_1 = Z_2 V_2$ for some Z_1 and Z_2, and any common left multiple of V_1 and V_2 is a left multiple of $\operatorname{lclm}(V_1, V_2)$.

For example, let $U_1 = abbbab + abbab - bbab + ab - 1$, $V_1 = babab + abab + ab - b$; $U_2 = abb + ab - b$, $V_2 = babbabab + bababab + babab + abab - babb - 1$. Then we have $U_1 V_1 = U_2 V_2 = abbbabbabab + abbabbabab + abbbababab + abbababab - bbabbabab + abbbabab - bbababab + 2abbabab - abbbabb + ababab - abbabb - bbabab - babab + bbabb - abb - ab + b$. For these string polynomials it can be shown that $\gcd(V_1, V_2) = ab + 1$, and $\operatorname{lclm}(V_1, V_2) = U_1 V_1$.

The division algorithm of exercise 17 may be restated thus: If V_1 and V_2 are string polynomials, with $V_2 \neq 0$, and if $U_1 \neq 0$ and U_2 satisfy the equation $U_1 V_1 = U_2 V_2$, then there exist string polynomials Q and R such that

$$V_1 = QV_2 + R, \qquad \text{where } \deg(R) < \deg(V_2).$$

It follows readily that Q and R are uniquely determined; they do not depend on the given U_1 and U_2. Furthermore the result is right-left symmetric, in the sense that

$$U_2 = U_1 Q + R', \qquad \text{where } \deg(R') = \deg(U_1) - \deg(V_2) + \deg(R) < \deg(U_1).$$

Show that this division algorithm can be extended to an algorithm that computes lclm(V_1, V_2) and gcrd(V_1, V_2); in fact, the extended algorithm finds string polynomials Z_1 and Z_2 such that $Z_1 V_1 + Z_2 V_2 = \text{gcrd}(V_1, V_2)$. [*Hint:* Use auxiliary variables u_1, u_2, v_1, v_2, w_1, w_2, w_1', w_2', z_1, z_2, z_1', z_2', whose values are string polynomials; start by setting $u_1 \leftarrow U_1$, $u_2 \leftarrow U_2$, $v_1 \leftarrow V_1$, $v_2 \leftarrow V_2$, and throughout the algorithm maintain the conditions

$$U_1 w_1 + U_2 w_2 = u_1, \qquad\qquad z_1 V_1 + z_2 V_2 = v_1,$$
$$U_1 w_1' + U_2 w_2' = u_2, \qquad\qquad z_1' V_1 + z_2' V_2 = v_2,$$
$$u_1 z_1 - u_2 z_1' = (-1)^n U_1, \qquad w_1 v_1 - w_1' v_2 = (-1)^n V_1,$$
$$-u_1 z_2 + u_2 z_2' = (-1)^n U_2, \qquad -w_2 v_1 + w_2' v_2 = (-1)^n V_2$$

at the nth iteration. This might be regarded as the "ultimate" extension of Euclid's algorithm.]

19. [*M39*] (*Common divisors of square matrices.*) Exercise 18 shows that the concept of greatest common right divisor can be meaningful when multiplication is not commutative. Prove that any two $n \times n$ matrices A and B of integers have a greatest common right matrix divisor D. [*Suggestion:* Design an algorithm whose inputs are A and B, and whose outputs are integer matrices D, P, Q, X, Y, where $A = PD$, $B = QD$, and $D = XA + YB$.] Find a greatest common right divisor of the matrices $\left(\begin{smallmatrix} 1 & 2 \\ 3 & 4 \end{smallmatrix}\right)$ and $\left(\begin{smallmatrix} 4 & 3 \\ 2 & 1 \end{smallmatrix}\right)$.

20. [*M40*] Investigate *approximate* polynomial gcds and the accuracy of Euclid's algorithm: What can be said about calculation of the greatest common divisor of polynomials whose coefficients are floating point numbers?

21. [*M25*] Prove that the computation time required by Algorithm C to compute the gcd of two nth degree polynomials over the integers is $O(n^4 (\log Nn)^2)$, if the coefficients of the given polynomials are bounded by N in absolute value.

22. [*M23*] Prove Sturm's theorem. [*Hint:* Some sign sequences are impossible.]

23. [*M22*] Prove that if $u(x)$ in (29) has deg(u) real roots, then we have deg$(u_{j+1}) = \text{deg}(u_j) - 1$ for $0 \le j \le k$.

24. [*M21*] Show that (19) simplifies to (20) and (23) simplifies to (24).

25. [*M24*] (W. S. Brown.) Prove that all the polynomials $u_j(x)$ in (16) for $j \ge 3$ are multiples of $\gcd(\ell(u), \ell(v))$, and explain how to improve Algorithm C accordingly.

▶ **26.** [*M26*] The purpose of this exercise is to give an analog for polynomials of the fact that continued fractions with positive integer entries give the best approximations to real numbers (exercise 4.5.3–42).

Let $u(x)$ and $v(x)$ be polynomials over a field, with deg$(u) > \text{deg}(v)$, and let $a_1(x)$, $a_2(x)$, ... be the quotient polynomials when Euclid's algorithm is applied to $u(x)$ and $v(x)$. For example, the sequence of quotients in (5) and (6) is $9x^2 + 7$, $5x^2 + 5$, $6x^3 + 5x^2 + 6x + 5$, $9x + 12$. We wish to show that the convergents $p_n(x)/q_n(x)$ of the continued fraction $/\!/ a_1(x), a_2(x), \dots /\!/$ are the "best approximations" of low degree to the rational function $v(x)/u(x)$, where we have $p_n(x) = K_{n-1}(a_2(x), \dots, a_n(x))$ and $q_n(x) = K_n(a_1(x), \dots, a_n(x))$ in terms of the continuant polynomials of Eq. 4.5.3–(4). By convention, we let $p_0(x) = q_{-1}(x) = 0$, $p_{-1}(x) = q_0(x) = 1$.

Prove that if $p(x)$ and $q(x)$ are polynomials such that deg$(q) < \text{deg}(q_n)$ and deg$(pu - qv) \le \text{deg}(p_{n-1}u - q_{n-1}v)$, for some $n \ge 1$, then $p(x) = cp_{n-1}(x)$ and $q(x) = cq_{n-1}(x)$ for some constant c. In particular, each $q_n(x)$ is a "record-breaking" polynomial in the sense that no nonzero polynomial $q(x)$ of smaller degree can make the quantity $p(x)u(x) - q(x)v(x)$, for any polynomial $p(x)$, achieve a degree as small as $p_n(x)u(x) - q_n(x)v(x)$.

27. [*M23*] Suggest a way to speed up the division of $u(x)$ by $v(x)$ when we know in advance that the remainder will be zero.

*4.6.2. Factorization of Polynomials

Let us now consider the problem of *factoring* polynomials, not merely finding the greatest common divisor of two or more of them.

Factoring modulo p. As in the case of integer numbers (Sections 4.5.2, 4.5.4), the problem of factoring seems to be more difficult than finding the greatest common divisor. But factorization of polynomials modulo a prime integer p is not as hard to do as we might expect. It is much easier to find the factors of an arbitrary polynomial of degree n, modulo 2, than to use any known method to find the factors of an arbitrary n-bit binary number. This surprising situation is a consequence of an instructive factorization algorithm discovered in 1967 by Elwyn R. Berlekamp [*Bell System Technical J.* **46** (1967), 1853–1859].

Let p be a prime number; all arithmetic on polynomials in the following discussion will be done modulo p. Suppose that someone has given us a polynomial $u(x)$, whose coefficients are chosen from the set $\{0, 1, \ldots, p-1\}$; we may assume that $u(x)$ is monic. Our goal is to express $u(x)$ in the form

$$u(x) = p_1(x)^{e_1} \ldots p_r(x)^{e_r}, \tag{1}$$

where $p_1(x), \ldots, p_r(x)$ are distinct, monic, irreducible polynomials.

As a first step, we can use a standard technique to determine whether any of the exponents $e_1, \ldots, e_r$ are greater than unity. If

$$u(x) = u_n x^n + \cdots + u_0 = v(x)^2 w(x), \tag{2}$$

then the derivative (formed in the usual way, but modulo p) is

$$u'(x) = n u_n x^{n-1} + \cdots + u_1 = 2v(x)v'(x)w(x) + v(x)^2 w'(x), \tag{3}$$

and this is a multiple of the squared factor $v(x)$. Therefore our first step in factoring $u(x)$ is to form

$$\gcd\big(u(x), u'(x)\big) = d(x). \tag{4}$$

If $d(x)$ is equal to 1, we know that $u(x)$ is *squarefree*, the product of distinct primes $p_1(x) \ldots p_r(x)$. If $d(x)$ is not equal to 1 and $d(x) \neq u(x)$, then $d(x)$ is a proper factor of $u(x)$; the relation between the factors of $d(x)$ and the factors of $u(x)/d(x)$ speeds up the factorization process nicely in this case (see exercises 34 and 36). Finally, if $d(x) = u(x)$, we must have $u'(x) = 0$; hence the coefficient u_k of x^k is nonzero only when k is a multiple of p. This means that $u(x)$ can be written as a polynomial of the form $v(x^p)$, and in such a case we have

$$u(x) = v(x^p) = \big(v(x)\big)^p; \tag{5}$$

the factorization process can be completed by finding the irreducible factors of $v(x)$ and raising them to the pth power.

Identity (5) may appear somewhat strange to the reader; it is an important fact that is basic to Berlekamp's algorithm and to several other methods we shall discuss. We can prove it as follows: If $v_1(x)$ and $v_2(x)$ are any polynomials modulo p, then

$$\big(v_1(x) + v_2(x)\big)^p = v_1(x)^p + \binom{p}{1}v_1(x)^{p-1}v_2(x) + \cdots + \binom{p}{p-1}v_1(x)v_2(x)^{p-1} + v_2(x)^p,$$
$$= v_1(x)^p + v_2(x)^p,$$

since the binomial coefficients $\binom{p}{1}$, $\ldots$, $\binom{p}{p-1}$ are all multiples of p. Furthermore if a is any integer, we have $a^p \equiv a$ (modulo p) by Fermat's theorem. Therefore when $v(x) = v_m x^m + v_{m-1}x^{m-1} + \cdots + v_0$, we find that

$$v(x)^p = (v_m x^m)^p + (v_{m-1}x^{m-1})^p + \cdots + (v_0)^p$$
$$= v_m x^{mp} + v_{m-1}x^{(m-1)p} + \cdots + v_0 = v(x^p).$$

The remarks above show that the problem of factoring a polynomial reduces to the problem of factoring a squarefree polynomial. Let us therefore assume that

$$u(x) = p_1(x)p_2(x)\ldots p_r(x) \tag{6}$$

is the product of distinct primes. How can we be clever enough to discover the $p_j(x)$'s when only $u(x)$ is given? Berlekamp's idea is to make use of the Chinese remainder theorem, which is valid for polynomials just as it is valid for integers (see exercise 3). If $(s_1, s_2, \ldots, s_r)$ is any r-tuple of integers mod p, the Chinese remainder theorem implies that *there is a unique polynomial $v(x)$ such that*

$$v(x) \equiv s_1 \ (\text{modulo } p_1(x)), \quad \ldots, \quad v(x) \equiv s_r \ (\text{modulo } p_r(x)),$$
$$\deg(v) < \deg(p_1) + \deg(p_2) + \cdots + \deg(p_r) = \deg(u). \tag{7}$$

The notation "$g(x) \equiv h(x) \ (\text{modulo } f(x))$" that appears here has the same meaning as "$g(x) \equiv h(x) \ (\text{modulo } f(x) \text{ and } p)$" in exercise 3.2.2–11, since we are considering polynomial arithmetic modulo p. The polynomial $v(x)$ in (7) gives us a way to get at the factors of $u(x)$, for if $r \geq 2$ and $s_1 \neq s_2$, we will have $\gcd\big(u(x), v(x) - s_1\big)$ divisible by $p_1(x)$ but not by $p_2(x)$.

Since this observation shows that we can get information about the factors of $u(x)$ from appropriate solutions $v(x)$ of (7), let us analyze (7) more closely. In the first place we can observe that the polynomial $v(x)$ satisfies the condition $v(x)^p \equiv s_j^p = s_j \equiv v(x) \ (\text{modulo } p_j(x))$ for $1 \leq j \leq r$; therefore

$$v(x)^p \equiv v(x) \ (\text{modulo } u(x)), \qquad \deg(v) < \deg(u). \tag{8}$$

In the second place we have the basic polynomial identity

$$x^p - x \equiv (x - 0)(x - 1)\ldots\big(x - (p-1)\big) \ (\text{modulo } p) \tag{9}$$

(see exercise 6); hence

$$v(x)^p - v(x) = \big(v(x) - 0\big)\big(v(x) - 1\big)\ldots\big(v(x) - (p-1)\big) \tag{10}$$

is an identity for any polynomial $v(x)$, when we are working modulo p. If $v(x)$ satisfies (8), it follows that $u(x)$ divides the left-hand side of (10), so every irreducible factor of $u(x)$ must divide one of the p relatively prime factors of the right-hand side of (10). In other words, *all* solutions of (8) must have the form of (7), for some $s_1, s_2, \ldots, s_r$; *there are exactly p^r solutions of (8).*

The solutions $v(x)$ to congruence (8) therefore provide a key to the factorization of $u(x)$. It may seem harder to find all solutions to (8) than to factor $u(x)$ in the first place, but in fact this is not true, since the set of solutions to (8) is closed under addition. Let $\deg(u) = n$; we can construct the $n \times n$ matrix

$$Q = \begin{pmatrix} q_{0,0} & q_{0,1} & \cdots & q_{0,n-1} \\ \vdots & \vdots & & \vdots \\ q_{n-1,0} & q_{n-1,1} & \cdots & q_{n-1,n-1} \end{pmatrix} \qquad (11)$$

where

$$x^{pk} \equiv q_{k,n-1}x^{n-1} + \cdots + q_{k,1}x + q_{k,0} \quad (\text{modulo } u(x)). \qquad (12)$$

Then $v(x) = v_{n-1}x^{n-1} + \cdots + v_1 x + v_0$ is a solution to (8) if and only if

$$(v_0, v_1, \ldots, v_{n-1})Q = (v_0, v_1, \ldots, v_{n-1}); \qquad (13)$$

for the latter equation holds if and only if

$$v(x) = \sum_j v_j x^j = \sum_j \sum_k v_k q_{k,j} x^j \equiv \sum_k v_k x^{pk} = v(x^p) \equiv v(x)^p \quad (\text{modulo } u(x)).$$

Berlekamp's factoring algorithm therefore proceeds as follows:

B1. [Remove duplicate factors.] Ensure that $u(x)$ is squarefree; in other words, if $\gcd\big(u(x), u'(x)\big) \neq 1$, reduce the problem of factoring $u(x)$, as stated earlier in this section.

B2. [Get Q.] Form the matrix Q defined by (11) and (12). This can be done in different ways, depending on the size of p, as explained below.

B3. [Find null space.] "Triangularize" the matrix $Q - I$, where $I = (\delta_{ij})$ is the $n \times n$ identity matrix, finding its rank $n - r$ and finding linearly independent vectors $v^{[1]}, \ldots, v^{[r]}$ such that $v^{[j]}(Q - I) = (0, 0, \ldots, 0)$ for $1 \le j \le r$. (The first vector $v^{[1]}$ may always be taken as $(1, 0, \ldots, 0)$, representing the trivial solution $v^{[1]}(x) = 1$ to (8). The computation can be done using appropriate column operations, as explained in Algorithm N below.) *At this point, r is the number of irreducible factors of $u(x)$,* because the solutions to (8) are the p^r polynomials corresponding to the vectors $t_1 v^{[1]} + \cdots + t_r v^{[r]}$ for all choices of integers $0 \le t_1, \ldots, t_r < p$. Therefore if $r = 1$ we know that $u(x)$ is irreducible, and the procedure terminates.

B4. [Split.] Calculate $\gcd\big(u(x), v^{[2]}(x) - s\big)$ for $0 \le s < p$, where $v^{[2]}(x)$ is the polynomial represented by vector $v^{[2]}$. The result will be a nontrivial factorization of $u(x)$, because $v^{[2]}(x) - s$ is nonzero and has degree less than $\deg(u)$, and by exercise 7 we have

$$u(x) = \prod_{0 \le s < p} \gcd\big(v(x) - s, \, u(x)\big) \qquad (14)$$

whenever $v(x)$ satisfies (8).

If the use of $v^{[2]}(x)$ does not succeed in splitting $u(x)$ into r factors, further factors can be obtained by calculating $\gcd\big(v^{[k]}(x) - s, w(x)\big)$ for $0 \le s < p$ and all factors $w(x)$ found so far, for $k = 3, 4, \ldots$, until r factors are obtained. (If we choose $s_i \ne s_j$ in (7), we obtain a solution $v(x)$ to (8) that distinguishes $p_i(x)$ from $p_j(x)$; some $v^{[k]}(x) - s$ will be divisible by $p_i(x)$ and not by $p_j(x)$, so this procedure will eventually find all of the factors.)

If p is 2 or 3, the calculations of this step are quite efficient; but if p is more than 25, say, there is a much better way to proceed, as we shall see later. ∎

Historical notes: M. C. R. Butler [*Quart. J. Math.* **5** (1954), 102–107] observed that the matrix $Q - I$ corresponding to a squarefree polynomial with r irreducible factors will have rank $n - r$, modulo p. Indeed, this fact was implicit in a more general result of K. Petr [*Časopis pro Pěstování Matematiky a Fysiky* **66** (1937), 85–94], who determined the characteristic polynomial of Q. See also Š. Schwarz, *Quart. J. Math.* **7** (1956), 110–124.

As an example of Algorithm B, let us now determine the factorization of

$$u(x) = x^8 + x^6 + 10x^4 + 10x^3 + 8x^2 + 2x + 8 \tag{15}$$

modulo 13. (This polynomial appears in several of the examples in Section 4.6.1.) A quick calculation using Algorithm 4.6.1E shows that $\gcd\big(u(x), u'(x)\big) = 1$; therefore $u(x)$ is squarefree, and we turn to step B2. Step B2 involves calculating the Q matrix, which in this case is an 8×8 array. The first row of Q is always $(1, 0, 0, \ldots, 0)$, representing the polynomial $x^0 \bmod u(x) = 1$. The second row represents $x^{13} \bmod u(x)$, and, in general, $x^k \bmod u(x)$ may readily be determined as follows (for relatively small values of k): If

$$u(x) = x^n + u_{n-1}x^{n-1} + \cdots + u_1 x + u_0$$

and if

$$x^k \equiv a_{k,n-1}x^{n-1} + \cdots + a_{k,1}x + a_{k,0} \pmod{u(x)},$$

then

$$\begin{aligned}
x^{k+1} &\equiv a_{k,n-1}x^n + \cdots + a_{k,1}x^2 + a_{k,0}x \\
&\equiv a_{k,n-1}(-u_{n-1}x^{n-1} - \cdots - u_1 x - u_0) + a_{k,n-2}x^{n-1} + \cdots + a_{k,0}x \\
&= a_{k+1,n-1}x^{n-1} + \cdots + a_{k+1,1}x + a_{k+1,0},
\end{aligned}$$

where

$$a_{k+1,j} = a_{k,j-1} - a_{k,n-1}u_j. \tag{16}$$

In this formula $a_{k,-1}$ is treated as zero, so that $a_{k+1,0} = -a_{k,n-1}u_0$. The simple "shift register" recurrence (16) makes it easy to calculate $x^k \bmod u(x)$ for $k = 1$, $2, 3, \ldots, (n-1)p$. Inside a computer, this calculation is of course generally done by maintaining a one-dimensional array $(a_{n-1}, \ldots, a_1, a_0)$ and repeatedly setting

$$t \leftarrow a_{n-1}, \quad a_{n-1} \leftarrow (a_{n-2} - tu_{n-1}) \bmod p, \quad \ldots, \quad a_1 \leftarrow (a_0 - tu_1) \bmod p,$$

and $a_0 \leftarrow (-tu_0) \bmod p$. (We have seen similar procedures in connection with random number generation, 3.2.2–(10).) For the example polynomial $u(x)$ in (15), we obtain the following sequence of coefficients of $x^k \bmod u(x)$, using arithmetic modulo 13:

k	$a_{k,7}$	$a_{k,6}$	$a_{k,5}$	$a_{k,4}$	$a_{k,3}$	$a_{k,2}$	$a_{k,1}$	$a_{k,0}$
0	0	0	0	0	0	0	0	1
1	0	0	0	0	0	0	1	0
2	0	0	0	0	0	1	0	0
3	0	0	0	0	1	0	0	0
4	0	0	0	1	0	0	0	0
5	0	0	1	0	0	0	0	0
6	0	1	0	0	0	0	0	0
7	1	0	0	0	0	0	0	0
8	0	12	0	3	3	5	11	5
9	12	0	3	3	5	11	5	0
10	0	4	3	2	8	0	2	8
11	4	3	2	8	0	2	8	0
12	3	11	8	12	1	2	5	7
13	11	5	12	10	11	7	1	2

Therefore the second row of Q is $(2, 1, 7, 11, 10, 12, 5, 11)$. Similarly we may determine $x^{26} \bmod u(x)$, ..., $x^{91} \bmod u(x)$, and we find that

$$Q = \begin{pmatrix} 1 & 0 & 0 & 0 & 0 & 0 & 0 & 0 \\ 2 & 1 & 7 & 11 & 10 & 12 & 5 & 11 \\ 3 & 6 & 4 & 3 & 0 & 4 & 7 & 2 \\ 4 & 3 & 6 & 5 & 1 & 6 & 2 & 3 \\ 2 & 11 & 8 & 8 & 3 & 1 & 3 & 11 \\ 6 & 11 & 8 & 6 & 2 & 7 & 10 & 9 \\ 5 & 11 & 7 & 10 & 0 & 11 & 7 & 12 \\ 3 & 3 & 12 & 5 & 0 & 11 & 9 & 12 \end{pmatrix},$$

$$Q - I = \begin{pmatrix} 0 & 0 & 0 & 0 & 0 & 0 & 0 & 0 \\ 2 & 0 & 7 & 11 & 10 & 12 & 5 & 11 \\ 3 & 6 & 3 & 3 & 0 & 4 & 7 & 2 \\ 4 & 3 & 6 & 4 & 1 & 6 & 2 & 3 \\ 2 & 11 & 8 & 8 & 2 & 1 & 3 & 11 \\ 6 & 11 & 8 & 6 & 2 & 6 & 10 & 9 \\ 5 & 11 & 7 & 10 & 0 & 11 & 6 & 12 \\ 3 & 3 & 12 & 5 & 0 & 11 & 9 & 11 \end{pmatrix}.$$

(17)

That finishes step B2; the next step of Berlekamp's procedure requires finding the "null space" of $Q - I$. In general, suppose that A is an $n \times n$ matrix over a field, whose rank $n - r$ is to be determined; suppose further that we wish to determine linearly independent vectors $v^{[1]}, v^{[2]}, \ldots, v^{[r]}$ such that $v^{[1]}A = v^{[2]}A = \cdots = v^{[r]}A = (0, \ldots, 0)$. An algorithm for this calculation can be based on the observation that any column of A may be multiplied by a nonzero quantity, and any multiple of one of its columns may be added to a different column, without changing the rank or the vectors $v^{[1]}, \ldots, v^{[r]}$. (These transformations amount to replacing A by AB, where B is a nonsingular matrix.) The following well-known "triangularization" procedure may therefore be used.

Algorithm N (*Null space algorithm*). Let A be an $n \times n$ matrix, whose elements a_{ij} belong to a field and have subscripts in the range $0 \le i, j < n$. This algorithm outputs r vectors $v^{[1]}, \ldots, v^{[r]}$, which are linearly independent over the field and satisfy $v^{[j]}A = (0, \ldots, 0)$, where $n - r$ is the rank of A.

N1. [Initialize.] Set $c_0 \leftarrow c_1 \leftarrow \cdots \leftarrow c_{n-1} \leftarrow -1$, $r \leftarrow 0$. (During the calculation we will have $c_j \ge 0$ only if $a_{c_j j} = -1$ and all other entries of row c_j are zero.)

N2. [Loop on k.] Do step N3 for $k = 0, 1, \ldots, n - 1$, then terminate the algorithm.

N3. [Scan row for dependence.] If there is some j in the range $0 \le j < n$ such that $a_{kj} \ne 0$ and $c_j < 0$, then do the following: Multiply column j of A by $-1/a_{kj}$ (so that a_{kj} becomes equal to -1); then add a_{ki} times column j to column i for all $i \ne j$; finally set $c_j \leftarrow k$. (Since it is not difficult to show that $a_{sj} = 0$ for all $s < k$, these operations have no effect on rows $0, 1, \ldots,$ $k - 1$ of A.)

On the other hand, if there is no j in the range $0 \le j < n$ such that $a_{kj} \ne 0$ and $c_j < 0$, then set $r \leftarrow r + 1$ and output the vector

$$v^{[r]} = (v_0, v_1, \ldots, v_{n-1})$$

defined by the rule

$$v_j = \begin{cases} a_{ks}, & \text{if } c_s = j \ge 0; \\ 1, & \text{if } j = k; \\ 0, & \text{otherwise.} \end{cases} \qquad (18)$$

An example will reveal the mechanism of this algorithm. Let A be the matrix $Q - I$ of (17) over the field of integers modulo 13. When $k = 0$, we output the vector $v^{[1]} = (1, 0, 0, 0, 0, 0, 0, 0)$. When $k = 1$, we may take j in step N3 to be either 0, 2, 3, 4, 5, 6, or 7; the choice here is completely arbitrary, although it affects the particular vectors that are chosen to be output by the algorithm. For hand calculation, it is most convenient to pick $j = 5$, since $a_{15} = 12 = -1$ already; the column operations of step N3 then change A to the matrix

$$\begin{pmatrix} 0 & 0 & 0 & 0 & 0 & 0 & 0 & 0 \\ 0 & 0 & 0 & 0 & 0 & ⑫ & 0 & 0 \\ 11 & 6 & 5 & 8 & 1 & 4 & 1 & 7 \\ 3 & 3 & 9 & 5 & 9 & 6 & 6 & 4 \\ 4 & 11 & 2 & 6 & 12 & 1 & 8 & 9 \\ 5 & 11 & 11 & 7 & 10 & 6 & 1 & 10 \\ 1 & 11 & 6 & 1 & 6 & 11 & 9 & 3 \\ 12 & 3 & 11 & 9 & 6 & 11 & 12 & 2 \end{pmatrix}.$$

(The circled element in column "5", row "1", is used here to indicate that $c_5 = 1$. Remember that Algorithm N numbers the rows and columns of the matrix starting with 0, not 1.) When $k = 2$, we may choose $j = 4$ and proceed in a similar way, obtaining the following matrices, which all have the same null space as $Q - I$:

$$k = 2$$

$$\begin{pmatrix}
0 & 0 & 0 & 0 & 0 & 0 & 0 & 0 \\
0 & 0 & 0 & 0 & 0 & ⑫ & 0 & 0 \\
0 & 0 & 0 & 0 & ⑫ & 0 & 0 & 0 \\
8 & 1 & 3 & 11 & 4 & 9 & 10 & 6 \\
2 & 4 & 7 & 1 & 1 & 5 & 9 & 3 \\
12 & 3 & 0 & 5 & 3 & 5 & 4 & 5 \\
0 & 1 & 2 & 5 & 7 & 0 & 3 & 0 \\
11 & 6 & 7 & 0 & 7 & 0 & 6 & 12
\end{pmatrix}$$

$$k = 3$$

$$\begin{pmatrix}
0 & 0 & 0 & 0 & 0 & 0 & 0 & 0 \\
0 & 0 & 0 & 0 & 0 & ⑫ & 0 & 0 \\
0 & 0 & 0 & 0 & ⑫ & 0 & 0 & 0 \\
0 & ⑫ & 0 & 0 & 0 & 0 & 0 & 0 \\
9 & 9 & 8 & 9 & 11 & 8 & 8 & 5 \\
1 & 10 & 4 & 11 & 4 & 4 & 0 & 0 \\
5 & 12 & 12 & 7 & 3 & 4 & 6 & 7 \\
2 & 7 & 2 & 12 & 9 & 11 & 11 & 2
\end{pmatrix}$$

$$k = 4$$

$$\begin{pmatrix}
0 & 0 & 0 & 0 & 0 & 0 & 0 & 0 \\
0 & 0 & 0 & 0 & 0 & ⑫ & 0 & 0 \\
0 & 0 & 0 & 0 & ⑫ & 0 & 0 & 0 \\
0 & ⑫ & 0 & 0 & 0 & 0 & 0 & 0 \\
0 & 0 & 0 & 0 & 0 & 0 & 0 & ⑫ \\
1 & 10 & 4 & 11 & 4 & 4 & 0 & 0 \\
8 & 2 & 6 & 10 & 11 & 11 & 0 & 9 \\
1 & 6 & 4 & 11 & 2 & 0 & 0 & 10
\end{pmatrix}$$

$$k = 5$$

$$\begin{pmatrix}
0 & 0 & 0 & 0 & 0 & 0 & 0 & 0 \\
0 & 0 & 0 & 0 & 0 & ⑫ & 0 & 0 \\
0 & 0 & 0 & 0 & ⑫ & 0 & 0 & 0 \\
0 & ⑫ & 0 & 0 & 0 & 0 & 0 & 0 \\
0 & 0 & 0 & 0 & 0 & 0 & 0 & ⑫ \\
⑫ & 0 & 0 & 0 & 0 & 0 & 0 & 0 \\
5 & 0 & 0 & 0 & 5 & 5 & 0 & 9 \\
12 & 9 & 0 & 0 & 11 & 9 & 0 & 10
\end{pmatrix}$$

Now every column that has no circled entry is completely zero; so when $k = 6$ and $k = 7$ the algorithm outputs two more vectors, namely

$$v^{[2]} = (0, 5, 5, 0, 9, 5, 1, 0), \qquad v^{[3]} = (0, 9, 11, 9, 10, 12, 0, 1).$$

From the form of matrix A after $k = 5$, it is evident that these vectors satisfy the equation $vA = (0, \ldots, 0)$. Since the computation has produced three linearly independent vectors, $u(x)$ must have exactly three irreducible factors.

Finally we can go to step B4 of the factoring procedure. The calculation of $\gcd\big(u(x), v^{[2]}(x) - s\big)$ for $0 \le s < 13$, where $v^{[2]}(x) = x^6 + 5x^5 + 9x^4 + 5x^2 + 5x$, gives $x^5 + 5x^4 + 9x^3 + 5x + 5$ as the answer when $s = 0$, and $x^3 + 8x^2 + 4x + 12$ when $s = 2$; the gcd is unity for other values of s. Therefore $v^{[2]}(x)$ gives us only two of the three factors. Turning to $\gcd\big(v^{[3]}(x) - s, x^5 + 5x^4 + 9x^3 + 5x + 5\big)$, where $v^{[3]}(x) = x^7 + 12x^5 + 10x^4 + 9x^3 + 11x^2 + 9x$, we obtain the factor $x^4 + 2x^3 + 3x^2 + 4x + 6$ when $s = 6$, $x + 3$ when $s = 8$, and unity otherwise. Thus the complete factorization is

$$u(x) = (x^4 + 2x^3 + 3x^2 + 4x + 6)(x^3 + 8x^2 + 4x + 12)(x + 3). \qquad (19)$$

Let us now estimate the running time of Berlekamp's method when an nth degree polynomial is factored modulo p. First assume that p is relatively small, so that the four arithmetic operations can be done modulo p in essentially a fixed length of time. (Division modulo p can be converted to multiplication, by storing a table of reciprocals as suggested in exercise 9; for example, when working modulo 13, we have $\frac{1}{2} = 7$, $\frac{1}{3} = 9$, etc.) The computation in step B1 takes $O(n^2)$ units of time; step B2 takes $O(pn^2)$. For step B3 we use Algorithm N, which requires $O(n^3)$ units of time at most. Finally, in step B4 we can observe that the calculation of $\gcd(f(x), g(x))$ by Euclid's algorithm takes $O(\deg(f)\deg(g))$ units of time; hence the calculation of $\gcd(v^{[j]}(x) - s, w(x))$ for fixed j and s and for all factors $w(x)$ of $u(x)$ found so far takes $O(n^2)$ units. Step B4 therefore requires $O(prn^2)$ units of time at most. *Berlekamp's procedure factors an arbitrary polynomial of degree n, modulo p, in $O(n^3+prn^2)$ steps,* when p is a small prime; and exercise 5 shows that the average number of factors, r, is approximately $\ln n$. Thus the algorithm is much faster than any known methods of factoring n-digit numbers in the p-ary number system.

Of course, when n and p are small, a trial-and-error factorization procedure analogous to Algorithm 4.5.4A will be even faster than Berlekamp's method. Exercise 1 implies that it is a good idea to cast out factors of small degree first when p is small, before going to any more complicated procedure, even when n is large.

When p is large, a different implementation of Berlekamp's procedure would be used for the calculations. Division modulo p would not be done with an auxiliary table of reciprocals; instead the method of exercise 4.5.2–16, which takes $O((\log p)^2)$ steps, would probably be used. Then step B1 would take $O(n^2(\log p)^2)$ units of time; similarly, step B3 would take $O(n^3(\log p)^2)$. In step B2, we can form $x^p \bmod u(x)$ in a more efficient way than (16) when p is large: Section 4.6.3 shows that this value can be obtained by essentially using $O(\log p)$ operations of squaring $\bmod\, u(x)$, going from $x^k \bmod u(x)$ to $x^{2k} \bmod u(x)$, together with the operation of multiplying by x. The squaring operation is relatively easy to perform if we first make an auxiliary table of $x^m \bmod u(x)$ for $m = n,\ n+1,\ \ldots,\ 2n-2$; if $x^k \bmod u(x) = c_{n-1}x^{n-1} + \cdots + c_1x + c_0$, then

$$x^{2k} \bmod u(x) = \left(c_{n-1}^2 x^{2n-2} + \cdots + (c_1c_0 + c_1c_0)x + c_0^2\right) \bmod u(x),$$

where $x^{2n-2},\ \ldots,\ x^n$ can be replaced by polynomials in the auxiliary table. The total time to compute $x^p \bmod u(x)$ comes to $O(n^2(\log p)^3)$ units, and we obtain the second row of Q. To get further rows of Q, we can compute $x^{2p} \bmod u(x)$, $x^{3p} \bmod u(x),\ \ldots$, simply by multiplying repeatedly by $x^p \bmod u(x)$, in a fashion analogous to squaring $\bmod\, u(x)$; step B2 is completed in $O(n^3(\log p)^2)$ additional units of time. Thus steps B1, B2, and B3 take a total of $O(n^2(\log p)^3+n^3(\log p)^2)$ time units; these three steps tell us the number of factors of $u(x)$.

But when p is large and we get to step B4, we are asked to calculate a greatest common divisor for p different values of s, and that is out of the question if p is even moderately large. This hurdle was first surmounted by Hans Zassenhaus [*J. Number Theory* **1** (1969), 291–311], who showed how to determine all of the "useful" values of s (see exercise 14); but an even better way to proceed was found by Zassenhaus and Cantor in 1980. If $v(x)$ is any solution to (8), we know that $u(x)$ divides $v(x)^p - v(x) = v(x) \cdot (v(x)^{(p-1)/2} + 1) \cdot (v(x)^{(p-1)/2} - 1)$. This suggests that we calculate

$$\gcd\left(u(x),\, v(x)^{(p-1)/2} - 1\right); \tag{20}$$

with a little bit of luck, (20) will be a nontrivial factor of $u(x)$. In fact, we can determine exactly how much luck is involved, by considering (7). Let $v(x) \equiv s_j$ (modulo $p_j(x)$) for $1 \leq j \leq r$; then $p_j(x)$ divides $v(x)^{(p-1)/2} - 1$ if and only if $s_j^{(p-1)/2} \equiv 1$ (modulo p). We know that exactly $(p-1)/2$ of the integers s in the range $0 \leq s < p$ satisfy $s^{(p-1)/2} \equiv 1$ (modulo p), hence about half of the $p_j(x)$ will appear in the gcd (20). More precisely, if $v(x)$ is a random solution of (8), where all p^r solutions are equally likely, the probability that the gcd (20) equals $u(x)$ is exactly

$$\big((p-1)/2p\big)^r,$$

and the probability that it equals 1 is $\big((p+1)/2p\big)^r$. The probability that a nontrivial factor will be obtained is therefore

$$1 - \left(\frac{p-1}{2p}\right)^r - \left(\frac{p+1}{2p}\right)^r = 1 - \frac{1}{2^{r-1}}\left(1 + \binom{r}{2}p^{-2} + \binom{r}{4}p^{-4} + \cdots\right) \geq \frac{4}{9},$$

for all $r \geq 2$ and $p \geq 3$.

It is therefore a good idea to replace step B4 by the following procedure, unless p is quite small: Set $v(x) \leftarrow a_1 v^{[1]}(x) + a_2 v^{[2]}(x) + \cdots + a_r v^{[r]}(x)$, where the coefficients a_j are randomly chosen in the range $0 \leq a_j < p$. Let the current partial factorization of $u(x)$ be $u_1(x) \ldots u_t(x)$ where t is initially 1. Compute

$$g_i(x) = \gcd\big(u_i(x),\, v(x)^{(p-1)/2} - 1\big)$$

for all i such that $\deg(u_i) > 1$; replace $u_i(x)$ by $g_i(x) \cdot \big(u_i(x)/g_i(x)\big)$ and increase the value of t, whenever a nontrivial gcd is found. Repeat this process for different choices of $v(x)$ until $t = r$.

If we assume (as we may) that only $O(\log r)$ random solutions $v(x)$ to (8) will be needed, we can give an upper bound on the time required to perform this alternative to step B4. It takes $O\big(rn(\log p)^2\big)$ steps to compute $v(x)$; and if $\deg(u_i) = d$, it takes $O\big(d^2(\log p)^3\big)$ steps to compute $v(x)^{(p-1)/2} \bmod u_i(x)$ and $O\big(d^2(\log p)^2\big)$ further steps to compute $\gcd\big(u_i(x),\, v(x)^{(p-1)/2} - 1\big)$. Thus the total time is $O(n^2(\log p)^3 \log r)$.

Distinct-degree factorization. We shall now turn to a somewhat simpler way to find factors modulo p. The ideas we have studied so far in this section involve many instructive insights into computational algebra, so the author does not apologize to the reader for presenting them; but it turns out that the problem of factorization modulo p can actually be solved without relying on so many concepts.

In the first place we can make use of the fact that an irreducible polynomial $q(x)$ of degree d is a divisor of $x^{p^d} - x$, and it is not a divisor of $x^{p^c} - x$ for $1 \leq c < d$; see exercise 16. We can therefore cast out the irreducible factors of each degree separately, by adopting the following strategy.

D1. [Go squarefree.] Rule out squared factors, as in Berlekamp's method. Also set $v(x) \leftarrow u(x)$, $w(x) \leftarrow$ "x", and $d \leftarrow 0$. (Here $v(x)$ and $w(x)$ are variables that have polynomials as values.)

D2. [If not done, take pth power.] (At this point $w(x) = x^{p^d} \bmod v(x)$; all of the irreducible factors of $v(x)$ are distinct and have degree $> d$.) If $d + 1 > \frac{1}{2}\deg(v)$, the procedure terminates since we either have $v(x) = 1$ or $v(x)$ is irreducible. Otherwise increase d by 1 and replace $w(x)$ by $w(x)^p \bmod v(x)$.

D3. [Extract factors.] Find $g_d(x) = \gcd\big(w(x) - x,\, v(x)\big)$. (This is the product of all the irreducible factors of $u(x)$ whose degree is d.) If $g_d(x) \neq 1$, replace $v(x)$ by $v(x)/g_d(x)$ and $w(x)$ by $w(x) \bmod v(x)$; and if the degree of $g_d(x)$ is greater than d, use the algorithm below to find its factors. Return to step D2. ∎

This procedure determines the product of all irreducible factors of each degree d, and therefore it tells us how many factors there are of each degree. Since the three factors of our example polynomial (19) have different degrees, they would all be discovered without any need to factorize the polynomials $g_d(x)$.

To complete the method, we need a way to split the polynomial $g_d(x)$ into its irreducible factors when $\deg(g_d) > d$. Michael Rabin pointed out in 1976 that this can be done by doing arithmetic in the field of p^d elements. David G. Cantor and Hans Zassenhaus discovered in 1979 that there is an even simpler way to proceed, based on the following identity: If p is any odd prime, we have

$$g_d(x) = \gcd\big(g_d(x), t(x)\big)\, \gcd\big(g_d(x),\, t(x)^{(p^d-1)/2}+1\big)\, \gcd\big(g_d(x),\, t(x)^{(p^d-1)/2}-1\big) \tag{21}$$

for all polynomials $t(x)$, since $t(x)^{p^d} - t(x)$ is a multiple of all irreducible polynomials of degree d. (We may regard $t(x)$ as an element of the field of size p^d, when that field consists of all polynomials modulo an irreducible $f(x)$ as in exercise 16.) Now exercise 29 shows that $\gcd\big(g_d(x), t(x)^{(p^d-1)/2} - 1\big)$ will be a nontrivial factor of $g_d(x)$ about 50 percent of the time, when $t(x)$ is a random polynomial of degree $\leq 2d - 1$; hence we will not need many random trials to discover all of the factors. We may assume without loss of generality that $t(x)$ is monic, since integer multiples of $t(x)$ make no difference except possibly to change $t(x)^{(p^d-1)/2}$ into its negative. Thus in the case $d = 1$, we can take $t(x) = x + s$, where s is chosen at random.

Sometimes this procedure will in fact succeed for $d > 1$ when only linear polynomials $t(x)$ are used. For example, there are eight irreducible polynomials $f(x)$ of degree 3, modulo 3, and they will all be distinguished by calculating $\gcd\big(f(x), (x+s)^{13} - 1\big)$ for $0 \leq s < 3$:

$f(x)$	$s = 0$	$s = 1$	$s = 2$
$x^3 + 2x + 1$	1	1	1
$x^3 + 2x + 2$	$f(x)$	$f(x)$	$f(x)$
$x^3 + x^2 + 2$	$f(x)$	$f(x)$	1
$x^3 + x^2 + x + 2$	$f(x)$	1	$f(x)$
$x^3 + x^2 + 2x + 1$	1	$f(x)$	$f(x)$
$x^3 + 2x^2 + 1$	1	$f(x)$	1
$x^3 + 2x^2 + x + 1$	1	1	$f(x)$
$x^3 + 2x^2 + 2x + 2$	$f(x)$	1	1

Exercise 31 contains a partial explanation of why linear polynomials can be effective. But when there are more than 2^p irreducible polynomials of degree d, some irreducibles must exist that cannot be distinguished by linear choices of $t(x)$.

An alternative to (21) that works when $p = 2$ is discussed in exercise 30. Faster algorithms for distinct-degree factorization when p is very large have been found by J. von zur Gathen, V. Shoup, and E. Kaltofen; the running time is $O(n^{2+\epsilon} + n^{1+\epsilon} \log p)$ arithmetic operations modulo p for numbers of practical size, and $O(n^{(5+\omega+\epsilon)/4} \log p)$ such operations as $n \to \infty$, when ω is the exponent of "fast" matrix multiplication in exercise 4.6.4–66. [See *Computational Complexity* **2** (1992), 187–224; *J. Symbolic Comp.* **20** (1995), 363–397; *Math. Comp.* **67** (1998), 1179–1197.]

Historical notes: The idea of finding all the linear factors of a squarefree polynomial $f(x)$ modulo p by first calculating $g(x) = \gcd(x^{p-1} - 1, f(x))$ and then calculating $\gcd(g(x), (x + s)^{(p-1)/2} \pm 1)$ for arbitrary s is due to A. M. Legendre, *Mémoires Acad. Sci.* (Paris, 1785), 484–490; his motive was to find all of the integer solutions to Diophantine equations of the form $f(x) = py$, that is, $f(x) \equiv 0$ (modulo p). The more general degree-separation technique embodied in Algorithm D was discovered by C. F. Gauss before 1800, but not published [see his *Werke* **2** (1876), 237], and then by Évariste Galois in the now-classic paper that launched the theory of finite fields [*Bulletin des Sciences Mathématiques, Physiques et Chimiques* **13** (1830), 428–435; reprinted in *J. de Math. Pures et Appliquées* **11** (1846), 398–407]. However, this work of Gauss and Galois was ahead of its time, and not well understood until J. A. Serret gave a detailed exposition somewhat later [*Mémoires Acad. Sci.*, series 2, **35** (Paris, 1866), 617–688; Algorithm D is in §7]. Special procedures for splitting $g_d(x)$ into irreducible factors were devised subsequently by various authors, but methods of full generality that would work efficiently for large p were apparently not discovered until the advent of computers made them desirable. The first such randomized algorithm with a rigorously analyzed running time was published by E. Berlekamp [*Math. Comp.* **24** (1970), 713–735]; it was refined and simplified by Robert T. Moenck [*Math. Comp.* **31** (1977), 235–250], M. O. Rabin [*SICOMP* **9** (1980), 273–280], D. G. Cantor and H. J. Zassenhaus [*Math. Comp.* **36** (1981), 587–592]. Paul Camion independently found a generalization to special classes of multivariate polynomials [*Comptes Rendus Acad. Sci.* **A291** (Paris, 1980), 479–482; *IEEE Trans.* **IT-29** (1983), 378–385].

The average number of operations needed to factor a random polynomial mod p has been analyzed by P. Flajolet, X. Gourdon, and D. Panario, *Lecture Notes in Comp. Sci.* **1099** (1996), 232–243.

Factoring over the integers. It is somewhat more difficult to find the complete factorization of polynomials with integer coefficients when we are *not* working modulo p, but some reasonably efficient methods are available for this purpose.

Isaac Newton gave a method for finding linear and quadratic factors of polynomials with integer coefficients in his *Arithmetica Universalis* (1707). His method was extended by N. Bernoulli in 1708 and, more explicitly, by an astronomer named Friedrich von Schubert in 1793, who showed how to find all factors of degree n in a finite number of steps; see M. Mignotte and D. Ştefănescu, *Revue d'Hist. Math.* **7** (2001), 67–89. L. Kronecker rediscovered their approach independently, about 90 years later; but unfortunately the method is very inefficient when n is five or more. Much better results can be obtained with the help of the "mod p" factorization methods presented above.

Suppose that we want to find the irreducible factors of a given polynomial

$$u(x) = u_n x^n + u_{n-1} x^{n-1} + \cdots + u_0, \qquad u_n \neq 0,$$

over the integers. As a first step, we can divide by the greatest common divisor of the coefficients; this leaves us with a *primitive* polynomial. We may also assume that $u(x)$ is squarefree, by dividing out $\gcd\bigl(u(x), u'(x)\bigr)$ as in exercise 34.

Now if $u(x) = v(x)w(x)$, where each of these polynomials has integer coefficients, we obviously have $u(x) \equiv v(x)w(x)$ (modulo p) for all primes p, so there is a nontrivial factorization modulo p unless p divides $\ell(u)$. An efficient algorithm for factoring $u(x)$ modulo p can therefore be used in an attempt to reconstruct possible factorizations of $u(x)$ over the integers.

For example, let

$$u(x) = x^8 + x^6 - 3x^4 - 3x^3 + 8x^2 + 2x - 5. \tag{22}$$

We have seen above in (19) that

$$u(x) \equiv (x^4 + 2x^3 + 3x^2 + 4x + 6)(x^3 + 8x^2 + 4x + 12)(x + 3) \text{ (modulo 13);} \tag{23}$$

and the complete factorization of $u(x)$ modulo 2 shows one factor of degree 6 and another of degree 2 (see exercise 10). From (23) we can see that $u(x)$ has no factor of degree 2, so it must be irreducible over the integers.

This particular example was perhaps too simple; experience shows that most irreducible polynomials can be recognized as such by examining their factors modulo a few primes, but it is *not* always so easy to establish irreducibility. For example, there are polynomials that can be properly factored modulo p for all primes p, with consistent degrees of the factors, yet they are irreducible over the integers (see exercise 12).

A large family of irreducible polynomials is exhibited in exercise 38, and exercise 27 proves that almost all polynomials are irreducible over the integers. But we usually aren't trying to factor a random polynomial; there is probably some reason to expect a nontrivial factor or else the calculation would not have been attempted in the first place. We need a method that identifies factors when they are there.

In general if we try to find the factors of $u(x)$ by considering its behavior modulo different primes, the results will not be easy to combine. For example, if $u(x)$ is actually the product of four quadratic polynomials, we will have trouble matching up their images with respect to different prime moduli. Therefore it is desirable to stick to a single prime and to see how much mileage we can get out of it, once we feel that the factors modulo this prime have the right degrees.

One idea is to work modulo a very *large* prime p, big enough so that the coefficients in any true factorization $u(x) = v(x)w(x)$ over the integers must actually lie between $-p/2$ and $p/2$. Then all possible integer factors can be read off from the factors that we know how to compute mod p.

Exercise 20 shows how to obtain fairly good bounds on the coefficients of polynomial factors. For example, if (22) were reducible it would have a factor $v(x)$ of degree ≤ 4, and the coefficients of v would be at most 34 in magnitude by the results of that exercise. So all potential factors of $u(x)$ will be fairly evident if we work modulo any prime $p > 68$. Indeed, the complete factorization modulo 71 is

$$(x + 12)(x + 25)(x^2 - 13x - 7)(x^4 - 24x^3 - 16x^2 + 31x - 12),$$

and we see immediately that none of these polynomials could be a factor of (22) over the integers since the constant terms do not divide 5; furthermore there is no way to obtain a divisor of (22) by grouping two of these factors, since none of the conceivable constant terms 12×25, $12 \times (-7)$, $12 \times (-12)$ is congruent to ± 1 or ± 5 (modulo 71).

Incidentally, it is not trivial to obtain good bounds on the coefficients of polynomial factors, since a lot of cancellation can occur when polynomials are multiplied. For example, the innocuous-looking polynomial $x^n - 1$ has irreducible factors whose coefficients exceed $\exp(n^{1/\lg \lg n})$ for infinitely many n. [See R. C. Vaughan, *Michigan Math. J.* **21** (1974), 289–295.] The factorization of $x^n - 1$ is discussed in exercise 32.

Instead of using a large prime p, which might need to be truly enormous if $u(x)$ has large degree or large coefficients, we can also make use of small p, provided that $u(x)$ is squarefree mod p. For in this case, an important construction known as Hensel's Lemma can be used to extend a factorization modulo p in a unique way to a factorization modulo p^e for arbitrarily high exponents e (see exercise 22). If we apply Hensel's Lemma to (23) with $p = 13$ and $e = 2$, we obtain the unique factorization

$$u(x) \equiv (x - 36)(x^3 - 18x^2 + 82x - 66)(x^4 + 54x^3 - 10x^2 + 69x + 84)$$

(modulo 169). Calling these factors $v_1(x)v_3(x)v_4(x)$, we see that $v_1(x)$ and $v_3(x)$ are not factors of $u(x)$ over the integers, nor is their product $v_1(x)v_3(x)$ when the coefficients have been reduced modulo 169 to the range $(-\frac{169}{2} .. \frac{169}{2})$. Thus we have exhausted all possibilities, proving once again that $u(x)$ is irreducible over the integers — this time using only its factorization modulo 13.

The example we have been considering is atypical in one important respect: We have been factoring the *monic* polynomial $u(x)$ in (22), so we could assume that all its factors were monic. What should we do if $u_n > 1$? In such a case, the leading coefficients of all but one of the polynomial factors can be varied almost arbitrarily modulo p^e; we certainly don't want to try all possibilities. Perhaps the reader has already noticed this problem. Fortunately there is a simple way out: The factorization $u(x) = v(x)w(x)$ implies a factorization $u_n u(x) = v_1(x)w_1(x)$ where $\ell(v_1) = \ell(w_1) = u_n = \ell(u)$. ("Excuse me, do you mind if I multiply your polynomial by its leading coefficient before I factor it?") We can proceed essentially as above, but using $p^e > 2B$ where B now bounds the maximum coefficient for factors of $u_n u(x)$ instead of $u(x)$. Another way to solve the leading coefficient problem is discussed in exercise 40.

Putting these observations all together results in the following procedure:

F1. [Factor modulo a prime power.] Find the unique squarefree factorization

$$u(x) \equiv \ell(u)v_1(x) \dots v_r(x) \pmod{p^e},$$

where p^e is sufficiently large as explained above, and where the $v_j(x)$ are monic. (This will be possible for all but a few primes p; see exercise 23.) Also set $d \leftarrow 1$.

F2. [Try the d-element subfactors.] For every combination of factors $v(x) = v_{i_1}(x) \dots v_{i_d}(x)$, with $i_1 = 1$ if $d = \frac{1}{2}r$, form the unique polynomial $\bar{v}(x) \equiv \ell(u)v(x) \pmod{p^e}$ whose coefficients all lie in the interval $[-\frac{1}{2}p^e \mathinner{.\,.} \frac{1}{2}p^e)$. If $\bar{v}(x)$ divides $\ell(u)u(x)$, output the factor $\text{pp}(\bar{v}(x))$, divide $u(x)$ by this factor, and remove the corresponding $v_i(x)$ from the list of factors modulo p^e; decrease r by the number of factors removed, and terminate if $d > \frac{1}{2}r$.

F3. [Loop on d.] Increase d by 1, and return to F2 if $d \leq \frac{1}{2}r$. ∎

At the conclusion of this process, the current value of $u(x)$ will be the final irreducible factor of the originally given polynomial. Notice that if $|u_0| < |u_n|$, it is preferable to do all of the work with the reverse polynomial $u_0 x^n + \dots + u_n$, whose factors are the reverses of the factors of $u(x)$.

The procedure as stated requires $p^e > 2B$, where B is a bound on the coefficients of *any* divisor of $u_n u(x)$, but we can use a much smaller value of B if we only guarantee it to be valid for divisors of degree $\leq \frac{1}{2}\deg(u)$. In this case the divisibility test in step F2 should be applied to $w(x) = v_1(x) \dots v_r(x)/v(x)$ instead of $v(x)$, whenever $\deg(v) > \frac{1}{2}\deg(u)$.

We can decrease B still more if we decide to guarantee only that B should bound the coefficients of *at least one* proper divisor of $u(x)$. (For example, when we're factoring a nonprime integer N instead of a polynomial, some of the divisors might be very large, but at least one will be $\leq \sqrt{N}$.) This idea, due to B. Beauzamy, V. Trevisan, and P. S. Wang [*J. Symbolic Comp.* **15** (1993), 393–413], is discussed in exercise 21. The divisibility test in step F2 must then be applied to both $v(x)$ and $w(x)$, but the computations are faster because p^e is often much smaller.

The algorithm above contains an obvious bottleneck: We may have to test as many as $2^{r-1} - 1$ potential factors $v(x)$. The average value of 2^r in a random situation is about n, or perhaps $n^{1.5}$ (see exercise 5), but in nonrandom situations we will want to speed up this part of the routine as much as we can. One way to rule out spurious factors quickly is to compute the trailing coefficient $\bar{v}(0)$ first, continuing only if this divides $\ell(u)u(0)$; the complications explained in the preceding paragraphs do not have to be considered unless this divisibility condition is satisfied, since such a test is valid even when $\deg(v) > \frac{1}{2}\deg(u)$.

Another important way to speed up the procedure is to reduce r so that it tends to reflect the true number of factors. The distinct degree factorization algorithm above can be applied for various small primes p_j, thus obtaining for each prime a set D_j of possible degrees of factors modulo p_j; see exercise 26. We can represent D_j as a string of n binary bits. Now we compute the intersection $\bigcap D_j$, namely the bitwise "and" of these strings, and we perform step F2 only for

$$\deg(v_{i_1}) + \cdots + \deg(v_{i_d}) \in \bigcap D_j.$$

Furthermore p is chosen to be that p_j having the smallest value of r. This technique is due to David R. Musser, whose experience suggests trying about five primes p_j [see *JACM* **25** (1978), 271–282]. Of course we would stop immediately if the current $\bigcap D_j$ shows that $u(x)$ is irreducible.

Musser has given a complete discussion of a factorization method similar to the steps above, in *JACM* **22** (1975), 291–308. Steps F1–F3 incorporate an improvement suggested in 1978 by G. E. Collins, namely to look for trial divisors by taking combinations of d factors at a time rather than combinations of total degree d. This improvement is important because of the statistical behavior of the modulo-p factors of polynomials that are irreducible over the rationals (see exercise 37).

A. K. Lenstra, H. W. Lenstra, Jr., and L. Lovász introduced their famous "LLL algorithm" in order to obtain rigorous worst-case bounds on the amount of computation needed to factor a polynomial over the integers [*Math. Annalen* **261** (1982), 515–534]. Their method requires no random numbers, and its running time for $u(x)$ of degree n is $O(n^{12} + n^9(\log \|u\|)^3)$ bit operations, where $\|u\|$ is defined in exercise 20. This estimate includes the time to search for a suitable prime number p and to find all factors modulo p with Algorithm B. Of course, heuristic methods that use randomization run noticeably faster in practice. Mark van Hoeij [*J. Number Theory* **95** (2002), 167–189] has found an efficient way to apply LLL when those heuristics fail; its running time depends on r, not n.

Greatest common divisors. Similar techniques can be used to calculate greatest common divisors of polynomials: If $\gcd(u(x), v(x)) = d(x)$ over the integers, and if $\gcd(u(x), v(x)) = q(x)$ (modulo p) where $q(x)$ is monic, then $d(x)$ is a common divisor of $u(x)$ and $v(x)$ modulo p; hence

$$d(x) \text{ divides } q(x) \text{ (modulo } p). \tag{24}$$

If p does not divide the leading coefficients of both u and v, it does not divide the leading coefficient of d; in such a case $\deg(d) \leq \deg(q)$. When $q(x) = 1$ for such a prime p, we must therefore have $\deg(d) = 0$, and $d(x) = \gcd(\text{cont}(u), \text{cont}(v))$. This justifies the remark made in Section 4.6.1 that the simple computation of $\gcd(u(x), v(x))$ modulo 13 in 4.6.1–(6) is enough to prove that $u(x)$ and $v(x)$ are relatively prime over the integers; the comparatively laborious calculations of Algorithm 4.6.1E or Algorithm 4.6.1C are unnecessary. Since two random primitive polynomials are almost always relatively prime over the integers, and since they are relatively prime modulo p with probability $1 - 1/p$ by exercise 4.6.1–5, it is usually a good idea to do the computations modulo p.

As remarked before, we need good methods also for the nonrandom polynomials that arise in practice. Therefore we wish to sharpen our techniques and discover how to find $\gcd(u(x), v(x))$ in general, over the integers, based entirely on information that we obtain working modulo primes p. We may assume that $u(x)$ and $v(x)$ are primitive.

Instead of calculating $\gcd\big(u(x), v(x)\big)$ directly, it will be convenient to search instead for the polynomial

$$\bar{d}(x) = c \cdot \gcd\big(u(x), v(x)\big), \qquad (25)$$

where the constant c is chosen so that

$$\ell(\bar{d}) = \gcd\big(\ell(u), \ell(v)\big). \qquad (26)$$

This condition will always hold for suitable c, since the leading coefficient of any common divisor of $u(x)$ and $v(x)$ must be a divisor of $\gcd\big(\ell(u), \ell(v)\big)$. Once $\bar{d}(x)$ has been found satisfying these conditions, we can readily compute $\mathrm{pp}\big(\bar{d}(x)\big)$, which is the true greatest common divisor of $u(x)$ and $v(x)$. Condition (26) conveniently avoids the uncertainty of unit multiples of the gcd; we have used essentially the same idea to control the leading coefficients in our factorization routine.

If p is a sufficiently large prime, based on the bounds for coefficients in exercise 20 applied either to $\ell(\bar{d})u(x)$ or $\ell(\bar{d})v(x)$, let us compute the unique polynomial $\bar{q}(x) \equiv \ell(\bar{d})q(x)$ (modulo p) having all coefficients in $[-\frac{1}{2}p \mathinner{.\,.} \frac{1}{2}p)$. When $\mathrm{pp}\big(\bar{q}(x)\big)$ divides both $u(x)$ and $v(x)$, it must equal $\gcd\big(u(x), v(x)\big)$ because of (24). On the other hand if it does not divide both $u(x)$ and $v(x)$ we must have $\deg(q) > \deg(d)$. A study of Algorithm 4.6.1E reveals that this will be the case only if p divides the leading coefficient of one of the nonzero remainders computed by that algorithm with exact integer arithmetic; otherwise Euclid's algorithm modulo p deals with precisely the same sequence of polynomials as Algorithm 4.6.1E except for nonzero constant multiples (modulo p). So only a small number of "unlucky" primes can cause us to miss the gcd, and we will soon find a lucky prime if we keep trying.

If the bound on coefficients is so large that single-precision primes p are insufficient, we can compute $\bar{d}(x)$ modulo several primes p until it has been determined via the Chinese remainder algorithm of Section 4.3.2. This approach, which is due to W. S. Brown and G. E. Collins, has been described in detail by Brown in *JACM* **18** (1971), 478–504. Alternatively, as suggested by J. Moses and D. Y. Y. Yun [*Proc. ACM Conf.* **28** (1973), 159–166], we can use Hensel's method to determine $\bar{d}(x)$ modulo p^e for sufficiently large e. Hensel's construction appears to be computationally superior to the Chinese remainder approach; but it is valid directly only when

$$d(x) \perp u(x)/d(x) \qquad \text{or} \qquad d(x) \perp v(x)/d(x), \qquad (27)$$

since the idea is to apply the techniques of exercise 22 to one of the factorizations $\ell(\bar{d})u(x) \equiv \bar{q}(x)u_1(x)$ or $\ell(\bar{d})v(x) \equiv \bar{q}(x)v_1(x)$ (modulo p). Exercises 34 and 35 show that it is possible to arrange things so that (27) holds whenever necessary. (The notation

$$u(x) \perp v(x) \qquad (28)$$

used in (27) means that $u(x)$ and $v(x)$ are relatively prime, by analogy with the notation used for relatively prime integers.)

The gcd algorithms sketched here are significantly faster than those of Section 4.6.1 except when the polynomial remainder sequence is very short. Perhaps the best general procedure would be to start with the computation of $\gcd\bigl(u(x), v(x)\bigr)$ modulo a fairly small prime p, not a divisor of both $\ell(u)$ and $\ell(v)$. If the result $q(x)$ is 1, we're done; if it has high degree, we use Algorithm 4.6.1C; otherwise we use one of the methods above, first computing a bound for the coefficients of $\bar{d}(x)$ based on the coefficients of $u(x)$ and $v(x)$, and on the (small) degree of $q(x)$. As in the factorization problem, we should apply this procedure to the reverses of $u(x), v(x)$ and reverse the result, if the trailing coefficients are simpler than the leading ones.

Multivariate polynomials. Similar techniques lead to useful algorithms for factorization or gcd calculations on multivariate polynomials with integer coefficients. It is convenient to deal with the polynomial $u(x_1, \ldots, x_t)$ by working modulo the irreducible polynomials $x_2 - a_2, \ldots, x_t - a_t$, which play the role of p in the discussion above. Since $v(x) \bmod (x - a) = v(a)$, the value of

$$u(x_1, \ldots, x_t) \bmod \{x_2 - a_2, \ldots, x_t - a_t\}$$

is the univariate polynomial $u(x_1, a_2, \ldots, a_t)$. When the integers $a_2, \ldots, a_t$ are chosen so that $u(x_1, a_2, \ldots, a_t)$ has the same degree in x_1 as the original polynomial $u(x_1, x_2, \ldots, x_t)$, an appropriate generalization of Hensel's construction will "lift" squarefree factorizations of this univariate polynomial to factorizations modulo $\{(x_2 - a_2)^{n_2}, \ldots, (x_t - a_t)^{n_t}\}$, where n_j is the degree of x_j in u; at the same time we can also work modulo an appropriate integer prime p. As many as possible of the a_j should be zero, so that sparseness of the intermediate results is retained. For details, see P. S. Wang, *Math. Comp.* **32** (1978), 1215–1231, in addition to the papers by Musser and by Moses and Yun cited earlier.

Significant computational experience has been accumulating since the days when the pioneering papers cited above were written. See R. E. Zippel, *Effective Polynomial Computation* (Boston: Kluwer, 1993) for a more recent survey. Moreover, it is now possible to factor polynomials that are given implicitly by a "black box" computational procedure, even when both input and output polynomials would fill the universe if they were written out explicitly [see E. Kaltofen and B. M. Trager, *J. Symbolic Comp.* **9** (1990), 301–320; Y. N. Lakshman and B. David Saunders, *SICOMP* **24** (1995), 387–397].

> *The asymptotically best algorithms frequently turn out*
> *to be worst on all problems for which they are used.*
> — D. G. CANTOR and H. ZASSENHAUS (1981)

EXERCISES

▶ **1.** [*M24*] Let p be prime, and let $u(x)$ be a random polynomial of degree n, assuming that each of the p^n monic polynomials is equally likely. Show that if $n \geq 2$, the probability that $u(x)$ has a linear factor mod p lies between $(1+p^{-1})/2$ and $(2+p^{-2})/3$, inclusive. Give a closed form for this probability when $n \geq p$. What is the average number of linear factors?

▶ **2.** [*M25*] (a) Show that any monic polynomial $u(x)$, over a unique factorization domain, may be expressed uniquely in the form

$$u(x) = v(x)^2 w(x),$$

where $w(x)$ is squarefree (has no factor of positive degree of the form $d(x)^2$) and both $v(x)$ and $w(x)$ are monic. (b) (E. R. Berlekamp.) How many monic polynomials of degree n are squarefree modulo p, when p is prime?

3. [*M25*] (*The Chinese remainder theorem for polynomials.*) Let $u_1(x), \ldots, u_r(x)$ be polynomials over a field S, with $u_j(x) \perp u_k(x)$ for all $j \neq k$. For any given polynomials $w_1(x), \ldots, w_r(x)$ over S, prove that there is a unique polynomial $v(x)$ over S such that $\deg(v) < \deg(u_1) + \cdots + \deg(u_r)$ and $v(x) \equiv w_j(x)$ (modulo $u_j(x)$) for $1 \leq j \leq r$. Does this result hold also when S is the set of all integers?

4. [*HM28*] Let a_{np} be the number of monic irreducible polynomials of degree n, modulo a prime p. Find a formula for the generating function $G_p(z) = \sum_n a_{np} z^n$. [*Hint:* Prove the following identity connecting power series: $f(z) = \sum_{j \geq 1} g(z^j)/j^t$ if and only if $g(z) = \sum_{n \geq 1} \mu(n) f(z^n)/n^t$.] What is $\lim_{p \to \infty} a_{np}/p^n$?

5. [*HM30*] Let A_{np} be the average number of irreducible factors of a randomly selected polynomial of degree n, modulo a prime p. Show that $\lim_{p \to \infty} A_{np} = H_n$. What is the limiting average value of 2^r, when r is the number of irreducible factors?

6. [*M21*] (J. L. Lagrange, 1771.) Prove the congruence (9). [*Hint:* Factor $x^p - x$ in the field of p elements.]

7. [*M22*] Prove Eq. (14).

8. [*HM20*] How can we be sure that the vectors output by Algorithm N are linearly independent?

9. [*20*] Explain how to construct a table of reciprocals mod 101 in a simple way, given that 2 is a primitive root of 101.

▶ **10.** [*21*] Find the complete factorization of the polynomial $u(x)$ in (22), modulo 2, using Berlekamp's procedure.

11. [*22*] Find the complete factorization of the polynomial $u(x)$ in (22), modulo 5.

▶ **12.** [*M22*] Use Berlekamp's algorithm to determine the number of factors of $u(x) = x^4 + 1$, modulo p, for all primes p. [*Hint:* Consider the cases $p = 2$, $p = 8k + 1$, $p = 8k + 3$, $p = 8k + 5$, $p = 8k + 7$ separately; what is the matrix Q? You need not discover the factors; just determine how many there are.]

13. [*M25*] Continuing the previous exercise, give an explicit formula for the factors of $x^4 + 1$, modulo p, for all odd primes p, in terms of the quantities $\sqrt{-1}, \sqrt{2}, \sqrt{-2}$ when such square roots exist modulo p.

14. [*M25*] (H. Zassenhaus.) Let $v(x)$ be a solution to (8), and let $w(x) = \prod(x - s)$ where the product is over all $0 \leq s < p$ such that $\gcd(u(x), v(x) - s) \neq 1$. Explain how to compute $w(x)$, given $u(x)$ and $v(x)$. [*Hint:* Eq. (14) implies that $w(x)$ is the polynomial of least degree such that $u(x)$ divides $w(v(x))$.]

▶ **15.** [*M27*] (*Square roots modulo a prime.*) Design an algorithm to calculate the square root of a given integer u modulo a given prime p, that is, to find an integer v such that $v^2 \equiv u$ (modulo p) whenever such a v exists. Your algorithm should be efficient even for very large primes p. (For $p \neq 2$, a solution to this problem leads to a procedure for solving any given quadratic equation modulo p, using the quadratic formula in the usual way.) *Hint:* Consider what happens when the factorization methods of this section are applied to the polynomial $x^2 - u$.

16. [*M30*] (*Finite fields.*) The purpose of this exercise is to prove basic properties of the fields introduced by É. Galois in 1830.

   a) Given that $f(x)$ is an irreducible polynomial modulo a prime p, of degree n, prove that the p^n polynomials of degree less than n form a field under arithmetic modulo $f(x)$ and p. [*Note:* The existence of irreducible polynomials of each degree is proved in exercise 4; therefore fields with p^n elements exist for all primes p and all $n \geq 1$.]

   b) Show that any field with p^n elements has a "primitive root" element ξ such that the elements of the field are $\{0, 1, \xi, \xi^2, \ldots, \xi^{p^n-2}\}$. [*Hint:* Exercise 3.2.1.2–16 provides a proof in the special case $n = 1$.]

   c) If $f(x)$ is an irreducible polynomial modulo p, of degree n, prove that $x^{p^m} - x$ is divisible by $f(x)$ if and only if m is a multiple of n. (It follows that we can test irreducibility rather quickly: A given nth degree polynomial $f(x)$ is irreducible modulo p if and only if $x^{p^n} - x$ is divisible by $f(x)$ and $x^{p^{n/q}} - x \perp f(x)$ for all primes q that divide n.)

17. [*M23*] Let F be a field with 13^2 elements. How many elements of F have order f, for each integer f with $1 \leq f < 13^2$? (The *order* of an element a is the least positive integer m such that $a^m = 1$.)

▶ **18.** [*M25*] Let $u(x) = u_n x^n + \cdots + u_0, u_n \neq 0$, be a primitive polynomial with integer coefficients, and let $v(x)$ be the monic polynomial defined by

$$v(x) = u_n^{n-1} \cdot u(x/u_n) = x^n + u_{n-1} x^{n-1} + u_{n-2} u_n x^{n-2} + \cdots + u_0 u_n^{n-1}.$$

(a) Given that $v(x)$ has the complete factorization $p_1(x) \ldots p_r(x)$ over the integers, where each $p_j(x)$ is monic, what is the complete factorization of $u(x)$ over the integers?
(b) If $w(x) = x^m + w_{m-1} x^{m-1} + \cdots + w_0$ is a factor of $v(x)$, prove that w_k is a multiple of u_n^{m-1-k} for $0 \leq k < m$.

19. [*M20*] (*Eisenstein's criterion.*) Perhaps the best-known class of irreducible polynomials over the integers was introduced by T. Schönemann in *Crelle* **32** (1846), 100, then popularized by G. Eisenstein in *Crelle* **39** (1850), 166–169: Let p be prime and let $u(x) = u_n x^n + \cdots + u_0$ have the following properties: (i) u_n is not divisible by p; (ii) $u_{n-1}, \ldots, u_0$ are divisible by p; (iii) u_0 is not divisible by p^2. Show that $u(x)$ is irreducible over the integers.

20. [*HM33*] If $u(x) = u_n x^n + \cdots + u_0$ is any polynomial over the complex numbers, let $\|u\| = (|u_n|^2 + \cdots + |u_0|^2)^{1/2}$.

   a) Let $u(x) = (x - \alpha) w(x)$ and $v(x) = (\bar{\alpha} x - 1) w(x)$, where α is any complex number and $\bar{\alpha}$ is its complex conjugate. Prove that $\|u\| = \|v\|$.

   b) Let $u_n(x - \alpha_1) \ldots (x - \alpha_n)$ be the complete factorization of $u(x)$ over the complex numbers, and write $M(u) = |u_n| \prod_{j=1}^{n} \max(1, |\alpha_j|)$. Prove that $M(u) \leq \|u\|$.

   c) Show that $|u_j| \leq \binom{n-1}{j} M(u) + \binom{n-1}{j-1} |u_n|$, for $0 \leq j \leq n$.

   d) Combine these results to prove that if $u(x) = v(x) w(x)$ and $v(x) = v_m x^m + \cdots + v_0$, where u, v, w all have integer coefficients, then the coefficients of v are bounded by

$$|v_j| \leq \binom{m-1}{j} \|u\| + \binom{m-1}{j-1} |u_n|.$$

21. [*HM32*] Continuing exercise 20, we can also derive useful bounds on the coefficients of *multivariate* polynomial factors over the integers. For convenience we will let
boldface letters stand for sequences of t integers; thus, instead of writing

$$u(x_1, \dots, x_t) = \sum_{j_1, \dots, j_t} u_{j_1 \dots j_t} x_1^{j_1} \dots x_t^{j_t}$$

we will write simply $u(\mathbf{x}) = \sum_{\mathbf{j}} u_{\mathbf{j}} \mathbf{x}^{\mathbf{j}}$. Notice the convention for $\mathbf{x}^{\mathbf{j}}$; we also write
$\mathbf{j}! = j_1! \dots j_t!$ and $\Sigma \mathbf{j} = j_1 + \dots + j_t$.

a) Prove the identity

$$\sum_{\mathbf{j},\mathbf{k}} \frac{1}{\mathbf{j}!\,\mathbf{k}!} \sum_{\mathbf{p},\mathbf{q}\geq 0} [\mathbf{p}-\mathbf{j}=\mathbf{q}-\mathbf{k}]\, a_{\mathbf{p}} b_{\mathbf{q}} \frac{\mathbf{p}!\,\mathbf{q}!}{(\mathbf{p}-\mathbf{j})!} \sum_{\mathbf{r},\mathbf{s}\geq 0} [\mathbf{r}-\mathbf{j}=\mathbf{s}-\mathbf{k}]\, c_{\mathbf{r}} d_{\mathbf{s}} \frac{\mathbf{r}!\,\mathbf{s}!}{(\mathbf{r}-\mathbf{j})!}$$

$$= \sum_{\mathbf{i}\geq 0} \mathbf{i}! \sum_{\mathbf{p},\mathbf{s}\geq 0} [\mathbf{p}+\mathbf{s}=\mathbf{i}]\, a_{\mathbf{p}} d_{\mathbf{s}} \sum_{\mathbf{q},\mathbf{r}\geq 0} [\mathbf{q}+\mathbf{r}=\mathbf{i}]\, b_{\mathbf{q}} c_{\mathbf{r}} .$$

b) The polynomial $u(\mathbf{x}) = \sum_{\mathbf{j}} u_{\mathbf{j}} \mathbf{x}^{\mathbf{j}}$ is called *homogeneous* of degree n if each term has
total degree n; thus we have $\Sigma \mathbf{j} = n$ whenever $u_{\mathbf{j}} \neq 0$. Consider the weighted sum
of coefficients $B(u) = \sum_{\mathbf{j}} \mathbf{j}! |u_{\mathbf{j}}|^2$. Use part (a) to show that $B(u) \geq B(v)B(w)$
whenever $u(\mathbf{x}) = v(\mathbf{x})w(\mathbf{x})$ is homogeneous.

c) The *Bombieri norm* $[u]$ of a polynomial $u(\mathbf{x})$ is defined to be $\sqrt{B(u)/n!}$ when u
is homogeneous of degree n. It is also defined for nonhomogeneous polynomials,
by adding a new variable x_{t+1} and multiplying each term by a power of x_{t+1}
so that u becomes homogeneous without increasing its maximum degree. For
example, let $u(x) = 4x^3 + x - 2$; the corresponding homogeneous polynomial is
$4x^3 + xy^2 - 2y^3$, and we have $[u]^2 = (3!\,0!\,4^2 + 1!\,2!\,1^2 + 0!\,3!\,2^2)/3! = 16 + \frac{1}{3} + 4$.
If $u(x, y, z) = 3xy^3 - z^2$ we have, similarly, $[u]^2 = (1!\,3!\,0!\,0!\,3^2 + 0!\,0!\,2!\,2!\,1^2)/4! = \frac{9}{4} + \frac{1}{6}$. What does part (b) tell us about the relation between $[u]$, $[v]$, and $[w]$,
when $u(\mathbf{x}) = v(\mathbf{x})w(\mathbf{x})$?

d) Prove that if $u(x)$ is a reducible polynomial of degree n in one variable, it has a
factor whose coefficients are at most $n!^{1/4}[u]^{1/2}/(n/4)!$ in absolute value. What is
the corresponding result for homogeneous polynomials in t variables?

e) Calculate $[u]$ both explicitly and asymptotically when $u(x) = (x^2 - 1)^n$.

f) Prove that $[u][v] \geq [uv]$.

g) Show that $2^{-n/2} M(u) \leq [u] \leq 2^{n/2} M(u)$, when $u(x)$ is a polynomial of degree n
and $M(u)$ is the quantity defined in exercise 20. (Therefore the bound in part (d)
is roughly the square root of the bound we obtained in that exercise.)

▶ **22.** [*M24*] (*Hensel's Lemma.*) Let $u(x), v_e(x), w_e(x), a(x), b(x)$ be polynomials with
integer coefficients, satisfying the relations

$$u(x) \equiv v_e(x) w_e(x) \pmod{p^e}, \qquad a(x)v_e(x) + b(x)w_e(x) \equiv 1 \pmod{p},$$

where p is prime, $e \geq 1$, $v_e(x)$ is monic, $\deg(a) < \deg(w_e)$, $\deg(b) < \deg(v_e)$, and
$\deg(u) = \deg(v_e) + \deg(w_e)$. Show how to compute polynomials $v_{e+1}(x) \equiv v_e(x)$ and
$w_{e+1}(x) \equiv w_e(x) \pmod{p^e}$, satisfying the same conditions with e increased by 1.
Furthermore, prove that $v_{e+1}(x)$ and $w_{e+1}(x)$ are unique, modulo p^{e+1}.

Use your method for $p = 2$ to prove that (22) is irreducible over the integers,
starting with its factorization modulo 2 found in exercise 10. (Note that Euclid's
extended algorithm, exercise 4.6.1–3, will get the process started for $e = 1$.)

23. [*HM23*] Let $u(x)$ be a squarefree polynomial with integer coefficients. Prove that there are only finitely many primes p such that $u(x)$ is not squarefree modulo p.

24. [*M20*] The text speaks only of factorization over the integers, not over the field of rational numbers. Explain how to find the complete factorization of a polynomial with rational coefficients, over the field of rational numbers.

25. [*M25*] What is the complete factorization of $x^5 + x^4 + x^2 + x + 2$ over the field of rational numbers?

26. [*20*] Let $d_1, \ldots, d_r$ be the degrees of the irreducible factors of $u(x)$ modulo p, with proper multiplicity, so that $d_1 + \cdots + d_r = n = \deg(u)$. Explain how to compute the set $\{\deg(v) \mid u(x) \equiv v(x)w(x) \pmod{p} \text{ for some } v(x), w(x)\}$ by performing $O(r)$ operations on binary bit strings of length n.

27. [*HM30*] Prove that a random primitive polynomial over the integers is "almost always" irreducible, in some appropriate sense.

28. [*M25*] The distinct-degree factorization procedure is "lucky" when there is at most one irreducible polynomial of each degree d; then $g_d(x)$ never needs to be broken into factors. What is the probability of such a lucky circumstance, when factoring a random polynomial of degree n, modulo p, for fixed n as $p \to \infty$?

29. [*M22*] Let $g(x)$ be a product of two or more distinct irreducible polynomials of degree d, modulo an odd prime p. Prove that $\gcd\left(g(x), t(x)^{(p^d-1)/2} - 1\right)$ will be a proper factor of $g(x)$ with probability $\geq 1/2 - 1/(2p^{2d})$, for any fixed $g(x)$, when $t(x)$ is selected at random from among the p^{2d} polynomials of degree $< 2d$ modulo p.

30. [*M25*] Prove that if $q(x)$ is an irreducible polynomial of degree d, modulo p, and if $t(x)$ is any polynomial, then the value of $\left(t(x) + t(x)^p + t(x)^{p^2} + \cdots + t(x)^{p^{d-1}}\right) \bmod q(x)$ is an integer (that is, a polynomial of degree ≤ 0). Use this fact to design a randomized algorithm for factoring a product $g_d(x)$ of degree-d irreducibles, analogous to (21), for the case $p = 2$.

31. [*HM30*] Let p be an odd prime and let $d \geq 1$. Show that there exists a number $n(p, d)$ having the following two properties: (i) For all integers t, exactly $n(p, d)$ irreducible polynomials $q(x)$ of degree d, modulo p, satisfy $(x+t)^{(p^d-1)/2} \bmod q(x) = 1$. (ii) For all integers $0 \leq t_1 < t_2 < p$, exactly $n(p, d)$ irreducible polynomials $q(x)$ of degree d, modulo p, satisfy $(x + t_1)^{(p^d-1)/2} \bmod q(x) = (x + t_2)^{(p^d-1)/2} \bmod q(x)$.

▶ **32.** [*M30*] (*Cyclotomic polynomials.*) Let $\Psi_n(x) = \prod_{1 \leq k \leq n,\, k \perp n}(x - \omega^k)$, where $\omega = e^{2\pi i/n}$; thus, the roots of $\Psi_n(x)$ are the complex nth roots of unity that aren't mth roots for $m < n$.

a) Prove that $\Psi_n(x)$ is a polynomial with integer coefficients, and that

$$x^n - 1 = \prod_{d \backslash n} \Psi_d(x); \qquad \Psi_n(x) = \prod_{d \backslash n}(x^d - 1)^{\mu(n/d)}.$$

(See exercises 4.5.2–10(b) and 4.5.3–28(c).)

b) Prove that $\Psi_n(x)$ is irreducible over the integers, hence the formula above is the complete factorization of $x^n - 1$ over the integers. [*Hint:* If $f(x)$ is an irreducible factor of $\Psi_n(x)$ over the integers, and if ζ is a complex number with $f(\zeta) = 0$, prove that $f(\zeta^p) = 0$ for all primes p not dividing n. It may help to use the fact that $x^n - 1$ is squarefree modulo p for all such primes.]

c) Discuss the calculation of $\Psi_n(x)$, and tabulate the values for $n \leq 15$.

33. [*M18*] True or false: If $u(x) \neq 0$ and the complete factorization of $u(x)$ modulo p is $p_1(x)^{e_1} \dots p_r(x)^{e_r}$, then $u(x)/\gcd(u(x), u'(x)) = p_1(x) \dots p_r(x)$.

▶ **34.** [*M25*] (*Squarefree factorization.*) It is clear that any primitive polynomial of a unique factorization domain can be expressed in the form $u(x) = u_1(x) u_2(x)^2 u_3(x)^3 \dots$, where the polynomials $u_i(x)$ are squarefree and relatively prime to each other. This representation, in which $u_j(x)$ is the product of all the irreducible polynomials that divide $u(x)$ exactly j times, is unique except for unit multiples; and it is a useful way to represent polynomials that participate in multiplication, division, and gcd operations.

Let $\mathrm{GCD}(u(x), v(x))$ be a procedure that returns three answers:

$$\mathrm{GCD}(u(x), v(x)) = (d(x), u(x)/d(x), v(x)/d(x)), \quad \text{where } d(x) = \gcd(u(x), v(x)).$$

The modular method described in the text following Eq. (25) always ends with a trial division of $u(x)/d(x)$ and $v(x)/d(x)$, to make sure that no "unlucky prime" has been used, so the quantities $u(x)/d(x)$ and $v(x)/d(x)$ are byproducts of the gcd computation; thus we can compute $\mathrm{GCD}(u(x), v(x))$ essentially as fast as $\gcd(u(x), v(x))$ when we are using a modular method.

Devise a procedure that obtains the squarefree representation $(u_1(x), u_2(x), \dots)$ of a given primitive polynomial $u(x)$ over the integers. Your algorithm should perform exactly e computations of a GCD, where e is the largest subscript with $u_e(x) \neq 1$; furthermore, each GCD calculation should satisfy (27), so that Hensel's construction can be used.

35. [*M22*] (D. Y. Y. Yun.) Design an algorithm that computes the squarefree representation $(w_1(x), w_2(x), \dots)$ of $w(x) = \gcd(u(x), v(x))$ over the integers, given the squarefree representations $(u_1(x), u_2(x), \dots)$ and $(v_1(x), v_2(x), \dots)$ of $u(x)$ and $v(x)$.

36. [*M27*] Extend the procedure of exercise 34 so that it will obtain the squarefree representation $(u_1(x), u_2(x), \dots)$ of a given polynomial $u(x)$ when the coefficient arithmetic is performed modulo p.

37. [*HM24*] (George E. Collins.) Let $d_1, \dots, d_r$ be positive integers whose sum is n, and let p be prime. What is the probability that the irreducible factors of a random nth-degree integer polynomial $u(x)$ have degrees $d_1, \dots, d_r$, when it is completely factored modulo p? Show that this probability is asymptotically the same as the probability that a random permutation on n elements has cycles of lengths $d_1, \dots, d_r$.

38. [*HM27*] (*Perron's criterion.*) Let $u(x) = x^n + u_{n-1}x^{n-1} + \dots + u_0$ be a polynomial with integer coefficients such that $u_0 \neq 0$ and either $|u_{n-1}| > 1 + |u_{n-2}| + \dots + |u_0|$ or $(u_{n-1} = 0$ and $u_{n-2} > 1 + |u_{n-3}| + \dots + |u_0|)$. Show that $u(x)$ is irreducible over the integers. [*Hint:* Prove that almost all of u's roots are less than 1 in absolute value.]

39. [*HM42*] (David G. Cantor.) Show that if the polynomial $u(x)$ is irreducible over the integers, it has a "succinct" proof of irreducibility, in the sense that the number of bits in the proof is at most a polynomial in $\deg(u)$ and the length of the coefficients. (Only a bound on the *length* of proof is requested here, as in exercise 4.5.4–17, not a bound on the time needed to find such a proof.) *Hint:* If $v(x)$ is irreducible and t is any polynomial over the integers, all factors of $v(t(x))$ have degree $\geq \deg(v)$. Perron's criterion gives a large supply of irreducible polynomials $v(x)$.

▶ **40.** [*M20*] (P. S. Wang.) If u_n is the leading coefficient of $u(x)$ and B is a bound on coefficients of some factor of u, the text's factorization algorithm requires us to find a factorization modulo p^e where $p^e > 2|u_n|B$. But $|u_n|$ might be larger than B, when B is chosen by the method of exercise 21. Show that if $u(x)$ is reducible, there is a way to recover one of its true factors from a factorization modulo p^e whenever $p^e \geq 2B^2$, by using the algorithm of exercise 4.5.3–51.

41. [*M47*] (Beauzamy, Trevisan, and Wang.) Prove or disprove: There is a constant c such that, if $f(x)$ is any integer polynomial with all coefficients $\leq B$ in absolute value, then one of its irreducible factors has coefficients bounded by cB.

4.6.3. Evaluation of Powers

In this section we shall study the interesting problem of computing x^n efficiently, given x and n, where n is a positive integer. Suppose, for example, that we need to compute x^{16}; we could simply start with x and multiply by x fifteen times. But it is possible to obtain the same answer with only four multiplications, if we repeatedly take the square of each partial result, successively forming x^2, x^4, x^8, x^{16}.

The same idea applies, in general, to any value of n, in the following way: Write n in the binary number system (suppressing zeros at the left). Then replace each "1" by the pair of letters SX, replace each "0" by S, and cross off the "SX" that now appears at the left. The result is a rule for computing x^n, if "S" is interpreted as the operation of *squaring*, and if "X" is interpreted as the operation of *multiplying by* x. For example, if $n = 23$, its binary representation is 10111; so we form the sequence SX S SX SX SX and remove the leading SX to obtain the rule SSXSXSX. This rule states that we should "square, square, multiply by x, square, multiply by x, square, and multiply by x"; in other words, we should successively compute x^2, x^4, x^5, x^{10}, x^{11}, x^{22}, x^{23}.

This binary method is easily justified by a consideration of the sequence of exponents in the calculation: If we reinterpret "S" as the operation of multiplying by 2 and "X" as the operation of adding 1, and if we start with 1 instead of x, the rule will lead to a computation of n because of the properties of the binary number system. The method is quite ancient; it appeared before A.D. 400 in Piṅgala's Hindu classic *Chandaḥśāstra* [see B. Datta and A. N. Singh, *History of Hindu Mathematics* **2** (Lahore: Motilal Banarsi Das, 1935), 76]. There seem to be no other references to this method outside of India during the next several centuries, but a clear discussion of how to compute 2^n efficiently for arbitrary n was given by al-Uqlīdisī of Damascus in A.D. 952; see *The Arithmetic of al-Uqlīdisī* by A. S. Saidan (Dordrecht: D. Reidel, 1975), 341–342, where the general ideas are illustrated for $n = 51$. See also al-Bīrūnī's *Chronology of Ancient Nations*, edited and translated by E. Sachau (London: 1879), 132–136; this eleventh-century Arabic work had great influence.

The S-and-X binary method for obtaining x^n requires no temporary storage except for x and the current partial result, so it is well suited for incorporation in the hardware of a binary computer. The method can also be readily programmed; but it requires that the binary representation of n be scanned from left to right. Computer programs generally prefer to go the other way, because the available operations of division by 2 and remainder mod 2 will deduce the binary representation from right to left. Therefore the following algorithm, based on a right-to-left scan of the number, is often more convenient:

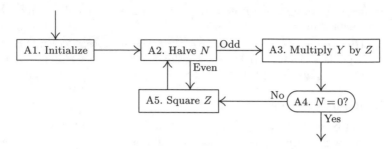

Fig. 13. Evaluation of x^n, based on a right-to-left scan of the binary notation for n.

Algorithm A (*Right-to-left binary method for exponentiation*). This algorithm evaluates x^n, where n is a positive integer. (Here x belongs to any algebraic system in which an associative multiplication, with identity element 1, has been defined.)

A1. [Initialize.] Set $N \leftarrow n$, $Y \leftarrow 1$, $Z \leftarrow x$.

A2. [Halve N.] (At this point, $x^n = Y Z^N$.) Set $t \leftarrow N \bmod 2$ and $N \leftarrow \lfloor N/2 \rfloor$. If $t = 0$, skip to step A5.

A3. [Multiply Y by Z.] Set $Y \leftarrow Z$ times Y.

A4. [$N = 0$?] If $N = 0$, the algorithm terminates, with Y as the answer.

A5. [Square Z.] Set $Z \leftarrow Z$ times Z, and return to step A2. ▌

As an example of Algorithm A, consider the steps in the evaluation of x^{23}:

	N	Y	Z
After step A1	23	1	x
After step A5	11	x	x^2
After step A5	5	x^3	x^4
After step A5	2	x^7	x^8
After step A5	1	x^7	x^{16}
After step A4	0	x^{23}	x^{16}

A MIX program corresponding to Algorithm A appears in exercise 2.

The great calculator al-Kāshī stated Algorithm A in A.D. 1427 [*Istoriko-Mat. Issledovaniiâ* **7** (1954), 256–257]. The method is closely related to a procedure for multiplication that was actually used by Egyptian mathematicians as early as 2000 B.C.; for if we change step A3 to "$Y \leftarrow Y + Z$" and step A5 to "$Z \leftarrow Z + Z$", and if we set Y to zero instead of unity in step A1, the algorithm terminates with $Y = nx$. [See A. B. Chace, *The Rhind Mathematical Papyrus* (1927); W. W. Struve, *Quellen und Studien zur Geschichte der Mathematik* **A1** (1930).] This is a practical method for multiplication by hand, since it involves only the simple operations of doubling, halving, and adding. It is often called the "Russian peasant method" of multiplication, since Western visitors to Russia in the nineteenth century found the method in wide use there.

The number of multiplications required by Algorithm A is

$$\lfloor \lg n \rfloor + \nu(n),$$

where $\nu(n)$ is the number of ones in the binary representation of n. This is one more multiplication than the left-to-right binary method mentioned at the beginning of this section would require, due to the fact that the first execution of step A3 is simply a multiplication by unity.

Because of the bookkeeping time required by this algorithm, the binary method is usually not of importance for small values of n, say $n \leq 10$, unless the time for a multiplication is comparatively large. If the value of n is known in advance, the left-to-right binary method is preferable. In some situations, such as the calculation of $x^n \bmod u(x)$ discussed in Section 4.6.2, it is much easier to multiply by x than to perform a general multiplication or to square a value, so binary methods for exponentiation are primarily suited for quite large n in such cases. If we wish to calculate the exact multiple-precision value of x^n, when x is an integer greater than the computer word size, binary methods are not much help unless n is so huge that the high-speed multiplication routines of Section 4.3.3 are involved; and such applications are rare. Similarly, binary methods are usually inappropriate for raising a polynomial to a power; see R. J. Fateman, *SICOMP* **3** (1974), 196–213, for a discussion of the extensive literature on polynomial exponentiation.

The point of these remarks is that binary methods are nice, but not a panacea. They are most applicable when the time to multiply $x^j \cdot x^k$ is essentially independent of j and k (for example, when we are doing floating point multiplication, or multiplication mod m); in such cases the running time is reduced from order n to order $\log n$.

Fewer multiplications. Several authors have published statements (without proof) that the binary method actually gives the *minimum* possible number of multiplications. But that is not true. The smallest counterexample is $n = 15$, when the binary method needs six multiplications, yet we can calculate $y = x^3$ in two multiplications and $x^{15} = y^5$ in three more, achieving the desired result with only five multiplications. Let us now discuss some other procedures for evaluating x^n, assuming that n is known in advance. Such procedures are of interest, for example, when an optimizing compiler is generating machine code.

The *factor method* is based on a factorization of n. If $n = pq$, where p is the smallest prime factor of n and $q > 1$, we may calculate x^n by first calculating x^p and then raising this quantity to the qth power. If n is prime, we may calculate x^{n-1} and multiply by x. And, of course, if $n = 1$, we have x^n with no calculation at all. Repeated application of these rules gives a procedure for evaluating x^n, given any value of n. For example, if we want to calculate x^{55}, we first evaluate $y = x^5 = x^4 x = (x^2)^2 x$; then we form $y^{11} = y^{10} y = (y^2)^5 y$. The whole process takes eight multiplications, while the binary method would have required nine. The factor method is better than the binary method on the average, but there are cases ($n = 33$ is the smallest example) where the binary method excels.

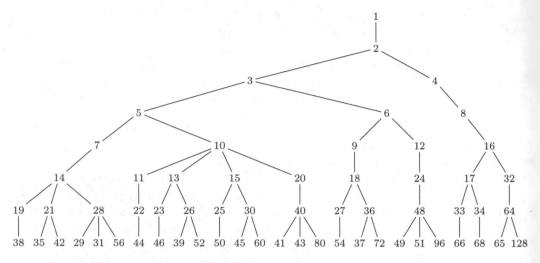

Fig. 14. The "power tree."

The binary method can be generalized to an *m-ary method* as follows: Let $n = d_0 m^t + d_1 m^{t-1} + \cdots + d_t$, where $0 \leq d_j < m$ for $0 \leq j \leq t$. The computation begins by forming $x, x^2, x^3, \ldots, x^{m-1}$. (Actually, only those powers x^{d_j} such that d_j appears in the representation of n are needed, and this observation often saves some of the work.) Then raise x^{d_0} to the mth power and multiply by x^{d_1}; we have computed $y_1 = x^{d_0 m + d_1}$. Next, raise y_1 to the mth power and multiply by x^{d_2}, obtaining $y_2 = x^{d_0 m^2 + d_1 m + d_2}$. The process continues in this way until $y_t = x^n$ has been computed. Whenever $d_j = 0$, it is of course unnecessary to multiply by x^{d_j}. Notice that this method reduces to the left-to-right binary method discussed earlier, when $m = 2$; there is also a less obvious right-to-left m-ary method that takes more memory but only a few more steps (see exercise 9). If m is a small prime, the m-ary method will be particularly efficient for calculating powers of one polynomial modulo another, when the coefficients are treated modulo m, because of Eq. 4.6.2–(5).

A systematic method that gives the minimum number of multiplications for all of the relatively small values of n (in particular, for most n that occur in practical applications) is indicated in Fig. 14. To calculate x^n, find n in this tree; then the path from the root to n indicates a sequence of exponents that occur in an efficient evaluation of x^n. The rule for generating this "power tree" appears in exercise 5. Computer tests have shown that the power tree gives optimum results for all of the n listed in the figure. But for large enough values of n the power tree method is not always optimum; the smallest examples are $n = 77, 154, 233$. The first case for which the power tree is superior to both the binary method and the factor method is $n = 23$. The first case for which the factor method beats the power tree method is $n = 19879 = 103 \cdot 193$; such cases are quite rare. (For $n \leq 100{,}000$ the power tree method is better than the factor method 88,803 times; it ties 11,191 times; and it loses only 6 times.)

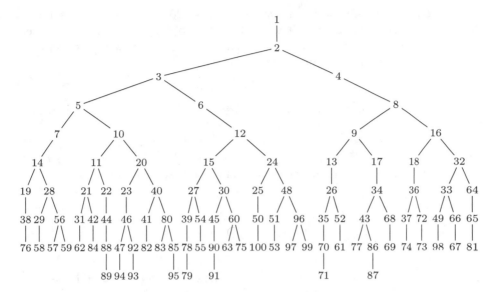

Fig. 15. A tree that minimizes the number of multiplications, for $n \leq 100$.

Addition chains. The most economical way to compute x^n by multiplication is a mathematical problem with an interesting history. We shall now examine it in detail, not only because it is classical and interesting in its own right, but because it is an excellent example of the theoretical questions that arise in the study of optimum methods of computation.

Although we are concerned with multiplication of powers of x, the problem can easily be reduced to addition, since the exponents are additive. This leads us to the following abstract formulation: An *addition chain for n* is a sequence of integers

$$1 = a_0, \quad a_1, \quad a_2, \quad \ldots, \quad a_r = n \tag{1}$$

with the property that

$$a_i = a_j + a_k, \qquad \text{for some } k \leq j < i, \tag{2}$$

for all $i = 1, 2, \ldots, r$. One way of looking at this definition is to consider a simple computer that has an accumulator and is capable of the three operations LDA, STA, and ADD; the machine begins with the number 1 in its accumulator, and it proceeds to compute the number n by adding together previous results. Notice that a_1 must equal 2, and a_2 is either 2, 3, or 4.

The shortest length, r, for which there exists an addition chain for n is denoted by $l(n)$. Thus $l(1) = 0$, $l(2) = 1$, $l(3) = l(4) = 2$, etc. Our goal in the remainder of this section is to discover as much as we can about this function $l(n)$. The values of $l(n)$ for small n are displayed in tree form in Fig. 15, which shows how to calculate x^n with the fewest possible multiplications for all $n \leq 100$.

The problem of determining $l(n)$ was apparently first raised by H. Dellac in 1894, and a partial solution by E. de Jonquières mentioned the factor method [see L'*Intermédiaire des Mathématiciens* **1** (1894), 20, 162–164]. In his solution, de Jonquières listed what he felt were the values of $l(p)$ for all prime numbers $p < 200$, but his table entries for $p = 107, 149, 163, 179, 199$ were one too high. The factor method tells us immediately that

$$l(mn) \leq l(m) + l(n),\tag{3}$$

since we can take the chains $1, a_1, \ldots, a_r = m$ and $1, b_1, \ldots, b_s = n$ and form the chain $1, a_1, \ldots, a_r, a_r b_1, \ldots, a_r b_s = mn$.

We can also recast the m-ary method into addition-chain terminology. Consider the case $m = 2^k$, and write $n = d_0 m^t + d_1 m^{t-1} + \cdots + d_t$ in the m-ary number system; the corresponding addition chain takes the form

$$
\begin{aligned}
&1, 2, 3, \ldots, m-2, m-1, \\
&\quad 2d_0, 4d_0, \ldots, md_0, md_0 + d_1, \\
&\qquad 2(md_0 + d_1), 4(md_0 + d_1), \ldots, m(md_0 + d_1), m^2 d_0 + md_1 + d_2, \\
&\qquad \ldots, \qquad m^t d_0 + m^{t-1} d_1 + \cdots + d_t.
\end{aligned}\tag{4}
$$

The length of this chain is $m - 2 + (k+1)t$; and it can often be reduced by deleting certain elements of the first row that do not occur among the coefficients d_j, plus elements among $2d_0$, $4d_0$, ... that already appear in the first row. Whenever digit d_j is zero, the step at the right end of the corresponding line may, of course, be dropped. Furthermore, we can omit all the even numbers (except 2) in the first row, if we bring values of the form $d_j / 2^e$ into the computation e steps earlier. [See E. Wattel and G. A. Jensen, *Math. Centrum Report* ZW1968-001 (1968), 18 pp.; E. G. Thurber, *Duke Math. J.* **40** (1973), 907–913.]

The simplest case of the m-ary method is the binary method ($m = 2$), when the general scheme (4) simplifies to the "S" and "X" rule mentioned at the beginning of this section: The binary addition chain for $2n$ is the binary chain for n followed by $2n$; for $2n + 1$ it is the binary chain for $2n$ followed by $2n + 1$. From the binary method we conclude that

$$l(2^{e_0} + 2^{e_1} + \cdots + 2^{e_t}) \leq e_0 + t, \qquad \text{if } e_0 > e_1 > \cdots > e_t \geq 0.\tag{5}$$

Let us now define two auxiliary functions for convenience in our subsequent discussion:

$$\lambda(n) = \lfloor \lg n \rfloor;\tag{6}$$

$$\nu(n) = \text{number of 1s in the binary representation of } n.\tag{7}$$

Thus $\lambda(17) = 4$, $\nu(17) = 2$; these functions may be defined by the recurrence relations

$$\lambda(1) = 0, \qquad \lambda(2n) = \lambda(2n + 1) = \lambda(n) + 1;\tag{8}$$

$$\nu(1) = 1, \qquad \nu(2n) = \nu(n), \qquad \nu(2n + 1) = \nu(n) + 1.\tag{9}$$

In terms of these functions, the binary addition chain for n requires exactly $\lambda(n) + \nu(n) - 1$ steps, and (5) becomes

$$l(n) \leq \lambda(n) + \nu(n) - 1.\tag{10}$$

Special classes of chains. We may assume without any loss of generality that an addition chain is *ascending*,

$$1 = a_0 < a_1 < a_2 < \cdots < a_r = n. \tag{11}$$

For if any two a's are equal, one of them may be dropped; and we can also rearrange the sequence (1) into ascending order and remove terms $> n$ without destroying the addition chain property (2). *From now on we shall consider only ascending chains*, without explicitly mentioning this assumption.

It is convenient at this point to define a few special terms relating to addition chains. By definition we have, for $1 \le i \le r$,

$$a_i = a_j + a_k \tag{12}$$

for some j and k, $0 \le k \le j < i$. If this relation holds for more than one pair (j, k), we let j be as large as possible. Let us say that step i of (11) is a *doubling*, if $j = k = i - 1$; then a_i has the maximum possible value $2a_{i-1}$ that can follow the ascending chain $1, a_1, \ldots, a_{i-1}$. If j (but not necessarily k) equals $i - 1$, let us say that step i is a *star step*. The importance of star steps is explained below. Finally let us say that step i is a *small step* if $\lambda(a_i) = \lambda(a_{i-1})$. Since $a_{i-1} < a_i \le 2a_{i-1}$, the quantity $\lambda(a_i)$ is always equal to either $\lambda(a_{i-1})$ or $\lambda(a_{i-1}) + 1$; it follows that, in any chain (11), *the length r is equal to $\lambda(n)$ plus the number of small steps.*

Several elementary relations hold between these types of steps: Step 1 is always a doubling. A doubling obviously is a star step, but never a small step. A doubling must be followed by a star step. Furthermore if step i is *not* a small step, then step $i + 1$ is either a small step or a star step, or both; putting this another way, if step $i + 1$ is neither small nor star, step i must have been small.

A *star chain* is an addition chain that involves only star steps. This means that each term a_i is the sum of a_{i-1} and a previous a_k; the simple "computer" discussed above after Eq. (2) makes use only of the two operations STA and ADD (not LDA) in a star chain, since each new term of the sequence utilizes the preceding result in the accumulator. Most of the addition chains we have discussed so far are star chains. The minimum length of a star chain for n is denoted by $l^*(n)$; clearly

$$l(n) \le l^*(n). \tag{13}$$

We are now ready to derive some nontrivial facts about addition chains. First we can show that there must be fairly many doublings if r is not far from $\lambda(n)$.

Theorem A. *If the addition chain* (11) *includes d doublings and $f = r - d$ nondoublings, then*

$$n \le 2^{d-1} F_{f+3}. \tag{14}$$

Proof. By induction on $r = d + f$, we see that (14) is certainly true when $r = 1$. When $r > 1$, there are three cases: If step r is a doubling, then $\frac{1}{2}n = a_{r-1} \le 2^{d-2} F_{f+3}$; hence (14) follows. If steps r and $r - 1$ are both nondoublings, then $a_{r-1} \le 2^{d-1} F_{f+2}$ and $a_{r-2} \le 2^{d-1} F_{f+1}$; hence $n = a_r \le$

$a_{r-1} + a_{r-2} \leq 2^{d-1}(F_{f+2} + F_{f+1}) = 2^{d-1}F_{f+3}$ by the definition of the Fibonacci sequence. Finally, if step r is a nondoubling but step $r-1$ is a doubling, then $a_{r-2} \leq 2^{d-2}F_{f+2}$ and $n = a_r \leq a_{r-1} + a_{r-2} = 3a_{r-2}$. Now $2F_{f+3} - 3F_{f+2} = F_{f+1} - F_f \geq 0$; hence $n \leq 2^{d-1}F_{f+3}$ in all cases. ∎

The method of proof we have used shows that inequality (14) is "best possible" under the stated assumptions; the addition chain

$$1, 2, \ldots, 2^{d-1}, 2^{d-1}F_3, 2^{d-1}F_4, \ldots, 2^{d-1}F_{f+3} \tag{15}$$

has d doublings and f nondoublings.

Corollary A. *If the addition chain* (11) *includes f nondoublings and s small steps, then*

$$s \leq f \leq 3.271s. \tag{16}$$

Proof. Obviously $s \leq f$. We have $2^{\lambda(n)} \leq n \leq 2^{d-1}F_{f+3} \leq 2^d \phi^f = 2^{\lambda(n)+s}(\phi/2)^f$, since $d + f = \lambda(n) + s$, and since $F_{f+3} \leq 2\phi^f$ when $f \geq 0$. Hence $0 \leq s \ln 2 + f \ln(\phi/2)$, and (16) follows from the fact that $\ln 2 / \ln(2/\phi) \approx 3.2706$. ∎

Values of $l(n)$ for special n. It is easy to show by induction that $a_i \leq 2^i$, and therefore $\lg n \leq r$ in any addition chain (11). Hence

$$l(n) \geq \lceil \lg n \rceil. \tag{17}$$

This lower bound, together with the upper bound (10) given by the binary method, gives us the values

$$l(2^A) = A; \tag{18}$$

$$l(2^A + 2^B) = A + 1, \qquad \text{if } A > B. \tag{19}$$

In other words, the binary method is optimum when $\nu(n) \leq 2$. With some further calculation we can extend these formulas to the case $\nu(n) = 3$:

Theorem B. $l(2^A + 2^B + 2^C) = A + 2, \qquad \text{if } A > B > C. \tag{20}$

Proof. We can, in fact, prove a stronger result that will be of use to us later in this section: *All addition chains with exactly one small step have one of the following six types* (where all steps indicated by "..." represent doublings):

Type 1. $1, \ldots, 2^A, 2^A + 2^B, \ldots, 2^{A+C} + 2^{B+C}; A > B \geq 0, C \geq 0.$

Type 2. $1, \ldots, 2^A, 2^A + 2^B, 2^{A+1} + 2^B, \ldots, 2^{A+C+1} + 2^{B+C}; A > B \geq 0, C \geq 0.$

Type 3. $1, \ldots, 2^A, 2^A + 2^{A-1}, 2^{A+1} + 2^{A-1}, 2^{A+2}, \ldots, 2^{A+C}; A > 0, C \geq 2.$

Type 4. $1, \ldots, 2^A, 2^A + 2^{A-1}, 2^{A+1} + 2^A, 2^{A+2}, \ldots, 2^{A+C}; A > 0, C \geq 2.$

Type 5. $1, \ldots, 2^A, 2^A + 2^{A-1}, \ldots, 2^{A+C} + 2^{A+C-1}, 2^{A+C+1} + 2^{A+C-2}, \ldots, 2^{A+C+D+1} + 2^{A+C+D-2}; A > 0, C > 0, D \geq 0.$

Type 6. $1, \ldots, 2^A, 2^A + 2^B, 2^{A+1}, \ldots, 2^{A+C}; A > B \geq 0, C \geq 1.$

A straightforward hand calculation shows that these six types exhaust all possibilities. By Corollary A, there are at most three nondoublings when there is one small step; this maximum occurs only in sequences of Type 3. All of the above are star chains, except Type 6 when $B < A - 1$.

The theorem now follows from the observation that

$$l(2^A + 2^B + 2^C) \leq A + 2;$$

and $l(2^A + 2^B + 2^C)$ must be greater than $A + 1$, since none of the six possible types have $\nu(n) > 2$. ∎

(E. de Jonquières stated without proof in 1894 that $l(n) \geq \lambda(n) + 2$ when $\nu(n) > 2$. The first published demonstration of Theorem B was by A. A. Gioia, M. V. Subbarao, and M. Sugunamma in *Duke Math. J.* **29** (1962), 481–487.)

The calculation of $l(2^A + 2^B + 2^C + 2^D)$, when $A > B > C > D$, is more involved. By the binary method it is at most $A+3$, and by the proof of Theorem B it is at least $A + 2$. The value $A + 2$ is possible, since we know that the binary method is not optimal when $n = 15$ or $n = 23$. The complete behavior when $\nu(n) = 4$ can be determined, as we shall now see.

Theorem C. *If $\nu(n) \geq 4$ then $l(n) \geq \lambda(n) + 3$, except in the following circumstances when $A > B > C > D$ and $l(2^A + 2^B + 2^C + 2^D)$ equals $A + 2$:*

Case 1. $A - B = C - D$. (Example: $n = 15$.)

Case 2. $A - B = C - D + 1$. (Example: $n = 23$.)

Case 3. $A - B = 3$, $C - D = 1$. (Example: $n = 39$.)

Case 4. $A - B = 5$, $B - C = C - D = 1$. (Example: $n = 135$.)

Proof. When $l(n) = \lambda(n) + 2$, there is an addition chain for n having just two small steps; such an addition chain starts out as one of the six types in the proof of Theorem B, followed by a small step, followed by a sequence of nonsmall steps. Let us say that n is "special" if $n = 2^A + 2^B + 2^C + 2^D$ for one of the four cases listed in the theorem. We can obtain addition chains of the required form for each special n, as shown in exercise 13; therefore it remains for us to prove that no chain with exactly two small steps contains any elements with $\nu(a_i) \geq 4$ except when a_i is special.

Let a "counterexample chain" be an addition chain with two small steps such that $\nu(a_r) \geq 4$, but a_r is not special. If counterexample chains exist, let $1 = a_0 < a_1 < \cdots < a_r = n$ be a counterexample chain of shortest possible length. Then step r is not a small step, since none of the six types in the proof of Theorem B can be followed by a small step with $\nu(n) \geq 4$ except when n is special. Furthermore, step r is not a doubling, otherwise $a_0, \ldots, a_{r-1}$ would be a shorter counterexample chain; and step r is a star step, otherwise $a_0, \ldots, a_{r-2}, a_r$ would be a shorter counterexample chain. Thus

$$a_r = a_{r-1} + a_{r-k}, \qquad k \geq 2; \qquad \text{and } \lambda(a_r) = \lambda(a_{r-1}) + 1. \qquad (21)$$

Let c be the number of carries that occur when a_{r-1} is added to a_{r-k} in the binary number system by Algorithm 4.3.1A. Using the fundamental relation

$$\nu(a_r) = \nu(a_{r-1}) + \nu(a_{r-k}) - c, \tag{22}$$

we can prove that *step $r-1$ is not a small step* (see exercise 14).

Let $m = \lambda(a_{r-1})$. Since neither r nor $r-1$ is a small step, $c \geq 2$; and $c = 2$ can hold only when $a_{r-1} \geq 2^m + 2^{m-1}$.

Now let us suppose that $r-1$ is not a star step. Then $r-2$ is a small step, and $a_0, \ldots, a_{r-3}, a_{r-1}$ is a chain with only one small step; hence $\nu(a_{r-1}) \leq 2$ and $\nu(a_{r-2}) \leq 4$. The relation (22) can now hold only if $\nu(a_r) = 4$, $\nu(a_{r-1}) = 2$, $k = 2$, $c = 2$, $\nu(a_{r-2}) = 4$. From $c = 2$ we conclude that $a_{r-1} = 2^m + 2^{m-1}$; hence $a_0, a_1, \ldots, a_{r-3} = 2^{m-1} + 2^{m-2}$ is an addition chain with only one small step, and it must be of Type 1, so a_r belongs to Case 3. Thus $r-1$ *is a star step.*

Now assume that $a_{r-1} = 2^t a_{r-k}$ for some t. If $\nu(a_{r-1}) \leq 3$, then by (22), $c = 2$, $k = 2$, and we see that a_r must belong to Case 3. On the other hand, if $\nu(a_{r-1}) = 4$ then a_{r-1} is special, and it is easy to see by considering each case that a_r also belongs to one of the four cases. (Case 4 arises, for example, when $a_{r-1} = 90$, $a_{r-k} = 45$; or $a_{r-1} = 120$, $a_{r-k} = 15$.) Therefore we may conclude that $a_{r-1} \neq 2^t a_{r-k}$ for any t.

We have proved that $a_{r-1} = a_{r-2} + a_{r-q}$ for some $q \geq 2$. If $k = 2$, then $q > 2$, and $a_0, a_1, \ldots, a_{r-2}, 2a_{r-2}, 2a_{r-2} + a_{r-q} = a_r$ is a counterexample sequence in which $k > 2$; therefore we may assume that $k > 2$.

Let us now suppose that $\lambda(a_{r-k}) = m - 1$; the case $\lambda(a_{r-k}) < m - 1$ may be ruled out by similar arguments, as shown in exercise 14. If $k = 4$, both $r-2$ and $r-3$ are small steps; hence $a_{r-4} = 2^{m-1}$, and (22) is impossible. Therefore $k = 3$; step $r-2$ is small, $\nu(a_{r-3}) = 2$, $c = 2$, $a_{r-1} \geq 2^m + 2^{m-1}$, and $\nu(a_{r-1}) = 4$. There must be at least two carries when a_{r-2} is added to $a_{r-1} - a_{r-2}$; hence $\nu(a_{r-2}) = 4$, and a_{r-2} (being special and $\geq \frac{1}{2}a_{r-1}$) has the form $2^{m-1} + 2^{m-2} + 2^{d+1} + 2^d$ for some d. Now a_{r-1} is either $2^m + 2^{m-1} + 2^{d+1} + 2^d$ or $2^m + 2^{m-1} + 2^{d+2} + 2^{d+1}$, and in both cases a_{r-3} must be $2^{m-1} + 2^{m-2}$, so a_r belongs to Case 3.   ∎

E. G. Thurber [*Pacific J. Math.* **49** (1973), 229–242] has extended Theorem C to show that $l(n) \geq \lambda(n) + 4$ when $\nu(n) > 8$. It seems reasonable to conjecture that $l(n) \geq \lambda(n) + \lg \nu(n)$ in general, since A. Schönhage has come very close to proving this (see exercise 28).

*Asymptotic values. Theorem C indicates that it is probably quite difficult to get exact values of $l(n)$ for large n, when $\nu(n) > 4$; however, we can determine the approximate behavior in the limit as $n \to \infty$.

Theorem D. [A. Brauer, *Bull. Amer. Math. Soc.* **45** (1939), 736–739.]

$$\lim_{n \to \infty} l^*(n)/\lambda(n) = \lim_{n \to \infty} l(n)/\lambda(n) = 1. \tag{23}$$

Proof. The addition chain (4) for the 2^k-ary method is a star chain if we delete the second occurrence of any element that appears twice in the chain; for if a_i

is the first element among $2d_0$, $4d_0$, ... of the second line that is not present in the first line, we have $a_i \leq 2(m-1)$; hence $a_i = (m-1) + a_j$ for some a_j in the first line. By totaling up the length of the chain, we have

$$\lambda(n) \leq l(n) \leq l^*(n) < (1 + 1/k) \lg n + 2^k \qquad (24)$$

for all $k \geq 1$. The theorem follows if we choose, say, $k = \lfloor \frac{1}{2} \lg \lambda(n) \rfloor$. ∎

If we let $k = \lambda\lambda(n) - 2\lambda\lambda\lambda(n)$ in (24) for large n, where $\lambda\lambda(n)$ denotes $\lambda(\lambda(n))$, we obtain the stronger asymptotic bound

$$l(n) \leq l^*(n) \leq \lambda(n) + \lambda(n)/\lambda\lambda(n) + O\big(\lambda(n)\lambda\lambda\lambda(n)/\lambda\lambda(n)^2\big). \qquad (25)$$

The second term $\lambda(n)/\lambda\lambda(n)$ is essentially the best that can be obtained from (24). A much deeper analysis of lower bounds can be carried out, to show that this term $\lambda(n)/\lambda\lambda(n)$ is, in fact, essential in (25). In order to see why this is so, let us consider the following fact:

Theorem E. [Paul Erdős, *Acta Arithmetica* **6** (1960), 77–81.] *Let ϵ be a positive real number. The number of addition chains* (11) *such that*

$$\lambda(n) = m, \qquad r \leq m + (1 - \epsilon)m/\lambda(m) \qquad (26)$$

is less than α^m, for some $\alpha < 2$, for all suitably large m. (In other words, the number of addition chains so short that (26) is satisfied is substantially less than the number of values of n such that $\lambda(n) = m$, when m is large.)

Proof. We want to estimate the number of possible addition chains, and for this purpose our first goal is to get an improvement of Theorem A that enables us to deal more satisfactorily with nondoublings.

Lemma P. *Let $\delta < \sqrt{2} - 1$ be a fixed positive real number. Call step i of an addition chain a "ministep" if it is not a doubling and if $a_i < a_j(1 + \delta)^{i-j}$ for some j, where $0 \leq j < i$. If the addition chain contains s small steps and t ministeps, then*

$$t \leq s/(1 - \theta), \qquad \text{where } (1 + \delta)^2 = 2^\theta. \qquad (27)$$

Proof. For each ministep i_k, $1 \leq k \leq t$, we have $a_{i_k} < a_{j_k}(1 + \delta)^{i_k - j_k}$ for some $j_k < i_k$. Let I_1, ..., I_t be the intervals $(j_1 .. i_1]$, ..., $(j_t .. i_t]$, where the notation $(j .. i]$ stands for the set of all integers k such that $j < k \leq i$. It is possible (see exercise 17) to find nonoverlapping intervals J_1, ..., $J_h = (j'_1 .. i'_1]$, ..., $(j'_h .. i'_h]$ such that

$$I_1 \cup \cdots \cup I_t = J_1 \cup \cdots \cup J_h,$$
$$a_{i'_k} < a_{j'_k}(1 + \delta)^{2(i'_k - j'_k)}, \qquad \text{for } 1 \leq k \leq h. \qquad (28)$$

Now for all steps i outside of the intervals J_1, ..., J_h we have $a_i \leq 2a_{i-1}$; hence if we let

$$q = (i'_1 - j'_1) + \cdots + (i'_h - j'_h),$$

we have $2^{\lambda(n)} \leq n \leq 2^{r-q}(1 + \delta)^{2q} = 2^{\lambda(n)+s-(1-\theta)q} \leq 2^{\lambda(n)+s-(1-\theta)t}$. ∎

Returning to the proof of Theorem E, let us choose $\delta = 2^{\epsilon/4} - 1$, and let us divide the r steps of each addition chain into three classes:

$$t \text{ ministeps,} \qquad u \text{ doublings,} \qquad v \text{ other steps,} \qquad t + u + v = r. \qquad (29)$$

Counting another way, we have s small steps, where $s + m = r$. By the hypotheses, Theorem A, and Lemma P, we obtain the relations

$$s \leq (1 - \epsilon)m/\lambda(m), \qquad t + v \leq 3.271s, \qquad t \leq s/(1 - \epsilon/2). \qquad (30)$$

Given s, t, u, v satisfying these conditions, there are

$$\binom{r}{t, u, v} = \binom{r}{t + v}\binom{t + v}{v} \qquad (31)$$

ways to assign the steps to the specified classes. Given such a distribution of the steps, let us consider how the non-ministeps can be selected: If step i is one of the "other" steps in (29), $a_i \geq (1 + \delta)a_{i-1}$, so $a_i = a_j + a_k$, where $\delta a_{i-1} \leq a_k \leq a_j \leq a_{i-1}$. Also $a_j \leq a_i/(1 + \delta)^{i-j} \leq 2a_{i-1}/(1 + \delta)^{i-j}$, so $\delta \leq 2/(1 + \delta)^{i-j}$. This gives at most β choices for j, where β is a constant that depends only on δ. There are also at most β choices for k, so the number of ways to assign j and k for each of the non-ministeps is at most

$$\beta^{2v}. \qquad (32)$$

Finally, once the "j" and "k" have been selected for each of the non-ministeps, there are fewer than

$$\binom{r^2}{t} \qquad (33)$$

ways to choose the j and the k for the ministeps: We select t distinct pairs $(j_1, k_1), \ldots, (j_t, k_t)$ of indices in the range $0 \leq k_h \leq j_h < r$, in fewer than (33) ways. Then for each ministep i, in turn, we use a pair of indices (j_h, k_h) such that

a) $j_h < i$;
b) $a_{j_h} + a_{k_h}$ is as small as possible among the pairs not already used for smaller ministeps i;
c) $a_i = a_{j_h} + a_{k_h}$ satisfies the definition of ministep.

If no such pair (j_h, k_h) exists, we get no addition chain; on the other hand, any addition chain with ministeps in the designated places must be selected in one of these ways, so (33) is an upper bound on the possibilities.

Thus the total number of possible addition chains satisfying (26) is bounded by (31) times (32) times (33), summed over all relevant s, t, u, and v. The proof of Theorem E can now be completed by means of a rather standard estimation of these functions (exercise 18). ∎

Corollary E. *The value of $l(n)$ is asymptotically $\lambda(n) + \lambda(n)/\lambda\lambda(n)$, for almost all n. More precisely, there is a function $f(n)$ such that $f(n) \to 0$ as $n \to \infty$, and*

$$\Pr\big(\,|l(n) - \lambda(n) - \lambda(n)/\lambda\lambda(n)| \geq f(n)\lambda(n)/\lambda\lambda(n)\,\big) = 0. \qquad (34)$$

(See Section 3.5 for the definition of this probability "Pr".)

Proof. The upper bound (25) shows that (34) holds without the absolute value signs. The lower bound comes from Theorem E, if we let $f(n)$ decrease to zero slowly enough so that, when $f(n) \leq \epsilon$, the value N is so large that at most ϵN values $n \leq N$ have $l(n) \leq \lambda(n) + (1 - \epsilon)\lambda(n)/\lambda\lambda(n)$. ∎

*Star chains. Optimistic people find it reasonable to suppose that $l(n) = l^*(n)$; given an addition chain of minimal length $l(n)$, it appears hard to believe that we cannot find one of the same length that satisfies the (apparently mild) star condition. But in 1958 Walter Hansen proved the remarkable theorem that, for certain large values of n, the value of $l(n)$ is definitely less than $l^*(n)$, and he also proved several related theorems that we shall now investigate.

Hansen's theorems begin with an investigation of the detailed structure of a star chain. Let $n = 2^{e_0} + 2^{e_1} + \cdots + 2^{e_t}$, where $e_0 > e_1 > \cdots > e_t \geq 0$, and let $1 = a_0 < a_1 < \cdots < a_r = n$ be a star chain for n. If there are d doublings in this chain, we define the auxiliary sequence

$$0 = d_0 \leq d_1 \leq d_2 \leq \cdots \leq d_r = d, \tag{35}$$

where d_i is the number of doublings among steps 1, 2, ..., i. We also define a sequence of "multisets" $S_0, S_1, \ldots, S_r$, which keep track of the powers of 2 present in the chain. (A *multiset* is a mathematical entity that is like a set, but it is allowed to contain repeated elements; an object may be an element of a multiset several times, and its multiplicity of occurrences is relevant. See exercise 19 for familiar examples of multisets.) The multisets S_i are defined by the rules

a) $S_0 = \{0\}$;

b) If $a_{i+1} = 2a_i$, then $S_{i+1} = S_i + 1 = \{x + 1 \mid x \in S_i\}$;

c) If $a_{i+1} = a_i + a_k$, $k < i$, then $S_{i+1} = S_i \uplus S_k$.

(The symbol $\uplus$ means that the multisets are combined, adding the multiplicities.) From this definition it follows that

$$a_i = \sum_{x \in S_i} 2^x, \tag{36}$$

where the terms in this sum are not necessarily distinct. In particular,

$$n = 2^{e_0} + 2^{e_1} + \cdots + 2^{e_t} = \sum_{x \in S_r} 2^x. \tag{37}$$

The number of elements in the latter sum is at most 2^f, where $f = r - d$ is the number of nondoublings.

Since n has two different binary representations in (37), we can partition the multiset S_r into multisets $M_0, M_1, \ldots, M_t$ such that

$$2^{e_j} = \sum_{x \in M_j} 2^x, \qquad 0 \leq j \leq t. \tag{38}$$

This can be done by arranging the elements of S_r into nondecreasing order $x_1 \leq x_2 \leq \cdots$ and taking $M_t = \{x_1, x_2, \ldots, x_k\}$, where $2^{x_1} + \cdots + 2^{x_k} = 2^{e_t}$.

This must be possible, since e_t is the smallest of the e's. Similarly, $M_{t-1} = \{x_{k+1}, x_{k+2}, \ldots, x_{k'}\}$, and so on; the process is easily visualized in binary notation. An example appears below.

Let M_j contain m_j elements (counting multiplicities); then $m_j \leq 2^f - t$, since S_r has at most 2^f elements and it has been partitioned into $t+1$ nonempty multisets. By Eq. (38), we can see that

$$e_j \geq x > e_j - m_j, \qquad \text{for all } x \in M_j. \tag{39}$$

Our examination of the star chain's structure is completed by forming the multisets M_{ij} that record the ancestral history of M_j. The multiset S_i is partitioned into $t+1$ multisets as follows:

a) $M_{rj} = M_j$;

b) If $a_{i+1} = 2a_i$, then $M_{ij} = M_{(i+1)j} - 1 = \{x - 1 \mid x \in M_{(i+1)j}\}$;

c) If $a_{i+1} = a_i + a_k$, $k < i$, then (since $S_{i+1} = S_i \uplus S_k$) we let $M_{ij} = M_{(i+1)j}$ minus S_k, that is, we remove the elements of S_k from $M_{(i+1)j}$. If some element of S_k appears in two or more different multisets $M_{(i+1)j}$, we remove it from the set with the largest possible value of j; this rule uniquely defines M_{ij} for each j, when i is fixed.

From this definition it follows that

$$e_j + d_i - d \geq x > e_j + d_i - d - m_j, \qquad \text{for all } x \in M_{ij}. \tag{40}$$

As an example of this detailed construction, let us consider the star chain 1, 2, 3, 5, 10, 20, 23, for which $t = 3$, $r = 6$, $d = 3$, $f = 3$. We obtain the following array of multisets:

$(d_0, d_1, \ldots, d_6)$:	0	1	1	1	2	3	3		
$(a_0, a_1, \ldots, a_6)$:	1	2	3	5	10	20	23		
$(M_{03}, M_{13}, \ldots, M_{63})$:							0	M_3	$e_3 = 0$, $m_3 = 1$
$(M_{02}, M_{12}, \ldots, M_{62})$:							1	M_2	$e_2 = 1$, $m_2 = 1$
$(M_{01}, M_{11}, \ldots, M_{61})$:			0	0	1	2	2	M_1	$e_1 = 2$, $m_1 = 1$
$(M_{00}, M_{10}, \ldots, M_{60})$:	0	1	1	1	2	3	3	M_0	$e_0 = 4$, $m_0 = 2$
					1	2	3	3	
	S_0	S_1	S_2	S_3	S_4	S_5	S_6		

Thus $M_{40} = \{2, 2\}$, etc. From the construction we can see that d_i is the largest element of S_i; hence

$$d_i \in M_{i0}. \tag{41}$$

The most important part of this structure comes from Eq. (40); one of its immediate consequences is

Lemma K. *If M_{ij} and M_{uv} both contain a common integer x, then*

$$-m_v < (e_j - e_v) - (d_u - d_i) < m_j. \quad \blacksquare \tag{42}$$

Although Lemma K may not look extremely powerful, it says (when m_j and m_v are reasonably small and when M_{ij} contains an element in common with M_{uv}) that the number of doublings between steps u and i is approximately equal to the difference between the exponents e_v and e_j. This imposes a certain amount of regularity on the addition chain; and it suggests that we might be able to prove a result analogous to Theorem B above, that $l^*(n) = e_0 + t$, if the exponents e_j are far enough apart. The next theorem shows how this can in fact be done.

Theorem H. [W. Hansen, *Crelle* **202** (1959), 129–136.] *Let* $n = 2^{e_0} + 2^{e_1} + \cdots + 2^{e_t}$, *where* $e_0 > e_1 > \cdots > e_t \geq 0$. *If*

$$e_0 > 2e_1 + 2.271(t-1) \qquad \text{and} \qquad e_{i-1} \geq e_i + 2m \quad \text{for } 1 \leq i \leq t, \tag{43}$$

where $m = 2^{\lfloor 3.271(t-1)\rfloor} - t$, *then* $l^*(n) = e_0 + t$.

Proof. We may assume that $t > 2$, since the result of the theorem is true without restriction on the e's when $t \leq 2$. Suppose that we have a star chain $1 = a_0 < a_1 < \cdots < a_r = n$ for n with $r \leq e_0 + t - 1$. Let the integers d, f, d_0, ..., d_r, and the multisets M_j, S_i, M_{ij} reflect the structure of this chain, as defined above. By Corollary A, we know that $f \leq \lfloor 3.271(t-1)\rfloor$; therefore the value of m is a bona fide upper bound for the number m_j of elements in each multiset M_j.

In the summation

$$a_i = \left(\sum_{x \in M_{i0}} 2^x\right) + \left(\sum_{x \in M_{i1}} 2^x\right) + \cdots + \left(\sum_{x \in M_{it}} 2^x\right),$$

no carries propagate from the term corresponding to M_{ij} to the term corresponding to $M_{i(j-1)}$, if we think of this sum as being carried out in the binary number system, since the e's are so far apart. (See (40).) In particular, the sum of all the terms for $j \neq 0$ will not carry up to affect the terms for $j = 0$, so we must have

$$a_i \geq \sum_{x \in M_{i0}} 2^x \geq 2^{\lambda(a_i)}, \qquad 0 \leq i \leq r. \tag{44}$$

In order to prove Theorem H, we would like to show that in some sense the t extra powers of n must be put in "one at a time," so we want to find a way to tell at which step each of these terms essentially enters the addition chain.

Let j be a number between 1 and t. Since M_{0j} is empty and $M_{rj} = M_j$ is nonempty, we can find the *first* step i for which M_{ij} is not empty.

From the way in which the M_{ij} are defined, we know that step i is a non-doubling: $a_i = a_{i-1} + a_u$ for some $u < i-1$. We also know that all the elements of M_{ij} are elements of S_u. We will prove that a_u must be relatively small compared to a_i.

Let x_j be an element of M_{ij}. Then since $x_j \in S_u$, there is some v for which $x_j \in M_{uv}$. It follows that

$$d_i - d_u > m, \tag{45}$$

that is, at least $m+1$ doublings occur between steps u and i. For if $d_i - d_u \leq m$, Lemma K tells us that $|e_j - e_v| < 2m$; hence $v = j$. But this is impossible, because M_{uj} is empty by our choice of step i.

All elements of S_u are less than or equal to $e_1 + d_i - d$. For if $x \in S_u \subseteq S_i$ and $x > e_1 + d_i - d$, then $x \in M_{u0}$ and $x \in M_{i0}$ by (40); so Lemma K implies that $|d_i - d_u| < m$, contradicting (45). In fact, this argument proves that M_{i0} has no elements in common with S_u, so $M_{(i-1)0} = M_{i0}$. From (44) we have $a_{i-1} \geq 2^{\lambda(a_i)}$, and therefore *step i is a small step*.

We can now deduce what is probably the key fact in this entire proof: *All elements of S_u are in M_{u0}.* For if not, let x be an element of S_u with $x \notin M_{u0}$. Since $x \geq 0$, (40) implies that $e_1 \geq d - d_u$, hence

$$e_0 = f + d - s \leq 2.271s + d \leq 2.271(t - 1) + e_1 + d_u.$$

By hypothesis (43), this implies $d_u > e_1$. But $d_u \in S_u$ by (41), and it cannot be in M_{i0}, hence $d_u \leq e_1 + d_i - d \leq e_1$, a contradiction.

Going back to our element x_j in M_{ij}, we have $x_j \in M_{uv}$; and we have proved that $v = 0$. Therefore, by equation (40) again,

$$e_0 + d_u - d \geq x_j > e_0 + d_u - d - m_0. \tag{46}$$

For all $j = 1, 2, \ldots, t$ we have determined a number x_j satisfying (46), and a small step i at which the term 2^{e_j} may be said to have entered into the addition chain. If $j \neq j'$, the step i at which this occurs cannot be the same for both j and j'; for (46) would tell us that $|x_j - x_{j'}| < m$, while elements of M_{ij} and $M_{ij'}$ must differ by more than m, since e_j and $e_{j'}$ are so far apart. We are forced to conclude that the chain contains at least t small steps; but this is a contradiction. ∎

Theorem F (W. Hansen).

$$l(2^A + xy) \leq A + \nu(x) + \nu(y) - 1, \qquad \text{if } \lambda(x) + \lambda(y) \leq A. \tag{47}$$

Proof. An addition chain (which is *not* a star chain in general) may be constructed by combining the binary and factor methods. Let $x = 2^{x_1} + \cdots + 2^{x_u}$ and $y = 2^{y_1} + \cdots + 2^{y_v}$, where $x_1 > \cdots > x_u \geq 0$ and $y_1 > \cdots > y_v \geq 0$.

The first steps of the chain form successive powers of 2, until 2^{A-y_1} is reached; in between these steps, the additional values $2^{x_{u-1}} + 2^{x_u}$, $2^{x_{u-2}} + 2^{x_{u-1}} + 2^{x_u}$, $\ldots$, and x are inserted in the appropriate places. After a chain up to $2^{A-y_i} + x(2^{y_1-y_i} + \cdots + 2^{y_{i-1}-y_i})$ has been formed, we continue by adding x and doubling the resulting sum $y_i - y_{i+1}$ times; this yields

$$2^{A-y_{i+1}} + x(2^{y_1-y_{i+1}} + \cdots + 2^{y_i-y_{i+1}}).$$

If this construction is done for $i = 1, 2, \ldots, v$, assuming for convenience that $y_{v+1} = 0$, we have an addition chain for $2^A + xy$ as desired. ∎

Theorem F enables us to find values of n for which $l(n) < l^*(n)$, since Theorem H gives an explicit value of $l^*(n)$ in certain cases. For example, let $x = 2^{1016} + 1$, $y = 2^{2032} + 1$, and let

$$n = 2^{6103} + xy = 2^{6103} + 2^{3048} + 2^{2032} + 2^{1016} + 1.$$

According to Theorem F, we have $l(n) \leq 6106$. But Theorem H also applies, with $m = 508$, and this proves that $l^*(n) = 6107$.

Computer calculations by the author in 1969 showed that $n = 12509$ is the smallest value with $l(n) < l^*(n)$. No star chain for this value of n is as short as the sequence 1, 2, 4, 8, 16, 17, 32, 64, 128, 256, 512, 1024, 1041, 2082, 4164, 8328, 8345, 12509. The smallest n with $\nu(n) = 5$ and $l(n) \neq l^*(n)$ is $16537 = 2^{14} + 9 \cdot 17$ (see exercise 15).

Jan van Leeuwen has generalized Theorem H to show that

$$l^*(k2^{e_0}) + t \leq l^*(kn) \leq l^*(k2^{e_t}) + e_0 - e_t + t$$

for all fixed $k \geq 1$, if the exponents $e_0 > \cdots > e_t$ are far enough apart [*Crelle* **295** (1977), 202–207].

Some conjectures. Although it was reasonable to guess at first glance that $l(n) = l^*(n)$, we have now seen that this is false. Another plausible conjecture [first made by A. Goulard, and supposedly "proved" by E. de Jonquières in *L'Interméd. des Math.* **2** (1895), 125–126] is that $l(2n) = l(n) + 1$; a doubling step is so efficient, it seems unlikely that there could be any shorter chain for $2n$ than to add a doubling step to the shortest chain for n. But computer calculations show that this conjecture also fails, since $l(191) = l(382) = 11$. (A star chain of length 11 for 382 is not hard to find; for example, 1, 2, 4, 5, 9, 14, 23, 46, 92, 184, 198, 382. The number 191 is minimal such that $l(n) = 11$, and it seems to be nontrivial to prove by hand that $l(191) > 10$. The author's computer-generated proof of this fact, using the backtrack method in a program called ACHAINO now on the Internet, involved a detailed examination of more than 100 cases.)

The smallest four values of n such that $l(2n) = l(n)$ are $n = 191$, 701, 743, 1111; E. G. Thurber proved in *Pacific J. Math.* **49** (1973), 229–242, that the third of these is a member of an infinite family of such n, namely $23 \cdot 2^k + 7$ for all $k \geq 5$. Neill Clift found in 2007 that $l(n) = l(2n) = l(4n) = 31$ when $n = 30958077$; and in 2008, astonishingly, he discovered that $l(n) > l(2n) = 34$ when $n = 375494703$. Kevin R. Hebb has shown that $l(n) - l(mn)$ can get arbitrarily large, for all fixed integers m not a power of 2 [*Notices Amer. Math. Soc.* **21** (1974), A–294]. The smallest case in which $l(n) > l(mn)$ is $l\big((2^{13} + 1)/3\big) = 15$.

Let $c(r)$ be the smallest value of n such that $l(n) = r$. The computation of $l(n)$ seems to be hardest for this sequence of n's, which begins as follows:

r	$c(r)$	r	$c(r)$	r	$c(r)$	r	$c(r)$
0	1	12	379	24	357887	36	550040063
1	2	13	607	25	685951	37	994660991
2	3	14	1087	26	1176431	38	1886023151
3	5	15	1903	27	2211837	39	3502562143
4	7	16	3583	28	4169527	40	6490123999
5	11	17	6271	29	7624319	41	11889505663
6	19	18	11231	30	14143037	42	22899028607
7	29	19	18287	31	25450463	43	41866170239
8	47	20	34303	32	46444543	44	76086635263
9	71	21	65131	33	89209343	45	142771387391
10	127	22	110591	34	155691199	46	257661019487
11	191	23	196591	35	298695487	47	498691112447

For $r \le 11$, the value of $c(r)$ is approximately equal to $c(r-1) + c(r-2)$, and this fact led to speculation by several people that $c(r)$ grows like the function ϕ^r; but the result of Theorem D (with $n = c(r)$) implies that $r/\lg c(r) \to 1$ as $r \to \infty$. The values of $c(r)$ listed here for $18 < r \le 28$ were discovered by Achim Flammenkamp before 1998, except that $c(24)$ was first computed by Daniel Bleichenbacher; $c(29)$ through $c(47)$ are due to Neill Clift, between 2004 and 2020. Notice that the formula $1 + r/(1 + 1/\lg r)$ gives a fairly good approximation to $\lg c(r)$ for $10 < r \le 47$; this agrees nicely with the upper bound (25).

Several people had conjectured at one time that $c(r)$ would always be a prime number, in view of the factor method; but $c(15)$, $c(18)$, and $c(21)$ are all divisible by 11. Perhaps no conjecture about addition chains is safe!

Tabulated values of $l(n)$ show that this function is surprisingly smooth; for example, $l(n) = 13$ for all n in the range $1125 \le n \le 1148$. The computer calculations show that a table of $l(n)$ may be prepared for $2 \le n \le 1000$ by using the formula

$$l(n) = \min(l(n-1) + 1, l_n) - \delta_n, \qquad (48)$$

where $l_n = \infty$ if n is prime, otherwise $l_n = l(p) + l(n/p)$ if p is the smallest prime dividing n; and $\delta_n = 1$ for n in Table 1, $\delta_n = 0$ otherwise.

Let $d(r)$ be the number of solutions n to the equation $l(n) = r$. The following table lists the first few values of $d(r)$, according to Flammenkamp and Clift:

r	$d(r)$	r	$d(r)$	r	$d(r)$	r	$d(r)$	r	$d(r)$	r	$d(r)$
1	1	6	15	11	246	16	4490	21	90371	26	1896704
2	2	7	26	12	432	17	8170	22	165432	27	3501029
3	3	8	44	13	772	18	14866	23	303475	28	6465774
4	5	9	78	14	1382	19	27128	24	558275	29	11947258
5	9	10	136	15	2481	20	49544	25	1028508	30	22087489

Surely $d(r)$ must be an increasing function of r, but there is no evident way to prove this seemingly simple assertion, much less to determine the asymptotic growth of $d(r)$ for large r. (Empirically, $d(r) \approx 1.7c(r)$ for $35 \le r \le 44$.)

The most famous problem about addition chains that is still outstanding is the *Scholz–Brauer conjecture*, which states that

$$l(2^n - 1) \le n - 1 + l(n). \qquad (49)$$

Notice that $2^n - 1$ is the worst case for the binary method, because $\nu(2^n - 1) = n$. E. G. Thurber [*Discrete Math.* **16** (1976), 279–289] has shown that several of these values, including the case $n = 32$, can actually be calculated by hand. Extensive computer calculations by Neill Clift [*Computing* **91** (2011), 265–284; also Thurber and Clift, *Discrete Math.* **344** (2021), #112200, 15 pp.] show that $l(2^n - 1)$ is in fact exactly *equal* to $n - 1 + l(n)$ whenever $l(n) \le 9$.

Arnold Scholz coined the name "addition chain" (in German) and posed (49) as a problem in 1937 [*Jahresbericht der Deutschen Mathematiker-Vereinigung, Abteilung II*, **47** (1937), 41–42]; Alfred Brauer proved in 1939 that

$$l^*(2^n - 1) \le n - 1 + l^*(n). \qquad (50)$$

Table 1

VALUES OF n FOR SPECIAL ADDITION CHAINS

23	163	229	319	371	413	453	553	599	645	707	741	813	849	903
43	165	233	323	373	419	455	557	611	659	709	749	825	863	905
59	179	281	347	377	421	457	561	619	667	711	759	835	869	923
77	203	283	349	381	423	479	569	623	669	713	779	837	887	941
83	211	293	355	382	429	503	571	631	677	715	787	839	893	947
107	213	311	359	395	437	509	573	637	683	717	803	841	899	955
149	227	317	367	403	451	551	581	643	691	739	809	845	901	983

Hansen's theorems show that $l(n)$ can be less than $l^*(n)$, so more work is definitely necessary in order to prove or disprove (49). As a step in this direction, Hansen has defined the concept of an l^0-*chain*, which lies "between" l-chains and l^*-chains. In an l^0-chain, some of the elements are underlined; the condition is that $a_i = a_j + a_k$, where a_j is the largest underlined element less than a_i.

As an example of an l^0-chain (certainly not a minimum one), consider

$$\underline{1}, 2, \underline{4}, 5, \underline{8}, 10, 12, \underline{18}; \tag{51}$$

it is easy to verify that the difference between each element and the previous underlined element is in the chain. We let $l^0(n)$ denote the minimum length of an l^0-chain for n. Clearly $l(n) \leq l^0(n) \leq l^*(n)$.

Hansen pointed out that the chain constructed in Theorem F is an l^0-chain (see exercise 22); and he also established the following improvement of Eq. (50):

Theorem G. $l^0(2^n - 1) \leq n - 1 + l^0(n)$.

Proof. Let $1 = a_0, a_1, \ldots, a_r = n$ be an l^0-chain of minimum length for n, and let $1 = b_0, b_1, \ldots, b_t = n$ be the subsequence of underlined elements. (We may assume that n is underlined.) Then we can get an l^0-chain for $2^n - 1$ as follows:

a) Include the $l^0(n) + 1$ numbers $2^{a_i} - 1$, for $0 \leq i \leq r$, underlined if and only if a_i is underlined.

b) Include the numbers $2^i(2^{b_j} - 1)$, for $0 \leq j < t$ and for $0 < i \leq b_{j+1} - b_j$, all underlined. (This is a total of $b_1 - b_0 + \cdots + b_t - b_{t-1} = n - 1$ numbers.)

c) Sort the numbers from (a) and (b) into ascending order.

We may easily verify that this gives an l^0-chain: The numbers of (b) are all equal to twice some other element of (a) or (b); furthermore, this element is the preceding underlined element. If $a_i = b_j + a_k$, where b_j is the largest underlined element less than a_i, then $a_k = a_i - b_j \leq b_{j+1} - b_j$, so $2^{a_k}(2^{b_j} - 1) = 2^{a_i} - 2^{a_k}$ appears underlined in the chain, just preceding $2^{a_i} - 1$. Since $2^{a_i} - 1$ is equal to $(2^{a_i} - 2^{a_k}) + (2^{a_k} - 1)$, where both of these values appear in the chain, we have an addition chain with the l^0 property. ∎

The chain corresponding to (51), constructed in the proof of Theorem G, is

$$\underline{1}, \underline{2}, \underline{3}, \underline{6}, \underline{12}, \underline{15}, \underline{30}, 31, \underline{60}, \underline{120}, \underline{240}, \underline{255}, \underline{510}, \underline{1020}, 1023, \underline{2040},$$
$$\underline{4080}, 4095, \underline{8160}, \underline{16320}, \underline{32640}, \underline{65280}, \underline{130560}, \underline{261120}, \underline{262143}.$$

Computations by Neill Clift have shown that $l(n) < l^0(n)$ when $n = 5784689$ (see exercise 42). This is the smallest case where Eq. (49) remains in doubt.

Graphical representation. An addition chain (1) corresponds in a natural way to a directed graph, where the vertices are labeled a_i for $0 \le i \le r$, and where we draw arcs from a_j to a_i and from a_k to a_i as a representation of each step $a_i = a_j + a_k$ in (2). For example, the addition chain 1, 2, 3, 6, 12, 15, 27, 39, 78, 79 that appears in Fig. 15 corresponds to the directed graph

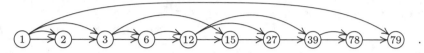

If $a_i = a_j + a_k$ for more than one pair of indices (j, k), we choose a definite j and k for purposes of this construction.

In general, all but the first vertex of such a directed graph will be at the head of exactly two arcs; however, this is not really an important property of the graph, because it conceals the fact that many different addition chains can be essentially equivalent. If a vertex has out-degree 1, it is used in only one later step, hence the later step is essentially a sum of three inputs $a_j + a_k + a_m$ that might be computed either as $(a_j + a_k) + a_m$ or as $a_j + (a_k + a_m)$ or as $a_k + (a_j + a_m)$. These three choices are immaterial, but the addition-chain conventions force us to distinguish between them. We can avoid such redundancy by deleting any vertex whose out-degree is 1 and attaching the arcs from its predecessors to its successor. For example, the graph above would become

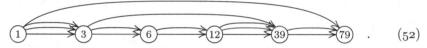   (52)

We can also delete any vertex whose out-degree is 0, except of course the final vertex a_r, since such a vertex corresponds to a useless step in the addition chain.

In this way every addition chain leads to a reduced directed graph that contains one "source" vertex (labeled 1) and one "sink" vertex (labeled n); every vertex but the source has in-degree ≥ 2 and every vertex but the sink has out-degree ≥ 2. Conversely, any such directed graph without oriented cycles corresponds to at least one addition chain, since we can topologically sort the vertices and write down $d - 1$ addition steps for each vertex of in-degree $d > 0$. The length of the addition chain, exclusive of useless steps, can be reconstructed by looking at the reduced graph; it is

$$\text{(number of arcs)} - \text{(number of vertices)} + 1, \qquad (53)$$

since deletion of a vertex of out-degree 1 also deletes one arc.

We say that two addition chains are *equivalent* if they have the same reduced directed graph. For example, the addition chain 1, 2, 3, 6, 12, 15, 24, 39, 40, 79 is equivalent to the chain we began with, since it also leads to (52). This example shows that a non-star chain can be equivalent to a star chain. An addition chain is equivalent to a star chain if and only if its reduced directed graph can be topologically sorted in only one way.

An important property of this graph representation has been pointed out by N. Pippenger: The label of each vertex is exactly equal to the number of oriented paths from the source to that vertex. Thus, the problem of finding an optimal addition chain for n is equivalent to minimizing the quantity (53) over all directed graphs that have one source vertex and one sink vertex and exactly n oriented paths from the source to the sink.

This characterization has a surprising corollary, because of the symmetry of the directed graph. If we reverse the directions of all the arcs, the source and the sink exchange roles, and we obtain another directed graph corresponding to a set of addition chains for the same n; these addition chains have the same length (53) as the chain we started with. For example, if we make the arrows in (52) run from right to left, and if we relabel the vertices according to the number of paths from the right-hand vertex, we get

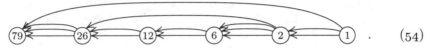

$$(54)$$

One of the star chains corresponding to this reduced directed graph is

$$1, 2, 4, 6, 12, 24, 26, 52, 78, 79;$$

we may call this a *dual* of the original addition chain.

Exercises 39 and 40 discuss important consequences of this graphical representation and the duality principle.

EXERCISES

1. [*15*] What is the value of Z when Algorithm A terminates?

2. [*24*] Write a MIX program for Algorithm A, to calculate $x^n \bmod w$ given integers n and x, where w is the word size. Assume that MIX has the binary operations SRB, JAE, etc., that are described in Section 4.5.2. Write another program that computes $x^n \bmod w$ in a serial manner (multiplying repeatedly by x), and compare the running times of these programs.

▶ **3.** [*22*] How is x^{975} calculated by (a) the binary method? (b) the ternary method? (c) the quaternary method? (d) the factor method?

4. [*M20*] Find a number n for which the octal (2^3-ary) method gives ten fewer multiplications than the binary method.

▶ **5.** [*24*] Figure 14 shows the first eight levels of the "power tree." The $(k+1)$st level of this tree is defined as follows, assuming that the first k levels have been constructed: Take each node n of the kth level, from left to right in turn, and attach below it the nodes

$$n + 1, \; n + a_1, \; n + a_2, \; \ldots, \; n + a_{k-1} = 2n$$

(in this order), where $1, a_1, a_2, \ldots, a_{k-1}$ is the path from the root of the tree to n; but discard any node that duplicates a number that has already appeared in the tree.

Design an efficient algorithm that constructs the first $r + 1$ levels of the power tree. [*Hint:* Make use of two sets of variables LINKU[j], LINKR[j] for $0 \le j \le 2^r$; these point upwards and to the right, respectively, if j is a number in the tree.]

6. [*M26*] If a slight change is made to the definition of the power tree that is given in exercise 5, so that the nodes below n are attached in *decreasing* order

$$n + a_{k-1}, \ \ldots, \ n + a_2, \ n + a_1, \ n + 1$$

instead of increasing order, we get a tree whose first five levels are

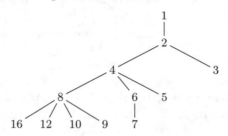

Show that this tree gives a method of computing x^n that requires exactly as many multiplications as the binary method; therefore it is not as good as the power tree, although it has been constructed in almost the same way.

7. [*M21*] Prove that there are infinitely many values of n

a) for which the factor method is better than the binary method;
b) for which the binary method is better than the factor method;
c) for which the power tree method is better than both the binary and factor methods.

(Here the "better" method is the one that computes x^n using fewer multiplications.)

8. [*M21*] Prove that the power tree (exercise 5) never gives more multiplications for the computation of x^n than the binary method.

▶ **9.** [*25*] Design an exponentiation procedure that is analogous to Algorithm A, but based on radix $m = 2^e$. Your method should perform approximately $\lg n + \nu + m$ multiplications, where ν is the number of nonzero digits in the m-ary representation of n.

10. [*10*] Figure 15 shows a tree that indicates one way to compute x^n with the fewest possible multiplications, for all $n \le 100$. How can this tree be conveniently represented within a computer, in just 100 memory locations?

▶ **11.** [*M26*] The tree of Fig. 15 depicts addition chains $a_0, a_1, \ldots, a_r$ having $l(a_i) = i$ for all a_i in the chain. Find all addition chains for n that have this property, when $n = 43$ and when $n = 77$. Show that any tree such as Fig. 15 must include either the path 1, 2, 4, 8, 9, 17, 34, 43, 77 or the path 1, 2, 4, 8, 9, 17, 34, 68, 77.

12. [*M10*] Is it possible to extend the tree shown in Fig. 15 to an infinite tree that yields a minimum-multiplication rule for computing x^n, for all positive integers n?

13. [*M21*] Find a star chain of length $A + 2$ for each of the four cases listed in Theorem C. (Consequently Theorem C holds also with l replaced by l^*.)

14. [*M29*] Complete the proof of Theorem C, by demonstrating that (a) step $r - 1$ is not a small step; and (b) $\lambda(a_{r-k})$ cannot be less than $m - 1$, where $m = \lambda(a_{r-1})$.

15. [*M43*] Write a computer program to extend Theorem C, characterizing all n such that $l(n) = \lambda(n) + 3$ and characterizing all n such that $l^*(n) = \lambda(n) + 3$.

16. [*HM15*] Show that Theorem D is not trivially true just because of the binary method; if $l^B(n)$ denotes the length of the addition chain for n produced by the binary S-and-X method, the ratio $l^B(n)/\lambda(n)$ does not approach a limit as $n \to \infty$.

17. [*M25*] Explain how to find the intervals $J_1, \ldots, J_h$ that are required in the proof of Lemma P.

18. [*HM24*] Let β be a positive constant. Show that there is a constant $\alpha < 2$ such that

$$\sum \binom{m+s}{t+v}\binom{t+v}{v}\beta^{2v}\binom{(m+s)^2}{t} < \alpha^m$$

for all large m, where the sum is over all s, t, v satisfying (30).

19. [*M23*] A "multiset" is like a set, but it may contain identical elements repeated a finite number of times. If A and B are multisets, we define new multisets $A \uplus B$, $A \cup B$, and $A \cap B$ in the following way: An element occurring exactly a times in A and b times in B occurs exactly $a + b$ times in $A \uplus B$, exactly $\max(a, b)$ times in $A \cup B$, and exactly $\min(a, b)$ times in $A \cap B$. (A "set" is a multiset that contains no elements more than once; if A and B are sets, so are $A \cup B$ and $A \cap B$, and the definitions given in this exercise agree with the customary definitions of set union and intersection.)

    a) The prime factorization of a positive integer n is a multiset N whose elements are primes, where $\prod_{p \in N} p = n$. The fact that every positive integer can be uniquely factored into primes gives us a one-to-one correspondence between the positive integers and the finite multisets of prime numbers; for example, if $n = 2^2 \cdot 3^3 \cdot 17$, the corresponding multiset is $N = \{2, 2, 3, 3, 3, 17\}$. If M and N are the multisets corresponding respectively to m and n, what multisets correspond to $\gcd(m, n)$, $\mathrm{lcm}(m, n)$, and mn?

    b) Every monic polynomial $f(z)$ over the complex numbers corresponds in a natural way to the multiset F of its "roots"; we have $f(z) = \prod_{\zeta \in F}(z - \zeta)$. If $f(z)$ and $g(z)$ are the polynomials corresponding to the finite multisets F and G of complex numbers, what polynomials correspond to $F \uplus G$, $F \cup G$, and $F \cap G$?

    c) Find as many interesting identities as you can that hold between multisets, with respect to the three operations $\uplus$, $\cup$, $\cap$.

20. [*M20*] What are the sequences S_i and M_{ij} ($0 \le i \le r$, $0 \le j \le t$) arising in Hansen's structural decomposition of star chains (a) of Type 3? (b) of Type 5? (The six "types" are defined in the proof of Theorem B.)

▶ **21.** [*M26*] (W. Hansen.) Let q be any positive integer. Find a value of n such that $l(n) \le l^*(n) - q$.

22. [*M20*] Prove that the addition chain constructed in the proof of Theorem F is an l^0-chain.

23. [*M20*] Prove Brauer's inequality (50).

▶ **24.** [*M22*] Generalize the proof of Theorem G to show that $l^0((B^n - 1)/(B - 1)) \le (n - 1)\,l^0(B) + l^0(n)$, for any integer $B > 1$; and prove that $l(2^{mn} - 1) \le l(2^m - 1) + mn - m + l^0(n)$.

25. [*20*] Let y be a fraction, $0 < y < 1$, expressed in the binary number system as $y = (.d_1 \ldots d_k)_2$. Design an algorithm to compute x^y using the operations of multiplication and square-root extraction.

▶ **26.** [*M25*] Design an efficient algorithm that computes the nth Fibonacci number F_n, modulo m, given large integers n and m.

27. [*M23*] (A. Flammenkamp.) What is the smallest n for which every addition chain contains at least eight small steps?

28. [*HM33*] (A. Schönhage.) The object of this exercise is to give a fairly short proof that $l(n) \geq \lambda(n) + \lg \nu(n) - O(\log \log(\nu(n) + 1))$.

   a) When $x = (x_k \ldots x_0.x_{-1} \ldots)_2$ and $y = (y_k \ldots y_0.y_{-1} \ldots)_2$ are real numbers written in binary notation, let us write $x \subseteq y$ if $x_j \leq y_j$ for all j. Give a simple rule for constructing the smallest number z with the property that $x' \subseteq x$ and $y' \subseteq y$ implies $x' + y' \subseteq z$. Denoting this number by $x \nabla y$, prove that $\nu(x \nabla y) \leq \nu(x) + \nu(y)$.

   b) Given any addition chain (11) with $r = l(n)$, let the sequence $d_0, d_1, \ldots, d_r$ be defined as in (35), and define the sequence $A_0, A_1, \ldots, A_r$ by the following rules: $A_0 = 1$; if $a_i = 2a_{i-1}$ then $A_i = 2A_{i-1}$; otherwise if $a_i = a_j + a_k$ for some $0 \leq k \leq j < i$, then $A_i = A_{i-1} \nabla (A_{i-1}/2^{d_j - d_k})$. Prove that this sequence "covers" the given chain, in the sense that $a_i \subseteq A_i$ for $0 \leq i \leq r$.

   c) Let δ be a positive integer (to be selected later). Call the nondoubling step $a_i = a_j + a_k$ a "baby step" if $d_j - d_k \geq \delta$, otherwise call it a "close step." Let $B_0 = 1$; $B_i = 2B_{i-1}$ if $a_i = 2a_{i-1}$; $B_i = B_{i-1} \nabla (B_{i-1}/2^{d_j - d_k})$ if $a_i = a_j + a_k$ is a baby step; and $B_i = \rho(2B_{i-1})$ otherwise, where $\rho(x)$ is the least number y such that $x/2^e \subseteq y$ for $0 \leq e \leq \delta$. Show that $A_i \subseteq B_i$ and $\nu(B_i) \leq (1 + \delta c_i)2^{b_i}$ for $0 \leq i \leq r$, where b_i and c_i respectively denote the number of baby steps and close steps $\leq i$. [*Hint:* Show that the 1s in B_i appear in consecutive blocks of size $\geq 1 + \delta c_i$.]

   d) We now have $l(n) = r = b_r + c_r + d_r$ and $\nu(n) \leq \nu(B_r) \leq (1 + \delta c_r)2^{b_r}$. Explain how to choose δ in order to obtain the inequality stated at the beginning of this exercise. [*Hint:* See (16), and note that $n \leq 2^r \alpha^{b_r}$ for some $\alpha < 1$ depending on δ.]

29. [*M49*] (K. B. Stolarsky, 1969.) Is $\nu(n) \leq 2^{l(n) - \lambda(n)}$ for all positive integers n? (If so, we have the lower bound $l(2^n - 1) \geq n - 1 + \lceil \lg n \rceil$; see (17) and (49).)

30. [*20*] An *addition-subtraction chain* has the rule $a_i = a_j \pm a_k$ in place of (2); the imaginary computer described in the text has a new operation code, SUB. (This corresponds in practice to evaluating x^n using both multiplications and divisions.) Find an addition-subtraction chain, for some n, that has fewer than $l(n)$ steps.

31. [*M46*] (D. H. Lehmer.) Explore the problem of minimizing $\epsilon q + (r - q)$ in an addition chain (1), where q is the number of "simple" steps in which $a_i = a_{i-1} + 1$, given a small positive "weight" ϵ. (This problem comes closer to reality for many calculations of x^n, if multiplication by x is simpler than a general multiplication; see the applications in Section 4.6.2.)

32. [*M30*] (A. C. Yao, F. F. Yao, R. L. Graham.) Associate the "cost" $a_j a_k$ with each step $a_i = a_j + a_k$ of an addition chain (1). Show that the left-to-right binary method yields a chain of minimum total cost, for all positive integers n.

33. [*15*] How many addition chains of length 9 have (52) as their reduced directed graph?

34. [*M23*] The binary addition chain for $n = 2^{e_0} + \cdots + 2^{e_t}$, when $e_0 > \cdots > e_t \geq 0$, is $1, 2, \ldots, 2^{e_0 - e_1}, 2^{e_0 - e_1} + 1, \ldots, 2^{e_0 - e_2} + 2^{e_1 - e_2}, 2^{e_0 - e_2} + 2^{e_1 - e_2} + 1, \ldots, n$. This corresponds to the S-and-X method described at the beginning of this section, while Algorithm A corresponds to the addition chain obtained by sorting the two sequences $(1, 2, 4, \ldots, 2^{e_0})$ and $(2^{e_t - 1} + 2^{e_t}, 2^{e_t - 2} + 2^{e_t - 1} + 2^{e_t}, \ldots, n)$ into increasing order. Prove or disprove: Each of these addition chains is a dual of the other.

35. [*M27*] How many addition chains without useless steps are equivalent to each of the addition chains discussed in exercise 34, when $e_0 > e_1 + 1$?

▶ **36.** [*25*] (E. G. Straus.) Find a way to compute a general *monomial* $x_1^{n_1} x_2^{n_2} \dots x_m^{n_m}$ in at most $2\lambda(\max(n_1, n_2, \dots, n_m)) + 2^m - m - 1$ multiplications.

37. [*HM30*] (A. C. Yao.) Let $l(n_1, \dots, n_m)$ be the length of the shortest addition chain that contains each of the numbers $n_1, \dots, n_m$. Generalizing (25), prove that $l(n_1, \dots, n_m) \le \lambda(n) + m\lambda(n)/\lambda\lambda(n) + O(\lambda(n) \lambda\lambda\lambda(n)/\lambda\lambda(n)^2)$, $n = \max\{n_1, \dots, n_m\}$.

38. [*M47*] What is the asymptotic value of $l(1, 4, 9, \dots, m^2) - m$, as $m \to \infty$, in the notation of exercise 37?

▶ **39.** [*M25*] (J. Olivos, 1979.) Let $l([n_1, n_2, \dots, n_m])$ be the minimum number of multiplications needed to evaluate the monomial $x_1^{n_1} x_2^{n_2} \dots x_m^{n_m}$ in the sense of exercise 36, where each n_i is a positive integer. Prove that this problem is equivalent to the problem of exercise 37, by showing that $l([n_1, n_2, \dots, n_m]) = l(n_1, n_2, \dots, n_m) + m - 1$. [*Hint:* Consider directed graphs like (52) that have more than one source vertex.]

▶ **40.** [*M21*] (J. Olivos.) Generalizing the factor method and Theorem F, prove that

$$l(m_1 n_1 + \dots + m_t n_t) \le l(m_1, \dots, m_t) + l(n_1, \dots, n_t) + t - 1,$$

where $l(n_1, \dots, n_t)$ is defined in exercise 37.

41. [*M40*] (P. Downey, B. Leong, R. Sethi.) Let G be a connected graph with n vertices $\{1, \dots, n\}$ and m edges, where the edges join u_j to v_j for $1 \le j \le m$. Prove that $l(1, 2, \dots, 2^{An}, 2^{Au_1} + 2^{Av_1} + 1, \dots, 2^{Au_m} + 2^{Av_m} + 1) = An + m + k$ for all sufficiently large A, where k is the minimum number of vertices in a vertex cover for G (namely a set that contains either u_j or v_j for $1 \le j \le m$).

42. [*22*] (Neill Clift, 2005.) Show that neither 1, 2, 4, 8, 16, 32, 64, 65, 97, 128, 256, 353, 706, 1412, 2824, 5648, 11296, 22592, 45184, 90368, 180736, 361472, 361537, 723074, 1446148, 2892296, 5784592, 5784689 nor its dual is an l^0-chain.

43. [*M50*] Is $l(2^n - 1) \le n - 1 + l(n)$ for all integers $n > 0$? Does equality always hold?

4.6.4. Evaluation of Polynomials

Now that we know efficient ways to evaluate the special polynomial x^n, let us consider the general problem of computing an nth degree polynomial

$$u(x) = u_n x^n + u_{n-1} x^{n-1} + \dots + u_1 x + u_0, \qquad u_n \ne 0, \qquad (1)$$

for given values of x. This problem arises frequently in practice.

In the following discussion we shall concentrate on minimizing the number of operations required to evaluate polynomials by computer, blithely assuming that all arithmetic operations are exact. Polynomials are most commonly evaluated using floating point arithmetic, which is not exact, and different schemes for the evaluation will, in general, give different answers. A numerical analysis of the accuracy achieved depends on the coefficients of the particular polynomial being considered, and is beyond the scope of this book; the reader should be careful to investigate the accuracy of any calculations undertaken with floating point arithmetic. In most cases the methods we shall describe turn out to be reasonably satisfactory from a numerical standpoint, but many bad examples can also be given. [See Webb Miller, *SICOMP* **4** (1975), 97–107, for a survey of the literature on stability of fast polynomial evaluation, and for a demonstration that certain kinds of numerical stability cannot be guaranteed for some families of high-speed algorithms.]

Throughout this section we will act as if the variable x were a single number. But it is important to keep in mind that most of the methods we will discuss are valid also when the variables are large objects like multiprecision numbers, polynomials, or matrices. In such cases efficient formulas lead to even bigger payoffs, especially when we can reduce the number of multiplications.

A beginning programmer will often evaluate the polynomial (1) in a manner that corresponds directly to its conventional textbook form: First $u_n x^n$ is calculated, then $u_{n-1} x^{n-1}$, ..., $u_1 x$, and finally all of the terms of (1) are added together. But even if the efficient methods of Section 4.6.3 are used to evaluate the powers of x in this approach, the resulting calculation is needlessly slow unless nearly all of the coefficients u_k are zero. If the coefficients are all nonzero, an obvious alternative would be to evaluate (1) from right to left, computing the values of x^k and $u_k x^k + \cdots + u_0$ for $k = 1, \ldots, n$. Such a process involves $2n - 1$ multiplications and n additions, and it might also require further instructions to store and retrieve intermediate results from memory.

Horner's rule. One of the first things a novice programmer is usually taught is an elegant way to rearrange this computation, by evaluating $u(x)$ as follows:

$$u(x) = \bigl(\ldots (u_n x + u_{n-1}) x + \cdots \bigr) x + u_0. \tag{2}$$

Start with u_n, multiply by x, add u_{n-1}, multiply by x, ..., multiply by x, add u_0. This form of the computation is usually called "Horner's rule"; we have already seen it used in connection with radix conversion in Section 4.4. The entire process requires n multiplications and n additions, minus one addition for each coefficient that is zero. Furthermore, there is no need to store partial results, since each quantity arising during the calculation is used immediately after it has been computed.

W. G. Horner gave this rule early in the nineteenth century [*Philosophical Transactions*, Royal Society of London **109** (1819), 308–335] in connection with a procedure for calculating polynomial roots. The fame of the latter method [see J. L. Coolidge, *Mathematics of Great Amateurs* (Oxford, 1949), Chapter 15] accounts for the fact that Horner's name has been attached to (2); but actually Isaac Newton had made use of the same idea more than 150 years earlier. For example, in a well-known work entitled *De Analysi per Æquationes Infinitas*, originally written in 1669, Newton wrote

$$\overline{\overline{y - 4 \times y} : + 5 \times y} : - 12 \times y : + 17$$

for the polynomial $y^4 - 4y^3 + 5y^2 - 12y + 17$, while illustrating what later came to be known as Newton's method for rootfinding. This clearly shows the idea of (2), since he often denoted grouping by using horizontal lines and colons instead of parentheses. Newton had been using the idea for several years in unpublished notes. [See *The Mathematical Papers of Isaac Newton*, edited by D. T. Whiteside, **1** (1967), 490, 531; **2** (1968), 222.] Independently, a method equivalent to Horner's had in fact been used in 13th-century China by Ch'in Chiu-Shao [see Y. Mikami, *The Development of Mathematics in China and Japan* (1913), 73–77].

Several generalizations of Horner's rule have been suggested. Let us first consider evaluating $u(z)$ when z is a complex number, while the coefficients u_k are real. In particular, when $z = e^{i\theta} = \cos\theta + i\sin\theta$, the polynomial $u(z)$ is essentially two Fourier series,

$$(u_0 + u_1 \cos\theta + \cdots + u_n \cos n\theta) + i(u_1 \sin\theta + \cdots + u_n \sin n\theta).$$

Complex addition and multiplication can obviously be reduced to a sequence of ordinary operations on real numbers:

real + complex	requires	1 addition
complex + complex	requires	2 additions
real × complex	requires	2 multiplications
complex × complex	requires	4 multiplications, 2 additions
	or	3 multiplications, 5 additions

(See exercise 41. Subtraction is considered here as if it were equivalent to addition.) Therefore Horner's rule (2) uses either $4n - 2$ multiplications and $3n - 2$ additions or $3n - 1$ multiplications and $6n - 5$ additions to evaluate $u(z)$ when $z = x + iy$ is complex. Actually $2n - 4$ of these additions can be saved, since we are multiplying by the same number z each time. An alternative procedure for evaluating $u(x + iy)$ is to let

$$a_1 = u_n, \qquad b_1 = u_{n-1}, \qquad r = x + x, \quad s = x^2 + y^2;$$
$$a_j = b_{j-1} + ra_{j-1}, \quad b_j = u_{n-j} - sa_{j-1}, \qquad 1 < j \le n. \tag{3}$$

Then it is easy to prove by induction that $u(z) = za_n + b_n$. This scheme [*BIT* **5** (1965), 142; see also G. Goertzel, *AMM* **65** (1958), 34–35] requires only $2n + 2$ multiplications and $2n + 1$ additions, so it is an improvement over Horner's rule when $n \ge 3$. In the case of Fourier series, when $z = e^{i\theta}$, we have $s = 1$, so the number of multiplications drops to $n + 1$. The moral of this story is that a good programmer does not make indiscriminate use of the built-in complex-arithmetic features of high-level programming languages.

Consider the process of dividing the polynomial $u(x)$ by $x - x_0$, using Algorithm 4.6.1D to obtain $u(x) = (x - x_0)q(x) + r(x)$; here $\deg(r) < 1$, so $r(x)$ is a constant independent of x, and $u(x_0) = 0 \cdot q(x_0) + r = r$. An examination of this division process reveals that the computation is essentially the same as Horner's rule for evaluating $u(x_0)$. Similarly, if we divide $u(z)$ by the polynomial $(z - z_0)(z - \bar{z}_0) = z^2 - 2x_0 z + x_0^2 + y_0^2$, the resulting computation turns out to be equivalent to (3); we obtain $u(z) = (z - z_0)(z - \bar{z}_0)q(z) + a_n z + b_n$, hence $u(z_0) = a_n z_0 + b_n$.

In general, if we divide $u(x)$ by $f(x)$ to obtain $u(x) = f(x)q(x) + r(x)$, and if $f(x_0) = 0$, we have $u(x_0) = r(x_0)$; this observation leads to further generalizations of Horner's rule. For example, we may let $f(x) = x^2 - x_0^2$; this yields the "second-order" Horner's rule

$$u(x) = \left(\ldots (u_{2\lfloor n/2\rfloor}x^2 + u_{2\lfloor n/2\rfloor-2})x^2 + \cdots\right)x^2 + u_0$$
$$+ \left((\ldots(u_{2\lceil n/2\rceil-1}x^2 + u_{2\lceil n/2\rceil-3})x^2 + \cdots)x^2 + u_1\right)x. \tag{4}$$

The second-order rule uses $n+1$ multiplications and n additions (see exercise 5); so it is no improvement over Horner's rule from this standpoint. But there are at least two circumstances in which (4) is useful: If we want to evaluate both $u(x)$ and $u(-x)$, this approach yields $u(-x)$ with just one more addition operation; two values can be obtained almost as cheaply as one. Moreover, if we have a computer that allows parallel computations, the two lines of (4) may be evaluated independently, so we save about half the running time.

When our computer allows parallel computation on k arithmetic units at once, a "kth-order" Horner's rule $\big($obtained in a similar manner from $f(x) = x^k - x_0^k\big)$ may be used. Another attractive method for parallel computation has been suggested by G. Estrin [*Proc. Western Joint Computing Conf.* **17** (1960), 33–40]; for $n = 7$, Estrin's method is:

Processor 1	Processor 2	Processor 3	Processor 4	Processor 5
$a_1 = u_7 x + u_6$	$b_1 = u_5 x + u_4$	$c_1 = u_3 x + u_2$	$d_1 = u_1 x + u_0$	x^2
$a_2 = a_1 x^2 + b_1$		$c_2 = c_1 x^2 + d_1$		x^4
$a_3 = a_2 x^4 + c_2$				

Here $a_3 = u(x)$. However, an interesting analysis by W. S. Dorn [*IBM J. Res. and Devel.* **6** (1962), 239–245] shows that these methods might not actually be an improvement over the second-order rule, if each arithmetic unit must access a memory that communicates with only one processor at a time.

Tabulating polynomial values. If we wish to evaluate an nth degree polynomial at many points in an arithmetic progression $\big($that is, if we want to calculate $u(x_0)$, $u(x_0 + h)$, $u(x_0 + 2h)$, $\ldots\big)$, the process can be reduced to addition only, after the first few steps. For if we start with any sequence of numbers $(\alpha_0, \alpha_1, \ldots, \alpha_n)$ and apply the transformation

$$\alpha_0 \leftarrow \alpha_0 + \alpha_1, \quad \alpha_1 \leftarrow \alpha_1 + \alpha_2, \quad \ldots, \quad \alpha_{n-1} \leftarrow \alpha_{n-1} + \alpha_n, \qquad (5)$$

we find that k applications of (5) yields

$$\alpha_j^{(k)} = \binom{k}{0}\beta_j + \binom{k}{1}\beta_{j+1} + \binom{k}{2}\beta_{j+2} + \cdots, \qquad 0 \le j \le n,$$

where β_j denotes the initial value of α_j and $\beta_j = 0$ for $j > n$. In particular,

$$\alpha_0^{(k)} = \binom{k}{0}\beta_0 + \binom{k}{1}\beta_1 + \cdots + \binom{k}{n}\beta_n \qquad (6)$$

is a polynomial of degree n in k. By properly choosing the β's, as shown in exercise 7, we can set things up so that this quantity $\alpha_0^{(k)}$ is the desired value $u(x_0 + kh)$, for all k. In other words, each execution of the n additions in (5) will produce the next value of the given polynomial.

Caution: Rounding errors can accumulate after many repetitions of (5), and an error in α_j produces a corresponding error in the coefficients of x^0, $\ldots$, x^j in the polynomial being computed. Therefore the values of the α's should be "refreshed" after a large number of iterations.

Derivatives and changes of variable. Sometimes we want to find the coefficients of $u(x+x_0)$, given a constant x_0 and the coefficients of $u(x)$. For example, if $u(x) = 3x^2 + 2x - 1$, then $u(x-2) = 3x^2 - 10x + 7$. This is analogous to a radix conversion problem, converting from base x to base $x + 2$. By Taylor's theorem, the new coefficients are given by the derivatives of $u(x)$ at $x = x_0$, namely

$$u(x + x_0) = u(x_0) + u'(x_0)x + \left(u''(x_0)/2!\right)x^2 + \cdots + \left(u^{(n)}(x_0)/n!\right)x^n, \qquad (7)$$

so the problem is equivalent to evaluating $u(x)$ and all its derivatives.

If we write $u(x) = q(x)(x - x_0) + r$, then $u(x + x_0) = q(x + x_0)x + r$; so r is the constant coefficient of $u(x+x_0)$, and the problem reduces to finding the coefficients of $q(x+x_0)$, where $q(x)$ is a known polynomial of degree $n - 1$. Thus the following algorithm is indicated:

H1. Set $v_j \leftarrow u_j$ for $0 \le j \le n$.

H2. For $k = 0, 1, \ldots, n - 1$ (in this order), set $v_j \leftarrow v_j + x_0 v_{j+1}$ for $j = n - 1$, $\ldots, k + 1, k$ (in this order). ∎

At the conclusion of step H2 we have $u(x + x_0) = v_n x^n + \cdots + v_1 x + v_0$. This procedure was a principal part of Horner's root-finding method, and when $k = 0$ it is exactly rule (2) for evaluating $u(x_0)$.

Horner's method requires $(n^2 + n)/2$ multiplications and $(n^2 + n)/2$ additions; but notice that if $x_0 = 1$ we avoid all of the multiplications. Fortunately we can reduce the general problem to the case $x_0 = 1$ by introducing comparatively few multiplications and divisions:

S1. Compute and store the values $x_0^2, \ldots, x_0^n$.

S2. Set $v_j \leftarrow u_j x_0^j$ for $0 \le j \le n$. $\left(\text{Now } v(x) = u(x_0 x).\right)$

S3. Perform step H2 but with $x_0 = 1$. $\left(\text{Now } v(x) = u\left(x_0(x+1)\right) = u(x_0 x + x_0).\right)$

S4. Set $v_j \leftarrow v_j / x_0^j$ for $0 < j \le n$. $\left(\text{Now } v(x) = u(x + x_0) \text{ as desired.}\right)$ ∎

This idea, due to M. Shaw and J. F. Traub [*JACM* **21** (1974), 161–167], has the same number of additions and the same numerical stability as Horner's method; but it needs only $2n - 1$ multiplications and $n - 1$ divisions, since $v_n = u_n$. About $\frac{1}{2}n$ of these multiplications can, in turn, be avoided (see exercise 6).

If we want only the first few or the last few derivatives, Shaw and Traub have observed that there are further ways to save time. For example, if we just want to evaluate $u(x)$ and $u'(x)$, we can do the job with $2n - 1$ additions and about $n + \sqrt{2n}$ multiplications/divisions as follows:

D1. Compute and store the values $x^2, x^3, \ldots, x^t, x^{2t}$, where $t = \lceil \sqrt{n/2} \rceil$.

D2. Set $v_j \leftarrow u_j x^{f(j)}$ for $0 \le j \le n$, where $f(j) = t - 1 - \left((n - 1 - j) \bmod 2t\right)$ for $0 \le j < n$, and $f(n) = t$.

D3. Set $v_j \leftarrow v_j + v_{j+1} x^{g(j)}$ for $j = n - 1, \ldots, 1, 0$; here $g(j) = 2t$ when $n - 1 - j$ is a positive multiple of $2t$, otherwise $g(j) = 0$ and the multiplication by $x^{g(j)}$ need not be done.

D4. Set $v_j \leftarrow v_j + v_{j+1} x^{g(j)}$ for $j = n - 1, \ldots, 2, 1$. Now $v_0 / x^{f(0)} = u(x)$ and $v_1 / x^{f(1)} = u'(x)$. ∎

Adaptation of coefficients. Let us now return to our original problem of evaluating a given polynomial $u(x)$ as rapidly as possible, for "random" values of x. The importance of this problem is due partly to the fact that standard functions such as $\sin x$, $\cos x$, e^x, etc., are usually computed by subroutines that rely on the evaluation of certain polynomials; such polynomials are evaluated so often, it is desirable to find the fastest possible way to do the computation.

Arbitrary polynomials of degree five and higher can be evaluated with fewer operations than Horner's rule requires, if we first "adapt" or "precondition" the coefficients u_0, u_1, ..., u_n. This adaptation process might involve a lot of work, as explained below; but the preliminary calculation is not wasted, since it must be done only once while the polynomial will be evaluated many times. For examples of "adapted" polynomials for standard functions, see V. Y. Pan, *USSR Computational Math. and Math. Physics* **2** (1963), 137–146.

The simplest case for which adaptation of coefficients is helpful occurs for a fourth degree polynomial:

$$u(x) = u_4 x^4 + u_3 x^3 + u_2 x^2 + u_1 x + u_0, \qquad u_4 \neq 0. \tag{8}$$

This equation can be rewritten in a form originally suggested by T. S. Motzkin,

$$y = (x + \alpha_0)x + \alpha_1, \qquad u(x) = \big((y + x + \alpha_2)y + \alpha_3\big)\alpha_4, \tag{9}$$

for suitably "adapted" coefficients α_0, α_1, α_2, α_3, α_4. The computation in this scheme involves three multiplications, five additions, and (on a one-accumulator machine like `MIX`) one instruction to store the partial result y into temporary storage. By comparison with Horner's rule, we have traded a multiplication for an addition and a possible storage command. Even this comparatively small change is worthwhile if the polynomial is to be evaluated often. (Of course, if the time for multiplication is comparable to the time for addition, (9) gives no improvement; we will see that a general fourth-degree polynomial always requires at least eight arithmetic operations for its evaluation.)

By equating coefficients in (8) and (9), we obtain formulas for computing the α_j's in terms of the u_k's:

$$
\begin{aligned}
&\alpha_0 = \tfrac{1}{2}(u_3/u_4 - 1), &&\beta = u_2/u_4 - \alpha_0(\alpha_0 + 1), &&\alpha_1 = u_1/u_4 - \alpha_0\beta, \\
&\alpha_2 = \beta - 2\alpha_1, &&\alpha_3 = u_0/u_4 - \alpha_1(\alpha_1 + \alpha_2), &&\alpha_4 = u_4.
\end{aligned} \tag{10}
$$

A similar scheme, which evaluates a fourth-degree polynomial in the same number of steps as (9), appears in exercise 18; this alternative method will give greater numerical accuracy than (9) in certain cases, although it yields poorer accuracy in others.

Polynomials that arise in practice often have a rather small leading coefficient, so that the division by u_4 in (10) leads to instability. In such a case it is usually preferable to replace x by $|u_4|^{1/4} x$ as the first step, reducing (8) to a polynomial whose leading coefficient is ± 1. A similar transformation applies to polynomials of higher degrees. This idea is due to C. T. Fike [*CACM* **10** (1967), 175–178], who has presented several interesting examples.

Any polynomial of the fifth degree may be evaluated using four multiplications, six additions, and one storing, by using the rule $u(x) = U(x)x + u_0$, where $U(x) = u_5x^4 + u_4x^3 + u_3x^2 + u_2x + u_1$ is evaluated as in (9). Alternatively, we can do the evaluation with four multiplications, five additions, and three storings, if the calculations take the form

$$y = (x + \alpha_0)^2, \qquad u(x) = \big(((y + \alpha_1)y + \alpha_2)(x + \alpha_3) + \alpha_4\big)\alpha_5. \qquad (11)$$

The determination of the α's this time requires the solution of a cubic equation (see exercise 19).

On many computers the number of "storing" operations required by (11) is less than 3; for example, we may be able to compute $(x + \alpha_0)^2$ without storing $x + \alpha_0$. In fact, most computers nowadays have more than one arithmetic register for floating point calculations, so we can avoid storing altogether. Because of the wide variety of features available for arithmetic on different computers, we shall henceforth in this section count only the arithmetic operations, not the operations of storing and loading an accumulator. The computation schemes can usually be adapted to any particular computer in a straightforward manner, so that very few of these auxiliary operations are necessary; on the other hand, it must be remembered that overhead costs might well overshadow the fact that we are saving a multiplication or two, especially if the machine code is being produced by a compiler that does not optimize.

A polynomial $u(x) = u_6x^6 + \cdots + u_1x + u_0$ of degree six can always be evaluated using four multiplications and seven additions, with the scheme

$$z = (x + \alpha_0)x + \alpha_1, \qquad w = (x + \alpha_2)z + \alpha_3,$$
$$u(x) = \big((w + z + \alpha_4)w + \alpha_5\big)\alpha_6. \qquad (12)$$

[See D. E. Knuth, *CACM* **5** (1962), 595–599.] This saves two of the six multiplications required by Horner's rule. Here again we must solve a cubic equation: Since $\alpha_6 = u_6$, we may assume that $u_6 = 1$. Under this assumption, let

$$\beta_1 = (u_5 - 1)/2, \qquad \beta_2 = u_4 - \beta_1(\beta_1 + 1),$$
$$\beta_3 = u_3 - \beta_1\beta_2, \qquad \beta_4 = \beta_1 - \beta_2, \qquad \beta_5 = u_2 - \beta_1\beta_3.$$

Let β_6 be a real root of the cubic equation

$$2y^3 + (2\beta_4 - \beta_2 + 1)y^2 + (2\beta_5 - \beta_2\beta_4 - \beta_3)y + (u_1 - \beta_2\beta_5) = 0. \qquad (13)$$

(This equation always has a real root, since the polynomial on the left approaches $+\infty$ for large positive y, and it approaches $-\infty$ for large negative y; it must assume the value zero somewhere in between.) Now if we define

$$\beta_7 = \beta_6^2 + \beta_4\beta_6 + \beta_5, \qquad \beta_8 = \beta_3 - \beta_6 - \beta_7,$$

we have finally

$$\alpha_0 = \beta_2 - 2\beta_6, \qquad \alpha_2 = \beta_1 - \alpha_0, \qquad \alpha_1 = \beta_6 - \alpha_0\alpha_2,$$
$$\alpha_3 = \beta_7 - \alpha_1\alpha_2, \qquad \alpha_4 = \beta_8 - \beta_7 - \alpha_1, \qquad \alpha_5 = u_0 - \beta_7\beta_8. \qquad (14)$$

We can illustrate this procedure with a contrived example: Suppose that we want to evaluate $x^6 + 13x^5 + 49x^4 + 33x^3 - 61x^2 - 37x + 3$. We obtain $\alpha_6 = 1$, $\beta_1 = 6$, $\beta_2 = 7$, $\beta_3 = -9$, $\beta_4 = -1$, $\beta_5 = -7$, and so we meet with the cubic equation

$$2y^3 - 8y^2 + 2y + 12 = 0. \tag{15}$$

This equation has $\beta_6 = 2$ as a root, and we continue to find

$$\beta_7 = -5, \qquad \beta_8 = -6,$$
$$\alpha_0 = 3, \quad \alpha_2 = 3, \quad \alpha_1 = -7, \quad \alpha_3 = 16, \quad \alpha_4 = 6, \quad \alpha_5 = -27.$$

The resulting scheme is therefore

$$z = (x+3)x - 7, \qquad w = (x+3)z + 16, \qquad u(x) = (w+z+6)w - 27.$$

By sheer coincidence the quantity $x + 3$ appears twice here, so we have found a method that uses three multiplications and six additions.

Another method for handling sixth-degree equations has been suggested by V. Y. Pan [*Problemy Kibernetiki* **5** (1961), 17–29]. His method requires one more addition operation, but it involves only rational operations in the preliminary steps; no cubic equation needs to be solved. We may proceed as follows:

$$z = (x + \alpha_0)x + \alpha_1, \qquad w = z + x + \alpha_2,$$
$$u(x) = \big(((z - x + \alpha_3)w + \alpha_4)z + \alpha_5\big)\alpha_6. \tag{16}$$

To determine the α's, we divide the polynomial once again by $u_6 = \alpha_6$ so that $u(x)$ becomes monic. It can then be verified that $\alpha_0 = u_5/3$ and that

$$\alpha_1 = (u_1 - \alpha_0 u_2 + \alpha_0^2 u_3 - \alpha_0^3 u_4 + 2\alpha_0^5)/(u_3 - 2\alpha_0 u_4 + 5\alpha_0^3). \tag{17}$$

Note that Pan's method requires that the denominator in (17) does not vanish. In other words, (16) can be used only when

$$27u_3 u_6^2 - 18u_6 u_5 u_4 + 5u_5^3 \neq 0; \tag{18}$$

in fact, this quantity should not be so small that α_1 becomes too large. Once α_1 has been determined, the remaining α's may be determined from the equations

$$\beta_1 = 2\alpha_0, \qquad\qquad\qquad\qquad \beta_2 = u_4 - \alpha_0\beta_1 - \alpha_1,$$
$$\beta_3 = u_3 - \alpha_0\beta_2 - \alpha_1\beta_1, \qquad\qquad \beta_4 = u_2 - \alpha_0\beta_3 - \alpha_1\beta_2,$$
$$\alpha_3 = \tfrac{1}{2}\big(\beta_3 - (\alpha_0 - 1)\beta_2 + (\alpha_0 - 1)(\alpha_0^2 - 1)\big) - \alpha_1,$$
$$\alpha_2 = \beta_2 - (\alpha_0^2 - 1) - \alpha_3 - 2\alpha_1, \qquad \alpha_4 = \beta_4 - (\alpha_2 + \alpha_1)(\alpha_3 + \alpha_1),$$
$$\alpha_5 = u_0 - \alpha_1\beta_4. \tag{19}$$

We have discussed the cases of degree $n = 4$, 5, 6 in detail because the smaller values of n arise most frequently in applications. Let us now consider a general evaluation scheme for nth degree polynomials, a method that involves at most $\lfloor n/2 \rfloor + 2$ multiplications and n additions.

Theorem E. *Every nth degree polynomial* (1) *with real coefficients, $n \geq 3$, can be evaluated by the scheme*

$$y = x + c, \qquad w = y^2; \qquad z = \begin{cases} (u_n y + \alpha_0)y + \beta_0, & n \text{ even,} \\ u_n y + \beta_0, & n \text{ odd,} \end{cases}$$

$$u(x) = (\ldots((z(w - \alpha_1) + \beta_1)(w - \alpha_2) + \beta_2)\ldots)(w - \alpha_m) + \beta_m, \qquad (20)$$

for suitable real parameters c, α_k and β_k, where $m = \lceil n/2 \rceil - 1$. In fact, it is possible to select these parameters so that $\beta_m = 0$.

Proof. Let us first examine the circumstances under which the α's and β's can be chosen in (20), if c is fixed. Let

$$p(x) = u(x - c) = a_n x^n + a_{n-1}x^{n-1} + \cdots + a_1 x + a_0. \qquad (21)$$

We want to show that $p(x)$ has the form $p_1(x)(x^2 - \alpha_m) + \beta_m$ for some polynomial $p_1(x)$ and some constants α_m, β_m. If we divide $p(x)$ by $x^2 - \alpha_m$, we can see that the remainder β_m is a constant only if the auxiliary polynomial

$$q(x) = a_{2m+1}x^m + a_{2m-1}x^{m-1} + \cdots + a_1, \qquad (22)$$

formed from every odd-numbered coefficient of $p(x)$, is a multiple of $x - \alpha_m$. Conversely, if $q(x)$ has $x - \alpha_m$ as a factor, then $p(x) = p_1(x)(x^2 - \alpha_m) + \beta_m$, for some constant β_m that may be determined by division.

Similarly, we want $p_1(x)$ to have the form $p_2(x)(x^2 - \alpha_{m-1}) + \beta_{m-1}$, and this is the same as saying that $q(x)/(x - \alpha_m)$ is a multiple of $x - \alpha_{m-1}$; for if $q_1(x)$ is the polynomial corresponding to $p_1(x)$ as $q(x)$ corresponds to $p(x)$, we have $q_1(x) = q(x)/(x - \alpha_m)$. Continuing in the same way, we find that the parameters $\alpha_1, \beta_1, \ldots, \alpha_m, \beta_m$ will exist if and only if

$$q(x) = a_{2m+1}(x - \alpha_1)\ldots(x - \alpha_m). \qquad (23)$$

In other words, either $q(x)$ is identically zero (and this can happen only when n is even), or else $q(x)$ is an mth degree polynomial having all real roots.

Now we have a surprising fact discovered by J. Eve [*Numer. Math.* **6** (1964), 17–21]: *If $p(x)$ has at least $n - 1$ complex roots whose real parts are all nonnegative, or all nonpositive, then the corresponding polynomial $q(x)$ is identically zero or has all real roots.* (See exercise 23.) Since $u(x) = 0$ if and only if $p(x + c) = 0$, we need merely choose the parameter c large enough that at least $n - 1$ of the roots of $u(x) = 0$ have a real part $\geq -c$, and (20) will apply whenever $a_{n-1} = u_{n-1} - ncu_n \neq 0$.

We can also determine c so that these conditions are fulfilled and also that $\beta_m = 0$. First the n roots of $u(x) = 0$ are determined. If $a + bi$ is a root having the largest or the smallest real part, and if $b \neq 0$, let $c = -a$ and $\alpha_m = -b^2$; then $x^2 - \alpha_m$ is a factor of $u(x - c)$. If the root with smallest or largest real part is real, but the root with *second* smallest (or second largest) real part is nonreal, the same transformation applies. If the two roots with smallest (or largest) real parts are both real, they can be expressed in the form $a - b$ and $a + b$, respectively; let $c = -a$ and $\alpha_m = b^2$. Again $x^2 - \alpha_m$ is a factor of $u(x - c)$. (Still other values of c are often possible; see exercise 24.) The coefficient a_{n-1} will be nonzero for at least one of these alternatives, unless $q(x)$ is identically zero. ∎

Note that this method of proof usually gives at least two values of c, and we also have the chance to permute $\alpha_1, \ldots, \alpha_{m-1}$ in $(m-1)!$ ways. Some of these alternatives may give more desirable numerical accuracy than others.

Questions of numerical accuracy do not arise, of course, when we are working with integers modulo m instead of with real numbers. Scheme (9) works for $n = 4$ when m is relatively prime to $2u_4$, and (16) works for $n = 6$ when m is relatively prime to $6u_6$ and to the denominator of (17). Exercise 44 shows that $n/2 + O(\log n)$ multiplications and $O(n)$ additions suffice for any monic nth degree polynomial modulo any m.

*Polynomial chains.   Now let us consider questions of optimality. What are the *best possible* schemes for evaluating polynomials of various degrees, in terms of the minimum possible number of arithmetic operations? This question was first analyzed by A. M. Ostrowski in the case that no preliminary adaptation of coefficients is allowed [*Studies in Mathematics and Mechanics Presented to R. von Mises* (New York: Academic Press, 1954), 40–48], and by T. S. Motzkin in the case of adapted coefficients [see *Bull. Amer. Math. Soc.* **61** (1955), 163].

In order to investigate this question, we can extend Section 4.6.3's concept of addition chains to the notion of *polynomial chains*. A polynomial chain is a sequence of the form

$$x = \lambda_0, \quad \lambda_1, \quad \ldots, \quad \lambda_r = u(x), \tag{24}$$

where $u(x)$ is some polynomial in x, and for $1 \le i \le r$

$$\text{either } \lambda_i = (\pm\lambda_j) \circ \lambda_k, \quad 0 \le j, k < i,$$
$$\text{or } \lambda_i = \alpha_j \circ \lambda_k, \quad 0 \le k < i. \tag{25}$$

Here "∘" denotes any of the three operations "+", "−", or "×", and α_j denotes a so-called parameter. Steps of the first kind are called *chain steps*, and steps of the second kind are called *parameter steps*. We shall assume that a different parameter α_j is used in each parameter step; if there are s parameter steps, they should involve $\alpha_1, \alpha_2, \ldots, \alpha_s$ in this order.

It follows that the polynomial $u(x)$ at the end of the chain has the form

$$u(x) = q_n x^n + \cdots + q_1 x + q_0, \tag{26}$$

where $q_n, \ldots, q_1, q_0$ are polynomials in $\alpha_1, \alpha_2, \ldots, \alpha_s$ with integer coefficients. We shall interpret the parameters $\alpha_1, \alpha_2, \ldots, \alpha_s$ as real numbers, and we shall therefore restrict ourselves to considering the evaluation of polynomials with real coefficients. The *result set* R of a polynomial chain is defined to be the set of all vectors $(q_n, \ldots, q_1, q_0)$ of real numbers that occur as $\alpha_1, \alpha_2, \ldots, \alpha_s$ independently assume all possible real values.

If for every choice of $t + 1$ distinct integers $j_0, \ldots, j_t \in \{0, 1, \ldots, n\}$ there is a nonzero multivariate polynomial $f_{j_0 \ldots j_t}$ with integer coefficients such that $f_{j_0 \ldots j_t}(q_{j_0}, \ldots, q_{j_t}) = 0$ for all $(q_n, \ldots, q_1, q_0)$ in R, let us say that the result set R has at most t *degrees of freedom*, and that the chain (24) has at most t degrees of freedom. We also say that the chain (24) *computes* a given polynomial $u(x) = u_n x^n + \cdots + u_1 x + u_0$ if $(u_n, \ldots, u_1, u_0)$ is in R. It follows that a polynomial chain with at most n degrees of freedom cannot compute all nth degree polynomials (see exercise 27).

As an example of a polynomial chain, consider the following chain corresponding to Theorem E, when n is odd:

$$\lambda_0 = x$$
$$\lambda_1 = \alpha_1 + \lambda_0$$
$$\lambda_2 = \lambda_1 \times \lambda_1$$
$$\lambda_3 = \alpha_2 \times \lambda_1 \tag{27}$$
$$\left.\begin{array}{l} \lambda_{1+3i} = \alpha_{1+2i} + \lambda_{3i} \\ \lambda_{2+3i} = \alpha_{2+2i} + \lambda_2 \\ \lambda_{3+3i} = \lambda_{1+3i} \times \lambda_{2+3i} \end{array}\right\} \quad 1 \le i < n/2.$$

There are $\lfloor n/2 \rfloor + 2$ multiplications and n additions; $\lfloor n/2 \rfloor + 1$ chain steps and $n+1$ parameter steps. By Theorem E, the result set R includes the set of all $(u_n, \ldots, u_1, u_0)$ with $u_n \ne 0$, so (27) computes all polynomials of degree n. We cannot prove that R has at most n degrees of freedom, since the result set has $n+1$ independent components.

A polynomial chain with s parameter steps has at most s degrees of freedom. In a sense, this is obvious: We can't compute a function with t degrees of freedom using fewer than t arbitrary parameters. But this intuitive fact is not easy to prove formally; for example, there are continuous functions ("space-filling curves") that map the real line onto a plane, and such functions map a single parameter into two independent parameters. For our purposes, we need to verify that no polynomial functions with integer coefficients can have such a property; a proof appears in exercise 28.

Given this fact, we can proceed to prove the results we seek:

Theorem M (T. S. Motzkin, 1954). *A polynomial chain with $m > 0$ multiplications has at most $2m$ degrees of freedom.*

Proof. Let $\mu_1, \mu_2, \ldots, \mu_m$ be the λ_i's of the chain that are multiplication operations. Then

$$\mu_i = S_{2i-1} \times S_{2i} \quad \text{for } 1 \le i \le m \qquad \text{and} \qquad u(x) = S_{2m+1}, \tag{28}$$

where each S_j is a certain sum of μ's, x's, and α's. Write $S_j = T_j + \beta_j$, where T_j is a sum of μ's and x's while β_j is a sum of α's.

Now $u(x)$ is expressible as a polynomial in x, $\beta_1, \ldots, \beta_{2m+1}$ with integer coefficients. Since the β's are expressible as linear functions of $\alpha_1, \ldots, \alpha_s$, the set of values represented by all real values of $\beta_1, \ldots, \beta_{2m+1}$ contains the result set of the chain. Therefore there are at most $2m+1$ degrees of freedom; this can be improved to $2m$ when $m > 0$, as shown in exercise 30. ∎

An example of the construction in the proof of Theorem M appears in exercise 25. A similar result can be proved for additions:

Theorem A (É. G. Belaga, 1958). *A polynomial chain containing q additions and subtractions has at most $q + 1$ degrees of freedom.*

Proof. [*Problemy Kibernetiki* **5** (1961), 7–15.] Let $\kappa_1, \ldots, \kappa_q$ be the λ_i's of the chain that correspond to addition or subtraction operations. Then

$$\kappa_i = \pm T_{2i-1} \pm T_{2i} \quad \text{for } 1 \le i \le q \qquad \text{and} \qquad u(x) = T_{2q+1}, \qquad (29)$$

where each T_j is a product of κ's, x's, and α's. We may write $T_j = A_j B_j$, where A_j is a product of α's and B_j is a product of κ's and x's. The following transformation may now be made to the chain, successively for $i = 1, 2, \ldots, q$: Let $\beta_i = A_{2i}/A_{2i-1}$, so that $\kappa_i = A_{2i-1}(\pm B_{2i-1} \pm \beta_i B_{2i})$. Then change κ_i to $\pm B_{2i-1} \pm \beta_i B_{2i}$, and replace each occurrence of κ_i in future formulas T_{2i+1}, $T_{2i+2}, \ldots, T_{2q+1}$ by $A_{2i-1}\kappa_i$. (This replacement may change the values of A_{2i+1}, $A_{2i+2}, \ldots, A_{2q+1}$.)

After the transformation has been done for all i, let $\beta_{q+1} = A_{2q+1}$; then $u(x)$ can be expressed as a polynomial in $\beta_1, \ldots, \beta_{q+1}$, and x, with integer coefficients. We are almost ready to complete the proof; but we must be careful because the polynomials that are obtained, as $\beta_1, \ldots, \beta_{q+1}$ range over all real values, may not include all polynomials that are representable by the original chain (see exercise 26). It is possible to have $A_{2i-1} = 0$, for some values of the α's, and that will make β_i undefined.

To complete the proof, let us observe that the result set R of the original chain can be written $R = R_1 \cup R_2 \cup \cdots \cup R_q \cup R'$, where R_i is the set of result vectors possible when $A_{2i-1} = 0$, and where R' is the set of result vectors possible when all α's are nonzero. The discussion above proves that R' has at most $q+1$ degrees of freedom. If $A_{2i-1} = 0$, then $T_{2i-1} = 0$, so addition step κ_i may be dropped to obtain another chain computing the result set R_i; by induction we see that each R_i has at most q degrees of freedom. Hence by exercise 29, R has at most $q + 1$ degrees of freedom. ∎

Theorem C. *If a polynomial chain (24) computes all nth degree polynomials $u(x) = u_n x^n + \cdots + u_0$, for some $n \ge 2$, then it includes at least $\lfloor n/2 \rfloor + 1$ multiplications and at least n addition-subtractions.*

Proof. Let there be m multiplication steps. By Theorem M, the chain has at most $2m$ degrees of freedom, so $2m \ge n + 1$. Similarly, by Theorem A there are $\ge n$ addition-subtractions. ∎

This theorem states that no *single* method having fewer than $\lfloor n/2 \rfloor + 1$ multiplications or fewer than n additions can evaluate all possible nth degree polynomials. The result of exercise 29 allows us to strengthen this and say that no finite collection of such polynomial chains will suffice for all polynomials of a given degree. Some special polynomials can, of course, be evaluated more efficiently; all we have really proved is that polynomials whose coefficients are *algebraically independent*, in the sense that they satisfy no nontrivial polynomial equation, require $\lfloor n/2 \rfloor + 1$ multiplications and n additions. Unfortunately the coefficients we deal with in computers are always rational numbers, so the theorems above don't really apply; in fact, exercise 42 shows that we can always get by with $O(\sqrt{n})$ multiplications (and a possibly huge number of additions). From a practical standpoint, the bounds of Theorem C apply to "almost all" coefficients, and they seem to apply to all reasonable schemes for evaluation. Furthermore it is possible to obtain lower bounds corresponding to those of Theorem C even in the rational case: By strengthening the proofs above, V. Strassen has shown, for example, that the polynomial

$$u(x) = \sum_{k=0}^{n} 2^{2^{kn^3}} x^k \tag{30}$$

cannot be evaluated by any polynomial chain of length $< n^2/\lg n$ unless the chain has at least $\frac{1}{2}n - 2$ multiplications and $n - 4$ additions [*SICOMP* **3** (1974), 128–149]. The coefficients of (30) are very large; but it is also possible to find polynomials whose coefficients are just 0s and 1s, such that every polynomial chain computing them involves at least $\sqrt{n}/(4\lg n)$ chain multiplications, for all sufficiently large n, even when the parameters α_j are allowed to be arbitrary complex numbers. [See R. J. Lipton, *SICOMP* **7** (1978), 61–69; C.-P. Schnorr, *Lecture Notes in Comp. Sci.* **53** (1977), 135–147.] Jean-Paul van de Wiele has shown that the evaluation of certain 0–1 polynomials requires a total of at least $cn/\log n$ arithmetic operations, for some $c > 0$ [*FOCS* **19** (1978), 159–165].

A gap still remains between the lower bounds of Theorem C and the actual operation counts known to be achievable, except in the trivial case $n = 2$. Theorem E gives $\lfloor n/2 \rfloor + 2$ multiplications, not $\lfloor n/2 \rfloor + 1$, although it does achieve the minimum number of additions. Our special methods for $n = 4$ and $n = 6$ have the minimum number of multiplications, but one extra addition. When n is odd, it is not difficult to prove that the lower bounds of Theorem C cannot be achieved simultaneously for both multiplications and additions; see exercise 33. For $n = 3$, 5, and 7, it is possible to show that at least $\lfloor n/2 \rfloor + 2$ multiplications are necessary. Exercises 35 and 36 show that the lower bounds of Theorem C cannot both be achieved when $n = 4$ or $n = 6$; thus the methods we have discussed are best possible, for $n < 8$. When n is even, Motzkin proved that $\lfloor n/2 \rfloor + 1$ multiplications are sufficient, but his construction involves an indeterminate number of additions (see exercise 39). An optimal scheme for $n = 8$ was found by V. Y. Pan, who showed that $n + 1$ additions are necessary and sufficient for this case when there are $\lfloor n/2 \rfloor + 1$ multiplications; he also showed that $\lfloor n/2 \rfloor + 1$ multiplications and $n + 2$ additions will suffice for all even $n \geq 10$. Pan's paper [*STOC* **10** (1978), 162–172] also establishes the exact minimum number of multiplications and additions needed when calculations are done entirely with complex numbers instead of reals, for all degrees n. Exercise 40 discusses the interesting situation that arises for odd values of $n \geq 9$.

It is clear that the results we have obtained about chains for polynomials in a single variable can be extended without difficulty to multivariate polynomials.

For example, if we want to find an optimum scheme for polynomial evaluation *without* adaptation of coefficients, we can regard $u(x)$ as a polynomial in the $n + 2$ variables x, u_n, $\ldots$, u_1, u_0; exercise 38 shows that n multiplications and n additions are necessary in this case. Indeed, A. Borodin [*Theory of Machines and Computations*, edited by Z. Kohavi and A. Paz (New York: Academic Press, 1971), 45–58] has proved that Horner's rule (2) is essentially the *only* way to compute $u(x)$ in $2n$ operations without preconditioning.

With minor variations, the methods above can be extended to chains involving division, that is, to rational functions as well as polynomials. Curiously, the continued-fraction analog of Horner's rule now turns out to be optimal from an operation-count standpoint, if multiplication and division speeds are equal, even when preconditioning is allowed (see exercise 37).

Sometimes division is helpful during the evaluation of polynomials, even though polynomials are defined only in terms of multiplication and addition; we have seen examples of this in the Shaw–Traub algorithms for polynomial derivatives. Another example is the polynomial

$$x^n + \cdots + x + 1;$$

since this polynomial can be written $(x^{n+1} - 1)/(x - 1)$, we can evaluate it with $l(n + 1)$ multiplications (see Section 4.6.3), two subtractions, and one division, while techniques that avoid division seem to require about three times as many operations (see exercise 43).

Special multivariate polynomials. The *determinant* of an $n \times n$ matrix may be considered to be a polynomial in n^2 variables x_{ij}, $1 \le i, j \le n$. If $x_{11} \ne 0$, we have

$$\det \begin{pmatrix} x_{11} & x_{12} & \ldots & x_{1n} \\ x_{21} & x_{22} & \ldots & x_{2n} \\ x_{31} & x_{32} & \ldots & x_{3n} \\ \vdots & \vdots & & \vdots \\ x_{n1} & x_{n2} & \ldots & x_{nn} \end{pmatrix} = x_{11} \det \begin{pmatrix} x_{22} - (x_{21}/x_{11})x_{12} & \ldots & x_{2n} - (x_{21}/x_{11})x_{1n} \\ x_{32} - (x_{31}/x_{11})x_{12} & \ldots & x_{3n} - (x_{31}/x_{11})x_{1n} \\ \vdots & & \vdots \\ x_{n2} - (x_{n1}/x_{11})x_{12} & \ldots & x_{nn} - (x_{n1}/x_{11})x_{1n} \end{pmatrix}. \tag{31}$$

The determinant of an $n \times n$ matrix may therefore be evaluated by evaluating the determinant of an $(n - 1) \times (n - 1)$ matrix and performing an additional $(n - 1)^2 + 1$ multiplications, $(n - 1)^2$ additions, and $n - 1$ divisions. Since a 2×2 determinant can be evaluated with two multiplications and one addition, we see that the determinant of almost all matrices (namely those for which no division by zero is needed) can be computed with at most $(2n^3 - 3n^2 + 7n - 6)/6$ multiplications, $(2n^3 - 3n^2 + n)/6$ additions, and $(n^2 - n - 2)/2$ divisions.

When zero occurs, the determinant is even easier to compute. For example, if $x_{11} = 0$ but $x_{21} \ne 0$, we have

$$\det \begin{pmatrix} 0 & x_{12} & \ldots & x_{1n} \\ x_{21} & x_{22} & \ldots & x_{2n} \\ x_{31} & x_{32} & \ldots & x_{3n} \\ \vdots & \vdots & & \vdots \\ x_{n1} & x_{n2} & \ldots & x_{nn} \end{pmatrix} = -x_{21} \det \begin{pmatrix} x_{12} & \ldots & x_{1n} \\ x_{32} - (x_{31}/x_{21})x_{22} & \ldots & x_{3n} - (x_{31}/x_{21})x_{2n} \\ \vdots & & \vdots \\ x_{n2} - (x_{n1}/x_{21})x_{22} & \ldots & x_{nn} - (x_{n1}/x_{21})x_{2n} \end{pmatrix}. \tag{32}$$

Here the reduction to an $(n-1) \times (n-1)$ determinant saves $n-1$ of the multiplications and $n-1$ of the additions used in (31), in compensation for the additional bookkeeping required to recognize this case. Thus any determinant can be evaluated with roughly $\frac{2}{3}n^3$ arithmetic operations (including division); this is remarkable, since it is a polynomial with $n!$ terms and n variables in each term.

If we want to evaluate the determinant of a matrix with *integer* elements, the procedure of (31) and (32) appears to be unattractive since it requires rational arithmetic. However, we can use the method to evaluate the determinant mod p, for any prime p, since division mod p is possible (exercise 4.5.2–16). If this is done for sufficiently many primes, the exact value of the determinant can be found as explained in Section 4.3.2, since Hadamard's inequality 4.6.1–(25) gives an upper bound on the magnitude.

The coefficients of the *characteristic polynomial* $\det(xI - X)$ of an $n \times n$ matrix X can also be computed in $O(n^3)$ steps; see J. H. Wilkinson, *The Algebraic Eigenvalue Problem* (Oxford: Clarendon Press, 1965), 353–355, 410–411. Exercise 70 discusses an interesting division-free method that involves $O(n^4)$ steps.

The *permanent* of a matrix is a polynomial that is very similar to the determinant; the only difference is that all of its nonzero coefficients are $+1$. Thus we have

$$\text{per} \begin{pmatrix} x_{11} & \cdots & x_{1n} \\ \vdots & & \vdots \\ x_{n1} & \cdots & x_{nn} \end{pmatrix} = \sum x_{1j_1} x_{2j_2} \cdots x_{nj_n}, \tag{33}$$

summed over all permutations $j_1 j_2 \ldots j_n$ of $\{1, 2, \ldots, n\}$. It would seem that this function should be even easier to compute than its more complicated-looking cousin, but no way to evaluate the permanent as efficiently as the determinant is known. Exercises 9 and 10 show that substantially fewer than $n!$ operations will suffice, for large n, but the execution time of all known methods still grows exponentially with the size of the matrix. In fact, Leslie G. Valiant has shown that it is as difficult to compute the permanent of a given 0–1 matrix as it is to count the number of accepting computations of a nondeterministic polynomial-time Turing machine, if we ignore polynomial factors in the running time of the calculation. Therefore a polynomial-time evaluation algorithm for permanents would imply that scores of other well known problems that have resisted efficient solution would be solvable in polynomial time. On the other hand, Valiant proved that the permanent of an $n \times n$ integer matrix can be evaluated modulo 2^k in $O(n^{4k-3})$ steps for all $k \geq 2$. [See *Theoretical Comp. Sci.* **8** (1979), 189–201.]

Another fundamental operation involving matrices is, of course, *matrix multiplication*: If $X = (x_{ij})$ is an $m \times n$ matrix, $Y = (y_{jk})$ is an $n \times s$ matrix, and $Z = (z_{ik})$ is an $m \times s$ matrix, then the formula $Z = XY$ means that

$$z_{ik} = \sum_{j=1}^{n} x_{ij} y_{jk}, \qquad 1 \leq i \leq m, \qquad 1 \leq k \leq s. \tag{34}$$

This equation may be regarded as the computation of ms simultaneous polynomials in $mn + ns$ variables; each polynomial is the "inner product" of two n-place vectors. A straightforward calculation would involve mns multiplications and $ms(n-1)$ additions; but S. Winograd discovered in 1967 that there is a way to trade about half of the multiplications for additions:

$$z_{ik} = \sum_{1 \le j \le n/2} (x_{i,2j} + y_{2j-1,k})(x_{i,2j-1} + y_{2j,k}) - a_i - b_k + x_{in}y_{nk} [n \text{ odd}];$$

$$a_i = \sum_{1 \le j \le n/2} x_{i,2j} x_{i,2j-1}; \qquad b_k = \sum_{1 \le j \le n/2} y_{2j-1,k} y_{2j,k}. \tag{35}$$

This scheme uses $\lceil n/2 \rceil ms + \lfloor n/2 \rfloor (m+s)$ multiplications and $(n+2)ms + (\lfloor n/2 \rfloor - 1)(ms + m + s)$ additions or subtractions; the total number of operations has increased slightly, but the number of multiplications has roughly been halved. [See *IEEE Trans.* **C-17** (1968), 693–694.] Winograd's surprising construction led many people to look more closely at the problem of matrix multiplication, and it touched off widespread speculation that $n^3/2$ multiplications might be necessary to multiply $n \times n$ matrices, because of the somewhat similar lower bound that was known to hold for polynomials in one variable.

An even better scheme for large n was discovered by Volker Strassen in 1968; he found a way to compute the product of 2×2 matrices with only seven multiplications, without relying on the commutativity of multiplication as in (35). Since $2n \times 2n$ matrices can be partitioned into four $n \times n$ matrices, his idea can be used recursively to obtain the product of $2^k \times 2^k$ matrices with only 7^k multiplications instead of $(2^k)^3 = 8^k$. The number of additions also grows as order 7^k. Strassen's original 2×2 identity [*Numer. Math.* **13** (1969), 354–356] used 7 multiplications and 18 additions; S. Winograd later discovered the following more economical formula:

$$\begin{pmatrix} a & b \\ c & d \end{pmatrix} \begin{pmatrix} A & C \\ B & D \end{pmatrix} = \begin{pmatrix} aA+bB & w+v+(a+b-c-d)D \\ w+u+d(B+C-A-D) & w+u+v \end{pmatrix}, \tag{36}$$

where $u = (c-a)(C-D)$, $v = (c+d)(C-A)$, $w = aA + (c+d-a)(A+D-C)$. If intermediate results are appropriately saved, this involves 7 multiplications and only 15 additions; by induction on k, we can multiply $2^k \times 2^k$ matrices with 7^k multiplications and $5(7^k - 4^k)$ additions. The total number of operations needed to multiply $n \times n$ matrices has therefore been reduced from order n^3 to $O(n^{\lg 7}) = O(n^{2.8074})$. A similar reduction applies also to the evaluation of determinants and matrix inverses; see J. R. Bunch and J. E. Hopcroft, *Math. Comp.* **28** (1974), 231–236.

Strassen's exponent $\lg 7$ resisted numerous attempts at improvement until 1978, when Viktor Pan discovered that it could be lowered to $\log_{70} 143640 \approx 2.795$ (see exercise 60). This new breakthrough led to further intensive analysis of the problem, and the combined efforts of D. Bini, M. Capovani, D. Coppersmith, G. Lotti, F. Romani, A. Schönhage, V. Pan, and S. Winograd, produced a dramatic reduction in the asymptotic running time. Exercises 60–67 discuss some of the interesting techniques by which such upper bounds have been established; in particular, exercise 66 contains a reasonably simple proof that $O(n^{2.55})$ operations suffice. Exercise 67 discusses how Coppersmith and Winograd [*SICOMP* **11** (1982), 472–492] lowered this further, eventually leading to $O(n^{2.373})$. By contrast, the best current lower bound is $3n^2 - O(n^2/\log n)$ (see exercise 12).

These theoretical results are quite striking, but from a practical standpoint they are of little use because n must be very large before we overcome the effect of additional bookkeeping costs. Richard Brent [Stanford Computer Science report CS157 (March 1970), see also *Numer. Math.* **16** (1970), 145–156] found that a careful implementation of Winograd's scheme (35), with appropriate scaling for numerical stability, became better than the conventional method only when $n \geq 40$, and it saved only about 7 percent of the running time when $n = 100$. For complex arithmetic the situation was somewhat different; scheme (35) became advantageous for $n > 20$, and saved 18 percent when $n = 100$. He estimated that Strassen's scheme (36) would not begin to excel over (35) until $n \approx 250$; and such enormous matrices rarely occur in practice unless they are very sparse, when other techniques apply. Furthermore, the known methods of order n^ω where $\omega < 2.7$ have such large constants of proportionality that they require more than 10^{23} multiplications before they start to beat (36).

By contrast, the methods we shall discuss next are eminently practical and have found wide use. The *discrete Fourier transform* f of a complex-valued function F of n variables, over respective domains of m_1, ..., m_n elements, is defined by the equation

$$f(s_1, \ldots, s_n) = \sum_{\substack{0 \leq t_1 < m_1 \\ \cdots \\ 0 \leq t_n < m_n}} \exp\left(2\pi i\left(\frac{s_1 t_1}{m_1} + \cdots + \frac{s_n t_n}{m_n}\right)\right) F(t_1, \ldots, t_n) \quad (37)$$

for $0 \leq s_1 < m_1$, ..., $0 \leq s_n < m_n$; the name "transform" is justified because we can recover the values $F(t_1, \ldots, t_n)$ from the values $f(s_1, \ldots, s_n)$, as shown in exercise 13. In the important special case that all $m_j = 2$, we have

$$f(s_1, \ldots, s_n) = \sum_{0 \leq t_1, \ldots, t_n \leq 1} (-1)^{s_1 t_1 + \cdots + s_n t_n} F(t_1, \ldots, t_n) \quad (38)$$

for $0 \leq s_1, \ldots, s_n \leq 1$, and this may be regarded as a simultaneous evaluation of 2^n linear polynomials in 2^n variables $F(t_1, \ldots, t_n)$. A well-known technique due to F. Yates [*The Design and Analysis of Factorial Experiments* (Harpenden: Imperial Bureau of Soil Sciences, 1937)] can be used to reduce the number of additions implied in (38) from $2^n(2^n - 1)$ to $n2^n$. Yates's method can be understood by considering the case $n = 3$: Let $X_{t_1 t_2 t_3} = F(t_1, t_2, t_3)$.

Given	First step	Second step	Third step
X_{000}	$X_{000}+X_{001}$	$X_{000}+X_{001}+X_{010}+X_{011}$	$X_{000}+X_{001}+X_{010}+X_{011}+X_{100}+X_{101}+X_{110}+X_{111}$
X_{001}	$X_{010}+X_{011}$	$X_{100}+X_{101}+X_{110}+X_{111}$	$X_{000}-X_{001}+X_{010}-X_{011}+X_{100}-X_{101}+X_{110}-X_{111}$
X_{010}	$X_{100}+X_{101}$	$X_{000}-X_{001}+X_{010}-X_{011}$	$X_{000}+X_{001}-X_{010}-X_{011}+X_{100}+X_{101}-X_{110}-X_{111}$
X_{011}	$X_{110}+X_{111}$	$X_{100}-X_{101}+X_{110}-X_{111}$	$X_{000}-X_{001}-X_{010}+X_{011}+X_{100}-X_{101}-X_{110}+X_{111}$
X_{100}	$X_{000}-X_{001}$	$X_{000}+X_{001}-X_{010}-X_{011}$	$X_{000}+X_{001}+X_{010}+X_{011}-X_{100}-X_{101}-X_{110}-X_{111}$
X_{101}	$X_{010}-X_{011}$	$X_{100}+X_{101}-X_{110}-X_{111}$	$X_{000}-X_{001}+X_{010}-X_{011}-X_{100}+X_{101}-X_{110}+X_{111}$
X_{110}	$X_{100}-X_{101}$	$X_{000}-X_{001}-X_{010}+X_{011}$	$X_{000}+X_{001}-X_{010}-X_{011}-X_{100}-X_{101}+X_{110}+X_{111}$
X_{111}	$X_{110}-X_{111}$	$X_{100}-X_{101}-X_{110}+X_{111}$	$X_{000}-X_{001}-X_{010}+X_{011}-X_{100}+X_{101}+X_{110}-X_{111}$

To get from the "Given" to the "First step" requires four additions and four subtractions; and the interesting feature of Yates's method is that exactly the same transformation that takes us from "Given" to "First step" will take us from "First step" to "Second step" and from "Second step" to "Third step." In each case we do four additions, then four subtractions; and after three steps we magically have the desired Fourier transform $f(s_1, s_2, s_3)$ in the place originally occupied by $F(s_1, s_2, s_3)$.

This special case is often called the *Hadamard transform* or the *Walsh transform* of 2^n data elements, since the corresponding pattern of signs was studied by J. Hadamard [*Bull. Sci. Math.* (2) **17** (1893), 240–246] and by J. L. Walsh [*Amer. J. Math.* **45** (1923), 5–24]. Notice that the number of sign changes from left to right in the "Third step" assumes the respective values

$$0, 7, 3, 4, 1, 6, 2, 5;$$

this is a permutation of the numbers $\{0, 1, 2, 3, 4, 5, 6, 7\}$. Walsh observed that there will be exactly $0, 1, \ldots, 2^n - 1$ sign changes in the general case, if we permute the transformed elements appropriately, so the coefficients provide discrete approximations to sine waves with various frequencies. (See Section 7.2.1.1 for further discussion of the Hadamard–Walsh coefficients.)

Yates's method can be generalized to the evaluation of any discrete Fourier transform, and, in fact, to the evaluation of any set of sums that can be written in the general form

$$f(s_1, s_2, \ldots, s_n) =$$

$$\sum_{\substack{0 \le t_1 < m_1 \\ \cdots \\ 0 \le t_n < m_n}} g_1(s_1, s_2, \ldots, s_n, t_1) g_2(s_2, \ldots, s_n, t_2) \ldots g_n(s_n, t_n) F(t_1, t_2, \ldots, t_n) \quad (39)$$

for $0 \le s_j < m_j$, given the functions $g_j(s_j, \ldots, s_n, t_j)$. We proceed as follows.

$$f_0(t_1, t_2, t_3, \ldots, t_n) = F(t_1, t_2, t_3, \ldots, t_n);$$

$$f_1(s_n, t_1, t_2, \ldots, t_{n-1}) = \sum_{0 \le t_n < m_n} g_n(s_n, t_n) f_0(t_1, t_2, \ldots, t_n);$$

$$f_2(s_{n-1}, s_n, t_1, \ldots, t_{n-2}) = \sum_{0 \le t_{n-1} < m_{n-1}} g_{n-1}(s_{n-1}, s_n, t_{n-1}) f_1(s_n, t_1, \ldots, t_{n-1});$$

$$\vdots$$

$$f_n(s_1, s_2, s_3, \ldots, s_n) = \sum_{0 \le t_1 < m_1} g_1(s_1, \ldots, s_n, t_1) f_{n-1}(s_2, s_3, \ldots, s_n, t_1);$$

$$f(s_1, s_2, s_3, \ldots, s_n) = f_n(s_1, s_2, s_3, \ldots, s_n). \quad (40)$$

For Yates's method as shown above, $g_j(s_j, \ldots, s_n, t_j) = (-1)^{s_j t_j}$; $f_0(t_1, t_2, t_3)$ represents the "Given"; $f_1(s_3, t_1, t_2)$ represents the "First step"; and so on. Whenever a desired set of sums can be put into the form of (39), for reasonably simple functions $g_j(s_j, \ldots, s_n, t_j)$, the scheme (40) will reduce the amount of computation from order N^2 to order $N \log N$ or thereabouts, where $N = m_1 \ldots m_n$ is the number of data points. Furthermore this scheme is ideally suited to parallel computation. The important special case of one-dimensional Fourier transforms is discussed in exercises 14 and 53; we have considered the one-dimensional case also in Section 4.3.3C.

Let us consider one more special case of polynomial evaluation. *Lagrange's interpolation polynomial* of order n, which we shall write as

$$u_{[n]}(x) = y_0 \frac{(x - x_1)(x - x_2) \ldots (x - x_n)}{(x_0 - x_1)(x_0 - x_2) \ldots (x_0 - x_n)} + y_1 \frac{(x - x_0)(x - x_2) \ldots (x - x_n)}{(x_1 - x_0)(x_1 - x_2) \ldots (x_1 - x_n)}$$
$$+ \cdots + y_n \frac{(x - x_0)(x - x_1) \ldots (x - x_{n-1})}{(x_n - x_0)(x_n - x_1) \ldots (x_n - x_{n-1})}, \quad (41)$$

is the only polynomial of degree $\leq n$ in x that takes on the respective values $y_0, y_1, \ldots, y_n$ at the $n + 1$ distinct points $x = x_0, x_1, \ldots, x_n$. (For it is evident from (41) that $u_{[n]}(x_k) = y_k$ for $0 \leq k \leq n$. If $f(x)$ is any such polynomial of degree $\leq n$, then $g(x) = f(x) - u_{[n]}(x)$ is of degree $\leq n$, and $g(x)$ is zero for $x = x_0, x_1, \ldots, x_n$; therefore $g(x)$ must be a multiple of the polynomial $(x - x_0)(x - x_1) \ldots (x - x_n)$. The degree of the latter polynomial is greater than n, so $g(x) = 0$.) If we assume that the values of a function in some table are well approximated by a polynomial, formula (41) may therefore be used to "interpolate" for values of the function at points x not appearing in the table. Lagrange presented (41) to his class at the Paris École Normale in 1795 [see his *Œuvres* **7** (Paris: 1877), 286]; but Edward Waring of Cambridge University actually deserves the credit, because he had already presented the same formula quite clearly and explicitly in *Philosophical Transactions* **69** (1779), 59–67.

There seem to be quite a few additions, subtractions, multiplications, and divisions in Waring and Lagrange's formula; in fact, there are exactly n additions, $2n^2 + 2n$ subtractions, $2n^2 + n - 1$ multiplications, and $n + 1$ divisions. But fortunately (as we might be conditioned to suspect by now), improvement is possible.

The basic idea for simplifying (41) is to exploit the fact that

$$u_{[n]}(x) - u_{[n-1]}(x) = 0 \qquad \text{for } x = x_0, \ldots, x_{n-1};$$

thus $u_{[n]}(x) - u_{[n-1]}(x)$ is a polynomial of degree n or less, and a multiple of $(x - x_0) \ldots (x - x_{n-1})$. We conclude that $u_{[n]}(x) = \alpha_n(x - x_0) \ldots (x - x_{n-1}) + u_{[n-1]}(x)$, where α_n is a constant. This leads us to *Newton's interpolation formula*

$$u_{[n]}(x) = \alpha_n(x - x_0)(x - x_1) \ldots (x - x_{n-1}) + \cdots$$
$$+ \alpha_2(x - x_0)(x - x_1) + \alpha_1(x - x_0) + \alpha_0, \quad (42)$$

where the α's are some coefficients that we want to determine from the given numbers $x_0, x_1, \ldots, x_n, y_0, y_1, \ldots, y_n$. Notice that this formula holds for all n; the coefficient α_k does not depend on $x_{k+1}, \ldots, x_n$, or on $y_{k+1}, \ldots, y_n$. Once the α's are known, Newton's interpolation formula is convenient for calculation, since we may generalize Horner's rule once again and write

$$u_{[n]}(x) = ((\ldots(\alpha_n(x-x_{n-1}) + \alpha_{n-1})(x-x_{n-2}) + \cdots)(x-x_0) + \alpha_0). \quad (43)$$

This requires n multiplications and $2n$ additions. Alternatively, we may evaluate each of the individual terms of (42) from right to left; with $2n-1$ multiplications and $2n$ additions we thereby calculate all of the values $u_{[0]}(x)$, $u_{[1]}(x)$, ..., $u_{[n]}(x)$, and this indicates whether or not an interpolation process is converging.

The coefficients α_k in Newton's formula may be found by computing the *divided differences* in the following tableau (shown for $n = 3$):

$$\begin{array}{l}
y_0 \\
\quad (y_1-y_0)/(x_1-x_0) = y_1' \\
y_1 \qquad\qquad\qquad\qquad (y_2'-y_1')/(x_2-x_0) = y_2'' \\
\quad (y_2-y_1)/(x_2-x_1) = y_2' \qquad\qquad\qquad\qquad (y_3''-y_2'')/(x_3-x_0) = y_3''' \\
y_2 \qquad\qquad\qquad\qquad (y_3'-y_2')/(x_3-x_1) = y_3'' \\
\quad (y_3-y_2)/(x_3-x_2) = y_3' \\
y_3
\end{array}$$
$$(44)$$

It is possible to prove that $\alpha_0 = y_0$, $\alpha_1 = y_1'$, $\alpha_2 = y_2''$, etc., and to show that the divided differences have important relations to the derivatives of the function being interpolated; see exercise 15. Therefore the following calculation (corresponding to (44)) may be used to obtain the α's:

Start with $(\alpha_0, \alpha_1, \ldots, \alpha_n) \leftarrow (y_0, y_1, \ldots, y_n)$;

then, for $k = 1, 2, \ldots, n$ (in this order),

set $\alpha_j \leftarrow (\alpha_j - \alpha_{j-1})/(x_j - x_{j-k})$ for $j = n, n-1, \ldots, k$ (in this order).

This process requires $\frac{1}{2}(n^2 + n)$ divisions and $n^2 + n$ subtractions, so about three-fourths of the work implied in (41) has been saved.

For example, suppose that we want to estimate 1.5! from the values of 0!, 1!, 2!, and 3!, using a cubic polynomial. The divided differences are

x	y	y'	y''	y'''
0	1			
		0		
1	1		$\frac{1}{2}$	
		1		$\frac{1}{3}$
2	2		$\frac{3}{2}$	
		4		
3	6			

so $u_{[0]}(x) = u_{[1]}(x) = 1$, $u_{[2]}(x) = \frac{1}{2}x(x-1) + 1$, $u_{[3]}(x) = \frac{1}{3}x(x-1)(x-2) + \frac{1}{2}x(x-1)+1$. Setting $x = 1.5$ in $u_{[3]}(x)$ gives $-.125+.375+1 = 1.25$; presumably the "correct" value is $\Gamma(2.5) = \frac{3}{4}\sqrt{\pi} \approx 1.33$. (But there are of course many other sequences that begin with the numbers 1, 1, 2, and 6.)

If we want to interpolate several polynomials that have the same interpolation points x_0, x_1, ..., x_n but varying values y_0, y_1, ..., y_n, it is desirable to rewrite (41) in a form suggested by W. J. Taylor [*J. Research Nat. Bur. Standards* **35** (1945), 151–155]:

$$u_{[n]}(x) = \left(\frac{y_0 w_0}{x - x_0} + \cdots + \frac{y_n w_n}{x - x_n}\right) \Big/ \left(\frac{w_0}{x - x_0} + \cdots + \frac{w_n}{x - x_n}\right), \quad (45)$$

when $x \notin \{x_0, x_1, \ldots, x_n\}$, where

$$w_k = 1/(x_k - x_0) \ldots (x_k - x_{k-1})(x_k - x_{k+1}) \ldots (x_k - x_n). \qquad (46)$$

This form is also recommended for its numerical stability [see P. Henrici, *Essentials of Numerical Analysis* (New York: Wiley, 1982), 237–243]. The denominator of (45) is the partial fraction expansion of $1/(x - x_0)(x - x_1) \ldots (x - x_n)$.

An important and somewhat surprising application of polynomial interpolation was discovered by Adi Shamir [*CACM* **22** (1979), 612–613], who observed that polynomials mod p can be used to "share a secret." This means that we can design a system of secret keys or passwords such that the knowledge of any $n + 1$ of the keys enables efficient calculation of a magic number N that unlocks a door (say), but the knowledge of any n of the keys gives no information whatsoever about N. Shamir's amazingly simple solution to this problem is to choose a random polynomial $u(x) = u_n x^n + \cdots + u_1 x + u_0$, where $0 \le u_i < p$ and p is a large prime number. Each part of the secret is an integer x in the range $0 < x < p$, together with the value of $u(x) \bmod p$; and the supersecret number N is the constant term u_0. Given $n + 1$ values $u(x_i)$, we can deduce N by interpolation. But if only n values of $u(x_i)$ are given, there is a unique polynomial $u(x)$ having a given constant term but the same values at x_1, ..., x_n; thus the n values do not make one particular N more likely than any other.

It is instructive to note that evaluation of the interpolation polynomial is just a special case of the Chinese remainder algorithm of Section 4.3.2 and exercise 4.6.2–3, since we know the values of $u_{[n]}(x)$ modulo the relatively prime polynomials $x - x_0$, ..., $x - x_n$. (As we have seen in Section 4.6.2 and in the discussion following (3), $f(x) \bmod (x - x_0) = f(x_0)$.) Under this interpretation, Newton's formula (42) is precisely the "mixed-radix representation" of Eq. 4.3.2–(25); and 4.3.2–(24) yields another way to compute α_0, ..., α_n using the same number of operations as (44).

By applying fast Fourier transforms, it is possible to reduce the running time for interpolation to $O(n (\log n)^2)$, and a similar reduction can also be made for related algorithms such as the solution to the Chinese remainder problem and the evaluation of an nth degree polynomial at n different points. [See E. Horowitz, *Inf. Proc. Letters* **1** (1972), 157–163; A. Borodin and R. Moenck, *J. Comp. Syst. Sci.* **8** (1974), 336–385; A. Borodin, *Complexity of Sequential and Parallel Numerical Algorithms*, edited by J. F. Traub (New York: Academic Press, 1973), 149–180; D. Bini and V. Pan, *Polynomial and Matrix Computations* **1** (Boston: Birkhäuser, 1994), Chapter 1.] However, these observations are primarily of theoretical interest, since the known algorithms have a rather large overhead factor that makes them unattractive unless n is quite large.

A remarkable extension of the method of divided differences, which applies to quotients of polynomials as well as to polynomials, was introduced by T. N. Thiele in 1909. Thiele's method of "reciprocal differences" is discussed in L. M. Milne-Thompson's *Calculus of Finite Differences* (London: MacMillan, 1933), Chapter 5; see also R. W. Floyd, *CACM* **3** (1960), 508.

*Bilinear forms. Several of the problems we have considered in this section are special cases of the general problem of evaluating a set of *bilinear forms*

$$z_k = \sum_{i=1}^{m} \sum_{j=1}^{n} t_{ijk} x_i y_j, \qquad \text{for } 1 \le k \le s, \tag{47}$$

where the t_{ijk} are specific coefficients belonging to some given field. The three-dimensional array (t_{ijk}) is called an $m \times n \times s$ *tensor*, and we can display it by writing down s matrices of size $m \times n$, one for each value of k. For example, the problem of multiplying complex numbers, namely the problem of evaluating

$$z_1 + iz_2 = (x_1 + ix_2)(y_1 + iy_2) = (x_1 y_1 - x_2 y_2) + i(x_1 y_2 + x_2 y_1), \tag{48}$$

is the problem of computing the bilinear form specified by the $2 \times 2 \times 2$ tensor

$$\begin{pmatrix} 1 & 0 \\ 0 & -1 \end{pmatrix} \begin{pmatrix} 0 & 1 \\ 1 & 0 \end{pmatrix}.$$

Matrix multiplication as defined in (34) is the problem of evaluating a set of bilinear forms corresponding to a particular $mn \times ns \times ms$ tensor. Fourier transforms (37) can also be cast in this mold, although they are linear instead of bilinear, if we let the x's be constant rather than variable.

The evaluation of bilinear forms is most easily studied if we restrict ourselves to what might be called *normal* evaluation schemes, in which all chain multiplications take place between a linear combination of the x's and a linear combination of the y's. Thus, we form r products

$$w_l = (a_{1l} x_1 + \cdots + a_{ml} x_m)(b_{1l} y_1 + \cdots + b_{nl} y_n), \qquad \text{for } 1 \le l \le r, \tag{49}$$

and obtain the z's as linear combinations of these products,

$$z_k = c_{k1} w_1 + \cdots + c_{kr} w_r, \qquad \text{for } 1 \le k \le s. \tag{50}$$

Here all the a's, b's, and c's belong to a given field of coefficients. By comparing (50) to (47), we see that a normal evaluation scheme is correct for the tensor (t_{ijk}) if and only if

$$t_{ijk} = a_{i1} b_{j1} c_{k1} + \cdots + a_{ir} b_{jr} c_{kr} \tag{51}$$

for $1 \le i \le m$, $1 \le j \le n$, and $1 \le k \le s$.

A nonzero tensor (t_{ijk}) is said to be of rank one if there are three vectors $(a_1, \ldots, a_m)$, $(b_1, \ldots, b_n)$, $(c_1, \ldots, c_s)$ such that $t_{ijk} = a_i b_j c_k$ for all i, j, k. We can extend this definition to all tensors by saying that *the rank of (t_{ijk}) is the minimum number r such that (t_{ijk}) is expressible as the sum of r rank-one tensors* in the given field. Comparing this definition with Eq. (51) shows that the rank of a tensor is the minimum number of chain multiplications in a normal evaluation of the corresponding bilinear forms. Incidentally, when $s = 1$ the tensor (t_{ijk}) is just an ordinary matrix, and the rank of (t_{ij1}) as a tensor is the same as its rank as a matrix (see exercise 49). The concept of tensor rank was introduced by F. L. Hitchcock in *J. Math. and Physics* **6** (1927), 164–189; its application to the complexity of polynomial evaluation was pointed out in an important paper by V. Strassen, *Crelle* **264** (1973), 184–202.

Winograd's scheme (35) for matrix multiplication is "abnormal" because it mixes x's and y's before multiplying them. The Strassen–Winograd scheme (36), on the other hand, does not rely on the commutativity of multiplication, so it is normal. In fact, (36) corresponds to the following way to represent the $4 \times 4 \times 4$ tensor for 2×2 matrix multiplication as a sum of seven rank-one tensors:

$$
\begin{pmatrix} 1000 \\ 0100 \\ 0000 \\ 0000 \end{pmatrix}
\begin{pmatrix} 0000 \\ 0000 \\ 1000 \\ 0100 \end{pmatrix}
\begin{pmatrix} 0010 \\ 0001 \\ 0000 \\ 0000 \end{pmatrix}
\begin{pmatrix} 0000 \\ 0000 \\ 0010 \\ 0001 \end{pmatrix}
=
\begin{pmatrix} 1000 \\ 0000 \\ 0000 \\ 0000 \end{pmatrix}
\begin{pmatrix} 1000 \\ 0000 \\ 0000 \\ 0000 \end{pmatrix}
\begin{pmatrix} 1000 \\ 0000 \\ 0000 \\ 0000 \end{pmatrix}
\begin{pmatrix} 1000 \\ 0000 \\ 0000 \\ 0000 \end{pmatrix}
$$

$$
+
\begin{pmatrix} 0000 \\ 0100 \\ 0000 \\ 0000 \end{pmatrix}
\begin{pmatrix} 0000 \\ 0000 \\ 0000 \\ 0000 \end{pmatrix}
\begin{pmatrix} 0000 \\ 0000 \\ 0000 \\ 0000 \end{pmatrix}
\begin{pmatrix} 0000 \\ 0000 \\ 0000 \\ 0000 \end{pmatrix}
+
\begin{pmatrix} 0000 \\ 0000 \\ 0000 \\ 0000 \end{pmatrix}
\begin{pmatrix} 00\bar{1}1 \\ 0000 \\ 001\bar{1} \\ 0000 \end{pmatrix}
\begin{pmatrix} 0000 \\ 0000 \\ 0000 \\ 0000 \end{pmatrix}
\begin{pmatrix} 00\bar{1}1 \\ 0000 \\ 001\bar{1} \\ 0000 \end{pmatrix}
$$

$$
+
\begin{pmatrix} 0000 \\ 0000 \\ 0000 \\ 0000 \end{pmatrix}
\begin{pmatrix} 0000 \\ 0000 \\ 0000 \\ \bar{1}11\bar{1} \end{pmatrix}
\begin{pmatrix} 0000 \\ 0000 \\ 0000 \\ 0000 \end{pmatrix}
\begin{pmatrix} 0000 \\ 0000 \\ 0000 \\ 0000 \end{pmatrix}
+
\begin{pmatrix} 0000 \\ 0000 \\ 0000 \\ 0000 \end{pmatrix}
\begin{pmatrix} 0000 \\ 0000 \\ 0000 \\ 0000 \end{pmatrix}
\begin{pmatrix} 0000 \\ 0000 \\ \bar{1}010 \\ \bar{1}010 \end{pmatrix}
\begin{pmatrix} 0000 \\ 0000 \\ \bar{1}010 \\ \bar{1}010 \end{pmatrix}
$$

$$
+
\begin{pmatrix} 0000 \\ 0000 \\ 0000 \\ 0000 \end{pmatrix}
\begin{pmatrix} 0000 \\ 0000 \\ 0000 \\ 0000 \end{pmatrix}
\begin{pmatrix} 0001 \\ 0001 \\ 000\bar{1} \\ 000\bar{1} \end{pmatrix}
\begin{pmatrix} 0000 \\ 0000 \\ 0000 \\ 0000 \end{pmatrix}
+
\begin{pmatrix} 0000 \\ 0000 \\ 0000 \\ 0000 \end{pmatrix}
\begin{pmatrix} \bar{1}01\bar{1} \\ 0000 \\ 10\bar{1}1 \\ 10\bar{1}1 \end{pmatrix}
\begin{pmatrix} \bar{1}01\bar{1} \\ 0000 \\ 10\bar{1}1 \\ 10\bar{1}1 \end{pmatrix}
\begin{pmatrix} \bar{1}01\bar{1} \\ 0000 \\ 10\bar{1}1 \\ 10\bar{1}1 \end{pmatrix} .
$$

$$(52)$$

(Here $\bar{1}$ stands for -1.)

The fact that (51) is symmetric in i, j, k and invariant under a variety of transformations makes the study of tensor rank mathematically tractable, and it also leads to some surprising consequences about bilinear forms. We can permute the indices i, j, k to obtain "transposed" bilinear forms, and the transposed tensor clearly has the same rank; but the corresponding bilinear forms are conceptually quite different. For example, a normal scheme for evaluating an $(m \times n)$ times $(n \times s)$ matrix product implies the existence of a normal scheme to evaluate an $(n \times s)$ times $(s \times m)$ matrix product, using the same number of chain multiplications. In matrix terms these two problems hardly seem to be related at all — they involve different numbers of dot products, on vectors of different sizes — but in tensor terms they are equivalent. [See V. Y. Pan, *Uspekhi Mat. Nauk* **27**, 5 (September–October 1972), 249–250; J. E. Hopcroft and J. Musinski, *SICOMP* **2** (1973), 159–173.]

When the tensor (t_{ijk}) can be represented as a sum (51) of r rank-one tensors, let A, B, C be the matrices (a_{il}), (b_{jl}), (c_{kl}) of respective sizes $m \times r$, $n \times r$, $s \times r$; we shall say that (A, B, C) is a *realization* of the tensor (t_{ijk}). For example, the realization of 2×2 matrix multiplication in (52) can be specified by the matrices

$$
A = \begin{pmatrix} 1\,0\,\bar{1}\,0\,0\,1\,\bar{1} \\ 0\,1\,0\,0\,0\,1\,0 \\ 0\,0\,1\,0\,1\,1\,1 \\ 0\,0\,0\,1\,1\,\bar{1}\,1 \end{pmatrix}, \quad
B = \begin{pmatrix} 1\,0\,0\,\bar{1}\,\bar{1}\,0\,1 \\ 0\,1\,0\,1\,0\,0\,0 \\ 0\,0\,1\,1\,1\,0\,\bar{1} \\ 0\,0\,\bar{1}\,\bar{1}\,0\,1\,1 \end{pmatrix}, \quad
C = \begin{pmatrix} 1\,1\,0\,0\,0\,0\,0 \\ 1\,0\,1\,1\,0\,0\,1 \\ 1\,0\,0\,0\,1\,1\,1 \\ 1\,0\,1\,0\,1\,0\,1 \end{pmatrix}.
\quad (53)
$$

An $m \times n \times s$ tensor (t_{ijk}) can also be represented as a matrix by grouping its subscripts together. We shall write $(t_{(ij)k})$ for the $mn \times s$ matrix whose rows are indexed by the pair of subscripts $\langle i, j \rangle$ and whose columns are indexed by k. Similarly, $(t_{k(ij)})$ stands for the $s \times mn$ matrix that contains t_{ijk} in row k and column $\langle i, j \rangle$; $(t_{(ik)j})$ is an $ms \times n$ matrix, and so on. The indices of an array need not be integers, and we are using ordered pairs as indices here. We can use this notation to derive the following simple but useful lower bound on the rank of a tensor.

Lemma T. *Let (A, B, C) be a realization of an $m \times n \times s$ tensor (t_{ijk}). Then* $\text{rank}(A) \geq \text{rank}(t_{i(jk)})$, $\text{rank}(B) \geq \text{rank}(t_{j(ik)})$, *and* $\text{rank}(C) \geq \text{rank}(t_{k(ij)})$; *consequently*

$$\text{rank}(t_{ijk}) \geq \max\big(\text{rank}(t_{i(jk)}), \text{rank}(t_{j(ik)}), \text{rank}(t_{k(ij)})\big).$$

Proof. It suffices by symmetry to show that $r \geq \text{rank}(A) \geq \text{rank}(t_{i(jk)})$. Since A is an $m \times r$ matrix, it is obvious that A cannot have rank greater than r. Furthermore, according to (51), the matrix $(t_{i(jk)})$ is equal to AQ, where Q is the $r \times ns$ matrix defined by $Q_{l\langle j,k \rangle} = b_{jl}c_{kl}$. If x is any row vector such that $xA = 0$ then $xAQ = 0$, hence all linear dependencies in A occur also in AQ. It follows that $\text{rank}(AQ) \leq \text{rank}(A)$. ∎

As an example of the use of Lemma T, let us consider the problem of polynomial multiplication. Suppose we want to multiply a general polynomial of degree 2 by a general polynomial of degree 3, obtaining the coefficients of the product:

$$(x_0 + x_1 u + x_2 u^2)(y_0 + y_1 u + y_2 u^2 + y_3 u^3)$$
$$= z_0 + z_1 u + z_2 u^2 + z_3 u^3 + z_4 u^4 + z_5 u^5. \quad (54)$$

This is the problem of evaluating six bilinear forms corresponding to the $3 \times 4 \times 6$ tensor

$$\begin{pmatrix} 1\,0\,0\,0 \\ 0\,0\,0\,0 \\ 0\,0\,0\,0 \end{pmatrix} \begin{pmatrix} 0\,1\,0\,0 \\ 1\,0\,0\,0 \\ 0\,0\,0\,0 \end{pmatrix} \begin{pmatrix} 0\,0\,1\,0 \\ 0\,1\,0\,0 \\ 1\,0\,0\,0 \end{pmatrix} \begin{pmatrix} 0\,0\,0\,1 \\ 0\,0\,1\,0 \\ 0\,1\,0\,0 \end{pmatrix} \begin{pmatrix} 0\,0\,0\,0 \\ 0\,0\,0\,1 \\ 0\,0\,1\,0 \end{pmatrix} \begin{pmatrix} 0\,0\,0\,0 \\ 0\,0\,0\,0 \\ 0\,0\,0\,1 \end{pmatrix}. \quad (55)$$

For brevity, we may write (54) as $x(u)y(u) = z(u)$, letting $x(u)$ denote the polynomial $x_0 + x_1 u + x_2 u^2$, etc. (We have come full circle from the way we began this section, since Eq. (1) refers to $u(x)$, not $x(u)$; the notation has changed because the *coefficients* of the polynomials are now the variables of interest to us.)

If each of the six matrices in (55) is regarded as a vector of length 12 indexed by $\langle i, j \rangle$, it is clear that the vectors are linearly independent, since they are nonzero in different positions; hence the rank of (55) is at least 6 by Lemma T. Conversely, it is possible to obtain the coefficients $z_0, z_1, \ldots, z_5$ by making only six chain multiplications, for example by computing

$$x(0)y(0), \; x(1)y(1), \; \ldots, \; x(5)y(5); \quad (56)$$

this gives the values of $z(0)$, $z(1)$, ..., $z(5)$, and the formulas developed above for interpolation will yield the coefficients of $z(u)$. The evaluation of $x(j)$

and $y(j)$ can be carried out entirely in terms of additions and/or parameter multiplications, and the interpolation formula merely takes linear combinations of these values. Thus, all of the chain multiplications are shown in (56), and the rank of (55) is 6. (We used essentially this same technique when multiplying high-precision numbers in Algorithm 4.3.3T.)

The realization (A, B, C) of (55) sketched in the paragraph above turns out to be

$$
\begin{pmatrix} 1 & 1 & 1 & 1 & 1 & 1 \\ 0 & 1 & 2 & 3 & 4 & 5 \\ 0 & 1 & 4 & 9 & 16 & 25 \end{pmatrix}, \quad
\begin{pmatrix} 1 & 1 & 1 & 1 & 1 & 1 \\ 0 & 1 & 2 & 3 & 4 & 5 \\ 0 & 1 & 4 & 9 & 16 & 25 \\ 0 & 1 & 8 & 27 & 64 & 125 \end{pmatrix}, \quad
\begin{pmatrix} 120 & 0 & 0 & 0 & 0 & 0 \\ -274 & 600 & -600 & 400 & -150 & 24 \\ 225 & -770 & 1070 & -780 & 305 & -50 \\ -85 & 355 & -590 & 490 & -205 & 35 \\ 15 & -70 & 130 & -120 & 55 & -10 \\ -1 & 5 & -10 & 10 & -5 & 1 \end{pmatrix} \times \frac{1}{120}.
\tag{57}
$$

Thus, the scheme does indeed achieve the minimum number of chain multiplications, but it is completely impractical because it involves so many additions and parameter multiplications. We shall now study a practical approach to the generation of more efficient schemes, introduced by S. Winograd.

In the first place, to evaluate the coefficients of $x(u)y(u)$ when $\deg(x) = m$ and $\deg(y) = n$, we can use the identity

$$
x(u)y(u) = \big(x(u)y(u) \bmod p(u)\big) + x_m y_n p(u),
\tag{58}
$$

when $p(u)$ is any monic polynomial of degree $m+n$. The polynomial $p(u)$ should be chosen so that the coefficients of $x(u)y(u) \bmod p(u)$ are easy to evaluate.

In the second place, to evaluate the coefficients of $x(u)y(u) \bmod p(u)$, when the polynomial $p(u)$ can be factored into $q(u)r(u)$ where $\gcd\big(q(u), r(u)\big) = 1$, we can use the identity

$$
x(u)y(u) \bmod q(u)r(u) = \big(a(u)r(u)(x(u)y(u) \bmod q(u))
$$
$$
+ b(u)q(u)(x(u)y(u) \bmod r(u))\big) \bmod q(u)r(u) \tag{59}
$$

where $a(u)r(u) + b(u)q(u) = 1$; this is essentially the Chinese remainder theorem applied to polynomials.

In the third place, we can always evaluate the coefficients of the polynomial $x(u)y(u) \bmod p(u)$ by using the trivial identity

$$
x(u)y(u) \bmod p(u) = \big(x(u) \bmod p(u)\big)\big(y(u) \bmod p(u)\big) \bmod p(u).
\tag{60}
$$

Repeated application of (58), (59), and (60) tends to produce efficient schemes, as we shall see.

For our example problem (54), let us choose $p(u) = u^5 - u$ and apply (58); the reason for this choice of $p(u)$ will appear as we proceed. Writing $p(u) = u(u^4 - 1)$, rule (59) reduces to

$$
x(u)y(u) \bmod u(u^4 - 1) = \big(-(u^4 - 1)x_0 y_0 + u^4(x(u)y(u) \bmod (u^4 - 1))\big)
$$
$$
\bmod (u^5 - u). \tag{61}
$$

Here we have used the fact that $x(u)y(u) \bmod u = x_0 y_0$; in general it is a good idea to choose $p(u)$ in such a way that $p(0) = 0$, so that this simplification can be used. If we could now determine the coefficients w_0, w_1, w_2, w_3 of the polynomial $x(u)y(u) \bmod (u^4 - 1) = w_0 + w_1 u + w_2 u^2 + w_3 u^3$, our problem would be solved, since

$$u^4 \big(x(u)y(u) \bmod (u^4 - 1)\big) \bmod (u^5 - u) = w_0 u^4 + w_1 u + w_2 u^2 + w_3 u^3,$$

and the combination of (58) and (61) would reduce to

$$x(u)y(u) = x_0 y_0 + (w_1 - x_2 y_3)u + w_2 u^2 + w_3 u^3 + (w_0 - x_0 y_0)u^4 + x_2 y_3 u^5. \quad (62)$$

(This formula can, of course, be verified directly.)

The problem remaining to be solved is to compute $x(u)y(u) \bmod (u^4 - 1)$; and this subproblem is interesting in itself. Let us momentarily allow $x(u)$ to be of degree 3 instead of degree 2. Then the coefficients of $x(u)y(u) \bmod (u^4 - 1)$ are respectively

$$x_0 y_0 + x_1 y_3 + x_2 y_2 + x_3 y_1, \quad x_0 y_1 + x_1 y_0 + x_2 y_3 + x_3 y_2,$$
$$x_0 y_2 + x_1 y_1 + x_2 y_0 + x_3 y_3, \quad x_0 y_3 + x_1 y_2 + x_2 y_1 + x_3 y_0,$$

and the corresponding tensor is

$$\begin{pmatrix} 1\,0\,0\,0 \\ 0\,0\,0\,1 \\ 0\,0\,1\,0 \\ 0\,1\,0\,0 \end{pmatrix} \begin{pmatrix} 0\,1\,0\,0 \\ 1\,0\,0\,0 \\ 0\,0\,0\,1 \\ 0\,0\,1\,0 \end{pmatrix} \begin{pmatrix} 0\,0\,1\,0 \\ 0\,1\,0\,0 \\ 1\,0\,0\,0 \\ 0\,0\,0\,1 \end{pmatrix} \begin{pmatrix} 0\,0\,0\,1 \\ 0\,0\,1\,0 \\ 0\,1\,0\,0 \\ 1\,0\,0\,0 \end{pmatrix}. \quad (63)$$

In general when $\deg(x) = \deg(y) = n-1$, the coefficients of $x(u)y(u) \bmod (u^n - 1)$ are called the *cyclic convolution* of $(x_0, x_1, \ldots, x_{n-1})$ and $(y_0, y_1, \ldots, y_{n-1})$. The kth coefficient w_k is the bilinear form $\sum x_i y_j$ summed over all i and j with $i + j \equiv k \pmod{n}$.

The cyclic convolution of degree 4 can be obtained by applying rule (59). The first step is to find the factors of $u^4 - 1$, namely $(u - 1)(u + 1)(u^2 + 1)$. We could write this as $(u^2 - 1)(u^2 + 1)$, then apply rule (59), then use (59) again on the part modulo $(u^2 - 1) = (u - 1)(u + 1)$; but it is easier to generalize the Chinese remainder rule (59) directly to the case of several relatively prime factors. For example, we have

$$x(u)y(u) \bmod q_1(u)q_2(u)q_3(u)$$
$$= \big(a_1(u)q_2(u)q_3(u)\big(x(u)y(u) \bmod q_1(u)\big) + a_2(u)q_1(u)q_3(u)\big(x(u)y(u) \bmod q_2(u)\big)$$
$$\qquad + a_3(u)q_1(u)q_2(u)\big(x(u)y(u) \bmod q_3(u)\big)\big) \bmod q_1(u)q_2(u)q_3(u), \quad (64)$$

where $a_1(u)q_2(u)q_3(u) + a_2(u)q_1(u)q_3(u) + a_3(u)q_1(u)q_2(u) = 1$. (This equation can also be understood in another way, by noting that the partial fraction expansion of $1/q_1(u)q_2(u)q_3(u)$ is $a_1(u)/q_1(u) + a_2(u)/q_2(u) + a_3(u)/q_3(u)$.) From (64) we obtain

$$x(u)y(u) \bmod (u^4 - 1) = \big(\tfrac{1}{4}(u^3 + u^2 + u + 1)x(1)y(1) - \tfrac{1}{4}(u^3 - u^2 + u - 1)x(-1)y(-1)$$
$$\qquad - \tfrac{1}{2}(u^2 - 1)\big(x(u)y(u) \bmod (u^2 + 1)\big)\big) \bmod (u^4 - 1). \quad (65)$$

The remaining problem is to evaluate $x(u)y(u) \bmod (u^2 + 1)$, and it is time to invoke rule (60). First we reduce $x(u)$ and $y(u) \bmod (u^2 + 1)$, obtaining

$X(u) = (x_0 - x_2) + (x_1 - x_3)u$, $Y(u) = (y_0 - y_2) + (y_1 - y_3)u$. Then (60) tells us to evaluate $X(u)Y(u) = Z_0 + Z_1u + Z_2u^2$, and to reduce this in turn modulo $(u^2 + 1)$, obtaining $(Z_0 - Z_2) + Z_1u$. The job of computing $X(u)Y(u)$ is simple; we can use rule (58) with $p(u) = u(u+1)$ and we get

$$Z_0 = X_0Y_0, \quad Z_1 = X_0Y_0 - (X_0 - X_1)(Y_0 - Y_1) + X_1Y_1, \quad Z_2 = X_1Y_1.$$

(We have thereby rediscovered the trick of Eq. 4.3.3–(2) in a more systematic way.) Putting everything together yields the following realization (A, B, C) of degree-4 cyclic convolution:

$$
\begin{pmatrix}
1 & 1 & 1 & 0 & 1 \\
1 & \bar{1} & 0 & 1 & \bar{1} \\
1 & 1 & \bar{1} & 0 & \bar{1} \\
1 & \bar{1} & 0 & \bar{1} & 1
\end{pmatrix},
\quad
\begin{pmatrix}
1 & 1 & 1 & 0 & 1 \\
1 & \bar{1} & 0 & 1 & 1 \\
1 & 1 & \bar{1} & 0 & \bar{1} \\
1 & \bar{1} & 0 & \bar{1} & 1
\end{pmatrix},
\quad
\begin{pmatrix}
1 & 1 & 2 & \bar{2} & 0 \\
1 & \bar{1} & 2 & 2 & \bar{2} \\
1 & 1 & \bar{2} & 2 & 0 \\
1 & \bar{1} & \bar{2} & \bar{2} & 2
\end{pmatrix}
\times \frac{1}{4}.
\tag{66}
$$

Here $\bar{1}$ stands for -1 and $\bar{2}$ stands for -2.

The tensor for cyclic convolution of degree n satisfies

$$t_{i,j,k} = t_{k,-j,i}, \tag{67}$$

treating the subscripts modulo n, since $t_{ijk} = 1$ if and only if $i + j \equiv k$ (modulo n). Thus if (a_{il}), (b_{jl}), (c_{kl}) is a realization of the cyclic convolution, so is (c_{kl}), $(b_{-j,l})$, (a_{il}); in particular, we can realize (63) by transforming (66) into

$$
\begin{pmatrix}
1 & 1 & 2 & \bar{2} & 0 \\
1 & \bar{1} & 2 & 2 & \bar{2} \\
1 & 1 & \bar{2} & 2 & 0 \\
1 & \bar{1} & \bar{2} & \bar{2} & 2
\end{pmatrix}
\times \frac{1}{4},
\quad
\begin{pmatrix}
1 & 1 & 1 & 0 & 1 \\
1 & \bar{1} & 0 & \bar{1} & 1 \\
1 & 1 & \bar{1} & 0 & \bar{1} \\
1 & \bar{1} & 0 & 1 & \bar{1}
\end{pmatrix},
\quad
\begin{pmatrix}
1 & 1 & 1 & 0 & 1 \\
1 & \bar{1} & 0 & 1 & \bar{1} \\
1 & 1 & \bar{1} & 0 & \bar{1} \\
1 & \bar{1} & 0 & \bar{1} & 1
\end{pmatrix}.
\tag{68}
$$

Now all of the complicated scalars appear in the A matrix. This is important in practice, since we often want to compute the convolution for many values of y_0, y_1, y_2, y_3 but for a fixed choice of x_0, x_1, x_2, x_3. In such a situation, the arithmetic on x's can be done once and for all, and we need not count it. Thus (68) leads to the following scheme for evaluating the cyclic convolution w_0, w_1, w_2, w_3 when x_0, x_1, x_2, x_3 are known in advance:

$$s_1 = y_0 + y_2, \quad s_2 = y_1 + y_3, \quad s_3 = s_1 + s_2, \quad s_4 = s_1 - s_2,$$
$$s_5 = y_0 - y_2, \quad s_6 = y_3 - y_1, \quad s_7 = s_5 - s_6;$$
$$m_1 = \tfrac{1}{4}(x_0 + x_1 + x_2 + x_3) \cdot s_3, \quad m_2 = \tfrac{1}{4}(x_0 - x_1 + x_2 - x_3) \cdot s_4,$$
$$m_3 = \tfrac{1}{2}(x_0 + x_1 - x_2 - x_3) \cdot s_5, \quad m_4 = \tfrac{1}{2}(-x_0 + x_1 + x_2 - x_3) \cdot s_6, \quad m_5 = \tfrac{1}{2}(x_3 - x_1) \cdot s_7;$$
$$t_1 = m_1 + m_2, \quad t_2 = m_3 + m_5, \quad t_3 = m_1 - m_2, \quad t_4 = m_4 - m_5;$$
$$w_0 = t_1 + t_2, \quad w_1 = t_3 + t_4, \quad w_2 = t_1 - t_2, \quad w_3 = t_3 - t_4. \tag{69}$$

There are 5 multiplications and 15 additions, while the definition of cyclic convolution involves 16 multiplications and 12 additions. We will prove later that 5 multiplications are necessary.

Going back to our original multiplication problem (54), using (62), we have derived the realization

$$
\begin{pmatrix} 4 & 0 & 1 & 1 & 2 & \bar{2} & 0 \\ 0 & 0 & 1 & \bar{1} & 2 & 2 & \bar{2} \\ 0 & 4 & 1 & 1 & \bar{2} & 2 & 0 \end{pmatrix} \times \frac{1}{4},
\quad
\begin{pmatrix} 1 & 0 & 1 & 1 & 1 & 0 & 1 \\ 0 & 0 & 1 & \bar{1} & 0 & \bar{1} & 1 \\ 0 & 0 & 1 & 1 & \bar{1} & 0 & \bar{1} \\ 0 & 1 & \bar{1} & 0 & 1 & 1 \end{pmatrix},
\quad
\begin{pmatrix} 1 & 0 & 0 & 0 & 0 & 0 & 0 \\ 0 & \bar{1} & 1 & \bar{1} & 0 & 1 & \bar{1} \\ 0 & 0 & 1 & 1 & \bar{1} & 0 & \bar{1} \\ 0 & 0 & 1 & \bar{1} & 0 & \bar{1} & 1 \\ \bar{1} & 0 & 1 & 1 & 1 & 0 & 1 \\ 0 & 1 & 0 & 0 & 0 & 0 & 0 \end{pmatrix}.
\tag{70}
$$

This scheme uses one more than the minimum number of chain multiplications, but it requires far fewer parameter multiplications than (57). Of course, it must be admitted that the scheme is still rather complicated: If our goal is simply to compute the coefficients z_0, z_1, ..., z_5 of the product of two given polynomials $(x_0 + x_1 u + x_2 u^2)(y_0 + y_1 u + y_2 u^2 + y_3 u^3)$, as a one-shot problem, our best bet may well be to use the obvious method that does 12 multiplications and 6 additions — unless (say) the x's and y's are matrices. Another reasonably attractive scheme, which requires 8 multiplications and 18 additions, appears in exercise 58(b). Notice that if the x's are fixed as the y's vary, (70) does the evaluation with 7 multiplications and 17 additions. Even though this scheme isn't especially useful as it stands, our derivation has illustrated important techniques that are useful in a variety of other situations. For example, Winograd has used this approach to compute Fourier transforms using significantly fewer multiplications than the fast Fourier transform algorithm needs (see exercise 53).

Let us conclude this section by determining the exact rank of the $n \times n \times n$ tensor that corresponds to the multiplication of two polynomials modulo a third,

$$
z_0 + z_1 u + \cdots + z_{n-1} u^{n-1}
$$
$$
= (x_0 + x_1 u + \cdots + x_{n-1} u^{n-1})(y_0 + y_1 u + \cdots + y_{n-1} u^{n-1}) \bmod p(u).
\tag{71}
$$

Here $p(u)$ stands for any given monic polynomial of degree n; in particular, $p(u)$ might be $u^n - 1$, so one of the results of our investigation will be to deduce the rank of the tensor corresponding to cyclic convolution of degree n. It will be convenient to write $p(u)$ in the form

$$
p(u) = u^n - p_{n-1} u^{n-1} - \cdots - p_1 u - p_0,
\tag{72}
$$

so that $u^n \equiv p_0 + p_1 u + \cdots + p_{n-1} u^{n-1}$ (modulo $p(u)$).

The tensor element t_{ijk} is the coefficient of u^k in $u^{i+j} \bmod p(u)$; and this is the element in row i, column k of the matrix P^j, where

$$
P = \begin{pmatrix} 0 & 1 & 0 & \cdots & 0 \\ 0 & 0 & 1 & \cdots & 0 \\ \vdots & \vdots & \vdots & & \vdots \\ 0 & 0 & 0 & \cdots & 1 \\ p_0 & p_1 & p_2 & \cdots & p_{n-1} \end{pmatrix}
\tag{73}
$$

is called the *companion matrix* of $p(u)$. (The indices i, j, k in our discussion will run from 0 to $n - 1$ instead of from 1 to n.) It is convenient to transpose the tensor, for if $T_{ijk} = t_{ikj}$ the individual layers of (T_{ijk}) for $k = 0, 1, 2, \ldots, n-1$ are simply given by the matrices

$$I \quad P \quad P^2 \quad \ldots \quad P^{n-1}. \tag{74}$$

The first rows of the matrices in (74) are respectively the unit vectors $(1, 0, 0, \ldots, 0)$, $(0, 1, 0, \ldots, 0)$, $(0, 0, 1, \ldots, 0)$, $\ldots$, $(0, 0, 0, \ldots, 1)$, hence a linear combination $\sum_{k=0}^{n-1} v_k P^k$ will be the zero matrix if and only if the coefficients v_k are all zero. Furthermore, most of these linear combinations are actually non-singular matrices, for we have

$$(w_0, w_1, \ldots, w_{n-1}) \sum_{k=0}^{n-1} v_k P^k = (0, 0, \ldots, 0)$$

$$\text{if and only if} \quad v(u)w(u) \equiv 0 \quad (\text{modulo } p(u)),$$

where $v(u) = v_0 + v_1 u + \cdots + v_{n-1} u^{n-1}$ and $w(u) = w_0 + w_1 u + \cdots + w_{n-1} u^{n-1}$. Thus, $\sum_{k=0}^{n-1} v_k P^k$ is a singular matrix if and only if the polynomial $v(u)$ is a multiple of some factor of $p(u)$. We are now ready to prove the desired result.

Theorem W (S. Winograd, 1975). *Let $p(u)$ be a monic polynomial of degree n whose complete factorization over a given infinite field is*

$$p(u) = p_1(u)^{e_1} \ldots p_q(u)^{e_q}. \tag{75}$$

Then the rank of the tensor (74) corresponding to the bilinear forms (71) is $2n - q$ over this field.

Proof. The bilinear forms can be evaluated with only $2n - q$ chain multiplications by using rules (58), (59), (60) in an appropriate fashion, so we must prove only that the rank r is $\geq 2n - q$. The discussion above establishes the fact that $\text{rank}(T_{(ij)k}) = n$; hence by Lemma T, any $n \times r$ realization (A, B, C) of (T_{ijk}) has $\text{rank}(C) = n$. Our strategy will be to use Lemma T again, by finding a vector $(v_0, v_1, \ldots, v_{n-1})$ that has the following two properties:

i) The vector $(v_0, v_1, \ldots, v_{n-1})C$ has at most $q + r - n$ nonzero coefficients.

ii) The matrix $v(P) = \sum_{k=0}^{n-1} v_k P^k$ is nonsingular.

This and Lemma T will prove that $q + r - n \geq n$, since the identity

$$\sum_{l=1}^{r} a_{il} b_{jl} \left(\sum_{k=0}^{n-1} v_k c_{kl} \right) = v(P)_{ij}$$

shows how to realize the $n \times n \times 1$ tensor $v(P)$ of rank n with $q + r - n$ chain multiplications.

We may assume for convenience that the first n columns of C are linearly independent. Let D be the $n \times n$ matrix such that the first n columns of DC are equal to the identity matrix. Our goal will be achieved if there is a linear combination $(v_0, v_1, \ldots, v_{n-1})$ of at most q rows of D, such that $v(P)$ is nonsingular; such a vector will satisfy conditions (i) and (ii).

Since the rows of D are linearly independent, no irreducible factor $p_\lambda(u)$ can divide the polynomials corresponding to every row. Given a vector

$$w = (w_0, w_1, \ldots, w_{n-1}),$$

let covered(w) be the set of all λ such that $w(u)$ is not a multiple of $p_\lambda(u)$. From two vectors v and w we can find a linear combination $v + \alpha w$ such that

$$\text{covered}(v + \alpha w) = \text{covered}(v) \cup \text{covered}(w), \tag{76}$$

for some α in the field. The reason is that if λ is covered by v or w but not both, then λ is covered by $v + \alpha w$ for all nonzero α; if λ is covered by both v and w but λ is not covered by $v + \alpha w$, then λ is covered by $v + \beta w$ for all $\beta \neq \alpha$. By trying $q+1$ different values of α, at least one must yield (76). In this way we can systematically construct a linear combination of at most q rows of D, covering all λ for $1 \leq \lambda \leq q$. ∎

One of the most important corollaries of Theorem W is that the rank of a tensor can depend on the field from which we draw the elements of the realization (A, B, C). For example, consider the tensor corresponding to cyclic convolution of degree 5; this is equivalent to multiplication of polynomials mod $p(u) = u^5 - 1$. Over the field of rational numbers, the complete factorization of $p(u)$ is $(u - 1) \times (u^4 + u^3 + u^2 + u + 1)$ by exercise 4.6.2–32, so the tensor rank is $10 - 2 = 8$. On the other hand, the complete factorization over the real numbers, in terms of the number $\phi = \frac{1}{2}(1 + \sqrt{5})$, is $(u - 1)(u^2 + \phi u + 1)(u^2 - \phi^{-1}u + 1)$; thus, the rank is only 7, if we allow arbitrary real numbers to appear in A, B, C. Over the complex numbers the rank is 5. This phenomenon does not occur in two-dimensional tensors (matrices), where the rank can be determined by evaluating determinants of submatrices and testing for 0. The rank of a matrix does not change when the field containing its elements is embedded in a larger field, but the rank of a tensor can decrease when the field gets larger.

In the paper that introduced Theorem W [*Math. Systems Theory* **10** (1977), 169–180], Winograd went on to show that *all* realizations of (71) in $2n - q$ chain multiplications correspond to the use of (59), when q is greater than 1. Furthermore he has shown that the only way to evaluate the coefficients of $x(u)y(u)$ in $\deg(x) + \deg(y) + 1$ chain multiplications is to use interpolation or to use (58) with a polynomial that splits into distinct linear factors in the field. Finally he has proved that the only way to evaluate $x(u)y(u) \bmod p(u)$ in $2n - 1$ chain multiplications when $q = 1$ is essentially to use (60). These results hold for *all* polynomial chains, not only "normal" ones. He has extended the results to multivariate polynomials in *SICOMP* **9** (1980), 225–229.

The tensor rank of an arbitrary $m \times n \times 2$ tensor in a suitably large field has been determined by Joseph Ja'Ja', *SICOMP* **8** (1979), 443–462; *JACM* **27** (1980), 822–830. See also his interesting discussion of commutative bilinear forms in *SICOMP* **9** (1980), 713–728. However, the problem of computing the tensor rank of an arbitrary $n \times n \times n$ tensor over any finite field is NP-complete [J. Håstad, *Journal of Algorithms* **11** (1990), 644–654].

For further reading. In this section we have barely scratched the surface of a very large subject in which many beautiful theories are emerging. Considerably more comprehensive treatments can be found in the books *Computational Complexity of Algebraic and Numeric Problems* by A. Borodin and I. Munro (New York: American Elsevier, 1975); *Polynomial and Matrix Computations* **1** by D. Bini and V. Pan (Boston: Birkhäuser, 1994); *Algebraic Complexity Theory* by P. Bürgisser, M. Clausen, and M. Amin Shokrollahi (Heidelberg: Springer, 1997).

EXERCISES

1. [*15*] What is a good way to evaluate an "odd" polynomial

$$u(x) = u_{2n+1}x^{2n+1} + u_{2n-1}x^{2n-1} + \cdots + u_1 x?$$

▶ **2.** [*M20*] Instead of computing $u(x + x_0)$ by steps H1 and H2 as in the text, discuss the application of Horner's rule (2) when *polynomial* multiplication and addition are used instead of arithmetic in the domain of coefficients.

3. [*20*] Give a method analogous to Horner's rule, for evaluating a polynomial in two variables $\sum_{i+j\le n} u_{ij} x^i y^j$. (This polynomial has $(n + 1)(n + 2)/2$ coefficients, and its "total degree" is n.) Count the number of additions and multiplications you use.

4. [*M20*] The text shows that scheme (3) is superior to Horner's rule when we are evaluating a polynomial with real coefficients at a complex point z. Compare (3) to Horner's rule when *both* the coefficients and the variable z are complex numbers; how many (real) multiplications and addition-subtractions are required by each method?

5. [*M15*] Count the number of multiplications and additions required by the second-order rule (4).

6. [*22*] (L. de Jong and J. van Leeuwen.) Show how to improve on steps S1, . . . , S4 of the Shaw–Traub algorithm by computing only about $\frac{1}{2}n$ powers of x_0.

7. [*M25*] How can β_0, . . . , β_n be calculated so that (6) has the value $u(x_0 + kh)$ for all integers k?

8. [*M20*] The factorial power $x^{\underline{k}}$ is defined to be $k!\binom{x}{k} = x(x - 1) \ldots (x - k + 1)$. Explain how to evaluate $u_n x^{\underline{n}} + \cdots + u_1 x^{\underline{1}} + u_0$ with at most n multiplications and $2n - 1$ additions, starting with x and the $n + 3$ constants u_n, . . . , u_0, 1, $n - 1$.

9. [*M25*] (H. J. Ryser.) Show that if $X = (x_{ij})$ is an $n \times n$ matrix, then

$$\text{per}(X) = \sum (-1)^{n-\epsilon_1-\cdots-\epsilon_n} \prod_{1\le i\le n} \sum_{1\le j\le n} \epsilon_j x_{ij}$$

summed over all 2^n choices of ϵ_1, . . . , ϵ_n equal to 0 or 1 independently. Count the number of addition and multiplication operations required to evaluate $\text{per}(X)$ by this formula.

10. [*M21*] The permanent of an $n \times n$ matrix $X = (x_{ij})$ may be calculated as follows: Start with the n quantities x_{11}, x_{12}, . . . , x_{1n}. For $1 \le k < n$, assume that the $\binom{n}{k}$ quantities A_{kS} have been computed, for all k-element subsets S of $\{1, 2, \ldots, n\}$, where $A_{kS} = \sum x_{1j_1} \ldots x_{kj_k}$ summed over all $k!$ permutations $j_1 \ldots j_k$ of the elements of S; then form all of the sums

$$A_{(k+1)S} = \sum_{j\in S} A_{k(S\setminus\{j\})} x_{(k+1)j}.$$

We have $\text{per}(X) = A_{n\{1,\ldots,n\}}$. How many additions and multiplications does this method require? How much temporary storage is needed?

11. [*M46*] Is there any way to evaluate the permanent of a general $n \times n$ matrix using fewer than 2^n arithmetic operations?

12. [*M50*] What is the minimum number of multiplications required to form the product of two $n \times n$ matrices? What is the smallest exponent ω such that $O(n^{\omega+\epsilon})$ multiplications are sufficient for all $\epsilon > 0$? (Find good upper and lower bounds for small n as well as large n.)

13. [*M23*] Find the inverse of the general discrete Fourier transform (37), by expressing $F(t_1, \ldots, t_n)$ in terms of the values of $f(s_1, \ldots, s_n)$. [*Hint:* See Eq. 1.2.9–(13).]

▶ **14.** [*HM28*] (*Fast Fourier transforms.*) Show that the scheme (40) can be used to evaluate the one-dimensional discrete Fourier transform

$$f(s) = \sum_{0 \le t < 2^n} F(t)\, \omega^{st}, \qquad \omega = e^{2\pi i/2^n}, \qquad 0 \le s < 2^n,$$

using arithmetic on complex numbers. Estimate the number of arithmetic operations performed.

▶ **15.** [*HM28*] The nth *divided difference* $f(x_0, x_1, \ldots, x_n)$ of a function $f(x)$ at $n+1$ distinct points $x_0, x_1, \ldots, x_n$ is defined by the formula

$$f(x_0, x_1, \ldots, x_n) = \big(f(x_0, x_1, \ldots, x_{n-1}) - f(x_1, \ldots, x_{n-1}, x_n)\big)/(x_0 - x_n),$$

for $n > 0$. Thus $f(x_0, x_1, \ldots, x_n) = \sum_{k=0}^{n} f(x_k)/ \prod_{0 \le j \le n,\, j \ne k}(x_k - x_j)$ is a symmetric function of its $n+1$ arguments. (a) Prove that $f(x_0, \ldots, x_n) = f^{(n)}(\theta)/n!$, for some θ between $\min(x_0, \ldots, x_n)$ and $\max(x_0, \ldots, x_n)$, if the nth derivative $f^{(n)}(x)$ exists and is continuous. [*Hint:* Prove the identity

$$f(x_0, x_1, \ldots, x_n) = \int_0^1 dt_1 \int_0^{t_1} dt_2 \ldots \int_0^{t_{n-1}} dt_n\, f^{(n)}\big(x_0(1 - t_1) + x_1(t_1 - t_2) + \cdots$$
$$+ x_{n-1}(t_{n-1} - t_n) + x_n(t_n - 0)\big).$$

This formula also defines $f(x_0, x_1, \ldots, x_n)$ in a useful manner when the x_j are not distinct.] (b) If $y_j = f(x_j)$, show that $\alpha_j = f(x_0, \ldots, x_j)$ in Newton's interpolation polynomial (42).

16. [*M22*] How can we readily compute the coefficients of $u_{[n]}(x) = u_n x^n + \cdots + u_0$, if we are given the values of $x_0, x_1, \ldots, x_{n-1}, \alpha_0, \alpha_1, \ldots, \alpha_n$ in Newton's interpolation polynomial (42)?

17. [*M20*] Show that the interpolation formula (45) reduces to a very simple expression involving binomial coefficients when $x_k = x_0 + kh$ for $0 \le k \le n$. [*Hint:* See exercise 1.2.6–48.]

18. [*M20*] If the fourth-degree scheme (9) were changed to

$$y = (x + \alpha_0)x + \alpha_1, \qquad u(x) = ((y - x + \alpha_2)y + \alpha_3)\alpha_4,$$

what formulas for computing the α_j's in terms of the u_k's would take the place of (10)?

▶ **19.** [*M24*] Explain how to determine the adapted coefficients $\alpha_0, \alpha_1, \ldots, \alpha_5$ in (11) from the coefficients $u_5, \ldots, u_1, u_0$ of $u(x)$, and find the α's for the particular polynomial $u(x) = x^5 + 5x^4 - 10x^3 - 50x^2 + 13x + 60$.

▶ **20.** [*21*] Write a MIX program that evaluates a fifth-degree polynomial according to scheme (11); try to make the program as efficient as possible, by making slight modifications to (11). Use MIX's floating point arithmetic operators FADD and FMUL, which are described in Section 4.2.1.

21. [20] Find two additional ways to evaluate the polynomial $x^6 + 13x^5 + 49x^4 + 33x^3 - 61x^2 - 37x + 3$ by scheme (12), using the two roots of (15) that were not considered in the text.

22. [18] What is the scheme for evaluating $x^6 - 3x^5 + x^4 - 2x^3 + x^2 - 3x - 1$, using Pan's method (16)?

23. [HM30] (J. Eve.) Let $f(z) = a_n z^n + a_{n-1} z^{n-1} + \cdots + a_0$ be a polynomial of degree n with real coefficients, having at least $n-1$ roots with a nonnegative real part. Let

$$g(z) = a_n z^n + a_{n-2} z^{n-2} + \cdots + a_{n \bmod 2} z^{n \bmod 2},$$

$$h(z) = a_{n-1} z^{n-1} + a_{n-3} z^{n-3} + \cdots + a_{(n-1) \bmod 2} z^{(n-1) \bmod 2}.$$

Assume that $h(z)$ is not identically zero.

a) Show that $g(z)$ has at least $n-2$ imaginary roots (that is, roots whose real part is zero), and $h(z)$ has at least $n-3$ imaginary roots. [Hint: Consider the number of times the path $f(z)$ circles the origin as z goes around the path shown in Fig. 16, for a sufficiently large radius R.]

b) Prove that the squares of the roots of $g(z) = 0$ and $h(z) = 0$ are all real.

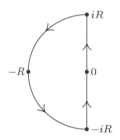

Fig. 16. Proof of Eve's theorem.

▸ **24.** [M24] Find values of c and α_k, β_k satisfying the conditions of Theorem E, for the polynomial $u(x) = (x + 7)(x^2 + 6x + 10)(x^2 + 4x + 5)(x + 1)$. Choose these values so that $\beta_2 = 0$. Give two different solutions.

25. [M20] When the construction in the proof of Theorem M is applied to the (inefficient) polynomial chain

$$\lambda_1 = \alpha_1 + \lambda_0, \qquad \lambda_2 = -\lambda_0 - \lambda_0, \qquad \lambda_3 = \lambda_1 + \lambda_1, \qquad \lambda_4 = \alpha_2 \times \lambda_3,$$

$$\lambda_5 = \lambda_0 - \lambda_0, \qquad \lambda_6 = \alpha_6 - \lambda_5, \qquad \lambda_7 = \alpha_7 \times \lambda_6, \qquad \lambda_8 = \lambda_7 \times \lambda_7,$$

$$\lambda_9 = \lambda_1 \times \lambda_4, \qquad \lambda_{10} = \alpha_8 - \lambda_9, \qquad \lambda_{11} = \lambda_3 - \lambda_{10},$$

how can $\beta_1, \beta_2, \ldots, \beta_9$ be expressed in terms of $\alpha_1, \ldots, \alpha_8$?

▸ **26.** [M21] (a) Give the polynomial chain corresponding to Horner's rule for evaluating polynomials of degree $n = 3$. (b) Using the construction that appears in the text's proof of Theorem A, express κ_1, κ_2, κ_3, and the result polynomial $u(x)$ in terms of β_1, β_2, β_3, β_4, and x. (c) Show that the result set obtained in (b), as β_1, β_2, β_3, and β_4 independently assume all real values, omits certain vectors in the result set of (a).

27. [M22] Let R be a set that includes all $(n+1)$-tuples $(q_n, \ldots, q_1, q_0)$ of real numbers such that $q_n \neq 0$; prove that R does not have at most n degrees of freedom.

28. [*HM20*] Show that if $f_0(\alpha_1, \ldots, \alpha_s)$, $\ldots$, $f_s(\alpha_1, \ldots, \alpha_s)$ are multivariate polynomials with integer coefficients, then there is a nonzero polynomial $g(x_0, \ldots, x_s)$ with integer coefficients such that $g(f_0(\alpha_1, \ldots, \alpha_s), \ldots, f_s(\alpha_1, \ldots, \alpha_s)) = 0$ for all real α_1, $\ldots$, α_s. (Hence any polynomial chain with s parameters has at most s degrees of freedom.) [*Hint:* Use the theorems about "algebraic dependence" that are found, for example, in B. L. van der Waerden's *Modern Algebra*, translated by Fred Blum (New York: Ungar, 1949), Section 64.]

▶ **29.** [*M20*] Let R_1, R_2, $\ldots$, R_m all be sets of $(n + 1)$-tuples of real numbers having at most t degrees of freedom. Show that the union $R_1 \cup R_2 \cup \cdots \cup R_m$ also has at most t degrees of freedom.

▶ **30.** [*M28*] Prove that a polynomial chain with m_c chain multiplications and m_p parameter multiplications has at most $2m_c + m_p + \delta_{0m_c}$ degrees of freedom. [*Hint:* Generalize Theorem M, showing that the first chain multiplication and each parameter multiplication can essentially introduce only one new parameter into the result set.]

31. [*M23*] Prove that a polynomial chain capable of computing all *monic* polynomials of degree n has at least $\lfloor n/2 \rfloor$ multiplications and at least n addition-subtractions.

32. [*M24*] Find a polynomial chain of minimum possible length that can compute all polynomials of the form $u_4 x^4 + u_2 x^2 + u_0$; and prove that its length is minimal.

▶ **33.** [*M25*] Let $n \geq 3$ be odd. Prove that a polynomial chain with $\lfloor n/2 \rfloor + 1$ multiplication steps cannot compute all polynomials of degree n unless it has at least $n + 2$ addition-subtraction steps. [*Hint:* See exercise 30.]

34. [*M26*] Let λ_0, λ_1, $\ldots$, λ_r be a polynomial chain in which all of the addition and subtraction steps are parameter steps, and in which there is at least one parameter multiplication. Assume that this scheme has m multiplications and $k = r - m$ addition-subtractions, and that the polynomial computed by the chain has maximum degree n. Prove that all polynomials computable by this chain, for which the coefficient of x^n is not zero, can be computed by another chain that has at most m multiplications and at most k additions, and no subtractions; furthermore the last step of the new chain should be the only parameter multiplication.

▶ **35.** [*M25*] Show that any polynomial chain that computes a general fourth-degree polynomial using three multiplications must have at least five addition-subtractions. [*Hint:* Assume that there are only four addition-subtractions, and show that exercise 34 applies; therefore the scheme must have a particular form that is incapable of representing all fourth-degree polynomials.]

36. [*M27*] Continuing the previous exercise, show that any polynomial chain that computes a general sixth-degree polynomial using only four multiplications must have at least seven addition-subtractions.

37. [*M21*] (T. S. Motzkin.) Show that "almost all" rational functions of the form

$$(u_n x^n + u_{n-1} x^{n-1} + \cdots + u_1 x + u_0)/(x^n + v_{n-1} x^{n-1} + \cdots + v_1 x + v_0),$$

with coefficients in a field S, can be evaluated using the scheme

$$\alpha_1 + \beta_1/(x + \alpha_2 + \beta_2/(x + \cdots + \beta_n/(x + \alpha_{n+1}) \ldots)),$$

for suitable α_j, β_j in S. (This continued fraction scheme has n divisions and $2n$ additions; by "almost all" rational functions we mean all except those whose coefficients satisfy some nontrivial polynomial equation.) Determine the α's and β's for the rational function $(x^2 + 10x + 29)/(x^2 + 8x + 19)$.

▶ **38.** [*HM32*] (V. Y. Pan, 1962.) The purpose of this exercise is to prove that Horner's rule is really optimal if no preliminary adaptation of coefficients is made; we need n multiplications and n additions to compute $u_n x^n + \cdots + u_1 x + u_0$, if the variables u_n, $\ldots$, u_1, u_0, x, and arbitrary constants are given. Consider chains that are as before except that u_n, $\ldots$, u_1, u_0, x are each considered to be variables; we may say, for example, that $\lambda_{-j-1} = u_j$, $\lambda_0 = x$. In order to show that Horner's rule is best, it is convenient to prove a somewhat more general theorem: Let $A = (a_{ij})$, $0 \le i \le m$, $0 \le j \le n$, be an $(m+1) \times (n+1)$ matrix of real numbers, of rank $n+1$; and let $B = (b_0, \ldots, b_m)$ be a vector of real numbers. Prove that *any polynomial chain that computes*

$$P(x; u_0, \ldots, u_n) = \sum_{i=0}^{m} (a_{i0} u_0 + \cdots + a_{in} u_n + b_i) x^i$$

involves at least n chain multiplications. (Note that this does not mean only that we are considering some fixed chain in which the parameters α_j are assigned values depending on A and B; it means that both the chain *and* the values of the α's may depend on the given matrix A and vector B. No matter how A, B, and the values of α_j are chosen, it is impossible to compute $P(x; u_0, \ldots, u_n)$ without doing n "chain-step" multiplications.) The assumption that A has rank $n+1$ implies that $m \ge n$. [*Hint:* Show that from any such scheme we can derive another that has fewer chain multiplications and that has n decreased by one.]

39. [*M29*] (T. S. Motzkin, 1954.) Show that schemes of the form

$$w_1 = x(x + \alpha_1) + \beta_1, \qquad w_k = w_{k-1}(w_1 + \gamma_k x + \alpha_k) + \delta_k x + \beta_k \quad \text{for } 1 < k \le m,$$

where the α_k, β_k are real and the γ_k, δ_k are integers, can be used to evaluate all monic polynomials of degree $2m$ over the real numbers. (We may have to choose α_k, β_k, γ_k, and δ_k differently for different polynomials.) Try to let $\delta_k = 0$ whenever possible.

40. [*M41*] Can the lower bound in the number of multiplications in Theorem C be raised from $\lfloor n/2 \rfloor + 1$ to $\lceil n/2 \rceil + 1$? (See exercise 33.)

41. [*22*] Show that the real and imaginary parts of $(a + bi)(c + di)$ can be obtained by doing 3 multiplications and 5 additions of real numbers, where two of the additions involve a and b only.

42. [*36*] (M. Paterson and L. Stockmeyer.) (a) Prove that a polynomial chain with $m \ge 2$ chain multiplications has at most $m^2 + 1$ degrees of freedom. (b) Show that for all $n \ge 2$ there exist polynomials of degree n, all of whose coefficients are 0 or 1, that cannot be evaluated by any polynomial chain with fewer than $\lfloor \sqrt{n} \rfloor$ multiplications, if we require all parameters α_j to be integers. (c) Show that any polynomial of degree n with integer coefficients can be evaluated by an all-integer algorithm that performs at most $2\lfloor \sqrt{n} \rfloor$ multiplications, if we don't care how many additions we do.

43. [*22*] Explain how to evaluate $x^n + \cdots + x + 1$ with $2l(n+1) - 2$ multiplications and $l(n+1)$ additions (no divisions or subtractions), where $l(n)$ is the function studied in Section 4.6.3.

▶ **44.** [*M25*] Show that any monic polynomial $u(x) = x^n + u_{n-1} x^{n-1} + \cdots + u_0$ can be evaluated with $\frac{1}{2} n + O(\log n)$ multiplications and $\le \frac{5}{4} n$ additions, using parameters α_1, α_2, $\ldots$ that are polynomials in u_{n-1}, u_{n-2}, $\ldots$ with integer coefficients. [*Hint:* Consider first the case $n = 2^l$.]

▶ **45.** [*HM22*] Let (t_{ijk}) be an $m \times n \times s$ tensor, and let F, G, H be nonsingular matrices of respective sizes $m \times m$, $n \times n$, $s \times s$. If

$$T_{ijk} = \sum_{i'=1}^{m} \sum_{j'=1}^{n} \sum_{k'=1}^{s} F_{ii'} G_{jj'} H_{kk'} t_{i'j'k'}$$

for all i, j, k, prove that the tensor (T_{ijk}) has the same rank as (t_{ijk}). [*Hint:* Consider what happens when F^{-1}, G^{-1}, H^{-1} are applied in the same way to (T_{ijk}).]

46. [*M28*] Prove that all pairs (z_1, z_2) of bilinear forms in (x_1, x_2) and (y_1, y_2) can be evaluated with at most three chain multiplications. In other words, show that every $2 \times 2 \times 2$ tensor has rank ≤ 3.

47. [*M25*] Prove that for all m, n, and s there exists an $m \times n \times s$ tensor whose rank is at least $\lceil mns/(m+n+s) \rceil$. Conversely, show that every $m \times n \times s$ tensor has rank at most $mns/\max(m, n, s)$.

48. [*M21*] If (t_{ijk}) and (t'_{ijk}) are tensors of sizes $m \times n \times s$ and $m' \times n' \times s'$, respectively, their *direct sum* $(t_{ijk}) \oplus (t'_{ijk}) = (t''_{ijk})$ is the $(m + m') \times (n + n') \times (s + s')$ tensor defined by $t''_{ijk} = t_{ijk}$ if $i \le m$, $j \le n$, $k \le s$; $t''_{ijk} = t'_{i-m, j-n, k-s}$ if $i > m$, $j > n$, $k > s$; and $t''_{ijk} = 0$ otherwise. Their *direct product* $(t_{ijk}) \otimes (t'_{ijk}) = (t'''_{ijk})$ is the $mm' \times nn' \times ss'$ tensor defined by $t_{\langle ii' \rangle \langle jj' \rangle \langle kk' \rangle} = t_{ijk} t'_{i'j'k'}$. Derive the upper bounds $\mathrm{rank}(t''_{ijk}) \le \mathrm{rank}(t_{ijk}) + \mathrm{rank}(t'_{ijk})$ and $\mathrm{rank}(t'''_{ijk}) \le \mathrm{rank}(t_{ijk}) \cdot \mathrm{rank}(t'_{ijk})$.

▶ **49.** [*HM25*] Show that the rank of an $m \times n \times 1$ tensor (t_{ijk}) is the same as its rank as an $m \times n$ matrix (t_{ij1}), according to the traditional definition of matrix rank as the maximum number of linearly independent rows.

50. [*HM20*] (S. Winograd.) Let (t_{ijk}) be the $mn \times n \times m$ tensor corresponding to multiplication of an $m \times n$ matrix by an $n \times 1$ column vector. Prove that the rank of (t_{ijk}) is mn.

▶ **51.** [*M24*] (S. Winograd.) Devise an algorithm for cyclic convolution of degree 2 that uses 2 multiplications and 4 additions, not counting operations on the x_i. Similarly, devise an algorithm for degree 3, using 4 multiplications and 11 additions. (See (69), which solves the analogous problem for degree 4.)

52. [*M25*] (S. Winograd.) Let $n = n'n''$ where $n' \perp n''$. Given normal schemes for cyclic convolutions of degrees n' and n'', using respectively (m', m'') chain multiplications, (p', p'') parameter multiplications, and (a', a'') additions, show how to construct a normal scheme for cyclic convolution of degree n using $m'm''$ chain multiplications, $p'n'' + m'p''$ parameter multiplications, and $a'n'' + m'a''$ additions.

53. [*HM40*] (S. Winograd.) Let ω be a complex mth root of unity, and consider the one-dimensional discrete Fourier transform

$$f(s) = \sum_{t=1}^{m} F(t)\, \omega^{st}, \qquad \text{for } 1 \le s \le m.$$

a) When $m = p^e$ is a power of an odd prime, show that efficient normal schemes for computing cyclic convolutions of degrees $(p - 1)p^k$, for $0 \le k < e$, will lead to efficient algorithms for computing the Fourier transform on m complex numbers. Give a similar construction for the case $p = 2$.

b) When $m = m'm''$ and $m' \perp m''$, show that Fourier transformation algorithms for m' and m'' can be combined to yield a Fourier transformation algorithm for m elements.

54. [*M23*] Theorem W refers to an infinite field. How many elements must a finite field have in order for the proof of Theorem W to be valid?

55. [*HM22*] Determine the rank of tensor (74) when P is an *arbitrary* $n \times n$ matrix.

56. [*M32*] (V. Strassen.) Show that any polynomial chain that evaluates a set of *quadratic forms* $\sum_{i=1}^{n} \sum_{j=1}^{n} \tau_{ijk} x_i x_j$ for $1 \le k \le s$ must use at least $\frac{1}{2}\text{rank}(\tau_{ijk} + \tau_{jik})$ chain multiplications altogether. [*Hint:* Show that the minimum number of chain multiplications is the minimum rank of (t_{ijk}) taken over all tensors (t_{ijk}) such that $t_{ijk} + t_{jik} = \tau_{ijk} + \tau_{jik}$ for all i, j, k.] Conclude that if a polynomial chain evaluates a set of bilinear forms (47) corresponding to a tensor (t_{ijk}), whether normal or abnormal, it must use at least $\frac{1}{2}\text{rank}(t_{ijk})$ chain multiplications.

57. [*M20*] Show that fast Fourier transforms can be used to compute the coefficients of the product $x(u)y(u)$ of two given polynomials of degree n, using $O(n \log n)$ operations of (exact) addition and multiplication of complex numbers. [*Hint:* Consider the product of Fourier transforms of the coefficients.]

58. [*HM28*] (a) Show that any realization (A, B, C) of the polynomial multiplication tensor (55) must have the following property: Any nonzero linear combination of the three rows of A must be a vector with at least four nonzero elements; and any nonzero linear combination of the four rows of B must have at least three nonzero elements. (b) Find a realization (A, B, C) of (55) that uses only 0, +1, and −1 as elements, where $r = 8$. Try to use as many 0s as possible.

▶ **59.** [*M40*] (H. J. Nussbaumer, 1980.) The text defines the cyclic convolution of two sequences $(x_0, x_1, \ldots, x_{n-1})$ and $(y_0, y_1, \ldots, y_{n-1})$ to be the sequence $(z_0, z_1, \ldots, z_{n-1})$ where $z_k = x_0 y_k + \cdots + x_k y_0 + x_{k+1} y_{n-1} + \cdots + x_{n-1} y_{k+1}$. Let us define the *negacyclic convolution* similarly, but with

$$z_k = x_0 y_k + \cdots + x_k y_0 - (x_{k+1} y_{n-1} + \cdots + x_{n-1} y_{k+1}).$$

Construct efficient algorithms for cyclic and negacyclic convolution over the integers when n is a power of 2. Your algorithms should deal entirely with integers, and they should perform at most $O(n \log n)$ multiplications and at most $O(n \log n \log \log n)$ additions or subtractions or divisions of even numbers by 2. [*Hint:* A cyclic convolution of order $2n$ can be reduced to cyclic and negacyclic convolutions of order n, using (59).]

60. [*M27*] (V. Y. Pan.) The problem of $(m \times n)$ times $(n \times s)$ matrix multiplication corresponds to an $mn \times ns \times sm$ tensor $(t_{\langle i,j'\rangle\langle j,k'\rangle\langle k,i'\rangle})$ where $t_{\langle i,j'\rangle\langle j,k'\rangle\langle k,i'\rangle} = 1$ if and only if $i' = i$ and $j' = j$ and $k' = k$. The rank of this tensor $T(m, n, s)$ is the smallest number r such that numbers $a_{ij'l}$, $b_{jk'l}$, $c_{ki'l}$ exist satisfying

$$\sum_{\substack{1 \le i \le m \\ 1 \le j \le n \\ 1 \le k \le s}} x_{ij} y_{jk} z_{ki} = \sum_{1 \le l \le r} \left(\sum_{\substack{1 \le i \le m \\ 1 \le j' \le n}} a_{ij'l} x_{ij'} \right) \left(\sum_{\substack{1 \le j \le n \\ 1 \le k' \le s}} b_{jk'l} y_{jk'} \right) \left(\sum_{\substack{1 \le k \le s \\ 1 \le i' \le m}} c_{ki'l} z_{ki'} \right).$$

Let $M(n)$ be the rank of $T(n, n, n)$. The purpose of this exercise is to exploit the symmetry of such a trilinear representation, obtaining efficient realizations of matrix multiplication over the integers when $m = n = s = 2\nu$. For convenience we divide the indices $\{1, \ldots, n\}$ into two subsets $O = \{1, 3, \ldots, n-1\}$ and $E = \{2, 4, \ldots, n\}$ of ν elements each, and we set up a one-to-one correspondence between O and E by the rule $\tilde{i} = i + 1$ if $i \in O$; $\tilde{i} = i - 1$ if $i \in E$. Thus we have $\tilde{\tilde{i}} = i$ for all indices i.

a) The identity

$$abc + ABC = (a + A)(b + B)(c + C) - (a + A)bC - A(b + B)c - aB(c + C)$$

implies that

$$\sum_{1 \leq i,j,k \leq n} x_{ij} y_{jk} z_{ki} = \sum_{(i,j,k) \in S} (x_{ij} + x_{\bar{k}\bar{i}})(y_{jk} + y_{\bar{i}\bar{j}})(z_{ki} + z_{\bar{j}\bar{k}}) - \Sigma_1 - \Sigma_2 - \Sigma_3,$$

where $S = E \times E \times E \cup E \times E \times O \cup E \times O \times E \cup O \times E \times E$ is the set of all triples of indices containing at most one odd index; Σ_1 is the sum of all terms of the form $(x_{ij} + x_{\bar{k}\bar{i}})y_{jk} z_{\bar{j}\bar{k}}$ for $(i,j,k) \in S$; and Σ_2, Σ_3 similarly are sums of the terms $x_{\bar{k}\bar{i}}(y_{jk} + y_{\bar{i}\bar{j}})z_{ki}$, $x_{ij} y_{\bar{i}\bar{j}}(z_{ki} + z_{\bar{j}\bar{k}})$. Clearly S has $4\nu^3 = \frac{1}{2}n^3$ terms. Show that each of $\Sigma_1, \Sigma_2, \Sigma_3$ can be realized as the sum of $3\nu^2$ trilinear terms; furthermore, if the 3ν triples of the forms $(i,i,\bar{i})$ and $(i,\bar{i},i)$ and $(\bar{i},i,i)$ are removed from S, we can modify $\Sigma_1, \Sigma_2,$ and Σ_3 in such a way that the identity is still valid, without adding any new trilinear terms. Thus $M(n) \leq \frac{1}{2}n^3 + \frac{9}{4}n^2 - \frac{3}{2}n$ when n is even.

b) Apply the method of (a) to show that two *independent* matrix multiplication problems of the respective sizes $m \times n \times s$ and $s \times m \times n$ can be performed with $mns + mn + ns + sm$ noncommutative multiplications.

61. [*M26*] Let (t_{ijk}) be a tensor over an arbitrary field. We define $\text{rank}_d(t_{ijk})$ as the minimum value of r such that there is a realization of the form

$$\sum_{l=1}^{r} a_{il}(u) b_{jl}(u) c_{kl}(u) = t_{ijk} u^d + O(u^{d+1}),$$

where $a_{il}(u)$, $b_{jl}(u)$, $c_{kl}(u)$ are polynomials in u over the field. Thus rank_0 is the ordinary rank of a tensor. Prove that

a) $\text{rank}_{d+1}(t_{ijk}) \leq \text{rank}_d(t_{ijk})$;

b) $\text{rank}(t_{ijk}) \leq \binom{d+2}{2} \text{rank}_d(t_{ijk})$;

c) $\text{rank}_d((t_{ijk}) \oplus (t'_{ijk})) \leq \text{rank}_d(t_{ijk}) + \text{rank}_d(t'_{ijk})$, in the sense of exercise 48;

d) $\text{rank}_{d+d'}((t_{ijk}) \otimes (t'_{ijk})) \leq \text{rank}_d(t_{ijk}) \cdot \text{rank}_{d'}(t'_{ijk})$;

e) $\text{rank}_{d+d'}((t_{ijk}) \otimes (t'_{ijk})) \leq \text{rank}_{d'}(r(t'_{ijk}))$, where $r = \text{rank}_d(t_{ijk})$ and rT denotes the direct sum $T \oplus \cdots \oplus T$ of r copies of T.

62. [*M24*] The *border rank* of (t_{ijk}), denoted by $\underline{\text{rank}}(t_{ijk})$, is $\min_{d \geq 0} \text{rank}_d(t_{ijk})$, where rank_d is defined in exercise 61. Prove that the tensor $\left(\begin{smallmatrix} 1 & 0 \\ 0 & 1 \end{smallmatrix}\right)\left(\begin{smallmatrix} 0 & 1 \\ 0 & 0 \end{smallmatrix}\right)$ has rank 3 but border rank 2, over every field.

63. [*HM30*] Let $T(m,n,s)$ be the tensor for matrix multiplication as in exercise 60, and let $M(N)$ be the rank of $T(N,N,N)$.

a) Show that $T(m,n,s) \otimes T(M,N,S) = T(mM,nN,sS)$.

b) Show that $\text{rank}_d(T(mN,nN,sN)) \leq \text{rank}_d(M(N)T(m,n,s))$ (see exercise 61(e)).

c) If $T(m,n,s)$ has rank $\leq r$, show that $M(N) = O(N^{\omega(m,n,s,r)})$ as $N \to \infty$, where $\omega(m,n,s,r) = 3 \log r / \log mns$.

d) If $T(m,n,s)$ has border rank $\leq r$, show that $M(N) = O(N^{\omega(m,n,s,r)}(\log N)^2)$.

64. [*M30*] (A. Schönhage.) Show that $\text{rank}_2(T(3,3,3)) \leq 21$, so $M(N) = O(N^{2.78})$.

▶ **65.** [*M27*] (A. Schönhage.) Show that $\text{rank}_2(T(m,1,n) \oplus T(1,(m-1)(n-1),1)) = mn + 1$. *Hint:* Consider the trilinear form

$$\sum_{i=1}^{m} \sum_{j=1}^{n} (x_i + u X_{ij})(y_j + u Y_{ij})(Z + u^2 z_{ij}) - (x_1 + \cdots + x_m)(y_1 + \cdots + y_n)Z$$

when $\sum_{i=1}^{m} X_{ij} = \sum_{j=1}^{n} Y_{ij} = 0$.

66. [*HM33*] We can now use the result of exercise 65 to sharpen the asymptotic bounds of exercise 63.

a) Prove that the limit $\omega = \lim_{n\to\infty} \log M(n)/\log n$ exists.

b) Prove that $(mns)^{\omega/3} \le \underline{\mathrm{rank}}(T(m,n,s))$.

c) Let t be the tensor $T(m,n,s) \oplus T(M,N,S)$. Prove that $(mns)^{\omega/3} + (MNS)^{\omega/3} \le \underline{\mathrm{rank}}(t)$. *Hint:* Consider direct products of t with itself.

d) Therefore $16^{\omega/3} + 9^{\omega/3} \le 17$, and we have $\omega < 2.55$.

67. [*HM40*] (D. Coppersmith and S. Winograd.) By generalizing exercises 65 and 66 we can obtain even better upper bounds on ω.

a) Say that the tensor (t_{ijk}) is *nondegenerate* if $\mathrm{rank}(t_{i(jk)}) = m$, $\mathrm{rank}(t_{j(ki)}) = n$, and $\mathrm{rank}(t_{k(ij)}) = s$, in the notation of Lemma T. Prove that the tensor $T(m,n,s)$ for $mn \times ns$ matrix multiplication is nondegenerate.

b) Show that the direct sum of nondegenerate tensors is nondegenerate.

c) An $m \times n \times s$ tensor t with realization (A, B, C) of length r is called *improvable* if it is nondegenerate and there are nonzero elements $d_1, \ldots, d_r$ such that $\sum_{l=1}^{r} a_{il}b_{jl}d_l = 0$ for $1 \le i \le m$ and $1 \le j \le n$. Prove that in such a case $t \oplus T(1,q,1)$ has border rank $\le r$, where $q = r - m - n$. *Hint:* There are $q \times r$ matrices V and W such that $\sum_{l=1}^{r} v_{il}b_{jl}d_l = \sum_{l=1}^{r} a_{il}w_{jl}d_l = 0$ and $\sum_{l=1}^{r} v_{il}w_{jl}d_l = \delta_{ij}$ for all relevant i and j.

d) Explain why the result of exercise 65 is a special of (c).

e) Prove that $\mathrm{rank}(T(m,n,s)) \le r$ implies
$$\mathrm{rank}_2\big(T(m,n,s) \oplus T(1, r - n(m+s-1), 1)\big) \le r + n.$$

f) Therefore ω is strictly less than $\log M(n)/\log n$ for all $n > 1$.

g) Generalize (c) to the case where (A, B, C) realizes t only in the weaker sense of exercise 61.

h) From (d) we have $\underline{\mathrm{rank}}(T(3,1,3) \oplus T(1,4,1)) \le 10$; thus by exercise 61(d) we also have $\underline{\mathrm{rank}}(T(9,1,9) \oplus 2T(3,4,3) \oplus T(1,16,1)) \le 100$. Prove that if we simply delete the rows of A and B that correspond to the $16 + 16$ variables of $T(1,16,1)$, we obtain a realization of $T(9,1,9) \oplus 2T(3,4,3)$ that is improvable. Therefore we have in fact $\underline{\mathrm{rank}}(T(9,1,9) \oplus 2T(3,4,3) \oplus T(1,34,1)) \le 100$.

i) Generalizing exercise 66(c), show that
$$\sum_{p=1}^{t} (m_p n_p s_p)^{\omega/3} \le \underline{\mathrm{rank}}\Big(\bigoplus_{p=1}^{t} T(m_p, n_p, s_p)\Big).$$

j) Therefore $\omega < 2.5$.

68. [*M46*] Is there a way to evaluate the polynomial
$$\sum_{1 \le i < j \le n} x_i x_j = x_1 x_2 + \cdots + x_{n-1} x_n$$

with fewer than $n - 1$ multiplications and $2n - 4$ additions? (There are $\binom{n}{2}$ terms.)

▶ **69.** [*HM27*] (V. Strassen, 1973.) Show that the determinant (31) of an $n \times n$ matrix can be evaluated by doing $O(n^5)$ multiplications and $O(n^5)$ additions or subtractions, and no divisions. [*Hint:* Consider $\det(I + Y)$ where $Y = X - I$.]

▶ **70.** [*HM25*] The *characteristic polynomial* $f_X(\lambda)$ of a matrix X is defined to be $\det(\lambda I - X)$. Prove that if $X = \left(\begin{smallmatrix} x & u \\ v & Y \end{smallmatrix}\right)$, where X, u, v, and Y are respectively of sizes $n \times n$, $1 \times (n-1)$, $(n-1) \times 1$, and $(n-1) \times (n-1)$, we have

$$f_X(\lambda) = f_Y(\lambda) \left(\lambda - x - \frac{uv}{\lambda} - \frac{uYv}{\lambda^2} - \frac{uY^2v}{\lambda^3} - \cdots \right).$$

Show that this relation allows us to compute the coefficients of f_X with about $\frac{1}{4}n^4$ multiplications, $\frac{1}{4}n^4$ addition-subtractions, and no divisions. *Hint:* Use the identity

$$\begin{pmatrix} A & B \\ C & D \end{pmatrix} = \begin{pmatrix} I & 0 \\ 0 & D \end{pmatrix} \begin{pmatrix} A - BD^{-1}C & B \\ 0 & I \end{pmatrix} \begin{pmatrix} I & 0 \\ D^{-1}C & I \end{pmatrix},$$

which holds for any matrices A, B, C, and D of respective sizes $l \times l$, $l \times m$, $m \times l$, and $m \times m$ when D is nonsingular.

▶ **71.** [*HM30*] A *quolynomial chain* is like a polynomial chain except that it allows division as well as addition, subtraction, and multiplication. Prove that if $f(x_1, \ldots, x_n)$ can be computed by a quolynomial chain that has m chain multiplications and d divisions, then $f(x_1, \ldots, x_n)$ and all n of its partial derivatives $\partial f(x_1, \ldots, x_n)/\partial x_k$ for $1 \le k \le n$ can be computed by a single quolynomial chain that has at most $3m+d$ chain multiplications and $2d$ divisions. (Consequently, for example, any efficient method for calculating the determinant of a matrix leads to an efficient method for calculating all of its cofactors, hence an efficient method for computing the inverse matrix.)

72. [*M48*] Is it possible to determine the rank of any given tensor (t_{ijk}) over, say, the field of rational numbers, in a finite number of steps?

73. [*HM25*] (J. Morgenstern, 1973.) Prove that any polynomial chain for the discrete Fourier transform (37) has at least $\frac{1}{2}m_1 \ldots m_n \lg m_1 \ldots m_n$ addition-subtractions, if there are no chain multiplications and if every parameter multiplication is by a complex-valued constant with $|\alpha_j| \le 1$. *Hint:* Consider the matrices of the linear transformations computed by the first k steps. How big can their determinants be?

74. [*HM35*] (A. Nozaki, 1978.) Most of the theory of polynomial evaluation is concerned with bounds on chain multiplications, but multiplication by noninteger constants can also be essential. The purpose of this exercise is to develop an appropriate theory of constants. Let us say that vectors v_1, $\ldots$, v_s of real numbers are *Z-dependent* if there are integers $(k_1, \ldots, k_s)$ such that $\gcd(k_1, \ldots, k_s) = 1$ and $k_1 v_1 + \cdots + k_s v_s$ is an all-integer vector. If no such $(k_1, \ldots, k_s)$ exist, the vectors v_1, $\ldots$, v_s are *Z-independent*.

  a) Prove that if the columns of an $r \times s$ matrix V are Z-independent, so are the columns of VU, when U is any $s \times s$ unimodular matrix (a matrix of integers whose determinant is ± 1).

  b) Let V be an $r \times s$ matrix with Z-independent columns. Prove that a polynomial chain to evaluate the elements of Vx from inputs x_1, $\ldots$, x_s, where $x = (x_1, \ldots, x_s)^T$, needs at least s multiplications.

  c) Let V be an $r \times t$ matrix having s columns that are Z-independent. Prove that a polynomial chain to evaluate the elements of Vx from inputs x_1, $\ldots$, x_t, where $x = (x_1, \ldots, x_t)^T$, needs at least s multiplications.

  d) Show how to compute the pair of values $\{x/2 + y, x + y/3\}$ from x and y using only one multiplication, although two multiplications are needed to compute the pair $\{x/2 + y, x + y/2\}$.

*4.7. MANIPULATION OF POWER SERIES

IF WE ARE GIVEN two power series

$$U(z) = U_0 + U_1 z + U_2 z^2 + \cdots, \qquad V(z) = V_0 + V_1 z + V_2 z^2 + \cdots, \qquad (1)$$

whose coefficients belong to a field, we can form their sum, their product, and sometimes their quotient, to obtain new power series. A polynomial is obviously a special case of a power series, in which there are only finitely many terms.

Of course, only a finite number of terms can be represented and stored within a computer, so it makes sense to ask whether power series arithmetic is even possible on computers; and if it is possible, what makes it different from polynomial arithmetic? The answer is that we work with only the first N coefficients of the power series, where N is a parameter that may in principle be arbitrarily large; instead of ordinary polynomial arithmetic, we are essentially doing polynomial arithmetic modulo z^N, and this often leads to a somewhat different point of view. Furthermore, special operations like "reversion" can be performed on power series but not on polynomials, since polynomials are not closed under those operations.

Manipulation of power series has many applications to numerical analysis, but perhaps its greatest use is the determination of asymptotic expansions (as we have seen in Section 1.2.11.3), or the calculation of quantities defined by certain generating functions. The latter applications make it desirable to calculate the coefficients exactly, instead of with floating point arithmetic. All of the algorithms in this section, with obvious exceptions, can be done using rational operations only, so the techniques of Section 4.5.1 can be used to obtain exact results when desired.

The calculation of $W(z) = U(z) \pm V(z)$ is, of course, trivial, since we have $W_n = [z^n] W(z) = U_n \pm V_n$ for $n = 0, 1, 2, \ldots$. It is also easy to calculate the coefficients of $W(z) = U(z)V(z)$, using the familiar convolution rule

$$W_n = \sum_{k=0}^{n} U_k V_{n-k} = U_0 V_n + U_1 V_{n-1} + \cdots + U_n V_0. \qquad (2)$$

The quotient $W(z) = U(z)/V(z)$, when $V_0 \neq 0$, can be obtained by interchanging U and W in (2); we obtain the rule

$$W_n = \left(U_n - \sum_{k=0}^{n-1} W_k V_{n-k} \right) \Big/ V_0$$

$$= (U_n - W_0 V_n - W_1 V_{n-1} - \cdots - W_{n-1} V_1)/V_0. \qquad (3)$$

This recurrence relation for the W's makes it easy to determine $W_0, W_1, W_2, \ldots$ successively, without inputting U_n and V_n until after W_{n-1} has been computed. A power series manipulation algorithm with that property is traditionally called *online*; with an online algorithm, we can determine N coefficients $W_0, W_1, \ldots, W_{N-1}$ of the result without knowing N in advance, so we could in principle run the algorithm indefinitely and compute the entire power series. We can also run an online algorithm until any desired condition is met. (The opposite of "online" is "offline.")

If the coefficients U_k and V_k are integers but the W_k are not, the recurrence relation (3) involves computation with fractions. This can be avoided by the all-integer approach described in exercise 2.

Let us now consider the operation of computing $W(z) = V(z)^\alpha$, where α is an "arbitrary" power. For example, we could calculate the square root of $V(z)$ by taking $\alpha = \frac{1}{2}$, or we could find $V(z)^{-10}$ or even $V(z)^\pi$. If V_m is the first nonzero coefficient of $V(z)$, we have

$$V(z) = V_m z^m \left(1 + (V_{m+1}/V_m)z + (V_{m+2}/V_m)z^2 + \cdots\right),$$
$$V(z)^\alpha = V_m^\alpha z^{\alpha m} \left(1 + (V_{m+1}/V_m)z + (V_{m+2}/V_m)z^2 + \cdots\right)^\alpha. \tag{4}$$

This will be a power series if and only if αm is a nonnegative integer. If α itself is not an integer, there's more than one possibility for $V_m^\alpha z^{\alpha m}$ here.

From (4) we can see that the problem of computing general powers can be reduced to the case that $V_0 = 1$; then the problem is to compute the coefficients of

$$W(z) = (1 + V_1 z + V_2 z^2 + V_3 z^3 + \cdots)^\alpha. \tag{5}$$

Clearly $W_0 = 1^\alpha = 1$.

The obvious way to find the coefficients of (5) is to use the binomial theorem, Eq. 1.2.9–(19), or (if α is a positive integer) to try repeated squaring as in Section 4.6.3. But Leonhard Euler discovered a much simpler and more efficient way to obtain power series powers [*Introductio in Analysin Infinitorum* **1** (1748), §76]: If $W(z) = V(z)^\alpha$, we have by differentiation

$$W_1 + 2W_2 z + 3W_3 z^2 + \cdots = W'(z) = \alpha V(z)^{\alpha-1} V'(z); \tag{6}$$

therefore

$$W'(z)V(z) = \alpha W(z)V'(z). \tag{7}$$

If we now equate the coefficients of z^{n-1} in (7), we find that

$$\sum_{k=0}^{n} k W_k V_{n-k} = \alpha \sum_{k=0}^{n} (n-k) W_k V_{n-k}, \tag{8}$$

and this gives us a useful computational rule valid for all $n \geq 1$:

$$W_n = \sum_{k=1}^{n} \left(\left(\frac{\alpha+1}{n}\right)k - 1\right) V_k W_{n-k}$$
$$= \left((\alpha+1-n)V_1 W_{n-1} + (2\alpha+2-n)V_2 W_{n-2} + \cdots + n\alpha V_n W_0\right)/n. \tag{9}$$

Equation (9) leads to a simple online algorithm by which we can successively determine $W_1, W_2, \ldots$, using approximately $2n$ multiplications to compute the nth coefficient. Notice the special case $\alpha = -1$, in which (9) becomes the special case $U(z) = V_0 = 1$ of (3).

A similar technique can be used to form $f(V(z))$ when f is any function that satisfies a simple differential equation. (For example, see exercise 4.) A comparatively straightforward "power series method" is often used to obtain

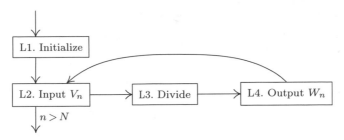

Fig. 17. Power series reversion by Algorithm L.

the solution of differential equations; this technique is explained in nearly all textbooks about differential equations.

Reversion of series. The transformation of power series that is perhaps of greatest interest is called "reversion of series." This problem is to solve the equation

$$z = t + V_2 t^2 + V_3 t^3 + V_4 t^4 + \cdots \tag{10}$$

for t, obtaining the coefficients of the power series

$$t = z + W_2 z^2 + W_3 z^3 + W_4 z^4 + \cdots. \tag{11}$$

Several interesting ways to achieve such a reversion are known. We might say that the "classical" method is one based on Lagrange's remarkable inversion formula [*Mémoires Acad. Royale des Sciences et Belles-Lettres de Berlin* **24** (1768), 251–326], which states that

$$W_n = \frac{1}{n} [t^{n-1}] (1 + V_2 t + V_3 t^2 + \cdots)^{-n}. \tag{12}$$

For example, we have $(1-t)^{-5} = \binom{4}{4} + \binom{5}{4}t + \binom{6}{4}t^2 + \cdots$; hence the fifth coefficient, W_5, in the reversion of $z = t - t^2$ is equal to $\binom{8}{4}/5 = 14$. This checks with the formulas for enumerating binary trees in Section 2.3.4.4.

Relation (12), which has a simple algorithmic proof (see exercise 16), shows that we can revert the series (10) if we successively compute the negative powers $(1 + V_2 t + V_3 t^2 + \cdots)^{-n}$ for $n = 1, 2, 3, \ldots$. A straightforward application of this idea would lead to an online reversion algorithm that uses approximately $N^3/2$ multiplications to find N coefficients, but Eq. (9) makes it possible to work with only the first n coefficients of $(1 + V_2 t + V_3 t^2 + \cdots)^{-n}$, obtaining an online algorithm that requires only about $N^3/6$ multiplications.

Algorithm L (*Lagrangian power series reversion*). This online algorithm inputs the value of V_n in (10) and outputs the value of W_n in (11), for $n = 2, 3, 4,$ $\ldots, N$. (The number N need not be specified in advance; any desired termination criterion may be substituted.)

L1. [Initialize.] Set $n \leftarrow 1$, $U_0 \leftarrow 1$. (The relation

$$(1 + V_2 t + V_3 t^2 + \cdots)^{-n} = U_0 + U_1 t + \cdots + U_{n-1} t^{n-1} + O(t^n) \tag{13}$$

will be maintained throughout this algorithm.)

L2. [Input V_n.] Increase n by 1. If $n > N$, the algorithm terminates; otherwise input the next coefficient, V_n.

L3. [Divide.] Set $U_k \leftarrow U_k - U_{k-1}V_2 - \cdots - U_1V_k - U_0V_{k+1}$, for $k = 1, 2, \ldots,$ $n - 2$ (in this order); then set

$$U_{n-1} \leftarrow -2U_{n-2}V_2 - 3U_{n-3}V_3 - \cdots - (n-1)U_1V_{n-1} - nU_0V_n.$$

$\big($We have thereby divided $U(z)$ by $V(z)/z$; see (3) and (9).$\big)$

L4. [Output W_n.] Output U_{n-1}/n (which is W_n) and return to L2.   ∎

When applied to the example $z = t - t^2$, Algorithm L computes

n	V_n	U_0	U_1	U_2	U_3	U_4	W_n
1	1	1					1
2	-1	1	2				1
3	0	1	3	6			2
4	0	1	4	10	20		5
5	0	1	5	15	35	70	14

Exercise 8 shows that a slight modification of Algorithm L will solve a considerably more general problem with only a little more effort.

Let us now consider solving the equation

$$U_1z + U_2z^2 + U_3z^3 + \cdots = t + V_2t^2 + V_3t^3 + \cdots \tag{14}$$

for t, obtaining the coefficients of the power series

$$t = W_1z + W_2z^2 + W_3z^3 + W_4z^4 + \cdots. \tag{15}$$

Eq. (10) is the special case $U_1 = 1$, $U_2 = U_3 = \cdots = 0$. If $U_1 \neq 0$, we may assume that $U_1 = 1$, if we replace z by (U_1z); but we shall consider the general equation (14), since U_1 might equal zero.

Algorithm T (*General power series reversion*). This online algorithm inputs the values of U_n and V_n in (14) and outputs the value of W_n in (15), for $n = 1, 2, 3, \ldots, N$. An auxiliary matrix T_{mn}, $1 \leq m \leq n \leq N$, is used in the calculations.

T1. [Initialize.] Set $n \leftarrow 1$. Let the first two inputs (namely, U_1 and V_1) be stored in T_{11} and V_1, respectively. (We must have $V_1 = 1$.)

T2. [Output W_n.] Output the value of T_{1n} (which is W_n).

T3. [Input U_n, V_n.] Increase n by 1. If $n > N$, the algorithm terminates; otherwise store the next two inputs (namely, U_n and V_n) in T_{1n} and V_n.

T4. [Multiply.] Set

$$T_{mn} \leftarrow T_{11}T_{m-1,n-1} + T_{12}T_{m-1,n-2} + \cdots + T_{1,n-m+1}T_{m-1,m-1}$$

and $T_{1n} \leftarrow T_{1n} - V_mT_{mn}$, for $2 \leq m \leq n$. (After this step we have

$$t^m = T_{mm}z^m + T_{m,m+1}z^{m+1} + \cdots + T_{mn}z^n + O(z^{n+1}), \tag{16}$$

for $1 \leq m \leq n$. It is easy to verify (16) by induction for $m \geq 2$, and when $m = 1$, we have $U_n = T_{1n} + V_2T_{2n} + \cdots + V_nT_{nn}$ by (14) and (16).) Return to step T2.   ∎

Equation (16) explains the mechanism of this algorithm, which is due to Henry C. Thacher, Jr. [*CACM* **9** (1966), 10–11]. The running time is essentially the same as Algorithm L, but considerably more storage space is required. An example of this algorithm is worked out in exercise 9.

Still another approach to power series reversion has been proposed by R. P. Brent and H. T. Kung [*JACM* **25** (1978), 581–595], based on the fact that standard iterative procedures used to find roots of equations over the real numbers can also be applied to equations over power series. In particular, we can consider Newton's method for computing approximations to a real number t such that $f(t) = 0$, given a function f that is well-behaved near t: If x is a good approximation to t, then $\phi(x) = x - f(x)/f'(x)$ will be even better, for if we write $x = t + \epsilon$ we have $f(x) = f(t) + \epsilon f'(t) + O(\epsilon^2)$, $f'(x) = f'(t) + O(\epsilon)$; consequently $\phi(x) = t + \epsilon - \big(0 + \epsilon f'(t) + O(\epsilon^2)\big)/\big(f'(t) + O(\epsilon)\big) = t + O(\epsilon^2)$. Applying this idea to power series, let $f(x) = V(x) - U(z)$, where U and V are the power series in Eq. (14). We wish to find the power series t in z such that $f(t) = 0$. Let $x = W_1 z + \cdots + W_{n-1} z^{n-1} = t + O(z^n)$ be an "approximation" to t of order n; then $\phi(x) = x - f(x)/f'(x)$ will be an approximation of order $2n$, since the assumptions of Newton's method hold for this f and t.

In other words, we can use the following procedure:

Algorithm N (*General power series reversion by Newton's method*). This "semi-online" algorithm inputs the values of U_n and V_n in (14) for $2^k \leq n < 2^{k+1}$ and then outputs the values of W_n in (15) for $2^k \leq n < 2^{k+1}$, thereby producing its answers in batches of 2^k at a time, for $k = 0, 1, 2, \ldots, K$.

N1. [Initialize.] Set $N \leftarrow 1$. (We will have $N = 2^k$.) Input the first coefficients U_1 and V_1 (where $V_1 = 1$), and set $W_1 \leftarrow U_1$.

N2. [Output.] Output W_n for $N \leq n < 2N$.

N3. [Input.] Set $N \leftarrow 2N$. If $N > 2^K$, the algorithm terminates; otherwise input the values U_n and V_n for $N \leq n < 2N$.

N4. [Newtonian step.] Use an algorithm for power series composition (see exercise 11) to evaluate the coefficients Q_j and R_j ($0 \leq j < N$) in the power series

$$U_1 z + \cdots + U_{2N-1} z^{2N-1} - V(W_1 z + \cdots + W_{N-1} z^{N-1})$$
$$= R_0 z^N + R_1 z^{N+1} + \cdots + R_{N-1} z^{2N-1} + O(z^{2N}),$$
$$V'(W_1 z + \cdots + W_{N-1} z^{N-1}) = Q_0 + Q_1 z + \cdots + Q_{N-1} z^{N-1} + O(z^N),$$

where $V(x) = x + V_2 x^2 + \cdots$ and $V'(x) = 1 + 2V_2 x + \cdots$. Then set $W_N, \ldots,$ W_{2N-1} to the coefficients in the power series

$$\frac{R_0 + R_1 z + \cdots + R_{N-1} z^{N-1}}{Q_0 + Q_1 z + \cdots + Q_{N-1} z^{N-1}} = W_N + \cdots + W_{2N-1} z^{N-1} + O(z^N)$$

and return to step N2.   ∎

The running time for this algorithm to obtain the coefficients up to $N = 2^K$ is $T(N)$, where

$$T(2N) = T(N) + (\text{time to do step N4}) + O(N). \qquad (17)$$

Straightforward algorithms for composition and division in step N4 will take order N^3 steps, so Algorithm N will run slower than Algorithm T. However, Brent and Kung have found a way to do the required composition of power series with $O(N \log N)^{3/2}$ arithmetic operations, and exercise 6 gives an even faster algorithm for division; hence (17) shows that power series reversion can be achieved by doing only $O(N \log N)^{3/2}$ operations as $N \to \infty$. (On the other hand the constant of proportionality is such that N must be really large before Algorithms L and T lose out to this "high-speed" method.)

Historical note: J. N. Bramhall and M. A. Chapple published the first $O(N^3)$ method for power series reversion in *CACM* **4** (1961), 317–318, 503. It was an offline algorithm essentially equivalent to the method of exercise 16, with running time approximately the same as that of Algorithms L and T.

Iteration of series. If we want to study the behavior of an iterative process $x_n \leftarrow f(x_{n-1})$, we are interested in studying the n-fold composition of a given function f with itself, namely $x_n = f\big(f(\ldots f(x_0)\ldots)\big)$. Let us define $f^{[0]}(x) = x$ and $f^{[n]}(x) = f\big(f^{[n-1]}(x)\big)$, so that

$$f^{[m+n]}(x) = f^{[m]}\big(f^{[n]}(x)\big) \qquad (18)$$

for all integers m, $n \geq 0$. In many cases the notation $f^{[n]}(x)$ makes sense also when n is a negative integer, namely if $f^{[n]}$ and $f^{[-n]}$ are inverse functions such that $x = f^{[n]}\big(f^{[-n]}(x)\big)$; if inverse functions are unique, (18) holds for *all* integers m and n. Reversion of series is essentially the operation of finding the inverse power series $f^{[-1]}(x)$; for example, Eqs. (10) and (11) essentially state that $z = V\big(W(z)\big)$ and that $t = W\big(V(t)\big)$, so $W = V^{[-1]}$.

Suppose we are given two power series $V(z) = z + V_2 z^2 + \cdots$ and $W(z) = z + W_2 z^2 + \cdots$ such that $W = V^{[-1]}$. Let u be any nonzero constant, and consider the function

$$U(z) = W\big(uV(z)\big). \qquad (19)$$

It is easy to see that $U\big(U(z)\big) = W\big(u^2 V(z)\big)$, and in general that

$$U^{[n]}(z) = W\big(u^n V(z)\big) \qquad (20)$$

for all integers n. Therefore we have a simple expression for the nth iterate $U^{[n]}$, which can be calculated with roughly the same amount of work for all n. Furthermore, we can even use (20) to define $U^{[n]}$ for noninteger values of n; the "half iterate" $U^{[1/2]}$, for example, is a function such that $U^{[1/2]}\big(U^{[1/2]}(z)\big) = U(z)$. (There are two such functions $U^{[1/2]}$, obtained by using $\sqrt{u}$ and $-\sqrt{u}$ as the value of $u^{1/2}$ in (20).)

We obtained the simple state of affairs in (20) by starting with V and u, then defining U. But in practice we generally want to go the other way: Starting with some given function U, we want to find V and u such that (19) holds, namely such that

$$V\big(U(z)\big) = u V(z). \tag{21}$$

Such a function V is called the *Schröder function* of U, because it was introduced by Ernst Schröder in *Math. Annalen* **3** (1871), 296–322. Let us now look at the problem of finding the Schröder function $V(z) = z + V_2 z^2 + \cdots$ of a given power series $U(z) = U_1 z + U_2 z^2 + \cdots$. Clearly $u = U_1$ if (21) is to hold.

Expanding (21) with $u = U_1$ and equating coefficients of z leads to a sequence of equations that begins

$$U_1^2 V_2 + U_2 = U_1 V_2,$$

$$U_1^3 V_3 + 2 U_1 U_2 V_2 + U_3 = U_1 V_3,$$

$$U_1^4 V_4 + 3 U_1^2 U_2 V_3 + 2 U_1 U_3 V_2 + U_2^2 V_2 + U_4 = U_1 V_4,$$

and so on. Clearly there is no solution when $U_1 = 0$ (unless trivially $U_2 = U_3 = \cdots = 0$); otherwise there is a unique solution unless U_1 is a root of unity. We might have expected that something funny would happen when $U_1^n = 1$, since Eq. (20) tells us that $U^{[n]}(z) = z$ if the Schröder function exists in that case. For the moment let us assume that U_1 is nonzero and not a root of unity; then the Schröder function does exist, and the next question is how to compute it without doing too much work.

The following procedure has been suggested by R. P. Brent and J. F. Traub. Equation (21) leads to subproblems of a similar but more complicated form, so we set ourselves a more general task whose subtasks have the same form: Let us try to find $V(z) = V_0 + V_1 z + \cdots + V_{n-1} z^{n-1}$ such that

$$V\big(U(z)\big) = W(z) V(z) + S(z) + O(z^n), \tag{22}$$

given $U(z)$, $W(z)$, $S(z)$, and n, where n is a power of 2 and $U(0) = 0$. If $n = 1$ we simply let $V_0 = S(0)/(1 - W(0))$, with $V_0 = 1$ if $S(0) = 0$ and $W(0) = 1$. Furthermore it is possible to go from n to $2n$: First we find $R(z)$ such that

$$V\big(U(z)\big) = W(z) V(z) + S(z) - z^n R(z) + O(z^{2n}). \tag{23}$$

Then we compute

$$\hat{W}(z) = W(z)\big(z/U(z)\big)^n + O(z^n), \qquad \hat{S}(z) = R(z)\big(z/U(z)\big)^n + O(z^n), \tag{24}$$

and find $\hat{V}(z) = V_n + V_{n+1} z + \cdots + V_{2n-1} z^{n-1}$ such that

$$\hat{V}\big(U(z)\big) = \hat{W}(z)\hat{V}(z) + \hat{S}(z) + O(z^n). \tag{25}$$

It follows that the function $V^*(z) = V(z) + z^n \hat{V}(z)$ satisfies

$$V^*\big(U(z)\big) = W(z) V^*(z) + S(z) + O(z^{2n}),$$

as desired.

The running time $T(n)$ of this procedure satisfies

$$T(2n) = 2T(n) + C(n), \tag{26}$$

where $C(n)$ is the time to compute $R(z)$, $\hat{W}(z)$, and $\hat{S}(z)$. The function $C(n)$ is dominated by the time to compute $V(U(z))$ modulo z^{2n}, and $C(n)$ presumably grows faster than order $n^{1+\epsilon}$; therefore the solution $T(n)$ to (26) will be of order $C(n)$. For example, if $C(n) = cn^3$ we have $T(n) \approx \frac{4}{3}cn^3$; or if $C(n)$ is $O(n\log n)^{3/2}$ using "fast" composition, we have $T(n) = O(n\log n)^{3/2}$.

The procedure breaks down when $W(0) = 1$ and $S(0) \neq 0$, so we need to investigate when this can happen. It is easy to prove by induction on n that the solution of (22) by the Brent–Traub method entails consideration of exactly n subproblems, in which the coefficient of $V(z)$ on the right-hand side takes the respective values $W(z)\bigl(z/U(z)\bigr)^j + O(z^n)$ for $0 \leq j < n$ in some order. If $W(0) = U_1$ and if U_1 is not a root of unity, we therefore have $W(0) = 1$ only when $j = 1$; the procedure will fail in this case only if (22) has no solution for $n = 2$.

Consequently the Schröder function for U can be found by solving (22) for $n = 2, 4, 8, 16, \ldots$, with $W(z) = U_1$ and $S(z) = 0$, whenever U_1 is nonzero and not a root of unity.

If $U_1 = 1$, there is no Schröder function unless $U(z) = z$. But Brent and Traub have found a fast way to compute $U^{[n]}(z)$ even when $U_1 = 1$, by making use of a function $V(z)$ such that

$$V\bigl(U(z)\bigr) = U'(z)V(z). \tag{27}$$

If two functions $U(z)$ and $\hat{U}(z)$ both satisfy (27), for the same V, it is easy to check that their composition $U\bigl(\hat{U}(z)\bigr)$ does too; therefore all iterates of $U(z)$ are solutions of (27). Suppose we have $U(z) = z + U_k z^k + U_{k+1}z^{k+1} + \cdots$ where $k \geq 2$ and $U_k \neq 0$. Then it can be shown that there is a unique power series of the form $V(z) = z^k + V_{k+1}z^{k+1} + V_{k+2}z^{k+2} + \cdots$ satisfying (27). Conversely if such a function $V(z)$ is given, and if $k \geq 2$ and U_k are given, then there is a unique power series of the form $U(z) = z + U_k z^k + U_{k+1}z^{k+1} + \cdots$ satisfying (27). The desired iterate $U^{[n]}(z)$ is the unique power series $P(z)$ satisfying

$$V\bigl(P(z)\bigr) = P'(z)V(z) \tag{28}$$

such that $P(z) = z + nU_k z^k + \cdots$. Both $V(z)$ and $P(z)$ can be found by appropriate algorithms (see exercise 14).

If U_1 is a kth root of unity, but not equal to 1, the same method can be applied to the function $U^{[k]}(z) = z + \cdots$, and $U^{[k]}(z)$ can be found from $U(z)$ by doing $l(k)$ composition operations (see Section 4.6.3). We can also handle the case $U_1 = 0$: If $U(z) = U_k z^k + U_{k+1}z^{k+1} + \cdots$ where $k \geq 2$ and $U_k \neq 0$, the idea is to find a solution to the equation $V\bigl(U(z)\bigr) = U_k V(z)^k$; then

$$U^{[n]}(z) = V^{[-1]}\bigl(U_k^{[(k^n-1)/(k-1)]}V(z)^{k^n}\bigr). \tag{29}$$

Finally, if $U(z) = U_0 + U_1 z + \cdots$ where $U_0 \neq 0$, let α be a "fixed point" such that $U(\alpha) = \alpha$, and let

$$\hat{U}(z) = U(\alpha + z) - \alpha = zU'(\alpha) + z^2U''(\alpha)/2! + \cdots; \tag{30}$$

then $U^{[n]}(z) = \hat{U}^{[n]}(z-\alpha)+\alpha$. Further details can be found in Brent and Traub's paper [*SICOMP* **9** (1980), 54–66]. The V function of (27) had previously been considered by M. Kuczma, *Functional Equations in a Single Variable* (Warsaw: PWN–Polish Scientific, 1968), Lemma 9.4, and implicitly by E. Jabotinsky a few years earlier (see exercise 23).

Algebraic functions. The coefficients of each power series $W(z)$ that satisfies a general equation of the form

$$A_n(z)W(z)^n + \cdots + A_1(z)W(z) + A_0(z) = 0, \tag{31}$$

where each $A_i(z)$ is a polynomial, can be computed efficiently by using methods due to H. T. Kung and J. F. Traub; see *JACM* **25** (1978), 245–260. See also D. V. Chudnovsky and G. V. Chudnovsky, *J. Complexity* **2** (1986), 271–294; **3** (1987), 1–25.

EXERCISES

1. [*M10*] The text explains how to divide $U(z)$ by $V(z)$ when $V_0 \neq 0$; how should the division be done when $V_0 = 0$?

2. [*20*] If the coefficients of $U(z)$ and $V(z)$ are integers and $V_0 \neq 0$, find a recurrence relation for the integers $V_0^{n+1}W_n$, where W_n is defined by (3). How could you use this for power series division?

3. [*M15*] Does formula (9) give the right results when $\alpha = 0$? When $\alpha = 1$?

▸ **4.** [*HM23*] Show that simple modifications of (9) can be used to calculate $e^{V(z)}$ when $V_0 = 0$, and $\ln V(z)$ when $V_0 = 1$.

5. [*M00*] What happens when a power series is reverted twice — that is, if the output of Algorithm L or T is reverted again?

▸ **6.** [*M21*] (H. T. Kung.) Apply Newton's method to the computation of $W(z) = 1/V(z)$, when $V(0) \neq 0$, by finding the power series root of the equation $f(x) = 0$, where $f(x) = x^{-1} - V(z)$.

7. [*M23*] Use Lagrange's inversion formula (12) to find a simple expression for the coefficient W_n in the reversion of $z = t - t^m$.

▸ **8.** [*M25*] If $W(z) = W_1 z + W_2 z^2 + W_3 z^3 + \cdots = G_1 t + G_2 t^2 + G_3 t^3 + \cdots = G(t)$, where $z = V_1 t + V_2 t^2 + V_3 t^3 + \cdots$ and $V_1 \neq 0$, Lagrange proved that

$$W_n = \frac{1}{n}[t^{n-1}]\, G'(t)/(V_1 + V_2 t + V_3 t^2 + \cdots)^n.$$

(Equation (12) is the special case $G_1 = V_1 = 1$, $G_2 = G_3 = \cdots = 0$.) Extend Algorithm L so that it obtains the coefficients $W_1, W_2, \ldots$ in this more general situation, without substantially increasing its running time.

9. [*11*] Find the values of T_{mn} computed by Algorithm T as it determines the first five coefficients in the reversion of $z = t - t^2$.

10. [*M20*] Given that $y = x^\alpha + a_1 x^{\alpha+1} + a_2 x^{\alpha+2} + \cdots$, $\alpha \neq 0$, show how to compute the coefficients in the expansion $x = y^{1/\alpha} + b_2 y^{2/\alpha} + b_3 y^{3/\alpha} + \cdots$.

▸ **11.** [*M25*] (*Composition of power series.*) Let

$$U(z) = U_0 + U_1 z + U_2 z^2 + \cdots \quad \text{and} \quad V(z) = V_1 z + V_2 z^2 + V_3 z^3 + \cdots.$$

Design an algorithm that computes the first N coefficients of $U(V(z))$.

12. [*M20*] Find a connection between polynomial division and power series division: Given polynomials $u(x)$ and $v(x)$ of respective degrees m and n over a field, show how to find the polynomials $q(x)$ and $r(x)$ such that $u(x) = q(x)v(x) + r(x)$ and $\deg(r) < n$, using only operations on power series.

13. [*M27*] (*Rational function approximation.*) It is occasionally desirable to find polynomials whose quotient has the same initial terms as a given power series. For example, if $W(z) = 1 + z + 3z^2 + 7z^3 + \cdots$, there are essentially four different ways to express $W(z)$ as $w_1(z)/w_2(z) + O(z^4)$ where $w_1(z)$ and $w_2(z)$ are polynomials with $\deg(w_1) + \deg(w_2) < 4$:

$$(1 + z + 3z^2 + 7z^3)/1 = 1 + z + 3z^2 + 7z^3 + 0z^4 + \cdots,$$
$$(3 - 4z + 2z^2)/(3 - 7z) = 1 + z + 3z^2 + 7z^3 + \tfrac{49}{3}z^4 + \cdots,$$
$$(1 - z)/(1 - 2z - z^2) = 1 + z + 3z^2 + 7z^3 + 17z^4 + \cdots,$$
$$1/(1 - z - 2z^2 - 2z^3) = 1 + z + 3z^2 + 7z^3 + 15z^4 + \cdots.$$

Rational functions of this kind are commonly called *Padé approximations*, since they were studied extensively by H. E. Padé [*Annales Scient. de l'École Normale Supérieure* (3) **9** (1892), S1–S93; (3) **16** (1899), 395–426].

Show that all Padé approximations $W(z) = w_1(z)/w_2(z) + O(z^N)$ with $\deg(w_1) + \deg(w_2) < N$ can be obtained by applying an extended Euclidean algorithm to the polynomials z^N and $W_0 + W_1 z + \cdots + W_{N-1} z^{N-1}$; and design an all-integer algorithm for the case that each W_i is an integer. [*Hint:* See exercise 4.6.1–26.]

▶ **14.** [*HM30*] Fill in the details of Brent and Traub's method for calculating $U^{[n]}(z)$ when $U(z) = z + U_k z^k + \cdots$, using (27) and (28).

15. [*HM20*] For what functions $U(z)$ does $V(z)$ have the simple form z^k in (27)? What do you deduce about the iterates of $U(z)$?

16. [*HM21*] Let $W(z) = G(t)$ as in exercise 8. The "obvious" way to find the coefficients W_1, W_2, W_3, ... is to proceed as follows: Set $n \leftarrow 1$ and $R_1(t) \leftarrow G(t)$. Then preserve the relation $W_n V(t) + W_{n+1} V(t)^2 + \cdots = R_n(t)$ by repeatedly setting $W_n \leftarrow [t] R_n(t)/V_1$, $R_{n+1}(t) \leftarrow R_n(t)/V(t) - W_n$, $n \leftarrow n + 1$.

Prove Lagrange's formula of exercise 8 by showing that

$$\frac{1}{n}[t^{n-1}] R'_{k+1}(t) t^n/V(t)^n = \frac{1}{n+1}[t^n] R'_k(t) t^{n+1}/V(t)^{n+1}, \quad \text{for all } n \geq 1 \text{ and } k \geq 1.$$

▶ **17.** [*M20*] Given the power series $V(z) = V_1 z + V_2 z^2 + V_3 z^3 + \cdots$, we define the *power matrix* of V as the infinite array of coefficients $v_{nk} = \frac{n!}{k!}[z^n]V(z)^k$; the nth *poweroid* of V is then defined to be $V_n(x) = v_{n0} + v_{n1}x + \cdots + v_{nn}x^n$. Prove that poweroids satisfy the general convolution law

$$V_n(x + y) = \sum_k \binom{n}{k} V_k(x) V_{n-k}(y).$$

(For example, when $V(z) = z$ we have $V_n(x) = x^n$, and this is the binomial theorem. When $V(z) = \ln(1/(1 - z))$ we have $v_{nk} = \begin{bmatrix} n \\ k \end{bmatrix}$ by Eq. 1.2.9–(26); hence the poweroid $V_n(x)$ is $x^{\overline{n}}$, and the identity is the result proved in exercise 1.2.6–33. When $V(z) = e^z - 1$ we have $V_n(x) = \sum_k \begin{Bmatrix} n \\ k \end{Bmatrix} x^k$ and the formula is equivalent to

$$\binom{l+m}{m}\begin{Bmatrix} n \\ l+m \end{Bmatrix} = \sum_k \binom{n}{k}\begin{Bmatrix} k \\ l \end{Bmatrix}\begin{Bmatrix} n-k \\ m \end{Bmatrix},$$

an identity we haven't seen before. Several other triangular arrays of coefficients that arise in combinatorial mathematics and the analysis of algorithms also turn out to be the power matrices of power series.)

18. [*HM22*] Continuing exercise 17, prove that poweroids also satisfy

$$xV_n(x+y) = (x+y)\sum_k \binom{n-1}{k-1} V_k(x)V_{n-k}(y).$$

[*Hint:* Consider the derivative of $e^{xV(z)}$.]

19. [*M25*] Continuing exercise 17, express all the numbers v_{nk} in terms of the numbers $v_n = v_{n1} = n!\,V_n$ of the first column, and find a simple recurrence by which all columns can be computed from the sequence $v_1, v_2, \ldots$. Show in particular that if all the v_n are integers, then all the v_{nk} are integers.

20. [*HM20*] Continuing exercise 17, suppose we have $W(z) = U(V(z))$ and $U_0 = 0$. Prove that the power matrix of W is the product of the power matrices of V and U: $w_{nk} = \sum_j v_{nj}u_{jk}$.

▸ **21.** [*HM27*] Continuing the previous exercises, suppose $V_1 \neq 0$ and let $W(z) = -V^{[-1]}(-z)$. The purpose of this exercise is to show that the power matrices of V and W are "dual" to each other; for example, when $V(z) = \ln(1/(1-z))$ we have $V^{[-1]}(z) = 1 - e^{-z}$, $W(z) = e^z - 1$, and the corresponding power matrices are the well-known Stirling triangles $v_{nk} = \left[{n \atop k}\right]$, $w_{nk} = \left\{{n \atop k}\right\}$.

a) Prove that the inversion formulas 1.2.6–(47) for Stirling numbers hold in general:

$$\sum_k v_{nk}w_{km}(-1)^{n-k} = \sum_k w_{nk}v_{km}(-1)^{n-k} = \delta_{mn}.$$

b) The relation $v_{n(n-k)} = n^{\underline{k}}\,[z^k]\,(V(z)/z)^{n-k}$ shows that, for fixed k, the quantity $v_{n(n-k)}/V_1^n$ is a polynomial in n of degree $\leq 2k$. We can therefore define

$$v_{\alpha(\alpha-k)} = \alpha^{\underline{k}}\,[z^k]\,(V(z)/z)^{\alpha-k}$$

for arbitrary α when k is a nonnegative integer, as we did for Stirling numbers in Section 1.2.6. Prove that $v_{(-k)(-n)} = w_{nk}$. (This generalizes Eq. 1.2.6–(58).)

▸ **22.** [*HM27*] Given $U(z) = U_0 + U_1 z + U_2 z^2 + \cdots$ with $U_0 \neq 0$, the αth *induced function* $U^{\{\alpha\}}(z)$ is the power series $V(z)$ defined implicitly by the equation

$$V(z) = U(zV(z)^\alpha).$$

a) Prove that $U^{\{0\}}(z) = U(z)$ and $U^{\{\alpha\}\{\beta\}}(z) = U^{\{\alpha+\beta\}}(z)$.

b) Let $B(z)$ be the simple binomial series $1 + z$. Where have we seen $B^{\{2\}}(z)$ before?

c) Prove that $[z^n]\,U^{\{\alpha\}}(z)^x = \frac{x}{x+n\alpha}\,[z^n]\,U(z)^{x+n\alpha}$. *Hint:* If $W(z) = z/U(z)^\alpha$, we have $U^{\{\alpha\}}(z) = (W^{[-1]}(z)/z)^{1/\alpha}$.

d) Consequently any poweroid $V_n(x)$ satisfies not only the identities of exercises 17 and 18, but also

$$\frac{(x+y)V_n(x+y+n\alpha)}{x+y+n\alpha} = \sum_k \binom{n}{k}\frac{xV_k(x+k\alpha)}{x+k\alpha}\frac{yV_{n-k}(y+(n-k)\alpha)}{y+(n-k)\alpha};$$

$$\frac{V_n(x+y)}{y-n\alpha} = (x+y)\sum_k \binom{n-1}{k-1}\frac{V_k(x+k\alpha)}{x+k\alpha}\frac{V_{n-k}(y-k\alpha)}{y-k\alpha}.$$

[Special cases include Abel's binomial theorem, Eq. 1.2.6–(16); Rothe's identities 1.2.6–(26) and 1.2.6–(30); Torelli's sum, exercise 1.2.6–34.]

23. [*HM35*] (E. Jabotinsky.) Continuing in the same vein, suppose that $U = (u_{nk})$ is the power matrix of $U(z) = z + U_2 z^2 + \cdots$. Let $u_n = u_{n1} = n! U_n$.

a) Explain how to compute a matrix $\ln U$ so that the power matrix of $U^{[\alpha]}(z)$ is $\exp(\alpha \ln U) = I + \alpha \ln U + (\alpha \ln U)^2/2! + \cdots$.

b) Let l_{nk} be the entry in row n and column k of $\ln U$, and let

$$l_n = l_{n1}, \qquad L(z) = l_2 \frac{z^2}{2!} + l_3 \frac{z^3}{3!} + l_4 \frac{z^4}{4!} + \cdots.$$

Prove that $l_{nk} = \binom{n}{k-1} l_{n+1-k}$ for $1 \le k \le n$. [*Hint:* $U^{[\epsilon]}(z) = z + \epsilon L(z) + O(\epsilon^2)$.]

c) Considering $U^{[\alpha]}(z)$ as a function of both α and z, prove that

$$\frac{\partial}{\partial \alpha} U^{[\alpha]}(z) = L(z) \frac{\partial}{\partial z} U^{[\alpha]}(z) = L(U^{[\alpha]}(z)).$$

(Consequently $L(z) = (l_k/k!)V(z)$, where $V(z)$ is the function in (27) and (28).)

d) Show that if $u_2 \ne 0$, the numbers l_n can be computed from the recurrence

$$l_2 = u_2, \qquad \sum_{k=2}^{n} \binom{n}{k} l_k u_{n+1-k} = \sum_{k=2}^{n} l_k u_{nk}.$$

How would you use this recurrence when $u_2 = 0$?

e) Prove the identity

$$u_n = \sum_{m=0}^{n-1} \frac{n!}{m!} \sum_{\substack{k_1 + \cdots + k_m = n+m-1 \\ k_1, \ldots, k_m \ge 2}} \frac{n_0}{k_1!} \frac{n_1}{k_2!} \cdots \frac{n_{m-1}}{k_m!} l_{k_1} l_{k_2} \ldots l_{k_m},$$

where $n_j = 1 + k_1 + \cdots + k_j - j$.

24. [*HM25*] Given the power series $U(z) = U_1 z + U_2 z^2 + \cdots$, where U_1 is not a root of unity, let $U = (u_{nk})$ be the power matrix of $U(z)$.

a) Explain how to compute a matrix $\ln U$ so that the power matrix of $U^{[\alpha]}(z)$ is $\exp(\alpha \ln U) = I + \alpha \ln U + (\alpha \ln U)^2/2! + \cdots$.

b) Show that if $W(z)$ is not identically zero and if $U(W(z)) = W(U(z))$, then $W(z) = U^{[\alpha]}(z)$ for some complex number α.

25. [*M24*] If $U(z) = z + U_k z^k + U_{k+1} z^{k+1} + \cdots$ and $V(z) = z + V_l z^l + V_{l+1} z^{l+1} + \cdots$, where $k \ge 2$, $l \ge 2$, $U_k \ne 0$, $V_l \ne 0$, and $U(V(z)) = V(U(z))$, prove that we must have $k = l$ and $V(z) = U^{[\alpha]}(z)$ for $\alpha = V_k/U_k$.

26. [*M22*] Show that if $U(z) = U_0 + U_1 z + U_2 z^2 + \cdots$ and $V(z) = V_1 z + V_2 z^2 + \cdots$ are power series with all coefficients 0 or 1, we can obtain the first N coefficients of $U(V(z)) \bmod 2$ in $O(N^{1+\epsilon})$ steps, for any $\epsilon > 0$.

27. [*M22*] (D. Zeilberger.) Find a recurrence analogous to (9) for computing the coefficients of $W(z) = V(z)V(qz)\ldots V(q^{m-1}z)$, given q, m, and the coefficients of $V(z) = 1 + V_1 z + V_2 z^2 + \cdots$. Assume that q is not a root of unity.

▶ **28.** [*HM26*] A *Dirichlet series* is a sum of the form $V(z) = V_1/1^z + V_2/2^z + V_3/3^z + \cdots$; the product $U(z)V(z)$ of two such series is the Dirichlet series $W(z)$ where

$$W_n = \sum_{d \backslash n} U_d V_{n/d}.$$

Ordinary power series are special cases of Dirichlet series, since we have $V_0 + V_1 z + V_2 z^2 + V_3 z^3 + \cdots = V_0/1^s + V_1/2^s + V_2/4^s + V_3/8^s + \cdots$ when $z = 2^{-s}$. In fact, Dirichlet series are essentially equivalent to power series $V(z_1, z_2, \dots)$ in arbitrarily many variables, where $z_k = p_k^{-s}$ and p_k is the kth prime number.

Find recurrence relations that generalize (9) and the formulas of exercise 4, assuming that a Dirichlet series $V(z)$ is given and that we want to calculate (a) $W(z) = V(z)^\alpha$ when $V_1 = 1$; (b) $W(z) = \exp V(z)$ when $V_1 = 0$; (c) $W(z) = \ln V(z)$ when $V_1 = 1$. [*Hint:* Let $t(n)$ be the total number of prime factors of n, including multiplicity, and let $\delta \sum_n V_n/n^z = \sum_n t(n) V_n/n^z$. Show that δ is analogous to a derivative; for example, $\delta e^{V(z)} = e^{V(z)} \delta V(z)$.]

> *It seems impossible that any thing*
> *should really alter the series of things,*
> *without the same power which first produced them.*
> — EDWARD STILLINGFLEET, *Origines Sacræ*, 2:3:2 (1662)

> *This business of series, the most disagreeable thing in mathematics,*
> *is no more than a game for the English;*
> *Stirling's book, and the one by de Moivre, are proof.*
> — PIERRE DE MAUPERTUIS, letter to d'Ortous de Mairan (30 Oct 1730)

> *He was daunted and bewildered by their almost infinite series.*
> — G. K. CHESTERTON, *The Man Who Was Thursday* (1907)

ANSWERS TO EXERCISES

This branch of mathematics is the only one, I believe,
in which good writers frequently get results entirely erroneous.
... It may be doubted if there is a single
extensive treatise on probabilities in existence
which does not contain solutions absolutely indefensible.

— C. S. PEIRCE, in *Popular Science Monthly* (1878)

NOTES ON THE EXERCISES

1. An average problem for a mathematically inclined reader.

3. (Solution by Roger Frye, after about 110 hours of computation on a Connection Machine in 1987.) $95800^4 + 217519^4 + 414560^4 = 422481^4$ and (therefore) $191600^4 + 435038^4 + 829120^4 = 844962^4$.

4. (One of the readers of the preliminary manuscript for this book reported that he had found a truly remarkable proof. But unfortunately the margin of his copy was too small to contain it.)

SECTION 3.1

1. (a) This will usually fail, since "round" telephone numbers are often selected by the telephone user when possible. In some communities, telephone numbers are perhaps assigned randomly. But it would be a mistake in any case to try to get several successive random numbers from the same page, since the same telephone number is often listed several times in a row.

(b) But do you use the left-hand page or the right-hand page? Say, use the left-hand page number, divide by 2, and take the units digit. The total number of pages should be a multiple of 20; but even so, this method will have some bias.

(c) The markings on the faces will slightly bias the die, but for practical purposes this method is quite satisfactory (and it has been used by the author in the preparation of several examples in this set of books). See *Math. Comp.* **15** (1961), 94–95, for further discussion of icosahedral dice.

(d) (This is a hard question thrown in purposely as a surprise.) The number is not quite uniformly random. If the average number of emissions per minute is m, the probability that the counter registers k is $e^{-m}m^k/k!$ (the Poisson distribution); so the digit 0 is selected with probability $e^{-m}\sum_{k\geq 0} m^{10k}/(10k)!$, etc. In particular, the units digit will be even with probability $e^{-m}\cosh m = \frac{1}{2} + \frac{1}{2}e^{-2m}$, and this is never equal to $\frac{1}{2}$ (although the error is negligibly small when m is large).

It is almost legitimate to take ten readings $(m_0, \ldots, m_9)$ and then to output j if m_j is strictly less than m_i for all $i \neq j$; try again if the minimum value appears more than once. (See (h).) However, the parameter m isn't really constant in the real world.

(e) Okay, provided that the time since the previous digit selected in this way is random. However, there is possible bias in borderline cases.

(f, g) No. People usually think of certain digits (like 7) with higher probability.

(h) Okay; your assignment of numbers to the horses had probability $\frac{1}{10}$ of assigning a given digit to the winning horse (unless you know, say, the jockey).

2. The number of such sequences is the multinomial coefficient $1000000!/(100000!)^{10}$; the probability is this number divided by $10^{1000000}$, the total number of sequences of a million digits. By Stirling's approximation we find that the probability is close to $1/(16\pi^4 10^{22}\sqrt{2\pi}) \approx 2.56 \times 10^{-26}$, roughly one chance in 4×10^{25}.

3. 3040504030.

4. (a) Step K11 can be entered only from step K10 or step K2, and in either case we find it impossible for X to be zero by a simple argument. If X could be zero at that point, the algorithm would not terminate.

(b) If X is initially 3830951656, the computation is like many of the steps that appear in Table 1 except that we reach step K11 with $Y = 3$ instead of $Y = 5$; hence 3830951656 $\rightarrow$ 5870802097. Similarly, 5870802097 $\rightarrow$ 1226919902 $\rightarrow$ 3172562687 $\rightarrow$ 3319967479 $\rightarrow$ 6065038420 $\rightarrow$ 6065038420 $\rightarrow$ $\cdots$.

5. Since only 10^{10} ten-digit numbers are possible, some value of X must be repeated during the first $10^{10}+1$ steps; and as soon as a value is repeated, the sequence continues to repeat its past behavior.

6. (a) Arguing as in the previous exercise, the sequence must eventually repeat a value; let this repetition occur for the first time at step $\mu + \lambda$, where $X_{\mu+\lambda} = X_\mu$. (This condition defines μ and λ.) We have $0 \leq \mu < m$, $0 < \lambda \leq m$, $\mu + \lambda \leq m$. The values $\mu = 0$, $\lambda = m$ are attained if and only if f is a cyclic permutation; and $\mu = m-1$, $\lambda = 1$ occurs, e.g., if $X_0 = 0$, $f(x) = x + 1$ for $x < m - 1$, and $f(m - 1) = m - 1$.

(b) We have, for $r > n$, $X_r = X_n$ if and only if $r - n$ is a multiple of λ and $n \geq \mu$. Hence $X_{2n} = X_n$ if and only if n is a multiple of λ and $n \geq \mu$. The desired results now follow immediately. [*Note:* Equivalently, the powers of an element in a finite semigroup include a unique idempotent element: Take $X_1 = a$, $f(x) = ax$. See G. Frobenius, *Sitzungsberichte preußische Akademie der Wissenschaften* (1895), 82–83.]

(c) Once n has been found, generate X_i and X_{n+i} for $i \geq 0$ until first finding $X_i = X_{n+i}$; then $\mu = i$. If none of the values of X_{n+i} for $0 < i < \mu$ is equal to X_n, it follows that $\lambda = n$, otherwise λ is the smallest such i.

7. (a) The least $n > 0$ such that $n - (\ell(n) - 1)$ is a multiple of λ and $\ell(n) - 1 \geq \mu$ is $n = 2^{\lceil \lg \max(\mu+1, \lambda) \rceil} - 1 + \lambda$. [This may be compared with the least $n > 0$ such that $X_{2n} = X_n$, namely $\lambda(\lceil \mu/\lambda \rceil + \delta_{\mu 0})$.]

(b) Start with $X = Y = X_0$, $k = m = 1$. (At key places in this algorithm we will have $X = X_{2m-k-1}$, $Y = X_{m-1}$, and $m = \ell(2m - k)$.) To generate the next random number, do the following steps: Set $X \leftarrow f(X)$ and $k \leftarrow k - 1$. If $X = Y$, stop (the period length λ is equal to $m - k$). Otherwise if $k = 0$, set $Y \leftarrow X$, $m \leftarrow 2m$, $k \leftarrow m$. Output X.

Notes: Brent has also considered a more general method in which the successive values of $Y = X_{n_i}$ satisfy $n_1 = 0$, $n_{i+1} = 1 + \lfloor p n_i \rfloor$ where p is any number greater than 1. He showed that the best choice of p, approximately 2.4771, saves about 3 percent of the iterations by comparison with $p = 2$. (See exercise 4.5.4–4.)

The method in part (b) has a serious deficiency, however, since it might generate a lot of nonrandom numbers before shutting off. For example, we might have a particularly bad case such as $\lambda = 1$, $\mu = 2^k$. A method based on Floyd's idea in exercise 6(b), namely one that maintains $Y = X_{2n}$ and $X = X_n$ for $n = 0, 1, 2, \ldots$, will require a few more function evaluations than Brent's method, but it will stop before any number has been output twice.

On the other hand, if f is unknown (for example, if we are receiving the values X_0, X_1, $\ldots$ online from an outside source) or if f is difficult to apply, the following cycle detection algorithm due to R. W. Gosper will be preferable: Maintain an auxiliary table T_0, T_1, $\ldots$, T_m, where $m = \lfloor \lg n \rfloor$ when receiving X_n. Initially $T_0 \leftarrow X_0$. For $n = 1, 2, \ldots$, compare X_n with each of T_0, $\ldots$, $T_{\lfloor \lg n \rfloor}$; if no match is found, set $T_{e(n)} \leftarrow X_n$, where $e(n) = \rho(n+1) = \max\{e \mid 2^e \text{ divides } n+1\}$. But if a match $X_n = T_k$ is found, then $\lambda = n - \max\{l \mid l < n \text{ and } e(l) = k\}$. After X_n has been stored in $T_{e(n)}$, it is subsequently compared with X_{n+1}, X_{n+2}, $\ldots$, $X_{n+2^{e(n)}+1}$. Therefore the procedure stops immediately after generating $X_{\mu+\lambda+j}$, where $j \geq 0$ is minimum with $e(\mu+j) \geq \lceil \lg \lambda \rceil - 1$. With this method, no X value is generated more than twice, and at most $\max(1, 2^{\lceil \lg \lambda \rceil - 1})$ values are generated more than once. [MIT AI Laboratory Memo 239 (29 February 1972), Hack 132.]

R. Sedgewick, T. G. Szymanski, and A. C. Yao have analyzed a more complex algorithm based on parameters $m \geq 2$ and $g \geq 1$: An auxiliary table of size m contains X_0, X_b, $\ldots$, X_{qb} at the moment that X_n is computed, where $b = 2^{\lceil \lg n/m \rceil}$ and $q = \lceil n/b \rceil - 1$. If $n \bmod gb < b$, X_n is compared to the entries in the table; eventually equality occurs, and we can reconstruct μ and λ after doing at most $(g+1)2^{\lceil \lg(\mu+\lambda) \rceil + 1}$ further evaluations of f. If the evaluation of f costs τ units of time, and if testing X_n for membership in the table costs σ units, then g can be chosen so that the total running time is $(\mu + \lambda)(\tau + O(\frac{\sigma\tau}{m})^{1/2})$; this is optimum if $\sigma/\tau = O(m)$. Moreover, X_n is not computed unless $\mu+\lambda > mn/(m+4g+2)$, so we can use this method "online" to output elements that are guaranteed to be distinct, making only $2+O(m^{-1/2})$ function evaluations per output. [*SICOMP* **11** (1982), 376–390.]

8. (a, b) $00, 00, \ldots$ [62 starting values]; $10, 10, \ldots$ [19]; $60, 60, \ldots$ [15]; $50, 50, \ldots$ [1]; $24, 57, 24, 57, \ldots$ [3]. (c) 42 or 69; these both lead to a set of fifteen distinct values, namely (42 or 69), 76, 77, 92, 46, 11, 12, 14, 19, 36, 29, 84, 05, 02, 00.

9. Since $X < b^n$, we have $X^2 < b^{2n}$, and the middle square is $\lfloor X^2/b^n \rfloor \leq X^2/b^n$. If $X > 0$, then $X^2/b^n < Xb^n/b^n = X$.

10. If $X = ab^n$, the next number of the sequence has the same form; it is equal to $(a^2 \bmod b^n)b^n$. If a is a multiple of all the prime factors of b, the sequence will soon degenerate to zero; if not, the sequence will degenerate into a cycle of numbers having the same general form as X.

Further facts about the middle-square method have been found by B. Jansson, *Random Number Generators* (Stockholm: Almqvist & Wiksell, 1966), Section 3A. Numerologists will be interested to learn that the number 3792 is self-reproducing in the four-digit middle-square method, since $3792^2 = 14379264$; furthermore (as Jansson observed), it is "self-reproducing" in another sense, too, since its prime factorization is $3 \cdot 79 \cdot 2^4$!

11. The probability that $\mu = 0$ and $\lambda = 1$ is the probability that $X_1 = X_0$, namely $1/m$. The probability that $(\mu, \lambda) = (1, 1)$ or that $(\mu, \lambda) = (0, 2)$ is the probability that $X_1 \neq X_0$ and that X_2 has a certain value, so it is $(1 - 1/m)(1/m)$. Similarly, the probability that the sequence has any given μ and λ is a function only of $\mu + \lambda$, namely

$$P(\mu, \lambda) = \frac{1}{m} \prod_{1 \le k < \mu + \lambda} \left(1 - \frac{k}{m}\right).$$

For the probability that $\lambda = 1$, we have

$$\sum_{\mu \ge 0} \frac{1}{m} \prod_{k=1}^{\mu} \left(1 - \frac{k}{m}\right) = \frac{1}{m} Q(m),$$

where $Q(m)$ is defined in Section 1.2.11.3, Eq. (2). By Eq. (25) in that section, the probability is approximately $\sqrt{\pi/2m} \approx 1.25/\sqrt{m}$. The chance of Algorithm K converging as it did is only about one in 80000; the author was decidedly unlucky. But see exercise 15 for further comments on the "colossalness."

12. $\displaystyle \sum_{\substack{1 \le \lambda \le m \\ 0 \le \mu < m}} \lambda P(\mu, \lambda) = \frac{1}{m}\left(1 + 3\left(1 - \frac{1}{m}\right) + 6\left(1 - \frac{1}{m}\right)\left(1 - \frac{2}{m}\right) + \cdots\right) = \frac{1 + Q(m)}{2}.$

(See the previous answer. In general if $f(a_0, a_1, \dots) = \sum_{n \ge 0} a_n \prod_{k=1}^{n}(1 - k/m)$ then $f(a_0, a_1, \dots) = a_0 + f(a_1, a_2, \dots) - f(a_1, 2a_2, \dots)/m$; apply this identity with $a_n = (n+1)/2$.) Therefore the average value of λ (and, by symmetry of $P(\mu, \lambda)$, also of $\mu + 1$) is approximately $\sqrt{\pi m/8} + \frac{1}{3}$. The average value of $\mu + \lambda$ is exactly $Q(m)$, approximately $\sqrt{\pi m/2} - \frac{1}{3}$. [For alternative derivations and further results, including asymptotic values for the moments, see A. Rapoport, *Bull. Math. Biophysics* **10** (1948), 145–157, and B. Harris, *Annals Math. Stat.* **31** (1960), 1045–1062; see also I. M. Sobol, *Theory of Probability and Its Applications* **9** (1964), 333–338. Sobol discusses the asymptotic period length for the more general sequence $X_{n+1} = f(X_n)$ if $n \not\equiv 0$ (modulo m), $X_{n+1} = g(X_n)$ if $n \equiv 0$ (modulo m), with both f and g random.]

13. [Paul Purdom and John Williams, *Trans. Amer. Math. Soc.* **133** (1968), 547–551.] Let T_{mn} be the number of functions that have n one-cycles and no cycles of length greater than one. Then

$$T_{mn} = \binom{m-1}{n-1} m^{m-n}.$$

(This is $\binom{m}{n} r(m, m-n)$ in exercise 2.3.4.4–25.) *Any* function is such a function followed by a permutation of the n elements that were the one-cycles. Hence $\sum_{n \ge 1} T_{mn} n! = m^m$.

Let P_{nk} be the number of permutations of n elements in which the longest cycle is of length k. Then the number of functions with a maximum cycle of length k is $\sum_{n \ge 1} T_{mn} P_{nk}$. To get the average value of k, we compute $\sum_{k \ge 1} \sum_{n \ge 1} k T_{mn} P_{nk}$, which by the result of exercise 1.3.3–23 is $\sum_{n \ge 1} T_{mn} n!(cn + \frac{1}{2}c + O(n^{-1}))$ where $c \approx .62433$. Summing, we get the average value $cQ(m) + \frac{1}{2}c + O(m^{1/2})$. (This is not substantially larger than the average value when X_0 is selected at random. The average value of $\max \mu$ is asymptotic to $Q(m) \ln 4$, and the average value of $\max(\mu + \lambda)$ is asymptotic to $1.9268 Q(m)$; see Flajolet and Odlyzko, *Lecture Notes in Comp. Sci.* **434** (1990), 329–354.)

14. Let $c_r(m)$ be the number of functions with exactly r different final cycles. From the recurrence $c_1(m) = (m-1)! - \sum_{k>0} \binom{m}{k}(-1)^k (m-k)^k c_1(m-k)$, which comes by counting the number of functions whose image contains at most $m - k$ elements, we find the solution $c_1(m) = m^{m-1} Q(m)$. (See exercise 1.2.11.3–16.) Another way to obtain the value of $c_1(m)$, which is perhaps more elegant and revealing, is given in exercise 2.3.4.4–17. The value of $c_r(m)$ may be determined as in exercise 13:

$$c_r(m) = \sum_{n \geq 1} T_{mn} \begin{bmatrix} n \\ r \end{bmatrix} = m^{m-1} \left(\frac{1}{0!} \begin{bmatrix} 1 \\ r \end{bmatrix} + \frac{1}{1!} \begin{bmatrix} 2 \\ r \end{bmatrix} \frac{m-1}{m} + \frac{1}{2!} \begin{bmatrix} 3 \\ r \end{bmatrix} \frac{m-1}{m} \frac{m-2}{m} + \cdots \right).$$

The desired average value can now be computed; it is (see exercise 12)

$$E_m = \frac{1}{m} \left(H_1 + 2H_2 \frac{m-1}{m} + 3H_3 \frac{m-1}{m} \frac{m-2}{m} + \cdots \right)$$
$$= 1 + \frac{1}{2} \frac{m-1}{m} + \frac{1}{3} \frac{m-1}{m} \frac{m-2}{m} + \cdots.$$

This latter formula was obtained by quite different means by Martin D. Kruskal, *AMM* **61** (1954), 392–397. Using the integral representation

$$E_m = \int_0^\infty \left(\left(1 + \frac{x}{m} \right)^m - 1 \right) e^{-x} \frac{dx}{x},$$

he proved the asymptotic relation $\lim_{m \to \infty} (E_m - \frac{1}{2} \ln m) = \frac{1}{2}(\gamma + \ln 2)$. For further results and references, see John Riordan, *Annals Math. Stat.* **33** (1962), 178–185.

15. The probability that $f(x) \neq x$ for all x is $(m-1)^m/m^m$, which is approximately $1/e$. The existence of a self-repeating value in an algorithm like Algorithm K is therefore not "colossal" at all — it occurs with probability $1 - 1/e \approx .63212$. The only "colossal" thing was that the author happened to hit such a value when X_0 was chosen at random (see exercise 11).

16. The sequence will repeat when a pair of successive elements occurs for the second time. The maximum period is m^2. (See the next exercise.)

17. After selecting $X_0, \ldots, X_{k-1}$ arbitrarily, let $X_{n+1} = f(X_n, \ldots, X_{n-k+1})$, where $0 \leq x_1, \ldots, x_k < m$ implies that $0 \leq f(x_1, \ldots, x_k) < m$. The maximum period is m^k. This is an obvious upper bound, but it is not obvious that it can be attained; for constructive proofs that it can always be attained for suitable f, see exercises 3.2.2–17 and 3.2.2–21, and for the number of ways to attain it see exercise 2.3.4.2–23.

18. Same as exercise 7, but use the k-tuple of elements $(X_n, \ldots, X_{n-k+1})$ in place of the single element X_n.

19. Clearly $\Pr(\text{no final cycle has length } 1) = (m-1)^m/m^m$. R. Pemantle [*J. Algorithms* **54** (2005), 72–84] has shown that $\Pr(\lambda = 1) = \Theta(m^{k/2})$, and that $\Pr((\mu + \lambda)^2 > 2m^k x$ and $\lambda/(\mu + \lambda) \leq y)$ rapidly approaches ye^{-x}, when $x > 0$, $0 < y < 1$, and $m \to \infty$. The k-dimensional analogs of exercises 13 and 14 remain unsolved.

20. It suffices to consider the simpler mapping $g(X)$ defined by steps K2–K13. Working backward from 6065038420, we obtain a total of 597 solutions; the smallest is 0009612809 and the largest is 9995371004.

21. We may work with $g(X)$ as in the previous exercise, but now we want to run the function forward instead of backward. There is an interesting tradeoff between time and space. Notice that the mechanism of step K1 tends to make the period length small. So does the existence of X's with large in-degree; for example, 512 choices of $X = *6********$ in step K2 will go to K10 with $X \leftarrow 0500000000$.

Scott Fluhrer has discovered *another* fixed point of Algorithm K, namely the value 5008502835(!). He also found the 3-cycle $0225923640 \to 2811514413 \to 0590051662 \to$

0225923640, making a total of seven cycles in all. Only 128 starting numbers lead to the repeating value 5008502835. Algorithm K is a *terrible* random number generator.

22. If f were truly random, this would be ideal; but how do we construct such f? The function defined by Algorithm K would work much better under this scheme, although it does have decidedly nonrandom properties (see the previous answer).

23. The function f permutes its cyclic elements; let $(x_0, \ldots, x_{k-1})$ be the "unusual" representation of the inverse of that permutation. Then proceed to define $x_k, \ldots, x_{m-1}$ as in exercise 2.3.4.4–18. [See *J. Combinatorial Theory* **8** (1970), 361–375.]

For example, if $m = 10$ and $(f(0), \ldots, f(9)) = (3, 1, 4, 1, 5, 9, 2, 6, 5, 4)$, we have $(x_0, \ldots, x_9) = (4, 9, 5, 1, 1, 3, 4, 2, 6, 5)$; if $(x_0, \ldots, x_9) = (3, 1, 4, 1, 5, 9, 2, 6, 5, 4)$, we have $(f(0), \ldots, f(9)) = (6, 4, 9, 3, 1, 1, 2, 5, 4, 5)$.

SECTION 3.2.1

1. Take X_0 even, a even, c odd. Then X_n is odd for $n > 0$.

2. Let X_r be the first repeated value in the sequence. If X_r were equal to X_k for some k where $0 < k < r$, we could prove that $X_{r-1} = X_{k-1}$, since X_n uniquely determines X_{n-1} when a is prime to m. Hence $k = 0$.

3. If d is the greatest common divisor of a and m, the quantity aX_n can take on at most m/d values. The situation can be even worse; for example, if $m = 2^e$ and if a is even, Eq. (6) shows that the sequence is eventually constant.

4. Induction on k.

5. If a is relatively prime to m, there is a number a' for which $aa' \equiv 1 \pmod{m}$. Then $X_{n-1} = (a'X_n - a'c) \bmod m$; and in general, if $b = a - 1$,

$$X_{n-k} = ((a')^k X_n - c(a' + \cdots + (a')^k)) \bmod m$$
$$= \left((a')^k X_n + ((a')^k - 1)c/b\right) \bmod m$$

when $k \geq 0$, $n - k \geq 0$. If a is not relatively prime to m, it is not possible to determine X_{n-1} when X_n is given; multiples of $m/\gcd(a, m)$ may be added to X_{n-1} without changing the value of X_n. (See also exercise 3.2.1.3–7.)

SECTION 3.2.1.1

1. Let c' be a solution to the congruence $ac' \equiv c \pmod{m}$. (Thus, $c' = a'c \bmod m$, if a' is the number in the answer to exercise 3.2.1–5.) Then we have

LDA X;   ADD CPRIME;   MUL A.

Overflow is possible on this addition operation. (From results derived later in the chapter, it is probably best to save a unit of time, taking $c = a$ and replacing the ADD instruction by 'INCA 1'. Then if $X_0 = 0$, overflow will not occur until the end of the period, so it won't occur in practice.)

```
2. RANDM STJ   1F                              1H      JNOV  *
         LDA   XRAND                                   JMP   *-1
         MUL   2F                              XRAND CON   X0
         SLAX  5                               2H      CON   a
         ADD   3F   (or, INCA c, if c is small) 3H     CON   c  ▌
         STA   XRAND
```

3. Let $a' = aw \bmod m$, and let m' be such that $mm' \equiv 1$ (modulo w). Set $y \leftarrow$ lomult(a',x), $z \leftarrow$ himult(a',x), $t \leftarrow$ lomult(m',y), $u \leftarrow$ himult(m,t). Then we have $mt \equiv a'x$ (modulo w), hence $a'x - mt = (z-u)w$, hence $ax \equiv z-u$ (modulo m); it follows that $ax \bmod m = z - u + [z<u]m$.

4. Define the operation $x \bmod 2^e = y$ if and only if $x \equiv y$ (modulo 2^e) and $-2^{e-1} \leq y < 2^{e-1}$. The congruential sequence $\langle Y_n \rangle$ defined by

$$Y_0 = X_0 \bmod 2^{32}, \qquad Y_{n+1} = (aY_n + c) \bmod 2^{32}$$

is easy to compute on 370-style machines, since the lower half of the product of y and z is $(yz) \bmod 2^{32}$ for all two's complement numbers y and z, and since addition ignoring overflow also delivers its result $\bmod 2^{32}$. This sequence has all the randomness properties of the standard linear congruential sequence $\langle X_n \rangle$, since $Y_n \equiv X_n$ (modulo 2^{32}). Indeed, the two's complement representation of Y_n is *identical* to the binary representation of X_n, for all n. [G. Marsaglia and T. A. Bray first pointed this out in *CACM* **11** (1968), 757–759.]

5. (a) Subtraction: `LDA X`; `SUB Y`; `JANN *+2`; `ADD M`. (b) Addition: `LDA X`; `SUB M`; `ADD Y`; `JANN *+2`; `ADD M`. (Note that if m is more than half the word size, the instruction 'SUB M' must precede the instruction 'ADD Y'.)

6. The sequences are not essentially different, since adding the constant $(m-c)$ has the same effect as subtracting the constant c. The operation must be combined with multiplication, so a subtractive process has little merit over the additive one (at least in `MIX`'s case), except when it is necessary to avoid affecting the overflow toggle.

7. The prime factors of $z^k - 1$ appear in the factorization of $z^{kr} - 1$. If r is odd, the prime factors of $z^k + 1$ appear in the factorization of $z^{kr} + 1$. And $z^{2k} - 1$ equals $(z^k - 1)(z^k + 1)$.

8.
```
JOV   *+1    (Ensure that overflow is off.)
LDA   X
MUL   A
STX   TEMP
ADD   TEMP   Add lower half to upper half.
JNOV  *+2    If ≥ w, subtract w − 1.
INCA  1      (Overflow is impossible in this step.)
```

Note: Since addition on an e-bit ones'-complement computer is $\bmod (2^e - 1)$, it is possible to combine the techniques of exercises 4 and 8, producing $(yz) \bmod (2^e - 1)$ by adding together the two e-bit halves of the product yz, for all ones' complement numbers y and z regardless of sign.

9. (a) Both sides equal $aq\lfloor x/q \rfloor$.

(b) Set $t \leftarrow a(x \bmod q) - r\lfloor x/q \rfloor$, where $r = m \bmod a$; the constants q and r can be precomputed. Then $ax \bmod m = t + [t<0]m$, because we can prove that $t > -m$: Clearly $a(x \bmod q) \leq a(q-1) < m$. Also $r\lfloor x/q \rfloor \leq r\lfloor (m-1)/q \rfloor = r\lfloor a + (r-1)/q \rfloor = ra \leq qa < m$ if $0 < r \leq q$; and $a^2 \leq m$ implies $r < a \leq q$. [This technique is implicit in a program published by B. A. Wichmann and I. D. Hill, *Applied Stat.* **31** (1982), 190.]

10. If $r > q$ and $x = m-1$ we have $r\lfloor x/q \rfloor \geq (q+1)(a+1) > m$. So the condition $r \leq q$ is necessary and sufficient for method 9(b) to be valid; this means $\frac{m}{q} - 1 \leq a \leq \frac{m}{q}$. Let $t = \lfloor \sqrt{m} \rfloor$. The intervals $[\frac{m}{q}-1 .. \frac{m}{q}]$ are disjoint for $1 \leq q \leq t$, and they include exactly 1 or 2 integers, depending on whether q is a divisor of m. These intervals account for all solutions with $a > \sqrt{m}$; they also include the case $a = t$, if $(\sqrt{m} \bmod 1) < \frac{1}{2}$, and the case $a = t - 1$ if $m = t^2$. Thus the total number of "lucky" multipliers is exactly $2\lfloor\sqrt{m}\rfloor + \lfloor d(m)/2\rfloor - [(\sqrt{m} \bmod 1) < \frac{1}{2}] - 1$, where $d(m)$ is the number of divisors of m.

11. We can assume that $a \le \frac{1}{2}m$; otherwise we can obtain $ax \bmod m$ from $(m - a)x$ $\bmod m$. Then we can represent $a = a'a'' - a'''$, where a', a'', and a''' are all less than $\sqrt{m}$; for example, we can take $a' \approx \sqrt{m} - 1$ and $a'' = \lceil a/a'\rceil$. It follows that $ax \bmod m$ is $(a'(a''x \bmod m) \bmod m - (a'''x \bmod m)) \bmod m$, and the inner three operations can all be handled by exercise 9.

When $m = 2^{31} - 1$ we can take advantage of the fact that $m - 1$ has 192 divisors to find cases in which $m = q'a' + 1$, simplifying the general method because $r' = 1$. It turns out that 86 of these divisors lead to lucky a'' and a''', when $a = 62089911$; the best such case is probably $a' = 3641$, $a'' = 17053$, $a''' = 62$, because 3641 and 62 both divide $m - 1$. This decomposition yields the scheme

$$t \leftarrow 17053(x \bmod 125929) - 16410\lfloor x/125929\rfloor,$$

$$t \leftarrow 3641(t \bmod 589806) - \lfloor t/589806\rfloor,$$

$$t \leftarrow t - (62(x \bmod 34636833) - \lfloor x/34636833\rfloor),$$

where "$-$" denotes subtraction mod m. The mod operations count as one multiplication and one subtraction, because $x \bmod q = x - q\lfloor x/q\rfloor$ and the operation $\lfloor x/q\rfloor$ has already been done; thus, we have performed seven multiplications, three divisions, and seven subtractions. But it's even better to notice that 62089911 itself has 24 divisors; they lead to five suitable factorizations with $a''' = 0$. For example, when $a' = 883$ and $a'' = 70317$ we need only six multiplications, two divisions, four subtractions:

$$t \leftarrow 883(x \bmod 2432031) - 274\lfloor x/2432031\rfloor,$$

$$t \leftarrow 70317(t \bmod 30540) - 2467\lfloor t/30540\rfloor.$$

[Can the worst-case number of multiplications plus divisions be reduced to at most 11, for all a and m, or is 12 the best upper bound? Another way to achieve 12 appears in exercise 4.3.3–19.]

12. (a) Let $m = 9999998999 = 10^{10} - 10^3 - 1$. To multiply $(x_9x_8 \dots x_0)_{10}$ by 10 modulo m, use the fact that $10^{10}x_9 \equiv 10^3x_9 + x_9$: Add $(x_9000)_{10}$ to $(x_8x_7 \dots x_0x_9)_{10}$. And to avoid circular shifting, imagine that the digits are arranged on a wheel: Just add the high-order digit x_9 to the digit x_2 three positions left, and point to x_8 as the new high-order digit. If $x_9 + x_2 \ge 10$, a carry propagates to the left. And if this carry ripples all the way to the left of x_8, it propagates not only to x_9 but also to the x_2 position; it may continue to propagate from both x_9 and x_2 before finally settling down. (The numbers might also become slightly larger than m. For example, 0999999900 goes to 9999999000 = $m + 1$, which goes to 9999999009 = $m + 10$. But a redundant representation isn't necessarily harmful.)

(b) This is the operation of *dividing* by 10, so we do the opposite of (a): Move the high-order digit pointer cyclically *left*, and *subtract* the new high-order digit from the digit three to its left. If the result of subtraction is negative, "borrow" in the usual fashion (Algorithm 4.3.1S); that is, decrease the preceding digit by 1. Borrowing may propagate as in (a), but never past the high-order digit position. This operation keeps the numbers nonnegative and less than m. (Thus, division by 10 turns out to be easier than multiplication by 10.)

(c) We can *remember* the borrow-bit instead of propagating it, because it can be incorporated into the subtraction on the next step. Thus, if we define digits x_n and borrow-bits b_n by the recurrence

$$x_n = (x_{n-10} - x_{n-3} - b_n) \bmod 10 = x_{n-10} - x_{n-3} - b_n + 10b_{n+1},$$

we have $999999900^n \bmod 9999998999 = X_n$ by induction on n, where

$$X_n = (x_{n-1}x_{n-2}x_{n-3}x_{n-4}x_{n-5}x_{n-6}x_{n-7}x_{n+2}x_{n+1}x_n)_{10} - 1000b_{n+3}$$
$$= (x_{n-1}x_{n-2}\dots x_{n-10})_{10} - (x_{n-1}x_{n-2}x_{n-3})_{10} - b_n,$$

provided that the initial conditions are set up to make $X_0 = 1$. Notice that $10X_{n+1} = (x_n x_{n-1}x_{n-2}x_{n-3}x_{n-4}x_{n-5}x_{n-6}x_{n+3}x_{n+2}x_{n+1}0)_{10} - 10000b_{n+4} = mx_n + X_n$; it follows that $0 \le X_n < m$ for all $n \ge 0$.

(d) If $0 \le U < m$, the first digit of the decimal representation of U/m is $\lfloor 10U/m \rfloor$, and the subsequent digits are the decimal representation of $(10U \bmod m)/m$; see, for example, Method 2a in Section 4.4. Thus $U/m = (.u_1 u_2 \dots)_{10}$ if we set $U_0 = U$ and $U_n = 10U_{n-1} \bmod m = 10U_{n-1} - mu_n$. Informally, the digits of $1/m$ are the leading digits of $10^n \bmod m$ for $n = 1, 2, \dots$, a sequence that is eventually periodic; these are the leading digits of $10^{-n} \bmod m$ in reverse order, so we have calculated them in (c).

A rigorous proof is, of course, preferable to handwaving. Let λ be the least positive integer with $10^\lambda \equiv 1$ (modulo m), and define $x_n = x_{n \bmod \lambda}$, $b_n = b_{n \bmod \lambda}$, $X_n = X_{n \bmod \lambda}$ for all $n < 0$. Then the recurrences for x_n, b_n, and X_n in (c) are valid for all integers n. If $U_0 = 1$ it follows that $U_n = X_{-n}$ and $u_n = x_{-n}$; hence

$$\frac{999999900^n \bmod 9999998999}{9999998999} = (.x_{n-1}x_{n-2}x_{n-3}\dots)_{10}.$$

(e) Let w be the computer's word size, and use the recurrence

$$x_n = (x_{n-k} - x_{n-l} - b_n) \bmod w = x_{n-k} - x_{n-l} - b_n + wb_{n+1},$$

where $0 < l < k$ and k is large. Then $(.x_{n-1}x_{n-2}x_{n-3}\dots)_w = X_n/m$, where $m = w^k - w^l - 1$ and $X_{n+1} = (w^{k-1} - w^{l-1})X_n \bmod m$. The relation

$$X_n = (x_{n-1}\dots x_{n-k})_w - (x_{n-1}\dots x_{n-l})_w - b_n$$

holds for $n \ge 0$; the values of $x_{-1}, \dots, x_{-k}$, and b_0 should be such that $0 \le X_0 < m$.

Such random number generators, and the similar ones in the following exercise, were introduced by G. Marsaglia and A. Zaman [*Annals of Applied Probability* **1** (1991), 462–480], who called the method *subtract-with-borrow*. Their starting point was the radix-w representation of fractions with denominator m. The relation to linear congruential sequences was noticed by Shu Tezuka, and analyzed in detail by Tezuka, L'Ecuyer, and Couture [*ACM Trans. Modeling and Computer Simulation* **3** (1993), 315–331]. The period length is discussed in exercise 3.2.1.2–22.

13. Multiplication by 10 now requires *negating* the digit that is added. For this purpose it is convenient to represent a number with its last three digits negated; for example, $9876543210 = (9876544\bar{7}\bar{9}\bar{0})_{10}$. Then 10 times $(x_9 \dots x_3 \bar{x}_2 \bar{x}_1 \bar{x}_0)_{10}$ is $(x_8 \dots x_3 x' \bar{x}_1 \bar{x}_0 \bar{x}_9)_{10}$ where $x' = x_9 - x_2$. Similarly, $(x_9 \dots x_3 \bar{x}_2 \bar{x}_1 \bar{x}_0)_{10}$ divided by 10 is $(x_0 x_9 \dots x_4 \bar{x}'' \bar{x}_2 \bar{x}_1)_{10}$ where $x'' = x_0 - x_3$. The recurrence

$$x_n = (x_{n-3} - x_{n-10} - b_n) \bmod 10 = x_{n-3} - x_{n-10} - b_n + 10b_{n+1}$$

yields $8999999101^n \bmod 9999999001 = X_n$ where

$$X_n = (x_{n-1}x_{n-2}x_{n-3}x_{n-4}x_{n-5}x_{n-6}x_{n-7}\bar{x}_{n+2}\bar{x}_{n+1}\bar{x}_n)_{10} + 1000b_{n+3}$$
$$= (x_{n-1}x_{n-2}\dots x_{n-10})_{10} - (x_{n-1}x_{n-2}x_{n-3})_{10} + b_n.$$

When the radix is generalized from 10 to w, we find that the inverse powers of w modulo $w^k - w^l + 1$ are generated by

$$x_n = (x_{n-l} - x_{n-k} - b_n) \bmod w = x_{n-l} - x_{n-k} - b_n + wb_{n+1}$$

(the same as in exercise 12 but with k and l interchanged).

14. Mild generalization: We can effectively divide by b modulo $b^k - b^l \pm 1$ for any b less than or equal to the word size w, since the recurrence for x_n is almost as efficient when $b < w$ as it is when $b = w$.

Strong generalization: The recurrence

$$x_n = (a_1 x_{n-1} + \cdots + a_k x_{n-k} + c_n) \bmod b, \quad c_{n+1} = \left\lfloor \frac{a_1 x_{n-1} + \cdots + a_k x_{n-k} + c_n}{b} \right\rfloor$$

is equivalent to $X_n = b^{-1} X_{n-1} \bmod |m|$ in the sense that $X_n/|m| = (.x_{n-1}x_{n-2}\ldots)_b$, if we define

$$m = a_k b^k + \cdots + a_1 b - 1 \quad \text{and} \quad X_n = \left(\sum_{j=1}^{k} a_j(x_{n-1}\ldots x_{n-j})_b + c_n \right)(\text{sign } m).$$

The initial values $x_{-1}\ldots x_{-k}$ and c_0 should be selected so that $0 \leq X_0 < |m|$; we will then have $x_n = (bX_{n+1} - X_n)/|m|$ for $n \geq 0$. The values of x_j for $j < 0$ that appear in the formula $X_n/|m| = (.x_{n-1}x_{n-2}\ldots)_b$ are properly regarded as $x_{j \bmod \lambda}$, where λ is the least positive integer with $b^\lambda \equiv 1$ (modulo m); these values may differ from the numbers $x_{-1}, \ldots, x_{-k}$ that were initially supplied. The carry digits c_n will satisfy

$$\sum_{j=1}^{k} \min(0, a_j) \leq c_n < \sum_{j=1}^{k} \max(0, a_j)$$

if the initial carry c_0 is in this range.

The special case $m = b^k + b^l - 1$, for which $a_j = \delta_{jl} + \delta_{jk}$, is of particular interest because it can be computed so easily; Marsaglia and Zaman called this the *add-with-carry* generator:

$$x_n = (x_{n-l} + x_{n-k} + c_n) \bmod b = x_{n-l} + x_{n-k} + c_n - b\,c_{n+1}.$$

Another potentially attractive possibility is to use $k = 2$ in a generator with, say, $b = 2^{31}$ and $m = 65430b^2 + b - 1$. This modulus m is prime, and the period length turns out to be $(m-1)/2$. The spectral test of Section 3.3.4 indicates that the spacing between planes is good (large ν values), although of course the multiplier b^{-1} is poor in comparison with other multipliers for this particular modulus m.

Exercise 3.2.1.2–22 contains additional information about subtract-with-borrow and add-with-carry moduli that lead to extremely long periods.

SECTION 3.2.1.2

1. Period length m, by Theorem A. (See exercise 3.)

2. Yes, these conditions imply the conditions in Theorem A, since the only prime divisor of 2^e is 2, and any odd number is relatively prime to 2^e. (In fact, the conditions of the exercise are *necessary* and sufficient.)

3. By Theorem A, we need $a \equiv 1$ (modulo 4) and $a \equiv 1$ (modulo 5). By Law D of Section 1.2.4, this is equivalent to $a \equiv 1$ (modulo 20).

4. We know $X_{2^{e-1}} \equiv 0$ (modulo 2^{e-1}) by using Theorem A in the case $m = 2^{e-1}$. Also using Theorem A for $m = 2^e$, we know that $X_{2^{e-1}} \not\equiv 0$ (modulo 2^e). It follows that $X_{2^{e-1}} = 2^{e-1}$. More generally, we can use Eq. 3.2.1–(6) to prove that the second half of the period is essentially like the first half, since $X_{n+2^{e-1}} = (X_n + 2^{e-1}) \bmod 2^e$. (The quarters are similar too, see exercise 21.)

5. We need $a \equiv 1$ (modulo p) for $p = 3, 11, 43, 281, 86171$. By Law D of Section 1.2.4, this is equivalent to $a \equiv 1$ (modulo $3 \cdot 11 \cdot 43 \cdot 281 \cdot 86171$), so the *only* solution is the terrible multiplier $a = 1$.

6. (See the previous exercise.) The congruence $a \equiv 1$ (modulo $3 \cdot 7 \cdot 11 \cdot 13 \cdot 37$) implies that the solutions are $a = 1 + 111111k$, for $0 \le k \le 8$.

7. Using the notation of the proof of Lemma Q, μ is the smallest value such that $X_{\mu+\lambda} = X_\mu$; so it is the smallest value such that $Y_{\mu+\lambda} = Y_\mu$ and $Z_{\mu+\lambda} = Z_\mu$. This shows that $\mu = \max(\mu_1, \ldots, \mu_t)$. The highest achievable μ is $\max(e_1, \ldots, e_t)$, but nobody really wants to achieve it.

8. We have $a^2 \equiv 1$ (modulo 8); so $a^4 \equiv 1$ (modulo 16), $a^8 \equiv 1$ (modulo 32), etc. If $a \bmod 4 = 3$, then $a - 1$ is twice an odd number; so $(a^{2^{e-1}} - 1)/(a-1) \equiv 0$ (modulo 2^e) if and only if $(a^{2^{e-1}} - 1)/2 \equiv 0$ (modulo $2^{e+1}/2$), which is true.

9. Substitute for X_n in terms of Y_n and simplify. If $X_0 \bmod 4 = 3$, the formulas of the exercise do not apply; but they do apply to the sequence $Z_n = (-X_n) \bmod 2^e$, which has essentially the same behavior.

10. Only when $m = 1, 2, 4, p^e$, and $2p^e$, for odd primes p. In all other cases, the result of Theorem B is an improvement over Euler's theorem (exercise 1.2.4–28).

11. (a) Either $x+1$ or $x-1$ (not both) will be a multiple of 4, so $x \mp 1 = q2^f$, where q is odd and f is greater than 1. (b) In the given circumstances, $f < e$ and so $e \ge 3$. We have $\pm x \equiv 1$ (modulo 2^f) and $\pm x \not\equiv 1$ (modulo 2^{f+1}) and $f > 1$. Hence, by applying Lemma P, we find that $(\pm x)^{2^{e-f-1}} \not\equiv 1$ (modulo 2^e), while $x^{2^{e-f}} = (\pm x)^{2^{e-f}} \equiv 1$ (modulo 2^e). So the order is a divisor of 2^{e-f}, but not a divisor of 2^{e-f-1}. (c) 1 has order 1; $2^e - 1$ has order 2. The maximum order when $e \ge 3$ is therefore 2^{e-2}, and for $e \ge 4$ it is necessary to have $f = 2$, that is, $x \equiv 4 \pm 1$ (modulo 8).

12. If k is a proper divisor of $p - 1$ and if $a^k \equiv 1$ (modulo p), then by Lemma P we have $a^{kp^{e-1}} \equiv 1$ (modulo p^e). Similarly, if $a^{p-1} \equiv 1$ (modulo p^2), we find that $a^{(p-1)p^{e-2}} \equiv 1$ (modulo p^e). So in these cases a is *not* primitive. Conversely, if $a^{p-1} \not\equiv 1$ (modulo p^2), Theorem 1.2.4F and Lemma P tell us that $a^{(p-1)p^{e-2}} \not\equiv 1$ (modulo p^e), but $a^{(p-1)p^{e-1}} \equiv 1$ (modulo p^e). So the order is a divisor of $(p - 1)p^{e-1}$ but not of $(p-1)p^{e-2}$; it therefore has the form kp^{e-1}, where k divides $p-1$. But if a is primitive modulo p, the congruence $a^{kp^{e-1}} \equiv a^k \equiv 1$ (modulo p) implies that $k = p - 1$.

13. Suppose $a \bmod p \ne 0$, and let λ be the order of a modulo p. By Theorem 1.2.4F, λ is a divisor of $p - 1$. If $\lambda < p - 1$, then $(p-1)/\lambda$ has a prime factor, q.

14. Let $0 < k < p$. If $a^{p-1} \equiv 1$ (modulo p^2), then $(a + kp)^{p-1} \equiv a^{p-1} + (p-1)a^{p-2}kp$ (modulo p^2); and this is $\not\equiv 1$, since $(p-1)a^{p-2}k$ is not a multiple of p. By exercise 12, $a + kp$ is primitive modulo p^e.

15. (a) If $\lambda_1 = p_1^{e_1} \ldots p_t^{e_t}$ and $\lambda_2 = p_1^{f_1} \ldots p_t^{f_t}$, let $\kappa_1 = p_1^{g_1} \ldots p_t^{g_t}$ and $\kappa_2 = p_1^{h_1} \ldots p_t^{h_t}$, where

$$g_j = e_j \quad \text{and} \quad h_j = 0, \qquad \text{if } e_j < f_j,$$
$$g_j = 0 \quad \text{and} \quad h_j = f_j, \qquad \text{if } e_j \ge f_j.$$

Now $a_1^{\kappa_1}$ and $a_2^{\kappa_2}$ have periods λ_1/κ_1 and λ_2/κ_2, and the latter are relatively prime. Furthermore $(\lambda_1/\kappa_1)(\lambda_2/\kappa_2) = \lambda$, so it suffices to consider the case when λ_1 is relatively prime to λ_2, that is, when $\lambda = \lambda_1\lambda_2$. Now let λ' be the order of a_1a_2. Since $(a_1a_2)^{\lambda'} \equiv 1$, we have $1 \equiv (a_1a_2)^{\lambda'\lambda_1} \equiv a_2^{\lambda'\lambda_1}$; hence $\lambda'\lambda_1$ is a multiple of λ_2. This implies that λ' is a multiple of λ_2, since λ_1 is relatively prime to λ_2. Similarly, λ' is a multiple of λ_1; hence λ' is a multiple of $\lambda_1\lambda_2$. But obviously $(a_1a_2)^{\lambda_1\lambda_2} \equiv 1$, so $\lambda' = \lambda_1\lambda_2$.

(b) If a_1 has order $\lambda(m)$ and if a_2 has order λ, by part (a) $\lambda(m)$ must be a multiple of λ, otherwise we could find an element of higher order, namely of order $\mathrm{lcm}(\lambda, \lambda(m))$.

16. (a) $f(x) = (x - a)(x^{n-1} + (a + c_1)x^{n-2} + \cdots + (a^{n-1} + \cdots + c_{n-1})) + f(a)$.
(b) The statement is clear when $n = 0$. If a is one root, $f(x) \equiv (x - a)q(x)$; therefore, if a' is any other root,

$$0 \equiv f(a') \equiv (a' - a)q(a'),$$

and since $a' - a$ is not a multiple of p, a' must be a root of $q(x)$. So if $f(x)$ has more than n distinct roots, $q(x)$ has more than $n - 1$ distinct roots. [J. L. Lagrange, *Mém. Acad. Roy. Sci. Berlin* **24** (1768), 181–250, §10.] (c) $\lambda(p) \geq p-1$, since $f(x)$ must have degree $\geq p-1$ in order to possess so many roots. But $\lambda(p) \leq p-1$ by Theorem 1.2.4F.

17. By Lemma P, $11^5 \equiv 1$ (modulo 25), $11^5 \not\equiv 1$ (modulo 125), etc.; so the order of 11 is 5^{e-1} (modulo 5^e), not the maximum value $\lambda(5^e) = 4 \cdot 5^{e-1}$. But by Lemma Q the total period length is the least common multiple of the period modulo 2^e (namely 2^{e-2}) and the period modulo 5^e (namely 5^{e-1}), and this is $2^{e-2}5^{e-1} = \lambda(10^e)$. The period modulo 5^e may be 5^{e-1} or $2 \cdot 5^{e-1}$ or $4 \cdot 5^{e-1}$, without affecting the length of period modulo 10^e, since the least common multiple is taken. The values that are primitive modulo 5^e are those congruent to 2, 3, 8, 12, 13, 17, 22, 23 modulo 25 (see exercise 12), namely 3, 13, 27, 37, 53, 67, 77, 83, 117, 123, 133, 147, 163, 173, 187, 197.

18. According to Theorem C, $a \bmod 8$ must be 3 or 5. Knowing the period of a modulo 5 and modulo 25 allows us to apply Lemma P to determine admissible values of $a \bmod 25$. Period $= 4 \cdot 5^{e-1}$: 2, 3, 8, 12, 13, 17, 22, 23; period $= 2 \cdot 5^{e-1}$: 4, 9, 14, 19; period $= 5^{e-1}$: 6, 11, 16, 21. Each of these 16 values yields one value of a, $0 \leq a < 200$, with $a \bmod 8 = 3$, and another value of a with $a \bmod 8 = 5$.

19. Several examples appear in lines 17–20 of Table 3.3.4–1.

20. (a) We have $AY_n + X_0 \equiv AY_{n+k} + X_0$ (modulo m) if and only if $Y_n \equiv Y_{n+k}$ (modulo m'). (b)(i) Obvious. (ii) Theorem A. (iii) $(a^n - 1)/(a - 1) \equiv 0$ (modulo 2^e) if and only if $a^n \equiv 1$ (modulo 2^{e+1}); if $a \not\equiv -1$, the order of a modulo 2^{e+1} is twice its order modulo 2^e. (iv) $(a^n - 1)/(a - 1) \equiv 0$ (modulo p^e) if and only if $a^n \equiv 1$.

21. $X_{n+s} \equiv X_n + X_s$ by Eq. 3.2.1–(6); and s is a divisor of m, since s is a power of p when m is a power of p. Hence a given integer q is a multiple of m/s if and only if $X_{qs} \equiv 0$, if and only if q is a multiple of $m/\gcd(X_s, m)$.

22. Algorithm 4.5.4P is able to test numbers of the form $m = b^k \pm b^l \pm 1$ for primality in a reasonable time when, say, $b \approx 2^{32}$ and $l < k \approx 100$; the calculations should be done in radix b so that the special form of m speeds up the operation of squaring mod m. (Consider, for example, squaring mod 9999998999 in decimal notation.) Algorithm 4.5.4P should, of course, be used only when m is known to have no small divisors.

Marsaglia and Zaman [*Annals of Applied Probability* **1** (1991), 474–475] showed that $m = b^{43} - b^{22} + 1$ is prime with primitive root b when b is the prime number $2^{32} - 5$. This required factoring $m - 1 = b^{22}(b-1)(b^6 + b^5 + b^4 + b^3 + b^2 + b + 1)(b^{14} + b^7 + 1)$ in order to establish the primitivity of b; one of the 17 prime factors of $m - 1$ has 99 decimal digits. As a result, we can be sure that the sequence $x_n = (x_{n-22} - x_{n-43} - c_n) \bmod b =$

$x_{n-22} - x_{n-43} - c_n + bc_{n+1}$ has period length $m - 1 \approx 10^{414}$ for every nonzero choice of seed values $0 \le x_{-1}, \ldots, x_{-43} < b$ when $c_0 = 0$.

However, 43 is still a rather small value for k from the standpoint of the birthday spacings test (see Section 3.3.2J), and 22 is rather near $43/2$. Considerations of "mixing" indicate that we prefer values of k and l for which the first few partial quotients in the continued fraction of l/k are small. To avoid potential problems with this generator, it's a good idea to discard some of the numbers, as recommended by Lüscher (see Section 3.2.2).

Here are some prime numbers of the form $b^k \pm b^l \pm 1$ that satisfy the mixing constraint when $b = 2^{32}$ and $50 < k \le 100$: For subtract-with-borrow, $b^{57} - b^{17} - 1$, $b^{73} - b^{17} - 1$, $b^{86} - b^{62} - 1$, $b^{88} - b^{52} - 1$, $b^{95} - b^{61} - 1$; $b^{58} - b^{33} + 1$, $b^{62} - b^{17} + 1$, $b^{69} - b^{24} + 1$, $b^{70} - b^{57} + 1$, $b^{87} - b^{24} + 1$. For add-with-carry, $b^{56} + b^{22} - 1$, $b^{61} + b^{44} - 1$, $b^{74} + b^{27} - 1$, $b^{90} + b^{65} - 1$. (Less desirable from a mixing standpoint are the primes $b^{56} - b^5 - 1$, $b^{56} - b^{32} - 1$, $b^{66} - b^{57} - 1$, $b^{76} - b^{15} - 1$, $b^{84} - b^{26} - 1$, $b^{90} - b^{42} - 1$, $b^{93} - b^{18} - 1$; $b^{52} - b^8 + 1$, $b^{60} - b^{12} + 1$, $b^{67} - b^8 + 1$, $b^{67} - b^{63} + 1$, $b^{83} - b^{14} + 1$; $b^{65} + b^2 - 1$, $b^{76} + b^{11} - 1$, $b^{88} + b^{30} - 1$, $b^{92} + b^{48} - 1$.)

To calculate the period of the resulting sequences, we need to know the factors of $m - 1$; but this isn't feasible for such large numbers unless we are extremely lucky. Suppose we do succeed in finding the prime factors $q_1, \ldots, q_t$; then the probability that $b^{(m-1)/q} \bmod m = 1$ is extremely small, only $1/q$, except for the very small primes q. Therefore we can be quite confident that the period of $b^n \bmod m$ is extremely long even though we cannot factor $m - 1$.

Indeed, the period is almost certainly very long even if m is not prime. Consider, for example, the case $k = 10$, $l = 3$, $b = 10$ (which is much too small for random number generation but small enough that we can easily compute the exact results). In this case $\langle 10^n \bmod m \rangle$ has period length $\text{lcm}(219, 11389520) = 2494304880$ when $m = 9999998999 = 439 \cdot 22779041$; 4999999500 when $m = 9999999001$; 5000000499 when $m = 10000000999$; and $\text{lcm}(1, 16, 2686, 12162) = 130668528$ when $m = 10000001001 = 3 \cdot 17 \cdot 2687 \cdot 72973$. Rare choices of the seed values may shorten the period when m is not prime. But we can hardly go wrong if we choose, say, $k = 1000$, $l = 619$, and $b = 2^{16}$.

SECTION 3.2.1.3

1. $c = 1$ is always relatively prime to B^5; and every prime dividing $m = B^5$ is a divisor of B, so it divides $b = B^2$ to at least the second power.

2. Only 3, so the generator is not recommended in spite of its long period.

3. The potency is 18 in both cases (see the next exercise).

4. Since $a \bmod 4 = 1$, we must have $a \bmod 8 = 1$ or 5, so $b \bmod 8 = 0$ or 4. If b is an odd multiple of 4, and if b_1 is a multiple of 8, clearly $b^s \equiv 0$ (modulo 2^e) implies that $b_1^s \equiv 0$ (modulo 2^e), so b_1 cannot have higher potency than b.

5. The potency is the smallest value of s such that $f_j s \ge e_j$ for all j.

6. The modulus must be divisible by 2^7 or by p^4 (for odd prime p) in order to have a potency as high as 4. The only values are $m = 2^{27} + 1$ and $10^9 - 1$.

7. $a' = (1 - b + b^2 - \cdots) \bmod m$, where the terms in b^s, b^{s+1}, etc., are dropped (if s is the potency).

8. Since X_n is always odd,

$$X_{n+2} = (2^{34} + 3 \cdot 2^{18} + 9)X_n \bmod 2^{35} = (2^{34} + 6X_{n+1} - 9X_n) \bmod 2^{35}.$$

Given Y_n and Y_{n+1}, the possibilities for

$$Y_{n+2} = (10 + 6(Y_{n+1} + \epsilon_1) - 9(Y_n + \epsilon_2)) \bmod 20,$$

with $0 \le \epsilon_1 < 1$, $0 \le \epsilon_2 < 1$, are limited and nonrandom.

Note: If the multiplier suggested in exercise 3 were, say, $2^{33} + 2^{18} + 2^2 + 1$, instead of $2^{23} + 2^{13} + 2^2 + 1$, we would similarly find $X_{n+2} - 10X_{n+1} + 25X_n \equiv$ constant (modulo 2^{35}). In general, we do not want $a \pm \delta$ to be divisible by high powers of 2 when δ is small, else we get "second-order impotency." See Section 3.3.4 for a more detailed discussion.

The generator that appears in this exercise is discussed in an article by MacLaren and Marsaglia, *JACM* **12** (1965), 83–89. The deficiencies of such generators were first demonstrated by M. Greenberger, *CACM* **8** (1965), 177–179. Yet generators like this were still in widespread use more than ten years later (see the discussion of RANDU in Section 3.3.4).

SECTION 3.2.2

1. The method is useful only with great caution. In the first place, aU_n is likely to be so large that the addition of c/m that follows will lose almost all significance, and the "mod 1" operation will nearly destroy any vestiges of significance that might remain. We conclude that double-precision floating point arithmetic is necessary. Even with double precision, one must be sure that no rounding, etc., occurs to affect the numbers of the sequence in any way, since that would destroy the theoretical grounds for the good behavior of the sequence. (But see exercise 23.)

2. X_{n+1} equals either $X_{n-1} + X_n$ or $X_{n-1} + X_n - m$. If $X_{n+1} < X_n$ we must have $X_{n+1} = X_{n-1} + X_n - m$; hence $X_{n+1} < X_{n-1}$.

3. (a) The underlined numbers are $V[j]$ after step M3.

Output: initial		
		0 4 5 6 2 0 3(2 7 4 1 6 3 0 5) and repeats.
$V[0]$:	0	4 <u>7</u> 7 7 7 7 7 7 <u>4</u> <u>7</u> 7 7 7 7 7 7 <u>4</u> <u>7</u> $\cdots$
$V[1]$:	3	3 3 3 3 3 3 <u>2</u> <u>5</u> 5 5 5 5 5 5 <u>2</u> <u>5</u> 5 5 $\cdots$
$V[2]$:	2	2 2 2 2 <u>0</u> <u>3</u> 3 3 3 3 3 3 <u>0</u> <u>3</u> 3 3 3 3 $\cdots$
$V[3]$:	5	5 5 <u>6</u> <u>1</u> 1 1 1 1 1 <u>6</u> <u>1</u> 1 1 1 1 1 $\cdots$
X:		4 7 6 1 0 3 2 5 4 7 6 1 0 3 2 5 4 7 $\cdots$
Y:		0 1 6 7 4 5 2 3 0 1 6 7 4 5 2 3 0 1 $\cdots$

So the potency has been reduced to 1! (See further comments in the answer to exercise 15.)

(b) The underlined numbers are $V[j]$ after step B2.

Output: initial		
		2 3 6 5 7 0 0 5 3 $\ldots$ 4 6(3 0 $\ldots$ 4 7)$\ldots$
$V[0]$:	0	0 0 0 0 0 0 <u>5</u> <u>4</u> 4 $\ldots$ 1 1 1 1 $\ldots$ 1 1 $\ldots$
$V[1]$:	3	3 <u>6</u> <u>1</u> 1 1 1 1 1 1 $\ldots$ 0 0 <u>4</u> $\ldots$ 0 0 $\ldots$
$V[2]$:	2	<u>7</u> 7 7 7 <u>3</u> 3 3 3 <u>7</u> $\ldots$ 6 <u>2</u> 2 2 $\ldots$ 7 <u>2</u> $\ldots$
$V[3]$:	5	5 5 5 <u>0</u> 0 <u>2</u> 2 2 2 $\ldots$ 3 3 <u>5</u> 5 $\ldots$ <u>3</u> 3 $\ldots$
X:	4	7 6 1 0 3 2 5 4 7 $\ldots$ 3 2 5 4 $\ldots$ 3 2 $\ldots$

In this case the output is considerably better than the input; it enters a repeating cycle of length 40 after 46 steps: 236570 05314 72632 40110 37564 76025 12541 73625 03746 (30175 24061 52317 46203 74531 60425 16753 02647). The cycle can be found easily by applying the method of exercise 3.1–7 to the array above until a column is repeated.

4. The low-order byte of many random sequences (e.g., linear congruential sequences with m = word size) is much less random than the high-order byte. See Section 3.2.1.1.

5. The randomizing effect would be quite minimized, because $V[j]$ would always contain a number in a certain range, essentially $j/k \leq V[j]/m < (j+1)/k$. However, some similar approaches could be used: We could take $Y_n = X_{n-1}$, or we could choose j from X_n by extracting some digits from the middle instead of at the extreme left. None of these suggestions would produce a lengthening of the period analogous to the behavior of Algorithm B. (Exercise 27 shows, however, that Algorithm B doesn't necessarily increase the period length.)

6. For example, if $X_n/m < \frac{1}{2}$, then $X_{n+1} = 2X_n$.

7. [W. Mantel, *Nieuw Archief voor Wiskunde* (2) **1** (1897), 172–184.]

The subsequence of
X values:

00...01	
00...10	
. . .	becomes:
10...00	
CONTENTS(A)	

00...01
00...10
. . .
10...00
00...00
CONTENTS(A)

8. We may assume that $X_0 = 0$ and $m = p^e$, as in the proof of Theorem 3.2.1.2A. First suppose that the sequence has period length p^e; it follows that the period of the sequence mod p^f has length p^f, for $1 \leq f \leq e$, otherwise some residues mod p^f would never occur. Clearly, c is not a multiple of p, for otherwise each X_n would be a multiple of p. If $p \leq 3$, it is easy to establish the necessity of conditions (iii) and (iv) by trial and error, so we may assume that $p \geq 5$. If $d \not\equiv 0$ (modulo p) then $dx^2 + ax + c \equiv d(x + a_1)^2 + c_1$ (modulo p^e) for some integers a_1 and c_1 and for all integers x; this quadratic takes the same value at the points x and $-x - 2a_1$, so it cannot assume all values modulo p^e. Hence $d \equiv 0$ (modulo p); and if $a \not\equiv 1$, we would have $dx^2 + ax + c \equiv x$ (modulo p) for some x, contradicting the fact that the sequence mod p has period length p.

To show the sufficiency of the conditions, we may assume by Theorem 3.2.1.2A and consideration of some trivial cases that $m = p^e$ where $e \geq 2$. If $p = 2$, we have $X_{n+2} \equiv X_n + 2$ (modulo 4), by trial; and if $p = 3$, we have $X_{n+3} \equiv X_n - d + 3c$ (modulo 9), using (i) and (ii). For $p \geq 5$, we can prove that $X_{n+p} \equiv X_n + pc$ (modulo p^2): Let $d = pr$, $a = 1 + ps$. Then if $X_n \equiv cn + pY_n$ (modulo p^2), we must have $Y_{n+1} \equiv n^2c^2r + ncs + Y_n$ (modulo p); hence $Y_n \equiv \binom{n}{3}2c^2r + \binom{n}{2}(c^2r + cs)$ (modulo p). Thus Y_p mod $p = 0$, and the desired relation has been proved.

Now we can prove that the sequence $\langle X_n \rangle$ of integers defined in the "hint" satisfies the relation

$$X_{n+p^f} \equiv X_n + tp^f \pmod{p^{f+1}}, \qquad n \geq 0,$$

for some t with $t \bmod p \neq 0$, and for all $f \geq 1$. This suffices to prove that the sequence $\langle X_n \bmod p^e \rangle$ has period length p^e, for the length of the period is a divisor of p^e but not a divisor of p^{e-1}. The relation above has already been established for $f = 1$, and for $f > 1$ it can be proved by induction in the following manner: Let

$$X_{n+p^f} \equiv X_n + tp^f + Z_n p^{f+1} \pmod{p^{f+2}};$$

then the quadratic law for generating the sequence, with $d = pr$, $a = 1 + ps$, yields $Z_{n+1} \equiv 2rtnc + st + Z_n$ (modulo p). It follows that $Z_{n+p} \equiv Z_n$ (modulo p); hence

$$X_{n+kp^f} \equiv X_n + k(tp^f + Z_n p^{f+1}) \pmod{p^{f+2}}$$

for $k = 1, 2, 3, \ldots$; setting $k = p$ completes the proof.

   Notes: If $f(x)$ is a polynomial of degree higher than 2 and $X_{n+1} = f(X_n)$, the analysis is more complicated, although we can use the fact that $f(m + p^k) = f(m) + p^k f'(m) + p^{2k} f''(m)/2! + \cdots$ to prove that many polynomial recurrences give the maximum period. For example, Coveyou has proved that the period is $m = 2^e$ if $f(0)$ is odd, $f'(j) \equiv 1$, $f''(j) \equiv 0$, and $f(j+1) \equiv f(j) + 1$ (modulo 4) for $j = 0, 1, 2, 3$. [*Studies in Applied Math.* **3** (Philadelphia: SIAM, 1969), 70–111.]

9. Let $X_n = 4Y_n + 2$; then the sequence Y_n satisfies the quadratic recurrence $Y_{n+1} = (4Y_n^2 + 5Y_n + 1) \bmod 2^{e-2}$.

10. *Case 1:* $X_0 = 0$, $X_1 = 1$; hence $X_n \equiv F_n$. We seek the smallest n for which $F_n \equiv 0$ and $F_{n+1} \equiv 1$ (modulo 2^e). Since $F_{2n} = F_n(F_{n-1} + F_{n+1})$, $F_{2n+1} = F_n^2 + F_{n+1}^2$, we find by induction on e that, for $e > 1$, $F_{3 \cdot 2^{e-1}} \equiv 0$ and $F_{3 \cdot 2^{e-1}+1} \equiv 2^e + 1$ (modulo 2^{e+1}). This implies that the period is a divisor of $3 \cdot 2^{e-1}$ but not a divisor of $3 \cdot 2^{e-2}$, so it is either $3 \cdot 2^{e-1}$ or 2^{e-1}. But F_{2^e-1} is always odd (since only F_{3n} is even).

   Case 2: $X_0 = a$, $X_1 = b$. Then $X_n \equiv aF_{n-1} + bF_n$; we need to find the smallest positive n with $a(F_{n+1} - F_n) + bF_n \equiv a$ and $aF_n + bF_{n+1} \equiv b$. This implies that $(b^2 - ab - a^2)F_n \equiv 0$, $(b^2 - ab - a^2)(F_{n+1} - 1) \equiv 0$. And $b^2 - ab - a^2$ is odd (that is, prime to m); so the condition is equivalent to $F_n \equiv 0$, $F_{n+1} \equiv 1$.

   Methods to determine the period of $\langle F_n \rangle$ for any modulus appear in an article by D. D. Wall, *AMM* **67** (1960), 525–532. Further facts about the Fibonacci sequence mod 2^e have been derived by B. Jansson [*Random Number Generators* (Stockholm: Almqvist & Wiksell, 1966), Section 3C1].

11. (a) We have $z^\lambda = 1 + f(z)u(z) + p^e v(z)$ for some $u(z)$ and $v(z)$, where $v(z) \not\equiv 0$ (modulo $f(z)$ and p). By the binomial theorem,

$$z^{\lambda p} = 1 + p^{e+1} v(z) + p^{2e+1} v(z)^2 (p-1)/2$$

plus further terms congruent to zero (modulo $f(z)$ and p^{e+2}). Since $p^e > 2$, we have $z^{\lambda p} \equiv 1 + p^{e+1} v(z)$ (modulo $f(z)$ and p^{e+2}). If $p^{e+1} v(z) \equiv 0$ (modulo $f(z)$ and p^{e+2}), there must exist polynomials $a(z)$ and $b(z)$ such that $p^{e+1}(v(z) + pa(z)) = f(z)b(z)$. Since $f(0) = 1$, this implies that $b(z)$ is a multiple of p^{e+1} (by Gauss's Lemma 4.6.1G); hence $v(z) \equiv 0$ (modulo $f(z)$ and p), a contradiction.

   (b) If $z^\lambda - 1 = f(z)u(z) + p^e v(z)$, then

$$G(z) = u(z)/(z^\lambda - 1) + p^e v(z)/f(z)(z^\lambda - 1);$$

hence $A_{n+\lambda} \equiv A_n$ (modulo p^e) for large n. Conversely, if $\langle A_n \rangle$ has the latter property then $G(z) = u(z) + v(z)/(1 - z^\lambda) + p^e H(z)$, for some polynomials $u(z)$ and $v(z)$, and some power series $H(z)$, all with integer coefficients. This implies the identity $1 - z^\lambda = u(z)f(z)(1 - z^\lambda) + v(z)f(z) + p^e H(z)f(z)(1 - z^\lambda)$; and $H(z)f(z)(1 - z^\lambda)$ is a polynomial since the other terms of the equation are polynomials.

   (c) It suffices to prove that $\lambda(p^e) \neq \lambda(p^{e+1})$ implies that $\lambda(p^{e+1}) = p\lambda(p^e) \neq \lambda(p^{e+2})$. Applying (a) and (b), we know that $\lambda(p^{e+2}) \neq p\lambda(p^e)$, and that $\lambda(p^{e+1})$ is a divisor of $p\lambda(p^e)$ but not of $\lambda(p^e)$. Hence if $\lambda(p^e) = p^f q$, where $q \bmod p \neq 0$, then $\lambda(p^{e+1})$ must be $p^{f+1}d$, where d is a divisor of q. But now $X_{n+p^{f+1}d} \equiv X_n$ (modulo p^e); hence $p^{f+1}d$ is a multiple of $p^f q$, hence $d = q$. [*Note:* The hypothesis $p^e > 2$ is

necessary; for example, let $a_1 = 4$, $a_2 = -1$, $k = 2$; then $\langle A_n \rangle = 1, 4, 15, 56, 209, 780,$
$\ldots$; $\lambda(2) = 2$, $\lambda(4) = 4$, $\lambda(8) = 4$.]

(d) $g(z) = X_0 + (X_1 - a_1 X_0)z + \cdots + (X_{k-1} - a_1 X_{k-2} - a_2 X_{k-3} - \cdots - a_{k-1}X_0)z^{k-1}$.

(e) The derivation in (b) can be generalized to the case $G(z) = g(z)/f(z)$; then
the assumption of period length λ implies that $g(z)(1 - z^\lambda) \equiv 0$ (modulo $f(z)$ and p^e);
we treated only the special case $g(z) = 1$ above. But both sides of this congruence can
be multiplied by Hensel's $b(z)$, and we obtain $1 - z^\lambda \equiv 0$ (modulo $f(z)$ and p^e).

Note: A more "elementary" proof of the result in (c) can be given without using
generating functions, using methods analogous to those in the answer to exercise 8: If
$A_{\lambda+n} = A_n + p^e B_n$, for $n = r, r+1, \ldots, r+k-1$ and some integers B_n, then this
same relation holds for *all* $n \geq r$ if we define $B_{r+k}, B_{r+k+1}, \ldots$ by the given recurrence
relation. Since the resulting sequence of B's is some linear combination of shifts of
the sequence of A's, we will have $B_{\lambda+n} \equiv B_n$ (modulo p^e) for all large enough values
of n. Now $\lambda(p^{e+1})$ must be some multiple of $\lambda = \lambda(p^e)$; for all large enough n we have
$A_{n+j\lambda} = A_n + p^e(B_n + B_{n+\lambda} + B_{n+2\lambda} + \cdots + B_{n+(j-1)\lambda}) \equiv A_n + jp^e B_n$ (modulo p^{2e})
for $j = 1, 2, 3, \ldots$. No k consecutive B's are multiples of p; hence $\lambda(p^{e+1}) = p\lambda(p^e) \neq$
$\lambda(p^{e+2})$ follows immediately when $e \geq 2$. We still must prove that $\lambda(p^{e+2}) \neq p\lambda(p^e)$
when p is odd and $e = 1$; here we let $B_{\lambda+n} = B_n + pC_n$, and observe that $C_{n+\lambda} \equiv C_n$
(modulo p) when n is large enough. Then $A_{n+p\lambda} \equiv A_n + p^2\left(B_n + \binom{p}{2}C_n\right)$ (modulo p^3),
and the proof is readily completed.

For the history of this problem, see Morgan Ward, *Trans. Amer. Math. Soc.* **35**
(1933), 600–628; see also D. W. Robinson, *AMM* **73** (1966), 619–621.

12. The period length mod 2 can be at most 4; and the period length mod 2^{e+1} is at
most twice the maximum length mod 2^e, by the considerations of the previous exercise.
So the maximum conceivable period length is 2^{e+1}; this is achievable, for example, in
the trivial case $a = 0$, $b = c = 1$.

13, 14. Clearly $Z_{n+\lambda} = Z_n$, so λ' is certainly a divisor of λ. Let the least common
multiple of λ' and λ_1 be λ_1', and define λ_2' similarly. We have $X_n + Y_n \equiv Z_n \equiv Z_{n+\lambda_1'} \equiv$
$X_n + Y_{n+\lambda_1'}$, so λ_1' is a multiple of λ_2. Similarly, λ_2' is a multiple of λ_1. This yields
the desired result. (The result is "best possible" in the sense that sequences for which
$\lambda' = \lambda_0$ can be constructed, as well as sequences for which $\lambda' = \lambda$.)

15. Algorithm M generates (X_{n+k}, Y_n) in step M1 and outputs $Z_n = X_{n+k-q_n}$ in step
M3, for all sufficiently large n. Thus $\langle Z_n \rangle$ has a period of length λ', where λ' is the
least positive integer such that $X_{n+k-q_n} = X_{n+\lambda'+k-q_{n+\lambda'}}$ for all large n. Since λ is a
multiple of λ_1 and λ_2, it follows that λ' is a divisor of λ. (These observations are due
to Alan G. Waterman.)

We also have $n + k - q_n \equiv n + \lambda' + k - q_{n+\lambda'}$ (modulo λ_1) for all large n, by the
distinctness of the X's. The bound on $\langle q_n \rangle$ implies that $q_{n+\lambda'} = q_n + c$ for all large n,
where $c \equiv \lambda'$ (modulo λ_1) and $|c| < \frac{1}{2}\lambda_1$. But c must be 0 since $\langle q_n \rangle$ is bounded. Hence
$\lambda' \equiv 0$ (modulo λ_1), and $q_{n+\lambda'} = q_n$ for all large n; it follows that λ' is a multiple of
λ_2 and λ_1, so $\lambda' = \lambda$.

Note: The answer to exercise 3.2.1.2–4 implies that when $\langle Y_n \rangle$ is a linear congruential sequence of maximum period modulo $m = 2^e$, the period length λ_2 will be at
most 2^{e-2} when k is a power of 2.

16. There are several methods of proof.

(1) Using the theory of finite fields. In the field with 2^k elements let ξ satisfy
$\xi^k = a_1\xi^{k-1} + \cdots + a_k$. Let $f(b_1\xi^{k-1} + \cdots + b_k) = b_k$, where each b_j is either zero

or one; this is a linear function. If word X in the generation algorithm is $(b_1 b_2 \ldots b_k)_2$ before (10) is executed, and if $b_1 \xi^{k-1} + \cdots + b_k \xi^0 = \xi^n$, then word X represents ξ^{n+1} after (10) is executed. Hence the sequence is $f(\xi^n)$, $f(\xi^{n+1})$, $f(\xi^{n+2})$, $\ldots$; and $f(\xi^{n+k}) = f(\xi^n \xi^k) = f(a_1 \xi^{n+k-1} + \cdots + a_k \xi^n) = a_1 f(\xi^{n+k-1}) + \cdots + a_k f(\xi^n)$.

(2) Using brute force, or elementary ingenuity. We are given a sequence X_{nj}, $n \geq 0$, $1 \leq j \leq k$, satisfying

$$X_{(n+1)j} \equiv X_{n(j+1)} + a_j X_{n1}, \quad 1 \leq j < k; \qquad X_{(n+1)k} \equiv a_k X_{n1} \text{ (modulo 2).}$$

We must show that this implies $X_{nk} \equiv a_1 X_{(n-1)k} + \cdots + a_k X_{(n-k)k}$, for $n \geq k$. Indeed, it implies $X_{nj} \equiv a_1 X_{(n-1)j} + \cdots + a_k X_{(n-k)j}$ when $1 \leq j \leq k \leq n$. This is clear for $j = 1$, since $X_{n1} \equiv a_1 X_{(n-1)1} + X_{(n-1)2} \equiv a_1 X_{(n-1)1} + a_2 X_{(n-2)1} + X_{(n-2)3}$, etc. For $j > 1$, we have by induction

$$X_{nj} \equiv X_{(n+1)(j-1)} - a_{j-1} X_{n1}$$

$$\equiv \sum_{1 \leq i \leq k} a_i X_{(n+1-i)(j-1)} - a_{j-1} \sum_{1 \leq i \leq k} a_i X_{(n-i)1}$$

$$\equiv \sum_{1 \leq i \leq k} a_i \left(X_{(n+1-i)(j-1)} - a_{j-1} X_{(n-i)1} \right)$$

$$\equiv a_1 X_{(n-1)j} + \cdots + a_k X_{(n-k)j}.$$

This proof does *not* depend on the fact that operations were done modulo 2, or modulo any prime number.

17. (a) When the sequence terminates, the $(k-1)$-tuple $(X_{n+1}, \ldots, X_{n+k-1})$ occurs for the $(m+1)$st time. A given $(k-1)$-tuple $(X_{r+1}, \ldots, X_{r+k-1})$ can have only m distinct predecessors X_r, so one of these occurrences must be for $r = 0$. (b) Since the $(k-1)$-tuple $(0, \ldots, 0)$ occurs $(m+1)$ times, each possible predecessor appears, so the k-tuple $(a_1, 0, \ldots, 0)$ appears for all a_1, $0 \leq a_1 < m$. Let $1 \leq s < k$ and suppose we have proved that all k-tuples $(a_1, \ldots, a_s, 0, \ldots, 0)$ appear in the sequence when $a_s \neq 0$. By the construction, this k-tuple would not be in the sequence unless $(a_1, \ldots, a_s, 0, \ldots, 0, y)$ had appeared earlier for $1 \leq y < m$. Hence the $(k-1)$-tuple $(a_1, \ldots, a_s, 0, \ldots, 0)$ has appeared m times, and all m possible predecessors appear; this means that $(a, a_1, \ldots, a_s, 0, \ldots, 0)$ appears for $0 \leq a < m$. The proof is now complete by induction.

The result also follows from Theorem 2.3.4.2D, using the directed graph of exercise 2.3.4.2–23. The arcs from $(x_1, \ldots, x_j, 0, \ldots, 0)$ to $(x_2, \ldots, x_j, 0, 0, \ldots, 0)$, where $x_j \neq 0$ and $1 \leq j \leq k$, form an oriented subtree related neatly to Dewey decimal notation.

18. By exercise 16, the most significant bit of U_{n+1} is completely determined by the first and third bits of U_n, so only 32 of the 64 possible pairs $(\lfloor 8U_n \rfloor, \lfloor 8U_{n+1} \rfloor)$ occur. [*Notes:* If we had used, say, 11-bit numbers $U_n = (.X_{11n} X_{11n+1} \cdots X_{11n+10})_2$, the sequence *would* be satisfactory for many applications. If another constant appears in A having more 1 bits, the generalized spectral test might give some indication of its suitability. See exercise 3.3.4–24; we could examine ν_t in dimensions $t = 36, 37, 38, \ldots$.]

20. For $k = 64$ one can use CONTENTS(A) = $(243F6A8885A308D3)_{16}$ (the bits of π!).

21. [*J. London Math. Society* (2) **21** (1946), 169–172.] Any sequence of period length $m^k - 1$ with no k consecutive zeros leads to a sequence of period length m^k by inserting a zero in the appropriate place, as in exercise 7; conversely, we can start with a sequence of period length m^k and delete an appropriate zero from the period, to form a sequence of the other type. Let us call these "(m, k) sequences" of types A and B. The hypothesis assures us of the existence of (p, k) sequences of type A, for all primes p and all $k \geq 1$; hence we have (p, k) sequences of type B for all such p and k.

To get a (p^e, k) sequence of type B, let $e = qr$, where q is a power of p and r is not a multiple of p. Start with a (p, qrk) sequence of type A, namely $X_0, X_1, X_2, \ldots$; then (using the p-ary number system) the grouped digits $(X_0 \ldots X_{q-1})_p, (X_q \ldots X_{2q-1})_p, \ldots$ form a (p^q, rk) sequence of type A, since q is relatively prime to $p^{qrk} - 1$ and the sequence therefore has a period length of $p^{qrk} - 1$. This leads to a (p^q, rk) sequence $\langle Y_n \rangle$ of type B; and $(Y_0 Y_1 \ldots Y_{r-1})_{p^q}, (Y_r Y_{r+1} \ldots Y_{2r-1})_{p^q}, \ldots$ is a (p^{qr}, k) sequence of type B by a similar argument, since r is relatively prime to p^{qk}.

To get an (m, k) sequence of type B for arbitrary m, we can combine (p^e, k) sequences for each of the prime power factors of m using the Chinese remainder theorem; but a simpler method is available. Let $\langle X_n \rangle$ be an (r, k) sequence of type B, and let $\langle Y_n \rangle$ be an (s, k) sequence of type B, where r and s are relatively prime; then $\langle (X_n + Y_n) \bmod rs \rangle$ is an (rs, k) sequence of type B, by exercise 13.

A simple, uniform construction that yields $(2, k)$ sequences for arbitrary k has been discovered by A. Lempel [*IEEE Trans.* **C-19** (1970), 1204–1209].

22. By the Chinese remainder theorem, we can find constants $a_1, \ldots, a_k$ having desired residues modulo each prime divisor of m. If $m = p_1 p_2 \ldots p_t$, the period length will be $\operatorname{lcm}(p_1^k - 1, \ldots, p_t^k - 1)$. In fact, we can achieve reasonably long periods for arbitrary m (not necessarily squarefree), as shown in exercise 11.

23. Subtraction may be faster than addition, see exercise 3.2.1.1–5; the period length is still $2^{e-1}(2^{55} - 1)$, by exercise 30. R. Brent has pointed out that the calculations can be done exactly on floating point numbers in $[0 \mathinner{.\,.} 1)$; see exercise 3.6–11.

24. Run the sequence backwards. In other words, if $Z_n = Y_{-n}$ we have $Z_n = (Z_{n-k+l} - Z_{n-k}) \bmod 2 = (Z_{n-k+l} + Z_{n-k}) \bmod 2$.

25. This idea can save most of the overhead of subroutine calls. For example, suppose Program A is invoked by calling `JMP RANDM`, where we have

```
RANDM  STJ  1F      ⎫
       LDA  Y,6     ⎪
        ⋮           ⎬  Program A
       ENT6 55      ⎪
1H     JMP  *       ⎭
```

The cost per random number is then $14 + \frac{2}{55}$ units of time. But suppose we generate random numbers by saying '`DEC6 1; J6Z RNGEN; LDA Y,6`' instead, with the subroutine

```
RNGEN  STJ  1F           ENT6 31
       ENT6 24           LDA  Y,6
       LDA  Y+31,6       ADD  Y+24,6
       ADD  Y,6          STA  Y,6
       STA  Y+31,6       DEC6 1
       DEC6 1            J6P  *-4
       J6P  *-4          ENT6 55
                    1H   JMP  *
```

The cost is now only $(12 + \frac{6}{55})u$. [A similar implementation, expressed in the C language, is used in *The Stanford GraphBase* (New York: ACM Press, 1994), GB_FLIP.] Indeed, many applications find it preferable to generate an array of random numbers all at once. Moreover, the latter approach is essentially mandatory when we enhance the randomness with Lüscher's method; see the C and FORTRAN routines in Section 3.6.

27. Let $J_n = \lfloor kX_n/m \rfloor$. **Lemma.** *After the $(k^2 + 7k - 2)/2$ consecutive values*

$$0^{k+2} \, 1 \, 0^{k+1} \, 2 \, 0^k \, \ldots \, (k-1) \, 0^3$$

occur in the $\langle J_n \rangle$ sequence, Algorithm B will have $V[j] < m/k$ for $0 \le j < k$, and also $Y < m/k$. Proof. Let S_n be the set of positions j such that $V[j] < m/k$ just before X_n is generated, and let j_n be the index such that $V[j_n] \leftarrow X_n$. If $j_n \notin S_n$ and $J_n = 0$, then $S_{n+1} = S_n \cup \{j_n\}$ and $j_{n+1} > 0$; if $j_n \in S_n$ and $J_n = 0$, then $S_{n+1} = S_n$ and $j_{n+1} = 0$. After $k+2$ successive 0s, we must therefore have $0 \in S_n$ and $j_{n+1} = 0$. Then after "1 0^{k+1}" we must have $\{0, 1\} \subseteq S_n$ and $j_{n+1} = 0$; after "2 0^k" we must have $\{0, 1, 2\} \subseteq S_n$ and $j_{n+1} = 0$; and so on.

    Corollary. *Let $l = (k^2 + 7k - 2)/2$. If $\lambda \ge lk^l$, either Algorithm B yields a period of length λ or the sequence $\langle X_n \rangle$ is poorly distributed. Proof.* The probability that any given length-l pattern of J's does not occur in a random sequence of length λ is less than $(1 - k^{-l})^{\lambda/l} < \exp(-k^{-l}\lambda/l) \le e^{-1}$; hence the stated pattern should appear. After it does, the subsequent behavior of Algorithm B will be the same each time it reaches this part of the period. (When $k > 4$, we are requiring $\lambda > 10^{21}$, so this result is purely academic. But smaller bounds may be possible.)

29. The following algorithm performs about k^2 operations in the worst case, but its average running time is much faster, perhaps $O(\log k)$ or even $O(1)$:

    X1. Set $(a_0, a_1, \ldots, a_k) \leftarrow (x_1, \ldots, x_k, m-1)$.

    X2. Let i be minimum with $a_i > 0$ and $i > 0$. Do subroutine Y for $j = i + 1$, $\ldots, k$, while $a_k > 0$.

    X3. If $a_0 > a_k$, $f(x_1, \ldots, x_k) = a_0$; otherwise if $a_0 > 0$, $f(x_1, \ldots, x_k) = a_0 - 1$; otherwise $f(x_1, \ldots, x_k) = a_k$.   ▌

    Y1. Set $l \leftarrow 0$. (The subroutine in steps Y1–Y3 essentially tests the lexicographic relation $(a_i, \ldots, a_{i+k-1}) \ge (a_j, \ldots, a_{j+k-1})$, decreasing a_k if necessary to make this inequality true. We assume that $a_{k+1} = a_1$, $a_{k+2} = a_2$, etc.)

    Y2. If $a_{i+l} > a_{j+l}$, exit the subroutine. Otherwise if $j + l = k$, set $a_k \leftarrow a_{i+l}$. Otherwise if $a_{i+l} = a_{j+l}$, go on to step Y3. Otherwise if $j + l > k$, decrease a_k by 1 and exit. Otherwise set $a_k \leftarrow 0$ and exit.

    Y3. Increase l by 1, and return to step Y2 if $l < k$.   ▌

    This problem was first solved by H. Fredricksen when $m = 2$ [*J. Combinatorial Theory* **9** (1970), 1–5; **A12** (1972), 153–154]; in that special case the algorithm is simpler and it can be done with k-bit registers. See also H. Fredricksen and J. Maiorana, *Discrete Math.* **23** (1978), 207–210, who essentially discovered Algorithm 7.2.1.1F.

30. (a) By exercise 11, it suffices to show that the period length mod 8 is $4(2^k - 1)$; this will be true if and only if $x^{2(2^k-1)} \not\equiv 1$ (modulo 8 and $f(x)$), if and only if $x^{2^k-1} \not\equiv 1$ (modulo 4 and $f(x)$). Write $f(x) = f_e(x^2) + xf_o(x^2)$, where $f_e(x^2) = \frac{1}{2}(f(x) + f(-x))$. Then $f(x)^2 + f(-x)^2 \equiv 2f(x^2)$ (modulo 8) if and only if $f_e(x)^2 + xf_o(x)^2 \equiv f(x)$ (modulo 4); and the latter condition holds if and only if $f_e(x)^2 \equiv -xf_o(x)^2$ (modulo 4 and $f(x)$), because $f_e(x)^2 + xf_o(x)^2 = f(x) + O(x^{k-1})$. Furthermore, working modulo 2 and $f(x)$, we have $f_e(x)^2 \equiv f_e(x^2) \equiv xf_o(x^2) \equiv x^{2^k}f_o(x)^2$, hence $f_e(x) \equiv x^{2^{k-1}}f_o(x)$. Therefore $f_e(x)^2 \equiv x^{2^k}f_o(x)^2$ (modulo 4 and $f(x)$), and the hint follows. A similar argument proves that $x^{2^k} \equiv x$ (modulo 4 and $f(x)$) if and only if $f(x)^2 + f(-x)^2 \equiv 2(-1)^k f(-x^2)$ (modulo 8).

    (b) The condition can hold only when l is odd and $k = 2l$. But then $f(x)$ is primitive modulo 2 only when $k = 2$. [*Math. Comp.* **63** (1994), 389–401.]

31. We have $X_n \equiv (-1)^{Y_n} 3^{Z_n} \bmod 2^e$ for some Y_n and Z_n, by Theorem 3.2.1.2C; hence $Y_n = (Y_{n-24} + Y_{n-55}) \bmod 2$ and $Z_n = (Z_{n-24} + Z_{n-55}) \bmod 2^{e-2}$. Since Z_k is odd if and only if $X_k \bmod 8 = 3$ or 5, the period length is $2^{e-3}(2^{55} - 1)$ by the previous exercise.

32. We can ignore the 'mod m' and put it back afterwards. The generating function $g(z) = \sum_n X_n z^n$ is a polynomial multiple of $1/(1 - z^{24} - z^{55})$; hence $\sum_n X_{2n} z^{2n} = \frac{1}{2}(g(z) + g(-z))$ is a polynomial divided by $(1 - z^{24} - z^{55})(1 - z^{24} + z^{55}) = 1 - 2z^{24} + z^{48} - z^{110}$. The first desired recurrence is therefore $X_{2n} = (2X_{2(n-12)} - X_{2(n-24)} + X_{2(n-55)}) \bmod m$. Similarly, $\sum_n X_{3n} z^{3n} = \frac{1}{3}(g(z) + g(\omega z) + g(\omega^2 z))$ where $\omega = e^{2\pi i/3}$, and we find $X_{3n} = (3X_{3(n-8)} - 3X_{3(n-16)} + X_{3(n-24)} + X_{3(n-55)}) \bmod m$.

33. (a) $g_{n+t}(z) \equiv z^t g_n(z)$ (modulo m and $1 + z^{31} - z^{55}$), by induction on t. (b) Since $z^{500} \bmod (1 + z^{31} - z^{55}) = 792z^2 + z^5 + 17z^6 + 715z^9 + 36z^{12} + z^{13} + 364z^{16} + 210z^{19} + 105z^{23} + 462z^{26} + 16z^{30} + 1287z^{33} + 9z^{36} + 18z^{37} + 1001z^{40} + 120z^{43} + z^{44} + 455z^{47} + 462z^{50} + 120z^{54}$ (see Algorithm 4.6.1D), we have $X_{500} = (792X_2 + X_5 + \cdots + 120X_{54}) \bmod m$.

[It is interesting to compare the similar formula $X_{165} = (X_0 + 3X_7 + X_{14} + 3X_{31} + 4X_{38} + X_{45}) \bmod m$ to the sparser recurrence for $\langle X_{3n} \rangle$ in the previous exercise. Lüscher's method of generating 165 numbers and using only the first 55 is clearly superior to the idea of generating 165 and using only $X_3, X_6, \ldots, X_{165}$.]

34. Let $q_0 = 0$, $q_1 = 1$, $q_{n+1} = cq_n + aq_{n-1}$. Then we have $\left(\begin{smallmatrix} 0 & 1 \\ a & c \end{smallmatrix}\right)^n = \left(\begin{smallmatrix} aq_{n-1} & q_n \\ aq_n & q_{n+1} \end{smallmatrix}\right)$, $X_n = (q_{n+1}X_0 + aq_n)/(q_n X_0 + aq_{n-1})$, and $x^n \bmod f(x) \equiv q_n x + aq_{n-1}$, for $n \geq 1$. Thus if $X_0 = 0$ we have $X_n = 0$ if and only if $x^n \bmod f(x)$ is a nonzero constant.

35. Conditions (i) and (ii) imply that $f(x)$ is irreducible. For if $f(x) = (x - r_1)(x - r_2)$ and $r_1 r_2 \neq 0$ we have $x^{p-1} \equiv 1$ if $r_1 \neq r_2$ and $x^p \equiv r_1$ if $r_1 = r_2$.

Let ξ be a primitive root of a field with p^2 elements, and suppose $\xi^{2k} = c_k \xi^k + a_k$. The quadratic polynomials we seek are precisely the polynomials $f_k(x) = x^2 - c_k x - a_k$ where $1 \leq k < p^2 - 1$ and $k \perp p + 1$. (See exercise 4.6.2–16.) Each polynomial occurs for two values of k; hence the number of solutions is $\frac{1}{2}(p^2 - 1) \prod_{q \backslash p+1, \, q \text{ prime}} (1 - 1/q)$.

36. In this case X_n is always odd, so X_n^{-1} exists mod 2^e. The sequence $\langle q_n \rangle$ defined in answer 34 is 0, 1, 2, 1, 0, 1, 2, 1, ... modulo 4. We also have $q_{2n} = q_n(q_{n+1} + aq_{n-1})$ and $q_{2n-1} = aq_{n-1}^2 + q_n^2$; hence $q_{2n+1} - aq_{2n-1} = (q_{n+1} - aq_{n-1})(q_{n+1} + aq_{n+1})$. Since $q_{n+1} + aq_{n+1} \equiv 2$ (modulo 4) when n is even, we deduce that q_{2^e} is an odd multiple of 2^e and $q_{2^e+1} - aq_{2^e-1}$ is an odd multiple of 2^{e+1}, for all $e \geq 0$. Therefore

$$q_{2^e} + aq_{2^e-1} \equiv q_{2^e+1} + aq_{2^e} + 2^{e+1} \pmod{2^{e+2}}.$$

And $X_{2^{e-2}} \equiv (q_{2^{e-2}+1} + aq_{2^{e-2}})/(q_{2^{e-2}} + aq_{2^{e-2}-1}) \not\equiv 1$ (modulo 2^e), while $X_{2^{e-1}} \equiv 1$. Conversely, we need $a \bmod 4 = 1$ and $c \bmod 4 = 2$; otherwise $X_{2n} \equiv 1$ (modulo 8). [Eichenauer, Lehn, and Topuzoğlu, *Math. Comp.* **51** (1988), 757–759.] The low-order bits of this sequence have a short period, so inversive generators with prime modulus are preferable.

37. We can assume that $b_1 = 0$. By exercise 34, a typical vector in V is

$$(x, (s_2' x + as_2)/(s_2 x + as_2''), \ldots, (s_d' x + as_d)/(s_d x + as_d'')),$$

where $s_j = q_{b_j}$, $s_j' = q_{b_j+1}$, $s_j'' = q_{b_j-1}$. This vector belongs to the hyperplane H if and only if

$$r_1 x + \frac{r_2 t_2}{x + u_2} + \cdots + \frac{r_d t_d}{x + u_d} \equiv r_0 - r_2 s_2' s_2^{-1} - \cdots - r_d s_d' s_d^{-1} \pmod{p},$$

where $t_j = a - a s_j' s_j'' s_j^{-2} = -(-a)^{b_j} s_j^{-2}$ and $u_j = a s_j'' s_j^{-1}$. But this relation is equivalent to a polynomial congruence of degree $\leq d$; so it cannot hold for $d+1$ values of x unless it holds for all x, including the distinct points $x = u_2, \ldots, x = u_d$. Hence $r_2 = \cdots = r_d \equiv 0$, and $r_1 \equiv 0$. [See J. Eichenauer-Herrmann, *Math. Comp.* **56** (1991), 297–301.]

   Notes: If we consider the $(p+1-d) \times (d+1)$ matrix M with rows $\{(1, v_1, \ldots, v_d) \mid (v_1, \ldots, v_d) \in V\}$, this exercise is equivalent to the assertion that any $d+1$ rows of M are linearly independent modulo p. It is interesting to plot the points (X_n, X_{n+1}) for $p \approx 1000$ and $0 \leq n \leq p$; traces of circles, rather than straight lines, meet the eye.

38. In fact [www10.plala.or.jp/h-nkzw/04eprsq1.pdf], $bX_n = mx_n + X_{n+1}$ for all n.

SECTION 3.3.1

1. There are $k = 11$ categories, so the line $\nu = 10$ should be used.

2. $\frac{2}{49}, \frac{3}{49}, \frac{4}{49}, \frac{5}{49}, \frac{6}{49}, \frac{9}{49}, \frac{6}{49}, \frac{5}{49}, \frac{4}{49}, \frac{3}{49}, \frac{2}{49}$.

3. $V = 7\frac{173}{240}$, only very slightly higher than that obtained from the good dice! There are two reasons why we do not detect the weighting: (a) The new probabilities (see exercise 2) are not really very far from the old ones in Eq. (1). The sum of the two dice tends to smooth out the probabilities; if we counted instead each of the 36 possible pairs of values, we would probably detect the difference quite rapidly (assuming that the two dice are distinguishable). (b) A far more important reason is that n is too small for a significant difference to be detected. If the same experiment is done for large enough n, the faulty dice will be discovered (see exercise 12).

4. $p_s = \frac{1}{12}$ for $2 \leq s \leq 12$ and $s \neq 7$; $p_7 = \frac{1}{6}$. The value of V is $16\frac{1}{2}$, which falls between the 75% and 95% entries in Table 1; so it is reasonable, in spite of the fact that not too many sevens actually turned up.

5. $K_{20}^+ = 1.15$; $K_{20}^- = 0.215$; these values do not differ significantly from random behavior (being at about the 94% and 86% levels), but they are mighty close. (The data values in this exercise come from Appendix A, Table 1.)

6. The probability that $X_j \leq x$ is $F(x)$, so we have the binomial distribution discussed in Section 1.2.10: $F_n(x) = s/n$ with probability $\binom{n}{s} F(x)^s (1 - F(x))^{n-s}$; the mean is $F(x)$; the standard deviation is $\sqrt{F(x)(1 - F(x))/n}$. [See Eq. 1.2.10–(19). This suggests that a slightly better statistic would be to define

$$K_n^+ = \sqrt{n} \max_{-\infty < x < \infty} (F_n(x) - F(x)) / \sqrt{F(x)(1 - F(x))};$$

see exercise 22. We can calculate the mean and standard deviation of $F_n(y) - F_n(x)$, for $x < y$, and obtain the covariance of $F_n(x)$ and $F_n(y)$. Using these facts, it can be shown that for large values of n the function $F_n(x)$ behaves as a "Brownian motion," and techniques from this branch of probability theory may be used to study it. The situation is exploited in articles by J. L. Doob and M. D. Donsker, *Annals Math. Stat.* **20** (1949), 393–403 and **23** (1952), 277–281; their approach is generally regarded as the most enlightening way to study the KS tests.]

7. Set $j = n$ in Eq. (13) to see that K_n^+ is never negative, and that it can get as high as $\sqrt{n}$. Similarly, set $j = 1$ to make the same observations about K_n^-.

8. The new KS statistic was computed for 20 observations. The distribution of K_{10}^+ was used as $F(x)$ when the KS statistic was computed.

9. The idea is erroneous, because all of the observations must be *independent*. There is a relation between the statistics K_n^+ and K_n^- on the same data, so each test should be judged separately. (A high value of one tends to give a low value of the other.) Similarly, the entries in Figs. 2 and 5, which show 15 tests for each generator, do not show 15 independent observations, because the maximum-of-5 test is not independent of the maximum-of-4 test. The three tests of each horizontal row are independent (because they were done on different parts of the sequence), but the five tests in a column are somewhat correlated. The net effect of this is that the 95-percent probability levels, etc., which apply to one test, cannot legitimately be applied to a whole group of tests on the same data. Moral: When testing a random number generator, we may expect it to "pass" each of several tests, like the frequency test, maximum test, and run test; but an array of data from several different tests should not be considered as a unit since the tests themselves may not be independent. The K_n^+ and K_n^- statistics should be considered as two separate tests; a good source of random numbers will pass both.

10. Each Y_s is doubled, and np_s is doubled, so the numerators of (6) are quadrupled while the denominators only double. Hence the new value of V is twice as high as the old one.

11. The empirical distribution function stays the same; the values of K_n^+ and K_n^- are multiplied by $\sqrt{2}$.

12. Let $Z_s = (Y_s - nq_s)/\sqrt{nq_s}$. The value of V is n times

$$\sum_{s=1}^{k} (q_s - p_s + \sqrt{q_s/n}\, Z_s)^2 / p_s,$$

and the latter quantity stays bounded away from zero as n increases (since $Z_s n^{-1/4}$ is bounded with probability 1). Hence the value of V will increase to a value that is extremely improbable under the p_s assumption.

For the KS test, let $F(x)$ be the assumed distribution, $G(x)$ the actual distribution, and let $h = \max|G(x) - F(x)|$. Take n large enough so that $|F_n(x) - G(x)| > h/2$ occurs with very small probability; then $|F_n(x) - F(x)|$ will be improbably high under the assumed distribution $F(x)$.

13. (The "max" notation should really be replaced by "sup" since a least upper bound is meant; however, "max" was used in the text to avoid confusing too many readers by the less familiar "sup" notation.) For convenience, let $X_0 = -\infty$, $X_{n+1} = +\infty$. When $X_j \leq x < X_{j+1}$, we have $F_n(x) = j/n$; therefore $\max(F_n(x) - F(x)) = j/n - F(X_j)$ and $\max(F(x) - F_n(x)) = F(X_{j+1}) - j/n$ in this interval. As j varies from 0 to n, all real values of x are considered; this proves that

$$K_n^+ = \sqrt{n} \max_{0 \leq j \leq n} \left(\frac{j}{n} - F(X_j) \right);$$

$$K_n^- = \sqrt{n} \max_{1 \leq j \leq n+1} \left(F(X_j) - \frac{j-1}{n} \right).$$

These equalities are equivalent to (13), since the extra term under the maximum signs is nonpositive and it must be redundant by exercise 7.

14. The logarithm of the left-hand side simplifies to

$$-\sum_{s=1}^{k} Y_s \ln\left(1 + \frac{Z_s}{\sqrt{np_s}}\right) + \frac{1-k}{2} \ln(2\pi n) - \frac{1}{2}\sum_{s=1}^{k} \ln p_s - \frac{1}{2}\sum_{s=1}^{k} \ln\left(1 + \frac{Z_s}{\sqrt{np_s}}\right) + O\left(\frac{1}{n}\right),$$

and this quantity simplifies further (upon expanding $\ln(1 + Z_s/\sqrt{np_s})$ and realizing that $\sum_{s=1}^{k} Z_s\sqrt{np_s} = 0$) to

$$-\frac{1}{2}\sum_{s=1}^{k} Z_s^2 + \frac{1-k}{2}\ln(2\pi n) - \frac{1}{2}\ln(p_1 \ldots p_k) + O\left(\frac{1}{\sqrt{n}}\right).$$

15. The corresponding Jacobian determinant is easily evaluated by (i) removing the factor r^{n-1} from the determinant, (ii) expanding the resulting determinant by the cofactors of the row containing "$\cos\theta_1 \; -\sin\theta_1 \; 0 \ldots 0$" (each of the cofactor determinants may be evaluated by induction), and (iii) recalling that $\sin^2\theta_1 + \cos^2\theta_1 = 1$.

16.
$$\int_0^{z\sqrt{2x}+y} \exp\left(-\frac{u^2}{2x} + \cdots\right) du = ye^{-z^2} + O\left(\frac{1}{\sqrt{x}}\right) + \int_0^{z\sqrt{2x}} \exp\left(-\frac{u^2}{2x} + \cdots\right) du.$$

The latter integral is

$$\int_0^{z\sqrt{2x}} e^{-u^2/2x}\, du + \frac{1}{3x^2}\int_0^{z\sqrt{2x}} e^{-u^2/2x} u^3\, du + O\left(\frac{1}{\sqrt{x}}\right).$$

When all is put together, the final result is

$$\frac{\gamma(x+1,\, x+z\sqrt{2x}+y)}{\Gamma(x+1)} = \frac{1}{\sqrt{2\pi}}\int_{-\infty}^{z\sqrt{2}} e^{-u^2/2}\, du + \frac{e^{-z^2}}{\sqrt{2\pi x}}(y - \tfrac{2}{3} - \tfrac{2}{3}z^2) + O\left(\frac{1}{x}\right).$$

If we set $z\sqrt{2} = x_p$ and write

$$\frac{1}{\sqrt{2\pi}}\int_{-\infty}^{z\sqrt{2}} e^{-u^2/2}\, du = p, \qquad x+1 = \frac{\nu}{2}, \qquad \gamma\left(\frac{\nu}{2}, \frac{t}{2}\right)\Big/\Gamma\left(\frac{\nu}{2}\right) = p,$$

where $t/2 = x + z\sqrt{2x} + y$, we can solve for y to obtain $y = \frac{2}{3}(1 + z^2) + O(1/\sqrt{x})$, which is consistent with the analysis above. The solution is therefore $t = \nu + 2\sqrt{\nu}z + \frac{4}{3}z^2 - \frac{2}{3} + O(1/\sqrt{\nu})$.

17. (a) Change of variable, $x_j \leftarrow x_j + t$.
    (b) Induction on n; by definition, $P_{n0}(x - t) = \int_n^x P_{(n-1)0}(x_n - t)\, dx_n$.
    (c) The left-hand side is

$$\int_n^{x+t} dx_n \ldots \int_{k+1}^{x_{k+2}} dx_{k+1} \quad \text{times} \quad \int_t^k dx_k \int_t^{x_k} dx_{k-1} \ldots \int_t^{x_2} dx_1.$$

    (d) From (b) and (c) we have $P_{nk}(x) = \sum_{r=0}^{k} \frac{(r-t)^r}{r!} \frac{(x+t-r)^{n-r-1}}{(n-r)!}(x+t-n)$.
The numerator in (24) is $P_{n\lfloor t\rfloor}(n)$.

18. We may assume that $F(x) = x$ for $0 \le x \le 1$, as remarked in the text's derivation of (24). If $0 \le X_1 \le \cdots \le X_n \le 1$, let $Z_j = 1 - X_{n+1-j}$. We have $0 \le Z_1 \le \cdots \le Z_n \le 1$; and K_n^+ evaluated for $X_1, \ldots, X_n$ equals K_n^- evaluated for $Z_1, \ldots, Z_n$. This symmetrical relation gives a one-to-one correspondence between sets of equal volume for which K_n^+ and K_n^- fall in a given range.

20. For example, the term $O(1/n)$ is $-(\frac{4}{9}s^4 - \frac{2}{3}s^2)/n + O(n^{-3/2})$. A complete expansion has been obtained by H. A. Lauwerier, *Zeitschrift für Wahrscheinlichkeitstheorie und verwandte Gebiete* **2** (1963), 61–68.

23. Let m be any number $\geq n$. (a) If $\lfloor mF(X_i)\rfloor = \lfloor mF(X_j)\rfloor$ and $i > j$, then $i/n - F(X_i) > j/n - F(X_j)$. (b) Start with $a_k = 1.0$, $b_k = 0.0$, and $c_k = 0$ for $0 \leq k < m$. Then do the following for each observation X_j: Set $Y \leftarrow F(X_j)$, $k \leftarrow \lfloor mY\rfloor$, $a_k \leftarrow \min(a_k, Y)$, $b_k \leftarrow \max(b_k, Y)$, $c_k \leftarrow c_k + 1$. (Assume that $F(X_j) < 1$ so that $k < m$.) Then set $j \leftarrow 0$, $r^+ \leftarrow r^- \leftarrow 0$, and for $k = 0, 1, \ldots, m-1$ (in this order) do the following whenever $c_k > 0$: Set $r^- \leftarrow \max(r^-, a_k - j/n)$, $j \leftarrow j + c_k$, $r^+ \leftarrow \max(r^+, j/n - b_k)$. Finally set $K_n^+ \leftarrow \sqrt{n}\, r^+$, $K_n^- \leftarrow \sqrt{n}\, r^-$. The time required is $O(m+n)$, and the precise value of n need not be known in advance. (If the estimate $(k + \frac{1}{2})/m$ is used for a_k and b_k, so that only the values c_k are actually computed for each k, we obtain estimates of K_n^+ and K_n^- good to within $\frac{1}{2}\sqrt{n}/m$, even when $m < n$.) [*ACM Trans. Math. Software* **3** (1977), 60–64.]

25. (a) Since $c_{ij} = \mathrm{E}(\sum_{k=1}^n a_{ik}X_k \sum_{l=1}^n a_{jl}X_l) = \sum_{k=1}^n a_{ik}a_{jk}$, we have $C = AA^T$.

(b) Consider the singular value decomposition $A = UDV^T$, where U and V are orthogonal of sizes $m \times m$ and $n \times n$, and D is $m \times n$ with entries $d_{ij} = [i{=}j]\sigma_j$; the singular values σ_j are all positive. [See, for example, Golub and Van Loan, *Matrix Computations* (1996), §2.5.3.] If $C\bar{C}C = C$ we have $SBS = S$, where $S = DD^T$ and $B = U^T\bar{C}U$. Thus $s_{ij} = [i{=}j]\sigma_j^2$, where we let $\sigma_{n+1} = \cdots = \sigma_m = 0$, and $s_{ij} = \sum_{k,l} s_{ik}b_{kl}s_{lj} = \sigma_i^2\sigma_j^2 b_{ij}$. Consequently $b_{ij} = [i{=}j]/\sigma_j^2$ if $i, j \leq n$, and we deduce that D^TBD is the $n \times n$ identity matrix. Let $Y = (Y_1 - \mu_1, \ldots, Y_m - \mu_m)^T$ and $X = (X_1, \ldots, X_n)^T$; it follows that $W = Y^T\bar{C}Y = X^TA^T\bar{C}AX = X^TVD^TBDV^TX = X^TX$.

SECTION 3.3.2

1. The observations for a chi-square test must be independent. In the second sequence, successive observations are manifestly dependent, since the second component of one equals the first component of the next.

2. Form t-tuples $(Y_{jt}, \ldots, Y_{jt+t-1})$, for $0 \leq j < n$, and count how many of them are equal to each possible value. Apply the chi-square test with $k = d^t$ and with probability $1/d^t$ in each category. The number of observations, n, should be at least $5d^t$.

3. The probability that exactly j values are examined, namely the probability that U_{j-1} is the nth element that lies in the range $\alpha \leq U_{j-1} < \beta$, is easily seen to be

$$\binom{j-1}{n-1} p^n (1-p)^{j-n},$$

by enumeration of the possible places in which the other $n-1$ occurrences can appear and by evaluation of the probability of such a pattern. The generating function is $G(z) = (pz/(1 - (1-p)z))^n$, which makes sense since the given distribution is the n-fold convolution of the same thing for $n = 1$. Hence the mean and variance are proportional to n; the number of U's to be examined is now easily found to have the characteristics $(\min n, \text{ave } n/p, \max \infty, \text{dev } \sqrt{n(1-p)}/p)$. A more detailed discussion of this probability distribution when $n = 1$ may be found in the answer to exercise 3.4.1–17; see also the considerably more general results of exercise 2.3.4.2–26.

4. The probability of a gap of length $\geq r$ is the probability that r consecutive U's lie outside the given range, namely $(1-p)^r$. The probability of a gap of length exactly r is the probability for length $\geq r$ minus the probability for length $\geq (r+1)$.

5. As N goes to infinity, so does n (with probability 1), hence this test is just the same as the gap test described in the text except for the length of the very last gap. And the text's gap test certainly is asymptotic to the chi-square distribution stated, since the length of each gap is independent of the length of the others. [*Notes:* A quite complicated proof of this result by E. Bofinger and V. J. Bofinger appears in *Annals Math. Stat.* **32** (1961), 524–534. Their paper is noteworthy because it discusses several interesting variations of the gap test; they show, for example, that the quantity

$$\sum_{0 \le r \le t} \frac{(Y_r - (Np)p_r)^2}{(Np)p_r}$$

does *not* approach a chi-square distribution, although others had suggested this statistic as a "stronger" test because Np is the expected value of n.]

7. 5, 3, 5, 6, 5, 5, 4.

8. See exercise 10, with $w = d$.

9. (Change d to w in steps C1 and C4.) We have

$$p_r = \frac{d(d-1)\dots(d-w+1)}{d^r} \left\{ \begin{matrix} r-1 \\ w-1 \end{matrix} \right\}, \qquad \text{for } w \le r < t;$$

$$p_t = 1 - \frac{d!}{d^{t-1}} \left(\frac{1}{0!} \left\{ \begin{matrix} t-1 \\ d \end{matrix} \right\} + \dots + \frac{1}{(d-w)!} \left\{ \begin{matrix} t-1 \\ w \end{matrix} \right\} \right).$$

10. As in exercise 3, we really need consider only the case $n = 1$. The generating function for the probability that a coupon set has length r is

$$G(z) = \frac{d!}{(d-w)!} \sum_{r>0} \left\{ \begin{matrix} r-1 \\ w-1 \end{matrix} \right\} \left(\frac{z}{d} \right)^r = z^w \left(\frac{d-1}{d-z} \right) \dots \left(\frac{d-w+1}{d-(w-1)z} \right)$$

by the previous exercise and Eq. 1.2.9–(28). The mean and variance are readily computed using Theorem 1.2.10A and exercise 3.4.1–17. We find that

$$\text{mean}(G) = w + \left(\frac{d}{d-1} - 1 \right) + \dots + \left(\frac{d}{d-w+1} - 1 \right) = d(H_d - H_{d-w}) = \mu;$$

$$\text{var}(G) = d^2(H_d^{(2)} - H_{d-w}^{(2)}) - d(H_d - H_{d-w}) = \sigma^2.$$

The number of U's examined, as the search for a coupon set is repeated n times, therefore has the characteristics (min wn, ave μn, max ∞, dev $\sigma\sqrt{n}$).

11. $\left| 1 \left| 2 \right| 9 \ 8 \ 5 \ 3 \left| 6 \right| 7 \ 0 \left| 4 \right| \right.$.

12. Algorithm R (*Data for run test*).

    R1. [Initialize.] Set $j \leftarrow -1$, and set COUNT[1] $\leftarrow$ COUNT[2] $\leftarrow \dots \leftarrow$ COUNT[6] $\leftarrow 0$. Also set $U_n \leftarrow U_{n-1}$, for convenience in terminating the algorithm.

    R2. [Set r zero.] Set $r \leftarrow 0$.

    R3. [Is $U_j < U_{j+1}$?] Increase r and j by 1. If $U_j < U_{j+1}$, repeat this step.

    R4. [Record the length.] If $r \ge 6$, increase COUNT[6] by one, otherwise increase COUNT[r] by one.

    R5. [Done?] If $j < n - 1$, return to step R2. ▮

13. There are $(p+q+1)\binom{p+q}{p}$ ways to have $U_{i-1} \gtrless U_i < \dots < U_{i+p-1} \gtrless U_{i+p} < \dots < U_{i+p+q-1}$; subtract $\binom{p+q+1}{p+1}$ for those ways in which $U_{i-1} < U_i$, and subtract $\binom{p+q+1}{1}$ for those in which $U_{i+p-1} < U_{i+p}$; then add in 1 for the case that both $U_{i-1} < U_i$ and $U_{i+p-1} < U_{i+p}$, since this case has been subtracted out twice. (This is a special case of the inclusion-exclusion principle, which is explained further in Section 1.3.3.)

14. A run of length r occurs with probability $1/r! - 1/(r+1)!$, assuming distinct U's. Therefore we use $p_r = 1/r! - 1/(r+1)!$ for $r < t$ and $p_t = 1/t!$ for runs of length $\geq t$.

15. This is always true of $F(X)$ when F is continuous and X has distribution F; see the remarks preceding Eq. 3.3.1–(24).

16. (a) $Z_{jt} = \max(Z_{j(t-1)}, Z_{(j+1)(t-1)})$. If the $Z_{j(t-1)}$ are stored in memory, it is therefore a simple matter to transform this array into the set of Z_{jt} with no auxiliary storage required. (b) With his "improvement," each of the V's should indeed have the stated distribution, but the observations are no longer independent. In fact, when U_j is a relatively large value, all of $Z_{jt}, Z_{(j-1)t}, \ldots, Z_{(j-t+1)t}$ will be equal to U_j; so we almost have the effect of repeating the same data t times (and that would multiply V by t, as in exercise 3.3.1–10).

17. (b) By Binet's identity, the difference is $\sum_{0 \leq k < j < n} (U'_k V'_j - U'_j V'_k)^2$, and this is certainly nonnegative. (c) Therefore if $D^2 = N^2$, we must have $U'_k V'_j - U'_j V'_k = 0$, for all pairs j, k. This means that the matrix

$$\begin{pmatrix} U'_0 & U'_1 & \cdots & U'_{n-1} \\ V'_0 & V'_1 & \cdots & V'_{n-1} \end{pmatrix}$$

has rank < 2, so its rows are linearly dependent. (A more elementary proof can be given, using the fact that $U'_0 V'_j - U'_j V'_0 = 0$ for $1 \leq j < n$ implies the existence of constants α, β such that $\alpha U'_j + \beta V'_j = 0$ for all j, provided that U'_0 and V'_0 are not both zero; the latter case can be avoided by a suitable renumbering.)

18. (a) The numerator is $-(U_0 - U_1)^2$, the denominator is $(U_0 - U_1)^2$. (b) The numerator in this case is $-(U_0^2 + U_1^2 + U_2^2 - U_0 U_1 - U_1 U_2 - U_2 U_0)$; the denominator is $2(U_0^2 + \cdots - U_2 U_0)$. (c) The denominator always equals $\sum_{0 \leq j < k < n} (U_j - U_k)^2$, by exercise 1.2.3–30 or 1.2.3–31.

19. The stated result holds, in fact, whenever the joint distribution of $U_0, \ldots, U_{n-1}$ is symmetrical (unchanged under permutations). Let $S_1 = U_0 + \cdots + U_{n-1}$, $S_2 = U_0^2 + \cdots + U_{n-1}^2$, $X = U_0 U_1 + \cdots + U_{n-2} U_{n-1} + U_{n-1} U_0$, and $D = n S_2 - S_1^2$. Also let $\mathrm{E}\, f(U_0, \ldots, U_{n-1})$ denote the expected value of $f(U_0, \ldots, U_{n-1})$ subject to the condition $D \neq 0$. Since D is a symmetric function, we have $\mathrm{E}\, f(U_0, \ldots, U_{n-1}) = \mathrm{E}\, f(U_{p(0)}, \ldots, U_{p(n-1)})$ for all permutations p of $\{0, \ldots, n-1\}$. Therefore $\mathrm{E}\, S_2/D = n\, \mathrm{E}\, U_0^2/D$, $\mathrm{E}\, S_1^2/D = n(n-1)\,\mathrm{E}(U_0 U_1/D) + n\,\mathrm{E}\, U_0^2/D$, and $\mathrm{E}\, X/D = n\,\mathrm{E}(U_0 U_1/D)$. It follows that $1 = \mathrm{E}\,(n S_2 - S_1^2)/D = -(n-1)\,\mathrm{E}\,(nX - S_1^2)/D$. (Strictly speaking, $\mathrm{E}\, S_2/D$ and $\mathrm{E}\, S_1^2/D$ might be infinite, so we should be careful to work only with linear combinations of expected values that are known to exist.)

20. Let $E_{1111}, E_{211}, E_{22}, E_{31}$, and E_4 denote the respective values $\mathrm{E}(U_0 U_1 U_2 U_3/D^2)$, $\mathrm{E}(U_0^2 U_1 U_2/D^2)$, $\mathrm{E}(U_0^2 U_1^2/D^2)$, $\mathrm{E}(U_0^3 U_1/D^2)$, $\mathrm{E}(U_0^4/D^2)$. Then we have $\mathrm{E}\, S_2^2/D^2 = n(n-1)E_{22} + nE_4$, $\mathrm{E}(S_2 S_1^2/D^2) = n(n-1)(n-2)E_{211} + n(n-1)E_{22} + 2n(n-1)E_{31} + nE_4$, $\mathrm{E}\, S_1^4/D^2 = n(n-1)(n-2)(n-3)E_{1111} + 6n(n-1)(n-2)E_{211} + 3n(n-1)E_{22} + 4n(n-1)E_{31} + nE_4$, $\mathrm{E}\, X^2/D^2 = n(n-3)E_{1111} + 2nE_{211} + nE_{22}$, $\mathrm{E}(XS_1^2/D^2) = n(n-2)(n-3)E_{1111} + 5n(n-2)E_{211} + 2nE_{22} + 2nE_{31}$, $\mathrm{E}((U_0 - U_1)^4/D^2) = 6E_{22} - 8E_{31} + 2E_4$, and the first result follows.

Let $\delta = \alpha((\ln n)/n)^{1/3}$, $M = \alpha^3/2 + 1/3$, and $m = \lceil 1/\delta \rceil$. If we divide the range of the distribution into m equiprobable parts, we can show that each part will contain between $n\delta(1 - \delta)$ and $n\delta(1 + \delta)$ points, with probability $\geq 1 - O(n^{-M})$, using the tail inequalities 1.2.10–(24) and (25). Hence, if the distribution is uniform, $D = \frac{1}{12} n^2 (1 + O(\delta))$ with at least this probability. If D is not in that range, we have

$0 \le (U_0 - U_1)^4/D^2 \le 1$. Since $\mathrm{E}((U_0 - U_1)^4) = \int_0^1 \int_0^1 (x - y)^4 \, dx \, dy = \frac{1}{15}$, we may conclude that $\mathrm{E}((U_0 - U_1)^4/D^2) = \frac{48}{5} n^{-4}(1 + O(\delta)) + O(n^{-M})$.

Note: Let N be the numerator of (23). When the variables all have the normal distribution, W. J. Dixon proved that the expected value of $e^{(wN+zD)/n}$ is

$$(1 - 2z - 2w)^{1/2}\left(1 - 2z + \sqrt{(1 - 2z)^2 - 4w^2}\,\right)^{-n/2} + O(w^n).$$

Differentiating with respect to w and integrating with respect to z, he found the moments $\mathrm{E}(N/D)^{2k-1} = (-\frac{1}{2})^{\overline{k}}/(n - \frac{1}{2})^{\overline{k}}$, $\mathrm{E}(N/D)^{2k} = (+\frac{1}{2})^{\overline{k}}/(n + \frac{1}{2})^{\overline{k}}$, when $n > 2k$. In particular, the variance in this case is exactly $1/(n + 1) - 1/(n - 1)^2$. [*Annals of Math. Stat.* **15** (1944), 119–144.]

21. The successive values of $c_{r-1} = s - 1$ in step P2 are 2, 3, 7, 6, 4, 2, 2, 1, 0; hence $f = 886862$.

22. $1024 = 6! + 2 \cdot 5! + 2 \cdot 4! + 2 \cdot 3! + 2 \cdot 2! + 0 \cdot 1!$, so we want the successive values of $s - 1$ in step P2 to be 0, 0, 0, 1, 2, 2, 2, 2, 0; working backwards, the permutation is $(9, 6, 5, 2, 3, 4, 0, 1, 7, 8)$.

23. Let $P'(x_1, \ldots, x_t) = \frac{1}{\lambda'} \sum_{n=0}^{\lambda'-1}[(Y'_n, \ldots, Y'_{n+t-1}) = (x_1, \ldots, x_t)]$. Then we have

$$Q(x_1, \ldots, x_t) = \sum_{(y_1, \ldots, y_t)} P'(y_1, \ldots, y_t)P((x_1 - y_1) \bmod d, \ldots, (x_t - y_t) \bmod d);$$

more compactly, $Q(x) = \sum_y P'(y)P(x - y)$. Hence, using the general inequality $(\mathrm{E}\,X)^2 \le \mathrm{E}\,X^2$, we have $\sum_x (Q(x) - d^{-t})^2 = \sum_x(\sum_y P'(y)(P(x - y) - d^{-t}))^2 \le \sum_x \sum_y P'(y)(P(x - y) - d^{-t})^2 = \sum_y P'(y)\sum_x(P(x) - d^{-t})^2 = \sum_x(P(x) - d^{-t})^2$. [See G. Marsaglia, *Comp. Sci. and Statistics: Symp. on the Interface* **16** (1984), 5–6. The result is of interest only when $d^t \le 2\lambda$, since each $P(x)$ is a multiple of $1/\lambda$.]

24. Write $k : \alpha$ and $\alpha : k$ for the first k and last k elements of string α. Let $K(\alpha, \beta) = [\alpha = \beta]/P(\alpha)$, and let $\bar{C}$ be the $d^t \times d^t$ matrix with entries $\bar{c}_{\alpha\beta} = K(\alpha, \beta) - K(t - 1 : \alpha, t - 1 : \beta)$. Let C be the covariance matrix of the random variables $N(\alpha)$ for $|\alpha| = t$, divided by n. These variables are subject to the constraint $\sum_{a=0}^{d-1} N(\alpha a) = \sum_{a=0}^{d-1} N(a\alpha)$ for each of d^{t-1} strings α, and we also have $\sum_{|\alpha|=t} N(\alpha) = n$; but all other linear constraints are derivable from these (see Theorem 2.3.4.2G). Therefore C has rank $d^t - d^{t-1}$, and by exercise 3.3.1–25 we need only show that $C\bar{C}C = C$.

It is not difficult to verify that $c_{\alpha\beta} = P(\alpha\beta)\sum_{|k|<t} T_k(\alpha, \beta)$, where $T_k(\alpha, \beta)$ is a term corresponding to the overlap that might occur when we superimpose β on α and slide it k positions to the right:

$$T_k(\alpha, \beta) = \begin{cases} K(t + k : \alpha, \ \beta : t + k) - 1, & \text{if } k \le 0; \\ K(\alpha : t - k, \ t - k : \beta) - 1, & \text{if } k \ge 0. \end{cases}$$

For example, if $d = 2$, $t = 5$, $\alpha = 01101$, and $\beta = 10101$, we have $c_{\alpha\beta} = P(0)^4 P(1)^6 \times (P(01)^{-1} + P(101)^{-1} + P(1)^{-1} - 9)$. Entry $\alpha\beta$ of $C\bar{C}C$ is therefore $P(\alpha\beta)$ times

$$\sum_{|\gamma|=t-1} \sum_{a,b=0}^{d-1} P(\gamma ab) \sum_{|k|<t} \sum_{|l|<t} T_k(\alpha, \gamma a)(K(a, b) - 1)T_l(\gamma b, \beta).$$

Given k and l, the product $T_k(\alpha, \gamma a)(K(a, b) - 1)T_l(\gamma b, \beta)$ expands to eight terms, each of which usually sums to ± 1 when multiplied by $P(\gamma ab)$ and summed over all γab. For example, the sum of $P(\gamma ab)K(2 : \alpha, \ \gamma a : 2)K(a, b)K(3 : \gamma b, \ \beta : 3)$, when $\alpha = a_1 \ldots a_t$,

$\beta = b_1 \ldots b_t$, $\gamma = c_1 \ldots c_{t-1}$, and $t \geq 5$, is the sum of $P(c_4 \ldots c_{t-2})$, which is 1. If $t = 4$, the same sum would be $K(a_1, b_4)$, but it would cancel with the sum of $P(\gamma ab) K(2 : \alpha, \gamma a : 2)(-1) K(3 : \gamma b, \beta : 3)$. The net result is therefore 0 unless $k \leq 0 \leq l$; otherwise it turns out to be $K(i : (\alpha : i - k), i : (\beta : i + l)) - K(i - 1 : (\alpha : i - k), i - 1 : (\beta : i + l))$, where $i = \min(t + k, t - l)$. The sum over k and l telescopes to $c_{\alpha\beta}$.

25. Empirical tests show, in fact, that when (22) is generalized to arbitrary t the ratios of corresponding elements of C_1^{-1} and $C_1^{-1} C_2 C_1^{-1}$ are very nearly $-t$, when $t \geq 5$. For example, when $t = 6$ they all lie between -6.039 and -6.111; when $t = 20$ they all lie between -20.039 and -20.045. This phenomenon demands an explanation.

26. (a) The vectors $(S_1, \ldots, S_n)$ are uniformly distributed points in the $(n - 1)$-dimensional polyhedron defined by the inequalities $S_1 \geq 0$, $\ldots$, $S_n \geq 0$ in the hyperplane $S_1 + \cdots + S_n = 1$. An easy induction proves that

$$\int_{s_1}^{\infty} dt_1 \int_{s_2}^{\infty} dt_2 \cdots \int_{s_{n-1}}^{\infty} dt_{n-1} \left[1 - t_1 - \cdots - t_{n-1} \geq s_n\right] = \frac{(1 - s_1 - s_2 - \cdots - s_n)_+^{n-1}}{(n-1)!}.$$

To get the probability, divide this integral by its value in the special case $s_1 = \cdots = s_n = 0$. [Bruno de Finetti, *Giornale Istituto Italiano degli Attuari* **27** (1964), 151–173.]

(b) The probability that $S_{(1)} \geq s$ is the probability that $S_1 \geq s$, $\ldots$, $S_n \geq s$.

(c) The probability that $S_{(k)} \geq s$ is the probability that at most $k - 1$ of the S_j are $< s$; hence $1 - F_k(s) = G_1(s) + \cdots + G_{k-1}(s)$, where $G_j(s)$ is the probability that exactly j spacings are $< s$. By symmetry, $G_j(s)$ is $\binom{n}{j}$ times the probability that $S_1 < s$, $\ldots$, $S_j < s$, $S_{j+1} \geq s$, $\ldots$, $S_n \geq s$; and the latter is $\Pr(S_1 < s, \ldots, S_{j-1} < s, S_j \geq 0, S_{j+1} \geq s, \ldots, S_n \geq s) - \Pr(S_1 < s, \ldots, S_{j-1} < s, S_j \geq s, \ldots, S_n \geq s)$. Repeated application of (a) shows that $G_j(s) = \binom{n}{j} \sum_l \binom{j}{l} (-1)^{j-l} (1 - (n - l)s)_+^{n-1}$; hence

$$1 - F_k(s) = \sum_l \binom{n}{l} \binom{n-l-1}{k-l-1} (-1)^{k-l-1} (1 - (n-l)s)_+^{n-1}.$$

In particular, the largest spacing $S_{(n)}$ has distribution

$$F_n(s) = 1 - \sum_l \binom{n}{l} \binom{n-l-1}{n-l-1} (-1)^{n-l-1} (1 - (n-l)s)_+^{n-1} = \sum_l \binom{n}{l} (-1)^l (1 - ls)_+^{n-1}.$$

[Incidentally, the similar quantity $x^{n-1}(n-1)!^{-1} F_n(x^{-1})$ turns out to be the *density* function for the *sum* $U_1 + \cdots + U_n$ of uniform deviates.]

(d) From the formulas $\mathrm{E}\, s^r = r \int_0^1 (1 - F(s)) s^{r-1}\, ds$ and $\int_0^1 s^r (1 - ks)_+^{n-1}\, ds = k^{-r-1} n^{-1} \binom{n+r}{r}^{-1}$, we find $\mathrm{E}\, S_{(k)} = n^{-1}(H_n - H_{n-k})$ and, with a bit of algebra, $\mathrm{E}\, S_{(k)}^2 = n^{-1}(n+1)^{-1}(H_n^{(2)} - H_{n-k}^{(2)} + (H_n - H_{n-k})^2)$. Thus the variance of $S_{(k)}$ is equal to $n^{-1}(n+1)^{-1}(H_n^{(2)} - H_{n-k}^{(2)} - (H_n - H_{n-k})^2/n)$.

[The distributions $F_k(s)$ were first found by W. A. Whitworth, in problem 667 of *DCC Exercises in Choice and Chance* (Cambridge, 1897). Whitworth also discovered an elegant way to compute the expected value of any polynomial in the functions $G_k(s) = F_k(s) - F_{k+1}(s)$; this was published in a booklet entitled *The Expectation of Parts* (Cambridge, 1898), and incorporated into the fifth edition of *Choice and Chance* (1901). Simplified expressions for the mean and variance and for a variety of more general spacing statistics were found by Barton and David, *J. Royal Stat. Soc.* **B18** (1956), 79–94. See R. Pyke, *J. Royal Stat. Soc.* **B27** (1965), 395–449, for a survey of the ways in which statisticians have traditionally analyzed spacings as clues to potential biases in data.]

27. Consider the polyhedron in the hyperplane $S_1 + \cdots + S_n = 1$ defined by the inequalities $S_1 \geq 0, \ldots, S_n \geq 0$. This polyhedron consists of $n!$ congruent subpolyhedra defined by the ordering of the S's (assuming that the S's are distinct), and the operation of sorting is an $n!$-to-1 folding of the large polyhedron to the subpolyhedron in which $S_1 \leq \cdots \leq S_n$. The transformation that takes $(S_{(1)}, \ldots, S_{(n)})$ to $(S'_1, \ldots, S'_n)$ is a 1-to-1 mapping that expands differential volumes by the factor $n!$. It takes the vertices $(\frac{1}{n}, \ldots, \frac{1}{n})$, $(0, \frac{1}{n-1}, \ldots, \frac{1}{n-1})$, $\ldots$, $(0, \ldots, 0, 1)$ of the subpolyhedron into the respective vertices $(1, 0, \ldots, 0)$, $(0, 1, 0, \ldots, 0)$, $\ldots$, $(0, \ldots, 0, 1)$, linearly stretching and distorting the overall shape in the process. (The Euclidean distance between vertices $(0, \ldots, 0, \frac{1}{j}, \ldots, \frac{1}{j})$ and $(0, \ldots, 0, \frac{1}{k}, \ldots, \frac{1}{k})$ in the subpolyhedron is $|j^{-1} - k^{-1}|^{1/2}$; the transformation produces a regular simplex in which all n vertices are $\sqrt{2}$ apart.)

The behavior of iterated spacings is easiest to understand if we examine the details graphically when $n = 3$. In this case the polyhedron is simply an equilateral triangle, whose points are represented with barycentric coordinates (x, y, z), $x + y + z = 1$. The accompanying diagram illustrates the first two levels of a recursive decomposition of this triangle. Each of the 6^2 subtriangles has been labeled with a two-digit code pq, where p represents the applicable permutation when $(x, y, z) = (S_1, S_2, S_3)$ is sorted into $(S_{(1)}, S_{(2)}, S_{(3)})$, and q represents the permutation in the next stage when S'_1, S'_2, and S'_3 are sorted, according to the following code:

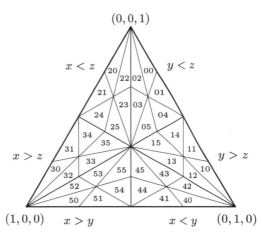

$$0: x<y<z, \quad 1: x<z<y, \quad 2: y<x<z, \quad 3: y<z<x, \quad 4: z<x<y, \quad 5: z<y<x.$$

For example, the points of subtriangle 34 have $S_2 < S_3 < S_1$ and $S'_3 < S'_1 < S'_2$. We can continue this process to infinitely many levels; all points of the triangle with irrational barycentric coordinates thereby acquire a unique representation as an infinite radix-6 expansion. A tetrahedron can be subdivided similarly into 24, 24^2, 24^3, $\ldots$ subtetrahedra, and in general this procedure constructs a radix-$n!$ expansion for the points of any $(n-1)$-dimensional simplex.

When $n = 2$ the process is especially simple: If $x \notin \{0, \frac{1}{2}, 1\}$, the transformation takes spacings $(x, 1-x) = (x, y)$ into either $(2x \bmod 1, 2y \bmod 1)$ or $(2y \bmod 1, 2x \bmod 1)$, depending on whether $x < y$ or $x > y$. Repeated tests therefore essentially shift the binary representation left one bit, possibly complementing the result. After at most $e+1$ iterations on e-bit numbers the process must converge to the fixed point $(0, 1)$. Permutation coding in the case $n = 2$ corresponds simply to folding and stretching a line; the first four levels of subdivision have the following four-bit codes:

$(0,1) \vdash\!\dashv (1,0)$

0000 0001 0011 0010 0110 0111 0101 0100 1100 1101 1111 1110 1010 1011 1001 1000

This sequence is exactly the Gray binary code studied in Section 7.2.1.1. In general, the radix-$n!$ permutation code for an n-simplex has the property that adjacent regions have identical codes except in one digit position. Each iteration of the spacing transformation shifts off the leftmost digit of the representation of each point. Note that equal birthday spacings are points near the boundary of the first-level decomposition.

This fundamental transformation from $(S_1, \ldots, S_n)$ to $(S_1', \ldots, S_n')$ is implicit in Whitworth's proof of Proposition LVI in the fifth edition of *Choice and Chance* (see the reference in answer 26). It was first studied explicitly by J. Durbin [*Biometrika* **48** (1961), 41–55], who was inspired by a similar construction of P. V. Sukhatme [*Annals of Eugenics* **8** (1937), 52–56]. The permutation coding for iterated spacings was introduced by H. E. Daniels [*Biometrika* **49** (1962), 139–149].

28. (a) The number of partitions of m into n distinct positive parts is $p_n(m - \binom{n+1}{2})$, by exercise 5.1.1–16. These partitions can be permuted in $n!$ ways to yield n-tuples $(y_1, \ldots, y_n)$ with $0 = y_1 < y_2 < \cdots < y_n < m$; and each of these n-tuples leads to $(n-1)!$ n-tuples that have $y_1 = 0$ and $0 < y_2, \ldots, y_n < m$. Now add a constant mod m to each y_j; this preserves the spacings. Hence $b_{n00}(m) = mn!\,(n-1)!\,p_n(m - \binom{n+1}{2})$.

(b) Zero spacings correspond to balls in the same urn, and they contribute $s - 1$ to the count of equal spacings. Therefore $b_{nrs}(m) = \{ {n \atop n-s} \} b_{(n-s)(r+1-s)0}(m)$.

(c) Since $\{ {n \atop n-1} \} = \binom{n}{2}$, the probability is

$$n!\,(n-1)!\,m^{1-n} \left(p_n\left(m - \binom{n+1}{2}\right) - \frac{1}{2} p_{n-1}\left(m - \binom{n}{2}\right) \right).$$

29. By the previous answer and exercise 5.1.1–15 we have $b_{n0}(z) = n!\,(n-1)!\,z^{\binom{n+1}{2}}/(1-z)\ldots(1-z^n)$. When $r = 1$, the $n!$ in our previous derivation becomes $n!/2$, and the number of solutions to $0 < s_1 < \cdots < s_k \le s_{k+1} < \cdots < s_n$ with $s_1 + \cdots + s_n = m$ is the number of solutions to $0 \le s_1 - 1 \le \cdots \le s_k - k \le s_{k+1} - k \le \cdots \le s_n - n + 1$ with $(s_1 - 1) + \cdots + (s_k - k) + (s_{k+1} - k) + \cdots + (s_n - n + 1) = m - \binom{n}{2} - k$. Hence $b_{n1}(z) = \frac{1}{2} n!\,(n-1)! \sum_{k=1}^{n} (z^k - z^n)\, z^{\binom{n}{2}}/(1-z)\ldots(1-z^n)$. A similar argument shows that

$$\frac{b_{n2}(z)}{n!\,(n-1)!} = \left(\frac{1}{2!\,2!} \sum_{1 \le j < k < n} (z^j - z^n)(z^k - z^{n-1}) + \frac{1}{3!} \sum_{1 \le k < n} (z^k - z^n)(z^k - z^{n-1}) \right)$$

$$\times \frac{z^{\binom{n-1}{2}}}{(1-z)\ldots(1-z^n)}.$$

We can obtain $b_{nr}(z)$ for general r from the formula

$$\frac{\sum_r b_{nr}(z) w^r}{n!\,(n-1)!\,z^n} = \sum_{0 \le b_1, \ldots, b_{n-1} \le 1} \frac{(z - b_1 z^n) \ldots (z^{n-1} - b_{n-1} z^n)}{c_1 \ldots c_{n-1} (1-z) \ldots (1-z^n)} \left(\frac{w}{z^{n-1}} \right)^{b_1} \ldots \left(\frac{w}{z^1} \right)^{b_{n-1}}$$

where $c_k = 1 + b_k + b_k b_{k-1} + \cdots + b_k \ldots b_2 b_1 = 1 + b_k c_{k-1}$. (The special case $w = 1$ is interesting because the left side sums to $(1-z)^{-n}/n!$ in that case.)

30. This is a good problem for the saddle point method [N. G. de Bruijn, *Asymptotic Methods in Analysis* (North-Holland, 1961), Chapter 5]. We have $p_n(m) = \frac{1}{2\pi i} \oint e^{f(z)} \frac{dz}{z}$, where $f(z) = -m \ln z - \sum_{k=1}^{n} \ln(1 - z^k)$. Let $\rho = n/m$ and $\delta = \sqrt{n}/m$; integrating on the path $z = e^{-\rho + it\delta}$ gives $p_n(m) = \frac{\delta}{2\pi} \int_{-\pi/\delta}^{\pi/\delta} \exp(f(e^{-\rho + it\delta}))\, dt$. It is convenient to use the identity

$$g(se^t) = \sum_{j=0}^{n} \frac{t^j}{j!} \vartheta^j g(s) + \int_0^t \frac{u^n}{n!} \vartheta^{n+1} g(se^{t-u}) \, du,$$

where $g = g(z)$ is any analytic function and ϑ is the operator $z\frac{d}{dz}$. When the function $\vartheta^j g$ is evaluated at e^z the result is the same as when $g(e^z)$ is differentiated j times with respect to z. This principle leads to the formula

$$\vartheta^j f(e^{-\rho}) = -m[j=1] + \frac{j! \, n}{\rho^j} + (-1)^j \sum_{k=1}^{n} \sum_{l \geq j} \frac{l^{\underline{j}} \, B_l}{l \cdot l!} (-k)^l \rho^{l-j},$$

because of another handy identity,

$$\ln\left(\frac{e^z - 1}{z}\right) = \sum_{n \geq 1} \frac{B_n z^n}{n \cdot n!}.$$

Therefore we obtain an asymptotic expansion of the integrand,

$$\exp f(e^{-\rho + it\delta}) = \exp\left(\sum_{j \geq 0} \frac{i^j \delta^j t^j}{j!} \vartheta^j f(e^{-\rho})\right) = e^{-t^2/2 + f(e^{-\rho})} \exp(ic_1 t - c_2 t^2 - ic_3 t^3 + \cdots),$$

where $c_1 = \left(-\frac{n(n+1)}{2} B_1 + \frac{n(n+1/2)(n+1)}{6} B_2 \rho\right)\delta + O(n^{-3})$, etc.; and it turns out that $c_j = O(n^{-3})$ for $j \geq 3$. Factoring out the constant term

$$\frac{\delta}{2\pi} e^{f(e^{-\rho})} = \frac{\delta}{2\pi \, n! \, \rho^n e^{-m\rho}} \exp\left(-\sum_{k=1}^{n} \sum_{l \geq 1} \frac{B_l}{l \cdot l!} (-k)^l \rho^l\right)$$

$$= \frac{\sqrt{n} \, m^{n-1} e^{n+\alpha/4}}{2\pi \, n! \, n^n} \left(1 + \frac{18\alpha - \alpha^2}{72n} + \frac{108\alpha^2 - 36\alpha^3 + \alpha^4}{10368n^2} + O(n^{-3})\right)$$

leaves us with an integral whose integrand is exponentially small when $|t| \geq n^\epsilon$. We can ignore larger values of t, because partial fraction expansion shows that the integrand is $O((m/n)^{n/2})$; none of the other roots of unity occurs more than $n/2$ times as a pole of the denominator. Hence we are allowed to "trade tails" [CMath, §9.4] and integrate over all t. The formulas $\int_{-\infty}^{\infty} e^{-t^2/2} t^j \, dt = (j-1)(j-3)\ldots(1)\sqrt{2\pi}$ [j even] and $n! = (n/e)^n \sqrt{2\pi n} \exp(\frac{1}{12} n^{-1} + O(n^{-3}))$ suffice to complete the evaluation.

With $q_n(m) = p_n(m - \binom{n+1}{2})$ in place of $p_n(m)$ the calculation proceeds in the same way but with c_1 increased by $\frac{1}{2}\alpha(n^{1/2} - n^{-1/2})$ and with the additional factor $\exp(-\rho\binom{n+1}{2})$. We get

$$q_n(m) = \frac{m^{n-1} e^{-\alpha/4}}{n! \, (n-1)!} \left(1 - \frac{13\alpha^2}{288n} + \frac{169\alpha^4 - 2016\alpha^3 - 1728\alpha^2 + 41472\alpha}{165888n^2} + O(n^{-3})\right);$$

this matches the formula for $p_n(m)$ except that α has been changed to $-\alpha$. (In fact, if we define $p_n(m) = r_n(2m + \binom{n+1}{2})$ and $q_n(m) = r_n(2m - \binom{n+1}{2})$, the generating function $R_n(z) = \sum_m r_n(z^m) = \prod_{k=1}^{n}(z^{-k} - z^k)^{-1}$ satisfies $R_n(1/z) = (-1)^n R_n(z)$. This implies a duality formula $r_n(-m) = (-1)^{n-1} r_n(m)$, in the sense that this equation is identically true when we express $r_n(m)$ as a polynomial in m and roots of unity. Therefore we may say that $q_n(m) = p_n(-m)$. A general treatment of such duality can be found in G. Pólya, Math. Zeitschrift 29 (1928), 549–640, §44.) For further information see G. Szekeres, *Quarterly J. Math. Oxford* **2** (1951), 85–108; **4** (1953), 96–111.

The exact value of $q_n(m)$ when $m = 2^{25}$ and $n = 512$ is 7.08069 34695 90264 094... $\times 10^{1514}$; our approximation gives the estimate $7.080693501 \times 10^{1514}$.

The probability that the birthday test finds $R = 0$ spacings is $b_{n00}(m)/m^n = n!\,(n-1)!\,m^{1-n}q_n(m) = e^{-\alpha/4} + O(n^{-1})$, by exercise 28, because the contribution from $b_{n01}(m)$ is $\approx \frac{\alpha}{2n}e^{-\alpha/4} = O(n^{-1})$. Inserting the factor $g_n(z) = \sum_{k=1}^{n-1}(z^{-k}-1)$ into the integrand for $q_n(m)$ has the effect of multiplying the result by $\frac{\alpha}{2} + O(n^{-1})$, because $g_n(e^{-\rho+it\delta}) = \binom{n}{2}\rho + O(n^3\rho^2) + itO(n^2\delta) - \frac{1}{2}t^2O(n^3\delta^2) + \cdots$. Similarly, the extra factor $\sum_{1 \le j < k < n}(z^{-j}-1)(z^{-k}-1)$ essentially multiplies by $\frac{1}{8}n^4\rho^2 = \frac{1}{8}\alpha^2$, plus $O(n^{-1})$; other contributions to the probability that $R = 2$ are $O(n^{-1})$. In this way we find that the probability of r equal spacings is $e^{-\alpha/4}(\alpha/4)^r/r! + O(n^{-1})$, a Poisson distribution; more complicated terms arise if we carry the expansion out to $O(n^{-2})$.

31. The 79 bits consist of 24 sets of three, $\{Y_n, Y_{n+31}, Y_{n+55}\}$, $\{Y_{n+1}, Y_{n+32}, Y_{n+56}\}$, ..., $\{Y_{n+23}, Y_{n+54}, Y_{n+78}\}$, plus 7 additional bits $Y_{n+24}, \ldots, Y_{n+30}$. The latter bits are equally likely to be 0 or 1, but in each group of three the probability is $\frac{1}{4}$ that the bits will be $\{0,0,0\}$ and $\frac{3}{4}$ that they will be $\{0,1,1\}$. Therefore the probability generating function for the sum of bits is $f(z) = \left(\frac{1+z}{2}\right)^7\left(\frac{1+3z^2}{4}\right)^{24}$, a polynomial of degree 55. (Well, not quite; strictly speaking, it is $(2^{55}f(z) - 1)/(2^{55} - 1)$, because the all-0 case is excluded.) The coefficients of $2^{55}f(z)$ are easily computed by machine, and we find that the probability of more 1s than 0s is $18509401282464000/(2^{55} - 1) \approx 0.51374$.

Notes: This exercise is based on the discovery by Vattulainen, Ala-Nissila, and Kankaala [*Physical Review Letters* **73** (1994), 2513–2516] that a lagged Fibonacci generator fails a more complicated two-dimensional random walk test. Notice that the sequence $Y_{2n}, Y_{2n+2}, \ldots$ will fail the test too, because it satisfies the same recurrence. The bias toward 1s also carries over into the subsequence consisting of the even-valued elements generated by $X_n = (X_{n-55} \pm X_{n-24}) \bmod 2^e$; we tend to have more occurrences of $(\ldots 10)_2$ than $(\ldots 00)_2$ in binary notation.

There's nothing magic about the number 79 in this test; experiments show that a significant bias towards a majority of 1s is present also in random walks of length 101 or 1001 or 10001. But a formal proof seems to be difficult. After 86 steps the generating function is $\left(\frac{1+3z^2}{4}\right)^{17}\left(\frac{1+2z^2+4z^3+z^4}{8}\right)^7$; then we get the factors $(1 + 2z^2 + 5z^3 + 5z^4 + 10z^5 + 8z^6 + z^7)/32$; then $(1 + 2z^2 + 7z^3 + 7z^4 + 15z^5 + 25z^6 + 29z^7 + 28z^8 + 13z^9 + z^{10})/128$, etc. The analysis becomes more and more complicated as the walks get longer.

Intuitively, the preponderance of 1s that arise in the first 79 steps ought to persist as long as the subsequent numbers are reasonably balanced between 0 and 1. The accompanying diagram shows the results of a much smaller case, the generator $Y_n = (Y_{n-2} + Y_{n-11}) \bmod 2$, which is easy to analyze exhaustively. In this case random walks of length 445 have a 64% chance of finishing to the right of the starting point; this bias disappears only when the length of the walk increases to half the period length (after which, of course, 0s are more likely, although the full period does lack one 0).

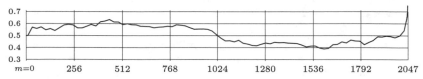

The probability that 1s outnumber 0s in random m-tuples when $Y_n = Y_{n-2} \oplus Y_{n-11}$.

Lüscher's discarding technique can be used to avoid the bias toward 1s (see the end of Section 3.2.2). For example, with lags 55 and 24, no deviation for randomness is observed for random walks of length 1001 when the numbers are generated in batches of 165, if only the first 55 numbers of each batch are used.

32. Not if, say, X and Y each take the values $(-n, m)$ with the respective probabilities $(m/(m+n), n/(m+n))$, where $m < n < (1 + \sqrt{2})m$. [Suppose two competitors differ by X after playing one round of golf. Then they are of equal strength based on their mean scores, but one might be more likely to win a one-round tournament while the other will more often win in two rounds. See T. M. Cover, *Amer. Statistician* **43** (1989), 277–278, for a discussion of similar phenomena.]

33. We essentially want $[z^{(k+l-1)/2}] \left(\frac{1+z}{2}\right)^{k-2l} \left(\frac{1+3z^2}{4}\right)^l /(1 - z)$. Let $m = k - 2l$ and $n = l$; the desired coefficient is $\frac{1}{2\pi i} \oint e^{g(z)} \frac{dz}{z(1-z)}$, where $g(z) = m \ln\left(\frac{1+z}{2}\right) + n \ln\left(\frac{1+3z^2}{4}\right) - \left(\frac{m+3n-1}{2}\right) \ln z$. It is convenient (and saddle-wise) to integrate along the path $z = e^{\epsilon u}$ where $\epsilon^2 = 4/(m + 3n)$ and $u = -1 + it$ for $-\infty < t < \infty$. We have $g(e^{\epsilon u}) = -\epsilon u/2 + u^2/2 + c_3 \epsilon u^3 + c_4 \epsilon^2 u^4 + \cdots$, where $c_k = \epsilon^2 \vartheta^k g(1)/k! = O(1)$. Also $1/(1 - e^{\epsilon u}) = \frac{-1}{\epsilon u} + \frac{1}{2} - B_2 \epsilon u/2! - \cdots$. Multiplying out the integrand and using the facts that $\frac{1}{2\pi i} \int_{1-i\infty}^{1+i\infty} e^{u^2/2} \frac{du}{u} = \frac{1}{2}$ and $\frac{1}{2\pi i} \int_{a-i\infty}^{a+i\infty} e^{u^2/2} u^{2k} du = (-1)^k (2k - 1)(2k - 3) \ldots (1) \sqrt{2\pi}$ yields the asymptotic formula $\frac{1}{2} + (2\pi)^{-1/2} n(m + 3n)^{-3/2} + O((m + 3n)^{-3/2})$. If $m + 3n$ is even, the same asymptotic formula holds, provided that we give half of the coefficient of $z^{(m+3n)/2}$ to the 1s and half to the 0s. (This coefficient is $\left(\frac{2}{\pi(m+3n)}\right)^{1/2} + O((m-3n)^{-3/2})$.)

34. The number of strings of length n that exclude a given two-letter substring or pair of substrings is the coefficient of z^n in an appropriate generating function, and it can be written $ce^{n\tau} m^n + O(1)$ where c and τ have series expansions in powers of $\epsilon = 1/m$:

Case	Excluded	Generating function	c	τ
1	aa	$(1+z)/p(z)$	$1 + \epsilon^2 - 2\epsilon^3 + \cdots$	$-\epsilon^2 + \epsilon^3 - \frac{5}{2}\epsilon^4 + \cdots$
2	ab	$1/(1 - mz + z^2)$	$1 + \epsilon^2 + 3\epsilon^4 + \cdots$	$-\epsilon^2 - \frac{3}{2}\epsilon^4 + \cdots$
3	aa, bb	$(1+z)/(p(z)+z^2)$	$1 + 2\epsilon^2 - 4\epsilon^3 + \cdots$	$-2\epsilon^2 + 2\epsilon^3 - 8\epsilon^4 + \cdots$
4	aa, bc	$(1+z)/(p(z)+z^2+z^3)$	$1 + 2\epsilon^2 - 2\epsilon^3 + \cdots$	$-2\epsilon^2 + \epsilon^3 - 7\epsilon^4 + \cdots$
5	ab, bc	$(1+z)/(1 - mz + 2z^2 - z^3)$	$1 + 2\epsilon^2 - 2\epsilon^3 + \cdots$	$-2\epsilon^2 + \epsilon^3 - 6\epsilon^4 + \cdots$
6	ab, cd	$1/(1 - mz + 2z^2)$	$1 + 2\epsilon^2 + 12\epsilon^4 + \cdots$	$-2\epsilon^2 - 6\epsilon^4 + \cdots$

(Here a, b, c, d denote distinct letters and $p(z) = 1 - (m - 1)(z + z^2)$. It turns out that the effect of excluding $\{ab, ba\}$ or $\{aa, ab\}$ is equivalent to excluding $\{aa, bb\}$; excluding $\{ab, ac\}$ is equivalent to excluding $\{ab, cd\}$.) Let $S_n^{(j)}$ be the coefficient of z^n in Case j and let X be the total number of two-letter combinations that do not appear. Then $EX = (mS_n^{(1)} + m^2 S_n^{(2)})/m^n$ and
$$EX^2 = (mS_n^{(1)} + m^2(S_n^{(2)} + 6S_n^{(3)}) + 2m^3(S_n^{(4)} + S_n^{(5)} + S_n^{(6)}) + m^4 S_n^{(6)})/m^n.$$

35. (a) $E S_m = N^{-1} \sum_{n=0}^{N-1} \sum_{j=0}^{m-1} Z_{n+j} = N^{-1} \sum_{j=0}^{m-1} \sum_{n=0}^{N-1} Z_{n+j} = m/N$, because $\sum_{n=0}^{N-1} Z_{n+j} = 2^{k-1} - (2^{k-1} - 1) = 1$.

(b) Let $\xi^k = a_1 \xi^{k-1} + \cdots + a_k$, and define the linear function f as in the first solution to exercise 3.2.2–16. Then $Y_n = f(\xi^n)$, and it follows that $Y_{n+i} + Y_{n+j} = f(\xi^{n+i}) + f(\xi^{n+j}) \equiv f(\xi^{n+i} + \xi^{n+j}) = f(\xi^n \alpha)$ (modulo 2), where α is nonzero when $i \ne j$ (modulo N). Hence $E S_m^2 = N^{-1} \sum_{i=0}^{m-1} \sum_{j=0}^{m-1} \sum_{n=0}^{N-1} Z_{n+i} Z_{n+j} = N^{-1}(\sum_{i=0}^{m-1} \sum_{n=0}^{N-1} Z_{n+i}^2 - 2\sum_{0 \le i < j < m} \sum_{n=0}^{N-1} Z_n) = m - m(m - 1)/N$.

(c) $E \sum_{j=0}^{m-1} Z_{n+j} = \sum_{j=0}^{m-1} E Z_{n+j} = 0$ and $E(\sum_{j=0}^{m-1} Z_{n+j})^2 = \sum_{j=0}^{m-1} E Z_{n+j}^2 + \sum_{0 \le i < j < m} (E Z_{n+i})(E Z_{n+j}) = m$ when each Z_n is truly random. Thus the mean and variance of S_m are very close to the correct values when $m \ll N$.

(d) $E S_m^3 = N^{-1} \sum_{h=0}^{m-1} \sum_{i=0}^{m-1} \sum_{j=0}^{m-1} \sum_{n=0}^{N-1} Z_{n+h} Z_{n+i} Z_{n+j}$. If any of h, i, or j are equal, the sum on n is 1; hence

$$E S_m^3 = \frac{1}{N} \left(m^3 - m^{\underline{3}} + 6 \sum_{0 \le h < i < j < m} \sum_{n=0}^{N-1} Z_{n+h} Z_{n+i} Z_{n+j} \right).$$

Arguing as in (b), we find that the sum on n will be 1 if $\xi^h + \xi^i + \xi^j \ne 0$; otherwise it will be $-N$. Thus $E S_m^3 = m^3 - 6B(N+1)/N$, where $B = \sum_{0 \le h < i < j < m} [\xi^h + \xi^i + \xi^j = 0] = \sum_{0 < i < j < m} [1 + \xi^i + \xi^j = 0] (m - j)$. Finally observe that $1 + \xi^i = \xi^j$ in the field if and only if $f(\xi^{i+l}) = f(\xi^{j+l})$ for $0 < l < k$, assuming that $0 < i < j < N$.

(e) The only nonzero term occurs for $i = 31$ and $j = 55$; hence $B = 79 - 55 = 24$. (The next nonzero term occurs when $i = 62$ and $j = 110$.) In a truly random situation, $E S_m^3$ should be zero, so this value $E S_{79}^3 \approx -144$ is distinctly nonrandom. Curiously it is negative, although exercise 31 showed that S_{79} is usually *positive*. The value of S_{79} tends to be more seriously negative when it does dip below zero.

Reference: IEEE Trans. **IT-14** (1968), 569–576. Experiments by M. Matsumoto and Y. Kurita [*ACM Trans. Modeling and Comp. Simul.* **2** (1992), 179–194; **4** (1994), 254–266] confirm that trinomial-based generators fail such distribution tests even when the lags are quite large. See also *ACM Trans. Modeling and Comp. Simul.* **6** (1996), 99–106, where they exhibit exponentially long subsequences of low density.

SECTION 3.3.3

1. $y((x/y)) + \frac{1}{2}y - \frac{1}{2}y\delta(x/y)$.

2. $((x)) = -\sum_{n \ge 1} \frac{1}{n\pi} \sin 2\pi n x$, which converges for all x. (The representation in Eq. (24) may be considered a "finite" Fourier series, for the case when x is rational.)

3. The sum is $((2^n x)) - ((x))$. [See *Trans. Amer. Math. Soc.* **65** (1949), 401.]

4. $d_{\max} = 2^{10} \cdot 5$. Note that we have $X_{n+1} < X_n$ with probability $\frac{1}{2} + \epsilon$, where

$$|\epsilon| < d/(2 \cdot 10^{10}) \le 1/(2 \cdot 5^9);$$

hence *every* potency-10 generator is respectable from the standpoint of Theorem P.

5. An intermediate result:

$$\sum_{0 \le x < m} \frac{x}{m} \frac{s(x)}{m} = \frac{1}{12}\sigma(a, m, c) + \frac{m}{4} - \frac{c}{2m} - \frac{x'}{2m}.$$

6. (a) Use induction and the formula

$$\left(\left(\frac{hj + c}{k} \right) \right) - \left(\left(\frac{hj + c - 1}{k} \right) \right) = \frac{1}{k} - \frac{1}{2}\delta \left(\frac{hj + c}{k} \right) - \frac{1}{2}\delta \left(\frac{hj + c - 1}{k} \right).$$

(b) Use the fact that $-\left(\left(\frac{h'j}{k} \right) \right) = -\left(\left(\frac{j}{hk} - \frac{k'j}{h} \right) \right) = \left(\left(\frac{k'j}{h} \right) \right) - \frac{j}{hk} + \frac{1}{2}\delta \left(\frac{k'j}{h} \right)$.

7. Take $m = h$, $n = k$, $k = 2$ in the second formula of exercise 1.2.4–45:

$$\sum_{0 < j < k} \left(\frac{hj}{k} - \left(\left(\frac{hj}{k} \right) \right) + \frac{1}{2} \right) \left(\frac{hj}{k} - \left(\left(\frac{hj}{k} \right) \right) - \frac{1}{2} \right) + 2 \sum_{0 < j < h} \left(\frac{kj}{h} - \left(\left(\frac{kj}{h} \right) \right) + \frac{1}{2} \right) j = kh(h-1).$$

The sums on the left simplify, and by standard manipulations we get

$$h^2k - hk - \frac{h}{2} + \frac{h^2}{6k} + \frac{k}{12} + \frac{1}{4} - \frac{h}{6}\sigma(h,k,0) - \frac{h}{6}\sigma(k,h,0) + \frac{1}{12}\sigma(1,k,0) = h^2k - hk.$$

Since $\sigma(1,k,0) = (k-1)(k-2)/k$, this reduces to the reciprocity law.

8. See *Duke Math. J.* **21** (1954), 391–397.

9. Begin with the interesting identity $\sum_{k=0}^{r-1}\lfloor kp/r\rfloor\lfloor kq/r\rfloor + \sum_{k=0}^{p-1}\lfloor kq/p\rfloor\lfloor kr/p\rfloor + \sum_{k=0}^{q-1}\lfloor kr/q\rfloor\lfloor kp/q\rfloor = (p-1)(q-1)(r-1)$, for which a simple geometric proof is possible, assuming that $p \perp q$, $q \perp r$, and $r \perp p$. [U. Dieter, *Abh. Math. Sem. Univ. Hamburg* **21** (1957), 109–125.]

10. Obviously $\sigma(k-h, k, c) = -\sigma(h,k,-c)$, by (8). Replace j by $k-j$ in definition (16), to deduce that $\sigma(h,k,c) = \sigma(h,k,-c)$.

11. (a) $\displaystyle\sum_{0 \le j < dk}\left(\left(\frac{j}{dk}\right)\right)\left(\left(\frac{hj+c}{k}\right)\right) = \sum_{\substack{0 \le i < d \\ 0 \le j < k}}\left(\left(\frac{ik+j}{dk}\right)\right)\left(\left(\frac{hj+c}{k}\right)\right);$ use (10) to sum on i.

(b) $\displaystyle\left(\left(\frac{hj+c+\theta}{k}\right)\right) = \left(\left(\frac{hj+c}{k}\right)\right) + \frac{\theta}{k} - \frac{1}{2}\delta\left(\frac{hj+c}{k}\right);$ now sum.

12. Since $\left(\left(\frac{hj+c}{k}\right)\right)$ runs through the same values as $\left(\left(\frac{j}{k}\right)\right)$ in some order, Cauchy's inequality implies that $\sigma(h,k,c)^2 \le \sigma(h,k,0)^2$; and $\sigma(1,k,0)$ may be summed directly, see exercise 7.

13. $\displaystyle\sigma(h,k,c) + \frac{3(k-1)}{k} = \frac{12}{k}\sum_{0 < j < k}\frac{\omega^{-cj}}{(\omega^{-hj}-1)(\omega^j-1)} + \frac{6}{k}(c \bmod k) - 6\left(\left(\frac{h'c}{k}\right)\right),$

if $hh' \equiv 1 \pmod{k}$.

14. $(2^{38} - 3 \cdot 2^{20} + 5)/(2^{70} - 1) \approx 2^{-32}$. An extremely satisfactory global value, in spite of the local nonrandomness!

15. Replace c^2 where it appears in (19) by $\lfloor c\rfloor\lceil c\rceil$.

16. The hinted identity is equivalent to $m_1 = p_r m_{r+1} + p_{r-1}m_{r+2}$ for $1 \le r \le t$; this follows by induction. (See also exercise 4.5.3–32.) Now replace c_j by $\sum_{j \le r \le t} b_r m_{r+1}$ and compare coefficients of $b_i b_j$ on both sides of the identity to be proved.

Note: For all exponents $e \ge 1$, a similar argument gives

$$\sum_{1 \le j \le t}(-1)^{j+1}\frac{c_j^e}{m_j m_{j+1}} = \frac{1}{m_1}\sum_{1 \le j \le t}(-1)^{j+1}b_j\frac{c_j^e - c_{j+1}^e}{c_j - c_{j+1}}p_{j-1}.$$

17. During this algorithm we will have $k = m_j$, $h = m_{j+1}$, $c = c_j$, $p = p_{j-1}$, $p' = p_{j-2}$, $s = (-1)^{j+1}$ for $j = 1, 2, \ldots, t+1$.

D1. [Initialize.] Set $A \leftarrow 0$, $B \leftarrow h$, $p \leftarrow 1$, $p' \leftarrow 0$, $s \leftarrow 1$.

D2. [Divide.] Set $a \leftarrow \lfloor k/h\rfloor$, $b \leftarrow \lfloor c/h\rfloor$, $r \leftarrow c \bmod h$. (Now $a = a_j$, $b = b_j$, and $r = c_{j+1}$.)

D3. [Accumulate.] Set $A \leftarrow A + (a - 6b)s$, $B \leftarrow B + 6bp(c+r)s$. If $r \ne 0$ or $c = 0$, set $A \leftarrow A - 3s$. If $h = 1$, set $B \leftarrow B + ps$. (This subtracts $3e(m_{j+1},c_j)$ and also takes care of the $\sum(-1)^{j+1}/m_j m_{j+1}$ terms.)

D4. [Prepare for next iteration.] Set $c \leftarrow r$, $s \leftarrow -s$; set $r \leftarrow k - ah$, $k \leftarrow h$, $h \leftarrow r$; set $r \leftarrow ap + p'$, $p' \leftarrow p$, $p \leftarrow r$. If $h > 0$, return to D2. ∎

At the conclusion of this algorithm, p will be equal to the original value k_0 of k, so the desired answer will be $A+B/p$. The final value of p' will be h' if $s < 0$, otherwise p' will be $k_0 - h'$. It would be possible to maintain B in the range $0 \le B < k_0$, by making appropriate adjustments to A, thereby requiring only single-precision operations (with double-precision products and dividends) if k_0 is a single-precision number.

18. A moment's thought shows that the formula

$$S(h, k, c, z) = \sum_{0 \le j < k} (\lfloor j/k \rfloor - \lfloor (j-z)/k \rfloor)(((hj+c)/k))$$

is in fact valid for all $z \ge 0$, not only when $k \ge z$. Writing $\lfloor j/k \rfloor - \lfloor (j-z)/k \rfloor = \frac{z}{k} + ((\frac{j-z}{k})) - ((\frac{j}{k})) + \frac{1}{2}\delta_{j0} - \frac{1}{2}\delta(\frac{j-z}{k})$ and carrying out the sums yields

$$S(h, k, c, z) = \frac{zd}{k}\left(\left(\frac{c}{d}\right)\right) + \frac{1}{12}\sigma(h, k, hz+c) - \frac{1}{12}\sigma(h, k, c) + \frac{1}{2}\left(\left(\frac{c}{k}\right)\right) - \frac{1}{2}\left(\left(\frac{hz+c}{k}\right)\right),$$

where $d = \gcd(h, k)$. [This formula allows us to express the probability that $X_{n+1} < X_n < \alpha$ in terms of generalized Dedekind sums, given α.]

19. The desired probability is

$$m^{-1}\sum_{x=0}^{m-1}\left(\left\lfloor\frac{x-\alpha}{m}\right\rfloor - \left\lfloor\frac{x-\beta}{m}\right\rfloor\right)\left(\left\lfloor\frac{s(x)-\alpha'}{m}\right\rfloor - \left\lfloor\frac{s(x)-\beta'}{m}\right\rfloor\right)$$

$$= m^{-1}\sum_{x=0}^{m-1}\left(\frac{\beta-\alpha}{m} + \left(\left(\frac{x-\beta}{m}\right)\right) - \left(\left(\frac{x-\alpha}{m}\right)\right) + \frac{1}{2}\delta\left(\frac{x-\alpha}{m}\right) - \frac{1}{2}\delta\left(\frac{x-\beta}{m}\right)\right)$$

$$\times \left(\frac{\beta'-\alpha'}{m} + \left(\left(\frac{s(x)-\beta'}{m}\right)\right) - \left(\left(\frac{s(x)-\alpha'}{m}\right)\right) + \frac{1}{2}\delta\left(\frac{s(x)-\alpha'}{m}\right) - \frac{1}{2}\delta\left(\frac{s(x)-\beta'}{m}\right)\right)$$

$$= \frac{\beta-\alpha}{m}\frac{\beta'-\alpha'}{m} + \frac{1}{12m}\Big(\sigma(a, m, c + a\alpha - \alpha') - \sigma(a, m, c + a\alpha - \beta')$$

$$+ \sigma(a, m, c + a\beta - \beta') - \sigma(a, m, c + a\beta - \alpha')\Big) + \epsilon,$$

where $|\epsilon| \le 2.5/m$.

[This approach is due to U. Dieter. The discrepancy between the true probability and the ideal value $\frac{\beta-\alpha}{m}\frac{\beta'-\alpha'}{m}$ is bounded by $\sum_{j=1}^{t} a_j/4m$, according to Theorem K; conversely, by choosing α, β, α', β' appropriately we will obtain a discrepancy of at least half this bound when there are large partial quotients, using the fact that Theorem K is "best possible." Note that when $a \approx \sqrt{m}$ the discrepancy cannot exceed $O(1/\sqrt{m})$, so even the locally nonrandom generator of exercise 14 will look good on the serial test over the full period; it appears that we should insist on an *extremely* small discrepancy.]

20. $\sum_{0 \le x < m}\lceil(x - s(x))/m\rceil\lceil(s(x) - s(s(x)))/m\rceil/m = \sum_{0 \le x < m}((x - s(x))/m + (((bx+c)/m)) + \frac{1}{2})((s(x) - s(s(x)))/m + ((a(bx+c)/m)) + \frac{1}{2})/m$; and $x/m = ((x/m)) + \frac{1}{2} - \frac{1}{2}\delta(x/m)$, $s(x)/m = (((ax + c)/m)) + \frac{1}{2} - \frac{1}{2}\delta((ax + c)/m)$, $s(s(x))/m = (((a^2x + ac + c)/m)) + \frac{1}{2} - \frac{1}{2}\delta((a^2x + ac + c)/m)$. Let $s(x') = s(s(x'')) = 0$ and $d = \gcd(b, m)$. The sum now reduces to

$$\frac{1}{4} + \frac{1}{12m}(S_1 - S_2 + S_3 - S_4 + S_5 - S_6 + S_7 - S_8 + S_9) + \frac{d}{m}\left(\left(\frac{c}{d}\right)\right)$$

$$+ \frac{1}{2m}\left(\left(\left(\frac{x'-x''}{m}\right)\right) - \left(\left(\frac{x'}{m}\right)\right) + \left(\left(\frac{x''}{m}\right)\right) + \left(\left(\frac{ac+c}{m}\right)\right) - \left(\left(\frac{ac}{m}\right)\right) - \left(\left(\frac{c}{m}\right)\right) - \frac{1}{2}\right),$$

where $S_1 = \sigma(a, m, c)$, $S_2 = \sigma(a^2, m, ac + c)$, $S_3 = \sigma(ab, m, ac)$, $S_4 = \sigma(1, m, 0) = (m-1)(m-2)/m$, $S_5 = \sigma(a, m, c)$, $S_6 = \sigma(b, m, c)$, $S_7 = -\sigma(a' - 1, m, a'c)$, and $S_8 = -\sigma(a'(a' - 1), m, (a')^2 c)$, if $a'a \equiv 1$ (modulo m); and finally

$$S_9 = 12 \sum_{0 \le x < m} \left(\left(\frac{bx + c}{m} \right) \right) \left(\left(\frac{a(bx + c)}{m} \right) \right)$$

$$= 12d \sum_{0 \le x < m/d} \left(\left(\frac{x + c_0/d}{m/d} \right) \right) \left(\left(\frac{a(x + c_0/d)}{m/d} \right) \right)$$

$$= 12d \sum_{0 \le x < m/d} \left(\left(\left(\frac{x}{m/d} \right) \right) + \frac{c_0}{m} - \frac{1}{2} \delta_{x0} \right) \left(\left(\frac{a(x + c_0/d)}{m/d} \right) \right)$$

$$= d \left(\sigma(ad, m, ac_0) + 12 \frac{c_0}{m} \left(\left(\frac{ac_0}{d} \right) \right) - 6 \left(\left(\frac{ac_0}{m} \right) \right) \right)$$

where $c_0 = c \bmod d$. The grand total will be near $\frac{1}{6}$ when d is small and when the fractions a/m, $(a^2 \bmod m)/m$, $(ab \bmod m)/m$, b/m, $(a' - 1)/m$, $(a'(a' - 1) \bmod m)/m$, $((ad) \bmod m)/m$ all have small partial quotients. (Note that $a' - 1 \equiv -b + b^2 - \cdots$, as in exercise 3.2.1.3–7.)

21. Notice first that the main integral decomposes nicely:

$$s_n = \int_{x_n}^{x_{n+1}} x\{ax + \theta\} \, dx = \frac{1}{a^2} \left(\frac{1}{3} - \frac{\theta}{2} + \frac{n}{2} \right), \qquad \text{if } x_n = \frac{n - \theta}{a};$$

$$s = \int_0^1 x\{ax + \theta\} \, dx = s_0 + s_1 + \cdots + s_{a-1} + \int_{-\theta/a}^0 (ax + \theta) \, dx = \frac{1}{3a} - \frac{\theta}{2a} + \frac{a - 1}{4a} + \frac{\theta^2}{2a}.$$

Therefore $C = (s - (\frac{1}{2})^2)/(\frac{1}{3} - (\frac{1}{2})^2) = (1 - 6\theta + 6\theta^2)/a$.

22. We have $s(x) < x$ in the disjoint intervals $[\frac{1-\theta}{a} \, .. \, \frac{1-\theta}{a-1}), [\frac{2-\theta}{a} \, .. \, \frac{2-\theta}{a-1}), \ldots, [\frac{a-\theta}{a} \, .. \, 1)$, which have total length

$$1 + \sum_{0 < j \le a-1} \left(\frac{j - \theta}{a - 1} \right) - \sum_{0 < j \le a} \left(\frac{j - \theta}{a} \right) = 1 + \frac{a}{2} - \theta - \frac{a + 1}{2} + \theta = \frac{1}{2}.$$

23. We have $s(s(x)) < s(x) < x$ when x is in $[\frac{k-\theta}{a} \, .. \, \frac{k-\theta}{a-1})$ and $ax + \theta - k$ is in $[\frac{j-\theta}{a} \, .. \, \frac{j-\theta}{a-1})$, for $0 < j \le k < a$; or when x is in $[\frac{a-\theta}{a} \, .. \, 1)$ and $ax + \theta - a$ is either in $[\frac{j-\theta}{a} \, .. \, \frac{j-\theta}{a-1})$ for $0 < j \le \lfloor a\theta \rfloor$ or in $[\frac{\lfloor a\theta \rfloor + 1 - \theta}{a} \, .. \, \theta)$. The desired probability is

$$\sum_{0 < j \le k < a} \frac{j - \theta}{a^2(a - 1)} + \sum_{0 < j \le \lfloor a\theta \rfloor} \frac{j - \theta}{a^2(a - 1)} + \frac{1}{a^2} \max(0, \{a\theta\} + \theta - 1)$$

$$= \frac{1}{6} + \frac{1}{6a} - \frac{\theta}{2a} + \frac{1}{a^2} \left(\frac{\lfloor a\theta \rfloor (\lfloor a\theta \rfloor + 1 - 2\theta)}{2(a - 1)} + \max(0, \{a\theta\} + \theta - 1) \right),$$

which is $\frac{1}{6} + (1 - 3\theta + 3\theta^2)/6a + O(1/a^2)$ for large a. Note that $1 - 3\theta + 3\theta^2 \ge \frac{1}{4}$, so θ can't be chosen to make this probability come out right.

24. Proceed as in the previous exercise; the sum of the interval lengths is

$$\sum_{0 < j_1 \le \cdots \le j_{t-1} < a} \frac{j_1}{a^{t-1}(a - 1)} = \frac{1}{a^{t-1}(a - 1)} \binom{a + t - 2}{t}.$$

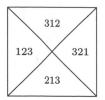

Fig. A–1. Permutation regions
for the Fibonacci generator.

Fig. A–2. Run-length regions
for the Fibonacci generator.

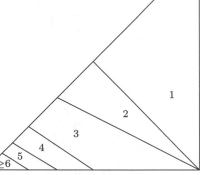

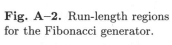

To compute the average length, let p_k be the probability of a run of length $\geq k$; the average is

$$\sum_{k \geq 1} p_k = \sum_{k \geq 1} \binom{a + k - 2}{k} \frac{1}{a^{k-1}(a - 1)} = \left(\frac{a}{a-1}\right)^a - \frac{a}{a-1}.$$

The value for a truly random sequence would be $e - 1$; and our value is $e - 1 + (e/2 - 1)/a + O(1/a^2)$. [*Note:* The same result holds for an ascending run, since we have $U_n > U_{n+1}$ if and only if $1 - U_n < 1 - U_{n+1}$. This would lead us to suspect that runs in linear congruential sequences might be slightly longer than normal, so the run test should be applied to such generators.]

25. x must be in the interval $[(k + \alpha' - \theta)/a \,..\, (k + \beta' - \theta)/a)$ for some k, and also in the interval $[\alpha \,..\, \beta)$. Let $k_0 = \lceil a\alpha + \theta - \beta' \rceil$, $k_1 = \lceil a\beta + \theta - \beta' \rceil$. With due regard to boundary conditions, we get the probability

$$(k_1 - k_0)(\beta' - \alpha')/a + \max(0, \beta - (k_1 + \alpha' - \theta)/a) - \max(0, \alpha - (k_0 + \alpha' - \theta)/a).$$

This is $(\beta - \alpha)(\beta' - \alpha') + \epsilon$, where $|\epsilon| < 2(\beta' - \alpha')/a$.

26. See Fig. A–1. The orderings $U_1 < U_3 < U_2$ and $U_2 < U_3 < U_1$ are impossible; the other four each have probability $\frac{1}{4}$.

27. $U_n = \{F_{n-1}U_0 + F_nU_1\}$. We need to have both $F_{k-1}U_0 + F_kU_1 < 1$ and $F_kU_0 + F_{k+1}U_1 > 1$. The half-unit-square in which $U_0 > U_1$ is broken up as shown in Fig. A–2, with various values of k indicated. The probability for a run of length k is $\frac{1}{2}$, if $k = 1$; it is $1/F_{k-1}F_{k+1} - 1/F_kF_{k+2}$, if $k > 1$. The corresponding probabilities for a random sequence are $2k/(k+1)! - 2(k+1)/(k+2)!$; the following table compares the first few values.

k:	1	2	3	4	5
Probability in Fibonacci case:	$\frac{1}{2}$	$\frac{1}{3}$	$\frac{1}{10}$	$\frac{1}{24}$	$\frac{1}{65}$
Probability in random case:	$\frac{1}{3}$	$\frac{5}{12}$	$\frac{11}{60}$	$\frac{19}{360}$	$\frac{29}{2520}$

28. Fig. A–3 shows the various regions in the general case. The "213" region means $U_2 < U_1 < U_3$, if U_1 and U_2 are chosen at random; the "321" region means that $U_3 < U_2 < U_1$, etc. The probabilities for 123 and 321 are $\frac{1}{4} - \alpha/2 + \alpha^2/2$; the probabilities for all other cases are $\frac{1}{8} + \alpha/4 - \alpha^2/4$. To have all equal to $\frac{1}{6}$, we must have

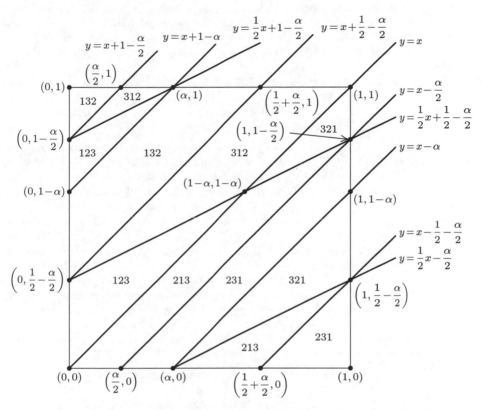

Fig. A–3. Permutation regions for a generator with potency 2; $\alpha = (a-1)c/m$.

$1 - 6\alpha + 6\alpha^2 = 0$. [This exercise establishes a theorem due to J. N. Franklin, *Math. Comp.* **17** (1963), 28–59, Theorem 13; other results of Franklin's paper are related to exercises 22 and 23.]

SECTION 3.3.4

1. For generators of maximum period, the 1-D accuracy ν_1 is always m, and $\mu_1 = 2$.

2. Let V be the matrix whose rows are $V_1, \ldots, V_t$. To minimize $Y \cdot Y$, subject to the condition that $Y \neq (0, \ldots, 0)$ and VY is an integer column vector X, is equivalent to minimizing $(V^{-1}X) \cdot (V^{-1}X)$, subject to the condition that X is a nonzero integer column vector. The columns of V^{-1} are $U_1, \ldots, U_t$.

3. $a^2 \equiv 2a - 1$ and $a^3 \equiv 3a - 2$ (modulo m). By considering all short solutions of (15), we find that $\nu_3^2 = 6$ and $\nu_4^2 = 4$, for the respective vectors $(1, -2, 1)$ and $(1, -1, -1, 1)$, except in the following cases:

$$m = 9, \quad a = 4 \text{ or } 7, \quad \nu_2^2 = \nu_3^2 = 5;$$
$$m = 9q, \quad a = 3q + 1 \text{ or } 6q + 1, \quad \nu_4^2 = 2.$$

4. (a) The unique choice for (x_1, x_2) is $\frac{1}{m}(y_1 u_{22} - y_2 u_{21}, -y_1 u_{12} + y_2 u_{11})$, and this is $\equiv \frac{1}{m}(y_1 u_{22} + y_2 a u_{22}, -y_1 u_{12} - y_2 a u_{12}) \equiv (0, 0)$ (modulo 1); that is, x_1 and x_2 are integers. (b) When $(x_1, x_2) \neq (0, 0)$, we have $(x_1 u_{11} + x_2 u_{21})^2 + (x_1 u_{12} + x_2 u_{22})^2 = x_1^2(u_{11}^2 + u_{12}^2) + x_2^2(u_{21}^2 + u_{22}^2) + 2x_1 x_2(u_{11} u_{21} + u_{12} u_{22})$, and by hypothesis this is $\geq (x_1^2 + x_2^2 - |x_1 x_2|)(u_{11}^2 + u_{12}^2) \geq u_{11}^2 + u_{12}^2$.

[Note that this is a stronger result than Lemma A, which tells us only that $x_1^2 \leq (u_{11}^2 + u_{12}^2)(u_{21}^2 + u_{22}^2)/m^2$ and that $x_2^2 \leq (u_{11}^2 + u_{12}^2)^2/m^2$, where the latter can be ≥ 1. The idea is essentially Gauss's notion of a reduced binary quadratic form, *Disquisitiones Arithmeticæ* (Leipzig: 1801), §171.]

5. Conditions (30) remain invariant; hence h cannot be zero in step S2, when a is relatively prime to m. Since h always decreases in that step, S2 eventually terminates with $u^2 + v^2 \geq s$. Notice that $pp' \leq 0$ throughout the calculation.

The hinted inequality surely holds the first time step S2 is encountered. The integer q' that minimizes $(h' - q'h)^2 + (p' - q'p)^2$ is $q' = \text{round}((h'h + p'p)/(h^2 + p^2))$, by Eq. (24). If $(h' - q'h)^2 + (p' - q'p)^2 < h^2 + p^2$ we must have $q' \neq 0$, $q' \neq -1$, hence $(p' - q'p)^2 \geq p^2$, hence $(h' - q'h)^2 < h^2$, i.e., $|h' - q'h| < h$, i.e., q' is q or $q+1$. We have $hu + pv \geq h(h' - q'h) + p(p' - q'p) \geq -\frac{1}{2}(h^2 + p^2)$, so if $u^2 + v^2 < s$ the next iteration of step S2 will preserve the assumption in the hint. If $u^2 + v^2 \geq s > (u - h)^2 + (v - p)^2$, we have $2|h(u - h) + p(v - p)| = 2(h(h - u) + p(p - v)) = (u - h)^2 + (v - p)^2 + h^2 + p^2 - (u^2 + v^2) \leq (u - h)^2 + (v - p)^2 \leq h^2 + p^2$, hence $(u - h)^2 + (v - p)^2$ is minimal by exercise 4. Finally if both $u^2 + v^2$ and $(u - h)^2 + (v - p)^2$ are $\geq s$, let $u' = h' - q'h$, $v' = p' - q'p$; then $2|hu' + pv'| \leq h^2 + p^2 \leq u'^2 + v'^2$, and $h^2 + p^2$ is minimal by exercise 4.

[Generalizations to finding the shortest 2-D vector with respect to other metrics are discussed by Kaib and Schnorr, *J. Algorithms* **21** (1996), 565–578.]

6. If $u^2 + v^2 \geq s > (u - h)^2 + (v - p)^2$ in the previous answer, we have $(v - p)^2 > v^2$, hence $(u - h)^2 < u^2$; and if $q = a_j$, so that $h' = a_j h + u$, we must have $a_{j+1} = 1$. It follows that $\nu_2^2 = \min_{0 \leq j < t}(m_j^2 + p_{j-1}^2)$, in the notation of exercise 3.3.3–16.

Now we have $m_0 = m_j p_j + m_{j+1} p_{j-1} = a_j m_j p_{j-1} + m_j p_{j-2} + m_{j+1} p_{j-1} < (a_j + 1 + 1/a_j) m_j p_{j-1} \leq (A + 1 + 1/A) m_j p_{j-1}$, and $m_j^2 + p_{j-1}^2 \geq 2 m_j p_{j-1}$, hence the result.

7. We shall prove, using condition (19), that $U_j \cdot U_k = 0$ for all $k \neq j$ if and only if $V_j \cdot V_k = 0$ for all $k \neq j$. Assume that $U_j \cdot U_k = 0$ for all $k \neq j$, and let $U_j = \alpha_1 V_1 + \cdots + \alpha_t V_t$. Then $U_j \cdot U_k = \alpha_k$ for all k, hence $U_j = \alpha_j V_j$, and $V_j \cdot V_k = \alpha_j^{-1}(U_j \cdot V_k) = 0$ for all $k \neq j$. A symmetric argument proves the converse.

8. Clearly $\nu_{t+1} \leq \nu_t$ (a fact used implicitly in Algorithm S, since s is not changed when t increases). For $t = 2$ this is equivalent to $(m\mu_2/\pi)^{1/2} \geq (\frac{3}{4}m\mu_3/\pi)^{1/3}$, i.e., $\mu_3 \leq \frac{4}{3}\sqrt{m/\pi}\,\mu_2^{3/2}$. This bound reduces to $\frac{4}{3}10^{-4}/\sqrt{\pi}$ with the given parameters, but for large m and fixed μ_2 the bound (40) is better.

9. Let $f(y_1, \ldots, y_t) = \theta$; then $\gcd(y_1, \ldots, y_t) = 1$, so there is an integer matrix W of determinant 1 having $(y_1, \ldots, y_t)$ as its first row. (Prove the latter fact by induction on the magnitude of the smallest nonzero entry in the row.) Now if $X = (x_1, \ldots, x_t)$ is a row vector, we have $XW = X'$ if and only if $X = X'W^{-1}$, and W^{-1} is an integer matrix of determinant 1, hence the form g defined by WU satisfies $g(x_1, \ldots, x_t) = f(x_1', \ldots, x_t')$; furthermore $g(1, 0, \ldots, 0) = \theta$.

Without loss of generality, assume that $f = g$. If now S is any orthogonal matrix, the matrix US defines the same form as U, since $(XUS)(XUS)^T = (XU)(XU)^T$. Choosing S so that its first column is a multiple of U_1^T and its other columns are any suitable vectors, we have

$$US = \begin{pmatrix} \alpha_1 & 0 & \cdots & 0 \\ \alpha_2 & & & \\ \vdots & & U' & \\ \alpha_t & & & \end{pmatrix}$$

for some $\alpha_1, \alpha_2, \ldots, \alpha_t$ and some $(t-1) \times (t-1)$ matrix U'. Hence $f(x_1, \ldots, x_t) = (\alpha_1 x_1 + \cdots + \alpha_t x_t)^2 + h(x_2, \ldots, x_t)$. It follows that $\alpha_1 = \sqrt{\theta}$ [in fact, $\alpha_j = (U_1 \cdot U_j)/\sqrt{\theta}$ for $1 \le j \le t$] and that h is a positive definite quadratic form defined by U', where $\det U' = (\det U)/\sqrt{\theta}$. By induction on t, there are integers $(x_2, \ldots, x_t)$ with

$$h(x_2, \ldots, x_t) \le (\tfrac{4}{3})^{(t-2)/2} |\det U|^{2/(t-1)}/\theta^{1/(t-1)},$$

and for these integer values we can choose x_1 so that $|x_1 + (\alpha_2 x_2 + \cdots + \alpha_t x_t)/\alpha_1| \le \tfrac{1}{2}$; equivalently, $(\alpha_1 x_1 + \cdots + \alpha_t x_t)^2 \le \tfrac{1}{4}\theta$. Hence

$$\theta \le f(x_1, \ldots, x_t) \le \tfrac{1}{4}\theta + (\tfrac{4}{3})^{(t-2)/2} |\det U|^{2/(t-1)}/\theta^{1/(t-1)}$$

and the desired inequality follows immediately.

[*Note:* For $t = 2$ the result is best possible. For general t, Hermite's theorem implies that $\mu_t \le \pi^{t/2}(4/3)^{t(t-1)/4}/(t/2)!$. A fundamental theorem due to Minkowski ("Every t-dimensional convex set symmetric about the origin with volume $\ge 2^t$ contains a nonzero integer point") gives $\mu_t \le 2^t$; this is stronger than Hermite's theorem for $t \ge 9$. Even stronger results are known, see (41).]

10. Since y_1 and y_2 are relatively prime, we can solve $u_1 y_2 - u_2 y_1 = m$; furthermore $(u_1 + q y_1)y_2 - (u_2 + q y_2)y_1 = m$ for all q, so we can ensure that $2|u_1 y_1 + u_2 y_2| \le y_1^2 + y_2^2$ by choosing an appropriate integer q. Now $y_2(u_1 + a u_2) \equiv y_2 u_1 - y_1 u_2 \equiv 0 \pmod{m}$, and y_2 must be relatively prime to m, hence $u_1 + a u_2 \equiv 0$. Finally let $|u_1 y_1 + u_2 y_2| = \alpha m$, $u_1^2 + u_2^2 = \beta m$, $y_1^2 + y_2^2 = \gamma m$; we have $0 \le \alpha \le \tfrac{1}{2}\gamma$, and it remains to be shown that $\alpha \le \tfrac{1}{2}\beta$ and $\beta\gamma \ge 1$. The identity $(u_1 y_2 - u_2 y_1)^2 + (u_1 y_1 + u_2 y_2)^2 = (u_1^2 + u_2^2)(y_1^2 + y_2^2)$ implies that $1 + \alpha^2 = \beta\gamma$. If $\alpha > \tfrac{1}{2}\beta$, we have $2\alpha\gamma > 1 + \alpha^2$, that is, $\gamma - \sqrt{\gamma^2 - 1} < \alpha \le \tfrac{1}{2}\gamma$. But $\tfrac{1}{2}\gamma < \sqrt{\gamma^2 - 1}$ implies that $\gamma^2 > \tfrac{4}{3}$, a contradiction.

11. Since a is odd, $y_1 + y_2$ must be even. To avoid solutions with y_1 and y_2 both even, let $y_1 = x_1 + x_2$, $y_2 = x_1 - x_2$, and solve $x_1^2 + x_2^2 = m/\sqrt{3} - \epsilon$, with $x_1 \perp x_2$ and x_1 even; the corresponding multiplier a will be the solution to $(x_2 - x_1)a \equiv x_2 + x_1 \pmod{2^e}$. It is not difficult to prove that $a \equiv 1 \pmod{2^{k+1}}$ if and only if $x_1 \equiv 0 \pmod{2^k}$, so we get the best potency when $x_1 \bmod 4 = 2$. The problem reduces to finding relatively prime solutions to $x_1^2 + x_2^2 = N$ where N is a large integer of the form $4k + 1$. By factoring N over the Gaussian integers, we can see that solutions exist if and only if each prime factor of N (over the usual integers) has the form $4k + 1$.

According to a famous theorem of Fermat, every prime p of the form $4k + 1$ can be written $p = u^2 + v^2 = (u + iv)(u - iv)$, v even, in a unique way except for the signs of u and v. The numbers u and v can be calculated efficiently by solving $x^2 \equiv -1 \pmod{p}$, then calculating $u + iv = \gcd(x + i, p)$ by Euclid's algorithm over the Gaussian integers. [We can take $x = n^{(p-1)/4} \bmod p$ for almost half of all integers n. This application of a Euclidean algorithm is essentially the same as finding the least nonzero $u^2 + v^2$ such that $u \pm xv \equiv 0 \pmod{p}$. The values of u and v also appear when Euclid's algorithm for integers is applied in the ordinary way to p and x; see J. A. Serret and C. Hermite, *J. de Math. Pures et Appl.* **13** (1848), 12–15.] If the prime factorization of N is $p_1^{e_1} \ldots p_r^{e_r} = (u_1 + iv_1)^{e_1}(u_1 - iv_1)^{e_1} \ldots (u_r + iv_r)^{e_r}(u_r - iv_r)^{e_r}$, we get 2^{r-1} distinct solutions to $x_1^2 + x_2^2 = N$, $x_1 \perp x_2$, x_1 even, by letting $|x_2| + i|x_1| = (u_1 + iv_1)^{e_1}(u_2 \pm iv_2)^{e_2} \ldots (u_r + iv_r)^{e_r}$; and all such solutions are obtained in this way.

Note: When $m = 10^e$, a similar procedure can be used, but it is five times as much work since we must keep trying until finding a solution with $x_1 \equiv 0 \pmod{10}$. For example, when $m = 10^{10}$ we have $\lfloor m/\sqrt{3} \rfloor = 5773502691$, and $5773502689 = 53 \cdot 108934013 = (7 + 2i)(7 - 2i)(2203 + 10202i)(2203 - 10202i)$. Of the two solutions $|x_2| + i|x_1| = (7 + 2i)(2203 + 10202i)$ or $(7 + 2i)(2203 - 10202i)$, the former gives $|x_1| = 67008$ (no good) and the latter gives $|x_1| = 75820$, $|x_2| = 4983$ (which is usable). Line 9 of Table 1 was obtained by taking $x_1 = 75820$, $x_2 = -4983$.

Line 14 of the table was obtained as follows: $\lfloor 2^{32}/\sqrt{3} \rfloor = 2479700524$; we drop down to $N = 2479700521$, which equals $37 \cdot 797 \cdot 84089$ and has four solutions $N = 4364^2 + 49605^2 = 26364^2 + 42245^2 = 38640^2 + 31411^2 = 11960^2 + 48339^2$. The corresponding multipliers are 2974037721, 2254986297, 4246248609, and 956772177. We try also $N - 4$, but it is ineligible because it is divisible by 3. On the other hand the prime number $N - 8 = 45088^2 + 21137^2$ leads to the multiplier 3825140801. Similarly, we get additional multipliers from $N - 20$, $N - 44$, $N - 48$, etc. The multiplier on line 14 is the best of the first sixteen multipliers found by this procedure; it's one of the four obtained from $N - 68$.

12. $U_j' \cdot U_j' = U_j \cdot U_j + 2 \sum_{i \neq j} q_i (U_i \cdot U_j) + \sum_{i \neq j} \sum_{k \neq j} q_i q_k (U_i \cdot U_k)$. The partial derivative with respect to q_k is twice the left-hand side of (26). If the minimum can be achieved, these partial derivatives must all vanish.

13. $u_{11} = 1$, $u_{21} =$ irrational, $u_{12} = u_{22} = 0$.

14. After three Euclidean steps we find $v_2^2 = 5^2 + 5^2$, then S4 produces

$$U = \begin{pmatrix} -5 & 5 & 0 \\ -18 & -2 & 0 \\ 1 & -2 & 1 \end{pmatrix}, \qquad V = \begin{pmatrix} -2 & 18 & 38 \\ -5 & -5 & -5 \\ 0 & 0 & 100 \end{pmatrix}.$$

Transformations $(j, q_1, q_2, q_3) = (1, *, 0, 2)$, $(2, -4, *, 1)$, $(3, 0, 0, *)$, $(1, *, 0, 0)$ result in

$$U = \begin{pmatrix} -3 & 1 & 2 \\ -5 & -8 & -7 \\ 1 & -2 & 1 \end{pmatrix}, \qquad V = \begin{pmatrix} -22 & -2 & 18 \\ -5 & -5 & -5 \\ 9 & -31 & 29 \end{pmatrix}, \qquad Z = (0 \quad 0 \quad 1).$$

Thus $v_3 = \sqrt{6}$, as we already knew from exercise 3.

15. The largest achievable q in (11), minus the smallest achievable, plus 1, is $|u_1| + \cdots + |u_t| - \delta$, where $\delta = 1$ if $u_i u_j < 0$ for some i and j, otherwise $\delta = 0$. For example if $t = 5$, $u_1 > 0$, $u_2 > 0$, $u_3 > 0$, $u_4 = 0$, and $u_5 < 0$, the largest achievable value is $q = u_1 + u_2 + u_3 - 1$ and the smallest is $q = u_5 + 1 = -|u_5| + 1$.

[Note that the number of hyperplanes is unchanged when c varies, hence the same answer applies to the problem of covering L instead of L_0. However, the stated formula is *not* always exact for covering L_0, since the hyperplanes that intersect the unit hypercube may not all contain points of L_0. In the example above, we can never achieve the value $q = u_1 + u_2 + u_3 - 1$ in L_0 if $u_1 + u_2 + u_3 > m$; it is achievable if and only if there is a solution to $m - u_1 - u_2 - u_3 = x_1 u_1 + x_2 u_2 + x_3 u_3 + x_4 |u_5|$ in nonnegative integers (x_1, x_2, x_3, x_4). It may be true that the stated limits are always achievable when $|u_1| + \cdots + |u_t|$ is minimal, but this does not appear to be obvious.]

16. It suffices to determine all solutions to (15) having minimum $|u_1| + \cdots + |u_t|$, subtracting 1 if any one of these solutions has components of opposite sign.

Instead of positive definite quadratic forms, we work with the somewhat similar function $f(x_1, \ldots, x_t) = |x_1 U_1 + \cdots + x_t U_t|$, defining $|Y| = |y_1| + \cdots + |y_t|$. Inequality (21) can be replaced by $|x_k| \leq f(y_1, \ldots, y_t)(\max_{1 \leq j \leq t} |v_{kj}|)$.

Thus a workable algorithm can be obtained as follows. Replace steps S1 through S3 by: "Set $U \leftarrow (m)$, $V \leftarrow (1)$, $r \leftarrow 1$, $s \leftarrow m$, $t \leftarrow 1$." (Here U and V are 1×1 matrices; thus the two-dimensional case will be handled by the general method. A special procedure for $t = 2$ could, of course, be used; see the reference following the answer to exercise 5.) In steps S4 and S7, set $s \leftarrow \min(s, |U_k|)$. In step S7, set $z_k \leftarrow \lfloor \max_{1 \leq j \leq t} |v_{kj}| s/m \rfloor$. In step S9, set $s \leftarrow \min(s, |Y| - \delta)$; and in step S10, output $s = N_t$. Otherwise leave the algorithm as it stands, since it already produces suitably short vectors. [*Math. Comp.* **29** (1975), 827–833.]

17. When $k > t$ in S9, and if $Y \cdot Y \leq s$, output Y and $-Y$; furthermore if $Y \cdot Y < s$, take back the previous output of vectors for this t. [In the author's experience preparing Table 1, there was exactly one vector (and its negative) output for each ν_t, except when $y_1 = 0$ or $y_t = 0$.]

18. (a) Let $x = m$, $y = (1 - m)/3$, $v_{ij} = y + x\delta_{ij}$, $u_{ij} = -y + \delta_{ij}$. Then $V_j \cdot V_k = \frac{1}{3}(m^2 - 1)$ for $j \neq k$, $V_k \cdot V_k = \frac{2}{3}(m^2 + \frac{1}{2})$, $U_j \cdot U_j = \frac{1}{3}(m^2 + 2)$, $z_k \approx \sqrt{\frac{2}{9}} m$. (This example satisfies (28) with $a = 1$ and works for all $m \equiv 1$ (modulo 3).)

(b) Interchange the roles of U and V in step S5. Also set $s \leftarrow \min(s, U_i \cdot U_i)$ for all U_i that change. For example, when $m = 64$ this transformation with $j = 1$, applied to the matrices of (a), reduces

$$V = \begin{pmatrix} 43 & -21 & -21 \\ -21 & 43 & -21 \\ -21 & -21 & 43 \end{pmatrix}, \quad U = \begin{pmatrix} 22 & 21 & 21 \\ 21 & 22 & 21 \\ 21 & 21 & 22 \end{pmatrix}$$

to

$$V = \begin{pmatrix} 1 & 1 & 1 \\ -21 & 43 & -21 \\ -21 & -21 & 43 \end{pmatrix}, \quad U = \begin{pmatrix} 22 & 21 & 21 \\ -1 & 1 & 0 \\ -1 & 0 & 1 \end{pmatrix}.$$

[Since the transformation can increase the length of V_j, an algorithm that incorporates both transformations must be careful to avoid infinite looping. See also exercise 23.]

19. No, since a product of non-identity matrices with all off-diagonal elements non-negative and all diagonal elements 1 cannot be the identity.

[However, looping would be possible if a subsequent transformation with $q = -1$ were performed when $-2V_i \cdot V_j = V_j \cdot V_j$; the rounding rule must be asymmetric with respect to sign if non-shortening transformations are allowed.]

20. When $a \bmod 8 = 5$, the points $2^{-e}(x, s(x), \ldots, s^{[t-1]}(x))$ for x in the period are the same as the points $2^{2-e}(y, \sigma(y), \ldots, \sigma^{t-1}(y))$ for $0 \leq y < 2^{e-2}$, plus $2^{-e}(t, \ldots, t)$, where $\sigma(y) = (ay + \lfloor a/4 \rfloor t) \bmod 2^{e-2}$ and $t = X_0 \bmod 4$. So in this case we should use Algorithm S with $m = 2^{e-2}$.

When $a \bmod 8 = 3$, the maximum distance between parallel hyperplanes that cover the points $2^{-e}(x, s(x), \ldots, s^{[t-1]}(x))$ modulo 1 is the same as the maximum distance covering the points $2^{-e}(x, -s(x), \ldots, (-1)^{t-1} s^{[t-1]}(x))$, because the negation of coordinates doesn't change distance. The latter points are $2^{2-e}(y, \sigma(y), \ldots, \sigma^{t-1}(y))$ where $\sigma(y) = (-ay - \lceil a/4 \rceil t) \bmod 2^{e-2}$, plus a constant offset. Again we apply Algorithm S with $m = 2^{e-2}$; changing a to $m - a$ has no effect on the result.

21. $X_{4n+4} \equiv X_{4n}$ (modulo 4), so it is now appropriate to let $V_1 = (4, 4a^2, 4a^3)/m$, $V_2 = (0, 1, 0)$, $V_3 = (0, 0, 1)$ define the corresponding lattice L_0.

24. Let $m = p$; an analysis paralleling the text can be given. For example, when $t = 4$ we have $X_{n+3} = ((a^2 + b)X_{n+1} + abX_n) \bmod m$, and we want to minimize $u_1^2 + u_2^2 + u_3^2 + u_4^2 \neq 0$ such that $u_1 + bu_3 + abu_4 \equiv u_2 + au_3 + (a^2 + b)u_4 \equiv 0$ (modulo m).

Replace steps S1 through S3 by the operations of setting

$$U \leftarrow \begin{pmatrix} m & 0 \\ 0 & m \end{pmatrix}, \qquad V \leftarrow \begin{pmatrix} 1 & 0 \\ 0 & 1 \end{pmatrix}, \qquad R \leftarrow \begin{pmatrix} 1 & 0 \\ 0 & 1 \end{pmatrix}, \qquad s \leftarrow m^2, \qquad t \leftarrow 2,$$

and outputting $\nu_2 = m$. Replace step S4 by

> **S4′.** [Advance t.] If $t = T$, the algorithm terminates. Otherwise set $t \leftarrow t + 1$ and $R \leftarrow R\left(\begin{smallmatrix} 0 & b \\ 1 & a \end{smallmatrix}\right) \bmod m$. Set U_t to the new row $(-r_{12}, -r_{22}, 0, \ldots, 0, 1)$ of t elements, and set $u_{it} \leftarrow 0$ for $1 \leq i < t$. Set V_t to the new row $(0, \ldots, 0, m)$. For $1 \leq i < t$, set $q \leftarrow \text{round}((v_{i1}r_{12} + v_{i2}r_{22})/m)$, $v_{it} \leftarrow v_{i1}r_{12} + v_{i2}r_{22} - qm$, and $U_t \leftarrow U_t + qU_i$. Finally set $s \leftarrow \min(s, U_t \cdot U_t)$, $k \leftarrow t$, $j \leftarrow 1$.

[A similar generalization applies to all sequences of length $p^k - 1$ that satisfy the linear recurrence 3.2.2–(8). Additional numerical examples have been given by A. Grube, *Zeitschrift für angewandte Math. und Mechanik* **53** (1973), T223–T225; L'Ecuyer, Blouin, and Couture, *ACM Trans. Modeling and Comp. Simul.* **3** (1993), 87–98.]

25. The given sum is at most twice the quantity $\sum_{0 \leq k \leq m/(2d)} r(dk) = 1 + \frac{1}{d}f(m/d)$, where

$$f(m) = \frac{1}{m} \sum_{1 \leq k \leq m/2} \csc(\pi k/m)$$

$$= \frac{1}{m} \int_1^{m/2} \csc(\pi x/m)\,dx + O\left(\frac{1}{m}\right) = \frac{1}{\pi}\ln\tan\left(\frac{\pi}{2m}x\right)\Big|_1^{m/2} + O\left(\frac{1}{m}\right).$$

[When $d = 1$, we have $\sum_{0 \leq k < m} r(k) = (2/\pi)\ln m + 1 + (2/\pi)\ln(2e/\pi) + O(1/m)$.]

26. If $\gcd(q, m) = d$, the same derivation goes through with m replaced by m/d. Suppose we have $m = p_1^{e_1} \ldots p_r^{e_r}$ and $\gcd(a - 1, m) = p_1^{f_1} \ldots p_r^{f_r}$ and $d = p_1^{d_1} \ldots p_r^{d_r}$. If m is replaced by m/d, then s is replaced by $p_1^{\max(0, e_1 - f_1 - d_1)} \ldots p_r^{\max(0, e_r - f_r - d_r)}$. Since $m/d > 1$, we can also replace N by $N \bmod (m/d)$.

27. It is convenient to use the following functions: $\rho(x) = 1$ if $x = 0$, $\rho(x) = x$ if $0 < x \leq m/2$, $\rho(x) = m - x$ if $m/2 < x < m$; $\text{trunc}(x) = \lfloor x/2 \rfloor$ if $0 \leq x \leq m/2$, $\text{trunc}(x) = m - \lfloor (m - x)/2 \rfloor$ if $m/2 < x < m$; $L(x) = 0$ if $x = 0$, $L(x) = \lfloor \lg x \rfloor + 1$ if $0 < x \leq m/2$, $L(x) = -(\lfloor \lg(m - x) \rfloor + 1)$ if $m/2 < x < m$; and $l(x) = \max(1, 2^{|x|-1})$. Note that $l(L(x)) \leq \rho(x) < 2l(L(x))$ and $2\rho(x) \leq 1/r(x) = m\sin(\pi x/m) < \pi\rho(x)$, for $0 < x < m$.

Say that a vector $(u_1, \ldots, u_t)$ is *bad* if it is nonzero and satisfies (15); and let $\rho_{\min}$ be the minimum value of $\rho(u_1) \ldots \rho(u_t)$ over all bad $(u_1, \ldots, u_t)$. The vector $(u_1, \ldots, u_t)$ is said to be in class $(L(u_1), \ldots, L(u_t))$. Thus there are at most $(2\lg m + 1)^t$ classes, and class $(L_1, \ldots, L_t)$ contains at most $l(L_1) \ldots l(L_t)$ vectors. Our proof is based on showing that the bad vectors in each fixed class contribute at most $2/\rho_{\min}$ to $\sum r(u_1, \ldots, u_t)$; this establishes the desired bound, since $1/\rho_{\min} < \pi^t r_{\max}$.

Let $\mu = \lfloor \lg \rho_{\min} \rfloor$. The μ-*fold truncation operator* on a vector is defined to be the following operation repeated μ times: "Let j be minimal such that $\rho(u_j) > 1$, and replace u_j by $\text{trunc}(u_j)$; but do nothing if $\rho(u_j) = 1$ for all j." (This operation essentially throws away one bit of information about $(u_1, \ldots, u_t)$.) If $(u_1', \ldots, u_t')$ and $(u_1'', \ldots, u_t'')$ are two vectors of the same class having the same μ-fold truncation, we say they are *similar*; in this case it follows that $\rho(u_1' - u_1'')\ldots\rho(u_t' - u_t'') < 2^\mu \le \rho_{\min}$. For example, any two vectors of the form $((1x_2x_1)_2, 0, m-(1x_3)_2, (101x_5x_4)_2, (1101)_2)$ are similar when m is large and $\mu = 5$; the μ-fold truncation operator successively removes x_1, x_2, x_3, x_4, x_5. Since the difference of two bad vectors satisfies (15), it is impossible for two unequal bad vectors to be similar. Therefore class $(L_1, \ldots, L_t)$ can contain at most $\max(1, l(L_1)\ldots l(L_t)/2^\mu)$ bad vectors. If class $(L_1, \ldots, L_t)$ contains exactly one bad vector $(u_1, \ldots, u_t)$, we have $r(u_1, \ldots, u_t) \le r_{\max} \le 1/\rho_{\min}$; if it contains $\le l(L_1)\ldots l(L_t)/2^\mu$ bad vectors, each of them has $r(u_1, \ldots, u_t) \le 1/\rho(u_1)\ldots\rho(u_t) \le 1/l(L_1)\ldots l(L_t)$, and we have $1/2^\mu < 2/\rho_{\min}$.

28. Let $\zeta = e^{2\pi i/(m-1)}$ and let $S_{kl} = \sum_{0 \le j < m-1} \omega^{x_j+l}\zeta^{jk}$. The analog of (51) is $|S_{k0}| = \sqrt{m}$, hence the analog of (53) is

$$\left| N^{-1} \sum_{0 \le n < N} \omega^{x_n} \right| = O((\sqrt{m}\log m)/N).$$

The analogous theorem now states that

$$D_N^{(t)} = O\left(\frac{\sqrt{m}\,(\log m)^{t+1}}{N}\right) + O\left((\log m)^t r_{\max}\right), \qquad D_{m-1}^{(t)} = O((\log m)^t r_{\max}).$$

In fact, $D_{m-1}^{(t)} \le \frac{m-2}{m-1}\sum r(u_1, \ldots, u_t)$ [summed over nonzero solutions of (15)] $+ \frac{1}{m-1}\sum r(u_1, \ldots, u_t)$ [summed over all nonzero $(u_1, \ldots, u_t)$]. The latter sum is $O(\log m)^t$ by exercise 25 with $d = 1$, and the former sum is treated as in exercise 27. Let us now consider the quantity $R(a) = \sum r(u_1, \ldots, u_t)$ summed over nonzero solutions of (15). Since m is prime, each $(u_1, \ldots, u_t)$ can be a solution to (15) for at most $t - 1$ values of a, hence $\sum_{0 < a < m} R(a) \le (t - 1)\sum r(u_1, \ldots, u_t) = O(t(\log m)^t)$. It follows that the average value of $R(a)$ taken over all $\varphi(m - 1)$ primitive roots is $O(t(\log m)^t/\varphi(m - 1))$.

Note: In general $1/\varphi(n) = O(\log\log n/n)$; we have therefore proved that *for all prime m and for all T there exists a primitive root a modulo m such that the linear congruential sequence $(1, a, 0, m)$ has discrepancy $D_{m-1}^{(t)} = O(m^{-1}T(\log m)^T \log\log m)$ for $1 \le t \le T$.* This method of proof does *not* extend to a similar result for linear congruential generators of period 2^e modulo 2^e, since for example the vector $(1, -3, 3, -1)$ solves (15) for about $2^{2e/3}$ values of a.

29. To get an upper bound, allow the nonzero components of $u = (u_1, \ldots, u_t)$ to be any real values $1 \le |u_j| \le \frac{1}{2}m$. If k components are nonzero, we have $r(u) \le 1/(2^k\rho(u))$ in the notation of the answer to exercise 27. And if $u_1^2 + \cdots + u_t^2$ has a given value ν^2, we minimize $\rho(u)$ by taking $u_1 = \cdots = u_{k-1} = 1$ and $u_k^2 = \nu^2 - k + 1$. Thus $r(u) \le 1/(2^k\sqrt{\nu^2 - k + 1})$. But $2^k\sqrt{\nu^2 - k + 1} \ge \sqrt{8}\nu$, since $\nu \ge k \ge 2$.

30. Let's first minimize $q|aq - mp|$ for $1 \le q < m$ and $0 \le p < a$. In the notation of exercise 4.5.3–42, we have $aq_n - mp_n = (-1)^n K_{s-n-1}(a_{n+2}, \ldots, a_s)$ for $0 \le n \le s$. In the range $q_{n-1} \le q < q_n$ we have $|aq - mp| \ge |aq_{n-1} - mp_{n-1}|$; consequently $q|aq - mp| \ge q_{n-1}|aq_{n-1} - mp_{n-1}|$, and the minimum is $\min_{0 \le n < s} q_n|aq_n - mp_n| = \min_{0 \le n < s} K_n(a_1, \ldots, a_n)K_{s-n-1}(a_{n+2}, \ldots, a_s)$. By exercise 4.5.3–32 we have $m = K_n(a_1, \ldots, a_n)a_{n+1}K_{s-n-1}(a_{n+2}, \ldots, a_s) + K_n(a_1, \ldots, a_n)K_{s-n-2}(a_{n+3}, \ldots, a_s) + K_{n-1}(a_1, \ldots, a_{n-1})K_{s-n-1}(a_{n+2}, \ldots, a_s)$; and our problem is essentially that of maximizing the quantity $m/K_n(a_1, \ldots, a_n)K_{s-n-1}(a_{n+2}, \ldots, a_s)$, which lies between a_{n+1} and $a_{n+1} + 2$.

Now let $A = \max(a_1, \ldots, a_s)$. Since $r(m - u) = r(u)$, we can assume that $r_{\max} = r(u)r(au \bmod m)$ for some u with $1 \le u \le \frac{1}{2}m$. Setting $u' = \min(au \bmod m, (-au) \bmod m)$, we have $r_{\max} = r(u)r(u')$. We know from the previous paragraph that $uu' \ge qq'$, where $A/m \le 1/qq' \le (A+2)/m$. Furthermore $2u \le r(u)^{-1} \le \pi u$ for $0 < u \le \frac{1}{2}m$, so $r_{\max} \le 1/(4uu')$. Hence we have $r_{\max} \le (A+2)/(4m)$. (There is a similar lower bound, namely $r_{\max} > A/(\pi^2 m)$.)

31. Equivalently, the conjecture is that all large m can be written $m = K_n(a_1, \ldots, a_n)$ for some n and some $a_i \in \{1, 2, 3\}$. For fixed n the 3^n numbers $K_n(a_1, \ldots, a_n)$ have an average value of order $(1 + \sqrt{2})^n$, and their standard deviation is of order $(2.51527)^n$; so the conjecture is almost surely true. S. K. Zaremba conjectured in 1972 that all m can be represented with $a_i \le 5$; T. W. Cusick made some early progress on this problem in *Mathematika* **24** (1977), 166–172, and an excellent survey of later work has been prepared by A. Kontorovich in *Bull. Amer. Math. Soc.* **50** (2013), 187–228. It appears that only the cases $m = 54$ and $m = 150$ require $a_i = 5$, and the largest m's that require 4s are 2052, 2370, 5052, and 6234; at least, the author has found representations with $a_i \le 3$ for all other integers less than 2000000. When we require $a_i \le 2$, the average of $K_n(a_1, \ldots, a_n)$ is $\frac{4}{5} 2^n + \frac{1}{5}(-2)^{-n}$, while the standard deviation grows as $(2.04033)^n$. The density of such numbers in the author's experiments (which considered 2^6 blocks of 2^{14} numbers each, for $m \le 2^{20}$) appears to vary between .50 and .65.

[See I. Borosh and H. Niederreiter, *BIT* **23** (1983), 65–74, for a computational method that finds multipliers with small partial quotients. They have found 2-bounded solutions with $m = 2^e$ for $25 \le e \le 35$.]

32. (a) $U_n - Z_n/m_1 \equiv (m_2 - m_1)Y_n/m_1 m_2$ (modulo 1), and $(m_1 - m_2)/m_1 m_2 \approx 2^{-54}$. (Therefore we can analyze the high-order bits of Z_n by analyzing U_n. The low-order bits are probably random too, but this argument does not apply to them.) (b) We have $U_n = W_n/m$ for all n. The Chinese remainder theorem tells us that we need only verify the congruences $W_n \equiv X_n m_2$ (modulo m_1) and $W_n \equiv -Y_n m_1$ (modulo m_2), because $m_1 \perp m_2$. [Pierre L'Ecuyer and Shu Tezuka, *Math. Comp.* **57** (1991), 735–746.]

SECTION 3.4.1

1. $\alpha + (\beta - \alpha)U$.

2. Let $U = X/m$; then $\lfloor kU \rfloor = r \iff r \le kX/m < r + 1 \iff mr/k \le X < m(r+1)/k \iff \lceil mr/k \rceil \le X < \lceil m(r+1)/k \rceil$. The exact probability is given by the formula $(1/m)(\lceil m(r+1)/k \rceil - \lceil mr/k \rceil) = 1/k + \epsilon$, where $|\epsilon| < 1/m$.

3. If full-word random numbers are given, the result will deviate from the correct distribution by at most $1/m$, as in exercise 2; but all of the excess is given to the smallest results. Thus if $k \approx m/3$, the result will be less than $k/2$ about $\frac{2}{3}$ of the time. It is much better to obtain a perfectly uniform distribution by rejecting U if $U \ge k\lfloor m/k \rfloor$; see D. E. Knuth, *The Stanford GraphBase* (New York: ACM Press, 1994), 221.

On the other hand, if a linear congruential sequence is used, k must be relatively prime to the modulus m, lest the numbers have a very short period, by the results of Section 3.2.1.1. For example, if $k = 2$ and m is even, the numbers will at best be alternately 0 and 1. The method is slower than (1) in nearly every case, so it is not recommended.

Unfortunately, however, the "himult" operation in (1) is not supported in many high-level languages; see exercise 3.2.1.1–3. Division by m/k may be best when himult is unavailable.

Fig. A–4. Region of "acceptance" for the algorithm of exercise 6.

4. $\max(X_1, X_2) \le x$ if and only if $X_1 \le x$ and $X_2 \le x$; $\min(X_1, X_2) \ge x$ if and only if $X_1 \ge x$ and $X_2 \ge x$. The probability that two independent events both happen is the product of the individual probabilities.

5. Obtain independent uniform deviates U_1 and U_2. Set $X \leftarrow U_2$. If $U_1 \ge p$, set $X \leftarrow \max(X, U_3)$, where U_3 is a third uniform deviate. If $U_1 \ge p + q$, also set $X \leftarrow \max(X, U_4)$, where U_4 is a fourth uniform deviate. This method can obviously be generalized to any polynomial, and indeed even to infinite power series (as shown for example in Algorithm S, which uses minimization instead of maximization).

We could also proceed as follows (suggested by M. D. MacLaren): If $U_1 < p$, set $X \leftarrow U_1/p$; otherwise if $U_1 < p + q$, set $X \leftarrow \max((U_1 - p)/q, U_2)$; otherwise set $X \leftarrow \max((U_1 - p - q)/r, U_2, U_3)$. This method requires less time than the other to obtain the uniform deviates, although it involves further arithmetical operations and it is slightly less stable numerically.

6. $F(x) = A_1/(A_1 + A_2)$, where A_1 and A_2 are the areas in Fig. A–4; so

$$F(x) = \frac{\int_0^x \sqrt{1 - y^2}\, dy}{\int_0^1 \sqrt{1 - y^2}\, dy} = \frac{2}{\pi} \arcsin x + \frac{2}{\pi} x \sqrt{1 - x^2}.$$

The probability of termination at step 2 is $p = \pi/4$, each time step 2 is encountered, so the number of executions of step 2 has the geometric distribution. The characteristics of this number are $(\min 1,\ \text{ave } 4/\pi,\ \max \infty,\ \text{dev } (4/\pi)\sqrt{1 - \pi/4})$, by exercise 17.

7. If $k = 1$, then $n_1 = n$ and the problem is trivial. Otherwise it is always possible to find $i \ne j$ such that $n_i \le n \le n_j$. Fill B_i with n_i cubes of color C_i and $n - n_i$ of color C_j, then decrease n_j by $n - n_i$ and eliminate color C_i. We are left with the same sort of problem but with k reduced by 1; by induction, it's possible.

The following algorithm can be used to compute the P and Y tables: Form a list of pairs $(p_1, 1) \ldots (p_k, k)$ and sort it by first components, obtaining a list $(q_1, a_1) \ldots (q_k, a_k)$ where $q_1 \le \cdots \le q_k$. Set $n \leftarrow k$; then repeat the following operations until $n = 0$: Set $P[a_1 - 1] \leftarrow kq_1$ and $Y[a_1 - 1] \leftarrow x_{a_n}$. Delete (q_1, a_1) and (q_n, a_n), then insert the new entry $(q_n - (1/k - q_1), a_n)$ into its proper place in the list and decrease n by 1.

(If $p_j < 1/k$ the algorithm will never put x_j in the Y table; this fact is used implicitly in Algorithm M. The algorithm attempts to maximize the probability that $V < P_K$ in (3), by always robbing from the richest remaining element and giving it to the poorest. However, it is very difficult to determine the absolute maximum of this probability, since such a task is at least as difficult as the "bin-packing problem"; see Section 7.9.)

8. Replace P_j by $(j + P_j)/k$ for $0 \le j < k$.

9. Consider the sign of $f''(x) = \sqrt{2/\pi}\,(x^2 - 1)e^{-x^2/2}$.

10. Let $S_j = (j-1)/5$ for $1 \le j \le 16$ and $p_{j+15} = F(S_{j+1}) - F(S_j) - p_j$ for $1 \le j \le 15$; also let $p_{31} = 1 - F(3)$ and $p_{32} = 0$. (Eq. (15) defines $p_1, \ldots, p_{15}$.) The algorithm of exercise 7 can now be used with $k = 32$ to compute P_j and Y_j, after which we will have $1 \le Y_j \le 15$ for $1 \le j \le 32$. Set $P_0 \leftarrow P_{32}$ (which is 0) and $Y_0 \leftarrow Y_{32}$. Then set $Z_j \leftarrow 1/(5 - 5P_j)$ and $Y_j \leftarrow \frac{1}{5}Y_j - Z_j$ for $0 \le j < 32$; $Q_j \leftarrow 1/(5P_j)$ for $1 \le j \le 15$.

Let $h = \frac{1}{5}$ and $f_{j+15}(x) = \sqrt{2/\pi}(e^{-x^2/2} - e^{-j^2/50})/p_{j+15}$ for $S_j \le x \le S_j + h$. Then let $a_j = f_{j+15}(S_j)$ for $1 \le j \le 5$, $b_j = f_{j+15}(S_j)$ for $6 \le j \le 15$; also $b_j = -hf'_{j+15}(S_j + h)$ for $1 \le j \le 5$, and $a_j = f_{j+15}(x_j) + (x_j - S_j)b_j/h$ for $6 \le j \le 15$, where x_j is the root of the equation $f'_{j+15}(x_j) = -b_j/h$. Finally set $D_{j+15} \leftarrow a_j/b_j$ for $1 \le j \le 15$ and $E_{j+15} \leftarrow 25/j$ for $1 \le j \le 5$, $E_{j+15} \leftarrow 1/(e^{(2j-1)/50} - 1)$ for $6 \le j \le 15$.

Table 1 was computed while making use of the following intermediate values: $(p_1, \ldots, p_{31}) = (.156, .147, .133, .116, .097, .078, .060, .044, .032, .022, .014, .009, .005,$ $.003, .002, .002, .005, .007, .009, .010, .009, .009, .008, .006, .005, .004, .002, .002, .001, .001,$ $.003)$; $(x_6, \ldots, x_{15}) = (1.115, 1.304, 1.502, 1.700, 1.899, 2.099, 2.298, 2.497, 2.697, 2.896)$; $(a_1, \ldots, a_{15}) = (7.5, 9.1, 9.5, 9.8, 9.9, 10.0, 10.0, 10.1, 10.1, 10.1, 10.1, 10.2, 10.2, 10.2, 10.2)$; $(b_1, \ldots, b_{15}) = (14.9, 11.7, 10.9, 10.4, 10.1, 10.1, 10.2, 10.3, 10.4, 10.5, 10.6, 10.7, 10.7, 10.8,$ $10.9)$.

11. Let $g(t) = e^{9/2}te^{-t^2/2}$ for $t \ge 3$. Since $G(x) = \int_3^x g(t)\,dt = 1 - e^{-(x^2-9)/2}$, a random variable X with density g can be computed by setting $X \leftarrow G^{[-1]}(1 - V) = \sqrt{9 - 2\ln V}$. Now $e^{-t^2/2} \le (t/3)e^{-t^2/2}$ for $t \ge 3$, so we obtain a valid rejection method if we accept X with probability $f(X)/cg(X) = 3/X$.

12. We have $f'(x) = xf(x) - 1 < 0$ for $x \ge 0$, since $f(x) = x^{-1} - e^{x^2/2}\int_x^\infty e^{-t^2/2}\,dt/t^2$ for $x > 0$. Let $x = a_{j-1}$ and $y^2 = x^2 + 2\ln 2$; then

$$\sqrt{2/\pi}\int_y^\infty e^{-t^2/2}\,dt = \tfrac{1}{2}\sqrt{2/\pi}\,e^{-x^2/2}f(y) < \tfrac{1}{2}\sqrt{2/\pi}\,e^{-x^2/2}f(x) = 2^{-j},$$

hence $y > a_j$.

13. Take $b_j = \mu_j$; consider now the problem with $\mu_j = 0$ for each j. In matrix notation, if $Y = AX$, where $A = (a_{ij})$, we need $AA^T = C = (c_{ij})$. (In other notation, if $Y_j = \sum a_{jk}X_k$, then the average value of Y_iY_j is $\sum a_{ik}a_{jk}$.) If this matrix equation can be solved for A, it can be solved when A is triangular, since $A = BU$ for some orthogonal matrix U and some triangular B, and $BB^T = C$. The desired triangular solution can be obtained by solving the equations $a_{11}^2 = c_{11}$, $a_{11}a_{21} = c_{12}$, $a_{21}^2 + a_{22}^2 = c_{22}$, $a_{11}a_{31} = c_{13}$, $a_{21}a_{31} + a_{22}a_{32} = c_{23}$, $\ldots$, successively for a_{11}, a_{21}, a_{22}, a_{31}, a_{32}, etc. [*Note:* The covariance matrix must be positive semidefinite, since the average value of $(\sum y_jY_j)^2$ is $\sum c_{ij}y_iy_j$, which must be nonnegative. And there is always a solution when C is positive semidefinite, since $C = U^{-1}\mathrm{diag}(\lambda_1, \ldots, \lambda_n)U$, where the eigenvalues λ_j are nonnegative, and $U^{-1}\mathrm{diag}(\sqrt{\lambda_1}, \ldots, \sqrt{\lambda_n})U$ is a solution.]

14. $F(x/c)$ if $c > 0$; the step function $[x \ge 0]$ if $c = 0$; or $1 - F(x/c)$ if $c < 0$.

15. Distribution $\int_{-\infty}^\infty F_1(x - t)\,dF_2(t)$. Density $\int_{-\infty}^\infty f_1(x - t)f_2(t)\,dt$. This is called the *convolution* of the given distributions.

16. It is clear that $f(t) \le cg(t)$ for all t as required. Since $\int_0^\infty g(t)\,dt = 1$ we have $g(t) = Ct^{a-1}$ for $0 \le t < 1$, Ce^{-t} for $t \ge 1$, where $C = ae/(a + e)$. A random variable with density g is easy to obtain as a mixture of two distributions, $G_1(x) = x^a$ for $0 \le x < 1$, and $G_2(x) = 1 - e^{1-x}$ for $x \ge 1$:

G1. [Initialize.] Set $p \leftarrow e/(a + e)$. (This is the probability that G_1 should be used.)

G2. [Generate G deviate.] Generate independent uniform deviates U and V, where $V \neq 0$. If $U < p$, set $X \leftarrow V^{1/a}$ and $q \leftarrow e^{-X}$; otherwise set $X \leftarrow 1 - \ln V$ and $q \leftarrow X^{a-1}$. (Now X has density g, and $q = f(X)/cg(X)$.)

G3. [Reject?] Generate a new uniform deviate U. If $U \geq q$, return to G2.   ∎

The average number of iterations is $c = (a + e)/(e\Gamma(a + 1)) < 1.4$.

It is possible to streamline this procedure in several ways. First, we can replace V by an exponential deviate Y of mean 1, generated by Algorithm S, say, and then we set $X \leftarrow e^{-Y/a}$ or $X \leftarrow 1 + Y$ in the two cases. Moreover, if we set $q \leftarrow pe^{-X}$ in the first case and $q \leftarrow p + (1 - p)X^{a-1}$ in the second, we can use the original U instead of a newly generated one in step G3. Finally if $U < p/e$ we can accept $V^{1/a}$ immediately, avoiding the calculation of q about 30 percent of the time.

17. (a) $F(x) = 1 - (1 - p)^{\lfloor x \rfloor}$, for $x \geq 0$. (b) $G(z) = pz/(1 - (1 - p)z)$. (c) Mean $1/p$, standard deviation $\sqrt{1-p}/p$. To do the latter calculation, observe that if $H(z) = q + (1 - q)z$, then $H'(1) = 1 - q$ and $H''(1) + H'(1) - (H'(1))^2 = q(1 - q)$, so the mean and variance of $1/H(z)$ are $q - 1$ and $q(q - 1)$, respectively. (See Section 1.2.10.) In this case, $q = 1/p$; the extra factor z in the numerator of $G(z)$ adds 1 to the mean.

18. Set $N \leftarrow N_1 + N_2 - 1$, where N_1 and N_2 independently have the geometric distribution for probability p. (Consider the generating function.)

19. Set $N \leftarrow N_1 + \cdots + N_t - t$, where the N_j have the geometric distribution for p. (This is the number of failures before the tth success, when a sequence of independent trials are made each of which succeeds with probability p.)

For $t = p = \frac{1}{2}$, and in general when the mean value (namely $t(1 - p)/p$) of the distribution is small, we can simply evaluate the probabilities $p_n = \binom{t-1+n}{n}p^t(1 - p)^n$ consecutively for $n = 0, 1, 2, \ldots$ as in the following algorithm:

N1. [Initialize.] Set $N \leftarrow 0$, $q \leftarrow p^t$, $r \leftarrow q$, and generate a random uniform deviate U. (We will have $q = p_N$ and $r = p_0 + \cdots + p_N$ during this algorithm, which stops as soon as $U < r$.)

N2. [Iterate.] If $U \geq r$, set $N \leftarrow N + 1$, $q \leftarrow q(1 - p)(t - 1 + N)/N$, $r \leftarrow r + q$, and repeat this step. Otherwise return N and terminate.   ∎

[An interesting technique for the negative binomial distribution, for arbitrarily large real values of t, has been suggested by R. Léger: First generate a random gamma deviate X of order t, then let N be a random Poisson deviate of mean $X(1 - p)/p$.]

20. R1 $= 1 + (1 - A/R) \cdot$ R1. When R2 is performed, the algorithm terminates with probability I/R; when R3 is performed, it goes to R1 with probability E/R. We have

R1	R/A	R/A	R/A	R/A
R2	0	R/A	0	R/A
R3	0	0	R/A	$R/A - I/A$
R4	R/A	$R/A - I/A$	$R/A - E/A$	$R/A - I/A - E/A$

21. $R = \sqrt{8/e} \approx 1.71553$; $A = \sqrt{2}\Gamma(3/2) = \sqrt{\pi/2} \approx 1.25331$. Since

$$\int u\sqrt{a - bu}\, du = (a - bu)^{3/2} \left(\tfrac{2}{5}(a - bu) - \tfrac{2}{3}a\right)/b^2,$$

we have $I = 2\int_0^{a/b} u\sqrt{a - bu}\, du = \frac{8}{15}a^{5/2}/b^2$ where $a = 4(1 + \ln c)$ and $b = 4c$; when $c = e^{1/4}$, I has its maximum value $\frac{5}{6}\sqrt{5/e} \approx 1.13020$. Finally the following integration formulas are needed for E:

$$\int\sqrt{bu - au^2}\, du = \tfrac{1}{8}b^2 a^{-3/2} \arcsin(2ua/b - 1) + \tfrac{1}{4}ba^{-1}\sqrt{bu - au^2}\,(2ua/b - 1),$$

$$\int\sqrt{bu + au^2}\, du = -\tfrac{1}{8}b^2 a^{-3/2}\ln(\sqrt{bu + au^2} + u\sqrt{a} + b/2\sqrt{a}) + \tfrac{1}{4}ba^{-1}\sqrt{bu + au^2}\,(2ua/b + 1),$$

where $a, b > 0$. Let the test in step R3 be "$X^2 \geq 4e^{x-1}/U - 4x$"; then the exterior region hits the top of the rectangle when $u = r(x) = (e^x - \sqrt{e^{2x} - 2ex})/2ex$. (Incidentally, $r(x)$ reaches its maximum value at $x = 1/2$, a point where it is *not* differentiable!) We have $E = 2\int_0^{r(x)}(\sqrt{2/e} - \sqrt{bu - au^2})\, du$ where $b = 4e^{x-1}$ and $a = 4x$. The maximum value of E occurs near $x = -.35$, where we have $E \approx .29410$.

22. (Solution by G. Marsaglia.) Consider the "continuous Poisson distribution" defined by $G(x) = \int_\mu^\infty e^{-t}t^{x-1}\, dt/\Gamma(x)$, for $x > 0$; if X has this distribution then $\lfloor X \rfloor$ is Poisson distributed, since $G(x + 1) - G(x) = e^{-\mu}\mu^x/x!$. If μ is large, G is approximately normal, hence $G^{[-1]}(F_\mu(x))$ is approximately linear, where $F_\mu(x)$ is the distribution function for a normal deviate with mean and variance μ; that is, $F_\mu(x) = F((x - \mu)/\sqrt{\mu})$, where $F(x)$ is the normal distribution function (10). Let $g(x)$ be an efficiently computable function such that $|G^{[-1]}(F_\mu(x)) - g(x)| < \epsilon$ for $-\infty < x < \infty$; we can now generate Poisson deviates efficiently as follows: Generate a normal deviate X, and set $Y \leftarrow g(\mu + \sqrt{\mu}\,X)$, $N \leftarrow \lfloor Y \rfloor$, $M \leftarrow \lfloor Y + \tfrac{1}{2}\rfloor$. Then if $|Y - M| > \epsilon$, output N; otherwise output $M - [G^{[-1]}(F(X)) < M]$.
   This approach applies also to the binomial distribution, with

$$G(x) = \int_p^1 u^{x-1}(1 - u)^{n-x}\, du\; \frac{\Gamma(t + 1)}{\Gamma(x)\,\Gamma(t + 1 - x)},$$

since $\lfloor G^{[-1]}(U) \rfloor$ is binomial with parameters (t, p) and G is approximately normal.
   [See also the alternative method proposed by Ahrens and Dieter in *Computing* **25** (1980), 193–208.]

23. Yes. The second method calculates $|\cos 2\theta|$, where θ is uniformly distributed between 0 and $\pi/2$. (Let $U = r\cos\theta$, $V = r\sin\theta$.)

25. $\frac{21}{32} = (.10101)_2$. In general, the binary representation is formed by using 1 for | and 0 for &, from left to right, then suffixing 1. This technique [see K. D. Tocher, *J. Roy. Stat. Soc.* **B16** (1954), 49] can lead to efficient generation of independent bits having a given probability p, and it can also be applied to the geometric and binomial distributions.

26. (a) True: $\sum_k \Pr(N_1 = k)\Pr(N_2 = n - k) = e^{-\mu_1 - \mu_2}(\mu_1 + \mu_2)^n/n!$. (b) False, unless $\mu_2 = 0$; otherwise $N_1 - N_2$ might be negative.

27. Let the binary representation of p be $(.b_1 b_2 b_3 \ldots)_2$, and proceed according to the following rules:

B1. [Initialize.] Set $m \leftarrow t$, $N \leftarrow 0$, $j \leftarrow 1$. (During this algorithm, m represents the number of simulated uniform deviates whose relation to p is still unknown, since they match p in their leading $j-1$ bits; and N is the number of simulated deviates known to be less than p.)

B2. [Look at next column of bits.] Generate a random integer M with the binomial distribution $(m, \tfrac{1}{2})$. (Now M represents the number of unknown deviates that fail to match b_j.) Set $m \leftarrow m - M$, and if $b_j = 1$ set $N \leftarrow N + M$.

B3. [Done?] If $m = 0$, or if the remaining bits $(.b_{j+1}b_{j+2}\ldots)_2$ of p are all zero, the algorithm terminates. Otherwise, set $j \leftarrow j+1$ and return to step B2. ∎

[When $b_j = 1$ for infinitely many j, the average number of iterations A_t satisfies

$$A_0 = 0; \qquad A_n = 1 + \frac{1}{2^n}\sum_k \binom{n}{k}A_k, \quad \text{for } n \geq 1.$$

Letting $A(z) = \sum A_n z^n/n!$, we have $A(z) = e^z - 1 + A(\tfrac{1}{2}z)e^{z/2}$. Therefore $A(z)e^{-z} = 1 - e^{-z} + A(\tfrac{1}{2}z)e^{-z/2} = \sum_{k\geq 0}(1 - e^{-z/2^k}) = 1 - e^{-z} - \sum_{n\geq 1}(-z)^n/(n!(2^n - 1))$, and

$$A_m = 1 + \sum_{k\geq 1}\binom{n}{k}\frac{(-1)^{k+1}}{2^k - 1} = 1 + \frac{V_{n+1}}{n+1} = \lg n + \frac{\gamma}{\ln 2} + \frac{1}{2} + f_0(n) + O(n^{-1})$$

in the notation of exercise 5.2.2–48.]

28. Generate a random point $(y_1,\ldots,y_n)$ on the unit sphere, and let $\rho = \sqrt{\sum a_k y_k^2}$. Generate an independent uniform deviate U, and if $\rho^{n+1}U < K\sqrt{\sum a_k^2 y_k^2}$, output the point $(y_1/\rho,\ldots,y_n/\rho)$; otherwise start over. Here $K^2 = \min\{(\sum a_k y_k^2)^{n+1}/(\sum a_k^2 y_k^2) \mid \sum y_k^2 = 1\} = a_n^{n-1}$ if $na_n \geq a_1$, $((n+1)/(a_1 + a_n))^{n+1}(a_1 a_n/n)^n$ otherwise.

29. Let $X_{n+1} = 1$, then set $X_k \leftarrow X_{k+1}U_k^{1/k}$ or $X_k \leftarrow X_{k+1}e^{-Y_k/k}$ for $k = n, n-1, \ldots, 1$, where U_k is uniform or Y_k is exponential. [*ACM Trans. Math. Software* **6** (1980), 359–364. This technique was introduced in the 1960s by David Seneschal; see *Amer. Statistician* **26**, 4 (October 1972), 56–57. The alternative of generating n uniform numbers and sorting them is probably faster, with an appropriate sorting method, but the method suggested here is particularly valuable if only a few of the largest or smallest X's are desired. Notice that $(F^{[-1]}(X_1),\ldots,F^{[-1]}(X_n))$ will be sorted deviates having distribution F.]

30. Generate random numbers $Z_1 = -\mu^{-1}\ln U_1$, $Z_2 = Z_1 - \mu^{-1}\ln U_2$, $\ldots$, until $Z_{m+1} \geq 1$. Output $(X_j, Y_j) = f(Z_j)$ for $1 \leq j \leq m$, where $f((.b_1 b_2 \ldots b_{2r})_2) = ((.b_1 b_2 \ldots b_r)_2, (.b_{r+1}b_{r+2}\ldots b_{2r})_2)$. If the less significant bits are significantly less random than the more significant bits, it's safer (but slower) to let $f((.b_1 b_2 \ldots b_{2r})_2) = ((.b_1 b_3 \ldots b_{2r-1})_2, (.b_2 b_4 \ldots b_{2r})_2)$.

31. (a) It suffices to consider the case $k = 2$, since $a_1 X_1 + \cdots + a_k X_k = X\cos\theta + Y\sin\theta$ when $X = X_1$, $\cos\theta = a_1$, and $Y = (a_2 X_2 + \cdots + a_k X_k)/\sin\theta$. And

$$\Pr(X\cos\theta + Y\sin\theta \leq x) = \frac{1}{2\pi}\int_{s,t} e^{-s^2/2 - t^2/2}\,ds\,dt\,[s\cos\theta + t\sin\theta \leq x]$$

$$= \frac{1}{2\pi}\int_{u,v} e^{-u^2/2 - v^2/2}\,du\,dv\,[u \leq x] = (10),$$

from the substitution $u = s\cos\theta + t\sin\theta$, $v = -s\sin\theta + t\cos\theta$.

(b) There are numbers $\alpha > 1$ and $\beta > 1$ such that $(\alpha^{-24} + \alpha^{-55})/\sqrt{2} = 1$ and $\frac{3}{5}\beta^{-24} + \frac{4}{5}\beta^{-55} = 1$; so the numbers X_n will grow exponentially with n, by the properties of linear recurrences.

If we break out of the linear recurrence mold by, say, using the recurrence $X_n = X_{n-24}\cos\theta_n + X_{n-55}\sin\theta_n$, where θ_n is chosen uniformly in $[0\mathinner{.\,.}2\pi)$, we probably will obtain decent results; but this alternative would involve much more computation.

(c) Start with, say, 2048 normal deviates $X_0, \ldots, X_{1023}, Y_0, \ldots, Y_{1023}$. After having used about 1/3 of them, generate 2048 more as follows: Choose integers a, b, c, and d uniformly in $[0 \, .. \, 1024)$, with a and c odd; then set

$$X'_j \leftarrow X_{(aj+b) \bmod 1024} \cos\theta + Y_{(cj+d) \bmod 1024} \sin\theta,$$
$$Y'_j \leftarrow -X_{(aj+b) \bmod 1024} \sin\theta + Y_{(cj+d) \bmod 1024} \cos\theta,$$

for $0 \le j < 1024$, where $\cos\theta$ and $\sin\theta$ are random ratios $(U^2 - V^2)/(U^2 + V^2)$ and $2UV/(U^2 + V^2)$, chosen as in exercise 23. We can reject U and V unless $|\cos\theta| \ge \frac{1}{2}$ and $|\sin\theta| \ge \frac{1}{2}$. The 2048 new deviates now replace the old ones. Notice that only a few operations were needed per new deviate.

This method does not diverge like the sequences considered in (b), because the sum of squares $\sum(X_j^2 + Y_j^2) = \sum((X'_j)^2 + (Y'_j)^2)$ remains at the constant value $S \approx 2048$, except for a slight roundoff error. On the other hand, the constancy of S is actually a defect of the method, because the sum of squares should really have the χ^2 distribution with 2048 degrees of freedom. To overcome this problem, the normal deviates actually delivered to the user should be not X_j but αX_j, where $\alpha^2 = \frac{1}{2}(Y_{1023} + \sqrt{4095})^2/S$ is a precomputed scale factor. (The quantity $\frac{1}{2}(Y_{1023} + \sqrt{4095})^2$ will be a reasonable approximation to the χ^2 deviate desired.)

References: C. S. Wallace [*ACM Trans. on Math. Software* **22** (1996), 119–127]; R. P. Brent [*Lecture Notes in Comp. Sci.* **1470** (1998), 1–20].

32. (a) This mapping $(X', Y') = f(X, Y)$ is a one-to-one correspondence from the set $\{x, y \ge 0\}$ to itself such that $x' + y' = x + y$ and $dx' \, dy' = dx \, dy$. We have

$$\frac{X'}{X' + Y'} = \left(\frac{X}{X + Y} - \lambda\right) \bmod 1, \qquad \frac{Y'}{X' + Y'} = \left(\frac{Y}{X + Y} + \lambda\right) \bmod 1.$$

(b) This mapping is a two-to-one correspondence such that $x' + y' = x + y$ and $dx' \, dy' = 2 \, dx \, dy$.

(c) It suffices to consider the "j-flip" transformation

$$X' = (\dots x_{j+2} x_{j+1} x_j y_{j-1} y_{j-2} y_{j-3} \dots)_2,$$
$$Y' = (\dots y_{j+2} y_{j+1} y_j x_{j-1} x_{j-2} x_{j-3} \dots)_2,$$

for a fixed integer j, and then to compose j-flips for $j = 0, 1, -1, 2, -2, \dots$, noticing that the joint probability distribution of X' and Y' converges as $|j| \to \infty$. Each j-flip is one-to-one, with $x' + y' = x + y$ and $dx' \, dy' = dx \, dy$.

33. Use U_1 as the seed for *another* random number generator (perhaps a linear congruential generator with a different multiplier); take $U_2, U_3, \dots$ from that one.

SECTION 3.4.2

1. There are $\binom{N-t}{n-m}$ ways to pick $n - m$ records from the last $N - t$, and $\binom{N-t-1}{n-m-1}$ ways to pick $n - m - 1$ from $N - t - 1$ after selecting the $(t+1)$st item.

2. Step S3 will never go to step S5 when the number of records left to be examined is equal to $n - m$.

3. We should not confuse conditional and unconditional probabilities. The quantity m depends randomly on the selections that took place among the first t elements; if we take the average over all possible choices that could have occurred among these elements, we will find that $(n - m)/(N - t)$ is exactly n/N on the average. For example, consider the second element; if the first element was selected in the sample (this happens with probability n/N), the second element is selected with probability $(n-1)/(N-1)$; if the first element was not selected, the second is selected with

probability $n/(N - 1)$. The overall probability of selecting the second element is
$(n/N)((n - 1)/(N - 1)) + (1 - n/N)(n/(N - 1)) = n/N$.

4. From the algorithm,

$$p(m, t + 1) = \left(1 - \frac{n - m}{N - t}\right) p(m, t) + \frac{n - (m - 1)}{N - t} p(m - 1, t).$$

The desired formula can be proved by induction on t. In particular, $p(n, N) = 1$.

5. In the notation of exercise 4, the probability that $t = k$ at termination is $q_k = p(n, k) - p(n, k - 1) = \binom{k-1}{n-1}/\binom{N}{n}$. The average is $\sum_{k=0}^{N} k q_k = (N + 1)n/(n + 1)$.

6. Similarly, $\sum_{k=0}^{N} k(k + 1)q_k = (N + 2)(N + 1)n/(n + 2)$; the variance is therefore $(N + 1)(N - n)n/(n + 2)(n + 1)^2$.

7. Suppose the choice is $1 \le x_1 < x_2 < \cdots < x_n \le N$. Let $x_0 = 0$, $x_{n+1} = N + 1$. The choice is obtained with probability $p = \prod_{1 \le t \le N} p_t$, where

$$p_t = \begin{cases} (N - (t - 1) - n + m)/(N - (t - 1)), & \text{for } x_m < t < x_{m+1}; \\ (n - m)/(N - (t - 1)), & \text{for } t = x_{m+1}. \end{cases}$$

The denominator of the product p is $N!$; the numerator contains the terms $N - n$, $N - n - 1$, $\ldots$, 1 for those t's that are not x's, and the terms n, $n - 1$, $\ldots$, 1 for those t's that *are* x's. Hence $p = (N - n)!n!/N!$.

Example: $n = 3$, $N = 8$, $(x_1, x_2, x_3) = (2, 3, 7)$; $p = \frac{5}{8}\frac{3}{7}\frac{2}{6}\frac{4}{5}\frac{3}{4}\frac{2}{3}\frac{1}{2}\frac{1}{1}$.

8. (a) $p(0, k) = \binom{N-k}{n}/\binom{N}{n} = \binom{N-n}{k}/\binom{N}{n}$ of the $\binom{N}{n}$ samples omit the first k records.
(b) Set $X \leftarrow k - 1$, where k is minimum with $U \ge \Pr(X \ge k)$. Thus, start with $X \leftarrow 0$, $p \leftarrow N - n$, $q \leftarrow N$, $R \leftarrow p/q$, and while $U < R$ set $X \leftarrow X + 1$, $p \leftarrow p - 1$, $q \leftarrow q - 1$, $R \leftarrow Rp/q$. (This method is good when n/N is, say, $\ge 1/5$. We can assume that $n/N \le 1/2$; otherwise it's better to select $N - n$ *unsampled* items.)
(c) $\Pr(\min(Y_N, \ldots, Y_{N-n+1}) \ge k) = \prod_{j=0}^{n-1} \Pr(Y_{N-j} \ge k) = \prod_{j=0}^{n-1}((N-j-k)/(N-j))$. (This method is good if, say, $n \le 5$.)
(d) (See exercise 3.4.1–29.) The value $X \leftarrow \lfloor N(1 - U^{1/n}) \rfloor$ needs to be rejected with probability only $O(n/N)$. Precise details are worked out carefully in *CACM* **27** (1984), 703–718, and a practical implementation appears in *ACM Trans. Math. Software* **13** (1987), 58–67. (This method is good when, say, $5 < n < \frac{1}{5}N$.)
   After skipping X records and selecting the next, we set $n \leftarrow n - 1$, $N \leftarrow N - X - 1$, and repeat the process until $n = 0$. A similar approach speeds up the reservoir method; see *ACM Trans. Math. Software* **11** (1985), 37–57.

9. The reservoir gets seven records: 1, 2, 3, 5, 9, 13, 16. The final sample consists of records 2, 5, 16.

10. Delete step R6 and the variable m. Replace the I table by a table of records, initialized to the first n records in step R1, and with the new record replacing the Mth table entry in step R4.

11. Arguing as in Section 1.2.10, which considers the special case $n = 1$, we see that the generating function is

$$G(z) = z^n \left(\frac{1}{n+1} + \frac{n}{n+1}z\right)\left(\frac{2}{n+2} + \frac{n}{n+2}z\right) \cdots \left(\frac{N - n}{N} + \frac{n}{N}z\right).$$

The mean is $n + \sum_{n < t \le N}(n/t) = n(1 + H_N - H_n)$; and the variance turns out to be $n(H_N - H_n) - n^2(H_N^{(2)} - H_n^{(2)})$.

12. (Note that $\pi^{-1} = (b_t t) \ldots (b_3 3)(b_2 2)$, so we seek an algorithm that goes from the representation of π to that for π^{-1}.) Set $b_j \leftarrow j$ for $1 \leq j \leq t$. Then for $j = 2, 3, \ldots, t$ (in this order), interchange $b_j \leftrightarrow b_{a_j}$. Finally for $j = t, \ldots, 3, 2$ (in this order), set $b_{a_j} \leftarrow b_j$. (The algorithm is based on the fact that $(a_t t)\pi_1 = \pi_1(b_t t)$.)

13. Renumbering the deck $0, 1, \ldots, 2n - 2$, we find that s takes card number x into card number $(2x) \bmod (2n - 1)$, while c takes card x into $(x - 1) \bmod (2n - 1)$. We have (c followed by s) $= cs = sc^2$. Therefore any product of c's and s's can be transformed into the form $s^i c^k$. Also $2^{\varphi(2n-1)} \equiv 1$ modulo $(2n - 1)$; since $s^{\varphi(2n-1)}$ and c^{2n-1} are the identity permutation, at most $(2n - 1)\varphi(2n - 1)$ arrangements are possible. (The *exact* number of different arrangements is $(2n-1)k$, where k is the order of 2 modulo $(2n-1)$. For if $s^k = c^j$, then c^j fixes the card 0, so $s^k = c^j =$ identity.) For further details, see *SIAM Review* **3** (1961), 293–297.

14. (a) ♛. We could have deduced this regardless of where he had moved it, unless he had put it into one of the first three or last two positions. (b) ♟. Three cut-and-riffles will produce an intermixture of at most eight cyclically increasing subsequences $a_{x_j} a_{(x_j+1) \bmod n} \cdots a_{(x_{j+1}-1) \bmod n}$; hence the subsequence ♦6 ♦5 ♦4 is a dead giveaway. [Several magic tricks are based on the fact that three cut-and-riffles are highly nonrandom; see Martin Gardner, *Mathematical Magic Show* (Knopf, 1977), Chapter 7.]

15. Set $Y_j \leftarrow j$ for $t - n < j \leq t$. Then for $j = t, t - 1, \ldots, t - n + 1$ do the following operations: Set $k \leftarrow \lfloor jU \rfloor + 1$. If $k > t - n$ then set $X_j \leftarrow Y_k$ and $Y_k \leftarrow Y_j$; otherwise if $k = X_i$ for some $i > j$ (a symbol table algorithm could be used), then set $X_j \leftarrow Y_i$ and $Y_i \leftarrow Y_j$; otherwise set $X_j \leftarrow k$. (The idea is to let $Y_{t-n+1}, \ldots, Y_j$ represent $X_{t-n+1}, \ldots, X_j$, and if $i > j$ and $X_i \leq t - n$ also to let Y_i represent X_{X_i}, in the execution of Algorithm P. It is interesting to prove the correctness of Dahl's algorithm. One basic observation is that, in step P2, $X_k \neq k$ implies $X_k > j$, for $1 \leq k \leq j$.)

16. We may assume that $n \leq \frac{1}{2}N$, otherwise it suffices to find the $N - n$ elements *not* in the sample. Using a hash table of size $2n$, the idea is to generate random numbers between 1 and N, storing them in the table and discarding duplicates, until n distinct numbers have been generated. The average number of random numbers generated is $N/N + N/(N - 1) + \cdots + N/(N - n + 1) < 2n$, by exercise 3.3.2–10, and the average time to process each number is $O(1)$. We want to output the results in increasing order, and this can be done as follows: Using an ordered hash table (exercise 6.4–66) with linear probing, the hash table will appear as if the values had been inserted in increasing order and the average total number of probes will be less than $\frac{5}{2}n$. Thus if we use a monotonic hash address such as $\lfloor 2n(k - 1)/N \rfloor$ for the key k, it will be a simple matter to output the keys in sorted order by making at most two passes over the table. [See *CACM* **29** (1986), 366–367.]

17. Show inductively that before step j, the set S is a random sample of $j - N - 1 + n$ integers from $\{1, \ldots, j - 1\}$. [*CACM* **30** (1987), 754–757. Floyd's method can be used to speed up the solution to exercise 16. It is essentially dual to Dahl's algorithm in exercise 15, which operates for *decreasing* values of j; see exercise 12.]

18. (a) Oriented trees that essentially merge $(1, 2, \ldots)$ with $(n, n - 1, \ldots)$, such as

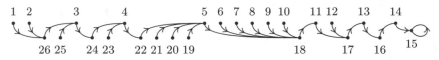

(b) Collections of 1-cycles and 2-cycles. (c) Binary search trees on the keys $(1, 2, \ldots, n)$, with k_j the parent of j (or j, at the root); see Section 6.2.2. The number of $(k_1, \ldots, k_n)$ in each case is (a) 2^{n-1}; (b) $t_n \geq \sqrt{n!}$, see 5.1.4–(40); (c) $\binom{2n}{n}\frac{1}{n+1}$. [Case (a) represents the least common permutation; case (b) represents the most common, when $n \geq 18$. See D. P. Robbins and E. D. Bolker, *Æquationes Mathematicæ* **22** (1981), 268–292; D. Goldstein and D. Moews, *Æquationes Mathematicæ* **65** (2003), 3–30.]

19. See N. Duffield, C. Lund, and M. Thorup, *JACM* **54** (2007), 32:1–32:37.

SECTION 3.5

1. A b-ary sequence, yes (see exercise 2); a $[0 .. 1)$ sequence, no (since only finitely many values are assumed by the elements).

2. It is 1-distributed and 2-distributed, but not 3-distributed (the binary number 111 never appears).

3. Repeat the sequence in exercise 3.2.2–17, with a period of length 27.

4. If $\nu_1(n)$, $\nu_2(n)$, $\nu_3(n)$, $\nu_4(n)$ are the counts for the four probabilities, we have $\nu_1(n)+\nu_2(n) = \nu_3(n)+\nu_4(n)$ for all n. So the desired result follows by addition of limits.

5. The sequence begins $\frac{1}{3}, \frac{2}{3}, \frac{2}{3}, \frac{1}{3}, \frac{1}{3}, \frac{1}{3}, \frac{1}{3}, \frac{2}{3}, \frac{2}{3}, \frac{2}{3}, \frac{2}{3}, \frac{2}{3}, \frac{2}{3}, \frac{2}{3}$, etc. When $n = 1, 3$, $7, 15, \ldots$ we have $\nu(n) = 1, 1, 5, 5, \ldots$ so that $\nu(2^{2k-1} - 1) = \nu(2^{2k} - 1) = (2^{2k} - 1)/3$; hence $\nu(n)/n$ oscillates between $\frac{1}{3}$ and approximately $\frac{2}{3}$, and no limit exists. The probability is undefined. [The methods of Section 4.2.4 show, however, that a numerical value *can* meaningfully be assigned to $\Pr(U_n < \frac{1}{2}) = \Pr(\text{leading digit of the radix-4}$ representation of $n + 1$ is 1), namely $\log_4 2 = \frac{1}{2}$.]

6. By exercise 4 and induction, $\Pr\bigl(S_j(n) \text{ for some } j, 1 \leq j \leq k\bigr) = \sum_{j=1}^{k} \Pr(S_j(n))$. As $k \to \infty$, the latter is a monotone sequence bounded by 1, so it converges; and $\underline{\Pr}\bigl(S_j(n) \text{ for some } j \geq 1\bigr) \geq \sum_{j=1}^{k} \Pr(S_j(n))$ for all k. For a counterexample to equality, it is not hard to arrange things so that $S_j(n)$ is always true for *some* j, yet $\Pr(S_j(n)) = 0$ for *all* j.

7. Let $p_i = \sum_{j \geq 1} \Pr(S_{ij}(n))$. The result of the preceding exercise can be generalized to $\underline{\Pr}\bigl(S_j(n) \text{ for some } j \geq 1\bigr) \geq \sum_{j \geq 1} \underline{\Pr}(S_j(n))$, for *any* disjoint statements $S_j(n)$. So we have $1 = \Pr\bigl(S_{ij}(n) \text{ for some } i, j \geq 1\bigr) \geq \sum_{i \geq 1} \underline{\Pr}\bigl(S_{ij}(n) \text{ for some } j \geq 1\bigr) \geq \sum_{i \geq 1} p_i = 1$, and hence $\underline{\Pr}\bigl(S_{ij}(n) \text{ for some } j \geq 1\bigr) = p_i$. Given $\epsilon > 0$, let I be large enough so that $\sum_{i=1}^{I} p_i \geq 1 - \epsilon$. Let

$$\phi_i(N) = \bigl(\text{number of } n < N \text{ with } S_{ij}(n) \text{ true for some } j \geq 1\bigr)/N.$$

Clearly $\sum_{i=1}^{I} \phi_i(N) \leq 1$, and for all large enough N we have $\sum_{i=2}^{I} \phi_i(N) \geq \sum_{i=2}^{I} p_i - \epsilon$; hence $\phi_1(N) \leq 1 - \phi_2(N) - \cdots - \phi_I(N) \leq 1 - p_2 - \cdots - p_I + \epsilon \leq 1 - (1 - \epsilon - p_1) + \epsilon = p_1 + 2\epsilon$. This proves that $\overline{\Pr}\bigl(S_{1j}(n) \text{ for some } j \geq 1\bigr) \leq p_1 + 2\epsilon$; hence $\Pr\bigl(S_{1j}(n) \text{ for some } j \geq 1\bigr) = p_1$, and the desired result holds for $i = 1$. By symmetry of the hypotheses, it holds for any value of i.

8. Add together the probabilities for j, $j + d$, $j + 2d$, $\ldots$, $m + j - d$ in Definition E.

9. $\limsup_{n \to \infty} (a_n + b_n) \leq \limsup_{n \to \infty} a_n + \limsup_{n \to \infty} b_n$; hence we find that

$$\limsup_{n \to \infty} \bigl((y_{1n} - \alpha)^2 + \cdots + (y_{mn} - \alpha)^2\bigr) \leq m\alpha^2 - 2m\alpha^2 + m\alpha^2 = 0,$$

and this can happen only if each $(y_{jn} - \alpha)$ tends to zero.

10. In the evaluation of the sum in Eq. (22).

11. $\langle U_{2n} \rangle$ is k-distributed if $\langle U_n \rangle$ is $(2, 2k - 1)$-distributed.

12. Apply Theorem B with $f(x_1, \ldots, x_k) = [u \le \max(x_1, \ldots, x_k) < v]$.

13. Let

$$p_k = \Pr(U_n \text{ begins a gap of length } k - 1)$$
$$= \Pr(U_{n-1} \in [\alpha \mathinner{..} \beta),\ U_n \notin [\alpha \mathinner{..} \beta),\ \ldots,\ U_{n+k-2} \notin [\alpha \mathinner{..} \beta),\ U_{n+k-1} \in [\alpha \mathinner{..} \beta))$$
$$= p^2(1 - p)^{k-1}.$$

It remains to translate this into the probability that $f(n) - f(n - 1) = k$. Let $\nu_k(n) =$ (number of $j \le n$ with $f(j) - f(j - 1) = k$); let $\mu_k(n) =$ (number of $j \le n$ with U_j the beginning of a gap of length $k-1$); and let $\mu(n)$ similarly count the number of $1 \le j \le n$ with $U_j \in [\alpha \mathinner{..} \beta)$. We have $\mu_k(f(n)) = \nu_k(n)$, $\mu(f(n)) = n$. As $n \to \infty$, we must have $f(n) \to \infty$, hence

$$\nu_k(n)/n = (\mu_k(f(n))/f(n)) \cdot (f(n)/\mu(f(n))) \to p_k/p = p(1 - p)^{k-1}.$$

[We have only made use of the fact that the sequence is $(k + 1)$-distributed.]

14. Let $p_k = \Pr(U_n \text{ begins a run of length } k)$

$$= \Pr(U_{n-1} > U_n < \cdots < U_{n+k-1} > U_{n+k})$$
$$= \frac{1}{(k+2)!} \left(\binom{k+2}{1}\binom{k+1}{1} - \binom{k+2}{1} - \binom{k+2}{1} + 1 \right) = \frac{k}{(k+1)!} - \frac{k+1}{(k+2)!}$$

(see exercise 3.3.2–13). Now proceed as in the previous exercise to transfer this to $\Pr(f(n) - f(n-1) = k)$. [We have assumed only that the sequence is $(k+2)$-distributed.]

15. For $s, t \ge 0$ let

$$p_{st} = \Pr(X_{n-2t-3} = X_{n-2t-2} \ne X_{n-2t-1} \ne \cdots \ne X_{n-1} \text{ and } X_n = \cdots = X_{n+s} \ne X_{n+s+1})$$
$$= 2^{-s-2t-3};$$

for $t \ge 0$ let $q_t = \Pr(X_{n-2t-2} = X_{n-2t-1} \ne \cdots \ne X_{n-1}) = 2^{-2t-1}$. By exercise 7,

$$\Pr(X_n \text{ is not the beginning of a coupon set}) = \sum_{t \ge 0} q_t = \tfrac{2}{3};$$
$$\Pr(X_n \text{ is the beginning of coupon set of length } s + 2) = \sum_{t \ge 0} p_{st} = \tfrac{1}{3} \cdot 2^{-s-1}.$$

Now proceed as in exercise 13.

16. (Solution by R. P. Stanley.) Whenever the subsequence $S = (b - 1), (b - 2), \ldots,$ $1, 0, 0, 1, \ldots, (b - 2), (b - 1)$ appears, a coupon set must end at the right of S, since some coupon set is completed in the first half of S. We now proceed to calculate the probability that a coupon set begins at position n by manipulating the probabilities that the last prior appearance of S ends at position $n - 1$, $n - 2$, etc., as in exercise 15.

18. Proceed as in the proof of Theorem A to calculate $\underline{\Pr}$ and $\overline{\Pr}$.

19. (Solution by T. Herzog.) Yes. For example, apply exercise 33 to the sequence $\langle U_{\lfloor n/2 \rfloor} \rangle$, when $\langle U_n \rangle$ satisfies R4 (or even its weaker version).

20. (a) 2 and $\frac{1}{2}$. (When n increases, we break $l_n^{(1)}$ in half.)

(b) Each new point breaks a single interval into two parts. Let ρ be equal to $\max_{k=0}^{n-1}((n + k)l_{n+k}^{(1)})$. Then $1 = \sum_{k=1}^{n} l_n^{(k)} \le \sum_{k=0}^{n-1} l_{n+k}^{(1)} \le \sum_{k=0}^{n-1} \rho/(n + k) = \rho \ln 2 + O(1/n)$. So infinitely many m have $m l_m^{(1)} \ge 1/\ln 2 + O(1/m)$.

(c) To verify the hint, let $l_{2n}^{(k)}$ come from the interval with endpoints U_m and $U_{m'}$, and set $a_k = \max(m-n, m'-n, 1)$. Then $\rho = \min_{m=n+1}^{2n} m l_m^{(m)}$ implies $1 = \sum_{k=1}^{2n} l_{2n}^{(k)} \ge \sum_{k=1}^{2n} \rho/(n + a_k) \ge 2\rho \sum_{k=1}^{n} 1/(n + k)$; hence $2\rho \le 1/(H_{2n} - H_n) = 1/\ln 2 + O(1/n)$.

(d) We have $(l_n^{(1)}, \ldots, l_n^{(n)}) = (\lg \frac{n+1}{n}, \lg \frac{n+2}{n+1}, \ldots, \lg \frac{2n}{2n-1})$, because the $(n+1)$st point always breaks the largest interval into intervals of length $\lg \frac{2n+1}{2n}$ and $\lg \frac{2n+2}{2n+1}$. [*Indagationes Math.* **11** (1949), 14–17.]

21. (a) No! We have $\overline{\Pr}(W_n < \frac{1}{2}) \geq \limsup_{n \to \infty} \nu(\lceil 2^{n-1/2} \rceil)/\lceil 2^{n-1/2} \rceil = 2 - \sqrt{2}$, and $\underline{\Pr}(W_n < \frac{1}{2}) \leq \liminf_{n \to \infty} \nu(2^n)/2^n = \sqrt{2} - 1$, because $\nu(\lceil 2^{n-1/2} \rceil) = \nu(2^n) = \frac{1}{2}\sum_{k=0}^{n}(2^{k+1/2} - 2^k) + O(n)$.

(b, c) See *Indagationes Math.* **40** (1978), 527–541.

22. If the sequence is k-distributed, the limit is zero by integration and Theorem B. Conversely, note that if $f(x_1, \ldots, x_k)$ has an absolutely convergent Fourier series

$$f(x_1, \ldots, x_k) = \sum_{-\infty < c_1, \ldots, c_k < \infty} a(c_1, \ldots, c_k) \exp(2\pi i(c_1 x_1 + \cdots + c_k x_k)),$$

we have $\lim_{N \to \infty} \frac{1}{N} \sum_{0 \leq n < N} f(U_n, \ldots, U_{n+k-1}) = a(0, \ldots, 0) + \epsilon_r$, where

$$|\epsilon_r| \leq \sum_{\max\{|c_1|, \ldots, |c_k|\} > r} |a(c_1, \ldots, c_k)|,$$

so ϵ_r can be made arbitrarily small. Hence this limit is equal to

$$a(0, \ldots, 0) = \int_0^1 \cdots \int_0^1 f(x_1, \ldots, x_k)\, dx_1 \ldots dx_k,$$

and Eq. (8) holds for all sufficiently smooth functions f. The remainder of the proof shows that the function in (9) can be approximated by smooth functions to any desired accuracy.

23. (a) This follows immediately from exercise 22. (b) Use a discrete Fourier transform in an analogous way; see D. E. Knuth, *AMM* **75** (1968), 260–264.

24. (a) Let c be any nonzero integer; we must show, by exercise 22, that

$$\frac{1}{N} \sum_{n=0}^{N-1} e^{2\pi i c U_n} \to 0 \qquad \text{as } N \to \infty.$$

This follows because, if K is any positive integer, we have $\sum_{k=0}^{K-1} \sum_{n=0}^{N-1} e^{2\pi i c U_{n+k}} = K \sum_{n=0}^{N-1} e^{2\pi i c U_n} + O(K^2)$. Hence, by Cauchy's inequality,

$$\frac{1}{N^2} \left| \sum_{n=0}^{N-1} e^{2\pi i c U_n} \right|^2 = \frac{1}{K^2 N^2} \left| \sum_{n=0}^{N-1} \sum_{k=0}^{K-1} e^{2\pi i c U_{n+k}} \right|^2 + O\left(\frac{K}{N}\right)$$

$$\leq \frac{1}{K^2 N} \sum_{n=0}^{N-1} \left| \sum_{k=0}^{K-1} e^{2\pi i c U_{n+k}} \right|^2 + O\left(\frac{K}{N}\right)$$

$$= \frac{1}{K} + \frac{2}{K^2 N} \Re\left(\sum_{0 \leq j < k < K} \sum_{n=0}^{N-1} e^{2\pi i c(U_{n+k} - U_{n+j})} \right) + O\left(\frac{K}{N}\right) \to \frac{1}{K}.$$

(b) When $d = 1$, exercise 22 tells us that $\langle (\alpha_1 n + \alpha_0) \bmod 1 \rangle$ is equidistributed if and only if α_1 is irrational. When $d > 1$, we can use (a) and induction on d. [*Acta Math.* **56** (1931), 373–456. The result in (b) had previously been obtained in a more complicated way by H. Weyl, *Nachr. Gesellschaft der Wiss. Göttingen, Math.-Phys. Kl.* (1914), 234–244. A similar argument proves that the polynomial sequence is equidistributed if at least one of the coefficients $\alpha_d, \ldots, \alpha_1$ is irrational.]

25. If the sequence is equidistributed, the denominator in Corollary S approaches $\frac{1}{12}$, and the numerator approaches the quantity in this exercise.

26. See *Math. Comp.* **17** (1963), 50–54. [Consider also the following example by A. G. Waterman: Let $\langle U_n \rangle$ be an equidistributed $[0 .. 1)$ sequence and $\langle X_n \rangle$ an ∞-distributed binary sequence. Let $V_n = U_{\lceil \sqrt{n} \rceil}$ or $1 - U_{\lceil \sqrt{n} \rceil}$ according as X_n is 0 or 1. Then $\langle V_n \rangle$ is equidistributed and white, but $\Pr(V_n = V_{n+1}) = \frac{1}{2}$. Let $W_n = (V_n - \epsilon_n) \bmod 1$ where $\langle \epsilon_n \rangle$ is any sequence that decreases monotonically to 0; then $\langle W_n \rangle$ is equidistributed and white, yet $\Pr(W_n < W_{n+1}) = \frac{3}{4}$.]

28. Let $\langle U_n \rangle$ be ∞-distributed, and consider the sequence $\langle \frac{1}{2}(X_n + U_n) \rangle$. This is 3-distributed, using the fact that $\langle U_n \rangle$ is $(16, 3)$-distributed.

29. If $x = x_1 x_2 \ldots x_t$ is any binary number, we can consider the number $\nu_x^E(n)$ of times $X_p \ldots X_{p+t-1} = x$, where $1 \le p \le n$ and p is even. Similarly, let $\nu_x^O(n)$ count the number of times when p is odd. Let $\nu_x^E(n) + \nu_x^O(n) = \nu_x(n)$. Now

$$\nu_0^E(n) = \sum \nu_{0**\ldots*}^E(n) \approx \sum \nu_{*0*\ldots*}^O(n) \approx \sum \nu_{**0\ldots*}^E(n) \approx \cdots \approx \sum \nu_{***\ldots0}^O(n)$$

where the ν's in these summations have $2k$ subscripts, $2k - 1$ of which are asterisks (meaning that they are being summed over — each sum is taken over 2^{2k-1} combinations of zeros and ones), and where "$\approx$" denotes approximate equality (except for an error of at most $2k$ due to end conditions). Therefore we find that

$$\frac{1}{n} 2k \nu_0^E(n) = \frac{1}{n} \left(\sum \nu_{*0*\ldots*}(n) + \cdots + \sum \nu_{***\ldots0}(n) \right) \frac{1}{n} \sum_x (r(x) - s(x)) \nu_x^E(n) + O\left(\frac{1}{n}\right),$$

where $x = x_1 \ldots x_{2k}$ contains $r(x)$ zeros in odd positions and $s(x)$ zeros in even positions. By $(2k)$-distribution, the parenthesized quantity tends to $k(2^{2k-1})/2^{2k} = k/2$. The remaining sum is clearly a maximum if $\nu_x^E(n) = \nu_x(n)$ when $r(x) > s(x)$, and $\nu_x^E(n) = 0$ when $r(x) < s(x)$. So the maximum of the right-hand side becomes

$$\frac{k}{2} + \sum_{0 \le s < r \le k} (r - s) \binom{k}{r} \binom{k}{s} \Big/ 2^{2k} = \frac{k}{2} + k \binom{2k - 1}{k} \Big/ 2^{2k}.$$

Now $\overline{\Pr}(X_{2n} = 0) \le \limsup_{n \to \infty} \nu_0^E(2n)/n$, so the proof is complete. Note that we have

$$\sum_{r,s} \binom{n}{r} \binom{n}{s} \max(r, s) = 2n2^{2n-2} + n \binom{2n - 1}{n};$$

$$\sum_{r,s} \binom{n}{r} \binom{n}{s} \min(r, s) = 2n2^{2n-2} - n \binom{2n - 1}{n}.$$

30. Construct a digraph with 2^{2k} nodes labeled $(E x_1 \ldots x_{2k-1})$ and $(O x_1 \ldots x_{2k-1})$, where each x_j is either 0 or 1. Let there be $1 + f(x_1, x_2, \ldots, x_{2k})$ directed arcs from $(E x_1 \ldots x_{2k-1})$ to $(O x_2 \ldots x_{2k})$, and $1 - f(x_1, x_2, \ldots, x_{2k})$ directed arcs leading from $(O x_1 \ldots x_{2k-1})$ to $(E x_2 \ldots x_{2k})$, where $f(x_1, x_2, \ldots, x_{2k}) = \text{sign}(x_1 - x_2 + x_3 - x_4 + \cdots - x_{2k})$. We find that each node has the same number of arcs leading into it as there are leading out; for example, $(E x_1 \ldots x_{2k-1})$ has $1 - f(0, x_1, \ldots, x_{2k-1}) + 1 - f(1, x_1, \ldots, x_{2k-1})$ leading in and $1 + f(x_1, \ldots, x_{2k-1}, 0) + 1 + f(x_1, \ldots, x_{2k-1}, 1)$ leading out, and $f(x, x_1, \ldots, x_{2k-1}) = -f(x_1, \ldots, x_{2k-1}, x)$. Drop all nodes that have no paths leading either in or out, namely $(E x_1 \ldots x_{2k-1})$ if $f(0, x_1, \ldots, x_{2k-1}) = +1$,

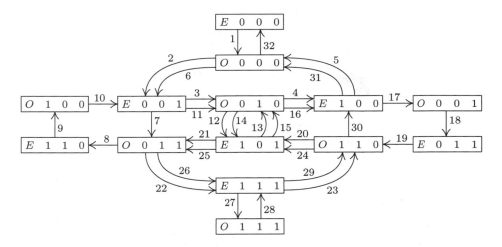

Fig. A–5. Directed graph for the construction in exercise 30.

or $(Ox_1 \ldots x_{2k-1})$ if $f(1, x_1, \ldots, x_{2k-1}) = -1$. The resulting directed graph is seen to be connected, since we can get from any node to $(E1010 \ldots 1)$ and from this to any desired node. By Theorem 2.3.4.2G, there is a cyclic path traversing each arc; this path has length 2^{2k+1}, and we may assume that it starts at node $(E00 \ldots 0)$. Construct a cyclic sequence with $X_1 = \cdots = X_{2k-1} = 0$, and $X_{n+2k-1} = x_{2k}$ if the nth arc of the path is from $(Ex_1 \ldots x_{2k-1})$ to $(Ox_2 \ldots x_{2k})$ or from $(Ox_1 \ldots x_{2k-1})$ to $(Ex_2 \ldots x_{2k})$. For example, the graph for $k = 2$ is shown in Fig. A–5; the arcs of the cyclic path are numbered from 1 to 32, and the cyclic sequence is

$$(00001000110010101001101110111110)(00001\ldots).$$

Notice that $\Pr(X_{2n} = 0) = \frac{11}{16}$ in this sequence. The sequence is clearly $(2k)$-distributed, since each $(2k)$-tuple $x_1 x_2 \ldots x_{2k}$ occurs

$$1 + f(x_1, \ldots, x_{2k}) + 1 - f(x_1, \ldots, x_{2k}) = 2$$

times in the cycle. The fact that $\Pr(X_{2n} = 0)$ has the desired value comes from the fact that the maximum value on the right-hand side in the proof of the preceding exercise has been achieved by this construction.

31. Use Algorithm W with rule $\mathcal{R}_1$ selecting the entire sequence. [For a generalization of this type of nonrandom behavior in R5-sequences, see Jean Ville, *Étude Critique de la Notion de Collectif* (Paris: 1939), 55–62. Perhaps R6 is also too weak, from this standpoint, but no such counterexample is presently known.]

32. If $\mathcal{R}, \mathcal{R}'$ are computable subsequence rules, so is $\mathcal{R}'' = \mathcal{R}\mathcal{R}'$ defined by the following functions: $f_n''(x_0, \ldots, x_{n-1}) = 1$ if and only if $\mathcal{R}$ defines the subsequence $x_{r_1}, \ldots, x_{r_k}$ of $x_0, \ldots, x_{n-1}$, where $k \geq 0$ and $0 \leq r_1 < \cdots < r_k < n$ and $f_k'(x_{r_1}, \ldots, x_{r_k}) = 1$.

Now $\langle X_n \rangle \mathcal{R}\mathcal{R}'$ is $(\langle X_n \rangle \mathcal{R})\mathcal{R}'$. The result follows immediately.

33. Given $\epsilon > 0$, find N_0 such that $N > N_0$ implies that both $|\nu_r(N)/N - p| < \epsilon$ and $|\nu_s(N)/N - p| < \epsilon$. Then find N_1 such that $N > N_1$ implies that t_N is r_M or s_M for some $M > N_0$. Now $N > N_1$ implies that

$$\left| \frac{\nu_t(N)}{N} - p \right| = \left| \frac{\nu_r(N_r) + \nu_s(N_s)}{N} - p \right| = \left| \frac{\nu_r(N_r) - pN_r + \nu_s(N_s) - pN_s}{N_r + N_s} \right| < \epsilon.$$

34. For example, if the binary representation of t is $(1\,0^{b-2}\,1\,0^{a_1}\,1\,1\,0^{a_2}\,1\,\ldots\,1\,0^{a_k})_2$, where "$0^a$" stands for a sequence of a consecutive zeros, let the rule $\mathcal{R}_t$ accept U_n if and only if $\lfloor bU_{n-k} \rfloor = a_1, \ldots, \lfloor bU_{n-1} \rfloor = a_k$.

35. Let $a_0 = s_0$ and $a_{m+1} = \max\{s_k \mid 0 \le k < 2^{a_m}\}$. Construct a subsequence rule that selects element X_n if and only if $n = s_k$ for some $k < 2^{a_m}$, when n is in the range $a_m \le n < a_{m+1}$. Then $\lim_{m \to \infty} \nu(a_m)/a_m = \frac{1}{2}$.

36. Let b and k be arbitrary but fixed integers greater than 1. Let $Y_n = \lfloor bU_n \rfloor$. An arbitrary infinite subsequence $\langle Z_n \rangle = \langle Y_{s_n} \rangle \mathcal{R}$ determined by algorithms $\mathcal{S}$ and $\mathcal{R}$ (as in the proof of Theorem M) corresponds in a straightforward but notationally hopeless manner to algorithms $\mathcal{S}'$ and $\mathcal{R}'$ that inspect $X_t, X_{t+1}, \ldots, X_{t+s}$ and/or select X_t, $X_{t+1}, \ldots, X_{t+\min(k-1,s)}$ of $\langle X_n \rangle$ if and only if $\mathcal{S}$ and $\mathcal{R}$ inspect and/or select Y_s, where $U_s = (0.X_t X_{t+1} \ldots X_{t+s})_2$. Algorithms $\mathcal{S}'$ and $\mathcal{R}'$ determine an infinite 1-distributed subsequence of $\langle X_n \rangle$ and in fact (as in exercise 32) this subsequence is ∞-distributed so it is $(k,1)$-distributed. Hence we find that $\underline{\Pr}(Z_n = a)$ and $\overline{\Pr}(Z_n = a)$ differ from $1/b$ by less than $1/2^k$.

[The result of this exercise is true if "R6" is replaced consistently by "R4" or "R5"; but it is false if "R1" is used, since $X_{\binom{n}{2}}$ might be identically zero.]

37. For $n \ge 2$ replace U_{n^2} by $\frac{1}{2}(U_{n^2} + \delta_n)$, where $\delta_n = 0$ or 1 according as the set $\{U_{(n-1)^2+1}, \ldots, U_{n^2-1}\}$ contains an even or odd number of elements less than $\frac{1}{2}$. [*Advances in Math.* **14** (1974), 333–334; see also the Ph.D. thesis of Thomas N. Herzog, Univ. of Maryland (1975).]

39. See *Acta Arithmetica* **21** (1972), 45–50. The best possible value of c is unknown.

40. Since F_k depends only on $B_1 \ldots B_k$, we have $P(A_k^P, \$_N) = \frac{1}{2}$. Let $q(B_1 \ldots B_k) = \Pr(B_{k+1} = 1 \mid B_1 \ldots B_k)$, where the probability is taken over all elements of S having $B_1 \ldots B_k$ as the first k bits. Similarly, let $q_b(B_1 \ldots B_k) = \Pr(F_k = 1$ and $B'_{k+1} = b \mid B_1 \ldots B_k)$. Then we have $\Pr(A_k^P = 1 \mid B_1 \ldots B_k) = \Pr((F_k + B_{k+1} + B'_{k+1}) \bmod 2 = 1 \mid B_1 \ldots B_k) = q \cdot (\frac{1}{2} - q_0 + q_1) + (1-q) \cdot (q_0 + \frac{1}{2} - q_1) = \frac{1}{2} - (q_0 + q_1) + 2(qq_1 + (1-q)q_0) = \frac{1}{2} - \Pr(F_k = 1 \mid B_1 \ldots B_k) + 2\Pr(F_k = 1$ and $B'_{k+1} = B_{k+1} \mid B_1 \ldots B_k)$. Hence $\Pr(A_k^P = 1) = \sum_{B_1 \ldots B_k} \Pr(B_1 \ldots B_k) \Pr(A_k^P = 1 \mid B_1 \ldots B_k) = \frac{1}{2} - \Pr(F_k = 1) + \Pr(F_{k+1} = 1)$. [See Theorem 4 of Goldreich, Goldwasser, and Micali in *JACM* **33** (1986), 792–807.]

41. Choose k uniformly from $\{0, \ldots, N-1\}$ and use the construction in the proof of Lemma P1. Then the proof of P1 shows that A' will be equal to 1 with probability $\sum_{k=0}^{N-1} (\frac{1}{2} - p_k + p_{k+1})/N$.

42. (a) Let $X = X_1 + \cdots + X_n$. Clearly $\mathrm{E}(X) = n\mu$; and we have $\mathrm{E}((X - n\mu)^2) = \mathrm{E}\,X^2 - n^2\mu^2 = n\,\mathrm{E}\,X_j^2 + 2\sum_{1 \le i < j \le n}(\mathrm{E}\,X_i)(\mathrm{E}\,X_j) - n^2\mu^2 = n\,\mathrm{E}\,X_j^2 - n\mu^2 = n\sigma^2$. Also $\mathrm{E}((X - n\mu)^2) = \sum_{x \ge 0} x\Pr((X - n\mu)^2 = x) \ge \sum_{x \ge tn\sigma^2} x\Pr((X - n\mu)^2 = x) \ge \sum_{x \ge tn\sigma^2} tn\sigma^2 \Pr((X - n\mu)^2 = x) = tn\sigma^2 \Pr((X - n\mu)^2 \ge tn\sigma^2)$.

(b) There is a position i where $c_i \ne c'_i$, say $c_i = 0$ and $c'_i = 1$. Then there's a position j where $c_j = 1$. For any fixed setting of B in the $k-2$ rows other than i or j, we have $(cB, c'B) = (d, d')$ if and only if rows i and j have particular values; this occurs with probability $1/2^{2R}$.

(c) In the notation of Algorithm L, take $n = 2^k - 1$ and $X_c = (-1)^{G(cB+e_i)}$; then $\mu = s$ and $\sigma^2 = 1 - s^2$. The probability that $X = \sum_{c \neq 0} X_c$ is negative is at most the probability that $(X - n\mu)^2 \geq n^2 \mu^2$. By (a) this is at most $\sigma^2 / (n\mu^2)$.

43. The conclusion for fixed M would be of no interest, since there obviously exists an algorithm to factor any fixed M (namely, an algorithm that knows the factors). The theory applies to *all* algorithms that have short running time, not only to algorithms that are effectively discoverable.

44. If every one-digit change to a random table yields a random table, all tables are random (or none are). If we don't allow degrees of randomness, the answer must therefore be, "Not always."

SECTION 3.6

1.
```
   RANDI STJ   9F              Store exit location.
         STA   8F              Store value of k.
         LDA   XRAND           rA ← X.
         MUL   7F              rAX ← aX.
         INCX  1009            rX ← (aX + c) mod m.
         JOV   *+1             Ensure that overflow is off.
         SLAX  5               rA ← (aX + c) mod m.
         STA   XRAND           Store X.
         MUL   8F              rA ← ⌊kX/m⌋.
         INCA  1               Add 1, so that 1 ≤ Y ≤ k.
9H       JMP   *               Return.
XRAND    CON   1               Value of X; X₀ = 1.
8H       CON   0               Temp storage of k.
7H       CON   3141592621      The multiplier a.   ▮
```

2. Putting a random number generator into a program makes the results essentially unpredictable to the programmer. If the behavior of the machine on each problem were known in advance, few programs would ever be written. As Turing has said, the actions of a computer quite often *do* surprise its programmer, especially when a program is being debugged.

So the world had better watch out.

7. In fact, you only need the 2-bit values $\lfloor X_n/2^{16} \rfloor \bmod 4$; see D. E. Knuth, *IEEE Trans.* **IT-31** (1985), 49–52. J. Reeds, *Cryptologia* **1** (1977), 20–26, **3** (1979), 83–95, initiated the study of related problems; see also J. Boyar, *J. Cryptology* **1** (1989), 177–184. In *SICOMP* **17** (1988), 262–280, Frieze, Håstad, Kannan, Lagarias, and Shamir discuss general techniques that are useful in problems like this.

8. We can, say, generate $X_{1000000}$ by making one million successive calls, and compare it to the correct value $(a^{1000000} X_0 + (a^{1000000} - 1)c/(a-1)) \bmod m$, which can also be expressed as $((a^{1000000}(X_0(a-1) + c) - c) \bmod (a-1)m)/(a-1)$. The latter can be evaluated quickly by an independent method (see Algorithm 4.6.3A). For example, $48271^{1000000} \bmod 2147483647 = 1263606197$. Most errors will be detected, because recurrence (1) is not self-correcting.

9. (a) The values of $X_0, X_1, \ldots, X_{99}$ are not all even. The polynomial $z^{100} + z^{37} + 1$ is primitive (see Section 3.2.2); hence there is a number $h(s)$ such that $P_0(z) \equiv z^{h(s)}$

(modulo 2 and $z^{100} + z^{37} + 1$). Now $zP_{n+1}(z) = P_n(z) - X_n z^{37} - X_{n+63} + X_{n+63} z^{100} + X_{n+100} z^{37} \equiv P_n(z) + X_{n+63}(z^{100} + z^{37} + 1)$ (modulo 2), so the result holds by induction.

(b) The operations "square" and "multiply by z" in ran_start change $p(z) = x_{99} z^{99} + \cdots + x_1 z + x_0$ to $p(z)^2$ and $zp(z)$, respectively, modulo 2 and $z^{100} + z^{37} + 1$, because $p(z)^2 \equiv p(z^2)$. (We consider here only the low-order bits. The other bits are manipulated in an ad hoc way that tends to preserve and/or enhance whatever disorder they already have.) Therefore if $s = (1s_j \ldots s_1 s_0)_2$ we have $h(s) = (1s_0 s_1 \ldots s_j 1)_2 \cdot 2^{69}$.

(c) $z^{h(s)-n} \equiv z^{h(s')-n'}$ (modulo 2 and $z^{100} + z^{37} + 1$) implies that $h(s) - n \equiv h(s') - n'$ (modulo $2^{100} - 1$). Since $2^{69} \le h(s) < 2^{100} - 2^{69}$, we have $|n - n'| \ge |h(s) - h(s')| \ge 2^{70}$.

[This method of initialization was inspired by comments of R. P. Brent, *Proc. Australian Supercomputer Conf.* **5** (1992), 95–104, although Brent's algorithm was completely different. In general if the lags are $k > l$, if $0 \le s < 2^e$, and if the separation parameter t satisfies $t + e \le k$, this method of proof shows that $|n - n'| \ge 2^t - 1$, with $2^t - 1$ occurring only if $\{s, s'\} = \{0, 2^e - 1\}$.]

10. The following code belongs to the simplified language Subset FORTRAN, as defined by the American National Standards Institute, except for its use of PARAMETER statements for readability.

```
         SUBROUTINE RNARRY(AA,N)
         IMPLICIT INTEGER (A-Z)
         DIMENSION AA(*)
         PARAMETER (KK=100)
         PARAMETER (LL=37)
         PARAMETER (MM=2**30)
         COMMON /RSTATE/ RANX(KK)
         SAVE /RSTATE/
         DO 1 J=1,KK
   1        AA(J)=RANX(J)
         DO 2 J=KK+1,N
            AA(J)=AA(J-KK)-AA(J-LL)
            IF (AA(J) .LT. 0) AA(J)=AA(J)+MM
   2     CONTINUE
         DO 3 J=1,LL
            RANX(J)=AA(N+J-KK)-AA(N+J-LL)
            IF (RANX(J) .LT. 0) RANX(J)=RANX(J)+MM
   3     CONTINUE
         DO 4 J=LL+1,KK
            RANX(J)=AA(N+J-KK)-RANX(J-LL)
            IF (RANX(J) .LT. 0) RANX(J)=RANX(J)+MM
   4     CONTINUE
         END

         SUBROUTINE RNSTRT(SEED)
         IMPLICIT INTEGER (A-Z)
         PARAMETER (KK=100)
         PARAMETER (LL=37)
         PARAMETER (MM=2**30)
         PARAMETER (TT=70)
```

```fortran
      PARAMETER (KKK=KK+KK-1)
      DIMENSION X(KKK)
      COMMON /RSTATE/ RANX(KK)
      SAVE /RSTATE/
      IF (SEED .LT. 0) THEN
         SSEED=MM-1-MOD(-1-SEED,MM)
      ELSE
         SSEED=MOD(SEED,MM)
      END IF
      SS=SSEED-MOD(SSEED,2)+2
      DO 1 J=1,KK
         X(J)=SS
         SS=SS+SS
         IF (SS .GE. MM) SS=SS-MM+2
1     CONTINUE
      X(2)=X(2)+1
      SS=SSEED
      T=TT-1
10    DO 12 J=KK,2,-1
         X(J+J-1)=X(J)
12       X(J+J-2)=0
      DO 14 J=KKK,KK+1,-1
         X(J-(KK-LL))=X(J-(KK-LL))-X(J)
         IF (X(J-(KK-LL)) .LT. 0) X(J-(KK-LL))=X(J-(KK-LL))+MM
         X(J-KK)=X(J-KK)-X(J)
         IF (X(J-KK) .LT. 0) X(J-KK)=X(J-KK)+MM
14    CONTINUE
      IF (MOD(SS,2) .EQ. 1) THEN
         DO 16 J=KK,1,-1
16          X(J+1)=X(J)
         X(1)=X(KK+1)
         X(LL+1)=X(LL+1)-X(KK+1)
         IF (X(LL+1) .LT. 0) X(LL+1)=X(LL+1)+MM
      END IF
      IF (SS .NE. 0) THEN
         SS=SS/2
      ELSE
         T=T-1
      END IF
      IF (T .GT. 0) GO TO 10
      DO 20 J=1,LL
20       RANX(J+KK-LL)=X(J)
      DO 21 J=LL+1,KK
21       RANX(J-LL)=X(J)
      DO 22 J=1,10
22       CALL RNARRY(X,KKK)
      END
```

11. Floating point arithmetic on 64-bit operands conforming to ANSI/IEEE Standard 754 allows us to compute $U_n = (U_{n-100} - U_{n-37}) \bmod 1$ with perfect accuracy for fractions U_n that are integer multiples of 2^{-53}. However, the following program uses the *additive* recurrence $U_n = (U_{n-100} + U_{n-37}) \bmod 1$ on integer multiples of 2^{-52} instead, because pipelined computers can subtract an integer part more quickly than they can branch conditionally on the sign of an intermediate result. The theory of exercise 9 applies equally well to this sequence.

A FORTRAN translation similar to the code in exercise 10 will generate exactly the same numbers as this C routine.

```c
#define KK 100                                    /* the long lag */
#define LL   37                                    /* the short lag */
#define mod_sum(x,y) (((x)+(y))-(int)((x)+(y)))    /* (x+y) mod 1.0 */

double ran_u[KK];                                  /* the generator state */

void ranf_array(double aa[],int n) { /* aa gets n random fractions */
  register int i,j;
  for (j=0;j<KK;j++) aa[j]=ran_u[j];
  for (;j<n;j++) aa[j]=mod_sum(aa[j-KK],aa[j-LL]);
  for (i=0;i<LL;i++,j++) ran_u[i]=mod_sum(aa[j-KK],aa[j-LL]);
  for (;i<KK;i++,j++) ran_u[i]=mod_sum(aa[j-KK],ran_u[i-LL]);
}

#define TT   70                 /* guaranteed separation between streams */
#define is_odd(s) ((s)&1)

void ranf_start(long seed) {      /* do this before using ranf_array */
  register int t,s,j;
  double u[KK+KK-1];
  double ulp=(1.0/(1L<<30))/(1L<<22);              /* 2 to the -52 */
  double ss=2.0*ulp*((seed&0x3fffffff)+2);

  for (j=0;j<KK;j++) {
    u[j]=ss;                                       /* bootstrap the buffer */
    ss+=ss;
    if (ss>=1.0) ss-=1.0-2*ulp;         /* cyclic shift of 51 bits */
  }
  u[1]+=ulp;                            /* make u[1] (and only u[1]) "odd" */
  for (s=seed&0x3fffffff,t=TT-1; t; ) {
    for (j=KK-1;j>0;j--)
      u[j+j]=u[j],u[j+j-1]=0.0;                         /* "square" */
    for (j=KK+KK-2;j>=KK;j--) {
      u[j-(KK-LL)]=mod_sum(u[j-(KK-LL)],u[j]);
      u[j-KK]=mod_sum(u[j-KK],u[j]);
    }
    if (is_odd(s)) {                                 /* "multiply by z" */
      for (j=KK;j>0;j--) u[j]=u[j-1];
      u[0]=u[KK];                    /* shift the buffer cyclically */
      u[LL]=mod_sum(u[LL],u[KK]);
    }
    if (s) s>>=1; else t--;
  }
}
```

```
    for (j=0;j<LL;j++) ran_u[j+KK-LL]=u[j];
    for (;j<KK;j++) ran_u[j-LL]=u[j];
    for (j=0;j<10;j++) ranf_array(u,KK+KK-1);    /* warm everything up */
  }
  int main() {                                   /* a rudimentary test */
    register int m;
    double a[2009];
    ranf_start(310952);
    for (m=0;m<2009;m++)
      ranf_array(a,1009);
    printf("%.20f\n", ran_u[0]);                 /* 0.36410514377569680455 */
    ranf_start(310952);
    for (m=0;m<1009;m++)
      ranf_array(a,2009);
    printf("%.20f\n", ran_u[0]);                 /* 0.36410514377569680455 */
    return 0;
  }
```

12. A simple linear congruential generator like (1) would fail, because m would be much too small. Good results are possible by combining three (not two) such generators, with multipliers and moduli $(157, 32363)$, $(146, 31727)$, $(142, 31657)$, as suggested by P. L'Ecuyer in *CACM* **31** (1988), 747–748. However, the best method is probably to use the C programs *ran_array* and *ran_start*, with the following changes to keep all numbers in range: 'long' becomes 'int'; 'MM' is defined to be '(1U<<15)'; and the type of variable ss should be **unsigned int**. This generates 15-bit integers, all of whose bits are usable. The seed is now restricted to the range $[0 . . 32765]$. The "rudimentary test routine" will print $X_{1009 \times 2009} = 24130$, given the seed 12509.

13. A program for subtract-with-borrow would be very similar to *ran_array*, but slower because of the carry maintenance. As in exercise 11, floating point arithmetic could be used with perfect accuracy. It is possible to guarantee disjointness of the sequences produced from different seeds s by initializing the generator with the $(-n)$th element of the sequence, where $n = 2^{70s}$; this requires computing $b^n \bmod (b^k - b^l \pm 1)$. Squaring a radix-$b$ number mod $b^k - b^l \pm 1$ is, however, considerably more complicated than the analogous operation in program *ran_start*, and for k in a practical range it takes about $k^{1.6}$ operations instead of $O(k)$.

     Both methods probably generate sequences of the same quality in practice, when they have roughly the same value of k. The only significant difference between them is a better theoretical guarantee and a provably immense period for the subtract-with-borrow method; the analysis of lagged Fibonacci generators is less complete. Experience shows that we should not reduce the value of k in subtract-with-borrow just because of these theoretical advantages. When all is said and done, lagged Fibonacci generators seem preferable from a practical standpoint; the subtract-with-borrow method is then valuable chiefly because of the insight it gives us into the excellent behavior of the simpler approach.

14. We have $X_{n+200} \equiv (X_n + X_{n+126})$ (modulo 2); see exercise 3.2.2–32. Hence $Y_{n+100} \equiv Y_n + Y_{n+26}$ when $n \bmod 100 > 73$. Similarly $X_{n+200} \equiv X_n + X_{n+26} + X_{n+89}$; hence $Y_{n+100} \equiv Y_n + Y_{n+26} + Y_{n+89}$ when $n \bmod 100 < 11$. Thus Y_{n+100} is a sum of only two or three elements of $\{Y_n, \ldots, Y_{n+99}\}$, in $26\% + 11\%$ of all cases; a preponderance of 0s will then tend to make $Y_{n+100} = 0$.

More precisely, consider the sequence $\langle u_1, u_2, \dots \rangle = \langle 126, 89, 152, 115, 78, \dots, 100, 63, 126, \dots \rangle$ where $u_{n+1} = u_n - 37 + 100[u_n < 100]$. Then we have

$$X_{n+200} = (X_n + X_{n+v_1} + \dots + X_{n+v_{k-2}} + X_{u_{k-1}}) \bmod 2,$$

where $v_j = u_j + (-1)^{[u_j \geq 100]} 100$; for example, $X_{n+200} \equiv X_n + X_{n+26} + X_{n+189} + X_{n+152} \equiv X_n + X_{n+26} + X_{n+189} + X_{n+52} + X_{n+115}$. If the subscripts are all $< n+t$ and $\geq n+100+t$, we obtain a k-term expression for Y_{n+100} when $n \bmod 100 = 100 - t$, for $1 \leq t \leq 100$. The case $t = 63$ is an exception, because $X_n + X_{n+1} + \dots + X_{n+62} + X_{n+163} + X_{n+164} + \dots + X_{n+199} \equiv 0$; in this case Y_{n+100} is independent of $\{Y_n, \dots, Y_{n+99}\}$. The case $t = 64$ is interesting because it gives the 99-term relation $Y_{n+100} \equiv Y_{n+1} + Y_{n+2} + \dots + Y_{n+99}$; this tends to be 0 in spite of the large number of terms, because most of the 100-tuples that have 40 or fewer 1s have even parity.

When there is a k-term relation, the probability that $Y_{n+100} = 1$ is

$$p_k = \sum_{l=0}^{40} \sum_{j=1}^{k} \binom{100-k}{l-j} \binom{k}{j} [j \text{ odd}] \bigg/ \sum_{l=0}^{40} \binom{100}{l}.$$

The quantity t takes the values 100, 99, ..., 1, 100, 99, ..., 1, ... as bits are printed; so we find that the expected number of 1s printed is $10^6 (26p_2 + 11p_3 + 26p_4 + 11p_6 + 11p_9 + 4p_{12} + 4p_{20} + 3p_{28} + p_{47} + p_{74} + p_{99} + 1/2)/100 \approx 14043$. The expected number of digits printed is $10^6 \sum_{l=0}^{40} \binom{100}{l}/2^{100} \approx 28444$, so the expected number of 0s is ≈ 14401.

The detectable bias goes away if more elements are discarded. For example, if we use only 100 elements of $ran\_array(a,300)$, the probability can be shown to be $(26p_5 + 22p_6 + 19p_{10} + \cdots)/100$; with $ran\_array(a,400)$ it is worse, $(15p_3 + 37p_6 + 15p_9 + \cdots)/100$, because $X_{n+400} \equiv X_n + X_{n+252}$. With $ran\_array(a,1009)$ as recommended in the text we have $(17p_7 + 10p_{11} + 2p_{12} + \cdots)/100$, which can only be detected by such experiments if the threshold for printing is raised from 60 to, say, 75; but then the expected number of outputs is only about 0.28 per million trials.

[This exercise is based on ideas of Y. Kurita, H. Leeb, and M. Matsumoto, communicated to the author in 1997.]

15. The following program makes it possible to obtain a new random integer quickly with the expression $ran\_arr\_next()$, once ran_start has been called to get things started:

```
#define QUALITY 1009    /* recommended quality level for high-res use */
#define KK 100                                        /* the long lag */
long ran_arr_buf[QUALITY];
long ran_arr_sentinel=-1;
long *ran_arr_ptr=&ran_arr_sentinel; /* the next random number, or -1 */

#define ran_arr_next() (*ran_arr_ptr>=0? *ran_arr_ptr++: ran_arr_cycle())
long ran_arr_cycle()
{
  ran_array(ran_arr_buf,QUALITY);
  ran_arr_buf[KK]=-1; ran_arr_ptr=ran_arr_buf+1;
  return ran_arr_buf[0];
}
```

Reset $ran\_arr\_ptr = \&ran\_arr\_sentinel$ if ran_start is used again.

SECTION 4.1

1. $(1010)_{-2}$, $(1011)_{-2}$, $(1000)_{-2}$, ..., $(11000)_{-2}$, $(11001)_{-2}$, $(11110)_{-2}$.

2. (a) $-(110001)_2$, $-(11.001001001001\ldots)_2$, $(11.00100100001111110110101\ldots)_2$.

(b) $(11010011)_{-2}$, $(1101.001011001011\ldots)_{-2}$, $(111.0110010001000000101\ldots)_{-2}$.

(c) $(\bar{1}11\bar{1}\bar{1})_3$, $(\bar{1}0.0\bar{1}\bar{1}0110\bar{1}\bar{1}011\ldots)_3$, $(10.011\bar{1}1111\bar{1}000\bar{1}011\bar{1}1101\bar{1}1111110\ldots)_3$.

(d) $-(9.4)_{1/10}$, $-(\ldots7582417582413)_{1/10}$, $(\ldots3462648323979853562951413)_{1/10}$.

3. $(1010113.2)_{2i}$.

4. (a) Between rA and rX. (b) The remainder in rX has radix point between bytes 3 and 4; the quotient in rA has radix point one byte to the right of the least significant portion of the register.

5. It has been subtracted from $999\ldots9 = 10^p - 1$, instead of from $1000\ldots0 = 10^p$.

6. (a, c) $2^{p-1} - 1$, $-(2^{p-1} - 1)$; (b) $2^{p-1} - 1$, -2^{p-1}.

7. A ten's complement representation for a negative number x can be obtained by considering $10^n + x$ (where n is large enough for this to be positive) and extending it on the left with infinitely many nines. The nines' complement representation can be obtained in the usual manner. (These two representations are equal for nonterminating decimals, otherwise the nines' complement representation has the form $\ldots(a)99999\ldots$ while the ten's complement representation has the form $\ldots(a+1)0000\ldots$) The representations may be considered sensible if we regard the value of the infinite sum $N = 9 + 90 + 900 + 9000 + \cdots$ as -1, since $N - 10N = 9$.

See also exercise 31, which considers p-adic number systems. The latter agree with the p's complement notations considered here, for numbers whose radix-p representation is terminating, but there is no simple relation between the field of p-adic numbers and the field of real numbers.

8. $\sum_j a_j b^j = \sum_j (a_{kj+k-1} b^{k-1} + \cdots + a_{kj}) b^{kj}$.

9. A BAD ADOBE FACADE FADED. [*Note:* Other possible "number sentences" would be DO A DEED A DECADE; A CAD FED A BABE BEEF, COCOA, COFFEE; BOB FACED A DEAD DODO.]

10. $\begin{bmatrix} \ldots, a_3, a_2, a_1, a_0; \; a_{-1}, a_{-2}, \ldots \\ \ldots, b_3, b_2, b_1, b_0; \; b_{-1}, b_{-2}, \ldots \end{bmatrix} = \begin{bmatrix} \ldots, A_3, A_2, A_1, A_0; \; A_{-1}, A_{-2}, \ldots \\ \ldots, B_3, B_2, B_1, B_0; \; B_{-1}, B_{-2}, \ldots \end{bmatrix}$, if

$$A_j = \begin{bmatrix} a_{k_{j+1}-1}, a_{k_{j+1}-2}, \ldots, a_{k_j} \\ b_{k_{j+1}-2}, \ldots, b_{k_j} \end{bmatrix}, \qquad B_j = b_{k_{j+1}-1} \ldots b_{k_j},$$

where $\langle k_n \rangle$ is any doubly infinite sequence of integers with $k_{j+1} > k_j$ and $k_0 = 0$.

11. (The following algorithm works both for addition or subtraction, depending on whether the plus or minus sign is chosen.)

Start by setting $k \leftarrow a_{n+1} \leftarrow a_{n+2} \leftarrow b_{n+1} \leftarrow b_{n+2} \leftarrow 0$; then for $m = 0, 1, \ldots, n+2$ do the following: Set $c_m \leftarrow a_m \pm b_m + k$; then if $c_m \geq 2$, set $k \leftarrow -1$ and $c_m \leftarrow c_m - 2$; otherwise if $c_m < 0$, set $k \leftarrow 1$ and $c_m \leftarrow c_m + 2$; otherwise (namely if $0 \leq c_m \leq 1$), set $k \leftarrow 0$.

12. (a) Subtract $\pm(\ldots a_3 0 a_1 0)_{-2}$ from $\pm(\ldots a_4 0 a_2 0 a_0)_{-2}$ in the negabinary system. (See also exercise 7.1.3–7 for a trickier solution that uses full-word bitwise operations.) (b) Subtract $(\ldots b_3 0 b_1 0)_2$ from $(\ldots b_4 0 b_2 0 b_0)_2$ in the binary system.

13. $(1.909090\ldots)_{-10} = (0.090909\ldots)_{-10} = \frac{1}{11}$.

14.

```
    1 1 3 2 1        [5 − 4i]
    1 1 3 2 1        [5 − 4i]
    1 1 3 2 1
    1 1 2 0 2
  1 2 1 2 3
  1 1 3 2 1
1 1 3 2 1
─────────────
0 1 0 3 1 1 2 0 1    [9 − 40i]
```

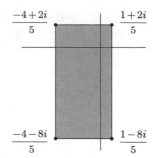

Fig. A–6. Fundamental region for quater-imaginary numbers.

15. $[-\frac{10}{11} .. \frac{1}{11}]$, and the rectangle on the right.

16. It is tempting to try to do this in a very simple way, by using the rule $2 = (1100)_{i-1}$ to take care of carries; but that leads to a nonterminating method if, for example, we try to add 1 to $(11101)_{i-1} = -1$.

The following solution does the job by providing four related algorithms (namely for adding or subtracting 1 or i). If α is a string of zeros and ones, let α^P be a string of zeros and ones such that $(\alpha^P)_{i-1} = (\alpha)_{i-1} + 1$; and let α^{-P}, α^Q, α^{-Q} be defined similarly, with -1, $+i$, and $-i$ respectively in place of $+1$. Then

$$(\alpha 0)^P = \alpha 1; \qquad (\alpha x 1)^P = \alpha^Q x 0. \qquad (\alpha 0)^Q = \alpha^P 1; \qquad (\alpha 1)^Q = \alpha^{-Q} 0.$$
$$(\alpha x 0)^{-P} = \alpha^{-Q} x 1; \qquad (\alpha 1)^{-P} = \alpha 0. \qquad (\alpha 0)^{-Q} = \alpha^Q 1; \qquad (\alpha 1)^{-Q} = \alpha^{-P} 0.$$

Here x stands for either 0 or 1, and the strings are extended on the left with zeros if necessary. The processes will clearly always terminate. Hence every number of the form $a + bi$ with a and b integers is representable in the $i - 1$ system.

17. No (in spite of exercise 28); the number -1 cannot be so represented. This can be proved by constructing a set S as in Fig. 1. We do have the representations $-i = (0.1111\ldots)_{1+i}$, $i = (100.1111\ldots)_{1+i}$.

18. Let S_0 be the set of points $(a_7 a_6 a_5 a_4 a_3 a_2 a_1 a_0)_{i-1}$, where each a_k is 0 or 1. (Thus, S_0 is given by the 256 interior dots shown in Fig. 1, if that picture is multiplied by 16.) We first show that S is closed: If $\{y_1, y_2, \ldots\}$ is an infinite subset of S, we have $y_n = \sum_{k=1}^{\infty} a_{nk} 16^{-k}$, where each a_{nk} is in S_0. Construct a tree whose nodes are $(a_{n1}, \ldots, a_{nr})$, for $1 \le r \le n$, and let a node of this tree be an ancestor of another node if it is an initial subsequence of that node. By the infinity lemma (Theorem 2.3.4.3K) this tree has an infinite path $(a_1, a_2, a_3, \ldots)$; consequently $\sum_{k \ge 1} a_k 16^{-k}$ is a limit point of $\{y_1, y_2, \ldots\}$ in S.

By the answer to exercise 16, all numbers of the form $(a+bi)/16^k$ are representable, when a and b are integers. Therefore if x and y are arbitrary reals and $k \ge 1$, the number $z_k = (\lfloor 16^k x \rfloor + \lfloor 16^k y \rfloor i)/16^k$ is in $S + m + ni$ for some integers m and n. It can be shown that $S + m + ni$ is bounded away from the origin when $(m, n) \ne (0, 0)$. Consequently if $|x|$ and $|y|$ are sufficiently small and k is sufficiently large, we have $z_k \in S$, and $\lim_{k \to \infty} z_k = x + yi$ is in S.

[B. Mandelbrot named S the "twindragon" because he noticed that it is essentially obtained by joining two "dragon curves" belly-to-belly; see his book *Fractals: Form, Chance, and Dimension* (San Francisco: Freeman, 1977), 313–314, where he also stated that the dimension of the boundary is $2 \lg x \approx 1.523627$, where $x = 1 + 2x^{-2} \approx 1.69562$. Other properties of the dragon curve are described in C. Davis and D. E. Knuth, *J. Recr.*

Math. **3** (1970), 66–81, 133–149. The sets S for digits $\{0, 1\}$ and other complex bases are illustrated and analyzed by D. Goffinet in *AMM* **98** (1991), 249–255.]

I. Kátai and J. Szabó have shown that the radix $-d+i$ yields a number system with digits $\{0, 1, \ldots, d^2\}$; see *Acta Scient. Math.* **37** (1975), 255–260. Further properties of such systems have been investigated by W. J. Gilbert, *Canadian J. Math.* **34** (1982), 1335–1348; *Math. Magazine* **57** (1984), 77–81. Another interesting case, with digits $\{0, 1, i, -1, -i\}$ and radix $2 + i$, has been suggested by V. Norton [*Math. Magazine* **57** (1984), 250–251]. For studies of number systems based on more general algebraic integers, see I. Kátai and B. Kovács, *Acta Math. Acad. Sci. Hung.* **37** (1981), 159–164, 405–407; B. Kovács, *Acta Math. Hung.* **58** (1991), 113–120; B. Kovács and A. Pethő, *Studia Scient. Math. Hung.* **27** (1992), 169–172.

19. If $m > u$ or $m < l$, find $a \in D$ such that $m \equiv a$ (modulo b); the desired representation will be a representation of $m' = (m - a)/b$ followed by a. Note that $m > u$ implies $l < m' < m$; $m < l$ implies $m < m' < u$; so the algorithm terminates.

[There are no solutions when $b = 2$. The representation will be unique if and only if $0 \in D$; nonunique representation occurs for example when $D = \{-3, -1, 7\}$, $b = 3$, since $(\alpha)_3 = (37\overline{7}3\alpha)_3$. When $b \geq 3$ it is not difficult to show that there are exactly 2^{b-3} solution sets D in which $|a| < b$ for all $a \in D$. Furthermore the set $D = \{0, 1, 2 - \epsilon_2 b^n, 3 - \epsilon_3 b^n, \ldots, b - 2 - \epsilon_{b-2} b^n, b - 1 - b^n\}$ gives unique representations, for all $b \geq 3$ and $n \geq 1$, when each ϵ_j is 0 or 1. *References: Proc. IEEE Symp. Comp. Arith.* **4** (1978), 1–9; *JACM* **29** (1982), 1131–1143.]

20. (a) $0.\overline{1}\overline{1}\overline{1} \ldots = \overline{1}.888 \ldots = \overline{1}8.\frac{111}{777} \ldots = \overline{1}8\frac{1}{7} \cdot \frac{222}{666} \ldots = \cdots = \overline{1}8\frac{123456}{765432} \cdot \frac{777}{111} \cdots$ has nine representations. (b) A "D-fraction" $.a_1 a_2 \ldots$ always lies between $-1/9$ and $+71/9$. Suppose x has ten or more D-decimal representations. Then for sufficiently large k, $10^k x$ has ten representations that differ to the left of the decimal point: $10^k x = n_1 + f_1 = \cdots = n_{10} + f_{10}$ where each f_j is a D-fraction. By uniqueness of integer representations, the n_j are distinct, say $n_1 < \cdots < n_{10}$, hence $n_{10} - n_1 \geq 9$; but this implies $f_1 - f_{10} \geq 9 > 71/9 - (-1/9)$, a contradiction. (c) Any number of the form $0.a_1 a_2 \ldots$, where each a_j is -1 or 8, equals $\overline{1}.a_1' a_2' \ldots$ where $a_j' = a_j + 9$ (and it even has six *more* representations $\overline{1}8.a_1'' a_2'' \ldots$, etc.).

21. We can convert to such a representation by using a method like that suggested in the text for converting to balanced ternary.

In contrast to the system of exercise 20, zero can be represented in infinitely many ways, all obtained from $\frac{1}{2} + \sum_{k \geq 1} (-4\frac{1}{2}) \cdot 10^{-k}$ (or from the negative of this representation) by multiplying it by a power of ten. The representations of unity are $1\frac{1}{2} - \frac{1}{2}*$, $\frac{1}{2} + \frac{1}{2}*$, $5 - 3\frac{1}{2} - \frac{1}{2}*$, $5 - 4\frac{1}{2} + \frac{1}{2}*$, $50 - 45 - 3\frac{1}{2} - \frac{1}{2}*$, $50 - 45 - 4\frac{1}{2} + \frac{1}{2}*$, etc., where $\pm \frac{1}{2}* = (\pm 4\frac{1}{2})(10^{-1} + 10^{-2} + \cdots)$. [*AMM* **57** (1950), 90–93.]

22. Given some approximation $b_n \ldots b_1 b_0$ with error $\sum_{k=0}^{n} b_k 10^k - x > 10^{-t}$ for $t > 0$, we will show how to reduce the error by approximately 10^{-t}. (The process can be started by finding a suitable $\sum_{k=0}^{n} b_k 10^k > x$; then a finite number of reductions of this type will make the error less than ϵ.) Simply choose $m > n$ so large that the decimal representation of $-10^m u$ has a one in position 10^{-t} and no ones in positions $10^{-t+1}, 10^{-t+2}, \ldots, 10^n$. Then $10^m \alpha + $ (a suitable sum of powers of 10 between 10^m and 10^n) $+ \sum_{k=0}^{n} b_k 10^k \approx \sum_{k=0}^{n} b_k 10^k - 10^{-t}$.

23. The set $S = \{\sum_{k \geq 1} a_k b^{-k} \mid a_k \in D\}$ is closed as in exercise 18, hence it is measurable, and in fact it has positive measure. Since $bS = \bigcup_{a \in D} (a + S)$, we have $b\mu(S) = \mu(bS) \leq \sum_{a \in D} \mu(a + S) = \sum_{a \in D} \mu(S) = b\mu(S)$, and we must therefore have

$\mu((a + S) \cap (a' + S)) = 0$ when $a \neq a' \in D$. Now T has measure zero if $0 \in D$, since T is a union of countably many sets of the form $b^k(n + ((a + S) \cap (a' + S)))$, $a \neq a'$, each of measure zero. On the other hand, as pointed out by K. A. Brakke, every real number has infinitely many representations in the number system of exercise 21.

[The set T cannot be empty, since the real numbers cannot be written as a countable union of disjoint, closed, bounded sets; see *AMM* **84** (1977), 827–828, and the more detailed analysis by Petkovšek in *AMM* **97** (1990), 408–411. If D has fewer than b elements, the set of numbers representable with radix b and digits from D has measure zero. If D has more than b elements and represents all reals, T has infinite measure.]

24. $\{2a \cdot 10^k + a' \mid 0 \le a < 5, 0 \le a' < 2\}$ or $\{5a' \cdot 10^k + a \mid 0 \le a < 5, 0 \le a' < 2\}$, for $k \ge 0$. [R. L. Graham has shown that there are no more sets of integer digits with these properties. And Andrew Odlyzko has shown that the restriction to integers is superfluous, in the sense that if the smallest two elements of D are 0 and 1, all the digits must be integers. *Proof.* Let $S = \{\sum_{k<0} a_k b^k \mid a_k \in D\}$ be the set of "fractions," and let $X = \{(a_n \ldots a_0)_b \mid a_k \in D\}$ be the set of "whole numbers"; then $[0 . . \infty) = \bigcup_{x \in X}(x + S)$, and $(x + S) \cap (x' + S)$ has measure zero for $x \neq x' \in X$. We have $(0 . . 1) \subseteq S$, and by induction on m we will prove that $(m . . m + 1) \subseteq x_m + S$ for some $x_m \in X$. Let $x_m \in X$ be such that $(m . . m + \epsilon) \cap (x_m + S)$ has positive measure for all $\epsilon > 0$. Then $x_m \le m$, and x_m must be an integer lest $x_{\lfloor x_m \rfloor} + S$ overlap $x_m + S$ too much. If $x_m > 0$, the fact that $(m - x_m . . m - x_m + 1) \cap S$ has positive measure implies by induction that this measure is 1, and $(m . . m+1) \subseteq x_m + S$ since S is closed. If $x_m = 0$ and $(m . . m + 1) \not\subseteq S$, we must have $m < x'_m < m + 1$ for some $x'_m \in X$, where $(m . . x'_m) \subseteq S$; but then $1 + S$ overlaps $x'_m + S$. See *Proc. London Math. Soc.* (3) **37** (1978), 213–229.]

Note: If we drop the restriction $0 \in D$, there *are* many other cases, some of which are quite interesting, especially $\{1, 2, 3, 4, 5, 6, 7, 8, 9, 10\}$, $\{1, 2, 3, 4, 5, 51, 52, 53, 54, 55\}$, and $\{2, 3, 4, 5, 6, 52, 53, 54, 55, 56\}$. Alternatively if we allow negative digits we obtain many other solutions by the method of exercise 19, plus further sets of unusual digits like $\{-1, 0, 1, 2, 3, 4, 5, 6, 7, 18\}$ that don't meet the conditions stated there. It appears hopeless to find a nice characterization of all solutions with negative digits.

25. A positive number whose radix-b representation has m consecutive $(b-1)$'s to the right of the radix point must have the form $c/b^n + (b^m - \theta)/b^{n+m}$, where c and n are nonnegative integers and $0 < \theta \le 1$. So if u/v has this form, we find that $b^{m+n}u = b^m cv + b^m v - \theta v$. Therefore θv is an integer that is a multiple of b^m. But $0 < \theta v \le v < b^m$. [There can be arbitrarily long runs of other digits a, if $0 \le a < b - 1$, for example in the representation of $a/(b-1)$.]

26. The proof of "sufficiency" is a straightforward generalization of the usual proof for base b, by successively constructing the desired representation. The proof of "necessity" breaks into two parts: If β_{n+1} is greater than $\sum_{k \le n} c_k \beta_k$ for some n, then $\beta_{n+1} - \epsilon$ has no representation for small ϵ. If $\beta_{n+1} \le \sum_{k \le n} c_k \beta_k$ for all n, but equality does not always hold, we can show that there are two representations for certain x. [See *Transactions of the Royal Society of Canada*, series III, **46** (1952), 45–55.]

27. Proof by induction on $|n|$: If n is even we must take $e_0 > 0$, and the result follows by induction, since $n/2$ has a unique such representation. If n is odd, we must take $e_0 = 0$, and the problem reduces to representing $-(n-1)/2$; if the latter quantity is either zero or one, there is obviously only one way to proceed, otherwise it has a unique reversing representation by induction. [A. D. Booth, in *Quarterly J. Mechanics and Applied Math.* **4** (1951), 236–240, applied this principle to two's complement multiplication.]

[It follows that every positive integer has exactly *two* such representations with *decreasing* exponents $e_0 > e_1 > \cdots > e_t$: one with t even and the other with t odd.]

28. A proof like that of exercise 27 may be given. Note that $a + bi$ is a multiple of $1 + i$ by a complex integer if and only if $a + b$ is even. This representation is intimately related to the dragon curve discussed in the answer to exercise 18.

29. It suffices to prove that any collection $\{T_0, T_1, T_2, \ldots\}$ satisfying Property B may be obtained by collapsing some collection $\{S_0, S_1, S_2, \ldots\}$, where $S_0 = \{0, 1, \ldots, b-1\}$ and all elements of $S_1, S_2, \ldots$ are multiples of b.

To prove the latter statement, we may assume that $1 \in T_0$ and that there is a least element $b > 1$ such that $b \notin T_0$. We will prove, by induction on n, that if $nb \notin T_0$, then $nb + 1$, $nb + 2$, ..., $nb + b - 1$ are not in any of the T_j's; but if $nb \in T_0$, then so are $nb + 1$, ..., $nb + b - 1$. The result then follows with $S_1 = \{nb \mid nb \in T_0\}$, $S_2 = T_1$, $S_3 = T_2$, etc.

If $nb \notin T_0$, then $nb = t_0 + t_1 + \cdots$, where t_1, t_2, ... are multiples of b; hence $t_0 < nb$ is a multiple of b. By induction, $(t_0 + k) + t_1 + t_2 + \cdots$ is the representation of $nb + k$, for $0 < k < b$; hence $nb + k \notin T_j$ for any j.

If $nb \in T_0$ and $0 < k < b$, let the representation of $nb + k$ be $t_0 + t_1 + \cdots$. We cannot have $t_j = nb + k$ for $j \geq 1$, lest $nb + b$ have two representations $(b - k) + \cdots + (nb + k) + \cdots = (nb) + \cdots + b + \cdots$. By induction, $t_0 \bmod b = k$; and the representation $nb = (t_0 - k) + t_1 + \cdots$ implies that $t_0 = nb + k$.

[*Reference: Nieuw Archief voor Wiskunde* (3) **4** (1956), 15–17. A finite analog of this result was derived by P. A. MacMahon, *Combinatory Analysis* **1** (1915), 217–223.]

30. (a) Let A_j be the set of numbers n whose representation does not involve b_j; then by the uniqueness property, $n \in A_j$ if and only if $n + b_j \notin A_j$. Consequently we have $n \in A_j$ if and only if $n + 2b_j \in A_j$. It follows that, for $j \neq k$, $n \in A_j \cap A_k$ if and only if $n + 2b_j b_k \in A_j \cap A_k$. Let m be the number of integers $n \in A_j \cap A_k$ such that $0 \leq n < 2b_j b_k$. Then this interval contains exactly m integers that are in A_j but not A_k, exactly m in A_k but not A_j, and exactly m in neither A_j nor A_k; hence $4m = 2b_j b_k$. Therefore b_j and b_k cannot both be odd. But at least one b_j is odd, of course, since odd numbers can be represented.

(b) According to (a) we can renumber the b's so that b_0 is odd and b_1, b_2, ... are even; then $\frac{1}{2}b_1$, $\frac{1}{2}b_2$, ... must also be a binary basis, and the process can be iterated.

(c) If it is a binary basis, we must have positive and negative d_k's for arbitrarily large k, in order to represent $\pm 2^n$ when n is large. Conversely, the following algorithm may be used:

S1. [Initialize.] Set $k \leftarrow 0$.

S2. [Done?] If $n = 0$, terminate.

S3. [Choose.] If n is even, set $n \leftarrow n/2$. Otherwise include $2^k d_k$ in the representation, and set $n \leftarrow (n - d_k)/2$.

S4. [Advance k.] Increase k by 1 and return to S2. ▮

At each step the choice is forced; furthermore step S3 always decreases $|n|$ unless $n = -d_k$, hence the algorithm must terminate.

(d) Two iterations of steps S2–S4 in the preceding algorithm will change $4m \to m$, $4m + 1 \to m + 5$, $4m + 2 \to m + 7$, $4m + 3 \to m - 1$. Arguing as in exercise 19, we need only show that the algorithm terminates for $-2 \leq n \leq 8$; all other values of n are moved toward this interval. In this range $3 \to -1 \to -2 \to 6 \to 8 \to 2 \to 7 \to 0$ and $4 \to 1 \to 5 \to 6$. Thus $1 = 7 \cdot 2^0 - 13 \cdot 2^1 + 7 \cdot 2^2 - 13 \cdot 2^3 - 13 \cdot 2^5 - 13 \cdot 2^9 + 7 \cdot 2^{10}$.

Note: The choice $d_0, d_1, d_2, \ldots = 5, -3, 3, 5, -3, 3, \ldots$ also yields a binary basis. For further details see *Math. Comp.* **18** (1964), 537–546; A. D. Sands, *Acta Math. Acad. Sci. Hung.* **8** (1957), 65–86.

31. (See also the related exercises 3.2.2–11, 4.3.2–13, 4.6.2–22.)

(a) By multiplying numerator and denominator by suitable powers of 2, we may assume that $u = (\ldots u_2 u_1 u_0)_2$ and $v = (\ldots v_2 v_1 v_0)_2$ are 2-adic integers, where $v_0 = 1$. The following computational method now determines w, using the notation $u^{(n)}$ to stand for the integer $(u_{n-1} \ldots u_0)_2 = u \bmod 2^n$ when $n > 0$:

Let $w_0 = u_0$ and $w^{(1)} = w_0$. For $n = 1, 2, \ldots$, assume that we have found an integer $w^{(n)} = (w_{n-1} \ldots w_0)_2$ such that $u^{(n)} \equiv v^{(n)} w^{(n)}$ (modulo 2^n). Then we have $u^{(n+1)} \equiv v^{(n+1)} w^{(n)}$ (modulo 2^n), hence $w_n = 0$ or 1 according as the quantity $(u^{(n+1)} - v^{(n+1)} w^{(n)}) \bmod 2^{n+1}$ is 0 or 2^n.

(b) Find the smallest integer k such that $2^k \equiv 1$ (modulo $2n + 1$). Then we have $1/(2n+1) = m/(2^k - 1)$ for some integer m, $1 \le m < 2^{k-1}$. Let α be the k-bit binary representation of m; then $(0.\alpha\alpha\alpha\ldots)_2$ times $2n + 1$ is $(0.111\ldots)_2 = 1$ in the binary system, and $(\ldots\alpha\alpha\alpha)_2$ times $2n + 1$ is $(\ldots 111)_2 = -1$ in the 2-adic system.

(c) If u is rational, say $u = m/(2^e n)$ where n is odd and positive, the 2-adic representation of u is periodic, because the set of numbers with periodic expansions includes $-1/n$ and is closed under the operations of negation, division by 2, and addition. Conversely, if $u_{N+\lambda} = u_N$ for all sufficiently large N, the 2-adic number $(2^\lambda - 1)2^r u$ is an integer for all sufficiently large r.

(d) The square of any number of the form $(\ldots u_2 u_1 1)_2$ has the form $(\ldots 001)_2$, hence the condition is necessary. To show the sufficiency, we can use the following procedure to compute $v = \sqrt{n}$ when $n \bmod 8 = 1$:

H1. [Initialize.] Set $m \leftarrow (n-1)/8$, $k \leftarrow 2$, $v_0 \leftarrow 1$, $v_1 \leftarrow 0$, $v \leftarrow 1$. (During this algorithm we will have $v = (v_{k-1} \ldots v_1 v_0)_2$ and $v^2 = n - 2^{k+1} m$.)

H2. [Transform.] If m is even, set $v_k \leftarrow 0$, $m \leftarrow m/2$. Otherwise set $v_k \leftarrow 1$, $m \leftarrow (m - v - 2^{k-1})/2$, $v \leftarrow v + 2^k$.

H3. [Advance k.] Increase k by 1 and return to H2. ∎

32. A more general result appears in *Math. Comp.* **29** (1975), 84–86.

33. Let K_n be the set of all such n-digit numbers, so that $k_n = |K_n|$. If S and T are any finite sets of integers, we shall say $S \sim T$ if $S = T + x$ for some integer x, and we shall write $k_n(S) = |\mathcal{K}_n(S)|$, where $\mathcal{K}_n(S)$ is the family of all subsets of K_n that are $\sim S$. When $n = 0$, we have $k_n(S) = 0$ unless $|S| \le 1$, since zero is the only "0-digit" number. When $n \ge 1$ and $S = \{s_1, \ldots, s_r\}$, we have

$$\mathcal{K}_n(S) = \bigcup_{0 \le j < b} \bigcup_{(a_1, \ldots, a_r)} \{\{t_1 b + a_1, \ldots, t_r b + a_r\} \mid$$

$$\{t_1, \ldots, t_r\} \in K_{n-1}(\{(s_i + j - a_i)/b \mid 1 \le i \le r\})\},$$

where the inner union is over all sequences of digits $(a_1, \ldots, a_r)$ satisfying the condition $a_i \equiv s_i + j$ (modulo b) for $1 \le i \le r$. In this formula we require $t_i - t_{i'} = (s_i - a_i)/b - (s_{i'} - a_{i'})/b$ for $1 \le i < i' \le r$, so that the naming of subscripts is uniquely determined. By the principle of inclusion and exclusion, therefore, we have $k_n(S) = \sum_{0 \le j < b} \sum_{m \ge 1} (-1)^{m-1} f(S, m, j)$, where $f(S, m, j)$ is the number of sets of integers that can be expressed as $\{t_1 b + a_1, \ldots, t_r b + a_r\}$ in the manner above for m different sequences $(a_1, \ldots, a_r)$, summed over all choices of m different sequences $(a_1, \ldots, a_r)$. Given m different sequences $(a_1^{(l)}, \ldots, a_r^{(l)})$ for $1 \le l \le m$, the number of such sets is $k_{n-1}(\{(s_i + j - a_i^{(l)})/b \mid 1 \leq i \leq r, 1 \leq l \leq m\})$. Thus there is a collection of sets $\mathcal{T}(S)$ such that

$$k_n(S) = \sum_{T \in \mathcal{T}(S)} c_T \, k_{n-1}(T),$$

where each c_T is an integer. Furthermore if $T \in \mathcal{T}(S)$, its elements are near those of S; we have $\min T \geq (\min S - \max D)/b$ and $\max T \leq (\max S + b - 1 - \min D)/b$. Thus we obtain simultaneous recurrence relations for the sequences $\langle k_n(S) \rangle$, where S runs through the nonempty integer subsets of $[l \mathrel{..} u+1]$, in the notation of exercise 19. Since $k_n = k_n(S)$ for any one-element set S, the sequence $\langle k_n \rangle$ appears among these recurrences. The coefficients c_T can be computed from the first few values of $k_n(S)$, so we can obtain a system of equations defining the generating functions $k_S(z) = \sum k_n(S) z^n = [|S| \leq 1] + z \sum_{T \in \mathcal{T}(S)} c_T k_T(z)$. [See *J. Algorithms* **2** (1981), 31–43.]

For example, when $D = \{-1, 0, 3\}$ and $b = 3$ we have $l = -\frac{3}{2}$ and $u = \frac{1}{2}$, so the relevant sets S are $\{0\}$, $\{0, 1\}$, $\{-1, 1\}$, and $\{-1, 0, 1\}$. The corresponding sequences for $n \leq 3$ are $\langle 1, 3, 8, 21 \rangle$, $\langle 0, 1, 3, 8 \rangle$, $\langle 0, 0, 1, 4 \rangle$, and $\langle 0, 0, 0, 0 \rangle$; so we obtain

$$k_0(z) = 1 + z\big(3k_0(z) - k_{01}(z)\big), \qquad\qquad k_{02}(z) = z\big(k_{01}(z) + k_{02}(z)\big),$$
$$k_{01}(z) = zk_0(z), \qquad\qquad\qquad\qquad\qquad k_{012}(z) = 0,$$

and $k(z) = 1/(1 - 3z + z^2)$. In this case $k_n = F_{2n+2}$ and $k_n(\{0, 2\}) = F_{2n-1} - 1$.

34. There is exactly one string α_n on the symbols $\{\bar{1}, 0, 1\}$ such that $n = (\alpha_n)_2$ and α_n has no leading zeros or consecutive nonzeros: α_0 is empty, otherwise $\alpha_{2n} = \alpha_n 0$, $\alpha_{4n+1} = \alpha_n 01$, $\alpha_{4n-1} = \alpha_n 0\bar{1}$. Any string that represents n can be converted to this "canonical signed bit representation" by using the reductions $1\bar{1} \to 01$, $\bar{1}1 \to 0\bar{1}$, $01\ldots11 \to 10\ldots0\bar{1}$, $0\bar{1}\ldots\bar{1}\bar{1} \to \bar{1}0\ldots01$, and inserting or deleting leading zeros. Since these reductions do not increase the number of nonzero digits, α_n has the fewest. [*Advances in Computers* **1** (1960), 244–260.] The number of nonzero digits in α_n, denoted by $\bar{\nu}(n)$, is the number of 1s in the ordinary representation that are immediately preceded by 0 or by the substring $00(10)^k1$ for some $k \geq 0$. (See exercise 7.1.3–35.)

A generalization to radix $b > 2$ has been given by J. von zur Gathen, *Computational Complexity* **1** (1991), 360–394.

SECTION 4.2.1

1. $N = (62, +.60\ 22\ 14\ 08)$; $h = (34, +.06\ 62\ 60\ 70)$. Note that the quantity $10h$ would be $(34, +.66\ 26\ 07\ 02)$.

2. $b^{E-q}(1 - b^{-p})$, b^{-q-p}; $b^{E-q}(1 - b^{-p})$, b^{-q-1}.

3. When e does not have its smallest value, the most significant "one" bit (which appears in all such normalized numbers) need not appear in the computer word.

4. $(51, +.10209877)$; $(50, +.12346000)$; $(53, +.99999999)$. The third answer would be $(54, +.10000000)$ if the first operand had been $(45, -.50000000)$, since $b/2$ is odd.

5. If $x \sim y$ and m is an integer then $mb + x \sim mb + y$. Furthermore $x \sim y$ implies $x/b \sim y/b$, by considering all possible cases. Another crucial property is that x and y will round to the same integer, whenever $bx \sim by$.

Now if $b^{-p-2}F_v \neq f_v$ we must have $(b^{p+2}f_v) \bmod b \neq 0$; hence the transformation leaves f_v unchanged unless $e_u - e_v \geq 2$. Since u was normalized, it is nonzero and $|f_u + f_v| > b^{-1} - b^{-2} \geq b^{-2}$: The leading nonzero digit of $f_u + f_v$ must be at most two places to the right of the radix point, and the rounding operation will convert

$b^{p+j}(f_u + f_v)$ to an integer, where $j \leq 1$. The proof will be complete if we can show that $b^{p+j+1}(f_u + f_v) \sim b^{p+j+1}(f_u + b^{-p-2}F_v)$. By the previous paragraph, we have $b^{p+2}(f_u + f_v) \sim b^{p+2}f_u + F_v = b^{p+2}(f_u + b^{-p-2}F_v)$, which implies the desired result for all $j \leq 1$. Similar remarks apply to step M2 of Algorithm M.

Note that, when $b > 2$ is even, such an integer F_v always exists; but when $b = 2$ we require $p+3$ bits (let $2F_v$ be an integer). When b is odd, an integer F_v always exists except in the case of division by Algorithm M, when a remainder of $\frac{1}{2}b$ is possible.

6. (Consider the case $e_u = e_v$, $f_u = -f_v$ in Program A.) Register A retains its previous sign, as in ADD.

7. Say that a number is normalized if and only if it is zero or its fraction part lies in the range $\frac{1}{6} < |f| < \frac{1}{2}$. A $(p+1)$-place accumulator suffices for addition and subtraction; rounding (except during division) is equivalent to truncation. A very pleasant system indeed! We might represent numbers with excess-zero exponent, inserted between the first and subsequent digits of the fraction, and complemented if the fraction is negative, so that the order of fixed point numbers is preserved.

8. (a) $(06, +.12345679) \oplus (06, -.12345678)$, $(01, +.10345678) \oplus (00, -.94000000)$;
(b) $(99, +.87654321) \oplus$ itself, $(99, +.99999999) \oplus (91, +.50000000)$.

9. $a = c = (-50, +.10000000)$, $b = (-41, +.20000000)$, $d = (-41, +.80000000)$, $y = (11, +.10000000)$.

10. $(50, +.99999000) \oplus (55, +.99999000)$.

11. $(50, +.10000001) \otimes (50, +.99999990)$.

12. If $0 < |f_u| < |f_v|$, then $|f_u| \leq |f_v| - b^{-p}$; hence $1/b < |f_u/f_v| \leq 1 - b^{-p}/|f_v| < 1 - b^{-p}$. If $0 < |f_v| \leq |f_u|$, we have $1/b \leq |f_u/f_v|/b \leq ((1 - b^{-p})/(1/b))/b = 1 - b^{-p}$.

13. See J. Michael Yohe, *IEEE Trans.* **C-22** (1973), 577–586; see also exercise 4.2.2–24.

14.
```
    FIX STJ   9F            Float-to-fix subroutine:
        STA   TEMP
        LD1   TEMP(EXP)     rI1 ← e.
        SLA   1             rA ← ±f f f f 0.
        JAZ   9F            Is input zero?
        DEC1  1
        CMPA  =0=(1:1)      If leading byte is zero,
        JE    *-4              shift left again.
        ENN1  -Q-4,1
        J1N   FIXOVFLO      Is magnitude too large?
        ENTX  0
        SRAX  0,1
        CMPX  =1//2=
        JL    9F
        JG    *+2
        JAO   9F            The ambiguous case becomes odd, since b/2 is even.
        STA   *+1(0:0)      Round, if necessary.
        INCA  1             Add ±1 (overflow is impossible).
    9H  JMP   *             Exit from subroutine.  ▌
```

15.
```
    FP  STJ   EXITF         Fractional part subroutine:
        JOV   OFLO          Ensure that overflow is off.
        STA   TEMP          TEMP ← u.
```

```
        ENTX 0
        SLA  1              rA ← f_u.
        LD2  TEMP(EXP)      rI2 ← e_u.
        DEC2 Q
        J2NP *+3
        SLA  0,2            Remove integer part of u.
        ENT2 0
        JANN 1F
        ENN2 0,2            Fraction is negative: Find
        SRAX 0,2              its complement.
        ENT2 0
        JXNZ *+3
        JAZ  *+2
        INCA 1
        ADD  WM1            Add word size minus one.
   1H   INC2 Q              Prepare to normalize the answer.
        JMP  NORM           Normalize, round, and exit.
   8H   EQU  1(1:1)
   WM1  CON  8B-1,8B-1(1:4) Word size minus one  ∎
```

16. If $|c| \geq |d|$, then set $r \leftarrow d \oslash c$, $s \leftarrow c \oplus (r \otimes d)$; $x \leftarrow (a \oplus (b \otimes r)) \oslash s$, $y \leftarrow (b \ominus (a \otimes r)) \oslash s$. Otherwise set $r \leftarrow c \oslash d$, $s \leftarrow d \oplus (r \otimes c)$; $x \leftarrow ((a \otimes r) \oplus b) \oslash s$, $y \leftarrow ((b \otimes r) \ominus a) \oslash s$. Then $x + iy$ is the desired approximation to $(a + bi)/(c + di)$. Computing $s' \leftarrow 1 \oslash s$ and multiplying twice by s' may be better than dividing twice by s. As with (11), gradual underflow is recommended for the calculation of r unless special precautions are taken. [*CACM* **5** (1962), 435. Other algorithms for complex arithmetic and function evaluation are given by P. Wynn, *BIT* **2** (1962), 232–255. For $|a + bi|$, see Paul Friedland, *CACM* **10** (1967), 665.]

17. See Robert Morris, *IEEE Trans.* **C-20** (1971), 1578–1579. Error analysis is more difficult with such systems, so interval arithmetic is correspondingly more desirable.

18. For positive numbers: Shift fraction left until $f_1 = 1$, then round, then if the fraction is zero (rounding overflow) shift it right again. For negative numbers: Shift fraction left until $f_1 = 0$, then round, then if the fraction is zero (rounding underflow) shift it right again.

19. $(73 - (5 - [\text{rounding digits are } \frac{b}{2} 0 \dots 0])(6 - [\text{magnitude is rounded up}]) + [e_v < e_u] +$ [first rounding digit is $\frac{b}{2}$] $- [\text{fraction overflow}] - 10[\text{result zero}] + 7[\text{rounding overflow}] +$ $7N + (3 + (16 + [\text{result negative}])[\text{opposite signs}])X)u$, where N is the number of left shifts during normalization, and X is the condition that rX receives nonzero digits and there is no fraction overflow. The maximum time of $84u$ occurs for example when

$$u = -50\ 01\ 00\ 00\ 00, \quad v = +45\ 49\ 99\ 99\ 99, \quad b = 100.$$

[The average time, considering the data in Section 4.2.4, will be less than $47u$.]

SECTION 4.2.2

1. $u \ominus v = u \oplus -v = -v \oplus u = -(v \oplus -u) = -(v \ominus u)$.

2. $u \oplus x \geq u \oplus 0 = u$, by (8), (2), (6); hence by (8) again, $(u \oplus x) \oplus v \geq u \oplus v$. Similarly, (8) and (6) together with (2) imply that $(u \oplus x) \oplus (v \oplus y) \geq (u \oplus x) \oplus v$.

3. $u = 8.0000001$, $v = 1.2500008$, $w = 8.0000008$; $(u \otimes v) \otimes w = 80.000064$, yet $u \otimes (v \otimes w) = 80.000057$.

4. Yes; let $1/u \approx v = w$, where v is large.

5. Not always; in decimal arithmetic take $u = v = 9$.

6. (a) Yes. (b) Only for $b + p \le 4$ (try $u = 1 - b^{-p}$). But see exercise 27.

7. If u and v are consecutive floating binary numbers, $u \oplus v = 2u$ or $2v$. When it is $2v$ we often have $u^{\text{②}} \oplus v^{\text{②}} < 2v^{\text{②}}$. For example, $u = (.10\ldots001)_2$, $v = (.10\ldots010)_2$, $u \oplus v = 2v$, and $u^{\text{②}} + v^{\text{②}} = (.10\ldots011)_2 = u^{\text{②}} \oplus v^{\text{②}}$.

8. (a) $\sim$, $\approx$; (b) $\sim$, $\approx$; (c) $\sim$, $\approx$; (d) $\sim$; (e) $\sim$.

9. $|u - w| \le |u - v| + |v - w| \le \epsilon_1 \min(b^{e_u - q}, b^{e_v - q}) + \epsilon_2 \min(b^{e_v - q}, b^{e_w - q}) \le \epsilon_1 b^{e_u - q} + \epsilon_2 b^{e_w - q} \le (\epsilon_1 + \epsilon_2) \max(b^{e_u - q}, b^{e_w - q})$. The result cannot be strengthened in general, since for example we might have e_u very small compared to both e_v and e_w, and this means that $u - w$ might be fairly large under the hypotheses.

10. We have $(.a_1 \ldots a_{p-1} a_p)_b \otimes (.9 \ldots 99)_b = (.a_1 \ldots a_{p-1}(a_p - 1))_b$ if $a_p \ge 1$ and $a_1 \ge \frac{b}{2}$; here "9" stands for $b - 1$. Furthermore, $(.a_1 \ldots a_{p-1} a_p)_b \otimes (1.0 \ldots 0)_b = (.a_1 \ldots a_{p-1} 0)_b$, so the multiplication is not monotone if $b > 2$ and $a_p \ge 1 + [a_1 \ge \frac{b}{2}]$. But when $b = 2$, this argument can be extended to show that multiplication *is* monotone; obviously the "certain computer" had $b > 2$.

11. Without loss of generality, let x be an integer, $0 \le x < b^p$. If $e \le 0$, then $t = 0$. If $0 < e \le p$, then $x - t$ has at most $p + 1$ digits, the least significant being zero. If $e > p$, then $x - t = 0$. [The result holds also under the weaker hypothesis $|t| < b^e$; in that case we might have $x - t = b^e$ when $e > p$.]

12. Assume that $e_u = p$, $e_v \le 0$, $u > 0$. Case 1, $u > b^{p-1}$. Case (1a), $w = u + 1$, $v \ge \frac{1}{2}$, $e_v = 0$. Then $u' = u$ or $u + 1$, $v' = 1$, $u'' = u$, $v'' = 1$ or 0. Case (1b), $w = u$, $|v| \le \frac{1}{2}$. Then $u' = u$, $v' = 0$, $u'' = u$, $v'' = 0$. If $|v| = \frac{1}{2}$ and more general rounding is permitted we might also have $u' = u \pm 1$, $v'' = \mp 1$. Case (1c), $w = u - 1$, $v \le -\frac{1}{2}$, $e_v = 0$. Then $u' = u$ or $u - 1$, $v' = -1$, $u'' = u$, $v'' = -1$ or 0. Case 2, $u = b^{p-1}$. Case (2a), $w = u + 1$, $v \ge \frac{1}{2}$, $e_v = 0$. Like (1a). Case (2b), $w = u$, $|v| \le \frac{1}{2}$, $u' \ge u$. Like (1b). Case (2c), $w = u$, $|v| \le \frac{1}{2}$, $u' < u$. Then $u' = u - j/b$ where $v = j/b + v_1$ and $|v_1| \le \frac{1}{2} b^{-1}$ for some positive integer $j \le \frac{1}{2} b$; we have $v' = 0$, $u'' = u$, $v'' = j/b$. Case (2d), $w < u$. Then $w = u - j/b$ where $v = -j/b + v_1$ and $|v_1| \le \frac{1}{2} b^{-1}$ for some positive integer $j \le b$; we have $(v', u'') = (-j/b, u)$, and $(u', v') = (u, -j/b)$ or $(u - 1/b, (1 - j)/b)$, the latter case only when $v_1 = \frac{1}{2} b^{-1}$. In all cases $u \ominus u' = u - u'$, $v \ominus v' = v - v'$, $u \ominus u'' = u - u''$, $v \ominus v'' = v - v''$, $\text{round}(w - u - v) = w - u - v$.

13. Since $\text{round}(x) = 0$ if and only if $x = 0$, we want to find a large set of integer pairs (m, n) with the property that $m \oslash n$ is an integer if and only if m/n is. Assume that $|m|, |n| < b^p$. If m/n is an integer, then $m \oslash n = m/n$ is also. Conversely if m/n is not an integer, but $m \oslash n$ is, we have $1/|n| \le |m \oslash n - m/n| < \frac{1}{2} |m/n| b^{1-p}$, hence $|m| > 2b^{p-1}$. Our answer is therefore to require $|m| \le 2b^{p-1}$ and $0 < |n| < b^p$. (Slightly weaker hypotheses are also possible.)

14. $|(u \otimes v) \otimes w - uvw| \le |(u \otimes v) \otimes w - (u \otimes v)w| + |w||u \otimes v - uv| \le \delta_{(u \otimes v) \otimes w} + b^{e_w - q - l_w} \delta_{u \otimes v} \le (1 + b) \delta_{(u \otimes v) \otimes w}$. Now $|e_{(u \otimes v) \otimes w} - e_{u \otimes (v \otimes w)}| \le 2$, so we may take $\epsilon = \frac{1}{2}(1 + b)(1 + b^2)b^{-p}$.

15. $u \le v$ implies that $(u \oplus u) \oslash 2 \le (u \oplus v) \oslash 2 \le (v \oplus v) \oslash 2$, so the condition holds for all u and v if and only if it holds whenever $u = v$. For base $b = 2$, the condition is therefore always satisfied (barring overflow); but for $b > 2$ there are numbers v such that $(v \oplus v) \oslash 2 \ne v$, hence the condition fails. [On the other hand, the formula $u \oplus ((v \ominus u) \oslash 2)$ does always give a midpoint in the correct range. *Proof.* It suffices to show that $u + (v \ominus u) \oslash 2 \le v$, i.e., $(v \ominus u) \oslash 2 \le v - u$; and it is easy to verify that round$(\frac{1}{2}\text{round}(x)) \le x$ for all $x \ge 0$.]

16. (a) Exponent changes occur at $\Sigma_{10} = 11.111111$, $\Sigma_{91} = 101.11110$, $\Sigma_{901} = 1001.1102$, $\Sigma_{9001} = 10001.020$, $\Sigma_{90009} = 100000.91$, $\Sigma_{900819} = 1000000.0$; therefore $\Sigma_{1000000} = 1109099.1$.

(b) After calculating $\sum_{k=1}^{n} 1.2345679 = 1224782.1$, (14) tries to take the square root of $-.0053187053$. But (15) and (16) are exact in this case. [If, however, $x_k = 1 + \lfloor (k-1)/2 \rfloor 10^{-7}$, (15) and (16) have errors of order n. See Chan and Lewis, *CACM* **22** (1979), 526–531, for further results on the accuracy of standard deviation calculations.]

(c) We need to show that $u \oplus ((v \ominus u) \oslash k)$ lies between u and v; see exercise 15.

17.
```
    FCMP  STJ   9F            Floating point comparison subroutine:
          JOV   OFLO          Ensure that overflow is off.
          STA   TEMP
          LDAN  TEMP          v ← −v.
    (Copy here lines 07–20 of Program 4.2.1A.)
          LDX   FV(0:0)       Set rX to zero with the sign of f_v.
          DEC1  5
          J1N   *+2
          ENT1  0             Replace large difference in exponents
          SRAX  5,1               by a smaller one.
          ADD   FU            rA ← difference of operands.
          JOV   7F            Fraction overflow: not ∼.
          CMPA  EPSILON(1:5)
          JG    8F            Jump if not ∼.
          JL    6F            Jump if ∼.
          JXZ   9F            Jump if ∼.
          JXP   1F            If |rA| = ε, check sign of rA × rX.
          JAP   9F            Jump if ∼. (rA ≠ 0)
          JMP   8F
7H        ENTX  1
          SRC   1             Make rA nonzero with same sign.
          JMP   8F
1H        JAP   8F            Jump if not ∼. (rA ≠ 0)
6H        ENTA  0
8H        CMPA  =0=           Set comparison indicator.
9H        JMP   *             Exit from subroutine. ∎
```

19. Let $\gamma_k = \delta_k = \eta_k = \sigma_k = 0$ for $k > n$. It suffices to find the coefficient of x_1, since the coefficient of x_k will be just the same except with all subscripts increased by $k - 1$. Let (f_k, g_k) denote the coefficient of x_1 in $(s_k - c_k, c_k)$ respectively. Then $f_1 = (1+\eta_1)(1-\gamma_1-\gamma_1\delta_1-\gamma_1\sigma_1-\delta_1\sigma_1-\gamma_1\delta_1\sigma_1)$, $g_1 = (1+\delta_1)(1+\eta_1)(\gamma_1+\sigma_1+\gamma_1\sigma_1)$, and $f_k = (1-\gamma_k\sigma_k-\delta_k\sigma_k-\gamma_k\delta_k\sigma_k)f_{k-1}+(\gamma_k-\eta_k+\gamma_k\delta_k+\gamma_k\eta_k+\gamma_k\delta_k\eta_k+\gamma_k\eta_k\sigma_k+\delta_k\eta_k\sigma_k+\gamma_k\delta_k\eta_k\sigma_k)g_{k-1}$, $g_k = \sigma_k(1+\gamma_k)(1+\delta_k)f_{k-1}-(1+\delta_k)(\gamma_k+\gamma_k\eta_k+\eta_k\sigma_k+\gamma_k\eta_k\sigma_k)g_{k-1}$, for $1 < k \le n$. Thus $f_n = 1 + \eta_1 - \gamma_1 + $ (4n terms of 2nd order) + (higher order terms) $= 1 + \eta_1 - \gamma_1 + O(n\epsilon^2)$ is sufficiently small. [The Kahan summation formula was first published in *CACM* **8** (1965), 40; see also *Proc. IFIP Congress* (1971), **2**, 1232, and further developments by K. Ozawa, *J. Information Proc.* **6** (1983), 226–230. Kahan observed that $s_n - c_n = \sum_{k=1}^{n}(1+\phi_k)x_k$ where $|\phi_k| \le 2\epsilon + O((n+1-k)\epsilon^2)$. For another approach to accurate summation, see R. J. Hanson, *CACM* **18** (1975), 57–58.

When some x's are negative and others are positive, we may be able to match them advantageously, as explained by T. O. Espelid, *SIAM Review* **37** (1995), 603–607. See also G. Bohlender, *IEEE Trans.* **C-26** (1977), 621–632, for algorithms that compute round$(x_1 + \cdots + x_n)$ and round$(x_1 \ldots x_n)$ *exactly*, given $\{x_1, \ldots, x_n\}$.]

20. By the proof of Theorem C, (47) fails for $e_w = p$ only if $|v| + \frac{1}{2} \geq |w - u| \geq b^{p-1} + b^{-1}$; hence $|f_u| \geq |f_v| \geq 1 - (\frac{1}{2}b - 1)b^{-p}$. We now find that a necessary and sufficient condition for failure is that $|f_w|$ is essentially rounded to 2 during the normalization process (actually to $2/b$ after scaling right for fraction overflow) — a very rare case indeed!

21. (Solution by G. W. Veltkamp.) Let $c = 2^{\lceil p/2 \rceil} + 1$; we may assume that $p \geq 2$, so c is representable. First compute $u' = u \otimes c$, $u_1 = (u \ominus u') \oplus u'$, $u_2 = u \ominus u_1$; similarly, $v' = v \otimes c$, $v_1 = (v \ominus v') \oplus v'$, $v_2 = v \ominus v_1$. Then set $w \leftarrow u \otimes v$, $w' \leftarrow (((u_1 \otimes v_1 \ominus w) \oplus (u_1 \otimes v_2)) \oplus (u_2 \otimes v_1)) \oplus (u_2 \otimes v_2)$.

It suffices to prove this when $u, v > 0$ and $e_u = e_v = p$, so that u and v are integers $\in [2^{p-1} .. 2^p)$. Then $u = u_1 + u_2$ where $2^{p-1} \leq u_1 \leq 2^p$, $u_1 \bmod 2^{\lceil p/2 \rceil} = 0$, and $|u_2| \leq 2^{\lceil p/2 \rceil - 1}$; similarly $v = v_1 + v_2$. The operations during the calculation of w' are exact, because $w - u_1 v_1$ is a multiple of 2^{p-1} such that $|w - u_1 v_1| \leq |w - uv| + |u_2 v_1 + u_1 v_2 + u_2 v_2| \leq 2^{p-1} + 2^{p+\lceil p/2 \rceil} + 2^{p-1}$; and similarly $|w - u_1 v_1 - u_1 v_2| \leq |w - uv| + |u_2 v| < 2^{p-1} + 2^{\lceil p/2 \rceil - 1 + p}$, where $w - u_1 v_1 - u_1 v_2$ is a multiple of $2^{\lceil p/2 \rceil}$.

22. We may assume that $b^{p-1} \leq u, v < b^p$. If $uv \leq b^{2p-1}$, then $x_1 = uv - r$ where $|r| \leq \frac{1}{2}b^{p-1}$, hence $x_2 = \text{round}(u - r/v) = x_0$ (since $|r/v| \leq \frac{1}{2}b^{p-1}/b^{p-1} \leq \frac{1}{2}$, and equality implies $v = b^{p-1}$ hence $r = 0$). If $uv > b^{2p-1}$, then $x_1 = uv - r$ where $|r| \leq \frac{1}{2}b^p$, hence $x_1/v = u - r/v < b^p + \frac{1}{2}b$ and $x_2 \leq b^p$. If $x_2 = b^p$, then $x_3 = x_1$ (since the condition $(b^p - \frac{1}{2})v \leq x_1$ implies that x_1 is a multiple of b^p, and we have $x_1 < b^p(v + \frac{1}{2})$). If $x_2 < b^p$ and $x_1 > b^{2p-1}$, then let $x_2 = x_1/v + q$ where $|q| \leq \frac{1}{2}$; we have $x_3 = \text{round}(x_1 + qv) = x_1$. Finally if $x_2 < b^p$, $x_1 = b^{2p-1}$, and $x_3 < b^{2p-1}$, then $x_4 = x_2$ by the first case above. This situation arises, for example, when $b = 10$, $p = 2$, $u = 19$, $v = 55$, $x_1 = 1000$, $x_2 = 18$, $x_3 = 990$.

23. If $u \geq 0$ or $u \leq -1$ we have $u \pmod 1 = u \bmod 1$, so the identity holds. If $-1 < u < 0$, then $u \pmod 1 = u \oplus 1 = u + 1 + r$ where $|r| \leq \frac{1}{2}b^{-p}$; the identity holds if and only if $\text{round}(1 + r) = 1$, so it always holds if we round to even. With the text's rounding rule the identity fails if and only if b is a multiple of 4 and $-1 < u < 0$ and $u \bmod 2b^{-p} = \frac{3}{2}b^{-p}$ (for example, $p = 3$, $b = 8$, $u = -(.0124)_8$).

24. Let $u = [u_l .. u_r]$, $v = [v_l .. v_r]$. Then $u \oplus v = [u_l \bigtriangledown v_l .. u_r \bigtriangleup v_r]$, where $x \bigtriangleup y = y \bigtriangleup x$, $x \bigtriangleup +0 = x$ for all x, $x \bigtriangleup -0 = x$ for all $x \neq +0$, $x \bigtriangleup +\infty = +\infty$ for all $x \neq -\infty$, and $x \bigtriangleup -\infty$ needn't be defined; $x \bigtriangledown y = -((-x) \bigtriangleup (-y))$. If $x \oplus y$ would overflow in normal floating point arithmetic because $x + y$ is too large, then $x \bigtriangleup y$ is $+\infty$ and $x \bigtriangledown y$ is the largest representable number.

For subtraction, let $u \ominus v = u \oplus (-v)$, where $-v = [-v_r .. -v_l]$.

Multiplication is somewhat more complicated. The correct procedure is to let $u \otimes v = [\min(u_l \bigtriangledown v_l, u_l \bigtriangledown v_r, u_r \bigtriangledown v_l, u_r \bigtriangledown v_r) .. \max(u_l \bigtriangleup v_l, u_l \bigtriangleup v_r, u_r \bigtriangleup v_l, u_r \bigtriangleup v_r)]$, where $x \bigtriangleup y = y \bigtriangleup x$, $x \bigtriangleup (-y) = -(x \bigtriangledown y) = (-x) \bigtriangleup y$; $x \bigtriangleup +0 = (+0$ for $x > 0$, -0 for $x < 0)$; $x \bigtriangleup -0 = -(x \bigtriangleup +0)$; $x \bigtriangleup +\infty = (+\infty$ for $x > +0$, $-\infty$ for $x < -0)$. (It is possible to determine the min and max simply by looking at the signs of u_l, u_r, v_l, and v_r, thereby computing only two of the eight products, except when $u_l < 0 < u_r$ and $v_l < 0 < v_r$; in the latter case we compute four products, and the answer is $[\min(u_l \bigtriangledown v_r, u_r \bigtriangledown v_l) .. \max(u_l \bigtriangleup v_l, u_r \bigtriangleup v_r)]$.)

Finally, $u \oslash v$ is undefined if $v_l < 0 < v_r$; otherwise we use the formulas for multiplication with v_l and v_r replaced respectively by v_r^{-1} and v_l^{-1}, where $x \mathbin{\triangle} y^{-1} = x \mathbin{\triangle} y$, $x \mathbin{\triangledown} y^{-1} = x \mathbin{\triangledown} y$, $(\pm 0)^{-1} = \pm\infty$, $(\pm\infty)^{-1} = \pm 0$.

[See E. R. Hansen, *Math. Comp.* **22** (1968), 374–384. An alternative scheme, in which division by 0 gives no error messages and intervals may be neighborhoods of ∞, has been proposed by W. M. Kahan. In Kahan's scheme, for example, the reciprocal of $[-1..+1]$ is $[+1..-1]$, and an attempt to multiply an interval containing 0 by an interval containing ∞ yields $[-\infty..+\infty]$, the set of all numbers. See *Numerical Analysis*, Univ. Michigan Engineering Summer Conf. Notes No. 6818 (1968).]

25. Cancellation reveals *previous* errors in the computation of u and v. For example, if ϵ is small, we often get poor accuracy when computing $f(x + \epsilon) \ominus f(x)$, because the rounded calculation of $f(x + \epsilon)$ destroys much of the information about ϵ. It is desirable to rewrite such formulas as $\epsilon \otimes g(x, \epsilon)$, where $g(x, \epsilon) = (f(x + \epsilon) - f(x))/\epsilon$ is first computed symbolically. Thus, if $f(x) = x^2$ then $g(x, \epsilon) = 2x + \epsilon$; if $f(x) = \sqrt{x}$ then $g(x, \epsilon) = 1/(\sqrt{x + \epsilon} + \sqrt{x})$.

26. Let $e = \max(e_u, e_{u'})$, $e' = \max(e_v, e_{v'})$, $e'' = \max(e_{u \oplus v}, e_{u' \oplus v'})$, and assume that $q = 0$. Then $(u \oplus v) - (u' \oplus v') \le u + v + \frac{1}{2} b^{e'' - p} - u' - v' + \frac{1}{2} b^{e'' - p} \le \epsilon b^e + \epsilon b^{e'} + b^{e'' - p}$, and $e'' \ge \max(e, e')$. Hence $u \oplus v \sim u' \oplus v'$ $(2\epsilon + b^{-p})$.

If $b = 2$ this estimate can be improved to $1.5\epsilon + b^{-p}$. For $\epsilon + b^{-p}$ is an upper bound if $u - u'$ and $v - v'$ have opposite signs, and in the other case we cannot have $e = e' = e''$.

27. The stated identity is a consequence of the fact that $1 \oslash (1 \oslash u) = u$ whenever $b^{-1} \le f_u \le b^{-1/2}$. If the latter were false, there would be integers x and y such that $b^{p-1} < x < b^{p-1/2}$ and either $y - \frac{1}{2} \le b^{2p-1}/x < b^{2p-1}/(x - \frac{1}{2}) \le y$ or $y \le b^{2p-1}/(x + \frac{1}{2}) < b^{2p-1}/x \le y + \frac{1}{2}$. But that is clearly impossible unless we have $x(x + \frac{1}{2}) > b^{2p-1}$, yet the latter condition implies $y = \lfloor b^{p-1/2} \rfloor = x$.

28. See *Math. Comp.* **32** (1978), 227–232.

29. When $b = 2$ and $p = 1$ and $x > 0$, we have $\operatorname{round}(x) = 2^{e(x)}$ where $e(x) = \lfloor \lg \frac{4}{3} x \rfloor$. Let $f(x) = x^\alpha$ and let $t(n) = \lfloor \lfloor \alpha n + \lg \frac{4}{3} \rfloor / \alpha + \lg \frac{4}{3} \rfloor$. Then $h(2^e) = 2^{t(e)}$. When $\alpha = .99$ we find $h(2^e) = 2^{e-1}$ for $41 < e \le 58$.

31. According to the theory in Section 4.5.3, the convergents to the continued fraction $\sqrt{3} = 1 + /\!/1, 2, 1, 2, \ldots /\!/$ are $p_n/q_n = K_{n+1}(1, 1, 2, 1, 2, \ldots)/K_n(1, 2, 1, 2, \ldots)$. These convergents are excellent approximations to $\sqrt{3}$, hence $3q_n^2 \approx p_n^2$; in fact, $3q_n^2 - p_n^2 = 2 - 3(n \bmod 2)$. The example given is $2p_{31}^2 + (3q_{31}^2 - p_{31}^2)(3q_{31}^2 + p_{31}^2) = 2p_{31}^2 - (p_{31}^2 - 1 + p_{31}^2) = 1$. Floating point subtraction of p_{31}^2 from $3q_{31}^2$ yields zero, unless we can represent $3q_{31}^2$ almost perfectly; subtracting p_{31}^4 from $9q_{31}^4$ generally gives rounding errors much larger than $2p_{31}^2$. Similar examples can be based on continued fraction approximations to any algebraic number.

32. (J. Ziegler Hunts, 2014.) $a = 1/2$ and $b \bmod 1 = 1/4$.

SECTION 4.2.3

1. First, $(w_m, w_l) = (.573, .248)$; then $w_m v_l / v_m = .290$; so the answer is $(.572, .958)$. This in fact is the correct result to six decimals.

2. The answer is not affected, since the normalization routine truncates to eight places and can never look at this particular byte position. (Scaling to the left occurs at most once during normalization, since the inputs are normalized.)

3. Overflow obviously cannot occur at line 09, since we are adding two-byte quantities, or at line 22, since we are adding four-byte quantities. In line 30 we are computing the sum of three four-byte quantities, so this cannot overflow. Finally, in line 32, overflow is impossible because the product $f_u f_v$ must be less than unity.

4. Insert 'JOV OFLO; ENT1 0' between lines 03 and 04. Also replace lines 21–22 by 'ADD TEMP(ABS); JNOV *+2; INC1 1', and change lines 28–31 to 'SLAX 5; ADD TEMP; JNOV *+2; INC1 1; ENTX 0,1; SRC 5'. This adds five lines of code and only 1, 2, or 3 units of execution time.

5. Insert 'JOV OFLO' after line 06. Change lines 23, 31, 39 respectively to 'SRAX 0,1', 'SLAX 5', 'ADD ACC'. Between lines 40 and 41, insert 'DEC2 1; JNOV DNORM; INC2 1; INCX 1; SRC 1'. (It's tempting to remove the 'DEC2 1' in favor of 'STZ EXPO', but then 'INC2 1' might overflow rI2!) This adds six lines of code; the running time *decreases* by $3u$, unless there is fraction overflow, when it increases by $7u$.

6.

```
  DOUBLE STJ   EXITDF      Convert to double precision:
         ENTX  0           Clear rX.
         STA   TEMP
         LD2   TEMP(EXP)   rI2 ← e.
         INC2  QQ-Q        Correct for difference in excess.
         STZ   EXPO        EXPO ← 0.
         SLAX  1           Remove exponent.
         JMP   DNORM       Normalize and exit.

  SINGLE STJ   EXITF       Convert to single precision:
         JOV   OFLO        Ensure that overflow is off.
         STA   TEMP
         LD2   TEMP(EXPD)  rI2 ← e.
         DEC2  QQ-Q        Correct for difference in excess.
         SLAX  2           Remove exponent.
         JMP   NORM        Normalize, round, and exit.  ▮
```

7. All three routines give zero as the answer if and only if the exact result would be zero, so we need not worry about zero denominators in the expressions for relative error. The worst case of the addition routine is pretty bad: Visualized in decimal notation, if the inputs are 1.0000000 and $-.99999999$, the answer is b^{-7} instead of b^{-8}; thus the maximum relative error δ_1 is $b - 1$, where b is the byte size.

For multiplication and division, we may assume that both operands are positive and have the same exponent QQ. The maximum error in multiplication is readily bounded by considering Fig. 4: When $uv \geq 1/b$, we have $0 \leq uv - u \otimes v < 3b^{-9} + (b-1)b^{-9}$, so the relative error is bounded by $(b+2)b^{-8}$. When $1/b^2 \leq uv < 1/b$, we have $0 \leq uv - u \otimes v < 3b^{-9}$, so the relative error in this case is bounded by $3b^{-9}/uv \leq 3b^{-7}$. We take δ_2 to be the larger of the two estimates, namely $3b^{-7}$.

Division requires a more careful analysis of Program D. The quantity actually computed by the subroutine is $\alpha - \delta - b\epsilon((\alpha - \delta'')(\beta - \delta') - \delta''') - \delta_n$ where $\alpha = (u_m + \epsilon u_l)/bv_m$, $\beta = v_l/bv_m$, and the nonnegative truncation errors $(\delta, \delta', \delta'', \delta''')$ are respectively less than $(b^{-10}, b^{-5}, b^{-5}, b^{-6})$; finally δ_n (the truncation during normalization) is nonnegative and less than either b^{-9} or b^{-8}, depending on whether scaling occurs or not. The actual value of the quotient is $\alpha/(1 + b\epsilon\beta) = \alpha - b\epsilon\alpha\beta + b^2\alpha\beta^2\delta''''$, where δ'''' is the nonnegative error due to truncation of the infinite series (2); here $\delta'''' < \epsilon^2 = b^{-10}$, since it is an alternating series. The relative error is therefore the absolute value of $(b\epsilon\delta' + b\epsilon\delta''\beta/\alpha + b\epsilon\delta'''/\alpha) - (\delta/\alpha + b\epsilon\delta'\delta''/\alpha + b^2\beta^2\delta'''' + \delta_n/\alpha)$, times

$(1 + b\epsilon\beta)$. The positive terms in this expression are bounded by $b^{-9} + b^{-8} + b^{-8}$, and the negative terms are bounded by $b^{-8} + b^{-12} + b^{-8}$ plus the contribution by the normalizing phase, which can be about b^{-7} in magnitude. It is therefore clear that the potentially greatest part of the relative error comes during the normalization phase, and that $\delta_3 = (b + 2)b^{-8}$ is a safe upper bound for the relative error.

8. Addition: If $e_u \leq e_v + 1$, the entire relative error occurs during the normalization phase, so it is bounded above by b^{-7}. If $e_u \geq e_v + 2$, and if the signs are the same, again the entire error may be ascribed to normalization; if the signs are opposite, the error due to shifting digits out of the register is in the opposite direction from the subsequent error introduced during normalization. Both of these errors are bounded by b^{-7}, hence $\delta_1 = b^{-7}$. (This is substantially better than the result in exercise 7.)

Multiplication: An analysis as in exercise 7 gives $\delta_2 = (b + 2)b^{-8}$.

SECTION 4.2.4

1. Since fraction overflow can occur only when the operands have the same sign, this is the probability that fraction overflow occurs divided by the probability that the operands have the same sign, namely, $7\%/(\frac{1}{2}(91\%)) \approx 15\%$.

3. $\log_{10} 2.4 - \log_{10} 2.3 \approx 1.84834\%$.

4. The pages would be uniformly gray.

5. The probability that $10f_U \leq r$ is $(r - 1)/10 + (r - 1)/100 + \cdots = (r - 1)/9$. So in this case the leading digits are *uniformly* distributed; for example, the leading digit is 1 with probability $\frac{1}{9}$.

6. The probability that there are three leading zero bits is $\log_{16} 2 = \frac{1}{4}$; the probability that there are two leading zero bits is $\log_{16} 4 - \log_{16} 2 = \frac{1}{4}$; and similarly for the other two cases. The "average" number of leading zero bits is $1\frac{1}{2}$, so the "average" number of "significant bits" is $p + \frac{1}{2}$. The worst case, $p - 1$ bits, occurs however with rather high probability. In practice, it is usually necessary to base error estimates on the worst case, since a chain of calculations is only as strong as its weakest link. In the error analysis of Section 4.2.2, the upper bound on relative rounding error for floating hex is 2^{1-p}. In the binary case we can have $p + 1$ significant bits in all normalized numbers (see exercise 4.2.1–3), with relative rounding errors bounded by 2^{-1-p}. Extensive computational experience confirms that floating binary produces significantly more accurate results than the equivalent floating hex, even when the binary numbers have a precision of p bits instead of $p + 1$.

Tables 1 and 2 show that hexadecimal arithmetic can be done a little faster, since fewer cycles are needed when scaling to the right or normalizing to the left. But this fact is insignificant compared to the substantial advantages of $b = 2$ over other radices (see also Theorem 4.2.2C and exercises 4.2.2–13, 15, 21), especially since floating binary can be made as fast as floating hex with only a tiny increase in total processor cost.

7. For example, suppose that $\sum_m (F(10^{km} \cdot 5^k) - F(10^{km})) = \log 5^k / \log 10^k$ and also that $\sum_m (F(10^{km} \cdot 4^k) - F(10^{km})) = \log 4^k / \log 10^k$; then

$$\sum_m (F(10^{km} \cdot 5^k) - F(10^{km} \cdot 4^k)) = \log_{10} \frac{5}{4}$$

for all k. But now let ϵ be a small positive number, and choose $\delta > 0$ so that $F(x) < \epsilon$ for $0 < x < \delta$, and choose $M > 0$ so that $F(x) > 1 - \epsilon$ for $x > M$. We can take k so large that $10^{-k} \cdot 5^k < \delta$ and $4^k > M$; hence by the monotonicity of F,

$$\sum_m \left(F(10^{km} \cdot 5^k) - F(10^{km} \cdot 4^k) \right)$$

$$\leq \sum_{m<0} \left(F(10^{km} \cdot 5^k) - F(10^{k(m-1)} \cdot 5^k) \right) + \sum_{m \geq 0} \left(F(10^{k(m+1)} \cdot 4^k) - F(10^{km} \cdot 4^k) \right)$$

$$= F(10^{-k} \cdot 5^k) + 1 - F(4^k) < 2\epsilon.$$

8. When $s > r$, $P_0(10^n s)$ is 1 for small n, and 0 when $\lfloor 10^n s \rfloor > \lfloor 10^n r \rfloor$. The least n for which this happens may be arbitrarily large, so no uniform bound can be given for $N_0(\epsilon)$ independent of s. (In general, calculus textbooks prove that such a uniform bound would imply that the limit function $S_0(s)$ would be continuous, and it isn't.)

9. Let q_1, q_2, ... be such that $P_0(n) = q_1 \binom{n-1}{0} + q_2 \binom{n-1}{1} + \cdots$ for all n. It follows that $P_m(n) = 1 - {}^m q_1 \binom{n-1}{0} + 2^{-m} q_2 \binom{n-1}{1} + \cdots$ for all m and n.

10. When $1 < r < 10$ the generating function $C(z)$ has simple poles at the points $1 + w_n$, where $w_n = 2\pi n i / \ln 10$, hence

$$C(z) = \frac{\log_{10} r - 1}{1 - z} + \sum_{n \neq 0} \frac{1 + w_n}{w_n} \frac{e^{-w_n \ln r} - 1}{(\ln 10)(z - 1 - w_n)} + E(z)$$

where $E(z)$ is analytic in the entire plane. Thus if $\theta = \arctan(2\pi / \ln 10)$,

$$c_m = \log_{10} r - 1 - \frac{2}{\ln 10} \sum_{n > 0} \Re \left(\frac{e^{-w_n \ln r} - 1}{w_n (1 + w_n)^m} \right) + e_m$$

$$= \log_{10} r - 1 + \frac{\sin(m\theta + 2\pi \log_{10} r) - \sin(m\theta)}{\pi (1 + 4\pi^2 / (\ln 10)^2)^{m/2}} + O\left(\frac{1}{(1 + 16\pi^2 / (\ln 10)^2)^{m/2}} \right).$$

11. When $(\log_b U) \bmod 1$ is uniformly distributed in $[0..1)$, so is $(\log_b 1/U) \bmod 1 = (1 - \log_b U) \bmod 1$.

12. We have

$$h(z) = \int_{1/b}^z f(x) \, dx \, g(z/bx)/bx + \int_z^1 f(x) \, dx \, g(z/x)/x;$$

consequently

$$\frac{h(z) - l(z)}{l(z)} = \int_{1/b}^z f(x) \, dx \, \frac{g(z/bx) - l(z/bx)}{l(z/bx)} + \int_z^1 f(x) \, dx \, \frac{g(z/x) - l(z/x)}{l(z/x)}.$$

Since $f(x) \geq 0$, $|(h(z) - l(z))/l(z)| \leq \int_{1/b}^z f(x) \, dx \, A(g) + \int_z^1 f(x) \, dx \, A(g)$ for all z, hence $A(h) \leq A(g)$. By symmetry, $A(h) \leq A(f)$. [*Bell System Tech. J.* **49** (1970), 1609–1625.]

13. Let $X = (\log_b U) \bmod 1$ and $Y = (\log_b V) \bmod 1$, so that X and Y are independently and uniformly distributed in $[0..1)$. No left shift is needed if and only if $X + Y \geq 1$, and that occurs with probability $1/2$.

(Similarly, the probability is $1/2$ that floating point division by Algorithm 4.2.1M needs no normalization shifts; this analysis needs only the weaker assumption that both of the operands independently have the *same* distribution.)

14. For convenience, the calculations are shown here for $b = 10$. If $k = 0$, the probability of a carry is

$$\left(\frac{1}{\ln 10}\right)^2 \int_{\substack{1 \le x, y \le 10 \\ x+y \ge 10}} \frac{dx}{x} \frac{dy}{y}.$$

(See Fig. A–7.) The value of the integral is

$$\int_0^{10} \frac{dy}{y} \int_{10-y}^{10} \frac{dx}{x} - 2 \int_0^1 \frac{dy}{y} \int_{10-y}^{10} \frac{dx}{x},$$

and

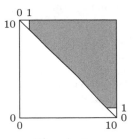

Fig. A–7.

$$\int_0^t \frac{dy}{y} \ln\left(\frac{1}{1 - y/10}\right) = \int_0^t \left(\frac{1}{10} + \frac{y}{200} + \frac{y^2}{3000} + \cdots\right) dy = \frac{t}{10} + \frac{t^2}{400} + \frac{t^3}{9000} + \cdots.$$

(The latter integral is essentially a "dilogarithm.") Hence the probability of a carry when $k = 0$ is $(1/\ln 10)^2 (\pi^2/6 - 2\sum_{n \ge 1} 1/n^2 10^n) \approx .27154$. [*Note:* When $b = 2$ and $k = 0$, fraction overflow *always* occurs, so this derivation proves that $\sum_{n \ge 1} 1/n^2 2^n = \pi^2/12 - (\ln 2)^2/2$.]

When $k > 0$, the probability is

$$\left(\frac{1}{\ln 10}\right)^2 \int_{10-k}^{10^{1-k}} \frac{dy}{y} \int_{10-y}^{10} \frac{dx}{x} = \left(\frac{1}{\ln 10}\right)^2 \left(\sum_{n \ge 1} \frac{1}{n^2 10^{nk}} - \sum_{n \ge 1} \frac{1}{n^2 10^{n(k+1)}}\right).$$

Thus when $b = 10$, fraction overflow should occur with approximate probability $.272p_0 + .017p_1 + .002p_2 + \cdots$. When $b = 2$ the corresponding figures are $p_0 + .655p_1 + .288p_2 + .137p_3 + .067p_4 + .033p_5 + .016p_6 + .008p_7 + .004p_8 + .002p_9 + .001p_{10} + \cdots$.

Now if we use the probabilities from Table 1, dividing by $.91$ to eliminate zero operands and assuming that the probabilities are independent of the operand signs, we predict a probability of about 14 percent when $b = 10$, instead of the 15 percent in exercise 1. For $b = 2$, we predict about 48 percent, while the table yields 44 percent. These results are certainly in agreement within the limits of experimental error.

15. When $k = 0$, the leading digit is 1 if and only if there is a carry. (It is possible for fraction overflow and subsequent rounding to yield a leading digit of 2, when $b \ge 4$, but we are ignoring rounding in this exercise.) The probability of fraction overflow is approximately $.272$, as shown in the previous exercise, and $.272 < \log_{10} 2$.

When $k > 0$, the leading digit is 1 with probability

$$\left(\frac{1}{\ln 10}\right)^2 \left(\int_{10-k}^{10^{1-k}} \frac{dy}{y} \int_{\substack{1 \le x < 2-y \\ \text{or } 10-y \le x < 10}} \frac{dx}{x}\right) < \left(\frac{1}{\ln 10}\right)^2 \left(\int_{10-k}^{10^{1-k}} \frac{dy}{y} \int_{1 \le x \le 2} \frac{dx}{x}\right) = \log_{10} 2.$$

16. To prove the hint [which is due to Landau, *Prace Matematyczno-Fizyczne* **21** (1910), 103–113], assume first that $\limsup a_n = \lambda > 0$. Let $\epsilon = \lambda/(\lambda + 4M)$ and choose N so that $|a_1 + \cdots + a_n| < \frac{1}{10}\epsilon\lambda n$ for all $n > N$. Let $n > N/(1 - \epsilon)$, $n > 5/\epsilon$ be such that $a_n > \frac{1}{2}\lambda$. Then, by induction, $a_{n-k} \ge a_n - kM/(n - \epsilon n) > \frac{1}{4}\lambda$ for $0 \le k < \epsilon n$, and $\sum_{n-\epsilon n < k \le n} a_k \ge \frac{1}{4}\lambda(\epsilon n - 1) > \frac{1}{5}\lambda\epsilon n$. But

$$\left|\sum_{n-\epsilon n < k \le n} a_k\right| = \left|\sum_{1 \le k \le n} a_k - \sum_{1 \le k \le n-\epsilon n} a_k\right| \le \frac{1}{5}\epsilon\lambda n$$

since $n - \epsilon n > N$. A similar contradiction applies if $\liminf a_n < 0$.

Assuming that $P_{m+1}(n) \to \lambda$ as $n \to \infty$, let $a_k = P_m(k) - \lambda$. If $m > 0$, the a_k satisfy the hypotheses of the hint (see Eq. 4.2.2–(15)), since $0 \le P_m(k) \le 1$; hence $P_m(n) \to \lambda$.

17. See *J. Math. Soc. Japan* **4** (1952), 313–322. (The fact that harmonic probability extends ordinary probability follows from a theorem of Cesàro, [*Atti della Reale Accademia dei Lincei, Rendiconti* (4) **4** (1888), 452–457]. Persi Diaconis [Ph.D. thesis (Harvard University, 1974)] has shown among other things that the definition of probability by repeated averaging is weaker than harmonic probability, in the following precise sense: If $\lim_{m\to\infty} \lim\inf_{n\to\infty} P_m(n) = \lim_{m\to\infty} \lim\sup_{n\to\infty} P_m(n) = \lambda$ then the harmonic probability is λ. On the other hand the statement "$10^{k^2} \le n < 10^{k^2+k}$ for some integer $k > 0$" has harmonic probability $\frac{1}{2}$, while repeated averaging never settles down to give it any particular probability.)

18. Let $p(a) = P(L_a)$ and $p(a, b) = \sum_{a \le k < b} p(k)$ for $1 \le a < b$. Since $L_a = L_{10a} \cup L_{10a+1} \cup \cdots \cup L_{10a+9}$ for all a, we have $p(a) = p(10a, 10(a+1))$ by (i). Furthermore since $P(S) = P(2S) + P(2S+1)$ by (i), (ii), (iii), we have $p(a) = p(2a, 2(a+1))$. It follows that $p(a, b) = p(2^m 10^n a, 2^m 10^n b)$ for all $m, n \ge 0$.

If $1 < b/a < b'/a'$, then $p(a, b) \le p(a', b')$. The reason is that there exist integers m, n, m', n' such that $2^{m'} 10^{n'} a' \le 2^m 10^n a < 2^m 10^n b \le 2^{m'} 10^{n'} b'$ as a consequence of the fact that $\log 2/\log 10$ is irrational, hence we can apply (v). (See exercise 3.5–22 with $k = 1$ and $U_n = n \log 2/\log 10$.) In particular, $p(a) \ge p(a+1)$, and it follows that $p(a, b)/p(a, b+1) \ge (b - a)/(b + 1 - a)$. (See Eq. 4.2.2–(15).)

Now we can prove that $p(a, b) = p(a', b')$ whenever $b/a = b'/a'$; for $p(a, b) = p(10^n a, 10^n b) \le c_n p(10^n a, 10^n b - 1) \le c_n p(a', b')$, for arbitrarily large values of n, where $c_n = 10^n (b - a)/(10^n (b - a) - 1) = 1 + O(10^{-n})$.

For any positive integer n we have $p(a^n, b^n) = p(a^n, ba^{n-1}) + p(ba^{n-1}, b^2 a^{n-2}) + \cdots + p(b^{n-1} a, b^n) = n p(a, b)$. If $10^m \le a^n \le 10^{m+1}$ and $10^{m'} \le b^n \le 10^{m'+1}$, then $p(10^{m+1}, 10^{m'}) \le p(a^n, b^n) \le p(10^m, 10^{m'+1})$ by (v). But $p(1, 10) = 1$ by (iv), hence $p(10^m, 10^{m'}) = m' - m$ for all $m' \ge m$. We conclude that $\lfloor \log_{10} b^n \rfloor - \lfloor \log_{10} a^n \rfloor - 1 \le n p(a, b) \le \lfloor \log_{10} b^n \rfloor + \lfloor \log_{10} a^n \rfloor + 1$ for all n, and $p(a, b) = \log_{10}(b/a)$.

[This exercise was inspired by D. I. A. Cohen, who proved a slightly weaker result in *J. Combinatorial Theory* **A20** (1976), 367–370.]

19. Equivalently, $\langle (\log_{10} F_n) \bmod 1 \rangle$ is equidistributed in the sense of Definition 3.5B. Since $\log_{10} F_n = n \log_{10} \phi - \log_{10} \sqrt{5} + O(\phi^{-2n})$ by 1.2.8–(14), this is equivalent to equidistribution of $\langle n \log_{10} \phi \rangle$, which follows from ex. 3.5–22. [*Fibonacci Quarterly* **5** (1967), 137–140.] The same proof shows that the sequences $\langle b^n \rangle$ obey the logarithmic law for all integers $b > 1$ that aren't powers of 10 [Yaglom and Yaglom, *Challenging Problems with Elementary Solutions* (Moscow: 1954; English translation, 1964), Problem 91b].

Notes: Many other sequences of integers have this property. For example, Persi Diaconis [*Annals of Probability* **5** (1977), 72–81] showed that $\langle n! \rangle$ is one such sequence, and that binomial coefficients obey the logarithmic law too, in the sense that

$$\lim_{n \to \infty} \frac{1}{n+1} \sum_{k=0}^{n} [10 f_{\binom{n}{k}} < r] = \log_{10} r.$$

P. Schatte [*Math. Nachrichten* **148** (1990), 137–144] proved that the denominators of continued fraction approximations have logarithmic fraction parts, whenever the partial quotients have a repeating pattern with polynomial variation as in exercise

4.5.3–16. One interesting open question is whether the sequence $\langle 2!, (2!)!, ((2!)!)!, \ldots \rangle$ has logarithmic fraction parts; see J. H. Conway and M. J. T. Guy, *Eureka* **25** (1962), 18–19.

SECTION 4.3.1

2. If the ith number to be added is $u_i = (u_{i(n-1)} \ldots u_{i1} u_{i0})_b$, use Algorithm A with step A2 changed to the following:

A2'. [Add digits.] Set

$$w_j \leftarrow (u_{1j} + \cdots + u_{mj} + k) \bmod b, \quad \text{and} \quad k \leftarrow \lfloor (u_{1j} + \cdots + u_{mj} + k)/b \rfloor.$$

(The maximum value of k is $m - 1$, so step A3 would have to be altered if $m > b$.)

3.

	ENN1 N	1	
	JOV OFLO	1	Ensure that overflow is off.
	ENTX 0	1	$k \leftarrow 0$.
2H	SLAX 5	N	(rX $\equiv$ next value of k)
	ENT3 M*N,1	N	$(\text{LOC}(u_{ij}) \equiv \text{U} + n(i-1) + j)$
3H	ADD U,3	MN	rA $\leftarrow$ rA $+ u_{ij}$.
	JNOV *+2	MN	
	INCX 1	K	Carry one.
	DEC3 N	MN	Repeat for $m \geq i \geq 1$.
	J3NN 3B	MN	(rI3 $\equiv n(i-1) + j$)
	STA W+N,1	N	$w_j \leftarrow$ rA.
	INC1 1	N	
	J1N 2B	N	Repeat for $0 \leq j < n$.
	STX W+N	1	Store final carry in w_n. $\blacksquare$

Running time, assuming that $K = \frac{1}{2}MN$, is $5.5MN + 7N + 4$ cycles.

4. We may make the following assertion before A1: "$n \geq 1$; and $0 \leq u_i, v_i < b$ for $0 \leq i < n$." Before A2, we assert: "$0 \leq j < n$; $0 \leq u_i, v_i < b$ for $0 \leq i < n$; $0 \leq w_i < b$ for $0 \leq i < j$; $0 \leq k \leq 1$; and $(u_{j-1} \ldots u_0)_b + (v_{j-1} \ldots v_0)_b = (k w_{j-1} \ldots w_0)_b$." The latter statement means more precisely that

$$\sum_{0 \leq l < j} u_l b^l + \sum_{0 \leq l < j} v_l b^l = k b^j + \sum_{0 \leq l < j} w_l b^l.$$

Before A3, we assert: "$0 \leq j < n$; $0 \leq u_i, v_i < b$ for $0 \leq i < n$; $0 \leq w_i < b$ for $0 \leq i \leq j$; $0 \leq k \leq 1$; and $(u_j \ldots u_0)_b + (v_j \ldots v_0)_b = (k w_j \ldots w_0)_b$." After A3, we assert that $0 \leq w_i < b$ for $0 \leq i < n$; $0 \leq w_n \leq 1$; and $(u_{n-1} \ldots u_0)_b + (v_{n-1} \ldots v_0)_b = (w_n \ldots w_0)_b$.

It is a simple matter to complete the proof by verifying the necessary implications between the assertions and by showing that the algorithm always terminates.

5. B1. Set $j \leftarrow n - 1$, $w_n \leftarrow 0$.

B2. Set $t \leftarrow u_j + v_j$, $w_j \leftarrow t \bmod b$, $i \leftarrow j$.

B3. If $t \geq b$, set $i \leftarrow i + 1$, $t \leftarrow w_i + 1$, $w_i \leftarrow t \bmod b$, and repeat this step until $t < b$.

B4. Decrease j by one, and if $j \geq 0$ go back to B2. $\blacksquare$

6. C1. Set $j \leftarrow n - 1$, $i \leftarrow n$, $r \leftarrow 0$.

C2. Set $t \leftarrow u_j + v_j$. If $t \geq b$, set $w_i \leftarrow r + 1$ and $w_k \leftarrow 0$ for $i > k > j$; then set $i \leftarrow j$ and $r \leftarrow t \bmod b$. Otherwise if $t < b - 1$, set $w_i \leftarrow r$ and $w_k \leftarrow b - 1$ for $i > k > j$; then set $i \leftarrow j$ and $r \leftarrow t$.

C3. Decrease j by one. If $j \geq 0$, go back to C2; otherwise set $w_i \leftarrow r$, and $w_k \leftarrow b - 1$ for $i > k \geq 0$. ∎

7. When $j = n - 3$, for example, we have $k = 0$ with probability $(b + 1)/2b$; $k = 1$ with probability $((b - 1)/2b)(1 - 1/b)$, namely the probability that a carry occurs and that the preceding digit wasn't $b - 1$; $k = 2$ with probability $((b-1)/2b)(1/b)(1-1/b)$; and $k = 3$ with probability $((b - 1)/2b)(1/b)(1/b)(1)$. For fixed k we may add the probabilities as j varies from $n - 1$ to 0; this gives the mean number of times the carry propagates back k places,

$$m_k = \frac{b - 1}{2b^k}\left((n + 1 - k)\left(1 - \frac{1}{b}\right) + \frac{1}{b}\right).$$

As a check, we find that the average number of carries is

$$m_1 + 2m_2 + \cdots + nm_n = \frac{1}{2}\left(n - \frac{1}{b - 1}\left(1 - \left(\frac{1}{b}\right)^n\right)\right),$$

in agreement with (6).

8.

	ENT1	N-1	1	3H	LDA	W,2	K
	JOV	OFLO	1		INCA	1	K
	STZ	W+N	1		STA	W,2	K
2H	LDA	U,1	N		INC2	1	K
	ADD	V,1	N		JOV	3B	K
	STA	W,1	N	4H	DEC1	1	N
	JNOV	4F	N		J1NN	2B	N ∎
	ENT2	1,1	L				

The running time depends on L, the number of positions in which $u_j + v_j \geq b$; and on K, the total number of carries. It is not difficult to see that K is the same quantity that appears in Program A. The analysis in the text shows that L has the average value $N((b - 1)/2b)$, and K has the average value $\frac{1}{2}(N - b^{-1} - b^{-2} - \cdots - b^{-n})$. So if we ignore terms of order $1/b$, the running time is $9N + L + 7K + 3 \approx 13N + 3$ cycles.

9. Replace "b" by "b_j" everywhere in step A2.

10. If lines 06 and 07 were interchanged, we would almost always have overflow, but register A might have a negative value at line 08, so this would not work. If the instructions on lines 05 and 06 were interchanged, the sequence of overflows occurring in the program would be slightly different in some cases, but the program would still be right.

11. This is equivalent to lexicographic comparison of strings: (i) Set $j \leftarrow n - 1$; (ii) if $u_j < v_j$, terminate $[u < v]$; if $u_j = v_j$ and $j = 0$, terminate $[u = v]$; if $u_j = v_j$ and $j > 0$, set $j \leftarrow j - 1$ and repeat (ii); if $u_j > v_j$, terminate $[u > v]$. This algorithm tends to be quite fast, since there is usually low probability that j will have to decrease very much before we encounter a case with $u_j \neq v_j$.

12. Use Algorithm S with $u_j = 0$ and $v_j = w_j$. Another borrow will occur at the end of the algorithm; this time it should be ignored.

13.

	ENN1	N	1	MUL	V	N	STA	W+N,1	N

```
13.    ENN1  N      1        MUL   V       N     STA  W+N,1  N
       JOV   OFLO   1        SLC   5       N     INC1 1      N
       ENTX  0      1        ADD   CARRY   N     J1N  2B     N
2H STX CARRY  N              JNOV  *+2     N     STX  W+N    1
       LDA   U+N,1  N        INCX  1       K
```

The running time is $23N + K + 5$ cycles, and K is roughly $\frac{1}{2}N$.

14. The key inductive assertion is the one that should be valid at the beginning of step M4; all others are readily filled in from this one, which is as follows: $0 \leq i < m$; $0 \leq j < n$; $0 \leq u_l < b$ for $0 \leq l < m$; $0 \leq v_l < b$ for $0 \leq l < n$; $0 \leq w_l < b$ for $0 \leq l < j + m$; $0 \leq k < b$; and, in the notation of the answer to exercise 4,

$$(w_{j+m-1} \ldots w_0)_b + kb^{i+j} = u \times (v_{j-1} \ldots v_0)_b + (u_{i-1} \ldots u_0)_b \times v_j b^j.$$

15. The error is nonnegative and less than $(n-2)b^{-n-1}$. [Similarly, if we ignore the products with $i + j > n + 3$, the error is bounded by $(n-3)b^{-n-2}$, etc.; but, in some cases, we must compute all of the products if we want to get the true rounded result. Further analysis shows that correctly rounded results of multiprecision floating point fractions can almost always be obtained by doing only about half the work needed to compute the full double-length product; moreover, a simple test will identify the rare cases for which full precision is needed. See W. Krandick and J. R. Johnson, *Proc. IEEE Symp. Computer Arithmetic* **11** (1993), 228–233.]

16. **Q1.** Set $r \leftarrow 0$, $j \leftarrow n - 1$.

Q2. Set $w_j \leftarrow \lfloor (rb + u_j)/v \rfloor$, $r \leftarrow (rb + u_j) \bmod v$.

Q3. Decrease j by 1, and return to Q2 if $j \geq 0$. ∎

17. $u/v > u_n b^n/(v_{n-1} + 1)b^{n-1} = b(1 - 1/(v_{n-1} + 1)) > b(1 - 1/(b/2)) = b - 2$.

18. $(u_n b + u_{n-1})/(v_{n-1} + 1) \leq u/(v_{n-1} + 1)b^{n-1} < u/v$.

19. $u - \hat{q}v \leq u - \hat{q}v_{n-1}b^{n-1} - \hat{q}v_{n-2}b^{n-2} = u_{n-2}b^{n-2} + \cdots + u_0 + \hat{r}b^{n-1} - \hat{q}v_{n-2}b^{n-2} < b^{n-2}(u_{n-2} + 1 + \hat{r}b - \hat{q}v_{n-2}) \leq 0$. Since $u - \hat{q}v < 0$, $q < \hat{q}$.

20. If $q \leq \hat{q} - 2$, then $u < (\hat{q} - 1)v < \hat{q}(v_{n-1}b^{n-1} + (v_{n-2} + 1)b^{n-2}) - v < \hat{q}v_{n-1}b^{n-1} + \hat{q}v_{n-2}b^{n-2} + b^{n-1} - v \leq \hat{q}v_{n-1}b^{n-1} + (b\hat{r} + u_{n-2})b^{n-2} + b^{n-1} - v = u_n b^n + u_{n-1}b^{n-1} + u_{n-2}b^{n-2} + b^{n-1} - v \leq u_n b^n + u_{n-1}b^{n-1} + u_{n-2}b^{n-2} \leq u$. In other words, $u < u$, and this is a contradiction.

21. (Solution by G. K. Goyal.) The inequality $\hat{q}v_{n-2} \leq b\hat{r} + u_{n-2}$ implies that we have $\hat{q} \leq (u_n b^2 + u_{n-1}b + u_{n-2})/(v_{n-1}b + v_{n-2}) \leq u/((v_{n-1}b + v_{n-2})b^{n-2})$. Now $u \bmod v = u - qv = v(1 - \alpha)$ where $0 < \alpha = 1 + q - u/v \leq \hat{q} - u/v \leq u(1/((v_{n-1}b + v_{n-2})b^{n-2}) - 1/v) = u(v_{n-3}b^{n-3} + \cdots)/((v_{n-1}b + v_{n-2})b^{n-2}v) < u/(v_{n-1}bv) \leq \hat{q}/(v_{n-1}b) \leq (b-1)/(v_{n-1}b)$, and this is at most $2/b$ since $v_{n-1} \geq \frac{1}{2}(b-1)$.

22. Let $u = 4100$, $v = 588$. We first try $\hat{q} = \lfloor \frac{41}{5} \rfloor = 8$, but $8 \cdot 8 > 10(41 - 40) + 0$. Then we set $\hat{q} = 7$, and now we find $7 \cdot 8 < 10(41 - 35) + 0$. But 7 times 588 equals 4116, so the true quotient is $q = 6$. (Incidentally, this example shows that Theorem B cannot be improved under the given hypotheses, when $b = 10$. Similarly, when $b = 2^{16}$ we can let $u = (7\text{fff}800100000000)_{16}$, $v = (800080020005)_{16}$.)

23. Obviously $v\lfloor b/(v+1) \rfloor < (v+1)\lfloor b/(v+1) \rfloor \leq b$; and the lower bound certainly holds if $v \geq b/2$. Otherwise $v\lfloor b/(v+1) \rfloor \geq v(b-v)/(v+1) \geq (b-1)/2 > \lfloor b/2 \rfloor - 1$.

24. The approximate probability is only $\log_b 2$, not $\frac{1}{2}$. (For example, if $b = 2^{32}$, the probability that $v_{n-1} \geq 2^{31}$ is approximately $\frac{1}{32}$; this is still high enough to warrant the special test for $d = 1$ in steps D1 and D8.)

25.

002		ENTA	1	1
003		ADD	V+N−1	1
004		STA	TEMP	1
005		ENTA	1	1
006		JOV	1F	1	Jump if $v_{n-1} = b - 1$.
007		ENTX	0	1
008		DIV	TEMP	1	Otherwise compute $\lfloor b/(v_{n-1}+1) \rfloor$.
009		JOV	DIVBYZERO	1	Jump if $v_{n-1} = 0$.
010	1H	STA	D	1
011		DECA	1	1
012		JANZ	*+3	1	Jump if $d \neq 1$.
013		STZ	U+M+N	$1 - A$	Set $u_{m+n} \leftarrow 0$.
014		JMP	D2	$1 - A$
015		ENN1	N	A	Multiply v by d.
016		ENTX	0	A
017	2H	STX	CARRY	AN
018		LDA	V+N,1	AN
019		MUL	D	AN
...					(as in exercise 13)
026		J1N	2B	AN
027		ENN1	M+N	A	(Now rX = 0.)
028	2H	STX	CARRY	$A(M + N)$	Multiply u by d.
029		LDA	U+M+N,1	$A(M + N)$
...					(as in exercise 13)
037		J1N	2B	$A(M + N)$
038		STX	U+M+N	A	∎

26. (See the algorithm of exercise 16.)

101	D8	LDA	D	1	(Remainder will be left in
102		DECA	1	1	locations U through U+N−1)
103		JAZ	DONE	1	Terminate if $d = 1$.
104		ENT1	N−1	A	rI1 $\equiv j$; $j \leftarrow n - 1$.
105		ENTA	0	A	$r \leftarrow 0$.
106	1H	LDX	U,1	AN	rAX $\leftarrow rb + u_j$.
107		DIV	D	AN
108		STA	U,1	AN
109		SLAX	5	AN	$(u_j, r) \leftarrow (\lfloor \text{rAX}/d \rfloor, \text{rAX} \bmod d)$.
110		DEC1	1	AN	$j \leftarrow j - 1$.
111		J1NN	1B	AN	Repeat for $n > j \geq 0$. ∎

At this point, the division routine is complete; and by the next exercise, rAX = 0.

27. It is $du \bmod dv = d(u \bmod v)$.

28. For convenience, let us assume that v has a decimal point at the left, i.e., $v = (v_n.v_{n-1}v_{n-2}\dots)_b$. After step N1 we have $\frac{1}{2} \leq v < 1 + 1/b$: For

$$v \left\lfloor \frac{b+1}{v_{n-1}+1} \right\rfloor \leq \frac{v(b+1)}{v_{n-1}+1} = \frac{v(1+1/b)}{(1/b)(v_{n-1}+1)} < 1 + \frac{1}{b},$$

and

$$v \left\lfloor \frac{b+1}{v_{n-1}+1} \right\rfloor \geq \frac{v(b+1-v_{n-1})}{v_{n-1}+1} \geq \frac{1}{b} \frac{v_{n-1}(b+1-v_{n-1})}{v_{n-1}+1}.$$

The latter quantity takes its smallest value when $v_{n-1} = 1$, since it is a concave function and the other extreme value is greater.

The formula in step N2 may be written $v \leftarrow \left\lfloor \dfrac{b(b+1)}{v_{n-1}+1} \right\rfloor \dfrac{v}{b}$, so we see as above that v will never become $\geq 1 + 1/b$.

The minimum value of v after one iteration of step N2 is $\geq$

$$\left(\frac{b(b+1) - v_{n-1}}{v_{n-1}+1}\right)\frac{v}{b} \geq \left(\frac{b(b+1) - v_{n-1}}{v_{n-1}+1}\right)\frac{v_{n-1}}{b^2} = \left(\frac{b(b+1)+1-t}{t}\right)\left(\frac{t-1}{b^2}\right)$$

$$= 1 + \frac{1}{b} + \frac{2}{b^2} - \frac{1}{b^2}\left(t + \frac{b(b+1)+1}{t}\right),$$

if $t = v_{n-1} + 1$. The minimum of this quantity occurs for $t = b/2 + 1$; a lower bound is $1 - 3/2b$. Hence $v_{n-1} \geq b - 2$, after one iteration of step N2. Finally, we have $(1 - 3/2b)(1 + 1/b)^2 > 1$, when $b \geq 5$, so at most two more iterations are needed. The assertion is easily verified when $b < 5$.

29. True, since $(u_{j+n} \ldots u_j)_b < v$.

30. In Algorithms A and S, such overlap is possible if the algorithms are rewritten slightly; for example, in Algorithm A we could rewrite step A2 thus: "Set $t \leftarrow u_j + v_j + k$, $w_j \leftarrow t \bmod b$, $k \leftarrow \lfloor t/b \rfloor$."

In Algorithm M, v_j may be in the same location as w_{j+n}. In Algorithm D, it is most convenient (as in Program D, exercise 26) to let $r_{n-1} \ldots r_0$ be the same as $u_{n-1} \ldots u_0$; and we can also let $q_m \ldots q_0$ be the same as $u_{m+n} \ldots u_n$, provided that no alteration of u_{j+n} is made in step D6. (Line 098 of Program D can safely be changed to 'J1N 2B', since u_{j+n} isn't used in the subsequent calculation.)

31. Consider the situation of Fig. 6 with $u = (u_{j+n} \ldots u_{j+1}u_j)_3$ as in Algorithm D. If the leading nonzero digits of u and v have the same sign, set $r \leftarrow u - v$, $q \leftarrow 1$; otherwise set $r \leftarrow u + v$, $q \leftarrow -1$. Now if $|r| > |u|$, or if $|r| = |u|$ and the first nonzero digit of $u_{j-1} \ldots u_0$ has the same sign as the first nonzero digit of r, set $q \leftarrow 0$; otherwise set $u_{j+n} \ldots u_j$ equal to the digits of r.

32. See M. Nadler, *CACM* **4** (1961), 192–193; Z. Pawlak and A. Wakulicz, *Bull. de l'Acad. Polonaise des Sciences*, Classe III, **5** (1957), 233–236 (see also pages 803–804); and exercise 4.1–15.

34. See, for example, R. E. Maeder, *The Mathematica Journal* **6**, 2 (Spring 1996), 32–40; **6**, 3 (Summer 1996), 37–43.

36. Given ϕ with an accuracy of $\pm 2^{-2n}$, we can successively compute ϕ^{-1}, ϕ^{-2}, $\ldots$ by subtraction until $\phi^{-k} < 2^{-n}$; the accumulated error will not exceed 2^{1-n}. Then we can use the series $\ln \phi = \ln((1 + \phi^{-3})/(1 - \phi^{-3})) = 2(\phi^{-3} + \frac{1}{3}\phi^{-9} + \frac{1}{5}\phi^{-15} + \cdots)$. [See William Schooling's article in *Napier Tercentenary Memorial*, edited by C. G. Knott (London: Longmans, 1915), 337–344.] An even better procedure, suggested in 1965 by J. W. Wrench, Jr., is to evaluate

$$\ln \phi = \frac{1}{2}\ln((1 + 5^{-1/2})/(1 - 5^{-1/2})) = (2\phi - 1)(5^{-1} + \frac{1}{3}5^{-2} + \frac{1}{5}5^{-3} + \cdots).$$

37. Let $d = 2^e$ so that $b > dv_{n-1} \geq b/2$. Instead of normalizing u and v in step D1, simply compute the two leading digits $v'v''$ of $2^e(v_{n-1}v_{n-2}v_{n-3})_b$ by shifting left e bits. In step D3, use (v', v'') instead of (v_{n-1}, v_{n-2}) and (u', u'', u''') instead of $(u_{j+n}, u_{j+n-1}, u_{j+n-2})$, where the digits $u'u''u'''$ are obtained from $(u_{j\mid n} \ldots u_{j+n-3})_b$ by shifting left e bits. Omit division by d in step D8. (In essence, u and v are being "virtually" shifted. This method saves computation when m is small compared to n.)

38. Set $k \leftarrow n$, $r \leftarrow 0$, $s \leftarrow 1$, $t \leftarrow 0$, $w \leftarrow u$; we will preserve the invariant relation $uv = 2^{2k}(r + s^2 - s) + 2^{2k-n}t + 2^{2k-2n}vw$ with $0 \leq t, w < 2^n$, and with $0 < r \leq 2s$ unless $(r, s) = (0, 1)$. While $k > 0$, let $4w = 2^n w' + w''$ and $4t + w'v = 2^n t' + t''$, where $0 \leq w'', t'' < 2^n$ and $0 \leq t' \leq 6$; then set $t \leftarrow t''$, $w \leftarrow w''$, $s \leftarrow 2s$, $r \leftarrow 4r + t' - s$, $k \leftarrow k - 1$. If $r \leq 0$, set $s \leftarrow s - 1$ and $r \leftarrow r + 2s$; otherwise, if $r > 2s$, set $r \leftarrow r - 2s$ and $s \leftarrow s + 1$ (this correction might need to be done twice). Repeat until $k = 0$. Then $uv = r + s^2 - s$, since w is always a multiple of 2^{2n-2k}. Consequently $r = 0$ if and only if $uv = 0$; otherwise the answer is s, because $uv - s \leq s^2 < uv + s$.

39. Let $S_j = \sum_{k \geq 0} 16^{-k}/(8k+j)$. We want to know whether or not $2^{n-1}\pi \bmod 1 < \frac{1}{2}$. Since $\pi = 4S_1 - 2S_4 - S_5 - S_6$, it suffices to have good estimates of $2^{n-1}S_j \bmod 1$. Now $2^{n-1}S_j$ is congruent (modulo 1) to $\sum_{0 \leq k < n/4} a_{njk}/(8k+j) + \sum_{k \geq n/4} 2^{n-1-4k}/(8k+j)$, where $a_{njk} = 2^{n-1-4k} \bmod (8k + j)$. Each term in the first sum can be approximated within 2^{-m} by computing a_{njk} in $O(\log n)$ operations (Section 4.6.3) and then finding the scaled quotient $\lfloor 2^m a_{njk}/(8k + j) \rfloor$. The second sum can be approximated within 2^{-m} by computing 2^m times its first $m/4$ terms. If $m \approx 2 \lg n$, the range of uncertainty will be $\approx 1/n$, and this will almost always be accurate enough. [*Math. Comp.* **66** (1997), 903–913.]

Notes: Let $\zeta = e^{\pi i/4} = (1 + i)/\sqrt{2}$ be an 8th root of unity, and consider the values $l_j = \ln(1 - \zeta^j/\sqrt{2})$. Then $l_0 = \ln(1 - 1/\sqrt{2})$, $l_1 = \bar{l}_7 = \frac{1}{2}\ln\frac{1}{2} - i\arctan 1$, $l_2 = \bar{l}_6 = \frac{1}{2}\ln\frac{3}{2} - i\arctan(1/\sqrt{2})$, $l_3 = \bar{l}_5 = \frac{1}{2}\ln\frac{5}{2} - i\arctan(1/3)$, $l_4 = \ln(1 + 1/\sqrt{2})$. Also $-S_j/2^{j/2} = \frac{1}{8}(l_0 + \zeta^{-j}l_1 + \cdots + \zeta^{-7j}l_7)$ for $1 \leq j \leq 8$ by 1.2.9–(13). Therefore $4S_1 - 2S_4 - S_5 - S_6 = 2l_0 - (2 - 2i)2l_1 + 2l_4 + (2 + 2i)l_7 = \pi$. Other identities of interest are:

$$\ln 2 = S_2 + \tfrac{1}{2}S_4 + \tfrac{1}{4}S_6 + \tfrac{1}{8}S_8;$$

$$\ln 3 = 2S_2 + \tfrac{1}{2}S_6;$$

$$\ln 5 = 2S_2 + 2S_4 + \tfrac{1}{2}S_6;$$

$$\sqrt{2}\ln(\sqrt{2} + 1) = S_1 + \tfrac{1}{2}S_3 + \tfrac{1}{4}S_5 + \tfrac{1}{8}S_7;$$

$$\sqrt{2}\arctan(1/\sqrt{2}) = S_1 - \tfrac{1}{2}S_3 + \tfrac{1}{4}S_5 - \tfrac{1}{8}S_7;$$

$$\arctan(1/3) = S_1 - S_2 - \tfrac{1}{2}S_4 - \tfrac{1}{4}S_5;$$

$$0 = 8S_1 - 8S_2 - 4S_3 - 8S_4 - 2S_5 - 2S_6 + S_7.$$

In general we have

$$\sum_{k \geq 0} \frac{z^{8k+1}}{8k + 1} = A + B + C + D, \qquad \sum_{k \geq 0} \frac{z^{8k+5}}{8k + 5} = A - B + C - D,$$

$$\sum_{k \geq 0} \frac{z^{8k+3}}{8k + 3} = A - B - C + D, \qquad \sum_{k \geq 0} \frac{z^{8k+7}}{8k + 7} = A + B - C - D,$$

where

$$A = \frac{1}{8}\ln\frac{1 + z}{1 - z}, \qquad B = \frac{1}{2^{7/2}}\ln\frac{1 + \sqrt{2}z + z^2}{1 - \sqrt{2}z + z^2},$$

$$C = \frac{1}{4}\arctan z, \qquad D = \frac{1}{2^{5/2}}\arctan\frac{\sqrt{2}z}{1 - z^2};$$

and

$$\sum_{k \geq 0} \frac{z^{mk+a}}{mk+a} = -\frac{1}{m}\left(\ln(1-z) + (-1)^a [m \text{ even}] \ln(1+z) + f_{am}(z)\right),$$

$$f_{am}(z) = \sum_{k=1}^{\lfloor (m-1)/2 \rfloor} \left(\cos\frac{2\pi ka}{m} \ln\left(1 - 2z\cos\frac{2\pi k}{m} + z^2\right)\right.$$

$$\left. - 2\sin\frac{2\pi ka}{m} \arctan\frac{z\sin(2\pi k/m)}{1 - z\cos(2\pi k/m)}\right).$$

40. To get the most significant $n/2$ places, we need about $\sum_{k=1}^{n/2} \approx \frac{1}{8}n^2$ basic operations (see exercise 15). And we can get the least significant $n/2$ places by using a b-adic method when b is a power of 2 (see exercise 4.1–31): The problem is easily reduced to the case where v is odd. Let $u = (\ldots u_2 u_1 u_0)_b$, $v = (\ldots v_2 v_1 v_0)_b$, and $w = (\ldots w_2 w_1 w_0)_b$, where we want to solve $u = vw$ (modulo $b^{n/2}$). Compute v' such that $v'v \bmod b = 1$ (see exercise 4.5.2–17). Then $w_0 = v'u_0 \bmod b$, and we can compute $u' = u - w_0 v$, $w_1 = v'u_0' \bmod b$, etc. The rightmost $n/2$ places are found after about $\frac{1}{8}n^2$ basic operations. So the total is $\frac{1}{4}n^2 + O(n)$, while Algorithm D needs about $n^2 + O(n)$. A pure right-to-left method for all n digits would require $\frac{1}{2}n^2 + O(n)$. [See A. Schönhage and E. Vetter, *Lecture Notes in Comp. Sci.* **855** (1994), 448–459; W. Krandick and T. Jebelean, *J. Symbolic Computation* **21** (1996), 441–455.]

41. (a) If $m = 0$, let $v = u$. Otherwise subtract xw from $(u_{m+n-1} \ldots u_1 u_0)_b$, where $x = u_0 w' \bmod b$; this zeroes out the units digit, so we have effectively reduced m by 1. (This operation is closely related to the computation of u/w in b-adic arithmetic, since $u/w = q + b^m v/w$ for some integer q; see exercise 4.1–31. It wins over ordinary division because we never have to correct a trial divisor. To compute w' when b is a power of 2, notice that if $w_0 w' \equiv 1$ (modulo 2^e) then $w_0 w'' \equiv 1$ (modulo 2^{2e}) when $w'' = (2 - w_0 w')w'$, by the 2-adic analog of "Newton's method.")

(b) Apply (a) to the product uv. Memory space is conserved if we interlace multiplication and modulation as follows: Set $k \leftarrow 0$, $t \leftarrow 0$. Then while $k < n$, preserve the invariant relation $b^k t \equiv (u_{k-1} \ldots u_0)v$ (modulo w) by setting $t \leftarrow t + u_k v$, $t \leftarrow (t - xw)/b$, $k \leftarrow k+1$, where $x = t_0 w' \bmod b$ is chosen to make $t - xw$ a multiple of b. This solution assumes that t, u, and v have a signed magnitude representation; we can work also with nonnegative numbers $< 2w$ or with complement notations, as discussed by Shand and Vuillemin and by Kornerup, [*IEEE Symp. Computer Arithmetic* **11** (1993), 252–259, 277–283]. If n is large, the techniques of Section 4.3.3 speed up the multiplication.

(c) Represent all numbers congruent to u (modulo w) by an internal value $r(u)$ where $r(u) \equiv b^n u$. Then addition and subtraction are handled as usual, while multiplication is $r(uv) = \text{bmult}(r(u), r(v))$, where bmult is the operation of (b). At the beginning of the computation, replace each operand u by $r(u) = \text{bmult}(u, a)$, using the precomputed constant $a = b^{2n} \bmod w$. At the end, replace each $r(u)$ by $u = \text{bmult}(r(u), 1)$. [In the application to RSA encryption, Section 4.5.4, we could redefine the coding scheme so that precomputation and postcomputation are unnecessary.]

42. An interesting analysis by J. M. Holte in *AMM* **104** (1997), 138–149, establishes the exact formula

$$P_{nk} = \frac{1}{m!} \sum_j \begin{bmatrix} m \\ m-j \end{bmatrix} b^{-jn} \sum_{r=0}^k \binom{m+1}{r}(k+1-r)^{m-j}.$$

The inner sum is $\sum_{r=0}^{k}(-1)^{r}\binom{m+1}{r}(k+1-r)^{m} = \left\langle\begin{smallmatrix}m\\k\end{smallmatrix}\right\rangle$ when $j = 0$. (Exercise 5.1.3–25 explains why Eulerian numbers arise in this connection.)

43. By exercise 1.2.4–35 we have $w = \lfloor W/2^{16}\rfloor$, where $W = (2^8+1)t = (2^8+1)(uv+2^7)$. Therefore if $uv/255 > c+\frac{1}{2}$, we have $c < 2^8$, hence $w \geq \lfloor(2^{16}(c+1)+2^8-c)/2^{16}\rfloor \geq c+1$; if $uv/255 < c + \frac{1}{2}$, we have $w \leq \lfloor(2^{16}(c + 1) - c - 1)/2^{16}\rfloor = c$. [See J. F. Blinn, *IEEE Computer Graphics and Applic.* **14**,6 (November 1994), 78–82.]

SECTION 4.3.2

1. The solution is unique since $7\cdot11\cdot13 = 1001$. The constructive proof of Theorem C tells us that the answer is $((11\cdot13)^6+6\cdot(7\cdot13)^{10}+5\cdot(7\cdot11)^{12})$ mod 1001. But this answer is perhaps not explicit enough! By (24) we have $v_1 = 1$, $v_2 = (6 - 1) \cdot 8$ mod $11 = 7$, $v_3 = ((5 - 1) \cdot 2 - 7) \cdot 6$ mod $13 = 6$, so $u = 6 \cdot 7 \cdot 11 + 7 \cdot 7 + 1 = 512$.

2. No. There is at most one such u; the additional condition $u_1 \equiv \cdots \equiv u_r$ (modulo 1) is necessary and sufficient, and it follows that such a generalization is not very interesting.

3. $u \equiv u_i$ (modulo m_i) implies that $u \equiv u_i$ (modulo $\gcd(m_i, m_j)$), so the condition $u_i \equiv u_j$ (modulo $\gcd(m_i, m_j)$) must surely hold if there is a solution. Furthermore if $u \equiv v$ (modulo m_j) for all j, then $u - v$ is a multiple of $\text{lcm}(m_1,\ldots,m_r) = m$; hence there is at most one solution.

The proof can now be completed in a nonconstructive manner by counting the number of different r-tuples $(u_1,\ldots,u_r)$ satisfying the conditions $0 \leq u_j < m_j$ and $u_i \equiv u_j$ (modulo $\gcd(m_i, m_j)$). If this number is m, there must be a solution since $(u \bmod m_1,\ldots, u \bmod m_r)$ takes on m distinct values as u goes from a to $a + m - 1$. Assume that $u_1, \ldots, u_{r-1}$ have been chosen satisfying the given conditions; we must now pick $u_r \equiv u_j$ (modulo $\gcd(m_j, m_r)$) for $1 \leq j < r$, and by the generalized Chinese remainder theorem for $r - 1$ elements there are

$$m_r/\text{lcm}(\gcd(m_1, m_r),\ldots,\gcd(m_{r-1}, m_r)) = m_r/\gcd(\text{lcm}(m_1,\ldots,m_{r-1}), m_r)$$
$$= \text{lcm}(m_1,\ldots,m_r)/\text{lcm}(m_1,\ldots,m_{r-1})$$

ways to do this. [This proof is based on identities (10), (11), (12), and (14) of Section 4.5.2.]

A constructive proof [A. S. Fraenkel, *Proc. Amer. Math. Soc.* **14** (1963), 790–791] generalizing (25) can be given as follows. Let $M_j = \text{lcm}(m_1,\ldots,m_j)$; we wish to find $u = v_r M_{r-1} + \cdots + v_2 M_1 + v_1$, where $0 \leq v_j < M_j/M_{j-1}$. Assume that $v_1, \ldots, v_{j-1}$ have already been determined; then we must solve the congruence

$$v_j M_{j-1} + v_{j-1}M_{j-2} + \cdots + v_1 \equiv u_j \pmod{m_j}.$$

Here $v_{j-1}M_{j-2} + \cdots + v_1 \equiv u_i \equiv u_j$ (modulo $\gcd(m_i, m_j)$) for $i < j$ by hypothesis, so $c = u_j - (v_{j-1}M_{j-2} + \cdots + v_1)$ is a multiple of

$$\text{lcm}(\gcd(m_1, m_j),\ldots,\gcd(m_{j-1}, m_j)) = \gcd(M_{j-1}, m_j) = d_j.$$

We therefore must solve $v_j M_{j-1} \equiv c$ (modulo m_j). By Euclid's algorithm there is a number c_j such that $c_j M_{j-1} \equiv d_j$ (modulo m_j); hence we may take

$$v_j = (c_j\, c)/d_j \bmod (m_j/d_j).$$

Notice that, as in the nonconstructive proof, we have $m_j/d_j = M_j/M_{j-1}$.

4. (After $m_4 = 91 = 7 \cdot 13$, we have used up all products of two or more odd primes that can be less than 100, so $m_5, \ldots$ must all be prime.) We find

$$m_7 = 79, \quad m_8 = 73, \quad m_9 = 71, \quad m_{10} = 67, \quad m_{11} = 61,$$
$$m_{12} = 59, \quad m_{13} = 53, \quad m_{14} = 47, \quad m_{15} = 43, \quad m_{16} = 41,$$
$$m_{17} = 37, \quad m_{18} = 31, \quad m_{19} = 29, \quad m_{20} = 23, \quad m_{21} = 17,$$

and then we are stuck ($m_{22} = 1$ does no good).

5. (a) No. The obvious upper bound,

$$3^4 5^2 7^2 11^1 \ldots = \prod_{\substack{p \text{ odd} \\ p \text{ prime}}} p^{\lfloor \log_p 100 \rfloor},$$

is attained if we choose $m_1 = 3^4$, $m_2 = 5^2$, etc. (It is more difficult, however, to maximize $m_1 \ldots m_r$ when r is fixed, or to maximize $e_1 + \cdots + e_r$ with relatively prime e_j as we would attempt to do when using moduli $2^{e_j} - 1$.) (b) Replacing 100 by 256 and allowing even moduli gives $2^8 3^5 5^3 \ldots 251^1 \approx 1.67 \cdot 10^{109}$.

6. (a) If $e = f + kg$, then $2^e = 2^f (2^g)^k \equiv 2^f \cdot 1^k$ (modulo $2^g - 1$). So if $2^e \equiv 2^f$ (modulo $2^g - 1$), we have $2^{e \bmod g} \equiv 2^{f \bmod g}$ (modulo $2^g - 1$); and since the latter quantities lie between zero and $2^g - 1$ we must have $e \bmod g = f \bmod g$. (b) By part (a), $(1 + 2^d + \cdots + 2^{(c-1)d}) \cdot (2^e - 1) \equiv (1 + 2^d + \cdots + 2^{(c-1)d}) \cdot (2^d - 1) = 2^{cd} - 1 \equiv 2^{ce} - 1 \equiv 2^1 - 1 = 1$ (modulo $2^f - 1$).

7. We have $v_j m_{j-1} \ldots m_1 \equiv u_j - (v_{j-1} m_{j-2} \ldots m_1 + \cdots + v_1)$ and $C_j m_{j-1} \ldots m_1 \equiv 1$ (modulo m_j) by (23), (25), and (26); see P. A. Pritchard, *CACM* **27** (1984), 57.

This method of rewriting the formulas uses the same number of arithmetic operations and fewer constants; but the number of constants is fewer only if we order the moduli so that $m_1 < m_2 < \cdots < m_r$, otherwise we would need a table of $m_i \bmod m_j$. This ordering of the moduli might seem to require more computation than if we made m_1 the largest, m_2 the next largest, etc., since there are many more operations to be done modulo m_r than modulo m_1; but since v_j can be as large as $m_j - 1$, we are better off with $m_1 < m_2 < \cdots < m_r$ in (24) also. So this idea appears to be preferable to the formulas in the text, although Section 4.3.3B shows that the formulas in the text are advantageous when the moduli have the form (14).

8. Modulo m_j: $m_{j-1} \ldots m_1 v_j \equiv m_{j-1} \ldots m_1 (\ldots ((u_j - v_1) c_{1j} - v_2) c_{2j} - \cdots - v_{j-1}) \times c_{(j-1)j} \equiv m_{j-2} \ldots m_1 (\ldots (u_j - v_1) c_{1j} - \cdots - v_{j-2}) c_{(j-2)j} - v_{j-1} m_{j-2} \ldots m_1 \equiv \cdots \equiv u_j - v_1 - v_2 m_1 - \cdots - v_{j-1} m_{j-2} \ldots m_1$.

9. $u_r \leftarrow ((\ldots (v_r m_{r-1} + v_{r-1}) m_{r-2} + \cdots) m_1 + v_1) \bmod m_r, \quad \ldots,$
$$u_2 \leftarrow (v_2 m_1 + v_1) \bmod m_2, \quad u_1 \leftarrow v_1 \bmod m_1.$$

(The computation should be done in this order, if we want to let u_j and v_j share the same memory locations, as they can in (24).)

10. If we redefine the "mod" operator so that it produces residues in the symmetrical range, the basic formulas (2), (3), (4) for arithmetic and (24), (25) for conversion remain the same, and the number u in (25) lies in the desired range (10). (Here (25) is a *balanced mixed-radix* notation, generalizing balanced ternary notation.) The comparison of two numbers may still be done from left to right, in the simple manner described in the text. Furthermore, it is possible to retain the value u_j in a single computer word, if we have signed magnitude representation within the computer, even if m_j is almost twice the word size. But the arithmetic operations analogous to (11) and (12) are more difficult, so it appears that this idea would result in slightly slower operation on most computers.

11. Multiply by $\frac{1}{2}(m+1) = \left(\frac{1}{2}(m_1+1), \ldots, \frac{1}{2}(m_r+1)\right)$. Note that $2t \cdot \frac{m+1}{2} \equiv t$ (modulo m). In general if v is relatively prime to m, then we can find (by Euclid's algorithm) a number $v' = (v'_1, \ldots, v'_r)$ such that $vv' \equiv 1$ (modulo m); and then if u is known to be a multiple of v we have $u/v = uv'$, where the latter is computed with modular multiplication. When v is not relatively prime to m, division is much harder.

12. Replace m_j by m in (11). [Another way to test for overflow, if m is odd, is to maintain extra bits $u_0 = u \bmod 2$ and $v_0 = v \bmod 2$. Then overflow has occurred if and only if $u_0 + v_0 \not\equiv w_1 + \cdots + w_r$ (modulo 2), where $(w_1, \ldots, w_r)$ are the mixed-radix digits corresponding to $u+v$.]

13. (a) $x^2 - x = (x-1)x \equiv 0$ (modulo 10^n) is equivalent to $(x-1)x \equiv 0$ (modulo p^n) for $p = 2$ and 5. Either x or $x-1$ must be a multiple of p, and then the other is relatively prime to p^n; so either x or $x-1$ must be a multiple of p^n. If $x \bmod 2^n = x \bmod 5^n = 0$ or 1, we must have $x \bmod 10^n = 0$ or 1; hence automorphs have $x \bmod 2^n \neq x \bmod 5^n$. (b) If $x = qp^n + r$, where $r = 0$ or 1, then $r \equiv r^2 \equiv r^3$, so $3x^2 - 2x^3 \equiv (6qp^n r + 3r) - (6qp^n r + 2r) \equiv r$ (modulo p^{2n}). (c) Let c' be $(3(cx)^2 - 2(cx)^3)/x^2 = 3c^2 - 2c^3 x$.

Note: Since the last k digits of an n-digit automorph form a k-digit automorph, it makes sense to speak of the two ∞-digit automorphs, x and $1-x$, which are 10-adic numbers (see exercise 4.1–31). The set of 10-adic numbers is equivalent under modular arithmetic to the set of ordered pairs (u_1, u_2), where u_1 is a 2-adic number and u_2 is a 5-adic number.

14. Find the cyclic convolution $(z_0, z_1, \ldots, z_{n-1})$ of floating point approximations to $(a_0 u_0, a_1 u_1, \ldots, a_{n-1} u_{n-1})$ and $(a_0 v_0, a_1 v_1, \ldots, a_{n-1} v_{n-1})$, where the constants $a_k = 2^{-(kq \bmod n)/n}$ have been precomputed. The identities $u = \sum_{k=0}^{n-1} u_k a_k 2^{kq/n}$ and $v = \sum_{k=0}^{n-1} v_k a_k 2^{kq/n}$ now imply that $w = \sum_{k=0}^{n-1} t_k a_k 2^{kq/n-1}$ where $t_k \approx 2z_k/a_k$. If sufficient accuracy has been maintained, each t_k will be very close to an integer. The representation of w can readily be found from those integers, although overlapping bit sequences must be added together before reducing mod $2^q - 1$. [R. Crandall and B. Fagin, *Math. Comp.* **62** (1994), 305–324. For improved error bounds, and extensions to moduli of the form $k \cdot 2^n \pm 1$, see Colin Percival, *Math. Comp.* **72** (2002), 387–395.]

SECTION 4.3.3

1.

$12 \times 23:$	$34 \times 41:$	$22 \times 18:$	$1234 \times 2341:$
02	12	02	0276
02	12	02	0276
-01	$+03$	$+00$	-0396
06	04	16	1394
06	04	16	1394
0276	1394	0396	2888794

2. $\sqrt{Q + \lfloor\sqrt{Q}\rfloor} \leq \sqrt{Q + \sqrt{Q}} < \sqrt{Q + 2\sqrt{Q} + 1} = \sqrt{Q} + 1$, so $\lfloor\sqrt{Q+R}\rfloor \leq \lfloor\sqrt{Q}\rfloor + 1$.

3. The result is true when $k \leq 2$, so assume that $k > 2$. Let $q_k = 2^{Q_k}$, $r_k = 2^{R_k}$, so that $R_k = \lfloor\sqrt{Q_k}\rfloor$ and $Q_k = Q_{k-1} + R_{k-1}$. We must show that $1 + (R_k+1)2^{R_k} \leq 2^{Q_{k-1}}$; this inequality isn't close at all. One way is to observe that $1 + (R_k+1)2^{R_k} \leq 1 + 2^{2R_k}$ and $2R_k < Q_{k-1}$ when $k > 2$. (The fact that $2R_k < Q_{k-1}$ is readily proved by induction since $R_{k+1} - R_k \leq 1$ and $Q_k - Q_{k-1} \geq 2$.)

4. For $j = 1, \ldots, r$, calculate $U_e(j^2)$, $jU_o(j^2)$, $V_e(j^2)$, $jV_o(j^2)$; and by recursively calling the multiplication algorithm, calculate

$$W(j) = (U_e(j^2) + jU_o(j^2))(V_e(j^2) + jV_o(j^2)),$$
$$W(-j) = (U_e(j^2) - jU_o(j^2))(V_e(j^2) - jV_o(j^2)).$$

Then we have $W_e(j^2) = (W(j) + W(-j))/2$, $W_o(j^2) = (W(j) - W(-j))/(2j)$. Also calculate $W_e(0) = U(0)V(0)$. Now construct difference tables for W_e and W_o, which are polynomials whose respective degrees are r and $r - 1$.

This method reduces the size of the numbers being handled, and reduces the number of additions and multiplications. Its only disadvantage is a longer program (since the control is somewhat more complex, and some of the calculations must be done with signed numbers).

Another possibility would perhaps be to evaluate W_e and W_o at 1^2, 2^2, 4^2, ..., $(2^r)^2$; although the numbers involved are larger, the calculations are faster, since all multiplications are replaced by shifting and all divisions are by binary numbers of the form $2^j(2^k - 1)$. (Simple procedures are available for dividing by such numbers.)

5. Start the q and r sequences out with q_0 and q_1 large enough so that the inequality in exercise 3 is valid. Then we will find in the formulas like those preceding Theorem B that we have $\eta_1 \to 0$ and $\eta_2 = (1 + 1/(2r_k))2^{1+\sqrt{2Q_k} - \sqrt{2Q_{k+1}}}(Q_k/Q_{k+1})$. The factor $Q_k/Q_{k+1} \to 1$ as $k \to \infty$, so we can ignore it if we want to show that $\eta_2 < 1 - \epsilon$ for all large k. Now $\sqrt{2Q_{k+1}} = \sqrt{2Q_k + 2\lceil\sqrt{2Q_k}\rceil + 2} \geq \sqrt{(2Q_k + 2\sqrt{2Q_k} + 1) + 1} \geq \sqrt{2Q_k} + 1 + 1/(3R_k)$. Hence $\eta_2 \leq (1 + 1/(2r_k))2^{-1/(3R_k)}$, and $\lg \eta_2 < 0$ for large enough k.

Note: Algorithm T can also be modified to define a sequence $q_0, q_1, \ldots$ of a similar type that is based on n, so that $n \approx q_k + q_{k+1}$ after step T1. This modification leads to the estimate (21).

6. Any common divisor of $6q + d_1$ and $6q + d_2$ must also divide their difference $d_2 - d_1$. The $\binom{6}{2}$ differences are 2, 3, 4, 6, 8, 1, 2, 4, 6, 1, 3, 5, 2, 4, 2, so we must only show that at most one of the given numbers is divisible by each of the primes 2, 3, 5. Clearly only $6q + 2$ is even, and only $6q + 3$ is a multiple of 3; and there is at most one multiple of 5, since $q_k \not\equiv 3$ (modulo 5).

7. Let $p_{k-1} < n \leq p_k$. We have $t_k \leq 6t_{k-1} + ck3^k$ for some constant c; so $t_k/6^k \leq t_{k-1}/6^{k-1} + ck/2^k \leq t_0 + c\sum_{j\geq 1}j/2^j = M$. Thus $t_k \leq M \cdot 6^k = O(p_k^{\log_3 6})$.

8. False. To see the fallacy, try it with $k = 2$.

9. $\tilde{u}_s = \hat{u}_{(qs) \bmod K}$. In particular, if $q = -1$ we get $\hat{u}_{(-r) \bmod K}$, which avoids data-flipping when computing inverse transforms.

10. $A^{[j]}(s_{k-1}, \ldots, s_{k-j}, t_{k-j-1}, \ldots, t_0)$ can be written

$$\sum_{0 \leq t_{k-1}, \ldots, t_{k-j} \leq 1} \omega^{2^{k-j}(s_{k-j}\cdots s_{k-1})_2 \cdot (t_{k-1}\cdots t_{k-j})_2} \left(\sum_{0 < p < K} \omega^{tp}u_p\right)\left(\sum_{0 \leq q < K} \omega^{tq}v_q\right),$$

and this is $\sum_{p,q} u_p v_q S(p, q)$, where $|S(p, q)| = 0$ or 2^j. We have $|S(p, q)| = 2^j$ for exactly $2^{2k}/2^j$ values of p and q.

11. An automaton cannot have $z_2 = 1$ until it has $c \geq 2$, and this occurs first for M_j at time $3j - 1$. It follows that M_j cannot have $z_2z_1z_0 \neq 000$ until time $3(j - 1)$. Furthermore, if M_j has $z_0 \neq 0$ at time t, we cannot change this to $z_0 = 0$ without affecting the output; but the output cannot be affected by this value of z_0 until at least time $t + j - 1$, so we must have $t + j - 1 \leq 2n$. Since the first argument we gave proves that $3(j - 1) \leq t$, we must have $4(j - 1) \leq 2n$, that is, $j - 1 \leq n/2$, i.e., $j \leq \lfloor n/2 \rfloor + 1$. This is the best possible bound, since the inputs $u = v = 2^n - 1$ require the use of M_j for all $j \leq \lfloor n/2 \rfloor + 1$. (For example, Table 2 shows that M_2 is needed to multiply two-bit numbers, at time 3.)

12. We can "sweep through" K lists of MIX-like instructions, executing the first instruction on each list, in $O(K + (N \log N)^2)$ steps as follows: (i) A radix list sort (Section 5.2.5) will group together all identical instructions, in time $O(K + N)$. (ii) Each set of j identical instructions can be performed in $O(\log N)^2 + O(j)$ steps, and there are $O(N^2)$ sets. A bounded number of sweeps will finish all the lists. The remaining details are straightforward; for example, arithmetic operations can be simulated by converting p and q to binary. [*SICOMP* **9** (1980), 490–508.]

13. If it takes $T(n)$ steps to multiply n-bit numbers, we can accomplish m-bit times n-bit multiplication by breaking the n-bit number into $\lceil n/m \rceil$ m-bit groups, using $\lceil n/m \rceil T(m) + O(n + m)$ operations. The results cited in the text therefore give an estimated running time of $O(n \log m \log \log m)$ on Turing machines, or $O(n \log m)$ on machines with random access to words of bounded size, or $O(n)$ on pointer machines.

15. M. J. Fischer and L. J. Stockmeyer achieved time $O(n(\log n)^2 \log \log n)$ [*J. Comp. and Syst. Sci.* **9** (1974), 317–331]; their construction works on multitape Turing machines, and it is $O(n \log n)$ on pointer machines. That upper bound was improved to $O(n \log n \, e^{\sqrt{\ln 4}\sqrt{\ln \ln n}} \sqrt{\ln \ln n})$ by J. van der Hoeven [*Int. Symp. Symbolic and Algeb. Comp.* **39** (2014), 405–412]. The best lower bound known is of order $n \log n/\log \log n$, due to M. S. Paterson, M. J. Fischer, and A. R. Meyer [*SIAM/AMS Proceedings* **7** (1974), 97–111]; this applies to multitape Turing machines but not to pointer machines.

16. Let 2^k be the smallest power of 2 that exceeds $2K$. Set $a_t \leftarrow \omega^{-t^2/2} u_t$ and $b_t \leftarrow \omega^{(2K-2-t)^2/2}$, where $u_t = 0$ for $t \geq K$. We want to evaluate the convolutions $c_r = \sum_{j=0}^{r} a_j b_{r-j}$ for $r = 2K - 2 - s$, when $0 \leq s < K$. The convolutions can be found by using three fast Fourier transformations of order 2^k, as in the text's multiplication procedure. [Note that this technique, sometimes called the "chirp transform," works for any complex number ω, not necessarily a root of unity. See L. I. Bluestein, *Northeast Electronics Res. and Eng. Meeting Record* **10** (1968), 218–219; D. H. Bailey and P. N. Swarztrauber, *SIAM Review* **33** (1991), 389–404.]

17. The quantity $D_n = K_{n+1} - K_n$ satisfies $D_1 = 2$, $D_{2n} = 2D_n$, and $D_{2n+1} = D_n$; hence $D_n = 2^{e_1-t+2}$ when n has the stated form. It follows that $K_n = 3^{e_1} + \sum_{l=2}^{t} 3^{e_l} 2^{e_1-e_l-l+3}$, by induction on n.

Incidentally, K_n is odd, and we can multiply an n-place integer by an $(n + 1)$-place integer with $(K_n + K_{n+1})/2$ 1-place multiplications. The generating function $K(z) = \sum_{n \geq 1} K_n z^n$ satisfies $zK(z) + z^2 = K(z^2)(z + 1)(z + 2)$; hence $K(-2) = 2$, $K(-1) = 1$, and $K(1) = \frac{1}{5}$, if we're cavalier about convergence.

18. The following scheme uses $3N + S_N$ places of working storage, where $S_1 = 0$, $S_{2n} = S_n$, and $S_{2n-1} = S_n + 1$, hence $S_n = e_1 - e_t - t + 2 - [t=1]$ in the notation of the previous exercise. Let $N = 2n - \epsilon$, where ϵ is 0 or 1, and assume that $N > 1$. Given N-place numbers $u = 2^n U_1 + U_0$ and $v = 2^n V_1 + V_0$, we first form $|U_0 - U_1|$ and $|V_0 - V_1|$ in two n-place areas starting at positions 0 and n of the $(3N + S_N)$-place working area. Then we place their product into the working area starting at position $3n + S_n$. The next step is to form the $2(n - \epsilon)$-place product $U_1 V_1$, starting in position 0; using that product, we change the $3n - 2\epsilon$ places starting at position $3n + S_n$ to the value of $U_1V_1 - (U_0 - U_1)(V_0 - V_1) + 2^n U_1 V_1$. (Notice that $3n - 2\epsilon + 3n + S_n = 3N + S_N$.) Finally, we form the $2n$-place product $U_0 V_0$ starting at position 0, and add it to the partial result starting at positions $2n + S_n$ and $3n + S_n$. We must also move the $2N$-place answer to its final position by shifting it down $2n + S_n$ positions.

The final move could be avoided by a trickier variation that cyclically rotates its output by a given amount within a designated working area. If the $2N$-place product is not allowed to be adjacent to the auxiliary working space, we need about N more places of memory (that is, a total of about $6N$ instead of $5N$ places, for the input, output, and temporary storage); see R. Maeder, *Lecture Notes in Comp. Sci.* **722** (1993), 59–65.

19. Let $m = s^2 + r$ where $-s < r \le s$. We can use (2) with $U_1 = \lfloor u/s \rfloor$, $U_0 = u \bmod s$, $V_1 = \lfloor v/s \rfloor$, $V_0 = v \bmod s$, and with s playing the role of 2^n. If we know the signs of $U_1 - U_0$ and $V_1 - V_0$ we know how to compute the product $|U_1 - U_0||V_1 - V_0|$, which is $< m$, and whether to add or subtract it. It remains to multiply by s and by $s^2 \equiv -r$. Each of these can be done with four multiplication/divisions, using exercise 3.2.1.1–9, but only seven are needed because one of the multiplications needed to compute $sx \bmod m$ is by r or $r+s$. Thus 14 multiplication/divisions are sufficient (or 12, in case $u = v$ or u is constant). Without the ability to compare operands, we can still do the job with one more multiplication, by computing $U_0 V_1$ and $U_1 V_0$ separately.

SECTION 4.4

1. We compute $(\ldots (a_m b_{m-1} + a_{m-1}) b_{m-2} + \cdots + a_1) b_0 + a_0$ by adding and multiplying in the B_J system.

	T.	$= 20$(cwt.	$= 8$(st.	$= 14$(lb.	$= 16$ oz.)))
Start with zero	0	0	0	0	0
Add 3	0	0	0	0	3
Multiply by 24	0	0	0	4	8
Add 9	0	0	0	5	1
Multiply by 60	0	2	5	9	12
Add 12	0	2	5	10	8
Multiply by 60	8	3	1	0	0
Add 37	8	3	1	2	5

(Addition and multiplication by a constant in a mixed-radix system are readily done using a simple generalization of the usual carry rule; see exercise 4.3.1–9.)

2. We compute $\lfloor u/B_0 \rfloor$, $\lfloor \lfloor u/B_0 \rfloor / B_1 \rfloor$, etc., and the remainders are A_0, A_1, etc. The division is done in the b_j system.

	d.	$= 24$(h.	$= 60$(m.	$= 60$ s.))	
Start with u	3	9	12	37	
Divide by 16	0	5	4	32	Remainder $= 5$
Divide by 14	0	0	21	45	Remainder $= 2$
Divide by 8	0	0	2	43	Remainder $= 1$
Divide by 20	0	0	0	8	Remainder $= 3$
Divide by ∞	0	0	0	0	Remainder $= 8$

Answer: 8 T. 3 cwt. 1 st. 2 lb. 5 oz.

3. The following procedure due to G. L. Steele Jr. and Jon L White generalizes Taranto's algorithm for $B = 2$ originally published in *CACM* **2**, 7 (July 1959), 27.

A1. [Initialize.] Set $M \leftarrow 0$, $U_0 \leftarrow 0$.

A2. [Done?] If $u < \epsilon$ or $u > 1 - \epsilon$, go to step A4. (Otherwise no M-place fraction will satisfy the given conditions.)

A3. [Transform.] Set $M \leftarrow M + 1$, $U_{-M} \leftarrow \lfloor Bu \rfloor$, $u \leftarrow Bu \bmod 1$, $\epsilon \leftarrow B\epsilon$, and return to A2. (This transformation returns us to essentially the same state we were in before; the remaining problem is to convert u to U with fewest radix-B places so that $|U - u| < \epsilon$. Note, however, that ϵ may now be ≥ 1; in this case we could go immediately to step A4 instead of storing the new value of ϵ.)

A4. [Round.] If $u \geq \frac{1}{2}$, increase U_{-M} by 1. (If $u = \frac{1}{2}$ exactly, another rounding rule such as "increase U_{-M} by 1 only when it is odd" might be preferred; see Section 4.2.2.) ∎

Step A4 will never increase U_{-M} from $B - 1$ to B; for if $U_{-M} = B - 1$ we must have $M > 0$, but no $(M - 1)$-place fraction was sufficiently accurate. Steele and White go on to consider floating point conversions in their paper [*SIGPLAN Notices* **25**, 6 (June 1990), 112–126]. See also D. E. Knuth in *Beauty is Our Business*, edited by W. H. J. Feijen et al. (New York: Springer, 1990), 233–242.

4. (a) $1/2^k = 5^k/10^k$. (b) Every prime divisor of b divides B.

5. If and only if $10^n - 1 \leq c < w$; see (3).

7. $\alpha u \leq ux \leq \alpha u + u/w < \alpha u + 1$, hence $\lfloor \alpha u \rfloor \leq \lfloor ux \rfloor \leq \lfloor \alpha u + 1 \rfloor$. Furthermore, in the special case cited we have $ux < \alpha u + \alpha$ and $\lfloor \alpha u \rfloor = \lfloor \alpha u + \alpha - \epsilon \rfloor$ for $0 < \epsilon \leq \alpha$.

8.

	ENT1	0		LDA	TEMP	(Can occur only on

```
8.      ENT1  0              LDA   TEMP     (Can occur only on
        LDA   U              DECA  1              the first iteration,
1H MUL  =1//10=              JMP   3B             by exercise 7.)
3H STA  TEMP           2H STA   ANSWER,1  (May be minus zero.)
        MUL   =-10=              LDA   TEMP
        SLAX  5              INC1  1
        ADD   U              JAP   1B            ∎
        JANN  2F
```

9. Let $p_k = 2^{2^{k+2}}$. By induction on k we have $v_k(u) \leq \frac{16}{5}(1 - 1/p_k)(\lfloor u/2 \rfloor + 1)$; hence $\lfloor v_k(u)/16 \rfloor \leq \lfloor \lfloor u/2 \rfloor/5 \rfloor = \lfloor u/10 \rfloor$ for all integers $u \geq 0$. Furthermore, since $v_k(u + 1) \geq v_k(u)$, the smallest counterexample to $\lfloor v_k(u)/16 \rfloor = \lfloor u/10 \rfloor$ must occur when u is a multiple of 10.

Now let $u = 10m$ be fixed, and suppose $v_k(u) \bmod p_k = r_k$ so that $v_{k+1}(u) = v_k(u) + (v_k(u) - r_k)/p_k$. The fact that $p_k^2 = p_{k+1}$ implies that there exist integers m_0, m_1, m_2, ... such that $m_0 = m$, $v_k(u) = (p_k - 1)m_k + x_k$, and $m_k = m_{k+1}p_k + x_k - r_k$, where $x_{k+1} = (p_k + 1)x_k - p_k r_k$. Unwinding this recurrence yields

$$v_k(u) = (p_k - 1)m_k + c_k - \sum_{j=0}^{k-1} p_j r_j \prod_{i=j+1}^{k-1} (p_i + 1), \qquad c_k = 3\frac{p_k - 1}{p_0 - 1}.$$

Furthermore $v_k(u) + m_k = v_{k+1}(u) + m_{k+1}$ is independent of k, and it follows that $v_k(u)/16 = m + (3 - m_k)/16$. So the minimal counterexample $u = 10y_k$ is obtained for $0 \leq k \leq 4$ by setting $m_k = 4$ and $r_j = p_j - 1$ in the formula $y_k = \frac{1}{16}(v_k + m_k - c_0)$. In hexadecimal notation, y_k turns out to be the final 2^k digits of 434243414342434.

Since $v_4(10y_4)$ is less than 2^{64}, the same counterexample is also minimal for all $k > 4$. One way to work with larger operands is to modify the method by starting with

$v_0(u) = 6\lfloor u/2 \rfloor + 6$ and letting $c_k = 6(p_k - 1)/(p_0 - 1)$, $m_0 = 2m$. (In effect, we are truncating one bit further to the right than before.) Then $\lfloor v_k(u)/32 \rfloor = \lfloor u/10 \rfloor$ when u is less than $10 z_k$, for $1 \le k \le 7$, where $z_k = \frac{1}{32}(v_k + m_k - 6)$ when $m_k = 7$, $r_0 = 14$, and $r_j = p_j - 1$ for $j > 0$. For example, $z_4 = $ 1c342c3424342c34. [This exercise is based on ideas of R. A. Vowels, *Australian Comp. J.* **24** (1992), 81–85.]

10. (i) Shift right one; (ii) Extract the left bit of each group; (iii) Shift the result of (ii) right two; (iv) Shift the result of (iii) right one, and add it to the result of (iii); (v) Subtract the result of (iv) from the result of (i).

11.

```
    2.1 4 4 6
  -   4
    1 7.4 4 6              8.9 9 8
  -   3 4              +   2 0
    1 4 0.4 6            1 3 1.9 8
  -   2 8 0            +   2 6 2
    1 1 2 4.6            1 6 0 3.8
  -   2 2 4 8          +   3 4 0 6
      8 9 9 8            2 1 4 4 6
```
$\qquad\qquad$ *Answer:* $(8998)_{10}$. $\qquad\qquad\qquad$ *Answer:* $(21446)_8$.

12. First convert the ternary number to nonary (radix 9) notation, then proceed as in octal-to-decimal conversion but without doubling. Decimal to nonary is similar. In the given example, we have

```
    1.7 6 4 7 2 3
  -   1
    1 6.6 4 7 2 3            9.8 7 6 5 4
  -   1 6                +       9
    1 5 0.4 7 2 3          1 1 8.7 6 5 4
  -   1 5 0              +     1 1 8
    1 3 5 4.7 2 3          1 3 1 6.6 5 4
  -   1 3 5 4            +     1 3 1 6
    1 2 1 9 3.2 3          1 4 4 8 3.5 4
  -   1 2 1 9 3          +     1 4 4 8 3
    1 0 9 7 3 9.3          1 6 0 4 2 8.4
  -   1 0 9 7 3 9        +     1 6 0 4 2 8
      9 8 7 6 5 4          1 7 6 4 7 2 3
```
$\qquad$ *Answer:* $(987654)_{10}$. $\qquad\qquad\qquad$ *Answer:* $(1764723)_9$.

13.

```
BUF     ALF  .⊔⊔⊔⊔              (Radix point on first line)
        ORIG *+39
START   JOV  OFLO              Ensure that overflow is off.
        ENT2 -40               Set buffer pointer.
8H      ENT3 10                Set loop counter.
1H      ENT1 m                 Begin multiplication routine.
        ENTX 0
2H      STX  CARRY
        . . .                  (See exercise 4.3.1–13, with
        J1P  2B                    v = 10⁹ and W = U.)
        SLAX 5                 rA ← next nine digits.
        CHAR
        STA  BUF+40,2(2:5)     Store next nine digits.
```

```
        STX   BUF+41,2
        INC2  2                           Increase buffer pointer.
        DEC3  1
        J3P   1B                          Repeat ten times.
        OUT   BUF+20,2(PRINTER)
        J2N   8B                          Repeat until both lines are printed.  ▌
```

14. Let $K(n)$ be the number of steps required to convert an n-digit decimal number to binary and at the same time to compute the binary representation of 10^n. Then we have $K(2n) \leq 2K(n) + O(M(n))$. *Proof.* Given the number $U = (u_{2n-1} \ldots u_0)_{10}$, compute $U_1 = (u_{2n-1} \ldots u_n)_{10}$ and $U_0 = (u_{n-1} \ldots u_0)_{10}$ and 10^n, in $2K(n)$ steps, then compute $U = 10^n U_1 + U_0$ and $10^{2n} = 10^n \cdot 10^n$ in $O(M(n))$ steps. It follows that $K(2^n) = O(M(2^n) + 2M(2^{n-1}) + 4M(2^{n-2}) + \cdots) = O(nM(2^n))$.

[Similarly, Schönhage has observed that we can convert a $(2^n \lg 10)$-bit number U from binary to decimal, in $O(nM(2^n))$ steps. First form $V = 10^{2^{n-1}}$ in $O(M(2^{n-1}) + M(2^{n-2}) + \cdots) = O(M(2^n))$ steps, then compute $U_0 = (U \bmod V)$ and $U_1 = \lfloor U/V \rfloor$ in $O(M(2^n))$ further steps, then convert U_0 and U_1.]

17. See W. D. Clinger, *SIGPLAN Notices* **25**, 6 (June 1990), 92–101, and the paper by Steele and White cited in the answer to exercise 3.

18. Let $U = \text{round}_B(u, P)$ and $v = \text{round}_b(U, p)$. We may assume that $u > 0$, so that $U > 0$ and $v > 0$. *Case 1: $v < u$.* Determine e and E such that $b^{e-1} < u \leq b^e$, $B^{E-1} \leq U < B^E$. Then $u \leq U + \frac{1}{2}B^{E-P}$ and $U \leq u - \frac{1}{2}b^{e-P}$; hence $B^{P-1} \leq B^{P-E}U < B^{P-E}u \leq b^{p-e}u \leq b^p$. *Case 2: $v > u$.* Determine e and E such that $b^{e-1} \leq u < b^e$, $B^{E-1} < U \leq B^E$. Then $u \geq U - \frac{1}{2}B^{E-P}$ and $U \geq u + \frac{1}{2}b^{e-P}$; hence $B^{P-1} \leq B^{P-E}(U - B^{E-P}) < B^{P-E}u \leq b^{p-e}u < b^p$. Thus we have proved that $B^{P-1} < b^p$ whenever $v \neq u$.

Conversely, if $B^{P-1} < b^p$, the proof above suggests that the most likely example for which $u \neq v$ will occur when u is a power of b and at the same time it is close to a power of B. We have $B^{P-1}b^p < B^{P-1}b^p + \frac{1}{2}b^p - \frac{1}{2}B^{P-1} - \frac{1}{4} = (B^{P-1} + \frac{1}{2})(b^p - \frac{1}{2})$; hence $1 < \alpha = 1/(1 - \frac{1}{2}b^{-p}) < 1 + \frac{1}{2}B^{1-P} = \beta$. There are integers e and E such that $\log_B \alpha < e\log_B b - E < \log_B \beta$, by exercise 4.5.3–50. Hence $\alpha < b^e/B^E < \beta$, for some e and E. Now we have $\text{round}_B(b^e, P) = B^E$, and $\text{round}_b(B^E, p) < b^e$. [*CACM* **11** (1968), 47–50; *Proc. Amer. Math. Soc.* **19** (1968), 716–723.]

For example, if $b^p = 2^{10}$ and $B^P = 10^4$, the number $u = 2^{6408} \approx .100049 \cdot 10^{1930}$ rounds down to $U = .1 \cdot 10^{1930} \approx (.1111111111101111111111)_2 \cdot 2^{6408}$, which rounds down to $2^{6408} - 2^{6398}$. (The *smallest* example is actually $\text{round}((.1111111001)_2 \cdot 2^{784}) = .1011 \cdot 10^{236}$, $\text{round}(.1011 \cdot 10^{235}) = (.11111110010)_2 \cdot 2^{784}$, found by Fred J. Tydeman.)

19. $m_1 = (\text{F0F0F0F0})_{16}$, $c_1 = 1 - 10/16$ makes $U = ((u_7u_6)_{10} \ldots (u_1u_0)_{10})_{256}$; then $m_2 = (\text{FF00FF00})_{16}$, $c_2 = 1 - 10^2/16^2$ makes $U = ((u_7u_6u_5u_4)_{10}(u_3u_2u_1u_0)_{10})_{65536}$; and $m_3 = (\text{FFFF0000})_{16}$, $c_3 = 1 - 10^4/16^4$ finishes the job. [Compare with Schönhage's algorithm in exercise 14. This technique is due to Roy A. Keir, circa 1958.]

SECTION 4.5.1

1. Test whether or not $uv' < u'v$, since the denominators are positive. (See also the answer to exercise 4.5.3–39.)

2. If $c > 1$ divides both u/d and v/d, then cd divides both u and v.

3. Let p be prime. If p^e is a divisor of uv and $u'v'$ for $e \geq 1$, then either $p^e \backslash u$ and $p^e \backslash v'$ or $p^e \backslash u'$ and $p^e \backslash v$; hence $p^e \backslash \gcd(u, v') \gcd(u', v)$. The converse follows by reversing the argument.

4. Let $d_1 = \gcd(u, v)$, $d_2 = \gcd(u', v')$; the answer is $w = (u/d_1)(v'/d_2)\operatorname{sign}(v)$, $w' = |(u'/d_2)(v/d_1)|$, with a "divide by zero" error message if $v = 0$.

5. $d_1 = 10$, $t = 17 \cdot 7 - 27 \cdot 12 = -205$, $d_2 = 5$, $w = -41$, $w' = 168$.

6. Let $u'' = u'/d_1$, $v'' = v'/d_1$; our goal is to show that $\gcd(uv'' + u''v, d_1) = \gcd(uv'' + u''v, d_1 u''v'')$. If p is a prime that divides u'', then p does not divide u or v'', so p does not divide $uv'' + u''v$. A similar argument holds for prime divisors of v'', so no prime divisors of $u''v''$ affect the given gcd.

7. $(N-1)^2 + (N-2)^2 = 2N^2 - (6N - 5)$. If the inputs are n-bit binary numbers, $2n + 1$ bits may be necessary to represent t.

8. For multiplication and division these quantities obey the rules $x/0 = \operatorname{sign}(x)\infty$, $(\pm\infty) \times x = x \times (\pm\infty) = (\pm\infty)/x = \pm\operatorname{sign}(x)\infty$, $x/(\pm\infty) = 0$, provided that x is finite and nonzero, without change to the algorithms described. Furthermore, the algorithms can readily be modified so that $0/0 = 0 \times (\pm\infty) = (\pm\infty) \times 0 = \text{"}(0/0)\text{"}$, where the latter is a representation of "undefined." If either operand is undefined the result should be undefined also.

Since the multiplication and division subroutines can yield these fairly natural rules of extended arithmetic, it is sometimes worthwhile to modify the addition and subtraction operations so that they satisfy the rules $x \pm \infty = \pm\infty$, $x \pm (-\infty) = \mp\infty$, for x finite; $(\pm\infty) + (\pm\infty) = \pm\infty - (\mp\infty) = \pm\infty$; furthermore $(\pm\infty) + (\mp\infty) = (\pm\infty) - (\pm\infty) = (0/0)$; and if either or both operands are $(0/0)$, the result should also be $(0/0)$. Equality tests and comparisons may be treated in a similar manner.

The remarks above are independent of "overflow" indications. If ∞ is being used to suggest overflow, it is incorrect to let $1/\infty$ be equal to zero, lest inaccurate results be regarded as true answers. It is far better to represent overflow by $(0/0)$, and to adhere to the convention that the result of any operation is undefined if at least one of the inputs is undefined. This type of overflow indication has the advantage that final results of an extended calculation reveal exactly which answers are defined and which are not.

9. If $u/u' \neq v/v'$, then $1 \leq |uv' - u'v| = u'v'|u/u' - v/v'| < |2^{2n}u/u' - 2^{2n}v/v'|$; two quantities differing by more than unity cannot have the same "floor." (In other words, the first $2n$ bits to the right of the binary point are enough to characterize the value of a binary fraction, when there are n-bit denominators. We cannot improve this to $2n - 1$ bits, for if $n = 4$ we have $\frac{1}{13} = (.00010011\ldots)_2$, $\frac{1}{14} = (.00010010\ldots)_2$.)

11. To divide by $(v + v'\sqrt{5})/v''$, when v and v' are not both zero, multiply by the reciprocal, $(v - v'\sqrt{5})v''/(v^2 - 5v'^2)$, and reduce to lowest terms.

12. $((2^{q-1} - 1)/1)$; $\operatorname{round}(x) = (0/1)$ if and only if $|x| \leq 2^{1-q}$. Similarly, $\operatorname{round}(x) = (1/0)$ if and only if $x \geq 2^{q-1}$.

13. One idea is to limit numerator and denominator to a total of 27 bits, where we need only store 26 of these bits (since the leading bit of the denominator is 1 unless the denominator has length 0). This leaves room for a sign and five bits to indicate the denominator size. Another idea is to use 28 bits for numerator and denominator, which are to have a total of at most seven hexadecimal digits, together with a sign and a 3-bit field to indicate the number of hexadecimal digits in the denominator.

[Using the formulas in the next exercise, the first alternative leads to exactly 2140040119 finite representable numbers, while the second leads to 1830986459. The first alternative is preferable because it represents more values, and because it is cleaner and makes smoother transitions between ranges. With 64-bit words we would, similarly, limit numerator and denominator to a total of at most $64 - 6 = 58$ bits.]

14. The number of multiples of n in the interval $(a \ldotp\ldotp b]$ is $\lfloor b/n \rfloor - \lfloor a/n \rfloor$. Hence, by inclusion and exclusion, the answer to this problem is $S_0 - S_1 + S_2 - \cdots$, where S_k is $\sum (\lfloor M_2/P \rfloor - \lfloor M_1/P \rfloor)(\lfloor N_2/P \rfloor - \lfloor N_1/P \rfloor)$, summed over all products P of k distinct primes. We can also express the answer as

$$\sum_{n=1}^{\min(M_2, N_2)} \mu(n) \left(\lfloor M_2/n \rfloor - \lfloor M_1/n \rfloor \right) \left(\lfloor N_2/n \rfloor - \lfloor N_1/n \rfloor \right).$$

SECTION 4.5.2

1. Substitute min, max, + consistently for gcd, lcm, ×, respectively (after making sure that the identities are correct when any variable is zero).

2. For prime p, let u_p, v_{1p}, $\ldots$, v_{np} be the exponents of p in the canonical factorizations of u, v_1, $\ldots$, v_n. By hypothesis, $u_p \le v_{1p} + \cdots + v_{np}$. We must show that $u_p \le \min(u_p, v_{1p}) + \cdots + \min(u_p, v_{np})$, and this is certainly true if u_p is greater than or equal to each v_{jp}, or if u_p is less than some v_{jp}.

3. *Solution 1:* If $n = p_1^{e_1} \ldots p_r^{e_r}$, the number in each case is $(2e_1 + 1) \ldots (2e_r + 1)$. *Solution 2:* A one-to-one correspondence is obtained if we set $u = \gcd(d, n)$ and $v = n^2/\operatorname{lcm}(d, n)$ for each divisor d of n^2. [E. Cesàro, *Annali di Matematica Pura ed Applicata* (2) **13** (1885), 235–250, §12.]

4. See exercise 3.2.1.2–15(a).

5. Shift u and v right until neither is a multiple of 3, remembering the proper power of 3 that will appear in the gcd. Each subsequent iteration sets $t \leftarrow u + v$ or $t \leftarrow u - v$ (whichever is a multiple of 3), shifts t right until it is not a multiple of 3, then replaces $\max(u, v)$ by the result.

u	v	t
13634	24140	10506, 3502;
13634	3502	17136, 5712, 1904;
1904	3502	5406, 1802;
1904	1802	102, 34;
34	1802	1836, 612, 204, 68;
34	68	102, 34;
34	34	0.

The evidence that $\gcd(40902, 24140) = 34$ is now overwhelming.

6. The probability that both u and v are even is $\frac{1}{4}$; the probability that both are multiples of four is $\frac{1}{16}$; etc. Thus A has the distribution given by the generating function

$$\frac{3}{4} + \frac{3}{16} z + \frac{3}{64} z^2 + \cdots = \frac{3/4}{1 - z/4}.$$

The mean is $\frac{1}{3}$, and the standard deviation is $\sqrt{\frac{2}{9} + \frac{1}{3} - \frac{1}{9}} = \frac{2}{3}$. If u and v are independently and uniformly distributed with $1 \le u, v < 2^N$, some small correction terms are needed; the mean is then actually

$$(2^N - 1)^{-2} \sum_{k=1}^{N} (2^{N-k} - 1)^2 = \frac{1}{3} - \frac{4}{3}(2^N - 1)^{-1} + N(2^N - 1)^{-2}.$$

7. When u and v are not both even, each of the cases (even, odd), (odd, even), (odd, odd) is equally probable, and $B = 1$, 0, 0 in these cases. Hence $B = \frac{1}{3}$ on the average. Actually, as in exercise 6, a small correction should be given to be strictly accurate when $1 \le u, v < 2^N$; the probability that $B = 1$ is actually

$$(2^N - 1)^{-2} \sum_{k=1}^{N} (2^{N-k} - 1)2^{N-k} = \frac{1}{3} - \frac{1}{3}(2^N - 1)^{-1}.$$

8. Let F be the number of subtraction steps in which $u > v$; then $E = F + B$. If we change the inputs from (u, v) to (v, u), the value of C stays unchanged, while F becomes $C - 1 - F$. Hence $E_{\text{ave}} = \frac{1}{2}(C_{\text{ave}} - 1) + B_{\text{ave}}$.

9. The binary algorithm first gets to B6 with $u = 1963$, $v = 1359$; then $t \leftarrow 604$, 302, 151, etc. The gcd is 302. Using Algorithm X we find that $2 \cdot 31408 - 23 \cdot 2718 = 302$.

10. (a) Two integers are relatively prime if and only if they are not both divisible by any prime number. (b) Rearrange the sum in (a), with denominators $k = p_1 \ldots p_r$. (Each of the sums in (a) and (b) is actually finite.) (c) Since $(n/k)^2 - \lfloor n/k \rfloor^2 = O(n/k)$, we have $q_n - \sum_{k=1}^{n} \mu(k)(n/k)^2 = \sum_{k=1}^{n} O(n/k) = O(nH_n)$. Furthermore $\sum_{k>n}(n/k)^2 = O(n)$. (d) $\sum_{d\backslash n} \mu(d) = \delta_{1n}$. [In fact, we have the more general result

$$\sum_{d\backslash n} \mu(d) \left(\frac{n}{d}\right)^s = n^s - \sum \left(\frac{n}{p}\right)^s + \sum \left(\frac{n}{pq}\right)^s - \cdots,$$

as in part (b), where the sums on the right are over the prime divisors of n, and this is equal to $n^s(1 - 1/p_1^s) \ldots (1 - 1/p_r^s)$ if $n = p_1^{e_1} \ldots p_r^{e_r}$.]

    Notes: Similarly, we find that a set of k integers is relatively prime with probability $1/\zeta(k) = 1/(\sum_{n\geq 1} 1/n^k)$. This proof of Theorem D is due to F. Mertens, *Crelle* **77** (1874), 289–291. The technique actually gives a much stronger result, namely that $6\pi^{-2}mn + O(n \log m)$ pairs of integers $u \in [f(m) .. f(m) + m)$, $v \in [g(n) .. g(n) + n)$ are relatively prime, when $m \le n$, $f(m) = O(m)$, and $g(n) = O(n)$.

11. (a) $6/\pi^2$ times $1 + \frac{1}{4} + \frac{1}{9}$, namely $49/(6\pi^2) \approx .82746$. (b) $6/\pi^2$ times $1/1 + 2/4 + 3/9 + \cdots$, namely ∞. (This is true in spite of the results of exercises 12 and 14.)

12. [*Annali di Mat.* (2) **13** (1885), 235–250, §3.] Let $\sigma(n)$ be the number of positive divisors of n. The answer is

$$\sum_{k\geq 1} \sigma(k) \cdot \frac{6}{\pi^2 k^2} = \frac{6}{\pi^2} \left(\sum_{k\geq 1} \frac{1}{k^2}\right)^2 = \frac{\pi^2}{6}.$$

[Thus, the average is *less* than 2, although there are always at least two common divisors when u and v are not relatively prime.]

13. $1 + \frac{1}{9} + \frac{1}{25} + \cdots = 1 + \frac{1}{4} + \frac{1}{9} + \cdots - \frac{1}{4}(1 + \frac{1}{4} + \frac{1}{9} + \cdots)$.

14. (a) $L = (6/\pi^2)\sum_{d\geq 1} d^{-2} \ln d = -\zeta'(2)/\zeta(2) = \sum_{p \text{ prime}}(\ln p)/(p^2 - 1) \approx 0.56996$. (b) $(8/\pi^2)\sum_{d\geq 1}[d \text{ odd}] d^{-2} \ln d = L - \frac{1}{3} \ln 2 \approx 0.33891$.

15. $v_1 = \pm v/u_3$, $v_2 = \mp u/u_3$ (the sign depends on whether the number of iterations is even or odd). This follows from the fact that v_1 and v_2 are relatively prime to each other (throughout the algorithm), and that $v_1 u = -v_2 v$. [Hence $v_1 u = \text{lcm}(u, v)$ at the close of the algorithm, but this is not an especially efficient way to compute the least common multiple. For a generalization, see exercise 4.6.1–18.]

    Further details can be found in exercise 4.5.3–48.

16. Apply Algorithm X to v and m, thus obtaining a value x such that $xv \equiv 1$ (modulo m). (This can be done by simplifying Algorithm X so that u_2, v_2, and t_2 are not computed, since they are never used in the answer.) Then set $w \leftarrow ux \bmod m$. [It follows, as in exercise 4.5.3–45, that this process requires $O(n^2)$ units of time, when it is applied to large n-bit numbers. See exercises 17 and 39 for alternatives to Algorithm X.]

17. We can let $u' = (2u - vu^2) \bmod 2^{2e}$, as in Newton's method (see the end of Section 4.3.1). Equivalently, if $uv \equiv 1 + 2^e w$ (modulo 2^{2e}), let $u' = u + 2^e((-uw) \bmod 2^e)$.

18. Let u_1, u_2, u_3, v_1, v_2, v_3 be multiprecision variables, in addition to u and v. The extended algorithm will act the same on u_3 and v_3 as Algorithm L does on u and v. New multiprecision operations are to set $t \leftarrow Au_j$, $t \leftarrow t + Bv_j$, $w \leftarrow Cu_j$, $w \leftarrow w + Dv_j$, $u_j \leftarrow t$, $v_j \leftarrow w$ for all j, in step L4; also if $B = 0$ in that step to set $t \leftarrow u_j - qv_j$, $u_j \leftarrow v_j$, $v_j \leftarrow t$ for all j and for $q = \lfloor u_3/v_3 \rfloor$. A similar modification is made to step L1 if v_3 is small. The inner loop (steps L2 and L3) is unchanged.

19. (a) Set $t_1 = x + 2y + 3z$; then $3t_1 + y + 2z = 1$, $5t_1 - 3y - 20z = 3$. Eliminate y, then $14t_1 - 14z = 6$: No solution. (b) This time $14t_1 - 14z = 0$. Divide by 14, eliminate t_1; the general solution is $x = 8z - 2$, $y = 1 - 5z$, z arbitrary.

20. We can assume that $m \geq n$. If $m > n = 0$ we get to $(m - t, 0)$ with probability 2^{-t} for $1 \leq t < m$, to $(0,0)$ with probability 2^{1-m}. *Valida vi*, the following values can be obtained for $n > 0$:

Case 1, $m = n$. From (n,n) we go to $(n-t, n)$ with probability $t/2^t - 5/2^{t+1} + 3/2^{2t}$, for $2 \leq t < n$. (These values are $\frac{1}{16}$, $\frac{7}{64}$, $\frac{27}{256}$, ...) To $(0,n)$ the probability is $n/2^{n-1} - 1/2^{n-2} + 1/2^{2n-2}$. To (n, k) the probability is the same as to (k,n). The algorithm terminates with probability $1/2^{n-1}$.

Case 2, $m = n+1$. From $(n+1, n)$ we get to (n,n) with probability $\frac{1}{8}$ when $n > 1$, or 0 when $n = 1$; to $(n - t, n)$ with probability $11/2^{t+3} - 3/2^{2t+1}$, for $1 \leq t < n - 1$. (These values are $\frac{5}{16}$, $\frac{1}{4}$, $\frac{19}{128}$, ...) We get to $(1,n)$ with probability $5/2^{n+1} - 3/2^{2n-1}$, for $n > 1$; to $(0,n)$ with probability $3/2^n - 1/2^{2n-1}$.

Case 3, $m \geq n + 2$. The probabilities are given by the following table:

$$
\begin{array}{ll}
(m - 1, n): & 1/2 - 3/2^{m-n+2} - \delta_{n1}/2^{m+1}; \\
(m - t, n): & 1/2^t + 3/2^{m-n+t+1}, \quad 1 < t < n; \\
(m - n, n): & 1/2^n + 1/2^m, \quad n > 1; \\
(m - n - t, n): & 1/2^{n+t} + \delta_{t1}/2^{m-1}, \quad 1 \leq t < m - n; \\
(0, n): & 1/2^{m-1}.
\end{array}
$$

The only thing interesting about these results is that they are so messy; but that makes them uninteresting.

21. Show that for fixed v and for $2^m < u < 2^{m+1}$, when m is large, each subtract-and-shift cycle of the algorithm reduces $\lfloor \lg u \rfloor$ by two, on the average.

22. Exactly $(N - m)2^{m-1+\delta_{m0}}$ integers u in the range $1 \leq u < 2^N$ have $\lfloor \lg u \rfloor = m$, after u has been shifted right until it is odd. Thus

$$(2^N - 1)^2 C = N^2 C_{00} + 2N \sum_{1 \leq n \leq N} (N - n)2^{n-1} C_{n0}$$

$$+ 2 \sum_{1 \leq n < m \leq N} (N - m)(N - n)2^{m+n-2} C_{mn} + \sum_{1 \leq n \leq N} (N - n)^2 2^{2n-2} C_{nn}.$$

(The same formula holds for D in terms of D_{mn}.)

The middle sum is $2^{2N-2} \sum_{0 \le m < n < N} mn2^{-m-n}((\alpha+\beta)N+\gamma-\alpha m-\beta n)$. Since

$$\sum_{0 \le m < n} m2^{-m} = 2 - (n+1)2^{1-n} \quad \text{and} \quad \sum_{0 \le m < n} m(m-1)2^{-m} = 4 - (n^2+n+2)2^{1-n},$$

the sum on m is

$$2^{2N-2} \sum_{0 \le n < N} n2^{-n} \Big((\gamma-\alpha-\beta n+(\alpha+\beta)N)(2-(n+1)2^{1-n}) - \alpha(4-(n^2+n+2)2^{1-n}) \Big)$$

$$= 2^{2N-2} \Big((\alpha+\beta)N \sum_{n \ge 0} n2^{-n}(2-(n+1)2^{1-n}) + O(1) \Big).$$

Thus the coefficient of $(\alpha+\beta)N$ in the answer is found to be $2^{-2}(4 - (\frac{4}{3})^3) = \frac{11}{27}$. A similar argument applies to the other sums.

Note: The *exact* value of the sums may be obtained after some tedious calculation by means of the general summation-by-parts formula

$$\sum_{0 \le k < n} k^{\underline{m}} z^k = \frac{m! \, z^m}{(1-z)^{m+1}} - \sum_{k=0}^{m} \frac{m^{\underline{k}} \, n^{\underline{m-k}} \, z^{n+k}}{(1-z)^{k+1}}.$$

23. If $x \le 1$ it is $\Pr(u \ge v \text{ and } v/u \le x) = \frac{1}{2}(1-G_n(x))$. And if $x \ge 1$ it is $\frac{1}{2}+\Pr(u \le v$ and $v/u \ge 1/x) = \frac{1}{2} + \frac{1}{2}G_n(1/x)$; this also equals $\frac{1}{2}(1 - G_n(x))$ by (40).

24. $\sum_{k \ge 1} 2^{-k}G(1/(2^k+1)) = S(1)$. This value, which has no obvious connection to classical constants, is approximately 0.5432582959.

25. Richard Brent has noted that $G(e^{-y})$ is an odd function that is analytic for all real values of y. If we let $G(e^{-y}) = \lambda_1 y + \lambda_3 y^3 + \lambda_5 y^5 + \cdots = \rho(e^{-y}-1)$, we have $-\rho_1 = \lambda_1 = \lambda$, $\rho_2 = \frac{1}{2}\lambda$, $-\rho_3 = \frac{1}{3}\lambda + \lambda_3$, $\rho_4 = \frac{1}{4}\lambda + \frac{3}{4}\lambda_3$, $-\rho_5 = \frac{1}{5}\lambda + \frac{7}{4}\lambda_3 + \lambda_5$;

$$(-1)^n \rho_n = \sum_k \begin{bmatrix} n \\ k \end{bmatrix} \frac{k!}{n!} \lambda_k; \qquad \lambda_n = -\sum_k \begin{Bmatrix} n \\ k \end{Bmatrix} \frac{k!}{n!} \rho_k.$$

The first few values are $\lambda_1 \approx .3979226812$, $\lambda_3 \approx -.0210096400$, $\lambda_5 \approx .0013749841$, $\lambda_7 \approx -.0000960351$. *Wild conjecture:* $\lim_{k \to \infty} (-\lambda_{2k+1}/\lambda_{2k-1}) = 1/\pi^2$.

26. The left side is $2S(1/x)-5S(1/2x)+2S(1/4x)-2S(x)+5S(2x)-2S(4x)$ by (39); the right side is $S(2x)-2S(4x)+2S(1/x)-S(1/2x)-2S(x)+4S(2x)-4S(1/2x)+2S(1/4x)$ by (44). The cases $x = 1$, $x = 1/\sqrt{2}$, and $x = \phi$ are perhaps the most interesting; for example, $x = \phi$ gives $2G(4\phi) - 5G(2\phi) + G(\phi^2/2) - G(\phi^3) = 2G(2\phi^2)$.

27. $2\psi_n = [z^n] z \sum_{k \ge 0} 2^{-2k} \sum_{j=0}^{2^k-1} \sum_{l \ge 0}(jz/2^k)^l = \sum_{k \ge 1} 2^{-k(n+1)} \sum_{j=0}^{2^k-1} j^{n-1} = \sum_{k \ge 1} 2^{-k(n+1)} \sum_{l=0}^{n-1} \binom{n}{l}(-1)^l B_l 2^{k(n-l)}/n$ by exercise 1.2.11.2–4, when $n > 1$; and of course $\sum_{k \ge 1} 2^{-k(l+1)} = 1/(2^{l+1} - 1)$.

28. Letting $S_n(m) = \sum_{k=1}^{m-1}(1 - k/m)^n$ and $T_n(m) = 1/(e^{n/m} - 1)$ as in exercise 6.3–34(b), we find $S_n(m) = T_n(m) + O(e^{-n/m} n/m^2)$ and $2\psi_{n+1} = \sum_{j \ge 1} 2^{-2j} S_n(2^j) = \tau_n + O(n^{-3})$, where $\tau_n = \sum_{j \ge 1} 2^{-2j} T_n(2^j)$. Since $\tau_{n+1} < \tau_n$ and $4\tau_{2n} - \tau_n = 1/(e^n - 1)$ is positive but exponentially small, it follows that $\tau_n = \Theta(n^{-2})$. More detailed information can be obtained by writing

$$\sum_{j \ge 1} \frac{1}{2^{2j}} \frac{1}{e^{n/2^j}-1} = \frac{1}{2\pi i} \sum_{j \ge 1} \int_{3/2-i\infty}^{3/2+i\infty} \frac{\zeta(z)\Gamma(z)n^{-z}}{2^j(2-z)} \, dz = \frac{1}{2\pi i} \int_{3/2-i\infty}^{3/2+i\infty} \frac{\zeta(z)\Gamma(z)n^{-z}}{2^{2-z}-1} \, dz.$$

The integral is the sum of the residues at the poles $2 + 2\pi i k/\ln 2$, namely n^{-2} times $\pi^2/(6\ln 2) + f(n)$, where

$$f(n) = 2\sum_{k\geq 1}\Re(\zeta(2 + 2\pi ik/\ln 2)\Gamma(2 + 2\pi ik/\ln 2)\exp(-2\pi ik\lg n)/\ln 2)$$

is a periodic function of $\lg n$ whose "average" value is zero.

29. (Solution by P. Flajolet and B. Vallée.) If $f(x) = \sum_{k\geq 1}2^{-k}g(2^kx)$ and $g^*(s) = \int_0^\infty g(x)x^{s-1}\,dx$, then $f^*(s) = \sum_{k\geq 1}2^{-k(s+1)}g^*(s) = g^*(s)/(2^{s+1} - 1)$, and $f(x) = \frac{1}{2\pi i}\int_{c-i\infty}^{c+i\infty}f^*(s)x^{-s}\,ds$ under appropriate conditions. Letting $g(x) = 1/(1+x)$, we find that the transform in this case is $g^*(s) = \pi/\sin\pi s$ when $0 < \Re s < 1$; hence

$$f(x) = \sum_{k=1}^\infty\frac{1}{2^k}\frac{1}{1 + 2^kx} = \frac{1}{2\pi i}\int_{1/2-i\infty}^{1/2+i\infty}\frac{\pi x^{-s}\,ds}{(2^{s+1} - 1)\sin\pi s}.$$

It follows that $f(x)$ is the sum of the residues of $\frac{\pi}{\sin\pi s}x^{-s}/(2^{s+1}-1)$ for $\Re s \leq 0$, namely $1 + x\lg x + \frac{1}{2}x + xP(\lg x) - \frac{1}{4}x^2 + \frac{4}{3}x^3 - \frac{8}{7}x^4 + \cdots$, where

$$P(t) = \frac{2\pi}{\ln 2}\sum_{m=1}^\infty\frac{\sin 2\pi mt}{\sinh(2m\pi^2/\ln 2)}$$

is a periodic function whose absolute value never exceeds 8×10^{-12}. (The fact that $P(t)$ is so small caused Brent to overlook it in his original paper.)

The Mellin transform of $f(1/x)$ is $f^*(-s) = \pi/((1 - 2^{1-s})\sin\pi s)$ for $-1 < \Re s < 0$; thus $f(1/x) = \frac{1}{2\pi i}\int_{-1/2-i\infty}^{-1/2+i\infty}\frac{\pi}{\sin\pi s}x^{-s}\,ds/(1 - 2^{1-s})$, and we now want the residues of the integrand with $\Re s \leq -1$: $f(1/x) = \frac{1}{3}x - \frac{1}{7}x^2 + \cdots$. [This formula could also have been obtained directly.] We have $S_1(x) = 1 - f(x)$, and it follows that

$$G_1(x) = f(x) - f(1/x) = x\lg x + \frac{1}{2}x + xP(\lg x) - \frac{x^2}{1 + x} + (1 - x^2)\phi(x),$$

where $\phi(x) = \sum_{k=0}^\infty(-1)^kx^k/(2^{k+1} - 1)$.

30. We have $G_2(x) = \Sigma_1(x) - \Sigma_1(1/x) + \Sigma_2(x) - \Sigma_2(1/x)$, where

$$\Sigma_1(x) = \sum_{k,l\geq 1}\frac{1}{2^{k+l}}\frac{1}{1 + 2^l(1 + 2^kx)}, \qquad \Sigma_2(x) = \sum_{k,l\geq 1}\frac{1}{2^k}\frac{1}{1 + 2^l + 2^kx}.$$

The Mellin transforms are $\Sigma_1^*(s) = \frac{\pi}{\sin\pi s}a(s)/(2^{s+1} - 1)$, $\Sigma_2^*(s) = \frac{\pi}{\sin\pi s}b(s)/(2^{s+1} - 1)$, where

$$a(s) = \sum_{l\geq 1}\frac{(1 + 2^{-l})^{s-1}}{2^{2l}} = \sum_{k\geq 0}\binom{s-1}{k}\frac{1}{2^{k+2} - 1},$$

$$b(s) = \sum_{l\geq 1}(2^l + 1)^{s-1} = \sum_{k\geq 0}\binom{s-1}{k}\frac{1}{2^{k+1-s} - 1}.$$

Therefore we obtain the following expansions for $0 \leq x \leq 1$:

$$\Sigma_1(x) = a(0) + a(-1)x(\lg x + \tfrac{1}{2}) - a'(1)x/\ln 2 + xA(\lg x) - \sum_{k\geq 2}\frac{2^{k-1}}{2^{k-1} - 1}a(-k)(-x)^k,$$

$$\Sigma_2(x) = b(0) + b(-1)x(\lg x + \tfrac{1}{2}) - b'(1)x/\ln 2 + xB(\lg x) - \sum_{k\geq 2}\frac{2^{k-1}}{2^{k-1} - 1}b(-k)(-x)^k,$$

$$\Sigma_1(1/x) = \sum_{k \geq 1} \frac{-a(k)(-x)^k}{2^{k+1} - 1},$$

$$\Sigma_2(1/x) = \sum_{k \geq 1} \frac{(-x)^k}{2^{k+1} - 1} \left(\lg x - \hat{b}(k) - \frac{1}{2} - \frac{1}{2^{k+1} - 1} + \frac{H_{k-1}}{\ln 2} + P_k(\lg x) \right),$$

$$\hat{b}(s) = \sum_{k=0}^{s-2} \binom{s-1}{k} \frac{1}{2^{k+1-s} - 1};$$

$$A(t) = \frac{1}{\ln 2} \sum_{m \geq 1} \Re \left(\frac{2\pi i}{\sinh(2m\pi^2/\ln 2)} \, a(-1 + 2m\pi i/\ln 2) \, e^{-2m\pi i t} \right),$$

$$B(t) = \frac{1}{\ln 2} \sum_{m \geq 1} \Re \left(\frac{2\pi i}{\sinh(2m\pi^2/\ln 2)} \, b(-1 + 2m\pi i/\ln 2) \, e^{-2m\pi i t} \right),$$

$$P_k(t) = \frac{1}{\ln 2} \sum_{m \geq 1} \Re \left(\frac{2\pi i}{\sinh(2m\pi^2/\ln 2)} \binom{k - 1 - 2m\pi i/\ln 2}{k - 1} e^{-2m\pi i t} \right).$$

32. Yes: See G. Maze, *J. Discrete Algorithms* **5** (2007), 176–186.

34. Ian D. Morris [*Advances in Mathematics* **290** (2016), 73–143, whose function $\xi(z)$ is $G'(z)$] has successfully resolved this long-standing problem by applying and extending delicate methods of dynamical systems theory. Thus the problem of analyzing the binary gcd algorithm, now solved rigorously by Valleé and Morris in two quite different ways, continues to lead to ever more tantalizing questions of higher mathematics.

35. By induction, the length is $m + \lfloor n/2 \rfloor + 1 - [m = n = 1]$ when $m \geq n$. But exercise 37 shows that the algorithm cannot go as slowly as this.

36. Let $a_n = (2^n - (-1)^n)/3$; then $a_0, a_1, a_2, \ldots = 0, 1, 1, 3, 5, 11, 21, \ldots$. (This sequence of numbers has an interesting pattern of zeros and ones in its binary representation, and it arises in diverse applications. See H. Brocard, *Nouvelle Corresp. Math.* **6** (1880), 146. Notice that $a_n = a_{n-1} + 2a_{n-2}$, and $a_n + a_{n+1} = 2^n$.) For $m > n$, let $u = 2^{m+1} - a_{n+2}$, $v = a_{n+2}$. For $m = n > 0$, let $u = a_{n+2}$ and $v = u + (-1)^n$. Another example for the case $m = n > 0$ is $u = 2^{n+1} - 2$, $v = 2^{n+1} - 1$; this choice takes more shifts, and gives $B = 1$, $C = n+1$, $D = 2n$, $E = n$, the worst case for Program B.

37. (Solution by J. O. Shallit.) This is a problem where it appears to be necessary to prove *more* than was asked just to prove what was asked. Let $S(u, v)$ be the number of subtraction steps taken by Algorithm B on inputs u and v. We will prove that $S(u, v) \leq \lg(u + v)$. This will imply that $S(u, v) \leq \lfloor \lg(u + v) \rfloor \leq \lfloor \lg 2 \max(u, v) \rfloor = 1 + \lfloor \lg \max(u, v) \rfloor$ as desired.

Notice that $S(u, v) = S(v, u)$. If u is even, $S(u, v) = S(u/2, v)$; hence we may assume that u and v are odd. We may also assume that $u > v$, since $S(u, u) = 1$. Then $S(u, v) = 1 + S((u - v)/2, v) \leq 1 + \lg((u - v)/2 + v) = \lg(u + v)$ by induction.

It follows, incidentally, that the smallest case requiring n subtraction steps is $u = 2^{n-1} + 1$, $v = 2^{n-1} - 1$.

38. Keep track of the most significant and least significant words of the operands (the most significant is used to guess the sign of t and the least significant is to determine the amount of right shift), while building a 2×2 matrix A of single-precision integers such that $A\binom{u}{v} = \binom{u'w}{v'w}$, where w is the computer word size and where u' and v' are smaller than u and v. (Instead of dividing the simulated even operand by 2, multiply the other one by 2, until obtaining multiples of w after exactly $\lg w$ shifts.) Experiments show this algorithm running four times as fast as Algorithm L, on at least one computer. With the similar algorithm of exercise 40 we don't need the most significant words.

A possibly faster binary algorithm has been described by J. Sorenson, *J. Algorithms* **16** (1994), 110–144; Shallit and Sorenson, *Lecture Notes in Comp. Sci.* **877** (1994), 169–183.

39. (Solution by Michael Penk.) Assume that u and v are positive.

Y1. [Find power of 2.] Same as step B1.

Y2. [Initialize.] Set $(u_1, u_2, u_3) \leftarrow (1, 0, u)$ and $(v_1, v_2, v_3) \leftarrow (v, 1 - u, v)$. If u is odd, set $(t_1, t_2, t_3) \leftarrow (0, -1, -v)$ and go to Y4. Otherwise set $(t_1, t_2, t_3) \leftarrow (1, 0, u)$.

Y3. [Halve t_3.] If t_1 and t_2 are both even, set $(t_1, t_2, t_3) \leftarrow (t_1, t_2, t_3)/2$; otherwise set $(t_1, t_2, t_3) \leftarrow (t_1 + v, t_2 - u, t_3)/2$. (In the latter case, $t_1 + v$ and $t_2 - u$ will both be even.)

Y4. [Is t_3 even?] If t_3 is even, go back to Y3.

Y5. [Reset $\max(u_3, v_3)$.] If t_3 is positive, set $(u_1, u_2, u_3) \leftarrow (t_1, t_2, t_3)$; otherwise set $(v_1, v_2, v_3) \leftarrow (v - t_1, -u - t_2, -t_3)$.

Y6. [Subtract.] Set $(t_1, t_2, t_3) \leftarrow (u_1, u_2, u_3) - (v_1, v_2, v_3)$. Then if $t_1 \leq 0$, set $(t_1, t_2) \leftarrow (t_1 + v, t_2 - u)$. If $t_3 \neq 0$, go back to Y3. Otherwise the algorithm terminates with $(u_1, u_2, u_3 \cdot 2^k)$ as the output. ∎

It is clear that the relations in (16) are preserved, and that $0 \leq u_1, v_1, t_1 \leq v$, $0 \geq u_2, v_2, t_2 \geq -u$, $0 < u_3 \leq u$, $0 < v_3 \leq v$ after each of steps Y2–Y6. If u is odd after step Y1, then step Y3 can be simplified, since t_1 and t_2 are both even if and only if t_2 is even; similarly, if v is odd, then t_1 and t_2 are both even if and only if t_1 is even. Thus, as in Algorithm X, it is possible to suppress all calculations involving u_2, v_2, and t_2, provided that v is odd after step Y1. This condition is often known in advance (for example, it holds when v is prime and we are trying to compute u^{-1} modulo v).

See also A. W. Bojanczyk and R. P. Brent, *Computers and Mathematics with Applications* **14** (1987), 233–238, for a similar extension of the algorithm in exercise 40.

40. Let $m = \lg \max(|u|, |v|)$. We can show inductively that $|u| \leq 2^{m-(s-c)/2}$, $|v| \leq 2^{m-(s+c)/2}$ after we have performed the operation $c \leftarrow c + 1$ in step K3 s times. Therefore $s \leq 2m$. If K2 is executed t times, we have $t \leq s + 2$, because s increases every time except the first and last. [See *VLSI '83* (North-Holland, 1983), 145–154.]

Notes: When $u = 1$ and $v = 3 \cdot 2^k - 1$ and $k \geq 2$, we have $m = k + 2$, $s = 2k$, $t = k + 4$. When $u = u_j$ and $v = 2u_{j-1}$ in the sequence defined by $u_0 = 3$, $u_1 = 1$, $u_{j+1} = \min(|3u_j - 16u_{j-1}|, |5u_j - 16u_{j-1}|)$, we have $s = 2j + 2$, $t = 2j + 3$, and (empirically) $m \approx \phi j$. Can t be asymptotically larger than $2m/\phi$?

41. In general, since $(a^u - 1) \bmod (a^v - 1) = a^{u \bmod v} - 1$ (see Eq. 4.3.2–(20)), we find that $\gcd(a^m - 1, a^n - 1) = a^{\gcd(m,n)} - 1$ for all positive integers a.

42. Subtract the kth column from the $2k$th, $3k$th, $4k$th, etc., for $k = 1, 2, 3, \ldots$. The result is a triangular matrix with x_k on the diagonal in column k, where $m = \sum_{d \backslash m} x_d$. It follows that $x_m = \varphi(m)$, so the determinant is $\varphi(1)\varphi(2)\ldots\varphi(n)$.

[In general, "Smith's determinant," in which the (i, j) element is $f(\gcd(i, j))$ for an arbitrary function f, is equal to $\prod_{m=1}^{n} \sum_{d \backslash m} \mu(m/d)f(d)$, by the same argument. See L. E. Dickson, *History of the Theory of Numbers 1* (Carnegie Inst. of Washington, 1919), 122–123.]

SECTION 4.5.3

1. The running time is about $19.02T + 6$, just a trifle slower than Program 4.5.2A.

2. $\begin{pmatrix} K_n(x_1, x_2, \ldots, x_{n-1}, x_n) & K_{n-1}(x_1, x_2, \ldots, x_{n-1}) \\ K_{n-1}(x_2, \ldots, x_{n-1}, x_n) & K_{n-2}(x_2, \ldots, x_{n-1}) \end{pmatrix}$.

3. $K_n(x_1, \ldots, x_n)$.

4. By induction, or by taking the determinant of the matrix product in exercise 2.

5. When the x's are positive, the q's of (9) are positive, and $q_{n+1} > q_{n-1}$; hence (9) is an alternating series of decreasing terms, and it converges if and only if $q_n q_{n+1} \to \infty$. By induction, if the x's are greater than ϵ, we have $q_n \geq (1 + \epsilon/2)^n c$, where c is chosen small enough to make this inequality valid for $n = 1$ and 2. But if $x_n = 1/2^n$, we have $q_n \leq 2 - 1/2^n$.

6. It suffices to prove that $A_1 = B_1$; and from the fact that $0 \leq /\!/x_1, \ldots, x_n/\!/ < 1$ whenever $x_1, \ldots, x_n$ are positive integers, we have $B_1 = \lfloor 1/X \rfloor = A_1$.

7. Only $1\,2 \ldots n$ and $n \ldots 2\,1$. (The variable x_k appears in exactly $F_k F_{n+1-k}$ terms; hence x_1 and x_n can only be permuted into x_1 and x_n. If x_1 and x_n are fixed by the permutation, it follows by induction that $x_2, \ldots, x_{n-1}$ are also fixed.)

8. This is equivalent to

$$\frac{K_{n-2}(A_{n-1}, \ldots, A_2) - X K_{n-1}(A_{n-1}, \ldots, A_1)}{K_{n-1}(A_n, \ldots, A_2) - X K_n(A_n, \ldots, A_1)} = -\frac{1}{X_n},$$

and by (6) it is equivalent to

$$X = \frac{K_{n-1}(A_2, \ldots, A_n) + X_n K_{n-2}(A_2, \ldots, A_{n-1})}{K_n(A_1, \ldots, A_n) + X_n K_{n-1}(A_1, \ldots, A_{n-1})}.$$

9. (a) By definition. (b, d) Prove this when $n = 1$, then apply (a) to get the result for general n. (c) Prove it when $n = k + 1$, then apply (a).

10. If $A_0 > 0$, then $B_0 = 0$, $B_1 = A_0$, $B_2 = A_1$, $B_3 = A_2$, $B_4 = A_3$, $B_5 = A_4$, $m = 5$. If $A_0 = 0$, then $B_0 = A_1$, $B_1 = A_2$, $B_2 = A_3$, $B_3 = A_4$, $m = 3$. If $A_0 = -1$ and $A_1 = 1$, then $B_0 = -(A_2 + 2)$, $B_1 = 1$, $B_2 = A_3 - 1$, $B_3 = A_4$, $m = 3$. If $A_0 = -1$ and $A_1 > 1$, then $B_0 = -2$, $B_1 = 1$, $B_2 = A_1 - 2$, $B_3 = A_2$, $B_4 = A_3$, $B_5 = A_4$, $m = 5$. If $A_0 < -1$, then $B_0 = -1$, $B_1 = 1$, $B_2 = -A_0 - 2$, $B_3 = 1$, $B_4 = A_1 - 1$, $B_5 = A_2$, $B_6 = A_3$, $B_7 = A_4$, $m = 7$. [Actually, the last three cases involve eight subcases; if any of the B's is set to zero, the values should be "collapsed together" by using the rule of exercise 9(c). For example, if $A_0 = -1$ and $A_1 = A_3 = 1$, we actually have $B_0 = -(A_2 + 2)$, $B_1 = A_4 + 1$, $m = 1$. Double collapsing occurs when $A_0 = -2$ and $A_1 = 1$.]

11. Let $q_n = K_n(A_1, \ldots, A_n)$, $q'_n = K_n(B_1, \ldots, B_n)$, $p_n = K_{n+1}(A_0, \ldots, A_n)$, $p'_n = K_{n+1}(B_0, \ldots, B_n)$. By (5) and (11) we have $X = (p_m + p_{m-1}X_m)/(q_m + q_{m-1}X_m)$, $Y = (p'_n + p'_{n-1}Y_n)/(q'_n + q'_{n-1}Y_n)$; therefore if $X_m = Y_n$, the stated relation between X and Y holds by (8). Conversely, if $X = (qY + r)/(sY + t)$ and $|qt - rs| = 1$, we may assume that $s \geq 0$, and we can show that the partial quotients of X and Y eventually agree, by induction on s. The result is clear when $s = 0$, by exercise 9(d). If $s > 0$, let $q = as + s'$, where $0 \leq s' < s$. Then $X = a + 1/((sY + t)/(s'Y + r - at))$; since $s(r - at) - ts' = sr - tq$, and $s' < s$, we know by induction and exercise 10 that the partial quotients of X and Y eventually agree. [*J. de Math. Pures et Appl.* **15** (1850), 153–155. The fact that m is always odd in exercise 10 shows, by a close inspection of this proof, that $X_m = Y_n$ if and only if $X = (qY + r)/(sY + t)$, where $qt - rs = (-1)^{m-n}$.]

12. (a) Since $V_n V_{n+1} = D - U_n^2$, we know that $D - U_{n+1}^2$ is a multiple of V_{n+1}; hence by induction $X_n = (\sqrt{D} - U_n)/V_n$, where U_n and V_n are integers. [*Notes:* An algorithm based on this process has many applications to the solution of quadratic equations in integers; see, for example, H. Davenport, *The Higher Arithmetic* (London: Hutchinson, 1952); W. J. LeVeque, *Topics in Number Theory* (Reading, Mass.: Addison–Wesley, 1956); and see also Section 4.5.4. By exercise 1.2.4–35, we have

$$A_{n+1} = \begin{cases} \lfloor (\lfloor \sqrt{D} \rfloor + U_n)/V_{n+1} \rfloor, & \text{if } V_{n+1} > 0, \\ \lfloor (\lfloor \sqrt{D} \rfloor + 1 + U_n)/V_{n+1} \rfloor, & \text{if } V_{n+1} < 0; \end{cases}$$

hence such an algorithm need only work with the positive integer $\lfloor \sqrt{D} \rfloor$. Moreover, the identity $V_{n+1} = A_n(U_{n-1} - U_n) + V_{n-1}$ makes it unnecessary to divide when V_{n+1} is being determined.]

(b) Let $Y = (-\sqrt{D} - U)/V$, $Y_n = (-\sqrt{D} - U_n)/V_n$. The stated identity obviously holds by replacing $\sqrt{D}$ by $-\sqrt{D}$ in the proof of (a). We have

$$Y = (p_n/Y_n + p_{n-1})/(q_n/Y_n + q_{n-1}),$$

where p_n and q_n are defined in part (c) of this exercise; hence

$$Y_n = (-q_n/q_{n-1})(Y - p_n/q_n)/(Y - p_{n-1}/q_{n-1}).$$

But by (12), p_{n-1}/q_{n-1} and p_n/q_n are extremely close to X; since $X \neq Y$, $Y - p_n/q_n$ and $Y - p_{n-1}/q_{n-1}$ will have the same sign as $Y - X$ for all large n. This proves that $Y_n < 0$ for all large n; hence $0 < X_n < X_n - Y_n = 2\sqrt{D}/V_n$; V_n must be positive. Also $U_n < \sqrt{D}$, since $X_n > 0$. Hence $V_n < 2\sqrt{D}$, since $V_n \leq A_n V_n < \sqrt{D} + U_{n-1}$.

Finally, we want to show that $U_n > 0$. Since $X_n < 1$, we have $U_n > \sqrt{D} - V_n$, so we need only consider the case $V_n > \sqrt{D}$. Then $U_n = A_n V_n - U_{n-1} \geq V_n - U_{n-1} > \sqrt{D} - U_{n-1}$, and this is positive as we have already observed.

Notes: In the repeating cycle, $\sqrt{D} + U_n = A_n V_n + (\sqrt{D} - U_{n-1}) > V_n$; hence $\lfloor (\sqrt{D} + U_{n+1})/V_{n+1} \rfloor = \lfloor A_{n+1} + V_n/(\sqrt{D} + U_n) \rfloor = A_{n+1} = \lfloor (\sqrt{D} + U_n)/V_{n+1} \rfloor$. In other words A_{n+1} is determined by U_{n+1} and V_{n+1}; we can determine (U_n, V_n) from its successor (U_{n+1}, V_{n+1}) in the period. In fact, when $0 < V_n < \sqrt{D} + U_n$ and $0 < U_n < \sqrt{D}$, the arguments above prove that $0 < V_{n+1} < \sqrt{D} + U_{n+1}$ and $0 < U_{n+1} < \sqrt{D}$; moreover, if the pair (U_{n+1}, V_{n+1}) follows (U', V') with $0 < V' < \sqrt{D} + U'$ and $0 < U' < \sqrt{D}$, then $U' = U_n$ and $V' = V_n$. Hence (U_n, V_n) is part of the cycle if and only if $0 < V_n < \sqrt{D} + U_n$ and $0 < U_n < \sqrt{D}$.

(c) $$\frac{-V_{n+1}}{V_n} = X_n Y_n = \frac{(q_n X - p_n)(q_n Y - p_n)}{(q_{n-1} X - p_{n-1})(q_{n-1} Y - p_{n-1})}.$$

There is also a companion identity, namely

$$V p_n p_{n-1} + U(p_n q_{n-1} + p_{n-1} q_n) + ((U^2 - D)/V)q_n q_{n-1} = (-1)^n U_n.$$

(d) If $X_n = X_m$ for some $n \neq m$, then X is an irrational number that satisfies the quadratic equation $(q_n X - p_n)/(q_{n-1} X - p_{n-1}) = (q_m X - p_m)/(q_{m-1} X - p_{m-1})$.

The ideas underlying this exercise go back at least to Jayadeva in India, prior to A.D. 1073; see K. S. Shukla, *Gaṇita* **5** (1954), 1–20; C.-O. Selenius, *Historia Math.* **2** (1975), 167–184. Some of its aspects had also been discovered in Japan before 1750; see Y. Mikami, *The Development of Mathematics in China and Japan* (1913), 223–229. But the main principles of the theory of continued fractions for quadratics are largely due to Euler [*Novi Comment. Acad. Sci. Petrop.* **11** (1765), 28–66] and Lagrange [*Hist. Acad. Sci.* **24** (Berlin: 1768), 111–180].

14. As in exercise 9, we need only verify the stated identities when c is the last partial quotient, and this verification is trivial. Now Hurwitz's rule gives $2/e = //1, 2, 1, 2, 0, 1, 1, 1, 1, 1, 0, 2, 3, 2, 0, 1, 1, 3, 1, 1, 0, 2, 5, \ldots //$. Taking the reciprocal, collapsing out the zeros as in exercise 9, and taking note of the pattern that appears, we find (see exercise 16) that $e/2 = 1 + // 2, \overline{2m+1, 3, 1, 2m+1, 1, 3}//$, $m \geq 0$. [*Schriften der phys.-ökon. Gesellschaft zu Königsberg* **32** (1891), 59–62. Hurwitz also explained how to multiply by an arbitrary positive integer, in *Vierteljahrsschrift der Naturforschenden Gesellschaft in Zürich* **41** (1896), Jubelband II, 34–64, §2.]

15. (This procedure maintains four integers (A, B, C, D) with the invariant meaning that "our remaining job is to output the continued fraction for $(Ay+B)/(Cy+D)$, where y is the input yet to come.") Initially set $j \leftarrow k \leftarrow 0$, $(A, B, C, D) \leftarrow (a, b, c, d)$; then input x_j and set $(A, B, C, D) \leftarrow (Ax_j+B, A, Cx_j+D, C)$, $j \leftarrow j+1$, one or more times until $C + D$ has the same sign as C. (When $j \geq 1$ and the input has not terminated, we know that $1 < y < \infty$; and when $C + D$ has the same sign as C we know therefore that $(Ay + B)/(Cy + D)$ lies between $(A + B)/(C + D)$ and A/C.) Now comes the general step: If no integer lies strictly between $(A+B)/(C+D)$ and A/C, output $X_k \leftarrow \min(\lfloor A/C \rfloor, \lfloor (A+B)/(C+D) \rfloor)$, and set $(A, B, C, D) \leftarrow (C, D, A - X_kC, B - X_kD)$, $k \leftarrow k + 1$; otherwise input x_j and set $(A, B, C, D) \leftarrow (Ax_j + B, A, Cx_j + D, C)$, $j \leftarrow j + 1$. The general step is repeated ad infinitum. However, if at any time the *final* x_j is input, the algorithm immediately switches gears: It outputs the continued fraction for $(Ax_j + B)/(Cx_j + D)$, using Euclid's algorithm, and terminates.

The following tableau solves the requested example, where the matrix $\begin{pmatrix} B & A \\ D & C \end{pmatrix}$ begins at the upper left corner, then shifts right one on input, down one on output:

x_j	-1	5	1	1	1	2	1	2	∞
X_k	39	97	-58	-193					
-2	-25	-62	37	123					
2			16	53					
3			5	17	22				
7			1	2	3	5			
1				3	1	4	5	14	
1					2	1	3	7	
1							2	7	9	25
12							1	0	1	2
2									1
∞									0

M. Mendès France has shown that the number of quotients output per quotient input is asymptotically bounded between $1/r$ and r, where $r = 2\lfloor L(|ad - bc|)/2 \rfloor + 1$ and L is the function defined in exercise 38; this bound is best possible. [*Topics in Number Theory*, edited by P. Turán, *Colloquia Math. Soc. János Bolyai* **13** (1976), 183–194.]

Gosper has also shown that the algorithm above can be generalized to compute the continued fraction for $(axy + bx + cy + d)/(Axy + Bx + Cy + D)$ from those of x and y (in particular, to compute sums and products). [MIT AI Laboratory Memo 239 (29 February 1972), Hack 101.] For further developments, see J. Vuillemin, *ACM Conf. LISP and Functional Programming* **5** (1988), 14–27.

16. It is not difficult to prove by induction that $f_n(z) = z/(2n+1) + O(z^3)$ is an odd function with a convergent power series in a neighborhood of the origin, and that it satisfies the given differential equation. Hence

$$f_0(z) = //z^{-1} + f_1(z)// = \cdots = //z^{-1}, 3z^{-1}, \ldots, (2n+1)z^{-1} + f_{n+1}(z)//.$$

It remains to prove that $\lim_{n \to \infty} //z^{-1}, 3z^{-1}, \ldots, (2n+1)z^{-1}// = f_0(z)$. [Actually Euler, age 24, obtained continued fraction expansions for the considerably more general differential equation $f_n'(z) = az^m + bf_n(z)z^{m-1} + cf_n(z)^2$; but he did not bother to prove convergence, since formal manipulation and intuition were good enough in the eighteenth century.]

There are several ways to prove the desired limiting equation. First, letting $f_n(z) = \sum_k a_{nk}z^k$, we can argue from the equation

$$(2n+1)a_{n1} + (2n+3)a_{n3}z^2 + (2n+5)a_{n5}z^4 + \cdots = 1 - (a_{n1}z + a_{n3}z^3 + a_{n5}z^5 + \cdots)^2$$

that $(-1)^k a_{n(2k+1)}$ is a sum of terms of the form $c_k/(2n+1)^{k+1}(2n+b_{k1})\ldots(2n+b_{kk})$, where the c_k and b_{km} are positive integers independent of n. For example, we have $-a_{n7} = 4/(2n+1)^4(2n+3)(2n+5)(2n+7) + 1/(2n+1)^4(2n+3)^2(2n+7)$. Thus $|a_{(n+1)k}| \le |a_{nk}|$, and $|f_n(z)| \le \tan|z|$ for $|z| < \pi/2$. This uniform bound on $f_n(z)$ makes the convergence proof very simple. Careful study of this argument reveals that the power series for $f_n(z)$ actually converges for $|z| < \pi\sqrt{2n+1}/2$; therefore the singularities of $f_n(z)$ get farther and farther away from the origin as n grows, and the continued fraction actually represents $\tanh z$ *throughout* the complex plane.

Another proof gives further information of a different kind: If we let

$$A_n(z) = n! \sum_{k=0}^{n} \binom{2n-k}{n} \frac{z^k}{k!} = \sum_{k \ge 0} \frac{(n+k)! \, z^{n-k}}{k! \, (n-k)!} = z^n \, {}_2F_0(n+1, -n; ; -1/z),$$

then

$$A_{n+1}(z) = \sum_{k \ge 0} \frac{(n+k-1)! \, ((4n+2)k + (n+1-k)(n-k))}{k! \, (n+1-k)!} z^{n+1-k}$$

$$= (4n+2) A_n(z) + z^2 A_{n-1}(z).$$

It follows, by induction, that

$$K_n\left(\frac{1}{z}, \frac{3}{z}, \ldots, \frac{2n-1}{z}\right) = \frac{A_n(2z) + A_n(-2z)}{2^{n+1}z^n},$$

$$K_{n-1}\left(\frac{3}{z}, \ldots, \frac{2n-1}{z}\right) = \frac{A_n(2z) - A_n(-2z)}{2^{n+1}z^n}.$$

Hence

$$//z^{-1}, 3z^{-1}, \ldots, (2n-1)z^{-1}// = \frac{A_n(2z) - A_n(-2z)}{A_n(2z) + A_n(-2z)},$$

and we want to show that this ratio approaches $\tanh z$. By Equations 1.2.9–(11) and 1.2.6–(24),

$$e^z A_n(-z) = n! \sum_{m \ge 0} \frac{z^m}{m!} \left(\sum_{k=0}^{n} \binom{m}{k} \binom{2n-k}{n} (-1)^k \right) = \sum_{m \ge 0} \binom{2n-m}{n} z^m \frac{n!}{m!}.$$

Hence

$$e^z A_n(-z) - A_n(z) = R_n(z) = (-1)^n z^{2n+1} \sum_{k \ge 0} \frac{(n+k)! \, z^k}{(2n+k+1)! \, k!}.$$

We now have $(e^{2z} - 1)(A_n(2z) + A_n(-2z)) - (e^{2z} + 1)(A_n(2z) - A_n(-2z)) = 2R_n(2z)$; hence

$$\tanh z - /\!/ z^{-1}, 3z^{-1}, \ldots, (2n-1)z^{-1} /\!/ = \frac{2R_n(2z)}{(A_n(2z) + A_n(-2z))(e^{2z} + 1)},$$

and we have an exact formula for the difference. When $|2z| \leq 1$, the factor $e^{2z} + 1$ is bounded away from zero, $|R_n(2z)| \leq e\, n!/(2n+1)!$, and

$$\frac{1}{2}|A_n(2z) + A_n(-2z)| \geq n! \left(\binom{2n}{n} - \binom{2n-2}{n} - \binom{2n-4}{n} - \binom{2n-6}{n} - \cdots \right)$$
$$\geq \frac{(2n)!}{n!} \left(1 - \frac{1}{4} - \frac{1}{16} - \frac{1}{64} - \cdots \right) = \frac{2}{3}\frac{(2n)!}{n!}.$$

Thus convergence is very rapid, even for complex values of z.

To go from this continued fraction to the continued fraction for e^z, we have $\tanh z = 1 - 2/(e^{2z} + 1)$; hence we get the continued-fraction representation for $(e^{2z} + 1)/2$ by simple manipulations. Hurwitz's rule gives the expansion of $e^{2z} + 1$, from which we may subtract unity. For n odd,

$$e^{-2/n} = /\!/ \overline{1, 3mn + \lfloor n/2 \rfloor, (12m + 6)n, (3m + 2)n + \lfloor n/2 \rfloor, 1} /\!/, \qquad m \geq 0.$$

Another derivation has been given by C. S. Davis, *J. London Math. Soc.* (2) **20** (1945), 194–198. The continued fraction for e was first found empirically by Roger Cotes, *Philosophical Transactions* **29** (1714), 5–45, Proposition 1, Scholium 3. Euler communicated his results in a letter to Goldbach on November 25, 1731 [*Correspondance Mathématique et Physique*, edited by P. H. Fuss, **1** (St. Petersburg: 1843), 56–60], and he eventually published fuller descriptions in *Commentarii Acad. Sci. Petropolitanæ* **9** (1737), 98–137; **11** (1739), 32–81.

17. (b) $/\!/ x_1 - 1, 1, x_2 - 2, 1, x_3 - 2, 1, \ldots, 1, x_{2n-1} - 2, 1, x_{2n} - 1 /\!/$. [*Note:* One can remove negative parameters from continuants by using the identity

$$K_{m+n+1}(x_1, \ldots, x_m, -x, y_n, \ldots, y_1)$$
$$= (-1)^{n-1} K_{m+n+2}(x_1, \ldots, x_{m-1}, x_m - 1, 1, x - 1, -y_n, \ldots, -y_1),$$

from which we obtain

$$K_{m+n+1}(x_1, \ldots, x_m, -x, y_n, \ldots, y_1)$$
$$= -K_{m+n+3}(x_1, \ldots, x_{m-1}, x_m - 1, 1, x - 2, 1, y_n - 1, y_{n-1}, \ldots, y_1)$$

after a second application. A similar identity appears in exercise 41.]

(c) $1 + /\!/ 1, 1, 3, 1, 5, 1, \ldots /\!/ = 1 + /\!/ \overline{2m + 1, 1} /\!/$, $m \geq 0$.

18. Since we have $K_m(a_1, a_2, \ldots, a_m) /\!/ a_1, a_2, \ldots, a_m, x /\!/ = K_{m-1}(a_2, \ldots, a_m) + (-1)^m/(K_{m-1}(a_1, \ldots, a_{m-1}) + K_m(a_1, a_2, \ldots, a_m)x)$ by Eqs. (5) and (8), we also have $K_m(a_1, a_2, \ldots, a_m) /\!/ a_1, a_2, \ldots, a_m, x_1, a_1, a_2, \ldots, a_m, x_2, a_1, a_2, \ldots, a_m, x_3, a_1, \ldots /\!/ = K_{m-1}(a_2, \ldots, a_m) + /\!/ (-1)^m(C + Ax_1), C + Ax_2, (-1)^m(C + Ax_3), \ldots /\!/$, where $A = K_m(a_1, a_2, \ldots, a_m)$ and $C = K_{m-1}(a_2, \ldots, a_m) + K_{m-1}(a_1, \ldots, a_{m-1})$. Consequently the stated difference is $(K_{m-1}(a_2, \ldots, a_m) - K_{m-1}(a_1, \ldots, a_{m-1}))/K_m(a_1, a_2, \ldots, a_m)$, by (6). [The case $m = 2$ was discussed by Euler in *Commentarii Acad. Sci. Petropolitanæ* **9** (1737), 98–137, §24–26.]

19. The sum for $1 \leq k \leq N$ is $\log_b((1 + x)(N + 1)/(N + 1 + x))$.

20. Let $H = SG$, $g(x) = (1+x)G'(x)$, $h(x) = (1+x)H'(x)$. Then (37) implies that $h(x+1)/(x+2) - h(x)/(x+1) = -(1+x)^{-2}g(1/(1+x))/(1+1/(1+x))$.

21. $\varphi(x) = c/(cx+1)^2 + (2-c)/((c-1)x+1)^2$, $U\varphi(x) = 1/(x+c)^2$. When $c \leq 1$, the minimum of $\varphi(x)/U\varphi(x)$ occurs at $x = 0$ and is $2c^2 \leq 2$. When $c \geq \phi$, the minimum occurs at $x = 1$ and is $\leq \phi^2$. When $c \approx 1.31266$ the values at $x = 0$ and $x = 1$ are nearly equal and the minimum is > 3.2; the bounds $(0.29)^n \varphi \leq U^n \varphi \leq (0.31)^n \varphi$ are obtained. Still better bounds come from well-chosen linear combinations of the form $Tg(x) = \sum a_j/(x+c_j)$.

23. By the interpolation formula of exercise 4.6.4–15 with $x_0 = 0$, $x_1 = x$, $x_2 = x + \epsilon$, letting $\epsilon \to 0$, we have the general identity $R_n'(x) = (R_n(x) - R_n(0))/x + \frac{1}{2}x R_n''(\theta_n(x))$ for some $\theta_n(x)$ between 0 and x, whenever R_n is a function with continuous second derivative. Hence in this case $R_n'(x) = O(2^{-n})$.

24. ∞. [A. Khinchin, in *Compos. Math.* **1** (1935), 361–382, proved that the sum $A_1 + \cdots + A_n$ of the first n partial quotients of a real number X will be asymptotically $n \lg n$, for almost all X. Exercise 35 shows that the behavior is different for rational X.]

25. Any union of intervals can be written as a union of disjoint intervals, since we have $\bigcup_{k \geq 1} I_k = \bigcup_{k \geq 1}(I_k \setminus \bigcup_{1 \leq j < k} I_j)$, and this is a disjoint union in which $I_k \setminus \bigcup_{1 \leq j < k} I_j$ can be expressed as a finite union of disjoint intervals. Therefore we may take $\mathcal{I} = \bigcup I_k$, where I_k is an interval of length $\epsilon/2^k$ containing the kth rational number in $[0..1]$, using some enumeration of the rationals. In this case $\mu(\mathcal{I}) \leq \epsilon$, but $|\mathcal{I} \cap P_n| = n$ for all n.

26. The continued fractions $/\!/A_1, \ldots, A_t/\!/$ that appear are precisely those for which $A_1 > 1$, $A_t > 1$, and $K_t(A_1, A_2, \ldots, A_t)$ is a divisor of n. Therefore (6) completes the proof. [*Note:* If $m_1/n = /\!/A_1, \ldots, A_t/\!/$ and $m_2/n = /\!/A_t, \ldots, A_1/\!/$, where m_1 and m_2 are relatively prime to n, then $m_1 m_2 \equiv \pm 1$ (modulo n); this rule defines the correspondence. When $A_1 = 1$ an analogous symmetry is valid, according to (46).]

27. First prove the result for $n = p^e$, then for $n = rs$, where r and s are relatively prime. Alternatively, use the formulas in the next exercise.

28. (a) The left-hand side is multiplicative (see exercise 1.2.4–31), and it is easily evaluated when n is a power of a prime. (c) From (a), we have *Möbius's inversion formula*: If $f(n) = \sum_{d \setminus n} g(d)$, then $g(n) = \sum_{d \setminus n} \mu(n/d) f(d)$.

29. We have $\sum_{n=1}^{N} n \ln n = \frac{1}{2}N^2 \ln N + O(N^2)$ by Euler's summation formula (see exercise 1.2.11.2–7). Also $\sum_{n=1}^{N} n \sum_{d \setminus n} \Lambda(d)/d = \sum_{d=1}^{N} \Lambda(d) \sum_{1 \leq k \leq N/d} k$, and this is $O(\sum_{d=1}^{N} \Lambda(d)N^2/d^2) = O(N^2)$. Indeed, $\sum_{d \geq 1} \Lambda(d)/d^2 = -\zeta'(2)/\zeta(2)$.

30. The modified algorithm affects the calculation if and only if the following division step in the unmodified algorithm would have the quotient 1, and in this case it avoids the following division step. The probability that a given division step is avoided is the probability that $A_k = 1$ and that this quotient is preceded by an even number of quotients equal to 1. By the symmetry condition, this is the probability that $A_k = 1$ and is *followed* by an even number of quotients equal to 1. The latter happens if and only if $X_{k-1} > \phi - 1 = 0.618\ldots$, where ϕ is the golden ratio: For $A_k = 1$ and $A_{k+1} > 1$ if and only if $\frac{2}{3} \leq X_{k-1} < 1$; $A_k = A_{k+1} = A_{k+2} = 1$ and $A_{k+3} > 1$ if and only if $\frac{5}{8} \leq X_{k-1} < \frac{2}{3}$; etc. Thus we save approximately $F_{k-1}(1) - F_{k-1}(\phi - 1) \approx 1 - \lg \phi \approx 0.306$ of the division steps. The average number of steps is approximately $((12 \ln \phi)/\pi^2) \ln n$, when $v = n$ and u is relatively prime to n.

K. Vahlen [*Crelle* **115** (1895), 221–233] considered all algorithms that replace (u, v) by $(v, (\pm u) \bmod v)$ at each iteration when $u \bmod v \neq 0$. If $u \perp v$ there are exactly v such algorithms, and they can be represented as a binary tree with v leaves. The shallowest leaves, which correspond to the shortest possible number of iterations over all such gcd algorithms, occur when the least remainder is taken at each step; the deepest leaves occur when the greatest remainder is always chosen. [Similar ideas had been considered by Lagrange in *Hist. Acad. Sci.* **23** (Berlin: 1768), 111–180, §58.] For further results see N. G. de Bruijn and W. M. Zaring, *Nieuw Archief voor Wiskunde* (3) **1** (1953), 105–112; G. J. Rieger, *Math. Nachr.* **82** (1978), 157–180.

On many computers, the modified algorithm makes each division step longer; the idea of exercise 1, which saves *all* division steps when the quotient is unity, would be preferable in such cases.

31. Let $a_0 = 0$, $a_1 = 1$, $a_{n+1} = 2a_n + a_{n-1}$; then $a_n = ((1 + \sqrt{2})^n - (1 - \sqrt{2})^n)/2\sqrt{2}$, and the worst case (in the sense of Theorem F) occurs when $u = a_n + a_{n-1}$, $v = a_n$, $n \geq 2$. This result is due to A. Dupré [*J. de Math.* **11** (1846), 41–64], who also investigated more general "look-ahead" procedures suggested by J. Binet.

32. (b) $K_{m-1}(x_1, \ldots, x_{m-1}) K_{n-1}(x_{m+2}, \ldots, x_{m+n})$ corresponds to those Morse code sequences of length $m + n$ in which a dash occupies positions m and $m + 1$; the other term corresponds to the opposite case. (Alternatively, use exercise 2. The more general identity

$$K_{m+n}(x_1, \ldots, x_{m+n}) K_k(x_{m+1}, \ldots, x_{m+k}) =$$
$$K_{m+k}(x_1, \ldots, x_{m+k}) K_n(x_{m+1}, \ldots, x_{m+n})$$
$$+ (-1)^k K_{m-1}(x_1, \ldots, x_{m-1}) K_{n-k-1}(x_{m+k+2}, \ldots, x_{m+n})$$

also appeared in Euler's paper. Incidentally, "Morse code" was really invented by F. C. Gerke in 1848; Morse's prototypes were quite different.)

33. (a) The new representations are $x = m/d$, $y = (n - m)/d$, $x' = y' = d = \gcd(m, n - m)$, for $\frac{1}{2}n < m < n$. (b) The relation $(n/x') - y \leq x < n/x'$ defines x. (c) Count the x' satisfying (b). (d) A pair of integers $x > y > 0$ with $x \perp y$ can be uniquely written in the form $x = K_m(x_1, \ldots, x_m)$, $y = K_{m-1}(x_1, \ldots, x_{m-1})$, where $x_1 \geq 2$ and $m \geq 1$; here $y/x = //x_m, \ldots, x_1//$. (e) It suffices to show that $\sum_{1 \leq k \leq n/2} T(k, n) = 2\lfloor n/2 \rfloor + h(n)$; this follows from exercise 26.

34. (a) Dividing x and y by $\gcd(x, y)$ yields $g(n) = \sum_{d\backslash n} h(n/d)$; apply exercise 28(c), and use the symmetry between primed and unprimed variables. (b) For fixed y and t, the representations with $xd \geq x'$ have $x' < \sqrt{nd}$; hence there are $O(\sqrt{nd}/y)$ such representations. Now sum for $0 < t \leq y < \sqrt{n/d}$. (c) If $s(y)$ is the given sum, then $\sum_{d\backslash y} s(d) = y(H_{2y} - H_y) = k(y)$, say; hence $s(y) = \sum_{d\backslash y} \mu(d) k(y/d)$. Now $k(y) = y \ln 2 - 1/4 + O(1/y)$. (d) $\sum_{y=1}^n \varphi(y)/y^2 = \sum_{y=1}^n \sum_{d\backslash y} \mu(d)/yd = \sum_{cd \leq n} \mu(d)/cd^2$. (Similarly, $\sum_{y=1}^n \sigma_{-1}(y)/y^2 = O(1)$.) (e) $\sum_{k=1}^n \mu(k)/k^2 = 6/\pi^2 + O(1/n)$ (see exercise 4.5.2–10(d)); and $\sum_{k=1}^n \mu(k) \log k/k^2 = O(1)$. Hence $h_d(n) = n((3 \ln 2)/\pi^2) \ln(n/d) + O(n)$ for $d \geq 1$. Finally $h(n) = 2 \sum_{cd\backslash n} \mu(d) h_c(n/cd) = ((6 \ln 2)/\pi^2) n(\ln n - \sum - \sum') + O(n\sigma_{-1}(n)^2)$, where the remaining sums are $\sum = \sum_{cd\backslash n} \mu(d) \ln(cd)/cd = 0$ and $\sum' = \sum_{cd\backslash n} \mu(d) \ln c/cd = \sum_{d\backslash n} \Lambda(d)/d$. [It is well known that $\sigma_{-1}(n) = O(\log \log n)$; see Hardy and Wright, *An Introduction to the Theory of Numbers*, §22.9.]

35. See *Proc. Nat. Acad. Sci.* **72** (1975), 4720–4722. M. L. V. Pitteway and C. M. A. Castle [*Bull. Inst. Math. and Its Applications* **24** (1988), 17–20] have found strong and tantalizing empirical evidence that the sum of all partial quotients is actually

$$\frac{\pi^2}{24(\ln 2)^2}\left(T_n + \frac{1}{2} - \frac{18(\ln 2)^2}{\pi^2}\right)^2 + \frac{6}{\pi^2}\sum_{\substack{p\text{ prime}\\ p^r\backslash n}}\left(\frac{4r}{p^r} - \frac{p+1}{p^{2r}}\frac{p^r-1}{p-1}\right)(\ln p)^2$$
$$- 2.542875 + O(n^{-1/2}).$$

36. Working the algorithm backwards, assuming that $t_k - 1$ divisions occur in step C2 for a given value of k, we obtain minimum u_n when $\gcd(u_{k+1}, \ldots, u_n) = F_{t_1} \ldots F_{t_k}$ and $u_k \equiv F_{t_1} \ldots F_{t_{k-1}} F_{t_k - 1}$ (modulo $\gcd(u_{k+1}, \ldots, u_n)$); here the t's are ≥ 2, $t_1 \geq 3$, and $t_1 + \cdots + t_{n-1} = N + n - 1$. One way to minimize $u_n = F_{t_1} \ldots F_{t_{n-1}}$ under these conditions is to take $t_1 = 3$, $t_2 = \cdots = t_{n-2} = 2$, $u_n = 2F_{N-n+2}$. If we stipulate also that $u_1 \geq u_2 \geq \cdots \geq u_n$, the solution $u_1 = 2F_{N-n+3} + 1$, $u_2 = \cdots = u_{n-1} = 2F_{N-n+3}$, $u_n = 2F_{N-n+2}$ has minimum u_1. [See *CACM* **13** (1970), 433–436, 447–448.]

37. See *Proc. Amer. Math. Soc.* **7** (1956), 1014–1021; see also exercise 6.1–18.

38. Let $m = \lceil n/\phi \rceil$, so that $m/n = \phi^{-1} + \epsilon = //a_1, a_2, \ldots //$ where $0 < \epsilon < 1/n$. Let k be minimal such that $a_k \geq 2$; then $(\phi^{1-k} + (-1)^k F_{k-1}\epsilon)/(\phi^{-k} - (-1)^k F_k\epsilon) \geq 2$, hence k is even and $\phi^{-2} = 2 - \phi \leq \phi^k F_{k+2}\epsilon = (\phi^{2k+2} - \phi^{-2})\epsilon/\sqrt{5}$. [*Ann. Polon. Math.* **1** (1954), 203–206.]

39. At least 287 at bats; $//2, 1, 95// = 96/287 \approx .33449477$, and no fraction with denominator < 287 lies in the interval

$$[.3335\ldots.3345] = [//2, 1, 666// .. //2, 1, 94, 1, 1, 3//].$$

To solve the general question of the fraction in $[a .. b]$ with smallest denominator, where $0 < a < b < 1$, note that in terms of regular continued-fraction representations we have $//x_1, x_2, \ldots // < //y_1, y_2, \ldots //$ if and only if $(-1)^j x_j < (-1)^j y_j$ for the smallest j with $x_j \neq y_j$, where we place "∞" after the last partial quotient of a rational number. Thus if $a = //x_1, x_2, \ldots //$ and $b = //y_1, y_2, \ldots //$, and if j is minimal with $x_j \neq y_j$, the fractions in $[a .. b]$ have the form $c = //x_1, \ldots, x_{j-1}, z_j, \ldots, z_m//$ where $//z_j, \ldots, z_m//$ lies between $//x_j, x_{j+1}, \ldots //$ and $//y_j, y_{j+1}, \ldots //$ inclusive. Let $K_{-1} = 0$. The denominator

$$K_{j-1}(x_1, \ldots, x_{j-1})K_{m-j+1}(z_j, \ldots, z_m) + K_{j-2}(x_1, \ldots, x_{j-2})K_{m-j}(z_{j+1}, \ldots, z_m)$$

of c is minimized when $m = j$ and $z_j = (j \text{ odd} \Rightarrow y_j + [y_{j+1} \neq \infty]; x_j + [x_{j+1} \neq \infty])$. [Another way to derive this method comes from the theory in the following exercise.]

40. One can prove by induction that $p_r q_l - p_l q_r = 1$ at each node, hence p_l and q_l are relatively prime. Since $p/q < p'/q'$ implies that $p/q < (p+p')/(q+q') < p'/q'$, it is also clear that the labels on all left descendants of p/q are less than p/q, while the labels on all its right descendants are greater. Therefore each rational number occurs at most once as a label.

It remains to show that each rational does appear. If $p/q = //a_1, \ldots, a_r, 1//$, where each a_i is a positive integer, one can show by induction that the node labeled p/q is found by going left a_1 times, then right a_2 times, then left a_3 times, etc.

[The sequence of labels on successive levels of this tree was first studied by G. Eisenstein, who described them on 14 January 1850 in a letter to his friend M. A. Stern [see Eisenstein's *Mathematische Werke* **2** (1975), 819]. Stern developed the ideas in *Crelle* **55** (1858), 193–220, although the relation to binary trees was not explicit in his paper. The notion of obtaining all possible fractions by successively interpolating $(p + p')/(q + q')$ between adjacent elements p/q and p'/q' goes back much further:

The essential ideas were published by Daniel Schwenter [*Deliciæ Physico-Mathematicæ* (Nürnberg: 1636), Part 1, Problem 87; *Geometria Practica*, 3rd edition (1641), 68; see M. Cantor, *Geschichte der Math.* **2** (1900), 763–765], and by John Wallis in his *Treatise of Algebra* (1685), Chapters 10–11. C. Huygens put such ideas to good use when designing the gear-wheels of his planetarium [see *Descriptio Automati Planetarii* (1703), published after his death]. Lagrange gave a full description in *Hist. Acad. Sci.* **23** (Berlin: 1767), 311–352, §24, and in his additions to the French translation of Euler's algebra (1774), §18–§20. See also exercise 1.3.2–19; A. Brocot, *Revue Chronométrique* **3** (1861), 186–194; D. H. Lehmer, *AMM* **36** (1929), 59–67.]

41. In fact, the regular continued fractions for numbers of the general form

$$\frac{1}{l_1} + \frac{(-1)^{e_1}}{l_1^2 l_2} + \frac{(-1)^{e_2}}{l_1^4 l_2^2 l_3} + \cdots$$

have an interesting pattern, based on the continuant identity

$$K_{m+n+1}(x_1, \ldots, x_{m-1}, x_m - 1, 1, y_n - 1, y_{n-1}, \ldots, y_1) =$$
$$x_m K_{m-1}(x_1, \ldots, x_{m-1}) K_n(y_n, \ldots, y_1)$$
$$+ (-1)^n K_{m+n}(x_1, \ldots, x_{m-1}, 0, -y_n, -y_{n-1}, \ldots, -y_1).$$

This identity is most interesting when $y_n = x_{m-1}$, $y_{n-1} = x_{m-2}$, etc., since

$$K_{n+1}(z_1, \ldots, z_k, 0, z_{k+1}, \ldots, z_n) = K_{n-1}(z_1, \ldots, z_{k-1}, z_k + z_{k+1}, z_{k+2}, \ldots, z_n).$$

In particular we find that if $p_n/q_n = K_{n-1}(x_2, \ldots, x_n)/K_n(x_1, \ldots, x_n) = /\!/x_1, \ldots, x_n/\!/$, then $p_n/q_n + (-1)^n/q_n^2 r = /\!/x_1, \ldots, x_n, r - 1, 1, x_n - 1, x_{n-1}, \ldots, x_1/\!/$. By changing $/\!/x_1, \ldots, x_n/\!/$ to $/\!/x_1, \ldots, x_{n-1}, x_n - 1, 1/\!/$, we can control the sign $(-1)^n$ as desired.

For example, the partial sums of the first series have the following continued fractions of even length: $/\!/1, 1/\!/$; $/\!/1, 1, 1, 1, 0, 1/\!/ = /\!/1, 1, 1, 2/\!/$; $/\!/1, 1, 1, 2, 1, 1, 1, 1, 1, 1/\!/$; $/\!/1, 1, 1, 2, 1, 1, 1, 1, 1, 1, 1, 0, 1, 1, 1, 1, 1, 2, 1, 1, 1/\!/ = /\!/1, 1, 1, 2, 1, 1, 1, 1, 1, 1, 1, 2, 1, 1, 1, 1, 2, 1, 1, 1/\!/$; and from this point on the sequence settles down and obeys a simple reflecting pattern. We find that the nth partial quotient a_n can be computed rapidly as follows, if $n - 1 = 20q + r$ where $0 \le r < 20$:

$$a_n = \begin{cases} 1, & \text{if } r = 0, 2, 4, 5, 6, 7, 9, 10, 12, 13, 14, 15, 17, \text{ or } 19; \\ 2, & \text{if } r = 3 \text{ or } 16; \\ 1 + (q + r) \bmod 2, & \text{if } r = 8 \text{ or } 11; \\ 2 - d_q, & \text{if } r = 1; \\ 1 + d_{q+1}, & \text{if } r = 18. \end{cases}$$

Here d_n is the "dragon sequence" defined by the rules $d_0 = 1$, $d_{2n} = d_n$, $d_{4n+1} = 0$, $d_{4n+3} = 1$; the Jacobi symbol $\left(\frac{-1}{n}\right)$ is $1 - 2d_n$. The dragon curve discussed in exercise 4.1–18 turns right at its nth step if and only if $d_n = 1$.

Liouville's numbers with $l \ge 3$ are equal to $/\!/l - 1, l + 1, l^2 - 1, 1, l, l - 1, l^{12} - 1, 1, l - 2, l, 1, 1, l^2 - 1, l + 1, l - 1, l^{72} - 1, \ldots /\!/$. The nth partial quotient a_n depends on the dragon sequence on $n \bmod 4$ as follows: If $n \bmod 4 = 1$ it is $l - 2 + d_{n-1} + (\lfloor n/2 \rfloor \bmod 4)$ and if $n \bmod 4 = 2$ it is $l + 2 - d_{n+2} - (\lfloor n/2 \rfloor \bmod 4)$; if $n \bmod 4 = 0$ it is 1 or $l^{k!(k-1)} - 1$, depending on whether or not $d_n = 0$ or 1, where k is the largest power of 2 dividing n; and if $n \bmod 4 = 3$ it is $l^{k!(k-1)} - 1$ or 1, depending on whether $d_{n+1} = 0$ or 1, where k is the largest power of 2 dividing $n + 1$. When $l = 2$ the same rules apply, except that 0s must be removed, so there is a more complicated pattern depending on $n \bmod 24$.

[*References:* J. O. Shallit, *J. Number Theory* **11** (1979), 209–217; Allouche, Lubiw, Mendès France, van der Poorten, and Shallit, *Acta Arithmetica* **77** (1996), 77–96.]

42. Suppose that $\|qX\| = |qX - p|$. We can always find integers u and v such that $q = uq_{n-1} + vq_n$ and $p = up_{n-1} + vp_n$, where $p_n = K_{n-1}(A_2, \ldots, A_n)$, since $q_n p_{n-1} - q_{n-1} p_n = \pm 1$. The result is clear if $v = 0$. Otherwise we must have $uv < 0$, hence $u(q_{n-1}X - p_{n-1})$ has the same sign as $v(q_n X - p_n)$, and $|qX - p|$ is equal to $|u| \, |q_{n-1}X - p_{n-1}| + |v| \, |q_n X - p_n|$. This completes the proof, since $u \neq 0$. See Theorem 6.4S for a generalization.

43. If x is representable, so is the parent of x in the Stern–Brocot tree of exercise 40; thus the representable numbers form a subtree of that binary tree. Let (u/u') and (v/v') be adjacent representable numbers. Then one is an ancestor of the other; say (u/u') is an ancestor of (v/v'), since the other case is similar. Then (u/u') is the nearest left ancestor of (v/v'), so all numbers between u/u' and v/v' are left descendants of (v/v') and the mediant $((u+v)/(u'+v'))$ is its left child. According to the relation between regular continued fractions and the binary tree, the mediant and all of its left descendants will have (u/u') as their last representable p_i/q_i, while all of the mediant's right descendants will have (v/v') as one of the p_i/q_i. (The numbers p_i/q_i label the *parents* of the "turning-point" nodes on the path to x.)

44. A counterexample for $M = N = 100$ is $(u/u') = \frac{1}{3}$, $(v/v') = \frac{67}{99}$. However, the identity is almost always true, because of (12); it fails only when $u/u' + v/v'$ is very nearly equal to a fraction that is simpler than (u/u').

45. To determine A and r such that $u = Av + r$, $0 \leq r < v$, using ordinary long division, takes $O((1 + \log A)(\log u))$ units of time. If the quotients during the algorithm are A_1, $A_2, \ldots, A_m$, then $A_1 A_2 \ldots A_m \leq u$, so $\log A_1 + \cdots + \log A_m \leq \log u$. Also $m = O(\log u)$ by Corollary L.

46. Yes, to $O(n(\log n)^2(\log \log n))$, even if we also need to compute the sequence of partial quotients that would be computed by Euclid's algorithm; see A. Schönhage, *Acta Informatica* **1** (1971), 139–144. Moreover, Schönhage's algorithm is asymptotically optimal for computing a continued fraction expansion, with respect to the multiplications and divisions it performs [V. Strassen, *SICOMP* **12** (1983), 1–27]. Algorithm 4.5.2L is better in practice unless n is quite large, but an efficient implementation for numbers exceeding about 1800 bits is sketched in the book *Fast Algorithms* by A. Schönhage, A. F. W. Grotefeld, and E. Vetter (Heidelberg: Spektrum Akademischer Verlag, 1994), §7.2.

48. $T_j = (K_{j-2}(-a_2, \ldots, -a_{j-1}), \ K_{j-1}(-a_1, \ldots, -a_{j-1}), \ K_{n-j}(a_{j+1}, \ldots, a_n)d) = ((-1)^j K_{j-2}(a_2, \ldots, a_{j-1}), (-1)^{j-1} K_{j-1}(a_1, \ldots, a_{j-1}), K_{n-j}(a_{j+1}, \ldots, a_n)d)$.

49. Since $\lambda x_1 + \mu z_1 = \mu v$ and $\lambda x_{n+1} + \mu z_{n+1} = -\lambda v/d$, there is an odd value of j such that $\lambda x_j + \mu z_j \geq 0$ and $\lambda x_{j+2} + \mu z_{j+2} \leq 0$. If $\lambda x_j + \mu z_j > \theta$ and $\lambda x_{j+2} + \mu z_{j+2} < -\theta$ we have $\mu > \theta/z_j$ and $\lambda > -\theta/x_{j+2}$. It follows that $0 < \lambda x_{j+1} + \mu z_{j+1} < \lambda \mu x_{j+1} z_j / \theta - \lambda \mu z_{j+1} x_{j+2} / \theta \leq 2\lambda \mu v / \theta = 2\theta$, because we have $|x_{k+1} z_k| = K_{k-1}(a_2, \ldots, a_k) K_{n-k}(a_{k+1}, \ldots, a_n) \leq K_{n-1}(a_2, \ldots, a_n) = v/d$ for all k. [H. W. Lenstra, Jr., *Math. Comp.* **42** (1984), 331–340.]

50. Let $k = \lceil \beta/\alpha \rceil$. If $k\alpha < \gamma$, the answer is k; otherwise it is

$$k - 1 + \left\lceil \frac{f((1/\alpha) \bmod 1, k - \gamma/\alpha, k - \beta/\alpha)}{\alpha} \right\rceil.$$

51. If $ax - mz = y$ and $x \perp y$ we have $x \perp mz$. Consider the Stern–Brocot tree of exercise 40, with an additional node labeled $0/1$. Attach the tag value $y = ax - mz$

together with each node label z/x. We want to find all nodes z/x whose tag y is at most $\theta = \sqrt{m/2}$ in absolute value and whose denominator x is also $\leq \theta$. The only possible path to such nodes keeps a positive tag to the left and a negative tag to the right. This rule defines a unique path, which moves to the right when the tag is positive and to the left when the tag is negative, stopping when the tag becomes zero. The same path is followed implicitly when Algorithm 4.5.2X is performed with $u = m$ and $v = a$, except that the algorithm skips ahead — it visits only nodes of the path just before the tag changes sign (the parents of the "turning point" nodes as in exercise 43).

Let z/x be the first node of the path whose tag y satisfies $|y| \leq \theta$. If $x > \theta$, there is no solution, since subsequent values on the path have even larger denominators. Otherwise $(\pm x, \mp y)$ is a solution, provided that $x \perp y$.

It is easy to see that there is no solution if $y = 0$, and that if $y \neq 0$ the tag on the next node of the path will not have the same sign as y. Therefore node z/x will be visited by Algorithm 4.5.2X, and we will have $x = x_j = K_{j-1}(a_1, \ldots, a_{j-1})$, $y = y_j = (-1)^{(j-1)} K_{n-j}(a_{j+1}, \ldots, a_n)d$, $z = z_j = K_{j-2}(a_2, \ldots, a_{j-1})$ for some j (see exercise 48). The next possibility for a solution will be the node labeled $z'/x' = (z_{j-1} + kz_j)/(x_{j-1} + kx_j)$ with tag $y' = y_{j-1} + ky_j$, where k is as small as possible such that $|y'| \leq \theta$; we have $y'y < 0$. However, x' must now exceed θ; otherwise we would have $m = K_n(a_1, \ldots, a_n)d = x'|y| + x|y'| \leq \theta^2 + \theta^2 = m$, and equality cannot hold.

This discussion proves that the problem can be solved efficiently by applying Algorithm 4.5.2X with $u = m$ and $v = a$, but with the following replacement for step X2: "If $v_3 \leq \sqrt{m/2}$, the algorithm terminates. The pair $(x, y) = (|v_2|, v_3 \, \mathrm{sign}(v_2))$ is then the unique solution, provided that $x \perp y$ and $x \leq \sqrt{m/2}$; otherwise there is no solution." [P. S. Wang, *Lecture Notes in Comp. Sci.* **162** (1983), 225–235; P. Kornerup and R. T. Gregory, *BIT* **23** (1983), 9–20.]

A similar method works if we require $0 < x \leq \theta_1$ and $|y| \leq \theta_2$, whenever $2\theta_1\theta_2 \leq m$.

52. Induction. [See *Abhandlungen Math. Sem. Hamburg* **1** (1922), 77–98, 249–250.]

SECTION 4.5.4

1. If d_k isn't prime, its prime factors are cast out before d_k is tried.

2. No; the algorithm would fail if $p_{t-1} = p_t$, giving "1" as a spurious prime factor.

3. Let P be the product of the first 168 primes. [*Note:* Although $P = 19590 \ldots 5910$ is a 416-digit number, such a gcd can be computed in much less time than it would take to do 168 divisions, if we just want to test whether or not n is prime.]

4. In the notation of exercise 3.1–11,

$$\sum_{\mu, \lambda} 2^{\lceil \lg \max(\mu+1, \lambda) \rceil} P(\mu, \lambda) = \frac{1}{m} \sum_{l \geq 1} f(l) \prod_{k=1}^{l-1} \left(1 - \frac{k}{m}\right),$$

where $f(l) = \sum_{1 \leq \lambda \leq l} 2^{\lceil \lg \max(l+1-\lambda, \lambda) \rceil}$. If $l = 2^{k+\theta}$, where $0 < \theta \leq 1$, we have

$$f(l) = l^2 (3 \cdot 2^{-\theta} - 2 \cdot 2^{-2\theta}),$$

where the function $3 \cdot 2^{-\theta} - 2 \cdot 2^{-2\theta}$ reaches a maximum of $\frac{9}{8}$ at $\theta = \lg(4/3)$ and has a minimum of 1 at $\theta = 0$ and 1. Therefore the average value of $2^{\lceil \lg \max(\mu+1, \lambda) \rceil}$ lies between 1.0 and 1.125 times the average value of $\mu + \lambda$, and the result follows.

Notes: Richard Brent has observed that, as $m \to \infty$, the density $\prod_{k=1}^{l-1}(1 - k/m) = \exp(-l(l-1)/2m + O(l^3/m^2))$ approaches a normal distribution, and we may assume that θ is uniformly distributed. Then $3 \cdot 2^{-\theta} - 2 \cdot 2^{-2\theta}$ takes the average value $3/(4 \ln 2)$, and the average number of iterations needed by Algorithm B comes to approximately

$(3/(4\ln 2) + \frac{1}{2})\sqrt{\pi m/2} \approx 1.98277\sqrt{m}$. A similar analysis of the more general method in the answer to exercise 3.1–7 gives $\approx 1.92600\sqrt{m}$, when $p \approx 2.4771366$ is chosen "optimally" as the root of $(p^2 - 1)\ln p = p^2 - p + 1$. See *BIT* **20** (1980), 176–184.

Algorithm B is a refinement of Pollard's original algorithm, which was based on exercise 3.1–6(b) instead of the yet undiscovered result in exercise 3.1–7. He showed that the least n such that $X_{2n} = X_n$ has average value $\sim (\pi^2/12)Q(m) \approx 1.0308\sqrt{m}$; this constant $\pi^2/12$ is explained by Eq. 4.5.3–(21). Hence the average amount of work needed by his original algorithm is about $1.03081\sqrt{m}$ gcds (or multiplications mod m) and $3.09243\sqrt{m}$ squarings. This will actually be *better* than Algorithm B when the cost of gcd is more than about 1.17 times the cost of squaring — as it usually is with large numbers.

Brent noticed, however, that Algorithm B can be improved by not checking the gcd when $k > l/2$; if step B4 is repeated until $k \le l/2$, we will still detect the cycle, after $\lambda\lfloor \ell(\mu)/\lambda \rfloor = \ell(\mu) - (\ell(\mu) \bmod \lambda)$ further iterations. The average cost now becomes approximately $(3/(4\ln 2))\sqrt{\pi m/2} \approx 1.35611\sqrt{m}$ iterations when we square without taking the gcd, plus $((\ln \pi - \gamma)/(4\ln 2) + \frac{1}{2})\sqrt{\pi m/2} \approx .88319\sqrt{m}$ iterations when we do both. [See the analysis by Henri Cohen in *A Course in Computational Algebraic Number Theory* (Berlin: Springer, 1993), §8.5.]

5. Remarkably, $11111 \equiv 8616460799$ (modulo $3 \cdot 7 \cdot 8 \cdot 11$), so (14) is correct also for $N = 11111$ except with respect to the modulus 5. Since the residues $(x^2 - N) \bmod 5$ are 4, 0, 3, 3, 0, we must have $x \bmod 5 = 0$, 1, or 4. The first $x \ge \lceil \sqrt{N} \rceil = 106$ that satisfies all the conditions is $x = 144$; but the square root of $144^2 - 11111 = 9625$ is not an integer. The next case, however, gives $156^2 - 11111 = 13225 = 115^2$, and $11111 = (156 - 115) \cdot (156 + 115) = 41 \cdot 271$.

6. Let us count the number of solutions (x, y) of the congruence $N \equiv (x - y)(x + y)$ (modulo p), where $0 \le x, y < p$. Since $N \not\equiv 0$ and p is prime, $x + y \not\equiv 0$. For each $v \not\equiv 0$ there is a unique u (modulo p) such that $N \equiv uv$. The congruences $x - y \equiv u$, $x + y \equiv v$ now uniquely determine $x \bmod p$ and $y \bmod p$, since p is odd. Thus the stated congruence has exactly $p - 1$ solutions (x, y). If (x, y) is a solution, so is $(x, p - y)$ if $y \ne 0$, since $(p - y)^2 \equiv y^2$; and if (x, y_1) and (x, y_2) are solutions with $y_1 \ne y_2$, we have $y_1^2 \equiv y_2^2$; hence $y_1 = p - y_2$. Thus the number of different x values among the solutions (x, y) is $(p - 1)/2$ if $N \equiv x^2$ has no solutions, or $(p + 1)/2$ if $N \equiv x^2$ has solutions.

7. One procedure is to keep two indices for each modulus, one for the current word position and one for the current bit position; loading two words of the table and doing an indexed shift command will bring the table entries into proper alignment. (Many computers have special facilities for such bit manipulation.)

8. (We may assume that $N = 2M$ is even.) The following algorithm uses an auxiliary table $X[1]$, $X[2]$, ..., $X[M - 1]$, where $X[k]$ represents the primality of $2k + 1$.

    S1. Set $X[k] \leftarrow 1$ for $1 \le k < M$. Also set $j \leftarrow 1$, $k \leftarrow 1$, $p \leftarrow 3$, $q \leftarrow 4$. (During this algorithm $p = 2j + 1$ and $q = 2j + 2j^2$.)

    S2. If $X[j] = 0$, go to S4. Otherwise output p, which is prime, and set $k \leftarrow q$.

    S3. If $k < M$, then set $X[k] \leftarrow 0$, $k \leftarrow k + p$, and repeat this step.

    S4. Set $j \leftarrow j + 1$, $p \leftarrow p + 2$, $q \leftarrow q + 2p - 2$. If $j < M$, return to S2. ∎

A major part of this calculation could be made noticeably faster if q (instead of j) were tested against M in step S4, and if a new loop were appended that outputs $2j + 1$ for all remaining $X[j]$ that equal 1, suppressing the manipulation of p and q.

Notes: The original sieve of Eratosthenes was described in Book 1, Chapter 13 of Nicomachus's *Introduction to Arithmetic*. It is well known that $\sum_{p\,\text{prime}}[p \le N]/p = \ln\ln N + M + O((\log N)^{-10000})$, where $M = \gamma + \sum_{k\ge2}\mu(k)\ln\zeta(k)/k$ is Mertens's constant $0.26149\,72128\,47642\,78375\,54268\,38608\,69585\,90516-$; see F. Mertens, *Crelle* **76** (1874), 46–62; Greene and Knuth, *Mathematics for the Analysis of Algorithms* (Boston: Birkhäuser, 1981), §4.2.3. In particular, the number of operations in the original algorithm described by Nicomachus is $N\ln\ln N + O(N)$. Improvements in the efficiency of sieve methods for generating primes are discussed in exercise 5.2.3–15 and in Section 7.1.3.

9. If p^2 is a divisor of n for some prime p, then p is a divisor of $\lambda(n)$, but not of $n-1$. If $n = p_1p_2$, where $p_1 < p_2$ are primes, then $p_2 - 1$ is a divisor of $\lambda(n)$ and therefore $p_1p_2 - 1 \equiv 0$ (modulo $p_2 - 1$). Since $p_2 \equiv 1$, this means $p_1 - 1$ is a multiple of $p_2 - 1$, contradicting the assumption $p_1 < p_2$. [Values of n for which $\lambda(n)$ properly divides $n - 1$ are called *Carmichael numbers*. For example, here are some small Carmichael numbers with up to six prime factors: $3\cdot11\cdot17$, $5\cdot13\cdot17$, $7\cdot11\cdot13\cdot41$, $5\cdot7\cdot17\cdot19\cdot73$, $5\cdot7\cdot17\cdot73\cdot89\cdot107$. There are 8241 Carmichael numbers less than 10^{12}, and there are at least $\Omega(N^{2/7})$ Carmichael numbers less than N; see W. R. Alford, A. Granville, and C. Pomerance, *Annals of Math.* (2) **139** (1994), 703–722.]

10. Let k_p be the order of x_p modulo n, and let λ be the least common multiple of all the k_p's. Then λ is a divisor of $n - 1$ but not of any $(n - 1)/p$, so $\lambda = n - 1$. Since $x_p^{\varphi(n)} \bmod n = 1$, $\varphi(n)$ is a multiple of k_p for all p, so $\varphi(n) \ge \lambda$. But $\varphi(n) < n - 1$ when n is not prime. (Another way to carry out the proof is to construct an element x of order $n - 1$ from the x_p's, by the method of exercise 3.2.1.2–15.)

11.

U	V	A	P	S	T	Output
1984	1	0	992	0	—	
1981	1981	1	992	1	1981	
1983	4	495	993	0	1	$993^2 \equiv +2^2$
1983	991	2	98109	1	991	
1981	4	495	2	0	1	$2^2 \equiv +2^2$
1984	1981	1	99099	1	1981	
1984	1	1984	99101	0	1	$99101^2 \equiv +2^0$

The factorization $199\cdot991$ is evident from the first or last outputs. The shortness of the cycle, and the appearance of the notorious number 1984, are probably just coincidences.

12. The following algorithm makes use of an auxiliary $(m + 1) \times (m + 1)$ matrix of integers E_{jk}, $0 \le j, k \le m$; a single-precision vector $(b_0, b_1, \ldots, b_m)$; and a multiple-precision vector $(x_0, x_1, \ldots, x_m)$ with entries in the range $0 \le x_k < N$.

F1. [Initialize.] Set $b_i \leftarrow -1$ for $0 \le i \le m$; then set $j \leftarrow 0$.

F2. [Next solution.] Get the next output $(x, e_0, e_1, \ldots, e_m)$ from Algorithm E. (It is convenient to regard Algorithms E and F as coroutines.) Set $k \leftarrow m$.

F3. [Search for odd.] If $k < 0$ go to step F5. Otherwise if e_k is even, set $k \leftarrow k - 1$ and repeat this step.

F4. [Linear dependence?] If $b_k \ge 0$, then set $i \leftarrow b_k$, $x \leftarrow (x_i x) \bmod N$, $e_r \leftarrow e_r + E_{ir}$ for $0 \le r \le m$; set $k \leftarrow k - 1$ and return to F3. Otherwise set $b_k \leftarrow j$, $x_j \leftarrow x$, $E_{jr} \leftarrow e_r$ for $0 \le r \le m$; set $j \leftarrow j + 1$ and return to F2. (In the latter case we have a new linearly independent solution, modulo 2, whose first odd component is e_k. The values E_{jr} are not guaranteed to remain single-precision, but they tend to remain small when k decreases from m to 0 as recommended by Morrison and Brillhart.)

F5. [Try to factor.] (Now e_0, e_1, $\ldots$, e_m are even.) Set

$$y \leftarrow \left((-1)^{e_0/2} p_1^{e_1/2} \ldots p_m^{e_m/2}\right) \bmod N.$$

If $x = y$ or if $x + y = N$, return to F2. Otherwise compute $\gcd(x - y, N)$, which is a proper factor of N, and terminate the algorithm. ∎

This algorithm finds a factor whenever it is possible to deduce one from the given outputs of Algorithm E. [*Proof.* Let the outputs of Algorithm E be $(X_i, E_{i0}, \ldots, E_{im})$ for $1 \le i \le t$, and suppose that we could find a factorization $N = N_1 N_2$ when $x \equiv X_1^{a_1} \ldots X_t^{a_t}$ and $y \equiv (-1)^{e_0/2} p_1^{e_1/2} \ldots p_m^{e_m/2}$ (modulo N), where $e_j = a_1 E_{1j} + \cdots + a_t E_{tj}$ is even for all j. Then $x \equiv \pm y$ (modulo N_1) and $x \equiv \mp y$ (modulo N_2). It is not difficult to see that this solution can be transformed into a pair (x, y) that appears in step F5, by a series of steps that systematically replace (x, y) by (xx', yy') where $x' \equiv \pm y'$ (modulo N).]

13. There are 2^d values of x having the same exponents $(e_0, \ldots, e_m)$, since we can choose the sign of x modulo $q_i^{f_i}$ arbitrarily when $N = q_1^{f_1} \ldots q_d^{f_d}$. Exactly two of these 2^d values will fail to yield a factor.

14. Since $P^2 \equiv kNQ^2$ (modulo p) for any prime divisor p of V, we get $1 \equiv P^{2(p-1)/2} \equiv (kNQ^2)^{(p-1)/2} \equiv (kN)^{(p-1)/2}$ (modulo p), if $P \not\equiv 0$.

15. $U_n = (a^n - b^n)/\sqrt{D}$, where $a = \frac{1}{2}(P + \sqrt{D})$, $b = \frac{1}{2}(P - \sqrt{D})$, $D = P^2 - 4Q$. Then $2^{n-1} U_n = \sum_k \binom{n}{2k+1} P^{n-2k-1} D^k$; so $U_p \equiv D^{(p-1)/2}$ (modulo p) if p is an odd prime. Similarly, if $V_n = a^n + b^n = U_{n+1} - QU_{n-1}$, then $2^{n-1} V_n = \sum_k \binom{n}{2k} P^{n-2k} D^k$, and $V_p \equiv P^p \equiv P$. Thus if $U_p \equiv -1$, we find that $U_{p+1} \bmod p = 0$. If $U_p \equiv 1$, we find that $(QU_{p-1}) \bmod p = 0$; here if Q is a multiple of p, $U_n \equiv P^{n-1}$ (modulo p) for $n > 0$, so U_n is never a multiple of p; if Q is not a multiple of p, $U_{p-1} \bmod p = 0$. Therefore as in Theorem L, $U_t \bmod N = 0$ if $N = p_1^{e_1} \ldots p_r^{e_r}$, $N \perp Q$, and $t = \operatorname{lcm}_{1 \le j \le r}\left(p_j^{e_j - 1}(p_j + \epsilon_j)\right)$. Under the assumptions of this exercise, the rank of apparition of N is $N + 1$; hence N is prime to Q and t is a multiple of $N + 1$. Also, the assumptions of this exercise imply that each p_j is odd and each ϵ_j is ± 1, so $t \le 2^{1-r} \prod p_j^{e_j - 1}(p_j + \frac{1}{3} p_j) = 2(\frac{2}{3})^r N$; hence $r = 1$ and $t = p_1^{e_1} + \epsilon_1 p_1^{e_1 - 1}$. Finally, therefore, $e_1 = 1$ and $\epsilon_1 = 1$.

Note: If this test for primality is to be any good, we must choose P and Q in such a way that the test will probably work. Lehmer suggests taking $P = 1$ so that $D = 1 - 4Q$, and choosing Q so that $N \perp QD$. (If the latter condition fails, we know already that N is not prime, unless $|QD| \ge N$.) Furthermore, the derivation above shows that we will want $\epsilon_1 = 1$, that is, $D^{(N-1)/2} \equiv -1$ (modulo N). This is another condition that determines the choice of Q. Furthermore, if D satisfies this condition, and if $U_{N+1} \bmod N \ne 0$, we know that N is *not* prime.

Example: If $P = 1$ and $Q = -1$, we have the Fibonacci sequence, with $D = 5$. Since $5^{11} \equiv -1$ (modulo 23), we might attempt to prove that 23 is prime by using the Fibonacci sequence:

$$\langle F_n \bmod 23 \rangle = 0, 1, 1, 2, 3, 5, 8, 13, 21, 11, 9, 20, 6, 3, 9, 12, 21, 10, 8, 18, 3, 21, 1, 22, 0, \ldots,$$

so 24 is the rank of apparition of 23 and the test works. However, the Fibonacci sequence cannot be used in this way to prove the primality of 13 or 17, since $F_7 \bmod$

$13 = 0$ and $F_9 \bmod 17 = 0$. When $p \equiv \pm 1$ (modulo 10), we have $5^{(p-1)/2} \bmod p = 1$, so F_{p-1} (not F_{p+1}) is divisible by p.

17. Let $f(q) = 2 \lg q - 1$. When $q = 2$ or 3, the tree has at most $f(q)$ nodes. When $q > 3$ is prime, let $q = 1 + q_1 \ldots q_t$ where $t \geq 2$ and $q_1, \ldots, q_t$ are prime. The size of the tree is $\leq 1 + \sum f(q_k) = 2 + f(q-1) - t < f(q)$. [*SICOMP* **4** (1975), 214–220.]

18. $x(G(\alpha) - F(\alpha))$ is the number of $n \leq x$ whose second-largest prime factor is $\leq x^\alpha$ and whose largest prime factor is $> x^\alpha$. Hence

$$xG'(t)\,dt = \big(\pi(x^{t+dt}) - \pi(x^t)\big) \cdot x^{1-t}\big(G(t/(1-t)) - F(t/(1-t))\big).$$

The probability that $p_{t-1} \leq \sqrt{p_t}$ is $\int_0^1 F(t/2(1-t))t^{-1}\,dt$. [Curiously, it can be shown that this also equals $\int_0^1 F(t/(1-t))\,dt$, the average value of $\log p_t / \log x$, and it also equals the Dickman–Golomb constant .62433 of exercises 1.3.3–23 and 3.1–13. The derivative $G'(0)$ can be shown to equal

$$\int_0^1 F(t/(1-t))t^{-2}\,dt = F(1) + 2F(\tfrac{1}{2}) + 3F(\tfrac{1}{3}) + \cdots = e^\gamma.$$

The third-largest prime factor has $H(\alpha) = \int_0^\alpha \big(H(t/(1-t)) - G(t/(1-t))\big)t^{-1}\,dt$ and $H'(0) = \infty$. See P. Billingsley, *Period. Math. Hungar.* **2** (1972), 283–289; J. Galambos, *Acta Arith.* **31** (1976), 213–218; D. E. Knuth and L. Trabb Pardo, *Theoretical Comp. Sci.* **3** (1976), 321–348; J. L. Hafner and K. S. McCurley, *J. Algorithms* **10** (1989), 531–556.]

19. $M = 2^D - 1$ is a multiple of all p for which the order of 2 modulo p divides D. To extend this idea, let $a_1 = 2$ and $a_{j+1} = a_j^{q_j} \bmod N$, where $q_j = p_j^{e_j}$, p_j is the jth prime, and $e_j = \lfloor \log 1000 / \log p_j \rfloor$; let $A = a_{169}$. Now compute $b_q = \gcd(A^q - 1, N)$ for all primes q between 10^3 and 10^5. One way to do this is to start with $A^{1009} \bmod N$ and then to multiply alternately by $A^4 \bmod N$ and $A^2 \bmod N$. (A similar method was used in the 1920s by D. N. Lehmer, but he didn't publish it.) As with Algorithm B we can avoid most of the gcds by batching; for example, since $b_{30r-k} = \gcd(A^{30r} - A^k, N)$, we might try batches of 8, computing $c_r = (A^{30r} - A^{29})(A^{30r} - A^{23}) \ldots (A^{30r} - A) \bmod N$, then $\gcd(c_r, N)$ for $33 < r \leq 3334$.

20. See H. C. Williams, *Math. Comp.* **39** (1982), 225–234.

21. Some interesting theory relevant to this conjecture has been introduced by Eric Bach, *Information and Computation* **90** (1991), 139–155.

22. Algorithm P fails only when the random number x does not reveal the fact that n is nonprime. Say x is *bad* if $x^q \bmod n = 1$ or if one of the numbers $x^{2^j q}$ is $\equiv -1$ (modulo n) for $0 \leq j < k$. Since 1 is bad, we have $p_n = [n \text{ nonprime}](b_n - 1)/(n-2) < [n \text{ nonprime}]b_n/(n-1)$, where b_n is the number of bad x such that $1 \leq x < n$.

Every bad x satisfies $x^{n-1} \equiv 1$ (modulo n). When p is prime, the number of solutions to the congruence $x^q \equiv 1$ (modulo p^e) for $1 \leq x < p^e$ is the same as the number of solutions of $qy \equiv 0$ (modulo $p^{e-1}(p-1)$) for $0 \leq y < p^{e-1}(p-1)$, namely $\gcd(q, p^{e-1}(p-1))$, since we may replace x by a^y where a is a primitive root.

Let $n = n_1^{e_1} \ldots n_r^{e_r}$, where the n_i are distinct primes. According to the Chinese remainder theorem, the number of solutions to the congruence $x^{n-1} \equiv 1$ (modulo n) is $\prod_{i=1}^r \gcd(n-1, n_i^{e_i-1}(n_i-1))$, and this is at most $\prod_{i=1}^r (n_i - 1)$ since n_i is relatively prime to $n-1$. If some $e_i > 1$, we have $n_i - 1 \leq \frac{2}{9}n_i^{e_i}$, hence the number of solutions is at most $\frac{2}{9}n$; in this case $b_n \leq \frac{2}{9}n \leq \frac{1}{4}(n-1)$, since $n \geq 9$.

Therefore we may assume that n is the product $n_1 \ldots n_r$ of distinct primes. Let $n_i = 1 + 2^{k_i}q_i$, where $k_1 \leq \cdots \leq k_r$. Then $\gcd(n-1, n_i - 1) = 2^{k_i'}q_i'$, where $k_i' =$

$\min(k, k_i)$ and $q_i' = \gcd(q, q_i)$. Modulo n_i, the number of x such that $x^q \equiv 1$ is q_i'; and the number of x such that $x^{2^j q} \equiv -1$ is $2^j q_i'$ for $0 \le j < k_i'$, otherwise 0. Since $k \ge k_1$, we have $b_n = q_1' \ldots q_r' \left(1 + \sum_{0 \le j < k_1} 2^{jr} \right)$.

To complete the proof, it suffices to show that $b_n \le \frac{1}{4} q_1 \ldots q_r 2^{k_1 + \cdots + k_r} = \frac{1}{4} \varphi(n)$, since $\varphi(n) < n - 1$. We have

$$\left(1 + \sum_{0 \le j < k_1} 2^{jr} \right) / 2^{k_1 + \cdots + k_r} \le \left(1 + \sum_{0 \le j < k_1} 2^{jr} \right) / 2^{k_1 r}$$
$$= 1/(2^r - 1) + (2^r - 2)/(2^{k_1 r}(2^r - 1)) \le 1/2^{r-1},$$

so the result follows unless $r = 2$ and $k_1 = k_2$. If $r = 2$, exercise 9 shows that $n - 1$ is not a multiple of both $n_1 - 1$ and $n_2 - 1$. Thus if $k_1 = k_2$ we cannot have both $q_1' = q_1$ and $q_2' = q_2$; it follows that $q_1' q_2' \le \frac{1}{3} q_1 q_2$ and $b_n \le \frac{1}{6} \varphi(n)$ in this case.

[*Reference: J. Number Theory* **12** (1980), 128–138.] This proof shows that p_n is near $\frac{1}{4}$ in only two cases, when n is $(1 + 2q_1)(1 + 4q_1)$ or a Carmichael number of the special form $(1 + 2q_1)(1 + 2q_2)(1 + 2q_3)$. For example, when $n = 49939 \cdot 99877$ we have $b_n = \frac{1}{4}(49938 \cdot 99876)$ and $p_n \approx .24999$; when $n = 1667 \cdot 2143 \cdot 4523$, we have $b_n = \frac{1}{4}(1666 \cdot 2142 \cdot 4522)$, $p_n \approx .24968$. See the next answer for further remarks.]

23. (a) The proofs are simple except perhaps for the reciprocity law. Let $p = p_1 \ldots p_s$ and $q = q_1 \ldots q_r$, where the p_i and q_j are prime. Then

$$\left(\frac{p}{q} \right) = \prod_{i,j} \left(\frac{p_i}{q_j} \right) = \prod_{i,j} (-1)^{(p_i - 1)(q_j - 1)/4} \left(\frac{q_j}{p_i} \right) = (-1)^{\sum_{i,j} (p_i - 1)(q_j - 1)/4} \left(\frac{q}{p} \right),$$

so we need only verify that $\sum_{i,j} (p_i - 1)(q_j - 1)/4 \equiv (p - 1)(q - 1)/4$ (modulo 2). But $\sum_{i,j} (p_i - 1)(q_j - 1)/4 = \left(\sum_i (p_i - 1)/2 \right) \left(\sum_j (q_j - 1)/2 \right)$ is odd if and only if an odd number of the p_i and an odd number of the q_j are $\equiv 3$ (modulo 4), and this holds if and only if $(p-1)(q-1)/4$ is odd. [C. G. J. Jacobi, *Bericht Königl. Preuß. Akad. Wiss. Berlin* **2** (1837), 127–136; V. A. Lebesgue, *J. Math. Pures Appl.* **12** (1847), 497–520, discussed the efficiency.]

(b) As in exercise 22, we may assume that $n = n_1 \ldots n_r$ where the $n_i = 1 + 2^{k_i} q_i$ are distinct primes, and $k_1 \le \cdots \le k_r$; we let $\gcd(n - 1, n_i - 1) = 2^{k_i'} q_i'$ and we call x *bad* if it falsely makes n look prime. Let $\Pi_n = \prod_{i=1}^r q_i' 2^{\min(k_i, k-1)}$ be the number of solutions of $x^{(n-1)/2} \equiv 1$. The number of bad x with $\left(\frac{x}{n} \right) = 1$ is Π_n, times an extra factor of $\frac{1}{2}$ if $k_1 < k$. (This factor $\frac{1}{2}$ is needed to ensure that $\left(\frac{x}{n_i} \right) = -1$ for an even number of the n_i with $k_i < k$.) The number of bad x with $\left(\frac{x}{n} \right) = -1$ is Π_n if $k_1 = k$, otherwise 0. [If $x^{(n-1)/2} \equiv -1$ (modulo n_i), we have $\left(\frac{x}{n_i} \right) = -1$ if $k_i = k$, $\left(\frac{x}{n_i} \right) = +1$ if $k_i > k$, and a contradiction if $k_i < k$. If $k_1 = k$, there are an odd number of k_i equal to k.]

Notes: The probability of a bad guess is $> \frac{1}{4}$ only if n is a Carmichael number with $k_r < k$; for example, $n = 7 \cdot 13 \cdot 19 = 1729$, a number made famous by Ramanujan in another context. Louis Monier has extended the analyses above to obtain the following closed formulas for the number of bad x in general:

$$b_n = \left(1 + \frac{2^{rk_1} - 1}{2^r - 1} \right) \prod_{i=1}^r q_i'; \qquad b_n' = \delta_n \prod_{i=1}^r \gcd \left(\frac{n-1}{2}, n_i - 1 \right).$$

Here b_n' is the number of bad x in this exercise, and δ_n is either 2 (if $k_1 = k$), or $\frac{1}{2}$ (if $k_i < k$ and e_i is odd for some i), or 1 (otherwise).

(c) If $x^q \bmod n = 1$, then $1 = \left(\frac{x^q}{n} \right) = \left(\frac{x}{n} \right)^q = \left(\frac{x}{n} \right)$. If $x^{2^j q} \equiv -1$ (modulo n), then the order of x modulo n_i must be an odd multiple of 2^{j+1} for all prime divisors n_i

of n. Let $n = n_1^{e_1} \ldots n_r^{e_r}$ and $n_i = 1 + 2^{j+1} q_i''$; then $\left(\frac{x}{n_i}\right) = (-1)^{q_i''}$, so $\left(\frac{x}{n}\right) = +1$ or -1 according as $\sum e_i q_i''$ is even or odd. Since $n \equiv (1 + 2^{j+1} \sum e_i q_i'') \pmod{2^{j+2}}$, the sum $\sum e_i q_i''$ is odd if and only if $j + 1 = k$. [*Theoretical Comp. Sci.* **12** (1980), 97–108.]

24. Let M_1 be a matrix having one row for each nonprime odd number n in the range $1 \le n \le N$ and having $N - 1$ columns numbered from 2 to N; the entry in row n column x is 1 if n fails the x test of Algorithm P, otherwise it is zero. When $N = qn + r$ and $0 \le r < n$, we know that row n contains at most $-1 + q(b_n + 1) + \min(b_n + 1, r) < q(\frac{1}{4}(n-1) + 1) + \min(b_n + 1, r) \le \frac{1}{3} qn + \min(\frac{1}{4}n, r) = \frac{1}{3}N + \min(\frac{1}{4}n - \frac{1}{3}r, \frac{2}{3}r) \le \frac{1}{3}N + \frac{1}{6}n \le \frac{1}{2}N$ entries equal to 0, so at least half of the entries in the matrix are 1. Thus, some column x_1 of M_1 has at least half of its entries equal to 1. Removing column x_1 and all rows in which this column contains 1 leaves a matrix M_2 having similar properties; a repetition of this construction produces matrix M_r with $N - r$ columns and fewer than $N/2^r$ rows, and with at least $\frac{1}{2}(N-1)$ entries per row equal to 1. [See *FOCS* **19** (1978), 78.]

[A similar proof implies the existence of a *single* infinite sequence $x_1 < x_2 < \cdots$ such that the number $n > 1$ is prime if and only if it passes the x test of Algorithm P for $x = x_1, \ldots, x = x_m$, where $m = \frac{1}{2}\lfloor \lg n \rfloor(\lfloor \lg n \rfloor - 1)$. Does there exist a sequence $x_1 < x_2 < \cdots$ having this property but with $m = O(\log n)$?]

25. This theorem was first proved rigorously by von Mangoldt [*Crelle* **114** (1895), 255–305], who showed in fact that the $O(1)$ term is $C + \int_x^\infty dt/((t^2 - 1)t \ln t)$, minus $1/2k$ if x is the kth power of a prime. The constant C is $\mathrm{li}\, 2 - \ln 2 = \gamma + \ln \ln 2 + \sum_{n \ge 2} (\ln 2)^n / nn! = 0.35201\ 65995\ 57547\ 47542\ 73567\ 67736\ 43656\ 84471+$.

[For a summary of developments during the 100 years following von Mangoldt's paper, see A. A. Karatsuba, *Complex Analysis in Number Theory* (CRC Press, 1995). See also Eric Bach and Jeffrey Shallit, *Algorithmic Number Theory* **1** (MIT Press, 1996), Chapter 8, for an excellent introduction to the connection between Riemann's hypothesis and concrete problems about integers.]

26. If N is not prime, it has a prime factor $q \le \sqrt{N}$. By hypothesis, every prime divisor p of f has an integer x_p such that the order of x_p modulo q is a divisor of $N - 1$ but not of $(N-1)/p$. Therefore if p^k divides f, the order of x_p modulo q is a multiple of p^k. Exercise 3.2.1.2–15 now tells us that there is an element x of order f modulo q. But this is impossible, since it implies that $q^2 \ge (f+1)^2 \ge (f+1)\,r \ge N$, and equality cannot hold. [*Proc. Camb. Phil. Soc.* **18** (1914), 29–30.]

27. If k is not divisible by 3 and if $k \le 2^n + 1$, the number $k \cdot 2^n + 1$ is prime if and only if $3^{2^{n-1}k} \equiv -1 \pmod{k \cdot 2^n + 1}$. For if this condition holds, $k \cdot 2^n + 1$ is prime by exercise 26; and if $k \cdot 2^n + 1$ is prime, the number 3 is a quadratic nonresidue mod $k \cdot 2^n + 1$ by the law of quadratic reciprocity, since $(k \cdot 2^n + 1) \bmod 12 = 5$. [This test was stated without proof by Proth in *Comptes Rendus Acad. Sci.* **87** (Paris, 1878), 926.]

To implement Proth's test with the necessary efficiency, we need to be able to compute $x^2 \bmod (k \cdot 2^n + 1)$ with about the same speed as we can compute the quantity $x^2 \bmod (2^n - 1)$. Let $x^2 = A \cdot 2^n + B$; then $x^2 \equiv B - \lfloor A/k \rfloor + 2^n(A \bmod k)$, so the remainder is easily obtained when k is small. (See also exercise 4.3.2–14.)

[To test numbers of the form $3 \cdot 2^n + 1$ for primality, the job is only slightly more difficult; we first try random single-precision numbers until finding one that is a quadratic nonresidue mod $3 \cdot 2^n + 1$ by the law of quadratic reciprocity, then use this number in place of "3" in the test above. If $n \bmod 4 \ne 0$, the number 5 can be used. It turns out that $3 \cdot 2^n + 1$ is prime when $n = 1, 2, 5, 6, 8, 12, 18, 30, 36, 41, 66, 189,$ $201, 209, 276, 353, 408, 438, 534, 2208, 2816, 3168, 3189, 3912, 20909, 34350, 42294,$

42665, 44685, 48150, 55182, 59973, 80190, 157169, 213321, and no other $n \le 300000$; and $5 \cdot 2^n + 1$ is prime when $n = 1, 3, 7, 13, 15, 25, 39, 55, 75, 85, 127, 1947, 3313, 4687, 5947, 13165, 23473, 26607, 125413, 209787, 240937$, and no other $n \le 300000$. See R. M. Robinson, *Proc. Amer. Math. Soc.* **9** (1958), 673–681; G. V. Cormack and H. C. Williams, *Math. Comp.* **35** (1980), 1419–1421; H. Dubner and W. Keller, *Math. Comp.* **64** (1995), 397–405; J. S. Young, *Math. Comp.* **67** (1998), 1735–1738.]

28. $f(p, p^2 d) = 2/(p+1) + f(p, d)/p$, since $1/(p+1)$ is the probability that A is a multiple of p. $f(p, pd) = 1/(p+1)$ when $d \bmod p \ne 0$. $f(2, 4k+3) = \frac{1}{3}$ since $A^2 - (4k+3)B^2$ cannot be a multiple of 4; $f(2, 8k+5) = \frac{2}{3}$ since $A^2 - (8k+5)B^2$ cannot be a multiple of 8; $f(2, 8k+1) = \frac{1}{3} + \frac{1}{3} + \frac{1}{3} + \frac{1}{6} + \frac{1}{12} + \cdots = \frac{4}{3}$. $f(p, d) = (2p/(p^2-1), 0)$ if $d^{(p-1)/2} \bmod p = (1, p-1)$, respectively, for odd p.

29. The number of solutions to the inequality $x_1 + \cdots + x_m \le r$ in nonnegative integers x_i is $\binom{m+r}{r} \ge m^r/r!$, and each of these corresponds to a unique integer $p_1^{x_1} \ldots p_m^{x_m} \le n$. [For sharper estimates, in the special case that p_j is the jth prime for all j, see N. G. de Bruijn, *Indag. Math.* **28** (1966), 240–247; H. Halberstam, *Proc. London Math. Soc.* (3) **21** (1970), 102–107.]

30. If $p_1^{e_1} \ldots p_m^{e_m} \equiv x_i^2$ (modulo q_i), we can find y_i such that $p_1^{e_1} \ldots p_m^{e_m} \equiv (\pm y_i)^2$ (modulo $q_i^{d_i}$), hence by the Chinese remainder theorem we obtain 2^d values of X such that $X^2 \equiv p_1^{e_1} \ldots p_m^{e_m}$ (modulo N). Such $(e_1, \ldots, e_m)$ correspond to at most $\binom{r}{r/2}$ pairs $(e'_1, \ldots, e'_m; e''_1, \ldots, e''_m)$ having the hinted properties. Now for each of the 2^d binary numbers $a = (a_1 \ldots a_d)_2$, let n_a be the number of exponents $(e'_1, \ldots, e'_m)$ such that $(p_1^{e'_1} \ldots p_m^{e'_m})^{(q_i-1)/2} \equiv (-1)^{a_i}$ (modulo q_i); we have proved that the required number of integers X is $\ge 2^d (\sum_a n_a^2)/\binom{r}{r/2}$. Since $\sum_a n_a$ is the number of ways to choose at most $r/2$ objects from a set of m objects with repetitions permitted, namely $\binom{m+r/2}{r/2}$, we have $\sum_a n_a^2 \ge \binom{m+r/2}{r/2}^2/2^d \ge m^r/(2^d(r/2)!^2)$. [See *J. Algorithms* **3** (1982), 101–127, where Schnorr presents many further refinements of Theorem D.]

31. Set $n = M$, $pM = 4m$, and $\epsilon M = 2m$ to show that $\Pr(X \le 2m) \le e^{-m/2}$.

32. Let $M = \lfloor \sqrt[3]{N} \rfloor$, and let the places x_i of each message be restricted to the range $0 \le x < M^3 - M^2$. If $x \ge M$, encode it as $x^3 \bmod N$ as before, but if $x < M$ change the encoding to $(x + yM)^3 \bmod N$, where y is a random number in the range $M^2 - M \le y < M^2$. To decode, first take the cube root; and if the result is $M^3 - M^2$ or more, take the remainder mod M.

34. Let P be the probability that $x^m \bmod p = 1$ and let Q be the probability that $x^m \bmod q = 1$. The probability that $\gcd(x^m - 1, N) = p$ or q is $P(1 - Q) + Q(1 - P) = P + Q - 2PQ$. If $P \le \frac{1}{2}$ or $Q \le \frac{1}{2}$, this probability is $\ge 2(10^{-6} - 10^{-12})$, so we have a good chance of finding a factor after about $10^6 \log m$ arithmetic operations modulo N. On the other hand if $P > \frac{1}{2}$ and $Q > \frac{1}{2}$ then $P \approx Q \approx 1$, since we have the general formula $P = \gcd(m, p-1)/p$; thus m is a multiple of $\mathrm{lcm}(p-1, q-1)$ in this case. Let $m = 2^k r$ where r is odd, and form the sequence $x^r \bmod N$, $x^{2r} \bmod N$, $\ldots$, $x^{2^k r} \bmod N$; we find as in Algorithm P that the first appearance of 1 is preceded by a value y other than $N - 1$ with probability $\ge \frac{1}{2}$, hence $\gcd(y - 1, N) = p$ or q.

35. Let $f = (p^{q-1} - q^{p-1}) \bmod N$. Since $p \bmod 4 = q \bmod 4 = 3$, we have $\left(\frac{-1}{p}\right) = \left(\frac{-1}{q}\right) = \left(\frac{f}{p}\right) = -\left(\frac{f}{q}\right) = -1$, and we also have $\left(\frac{2}{p}\right) = -\left(\frac{2}{q}\right) = -1$. Given a message x in the range $0 \le x \le \frac{1}{8}(N-5)$, let $\bar{x} = 4x+2$ or $8x+4$, whichever satisfies $\left(\frac{\bar{x}}{N}\right) \ge 0$; then transmit the message $\bar{x}^2 \bmod N$.

To decode this message, we first use a SQRT box to find the unique number y such that $y^2 \equiv \bar{x}^2 \bmod N$ and $\left(\frac{y}{N}\right) \geq 0$ and y is even. Then $y = \bar{x}$, since the other square roots of $\bar{x}^2$ are $N - \bar{x}$ and $(\pm f\bar{x}) \bmod N$; the first of these is odd, and the other two either have negative Jacobi symbols or are simply $\bar{x}$ and $N - \bar{x}$. The decoding is now completed by setting $x \leftarrow \lfloor y/4 \rfloor$ if $y \bmod 4 = 2$, otherwise $x \leftarrow \lfloor y/8 \rfloor$.

Anybody who can decode such encodings can also find the factors of N, because the decoding of a false message $\bar{x}^2 \bmod N$ when $\left(\frac{\bar{x}}{N}\right) = -1$ reveals $(\pm f) \bmod N$, and $((\pm f) \bmod N) - 1$ has a nontrivial gcd with N. [*Reference: IEEE Transactions* **IT-26** (1980), 726–729.]

36. The mth prime equals $m \ln m + m \ln \ln m - m + m \ln \ln m/\ln m - 2m/\ln m + O(m(\log \log m)^2 (\log m)^{-2})$, by (4), although for this problem we need only the weaker estimate $p_m = m \ln m + O(m \log \log m)$. (We will assume that p_m is the mth prime, since this corresponds to the assumption that V is uniformly distributed.) If we choose $\ln m = \frac{1}{2}c\sqrt{\ln N \ln \ln N}$, where $c = O(1)$, we find that $r = c^{-1}\sqrt{\ln N/\ln \ln N} - c^{-2} - c^{-2}(\ln \ln \ln N/\ln \ln N) - 2c^{-2}(\ln \frac{1}{2}c)/\ln \ln N + O(\sqrt{\ln \ln N/\ln N})$. The estimated running time (22) now simplifies somewhat surprisingly to $\exp(f(c,N)\sqrt{\ln N \ln \ln N} + O(\log \log N))$, where we have $f(c,N) = c + (1 - (1 + \ln 2)/\ln \ln N)c^{-1}$. The value of c that minimizes $f(c,N)$ is $\sqrt{1 - (1 + \ln 2)/\ln \ln N}$, so we obtain the estimate

$$\exp(2\sqrt{\ln N \ln \ln N}\sqrt{1 - (1 + \ln 2)/\ln \ln N} + O(\log \log N)).$$

When $N = 10^{50}$ this gives $\epsilon(N) \approx .33$, which is still much larger than the observed behavior.

Note: The partial quotients of $\sqrt{D}$ seem to behave according to the distribution obtained for random real numbers in Section 4.5.3. For example, the first million partial quotients of the square root of the number $10^{18} + 314159$ include exactly $(415236, 169719, 93180, 58606)$ cases where A_n is respectively $(1,2,3,4)$. Moreover, we have $V_{n+1} = |p_n^2 - Dq_n^2| = 2\sqrt{D}q_n|p_n - \sqrt{D}q_n| + O(q_n^{-2})$ by exercise 4.5.3–12(c) and Eq. 4.5.3–(12). Therefore we can expect $V_n/2\sqrt{D}$ to behave essentially like the quantity $\theta_n(x) = q_n|p_n - xq_n|$, where x is a random real number. The random variable θ_n is known to have the approximate density $\min(1, \theta^{-1} - 1)/\ln 2$ for $0 \leq \theta \leq 1$ [see Bosma, Jager, and Wiedijk, *Indag. Math.* **45** (1983), 281–299], which is uniform when $\theta \leq 1/2$. So something besides the size of V_n must account for the unreasonable effectiveness of Algorithm E.

37. Apply exercise 4.5.3–12 to the number $\sqrt{D} + R$, to see that the periodic part begins immediately, and run the period backwards to verify the palindromic property. [It follows that the second half of the period gives the same V's as the first, and Algorithm E could be shut down earlier by terminating it when $U = U'$ or $V = V'$ in step E5. However, the period is generally so long, we never even get close to halfway through it, so there is no point in making the algorithm more complicated.]

38. Let $r = (10^{50} - 1)/9$. Then $P_0 = 10^{49} + 9$; $P_1 = r + 3 \cdot 10^{46}$; $P_2 = 2r + 3 \cdot 10^{47} + 7$; $P_3 = 3r + 2 \cdot 10^{49}$; $P_4 = 4r + 2 \cdot 10^{49} - 3$; $P_5 = 5r + 3 \cdot 10^{49} + 4$; $P_6 = 6r + 2 \cdot 10^{48} + 3$; $P_7 = 7r + 2 \cdot 10^{25}$ (very pretty); $P_8 = 8r + 10^{38} - 7$; $P_9 = 9r - 8000$.

39. Notice that it's easy to prove the primality of q when $q-1$ has just 2 and p as prime factors. The only successors of 2 are Fermat primes, and the existence or nonexistence of a sixth Fermat prime is one of the most famous unsolved problems of number theory. Thus we probably will never know how to determine whether or not an arbitrary integer has any successors. But it's sometimes possible; for example, John Selfridge proved in 1962 that 78557 and 271129 have none [see *AMM* **70** (1963), 101–102], after W. Sierpiński had proved the existence of infinitely many odd numbers without a successor [*Elemente der Math.* **15** (1960), 73–74]. Perhaps 78557 is the smallest of these, although 69 other contenders for that honor still existed in 1983, according to G. Jaeschke and W. Keller [*Math. Comp.* **40** (1983), 381–384, 661–673; **45** (1985), 637].

For information on the more traditional "Cunningham" form of prime chain, in which the transitions are $p \to 2p \pm 1$, see Günter Löh, *Math. Comp.* **53** (1989), 751–759. In particular, Löh found that $554688278430 \cdot 2^k - 1$ is prime for $0 \le k < 12$.

40. [*Inf. Proc. Letters* **8** (1979), 28–31.] Notice that $x \bmod y = x - y \lfloor x/y \rfloor$ can be computed easily on such a machine, and we can get simple constants like $0 = x - x$, $1 = \lfloor x/x \rfloor$, $2 = 1 + 1$; we can test $x > 0$ by testing whether $x = 1$ or $\lfloor x/(x - 1) \rfloor \ne 0$.

(a) First compute $l = \lfloor \lg n \rfloor$ in $O(\log n)$ steps, by repeatedly dividing by 2; at the same time compute $k = 2^l$ and $A = 2^{2^{l+1}}$ in $O(\log n)$ steps by repeatedly setting $k \leftarrow 2k$, $A \leftarrow A^2$. For the main computation, suppose we know that $t = A^m$, $u = (A+1)^m$, and $v = m!$; then we can increase the value of m by 1 by setting $m \leftarrow m+1$, $t \leftarrow At$, $u \leftarrow (A+1)u$, $v \leftarrow vm$; and we can *double* the value of m by setting $m \leftarrow 2m$, $u \leftarrow u^2$, $v \leftarrow (\lfloor u/t \rfloor \bmod A)v^2$, $t \leftarrow t^2$, provided that A is sufficiently large. (Consider the number u in radix-A notation; A must be greater than $\binom{2m}{m}$.) Now if $n = (a_l \ldots a_0)_2$, let $n_j = (a_l \ldots a_j)_2$; if $m = n_j$ and $k = 2^j$ and $j > 0$ we can decrease j by 1 by setting $k \leftarrow \lfloor k/2 \rfloor$, $m \leftarrow 2m + (\lfloor n/k \rfloor \bmod 2)$. Hence we can compute $n_j!$ for $j = l$, $l-1, \ldots, 0$ in $O(\log n)$ steps. [Another solution, due to Julia Robinson, is to compute $n! = \lfloor B^n / \binom{B}{n} \rfloor$ when $B > (2n)^{n+1}$; see *AMM* **80** (1973), 250–251, 266.]

(b) First compute $A = 2^{2^{l+2}}$ as in (a), then find the least $k \ge 0$ such that $2^{k+1}! \bmod n = 0$. If $\gcd(n, 2^k!) \ne 1$, let $f(n)$ be this value; note that this gcd can be computed in $O(\log n)$ steps by Euclid's algorithm. Otherwise we will find the least integer m such that $\binom{m}{\lfloor m/2 \rfloor} \bmod n = 0$, and let $f(n) = \gcd(m, n)$. (Note that in this case $2^k < m \le 2^{k+1}$, hence $\lceil m/2 \rceil \le 2^k$ and $\lceil m/2 \rceil!$ is relatively prime to n; therefore $\binom{m}{\lfloor m/2 \rfloor} \bmod n = 0$ if and only if $m! \bmod n = 0$. Furthermore $n \ne 4$.)

To compute m with a bounded number of registers, we can use Fibonacci numbers (see Algorithm 6.2.1F). Suppose we know that $s = F_j$, $s' = F_{j+1}$, $t = A^{F_j}$, $t' = A^{F_{j+1}}$, $u = (A+1)^{2F_j}$, $u' = (A+1)^{2F_{j+1}}$, $v = A^m$, $w = (A+1)^{2m}$, $\binom{2m}{m} \bmod n \ne 0$, and $\binom{2(m+s)}{m+s} \bmod n = 0$. It is easy to reach this state of affairs with $m = F_{j+1}$, for suitably large j, in $O(\log n)$ steps; furthermore A will be larger than $2^{2(m+s)}$. If $s = 1$, we set $f(n) = \gcd(2m+1, n)$ or $\gcd(2m+2, n)$, whichever is $\ne 1$, and terminate the algorithm. Otherwise we reduce j by 1 as follows: Set $r \leftarrow s$, $s \leftarrow s' - s$, $s' \leftarrow r$, $r \leftarrow t$, $t \leftarrow \lfloor t'/t \rfloor$, $t' \leftarrow r$, $r \leftarrow u$, $u \leftarrow \lfloor u'/u \rfloor$, $u' \leftarrow r$; then if $(\lfloor wu/vt \rfloor \bmod A) \bmod n \ne 0$, set $m \leftarrow m+s$, $w \leftarrow wu$, $v \leftarrow vt$.

[Can this problem be solved with fewer than $O(\log n)$ operations? Can the smallest, or the largest, prime factor of n be computed in $O(\log n)$ operations?]

41. (a) Clearly $\pi(x) = \pi(m) + f_1(x, m) = \pi(m) + f(x, m) - f_0(x, m) - f_2(x, m) - f_3(x, m) - \cdots$ when $1 \le m \le x$. Set $x = N^3$, $m = N$, and note that $f_k(N^3, N) = 0$ for $k > 2$.

(b) We have $f_2(N^3, N) = \sum_{N < p \le q}[pq \le N^3] = \sum_{N < p \le N^{3/2}} (\pi(N^3/p) - \pi(p) + 1) = \sum_{N < p \le N^{3/2}} \pi(N^3/p) - \binom{\pi(N^{3/2})}{2} + \binom{\pi(N)}{2}$, where p and q range over primes. Hence $f_2(1000, 10) = \pi(\frac{1000}{11}) + \pi(\frac{1000}{13}) + \pi(\frac{1000}{17}) + \pi(\frac{1000}{19}) + \pi(\frac{1000}{23}) + \pi(\frac{1000}{29}) + \pi(\frac{1000}{31}) - \binom{\pi(31)}{2} + \binom{\pi(10)}{2} = 24 + 21 + 16 + 15 + 14 + 11 + 11 - 55 + 6 = 63$.

(c) The hinted identity says simply that a p_j-survivor is a p_{j-1}-survivor that isn't a multiple of p_j. Clearly $f(N^3, N) = f(N^3, p_{\pi(N)})$. Apply the identity until reaching terms $f(x, p_j)$ where either $j = 0$ or $x \le N^2$; the result is

$$f(N^3, N) = \sum_{k=1}^{N-1} \mu(k) f\left(\frac{N^3}{k}, 1\right) - \sum_{j=1}^{\pi(N)} \sum_{N/p_j \le k < N} \mu(k) f\left(\frac{N^3}{kp_j}, p_{j-1}\right) [k \text{ is a } p_j\text{-survivor}].$$

Now $f(x, 1) = \lfloor x \rfloor$, so the first sum is $1000 - 500 - 333 - 200 + 166 - 142 = -9$ when $N = 10$. The second sum is $-f(\frac{1000}{10}, 1) - f(\frac{1000}{14}, 1) - f(\frac{1000}{15}, 2) - f(\frac{1000}{21}, 2) - f(\frac{1000}{35}, 3) = -100 - 71 - 33 - 24 - 9 = -237$. Hence $f(1000, 10) = -9 + 237 = 228$, and $\pi(1000) = 4 + 228 - 1 - 63 = 168$.

(d) If $N^2 \le 2^m$ we can construct an array in which $a_{2^m - 1 + n} = [n + 1$ is a p_j-survivor] for $1 \le n \le N^2$ represents a sieve after j passes, and $a_n = a_{2n} + a_{2n+1}$ for $1 \le n < 2^m$. Then it is easy to compute $f(x, p_j)$ in $O(m)$ steps when $x \le N^2$, and to remove multiples of p from the sieve in $O(N^2 m/p)$ steps. The total running time to compute $f(N^3, N)$ will come to $O(N^2 \log N \log \log N)$, because $\sum_{j=1}^{\pi(N)} 1/p_j = O(\log \log N)$.

The storage requirement can be reduced from $2N^2 m$ to $2Nm$ if we break the sieve into N parts of size N and work on each part separately. Auxiliary tables of p_j for $1 \le j \le \pi(N)$, and of $\mu(k)$ and the least prime factor of k for $1 \le k \le N$, are helpful and easily constructed before the main computation begins.

[See *Math. Comp.* **44** (1985), 537–560. A similar procedure was first introduced by D. F. E. Meissel, *Math. Annalen* **2** (1870), 636–642; **3** (1871), 523–525; **21** (1883), 304; **25** (1885), 251–257. D. H. Lehmer made several refinements in *Illinois J. Math.* **3** (1959), 381–388. Neither Meissel nor Lehmer had a stopping rule for the recurrence that was as efficient as the method described above. Further refinements due to numerous other researchers have made it possible to go much higher; the current record, due to David Baugh and Kim Walisch in 2022, is $\pi(10^{29}) = 1520698109714272166094258063$. (See OEIS sequence A006880.) Lagarias and Odlyzko also developed a completely different approach whereby $\pi(N)$ can be evaluated in $O(N^{1/2+\epsilon})$ steps, using principles of analytic number theory; see *J. Algorithms* **8** (1987), 173–191. But the constant in that O is impracticably large. See also the elementary method of D. Hirsch, I. Kessler, and U. Mendlovic, arXiv:2212.09857 [math.NT] (2022), 60 pages.]

42. L1. [Initialize.] Find $\bar{r}$ such that $r\bar{r} \equiv 1$ (modulo s); then set $r' \leftarrow n\bar{r} \bmod s$, $u \leftarrow r'\bar{r} \bmod s$, $v \leftarrow s$, $w \leftarrow (n - rr')\bar{r}/s \bmod s$, $\theta \leftarrow \lfloor \sqrt{N/s} \rfloor$, $(u_1, u_3) \leftarrow (1, u)$, $(v_1, v_3) \leftarrow (0, v)$. (We want to find all pairs of integers (λ, μ) such that $(\lambda s + r)(\mu s + r') = N$; this implies $\lambda u + \mu \equiv w$ (modulo s) and $\sqrt{\lambda \mu v} \le \theta$. We will perform Algorithm 4.5.2X with t_2, u_2, v_2 suppressed; the relations

$$\lambda t_3 + \mu t_1 \equiv w t_1, \qquad \lambda u_3 + \mu u_1 \equiv w u_1, \qquad \lambda v_3 + \mu v_1 \equiv w v_1 \qquad (\text{modulo } s)$$

will remain invariant.)

L2. [Try for divisors.] If $v_1 = 0$, output $\lambda s + r$ whenever $\lambda s + r$ divides N and $0 \le \lambda \le \theta/s$. If $v_3 = 0$, output $N/(\mu s + r')$ whenever $\mu s + r'$ divides N and $0 \le \mu \le \theta/s$. Otherwise, for all k such that $|wv_1 + ks| \le \theta$ if $v_1 < 0$, or $0 < wv_1 + ks \le 2\theta$ if $v_1 > 0$, and for $\sigma = +1$ and -1, output $\lambda s + r$ if $d = (wv_1 s + ks^2 + v_3 r + v_1 r')^2 - 4v_1 v_3 N$ is a perfect square and if the numbers

$$\lambda = \frac{wv_1 s + ks^2 - v_3 r + v_1 r' + \sigma\sqrt{d}}{2v_3 s}, \qquad \mu = \frac{wv_1 s + ks^2 + v_3 r - v_1 r' - \sigma\sqrt{d}}{2v_3 s}$$

are positive integers. (These are the solutions to $\lambda v_3 + \mu v_1 = wv_1 + ks$, $(\lambda s + r)(\mu s + r') = N$.)

L3. [Done?] If $v_3 = 0$, the algorithm terminates.

L4. [Divide and subtract.] Set $q \leftarrow \lfloor u_3/v_3 \rfloor$. If $u_3 = qv_3$ and $v_1 < 0$, decrease q by 1. Then set

$$(t_1, t_3) \leftarrow (u_1, u_3) - (v_1, v_3)q, \quad (u_1, u_3) \leftarrow (v_1, v_3), \quad (v_1, v_3) \leftarrow (t_1, t_3)$$

and return to step L2. ∎

[See *Math. Comp.* **42** (1984), 331–340. The bounds in step L2 can be sharpened, for example to ensure that $d \geq 0$. Some factors may be output more than once.]

43. (a) First make sure that the Jacobi symbol $\left(\frac{y}{m}\right)$ is $+1$. (If it's 0, the task is easy; if it's -1, then $y \notin Q_m$.) Then choose random integers $x_1, \ldots, x_n$ in $[0 \mathinner{.\,.} m)$ and let $X_j = \left[G(y^2 x_j^4 \bmod m) = (yx_j^2 \bmod m) \bmod 2 \right]$. If $y \in Q_m$ we have $\mathrm{E}\, X_j \geq \frac{1}{2} + \epsilon$; otherwise $m - y \in Q_m$ and $\mathrm{E}\, X_j \leq \frac{1}{2} - \epsilon$. Report that $y \in Q_m$ if $X_1 + \cdots + X_n \geq \frac{1}{2}n$. The probability of failure is at most $e^{-2\epsilon^2 n}$, by exercise 1.2.10–21. Therefore we choose $n = \lceil \frac{1}{2}\epsilon^{-2} \ln \delta^{-1} \rceil$.

(b) Find an x with Jacobi symbol $\left(\frac{x}{m}\right) = -1$, and set $y \leftarrow x^2 \bmod m$. Then the prime factors of m are $\gcd(x + \sqrt{y}, m)$ and $\gcd(x - \sqrt{y}, m)$, so our task is to find $\pm\sqrt{y}$ when $y \in Q_m$ is given. If we can find τv for any nonzero v, we are done, since $\sqrt{y} = (v^{-1}\tau v) \bmod m$ unless $\gcd(v, m)$ is a factor of m.

Assume that $\epsilon = 2^{-e}$ for some $e \geq 1$. Choose random integers a and b in $[0 \mathinner{.\,.} m)$, and assume that we know the binary fractions α_0 and β_0 such that

$$\left| \frac{\tau a}{m} - \alpha_0 \right| < \frac{\epsilon}{64}, \qquad \left| \frac{\tau b}{m} - \beta_0 \right| < \frac{\epsilon^3}{64};$$

here α_0 is an odd multiple of $\epsilon/64$, while β_0 is an odd multiple of $\epsilon^3/64$. Assume also that we know λa and λb. Of course we don't really know α_0, β_0, λa, or λb, but we will try all $32\epsilon^{-1} \times 32\epsilon^{-3} \times 2 \times 2$ possibilities. Spurious branches of the program, which operate under incorrect assumptions, will cause no harm.

Define the numbers $u_{tj} = 2^{-t}(a + (j + \frac{1}{2})b) \bmod m$ and $v_{tj} = 2^{-t-1}(a + jb) \bmod m$. Both u_{tj} and v_{tj} are uniformly distributed in $[0 \mathinner{.\,.} m)$, because a and b were chosen at random. Furthermore, for fixed t, the numbers u_{tj} for $j_0 \leq j < j_0 + l$ are *pairwise independent*, and so are the numbers v_{tj} for $j_0 \leq j < j_0 + l$, as long as l does not exceed the smallest prime factor of m. We will make use of u_{tj} and v_{tj} only for $-2r\epsilon^{-2} \leq j < 2r\epsilon^{-2}$; if any of these values has a nonzero factor in common with m, we're done.

For all $v \perp m$ we define $\chi v = +1$ if $v \in Q_m$, $\chi v = -1$ if $-v \in Q_m$, and $\chi v = 0$ if $\left(\frac{v}{m}\right) = -1$. Notice that $\chi u_{(t+2)j} = \chi u_{tj}$, since $u_{tj} = (2^2 u_{(t+2)j}) \bmod m$. Therefore we can determine χu_{tj} and χv_{tj} for all t and j by applying algorithm A to u_{tj} and v_{tj} for $0 \leq t \leq 1$ and $-2r\epsilon^{-2} \leq j < 2r\epsilon^{-2}$. Setting $\delta = \frac{1}{1440}\epsilon^2 r^{-1}$ in that algorithm will ensure that all χ values are correct with probability $\geq 1 - \frac{1}{90}$.

The algorithm works in at most r stages. At the beginning of stage t, for $0 \leq t < r$, we assume that we know $\lambda 2^{-t}a$, $\lambda 2^{-t}b$, and fractions α_t, β_t such that

$$\left| \frac{\tau 2^{-t}a}{m} - \alpha_t \right| < \frac{\epsilon}{2^{t+6}}, \qquad \left| \frac{\tau 2^{-t}b}{m} - \beta_t \right| < \frac{\epsilon^3}{2^{t+6}}.$$

Define $\alpha_{t+1} = \frac{1}{2}(\alpha_t + \lambda 2^{-t}a)$ and $\beta_{t+1} = \frac{1}{2}(\beta_t + \lambda 2^{-t}b)$; this preserves the inequalities. The next step is to find $\lambda 2^{-t-1}b$, which satisfies

$$\lambda u_{tj} + \lambda 2^{-t}a + j\lambda 2^{-t}b + \lambda 2^{-t-1}b + \left\lfloor \frac{\tau 2^{-t}a + j\tau 2^{-t}b + \tau 2^{-t-1}b}{m} \right\rfloor \equiv 0 \pmod 2.$$

Let $n = 4\min(r, 2^t)\epsilon^{-2}$; then when $|j| \leq \frac{n}{2}$ we have

$$\left| \frac{\tau 2^{-t}a}{m} + j\frac{\tau 2^{-t}b}{m} + \frac{\tau 2^{-t-1}b}{m} - (\alpha_t + j\beta_t + \beta_{t+1}) \right| < \frac{\epsilon}{16}.$$

Therefore if $\chi u_{tj} = 1$ it is likely that $\lambda 2^{-t-1}b = G_j$, where $G_j = (G(u_{tj}^2 y \bmod m) + \lambda 2^{-t}a + j\lambda 2^{-t}b + \lfloor \alpha_t j\beta_t + \beta_{t+1} \rfloor) \bmod 2$. More precisely, we will have

$$\lfloor (\tau 2^{-t}a + j\tau 2^{-t}b + \tau 2^{-t-1}b)/m \rfloor = \lfloor \alpha_t + j\beta_t + \beta_{t+1} \rfloor$$

unless $\tau u_{tj} < \frac{\epsilon}{16}m$ or $\tau u_{tj} > (1 - \frac{\epsilon}{16})m$. Let $Y_j = (2G_j - 1)\chi u_{tj}$. If $Y_j = +1$, it is a vote for $\lambda 2^{-t-1}b = 1$; if $Y_j = -1$, it is a vote for $\lambda 2^{-t-1}b = 0$; if $Y_j = 0$, it is an abstention. We will be democratic and set $\lambda 2^{-t-1}b = [\sum_{j=-n/2}^{n/2-1} Y_j \geq 0]$.

What is the probability that $\lambda 2^{-t-1}b$ is correct? Let $Z_j = -1$ if $\chi u_{tj} \neq 0$ and $(\tau u_{tj} < \frac{\epsilon}{16}m$ or $\tau u_{tj} > (1 - \frac{\epsilon}{16})m$ or $G(u_{tj}^2 y \bmod m) \neq \lambda u_{tj})$; otherwise let $Z_j = |\chi u_{tj}|$. Since Z_j is a function of u_{tj}, the random variables Z_j are pairwise independent and have the same distribution. Let $Z = \sum_{j=-n/2}^{n/2-1} Z_j$; if $Z > 0$, the value of $\lambda 2^{-t-1}b$ will be correct. The probability that $Z_j = 0$ is $\frac{1}{2}$, and the probability that $Z_j = +1$ is $\geq \frac{1}{4} + \frac{\epsilon}{2} - \frac{\epsilon}{8}$; therefore $\mathrm{E}\, Z_j \geq \frac{3}{4}\epsilon$. Clearly $\mathrm{var}(Z_j) \leq \frac{1}{2}$. So the chance of error, in the branch of the program that has the correct assumptions, is at most $\Pr(Z \leq 0) \leq \Pr((Z - n\,\mathrm{E}\, Z_j)^2 \geq \frac{9}{16}n^2\epsilon^2) \leq \frac{8}{9}n^{-1}\epsilon^2 = \frac{2}{9}\min(r, 2^t)^{-1}$, by Chebyshev's inequality (exercise 3.5–42).

A similar method, with v_{tj} in place of u_{tj}, can be used to determine $\lambda 2^{-t-1}a$ with error $\leq \frac{2}{9}\min(r, 2^t)^{-1}$. Eventually we will have $\epsilon^3/2^{t+6} < 1/(2m)$, so $\tau 2^{-t}b$ will be the nearest integer to $m\beta_t$. Then we can compute $\sqrt{y} = (2^t b^{-1} \tau 2^{-t}b) \bmod m$; squaring this quantity will tell us if we are correct.

The total chance of making a mistake is bounded by $\frac{4}{9}\sum_{t \geq 1} 2^{-t} = \frac{4}{9}$ in stages $t < \lg n$, and by $\frac{4}{9}\sum_{t \leq r} r^{-1} = \frac{4}{9}$ in subsequent stages. So the total chance of error, including the possibility that the χ values were not all correct, is at most $\frac{4}{9} + \frac{4}{9} + \frac{1}{90} = \frac{9}{10}$. At least $\frac{1}{10}$ of all runs of the program will succeed in finding $\sqrt{y}$; hence the factors of m will be found after repeating the process at most 10 times, on the average.

The total running time is dominated by $O(r\epsilon^{-4}\log(r\epsilon^{-2})T(G))$ for the χ computation, plus $O(r^2\epsilon^{-2}T(G))$ for subsequent guessing, plus $O(r^2\epsilon^{-6})$ for the calculations of α_t, β_t, $\lambda 2^{-t}a$, and $\lambda 2^{-t}b$ in all branches.

This procedure, which nicely illustrates many of the basic paradigms of randomized algorithms, is due to R. Fischlin and C. P. Schnorr [*J. Cryptology* **13** (2000), 221–244], who derived it from earlier approaches by Alexi, Chor, Goldreich, and Schnorr [*SICOMP* **17** (1988), 194–209] and by Ben-Or, Chor, and Shamir [*STOC* **15** (1983), 421–430]. When we combine it with Lemma 3.5P4, we get a theorem analogous to Theorem 3.5P, but with the sequence 3.2.2–(16) instead of 3.2.2–(17). Fischlin and Schnorr showed how to streamline the calculations so that their factoring algorithm takes $O(r\epsilon^{-4}\log(r\epsilon^{-1})T(G))$ steps; the resulting time bound for "cracking" 3.2.2–(16) is $T(F) = O(RN^4\epsilon^{-4}\log(RN\epsilon^{-1})(T(G) + R^2))$. The constant factor implied by this O is rather large, but not enormous. A similar method finds x from the RSA function $y = x^a \bmod m$ when $a \perp \varphi(m)$, if we can guess $y^{1/a} \bmod 2$ with probability $\geq \frac{1}{2} + \epsilon$.

44. Suppose $\sum_{j=0}^{d-1} a_{ij}x^j \equiv 0$ (modulo m_i), $\gcd(a_{i0}, a_{i1}, \ldots, a_{i(d-1)}, m_i) = 1$, and $|x| < m_i$ for $1 \leq i \leq k = d(d-1)/2 + 1$, where $m_i \perp m_j$ for $1 \leq i < j \leq k$. Also assume that $m = \min\{m_1, \ldots, m_k\} > n^{n/2}2^{n^2/2}d^d$, where $n = d + k$. First find

$u_1, \ldots, u_k$ such that $u_j \bmod m_i = \delta_{ij}$. Then set up the $n \times n$ matrix

$$
L = \begin{pmatrix}
M & & & & & & & \\
0 & mM & & & & & & \\
\vdots & \vdots & \ddots & & & & & \\
0 & 0 & \cdots & m^{d-1}M & & & & \\
a_{10}u_1 & ma_{11}u_1 & \cdots & m^{d-1}a_{1(d-1)}u_1 & M/m_1 d & & & \\
a_{20}u_2 & ma_{21}u_2 & \cdots & m^{d-1}a_{2(d-1)}u_2 & 0 & M/m_2 d & & \\
\vdots & \vdots & & \vdots & \vdots & \vdots & \ddots & \\
a_{k0}u_k & ma_{k1}u_k & \cdots & m^{d-1}a_{k(d-1)}u_k & 0 & 0 & \cdots & M/m_k d
\end{pmatrix}
$$

where $M = m_1 m_2 \ldots m_k$; all entries above the diagonal are zero, hence $\det L = M^{n-1}m^{k-1}d^{-k}$. Now let $v = (t_0, \ldots, t_{d-1}, v_1, \ldots, v_k)$ be a nonzero integer vector with $\text{length}(vL) \leq \sqrt{n}2^n M^{(n-1)/n}m^{(k-1)/n}d^{-k/n}$. Since $M^{(n-1)/n} < M/m^{k/n}$, we have $\text{length}(vL) < M/d$. Let $c_j = t_j M + \sum_{i=1}^{k} a_{ij}u_i v_i$ and $P(x) = c_0 + c_1 x + \cdots + c_{d-1}x^{d-1}$. Then $P(x) \equiv v_i(a_{i0} + a_{i1}x + \cdots + a_{i(d-1)}x^{d-1}) \equiv 0$ (modulo m_i), for $1 \leq i \leq k$; hence $P(x) \equiv 0$ (modulo M). Also $|m^j c_j| < M/d$; it follows that $P(x) = 0$. But $P(x)$ is not identically zero, because the conditions $v_i a_{ij} \equiv 0$ (modulo m_i) and $\gcd(a_{i0}, \ldots, a_{i(d-1)}, m_i) = 1$ imply $v_i \equiv 0$ (modulo m_i), while $|v_i M/m_i d| < M/d$ implies $|v_i| < m_i$; we cannot have $v_1 = \cdots = v_k = 0$. Thus we can find x (more precisely, at most $d-1$ possibilities for x), and the total running time is polynomial in $\lg M$. [*Lecture Notes in Comp. Sci.* **218** (1985), 403–408.]

45. Fact 1. A solution always exists. Suppose first that n is prime. If $\left(\frac{b}{n}\right) = 1$, there is a solution with $y = 0$. If $\left(\frac{b}{n}\right) = -1$, let $j > 0$ be minimum such that we have $\left(\frac{-ja}{n}\right) = -1$; then $x_0^2 - a \equiv -ja$ and $b \equiv -ja(y_0)^2$ for some x_0 and y_0 (modulo n), hence $(x_0 y_0)^2 - a y_0^2 \equiv b$. Suppose next that we have found a solution $x^2 - ay^2 \equiv b$ (modulo n) and we want to extend this to a solution modulo n^2. We can always find c and d such that $(x+cn)^2 - a(y+dn)^2 \equiv b$ (modulo n^2), because $(x+cn)^2 - a(y+dn)^2 \equiv x^2 - ay^2 + (2cx - 2ayd)n$ and $\gcd(2x, 2ay) \perp n$. Thus a solution always exists when n is a power of an odd prime. (We need to assume that n is odd because, for example, there is no solution to $x^2 + y^2 \equiv 3$ (modulo 8).) Finally, a solution exists for all odd n, by the Chinese remainder theorem.

Fact 2. The number of solutions, given a and n with $a \perp n$, is the same for all $b \perp n$. This follows from the hinted identity and Fact 1, for if $x_1^2 - ay_1^2 \equiv b$ then $(x_1 x_2 - ay_1 y_2, x_1 y_2 + x_2 y_1)$ runs through all solutions of $x^2 - ay^2 \equiv b$ as (x_2, y_2) runs through all solutions of $x^2 - ay^2 \equiv 1$. In other words, (x_2, y_2) is uniquely determined by (x_1, y_1) and (x, y), when $x_1^2 - ay_1^2 \perp n$.

Fact 3. Given integers (a, s, z) such that $z^2 \equiv a$ (modulo s), we can find integers (x, y, m, t) with $x^2 - ay^2 = m^2 st$, where $(x, y) \neq (0, 0)$ and $t^2 \leq \frac{4}{3}|a|$. For if $z^2 = a + ms$, let (u, v) be a nonzero pair of integers that minimizes $(zu + mv)^2 + |a|u^2$. We can find (u, v) efficiently using the methods of Section 3.3.4, and $(zu + mv)^2 + |a|u^2 \leq (\frac{4}{3}|a|)^{1/2}$ by exercise 3.3.4–9. Therefore $(zu + mv)^2 - au^2 = mt$ where $t^2 \leq \frac{4}{3}|a|$. The hinted identity now solves $x^2 - ay^2 = (ms)(mt)$.

Fact 4. It is easy to solve $x^2 - y^2 \equiv b$ (modulo n): Let $x = (b+1)/2$, $y = (b-1)/2$.

Fact 5. It is not difficult to solve $x^2 + y^2 \equiv b$ (modulo n), because the method in exercise 3.3.4–11 solves $x^2 + y^2 = p$ when p is prime and $p \bmod 4 = 1$; one of the numbers b, $b+n$, $b+2n$, $\ldots$ will be such a prime.

Now to solve the stated problem when $|a| > 1$ we can proceed as follows. Choose u and v at random between 1 and $n - 1$, then compute $w = (u^2 - av^2) \bmod n$ and

$d = \gcd(w, n)$. If $1 < d < n$ or if $\gcd(v, n) > 1$ we can reduce n; the methods used to prove Fact 1 will lift solutions for factors of n to solutions for n itself. If $d = n$ and $v \perp n$, we have $(u/v)^2 \equiv a$ (modulo n), hence we can reduce a to 1. Otherwise $d = 1$; let $s = bw \bmod n$. This number s is uniformly distributed among the numbers prime to n, by Fact 2. If $\left(\frac{a}{s}\right) = 1$, try to solve $z^2 \equiv a$ (modulo s), assuming that s is prime (exercise 4.6.2–15). If unsuccessful, start over with another random choice of u and v. If successful, let $z^2 = a + ms$ and compute $d = \gcd(ms, n)$. If $d > 1$, reduce the problem as before. Otherwise use Fact 3 to find $x^2 - ay^2 = m^2 st$ with $t^2 \leq \frac{4}{3}|a|$; this makes $(x/m)^2 - a(y/m)^2 \equiv st$ (modulo n). If $t = 0$, reduce a to 1. Otherwise apply the algorithm recursively to solve $X^2 - tY^2 \equiv a$ (modulo n). (Since t is much smaller than a, only $O(\log \log n)$ levels of recursion will be necessary.) If $\gcd(Y, n) > 1$ we can reduce n or a; otherwise $(X/Y)^2 - a(1/Y)^2 \equiv t$ (modulo n). Finally the hinted identity yields a solution to $x'^2 - ay'^2 \equiv s$ (see Fact 2), which leads in turn to the desired solution because $u^2 - av^2 \equiv s/b$.

In practice only $O(\log n)$ random trials are needed before the assumptions about prime numbers made in this algorithm turn out to be true. But a formal proof would require us to assume the Extended Riemann Hypothesis [*IEEE Trans.* **IT-33** (1987), 702–709]. Adleman, Estes, and McCurley [*Math. Comp.* **48** (1987), 17–28] have developed a slower and more complicated algorithm that does not rely on any unproved hypotheses.

46. [*FOCS* **20** (1979), 55–60.] After finding $a^{n_i} \bmod p = \prod_{j=1}^{m} p_j^{e_{ij}}$ for enough n_i, we can solve $\sum_i x_{ijk} e_{ij} + (p-1)t_{jk} = \delta_{jk}$ in integers x_{ijk}, t_{jk} for $1 \leq j, k \leq m$ (for example, as in 4.5.2–(23)), thereby knowing the solutions $N_j = (\sum_i x_{ijk} e_{jk}) \bmod (p-1)$ to $a^{N_j} \bmod p = p_j$. Then if $ba^{n'} \bmod p = \prod_{j=1}^{m} p_j^{e'_j}$, we have $n + n' \equiv \sum_{j=1}^{m} e'_j N_j$ (modulo $p - 1$). [Improved algorithms are known; see, for example, Coppersmith, Odlyzko, and Schroeppel, *Algorithmica* **1** (1986), 1–15.]

47. Earlier printings of this book had a 211-digit N, which was cracked in 2012 using the elliptic curve method and the general number field method by Greg Childers and about 500 volunteers(!).

SECTION 4.6

1. $9x^2 + 7x + 7$; $5x^3 + 7x^2 + 2x + 6$.

2. (a) True. (b) False if the algebraic system S contains *zero divisors*, that is, nonzero numbers whose product is zero, as in exercise 1; otherwise true. (c) True when $m \neq n$, but false in general when $m = n$, since the leading coefficients might cancel.

3. Assume that $r \leq s$. For $0 \leq k \leq r$ the maximum is $m_1 m_2 (k + 1)$; for $r \leq k \leq s$ it is $m_1 m_2 (r + 1)$; for $s \leq k \leq r + s$ it is $m_1 m_2 (r + s + 1 - k)$. The least upper bound valid for all k is $m_1 m_2 (r + 1)$. (The solver of this exercise will know how to factor the polynomial $x^7 + 2x^6 + 3x^5 + 3x^4 + 3x^3 + 3x^2 + 2x + 1$.)

4. If one of the polynomials has fewer than 2^t nonzero coefficients, the product can be formed by putting exactly $t - 1$ zeros between each of the coefficients, then multiplying in the binary number system, and finally using a bitwise AND instruction (present on most binary computers, see Algorithm 4.5.4D) to zero out the extra bits. For example, if $t = 3$, the multiplication in the text would become $(1001000001)_2 \times (1000001001)_2 = (1001001011001001001)_2$; the desired answer is obtained if we AND this result with the constant $(1001001 \ldots 1001)_2$. A similar technique can be used to multiply polynomials with nonnegative coefficients that are not too large.

5. Polynomials of degree $\leq 2n$ can be written $U_1(x)x^n + U_0(x)$ where $\deg(U_1) \leq n$ and $\deg(U_0) \leq n$; and $(U_1(x)x^n + U_0(x))(V_1(x)x^n + V_0(x)) = U_1(x)V_1(x)(x^{2n} + x^n) +$

$(U_1(x) + U_0(x))(V_1(x) + V_0(x))x^n + U_0(x)V_0(x)(x^n + 1)$. (This equation assumes that arithmetic is being done modulo 2.) Thus Eqs. 4.3.3–(3) and 4.3.3–(5) hold.

Notes: S. A. Cook has shown that Algorithm 4.3.3T can be extended in a similar way; and A. Schönhage [*Acta Informatica* **7** (1977), 395–398] has explained how to multiply polynomials mod 2 with only $O(n \log n \log \log n)$ bit operations. In fact, polynomials over any ring S can be multiplied with only $O(n \log n \log \log n)$ algebraic operations, even when S is an algebraic system in which multiplication need not be commutative or associative [D. G. Cantor and E. Kaltofen, *Acta Informatica* **28** (1991), 693–701]. See also exercises 4.6.4–57 and 4.6.4–58. But these ideas are not useful for sparse polynomials (having mostly zero coefficients).

SECTION 4.6.1

1. $q(x) = 1 \cdot 2^3 x^3 + 0 \cdot 2^2 x^2 - 2 \cdot 2x + 8 = 8x^3 - 4x + 8$; $r(x) = 28x^2 + 4x + 8$.

2. The monic sequence of polynomials produced during Euclid's algorithm has the coefficients $(1, 5, 6, 6, 1, 6, 3)$, $(1, 2, 5, 2, 2, 4, 5)$, $(1, 5, 6, 2, 3, 4)$, $(1, 3, 4, 6)$, 0. Hence the greatest common divisor is $x^3 + 3x^2 + 4x + 6$. (The greatest common divisor of a polynomial and its reverse is always symmetric, in the sense that it is a unit multiple of its own reverse.)

3. The procedure of Algorithm 4.5.2X is valid, with polynomials over S substituted for integers. When the algorithm terminates, we have $U(x) = u_2(x)$, $V(x) = u_1(x)$. Let $m = \deg(u)$, $n = \deg(v)$. It is easy to prove by induction that $\deg(u_3) + \deg(v_1) = n$, $\deg(u_3) + \deg(v_2) = m$, after step X3, throughout the execution of the algorithm, provided that $m \geq n$. Hence if m and n are greater than $d = \deg(\gcd(u, v))$ we have $\deg(U) < m - d$, $\deg(V) < n - d$; the exact degrees are $m - d_1$ and $n - d_1$, where d_1 is the degree of the next-to-last nonzero remainder. If $d = \min(m, n)$, say $d = n$, we have $U(x) = 0$ and $V(x) = 1$.

When $u(x) = x^m - 1$ and $v(x) = x^n - 1$, the identity $(x^m - 1) \bmod (x^n - 1) = x^{m \bmod n} - 1$ shows that all polynomials occurring during the calculation are monic, with integer coefficients. When $u(x) = x^{21} - 1$ and $v(x) = x^{13} - 1$, we have $V(x) = x^{11} + x^8 + x^6 + x^3 + 1$ and $U(x) = -(x^{19} + x^{16} + x^{14} + x^{11} + x^8 + x^6 + x^3 + x)$. [See also Eq. 3.3.3–(29), which gives an alternative formula for $U(x)$ and $V(x)$. See also exercise 4.3.2–6, with 2 replaced by x.]

4. Since the quotient $q(x)$ depends only on $v(x)$ and the first $m-n$ coefficients of $u(x)$, the remainder $r(x) = u(x) - q(x)v(x)$ is uniformly distributed and independent of $v(x)$. Hence each step of the algorithm may be regarded as independent of the others; this algorithm is much more well-behaved than Euclid's algorithm over the integers.

The probability that $n_1 = n - k$ is $p^{1-k}(1 - 1/p)$, and $t = 0$ with probability p^{-n}. Each succeeding step has essentially the same behavior; hence we can see that any given sequence of degrees $n, n_1, \ldots, n_t, -\infty$ occurs with probability $(p - 1)^t/p^n$. To find the average value of $f(n_1, \ldots, n_t)$, let S_t be the sum of $f(n_1, \ldots, n_t)$ over all sequences $n > n_1 > \cdots > n_t \geq 0$ having a given value of t; then the average is $\sum_t S_t (p - 1)^t/p^n$.

Let $f(n_1, \ldots, n_t) = t$; then $S_t = \binom{n}{t}t$, so the average is $n(1 - 1/p)$. Similarly, if $f(n_1, \ldots, n_t) = n_1 + \cdots + n_t$, then $S_t = \binom{n}{2}\binom{n-1}{t-1}$, and the average is $\binom{n}{2}(1 - 1/p)$. Finally, if $f(n_1, \ldots, n_t) = (n - n_1)n_1 + \cdots + (n_{t-1} - n_t)n_t$, then

$$S_t = \binom{n+2}{t+2} - (n + 1)\binom{n+1}{t+1} + \binom{n+1}{2}\binom{n}{t},$$

and the average is $\binom{n+1}{2} - (n + 1)p/(p - 1) + (p/(p - 1))^2(1 - 1/p^{n+1})$.

(The probability that $n_{j+1} = n_j - 1$ for $1 \le j \le t = n$ is $(1 - 1/p)^n$, obtained by setting $S_t = [t = n]$; so this probability approaches 1 as $p \to \infty$. As a consequence we have further evidence for the text's claim that Algorithm C almost always finds $\delta_2 = \delta_3 = \cdots = 1$, because any polynomials that fail the latter condition will fail the former condition modulo p for all p.)

5. Using the formulas developed in exercise 4, with $f(n_1, \ldots, n_t) = [n_t = 0]$, we find that the probability is $1 - 1/p$ if $n > 0$, 1 if $n = 0$.

6. Assuming that the constant terms $u(0)$ and $v(0)$ are nonzero, imagine a "right-to-left" division algorithm, $u(x) = v(x)q(x) + x^{m-n}r(x)$, where $\deg(r) < \deg(v)$. We obtain a gcd algorithm analogous to Algorithm 4.5.2B, which is essentially Euclid's algorithm applied to the "reverse" of the original inputs (see exercise 2), afterwards reversing the answer and multiplying by an appropriate power of x.

There is a similar algorithm analogous to the method of exercise 4.5.2–40. The average number of iterations for both algorithms has been found by G. H. Norton, *SICOMP* **18** (1989), 608–624; K. Ma and J. von zur Gathen, *J. Symbolic Comp.* **9** (1990), 429–455.

7. The units of S (as polynomials of degree zero).

8. If $u(x) = v(x)w(x)$, where $u(x)$ has integer coefficients while $v(x)$ and $w(x)$ have rational coefficients, there are nonzero integers m and n such that $m \cdot v(x)$ and $n \cdot w(x)$ have integer coefficients. Now $u(x)$ is primitive, so Eq. (4) implies that

$$u(x) = \mathrm{pp}((m \cdot v(x))(n \cdot w(x))) = \pm \mathrm{pp}(m \cdot v(x)) \, \mathrm{pp}(n \cdot w(x)).$$

9. We can extend Algorithm E as follows: Let $(u_1(x), u_2(x), u_3, u_4(x))$ and $(v_1(x), v_2(x), v_3, v_4(x))$ be quadruples that satisfy the relations $u_1(x)u(x) + u_2(x)v(x) = u_3u_4(x)$ and $v_1(x)u(x) + v_2(x)v(x) = v_3v_4(x)$. The extended algorithm starts with the quadruples $(1, 0, \mathrm{cont}(u), \mathrm{pp}(u(x)))$ and $(0, 1, \mathrm{cont}(v), \mathrm{pp}(v(x)))$ and manipulates them in such a way as to preserve the conditions above, where $u_4(x)$ and $v_4(x)$ run through the same sequence as $u(x)$ and $v(x)$ do in Algorithm E. If $au_4(x) = q(x)v_4(x) + br(x)$, we have $av_3(u_1(x), u_2(x)) - q(x)u_3(v_1(x), v_2(x)) = (r_1(x), r_2(x))$, where $r_1(x)u(x) + r_2(x)v(x) = bu_3v_3r(x)$, so the extended algorithm can preserve the desired relations. If $u(x)$ and $v(x)$ are relatively prime, the extended algorithm eventually finds $r(x)$ of degree zero, and we obtain $U(x) = r_2(x)$, $V(x) = r_1(x)$ as desired. (In practice we would divide $r_1(x)$, $r_2(x)$, and bu_3v_3 by $\gcd(\mathrm{cont}(r_1), \mathrm{cont}(r_2))$.) Conversely, if such $U(x)$ and $V(x)$ exist, then $u(x)$ and $v(x)$ have no common prime divisors, since they are primitive and have no common divisors of positive degree.

10. By successively factoring reducible polynomials into polynomials of smaller degree, we must obtain a finite factorization of any polynomial into irreducibles. The factorization of the *content* is unique. To show that there is at most one factorization of the primitive part, the key result is to prove that if $u(x)$ is an irreducible factor of $v(x)w(x)$, but not a unit multiple of the irreducible polynomial $v(x)$, then $u(x)$ is a factor of $w(x)$. This can be proved by observing that $u(x)$ is a factor of $v(x)w(x)U(x) = rw(x) - w(x)u(x)V(x)$ by the result of exercise 9, where r is a nonzero constant.

11. The only row names needed would be A_1, A_0, B_4, B_3, B_2, B_1, B_0, C_1, C_0, D_0. In general, let $u_{j+2}(x) = 0$; then the rows needed for the proof are $A_{n_2 - n_j}$ through A_0, $B_{n_1 - n_j}$ through B_0, $C_{n_2 - n_j}$ through C_0, $D_{n_3 - n_j}$ through D_0, etc.

12. If $n_k = 0$, the text's proof of (24) shows that the value of the determinant is $\pm h_k$, and this equals $\pm \prod_{j=2}^{k} \ell_j^{e_j}$, where $e_j = \delta_{j-1} \prod_{i=j}^{k-1}(1 - \delta_i)$, $\delta_i = \deg(u_i) - \deg(u_{i+1})$.

If the polynomials have a factor of positive degree, we can artificially assume that the polynomial zero has degree zero and use the same formula with $\ell_k = 0$.

Notes: The value $R(u, v)$ of Sylvester's determinant is called the *resultant* of u and v, and the quantity $(-1)^{\deg(u)(\deg(u)-1)/2} \ell(u)^{-1} R(u, u')$ is called the *discriminant* of u, where u' is the derivative of u. If $u(x)$ has the factored form $a(x - \alpha_1) \ldots (x - \alpha_m)$, and if $v(x) = b(x - \beta_1) \ldots (x - \beta_n)$, the resultant $R(u, v)$ is $a^n v(\alpha_1) \ldots v(\alpha_m) = (-1)^{mn} b^m u(\beta_1) \ldots u(\beta_n) = a^n b^m \prod_{i=1}^{m} \prod_{j=1}^{n} (\alpha_i - \beta_j)$. It follows that the polynomials of degree mn in y defined as the respective resultants with $v(x)$ of $u(y - x)$, $u(y + x)$, $x^m u(y/x)$, and $u(yx)$ have as respective roots the sums $\alpha_i + \beta_j$, differences $\alpha_i - \beta_j$, products $\alpha_i \beta_j$, and quotients α_i / β_j (when $v(0) \neq 0$). This idea has been used by R. G. K. Loos to construct algorithms for arithmetic on algebraic numbers [*Computing, Supplement* **4** (1982), 173–187].

If we replace each row A_i in Sylvester's matrix by

$$(b_0 A_i + b_1 A_{i+1} + \cdots + b_{n_2-1-i} A_{n_2-1}) - (a_0 B_i + a_1 B_{i+1} + \cdots + a_{n_2-1-i} B_{n_2-1}),$$

and then delete rows B_{n_2-1} through B_0 and the last n_2 columns, we obtain an $n_1 \times n_1$ determinant for the resultant instead of the original $(n_1 + n_2) \times (n_1 + n_2)$ determinant. In some cases the resultant can be evaluated efficiently by means of this determinant; see *CACM* **12** (1969), 23–30, 302–303.

J. T. Schwartz has shown that it is possible to evaluate resultants and Sturm sequences for polynomials of degree n with a total of $O(n(\log n)^2)$ arithmetic operations as $n \to \infty$. [See *JACM* **27** (1980), 701–717.]

13. One can show by induction on j that the values of $(u_{j+1}(x), g_{j+1}, h_j)$ are replaced respectively by $(\ell^{1+p_j} w(x) u_j(x), \ell^{2+p_j} g_j, \ell^{p_j} h_j)$ for $j \geq 2$, where $p_j = n_1 + n_2 - 2n_j$. [In spite of this growth, the bound (26) remains valid.]

14. Let p be a prime of the domain, and let j, k be maximum such that $p^k \backslash v_n = \ell(v)$, $p^j \backslash v_{n-1}$. Let $P = p^k$. By Algorithm R we may write $q(x) = a_0 + P a_1 x + \cdots + P^s a_s x^s$, where $s = m - n \geq 2$. Let us look at the coefficients of x^{n+1}, x^n, and x^{n-1} in $v(x)q(x)$, namely $P a_1 v_n + P^2 a_2 v_{n-1} + \cdots$, $a_0 v_n + P a_1 v_{n-1} + \cdots$, and $a_0 v_{n-1} + P a_1 v_{n-2} + \cdots$, each of which is a multiple of P^3. We conclude from the first that $p^j \backslash a_1$, from the second that $p^{\min(k, 2j)} \backslash a_0$, then from the third that $P \backslash a_0$. Hence $P \backslash r(x)$. [If m were only $n + 1$, the best we could prove would be that $p^{\lceil k/2 \rceil}$ divides $r(x)$; for example, consider $u(x) = x^3 + 1$, $v(x) = 4x^2 + 2x + 1$, $r(x) = 18$. On the other hand, an argument based on determinants of matrices like (21) and (22) can be used to show that $\ell(r)^{\deg(v)-\deg(r)-1} r(x)$ is always a multiple of $\ell(v)^{(\deg(u)-\deg(v))(\deg(v)-\deg(r)-1)}$.]

15. Let $c_{ij} = a_{i1} a_{j1} + \cdots + a_{in} a_{jn}$; we may assume that $c_{ii} > 0$ for all i. If $c_{ij} \neq 0$ for some $i \neq j$, we can replace row i and column i by $(c_{i1} - t c_{j1}, \ldots, c_{in} - t c_{jn})$, where $t = c_{ij}/c_{jj}$; this does not change the value of $\det C$, and it decreases the value of the upper bound we wish to prove, since c_{ii} is replaced by $c_{ii} - c_{ij}^2/c_{jj}$. Such replacements can be done in a systematic way for increasing i and for $j < i$, until $c_{ij} = 0$ for all $i \neq j$. [The latter algorithm is called the *Gram–Schmidt orthogonalization process*: See *Crelle* **94** (1883), 41–73; *Math. Annalen* **63** (1907), 442.] Then $\det(A)^2 = \det(AA^T) = c_{11} \ldots c_{nn}$.

16. A univariate polynomial of degree d over any unique factorization domain has at most d roots (see exercise 3.2.1.2–16(b)); so if $n = 1$ it is clear that $|r(S_1)| \leq d_1$. If $n > 1$ we have $f(x_1, \ldots, x_n) = g_0(x_2, \ldots, x_n) + x_1 g_1(x_2, \ldots, x_n) + \cdots + x_1^{d_1} g_{d_1}(x_2, \ldots, x_n)$ where g_k is nonzero for at least one k. Given $(x_2, \ldots, x_n)$, it follows that $f(x_1, \ldots, x_n)$ is zero for at most d_1 choices of x_1, unless $g_k(x_2, \ldots, x_n) = 0$; hence $|r(S_1, \ldots, S_n)| \leq$

$d_1(|S_2|-d_2)\ldots(|S_n|-d_n)+|S_1|(|S_2|\ldots|S_n|-(|S_2|-d_2)\ldots(|S_n|-d_n))$. [R. A. DeMillo and R. J. Lipton, *Inf. Proc. Letters* **7** (1978), 193–195.]

Notes: The stated upper bound is best possible, because equality occurs for the polynomial $f(x_1,\ldots,x_n) = \prod\{x_j - s_{jk} \mid s_{jk} \in S_j,\ 1 \le k \le d_j,\ 1 \le j \le n\}$. But there is another sense in which the upper bound can be significantly improved: Let $f_1(x_1,\ldots,x_n) = f(x_1,\ldots,x_n)$, and let $f_{j+1}(x_{j+1},\ldots,x_n)$ be any nonzero coefficient of a power of x_j in $f_j(x_j,\ldots,x_n)$. Then we can let d_j be the degree of x_j in f_j instead of the (often much larger) degree of x_j in f. For example, we could let $d_1 = 3$ and $d_2 = 1$ in the polynomial $x_1^3 x_2^9 - 3x_1^2 x_2 + x_2^{100} + 5$. This observation ensures that $d_1 + \cdots + d_n \le d$ when each term of f has total degree $\le d$; hence the probability in such cases is

$$\frac{|r(S,\ldots,S)|}{|S|} \le 1 - \left(1 - \frac{d_1}{|S|}\right)\ldots\left(1 - \frac{d_n}{|S|}\right) \le \frac{d_1 + \cdots + d_n}{|S|} \le \frac{d}{|S|}$$

when all sets S_j are equal. If this probability is $\le \frac{1}{2}$, and if $f(x_1,\ldots,x_n)$ turns out to be zero for 50 randomly selected vectors $(x_1,\ldots,x_n)$, then $f(x_1,\ldots,x_n)$ is identically zero with probability at least $1 - 2^{-50}$.

Moreover, if $f_j(x_j,\ldots,x_n)$ has the special form $x_j^{e_j} f_{j+1}(x_{j+1},\ldots,x_n)$ with $e_j > 0$ we can take $d_j = 1$, because x_j must then be 0 when $f_{j+1}(x_{j+1},\ldots,x_n) \ne 0$. A sparse polynomial with only m nonzero terms will therefore have $d_j \le 1$ for at least $n - \lg m$ values of j.

Applications of this inequality to gcd calculation and other operations on sparse multivariate polynomials were introduced by R. Zippel, *Lecture Notes in Comp. Sci.* **72** (1979), 216–226. J. T. Schwartz [*JACM* **27** (1980), 701–717] gave further extensions, including a way to avoid large numbers by means of modular arithmetic: If the coefficients of f are integers, if P is a set of prime numbers all $\ge q$, and if $|f(x_1,\ldots,x_n)| \le L$ whenever each $x_j \in S_j$, then the number of solutions to $f(x_1,\ldots,x_n) \equiv 0$ (modulo p) for $p \in P$ is at most

$$|S_1|\ldots|S_n||P| - (|S_1| - d_1)\ldots(|S_n| - d_n)(|P| - \log_q L).$$

17. (a) For convenience, let us describe the algorithm only for $A = \{a, b\}$. The hypotheses imply that $\deg(Q_1 U) = \deg(Q_2 V) \ge 0$, $\deg(Q_1) \le \deg(Q_2)$. If $\deg(Q_1) = 0$, then Q_1 is just a nonzero rational number, so we set $Q = Q_2/Q_1$. Otherwise we let $Q_1 = aQ_{11} + bQ_{12} + r_1$, $Q_2 = aQ_{21} + bQ_{22} + r_2$, where r_1 and r_2 are rational numbers; it follows that

$$Q_1 U - Q_2 V = a(Q_{11}U - Q_{21}V) + b(Q_{12}U - Q_{22}V) + r_1 U - r_2 V.$$

We must have either $\deg(Q_{11}) = \deg(Q_1) - 1$ or $\deg(Q_{12}) = \deg(Q_1) - 1$. In the former case, $\deg(Q_{11}U - Q_{21}V) < \deg(Q_{11}U)$, by considering the terms of highest degree that start with a; so we may replace Q_1 by Q_{11}, Q_2 by Q_{21}, and repeat the process. Similarly in the latter case, we may replace (Q_1, Q_2) by (Q_{12}, Q_{22}) and repeat the process.

(b) We may assume that $\deg(U) \ge \deg(V)$. If $\deg(R) \ge \deg(V)$, note that $Q_1 U - Q_2 V = Q_1 R - (Q_2 - Q_1 Q)V$ has degree less than $\deg(V) \le \deg(Q_1 R)$, so we can repeat the process with U replaced by R; we obtain $R = Q'V + R'$, $U = (Q + Q')V + R'$, where $\deg(R') < \deg(R)$, so eventually a solution will be obtained.

(c) The algorithm of (b) gives $V_1 = UV_2 + R$, $\deg(R) < \deg(V_2)$; by homogeneity, $R = 0$ and U is homogeneous.

(d) We may assume that $\deg(V) \leq \deg(U)$. If $\deg(V) = 0$, set $W \leftarrow U$; otherwise use (c) to find $U = QV$, so that $QVV = VQV$, $(QV - VQ)V = 0$. This implies that $QV = VQ$, so we can set $U \leftarrow V$, $V \leftarrow Q$ and repeat the process.

For further details about the subject of this exercise, see P. M. Cohn, *Proc. Cambridge Phil. Soc.* **57** (1961), 18–30. The considerably more difficult problem of characterizing *all* string polynomials such that $UV = VU$ has been solved by G. M. Bergman [Ph.D. thesis (Harvard University, 1967)].

18. [P. M. Cohn, *Transactions of the Amer. Math. Soc.* **109** (1963), 332–356.]

S1. Set $u_1 \leftarrow U_1$, $u_2 \leftarrow U_2$, $v_1 \leftarrow V_1$, $v_2 \leftarrow V_2$, $z_1 \leftarrow z_2' \leftarrow w_1 \leftarrow w_2' \leftarrow 1$, $z_1' \leftarrow z_2 \leftarrow w_1' \leftarrow w_2 \leftarrow 0$, $n \leftarrow 0$.

S2. (At this point the identities given in the exercise hold, and $u_1 v_1 = u_2 v_2$; $v_2 = 0$ if and only if $u_1 = 0$.) If $v_2 = 0$, the algorithm terminates with $\gcd(V_1, V_2) = v_1$, $\operatorname{lclm}(V_1, V_2) = z_1' V_1 = -z_2' V_2$. (Also, by symmetry, we have $\operatorname{gcld}(U_1, U_2) = u_2$ and $\operatorname{lcrm}(U_1, U_2) = U_1 w_1 = -U_2 w_2$.)

S3. Find Q and R such that $v_1 = Qv_2 + R$, where $\deg(R) < \deg(v_2)$. (We have $u_1(Qv_2 + R) = u_2 v_2$, so $u_1 R = (u_2 - u_1 Q)v_2 = R'v_2$.)

S4. Set $(w_1, w_2, w_1', w_2', z_1, z_2, z_1', z_2', u_1, u_2, v_1, v_2) \leftarrow (w_1' - w_1 Q, w_2' - w_2 Q, w_1, w_2, z_1', z_2', z_1 - Qz_1', z_2 - Qz_2', u_2 - u_1 Q, u_1, v_2, v_1 - Qv_2)$ and $n \leftarrow n+1$. Go back to S2.   ∎

This extension of Euclid's algorithm includes most of the features we have seen in previous extensions, all at the same time, so it provides new insight into the special cases already considered. To prove that it is valid, note first that $\deg(v_2)$ decreases in step S4, so the algorithm certainly terminates. At the conclusion of the algorithm, v_1 is a common right divisor of V_1 and V_2, since $w_1 v_1 = (-1)^n V_1$ and $-w_2 v_1 = (-1)^n V_2$; also if d is any common right divisor of V_1 and V_2, it is a right divisor of $z_1 V_1 + z_2 V_2 = v_1$. Hence $v_1 = \gcd(V_1, V_2)$. Also if m is any common left multiple of V_1 and V_2, we may assume without loss of generality that $m = U_1 V_1 = U_2 V_2$, since the sequence of values of Q does not depend on U_1 and U_2. Hence $m = (-1)^n(-u_2 z_1')V_1 = (-1)^n(u_2 z_2')V_2$ is a multiple of $z_1' V_1$.

In practice, if we just want to calculate $\gcd(V_1, V_2)$, we may suppress the computation of n, w_1, w_2, w_1', w_2', z_1, z_2, z_1', z_2'. These additional quantities were added to the algorithm primarily to make its validity more readily established.

Note: Nontrivial factorizations of string polynomials, such as the example given with this exercise, can be found from matrix identities such as

$$\begin{pmatrix} a & 1 \\ 1 & 0 \end{pmatrix}\begin{pmatrix} b & 1 \\ 1 & 0 \end{pmatrix}\begin{pmatrix} c & 1 \\ 1 & 0 \end{pmatrix}\begin{pmatrix} 0 & 1 \\ 1 & -c \end{pmatrix}\begin{pmatrix} 0 & 1 \\ 1 & -b \end{pmatrix}\begin{pmatrix} 0 & 1 \\ 1 & -a \end{pmatrix} = \begin{pmatrix} 1 & 0 \\ 0 & 1 \end{pmatrix},$$

since these identities hold even when multiplication is not commutative. For example,

$$(abc + a + c)(1 + ba) = (ab + 1)(cba + a + c).$$

(Compare this with the continuant polynomials of Section 4.5.3.)

19. [See Eugène Cahen, *Théorie des Nombres* **1** (Paris: 1914), 336–338.] If such an algorithm exists, D is a gcrd by the argument in exercise 18. Let us regard A and B as a single $2n \times n$ matrix C whose first n rows are those of A, and whose second n rows are those of B. Similarly, P and Q can be combined into a $2n \times n$ matrix R; X and Y can be combined into an $n \times 2n$ matrix Z. The desired conditions now reduce to two equations $C = RD$, $D = ZC$. If we can find a $2n \times 2n$ integer matrix U

with determinant ± 1 such that the last n rows of $U^{-1}C$ are all zero, then $R =$ (first n columns of U), $D =$ (first n rows of $U^{-1}C$), $Z =$ (first n rows of U^{-1}) solves the desired conditions. Hence, for example, the following algorithm may be used (with $m = 2n$):

Algorithm T (*Triangularization*). Let C be an $m \times n$ matrix of integers. This algorithm finds $m \times m$ integer matrices U and V such that $UV = I$ and VC is *upper triangular*. (This means that the entry in row i and column j of VC is zero if $i > j$.)

T1. [Initialize.] Set $U \leftarrow V \leftarrow I$, the $m \times m$ identity matrix; and set $T \leftarrow C$. (Throughout the algorithm we will have $T = VC$ and $UV = I$.)

T2. [Iterate on j.] Do step T3 for $j = 1, 2, \ldots, \min(m, n)$, then terminate the algorithm.

T3. [Zero out column j.] Perform the following actions zero or more times until T_{ij} is zero for all $i > j$: Let T_{kj} be a nonzero element of $\{T_{ij}, T_{(i+1)j}, \ldots, T_{mj}\}$ having the smallest absolute value. Interchange rows k and j of T and of V; interchange columns k and j of U. Then subtract $\lfloor T_{ij}/T_{jj} \rfloor$ times row j from row i, in matrices T and V, and add the same multiple of column i to column j in matrix U, for $j < i \leq m$. ∎

For the stated example, the algorithm yields $\left(\begin{smallmatrix} 1 & 2 \\ 3 & 4 \end{smallmatrix}\right) = \left(\begin{smallmatrix} 1 & 0 \\ 3 & 2 \end{smallmatrix}\right)\left(\begin{smallmatrix} 1 & 2 \\ 0 & -1 \end{smallmatrix}\right)$, $\left(\begin{smallmatrix} 4 & 3 \\ 2 & 1 \end{smallmatrix}\right) = \left(\begin{smallmatrix} 4 & 5 \\ 2 & 3 \end{smallmatrix}\right)\left(\begin{smallmatrix} 1 & 2 \\ 0 & -1 \end{smallmatrix}\right)$, $\left(\begin{smallmatrix} 1 & 2 \\ 0 & -1 \end{smallmatrix}\right) = \left(\begin{smallmatrix} 1 & 0 \\ 2 & -2 \end{smallmatrix}\right)\left(\begin{smallmatrix} 1 & 2 \\ 3 & 4 \end{smallmatrix}\right) + \left(\begin{smallmatrix} 0 & 0 \\ 1 & 0 \end{smallmatrix}\right)\left(\begin{smallmatrix} 4 & 3 \\ 2 & 1 \end{smallmatrix}\right)$. (Actually *any* matrix with determinant ± 1 would be a gcrd in this particular case.)

20. See V. Y. Pan, *Information and Computation* **167** (2001), 71–85.

21. To get an upper bound, we may assume that Algorithm R is used only when $m - n \leq 1$; furthermore, the coefficients are bounded by (26) with $m = n$. [The stated formula is, in fact, the execution time observed in practice, not merely an upper bound. For more detailed information see G. E. Collins, *Proc. 1968 Summer Inst. on Symbolic Mathematical Computation*, edited by Robert G. Tobey (IBM Federal Systems Center: June 1969), 195–231.]

22. A sequence of signs cannot contain two consecutive zeros, since $u_{k+1}(x)$ is a nonzero constant in (29). Moreover we cannot have "+, 0, +" or "−, 0, −" as subsequences. The formula $V(u, a) - V(u, b)$ is clearly valid when $b = a$, so we must only verify it as b increases. The polynomials $u_j(x)$ have finitely many roots, and $V(u, b)$ changes only when b encounters or passes such roots. Let x be a root of some (possibly several) u_j. When b increases from $x - \epsilon$ to x, the sign sequence near j goes from "+, ±, −" to "+, 0, −" or from "−, ±, +" to "−, 0, +" if $j > 0$; and from "+, −" to "0, −" or from "−, +" to "0, +" if $j = 0$. (Since $u'(x)$ is the derivative, $u'(x)$ is negative when $u(x)$ is decreasing.) Thus the net change in V is $-\delta_{j0}$. When b increases from x to $x + \epsilon$, a similar argument shows that V remains unchanged.

[L. E. Heindel, *JACM* **18** (1971), 533–548, has applied these ideas to construct algorithms for isolating the real zeros of a given polynomial $u(x)$, in time bounded by a polynomial in $\deg(u)$ and $\log N$, where all coefficients y_j are integers with $|u_j| \leq N$, and all operations are guaranteed to be exact.]

23. If v has $n-1$ real roots occurring between the n real roots of u, then (by considering sign changes) $u(x) \bmod v(x)$ has $n - 2$ real roots lying between the $n - 1$ roots of v.

24. First show that $h_j = g_j^{\delta_j - 1} g_{j-1}^{\delta_{j-2}(1 - \delta_{j-1})} \cdots g_2^{\delta_1(1 - \delta_2) \ldots (1 - \delta_{j-1})}$. Then show that the exponent of g_2 on the left-hand side of (18) has the form $\delta_2 + \delta_1 x$, where $x =$

$\delta_2 + \cdots + \delta_{j-1} + 1 - \delta_2(\delta_3 + \cdots + \delta_{j-1} + 1) - \delta_3(1 - \delta_2)(\delta_4 + \cdots + \delta_{j-1} + 1) - \cdots - \delta_{j-1}(1 - \delta_2) \ldots (1 - \delta_{j-2})(1)$. But $x = 1$, since it is seen to be independent of δ_{j-1} and we can set $\delta_{j-1} = 0$, etc. A similar derivation works for $g_3, g_4, \ldots$, and a simpler derivation works for (23).

25. Each coefficient of $u_j(x)$ can be expressed as a determinant in which one column contains only $\ell(u)$, $\ell(v)$, and zeros. To use this fact, modify Algorithm C as follows: In step C1, set $g \leftarrow \gcd(\ell(u), \ell(v))$ and $h \leftarrow 0$. In step C3, if $h = 0$, set $u(x) \leftarrow v(x)$, $v(x) \leftarrow r(x)/g$, $h \leftarrow \ell(u)^\delta/g$, $g \leftarrow \ell(u)$, and return to C2; otherwise proceed as in the unmodified algorithm. The effect of this new initialization is simply to replace $u_j(x)$ by $u_j(x)/\gcd(\ell(u), \ell(v))$ for all $j \geq 3$; thus, ℓ^{2j-4} will become ℓ^{2j-5} in (28).

26. In fact, even more is true. Note that the algorithm in exercise 3 computes $\pm p_n(x)$ and $\mp q_n(x)$ for $n \geq -1$. Let $e_n = \deg(q_n)$ and $d_n = \deg(p_n u - q_n v)$; we observed in exercise 3 that $d_{n-1} + e_n = \deg(u)$ for $n \geq 0$. We shall prove that the conditions $\deg(q) < e_n$ and $\deg(pu - qv) < d_{n-2}$ imply that $p(x) = c(x)p_{n-1}(x)$ and $q(x) = c(x)q_{n-1}(x)$: Given such p and q, we can find $c(x)$ and $d(x)$ such that $p(x) = c(x)p_{n-1}(x) + d(x)p_n(x)$ and $q(x) = c(x)q_{n-1}(x) + d(x)q_n(x)$, since $p_{n-1}(x)q_n(x) - p_n(x)q_{n-1}(x) = \pm 1$. Hence $pu - qv = c(p_{n-1}u - q_{n-1}v) + d(p_n u - q_n v)$. If $d(x) \neq 0$, we must have $\deg(c) + e_{n-1} = \deg(d) + e_n$, since $\deg(q) < \deg(q_n)$; it follows that $\deg(c) + d_{n-1} > \deg(d) + d_n$, since this is surely true if $d_n = -\infty$ and otherwise we have $d_{n-1} + e_n = d_n + e_{n+1} > d_n + e_{n-1}$. Therefore $\deg(pu - qv) = \deg(c) + d_{n-1}$. But we have assumed that $\deg(pu - qv) < d_{n-2} = d_{n-1} + e_n - e_{n-1}$; so $\deg(c) < e_n - e_{n-1}$ and $\deg(d) < 0$, a contradiction.

[This result is essentially due to L. Kronecker, *Monatsberichte Königl. preuß. Akad. Wiss.* (Berlin: 1881), 535–600. It implies the following theorem: "Let $u(x)$ and $v(x)$ be relatively prime polynomials over a field and let $d \leq \deg(v) < \deg(u)$. If $q(x)$ is a polynomial of least degree such that there exist polynomials $p(x)$ and $r(x)$ with $p(x)u(x) - q(x)v(x) = r(x)$ and $\deg(r) = d$, then $p(x)/q(x) = p_n(x)/q_n(x)$ for some n." For if $d_{n-2} > d \geq d_{n-1}$, there are solutions $q(x)$ with $\deg(q) = e_{n-1} + d - d_{n-1} < e_n$, and we have proved that all solutions of such low degree have the stated property.]

27. The ideas of answer 4.3.1–40 apply, but in simpler fashion because polynomial arithmetic is carry-free; right-to-left division uses 4.7–(3). Alternatively, with large values of n, we could divide Fourier transforms of the coefficients, using exercise 4.6.4–57 in reverse.

SECTION 4.6.2

1. For any choice of $k \leq n$ distinct roots, there are p^{n-k} monic polynomials having those roots at least once. Therefore by the principle of inclusion and exclusion (Section 1.3.3), the number of polynomials without linear factors is $\sum_{k \leq n} \binom{p}{k} p^{n-k}(-1)^k$, and it is alternately $\leq$ and $\geq$ the partial sums of this series. The stated bounds correspond to $k \leq 2$ and $k \leq 3$. When $n \geq p$ the probability of at least one linear factor is $1 - (1 - 1/p)^p$. The average number of linear factors is p times the average number of times x divides $u(x)$, so it is $1 + p^{-1} + \cdots + p^{1-n} = \frac{p}{p-1}(1 - p^{-n})$.

[In a similar way, we find that there is an irreducible factor of degree 2 with probability $\sum_{k \leq n/2} \binom{p(p-1)/2}{k}(-1)^k p^{-2k}$; this probability lies between $\frac{3}{8} - \frac{1}{4}p^{-1}$ and $\frac{1}{2} - \frac{1}{2}p^{-1}$ when $n \geq 2$ and it approaches $1 - e^{-1/2}(1 + \frac{1}{2}p^{-1}) + O(p^{-2})$ as $n \to \infty$. The average number of such factors is $\frac{1}{2} - \frac{1}{2}p^{-2\lfloor n/2 \rfloor}$.]

Note: Let $u(x)$ be a fixed polynomial with integer coefficients. Peter Weinberger has observed that, if $u(x)$ is irreducible over the integers, the average number of linear factors of $u(x)$ modulo p approaches 1 as $p \to \infty$, because the Galois group of $u(x)$ is transitive and the average number of 1-cycles in a randomly chosen element of any transitive permutation group is 1. Thus, *the average number of linear factors of $u(x)$ modulo p is the number of irreducible factors of $u(x)$ over the integers, as $p \to \infty$.* [See the remarks in the answer to exercise 37, and *Proc. Symp. Pure Math.* **24** (Amer. Math. Soc., 1972), 321–332.]

2. (a) We know that $u(x)$ has a representation as a product of irreducible polynomials; and the leading coefficients of these polynomials must be units, since they divide the leading coefficient of $u(x)$. Therefore we may assume that $u(x)$ has a representation as a product of monic irreducible polynomials $p_1(x)^{e_1} \ldots p_r(x)^{e_r}$, where $p_1(x), \ldots, p_r(x)$ are distinct. This representation is unique, except for the order of the factors, so the conditions on $u(x)$, $v(x)$, $w(x)$ are satisfied if and only if

$$v(x) = p_1(x)^{\lfloor e_1/2 \rfloor} \ldots p_r(x)^{\lfloor e_r/2 \rfloor}, \qquad w(x) = p_1(x)^{e_1 \bmod 2} \ldots p_r(x)^{e_r \bmod 2}.$$

(b) The generating function for the number of monic polynomials of degree n is $1 + pz + p^2 z^2 + \cdots = 1/(1-pz)$. The generating function for the number of polynomials of degree n having the form $v(x)^2$, where $v(x)$ is monic, is $1 + pz^2 + p^2 z^4 + \cdots = 1/(1-pz^2)$. If the generating function for the number of monic squarefree polynomials of degree n is $g(z)$, then we must have $1/(1-pz) = g(z)/(1-pz^2)$ by part (a). Hence $g(z) = (1-pz^2)/(1-pz) = 1 + pz + (p^2-p)z^2 + (p^3-p^2)z^3 + \cdots$. The answer is $p^n - p^{n-1}$ for $n \geq 2$. [Curiously, this proves that $u(x) \perp u'(x)$ with probability $1 - 1/p$; it is the same as the probability that $u(x) \perp v(x)$ when $u(x)$ and $v(x)$ are *independent*, by exercise 4.6.1–5.]

Note: By a similar argument, every $u(x)$ has a unique representation $v(x)w(x)^r$, where $v(x)$ is not divisible by the rth power of any irreducible; the number of such monic polynomials $v(x)$ is $p^n - p^{n-r+1}$ for $n \geq r$.

3. Let $u(x) = u_1(x) \ldots u_r(x)$. There is *at most* one such $v(x)$, by the argument of Theorem 4.3.2C. There is *at least* one if, for each j, we can solve the system with $w_j(x) = 1$ and $w_k(x) = 0$ for $k \neq j$. A solution to the latter is $v_1(x) \prod_{k \neq j} u_k(x)$, where $v_1(x)$ and $v_2(x)$ can be found satisfying

$$v_1(x) \prod_{k \neq j} u_k(x) + v_2(x)u_j(x) = 1, \qquad \deg(v_1) < \deg(u_j),$$

by the extension of Euclid's algorithm (exercise 4.6.1–3).

Over the integers we cannot make $v(x) \equiv 1$ (modulo x) and $v(x) \equiv 0$ (modulo $x-2$) when $\deg(v) < 2$.

4. By unique factorization, we have $(1 - pz)^{-1} = \prod_{n \geq 1}(1 - z^n)^{-a_{np}}$; after taking logarithms, this can be rewritten

$$\ln\big(1/(1-pz)\big) = \sum_{k,j \geq 1} a_{kp} z^{kj}/j = \sum_{j \geq 1} G_p(z^j)/j.$$

The stated identity now yields the answer $G_p(z) = \sum_{m \geq 1} \mu(m)m^{-1} \ln(1/(1 - pz^m))$, from which we obtain $a_{np} = \sum_{d \backslash n} \mu(n/d)p^d/n$; thus $\lim_{p \to \infty} a_{np}/p^n = 1/n$.

To prove the stated identity, note that

$$\sum_{n,j \geq 1} \mu(n)g(z^{nj})n^{-t}j^{-t} = \sum_{m \geq 1} g(z^m)m^{-t} \sum_{n \backslash m} \mu(n) = g(z).$$

[The numbers a_{np} were first found by Gauss; see his *Werke* **2**, 219–222.]

5. Let a_{npr} be the number of monic polynomials of degree n modulo p having exactly r irreducible factors. Then $\mathcal{G}_p(z,w) = \sum_{n,r \geq 0} a_{npr} z^n w^r = \exp(\sum_{k \geq 1} G_p(z^k) w^k / k) = \exp(\sum_{m \geq 1} a_{mw} \ln(1/(1 - pz^{-m})))$; see Eq. 1.2.9–(38). We have

$$\sum_{n \geq 0} A_{np} z^n = d\mathcal{G}_p(z/p, w)/dw \,|_{w=1} = \left(\sum_{k \geq 1} G_p(z^k/p^k)\right) \mathcal{G}_p(z/p, 1)$$
$$= \left(\sum_{n \geq 1} \ln(1/(1 - p^{1-n} z^n))\right) \varphi(n)/n)/(1 - z),$$

hence $A_{np} = H_n + 1/2p + O(p^{-2})$ for $n \geq 2$. The average value of 2^r is $[z^n] \mathcal{G}_p(z/p, 2) = n + 1 + (n-1)/p + O(np^{-2})$. (The variance is of order n^3, however: Set $w = 4$.)

6. For $0 \leq s < p$, $x - s$ is a factor of $x^p - x$ (modulo p) by Fermat's theorem. So $x^p - x$ is a multiple of $\mathrm{lcm}(x - 0, x - 1, \ldots, x - (p-1)) = x^{\underline{p}}$. [*Note:* Therefore the Stirling numbers $\left[{p \atop k}\right]$ are multiples of p except when $k = 1$ or $k = p$. Equation 1.2.6–(45) shows that the same statement is valid for Stirling numbers $\left\{{p \atop k}\right\}$ of the other kind.]

7. The factors on the right are relatively prime, and each is a divisor of $u(x)$, so their product divides $u(x)$. On the other hand, $u(x)$ divides

$$v(x)^p - v(x) = \prod_{0 \leq s < p}(v(x) - s),$$

so it divides the right-hand side by exercise 4.5.2–2.

8. The vector (18) is the only output whose kth component is nonzero.

9. For example, start with $x \leftarrow 1$ and $y \leftarrow 1$; then repeatedly set $R[x] \leftarrow y$, $x \leftarrow 2x \bmod 101$, $y \leftarrow 51y \bmod 101$, one hundred times.

10. The matrix $Q - I$ below has a null space generated by the two vectors $v^{[1]} = (1,0,0,0,0,0,0,0)$, $v^{[2]} = (0,1,1,0,0,1,1,1)$. The factorization is

$$(x^6 + x^5 + x^4 + x + 1)(x^2 + x + 1).$$

$$p = 2$$

$$\begin{pmatrix} 0 & 0 & 0 & 0 & 0 & 0 & 0 & 0 \\ 0 & 1 & 1 & 0 & 0 & 0 & 0 & 0 \\ 0 & 0 & 1 & 0 & 1 & 0 & 0 & 0 \\ 0 & 0 & 0 & 1 & 0 & 0 & 1 & 0 \\ 1 & 0 & 0 & 1 & 0 & 0 & 1 & 0 \\ 1 & 0 & 1 & 1 & 1 & 0 & 0 & 0 \\ 0 & 0 & 1 & 0 & 1 & 1 & 0 & 1 \\ 1 & 1 & 0 & 1 & 1 & 1 & 0 & 1 \end{pmatrix}$$

$$p = 5$$

$$\begin{pmatrix} 0 & 0 & 0 & 0 & 0 & 0 & 0 \\ 0 & 4 & 0 & 0 & 0 & 1 & 0 \\ 0 & 2 & 2 & 0 & 4 & 3 & 4 \\ 0 & 1 & 4 & 4 & 4 & 2 & 1 \\ 2 & 2 & 2 & 3 & 4 & 3 & 2 \\ 0 & 0 & 4 & 0 & 1 & 3 & 2 \\ 3 & 0 & 2 & 1 & 4 & 2 & 1 \end{pmatrix}$$

11. Removing the trivial factor x, the matrix $Q - I$ above has a null space generated by $(1,0,0,0,0,0,0)$ and $(0,3,1,4,1,2,1)$. The factorization is

$$x(x^2 + 3x + 4)(x^5 + 2x^4 + x^3 + 4x^2 + x + 3).$$

12. If $p = 2$, $(x+1)^4 = x^4 + 1$. If $p = 8k + 1$, $Q - I$ is the zero matrix, so there are four factors. For other values of p we have

$$p = 8k + 3 \qquad\qquad p = 8k + 5 \qquad\qquad p = 8k + 7$$

$$Q - I = \begin{pmatrix} 0 & 0 & 0 & 0 \\ 0 & -1 & 0 & 1 \\ 0 & 0 & -2 & 0 \\ 0 & 1 & 0 & -1 \end{pmatrix} \begin{pmatrix} 0 & 0 & 0 & 0 \\ 0 & -2 & 0 & 0 \\ 0 & 0 & 0 & 0 \\ 0 & 0 & 0 & -2 \end{pmatrix} \begin{pmatrix} 0 & 0 & 0 & 0 \\ 0 & -1 & 0 & -1 \\ 0 & 0 & -2 & 0 \\ 0 & -1 & 0 & -1 \end{pmatrix}.$$

Here $Q - I$ has rank 2, so there are $4 - 2 = 2$ factors. [But it is easy to prove that $x^4 + 1$ is irreducible over the integers, since it has no linear factors and the coefficient of x in any factor of degree two must be less than or equal to 2 in absolute value by exercise 20. (See also exercise 32, since $x^4 + 1 = \Psi_8(x)$.) For all $k \geq 2$, H. P. F. Swinnerton-Dyer has exhibited polynomials of degree 2^k that are irreducible over the integers, but they split completely into linear and quadratic factors modulo every prime. For degree 8, his example is $x^8 - 16x^6 + 88x^4 + 192x^2 + 144$, having roots $\pm\sqrt{2}\pm\sqrt{3}\pm i$ [see *Math. Comp.* **24** (1970), 733–734]. According to the theorem of Frobenius cited in exercise 37, any irreducible polynomial of degree n whose Galois group contains no n-cycles will have factors modulo almost all primes.]

13. Case $p = 8k+1$: $(x + (1 + \sqrt{-1})/\sqrt{2})(x + (1 - \sqrt{-1})/\sqrt{2})(x - (1+\sqrt{-1})/\sqrt{2}) \times$ $(x - (1 - \sqrt{-1})/\sqrt{2})$. Case $p = 8k + 3$: $(x^2 + \sqrt{-2}x - 1)(x^2 - \sqrt{-2}x - 1)$. Case $p = 8k+5$: $(x^2 + \sqrt{-1})(x^2 - \sqrt{-1})$. Case $p = 8k+7$: $(x^2 + \sqrt{2}x + 1)(x^2 - \sqrt{2}x + 1)$. The factorization for $p = 8k + 7$ also holds over the field of real numbers.

14. Algorithm N can be adapted to find the coefficients of w: Let A be the $(r+1) \times n$ matrix whose kth row contains the coefficients of $v(x)^k \bmod u(x)$, for $0 \leq k \leq r$. Apply the method of Algorithm N until the first dependence is found in step N3; then the algorithm terminates with $w(x) = v_0 + v_1 x + \cdots + v_k x^k$, where v_j is defined in (18). At this point $2 \leq k \leq r$; it is not necessary to know r in advance, since we can check for dependency after generating each row of A.

15. We may assume that $u \neq 0$ and that p is odd. Berlekamp's method applied to the polynomial $x^2 - u$ tells us that a square root exists if and only if $Q - I = O$ if and only if $u^{(p-1)/2} \bmod p = 1$; but we already knew that. The method of Cantor and Zassenhaus suggests that $\gcd(x^2 - u, (sx+t)^{(p-1)/2} - 1)$ will often be a nontrivial factor; and indeed one can show that $(p-1)/2 + (0, 1, \text{or } 2)$ values of s will succeed. In practice, sequential choices seem to work just as well as random choices, so we obtain the following algorithm: "Evaluate $\gcd(x^2 - u, x^{(p-1)/2} - 1)$, $\gcd(x^2 - u, (x+1)^{(p-1)/2} - 1)$, $\gcd(x^2 - u, (x + 2)^{(p-1)/2} - 1)$, $\ldots$, until finding the first case where the gcd has the form $x + v$. Then $\sqrt{u} = \pm v$." The expected running time (with random s) will be $O(\log p)^3$ for large p.

A closer look shows that the first step of this algorithm succeeds if and only if $p \bmod 4 = 3$. For if $p = 2q + 1$ where q is odd, we have $x^q \bmod (x^2 - u) = u^{(q-1)/2}x$, and $\gcd(x^2 - u, x^q - 1) \equiv x - u^{(q+1)/2}$ since $u^q \equiv 1$ (modulo p). In fact, we see that the formula $\sqrt{u} = \pm u^{(p+1)/4} \bmod p$ gives the square root directly whenever $p \bmod 4 = 3$.

But when $p \bmod 4 = 1$, we will have $x^{(p-1)/2} \bmod (x^2 - u) = u^{(p-1)/4}$, and the gcd will be 1. The algorithm above should therefore be used only when $p \bmod 4 = 1$, and the first gcd should then be omitted.

A direct method that works nicely when $p \bmod 8 = 5$ was discovered in the 1990s by A. O. L. Atkin, based on the fact that $2^{(p-1)/2} \equiv -1$ in that case: Set $v \leftarrow (2u)^{(p-5)/8} \bmod p$ and $i \leftarrow (2uv^2) \bmod p$; then $\sqrt{u} = \pm(uv(i - 1)) \bmod p$, and we also have $\sqrt{-1} = \pm i$. [*Computational Perspectives on Number Theory* (Cambridge, Mass.: International Press, 1998), 1–11; see also H. C. Pocklington, *Proc. Camb. Phil. Soc.* **19** (1917), 57–59.]

When $p \bmod 8 = 1$, a trial-and-error method seems to be necessary. The following procedure due to Daniel Shanks often outperforms all other known algorithms in such cases: Suppose $p = 2^e q + 1$ where $e \geq 3$.

S1. Choose x at random in the range $1 < x < p$, and set $z = x^q \bmod p$. If $z^{2^{e-1}} \bmod p = 1$, repeat this step. (The average number of repetitions will be less than 2. Random numbers will not be needed in steps S2 and S3. In practice we can save time by trying small odd prime numbers x, and stopping with $z = x^q \bmod p$ when $p^{(x-1)/2} \bmod x = x - 1$; see exercise 1.2.4–47.)

S2. Set $y \leftarrow z$, $r \leftarrow e$, $x \leftarrow u^{(q-1)/2} \bmod p$, $v \leftarrow ux \bmod p$, $w \leftarrow ux^2 \bmod p$.

S3. If $w = 1$, stop; v is the answer. Otherwise find the smallest k such that $w^{2^k} \bmod p$ is equal to 1. If $k = r$, stop (there is no answer); otherwise set $(y, r, v, w) \leftarrow (y^{2^{r-k}}, k, vy^{2^{r-k-1}}, wy^{2^{r-k}})$ and repeat step S3. ∎

The validity of this algorithm follows from the invariant congruences $uw \equiv v^2$, $y^{2^{r-1}} \equiv -1$, $w^{2^{r-1}} \equiv 1$ (modulo p). When $w \neq 1$, step S3 performs $r+2$ multiplications mod p; hence the maximum number of multiplications in that step is less than $\binom{e+3}{2}$, and the average number is less than $\frac{1}{2}\binom{e+4}{2}$. Thus the running time is $O(\log p)^3$ for steps S1 and S2 plus order $e^2 (\log p)^2$ for step S3, compared to just $O(\log p)^3$ for the randomized method based on (21). But the constant factors in Shanks's method are small. [*Congressus Numerantium* **7**(1972), 58–62. A related but less efficient method was published by A. Tonelli, *Göttinger Nachrichten* (1891), 344–346. The first person to discover a square root algorithm with expected running time $O(\log p)^3$ was M. Cipolla, *Rendiconti Accad. Sci. Fis. Mat. Napoli* **9** (1903), 154–163.]

16. (a) Substitute polynomials modulo p for integers, in the proof for $n = 1$. (b) The proof for $n = 1$ carries over to any finite field. (c) Since $x = \xi^k$ for some k, $x^{p^n} = x$ in the field defined by $f(x)$. Furthermore, the elements y that satisfy the equation $y^{p^m} = y$ in the field are closed under addition, and closed under multiplication; so if $x^{p^m} = x$, then ξ (being a polynomial in x with integer coefficients) satisfies $\xi^{p^m} = \xi$.

17. If ξ is a primitive root, each nonzero element is some power of ξ. Hence the order must be a divisor of $13^2 - 1 = 2^3 \cdot 3 \cdot 7$, and $\varphi(f)$ elements have order f.

f	$\varphi(f)$	f	$\varphi(f)$	f	$\varphi(f)$	f	$\varphi(f)$
1	1	3	2	7	6	21	12
2	1	6	2	14	6	42	12
4	2	12	4	28	12	84	24
8	4	24	8	56	24	168	48

18. (a) $\text{pp}(p_1(u_n x)) \dots \text{pp}(p_r(u_n x))$, by Gauss's lemma. For example, let

$$u(x) = 6x^3 - 3x^2 + 2x - 1, \qquad v(x) = x^3 - 3x^2 + 12x - 36 = (x^2 + 12)(x - 3);$$

then $\text{pp}(36x^2 + 12) = 3x^2 + 1$, $\text{pp}(6x - 3) = 2x - 1$. (This is a modern version of a fourteenth-century trick used for many years to help solve algebraic equations.)

(b) Let $\text{pp}(w(u_n x)) = \bar{w}_m x^m + \dots + \bar{w}_0 = w(u_n x)/c$, where c is the content of $w(u_n x)$ as a polynomial in x. Then $w(x) = (c\bar{w}/u_n^m)x^m + \dots + c\bar{w}_0$, hence $c\bar{w}_m = u_n^m$; since $\bar{w}_m$ is a divisor of u_n, c is a multiple of u_n^{m-1}.

19. If $u(x) = v(x)w(x)$ with $\deg(v)\deg(w) \geq 1$, then $u_n x^n \equiv v(x)w(x)$ (modulo p). By unique factorization modulo p, all but the leading coefficients of v and w are multiples of p, and p^2 divides $v_0 w_0 = u_0$.

20. (a) $\sum(\alpha u_j - u_{j-1})(\bar{\alpha}\bar{u}_j - \bar{u}_{j-1}) = \sum(u_j - \bar{\alpha}u_{j-1})(\bar{u}_j - \alpha\bar{u}_{j-1})$. (b) We may assume that $u_0 \neq 0$. Let $m(u) = \prod_{j=1}^n \min(1, |\alpha_j|) = |u_0|/M(u)$. Whenever $|\alpha_j| < 1$, change the factor $x - \alpha_j$ to $\bar{\alpha}_j x - 1$ in $u(x)$; this doesn't affect $\|u\|$, but it changes $|u_0|$ to $M(u)$. (c) $u_j = \pm u_n \sum \alpha_{i_1} \dots \alpha_{i_{n-j}}$, an elementary symmetric function, hence $|u_j| \leq |u_n| \sum \beta_{i_1} \dots \beta_{i_{n-j}}$ where $\beta_i = \max(1, |\alpha_i|)$. We complete the proof by showing that when $x_1 \geq 1, \dots, x_n \geq 1$, and $x_1 \dots x_n = M$, the elementary symmetric function

$\sigma_{nk} = \sum x_{i_1} \dots x_{i_k}$ is $\leq \binom{n-1}{k-1} M + \binom{n-1}{k}$, the value assumed when $x_1 = \dots = x_{n-1} = 1$ and $x_n = M$. (For if $x_1 \leq \dots \leq x_n < M$, the transformation $x_n \leftarrow x_{n-1}x_n$, $x_{n-1} \leftarrow 1$ increases σ_{nk} by $\sigma_{(n-2)(k-1)}(x_n - 1)(x_{n-1} - 1)$, which is positive.) (d) $|v_j| \leq \binom{m-1}{j} M(v) + \binom{m-1}{j-1} |v_m| \leq \binom{m-1}{j} M(u) + \binom{m-1}{j-1} |u_n|$ since $M(v) \leq M(u)$ and $|v_m| \leq |u_n|$. [M. Mignotte, *Math. Comp.* **28** (1974), 1153–1157.]

Notes: This solution shows that $\binom{m-1}{j} M(u) + \binom{m-1}{j-1} |u_n|$ is an upper bound, so we would like to have a better estimate of $M(u)$. Several methods are known [W. Specht, *Math. Zeit.* **53** (1950), 357–363; Cerlienco, Mignotte, and Piras, *J. Symbolic Comp.* **4** (1987), 21–33]. The simplest and most rapidly convergent is perhaps the following procedure [see C. H. Gräffe, *Die Auflösung der höheren numerischen Gleichungen* (Zürich: 1837)]: Assuming that $u(x) = u_n(x - \alpha_1) \dots (x - \alpha_n)$, let $\hat{u}(x) = u(\sqrt{x})u(-\sqrt{x}) = (-1)^n u_n^2 (x - \alpha_1^2) \dots (x - \alpha_n^2)$. Then $M(u)^2 = M(\hat{u}) \leq \|\hat{u}\|$. Hence we may set $c \leftarrow \|u\|$, $v \leftarrow u/c$, $t \leftarrow 0$, and then repeatedly set $t \leftarrow t + 1$, $c \leftarrow \|\hat{v}\|^{1/2^t} c$, $v \leftarrow \hat{v}/\|\hat{v}\|$. The invariant relations $M(u) = cM(v)^{1/2^t}$ and $\|v\| = 1$ guarantee that $M(u) \leq c$ at each step of the iteration. Notice that when $v(x) = v_0(x^2) + xv_1(x^2)$, we have $\hat{v}(x) = v_0(x)^2 - xv_1(x)^2$. It can be shown that if each $|\alpha_j|$ is $\leq \rho$ or $\geq 1/\rho$, then $M(u) = \|u\|(1 + O(\rho))$; hence c will be $M(u)(1 + O(\rho^{2^t}))$ after t steps.

For example, if $u(x)$ is the polynomial of (22), the successive values of c for $t = 0$, 1, 2, ... turn out to be 10.63, 12.42, 6.85, 6.64, 6.65, 6.6228, 6.62246, 6.62246, ... In this example $\rho \approx .90982$. Notice that convergence is not monotonic. Eventually $v(x)$ will converge to the monomial x^m, where m is the number of roots with $|\alpha_j| < 1$, assuming that $|\alpha_j| \neq 1$ for all j; in general, if there are k roots with $|\alpha_j| = 1$, the coefficients of x^m and x^{m+k} will not approach zero, while the coefficients of higher and lower powers of x will.

A famous formula due to Jensen [*Acta Math.* **22** (1899), 359–364] proves that $M(u)$ is the geometric mean of $|u(x)|$ on the unit circle, namely $\exp(\frac{1}{2\pi} \int_0^{2\pi} \ln|f(e^{i\theta})| \, d\theta)$. Exercise 21(a) will show, similarly, that $\|u\|$ is the root-mean-square of $|u(x)|$ on the unit circle. The inequality $M(u) \leq \|u\|$, which goes back to E. Landau [*Bull. Soc. Math. de France* **33** (1905), 251–261], can therefore be understood as a relation between mean values. The number $M(u)$ is often called the *Mahler measure* of a polynomial, because Kurt Mahler used it in *Mathematika* **7** (1960), 98–100. Incidentally, Jensen also proved that $\frac{1}{2\pi} \int_0^{2\pi} e^{im\theta} \ln|f(e^{i\theta})| \, d\theta = -\sum_{j=1}^n \alpha_j^m / (2m \max(|\alpha_j|, 1)^{2m})$ when $m > 0$.

21. (a) The coefficient of $a_p b_q c_r d_s$ is zero on both sides unless $\mathbf{p} + \mathbf{s} = \mathbf{q} + \mathbf{r}$. And when this condition holds, the coefficient on the right is $(\mathbf{p} + \mathbf{s})!$; on the left it is

$$\sum_j \binom{\mathbf{p}}{\mathbf{j}} \binom{\mathbf{s}}{\mathbf{r} - \mathbf{j}} \mathbf{q}! \, \mathbf{r}! = \binom{\mathbf{p} + \mathbf{s}}{\mathbf{r}} \mathbf{q}! \, \mathbf{r}! = (\mathbf{q} + \mathbf{r})! \, .$$

[B. Beauzamy and J. Dégot, *Trans. Amer. Math. Soc.* **345** (1995), 2607–2619; D. Zeilberger, *AMM* **101** (1994), 894–896.]

(b) Let $a_p = v_p$, $b_q = w_q$, $c_r = \overline{v}_r$, $d_s = \overline{w}_s$. Then the right side of (a) is $B(u)$, and the left side is a sum of nonnegative terms for each $\mathbf{j}$ and $\mathbf{k}$. If we consider only the terms where $\Sigma \mathbf{j}$ is the degree of v, the terms $v_p/(\mathbf{p} - \mathbf{j})!$ vanish except when $\mathbf{p} = \mathbf{j}$. Those terms therefore reduce to

$$\sum_{\mathbf{j}, \mathbf{k}} \frac{1}{\mathbf{j}! \, \mathbf{k}!} \left| v_{\mathbf{j}} w_{\mathbf{k}} \mathbf{j}! \, \mathbf{k}! \right|^2 = B(v)B(w) \, .$$

[B. Beauzamy, E. Bombieri, P. Enflo, and H. Montgomery, *J. Number Theory* **36** (1990), 219–245.]

(c) Adding a new variable, if needed to make everything homogeneous, does not change the relation $u = vw$. Thus if v and w have total degrees m and n, respectively, we have $(m+n)!\,[u]^2 \geq m!\,[v]^2\,n!\,[w]^2$; in other words, $[v][w] \leq \binom{m+n}{m}^{1/2}[u]$.

Incidentally, one nice way to think of the Bombieri norm is to imagine that the variables are noncommutative. For example, instead of $3xy^3 - z^2w^2$ we could write $\frac{3}{4}xyyy + \frac{3}{4}yxyy + \frac{3}{4}yyxy + \frac{3}{4}yyyx - \frac{1}{6}zzww - \frac{1}{6}zwzw - \frac{1}{6}zwwz - \frac{1}{6}wzzw - \frac{1}{6}wzwz - \frac{1}{6}wwzz$. Then the Bombieri norm is the $\|\ \|$ norm on the new coefficients. Another interesting formula, when u is homogeneous of degree n, is

$$[u]^2 = \frac{1}{n!\,\pi^n}\int_{\mathbf{x}}\int_{\mathbf{y}} e^{-x_1^2 - \cdots - x_t^2 - y_1^2 - \cdots - y_t^2}\,|u(\mathbf{x} + i\mathbf{y})|^2\,d\mathbf{x}\,d\mathbf{y}\,.$$

(d) The one-variable case corresponds to $t = 2$. Suppose $u = vw$ where v is homogeneous of degree m in t variables. Then $|v_{\mathbf{k}}|^2\,\mathbf{k}!/m! \leq [v]^2$ for all $\mathbf{k}$, and $\mathbf{k}! \geq (m/t)!^t$ since $\log\Gamma(x)$ is convex for $x > 0$; therefore $|v_{\mathbf{k}}|^2 \leq m!\,[v]^2/(m/t)!^t$. We can assume that $m!\,[v]^2/(m/t)!^t \leq m'!\,[w]^2/(m'/t)!^t$, where $m' = n - m$ is the degree of w. Then

$$|v_{\mathbf{k}}|^2 \leq m!\,[v]^2/(m/t)!^t \leq m!^{1/2}m'!^{1/2}\,[v][w]/(m/t)!^{t/2}(m'/t)!^{t/2} \leq n!^{1/2}\,[u]/(n/2t)!^t\,.$$

(A better bound is obtained if we maximize the next-to-last expression over all degrees m for which a factor has not been ruled out.) The quantity $n!^{1/4}/(n/2t)!^{t/2}$ is $c_t(2t)^{n/4}n^{-(2t-1)/8}(1 + O(\frac{1}{n}))$, where $c_t = 2^{1/8}\pi^{-(2t-1)/8}t^{t/4}$ is ≈ 1.004 when $t = 2$.

Notice that we have not demonstrated the existence of an *irreducible* factor with such small coefficients; further splitting may be needed. See exercise 41.

(e) $[u]^2 = \sum_k \binom{n}{k}^2/\binom{2n}{2k} = \sum_k \binom{2k}{k}\binom{2n-2k}{n-k}/\binom{2n}{n} = 4^n/\binom{2n}{n} = \sqrt{\pi n} + O(n^{-1/2})$. If $v(x) = (x-1)^n$ and $w(x) = (x+1)^n$, we have $[v]^2 = [w]^2 = 2^n$; hence the inequality of (c) is an equality in this case.

(f) Let u and v be homogeneous of degree m and n. Then

$$[uv]^2 \leq \sum_{\mathbf{k}} \frac{(\sum_{\mathbf{j}} |u_{\mathbf{j}}v_{\mathbf{k}-\mathbf{j}}|)^2}{\binom{m+n}{\mathbf{k}}} \leq \sum_{\mathbf{k}}\left(\sum_{\mathbf{j}} \frac{|u_{\mathbf{j}}|^2}{\binom{m}{\mathbf{j}}}\frac{|v_{\mathbf{k}-\mathbf{j}}|^2}{\binom{n}{\mathbf{k}-\mathbf{j}}}\right)\left(\sum_{\mathbf{j}} \frac{\binom{m}{\mathbf{j}}\binom{n}{\mathbf{k}-\mathbf{j}}}{\binom{m+n}{\mathbf{k}}}\right) = [u]^2[v]^2$$

by Cauchy's inequality. [B. Beauzamy, *J. Symbolic Comp.* **13** (1992), 465–472, Proposition 5.]

(g) By exercise 20, $\binom{n}{\lfloor n/2\rfloor}^{-1}M(u)^2 \leq \binom{n}{\lfloor n/2\rfloor}^{-1}\|u\|^2 = \binom{n}{\lfloor n/2\rfloor}^{-1}\sum_j |u_j|^2 \leq [u]^2 = \sum_j \binom{n}{j}^{-1}|u_j|^2 \leq \sum_j \binom{n}{j}^{-1}M(u)^2 = 2^n M(u)^2$. The upper inequality also follows from (f), for if $u(x) = u_n\prod_{j=1}^n(x - \alpha_j)$ we have $[u]^2 \leq |u_n|^2\prod_{j=1}^n[x - \alpha_j]^2 = |u_n|^2\prod_{j=1}^n(1 + |\alpha_j|^2) \leq |u_n|^2\prod_{j=1}^n(2\max(1, |\alpha_j|)^2) = 2^n M(u)^2$.

22. More generally, assume that $u(x) \equiv v(x)w(x)$ (modulo q), $a(x)v(x) + b(x)w(x) \equiv 1$ (modulo p), $c \cdot \ell(v) \equiv 1$ (modulo r), $\deg(a) < \deg(w)$, $\deg(b) < \deg(v)$, and $\deg(u) = \deg(v) + \deg(w)$, where $r = \gcd(p, q)$ and p, q needn't be prime. We shall construct polynomials $V(x) \equiv v(x)$ and $W(x) \equiv w(x)$ (modulo q) such that $u(x) \equiv V(x)W(x)$ (modulo qr), $\ell(V) = \ell(v)$, $\deg(V) = \deg(v)$, $\deg(W) = \deg(w)$; furthermore, if r is prime, the results will be unique modulo qr.

The problem asks us to find $\bar{v}(x)$ and $\bar{w}(x)$ with $V(x) = v(x) + q\bar{v}(x)$, $W(x) = w(x) + q\bar{w}(x)$, $\deg(\bar{v}) < \deg(v)$, $\deg(\bar{w}) \leq \deg(w)$; and the other condition

$$(v(x) + q\bar{v}(x))(w(x) + q\bar{w}(x)) \equiv u(x) \pmod{qr}$$

is equivalent to $\bar{w}(x)v(x) + \bar{v}(x)w(x) \equiv f(x)$ (modulo r), where $f(x)$ satisfies $u(x) \equiv v(x)w(x) + qf(x)$ (modulo qr). We have

$$(a(x)f(x) + t(x)w(x))v(x) + (b(x)f(x) - t(x)v(x))w(x) \equiv f(x) \text{ (modulo } r)$$

for all $t(x)$. Since $\ell(v)$ has an inverse modulo r, we can find a quotient $t(x)$ by Algorithm 4.6.1D such that $\deg(bf - tv) < \deg(v)$; for this $t(x)$, $\deg(af + tw) \leq \deg(w)$, since we have $\deg(f) \leq \deg(u) = \deg(v) + \deg(w)$. Thus the desired solution is $\bar{v}(x) = b(x)f(x) - t(x)v(x) = b(x)f(x) \bmod v(x)$, $\bar{w}(x) = a(x)f(x) + t(x)w(x)$. If $(\bar{\bar{v}}(x), \bar{\bar{w}}(x))$ is another solution, we have $(\bar{w}(x) - \bar{\bar{w}}(x))v(x) \equiv (\bar{\bar{v}}(x) - \bar{v}(x))w(x)$ (modulo r). Thus if r is prime, $v(x)$ must divide $\bar{\bar{v}}(x) - \bar{v}(x)$; but $\deg(\bar{\bar{v}} - \bar{v}) < \deg(v)$, so $\bar{\bar{v}}(x) = \bar{v}(x)$ and $\bar{\bar{w}}(x) = \bar{w}(x)$.

If p divides q, so that $r = p$, our choices of $V(x)$ and $W(x)$ also satisfy $a(x)V(x) + b(x)W(x) \equiv 1$ (modulo p), as required by Hensel's Lemma.

For $p = 2$, the factorization proceeds as follows (writing only the coefficients, and using bars for negative digits): Exercise 10 says that $v_1(x) = (1\bar{1}\bar{1})$, $w_1(x) = (\bar{1}\bar{1}\bar{1}00\bar{1}\bar{1})$ in one-bit two's complement notation. Euclid's extended algorithm yields $a(x) = (100001)$, $b(x) = (10)$. The factor $v(x) = x^2 + c_1 x + c_0$ must have $|c_1| \leq \lfloor 1 + \sqrt{113} \rfloor = 11$, $|c_0| \leq 10$, by exercise 20. Three applications of Hensel's lemma yield $v_4(x) = (13\bar{1})$, $w_4(x) = (1\bar{3}\bar{5}\bar{4}4\bar{3}5)$. Thus $c_1 \equiv 3$ and $c_0 \equiv -1$ (modulo 16); the only possible quadratic factor of $u(x)$ is $x^2 + 3x - 1$. Division fails, so $u(x)$ is irreducible. (Since we have now proved the irreducibility of this beloved polynomial by four separate methods, it is unlikely that it has any factors.)

Hans Zassenhaus has observed that we can often speed up such calculations by increasing p as well as q: When $r = p$ in the notation above, we can find $A(x)$, $B(x)$ such that $A(x)V(x) + B(x)W(x) \equiv 1$ (modulo p^2), namely by taking $A(x) = a(x) + p\bar{a}(x)$, $B(x) = b(x) + p\bar{b}(x)$, where $\bar{a}(x)V(x) + \bar{b}(x)W(x) \equiv g(x)$ (modulo p), $a(x)V(x) + b(x)W(x) \equiv 1 - pg(x)$ (modulo p^2). We can also find C with $\ell(V)C \equiv 1$ (modulo p^2). In this way we can lift a squarefree factorization $u(x) \equiv v(x)w(x)$ (modulo p) to its unique extensions modulo p^2, p^4, p^8, p^{16}, etc. However, this "accelerated" procedure reaches a point of diminishing returns in practice, as soon as we get to double-precision moduli, since the time for multiplying multiprecision numbers in practical ranges outweighs the advantage of squaring the modulus directly. From a computational standpoint it seems best to work with the successive moduli p, p^2, p^4, p^8, ..., p^E, p^{E+e}, p^{E+2e}, p^{E+3e}, ..., where E is the smallest power of 2 with p^E greater than single precision and e is the largest integer such that p^e has single precision.

"Hensel's Lemma" was actually invented by C. F. Gauss about 1799, in the draft of an unfinished book called *Analysis Residuorum*, §373–374. Gauss incorporated most of the material from that manuscript into his *Disquisitiones Arithmeticæ* (1801), but his ideas about polynomial factorization were not published until after his death [see his *Werke* **2** (Göttingen, 1863), 238]. Meanwhile T. Schönemann had independently discovered the lemma and proved uniqueness [*Crelle* **32** (1846), 93–105, §59]. Hensel's name was attached to the method because it is basic to the theory of p-adic numbers (see exercise 4.1–31). The lemma can be generalized in several ways. First, if there are more factors, say $u(x) \equiv v_1(x)v_2(x)v_3(x)$ (modulo p), we can find $a_1(x)$, $a_2(x)$, $a_3(x)$ such that $a_1(x)v_2(x)v_3(x) + a_2(x)v_1(x)v_3(x) + a_3(x)v_1(x)v_2(x) \equiv 1$ (modulo p) and $\deg(a_i) < \deg(v_i)$. (In essence, $1/u(x)$ is expanded in partial fractions as $\sum a_i(x)/v_i(x)$.) An exactly analogous construction now allows us to lift the factorization without changing the leading coefficients of v_1 and v_2; we take $\bar{v}_1(x) = a_1(x)f(x) \bmod v_1(x)$, $\bar{v}_2(x) = a_2(x)f(x) \bmod v_2(x)$, etc. Another important generalization is to several simultaneous moduli, of the respective forms p^e, $(x_2 - a_2)^{n_2}$, ..., $(x_t - a_t)^{n_t}$, when performing multivariate gcds and factorizations. See D. Y. Y. Yun, Ph.D. Thesis (M.I.T., 1974).

23. The discriminant of $pp(u(x))$ is a nonzero integer (see exercise 4.6.1–12), and there are multiple factors modulo p if and only if p divides the discriminant. [The factorization of (22) modulo 3 is $(x+1)(x^2 - x - 1)^2(x^3 + x^2 - x + 1)$; squared factors for this polynomial occur only for $p = 3$, 23, 233, and 121702457. It is not difficult to prove that the smallest prime that is not unlucky is at most $O(n \log Nn)$, if $n = \deg(u)$ and if N bounds the coefficients of $u(x)$.]

24. Multiply a monic polynomial with rational coefficients by a suitable nonzero integer, to get a primitive polynomial over the integers. Factor this polynomial over the integers, and then convert the factors back to monic. (No factorizations are lost in this way; see exercise 4.6.1–8.)

25. Consideration of the constant term shows there are no factors of degree 1, so if the polynomial is reducible, it must have one factor of degree 2 and one of degree 3. Modulo 2 the factors are $x(x+1)^2(x^2 + x + 1)$; this is not much help. Modulo 3 the factors are $(x+2)^2(x^3 + 2x + 2)$. Modulo 5 they are $(x^2 + x + 1)(x^3 + 4x + 2)$. So we see that the answer is $(x^2 + x + 1)(x^3 - x + 2)$.

26. Begin with $D \leftarrow (0\ldots01)$, representing the set $\{0\}$. Then for $1 \le j \le r$, set $D \leftarrow D \mid (D \ll d_j)$, where $\mid$ denotes bitwise "or" and $D \ll d$ denotes D shifted left d bit positions. (Actually we need only work with a bit vector of length $\lceil (n+1)/2 \rceil$, since $n - m$ is in the set if and only if m is.)

27. Exercise 4 says that a random polynomial of degree n is irreducible modulo p with rather low probability, about $1/n$. But the Chinese remainder theorem implies that a random monic polynomial of degree n over the integers will be reducible with respect to each of k distinct primes with probability about $(1 - 1/n)^k$, and this approaches zero as $k \to \infty$. Hence almost all polynomials over the integers are irreducible with respect to infinitely many primes; and almost all primitive polynomials over the integers are irreducible. [Another proof has been given by W. S. Brown, *AMM* **70** (1963), 965–969.]

28. See exercise 4; the probability is $[z^n](1 + a_{1p}z/p)(1 + a_{2p}z^2/p^2)(1 + a_{3p}z^3/p^3)\cdots$, which has the limiting value $g(z) = (1+z)(1 + \frac{1}{2}z^2)(1 + \frac{1}{3}z^3)\ldots$. For $1 \le n \le 10$ the answers are 1, $\frac{1}{2}$, $\frac{5}{6}$, $\frac{7}{12}$, $\frac{37}{60}$, $\frac{79}{120}$, $\frac{173}{280}$, $\frac{101}{168}$, $\frac{127}{210}$, $\frac{1033}{1680}$. [Let $f(y) = \ln(1+y) - y = O(y^2)$. We have
$$g(z) = \exp\left(\sum_{n \ge 1} z^n/n + \sum_{n \ge 1} f(z^n/n)\right) = h(z)/(1-z),$$
and it can be shown that the limiting probability is $h(1) = \exp(\sum_{n \ge 1} f(1/n)) = e^{-\gamma} \approx .56146$ as $n \to \infty$. Indeed, N. G. de Bruijn has established the asymptotic formula $\lim_{p \to \infty} a_{np} = e^{-\gamma} + e^{-\gamma}/n + O(n^{-2} \log n)$. [See D. H. Lehmer, *Acta Arith.* **21** (1972), 379–388; D. H. Greene and D. E. Knuth, *Math. for the Analysis of Algorithms* (Boston: Birkhäuser, 1981), §4.1.6.] On the other hand the answers for $1 \le n \le 10$ when $p = 2$ are smaller: 1, $\frac{1}{4}$, $\frac{1}{2}$, $\frac{7}{16}$, $\frac{7}{16}$, $\frac{7}{16}$, $\frac{27}{64}$, $\frac{111}{256}$, $\frac{109}{256}$, $\frac{109}{256}$. A. Knopfmacher and R. Warlimont [*Trans. Amer. Math. Soc.* **347** (1995), 2235–2243] have shown that for fixed p the probability is $c_p + O(1/n)$, where $c_p = \prod_{m \ge 1} e^{-1/m}(1 + a_{mp}/p^m)$, $c_2 \approx .397$.]

29. Let $q_1(x)$ and $q_2(x)$ be any two of the irreducible divisors of $g(x)$. By the Chinese remainder theorem (exercise 3), choosing a random polynomial $t(x)$ of degree $< 2d$ is equivalent to choosing two random polynomials $t_1(x)$ and $t_2(x)$ of degrees $< d$, where $t_i(x) = t(x) \bmod q_i(x)$. The gcd will be a proper factor if $t_1(x)^{(p^d - 1)/2} \bmod q_1(x) = 1$

and $t_2(x)^{(p^d-1)/2} \bmod q_1(x) \neq 1$, or vice versa, and this condition holds for exactly $2((p^d-1)/2)((p^d+1)/2) = (p^{2d}-1)/2$ choices of $t_1(x)$ and $t_2(x)$.

Notes: We are considering here only the behavior with respect to two irreducible factors, but the true behavior is probably much better. Suppose that each irreducible factor $q_i(x)$ has probability $\frac{1}{2}$ of dividing $t(x)^{(p^d-1)/2} - 1$ for each $t(x)$, independent of the behavior for other $q_j(x)$ and $t(x)$; and assume that $g(x)$ has r irreducible factors in all. Then if we encode each $q_i(x)$ by a sequence of 0s and 1s according as $q_i(x)$ does or doesn't divide $t(x)^{(p^d-1)/2} - 1$ for the successive t's tried, we obtain a random binary trie with r lieves (see Section 6.3). The cost associated with an internal node of this trie, having m lieves as descendants, is $O(m^2(\log p))$; and the solution to the recurrence $A_n = \binom{n}{2} + 2^{1-n}\sum\binom{n}{k}A_k$ is $A_n = 2\binom{n}{2}$, by exercise 5.2.2–36. Hence the sum of costs in the given random trie — representing the expected time to factor $g(x)$ *completely* — is $O(r^2(\log p)^3)$ under this plausible assumption. The plausible assumption becomes rigorously true if we choose $t(x)$ at random of degree $< rd$ instead of restricting it to degree $< 2d$.

30. Let $T(x) = x + x^p + \cdots + x^{p^{d-1}}$ be the *trace* of x and let $v(x) = T(t(x)) \bmod q(x)$. Since $t(x)^{p^d} = t(x)$ in the field of polynomial remainders modulo $q(x)$, we have $v(x)^p = v(x)$ in that field; in other words, $v(x)$ is one of the p roots of the equation $y^p - y = 0$. Hence $v(x)$ is an integer.

It follows that $\prod_{s=0}^{p-1} \gcd(g_d(x), T(t(x)) - s) = g_d(x)$. In particular, when $p = 2$ we can argue as in exercise 29 that $\gcd(g_d(x), T(t(x)))$ will be a proper factor of $g_d(x)$ with probability $\geq \frac{1}{2}$ when $g_d(x)$ has at least two irreducible factors and $t(x)$ is a random binary polynomial of degree $< 2d$.

[Note that $T(t(x)) \bmod g(x)$ can be computed by starting with $u(x) \leftarrow t(x)$ and setting $u(x) \leftarrow (t(x) + u(x)^p) \bmod g(x)$ repeatedly, $d - 1$ times. The method of this exercise is based on the polynomial factorization $x^{p^d} - x = \prod_{s=0}^{p-1}(T(x) - s)$, which holds for any p, while formula (21) is based on the polynomial factorization $x^{p^d} - x = x(x^{(p^d-1)/2} + 1)(x^{(p^d-1)/2} - 1)$ for odd p.]

The trace was introduced by Richard Dedekind, *Abhandlungen der Königl. Gesellschaft der Wissenschaften zu Göttingen* **29** (1882), 1–56. The technique of calculating $\gcd(f(x), T(x) - s)$ to find factors of $f(x)$ can be traced to A. Arwin, *Arkiv för Mat., Astr. och Fys.* **14**, 7 (1918), 1–46; but his method was incomplete because he did not consider $T(t(x))$ for $t(x) \neq x$. A complete factorization algorithm using traces was devised later by R. J. McEliece, *Math. Comp.* **23** (1969), 861–867; see also von zur Gathen and Shoup, *Computational Complexity* **2** (1992), 187–224, Algorithm 3.6, for asymptotically fast results.

Henri Cohen has observed that for $p = 2$ it suffices to test at most d special cases $t(x) = x, x^3, \ldots, x^{2d-1}$ when applying this method. One of these choices of $t(x)$ is guaranteed to split $g_d(x)$ whenever g_d is reducible, because we can obtain the effects of all polynomials $t(x)$ of degree $< 2d$ from these special cases using the facts that $T(t(x)^p) \equiv T(t(x))$ and $T(u(x)+t(x)) \equiv T(u(x))+T(t(x))$ (modulo $g_d(x)$). [*A Course in Computational Algebraic Number Theory* (Springer, 1993), Algorithm 3.4.8.]

31. If α is an element of the field of p^d elements, let $d(\alpha)$ be the *degree* of α, namely the smallest exponent e such that $\alpha^{p^e} = \alpha$. Then consider the polynomial

$$P_\alpha(x) = (x - \alpha)(x - \alpha^p)\ldots(x - \alpha^{p^{d-1}}) = q_\alpha(x)^{d/d(\alpha)},$$

where $q_\alpha(x)$ is an irreducible polynomial of degree $d(\alpha)$. As α runs through all elements of the field, the corresponding $q_\alpha(x)$ runs through every irreducible polynomial of degree e dividing d, where every such irreducible occurs exactly e times. We have $(x + t)^{(p^d-1)/2} \bmod q_\alpha(x) = 1$ if and only if $(\alpha + t)^{(p^d-1)/2} = 1$ in the field. If t is an integer, we have $d(\alpha + t) = d(\alpha)$, hence $n(p, d)$ is d^{-1} times the number of elements α of degree d such that $\alpha^{(p^d-1)/2} = 1$. Similarly, if $t_1 \neq t_2$ we want to count the number of elements of degree d such that $(\alpha + t_1)^{(p^d-1)/2} = (\alpha + t_2)^{(p^d-1)/2}$, or equivalently $((\alpha+t_1)/(\alpha+t_2))^{(p^d-1)/2} = 1$. As α runs through all the elements of degree d, so does the quantity $(\alpha + t_1)/(\alpha + t_2) = 1 + (t_1 - t_2)/(\alpha + t_2)$.

[We have $n(p, d) = \frac14 d^{-1} \sum_{c \backslash d}(3 + (-1)^c)\mu(c)(p^{d/c} - 1)$, which is about half the total number of irreducibles — exactly half, in fact, when d is odd. This proves that $\gcd(g_d(x), (x + t)^{(p^d-1)/2} - 1)$ has a good chance of finding factors of $g_d(x)$ when t is fixed and $g_d(x)$ is chosen at random; but a randomized algorithm is supposed to work with guaranteed probability for *fixed* $g_d(x)$ and *random* t, as in exercise 29.]

32. (a) Clearly $x^n - 1 = \prod_{d \backslash n} \Psi_d(x)$, since every complex nth root of unity is a primitive dth root for some unique $d \backslash n$. The second identity follows from the first; and $\Psi_n(x)$ has integer coefficients since it is expressed in terms of products and quotients of monic polynomials with integer coefficients.

(b) The condition in the hint suffices to prove that $f(x) = \Psi_n(x)$, so we shall take the hint. When p does not divide n, we have $x^n - 1 \perp nx^{n-1}$ modulo p, hence $x^n - 1$ is squarefree modulo p. Given $f(x)$ and ζ as in the hint, let $g(x)$ be the irreducible factor of $\Psi_n(x)$ such that $g(\zeta^p) = 0$. If $g(x) \neq f(x)$ then $f(x)$ and $g(x)$ are distinct factors of $\Psi_n(x)$, hence they are distinct factors of $x^n - 1$, hence they have no irreducible factors in common modulo p. However, ζ is a root of $g(x^p)$, so $\gcd(f(x), g(x^p)) \neq 1$ over the integers, hence $f(x)$ is a divisor of $g(x^p)$. By (5), $f(x)$ is a divisor of $g(x)^p$, modulo p, contradicting the assumption that $f(x)$ and $g(x)$ have no irreducible factors in common. Therefore $f(x) = g(x)$. [The irreducibility of $\Psi_n(x)$ was first proved for prime n by C. F. Gauss in *Disquisitiones Arithmeticæ* (Leipzig: 1801), Art. 341, and for general n by L. Kronecker, *J. de Math. Pures et Appliquées* **19** (1854), 177–192.]

(c) $\Psi_1(x) = x - 1$; and when p is prime, $\Psi_p(x) = 1 + x + \cdots + x^{p-1}$. If $n > 1$ is odd, it is not difficult to prove that $\Psi_{2n}(x) = \Psi_n(-x)$. If p divides n, the second identity in (a) shows that $\Psi_{pn}(x) = \Psi_n(x^p)$. If p does not divide n, we have $\Psi_{pn}(x) = \Psi_n(x^p)/\Psi_n(x)$. For nonprime $n \leq 15$ we have $\Psi_4(x) = x^2 + 1$, $\Psi_6(x) = x^2 - x + 1$, $\Psi_8(x) = x^4 + 1$, $\Psi_9(x) = x^6 + x^3 + 1$, $\Psi_{10}(x) = x^4 - x^3 + x^2 - x + 1$, $\Psi_{12}(x) = x^4 - x^2 + 1$, $\Psi_{14}(x) = x^6 - x^5 + x^4 - x^3 + x^2 - x + 1$, $\Psi_{15}(x) = x^8 - x^7 + x^5 - x^4 + x^3 - x + 1$. [The formula $\Psi_{pq}(x) = (1 + x^p + \cdots + x^{(q-1)p})(x - 1)/(x^q - 1)$ can be used to show that $\Psi_{pq}(x)$ has all coefficients ± 1 or 0 when p and q are prime; but the coefficients of $\Psi_{pqr}(x)$ can be arbitrarily large.]

33. False; we lose all p_j with e_j divisible by p. True if $p > \deg(u)$. [See exercise 36.]

34. [D. Y. Y. Yun, *Proc. ACM Symp. Symbolic and Algebraic Comp.* (1976), 26–35.] Set $(t(x), v_1(x), w_1(x)) \leftarrow \mathrm{GCD}(u(x), u'(x))$. If $t(x) = 1$, set $e \leftarrow 1$; otherwise set $(u_i(x), v_{i+1}(x), w_{i+1}(x)) \leftarrow \mathrm{GCD}(v_i(x), w_i(x) - v_i'(x))$ for $i = 1, 2, \ldots, e - 1$, until finding $w_e(x) - v_e'(x) = 0$. Finally set $u_e(x) \leftarrow v_e(x)$.

To prove the validity of this algorithm, we observe that it computes the polynomials $t(x) = u_2(x)u_3(x)^2 u_4(x)^3 \ldots$, $v_i(x) = u_i(x)u_{i+1}(x)u_{i+2}(x) \ldots$, and

$$w_i(x) = u_i'(x)u_{i+1}(x)u_{i+2}(x) \ldots + 2u_i(x)u_{i+1}'(x)u_{i+2}(x) \ldots + 3u_i(x)u_{i+1}(x)u_{i+2}'(x) \ldots + \cdots.$$

We have $t(x) \perp w_1(x)$, since an irreducible factor of $u_i(x)$ divides all but the ith term of $w_1(x)$, and it is relatively prime to that term. Furthermore we clearly have $u_i(x) \perp v_{i+1}(x)$.

[Although exercise 2(b) proves that most polynomials are squarefree, nonsquarefree polynomials actually occur often in practice; hence this method turns out to be quite important. See Paul S. Wang and Barry M. Trager, *SICOMP* **8** (1979), 300–305, for suggestions on how to improve the efficiency. Squarefree factorization modulo p is discussed by Bach and Shallit, *Algorithmic Number Theory* **1** (MIT Press, 1996), answer to exercise 7.27.]

35. We have $w_j(x) = \gcd(u_j(x), v_j^*(x)) \cdot \gcd(u_{j+1}^*(x), v_j(x))$, where

$$u_j^*(x) = u_j(x)u_{j+1}(x)\ldots \quad \text{and} \quad v_j^*(x) = v_j(x)v_{j+1}(x)\ldots .$$

[Yun notes that the running time for squarefree factorization by the method of exercise 34 is at most about twice the running time to calculate $\gcd(u(x), u'(x))$. Furthermore if we are given an arbitrary method for discovering squarefree factorization, the method of this exercise leads to a gcd procedure. (When $u(x)$ and $v(x)$ are squarefree, their gcd is simply $w_2(x)$ where $w(x) = u(x)v(x) = w_1(x)w_2(x)^2$; the polynomials $u_j(x)$, $v_j(x)$, $u_j^*(x)$, and $v_j^*(x)$ are all squarefree.) Hence the problem of converting a primitive polynomial of degree n to its squarefree representation is computationally *equivalent* to the problem of calculating the gcd of two nth degree polynomials, in the sense of asymptotic worst-case running time.]

36. Let $U_j(x)$ be the value computed for "$u_j(x)$" by the procedure of exercise 34. If $\deg(U_1) + 2\deg(U_2) + \cdots = \deg(u)$, then $u_j(x) = U_j(x)$ for all j. But in general we will have $e < p$ and $U_j(x) = \prod_{k \geq 0} u_{j+pk}(x)$ for $1 \leq j < p$. To separate these factors further, we can calculate $t(x)/(U_2(x)U_3(x)^2 \ldots U_{p-1}(x)^{p-2}) = \prod_{j \geq p} u_j(x)^{p\lfloor j/p \rfloor} = z(x^p)$. After recursively finding the squarefree representation of $z(x) = (z_1(x), z_2(x), \ldots)$, we will have $z_k(x) = \prod_{0 \leq j < p} u_{j+pk}(x)$, so we can calculate the individual $u_i(x)$ by the formula $\gcd(U_j(x), z_k(x)) = u_{j+pk}(x)$ for $1 \leq j < p$. The polynomial $u_{pk}(x)$ will be left when the other factors of $z_k(x)$ have been removed.

Note: This procedure is fairly simple but the program is lengthy. If one's goal is to have a short program for complete factorization modulo p, rather than an extremely efficient one, it is probably easiest to modify the distinct-degree factorization routine so that it casts out $\gcd(x^{p^d} - x, u(x))$ several times for the same value of d until the gcd is 1. In this case you needn't begin by calculating $\gcd(u(x), u'(x))$ and removing multiple factors as suggested in the text, since the polynomial $x^{p^d} - x$ is squarefree.

37. The exact probability is $\prod_{j \geq 1} (a_{jp}/p^j)^{k_j}/k_j!$, where k_j is the number of d_i that are equal to j. Since $a_{jp}/p^j \approx 1/j$ by exercise 4, we get the formula of exercise 1.3.3–21.

Notes: This exercise says that if we fix the prime p and let the polynomial $u(x)$ be random, it will have a certain probability of splitting in a given way modulo p. A much harder problem is to fix the polynomial $u(x)$ and to let p be "random"; it turns out that the same asymptotic result holds for almost all $u(x)$. G. Frobenius proved in 1880 that the integer polynomial $u(x)$ splits modulo p into factors of degrees $d_1, \ldots, d_r$, when p is a large prime chosen at random, with probability equal to the number of permutations in the Galois group G of $u(x)$ having cycle lengths $\{d_1, \ldots, d_r\}$ divided by the total number of permutations in G. [If $u(x)$ has rational coefficients and distinct roots $\xi_1, \ldots, \xi_n$ over the complex numbers, its Galois group is the (unique) group G of permutations such that the polynomial $\prod_{p(1)\ldots p(n) \in G}(z + \xi_{p(1)}y_1 + \cdots + \xi_{p(n)}y_n) = U(z, y_1, \ldots, y_n)$ has rational coefficients and is irreducible over the rationals; see G. Frobenius, *Sitzungsberichte Königl. preuß. Akad. Wiss.* (Berlin: 1896), 689–703. The linear mapping $x \mapsto x^p$ is traditionally called the Frobenius automorphism because of this famous paper.] Furthermore B. L. van der Waerden proved in 1934 that almost all polynomials of degree n have the set of all $n!$ permutations as their Galois group [*Math. Annalen* **109** (1934), 13–16]. Therefore almost all fixed irreducible polynomials $u(x)$ will factor as we might expect them to, with respect to randomly chosen large primes p. See also N. Chebotarev, *Math. Annalen* **95** (1926), for a generalization of Frobenius's theorem to conjugacy classes of the Galois group.

38. The conditions imply that when $|z| = 1$ we have either $|u_{n-2}z^{n-2} + \cdots + u_0| < |u_{n-1}| - 1 \le |z^n + u_{n-1}z^{n-1}|$ or $|u_{n-3}z^{n-3} + \cdots + u_0| < u_{n-2} - 1 \le |z^n + u_{n-2}z^{n-2}|$. Therefore by Rouché's theorem [*J. École Polytechnique* **21**, 37 (1858), 1–34], $u(z)$ has at least $n - 1$ or $n - 2$ roots inside the circle $|z| = 1$. If $u(z)$ is reducible, it can be written $v(z)w(z)$ where v and w are monic integer polynomials. The products of the roots of v and of w are nonzero integers, so each factor has a root of absolute value ≥ 1. Hence the only possibility is that v and w both have exactly one such root and that $u_{n-1} = 0$. These roots must be real, since the complex conjugates are roots; hence $u(z)$ has a real root z_0 with $|z_0| \ge 1$. But this cannot be, for if $r = 1/z_0$ we have $0 = |1 + u_{n-2}r^2 + \cdots + u_0r^n| \ge 1 + u_{n-2}r^2 - |u_{n-3}|r^3 - \cdots - |u_0|r^n > 1$. [O. Perron, *Crelle* **132** (1907), 288–307; for generalizations, see A. Brauer, *Amer. J. Math.* **70** (1948), 423–432, **73** (1951), 717–720.]

39. First we prove the hint: Let $u(x) = a(x - \alpha_1) \ldots (x - \alpha_n)$ have integer coefficients. The resultant of $u(x)$ with the polynomial $y - t(x)$ is a determinant, so it is a polynomial $r_t(y) = a^{\deg(t)}(y - t(\alpha_1)) \ldots (y - t(\alpha_n))$ with integer coefficients (see exercise 4.6.1–12). If $u(x)$ divides $v(t(x))$ then $v(t(\alpha_1)) = 0$, hence $r_t(y)$ has a factor in common with $v(y)$. So if v is irreducible, we have $\deg(u) = \deg(r_t) \ge \deg(v)$.

Given an irreducible polynomial $u(x)$ for which a short proof of irreducibility is desired, we may assume that $u(x)$ is monic, by exercise 18, and that $\deg(u) \ge 3$. The idea is to show the existence of a polynomial $t(x)$ such that $v(y) = r_t(y)$ is irreducible by the criterion of exercise 38. Then all factors of $u(x)$ divide the polynomial $v(t(x))$, and this will prove that $u(x)$ is irreducible. The proof will be succinct if the coefficients of $t(x)$ are suitably small.

The polynomial $v(y) = (y - \beta_1) \ldots (y - \beta_n)$ can be shown to satisfy the criterion of exercise 38 if $n \ge 3$ and $\beta_1 \ldots \beta_n \ne 0$, and if the following "smallness condition" holds: $|\beta_j| \le 1/(4n)$ except when $j = n$ or when $\beta_j = \overline{\beta_n}$ and $|\Re\beta_j| \le 1/(4n)$. The calculations are straightforward, using the fact that $|v_0| + \cdots + |v_n| \le (1 + |\beta_1|) \ldots (1 + |\beta_n|)$.

Let $\alpha_1, \ldots, \alpha_r$ be real and $\alpha_{r+1}, \ldots, \alpha_{r+s}$ be complex, where $n = r + 2s$ and $\alpha_{r+s+j} = \overline{\alpha}_{r+j}$ for $1 \le j \le s$. Consider the linear expressions $S_j(a_0, \ldots, a_{n-1})$ defined to be $\Re(\sum_{i=0}^{n-1} a_i\alpha_j^i)$ for $1 \le j \le r + s$ and $\Im(\sum_{i=0}^{n-1} a_i\alpha_j^i)$ for $r + s < j \le n$. If $0 \le a_i < b$ and $B = \lceil \max_{j=1}^{n-1} \sum_{i=0}^{n-1} |\alpha_i|^j \rceil$, we have $|S_j(a_1, \ldots, a_{n-1})| < bB$. Thus if we choose $b > (16nB)^{n-1}$, there must be distinct vectors $(a_0, \ldots, a_{n-1})$ and $(a_0', \ldots, a_{n-1}')$ such that $\lfloor 8nS_j(a_0, \ldots, a_{n-1}) \rfloor = \lfloor 8nS_j(a_0', \ldots, a_{n-1}') \rfloor$ for $1 \le j < n$, since there are b^n vectors but at most $(16nbB)^{n-1} < b^n$ possible $(n-1)$-tuples of values. Let $t(x) = (a_0 - a_0') + \cdots + (a_{n-1} - a_{n-1}')x^{n-1}$ and $\beta_j = t(\alpha_j)$. Then the smallness condition is satisfied. Furthermore $\beta_j \ne 0$; otherwise $t(x)$ would divide $u(x)$. [*J. Algorithms* **2** (1981), 385–392.]

40. Given a candidate factor $v(x) = x^d + a_{d-1}x^{d-1} + \cdots + a_0$, change each a_j to a rational fraction (modulo p^e), with numerators and denominators $\le B$. Then multiply by the least common denominator, and see if the resulting polynomial divides $u(x)$ over the integers. If not, no factor of $u(x)$ with coefficients bounded by B is congruent modulo p^e to a multiple of $v(x)$.

41. David Boyd notes that $4x^8 + 4x^6 + x^4 + 4x^2 + 4 = (2x^4 + 4x^3 + 5x^2 + 4x + 2) \times (2x^4 - 4x^3 + 5x^2 - 4x + 2)$, and he has found examples of higher degree to prove that c must be > 2 if it exists.

SECTION 4.6.3

1. x^m, where $m = 2^{\lfloor \lg n \rfloor}$ is the highest power of 2 less than or equal to n.

2. Assume that x is input in register A, and n in location NN; the output is in register X.

01	A1	ENTX	1	1	*A1. Initialize.*
02		STX	Y	1	$Y \leftarrow 1$.
03		STA	Z	1	$Z \leftarrow x$.
04		LDA	NN	1	$N \leftarrow n$.
05		JAP	2F	1	To A2.
06		JMP	DONE	0	Otherwise the answer is 1.
07	5H	SRB	1	$L + 1 - K$	
08		STA	N	$L + 1 - K$	$N \leftarrow \lfloor N/2 \rfloor$.
09	A5	LDA	Z	L	*A5. Square Z.*
10		MUL	Z	L	
11		STX	Z	L	$Z \leftarrow Z \times Z \bmod w$.
12	A2	LDA	N	L	*A2. Halve N.*
13	2H	JAE	5B	$L + 1$	To A5 if N is even.
14		SRB	1	K	
15	A4	JAZ	4F	K	Jump if $N = 1$.
16		STA	N	$K - 1$	$N \leftarrow \lfloor N/2 \rfloor$.
17	A3	LDA	Z	$K - 1$	*A3. Multiply Y by Z.*
18		MUL	Y	$K - 1$	
19		STX	Y	$K - 1$	$Y \leftarrow Z \times Y \bmod w$.
20		JMP	A5	$K - 1$	To A5.
21	4H	LDA	Z	1	
22		MUL	Y	1	Do the final multiplication. ∎

The running time is $21L + 16K + 8$, where $L = \lambda n = \lfloor \lg n \rfloor$ is one less than the number of bits in the binary representation of n, and $K = \nu n$ is the number of 1-bits in that representation.

For the serial program, we may assume that n is small enough to fit in an index register; otherwise serial exponentiation is out of the question. The following program leaves the output in register A:

01	S1	LD1	NN	1	$rI1 \leftarrow n$.
02		STA	X	1	$X \leftarrow x$.
03		JMP	2F	1	
04	1H	MUL	X	$N - 1$	$rA \times X \bmod w$
05		SLAX	5	$N - 1$	$\rightarrow rA$.
06	2H	DEC1	1	N	$rI1 \leftarrow rI1 - 1$.
07		J1P	1B	N	Multiply again if $rI1 > 0$. ∎

The running time for this program is $14N - 7$; it is faster than the previous program when $n \leq 7$, slower when $n \geq 8$.

3. The sequences of exponents are: (a) 1, 2, 3, 6, 7, 14, 15, 30, 60, 120, 121, 242, 243, 486, 487, 974, 975 [16 multiplications]; (b) 1, 2, 3, 4, 8, 12, 24, 36, 72, 108, 216, 324, 325, 650, 975 [14 multiplications]; (c) 1, 2, 3, 6, 12, 15, 30, 60, 120, 240, 243, 486, 972, 975 [13 multiplications]; (d) 1, 2, 3, 6, 12, 15, 30, 60, 75, 150, 300, 600, 900, 975 [13 multiplications]. [The smallest possible number of multiplications is 12; this is obtainable by combining the factor method with the binary method, since $975 = 15 \cdot (2^6 + 1)$.]

4. $(777777)_8 = 2^{18} - 1$.

5. **T1.** [Initialize.] Set $\mathtt{LINKU}[j] \leftarrow 0$ for $0 \le j \le 2^r$, and set $k \leftarrow 0$, $\mathtt{LINKR}[0] \leftarrow 1$, $\mathtt{LINKR}[1] \leftarrow 0$.

T2. [Change level.] (Now level k of the tree has been linked together from left to right, starting at $\mathtt{LINKR}[0]$.) If $k = r$, the algorithm terminates. Otherwise set $n \leftarrow \mathtt{LINKR}[0]$, $m \leftarrow 0$.

T3. [Prepare for n.] (Now n is a node on level k, and m points to the rightmost node currently on level $k + 1$.) Set $q \leftarrow 0$, $s \leftarrow n$.

T4. [Already in tree?] (Now s is a node in the path from the root to n.) If $\mathtt{LINKU}[n + s] \ne 0$, go to T6 (the value $n + s$ is already in the tree).

T5. [Insert below n.] If $q = 0$, set $m' \leftarrow n + s$. Then set $\mathtt{LINKR}[n + s] \leftarrow q$, $\mathtt{LINKU}[n + s] \leftarrow n$, $q \leftarrow n + s$.

T6. [Move up.] Set $s \leftarrow \mathtt{LINKU}[s]$. If $s \ne 0$, return to T4.

T7. [Attach group.] If $q \ne 0$, set $\mathtt{LINKR}[m] \leftarrow q$, $m \leftarrow m'$.

T8. [Move n.] Set $n \leftarrow \mathtt{LINKR}[n]$. If $n \ne 0$, return to T3.

T9. [End of level.] Set $\mathtt{LINKR}[m] \leftarrow 0$, $k \leftarrow k + 1$, and return to T2. ∎

6. Prove by induction that the path to the number $2^{e_0} + 2^{e_1} + \cdots + 2^{e_t}$, if $e_0 > e_1 > \cdots > e_t \ge 0$, is 1, 2, 2^2, ..., 2^{e_0}, $2^{e_0} + 2^{e_1}$, ..., $2^{e_0} + 2^{e_1} + \cdots + 2^{e_t}$; furthermore, the sequences of exponents on each level are in decreasing lexicographic order.

7. The binary and factor methods require one more step to compute x^{2n} than x^n; the power tree method requires at most one more step. Hence (a) $15 \cdot 2^k$; (b) $33 \cdot 2^k$; (c) $23 \cdot 2^k$; $k = 0, 1, 2, 3, \ldots$.

8. The power tree always includes the node $2m$ at one level below m, unless it occurs at the same level or an earlier level; and it always includes the node $2m + 1$ at one level below $2m$, unless it occurs at the same level or an earlier level. [It is not true that $2m$ is a child of m in the power tree for all m; the smallest example where this fails is $m = 2138$, which appears on level 15, while 4276 appears elsewhere on level 16. In fact, $2m$ sometimes occurs on the same level as m; the smallest example is $m = 6029$.]

9. Start with $N \leftarrow n$, $Z \leftarrow x$, and $Y_q \leftarrow 1$ for $1 \le q < m$, q odd; in general we will have $x^n = Y_1 Y_3^3 Y_5^5 \ldots Y_{m-1}^{m-1} Z^N$ as the algorithm proceeds. Assuming that $N > 0$, set $k \leftarrow N \bmod m$, $N \leftarrow \lfloor N/m \rfloor$. Then if $k = 0$, set $Z \leftarrow Z^m$ and repeat; otherwise if $k = 2^p q$ where q is odd, set $Z \leftarrow Z^{2^p}$, $Y_q \leftarrow Y_q \cdot Z$, and if $N > 0$ set $Z \leftarrow Z^{2^{e-p}}$ and repeat. Finally set $Y_k \leftarrow Y_k \cdot Y_{k+2}$ for $k = m - 3, m - 5, \ldots, 1$; the answer is $Y_1 (Y_3 Y_5 \ldots Y_{m-1})^2$. (About $m/2$ of the multiplications are by 1.)

10. By using the "**PARENT**" representation discussed in Section 2.3.3: Make use of a table $p[j]$, $1 \le j \le 100$, such that $p[1] = 0$ and $p[j]$ is the number of the node just above j for $j \ge 2$. (The fact that each node of this tree has degree at most two has no effect on the efficiency of this representation; it just makes the tree look prettier as an illustration.)

11. 1, 2, 3, 5, 10, 20, (23 or 40), 43; 1, 2, 4, 8, 9, 17, (26 or 34), 43; 1, 2, 4, 8, 9, 17, 34, (43 or 68), 77; 1, 2, 4, 5, 9, 18, 36, (41 or 72), 77. If either of the last two paths were in the tree we would have no possibility for $n = 43$, since the tree must contain either 1, 2, 3, 5 or 1, 2, 4, 8, 9.

12. No such infinite tree can exist, since $l(n) \neq l^*(n)$ for some n.

13. For Case 1, use a Type-1 chain followed by $2^{A+C} + 2^{B+C} + 2^A + 2^B$; or use the factor method. For Case 2, use a Type-2 chain followed by $2^{A+C+1} + 2^{B+C} + 2^A + 2^B$. For Case 3, use a Type-5 chain followed by addition of $2^A + 2^{A-1}$, or use the factor method. For Case 4, $n = 135 \cdot 2^D$, so we may use the factor method.

14. (a) It is easy to verify that steps $r - 1$ and $r - 2$ are not both small, so let us assume that step $r - 1$ is small and step $r - 2$ is not. If $c = 1$, then $\lambda(a_{r-1}) = \lambda(a_{r-k})$, so $k = 2$; and since $4 \leq \nu(a_r) = \nu(a_{r-1}) + \nu(a_{r-k}) - 1 \leq \nu(a_{r-1}) + 1$, we have $\nu(a_{r-1}) \geq 3$, making $r - 1$ a star step (lest $a_0, a_1, \ldots, a_{r-3}, a_{r-1}$ include only one small step). Then $a_{r-1} = a_{r-2} + a_{r-q}$ for some q, and if we replace a_{r-2}, a_{r-1}, a_r by $a_{r-2}, 2a_{r-2}, 2a_{r-2} + a_{r-q} = a_r$, we obtain another counterexample chain in which step r is small; but this is impossible. On the other hand, if $c \geq 2$, then $4 \leq \nu(a_r) \leq \nu(a_{r-1}) + \nu(a_{r-k}) - 2 \leq \nu(a_{r-1})$; hence $\nu(a_{r-1}) = 4$, $\nu(a_{r-k}) = 2$, and $c = 2$. This leads readily to an impossible situation by a consideration of the six types in the proof of Theorem B.

(b) If $\lambda(a_{r-k}) < m - 1$, we have $c \geq 3$, so $\nu(a_{r-k}) + \nu(a_{r-1}) \geq 7$ by (22); therefore both $\nu(a_{r-k})$ and $\nu(a_{r-1})$ are ≥ 3. All small steps must be $\leq r - k$, and $\lambda(a_{r-k}) = m - k + 1$. If $k \geq 4$, we must have $c = 4$, $k = 4$, $\nu(a_{r-1}) = \nu(a_{r-4}) = 4$; thus $a_{r-1} \geq 2^m + 2^{m-1} + 2^{m-2}$, and a_{r-1} must equal $2^m + 2^{m-1} + 2^{m-2} + 2^{m-3}$; but $a_{r-4} \geq \frac{1}{8}a_{r-1}$ now implies that $a_{r-1} = 8a_{r-4}$. Thus $k = 3$ and $a_{r-1} > 2^m + 2^{m-1}$. Since $a_{r-2} < 2^m$ and $a_{r-3} < 2^{m-1}$, step $r - 1$ must be a doubling; but step $r - 2$ is a nondoubling, since $a_{r-1} \neq 4a_{r-3}$. Furthermore, since $\nu(a_{r-3}) \geq 3$, $r - 3$ is a star step; and $a_{r-2} = a_{r-3} + a_{r-5}$ would imply that $a_{r-5} = 2^{m-2}$, hence we must have $a_{r-2} = a_{r-3} + a_{r-4}$. As in a similar case treated in the text, the only possibility is now seen to be $a_{r-4} = 2^{m-2} + 2^{m-3}$, $a_{r-3} = 2^{m-2} + 2^{m-3} + 2^{d+1} + 2^d$, $a_{r-1} = 2^m + 2^{m-1} + 2^{d+2} + 2^{d+1}$, and even this possibility is impossible.

15. Achim Flammenkamp [Diplomarbeit in Mathematics (Bielefeld University, 1991), Part 1] has shown that the numbers n with $\lambda(n) + 3 = l(n) < l^*(n)$ all have the form $2^A + 2^B + 2^C + 2^D + 2^E$ where $A > B > C > D > E$ and $B + E = C + D$; moreover, they are described precisely by not matching any of the following eight patterns where $|\epsilon| \leq 1$: $2^A + 2^{A-3} + 2^C + 2^{C-1} + 2^{2C+2-A}$, $2^A + 2^{A-1} + 2^C + 2^D + 2^{C+D+1-A}$, $2^A + 2^B + 2^{2B-A+3} + 2^{2B+2-A} + 2^{3B+5-2A}$, $2^A + 2^B + 2^{2B-A+\epsilon} + 2^D + 2^{B+D+\epsilon-A}$, $2^A + 2^B + 2^{B-1} + 2^D + 2^{D-1}$, $2^A + 2^B + 2^{B-2} + 2^D + 2^{D-2}$ $(A > B+1)$, $2^A + 2^B + 2^C + 2^{2B+\epsilon-A} + 2^{B+C+\epsilon-A}$, $2^A + 2^B + 2^C + 2^{B+C+\epsilon-A} + 2^{2C+\epsilon-A}$. And Neill Clift has characterized all n with $l(n) = \lambda(n) + 4$: See http://additionchains.com/FourStep.html.

16. $l^B(n) = \lambda(n) + \nu(n) - 1$; so if $n = 2^k$, $l^B(n)/\lambda(n) = 1$, but if $n = 2^{k+1} - 1$, $l^B(n)/\lambda(n) = 2$.

17. Let $i_1 < \cdots < i_t$. Delete any intervals I_k that can be removed without affecting the union $I_1 \cup \cdots \cup I_t$. (The interval $(j_k \mathinner{\ldotp\ldotp} i_k]$ may be dropped out if either $j_{k+1} \leq j_k$ or $j_1 < j_2 < \cdots$ and $j_{k+1} \leq i_{k-1}$.) Now combine overlapping intervals $(j_1 \mathinner{\ldotp\ldotp} i_1], \ldots, (j_d \mathinner{\ldotp\ldotp} i_d]$ into an interval $(j' \mathinner{\ldotp\ldotp} i'] = (j_1 \mathinner{\ldotp\ldotp} i_d]$ and note that

$$a_{i'} < a_{j'}(1 + \delta)^{i_1 - j_1 + \cdots + i_d - j_d} \leq a_{j'}(1 + \delta)^{2(i' - j')},$$

since each point of $(j' \mathinner{\ldotp\ldotp} i']$ is covered at most twice in $(j_1 \mathinner{\ldotp\ldotp} i_1] \cup \cdots \cup (j_d \mathinner{\ldotp\ldotp} i_d]$.

18. Call $f(m)$ a "nice" function if $(\log f(m))/m \to 0$ as $m \to \infty$. A polynomial in m is nice. The product of nice functions is nice. If $g(m) \to 0$ and c is a positive constant, then $c^{mg(m)}$ is nice; also $\binom{2m}{mg(m)}$ is nice, for by Stirling's approximation this is equivalent to saying that $g(m) \log(1/g(m)) \to 0$.

Now replace each term of the summation by the maximum term that is attained for any s, t, v. The total number of terms is nice, and so are $\binom{m+s}{t+v}$, $\binom{t+v}{v} \le 2^{t+v}$, and β^{2v}, because $(t+v)/m \to 0$. Finally, $\binom{(m+s)^2}{t} \le (2m)^{2t}/t! < (4em^2/t)^t$, where $(4e)^t$ is nice. Replacing t by its upper bound $(1-\epsilon/2)m/\lambda(m)$ shows that $(m^2/t)^t \le 2^{m(1-\epsilon/2)}f(m)$, where $f(m)$ is nice. Hence the entire sum is less than α^m for large m if $\alpha = 2^{1-\eta}$, where $0 < \eta < \frac{1}{2}\epsilon$.

19. (a) $M \cap N$, $M \cup N$, $M \uplus N$, respectively; see Eqs. 4.5.2–(6), 4.5.2–(7).

(b) $f(z)g(z)$, $\mathrm{lcm}(f(z), g(z))$, $\gcd(f(z), g(z))$. (For the same reasons as (a), because the monic irreducible polynomials over the complex numbers are precisely the polynomials $z - \zeta$.)

(c) Commutative laws $A \uplus B = B \uplus A$, $A \cup B = B \cup A$, $A \cap B = B \cap A$. Associative laws $A \uplus (B \uplus C) = (A \uplus B) \uplus C$, $A \cup (B \cup C) = (A \cup B) \cup C$, $A \cap (B \cap C) = (A \cap B) \cap C$. Distributive laws $A \cup (B \cap C) = (A \cup B) \cap (A \cup C)$, $A \cap (B \cup C) = (A \cap B) \cup (A \cap C)$, $A \uplus (B \cup C) = (A \uplus B) \cup (A \uplus C)$, $A \uplus (B \cap C) = (A \uplus B) \cap (A \uplus C)$. Idempotent laws $A \cup A = A$, $A \cap A = A$. Absorption laws $A \cup (A \cap B) = A$, $A \cap (A \cup B) = A$, $A \cap (A \uplus B) = A$, $A \cup (A \uplus B) = A \uplus B$. Identity and zero laws $\emptyset \uplus A = A$, $\emptyset \cup A = A$, $\emptyset \cap A = \emptyset$, where $\emptyset$ is the empty multiset. Counting law $A \uplus B = (A \cup B) \uplus (A \cap B)$. Further properties analogous to those of sets come from the partial ordering defined by the rule $A \subseteq B$ if and only if $A \cap B = A$ (if and only if $A \cup B = B$).

Notes: Other common applications of multisets are zeros and poles of meromorphic functions, invariants of matrices in canonical form, invariants of finite Abelian groups, etc.; multisets can be useful in combinatorial counting arguments and in the development of measure theory. The terminal strings of a noncircular context-free grammar form a multiset that is a set if and only if the grammar is unambiguous. The author's paper in *Theoretical Studies in Computer Science*, edited by J. D. Ullman (Academic Press, 1992), 1–13, discusses further applications to context-free grammars, and introduces the operation $A \cap B$, where each element that occurs a times in A and b times in B occurs ab times in $A \cap B$.

Although multisets appear frequently in mathematics, they often must be treated rather clumsily because there is currently no standard way to treat sets with repeated elements. Several mathematicians have voiced their belief that the lack of adequate terminology and notation for this common concept has been a definite handicap to the development of mathematics. (A multiset is, of course, formally equivalent to a mapping from a set into the nonnegative integers, but this formal equivalence is of little or no practical value for creative mathematical reasoning.) The author discussed this matter with many people during the 1960s in an attempt to find a good remedy. Some of the names suggested for the concept were list, bunch, bag, heap, sample, weighted set, collection, suite; but these words either conflicted with present terminology, had an improper connotation, or were too much of a mouthful to say and to write conveniently. Finally it became clear that such an important concept deserves a name of its own, and the word "multiset" was coined by N. G. de Bruijn. His suggestion was widely adopted during the 1970s, and it is now standard terminology.

The notation "$A \uplus B$" has been selected by the author to avoid conflict with existing notations and to stress the analogy with set union. It would not be as desirable to use

"$A+B$" for this purpose, since algebraists have found that $A+B$ is a good notation for the multiset $\{\alpha + \beta \mid \alpha \in A \text{ and } \beta \in B\}$. If A is a multiset of nonnegative integers, let $G(z) = \sum_{n \in A} z^n$ be a generating function corresponding to A. (Generating functions with nonnegative integer coefficients obviously correspond one-to-one with multisets of nonnegative integers.) If $G(z)$ corresponds to A and $H(z)$ to B, then $G(z) + H(z)$ corresponds to $A \uplus B$ and $G(z) H(z)$ corresponds to $A + B$. If we form "Dirichlet" generating functions $g(z) = \sum_{n \in A} 1/n^z$, $h(z) = \sum_{n \in B} 1/n^z$, then the product $g(z) h(z)$ corresponds to the multiset product AB.

20. Type 3: $(S_0, \ldots, S_r) = (M_{00}, \ldots, M_{r0}) = (\{0\}, \ldots, \{A\}, \{A-1, A\}, \{A-1, A, A\}, \{A-1, A-1, A, A, A\}, \ldots, \{A+C-3, A+C-3, A+C-2, A+C-2, A+C-2\})$. Type 5: $(M_{00}, \ldots, M_{r0}) = (\{0\}, \ldots, \{A\}, \{A-1, A\}, \ldots, \{A+C-1, A+C\}, \{A+C-1, A+C-1, A+C\}, \ldots, \{A+C+D-1, A+C+D-1, A+C+D\})$; $(M_{01}, \ldots, M_{r1}) = (\emptyset, \ldots, \emptyset, \emptyset, \ldots, \emptyset, \{A+C-2\}, \ldots, \{A+C+D-2\})$, $S_i = M_{i0} \uplus M_{i1}$.

21. For example, let $u = 2^{8q+5}$, $x = (2^{(q+1)u} - 1)/(2^u - 1) = 2^{qu} + \cdots + 2^u + 1$, $y = 2^{(q+1)u} + 1$. Then $xy = (2^{2(q+1)u} - 1)/(2^u - 1)$. If $n = 2^{4(q+1)u} + xy$, we have $l(n) \le 4(q+1)u + q + 2$ by Theorem F, but $l^*(n) = 4(q+1)u + 2q + 2$ by Theorem H.

22. Underline everything except the $u - 1$ insertions used in the calculation of x.

23. Theorem G (everything underlined).

24. Use the numbers $(B^{a_i} - 1)/(B - 1)$, $0 \le i \le r$, underlined when a_i is underlined; and $c_k B^{i-1}(B^{b_j} - 1)/(B-1)$ for $0 \le j < t$, $0 < i \le b_{j+1} - b_j$, $1 \le k \le l^0(B)$, underlined when c_k is underlined, where $c_0, c_1, \ldots$ is a minimum length l^0-chain for B. To prove the second inequality, let $B = 2^m$ and use (3). (The second inequality is rarely, if ever, an improvement on Theorem G.)

25. We may assume that $d_k = 1$. Use the rule R $A_{k-1} \ldots A_1$, where $A_j = $ "XR" if $d_j = 1$, $A_j = $ "R" otherwise, and where "R" means take the square root, "X" means multiply by x. For example, if $y = (.1101101)_2$, the rule is R R XR XR R XR XR. (There exist binary square-root extraction algorithms suitable for computer hardware, requiring an execution time comparable to that of division; computers with such hardware could therefore calculate more general fractional powers using the technique in this exercise.)

26. If we know the pair (F_k, F_{k-1}), then we have $(F_{k+1}, F_k) = (F_k + F_{k-1}, F_k)$ and $(F_{2k}, F_{2k-1}) = (F_k^2 + 2F_k F_{k-1}, F_k^2 + F_{k-1}^2)$; so a binary method can be used to calculate (F_n, F_{n-1}), using $O(\log n)$ arithmetic operations. Perhaps better is to use the pair of values (F_k, L_k), where $L_k = F_{k-1} + F_{k+1}$ (see exercise 4.5.4–15); then we have $(F_{k+1}, L_{k+1}) = (\frac{1}{2}(F_k + L_k), \frac{1}{2}(5F_k + L_k))$, $(F_{2k}, L_{2k}) = (F_k L_k, L_k^2 - 2(-1)^k)$.

For the general linear recurrence $x_n = a_1 x_{n-1} + \cdots + a_d x_{n-d}$, we can compute x_n in $O(d^3 \log n)$ arithmetic operations by computing the nth power of an appropriate $d \times d$ matrix. [This observation is due to J. C. P. Miller and D. J. Spencer Brown, *Comp. J.* **9** (1966), 188–190.] In fact, as Richard Brent has observed, the number of operations can be reduced to $O(d^2 \log n)$, or even to $O(d \log d \log n)$ using exercise 4.7–6, if we first compute $x^n \bmod (x^d - a_1 x^{d-1} - \cdots - a_d)$ and then replace x^j by x_j.

27. The smallest n requiring s small steps must be $c(r)$ for some r. For if $c(r) < n < c(r+1)$ we have $l(n) - \lambda(n) \le r - \lambda(c(r)) = l(c(r)) - \lambda(c(r))$. The answers for $1 \le s \le 8$ are therefore 3, 7, 29, 127, 1903, 65131, 4169527, 994660991.

28. (a) $x \nabla y = x \mid y \mid (x + y)$, where "$\mid$" is bitwise "or", see exercise 4.6.2–26; clearly $\nu(x \nabla y) \le \nu(x \mid y) + \nu(x \& y) = \nu(x) + \nu(y)$. (b) Note first that $A_{i-1}/2^{d_{i-1}} \subseteq A_i/2^{d_i}$ for $1 \le i \le r$. Secondly, note that $d_j = d_{i-1}$ in a nondoubling; for otherwise $a_{i-1} \ge 2a_j \ge$

$a_j + a_k = a_i$. Hence $A_j \subseteq A_{i-1}$ and $A_k \subseteq A_{i-1}/2^{d_j-d_k}$. (c) An easy induction on i, except that close steps need closer attention. Let us say that m has property $P(\alpha)$ if the 1s in its binary representation all appear in consecutive blocks of $\geq \alpha$ in a row. If m and m' have $P(\alpha)$, so does $m \nabla m'$; if m has $P(\alpha)$ then $\rho(m)$ has $P(\alpha + \delta)$. Hence B_i has $P(1 + \delta c_i)$. Finally if m has $P(\alpha)$ then $\nu(\rho(m)) \leq (\alpha + \delta)\nu(m)/\alpha$; for $\nu(m) = \nu_1 + \cdots + \nu_q$, where each block size ν_j is $\geq \alpha$, hence $\nu(\rho(m)) \leq (\nu_1 + \delta) + \cdots + (\nu_q + \delta) \leq (1 + \delta/\alpha)\nu_1 + \cdots + (1 + \delta/\alpha)\nu_q$. (d) Let $f = b_r + c_r$ be the number of nondoublings and s the number of small steps. If $f \geq 3.271 \lg \nu(n)$ we have $s \geq \lg \nu(n)$ as desired, by (16). Otherwise we have $a_i \leq (1 + 2^{-\delta})^{b_i} 2^{c_i + d_i}$ for $0 \leq i \leq r$, hence $n \leq ((1 + 2^{-\delta})/2)^{b_r} 2^r$, and $r \geq \lg n + b_r - b_r \lg(1 + 2^{-\delta}) \geq \lg n + \lg \nu(n) - \lg(1 + \delta c_r) - b_r \lg(1 + 2^{-\delta})$. Let $\delta = \lceil \lg(f + 1) \rceil$; then $\ln(1 + 2^{-\delta}) \leq \ln(1 + 1/(f + 1)) \leq 1/(f + 1) \leq \delta/(1 + \delta f)$, and it follows that $\lg(1 + \delta x) + (f - x)\lg(1 + 2^{-\delta}) \leq \lg(1 + \delta f)$ for $0 \leq x \leq f$. Hence finally $l(n) \geq \lg n + \lg \nu(n) - \lg(1 + (3.271 \lg \nu(n))\lceil \lg(1 + 3.271 \lg \nu(n)) \rceil)$. [*Theoretical Comp. Sci.* **1** (1975), 1–12.]

29. [*Canadian J. Math.* **21** (1969), 675–683. Schönhage refined the method of exercise 28 to prove that $l(n) \geq \lg n + \lg \nu(n) - 2.13$. Can the remaining gap be closed?]

30. $n = 31$ is the smallest example; $l(31) = 7$, but 1, 2, 4, 8, 16, 32, 31 is an addition-subtraction chain of length 6. [After proving Theorem E, Erdős stated that the same result holds also for addition-subtraction chains. Schönhage has extended the lower bound of exercise 28 to addition-subtraction chains, with $\nu(n)$ replaced by $\bar{\nu}(n)$ as defined in exercise 4.1–34. A generalized right-to-left binary method for exponentiation, which uses $\lambda(n) + \bar{\nu}(n) - 1$ multiplications when both x and x^{-1} are given, can be based on the representation α_n of that exercise.]

32. See *Discrete Math.* **23** (1978), 115–119. [This cost model corresponds to multiplication of large numbers by a classical method like Algorithm 4.3.1M. Empirical results with a more general model in which the cost is $(a_j a_k)^{\beta/2}$ have been obtained by D. P. McCarthy, *Math. Comp.* **46** (1986), 603–608; this model comes closer to the "fast multiplication" methods of Section 4.3.3, when two n-bit numbers are multiplied in $O(n^\beta)$ steps, but the cost function $a_j a_k^{\beta-1}$ would actually be more appropriate (see exercise 4.3.3–13). H. Zantema has analyzed the analogous problem when the cost of step i is $a_j + a_k$ instead of $a_j a_k$; see *J. Algorithms* **12** (1991), 281–307. In this case the optimum chains have total cost $\frac{5}{2}n + O(n^{1/2})$. Furthermore the optimum additive cost when n is odd is at least $\frac{5}{2}(n - 1)$, with equality if and only if n can be written as a product of numbers of the form $2^k + 1$.]

33. Eight; there are four ways to compute $39 = 12 + 12 + 12 + 3$ and two ways to compute $79 = 39 + 39 + 1$.

34. The statement is true. The labels in the reduced graph of the binary chain are $\lfloor n/2^k \rfloor$ for $k = e_0, \ldots, 0$; they are 1, 2, $\ldots$, 2^{e_0}, n in the dual graph. [Similarly, the right-to-left m-ary method of exercise 9 is the dual of the left-to-right method.]

35. 2^t are equivalent to the binary chain; it would be 2^{t-1} if $e_0 = e_1 + 1$. The number of chains equivalent to the scheme of Algorithm A is the number of ways to compute the sum of $t + 2$ numbers of which two are identical. This is $\frac{1}{2}f_{t+1} + \frac{1}{2}f_t$, where f_m is the number of ways to compute the sum of $m + 1$ distinct numbers. When we take commutativity into account, we see that f_m is 2^{-m} times $(m + 1)!$ times the number of binary trees on m nodes, so $f_m = (2m - 1)(2m - 3) \ldots 1$.

36. First form the $2^m - m - 1$ products $x_1^{e_1} \ldots x_m^{e_m}$, for all sequences of exponents such that $0 \leq e_k \leq 1$ and $e_1 + \cdots + e_m \geq 2$. Let $n_k = (d_{k\lambda} \ldots d_{k1} d_{k0})_2$; to complete the calculation, take $x_1^{d_1\lambda} \ldots x_m^{d_m\lambda}$, then square and multiply by $x_1^{d_{1i}} \ldots x_m^{d_{mi}}$, for $i = \lambda - 1$, $\ldots$, 1, 0. [Straus showed in *AMM* **71** (1964), 807–808, that $2\lambda(n)$ may be replaced by $(1+\epsilon)\lambda(n)$ for any $\epsilon > 0$, by generalizing this binary method to 2^k-ary as in Theorem D.]

37. (Solution by D. J. Bernstein.) Let $n = n_m$. First compute 2^e for $1 \le e \le \lambda(n)$. Then compute each n_j in $\lambda(n)/\lambda\lambda(n) + O(\lambda(n)\lambda\lambda\lambda(n)/\lambda\lambda(n)^2)$ further steps by the following variant of the 2^k-ary method, where $k = \lfloor \lg \lg n - 2 \lg \lg \lg n \rfloor$: For all odd $q < 2^k$, compute $y_q = \sum\{2^{kt+e} \mid d_t = 2^e q\}$ where $n_j = (\ldots d_1 d_0)_{2^k}$, in at most $\lfloor \frac{1}{k} \lg n \rfloor$ steps; then use the method in the final stages of answer 9 to compute $n_j = \sum q y_q$ with at most $2^k - 1$ further additions.

[A generalization of Theorem E gives the corresponding lower bound. *Reference: SICOMP* **5** (1976), 100–103.]

38. The following construction due to D. J. Newman provides the best upper bound currently known: Let $k = p_1 \ldots p_r$ be the product of the first r primes. Compute k and all quadratic residues mod k in $O(2^{-r}k \log k)$ steps (because there are approximately $2^{-r}k$ quadratic residues). Also compute all multiples of k that are $\le m^2$, in about m^2/k further steps. Now m additions suffice to compute $1^2, 2^2, \ldots, m^2$. We have $k = \exp(p_r + O(p_r/(\log p_r)^{1000}))$ where p_r is given by the formula in the answer to exercise 4.5.4–36; see, for example, Greene and Knuth, *Math. for the Analysis of Algorithms* (Boston: Birkhäuser, 1981), §4.1.6. So by choosing

$$r = \lfloor (1 + \tfrac{1}{2} \ln 2/\lg \lg m) \ln m/\ln \ln m \rfloor$$

it follows that $l(1^2, \ldots, m^2) = m + O(m \cdot \exp(-(\tfrac{1}{2} \ln 2 - \epsilon) \ln m/\ln \ln m))$.

On the other hand, D. Dobkin and R. Lipton have shown that, for any $\epsilon > 0$, $l(1^2, \ldots, m^2) > m + m^{2/3-\epsilon}$ when m is sufficiently large [*SICOMP* **9** (1980), 121–125].

39. The quantity $l([n_1, n_2, \ldots, n_m])$ is the minimum of arcs $-$ vertices $+ m$ taken over all directed graphs having m vertices s_j whose in-degree is zero and one vertex t whose out-degree is zero, where there are exactly n_j oriented paths from s_j to t for $1 \le j \le m$. The quantity $l(n_1, n_2, \ldots, n_m)$ is the minimum of arcs $-$ vertices $+ 1$ taken over all directed graphs having one vertex s whose in-degree is zero and m vertices t_j whose out-degree is zero, where there are exactly n_j oriented paths from s to t_j for $1 \le j \le m$. Those problems are dual to each other, if we change the direction of all the arcs. [See *J. Algorithms* **2** (1981), 13–21.] In this argument $\{n_1, n_2, \ldots, n_m\}$ can be any *multiset*.

Note: C. H. Papadimitriou has observed that this is a special case of a much more general theorem. Let $N = (n_{ij})$ be an $m \times p$ matrix of nonnegative integers having no row or column entirely zero. We can define $l(N)$ to be the minimum number of multiplications needed to compute the set of monomials $\{x_1^{n_{1j}} \ldots x_m^{n_{mj}} \mid 1 \le j \le p\}$. Now $l(N)$ is also the minimum of arcs $-$ vertices $+ m$ taken over all directed graphs having m vertices s_i whose in-degree is zero and p vertices t_j whose out-degree is zero, where there are exactly n_{ij} oriented paths from s_i to t_j for each i and j. By duality we have $l(N) = l(N^T) + m - p$. [*Bulletin of the EATCS* **13** (February 1981), 2–4.]

N. Pippenger has considerably extended the results of exercises 36 and 37. For example, if $L(m, p, n)$ is the maximum of $l(N)$ taken over all $m \times p$ matrices N of nonnegative integers $n_{ij} \le n$, he showed that $L(m, p, n) = \min(m, p) \lg n + H/\lg H + O(m + p + H(\log \log H)^{1/2}(\log H)^{-3/2})$, where $H = mp \lg(n + 1)$. [See *SICOMP* **9** (1980), 230–250.]

40. By exercise 39, it suffices to show that $l(m_1 n_1 + \cdots + m_t n_t) \le l(m_1, \ldots, m_t) + l([n_1, \ldots, n_t])$. But this is clear, since we can first form $\{x^{m_1}, \ldots, x^{m_t}\}$ and then compute the monomial $(x^{m_1})^{n_1} \ldots (x^{m_t})^{n_t}$.

Note: One strong way to state Olivos's theorem is that if a_0, ..., a_r and b_0, ..., b_s are any addition chains, then $l(\sum c_{ij}a_ib_j) \leq r + s + \sum c_{ij} - 1$ for any nonzero $(r + 1) \times (s + 1)$ matrix of nonnegative integers c_{ij}.

41. [*SICOMP* **10** (1981), 638–646.] The stated formula can be proved whenever $A \geq 9m^2$. Since this is a polynomial in m, and since the problem of finding a minimum vertex cover is NP-hard (see Section 7.9), the problem of computing $l(n_1, \ldots, n_m)$ is NP-complete. [It is unknown whether or not the problem of computing $l(n)$ is NP-complete. But it seems plausible that an optimum chain for, say, $\sum_{k=0}^{m-1} n_{k+1}2^{Ak^2}$ would entail an optimum chain for odd numbers $\{n_1, \ldots, n_m\}$, when A is sufficiently large.]

42. The condition fails at 128 (and in the dual 1, 2, ..., 16384, 16385, 16401, 32768, ... at 32768). Only two reduced digraphs of cost 27 exist; hence $l^0(5784689) = 28$. Furthermore, Clift's programs proved that $l^0(n) = l(n)$ for all smaller values of n.

SECTION 4.6.4

1. Set $y \leftarrow x^2$, then compute $((\ldots(u_{2n+1}y + u_{2n-1})y + \cdots)y + u_1)x$.

2. Replacing x in (2) by the polynomial $x + x_0$ leads to the following procedure:

> **G1.** Do step G2 for $k = n, n - 1, \ldots, 0$ (in this order), and stop.
>
> **G2.** Set $v_k \leftarrow u_k$, and then set $v_j \leftarrow v_j + x_0v_{j+1}$ for $j = k, k + 1, \ldots, n - 1$. (When $k = n$, this step simply sets $v_n \leftarrow u_n$.) ∎

The computations turn out to be identical to those in H1 and H2, but performed in a different order. (This process was Newton's original motivation for using scheme (2).)

3. The coefficient of x^k is a polynomial in y that may be evaluated by Horner's rule: $(\ldots(u_{n,0}x + (u_{n-1,1}y + u_{n-1,0}))x + \cdots)x + ((\ldots(u_{0,n}y + u_{0,n-1})y + \cdots)y + u_{0,0})$. [For a "homogeneous" polynomial, such as $u_nx^n + u_{n-1}x^{n-1}y + \cdots + u_1xy^{n-1} + u_0y^n$, another scheme is more efficient: If $0 < |x| \leq |y|$, first divide x by y, evaluate a polynomial in x/y, then multiply by y^n.]

4. Rule (2) involves $4n$ or $3n$ real multiplications and $4n$ or $7n$ real additions; (3) is worse, it takes $4n + 2$ or $4n + 1$ multiplications, $4n + 2$ or $4n + 5$ additions.

5. One multiplication to compute x^2; $\lfloor n/2 \rfloor$ multiplications and $\lfloor n/2 \rfloor$ additions to evaluate the first line; $\lceil n/2 \rceil$ multiplications and $\lceil n/2 \rceil - 1$ additions to evaluate the second line; and one addition to add the two lines together. Total: $n+1$ multiplications and n additions.

6. **J1.** Compute and store the values $x_0^2, x_0^3, \ldots, x_0^{\lceil n/2 \rceil}$.

> **J2.** Set $v_j \leftarrow u_jx_0^{j-\lfloor n/2 \rfloor}$ for $0 \leq j \leq n$.
>
> **J3.** For $k = 0, 1, \ldots, n - 1$, set $v_j \leftarrow v_j + v_{j+1}$ for $j = n - 1, \ldots, k + 1, k$.
>
> **J4.** Set $v_j \leftarrow v_jx_0^{\lfloor n/2 \rfloor - j}$ for $0 \leq j \leq n$. ∎

There are $(n^2 + n)/2$ additions, $n + \lceil n/2 \rceil - 1$ multiplications, n divisions. Another multiplication and division can be saved by treating v_n and v_0 as special cases. *Reference: SIGACT News* **7**, 3 (Summer 1975), 32–34.

7. Let $x_j = x_0 + jh$, and consider (42) and (44). Set $y_j \leftarrow u(x_j)$ for $0 \leq j \leq n$. For $k = 1, 2, \ldots, n$ (in this order), set $y_j \leftarrow y_j - y_{j-1}$ for $j = n, n - 1, \ldots, k$ (in this order). Now set $\beta_j \leftarrow y_j$ for all j.

However, rounding errors will accumulate as explained in the text, even if the operations of (5) are done with perfect accuracy. A better way to do the initialization, when (5) is performed with fixed point arithmetic, is to choose $\beta_0, \ldots, \beta_n$ so that

$$
\begin{pmatrix}
\binom{0}{0} & \binom{0}{1} & \cdots & \binom{0}{n} \\
\binom{d}{0} & \binom{d}{1} & \cdots & \binom{d}{n} \\
\vdots & \vdots & & \vdots \\
\binom{nd}{0} & \binom{nd}{1} & \cdots & \binom{nd}{n}
\end{pmatrix}
\begin{pmatrix}
\beta_0 \\
\beta_1 \\
\vdots \\
\beta_n
\end{pmatrix}
=
\begin{pmatrix}
u(x_0) \\
u(x_d) \\
\vdots \\
u(x_{nd})
\end{pmatrix}
+
\begin{pmatrix}
\epsilon_0 \\
\epsilon_1 \\
\vdots \\
\epsilon_n
\end{pmatrix},
$$

where $|\epsilon_0|, |\epsilon_1|, \ldots, |\epsilon_n|$ are as small as possible. [H. Hassler, *Proc. 12th Spring Conf. Computer Graphics* (Bratislava: Comenius University, 1996), 55–66.]

8. See (43).

9. [*Combinatorial Mathematics* (Buffalo: Math. Assoc. of America, 1963), 26–28.] This formula can be regarded as an application of the principle of inclusion and exclusion (Section 1.3.3), since the sum of the terms for $n - \epsilon_1 - \cdots - \epsilon_n = k$ is the sum of all $x_{1j_1} x_{2j_2} \ldots x_{nj_n}$ for which k values of the j_i do not appear. A direct proof can be given by observing that the coefficient of $x_{1j_1} \ldots x_{nj_n}$ is

$$\sum (-1)^{n - \epsilon_1 - \cdots - \epsilon_n} \epsilon_{j_1} \ldots \epsilon_{j_n};$$

if the j's are distinct, this equals unity, but if $j_1, \ldots, j_n \neq k$ then it is zero, since the terms for $\epsilon_k = 0$ cancel the terms for $\epsilon_k = 1$.

To evaluate the sum efficiently, we can start with $\epsilon_1 = 1$, $\epsilon_2 = \cdots = \epsilon_n = 0$, and we can then proceed through all combinations of the ϵ's in such a way that only one ϵ changes from one term to the next. (See "Gray binary code" in Section 7.2.1.1.) The first term costs $n - 1$ multiplications; the subsequent $2^n - 2$ terms each involve n additions, then $n - 1$ multiplications, then one more addition. Total: $(2^n - 1)(n - 1)$ multiplications, and $(2^n - 2)(n + 1)$ additions. Only $n + 1$ temporary storage locations are needed, one for the main partial sum and one for each factor of the current product.

10. $\sum_{1 \leq k < n} (k + 1)\binom{n}{k+1} = n(2^{n-1} - 1)$ multiplications and $\sum_{1 \leq k < n} k\binom{n}{k+1} = n 2^{n-1} - 2^n + 1$ additions. This is approximately half as many arithmetic operations as the method of exercise 9, although it requires a more complicated program to control the sequence. Approximately $\binom{n}{\lceil n/2 \rceil} + \binom{n}{\lceil n/2 \rceil - 1}$ temporary storage locations must be used, and this grows exponentially large (on the order of $2^n / \sqrt{n}$).

The method in this exercise is equivalent to the unusual matrix factorization of the permanent function given by Jurkat and Ryser in *J. Algebra* **3** (1966), 1–27. It may also be regarded as an application of (39) and (40), in an appropriate sense.

11. Efficient methods are known for computing an approximate value, if the matrix is sufficiently dense; see A. Sinclair, *Algorithms for Random Generation and Counting* (Boston: Birkhäuser, 1993). But this problem asks for the exact value. There may be a way to evaluate the permanent with $O(c^n)$ operations for some $c < 2$.

12. Here is a brief summary of progress on this famous research problem: J. Hopcroft and L. R. Kerr proved, among other things, that seven multiplications are necessary in 2×2 matrix multiplication modulo 2 [*SIAM J. Appl. Math.* **20** (1971), 30–36]. R. L. Probert showed that all 7-multiplication schemes, in which each multiplication takes a linear combination of elements from one matrix and multiplies by a linear combination of elements from the other, must have at least 15 additions [*SICOMP* **5** (1976), 187–203]. The tensor rank of 2×2 matrix multiplication is 7 over every field [V. Y. Pan, *J. Algorithms* **2** (1981), 301–310]; the rank of $T(2, 3, 2)$, the tensor for the product of a 2×3 matrix by a 3×2 matrix, is 11 [V. B. Alekseyev, *J. Algorithms* **6** (1985),

71–85]. For $n \times n$ matrix multiplication, the best upper bound known when $n = 3$ is due to J. D. Laderman [*Bull. Amer. Math. Soc.* **82** (1976), 126–128], who showed that 23 noncommutative multiplications suffice. His construction has been generalized by Ondrej Sýkora, who exhibited a method requiring $n^3 - (n-1)^2$ noncommutative multiplications and $n^3 - n^2 + 11(n-1)^2$ additions; this result also reduces to (36) when $n = 2$ [*Lecture Notes in Comp. Sci.* **53** (1977), 504–512]. For $n = 5$, the current record is 98 noncommutative multiplications, by A. Sedoglavic and A. V. Smirnov [see arXiv:2101.12568 [cs.CC] (2021), 8 pages]. The best lower bound known so far is due to J. M. Landsberg, A. Massarenti, and E. Raviolo, who showed that $m \times n$ by $n \times n$ multiplication requires at least $(2 - 1/p)mn + n^2 - (2\binom{2p-2}{p}) - \binom{2p-4}{p-2} + 2)n$ nonscalar multiplications, for any $p \le n$. [See *SICOMP* **43** (2014), 144–149; *Linear Algebra and Its Applications* **438** (2013), 4500–4509.] Setting $m = n$ and $p \approx \frac{1}{2}\lg(n/\lg n)$ gives the asymptotic lower bound $3n^2 - O(n^2/\log n)$.

The best upper bounds known for large n are discussed in answer 67.

13. By summing geometric series, we find that $F(t_1, \ldots, t_n)$ equals

$$\sum_{0 \le s_1 < m_1, \ldots, 0 \le s_n < m_n} \exp(-2\pi i(s_1 t_1/m_1 + \cdots + s_n t_n/m_n) f(s_1, \ldots, s_n))/m_1 \ldots m_n.$$

The inverse transform times $m_1 \ldots m_n$ can be found by doing a regular transform and interchanging t_j with $m_j - t_j$ when $t_j \ne 0$; see exercise 4.3.3–9.

[If we regard $F(t_1, \ldots, t_n)$ as the coefficient of $x_1^{t_1} \ldots x_n^{t_n}$ in a multivariate polynomial, the discrete Fourier transform amounts to evaluation of this polynomial at roots of unity, and the inverse transform amounts to finding the interpolating polynomial.]

14. Let $m_1 = \cdots = m_n = 2$, $F(t_1, t_2, \ldots, t_n) = F(2^{n-1}t_n + \cdots + 2t_2 + t_1)$, and $f(s_1, s_2, \ldots, s_n) = f(2^{n-1}s_1 + 2^{n-2}s_2 + \cdots + s_n)$; note the reversal between t's and s's. Also let $g_k(s_k, \ldots, s_n, t_k)$ be ω raised to the $2^{k-1}t_k(s_n + 2s_{n-1} + \cdots + 2^{n-k}s_k)$ power. Replace $f_k(s_{n-k+1}, \ldots, s_n, t_1, \ldots, t_{n-k})$ by $f_k(t_1, \ldots, t_{n-k}, s_{n-k+1}, \ldots, s_n)$ in (40) if you prefer to work *in situ*.

At each iteration we essentially take 2^{n-1} pairs of complex numbers (α, β) and replace them by $(\alpha + \zeta\beta, \alpha - \zeta\beta)$, where ζ is a suitable power of ω, hence $\zeta = \cos\theta + i\sin\theta$ for some θ. If we take advantage of simplifications when $\zeta = \pm 1$ or $\pm i$, the total work comes to $((n-3) \cdot 2^{n-1} + 2)$ complex multiplications and $n \cdot 2^n$ complex additions; the techniques of exercise 41 can be used to reduce the real multiplications and additions used to implement these complex operations.

The number of complex multiplications can be reduced about 25 percent without changing the number of additions by combining passes k and $k+1$ for $k = 1, 3, \ldots$; this means that 2^{n-2} quadruples $(\alpha, \beta, \gamma, \delta)$ are being replaced by

$$(\alpha + \zeta\beta + \zeta^2\gamma + \zeta^3\delta, \ \alpha + i\zeta\beta - \zeta^2\gamma - i\zeta^3\delta, \ \alpha - \zeta\beta + \zeta^2\gamma - \zeta^3\delta, \ \alpha - i\zeta\beta - \zeta^2\gamma + i\zeta^3\delta).$$

The total number of complex multiplications when n is even is thereby reduced to $(3n-2)2^{n-3} - 5\lfloor 2^{n-1}/3 \rfloor$.

These calculations assume that the given numbers $F(t)$ are complex. If the $F(t)$ are real, then $f(s)$ is the complex conjugate of $f(2^n - s)$, so we can avoid the redundancy by computing only the 2^n independent real numbers $f(0)$, $\Re f(1)$, $\ldots$, $\Re f(2^{n-1} - 1)$, $f(2^{n-1})$, $\Im f(1)$, $\ldots$, $\Im f(2^{n-1} - 1)$. The entire calculation in this case can be done by working with 2^n real values, using the fact that $f_k(s_{n-k+1}, \ldots, s_n, t_1, \ldots, t_{n-k})$ will be the complex conjugate of $f_k(s'_{n-k+1}, \ldots, s'_n, t_1, \ldots, t_{n-k})$ when $(s_1 \ldots s_n)_2 + (s'_1 \ldots s'_n)_2 \equiv 0 \pmod{2^n}$. About half as many multiplications and additions are needed as in the complex case.

[The fast Fourier transform algorithm was discovered by C. F. Gauss in 1805 and independently rediscovered many times since, most notably by J. W. Cooley and J. W. Tukey, *Math. Comp.* **19** (1965), 297–301. Its interesting history has been traced by J. W. Cooley, P. A. W. Lewis, and P. D. Welch, *Proc. IEEE* **55** (1967), 1675–1677; M. T. Heideman, D. H. Johnson, and C. S. Burrus, *IEEE ASSP Magazine* **1**, 4 (October 1984), 14–21. Details concerning its use have been discussed by hundreds of authors, admirably summarized by Charles Van Loan, *Computational Frameworks for the Fast Fourier Transform* (Philadelphia: SIAM, 1992). For a survey of fast Fourier transforms on finite groups, see M. Clausen and U. Baum, *Fast Fourier Transforms* (Mannheim: Bibliographisches Institut Wissenschaftsverlag, 1993).]

15. (a) The hint follows by integration and induction. Let $f^{(n)}(\theta)$ take on all values between A and B inclusive, as θ varies from $\min(x_0, \ldots, x_n)$ to $\max(x_0, \ldots, x_n)$. Replacing $f^{(n)}$ by each of these bounds, in the stated integral, yields $A/n! \leq f(x_0, \ldots, x_n) \leq B/n!$. (b) It suffices to prove this for $j = n$. Let f be Newton's interpolation polynomial, then $f^{(n)}$ is the constant $n!\, \alpha_n$. [See *The Mathematical Papers of Isaac Newton*, edited by D. T. Whiteside, **4** (1971), 36–51, 70–73.]

16. Carry out the multiplications and additions of (43) as operations on polynomials. (The special case $x_0 = x_1 = \cdots = x_n$ is considered in exercise 2. We have used this method in step T8 of Algorithm 4.3.3T.)

17. For example, when $n = 5$ we have

$$u_{[5]}(x) = \cfrac{\cfrac{y_0}{x - x_0} - \cfrac{5y_1}{x - x_1} + \cfrac{10y_2}{x - x_2} - \cfrac{10y_3}{x - x_3} + \cfrac{5y_4}{x - x_4} - \cfrac{y_5}{x - x_5}}{\cfrac{1}{x - x_0} - \cfrac{5}{x - x_1} + \cfrac{10}{x - x_2} - \cfrac{10}{x - x_3} + \cfrac{5}{x - x_4} - \cfrac{1}{x - x_5}},$$

independent of the value of h.

18. $\alpha_0 = \frac{1}{2}(u_3/u_4 + 1)$, $\beta = u_2/u_4 - \alpha_0(\alpha_0 - 1)$, $\alpha_1 = \alpha_0\beta - u_1/u_4$, $\alpha_2 = \beta - 2\alpha_1$, $\alpha_3 = u_0/u_4 - \alpha_1(\alpha_1 + \alpha_2)$, $\alpha_4 = u_4$.

19. Since α_5 is the leading coefficient, we may assume without loss of generality that $u(x)$ is monic (namely that $u_5 = 1$). Then α_0 is a root of the equation $40z^3 - 24u_4z^2 + (4u_4^2 + 2u_3)z + (u_2 - u_3u_4) = 0$; this equation always has at least one real root, and it may have three. Once α_0 is determined, we have $\alpha_3 = u_4 - 4\alpha_0$, $\alpha_1 = u_3 - 4\alpha_0\alpha_3 - 6\alpha_0^2$, $\alpha_2 = u_1 - \alpha_0(\alpha_0\alpha_1 + 4\alpha_0^2\alpha_3 + 2\alpha_1\alpha_3 + \alpha_0^3)$, $\alpha_4 = u_0 - \alpha_3(\alpha_0^4 + \alpha_1\alpha_0^2 + \alpha_2)$.

For the given polynomial we are to solve the cubic equation $40z^3 - 120z^2 + 80z = 0$; this leads to three solutions $(\alpha_0, \alpha_1, \alpha_2, \alpha_3, \alpha_4, \alpha_5) = (0, -10, 13, 5, -5, 1)$, $(1, -20, 68, 1, 11, 1)$, $(2, -10, 13, -3, 27, 1)$.

20.

LDA	X	STA	TEMP2	FADD	$=\alpha_1=$	FMUL	TEMP1
FADD	$=\alpha_3=$	FMUL	TEMP2	FMUL	TEMP2	FADD	$=\alpha_4=$
STA	TEMP1	STA	TEMP2	FADD	$=\alpha_2=$	FMUL	$=\alpha_5=$ █
FADD	$=\alpha_0-\alpha_3=$						

21. $z = (x+1)x - 2$, $w = (x+5)z + 9$, $u(x) = (w+z-8)w - 8$; or $z = (x+9)x + 26$, $w = (x-3)z + 73$, $u(x) = (w+z-24)w - 12$.

22. $\alpha_6 = 1$, $\alpha_0 = -1$, $\alpha_1 = 1$, $\beta_1 = -2$, $\beta_2 = -2$, $\beta_3 = -2$, $\beta_4 = 1$, $\alpha_3 = -4$, $\alpha_2 = 0$, $\alpha_4 = 4$, $\alpha_5 = -2$. We form $z = (x-1)x + 1$, $w = z + x$, and $u(x) = ((z-x-4)w + 4)z - 2$. Here one of the seven additions can be saved if we compute $w = x^2 + 1$, $z = w - x$.

23. (a) We may use induction on n; the result is trivial if $n < 2$. If $f(0) = 0$, then the result is true for the polynomial $f(z)/z$, so it holds for $f(z)$. If $f(iy) = 0$ for some real $y \neq 0$, then $g(\pm iy) = h(\pm iy) = 0$; since the result is true for $f(z)/(z^2 + y^2)$, it holds also for $f(z)$. Therefore we may assume that $f(z)$ has no roots whose real part is zero. Now the net number of times the given path circles the origin is the number of roots of $f(z)$ inside the region, which is at most 1. When R is large, the path $f(Re^{it})$ for $\pi/2 \leq t \leq 3\pi/2$ will circle the origin clockwise approximately $n/2$ times; so the path $f(it)$ for $-R \leq t \leq R$ must go counterclockwise around the origin at least $n/2 - 1$ times. For n even, this implies that $f(it)$ crosses the imaginary axis at least $n - 2$ times, and the real axis at least $n - 3$ times; for n odd, $f(it)$ crosses the real axis at least $n - 2$ times and the imaginary axis at least $n - 3$ times. These are roots respectively of $g(it) = 0$, $h(it) = 0$.

(b) If not, g or h would have a root of the form $a + bi$ with $a \neq 0$ and $b \neq 0$. But this would imply the existence of at least three other such roots, namely $a - bi$ and $-a \pm bi$, while $g(z)$ and $h(z)$ have at most n roots.

24. The roots of u are -7, $-3 \pm i$, $-2 \pm i$, and -1; permissible values of c are 2 and 4 (but *not* 3, since $c = 3$ makes the sum of the roots equal to zero). *Case 1: $c = 2$.* Then $p(x) = (x + 5)(x^2 + 2x + 2)(x^2 + 1)(x - 1) = x^6 + 6x^5 + 6x^4 + 4x^3 - 5x^2 - 2x - 10$; $q(x) = 6x^2 + 4x - 2 = 6(x + 1)(x - \frac{1}{3})$. Let $\alpha_2 = -1$, $\alpha_1 = \frac{1}{3}$; $p_1(x) = x^4 + 6x^3 + 5x^2 - 2x - 10 = (x^2 + 6x + \frac{16}{3})(x^2 - \frac{1}{3}) - \frac{74}{9}$; $\alpha_0 = 6$, $\beta_0 = \frac{16}{3}$, $\beta_1 = -\frac{74}{9}$. *Case 2: $c = 4$.* A similar analysis gives $\alpha_2 = 9$, $\alpha_1 = -3$, $\alpha_0 = -6$, $\beta_0 = 12$, $\beta_1 = -26$.

25. $\beta_1 = \alpha_2$, $\beta_2 = 2\alpha_1$, $\beta_3 = \alpha_7$, $\beta_4 = \alpha_6$, $\beta_5 = \beta_6 = 0$, $\beta_7 = \alpha_1$, $\beta_8 = 0$, $\beta_9 = 2\alpha_1 - \alpha_8$.

26. (a) $\lambda_1 = \alpha_1 \times \lambda_0$, $\lambda_2 = \alpha_2 + \lambda_1$, $\lambda_3 = \lambda_2 \times \lambda_0$, $\lambda_4 = \alpha_3 + \lambda_3$, $\lambda_5 = \lambda_4 \times \lambda_0$, $\lambda_6 = \alpha_4 + \lambda_5$. (b) $\kappa_1 = 1 + \beta_1 x$, $\kappa_2 = 1 + \beta_2 \kappa_1 x$, $\kappa_3 = 1 + \beta_3 \kappa_2 x$, $u(x) = \beta_4 \kappa_3 = \beta_1 \beta_2 \beta_3 \beta_4 x^3 + \beta_2 \beta_3 \beta_4 x^2 + \beta_3 \beta_4 x + \beta_4$. (c) If any coefficient is zero, the coefficient of x^3 must also be zero in (b), while (a) yields an arbitrary polynomial $\alpha_1 x^3 + \alpha_2 x^2 + \alpha_3 x + \alpha_4$ of degree ≤ 3.

27. Otherwise there would be a nonzero polynomial $f(q_n, \ldots, q_1, q_0)$ with integer coefficients such that $q_n \cdot f(q_n, \ldots, q_1, q_0) = 0$ for all sets $(q_n, \ldots, q_0)$ of real numbers. This cannot happen, since it is easy to prove by induction on n that a nonzero polynomial always takes on some nonzero value. (See exercise 4.6.1–16. However, this result is false for *finite* fields in place of the real numbers.)

28. The indeterminate quantities $\alpha_1, \ldots, \alpha_s$ form an algebraic basis for the polynomial domain $Q[\alpha_1, \ldots, \alpha_s]$, where Q is the field of rational numbers. Since $s + 1$ is greater than the number of elements in a basis, the polynomials $f_j(\alpha_1, \ldots, \alpha_s)$ are algebraically dependent; this means that there is a nonzero polynomial g with rational coefficients such that $g(f_0(\alpha_1, \ldots, \alpha_s), \ldots, f_s(\alpha_1, \ldots, \alpha_s))$ is identically zero.

29. Given $j_0, \ldots, j_t \in \{0, 1, \ldots, n\}$, there are nonzero polynomials with integer coefficients such that $g_j(q_{j_0}, \ldots, q_{j_t}) = 0$ for all $(q_n, \ldots, q_0)$ in R_j, $1 \leq j \leq m$. The product $g_1 g_2 \ldots g_m$ is therefore zero for all $(q_n, \ldots, q_0)$ in $R_1 \cup \cdots \cup R_m$.

30. Starting with the construction in Theorem M, we will prove that $m_p + (1 - \delta_{0m_c})$ of the β's may effectively be eliminated: If μ_i corresponds to a parameter multiplication, we have $\mu_i = \beta_{2i-1} \times (T_{2i} + \beta_{2i})$; add $c\beta_{2i-1}\beta_{2i}$ to each β_j for which $c\mu_i$ occurs in T_j, and replace β_{2i} by zero. This removes one parameter for each parameter multiplication. If μ_i is the first chain multiplication, then $\mu_i = (\gamma_1 x + \theta_1 + \beta_{2i-1}) \times (\gamma_2 x + \theta_2 + \beta_{2i})$, where γ_1, γ_2, θ_1, θ_2 are polynomials in $\beta_1, \ldots, \beta_{2i-2}$ with integer coefficients. Here θ_1 and θ_2 can be "absorbed" into β_{2i-1} and β_{2i}, respectively, so we may assume that

$\theta_1 = \theta_2 = 0$. Now add $c\beta_{2i-1}\beta_{2i}$ to each β_j for which $c\mu_i$ occurs in T_j; add $\beta_{2i-1}\gamma_2/\gamma_1$ to β_{2i}; and set β_{2i-1} to zero. The result set is unchanged by this elimination of β_{2i-1}, except for the values of $\alpha_1, \ldots, \alpha_s$ such that γ_1 is zero. [This proof is essentially due to V. Y. Pan, *Uspekhi Mat. Nauk* **21**, 1 (January–February 1966), 103–134.] The latter case can be handled as in the proof of Theorem A, since the polynomials with $\gamma_1 = 0$ can be evaluated by eliminating β_{2i} (as in the first construction, where μ_i corresponds to a parameter multiplication).

31. Otherwise we could add one parameter multiplication as a final step, and violate Theorem C. (The exercise is an improvement over Theorem A, in this special case, since there are only n degrees of freedom in the coefficients of a monic polynomial of degree n.)

32. $\lambda_1 = \lambda_0 \times \lambda_0$, $\lambda_2 = \alpha_1 \times \lambda_1$, $\lambda_3 = \alpha_2 + \lambda_2$, $\lambda_4 = \lambda_3 \times \lambda_1$, $\lambda_5 = \alpha_3 + \lambda_4$. We need at least three multiplications to compute $u_4 x^4$ (see Section 4.6.3), and at least two additions by Theorem A.

33. We must have $n+1 \le 2m_c + m_p + \delta_{0m_c}$, and $m_c + m_p = (n+1)/2$; so there are no parameter multiplications. Now the first λ_i whose leading coefficient (as a polynomial in x) is not an integer must be obtained by a chain addition; and there must be at least $n+1$ parameters, so there are at least $n+1$ parameter additions.

34. Transform the given chain step by step, and also define the "content" c_i of λ_i, as follows: (Intuitively, c_i is the leading coefficient of λ_i.) Define $c_0 = 1$. (a) If the step has the form $\lambda_i = \alpha_j + \lambda_k$, replace it by $\lambda_i = \beta_j + \lambda_k$, where $\beta_j = \alpha_j/c_k$; and define $c_i = c_k$. (b) If the step has the form $\lambda_i = \alpha_j - \lambda_k$, replace it by $\lambda_i = \beta_j + \lambda_k$, where $\beta_j = -\alpha_j/c_k$; and define $c_i = -c_k$. (c) If the step has the form $\lambda_i = \alpha_j \times \lambda_k$, replace it by $\lambda_i = \lambda_k$ (the step will be deleted later); and define $c_i = \alpha_j c_k$. (d) If the step has the form $\lambda_i = \lambda_j \times \lambda_k$, leave it unchanged; and define $c_i = c_j c_k$.

After this process is finished, delete all steps of the form $\lambda_i = \lambda_k$, replacing λ_i by λ_k in each future step that uses λ_i. Then add a final step $\lambda_{r+1} = \beta \times \lambda_r$, where $\beta = c_r$. This is the desired scheme, since it is easy to verify that the new λ_i are just the old ones divided by the factor c_i. The β's are given functions of the α's; division by zero is no problem, because if any $c_k = 0$ we must have $c_r = 0$ (hence the coefficient of x^n is zero), or else λ_k never contributes to the final result.

35. Since there are at least five parameter steps, the result is trivial unless there is at least one parameter multiplication; considering the ways in which three multiplications can form $u_4 x^4$, we see that there must be one parameter multiplication and two chain multiplications. Therefore the four addition-subtractions must each be parameter steps, and exercise 34 applies. We can now assume that only additions are used, and that we have a chain to compute a general *monic* fourth-degree polynomial with *two* chain multiplications and four parameter additions. The only possible scheme of this type that calculates a fourth-degree polynomial has the form

$$\lambda_1 = \alpha_1 + \lambda_0$$
$$\lambda_2 = \alpha_2 + \lambda_0$$
$$\lambda_3 = \lambda_1 \times \lambda_2$$
$$\lambda_4 = \alpha_3 + \lambda_3$$
$$\lambda_5 = \alpha_4 + \lambda_3$$
$$\lambda_6 = \lambda_4 \times \lambda_5$$
$$\lambda_7 = \alpha_5 + \lambda_6.$$

Actually this chain has one addition too many, but any correct scheme can be put into this form if we restrict some of the α's to be functions of the others. Now λ_7 has the form $(x^2 + Ax + B)(x^2 + Ax + C) + D = x^4 + 2Ax^3 + (E + A^2)x^2 + EAx + F$, where $A = \alpha_1 + \alpha_2$, $B = \alpha_1\alpha_2 + \alpha_3$, $C = \alpha_1\alpha_2 + \alpha_4$, $D = \alpha_6$, $E = B + C$, $F = BC + D$; and since this involves only three independent parameters it cannot represent a general monic fourth-degree polynomial.

36. As in the solution to exercise 35, we may assume that the chain computes a general monic polynomial of degree six, using only three chain multiplications and six parameter additions. The computation must take one of two general forms

<table>
<tr><td>$\lambda_1 = \alpha_1 + \lambda_0$</td><td>$\lambda_1 = \alpha_1 + \lambda_0$</td></tr>
<tr><td>$\lambda_2 = \alpha_2 + \lambda_0$</td><td>$\lambda_2 = \alpha_2 + \lambda_0$</td></tr>
<tr><td>$\lambda_3 = \lambda_1 \times \lambda_2$</td><td>$\lambda_3 = \lambda_1 \times \lambda_2$</td></tr>
<tr><td>$\lambda_4 = \alpha_3 + \lambda_0$</td><td>$\lambda_4 = \alpha_3 + \lambda_3$</td></tr>
<tr><td>$\lambda_5 = \alpha_4 + \lambda_3$</td><td>$\lambda_5 = \alpha_4 + \lambda_3$</td></tr>
<tr><td>$\lambda_6 = \lambda_4 \times \lambda_5$</td><td>$\lambda_6 = \lambda_4 \times \lambda_5$</td></tr>
<tr><td>$\lambda_7 = \alpha_5 + \lambda_6$</td><td>$\lambda_7 = \alpha_5 + \lambda_3$</td></tr>
<tr><td>$\lambda_8 = \alpha_6 + \lambda_6$</td><td>$\lambda_8 = \alpha_6 + \lambda_6$</td></tr>
<tr><td>$\lambda_9 = \lambda_7 \times \lambda_8$</td><td>$\lambda_9 = \lambda_7 \times \lambda_8$</td></tr>
<tr><td>$\lambda_{10} = \alpha_7 + \lambda_9$</td><td>$\lambda_{10} = \alpha_7 + \lambda_9$</td></tr>
</table>

where, as in exercise 35, an extra addition has been inserted to cover a more general case. Neither of these schemes can calculate a general sixth-degree monic polynomial, since the first case is a polynomial of the form

$$(x^3 + Ax^2 + Bx + C)(x^3 + Ax^2 + Bx + D) + E,$$

and the second case is a polynomial of the form

$$(x^4 + 2Ax^3 + (E + A^2)x^2 + EAx + F)(x^2 + Ax + G) + H;$$

both of these involve only five independent parameters.

37. Let $p_0(x) = u_n x^n + u_{n-1}x^{n-1} + \cdots + u_0$ and $q_0(x) = x^n + v_{n-1}x^{n-1} + \cdots + v_0$. For $1 \le j \le n$, divide $p_{j-1}(x)$ by the monic polynomial $q_{j-1}(x)$, obtaining $p_{j-1}(x) = \alpha_j q_{j-1}(x) + \beta_j q_j(x)$. Assume that a monic polynomial $q_j(x)$ of degree $n - j$ exists satisfying this relation; this will be true for almost all rational functions. Let $p_j(x) = q_{j-1}(x) - xv q_j(x)$. These definitions imply that $\deg(p_n) < 1$, so we may let $\alpha_{n+1} = p_n(x)$.

For the given rational function we have

j	α_j	β_j	$q_j(x)$	$p_j(x)$
0			$x^2 + 8x + 19$	$x^2 + 10x + 29$
1	1	2	$x + 5$	$3x + 19$
2	3	4	1	5

so $u(x)/v(x) = p_0(x)/q_0(x) = 1 + 2/(x + 3 + 4/(x + 5))$.

Notes: A general rational function of the stated form has $2n + 1$ "degrees of freedom," in the sense that it can be shown to have $2n + 1$ essentially independent parameters. If we generalize polynomial chains to quolynomial chains, which allow division operations as well as addition, subtraction, and multiplication (see exercise 71), we can obtain the following results with slight modifications to the proofs of Theorems A and M: *A quolynomial chain with q addition-subtraction steps has at most $q + 1$*

degrees of freedom. A quolynomial chain with m multiplication-division steps has at most $2m + 1$ degrees of freedom. Therefore a quolynomial chain that computes almost all rational functions of the stated form must have at least $2n$ addition-subtractions, and n multiplication-divisions; the method in this exercise is optimal.

38. The theorem is certainly true if $n = 0$. Assume that n is positive, and that a polynomial chain computing $P(x; u_0, \ldots, u_n)$ is given, where each of the parameters α_j has been replaced by a real number. Let $\lambda_i = \lambda_j \times \lambda_k$ be the first chain multiplication step that involves one of $u_0, \ldots, u_n$; such a step must exist because of the rank of A. Without loss of generality, we may assume that λ_j involves u_n; thus, λ_j has the form $h_0 u_0 + \cdots + h_n u_n + f(x)$, where $h_0, \ldots, h_n$ are real, $h_n \neq 0$, and $f(x)$ is a polynomial with real coefficients. (The h's and the coefficients of $f(x)$ are derived from the values assigned to the α's.)

Now change step i to $\lambda_i = \alpha \times \lambda_k$, where α is an arbitrary real number. (We could take $\alpha = 0$; general α is used here merely to show that there is a certain amount of flexibility available in the proof.) Add further steps to calculate

$$\lambda = (\alpha - f(x) - h_0 u_0 - \cdots - h_{n-1} u_{n-1})/h_n;$$

these new steps involve only additions and parameter multiplications (by suitable new parameters). Finally, replace $\lambda_{-n-1} = u_n$ everywhere in the chain by this new element λ. The result is a chain that calculates

$$Q(x; u_0, \ldots, u_{n-1}) = P\big(x; u_0, \ldots, u_{n-1}, (\alpha - f(x) - h_0 u_0 - \cdots - h_{n-1} u_{n-1})/h_n\big);$$

and this chain has one less chain multiplication. The proof will be complete if we can show that Q satisfies the hypotheses. The quantity $(\alpha - f(x))/h_n$ leads to a possibly increased value of m, and a new vector B'. If the columns of A are $A_0, A_1, \ldots, A_n$ (these vectors being linearly independent over the reals), the new matrix A' corresponding to Q has the column vectors

$$A_0 - (h_0/h_n) A_n, \qquad \ldots, \qquad A_{n-1} - (h_{n-1}/h_n) A_n,$$

plus perhaps a few rows of zeros to account for an increased value of m, and these columns are clearly also linearly independent. By induction, the chain that computes Q has at least $n - 1$ chain multiplications, so the original chain has at least n.

[Pan showed also that the use of division would give no improvement; see *Problemy Kibernetiki* **7** (1962), 21–30. Generalizations to the computation of several polynomials in several variables, with and without various kinds of preconditioning, have been given by S. Winograd, *Comm. Pure and Applied Math.* **23** (1970), 165–179.]

39. By induction on m. Let $w_m(x) = x^{2m} + u_{2m-1} x^{2m-1} + \cdots + u_0$, $w_{m-1}(x) = x^{2m-2} + v_{2m-3} x^{2m-3} + \cdots + v_0$, $a = \alpha_1 + \gamma_m$, $b = \alpha_m$, and let

$$f(r) = \sum_{i,j \geq 0} (-1)^{i+j} \binom{i+j}{j} u_{r+i+2j} a^i b^j.$$

It follows that $v_r = f(r + 2)$ for $r \geq 0$, and $\delta_m = f(1)$. If $\delta_m = 0$ and a is given, we have a polynomial of degree $m - 1$ in b, with leading coefficient $\pm(u_{2m-1} - ma) = \pm(\gamma_2 + \cdots + \gamma_m - m\gamma_m)$.

In Motzkin's unpublished notes he arranged to make $\delta_k = 0$ almost always, by choosing γ's so that this leading coefficient is $\neq 0$ when m is even and $= 0$ when m is odd; then we can almost always let b be a (real) root of an odd-degree polynomial.

40. No; S. Winograd found a way to compute all polynomials of degree 13 with only 7 (possibly complex) multiplications [*Comm. Pure and Applied Math.* **25** (1972), 455–457]. L. Revah found schemes that evaluate almost all polynomials of degree $n \geq 9$ with $\lfloor n/2 \rfloor + 1$ (possibly complex) multiplications [*SICOMP* **4** (1975), 381–392]; she also showed that when $n = 9$ it is possible to achieve $\lfloor n/2 \rfloor + 1$ multiplications only with at least $n + 3$ additions. By appending sufficiently many additions (see exercise 39), the "almost all" and "possibly complex" provisos disappear. V. Y. Pan [*STOC* **10** (1978), 162–172; IBM Research Report RC7754 (1979)] found schemes with $\lfloor n/2 \rfloor + 1$ (complex) multiplications and the minimum number $n + 2 + \delta_{n9}$ of (complex) additions, for all odd $n \geq 9$; his method for $n = 9$ is

$$v(x) = ((x + \alpha)^2 + \beta)(x + \gamma), \qquad w(x) = v(x) + x,$$
$$t_1(x) = (v(x) + \delta_1)(w(x) + \epsilon_1), \qquad t_2(x) = (v(x) + \delta_2)(w(x) + \epsilon_2),$$
$$u(x) = (t_1(x) + \zeta)(t_2(x) - t_1(x) + \eta) + \kappa.$$

The minimum number of *real* additions necessary, when the minimum number of (real) multiplications is achieved, remains unknown for $n \geq 9$.

41. $a(c+d) - (a+b)d + i(a(c+d) + (b-a)c)$. [Beware of numerical instability. Three multiplications are necessary, since complex multiplication is a special case of (71) with $p(u) = u^2 + 1$. Without the restriction on additions there are other possibilities. For example, the symmetric formula $ac - bd + i((a+b)(c+d) - ac - bd)$ was suggested by Peter Ungar in 1963; Eq. 4.3.3–(2) is similar, with 2^n in the role of i. See I. Munro, *STOC* **3** (1971), 40–44; S. Winograd, *Linear Algebra and Its Applications* **4** (1971), 381–388.]

Alternatively, if $a^2 + b^2 = 1$ and $t = (1-a)/b = b/(1+a)$, the algorithm "$w = c - td$, $v = d + bw$, $u = w - tv$" for calculating the product $(a + bi)(c + di) = u + iv$ has been suggested by Oscar Buneman [*J. Comp. Phys.* **12** (1973), 127–128]. In this method if $a = \cos\theta$ and $b = \sin\theta$, we have $t = \tan(\theta/2)$.

Helmut Alt and Jan van Leeuwen [*Computing* **27** (1981), 205–215] have shown that four real multiplications or divisions are necessary for computing $1/(a + bi)$, and four are sufficient for computing

$$\frac{a}{b + ci} = \frac{a}{b + c(c/b)} - i\frac{(c/b)a}{b + c(c/b)}.$$

Six multiplication-division operations and three addition-subtractions are necessary and sufficient to compute $(a + bi)/(c + di)$. [T. Lickteig, *SICOMP* **16** (1987), 278–311].

In spite of these lower bounds, one should remember that complex arithmetic need not be implemented in terms of real arithmetic. For example, the time needed to multiply two n-place complex numbers is asymptotically only about twice the time to multiply two n-place real numbers, using fast Fourier transforms.

42. (a) Let $\pi_1, \ldots, \pi_m$ be the λ_i's that correspond to chain multiplications; then $\pi_i = P_{2i-1} \times P_{2i}$ and $u(x) = P_{2m+1}$, where each P_j has the form $\beta_j + \beta_{j0}x + \beta_{j1}\pi_1 + \cdots + \beta_{jr(j)}\pi_{r(j)}$, where $r(j) \leq \lceil j/2 \rceil - 1$ and each of the β_j and β_{jk} is a polynomial in the α's with integer coefficients. We can systematically modify the chain (see exercise 30) so that $\beta_j = 0$ and $\beta_{jr(j)} = 1$, for $1 \leq j \leq 2m$; furthermore we can assume that $\beta_{30} = 0$. The result set now has at most $m + 1 + \sum_{j=1}^{2m}(\lceil j/2 \rceil - 1) = m^2 + 1$ degrees of freedom.

(b) Any such polynomial chain with at most m chain multiplications can be simulated by one with the form considered in (a), except that now we let $r(j) = \lceil j/2 \rceil - 1$ for $1 \leq j \leq 2m + 1$, and we do not assume that $\beta_{30} = 0$ or that $\beta_{jr(j)} = 1$ for $j \geq 3$.

This single canonical form involves $m^2 + 2m$ parameters. As the α's run through all integers and as we run through all chains, the β's run through at most 2^{m^2+2m} sets of values mod 2, hence the result set does also. In order to obtain all 2^n polynomials of degree n with 0–1 coefficients, we need $m^2 + 2m \geq n$.

(c) Set $m \leftarrow \lfloor \sqrt{n} \rfloor$ and compute $x^2, x^3, \ldots, x^m$. Let $u(x) = u_{m+1}(x)x^{(m+1)m} + \cdots + u_1(x)x^m + u_0(x)$, where each $u_j(x)$ is a polynomial of degree $\leq m$ with integer coefficients (hence it can be evaluated without any more multiplications). Now evaluate $u(x)$ by rule (2) as a polynomial in x^m with known coefficients. (The number of additions used is approximately the sum of the absolute values of the coefficients, so this algorithm is efficient on 0–1 polynomials. Paterson and Stockmeyer also gave another algorithm that uses about $\sqrt{2n}$ multiplications.)

References: SICOMP **2** (1973), 60–66; see also J. E. Savage, *SICOMP* **3** (1974), 150–158; J. Ganz, *SICOMP* **24** (1995), 473–483. For analogous results about additions, see Borodin and Cook, *SICOMP* **5** (1976), 146–157; Rivest and Van de Wiele, *Inf. Proc. Letters* **8** (1979), 178–180.

43. When $a_i = a_j + a_k$ is a step in some optimal addition chain for $n + 1$, compute $x^i = x^j x^k$ and $p_i = p_k x^j + p_j$, where $p_i = x^{i-1} + \cdots + x + 1$; omit the final calculation of x^{n+1}. We save one multiplication whenever $a_k = 1$, in particular when $i = 1$. (See exercise 4.6.3–31 with $\epsilon = \frac{1}{2}$.)

44. Let $l = \lfloor \lg n \rfloor$, and suppose $x, x^2, x^4, \ldots, x^{2^l}$ have been precomputed. If $u(x)$ is monic of degree $n = 2m + 1$, we can write $u(x) = (x^{m+1} + a)v(x) + w(x)$, where $v(x)$ and $w(x)$ are monic of degree m. This yields a method for $n = 2^{l+1} - 1 \geq 3$ that requires $2^l - 1$ further multiplications and $2^{l+1} + 2^{l-1} - 2$ additions. If $n = 2^l$ we can apply Horner's rule to reduce n by 1. And if $m = 2^l < n < 2^{l+1} - 1$, we can write $u(x) = x^m v(x) + w(x)$ where v and w are monic of degrees $n - m$ and m, respectively; by induction on l, this requires at most $\frac{1}{2}n + l - 1$ multiplications and $\frac{5}{4}n$ additions, after the precomputation. [See S. Winograd, *IBM Tech. Disclosure Bull.* **13** (1970), 1133–1135.]

Note: It is also possible to evaluate $u(x)$ with $\frac{1}{2}n + O(\sqrt{n})$ multiplications and $n + O(\sqrt{n})$ additions, under the same ground rules, if our goal is to minimize multiplications + additions. The generic polynomial

$$p_{jkm}(x) = \left(\left(\cdots \left(\left((x^m + \alpha_0)(x^{j+1} + \beta_1) + \alpha_1 \right)(x^{j+2} + \beta_2) \right. \right. \right.$$

$$\left. \left. \left. + \alpha_2 \right) \cdots \right)(x^k + \beta_{k-j}) + \alpha_{k-j} \right)(x^j + \beta_0)$$

"covers" the coefficients of exponents $\{j, j + k, j + k + (k - 1), \ldots, j + k + (k - 1) + \cdots + (j + 1), m' - k, m' - k + 1, \ldots, m' - j\}$, where

$$m' = m + j + (j + 1) + \cdots + k = m + \binom{k+1}{2} - \binom{j}{2}.$$

By adding together such polynomials $p_{1km_1}(x), p_{2km_2}(x), \ldots, p_{kkm_k}(x)$ for $m_j = \binom{j+1}{2} + \binom{k-j+2}{2}$, we obtain an arbitrary monic polynomial of degree $k^2 + k + 1$. [Rabin and Winograd, *Comm. on Pure and Applied Math.* **25** (1972), 433–458, §2; this paper also proves that constructions with $\frac{1}{2}n + O(\log n)$ multiplications and $\leq (1 + \epsilon)n$ additions are possible for all $\epsilon > 0$, if n is large enough.]

45. It suffices to show that (T_{ijk})'s rank is *at most* that of (t_{ijk}), since we can obtain (t_{ijk}) back from (T_{ijk}) by transforming it in the same way with F^{-1}, G^{-1}, H^{-1}. If

$t_{ijk} = \sum_{l=1}^{r} a_{il} b_{jl} c_{kl}$ then it follows immediately that

$$T_{ijk} = \sum_{1 \le l \le r} \left(\sum_{i'=1}^{m} F_{ii'} a_{i'l}\right)\left(\sum_{j'=1}^{n} G_{jj'} b_{j'l}\right)\left(\sum_{k'=1}^{s} H_{kk'} c_{k'l}\right).$$

[H. F. de Groote has proved that all normal schemes that yield 2×2 matrix products with seven chain multiplications are equivalent, in the sense that they can be obtained from each other by nonsingular matrix multiplication as in this exercise. In this sense Strassen's algorithm is unique. See *Theor. Comp. Sci.* **7** (1978), 127–148.]

46. By exercise 45 we can add any multiple of a row, column, or plane to another one without changing the rank; we can also multiply a row, column, or plane by a nonzero constant, or transpose the tensor. A sequence of such operations can always be found to reduce a given $2 \times 2 \times 2$ tensor to one of the forms $\left(\begin{smallmatrix} 0\,0 \\ 0\,0 \end{smallmatrix}\right) \left(\begin{smallmatrix} 0\,0 \\ 0\,0 \end{smallmatrix}\right)$, $\left(\begin{smallmatrix} 1\,0 \\ 0\,0 \end{smallmatrix}\right) \left(\begin{smallmatrix} 0\,0 \\ 0\,0 \end{smallmatrix}\right)$, $\left(\begin{smallmatrix} 1\,0 \\ 0\,1 \end{smallmatrix}\right) \left(\begin{smallmatrix} 0\,0 \\ 0\,0 \end{smallmatrix}\right)$, $\left(\begin{smallmatrix} 1\,0 \\ 0\,0 \end{smallmatrix}\right) \left(\begin{smallmatrix} 0\,0 \\ 0\,1 \end{smallmatrix}\right)$, $\left(\begin{smallmatrix} 1\,0 \\ 0\,1 \end{smallmatrix}\right) \left(\begin{smallmatrix} 0\,1 \\ q\,r \end{smallmatrix}\right)$. The last tensor has rank 3 or 2 according as the polynomial $u^2 - ru - q$ has one or two irreducible factors in the field of interest, by Theorem W (see (74)).

47. A general $m \times n \times s$ tensor has mns degrees of freedom. By exercise 28 it is impossible to express all $m \times n \times s$ tensors in terms of the $(m + n + s)r$ elements of a realization (A, B, C) unless $(m + n + s)r \ge mns$. On the other hand, assume that $m \ge n \ge s$. The rank of an $m \times n$ matrix is at most n, so we can realize any tensor in ns chain multiplications by realizing each matrix plane separately. [Exercise 46 shows that this lower bound on the maximum tensor rank is not best possible, nor is the upper bound. Thomas D. Howell [Ph.D. thesis (Cornell Univ., 1976)] has shown that there are tensors of rank $\ge \lceil mns/(m + n + s - 2) \rceil$ over the complex numbers.]

48. If (A, B, C) and (A', B', C') are realizations of (t_{ijk}) and (t'_{ijk}) of respective lengths r and r', then $A'' = A \oplus A'$, $B'' = B \oplus B'$, $C'' = C \oplus C'$, and $A''' = A \otimes A'$, $B''' = B \otimes B'$, $C''' = C \otimes C'$, are realizations of (t''_{ijk}) and (t'''_{ijk}) of respective lengths $r + r'$ and $r \cdot r'$.

Note: Many people have made the natural conjecture that $\text{rank}((t_{ijk}) \oplus (t'_{ijk})) = \text{rank}(t_{ijk}) + \text{rank}(t'_{ijk})$, but the constructions in exercise 60(b) and exercise 65 make this seem much less plausible than it once was.

49. By Lemma T, $\text{rank}(t_{ijk}) \ge \text{rank}(t_{i(jk)})$. Conversely if M is a matrix of rank r we can transform it by row and column operations, finding nonsingular matrices F and G such that FMG has all entries 0 except for r diagonal elements that are 1; see Algorithm 4.6.2N. The tensor rank of FMG is therefore $\le r$; and it is the same as the tensor rank of M, by exercise 45.

50. Let $i = \langle i', i'' \rangle$ where $1 \le i' \le m$ and $1 \le i'' \le n$; then $t_{\langle i', i'' \rangle jk} = \delta_{i''j} \delta_{i'k}$, and it is clear that $\text{rank}(t_{i(jk)}) = mn$ since $(t_{i(jk)})$ is a permutation matrix. By Lemma L, $\text{rank}(t_{ijk}) \ge mn$. Conversely, since (t_{ijk}) has only mn nonzero entries, its rank is clearly $\le mn$. (There is consequently no normal scheme requiring fewer than the mn obvious multiplications. There is no such abnormal scheme either [*Comm. Pure and Appl. Math.* **3** (1970), 165–179]. But some savings can be achieved if the same matrix is used with $s > 1$ different column vectors, since this is equivalent to $(m \times n)$ times $(n \times s)$ matrix multiplication.)

51. (a) $s_1 = y_0 + y_1$, $s_2 = y_0 - y_1$; $m_1 = \frac{1}{2}(x_0 + x_1)s_1$, $m_2 = \frac{1}{2}(x_0 - x_1)s_2$; $w_0 = m_1 + m_2$, $w_1 = m_1 - m_2$. (b) Here are some intermediate steps, using the methodology in the text: $((x_0 - x_2) + (x_1 - x_2)u)((y_0 - y_2) + (y_1 - y_2)u) \bmod (u^2 + u + 1) = ((x_0 - x_2)(y_0 - y_2) - (x_1 - x_2)(y_1 - y_2)) + ((x_0 - x_2)(y_0 - y_2) - (x_1 - x_0)(y_1 - y_0))u$. The first realization is

$$\begin{pmatrix} 1 & 1 & \bar{1} & 0 \\ 1 & 0 & 1 & 1 \\ 1 & \bar{1} & 0 & \bar{1} \end{pmatrix}, \qquad \begin{pmatrix} 1 & 1 & \bar{1} & 0 \\ 1 & 0 & 1 & 1 \\ 1 & \bar{1} & 0 & \bar{1} \end{pmatrix}, \qquad \begin{pmatrix} 1 & 1 & 1 & \bar{2} \\ 1 & 1 & \bar{2} & 1 \\ 1 & \bar{2} & 1 & 1 \end{pmatrix} \times \frac{1}{3}.$$

The second realization is

$$\begin{pmatrix} 1 & 1 & 1 & \bar{2} \\ 1 & 1 & \bar{2} & 1 \\ 1 & \bar{2} & 1 & 1 \end{pmatrix} \times \frac{1}{3}, \qquad \begin{pmatrix} 1 & 1 & \bar{1} & 0 \\ 1 & \bar{1} & 0 & \bar{1} \\ 1 & 0 & 1 & 1 \end{pmatrix}, \qquad \begin{pmatrix} 1 & 1 & \bar{1} & 0 \\ 1 & 0 & 1 & 1 \\ 1 & \bar{1} & 0 & \bar{1} \end{pmatrix}.$$

The resulting algorithm computes $s_1 = y_0 + y_1$, $s_2 = y_0 - y_1$, $s_3 = y_2 - y_0$, $s_4 = y_2 - y_1$, $s_5 = s_1 + y_2$; $m_1 = \frac{1}{3}(x_0 + x_1 + x_2)s_5$, $m_2 = \frac{1}{3}(x_0 + x_1 - 2x_2)s_2$, $m_3 = \frac{1}{3}(x_0 - 2x_1 + x_2)s_3$, $m_4 = \frac{1}{3}(-2x_0 + x_1 + x_2)s_4$; $t_1 = m_1 + m_2$, $t_2 = m_1 - m_2$, $t_3 = m_1 + m_3$, $w_0 = t_1 - m_3$, $w_1 = t_3 + m_4$, $w_2 = t_2 - m_4$.

52. Let $k = \langle k', k'' \rangle$ when $k \bmod n' = k'$ and $k \bmod n'' = k''$. Then we wish to compute $w_{\langle k', k'' \rangle} = \sum x_{\langle i', i'' \rangle} y_{\langle j', j'' \rangle}$ summed for $i' + j' \equiv k'$ (modulo n') and $i'' + j'' \equiv k''$ (modulo n''). This can be done by applying the n' algorithm to the $2n'$ vectors $X_{i'}$ and $Y_{j'}$ of length n'', obtaining the n' vectors $W_{k'}$. Each vector addition becomes n'' additions, each parameter multiplication becomes n'' parameter multiplications, and each chain multiplication of vectors is replaced by a cyclic convolution of degree n''. [If the subalgorithms use the minimum number of chain multiplications over the rationals, this algorithm uses $2(n' - d(n'))(n'' - d(n''))$ more than the minimum, where $d(n)$ is the number of divisors of n, because of exercise 4.6.2–32 and Theorem W.]

53. (a) Let $n(k) = (p - 1)p^{e-k-1} = \varphi(p^{e-k})$ for $0 \le k < e$, and $n(k) = 1$ for $k \ge e$. Represent the numbers $\{1, \ldots, m\}$ in the form $a^i p^k$ (modulo m), where $0 \le k \le e$ and $0 \le i < n(k)$, and a is a fixed primitive element modulo p^e. For example, when $m = 9$ we can let $a = 2$; the values are $\{2^0 3^0, 2^1 3^0, 2^0 3^1, 2^2 3^0, 2^5 3^0, 2^1 3^1, 2^4 3^0, 2^3 3^0, 2^0 3^2\}$. Then $f(a^i p^k) = \sum_{0 \le l \le e} \sum_{0 \le j < n(l)} \omega^{g(i,j,k,l)} F(a^j p^l)$ where $g(i, j, k, l) = a^{i+j} p^{k+l}$.

We shall compute $f_{ikl} = \sum_{0 \le j < n(l)} \omega^{g(i,j,k,l)} F(a^j p^l)$ for $0 \le i < n(k)$ and for each k and l. This is a cyclic convolution of degree $n(k + l)$ on the values $x_i = \omega^{a^i p^{k+l}}$ and $y_s = \sum_{0 \le j < n(l)}[s + j \equiv 0 \pmod{n(k + l)}] F(a^j p^l)$, since f_{ikl} is $\sum x_r y_s$ summed over $r + s \equiv i \pmod{n(k+l)}$. The Fourier transform is obtained by summing appropriate f_{ikl}'s. [*Note:* When linear combinations of the x_i are formed, for example as in (69), the result will be purely real or purely imaginary, when the cyclic convolution algorithm has been constructed by using rule (59) with $u^{n(k)} - 1 = (u^{n(k)/2} - 1)(u^{n(k)/2} + 1)$. The reason is that reduction mod $(u^{n(k)/2} - 1)$ produces a polynomial with real coefficients $\omega^j + \omega^{-j}$ while reduction mod $(u^{n(k)/2} + 1)$ produces a polynomial with imaginary coefficients $\omega^j - \omega^{-j}$.]

When $p = 2$ an analogous construction applies, using the representation $(-1)^i a^j 2^k$ (modulo m), where $0 \le k \le e$ and $0 \le i \le \min(e - k, 1)$ and $0 \le j < 2^{e-k-2}$. In this case we use the construction of exercise 52 with $n' = 2$ and $n'' = 2^{e-k-2}$; although these numbers are not relatively prime, the construction does yield the desired direct product of cyclic convolutions.

(b) Let $a'm' + a''m'' = 1$; and let $\omega' = \omega^{a''m''}$, $\omega'' = \omega^{a'm'}$. Define $s' = s \bmod m'$, $s'' = s \bmod m''$, $t' = t \bmod m'$, $t'' = t \bmod m''$, so that $\omega^{st} = (\omega')^{s't'}(\omega'')^{s''t''}$. It follows that $f(s', s'') = \sum_{t'=0}^{m'-1} \sum_{t''=0}^{m''-1} (\omega')^{s't'}(\omega'')^{s''t''} F(t', t'')$; in other words, the one-dimensional Fourier transform on m elements is actually a two-dimensional Fourier transform on $m' \times m''$ elements, in slight disguise.

We shall deal with "normal" algorithms consisting of (i) a number of sums s_i of the F's and s's; followed by (ii) a number of products m_j, each of which is obtained by multiplying one of the F's or s's by a real or imaginary number α_j; followed by (iii) a number of further sums t_k, each of which is formed from m's or t's (not F's or s's). The final values must be m's or t's. For example, the "normal" Fourier transform

scheme for $m = 5$ constructed from (69) and the method of part (a) is as follows:
$s_1 = F(1) + F(4)$, $s_2 = F(3) + F(2)$, $s_3 = s_1 + s_2$, $s_4 = s_1 - s_2$, $s_5 = F(1) - F(4)$,
$s_6 = F(2) - F(3)$, $s_7 = s_5 - s_6$; $m_1 = \frac{1}{4}(\omega + \omega^2 + \omega^4 + \omega^3)s_3$, $m_2 = \frac{1}{4}(\omega - \omega^2 + \omega^4 - \omega^3)s_4$,
$m_3 = \frac{1}{2}(\omega + \omega^2 - \omega^4 - \omega^3)s_5$, $m_4 = \frac{1}{2}(-\omega + \omega^2 + \omega^4 - \omega^3)s_6$, $m_5 = \frac{1}{2}(\omega^3 - \omega^2)s_7$,
$m_6 = 1 \cdot F(5)$, $m_7 = 1 \cdot s_3$; $t_0 = m_1 + m_6$, $t_1 = t_0 + m_2$, $t_2 = m_3 + m_5$, $t_3 = t_0 - m_2$,
$t_4 = m_4 - m_5$, $t_5 = t_1 + t_2$, $t_6 = t_3 + t_4$, $t_7 = t_1 - t_2$, $t_8 = t_3 - t_4$, $t_9 = m_6 + m_7$.
Note the multiplication by 1 shown in m_6 and m_7; this is required by our conventions,
and it is important to include such cases for use in recursive constructions (although
the multiplications need not really be done). Here $m_6 = f_{001}$, $m_7 = f_{010}$, $t_5 = f_{000} + f_{001} = f(2^0)$, $t_6 = f_{100} + f_{101} = f(2^1)$, etc. We can improve the scheme by
introducing $s_8 = s_3 + F(5)$, replacing m_1 by $(\frac{1}{4}(\omega + \omega^2 + \omega^4 + \omega^3) - 1)s_3$ [this is $-\frac{5}{4}s_3$],
replacing m_6 by $1 \cdot s_8$, and deleting m_7 and t_9; this saves one of the trivial multiplications
by 1, and it will be advantageous when the scheme is used to build larger ones. In the
improved scheme, $f(5) = m_6$, $f(1) = t_5$, $f(2) = t_6$, $f(3) = t_8$, $f(4) = t_7$.

Now suppose we have normal one-dimensional schemes for m' and m'', using
respectively (a', a'') complex additions, (t', t'') trivial multiplications by ± 1 or $\pm i$, and
a total of (c', c'') complex multiplications including the trivial ones. (The nontrivial
complex multiplications are all "simple" since they involve only two real multiplications
and no real additions.) We can construct a normal scheme for the two-dimensional
$m' \times m''$ case by applying the m' scheme to vectors $F(t', *)$ of length m''. Each s_i
step becomes m'' additions; each m_j becomes a Fourier transform on m'' elements,
but with all of the α's in this algorithm multiplied by α_j; and each t_k becomes m''
additions. Thus the new algorithm has $(a'm'' + c'a'')$ complex additions, $t't''$ trivial
multiplications, and a total of $c'c''$ complex multiplications.

Using these techniques, Winograd has found normal one-dimensional schemes for
the following small values of m with the following costs (a, t, c):

$m = 2$ $(2, 2, 2)$		$m = 7$ $(36, 1, 9)$
$m = 3$ $(6, 1, 3)$		$m = 8$ $(26, 6, 8)$
$m = 4$ $(8, 4, 4)$		$m = 9$ $(46, 1, 12)$
$m = 5$ $(17, 1, 6)$		$m = 16$ $(74, 8, 18)$

By combining these schemes as described above, we obtain methods that use fewer
arithmetic operations than the "fast Fourier transform" (FFT) discussed in exercise 14.
For example, when $m = 1008 = 7 \cdot 9 \cdot 16$, the costs come to $(17946, 8, 1944)$, so we can do
a Fourier transform on 1008 complex numbers with 3872 real multiplications and 35892
real additions. It is possible to improve on Winograd's method for combining relatively
prime moduli by using multidimensional convolutions, as shown by Nussbaumer and
Quandalle in *IBM J. Res. and Devel.* **22** (1978), 134–144; their ingenious approach
reduces the amount of computation needed for 1008-point complex Fourier transforms
to 3084 real multiplications and 34668 real additions. By contrast, the FFT on 1024
complex numbers involves 14344 real multiplications and 27652 real additions. If the
two-passes-at-once improvement in the answer to exercise 14 is used, however, the FFT
on 1024 complex numbers needs only 10936 real multiplications and 25948 additions,
and it is not difficult to implement. Therefore the subtler methods are faster only on
machines that take significantly longer to multiply than to add.

[*References: Proc. Nat. Acad. Sci. USA* **73** (1976), 1005–1006; *Math. Comp.* **32**
(1978), 175–199; *Advances in Math.* **32** (1979), 83–117; *IEEE Trans.* **ASSP-27** (1979),
169–181.]

54. $\max(2e_1\deg(p_1) - 1, \ldots, 2e_q\deg(p_q) - 1, q + 1)$.

55. $2n' - q'$, where n' is the degree of the minimum polynomial of P (the monic polynomial μ of least degree such that $\mu(P)$ is the zero matrix) and q' is the number of distinct irreducible factors it has. (Reduce P by similarity transformations.)

56. Let $t_{ijk} + t_{jik} = \tau_{ijk} + \tau_{jik}$, for all i, j, k. If (A, B, C) is a realization of (t_{ijk}) of rank r, then $\sum_{l=1}^{r} c_{kl} (\sum_i a_{il} x_i)(\sum_j b_{jl} x_j) = \sum_{i,j} t_{ijk} x_i x_j = \sum_{i,j} \tau_{ijk} x_i x_j$ for all k. Conversely, let the lth chain multiplication of a polynomial chain, for $1 \le l \le r$, be the product $(\alpha_l + \sum_i \alpha_{il} x_i)(\beta_l + \sum_j \beta_{jl} x_j)$, where α_l and β_l denote possible constant terms and/or nonlinear terms. All terms of degree 2 appearing at any step of the chain can be expressed as a linear combination $\sum_{l=1}^{r} c_l (\sum_i a_{il} x_i)(\sum_j b_{jl} x_j)$; hence the chain defines a tensor (t_{ijk}) of rank $\le r$ such that $t_{ijk} + t_{jik} = \tau_{ijk} + \tau_{jik}$. This establishes the hint. Now $\mathrm{rank}(\tau_{ijk} + \tau_{jik}) = \mathrm{rank}(t_{ijk} + t_{jik}) \le \mathrm{rank}(t_{ijk}) + \mathrm{rank}(t_{jik}) = 2\,\mathrm{rank}(t_{ijk})$.

A bilinear form in $x_1, \ldots, x_m, y_1, \ldots, y_n$ is a quadratic form in $m + n$ variables, where $\tau_{ijk} = t_{i,j-m,k}$ for $i \le m$ and $j > m$, otherwise $\tau_{ijk} = 0$. Now $\mathrm{rank}(\tau_{ijk}) + \mathrm{rank}(\tau_{jik}) \ge \mathrm{rank}(t_{ijk})$, since we obtain a realization of (t_{ijk}) by suppressing the last n rows of A and the first m rows of B in a realization (A, B, C) of $(\tau_{ijk} + \tau_{jik})$.

57. Let N be the smallest power of 2 that exceeds $2n$, and let $u_{n+1} = \cdots = u_{N-1} = v_{n+1} = \cdots = v_{N-1} = 0$. If $U_s = \sum_{t=0}^{N-1} \omega^{st} u_t$ and $V_s = \sum_{t=0}^{N-1} \omega^{st} v_t$ for $0 \le s < N$, where $\omega = e^{2\pi i/N}$, then $\sum_{s=0}^{N-1} \omega^{-st} U_s V_s = N \sum u_{t_1} v_{t_2}$, where the latter sum is taken over all t_1 and t_2 with $0 \le t_1, t_2 < N$, $t_1 + t_2 \equiv t$ (modulo N). The terms vanish unless $t_1 \le n$ and $t_2 \le n$, so $t_1 + t_2 < N$; thus the sum is the coefficient of z^t in the product $u(z)v(z)$. If we use the method of exercise 14 to compute the Fourier transforms and the inverse transforms, the number of complex operations is $O(N \log N) + O(N \log N) + O(N) + O(N \log N)$; and $N \le 4n$. [See Section 4.3.3C and the paper by J. M. Pollard, *Math. Comp.* **25** (1971), 365–374.]

When multiplying integer polynomials, it is possible to use an *integer* number ω that is of order 2^t modulo a prime p, and to determine the results modulo sufficiently many primes. Useful primes in this regard, together with their least primitive roots r (from which we take $\omega = r^{(p-1)/2^t} \bmod p$ when $p \bmod 2^t = 1$), can be found as described in Section 4.5.4. For $t = 9$, the ten largest cases $< 2^{35}$ are $p = 2^{35} - 512a + 1$, where $(a, r) = (28, 7)$, $(31, 10)$, $(34, 13)$, $(56, 3)$, $(58, 10)$, $(76, 5)$, $(80, 3)$, $(85, 11)$, $(91, 5)$, $(101, 3)$; the ten largest cases $< 2^{31}$ are $p = 2^{31} - 512a + 1$, where $(a, r) = (1, 10)$, $(11, 3)$, $(19, 11)$, $(20, 3)$, $(29, 3)$, $(35, 3)$, $(55, 19)$, $(65, 6)$, $(95, 3)$, $(121, 10)$. For larger t, all primes p of the form $2^t q + 1$ where $q < 32$ is odd and $2^{24} < p < 2^{36}$ are given by $(p - 1, r) = (11 \cdot 2^{21}, 3)$, $(25 \cdot 2^{20}, 3)$, $(27 \cdot 2^{20}, 5)$, $(25 \cdot 2^{22}, 3)$, $(27 \cdot 2^{22}, 7)$, $(5 \cdot 2^{25}, 3)$, $(7 \cdot 2^{26}, 3)$, $(27 \cdot 2^{26}, 13)$, $(15 \cdot 2^{27}, 31)$, $(17 \cdot 2^{27}, 3)$, $(3 \cdot 2^{30}, 5)$, $(13 \cdot 2^{28}, 3)$, $(29 \cdot 2^{27}, 3)$, $(23 \cdot 2^{29}, 5)$. Some of the latter primes can be used with $\omega = 2^e$ for appropriate small e. For a discussion of such primes, see R. M. Robinson, *Proc. Amer. Math. Soc.* **9** (1958), 673–681; S. W. Golomb, *Math. Comp.* **30** (1976), 657–663. Additional all-integer methods are cited in the answer to exercise 4.6–5.

However, the method of exercise 59 will almost always be preferable in practice.

58. (a) In general if (A, B, C) realizes (t_{ijk}), then $((x_1, \ldots, x_m)A, B, C)$ is a realization of the $1 \times n \times s$ matrix whose entry in row j, column k is $\sum x_i t_{ijk}$. So there must be at least as many nonzero elements in $(x_1, \ldots, x_m)A$ as the rank of this matrix. In the case of the $m \times n \times (m+n-1)$ tensor corresponding to polynomial multiplication of degree $m - 1$ by degree $n - 1$, the corresponding matrix has rank n whenever $(x_1, \ldots, x_m) \ne (0, \ldots, 0)$. A similar statement holds with $A \leftrightarrow B$ and $m \leftrightarrow n$.

Notes: In particular, if we work over the field of 2 elements, this says that the rows of A modulo 2 form a "linear code" of m vectors having distance at least n, whenever (A, B, C) is a realization consisting entirely of integers. This observation, due to R. W. Brockett and D. Dobkin [*Linear Algebra and Its Applications* **19** (1978), 207–235, Theorem 14; see also Lempel and Winograd, *IEEE Trans.* **IT-23** (1977), 503–508; Lempel, Seroussi, and Winograd, *Theoretical Comp. Sci.* **22** (1983), 285–296], can be used to obtain nontrivial lower bounds on the rank over the integers. For example, M. R. Brown and D. Dobkin [*IEEE Trans.* **C-29** (1980), 337–340] have used it to show that realizations of $n \times n$ polynomial multiplication over the integers must have rank $\geq \alpha n$ for all sufficiently large n, when α is any real number less than

$$\alpha_{\min} = 3.52762\,68026\,32407\,48061\,54754\,08128\,07512\,70182+;$$

here $\alpha_{\min} = 1/H(\sin^2 \theta, \cos^2 \theta)$, where $H(p, q) = p \lg(1/p) + q \lg(1/q)$ is the binary entropy function and $\theta \approx 1.34686$ is the root of $\sin^2(\theta - \pi/4) = H(\sin^2 \theta, \cos^2 \theta)$. An all-integer realization of rank $O(n \log n)$, based on cyclotomic polynomials, has been constructed by M. Kaminski [*J. Algorithms* **9** (1988), 137–147].

$$(b) \begin{pmatrix} 1\,0\,0\,0\,0\,1\,1\,1 \\ 0\,1\,0\,0\,1\,1\,0\,1 \\ 0\,0\,1\,1\,0\,0\,1\,1 \end{pmatrix}, \begin{pmatrix} 1\,0\,0\,0\,0\,1\,1\,1 \\ 0\,1\,0\,0\,0\,1\,0\,1 \\ 0\,0\,1\,0\,0\,0\,1\,1 \\ 0\,0\,0\,1\,1\,0\,0\,1 \end{pmatrix}, \begin{pmatrix} 1\,0\,0\,0\,0\,0\,0\,0 \\ \bar{1}\,\bar{1}\,0\,0\,0\,1\,0\,0 \\ \bar{1}\,1\,\bar{1}\,0\,0\,0\,1\,0 \\ 1\,0\,0\,\bar{1}\,\bar{1}\,\bar{1}\,\bar{1}\,1 \\ 0\,0\,1\,0\,1\,0\,0\,0 \\ 0\,0\,0\,1\,0\,0\,0\,0 \end{pmatrix}.$$

The following economical ways to realize the multiplication of general polynomials of degrees 2, 3, and 4 have been presented by H. Cohen and A. K. Lenstra [see *Math. Comp.* **48** (1987), S1–S2]:

$$\begin{pmatrix} 1\,0\,0\,1\,1\,0 \\ 0\,1\,0\,1\,0\,1 \\ 0\,0\,1\,0\,1\,1 \end{pmatrix}, \quad \text{same,} \quad \begin{pmatrix} 1\,0\,0\,0\,0\,0 \\ \bar{1}\,\bar{1}\,0\,1\,0\,0 \\ \bar{1}\,1\,\bar{1}\,0\,1\,0 \\ 0\,\bar{1}\,\bar{1}\,0\,0\,1 \\ 0\,0\,1\,0\,0\,0 \end{pmatrix};$$

$$\begin{pmatrix} 1\,0\,0\,0\,1\,1\,0\,0\,1 \\ 0\,1\,0\,0\,1\,0\,0\,1\,1 \\ 0\,0\,1\,0\,0\,1\,1\,0\,1 \\ 0\,0\,0\,1\,0\,0\,1\,1\,1 \end{pmatrix}, \quad \text{same,} \quad \begin{pmatrix} 1\,0\,0\,0\,0\,0\,0\,0\,0 \\ \bar{1}\,\bar{1}\,0\,0\,1\,0\,0\,0\,0 \\ \bar{1}\,1\,\bar{1}\,0\,0\,1\,0\,0\,0 \\ 1\,1\,1\,1\,\bar{1}\,\bar{1}\,\bar{1}\,\bar{1}\,1 \\ 0\,\bar{1}\,1\,\bar{1}\,0\,0\,0\,1\,0 \\ 0\,0\,\bar{1}\,\bar{1}\,0\,0\,1\,0\,0 \\ 0\,0\,0\,1\,0\,0\,0\,0\,0 \end{pmatrix};$$

$$\begin{pmatrix} 1\,0\,0\,1\,1\,0\,1\,0\,1\,1\,0\,0\,0\,0 \\ 0\,1\,0\,1\,0\,1\,0\,1\,1\,0\,1\,0\,0\,0 \\ 0\,0\,1\,0\,1\,1\,0\,0\,0\,1\,1\,0\,0\,0 \\ 0\,0\,0\,0\,0\,0\,1\,0\,1\,1\,0\,1\,0\,1 \\ 0\,0\,0\,0\,0\,0\,0\,1\,1\,0\,1\,0\,1\,1 \end{pmatrix}, \quad \text{same,} \quad \begin{pmatrix} 1\,0\,0\,0\,0\,0\,0\,0\,0\,0\,0\,0\,0\,0 \\ \bar{1}\,\bar{1}\,0\,1\,0\,0\,0\,0\,0\,0\,0\,0\,0\,0 \\ \bar{1}\,1\,\bar{1}\,0\,1\,0\,0\,0\,0\,0\,0\,0\,0\,0 \\ \bar{1}\,\bar{1}\,\bar{1}\,0\,0\,1\,1\,0\,0\,0\,0\,\bar{1}\,0\,0 \\ 1\,1\,1\,\bar{1}\,0\,0\,\bar{1}\,\bar{1}\,1\,0\,0\,1\,1\,\bar{1} \\ 1\,\bar{1}\,0\,0\,\bar{1}\,0\,\bar{1}\,1\,0\,1\,0\,0\,\bar{1}\,0 \\ 0\,1\,0\,0\,0\,\bar{1}\,0\,\bar{1}\,0\,0\,1\,1\,0\,0 \\ 0\,0\,0\,0\,0\,0\,0\,0\,0\,0\,0\,\bar{1}\,\bar{1}\,1 \\ 0\,0\,0\,0\,0\,0\,0\,0\,0\,0\,0\,0\,1\,0 \end{pmatrix}.$$

In each case the A and B matrices are identical.

59. [*IEEE Trans.* **ASSP-28** (1980), 205–215.] Note that cyclic convolution is polynomial multiplication mod $u^n - 1$, and negacyclic convolution is polynomial multiplication mod $u^n + 1$. Let us now change notation, replacing n by 2^n; we shall consider recursive algorithms for cyclic and negacyclic convolution $(z_0, \ldots, z_{2^n-1})$ of $(x_0, \ldots, x_{2^n-1})$ with $(y_0, \ldots, y_{2^n-1})$. The algorithms are presented in unoptimized form, for brevity and ease in exposition; readers who implement them will notice that many things can be streamlined. For example, the final value of $Z_{2m-1}(w)$ in step N5 will always be zero.

C1. [Test for simple case.] If $n = 1$, set

$$z_0 \leftarrow x_0 y_0 + x_1 y_1, \qquad z_1 \leftarrow (x_0 + x_1)(y_0 + y_1) - z_0,$$

and terminate. Otherwise set $m \leftarrow 2^{n-1}$.

C2. [Remainderize.] For $0 \le k < m$, set $(x_k, x_{m+k}) \leftarrow (x_k + x_{m+k}, x_k - x_{m+k})$ and $(y_k, y_{m+k}) \leftarrow (y_k + y_{m+k}, y_k - y_{m+k})$. (Now we have $x(u) \bmod (u^m - 1) = x_0 + \cdots + x_{m-1}u^{m-1}$ and $x(u) \bmod (u^m + 1) = x_m + \cdots + x_{2m-1}u^{m-1}$; we will compute $x(u)y(u) \bmod (u^m - 1)$ and $x(u)y(u) \bmod (u^m + 1)$, then we will combine the results by (59).)

C3. [Recurse.] Set $(z_0, \ldots, z_{m-1})$ to the cyclic convolution of $(x_0, \ldots, x_{m-1})$ with $(y_0, \ldots, y_{m-1})$. Also set $(z_m, \ldots, z_{2m-1})$ to the negacyclic convolution of $(x_m, \ldots, x_{2m-1})$ with $(y_m, \ldots, y_{2m-1})$.

C4. [Unremainderize.] For $0 \le k < m$, set $(z_k, z_{m+k}) \leftarrow \frac{1}{2}(z_k + z_{m+k}, z_k - z_{m+k})$. Now $(z_0, \ldots, z_{2m-1})$ is the desired answer. ∎

N1. [Test for simple case.] If $n = 1$, set $t \leftarrow x_0(y_0 + y_1)$, $z_0 \leftarrow t - (x_0 + x_1)y_1$, $z_1 \leftarrow t + (x_1 - x_0)y_0$, and terminate. Otherwise set $m \leftarrow 2^{\lfloor n/2 \rfloor}$ and $r \leftarrow 2^{\lceil n/2 \rceil}$. (The following steps use 2^{n+1} auxiliary variables X_{ij} for $0 \le i < 2m$ and $0 \le j < r$, to represent $2m$ polynomials $X_i(w) = X_{i0} + X_{i1}w + \cdots + X_{i(r-1)}w^{r-1}$; similarly, there are 2^{n+1} auxiliary variables Y_{ij}.)

N2. [Initialize auxiliary polynomials.] Set $X_{ij} \leftarrow X_{(i+m)j} \leftarrow x_{mj+i}$, $Y_{ij} \leftarrow Y_{(i+m)j} \leftarrow y_{mj+i}$, for $0 \le i < m$ and $0 \le j < r$. (At this point we have $x(u) = X_0(u^m) + uX_1(u^m) + \cdots + u^{m-1}X_{m-1}(u^m)$, and a similar formula holds for $y(u)$. Our strategy will be to multiply these polynomials modulo $(u^{mr} + 1) = (u^{2^n} + 1)$, by operating modulo $(w^r + 1)$ on the polynomials $X(w)$ and $Y(w)$, finding their cyclic convolution of length $2m$ and thereby obtaining $x(u)y(u) \equiv Z_0(u^m) + uZ_1(u^m) + \cdots + u^{2m-1}Z_{2m-1}(u^m)$.)

N3. [Transform.] (Now we will essentially do a fast Fourier transform on the polynomials $(X_0, \ldots, X_{m-1}, 0, \ldots, 0)$ and $(Y_0, \ldots, Y_{m-1}, 0, \ldots, 0)$, using $w^{r/m}$ as a $(2m)$th root of unity. This is efficient, because multiplication by a power of w is not really a multiplication at all.) For $j = \lfloor n/2 \rfloor - 1, \ldots, 1, 0$ (in this order), do the following for all m binary numbers $s + t = (s_{\lfloor n/2 \rfloor} \ldots s_{j+1} 0 \ldots 0)_2 + (0 \ldots 0 t_{j-1} \ldots t_0)_2$: Replace $(X_{s+t}(w), X_{s+t+2^j}(w))$ by the pair of polynomials $(X_{s+t}(w) + w^{(r/m)s'}X_{s+t+2^j}(w), X_{s+t}(w) - w^{(r/m)s'}X_{s+t+2^j}(w))$, where $s' = 2^j(s_{j+1} \ldots s_{\lfloor n/2 \rfloor})_2$. (We are evaluating 4.3.3–(39), with $K = 2m$ and $\omega = w^{r/m}$; notice the bit-reversal in s'. The polynomial operation $X_i(w) \leftarrow X_i(w) + w^k X_l(w)$ means, more precisely, that we set $X_{ij} \leftarrow X_{ij} + X_{l(j-k)}$ for $k \le j < r$, and $X_{ij} \leftarrow X_{ij} - X_{l(j-k+r)}$ for $0 \le j < k$. A copy of $X_l(w)$ can be made without wasting much space.) Do the same transformation on the Y's.

N4. [Recurse.] For $0 \leq i < 2m$, set $(Z_{i0}, \ldots, Z_{i(r-1)})$ to the negacyclic convolution of $(X_{i0}, \ldots, X_{i(r-1)})$ and $(Y_{i0}, \ldots, Y_{i(r-1)})$.

N5. [Untransform.] For $j = 0, 1, \ldots, \lfloor n/2 \rfloor$ (in this order), and for all m choices of s and t as in steps N3, set $\left(Z_{s+t}(w), Z_{s+t+2^j}(w)\right)$ to

$$\tfrac{1}{2}\left(Z_{s+t}(w) + Z_{s+t+2^j}(w), \; w^{-(r/m)s'}(Z_{s+t}(w) - Z_{s+t+2^j}(w))\right).$$

N6. [Repack.] (Now we have accomplished the goal stated at the end of step N2, since it is easy to show that the transform of the Z's is the product of the transforms of the X's and the Y's.) Set $z_i \leftarrow Z_{i0} - Z_{(m+i)(r-1)}$ and $z_{mj+i} \leftarrow Z_{ij} + Z_{(m+i)(j-1)}$ for $0 < j < r$, for $0 \leq i < m$. ∎

It is easy to verify that at most n extra bits of precision are needed for the intermediate variables in this calculation; for example, if $|x_i| \leq M$ for $0 \leq i < 2^n$ at the beginning of the algorithm, then all of the x and X variables will be bounded by $2^n M$ throughout. All of the z and Z variables will be bounded by $(2^n M)^2$, which is n more bits than required to hold the final convolution.

Algorithm N performs A_n addition-subtractions, D_n halvings, and M_n multiplications, where $A_1 = 5$, $D_1 = 0$, $M_1 = 3$; for $n > 1$ we have $A_n = \lfloor n/2 \rfloor 2^{n+2} + 2^{\lfloor n/2 \rfloor + 1} A_{\lceil n/2 \rceil} + (\lfloor n/2 \rfloor + 1)2^{n+1} + 2^n$, $D_n = 2^{\lfloor n/2 \rfloor + 1} D_{\lceil n/2 \rceil} + (\lfloor n/2 \rfloor + 1)2^{n+1}$, and $M_n = 2^{\lfloor n/2 \rfloor + 1} M_{\lceil n/2 \rceil}$. The solutions are $A_n = 11 \cdot 2^{n-1+\lceil \lg n \rceil} - 3 \cdot 2^n + 6 \cdot 2^n S_n$, $D_n = 4 \cdot 2^{n-1+\lceil \lg n \rceil} - 2 \cdot 2^n + 2 \cdot 2^n S_n$, $M_n = 3 \cdot 2^{n-1+\lceil \lg n \rceil}$; here S_n satisfies the recurrence $S_1 = 0$, $S_n = 2S_{\lceil n/2 \rceil} + \lfloor n/2 \rfloor$, and it is not difficult to prove the inequalities $\tfrac{1}{2} n \lceil \lg n \rceil \leq S_n \leq S_{n+1} \leq \tfrac{1}{2} n \lg n + n$ for all $n \geq 1$. Algorithm C does approximately the same amount of work as Algorithm N.

60. (a) In Σ_1, for example, we can group all terms having a common value of j and k into a single trilinear term; this gives ν^2 trilinear terms when $(j, k) \in E \times E$, plus ν^2 when $(j, k) \in E \times O$ and ν^2 when $(j, k) \in O \times E$. When $\hat{\jmath} = k$ we can also include $-x_{jj} y_{\hat{\jmath}\hat{\jmath}} z_{\hat{\jmath}\hat{\jmath}}$ in Σ_1, free of charge. [In the case $n = 10$, the method multiplies 10×10 matrices with 710 noncommutative multiplications; this is almost as good as seven 5×5 multiplications by the method of Sedoglavic and Smirnov cited in the answer to exercise 12, although Winograd's scheme (35) uses only 600 when commutativity is allowed. With a similar scheme, Pan showed for the first time that $M(n) < n^{2.8}$ for all large n, and this awakened great interest in the problem. See *SICOMP* **9** (1980), 321–342.]

(b) Here we simply let S be all the indices (i, j, k) of one problem, $\tilde{S}$ the indices $[k, i, j]$ of the other, and work with an $(mn+sm) \times (ns+mn) \times (sm+ns)$ tensor. [When $m = n = s = 10$, the result is quite surprising: We can multiply two separate 10×10 matrices with 1300 noncommutative multiplications, while no scheme is known that would multiply each of them with 650.]

61. (a) Replace $a_{il}(u)$ by $ua_{il}(u)$. (b) Let $a_{il}(u) = \sum_\mu a_{il\mu} u^\mu$, etc., in a polynomial realization of length $r = \mathrm{rank}_d(t_{ijk})$. Then $t_{ijk} = \sum_{\mu+\nu+\sigma=d} \sum_{l=1}^r a_{il\mu} b_{jl\nu} c_{kl\sigma}$. [This result can be improved to $\mathrm{rank}(t_{ijk}) \leq (2d+1)\,\mathrm{rank}_d(t_{ijk})$ in an infinite field, because the trilinear form $\sum_{\mu+\nu+\sigma=d} a_\mu b_\nu c_\sigma$ corresponds to multiplication of polynomials modulo u^{d+1}, as pointed out by Bini and Pan. See *Calcolo* **17** (1980), 87–97.] (c, d) This is clear from the realizations in exercise 48.

(e) Suppose we have realizations of t and rt' such that $\sum_{l=1}^r a_{il} b_{jl} c_{kl} = t_{ijk} u^d + O(u^{d+1})$ and $\sum_{L=1}^R A_{\langle ii' \rangle L} B_{\langle jj' \rangle L} C_{\langle kk' \rangle L} = [i = j = k]\, t'_{i'j'k'} u^{d'} + O(u^{d'+1})$. Then

$$\sum_{L=1}^R \sum_{l=1}^r a_{il} A_{\langle li' \rangle L} \sum_{m=1}^r b_{jm} B_{\langle mj' \rangle L} \sum_{n=1}^r c_{kn} C_{\langle nk' \rangle L} = t_{ijk} t'_{i'j'k'} u^{d+d'} + O(u^{d+d'+1}).$$

62. The rank is 3, by the method of proof in Theorem W with $P = \left(\begin{smallmatrix} 0 & 1 \\ 0 & 0 \end{smallmatrix}\right)$. The border rank cannot be 1, since we cannot have $a_1(u)b_1(u)c_1(u) \equiv a_1(u)b_2(u)c_2(u) \equiv u^d$ and $a_1(u)b_2(u)c_1(u) \equiv a_1(u)b_1(u)c_2(u) \equiv 0$ (modulo u^{d+1}). The border rank is 2 because of the realization $\left(\begin{smallmatrix} 1 & 1 \\ u & 0 \end{smallmatrix}\right)$, $\left(\begin{smallmatrix} u & 0 \\ 1 & 1 \end{smallmatrix}\right)$, $\left(\begin{smallmatrix} 1 & -1 \\ 0 & u \end{smallmatrix}\right)$.

The notion of border rank was introduced by Bini, Capovani, Lotti, and Romani in *Information Processing Letters* **8** (1979), 234–235. For a modern treatment, including proofs that $\underline{\text{rank}}(T(2,2,3)) = 10$ and $\underline{\text{rank}}(T(2,3,3)) = 14$, see A. Conner, A. Harper, and J. M. Landsberg, *Forum of Mathematics, Pi* **11** (2023), e17:1–30.

63. (a) Let the elements of $T(m,n,s)$ and $T(M,N,S)$ be denoted by $t_{\langle i,j'\rangle\langle j,k'\rangle\langle k,i'\rangle}$ and $T_{\langle I,J'\rangle\langle J,K'\rangle\langle K,I'\rangle}$, respectively. Each element $\mathcal{T}_{\langle \mathcal{I},\mathcal{J}'\rangle\langle \mathcal{J},\mathcal{K}'\rangle\langle \mathcal{K},\mathcal{I}'\rangle}$ of the direct product, where $\mathcal{I} = \langle i,I\rangle$, $\mathcal{J} = \langle j,J\rangle$, and $\mathcal{K} = \langle k,K\rangle$, is equal to $t_{\langle i,j'\rangle\langle j,k'\rangle\langle k,i'\rangle} \times T_{\langle I,J'\rangle\langle J,K'\rangle\langle K,I'\rangle}$ by definition, so it is $[\mathcal{I}' = \mathcal{I}$ and $\mathcal{J}' = \mathcal{J}$ and $\mathcal{K}' = \mathcal{K}]$.

(b) Apply exercise 61(e) with $M(N) = \text{rank}_0(T(N,N,N))$.

(c) We have $M(mns) \le r^3$, since $T(mns,mns,mns) = T(m,n,s) \otimes T(n,s,m) \otimes T(s,m,n)$. If $M(n) \le R$ we have $M(n^h) \le R^h$ for all h, and it follows that $M(N) \le M(n^{\lceil \log_n N\rceil}) \le R^{\lceil \log_n N\rceil} \le RN^{\log R/\log n}$. [This result appears in Pan's paper of 1972.]

(d) We have $M_d(mns) \le r^3$ for some d, where $M_d(n) = \text{rank}_d(T(n,n,n))$. If $M_d(n) \le R$ we have $M_{hd}(n^h) \le R^h$ for all h, and the stated formula follows since $M(n^h) \le \binom{hd+2}{2}R^h$ by exercise 61(b). In an infinite field we save a factor of $\log N$. [This result is due to Bini and Schönhage, 1979.]

64. We have $\sum_k (f_k(u) + \sum_{j \ne k} g_{j,k}(u)) = u^2\sum_{1 \le i,j,k \le 3} x_{ij}y_{jk}z_{ki} + O(u^3)$, when $f_k(u) = (x_{k1} + u^2x_{k2})(y_{2k} + u^2y_{1k})z_{kk} + (x_{k1} + u^2x_{k3})y_{3k}\big((1+u)z_{kk} - u(z_{1k} + z_{2k} + z_{3k})\big) - x_{k1}(y_{2k}+y_{3k})(z_{k1}+z_{k2}+z_{k3})$ and $g_{jk}(u) = (x_{k1}+u^2x_{j3})(y_{3k}+uy_{1j})(z_{kj}+uz_{jk}) + (x_{k1}+u^2x_{j2})(y_{2k}-uy_{1j})z_{kj}$. [The best upper bound known for $\text{rank}(T(3,3,3))$ is 23; see the answer to exercise 12. The paper cited in answer 62 proves that $\underline{\text{rank}}(T(2,2,2)) = 7$ and $\underline{\text{rank}}(T(3,3,3)) \ge 17$.]

65. The polynomial in the hint is $u^2 \sum_{i=1}^m \sum_{j=1}^n (x_iy_jz_{ij} + X_{ij}Y_{ij}Z) + O(u^3)$. Let X_{ij} and Y_{ij} be indeterminates for $1 \le i < m$ and $1 \le j < n$; also set $X_{in} = Y_{mj} = 0$, $X_{mj} = -\sum_{i=1}^{m-1} X_{ij}$, $Y_{in} = -\sum_{j=1}^{n-1} Y_{ij}$. Thus with $mn + 1$ multiplications of polynomials in the indeterminates we can compute x_iy_j for each i and j and also $\sum_{i=1}^m \sum_{j=1}^n X_{ij}Y_{ij} = \sum_{i=1}^{m-1} \sum_{j=1}^{n-1} X_{ij}Y_{ij}$. [*SICOMP* **10** (1981), 434–455. In this classic paper Schönhage also derived, among other things, the results of exercises 64, 66, and 67(i).]

66. (a) Let $\omega = \liminf_{n\to\infty} \log M(n)/\log n$; we have $\omega \ge 2$ by Lemma T. For all $\epsilon > 0$, there is an N with $M(N) < N^{\omega+\epsilon}$. The argument of exercise 63(c) now shows that $\log M(n)/\log n < \omega + 2\epsilon$ for all sufficiently large n.

(b) This is an immediate consequence of exercise 63(d).

(c) Let $r = \text{rank}(t)$, $q = (mns)^{\omega/3}$, $Q = (MNS)^{\omega/3}$. Given $\epsilon > 0$, there is an integer constant c_ϵ such that $M(p) \le c_\epsilon p^{\omega+\epsilon}$ for all positive integers p. For every integer $h > 0$ we have $t^h = \bigoplus_k \binom{h}{k}T(m^kM^{h-k}, n^kN^{h-k}, s^kS^{h-k})$, and $\text{rank}(t^h) \le r^h$. Given h and k, let $p = \lfloor\binom{h}{k}^{1/(\omega+\epsilon)}\rfloor$. Then

$$\underline{\text{rank}}(T(pm^kM^{h-k}, pn^kN^{h-k}, ps^kS^{h-k})) \le \underline{\text{rank}}(M(p)T(m^kM^{h-k}, n^kN^{h-k}, s^kS^{h-k}))$$
$$\le \underline{\text{rank}}(c_\epsilon\binom{h}{k}T(m^kM^{h-k}, n^kN^{h-k}, s^kS^{h-k}))$$
$$\le c_\epsilon r^h$$

by exercise 63(b), and it follows from part (b) that

$$p^\omega q^k Q^{h-k} = (pm^kM^{h-k}pn^kN^{h-k}ps^kS^{h-k})^{\omega/3} \le c_\epsilon r^h.$$

Since $p \geq \binom{h}{k}^{1/(\omega+\epsilon)}/2$ we have

$$\binom{h}{k} q^k Q^{h-k} \leq \binom{h}{k}^{\epsilon/(\omega+\epsilon)} (2p)^\omega q^k Q^{h-k} \leq 2^{\epsilon h/(\omega+\epsilon)} 2^\omega c_\epsilon r^h.$$

Therefore $(q + Q)^h \leq (h + 1) 2^{\epsilon h/(\omega+\epsilon)} 2^\omega c_\epsilon r^h$ for all h. And it follows that we must have $q + Q \leq 2^{\epsilon/(\omega+\epsilon)} r$ for all $\epsilon > 0$.

(d) Set $m = n = 4$ in exercise 65, and note that $16^{0.85} + 9^{0.85} > 17$.

67. (a) The $mn \times mns^2$ matrix $(t_{\langle ij'\rangle(\langle jk'\rangle\langle ki'\rangle)})$ has rank mn because it is a permutation matrix when restricted to the mn rows for which $k = k' = 1$.

(b) $((t \oplus t')_{i(jk)})$ is essentially $(t_{i(jk)}) \oplus (t'_{i(jk)})$, plus $n's + sn'$ additional columns of zeros. [Similarly we have $((t \otimes t')_{i(jk)}) = (t_{i(jk)}) \otimes (t'_{i(jk)})$ for the direct product.]

(c) Let D be the diagonal matrix $\mathrm{diag}(d_1, \ldots, d_r)$, so that $ADB^T = O$. We know by Lemma T that $\mathrm{rank}(A) = m$ and $\mathrm{rank}(B) = n$; hence $\mathrm{rank}(AD) = m$ and $\mathrm{rank}(DB^T) = n$. We can assume without loss of generality that the first m columns of A are linearly independent. Since the columns of B^T are in the null space of AD, we may also assume that the last n columns of B are linearly independent. Write A in the partitioned form $(A_1 \, A_2 \, A_3)$ where A_1 is $m \times m$ (and nonsingular), A_2 is $m \times q$, and A_3 is $m \times n$. Also partition D so that $AD = (A_1 D_1 \, A_2 D_2 \, A_3 D_3)$. Then there is a $q \times r$ matrix $W = (W_1 \, I \, O)$ such that $ADW^T = O$, namely $W_1 = -D_2 A_2^T A_1^{-T} D_1^{-1}$. Similarly, we may write $B = (B_1 \, B_2 \, B_3)$, and we find $VDB^T = O$ when $V = (O \, I \, V_3)$ is the $q \times r$ matrix with $V_3 = -D_2 B_2^T B_3^{-T} D_3^{-1}$. Notice that $UDV^T = D_2$, so the hint is established (more or less — after all, it was just a hint).

Now we let $A_{il}(u) = a_{il}$ for $1 \leq i \leq m$, $A_{(m+i)l}(u) = uv_{il}/d_{m+i}$; $B_{jl}(u) = b_{jl}$ for $1 \leq j \leq n$, $B_{(n+j)l}(u) = w_{jl}u$; $C_{kl}(u) = u^2 c_{kl}$ for $1 \leq k \leq s$, $C_{(s+1)l}(u) = d_l$. It follows that $\sum_{l=1}^r A_{il}(u) B_{jl}(u) C_{kl}(u) = u^2 t_{ijk} + O(u^3)$ if $k \leq s$, $u^2[i > m][j > n]$ if $k = s + 1$. [In this proof we did not need to assume that t is nondegenerate with respect to C.]

(d) Consider the following realization of $T(m, 1, n)$ with $r = mn+1$: $a_{il} = [\lfloor l/n \rfloor = i - 1]$, $b_{jl} = [l \bmod n = j]$, $b_{\langle ij\rangle l} = [l = (i-1)n + j]$, if $l \leq mn$; $a_{ir} = 1$, $b_{jr} = -1$, $c_{\langle ij\rangle r} = 0$. This is improvable with $d_l = 1$ for $1 \leq l \leq r$.

(e) The idea is to find an improvable realization of $T(m, n, s)$. Suppose (A, B, C) is a realization of length r. Given arbitrary integers $\alpha_1, \ldots, \alpha_m, \beta_1, \ldots, \beta_s$, extend A, B, and C by defining

$$A_{\langle ij'\rangle(r+p)} = \alpha_i[j' = p], \quad B_{\langle jk'\rangle(r+p)} = \beta_{k'}[j = p], \quad C_{\langle ki'\rangle(r+p)} = 0, \quad \text{for } 1 \leq p \leq n.$$

If $d_l = \sum_{i'=1}^m \sum_{k=1}^s \alpha_{i'} \beta_k c_{\langle ki'\rangle l}$ for $l \leq r$ and $d_l = -1$ otherwise, we have

$$\sum_{l=1}^{r+n} A_{\langle ij'\rangle l} B_{\langle jk'\rangle l} d_l = \sum_{i'=1}^m \sum_{k=1}^s \alpha_{i'} \beta_k \sum_{l=1}^r A_{\langle ij'\rangle l} B_{\langle jk'\rangle l} C_{\langle ki'\rangle l} - \sum_{p=1}^n \alpha_i[j' = p] \beta_{k'}[j = p]$$

$$= [j = j'] \alpha_i \beta_{k'} - [j = j'] \alpha_i \beta_{k'} = 0;$$

so this is improvable if $d_1 \ldots d_r \neq 0$. But $d_1 \ldots d_r$ is a polynomial in $(\alpha_1, \ldots, \alpha_m, \beta_1, \ldots, \beta_s)$, not identically zero, since we can assume without loss of generality that C has no all-zero columns. Therefore some choice of α's and β's will work.

(f) If $M(n) = n^\omega$ we have $M(n^h) = n^{h\omega}$, hence

$$\mathrm{rank}(T(n^h, n^h, n^h) \oplus T(1, n^{h\omega} - n^h(2n^h - 1), 1)) \leq n^{h\omega} + n^h.$$

Exercise 66(c) now implies that $n^{h\omega} + (n^{h\omega} - 2n^{2h} + n^h)^{\omega/3} \leq n^{h\omega} + n^h$ for all h. Therefore $\omega = 2$; but this contradicts the lower bound $2n^2 - 1$ (see the answer to exercise 12).

(g) Let $f(u)$ and $g(u)$ be polynomials such that the elements of $Vf(u)$ and $Wg(u)$ are polynomials. Then we redefine

$$A_{(i+m)l} = u^{d+1}v_{il}f(u)/d_{i+m}, \quad B_{(j+n)l} = u^{d+1}w_{jl}g(u)/p, \quad C_{kl} = u^{d+e+2}c_{kl},$$

where $f(u)g(u) = pu^e + O(u^{e+1})$. It follows that $\sum_{l=1}^{r} A_{il}(u)B_{jl}(u)C_{kl}(u)$ is equal to $u^{d+e+2}t_{ijk} + O(u^{d+e+3})$ if $k \le s$, $u^{d+e+2}[i > m][j > n]$ if $k = s + 1$. [*Note:* The result of (e) therefore holds over any field, if rank$_2$ is replaced by <u>rank</u>, since we can choose the α's and β's to be polynomials of the form $1 + O(u)$.]

(h) Let row p of C refer to the component $T(1, 16, 1)$. The key point is that $\sum_{l=1}^{r} a_{il}(u)b_{jl}(u)c_{pl}(u)$ is zero (not simply $O(u^{d+1})$) for all i and j that remain after deletion; moreover, $c_{pl}(u) \ne 0$ for all l. These properties are true in the constructions of parts (c) and (g), and they remain true when we take direct products.

(i) The proof generalizes from binomials to multinomials in a straightforward way.

(j) After part (h) we have $81^{\omega/3} + 2(36^{\omega/3}) + 34^{\omega/3} \le 100$, so $\omega < 2.52$. Squaring once again gives <u>rank</u>$(T(81, 1, 81) \oplus 4T(27, 4, 27) \oplus 2T(9, 34, 9) \oplus 4T(9, 16, 9) \oplus 4T(3, 136, 3) \oplus T(1, 3334, 1)) \le 10000$; this yields $\omega < 2.4999$. Success! Continued squaring leads to better and better bounds that converge rapidly to $2.497723729083\ldots$. If we had started with $T(4, 1, 4) \oplus T(1, 9, 1)$ instead of $T(3, 1, 3) \oplus T(1, 4, 1)$, the limiting bound would have been $2.51096309\ldots$.

[Sophisticated refinements yield $\omega < 2.3729$. See *J. Symbolic Comp.* **9** (1990), 251–280; A. Ambainis, Y. Filmus, and F. Le Gall, *STOC* **47** (2015), 585–593; J. Alman and V. Vassilevska Williams, *SODA* **32** (2021), 522–539.]

68. T. M. Vari has shown that $n - 1$ multiplications are necessary, by proving that n multiplications are necessary to compute $x_1^2 + \cdots + x_n^2$ [Cornell Computer Science Report 120 (1972)]. C. Pandu Rangan showed that if we compute the polynomial as $L_1 R_1 + \cdots + L_{n-1}R_{n-1}$, where the L's and R's are linear combinations of the x's, at least $n - 2$ additions are needed to form the L's and R's [*J. Algorithms* **4** (1983), 282–285]. But his lower bound does not obviously apply to all polynomial chains.

69. Let $y_{ij} = x_{ij} - [i = j]$, and apply the recursive construction (31) to the matrix $I + Y$, using arithmetic on power series in the n^2 variables y_{ij} but ignoring all terms of total degree $> n$. Each entry h of the array is represented as a sum $h_0 + h_1 + \cdots + h_n$, where h_k is the value of a homogeneous polynomial of degree k. Then every addition step becomes $n + 1$ additions, and every multiplication step becomes $\approx \frac{1}{2}n^2$ multiplications and $\approx \frac{1}{2}n^2$ additions. Furthermore, every division is by a quantity of the form $1 + h_1 + \cdots + h_n$, since all divisions in the recursive construction are by 1 when the y_{ij} are entirely zero; therefore division is slightly easier than multiplication (see Eq. 4.7–(3) when $V_0 = 1$). Since we stop when reaching a 2×2 determinant, we need not subtract 1 from y_{jj} when $j > n - 2$. It turns out that when redundant computations are suppressed, this method requires $20\binom{n}{5} + 8\binom{n}{4} + 12\binom{n}{3} - 4\binom{n}{2} + 5n - 4$ multiplications and $20\binom{n}{5} + 8\binom{n}{4} + 4\binom{n}{3} + 24\binom{n}{2} - n$ additions, thus $\frac{1}{6}n^5 - O(n^4)$ of each. A similar method can be used to eliminate division in many other cases; see *Crelle* **264** (1973), 184–202. (But the next exercise constructs an even faster divisionless scheme for determinants.)

70. Set $A = \lambda - x$, $B = -u$, $C = -v$, and $D = \lambda I - Y$ in the hinted identity, then take the determinant of both sides, using the fact that $I/\lambda + Y/\lambda^2 + Y^2/\lambda^3 + \cdots$ is the inverse of D as a formal power series in $1/\lambda$. We need to compute $uY^k v$ only for $0 \le k \le n - 2$, because we know that $f_X(\lambda)$ is a polynomial of degree n; thus, only $n^3 + O(n^2)$ multiplications and $n^3 + O(n^2)$ additions are needed to advance from degree

$n - 1$ to degree n. Proceeding recursively, we obtain the coefficients of f_X from the elements of X after doing $6\binom{n}{4} + 7\binom{n}{3} + 2\binom{n}{2}$ multiplications and $6\binom{n}{4} + 5\binom{n}{3} + 2\binom{n}{2}$ addition-subtractions.

If we only want to compute $\det X = (-1)^n f_X(0)$, we save $3\binom{n}{2} - n + 1$ multiplications and $\binom{n}{2}$ additions. This division-free method is in fact quite economical when n has a moderate size; it beats the obvious cofactor expansion scheme when $n > 4$.

If ω is the exponent of matrix multiplication in exercise 66, the same approach leads to a division-free computation in $O(n^{\omega+1+\epsilon})$ steps, because the vectors uY^k for $0 \le k < n$ can be evaluated in $O(M(n) \log n)$ steps: Take a matrix whose first 2^l rows are uY^k for $0 \le k < 2^l$ and multiply it by Y^{2^l}; then the first 2^l rows of the product are uY^k for $2^l \le k < 2^{l+1}$. [See S. J. Berkowitz, *Inf. Processing Letters* **18** (1984), 147–150.] Of course such asymptotically "fast" matrix multiplication is strictly of theoretical interest. E. Kaltofen has shown how to evaluate determinants with only $O(n^{2+\epsilon}\sqrt{M(n)})$ additions, subtractions, and multiplications [*Proc. Int. Symp. Symb. Alg. Comp.* **17** (1992), 342–349]; his method is interesting even with $M(n) = n^3$.

71. Suppose $g_1 = u_1 \circ v_1, \ldots, g_r = u_r \circ v_r$, and $f = \alpha_1 g_1 + \cdots + \alpha_r g_r + p_0$, where $u_k = \beta_{k1}g_1 + \cdots + \beta_{k(k-1)}g_{k-1} + p_k$, $v_k = \gamma_{k1}g_1 + \cdots + \gamma_{k(k-1)}g_{k-1} + q_k$, each $\circ$ is "$\times$" or "$/$", and each p_j or q_j is a polynomial of degree ≤ 1 in $x_1, \ldots, x_n$. Compute auxiliary quantities w_k, y_k, z_k for $k = r$, $r - 1$, $\ldots$, 1 as follows: $w_k = \alpha_k + \beta_{(k+1)k}y_{k+1} + \gamma_{(k+1)k}z_{k+1} + \cdots + \beta_{rk}y_r + \gamma_{rk}z_r$, and

$$y_k = w_k \times v_k, \quad z_k = w_k \times u_k, \qquad \text{if } g_k = u_k \times v_k;$$
$$y_k = w_k/v_k, \quad z_k = -y_k \times g_k, \qquad \text{if } g_k = u_k/v_k.$$

Then $f' = p'_0 + p'_1 y_r + q'_1 z_1 + \cdots + p'_r y_r + q'_r z_r$, where $'$ denotes the derivative with respect to any of $x_1, \ldots, x_n$. [W. Baur and V. Strassen, *Theoretical Comp. Sci.* **22** (1983), 317–330. A related method had been published by S. Linnainmaa, *BIT* **16** (1976), 146–160, who applied it to analysis of rounding errors.] We save two chain multiplications if $g_r = u_r \times v_r$, since $w_r = \alpha_r$. Repeating the construction gives all second partial derivatives with at most $9m + 3d$ chain multiplications and $4d$ divisions.

72. There is an algorithm to compute the tensor rank over algebraically closed fields like the complex numbers, since this is a special case of the results of Alfred Tarski, *A Decision Method for Elementary Algebra and Geometry*, 2nd edition (Berkeley, California: Univ. of California Press, 1951); but the known methods do not make this computation really feasible except for very small tensors. Over the field of rational numbers, the problem isn't even known to be solvable in finite time.

73. In such a polynomial chain on N variables, the determinant of any $N \times N$ matrix for N of the linear forms known after l addition-subtraction steps is at most 2^l. And in the discrete Fourier transform, the matrix of the final $N = m_1 \ldots m_n$ linear forms has determinant $N^{N/2}$, since its square is N times a permutation matrix by exercise 13. [*JACM* **20** (1973), 305–306.]

74. (a) If $k = (k_1, \ldots, k_s)^T$ is a vector of relatively prime integers, so is Uk, since any common divisor of the elements of Uk divides all elements of $k = U^{-1}Uk$. Therefore VUk cannot have all integer components.

(b) Suppose there is a polynomial chain for Vx with t multiplications. If $t = 0$, the entries of V must all be integers, so $s = 0$. Otherwise let $\lambda_i = \alpha \times \lambda_k$ or $\lambda_i = \lambda_j \times \lambda_k$ be the first multiplication step. We can assume that $\lambda_k = n_1 x_1 + \cdots + n_s x_s + \beta$ where $n_1, \ldots, n_s$ are integers, not all zero, and β is constant. Find a unimodular matrix U such that $(n_1, \ldots, n_s)U = (0, \ldots, 0, d)$, where $d = \gcd(n_1, \ldots, n_s)$. (The algorithm discussed before Eq. 4.5.2–(14) implicitly defines such a U.) Construct a new polynomial chain with inputs $y_1, \ldots, y_{s-1}$ as follows: First calculate $x = (x_1, \ldots, x_s)^T = U(y_1, \ldots, y_{s-1}, -\beta/d)^T$, then continue with the assumed polynomial chain for Vx. When step i of that chain is reached, we will have $\lambda_k = (n_1, \ldots, n_s)x + \beta = 0$, so we can simply set $\lambda_i = 0$ instead of multiplying. After Vx has been evaluated, add the constant vector $w\beta/d$ to the result, where w is the rightmost column of VU, and let W be the other $s - 1$ columns of VU. The new polynomial chain has computed $Vx + w\beta/d = VU(y_1, \ldots, y_{s-1}, -\beta/d)^T + w\beta/d = W(y_1, \ldots, y_{s-1})^T$, with $t - 1$ multiplications. But the columns of W are Z-independent, by part (a); hence $t - 1 \geq s - 1$, by induction on s, and we have $t \geq s$.

(c) Let $x_j = 0$ for the $t - s$ values of j that aren't in the set of Z-independent columns. Any chain for Vx then evaluates $V'x'$ for a matrix V' to which part (b) applies.

(d) $\lambda_1 = x - y$, $\lambda_2 = \lambda_1 + \lambda_1$, $\lambda_3 = \lambda_2 + x$, $\lambda_4 = (1/6) \times \lambda_3$, $\lambda_5 = \lambda_4 + \lambda_4$, $\lambda_6 = \lambda_5 + y$ $(= x + y/3)$, $\lambda_7 = \lambda_6 - \lambda_1$, $\lambda_8 = \lambda_7 + \lambda_4$ $(= x/2 + y)$. But $\{x/2 + y, x + y/2\}$ needs two multiplications, since the columns of $\left(\begin{smallmatrix} 1/2 & 1 \\ 1 & 1/2 \end{smallmatrix}\right)$ are Z-independent. [*Journal of Information Processing* **1** (1978), 125–129.]

SECTION 4.7

1. Find the first nonzero coefficient V_m, as in (4), and divide both $U(z)$ and $V(z)$ by z^m (shifting the coefficients m places to the left). The quotient will be a power series if and only if $U_0 = \cdots = U_{m-1} = 0$.

2. We have $V_0^{n+1}W_n = V_0^n U_n - (V_0^1 W_0)(V_0^{n-1}V_n) - (V_0^2 W_1)(V_0^{n-2}V_{n-1}) - \cdots - (V_0^n W_{n-1})(V_0^0 V_1)$. Thus, we can start by replacing (U_j, V_j) by $(V_0^j U_j, V_0^{j-1}V_j)$ for $j \geq 1$, then set $W_n \leftarrow U_n - \sum_{k=0}^{n-1} W_k V_{n-k}$ for $n \geq 0$, finally replace W_j by W_j/V_0^{j+1} for $j \geq 0$. Similar techniques are possible in connection with other algorithms in this section.

3. Yes. When $\alpha = 0$, it is easy to prove by induction that $W_1 = W_2 = \cdots = 0$. When $\alpha = 1$, we find $W_n = V_n$, by the cute identity

$$\sum_{k=1}^{n} \left(\frac{k - (n - k)}{n}\right) V_k V_{n-k} = V_n V_0.$$

4. If $W(z) = e^{V(z)}$, then $W'(z) = V'(z)W(z)$; we find $W_0 = e^{V_0}$, and

$$W_n = \sum_{k=1}^{n} \frac{k}{n} V_k W_{n-k}, \qquad \text{for } n \geq 1.$$

If $W(z) = \ln V(z)$, the roles of V and W are reversed; hence when $V_0 = 1$ the rule is $W_0 = 0$ and $W_n = V_n + \sum_{k=1}^{n-1}(k/n - 1)V_k W_{n-k}$ for $n \geq 1$.

[By exercise 6, the logarithm can be obtained to order n in $O(n \log n)$ operations. R. P. Brent observes that $\exp(V(z))$ can also be calculated with this asymptotic speed by applying Newton's method to $f(x) = \ln x - V(z)$; therefore general exponentiation $(1+V(z))^\alpha = \exp(\alpha \ln(1+V(z)))$ is $O(n \log n)$ too. *Reference: Analytic Computational Complexity*, edited by J. F. Traub (New York: Academic Press, 1975), 172–176.]

5. We get the original series back. This can be used to test a reversion algorithm.

6. $\phi(x) = x + x(1 - xV(z))$; see Algorithm 4.3.3R. Thus after $W_0, \ldots, W_{N-1}$ are known, the idea is to input $V_N, \ldots, V_{2N-1}$, compute $(W_0 + \cdots + W_{N-1}z^{N-1}) \times (V_0 + \cdots + V_{2N-1}z^{2N-1}) = 1 + R_0 z^N + \cdots + R_{N-1}z^{2N-1} + O(z^{2N})$, and let $W_N + \cdots + W_{2N-1}z^{N-1} = -(W_0 + \cdots + W_{N-1}z^{N-1})(R_0 + \cdots + R_{N-1}z^{N-1}) + O(z^N)$.

[*Numer. Math.* **22** (1974), 341–348; this algorithm was, in essence, first published by M. Sieveking, *Computing* **10** (1972), 153–156.] Note that the total time for N coefficients is $O(N \log N)$ arithmetic operations if we use "fast" polynomial multiplication (exercise 4.6.4–57).

7. $W_n = \binom{mk}{k}/n$ when $n = (m-1)k+1$, otherwise 0. (See exercise 2.3.4.4–11.)

8. G1. Input G_1 and V_1; set $n \leftarrow 1$, $U_0 \leftarrow 1/V_1$; output $W_1 = G_1 U_0$.

G2. Increase n by 1. Terminate the algorithm if $n > N$; otherwise input V_n and G_n.

G3. Set $U_k \leftarrow (U_k - \sum_{j=1}^{k} U_{k-j} V_{j+1})/V_1$ for $k = 0, 1, \ldots, n-2$ (in this order); then set $U_{n-1} \leftarrow -\sum_{k=2}^{n} k U_{n-k} V_k / V_1$.

G4. Output $W_n = \sum_{k=1}^{n} k U_{n-k} G_k / n$ and return to G2. ∎

(The running time of the order N^3 algorithm is hereby increased by only order N^2.)

Note: Algorithms T and N determine $V^{[-1]}(U(z))$; the algorithm in this exercise determines $G(V^{[-1]}(z))$, which is somewhat different. Of course, the results can all be obtained by a sequence of operations of reversion and composition (exercise 11), but it is helpful to have more direct algorithms for each case.

9.

	$n=1$	$n=2$	$n=3$	$n=4$	$n=5$
T_{1n}	1	1	2	5	14
T_{2n}		1	2	5	14
T_{3n}			1	3	9
T_{4n}				1	4
T_{5n}					1

10. Form $y^{1/\alpha} = x(1 + a_1 x + a_2 x^2 + \cdots)^{1/\alpha} = x(1 + c_1 x + c_2 x^2 + \cdots)$ by means of Eq. (9); then revert the latter series. (See the remarks following Eq. 1.2.11.3–(11).)

11. Set $W_0 \leftarrow U_0$, and set $(T_k, W_k) \leftarrow (V_k, 0)$ for $1 \leq k \leq N$. Then for $n = 1$, 2, $\ldots$, N, do the following: Set $W_j \leftarrow W_j + U_n T_j$ for $n \leq j \leq N$; and then set $T_j \leftarrow T_{j-1} V_1 + \cdots + T_n V_{j-n}$ for $j = N, N-1, \ldots, n+1$.

Here $T(z)$ represents $V(z)^N$. An *online* power series algorithm for this problem, analogous to Algorithm T, could be constructed, but it would require about $N^2/2$ storage locations. There is also an online algorithm that solves this exercise and needs only $O(N)$ storage locations: We may assume that $V_1 = 1$, if U_k is replaced by $U_k V_1^k$ and V_k is replaced by V_k/V_1 for all k. Then we may revert $V(z)$ by Algorithm L, and use its output as input to the algorithm of exercise 8 with $G_1 = U_1$, $G_2 = U_2$, etc., thus computing $U(V^{[-1][-1]}(z)) - U_0$. See also exercise 20.

Brent and Kung have constructed several algorithms that are asymptotically faster. For example, we can evaluate $U(x)$ for $x = V(z)$ by a slight variant of exercise 4.6.4–42(c), doing about $2\sqrt{N}$ chain multiplications of cost $M(N)$ and about N parameter multiplications of cost N, where $M(N)$ is the number of operations needed to multiply power series to order N; the total time is therefore $O(\sqrt{N} M(N) + N^2) = O(N^2)$. A still faster method can be based on the identity $U(V_0(z) + z^m V_1(z)) = U(V_0(z)) + z^m U'(V_0(z))V_1(z) + z^{2m} U''(V_0(z))V_1(z)^2/2! + \cdots$, extending to about N/m terms, where we choose $m \approx \sqrt{N/\log N}$; the first term $U(V_0(z))$ is evaluated in $O(mN(\log N)^2)$ operations using a method somewhat like that in exercise 4.6.4–43. Since we can go from $U^{(k)}(V_0(z))$ to $U^{(k+1)}(V_0(z))$ in $O(N \log N)$ operations by differentiating and dividing by $V_0'(z)$, the entire procedure takes $O(mN(\log N)^2 + (N/m) N \log N) = O(N \log N)^{3/2}$ operations. [*JACM* **25** (1978), 581–595.]

When the polynomials have m-bit integer coefficients, this algorithm involves roughly $N^{3/2+\epsilon}$ multiplications of $(N \lg m)$-bit numbers, so the total running time will be more than $N^{5/2}$. An alternative approach with asymptotic running time $O(N^{2+\epsilon})$ has been developed by P. Ritzmann [*Theoretical Comp. Sci.* **44** (1986), 1–16]. Composition can be done much faster modulo a small prime p (see exercise 26).

12. Polynomial division is trivial unless $m \geq n \geq 1$. Assuming the latter, the equation $u(x) = q(x)v(x) + r(x)$ is equivalent to $U(z) = Q(z)V(z) + z^{m-n+1}R(z)$ where $U(x) = x^m u(x^{-1})$, $V(x) = x^n v(x^{-1})$, $Q(x) = x^{m-n}q(x^{-1})$, and $R(x) = x^{n-1}r(x^{-1})$ are the "reverse" polynomials of u, v, q, and r.

To find $q(x)$ and $r(x)$, compute the first $m - n + 1$ coefficients of the power series $U(z)/V(z) = W(z) + O(z^{m-n+1})$; then compute the power series $U(z) - V(z)W(z)$, which has the form $z^{m-n+1}T(z)$ where $T(z) = T_0 + T_1 z + \cdots$. Note that $T_j = 0$ for all $j \geq n$; hence $Q(z) = W(z)$ and $R(z) = T(z)$ satisfy the requirements.

13. Apply exercise 4.6.1–3 with $u(z) = z^N$ and $v(z) = W_0 + \cdots + W_{N-1}z^{N-1}$; the desired approximations are the values of $v_3(z)/v_2(z)$ obtained during the course of the algorithm. Exercise 4.6.1–26 tells us that there are no further possibilities with relatively prime numerator and denominator. If each W_i is an integer, an all-integer extension of Algorithm 4.6.1C will have the desired properties.

Notes: See the book *History of Continued Fractions and Padé Approximants* by Claude Brezinski (Berlin: Springer, 1991) for further information. The case $N = 2n+1$ and $\deg(w_1) = \deg(w_2) = n$ is of particular interest, since it is equivalent to a so-called Toeplitz system; asymptotically fast methods for Toeplitz systems are surveyed in Bini and Pan, *Polynomial and Matrix Computations* **1** (Boston: Birkhäuser, 1994), §2.5. The method of this exercise can be generalized to arbitrary rational interpolation of the form $W(z) \equiv p(z)/q(z)$ (modulo $(z - z_1) \ldots (z - z_N)$), where the z_i's need not be distinct; thus, we can specify the value of $W(z)$ and some of its derivatives at several points. See Richard P. Brent, Fred G. Gustavson, and David Y. Y. Yun, *J. Algorithms* **1** (1980), 259–295.

14. If $U(z) = z + U_k z^k + \cdots$ and $V(z) = z^k + V_{k+1}z^{k+1} + \cdots$, we find that the difference $V(U(z)) - U'(z)V(z)$ is $\sum_{j\geq 1} z^{2k+j-1}j(U_k V_{k+j} - U_{k+j} + (\text{polynomial involving only } U_k, \ldots, U_{k+j-1}, V_{k+1}, \ldots, V_{k+j-1}))$; hence $V(z)$ is unique if $U(z)$ is given and $U(z)$ is unique if $V(z)$ and U_k are given.

The solution depends on two auxiliary algorithms, the first of which solves the equation $V(z + z^k U(z)) = (1 + z^{k-1}W(z))V(z) + z^{k-1}S(z) + O(z^{k-1+n})$ for $V(z) = V_0 + V_1 z + \cdots + V_{n-1}z^{n-1}$, given $U(z)$, $W(z)$, $S(z)$, and n. If $n = 1$, let $V_0 = -S(0)/W(0)$; or let V_0 be arbitrary when $S(0) = W(0) = 0$. To go from n to $2n$, let

$$V(z + z^k U(z)) = (1 + z^{k-1}W(z))V(z) + z^{k-1}S(z) - z^{k-1+n}R(z) + O(z^{k-1+2n}),$$
$$1 + z^{k-1}\hat{W}(z) = (z/(z + z^k U(z)))^n (1 + z^{k-1}W(z)) + O(z^{k-1+n}),$$
$$\hat{S}(z) = (z/(z + z^k U(z)))^n R(z) + O(z^n),$$

and let $\hat{V}(z) = V_n + V_{n+1}z + \cdots + V_{2n-1}z^{n-1}$ satisfy

$$\hat{V}(z + z^k U(z)) = (1 + z^{k-1}\hat{W}(z))\hat{V}(z) + z^{k-1}\hat{S}(z) + O(z^{k-1+n}).$$

The second algorithm solves $W(z)U(z) + zU'(z) = V(z) + O(z^n)$ for $U(z) = U_0 + U_1 z + \cdots + U_{n-1}z^{n-1}$, given $V(z)$, $W(z)$, and n. If $n = 1$, let $U_0 = V(0)/W(0)$, or let U_0 be arbitrary in case $V(0) = W(0) = 0$. To go from n to $2n$, let $W(z)U(z) + zU'(z) = $

$V(z) - z^n R(z) + O(z^{2n})$, and let $\hat{U}(z) = U_n + \cdots + U_{2n-1}z^{n-1}$ be a solution to the equation $(n + W(z))\hat{U}(z) + z\hat{U}'(z) = R(z) + O(z^n)$.

Resuming the notation of (27), the first algorithm can be used to solve $\hat{V}(U(z)) = U'(z)(z/U(z))^k \hat{V}(z)$ to any desired accuracy, and we set $V(z) = z^k \hat{V}(z)$. To find $P(z)$, suppose we have $V(P(z)) = P'(z)V(z) + O(z^{2k-1+n})$, an equation that holds for $n = 1$ when $P(z) = z + \alpha z^k$ and α is arbitrary. We can go from n to $2n$ by letting $V(P(z)) = P'(z)V(z) + z^{2k-1+n}R(z) + O(z^{2k-1+2n})$ and replacing $P(z)$ by $P(z) + z^{k+n}\hat{P}(z)$, where the second algorithm is used to find the polynomial $\hat{P}(z)$ such that $(k + n - zV'(P(z))/V(z))\hat{P}(z) + z\hat{P}'(z) = (z^k/V(z))R(z) + O(z^n)$.

15. The differential equation $U'(z)/U(z)^k = 1/z^k$ implies that $U(z)^{1-k} = z^{1-k} + c$ for some constant c. So we find $U^{[n]}(z) = z/(1 + cnz^{1-k})^{1/(k-1)}$.

A similar argument solves (27) for arbitrary $V(z)$: If $W'(z) = 1/V(z)$, we have $W(U^{[n]}(z)) = W(z) + nc$ for some c.

16. We want to show that $[t^n] t^{n+1}((n+1)R'_{k+1}(t)/V(t)^n - nR'_k(t)/V(t)^{n+1}) = 0$. This follows since $(n + 1)R'_{k+1}(t)/V(t)^n - nR'_k(t)/V(t)^{n+1} = \frac{d}{dt}(R_k(t)/V(t)^{n+1})$. Consequently we have $n^{-1}[t^{n-1}] R'_1(t) t^n/V(t)^n = (n - 1)^{-1}[t^{n-2}] R'_2(t) t^{n-1}/V(t)^{n-1} = \cdots = 1^{-1}[t^0] R'_n(t) t/V(t) = [t] R_n(t)/V_1 = W_n$.

17. Equating coefficients of $x^l y^m$, the convolution formula states that $\binom{l+m}{m}v_{n(l+m)} = \sum_k \binom{n}{k}v_{kl}v_{(n-k)m}$, which is the same as $[z^n] V(z)^{l+m} = \sum_k ([z^k]V(z)^l)([z^{n-k}] V(z)^m)$, which is a special case of (2).

Notes: The name "poweroid" was introduced by J. F. Steffensen, who was the first of many authors to study the striking properties of these polynomials in general [*Acta Mathematica* **73** (1941), 333–366]. For a review of the literature, and for further discussion of the topics in the next several exercises, see D. E. Knuth, *The Mathematica Journal* **2** (1992), 67–78. One of the results proved in that paper is the asymptotic formula $V_n(x) = e^{xV(s)}\left(\frac{n}{es}\right)^n\left(1 - V_2 y + O(y^2) + O(x^{-1})\right)$, if $V_1 = 1$ and $sV'(s) = y$ and $y = n/x$ is bounded as $x \to \infty$ and $n \to \infty$.

18. We have $V_n(x) = \sum_k x^k n! [z^n] V(z)^k/k! = n! [z^n] e^{xV(z)}$. Consequently $V_n(x)/x = (n - 1)! [z^{n-1}] V'(z) e^{xV(z)}$ when $n > 0$. We get the stated identity by equating the coefficients of z^{n-1} in $V'(z) e^{(x+y)V(z)} = V'(z) e^{xV(z)}e^{yV(z)}$.

19. We have

$$v_{nm} = \frac{n!}{m!} [z^n] \left(\frac{v_1}{1!}z + \frac{v_2}{2!}z^2 + \frac{v_3}{3!}z^3 + \cdots\right)^m$$

$$= \sum_{\substack{k_1+k_2+\cdots+k_n=m \\ k_1+2k_2+\cdots+nk_n=n \\ k_1,k_2,\ldots,k_n\geq 0}} \frac{n!}{k_1! k_2! \ldots k_n!} \left(\frac{v_1}{1!}\right)^{k_1} \left(\frac{v_2}{2!}\right)^{k_2} \cdots \left(\frac{v_n}{n!}\right)^{k_n}$$

by the multinomial theorem 1.2.6–(42). These coefficients, called partial Bell polynomials [see *Annals of Math.* (2) **35** (1934), 258–277], arise also in Arbogast's formula, exercise 1.2.5–21, and we can associate the terms with set partitions as explained in the answer to that exercise. The recurrence

$$v_{nk} = \sum_j \binom{n-1}{j-1}v_j v_{(n-j)(k-1)}$$

shows how to calculate column k from columns 1 and $k-1$; it is readily interpreted with respect to partitions of $\{1, \ldots, n\}$, since there are $\binom{n-1}{j-1}$ ways to include the element n

in a subset of size j. The first few rows of the matrix are

$$
\begin{array}{lllll}
v_1 & & & & \\
v_2 & v_1^2 & & & \\
v_3 & 3v_1v_2 & v_1^3 & & \\
v_4 & 4v_1v_3 + 3v_2^2 & 6v_1^2v_2 & v_1^4 & \\
v_5 & 5v_1v_4 + 10v_2v_3 & 15v_1v_2^2 + 10v_1^2v_3 & 10v_1^3v_2 & v_1^5
\end{array}
$$

20. $[z^n] W(z)^k = \sum_j ([z^j] U(z)^k)([z^n] V(z)^j)$; hence $w_{nk} = (n!/k!) \sum_j ((k!/j!) u_{jk}) \times ((j!/n!) v_{nj})$. [E. Jabotinsky, *Comptes Rendus Acad. Sci.* **224** (Paris, 1947), 323–324.]

21. (a) If $U(z) = \alpha W(\beta z)$ we have $u_{nk} = \frac{n!}{k!} [z^n] (\alpha W(\beta(z))^k = \alpha^k \beta^n w_{nk}$; in particular, if $U(z) = V^{[-1]}(z) = -W(-z)$ we have $u_{nk} = (-1)^{n-k} w_{nk}$. So $\sum_k u_{nk} v_{km}$ and $\sum_k v_{nk} u_{km}$ correspond to the identity function z, by exercise 20.

(b) [Solution by Ira Gessel.] This identity is, in fact, equivalent to Lagrange's inversion formula: We have $w_{nk} = (-1)^{n-k} u_{nk} = (-1)^{n-k} \frac{n!}{k!} [z^n] V^{[-1]}(z)^k$, and the coefficient of z^n in $V^{[-1]}(z)^k$ is $n^{-1} [t^{n-1}] k t^{n+k-1}/V(t)^n$ by exercise 16. On the other hand we have defined $v_{(-k)(-n)}$ to be $(-k)\frac{n-k}{} [z^{n-k}] (V(z)/z))^{-n}$, which equals $(-1)^{n-k}(n-1)\dots(k+1)k [z^{n-1}] z^{n+k-1}/V(z)^n$.

22. (a) If $V(z) = U^{\{\alpha\}}(z)$ and $W(z) = V^{\{\beta\}}(z)$, we have $W(z) = V(zW(z)^\beta) = U(zW(z)^\beta V(zW(z)^\beta)^\alpha) = U(zW(z)^{\alpha+\beta})$. (Notice the contrast between this law and the similar formulas $U^{[1]}(z) = U(z)$, $U^{[\alpha][\beta]}(z) = U^{[\alpha\beta]}(z)$ that apply to iteration.)

(b) $B^{\{2\}}(z)$ is the generating function for binary trees, 2.3.4.4–(12), which is $W(z)/z$ in the example $z = t - t^2$ following Algorithm L. Moreover, $B^{\{t\}}(z)$ is the generating function for t-ary trees, exercise 2.3.4.4–11.

(c) The hint is equivalent to $zU^{\{\alpha\}}(z)^\alpha = W^{[-1]}(z)$, which is equivalent to the formula $zU^{\{\alpha\}}(z)^\alpha/U(zU^{\{\alpha\}}(z)^\alpha)^\alpha = z$. Now Lagrange's inversion theorem (exercise 8) says that $[z^n] W^{[-1]}(z)^x = \frac{x}{n}[z^{-x}] W(z)^{-n}$ when x is a positive integer. (Here $W(z)^{-n}$ is a Laurent series — a power series divided by a power of z; we can use the notation $[z^m] V(z)$ for Laurent series as well as for power series.) Therefore $[z^n] U^{\{\alpha\}}(z)^x = [z^n] (W^{[-1]}(z)/z)^{x/\alpha} = [z^{n+x/\alpha}] W^{[-1]}(z)^{x/\alpha}$ is equal to $\frac{x/\alpha}{n+x/\alpha} [z^{-x/\alpha}] W(z)^{-n-x/\alpha} = \frac{x}{x+n\alpha} [z^{-x/\alpha}] z^{-n-x/\alpha} U(z)^{x+n\alpha}$ when x/α is a positive integer. We have verified the result for infinitely many α; that is sufficient, since the coefficients of $U^{\{\alpha\}}(z)^x$ are polynomials in α.

We've seen special cases of this result in exercises 1.2.6–25 and 2.3.4.4–29. One memorable consequence of the hint is the case $\alpha = -1$:

$$W(z) = zU(z) \qquad \text{if and only if} \qquad W^{[-1]}(z) = z/U^{\{-1\}}(z).$$

(d) If $U_0 = 1$ and $V_n(x)$ is the poweroid for $V(z) = \ln U(z)$, we've just proved that $xV_n(x + n\alpha)/(x + n\alpha)$ is the poweroid for $\ln U^{\{\alpha\}}(z)$. So we can plug this poweroid into the former identities, changing y to $y - \alpha n$ in the second formula.

23. (a) We have $U = I + T$ where T^n is zero in rows $\le n$. Hence $\ln U = T - \frac{1}{2}T^2 + \frac{1}{3}T^3 - \cdots$ will have the property that $\exp(\alpha \ln U) = I + \binom{\alpha}{1}T + \binom{\alpha}{2}T^2 + \cdots = U^\alpha$. Each entry of U^α is a polynomial in α, and the relations of exercise 19 hold whenever α is a positive integer; therefore U^α is a power matrix for all α, and its first column defines $U^{[\alpha]}(z)$. (In particular, U^{-1} is a power matrix; this is another way to revert $U(z)$.)

(b) Since $U^\epsilon = I + \epsilon \ln U + O(\epsilon^2)$, we have

$$l_{nk} = [\epsilon] u_{nk}^{[\epsilon]} = \frac{n!}{k!} [z^n][\epsilon] (z + \epsilon L(z) + O(\epsilon^2))^k = \frac{n!}{k!} [z^n] k z^{k-1} L(z).$$

(c) $\frac{\partial}{\partial\alpha}U^{[\alpha]}(z) = [\epsilon]U^{[\alpha+\epsilon]}(z)$, and we have

$$U^{[\alpha+\epsilon]}(z) = U^{[\alpha]}(U^{[\epsilon]}(z)) = U^{[\alpha]}(z + \epsilon L(z) + O(\epsilon^2)).$$

Also $U^{[\alpha+\epsilon]}(z) = U^{[\epsilon]}(U^{[\alpha]}(z)) = U^{[\alpha]}(z) + \epsilon L(U^{[\alpha]}(z)) + O(\epsilon^2)$.

(d) The identity follows from the fact that U commutes with $\ln U$. It determines l_{n-1} when $n \geq 4$, because the coefficient of l_{n-1} on the left is nu_2, while the coefficient on the right is $u_{n(n-1)} = \binom{n}{2}u_2$. Similarly, if $u_2 = \cdots = u_{k-1} = 0$ and $u_k \neq 0$, we have $l_k = u_k$ and the recurrence for $n \geq 2k$ determines $l_{k+1}, l_{k+2}, \ldots$: The left side has the form $l_n + \binom{n}{k-1}l_{n+1-k}u_k + \cdots$ and the right side has the form $l_n + \binom{n}{k}l_{n+1-k}u_k + \cdots$. In general, $l_2 = u_2$, $l_3 = u_3 - \frac{3}{2}u_2^2$, $l_4 = u_4 - 5u_2u_3 + \frac{9}{2}u_2^3$, $l_5 = u_5 - \frac{15}{2}u_2u_4 - 5u_3^2 + \frac{185}{6}u_2^2u_3 - 20u_2^4$.

(e) We have $U = \sum_m (\ln U)^m/m!$, and for fixed m the contribution to $u_n = u_{n1}$ from the mth term is $\sum l_{n_mn_{m-1}}\ldots l_{n_2n_1}l_{n_1n_0}$ summed over $n = n_m > \cdots > n_1 > n_0 = 1$. Now apply the result of part (b). [See *Trans. Amer. Math. Soc.* **108** (1963), 457–477.]

24. (a) By (21) and exercise 20, we have $U = VDV^{-1}$ where V is the power matrix of the Schröder function and D is the diagonal matrix $\mathrm{diag}(u, u^2, u^3, \ldots)$. So we may take $\ln U = V\mathrm{diag}(\ln u, 2\ln u, 3\ln u, \ldots)V^{-1}$. (b) The equation $WVDV^{-1} = VDV^{-1}W$ implies $(V^{-1}WV)D = D(V^{-1}WV)$. The diagonal entries of D are distinct, so $V^{-1}WV$ must be a diagonal matrix D'. Thus $W = VD'V^{-1}$, and W has the same Schröder function as U. It follows that $W_1 \neq 0$ and $W = VD^\alpha V^{-1}$, where $\alpha = (\ln W_1)/(\ln U_1)$.

25. We must have $k = l$ because $[z^{k+l-1}]U(V(z)) = U_{k+l-1} + V_{k+l-1} + kU_kV_l$. To complete the proof it suffices to show that $U_k = V_k$ and $U(V(z)) = V(U(z))$ implies $U(z) = V(z)$. Suppose l is minimal with $U_l \neq V_l$, and let $n = k + l - 1$. Then we have $u_{nk} - v_{nk} = \binom{n}{l}(u_l - v_l)$; $u_{nj} = v_{nj}$ for all $j > k$; $u_{nl} = \binom{n}{k}u_k$; and $u_{nj} = 0$ for $l < j < n$. Now the sum $\sum_j u_{nj}v_j = u_n + u_{nk}v_k + \cdots + u_{nl}v_l + v_n$ must be equal to $\sum_j v_{nj}u_j$; so we find $\binom{n}{l}(u_l - v_l)v_k = \binom{n}{k}v_k(u_l - v_l)$. But we have $\binom{k+l-1}{k} = \binom{k+l-1}{l}$ if and only if $k = l$.

[From this exercise and the previous one, we might suspect that $U(V(z)) = V(U(z))$ only when one of U and V is an iterate of the other. But this is not necessarily true when U_1 and V_1 are roots of unity. For example, if $V_1 = -1$ and $U(z) = V^{[2]}(z)$, V is not an iterate of $U^{[1/2]}$, nor is $U^{[1/2]}$ an iterate of V.]

26. Writing $U(z) = U_{[0]}(z^2) + zU_{[1]}(z^2)$, we have $U(V(z)) \equiv U_{[0]}(V_1z^2 + V_2z^4 + \cdots) + V(z)U_{[1]}(V_1z^2 + V_2z^4 + \cdots)$ (modulo 2). The running time satisfies $T(N) = 2T(N/2) + C(N)$, where $C(N)$ is essentially the time for polynomial multiplication mod z^N. We can make $C(N) = O(N^{1+\epsilon})$ by the method of, say, exercise 4.6.4–59; see also the answer to exercise 4.6–5.

A similar method works mod p in time $O(pN^{1+\epsilon})$. [D. J. Bernstein, *J. Symbolic Computation* **26** (1998), 339–341.]

27. From $(W(qz) - W(z))V(z) = W(z)(V(q^mz) - V(z))$ we obtain the recurrence $W_n = \sum_{k=1}^{n} V_kW_{n-k}(q^{km} - q^{n-k})/(q^n - 1)$. [*J. Difference Eqs. and Applics.* **1** (1995), 57–60.]

28. Note first that $\delta(U(z)V(z)) = (\delta U(z))V(z) + U(z)(\delta V(z))$, because $t(mn) = t(m) + t(n)$. Therefore $\delta(V(z)^n) = nV(z)^{n-1}\delta V(z)$ for all $n \geq 0$, by induction on n; and this is the identity we need to show that $\delta e^{V(z)} = \sum_{n\geq 0} \delta(V(z)^n/n!) = e^{V(z)}\delta V(z)$. Replacing $V(z)$ by $\ln V(z)$ in this equation gives $V(z)\delta\ln V(z) = \delta V(z)$;

hence $\delta(V(z)^{\alpha}) = \delta e^{\alpha \ln V(z)} = e^{\alpha \ln V(z)} \delta(\alpha \ln V(z)) = \alpha V(z)^{\alpha - 1}$ for all complex numbers α.

It follows that the desired recurrences are

    (a) $W_1 = 1$, $W_n = \sum_{d\backslash n, d>1}((\alpha + 1)t(d)/t(n) - 1)V_d W_{n/d}$;

    (b) $W_1 = 1$, $W_n = \sum_{d\backslash n, d>1}(t(d)/t(n))V_d W_{n/d}$;

    (c) $W_1 = 0$, $W_n = V_n + \sum_{d\backslash n, d>1}(t(d)/t(n) - 1)V_d W_{n/d}$.

[See H. W. Gould, *AMM* **81** (1974), 3–14. These formulas hold when t is any function such that $t(m) + t(n) = t(mn)$ and $t(n) = 0$ if and only if $n = 1$, but the suggested t is simplest. The method discussed here works also for power series in arbitrarily many variables; then t is the total degree of a term.]

"It is certainly an idea you have there," said Poirot, with some interest.
"Yes, yes, I play the part of the computer.
One feeds in the information — "

"And supposing you come up with all the wrong answers?" said Mrs. Oliver.

"That would be impossible," said Hercule Poirot.
"Computers do not do that sort of a thing."

"They're not supposed to," said Mrs. Oliver,
"but you'd be surprised at the things that happen sometimes."

— AGATHA CHRISTIE, Hallowe'en Party (1969)

APPENDIX A

TABLES OF NUMERICAL QUANTITIES

Table 1

QUANTITIES THAT ARE FREQUENTLY USED IN STANDARD SUBROUTINES
AND IN ANALYSIS OF COMPUTER PROGRAMS (40 DECIMAL PLACES)

$$\sqrt{2} = 1.41421\ 35623\ 73095\ 04880\ 16887\ 24209\ 69807\ 85697-$$
$$\sqrt{3} = 1.73205\ 08075\ 68877\ 29352\ 74463\ 41505\ 87236\ 69428+$$
$$\sqrt{5} = 2.23606\ 79774\ 99789\ 69640\ 91736\ 68731\ 27623\ 54406+$$
$$\sqrt{10} = 3.16227\ 76601\ 68379\ 33199\ 88935\ 44432\ 71853\ 37196-$$
$$\sqrt[3]{2} = 1.25992\ 10498\ 94873\ 16476\ 72106\ 07278\ 22835\ 05703-$$
$$\sqrt[3]{3} = 1.44224\ 95703\ 07408\ 38232\ 16383\ 10780\ 10958\ 83919-$$
$$\sqrt[4]{2} = 1.18920\ 71150\ 02721\ 06671\ 74999\ 70560\ 47591\ 52930-$$
$$\ln 2 = 0.69314\ 71805\ 59945\ 30941\ 72321\ 21458\ 17656\ 80755+$$
$$\ln 3 = 1.09861\ 22886\ 68109\ 69139\ 52452\ 36922\ 52570\ 46475-$$
$$\ln 10 = 2.30258\ 50929\ 94045\ 68401\ 79914\ 54684\ 36420\ 76011+$$
$$1/\ln 2 = 1.44269\ 50408\ 88963\ 40735\ 99246\ 81001\ 89213\ 74266+$$
$$1/\ln 10 = 0.43429\ 44819\ 03251\ 82765\ 11289\ 18916\ 60508\ 22944-$$
$$\pi = 3.14159\ 26535\ 89793\ 23846\ 26433\ 83279\ 50288\ 41972-$$
$$1° = \pi/180 = 0.01745\ 32925\ 19943\ 29576\ 92369\ 07684\ 88612\ 71344+$$
$$1/\pi = 0.31830\ 98861\ 83790\ 67153\ 77675\ 26745\ 02872\ 40689+$$
$$\pi^2 = 9.86960\ 44010\ 89358\ 61883\ 44909\ 99876\ 15113\ 53137-$$
$$\sqrt{\pi} = \Gamma(1/2) = 1.77245\ 38509\ 05516\ 02729\ 81674\ 83341\ 14518\ 27975+$$
$$\Gamma(1/3) = 2.67893\ 85347\ 07747\ 63365\ 56929\ 40974\ 67764\ 41287-$$
$$\Gamma(2/3) = 1.35411\ 79394\ 26400\ 41694\ 52880\ 28154\ 51378\ 55193+$$
$$e = 2.71828\ 18284\ 59045\ 23536\ 02874\ 71352\ 66249\ 77572+$$
$$1/e = 0.36787\ 94411\ 71442\ 32159\ 55237\ 70161\ 46086\ 74458+$$
$$e^2 = 7.38905\ 60989\ 30650\ 22723\ 04274\ 60575\ 00781\ 31803+$$
$$\gamma = 0.57721\ 56649\ 01532\ 86060\ 65120\ 90082\ 40243\ 10422-$$
$$\ln \pi = 1.14472\ 98858\ 49400\ 17414\ 34273\ 51353\ 05871\ 16473-$$
$$\phi = 1.61803\ 39887\ 49894\ 84820\ 45868\ 34365\ 63811\ 77203+$$
$$e^\gamma = 1.78107\ 24179\ 90197\ 98523\ 65041\ 03107\ 17954\ 91696+$$
$$e^{\pi/4} = 2.19328\ 00507\ 38015\ 45655\ 97696\ 59278\ 73822\ 34616+$$
$$\sin 1 = 0.84147\ 09848\ 07896\ 50665\ 25023\ 21630\ 29899\ 96226-$$
$$\cos 1 = 0.54030\ 23058\ 68139\ 71740\ 09366\ 07442\ 97660\ 37323+$$
$$-\zeta'(2) = 0.93754\ 82543\ 15843\ 75370\ 25740\ 94567\ 86497\ 78979-$$
$$\zeta(3) = 1.20205\ 69031\ 59594\ 28539\ 97381\ 61511\ 44999\ 07650-$$
$$\ln \phi = 0.48121\ 18250\ 59603\ 44749\ 77589\ 13424\ 36842\ 31352-$$
$$1/\ln \phi = 2.07808\ 69212\ 35027\ 53760\ 13226\ 06117\ 79576\ 77422-$$
$$-\ln \ln 2 = 0.36651\ 29205\ 81664\ 32701\ 24391\ 58232\ 66946\ 94543-$$

Table 2

QUANTITIES THAT ARE FREQUENTLY USED IN STANDARD SUBROUTINES
AND IN ANALYSIS OF COMPUTER PROGRAMS (45 OCTAL PLACES)

The names at the left of the "=" signs are given in decimal notation.

$0.1 =$	$0.06314\ 63146\ 31463\ 14631\ 46314\ 63146\ 31463\ 14631\ 46315-$
$0.01 =$	$0.00507\ 53412\ 17270\ 24365\ 60507\ 53412\ 17270\ 24365\ 60510-$
$0.001 =$	$0.00040\ 61115\ 64570\ 65176\ 76355\ 44264\ 16254\ 02030\ 44672+$
$0.0001 =$	$0.00003\ 21556\ 13530\ 70414\ 54512\ 75170\ 33021\ 15002\ 35223-$
$0.00001 =$	$0.00000\ 24761\ 32610\ 70664\ 36041\ 06077\ 17401\ 56063\ 34417-$
$0.000001 =$	$0.00000\ 02061\ 57364\ 05536\ 66151\ 55323\ 07746\ 44470\ 26033+$
$0.0000001 =$	$0.00000\ 00153\ 27745\ 15274\ 53644\ 12741\ 72312\ 20354\ 02151+$
$0.00000001 =$	$0.00000\ 00012\ 57143\ 56106\ 04303\ 47374\ 77341\ 01512\ 63327+$
$0.000000001 =$	$0.00000\ 00001\ 04560\ 27640\ 46655\ 12262\ 71426\ 40124\ 21742+$
$0.0000000001 =$	$0.00000\ 00000\ 06676\ 33766\ 35367\ 55653\ 37265\ 34642\ 01627-$
$\sqrt{2} =$	$1.32404\ 74631\ 77167\ 46220\ 42627\ 66115\ 46725\ 12575\ 17435+$
$\sqrt{3} =$	$1.56663\ 65641\ 30231\ 25163\ 54453\ 50265\ 60361\ 34073\ 42223-$
$\sqrt{5} =$	$2.17067\ 36334\ 57722\ 47602\ 57471\ 63003\ 00563\ 55620\ 32021-$
$\sqrt{10} =$	$3.12305\ 40726\ 64555\ 22444\ 02242\ 57101\ 41466\ 33775\ 22532+$
$\sqrt[3]{2} =$	$1.20505\ 05746\ 15345\ 05342\ 10756\ 65334\ 25574\ 22415\ 03024+$
$\sqrt[3]{3} =$	$1.34233\ 50444\ 22175\ 73134\ 67363\ 76133\ 05334\ 31147\ 60121-$
$\sqrt[4]{2} =$	$1.14067\ 74050\ 61556\ 12455\ 72152\ 64430\ 60271\ 02755\ 73136+$
$\ln 2 =$	$0.54271\ 02775\ 75071\ 73632\ 57117\ 07316\ 30007\ 71366\ 53640+$
$\ln 3 =$	$1.06237\ 24752\ 55006\ 05227\ 32440\ 63065\ 25012\ 35574\ 55337+$
$\ln 10 =$	$2.23273\ 06735\ 52524\ 25405\ 56512\ 66542\ 56026\ 46050\ 50705+$
$1/\ln 2 =$	$1.34252\ 16624\ 53405\ 77027\ 35750\ 37766\ 40644\ 35175\ 04353+$
$1/\ln 10 =$	$0.33626\ 75425\ 11562\ 41614\ 52325\ 33525\ 27655\ 14756\ 06220-$
$\pi =$	$3.11037\ 55242\ 10264\ 30215\ 14230\ 63050\ 56006\ 70163\ 21122+$
$1° = \pi/180 =$	$0.01073\ 72152\ 11224\ 72344\ 25603\ 54276\ 63351\ 22056\ 11544+$
$1/\pi =$	$0.24276\ 30155\ 62344\ 20251\ 23760\ 47257\ 50765\ 15156\ 70067-$
$\pi^2 =$	$11.67517\ 14467\ 62135\ 71322\ 25561\ 15466\ 30021\ 40654\ 34103-$
$\sqrt{\pi} = \Gamma(1/2) =$	$1.61337\ 61106\ 64736\ 65247\ 47035\ 40510\ 15273\ 34470\ 17762-$
$\Gamma(1/3) =$	$2.53347\ 35234\ 51013\ 61316\ 73106\ 47644\ 54653\ 00106\ 66046-$
$\Gamma(2/3) =$	$1.26523\ 57112\ 14154\ 74312\ 54572\ 37655\ 60126\ 23231\ 02452+$
$e =$	$2.55760\ 52130\ 50535\ 51246\ 52773\ 42542\ 00471\ 72363\ 61661+$
$1/e =$	$0.27426\ 53066\ 13167\ 46761\ 52726\ 75436\ 02440\ 52371\ 03355+$
$e^2 =$	$7.30714\ 45615\ 23355\ 33460\ 63507\ 35040\ 32664\ 25356\ 50217+$
$\gamma =$	$0.44742\ 14770\ 67666\ 06172\ 23215\ 74376\ 01002\ 51313\ 25521-$
$\ln \pi =$	$1.11206\ 40443\ 47503\ 36413\ 65374\ 52661\ 52410\ 37511\ 46057+$
$\phi =$	$1.47433\ 57156\ 27751\ 23701\ 27634\ 71401\ 40271\ 66710\ 15010+$
$e^\gamma =$	$1.61772\ 13452\ 61152\ 65761\ 22477\ 36553\ 53327\ 17554\ 21260+$
$e^{\pi/4} =$	$2.14275\ 31512\ 16162\ 52370\ 35530\ 11342\ 53525\ 44307\ 02171-$
$\sin 1 =$	$0.65665\ 24436\ 04414\ 73402\ 03067\ 23644\ 11612\ 07474\ 14505-$
$\cos 1 =$	$0.42450\ 50037\ 32406\ 42711\ 07022\ 14666\ 27320\ 70675\ 12321+$
$-\zeta'(2) =$	$0.74001\ 45144\ 53253\ 42362\ 42107\ 23350\ 50074\ 46100\ 27706+$
$\zeta(3) =$	$1.14735\ 00023\ 60014\ 20470\ 15613\ 42561\ 31715\ 10177\ 06614+$
$\ln \phi =$	$0.36630\ 26256\ 61213\ 01145\ 13700\ 41004\ 52264\ 30700\ 40646+$
$1/\ln \phi =$	$2.04776\ 60111\ 17144\ 41512\ 11436\ 16575\ 00355\ 43630\ 40651+$
$-\ln \ln 2 =$	$0.27351\ 71233\ 67265\ 63650\ 17401\ 56637\ 26334\ 31455\ 57005-$

Several of the 40-digit values in Table 1 were computed on a desk calculator by John W. Wrench, Jr., for the first edition of this book. When computer software for such calculations became available during the 1970s, all of his contributions proved to be correct. The 40-digit values of other fundamental constants can be found in Eqs. 4.5.2–(60), 4.5.3–(26), 4.5.3–(41), 4.5.4–(9), and the answers to exercises 4.5.4–8, 4.5.4–25, 4.6.4–58.

Table 3

VALUES OF HARMONIC NUMBERS, BERNOULLI NUMBERS,
AND FIBONACCI NUMBERS, FOR SMALL VALUES OF n

n	H_n	B_n	F_n	n
0	0	1	0	0
1	1	1/2	1	1
2	3/2	1/6	1	2
3	11/6	0	2	3
4	25/12	−1/30	3	4
5	137/60	0	5	5
6	49/20	1/42	8	6
7	363/140	0	13	7
8	761/280	−1/30	21	8
9	7129/2520	0	34	9
10	7381/2520	5/66	55	10
11	83711/27720	0	89	11
12	86021/27720	−691/2730	144	12
13	1145993/360360	0	233	13
14	1171733/360360	7/6	377	14
15	1195757/360360	0	610	15
16	2436559/720720	−3617/510	987	16
17	42142223/12252240	0	1597	17
18	14274301/4084080	43867/798	2584	18
19	275295799/77597520	0	4181	19
20	55835135/15519504	−174611/330	6765	20
21	18858053/5173168	0	10946	21
22	19093197/5173168	854513/138	17711	22
23	444316699/118982864	0	28657	23
24	1347822955/356948592	−236364091/2730	46368	24
25	34052522467/8923714800	0	75025	25
26	34395742267/8923714800	8553103/6	121393	26
27	312536252003/80313433200	0	196418	27
28	315404588903/80313433200	−23749461029/870	317811	28
29	9227046511387/2329089562800	0	514229	29
30	9304682830147/2329089562800	8615841276005/14322	832040	30

For any x, let $H_x = \sum_{n \geq 1} \left(\dfrac{1}{n} - \dfrac{1}{n+x} \right)$. Then

$$H_{1/2} = 2 - 2\ln 2,$$

$$H_{1/3} = 3 - \tfrac{1}{2}\pi/\sqrt{3} - \tfrac{3}{2}\ln 3,$$

$$H_{2/3} = \tfrac{3}{2} + \tfrac{1}{2}\pi/\sqrt{3} - \tfrac{3}{2}\ln 3,$$

$$H_{1/4} = 4 - \tfrac{1}{2}\pi - 3\ln 2,$$

$$H_{3/4} = \tfrac{4}{3} + \tfrac{1}{2}\pi - 3\ln 2,$$

$$H_{1/5} = 5 - \tfrac{1}{2}\pi\phi^{3/2}5^{-1/4} - \tfrac{5}{4}\ln 5 - \tfrac{1}{2}\sqrt{5}\ln \phi,$$

$$H_{2/5} = \tfrac{5}{2} - \tfrac{1}{2}\pi\phi^{-3/2}5^{-1/4} - \tfrac{5}{4}\ln 5 + \tfrac{1}{2}\sqrt{5}\ln \phi,$$

$$H_{3/5} = \tfrac{5}{3} + \tfrac{1}{2}\pi\phi^{-3/2}5^{-1/4} - \tfrac{5}{4}\ln 5 + \tfrac{1}{2}\sqrt{5}\ln \phi,$$

$$H_{4/5} = \tfrac{5}{4} + \tfrac{1}{2}\pi\phi^{3/2}5^{-1/4} - \tfrac{5}{4}\ln 5 - \tfrac{1}{2}\sqrt{5}\ln \phi,$$

$$H_{1/6} = 6 - \tfrac{1}{2}\pi\sqrt{3} - 2\ln 2 - \tfrac{3}{2}\ln 3,$$

$$H_{5/6} = \tfrac{6}{5} + \tfrac{1}{2}\pi\sqrt{3} - 2\ln 2 - \tfrac{3}{2}\ln 3,$$

and, in general, when $0 < p < q$ (see exercise 1.2.9–19),

$$H_{p/q} = \frac{q}{p} - \frac{\pi}{2}\cot\frac{p}{q}\pi - \ln 2q + 2 \sum_{1 \leq n < q/2} \cos\frac{2pn}{q}\pi \cdot \ln\sin\frac{n}{q}\pi.$$

INDEX TO NOTATIONS

In the following formulas, letters that are not further qualified have the following significance:

j, k integer-valued arithmetic expression

m, n nonnegative integer-valued arithmetic expression

x, y real-valued arithmetic expression

z complex-valued arithmetic expression

f real-valued or complex-valued function

S, T set or multiset

Formal symbolism	Meaning	Where defined
∎	end of algorithm, program, or proof	1.1
A_n or $A[n]$	the nth element of linear array A	1.1
A_{mn} or $A[m, n]$	the element in row m and column n of rectangular array A	1.1
$V \leftarrow E$	give variable V the value of expression E	1.1
$U \leftrightarrow V$	interchange the values of variables U and V	1.1
$(R?\ a{:}\ b)$	conditional expression: denotes a if relation R is true, b if R is false	
$[R]$	characteristic function of relation R: $(R?\ 1{:}\ 0)$	1.2.3
δ_{kj}	Kronecker delta: $[j = k]$	1.2.3
$[z^n]\, g(z)$	coefficient of z^n in power series $g(z)$	1.2.9
$\displaystyle\sum_{R(k)} f(k)$	sum of all $f(k)$ such that the variable k is an integer and relation $R(k)$ is true	1.2.3
$\displaystyle\prod_{R(k)} f(k)$	product of all $f(k)$ such that the variable k is an integer and relation $R(k)$ is true	1.2.3
$\displaystyle\min_{R(k)} f(k)$	minimum value of all $f(k)$ such that the variable k is an integer and relation $R(k)$ is true	1.2.3
$\displaystyle\max_{R(k)} f(k)$	maximum value of all $f(k)$ such that the variable k is an integer and relation $R(k)$ is true	1.2.3

Formal symbolism	Meaning	Where defined
$\Re z$	real part of z	1.2.2
$\Im z$	imaginary part of z	1.2.2
$\bar{z}$	complex conjugate: $\Re z - i\Im z$	1.2.2
A^T	transpose of rectangular array A: $$A^T[j,k] = A[k,j]$$	
x^y	x to the y power (when x is positive)	1.2.2
x^k	x to the kth power: $$\left(k \geq 0?\ \prod_{0 \leq j < k} x:\ 1/x^{-k}\right)$$	1.2.2
$x^{\bar{k}}$	x to the k rising: $\Gamma(x+k)/\Gamma(x) =$ $$\left(k \geq 0?\ \prod_{0 \leq j < k} (x+j):\ 1/(x+k)^{\overline{-k}}\right)$$	1.2.5
$x^{\underline{k}}$	x to the k falling: $x!/(x-k)! =$ $$\left(k \geq 0?\ \prod_{0 \leq j < k} (x-j):\ 1/(x-k)^{\underline{-k}}\right)$$	1.2.5
$n!$	n factorial: $\Gamma(n+1) = n^{\underline{n}}$	1.2.5
$f'(x)$	derivative of f at x	1.2.9
$f''(x)$	second derivative of f at x	1.2.10
$f^{(n)}(x)$	nth derivative: $\big(n = 0?\ f(x):\ g'(x)\big)$, where $g(x) = f^{(n-1)}(x)$	1.2.11.2
$f^{[n]}(x)$	nth iterate: $\big(n = 0?\ x:\ f(f^{[n-1]}(x))\big)$	4.7
$f^{\{n\}}(x)$	nth induced function: $$f^{\{n\}}(x) = f\big(x f^{\{n\}}(x)^n\big)$$	4.7
$H_n^{(x)}$	harmonic number of order x: $\displaystyle\sum_{1 \leq k \leq n} 1/k^x$	1.2.7
H_n	harmonic number: $H_n^{(1)}$	1.2.7
F_n	Fibonacci number: $$(n \leq 1?\ n:\ F_{n-1} + F_{n-2})$$	1.2.8
B_n	Bernoulli number: $n!\,[z^n]\,z/(1-e^{-z})$	1.2.11.2
$X \cdot Y$	dot product of vectors $X = (x_1, \dots, x_n)$ and $Y = (y_1, \dots, y_n)$: $x_1 y_1 + \cdots + x_n y_n$	3.3.4
$j \backslash k$	j divides k: $k \bmod j = 0$ and $j > 0$	1.2.4
$S \setminus T$	set difference: $\{a \mid a$ in S and a not in $T\}$	
$\oplus \ominus \otimes \oslash$	rounded or special operations	4.2.1

Formal symbolism	Meaning	Where defined
$(\ldots a_1 a_0 . a_{-1} \ldots)_b$	radix-b positional notation: $\sum_k a_k b^k$	4.1
$/\!/x_1, x_2, \ldots, x_n/\!/$	continued fraction: $$1/(x_1 + 1/(x_2 + 1/(\cdots + 1/(x_n)\ldots)))$$	4.5.3
$\binom{x}{k}$	binomial coefficient: $(k < 0?\ 0\!:\ x^{\underline{k}}/k!)$	1.2.6
$\binom{n}{n_1, n_2, \ldots, n_m}$	multinomial coefficient (defined only when $n = n_1 + n_2 + \cdots + n_m$)	1.2.6
$\begin{bmatrix} n \\ m \end{bmatrix}$	Stirling number of the first kind: $$\sum_{0 < k_1 < k_2 < \cdots < k_{n-m} < n} k_1 k_2 \ldots k_{n-m}$$	1.2.6
$\begin{Bmatrix} n \\ m \end{Bmatrix}$	Stirling number of the second kind: $$\sum_{1 \leq k_1 \leq k_2 \leq \cdots \leq k_{n-m} \leq m} k_1 k_2 \ldots k_{n-m}$$	1.2.6
$\{a \mid R(a)\}$	set of all a such that the relation $R(a)$ is true	
$\{a_1, \ldots, a_n\}$	the set or multiset $\{a_k \mid 1 \leq k \leq n\}$	
$\{x\}$	fractional part (used in contexts where a real value, not a set, is implied): $x - \lfloor x \rfloor$	1.2.11.2
$[a \mathinner{\ldotp\ldotp} b]$	closed interval: $\{x \mid a \leq x \leq b\}$	1.2.2
$(a \mathinner{\ldotp\ldotp} b)$	open interval: $\{x \mid a < x < b\}$	1.2.2
$[a \mathinner{\ldotp\ldotp} b)$	half-open interval: $\{x \mid a \leq x < b\}$	1.2.2
$(a \mathinner{\ldotp\ldotp} b]$	half-closed interval: $\{x \mid a < x \leq b\}$	1.2.2
$\lvert S \rvert$	cardinality: the number of elements in set S	
$\lvert x \rvert$	absolute value of x: $(x \geq 0?\ x\!:\ -x)$	
$\lvert z \rvert$	absolute value of z: $\sqrt{z\bar{z}}$	1.2.2
$\lfloor x \rfloor$	floor of x, greatest integer function: $\max_{k \leq x} k$	1.2.4
$\lceil x \rceil$	ceiling of x, least integer function: $\min_{k \geq x} k$	1.2.4
$((x))$	sawtooth function	3.3.3
$\langle X_n \rangle$	the infinite sequence $X_0, X_1, X_2, \ldots$ (here the letter n is part of the symbolism)	1.2.9

Formal symbolism	Meaning	Where defined
γ	Euler's constant: $\lim_{n\to\infty}(H_n - \ln n)$	1.2.7
$\gamma(x,y)$	incomplete gamma function: $\int_0^y e^{-t}t^{x-1}\,dt$	1.2.11.3
$\Gamma(x)$	gamma function: $(x-1)! = \gamma(x,\infty)$	1.2.5
$\delta(x)$	characteristic function of the integers	3.3.3
e	base of natural logarithms: $\sum_{n\geq 0} 1/n!$	1.2.2
$\zeta(x)$	zeta function: $\lim_{n\to\infty} H_n^{(x)}$ (when $x > 1$)	1.2.7
$K_n(x_1,\ldots,x_n)$	continuant polynomial	4.5.3
$\ell(u)$	leading coefficient of polynomial u	4.6
$l(n)$	length of shortest addition chain for n	4.6.3
$\Lambda(n)$	von Mangoldt's function	4.5.3
$\mu(n)$	Möbius function	4.5.2
$\nu(n)$	sideways sum	4.6.3
$O\big(f(n)\big)$	big-oh of $f(n)$, as the variable $n \to \infty$	1.2.11.1
$O\big(f(z)\big)$	big-oh of $f(z)$, as the variable $z \to 0$	1.2.11.1
$\Omega\big(f(n)\big)$	big-omega of $f(n)$, as the variable $n \to \infty$	1.2.11.1
$\Theta\big(f(n)\big)$	big-theta of $f(n)$, as the variable $n \to \infty$	1.2.11.1
$\pi(x)$	prime count: $\sum_{n\leq x}[n \text{ is prime}]$	4.5.4
π	circle ratio: $4\sum_{n\geq 0} (-1)^n/(2n+1)$	4.3.1
ϕ	golden ratio: $\frac{1}{2}\big(1 + \sqrt{5}\big)$	1.2.8
$\emptyset$	empty set: $\{x \mid 0 = 1\}$	
$\varphi(n)$	Euler's totient function: $\sum_{0\leq k<n}[k \perp n]$	1.2.4
∞	infinity: larger than any number	4.2.2
$\det(A)$	determinant of square matrix A	1.2.3
$\text{sign}(x)$	sign of x: $\big(x = 0?\ 0{:}\ x/|x|\big)$	
$\deg(u)$	degree of polynomial u	4.6
$\text{cont}(u)$	content of polynomial u	4.6.1
$\text{pp}\big(u(x)\big)$	primitive part of polynomial u	4.6.1
$\log_b x$	logarithm, base b, of x (when $x > 0$, $b > 0$, and $b \neq 1$): the y such that $x = b^y$	1.2.2
$\ln x$	natural logarithm: $\log_e x$	1.2.2
$\lg x$	binary logarithm: $\log_2 x$	1.2.2
$\exp x$	exponential of x: e^x	1.2.9
$j \perp k$	j is relatively prime to k: $\gcd(j,k) = 1$	1.2.4

Formal symbolism	Meaning	Where defined
$\gcd(j, k)$	greatest common divisor of j and k: $$\left(j = k = 0?\ 0:\ \max_{d\backslash j,\, d\backslash k} d\right)$$	4.5.2
$\mathrm{lcm}(j, k)$	least common multiple of j and k: $$\left(jk = 0?\ 0:\ \min_{d>0,\, j\backslash d,\, k\backslash d} d\right)$$	4.5.2
$x \bmod y$	mod function: $\left(y = 0?\ x:\ x - y\lfloor x/y\rfloor\right)$	1.2.4
$u(x) \bmod v(x)$	remainder of polynomial u after division by polynomial v	4.6.1
$x \equiv x'\ (\text{modulo } y)$	relation of congruence: $x \bmod y = x' \bmod y$	1.2.4
$x \approx y$	x is approximately equal to y	3.5, 4.2.2
$\Pr\big(S(n)\big)$	probability that statement $S(n)$ is true, for random positive integers n	3.5
$\Pr\big(S(X)\big)$	probability that statement $S(X)$ is true, for random values of X	1.2.10
$\mathrm{E}\,X$	expected value of X: $\sum_x x \Pr(X = x)$	1.2.10
$\mathrm{mean}(g)$	mean value of the probability distribution represented by generating function g: $g'(1)$	1.2.10
$\mathrm{var}(g)$	variance of the probability distribution represented by generating function g: $$g''(1) + g'(1) - g'(1)^2$$	1.2.10
$(\min x_1, \text{ ave } x_2,$ $\max x_3, \text{ dev } x_4)$	a random variable having minimum value x_1, average (expected) value x_2, maximum value x_3, standard deviation x_4	1.2.10
␣	one blank space	1.3.1
rA	register A (accumulator) of MIX	1.3.1
rX	register X (extension) of MIX	1.3.1
$\mathrm{rI}1, \ldots, \mathrm{rI}6$	(index) registers I1, ..., I6 of MIX	1.3.1
rJ	(jump) register J of MIX	1.3.1
(L:R)	partial field of MIX word, $0 \le \mathtt{L} \le \mathtt{R} \le 5$	1.3.1
OP ADDRESS,I(F)	notation for MIX instruction	1.3.1, 1.3.2
u	unit of time in MIX	1.3.1
*	"self" in MIXAL	1.3.2
OF, 1F, 2F, ..., 9F	"forward" local symbol in MIXAL	1.3.2
OB, 1B, 2B, ..., 9B	"backward" local symbol in MIXAL	1.3.2
OH, 1H, 2H, ..., 9H	"here" local symbol in MIXAL	1.3.2

APPENDIX C

INDEX TO ALGORITHMS AND THEOREMS

At any step, arbitrary combinations of algorithms and theorems
can be applied to solve a given problem.
— KARSTEN HOMANN and JACQUES CALMET (1995)

INDEX AND GLOSSARY

Seek and ye shall find.
— Matthew 7:7

When an index entry refers to a page containing a relevant exercise, see also the *answer* to that exercise for further information. An answer page is not indexed here unless it refers to a topic not included in the statement of the exercise.

Mitchell, Gerard Joseph Francis Xavier, 27, 32.
MIX computer, vi, 210.
  binary version, 202–204, 339, 389–390, 481.
  floating point attachment, 215, 223–225, 516.
Mixed congruential method, 11, see Linear congruential sequence.
Mixed-radix number systems, 66, 199, 208–211, 290, 293, 505.
  addition and subtraction, 209, 281.
  balanced, 103, 293, 631.
  comparison, 290.
  counting by 1s, 103.
  multiplication and division, 209.
  radix conversion, 327.
Mixture of distribution functions, 123–124, 138.
Möbius, August Ferdinand, function, 354, 376, 456, 459.
  inversion formula, 456, 652.
mod, 228, 421, 544, 734.
mod m arithmetic,
  addition, 12, 15, 203, 287–288.
  division, 354, 445, 499; see also Inverse modulo m.
  halving, 293.
  multiplication, 12–16, 284, 287–288, 294, 318, 663.
  on polynomial coefficients, 418–420.
  square root, 406–407, 415, 456–457, 681–682.
  subtraction, 15, 186, 203, 287–288.
Model V computer, 225.
Modular arithmetic, 284–294, 302–305, 450, 454, 499.
  complex, 292.
Modular method for polynomial gcd, 453, 460.
Modulus in a linear congruential sequence, 10–16, 23, 184.
Moenck, Robert Thomas, 449, 505.
Moews, David John, 593.
Moivre, Abraham de, 537.
Möller, Niels Gunnar Landgren, 279.
Møller, Ole, 242.
Monahan, John Francis, 130, 131, 135.
Monic polynomial, 418, 420, 421, 425, 435, 452, 457, 518.
Monier, Louis Marcel Gino, 414, 662.
Monkey tests, 75.
Monomials, evaluation of, 485, 697.
Monotonicity, 230, 243.
Monte Carlo, 2, 29, 55, 114, 185, 189.
Monte Carlo method: Any computational method that uses random numbers (possibly not producing a correct answer); see also Las Vegas algorithms, Randomized algorithms.
Montgomery, Hugh Lowell, 683.

Montgomery, Peter Lawrence, 284, 322, 327.
  multiplication mod m, 284, 386, 396.
Moore, Donald Philip, 27, 32.
Moore, Louis Robert, III, 108.
Moore, Ramon Edgar, 242.
Moore School of Electrical Engineering, 208, 225.
Morain, François Jean, 390.
Morgenstern, Jacques, 524.
Morley, Frank Vigor, 199.
Morris, Ian David, 352, 645.
Morris, Robert, 613.
Morrison, Michael Allan, 396, 400, 660.
Morse, Harrison Reed, III, 192.
Morse, Samuel Finley Breese, code, 377.
Moses, Joel, 454–455.
Most significant digit, 195.
Motzkin, Theodor (= Theodore) Samuel (תיאודור שמואל מוצקין), 378, 490, 494, 495, 497, 518, 519, 705.
Muddle-square method, 36, 174–176, 179.
Muller, Mervin Edgar, 122, 143.
Multinomial coefficients, 539.
Multinomial theorem, 722.
Multiple-precision arithmetic, 58, 202, 265–318, 419, 486.
  addition, 266–267, 276–278, 281, 283.
  comparison, 281.
  division, 270–275, 278–279, 282–283, 311–313.
  greatest common divisor, 345–348, 354, 355, 379, 656.
  multiplication, 268–270, 283, 294–318.
  radix conversion, 326, 328.
  subtraction, 267–268, 276, 281, 283.
Multiple-precision constants, 352, 362, 366, 384, 659, 663, 712, 726–728.
Multiples, 422.
Multiples of an irrational number mod 1, 164, 379, 622.
Multiplication, 194, 207–208, 265, 294, 462.
  complex, 205, 307–310, 487, 506, 519, 706.
  double-precision, 249–250, 252, 295.
  fast (asymptotically), 294–318.
  floating point, 220, 230–231, 243, 263–264.
  fractions, 282, 330.
  matrix, 499–501, 506–507, 516, 520–523, 699.
  Mersenne, 294.
  mixed-radix, 209.
  mod m, 12–16, 284, 287–288, 294, 318, 663.
  mod $u(x)$, 446.
  modular, 285–286, 302–305.
  multiprecision, 268–270, 283, 294–318.
  multiprecision by single-precision, 281.
  polynomial, 418–420, 508, 512, 521, 712, 713.
  power series, 525.
  two's complement, 608.

THIS BOOK was composed on a Sun SPARCstation with Computer Modern typefaces, using the TeX and METAFONT software as described in the author's books *Computers & Typesetting* (Reading, Mass.: Addison–Wesley, 1986), Volumes A–E. The illustrations were produced with John Hobby's METAPOST system. Some names in the index were typeset with additional fonts developed by Yannis Haralambous (Greek, Hebrew, Arabic), Olga G. Lapko (Cyrillic), Frans J. Velthuis (Devanagari), Masatoshi Watanabe (Japanese), and Linbo Zhang (Chinese).